Special Edition

USING
THE INTERNET
THIRD EDITION

Special Edition

USING

THE INTERNET

THIRD EDITION

Written by Jerry Honeycutt and Mary Ann Pike with

*Bill Brandon • Mark R. Brown • James Bryce • Dick Cravens
David Gunter • Faisal Jawdat • Dennis Jones • John Jung
Peter Kent • Joe Kraynak • Lori Leonardo • Ralph Losey
Jim Minatel • James O'Donnell • Mike O'Mara • Tim Parker
Tod Pike • Neil Randall • Eric C. Richardson • Joe Schepis
David Schramm • Mark Surfas • Scott Walter • Craig Zacker*

Special Edition Using the Internet, Third Edition

Library of Congress Catalog No.: 96-69965

ISBN: 0-7897-0846-9

98 97 96   6 5 4 3 2 1

Interpretation of the printing code: the rightmost double-digit number is the year of the book's printing; the rightmost single-digit number, the number of the book's printing. For example, a printing code of 96-1 shows that the first printing of the book occurred in 1996.

Screen reproductions in this book were created using Collage Plus from Inner Media, Inc., Hollis, NH.

Credits

PRESIDENT
Roland Elgey

PUBLISHER
Joseph B. Wikert

PUBLISHING MANAGER
Jim Minatel

TITLE MANAGER
Steven M. Schafer

EDITORIAL SERVICES DIRECTOR
Elizabeth Keaffaber

MANAGING EDITOR
Sandy Doell

DIRECTOR OF MARKETING
Lynn E. Zingraf

ACQUISITIONS MANAGER
Cheryl D. Willoughby

ACQUISITIONS EDITOR
Stephanie J. McComb

PRODUCTION EDITOR
Caroline D. Roop

EDITORS
Sean Dixon
Judith Goode
Sydney Jones
Bill McManus
Mike LaBonne
Bonnie Lawler
Jeannie Terheide Lemen
Jan Loveland
Mary Ann Sharbaugh
Jeannie Smith

PRODUCT MARKETING MANAGER
Kim Margolius

ASSISTANT PRODUCT MARKETING MANAGER
Christy M. Miller

STRATEGIC MARKETING MANAGER
Barry Pruett

TECHNICAL EDITORS
Matthew Brown
Bill Bruns
Kyle Bryant
Nanci Jacobs
Russ Jacobs
Faisal Jawdat
Greg Landes
Henry Staples
David Wolfe

TECHNICAL SUPPORT SPECIALIST
Nadeem Muhammed

ACQUISITIONS COORDINATOR
Jane K. Brownlow

SOFTWARE RELATIONS COORDINATOR
Patty Brooks

EDITORIAL ASSISTANT
Andrea Duvall

BOOK DESIGNER
Ruth Harvey

COVER DESIGNER
Dan Armstrong

PRODUCTION TEAM
Marcia Brizendine, Jason Carr, Kay Hoskin,
Daryl Kessler, Steph Mineart, Sossity Smith

INDEXER
Tim Tate

Composed in *Century Old Style* and *ITC Franklin Gothic* by Que Corporation.

Alex and Tricia Orta: many thanks for your friendship.

—Jerry Honeycutt

Acknowledgments

A book this massive requires the talents of many different individuals. Authors crank out chapters, only to find that the latest beta release forces them to rewrite much of their work. Development editors try hard to make sure that the book contains the information you need. Production editors keep track of all the pesky details such as coordinating the work of the authors, editors, and production staff. The editors? I feel for them. They have to take the gibberish that technical types produce and make real English sentences from it. Tough work sometimes.

I can't acknowledge everyone who worked on this book. For that you can flip a few pages back to see the name and contribution of each person—every one of which was a key part of the team. I do have a few special people that I'd like to point out to you. I worked with these folks on a daily basis. They made this book a most enjoyable project.

- ■ Cheryl Willoughby puts up with more rubbish than most folks. I get a real sense that she enjoys it, though.
- ■ Stephanie McComb's job is the most difficult. She has to get authors to deliver manuscripts on time—ouch.
- ■ Steve Schafer is a very warm and friendly person who is very focused on delivering the right material.
- ■ Caroline Roop is the production editor for this book. She keeps the authors honest and the work flowing.

—Jerry Honeycutt

About the Authors

Jerry Honeycutt provides business-oriented technical leadership to the Internet community and software development industry. He has served companies such as The Travelers, IBM, Nielsen North America, IRM, Howard Systems International, and NCR. Jerry has participated in the industry since before the days of Microsoft Windows 1.0 and is completely hooked on Windows 95 and the Internet.

Jerry is the author of *Using Microsoft Plus!*; *Using the Internet with Windows 95*; *Windows 95 Registry & Customization Handbook*; *Special Edition Using the Windows 95 Registry*; and *VBScript by Example*, published by Que. He is also a contributing author on *Special Edition Using Windows 95*; *Special Edition Using Netscape*; *Platinum Edition Using Windows 95*; and *Visual Basic for Applications Database Solutions,* published by Que. He has been printed in *Computer Language* magazine and is a regular speaker at the Windows World and Comdex trade shows on topics related to software development, Windows 95, and the Internet.

Jerry graduated from the University of Texas at Dallas in 1992 with a B.S. degree in computer science. He currently lives in the Dallas suburb of Frisco, Texas with Becky, two Westies, Corky and Turbo, and a cat called Scratches. Please feel free to contact Jerry on the Internet at **jerry@honeycutt.com**.

Mary Ann Pike has a B.S. in electrical engineering and an M.A. in professional writing from Carnegie Mellon University. She has experience in software design and development, and is currently working as a technical writer at the Software Engineering Institute at Carnegie Mellon University. She has authored several other Que Internet books, including *Special Edition Using the Internet*, Second Edition; *Using Mosaic*; and *Special Edition Using the World Wide Web and Mosaic*. Several of her books have won awards from the Society for Technical Communication.

Bill Brandon is a human performance technologist: a designer of human systems to support mission-critical business outcomes. He has coauthored seven books for Que since 1995, including *Building Multimedia Applications with Visual Basic 4*, *Special Edition Using HTML*, 2nd Edition, and *The Computer Trainer's Personal Training Guide*. Bill lives near Dallas with his wife of 26 years; they have two daughters and one granddaughter. Bill's e-mail address is **bill_brandon@msn.com**. You can also reach him at **71316,516** on CompuServe.

Faisal Jawdat is an Internet business specialist with TeleGlobal Media and is the co-moderator of the (unofficial) JavaScript Mailing List. He can be reached on the Internet at **faisal@tgm.com**.

Lori Leonardo is owner of L. Leonardo Consulting, a computer services company that provides Internet consulting and training. She is also an instructor at Brown University Learning Community where she teaches "Personal Finance: How to Capitalize on the Web" and "For KIDS" Web Ventures—Cyber Out on the Web." She can be reached at **lorileo@aol.com**.

Ralph Losey is an attorney and legal counselor with an office in Orlando, Florida, and in cyberspace at **http://seamless.com/rcl/**. He is also the provider of the Information Law Web located on the Internet at **http://seamless.com/rcl/infolaw.html**. Ralph is a partner in the law firm of Subin, Rosenbluth, Losey, Brennan, Bittman & Morse, P.A. When not working or attempting Aquality time@ with his wife, Molly, and their two kids, Eva and Adam, Ralph studies, writes, and teaches philosophy. He is the Webmaster of the popular School of Wisdom Web site found at **http://ddi.digital.net/~wisdom/welcome.html/**.

James O'Donnell, Ph.D., was born on October 17, 1963, in Pittsburgh, Pennsylvania (you may forward birthday greetings to **odonnj@rpi.edu**). After a number of unproductive years, he began his studies in electrical engineering at Rensselaer Polytechnic Institute. He can now be found plying his trade at the NASA Goddard Space Flight Center.

Mike O'Mara is a freelance author and technical writer. Previously, he was a staff author with The Cobb Group where he wrote innumerable articles about leading computer software programs and served as editor-in-chief of several monthly software journals. He has coauthored or contributed to many Que books. He can be reached at **76376.3441@compuserve.com**.

Mark Surfas has been involved in computer networks and online computing for over 10 years through both entrepreneurial startups and corporate positions. Mark is currently technical director for Critical Mass Communications, an online services company that consults on Internet, intranet, and online communications and develops new online technologies. Visit Mark's Web home at **www.criticalmass.com** or e-mail him at **mark@criticalmass.com**.

Craig Zacker has done PC and network support onsite, in the field, and over the phone for more than 5 years, and now works for a large manufacturer of networking software on the East coast, as a technical editor and online services engineer.

Mark R. Brown has been writing computer books, magazine articles, and software manuals for over 13 years. He's now a full-time freelance writer who has contributed to over a half-dozen Que books, and is the author of Que's *Special Edition Using Netscape 2* and *Special Edition Using HTML* (with John Jung). He is Webmaster of a Web site devoted to the topic of airships at **http://www2.giant.net/people/mbrown**, and can be reached via e-mail at **mbrown@avalon.net**.

James Y. Bryce is a writer, speaker, and consultant on communications systems and future technologies. He has a B.A. in philosophy and mathematics and a J.D. in law. He practiced law for ten years prior to studying computer science and installing the first commercial Ethernet using IBM PCs. He has worked with many of the major network operating systems from their inceptions. He resides in Austin, Texas. His Internet address is **bryce@bryce.com**.

Dick Cravens lives and works in Columbia, Missouri, where he is a product manager who designs the Next Big Thing from DATASTORM TECHNOLOGIES, Inc., a publisher of fax, data, and TCP/IP communications software for Windows PCs.

David Gunter is a consultant and computer author based in Cary, North Carolina. His areas of interest include UNIX systems management, and network and systems programming. David holds a master's degree in computer science from the University of Tennessee. During his free time, David enjoys traveling, reading, and spending as much time as possible with his wonderful wife.

Dennis Jones is a freelance writer, software trainer, and novelist. He also teaches creative writing at the University of Waterloo. He lives in Waterloo, Canada.

John Jung has been a contributing author for almost half a dozen books. When he's not working on books, he has a day job that he thoroughly enjoys. As a professional systems administrator for a world-wide information services company, he's around computers all day. He takes a break from writing and working by watching TV, surfing the Net, and generally goofing off. You can reach John at **jjung@netcom.com**.

Peter Kent lives in Lakewood, Colorado. He's been training computer users, documenting software, and designing user interfaces for the last 14 years. Working as an independent consultant for the last nine years, Peter has worked for companies such as MasterCard, Amgen, Data General, and Dvorak Development and Publishing. Peter is the author of several books by Que. He can be reached via CompuServe at **71601,1266** and the Internet at **pkent@lab-press.com**.

Joe Kraynak is a freelance writer with an affinity for computer documentation. During the last six years, Joe has written over 20 successful computer books, including *Internet Explorer 3 Unleashed*, *Windows 95 Cheat Sheet*, *The Complete Idiot's Guide to Netscape Navigator*, and *Your First Book on Personal Computing*. He can be reached at **kraynak@iquest.net**.

Jim Minatel is a title manager working for Que. His areas of expertise include the Internet and new technologies. He is the author of Que's *Easy World Wide Web with Netscape* and has contributed to several other books. Before coming to Que, he developed college math texts, earned a M.S. in mathematics from Chicago State University, and a B.A. in mathematics and physics from Wabash College.

Tim Parker started programming computers 20 years ago and started writing about them five years later. Since then he has published over 500 articles and ten books on the subject. He has held roles as columnist and editor with some of the most popular computer magazines and newsletters. He is the president of his own consulting company that specializes in technical writing and training, software development, and software quality testing.

Tod Pike is a graduate of Carnegie Mellon University, where he first became familiar with the Internet. A system administrator for almost ten years, he works daily with UNIX, Usenet, and Internet mail. He can be reached on the Internet at **tgp@cmu.edu**.

Neil Randall is the author or coauthor of several books about the Internet, including *Teach Yourself the Internet* and *The World Wide Web Unleashed*. In addition, he has written about the Internet and multimedia software in magazines such as *PC/Computing*, *PC Magazine*, *The Net*, *Internet World*, *I*Way*, *CD-ROM Today*, and *Windows*. In his real life, he's a professor at the University of Waterloo in Canada. He researches multimedia design and human-computer interaction, and he's a long-time fan of just about every game ever published—computerized or not.

Eric C. Richardson (**eric@rconsult.com**) has 21 years experience with computers. He attended the Pennsylvania State University and LaSalle University for his degree in comptuer science. He now is a coowner of Richardson Consulting with his wife, Stacie. As a consultant he works with companies in Internet integration. He doubles as Richardson Consulting's Webmaster writing the HTML and CGI programs for the Web site (**http://www.rconsult.com**).

Joe Schepis has been involved with computing, programming, and engineering since 1979. Since 1982, he has been employed at NASA's Goddard Space Flight Center where he acts as his branch's network administrator. Joe has been the author of many official NASA Web pages for both Internet and "Intranet" use, as well as consulting on Web page authoring and design. He is married to a woman who tolerates his computing hobbies and the father of two children with whom he prolongs his own childhood. He can be reached on the Internet at **jschepis@div720.gsfc.nasa.gov**.

David Schramm is the founder and president of Internet Productions, Inc. of Florida. He has over 25 years experience in advanced information systems technologies. He has been instrumental in the delivery of object-oriented business systems in manufacturing, healthcare, automotive, and services industries. He has over fours years of experience running his own company and an MBA degree with high honors. Additional information about Internet Productions can be found at **http://www.ipworld.com/company/about.htm**.

Scott Walter has worked for a Minnesota-based software publisher since 1986 where he has been developing retail software. He has coauthored (and continues to host the Web site for) *The Completed Idiot's Guide to JavaScript*. Scott's current penchants are for Java, JavaScript, VBScript, ActiveX, UNIX, Windows, C++, Delphi, and other budding development technologies. He is currently a "consultant at large" in the Minneapolis area. You can contact him at **sjwalter@winternet.com** or through his home page at **http://www.winternet.com/~sjwalter/**.

We'd Like to Hear from You!

As part of our continuing effort to produce books of the highest possible quality, Que would like to hear your comments. To stay competitive, we *really* want you, as a computer book reader and user, to let us know what you like or dislike most about this book or other Que products.

You can mail comments, ideas, or suggestions for improving future editions to the address below, or send us a fax at (317) 581-4663. For the online inclined, Macmillan Computer Publishing has a forum on CompuServe (type **GO QUEBOOKS** at any prompt) through which our staff and authors are available for questions and comments. The address of our Internet site is **http://www.mcp.com**.

In addition to exploring our forum, please feel free to contact me personally to discuss your opinions of this book: I'm **71034,3406** on CompuServe, and I'm **sschafer@que.mcp.com** on the Internet.

Thanks in advance—your comments will help us to continue publishing the best books available on computer topics in today's market.

Steve Schafer
Product Development Specialist
Que Corporation
201 W. 103rd Street
Indianapolis, Indiana 46290
USA

NOTE Although we cannot provide general technical support, we're happy to help you resolve problems you encounter related to our books, disks, or other products. If you need such assistance, please contact our Tech Support department at 800-545-5914, ext. 3833.

To order other Que or Macmillan Computer Publishing books or products, please call our Customer Service department at 800-835-3202, ext. 666. ▓

Contents at a Glance

Table of Contents

III | Using Internet E-mail

VII | Interactive Communication

IX | Web Server

Introduction

These days it seems that everyone is talking about the Internet. People can't help it. They're bombarded with it almost every day. The five o'clock news proudly boasts about its Web site. The morning paper contains Internet business news. And many advertisers have revised their television commercials to include the address of their Web sites. For that matter, folks who have never used a personal computer in their life regularly ask me about the Internet.

The Internet used to be a network of computers reserved for a select few scientific, government, and academic types. They used the Internet to exchange research information with colleagues. Now it's available to businesses (large and small) and individual users such as yourself. You can do a lot with the Internet, including the following:

- Exchange electronic messages with business associates and friends. In fact, you can strike up great dialogues with people you've never met before.

- Browse a vast universe of information, including news, research topics, sports, and entertainment. There is no subject so elusive that you can't find it on the Internet.

- Download programs and other files to your computer from other computers all over the world. You'll find large numbers of programs specific to your needs that you can try out free of charge.

- Exchange opinions and ideas with people from all over the world. You don't have to get really personal or serious, either—you can just chat if you want.

- Get help and advice about anything that you can imagine, including using a program, dealing with your 13-year-old child, or starting your own business. ■

Why You Need This Book

Face it. The Internet was not originally designed for you or me. It was designed for those highly skilled research types. Thus, the concepts behind the Internet and the tools used to access it weren't always easy to understand and use. Yes, graphical Internet tools have replaced the command line tools that were reminiscent of the old UNIX system. Still, the Internet can quickly frustrate you.

If you're new to the Internet, for example, you can quickly become overloaded with so much information that you can't find anything at all. And the tools that you use to access the Internet probably don't make much sense, either. This book shows you the concepts behind these tools and how to use them to get the best results. It doesn't waste your time with a lot of background information or basic computer skills. Instead, it cuts straight to the heart of the matter and shows you how to use the Internet like a pro.

If you already possess Internet savvy, on the other hand, you may find the Internet just as frustrating because of the quick pace at which it is evolving, as Microsoft has burst upon the scene, introducing new technologies and services almost weekly; not to be outdone, Netscape and a host of other companies are following suit with their own technologies and services. This book will help you keep up with the Internet race, because it contains information about the latest Internet goodies.

So, is this book right for you? Read the following list to yourself, and if any one item strikes you as familiar, the answer is yes—this book is right for you.

- I'm a new Internet user and want to learn about the various parts of the Internet at my own pace.

- I'm a computing professional and need to learn more about the Internet to enhance my career.

- I'm already an Internet junky, but I need to catch up with all the latest changes.

- My children are using the Internet, and I want to learn more about what they're doing.

- I'm a casual Internet user who has decided that it's time to learn more about what makes it tick.

- I'm just curious about the Internet.

What's Changed in the Third Edition

It took a year to produce the second edition of *Special Edition Using the Internet*. The quickened pace of the Internet has lit a fire under our feet, however, so that you don't have to wait that long for the third edition. Here's what we've changed in this edition:

■ We've expanded this book to include Windows 3.*x*, Windows 95, and Windows NT. One book covers all the platforms you use.

■ We've removed information about using the Internet with online services such as CompuServe or America Online. Using the Internet with these services is now indistinguishable from using it with any other Internet service provider.

■ We've added new coverage of the latest Internet programs such as Microsoft Internet Explorer 3.0, Netscape Navigator 3.0, Microsoft Internet Mail, and Microsoft News.

On the CD

■ We've removed the site listings (Hot Web Sites, Hot Mailing Lists, and Hot Newsgroups) from the book and put them on the companion CD-ROM (NetCD).

■ We've added information about the latest Web publishing tools such as Microsoft FrontPage, Microsoft Internet Studio, ActiveX, Java, and Visual Basic Scripting Edition.

■ We've added extensive coverage about using Windows NT as an Internet server using the Internet Information Server.

Aside from the more dramatic changes we've made to this edition, each and every chapter has gone through more subtle changes. We've updated each chapter with new tips. Outdated information has been replaced with new information. And each chapter has been updated with the latest versions of each program.

How This Book Is Organized

Special Edition Using the Internet, Third Edition, provides comprehensive information about the Internet. You'll find information about all of the Internet services, along with the interfaces to these services. The new edition has 9 parts, 48 chapters, and 1 appendix. Each part is dedicated to a particular Internet resource. What follows is an overview of topics you'll find in each part of this book:

■ Part I, "About the Internet," provides a brief history of the Internet and an overview of Internet services. The Internet services discussed in this book are introduced here.

■ Part II, "Getting Connected," tells you how to get connected to the Internet. This part discusses the different types of Internet accounts, along with the pros and cons of using each particular type of Internet service provider.

■ Part III, "Using Internet E-mail," shows you how to use Internet e-mail, the service that lets you communicate with more than 40 million people around the world. Learn about the most popular Internet mail programs and how to connect your business e-mail system to the Internet.

■ Part IV, "The World Wide Web," discusses the World Wide Web, one of the most exciting Internet services yet developed. If you want to learn the easiest way to interface with the Internet, don't miss this section.

■ Part V, "UseNet Newsgroups," provides information about the largest collection of discussion groups in cyberspace. You can talk to people all over the world about almost any subject you can imagine.

■ Part VI, "Locating and Retrieving Information," delves into the Internet's wealth of information. Learn how to look for the information of interest to you and get it to your computer.

■ Part VII, "Interactive Communication," talks about how the Internet connects you to people all over the world—live. Learn how to use Internet Relay Chat and WebChat to have real-time online conferences with others who have the same interests. Discover how you can use the Net to phone home and send live video.

■ Part VIII, "Internet Security," discusses how the Internet's ability to provide access to a tremendous amount of information has created significant security issues. The Internet was designed originally as an academic/research network, and security measures were not part of its initial development. Learn about security problems you may encounter, and what you can do to make your data and communications safe.

■ Part IX, "Web Server," shows you how to set up your own Internet server using Windows 3.1, Windows 95, or Windows NT. You'll learn about using Microsoft's Internet Information Server, and about managing a large, complex Web site.

How to Use This Book

Special Edition Using the Internet, Third Edition, is a tell-all book about the Internet. It covers all the current Windows platforms and the prevalent Internet programs that run on them. In short, you can use this book to learn about the Internet for the first time, or you can use this book as a complete reference for the Internet.

With that in mind, here are some suggestions to follow when using this book:

■ If you're not yet connected to the Internet, start by reading Part I to get familiar with what the Internet offers you. Then, read Part II to learn how to get connected to the Internet.

■ If you're already connected to the Internet, you can look up specific information about each Internet service in Parts III through VII.

■ If you want to learn how to publish great Web pages on the Internet, read Chapters 20 through 24 to learn about HTML, HTML editors, and scripting languages such as Visual Basic Scripting Edition.

■ If you want to learn about setting up your own Internet server, read Part IX to learn about setting up and managing an Internet server on Windows 3.1, Windows 95, or Windows NT.

Other Books of Interest

This book focuses on using the Internet with Windows. Que also publishes books in other specific, but related areas, as well as more introductory books about the Internet. Here are some you might find useful:

- *Using the Internet with Windows 95* is a basic level book about using the Internet.
- *Special Edition Using Netscape* shows you how to get the absolute most out of Netscape. This is a must-have book for avid Netscape users.
- *Special Edition Using HTML* shows you how to create your own Web pages using HTML. You won't find better information about publishing Web pages anywhere else.
- *Special Edition Using Windows 95* is a tell-all book about Windows 95. If you can buy just one book about Windows 95, this should be it.
- *Special Edition Using Windows NT* is a similar tell-all book about Windows NT. Again, if you can buy just one book about Windows NT, this should be it.
- *Special Edition Using Windows* is a similar book about Windows 3.*x* and Windows for Workgroups.

Special Features in this Book

This book contains a variety of special features to help you find the information you need—fast. Formatting conventions are used to make important keywords or special text obvious. Specific language is used so as to make keyboard and mouse actions clear. And a variety of visual elements are used to make important and useful information stand out. The following sections describe the special features used in this book.

Chapter Roadmaps

Each chapter begins with a brief introduction and a list of the topics you'll find covered in that chapter. You know what you'll be reading about before you start.

Visual Aids

Notes, Tips, Cautions, and other visual aids give you useful information. The following are descriptions of each element.

NOTE Notes provide useful information that isn't essential to the discussion. They usually contain more technical information, but can also contain interesting but non-vital technical or non-technical information. ■

 TIP Tips enhance your experience with Windows 95 by providing hints and tricks you won't find elsewhere.

CAUTION

Cautions warn you that a particular action can cause severe harm to your configuration. Given the consequences of editing your Registry, you shouldn't skip the cautions in this book.

TROUBLESHOOTING.

Troubleshooting elements anticipate the problems you might have and provide a solution. Cross references point you to specific sections within other chapters so that you can get more information that's related to the topic you're reading about. Here is what a cross reference looks like:

▶ **See** "Files," **p. 231**

Sidebars Are Interesting Nuggets of Information

Sidebars are detours from the main text. They usually provide background or interesting information that is relevant but not essential reading. You might find information that's a bit more technical than the surrounding text, or you might find a brief diversion into the historical aspects of the text.

Keyboard Conventions

In addition to the special features that help you find what you need, this book uses some special conventions to make it easier to read:

Feature	Convention
Hot keys	Hot keys are underlined in this book, just as they appear in Windows 95 menus. To use a hot key, press Alt and the underlined key. For example, the F in File is a hot key that represents the File menu.
Key combinations	Key combinations are joined with the plus sign (+). Alt+F, for example, means hold down the Alt key, press the F key, and then release both keys.
Menu commands	A comma is used to separate the parts of a pull-down menu command. For example, choosing File, New means to open the File menu and select the New option.

In most cases, special-purpose keys are referred to by the text that actually appears on them on a standard 101-key keyboard. For example, press Esc, press F1, or press Enter. Some of the keys on your keyboard don't actually have words on them. So here are the conventions used in this book for those keys:

■ The Backspace key, which is labeled with a left arrow, usually is located directly above the Enter key. The Tab key usually is labeled with two arrows pointing to lines, with one arrow pointing right and the other arrow pointing left.

- The cursor keys, labeled on most keyboards with arrows pointing up, down, right, and left, are called the up-arrow key, down-arrow key, right-arrow key, and left-arrow key.

- Case is not important unless explicitly stated. So "Press A" and "press a" mean the same thing.

Formatting Conventions

This book also uses some special typeface conventions to help you understand what you're reading:

Convention	Description
Italic	Italics indicate new terms. They also indicate placeholders in commands and addresses.
Bold	Bold indicates text you type. It also indicates addresses on the Internet.
Monospace	This typeface is used for on-screen messages and commands that you type.
Myfile.doc	Windows file names and folders are capitalized to help you distinguish them from regular text.

NetCD—Your Free Source for Internet Software

What is NetCD? If you turn to the inside back cover of the book, you'll find Que's NetCD. It provides you with all the software and documentation that you need to get started on the road to Internet success:

- You'll find a wide variety of software for use with the Internet on NetCD. We've spent hours online over the past few months to gather the best freeware, shareware, and public domain software available. I hope these efforts will save you online time and money.

- In addition to software that is available on the Net, we've made special arrangements to bring you commercial products that aren't available for downloading on the Net. Included is Internet Explorer 3.0, the software to connect to several major Internet service providers, and some special versions of shareware that were tweaked especially for this book. In some cases, this software can't be obtained free of charge anywhere other than on NetCD. In other cases, the program may be free, but not easy to get.

- Finally, we've included a large collection of useful documents about the Internet. You'll find RFCs, STDs, and FYIs on NetCD. We've also included lists of service providers, some selected FAQs, and other documents of special interest.

You'll see the NetCD icon in the margins throughout the book, indicating that the text is discussing software or a document on the NetCD. Appendix A describes the contents of NetCD and how to install it.

About the Internet

The Various Parts of the Internet

by Jerry Honeycutt and Mary Ann Pike

In the early days of the Internet, there were a small number of hosts. Most people who were on the Internet knew where to find the information they needed (often data or programs connected with their research). Today, there are many thousands of personal and commercial sites on the Internet. These sites provide services that businesses and individuals can use on a daily basis if they know they exist (for example, database searches and product ordering information). How do you find and retrieve the information you need?

A number of different services have developed over the years to facilitate the sharing of information between the many sites on the Internet. Because the Internet was originally research-oriented, many of these services were hard to use and poorly documented. Now that the Internet has been opened to commercial and private sites, new services are being developed that are easier to use, and new interfaces to the older services make them more friendly. ■

Communication

E-mail, Telnet, UseNet, and IRC let you communicate with people and computers all over the world.

Multimedia information

The World Wide Web gives you access to a huge variety of information and multimedia.

Information search and retrieval

You can use WAIS, Archie, and Veronica to search for documents and files. Then, download files with FTP and review documents using Gopher.

Real-time conferencing

You can communicate with other Internet users in real-time with video conferencing and virtual chat.

Recreation

Let your hair down with MUDs, MOOs, and MUSHes.

Electronic Mail

Electronic mail (e-mail) was one of the first Internet services developed. Although the original intent of having a network connecting physically remote sites was to exchange files and to use computing resources, the designers of the network discovered that one of the most popular services involved personal communications (e-mail). Today, e-mail is an important service on any computer network, not just the Internet. (Part III, "Using Internet E-mail," covers Internet e-mail in considerable detail.)

▶ **See** "Files," **p. 231**

E-mail involves sending a message from one computer account to another. It enables people to communicate quickly across vast distances. E-mail can be used to send important information about projects or products; it can be used to say hello to your cousin. It can even be used to send files directly to someone, although if the files are executable, they must be encoded into ASCII with one of many available programs because Internet e-mail can only handle ASCII information.

Getting E-mail to Work for You

There are many different e-mail standards, developed for different types of networks, or large self-contained user communities such as the commercial online services. This variety of standards makes it difficult to write a general purpose application to read and send e-mail, because the application would have to understand every different e-mail standard. However, there are a number of companies coming out with e-mail gateways that handle mail from many different e-mail systems (such as between cc:Mail and the Internet). Windows 95 and Windows NT come with Microsoft Exchange, a mail client that will allow you to send Microsoft Mail or Internet mail. If you're only interested in sending Internet mail, you can use Microsoft Internet Mail or Eudora.

▶ **See** "Sending E-mail to Online Service Users," **p. 238**
▶ **See** "Installing Exchange," **p. 252**
▶ **See** "Installing Internet Mail," **p. 283**
▶ **See** "Using Eudora," **p. 303**

E-mail can be exchanged between the Internet and all of the commercial online services, including America Online, CompuServe, and Prodigy. Gateways have been set up so that you can send e-mail to people on these services as easily as you can send e-mail to another Internet user. Chapter 10, "How Internet E-mail Works," tells you how to address your e-mail to these online services and other non-Internet destinations.

E-mail is becoming a popular way to conduct business over long distances. People can now use e-mail to report problems or request information about products and services. Using e-mail to contact a business associate can be better than using the phone because the recipient can read it at a convenient time, and the sender can include as much information as needed to explain the situation.

Care must be taken, though, to express yourself clearly, because all the recipient has to go on is your words. All subtle communication clues such as voice inflection and facial expression are missing in written communications. And the Internet may not be the best means of sending sensitive information because security on the Net is still under development. However, the Internet does provide one of the fastest ways to communicate with someone halfway around the world.

Mailing Lists

One of the most popular Internet services is based on e-mail. The mailing list is a way for a group of people with a common interest to have discussions. There are several ways of running a mailing list. The original way of doing it (and the way you can still do it if your list is small) is to have each person keep a list of the members of the mailing list. Then, when someone wants to submit a message for discussion, that person just sends the message to everyone on the list. The disadvantage to this method of having a mailing list is that everyone on the list has to remember to add and delete people from the list as the membership changes. Also, the machine of each person sending a message is tied up while the message is sent to everyone on the list.

Better ways of managing mailing lists have developed over the years. There are now several programs that automate the administration of mailing lists. The members of a list can number in the hundreds or thousands, but now the master list of e-mail addresses can be kept on the host that runs the mailing list program. All requests for information, or messages to subscribe (participate) or unsubscribe (drop out) are automatically handled by the mailing-list software. All messages to the participants are sent to the central host, where the mailing-list software then distributes them to all of the members of the list (thus limiting the workload to that central machine). Mailing lists still have human administrators, but they only need to take care of unusual problems that arise.

Most mailing lists consist of people who have agreed to discuss a particular topic, so there is no need to restrict the distribution of messages, and every message sent to the list is simply re-sent to every member of the list. Some mailing lists that discuss controversial topics (such as religion or politics) are moderated. In a moderated mailing list, a person reads every message that is sent to the list to make sure the contents of the messages are within the agreed-upon guidelines for that list. If a message is within the guidelines, it is sent on to the members. If not, it is deleted.

▶ **See** "Available Lists," **p. 334**

▶ **See** "Finding Majordomo Lists," **p. 342**

There are thousands of mailing lists to which you can subscribe. Some of them discuss topics that are also found in the UseNet discussion groups, because not everyone who has an e-mail address has access to UseNet (UseNet is explained in the section, "Internet Newsgroups (UseNet)," later in this chapter.)

Ask your friends with similar interests if they belong to any mailing lists. It's an easy way to find one.

World Wide Web

The World Wide Web (WWW) is one of the newest client/server-based Internet services. In the late 1980s, CERN (the European Laboratory for Particle Physics) began experimenting with a service that would allow anyone to easily access and display documents that were stored on a server anywhere on the Internet. To do this, they developed a standard format for the documents that enabled them to be easily displayed by any type of display device, and allowed links to other documents to be placed within documents. (Part IV, "The World Wide Web," covers the Web in detail.)

Although the WWW was developed for the CERN researchers to use, after the service was made public, it became tremendously popular. A number of different client applications (the ones that actually display the documents on-screen) were developed to read WWW documents. There are graphical-based clients (some of the most popular of these are Netscape, Mosaic, and the Microsoft Web browser, Internet Explorer), and terminal-based clients. Figure 1.1 shows an example of a graphical Web browser.

FIG. 1.1
Internet Explorer is a popular Web browser, allowing you to view, save, and print Web documents.

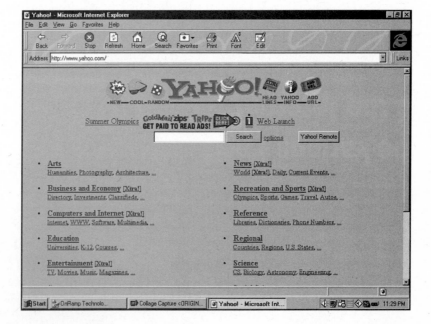

Most WWW clients also allow you to use the same interface to access other Internet services, such as FTP and Gopher. In addition, some WWW clients display multimedia files (such as movies and sounds) through multimedia player programs that you have installed on your computer.

What Are WWW Documents?

WWW documents are not ASCII text documents. They are ASCII documents that contain commands from a language called HTML (HyperText Markup Language). HTML commands allow you to tag passages of text (see Fig. 1.2). This tagging allows each WWW client to format the text in a way that is appropriate for the display that the client is using, providing for effective use of text formatting (larger text for heading, bold or italic text for emphasis, and so on). HTML also enables you to include inline images (pictures) in documents that can be displayed by the graphical WWW clients.

▶ **See** "Important WWW Concepts," **p. 366**

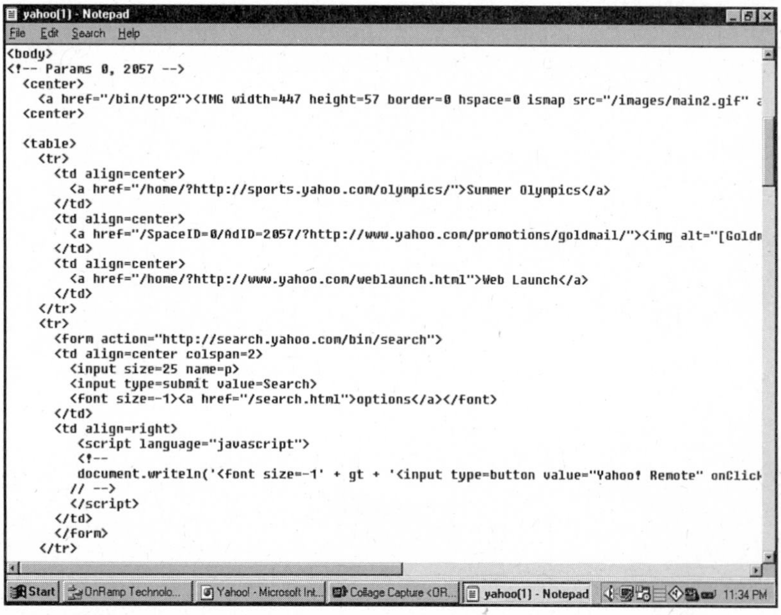

```
<body>
<!-- Params 0, 2057 -->
  <center>
    <a href="/bin/top2"><IMG width=447 height=57 border=0 hspace=0 ismap src="/images/main2.gif" a
  <center>

  <table>
    <tr>
      <td align=center>
        <a href="/home/?http://sports.yahoo.com/olympics/">Summer Olympics</a>
      </td>
      <td align=center>
        <a href="/SpaceID=0/AdID=2057/?http://www.yahoo.com/promotions/goldmail/"><img alt="[Goldm
      </td>
      <td align=center>
        <a href="/home/?http://www.yahoo.com/weblaunch.html">Web Launch</a>
      </td>
    </tr>
    <tr>
      <form action="http://search.yahoo.com/bin/search">
      <td align=center colspan=2>
        <input size=25 name=p>
        <input type=submit value=Search>
        <font size=-1><a href="/search.html">options</a></font>
      </td>
      <td align=right>
         <script language="javascript">
         <!--
         document.writeln('<font size=-1' + gt + '<input type=button value="Yahoo! Remote" onClick
        // -->
        </script>
      </td>
      </form>
    </tr>
```


FIG. 1.2
HTML lets you create Web documents that can be displayed differently depending on the Web browser you are using.

One of the main features of HTML is its ability to insert hypertext links into a document. Hypertext links enable you to load another WWW document into your WWW client simply by clicking a link area on-screen. A document may contain links to many other related documents. The related documents may be on the same computer as the first document, or they may be on a computer halfway around the world. A link area may be a word or group of words, or even a picture. And the document that you retrieve can be a text file, a graphic file, a sound file, an animation, or almost any other type of file.

Finding WWW Documents

There are thousands of WWW servers on the Internet today. Some have personal information on them, some have academic or government information on them, and many now have commercial information about them. You can find recipes for chicken casserole or fact sheets for a new printer on the Web. Many universities are putting their campus directories on the Web, and the government has everything from the text of congressional legislation to a tour of the White House. But how do you find these things?

If you know where you want to look for something, one thing that you can do is simply guess at the name of the WWW server. The convention for naming Web servers is to start the server name with "www." If, for example, you want to look for information about products from Kodak, you could try looking at the site **www.kodak.com** (.com denotes a commercial Internet address). That's great if you know where you can find the information that you want.

▶ **See** "Searching for Information on the Internet," **p. 871**

When the Web started to expand so dramatically in the mid-nineties, a number of people realized that it was fast becoming impossible to keep track of everything that's out there. So they designed programs to go out and search the Web, find all of the servers that exist, and build databases of the information that's on those servers (see Fig. 1.3). These Web search facilities (such as Yahoo and Lycos) are great resources.

FIG. 1.3

Lycos is one of the most popular of the World Wide Web search facilities.

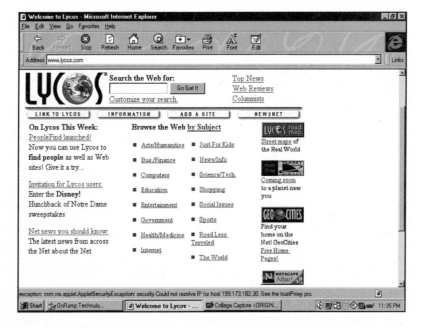

N O T E Many people are trying to collect and organize the overwhelming amount of information you can access from the Web. You can find a number of Web pages that are devoted to a particular topic. For example, at **http://www.interlog.com/~ohi/www/writesource.html**, you can find links to resources for all type of writers. ■

Lately, the search services have become serious business. Many of them have had very successful IPOs (Initial Public Offering). Yahoo! is a good example. The injection of funds into these organizations have already produced remarkable changes in their quality. In Yahoo!'s case, they've grown from a simple service that only offered a user-maintained index, to a complete search service that indexes and catalogs Web pages, UseNet newsgroups, and e-mail addresses. Other organizations offer even more value added services. Excite offers professionally written and edited reviews of thousands of Web sites, for example.

Recent Web Developments

The Web is the most competitive portion of the Internet. It gets the lion's share of attention from the media, capitalists, and big corporations such as Microsoft. These organizations have targeted the Web as the frontier with the most opportunity for growth (revenue). The next PC revolution. Thus, they don't want to be caught on the sidelines without driving the technology and standards that will determine the shape of the Web. As Microsoft has demonstrated, those organizations that drive the standards have the greatest amount of control over the technology. If you doubt this statement, look at Windows 95.

The result is an onslaught of new technology from Microsoft and Netscape over the last several months. While the decisions these organizations make can break their bank accounts, they're good for you, no matter how you slice it up. They're causing the Internet to advance at a faster pace than expected, so that you get the prize sooner. What is the prize? Take a look at the following list of recent advances:

■ Scripting tools such as Visual Basic Scripting Edition and Java that bring a Web page to life.

■ Objects such as ActiveX components embedded in Web pages that allow more complex forms and applications to be distributed over the Web.

■ Enhanced security that allows you to make secure transactions across the Internet or download a file without worrying about whether or not someone has tampered with it.

■ Integration of the Web and the desktop so that you only have one paradigm to learn. That's one look and feel for the resources on your desktop and the Internet.

■ 3D worlds using VRML that let you explore spaces in ways never before possible.

The technological advances are only part of the story, however. The content and services you'll find on the Web lately are much better than even just a few months ago. Many organizations aptly predict that the greatest opportunity for revenue is for those organizations that control the content. We've seen this trend before. The big broadcast networks control the content of television. The manufacturers produce the technology that makes it possible. While manufacturers are certainly doing well, if I had to pick the pockets of one or the other, I'd pick the pockets of the broadcast networks first. Here are some of the new and improved services:

- News feeds have gotten much better than they used to be. Microsoft Network's Web news service is a perfect example of what you should expect. Check it out at **http://www.msn.com/news**.

- Many, many services such as Federal Express's online tracking system are springing up (**www.fedex.com**). The scary part is that they're actually useful.

- Phone books are popping up all over the place. AT&T lets you search the 800 number listings (**http://www.tollfree.att.net/**). Other phone books are popping up that let you search residential and business pages all over the nation.

- Online magazines are becoming quite impressive. Web designers are finally figuring out how to present a range of information so that it's accessible on the Web. Check out my favorite online magazine at **http://homearts.com**.

Future Web Developments

Hypermedia is only the beginning of the exciting onslaught of information that will be brought to us on the Web. Developments in current Web technology include a language that will allow three-dimensional images to be included in Web documents, and the inclusion of live audio and video carried over the Web. One new application allows you to walk into a room, see a representation of another person in the room, and carry on a conversation with the person. Other applications under development will allow you to do things like take a walking tour through a 3D representation of a building.

▶ **See** "Keeping Up with New Technology," **p. 710**

Internet Newsgroups (UseNet)

Internet newsgroups are online discussions (via posted messages) on thousands of different topics. In addition to the mechanics of reading and posting to newsgroups, you should be aware of some of the social aspects of participating in newsgroup discussions. (Part V, "UseNet Newsgroups," provides extensive coverage of UseNet newsgroups.)

What Is UseNet?

UseNet (which is short for users' network) is made up of all the machines that receive network newsgroups, which are computer discussion groups or forums. The network news (commonly referred to as netnews) is the mechanism that sends the individual messages (called articles) from your local computer to all the computers that participate in UseNet.

▶ **See** "What Is UseNet?" **p. 716**

While you don't have to understand the exact details of how UseNet works, a broad outline helps you to understand what makes UseNet a powerful means for reaching lots of people. The basic idea with UseNet is that when you post an article on your local computer, the article is stored on your computer's disk, and then the article is sent to other computers that have agreed to exchange netnews articles with your computer. These computers, in turn, send your article to other machines, who send it to others; this continues until your article has reached every computer that participates in UseNet. Because each machine can send articles to many other machines, your article can reach the majority of UseNet computers within a few hours.

A news article is very similar to an e-mail message. It has some information at the top of the article in the header lines and the content of the article in the message body. Just as in an e-mail message, the header lines give information to the netnews software that puts the article in the right newsgroup or groups) and to identify the sender of the article. An article can appear in more than one group at the same time—this is called cross-posting the article.

The message body of the article contains the information that the sender of the article wrote. In many cases, the article ends with a signature; this is often a witty comment or some information about the author. Many news readers allow you to set up a file that contains your signature; this file is automatically included by your newsreader at the end of each article you post.

Newsgroups and Topics

The information carried by UseNet is divided into newsgroups, which are areas of discussion that can be compared to bulletin boards (the cork kind) with messages tacked all over them. Each newsgroup is devoted to a particular topic, although the discussion in these groups can be far-reaching (see Fig. 1.4). There is a newsgroup for almost every topic you can imagine— many large UseNet sites carry well over 15,000 newsgroups!

▶ See "Newsgroup Names," **p. 717**

FIG. 1.4

Free Agent is a very popular UseNet interface, allowing you to read and post articles, reply to the newsgroup or the author of an article, and save and print articles.

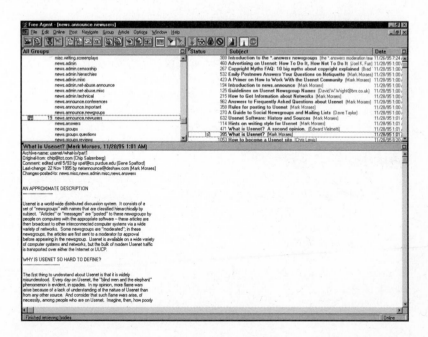

To get an idea of how discussion happens in newsgroups, you might think of UseNet as a large building, and each newsgroup as a room in that building. Each room has a name on the door, and a brief description of the topic of discussion in that room. In some of these rooms, you'll find a small number of people politely discussing a serious topic. You can come in, ask a question, and join in the discussion.

In other rooms, you may find a loud, raucous group of people discussing a heated topic. Each person is shouting out his or her opinion loudly, with little regard for the shouting from the people around them. You try to enter the conversation, but you either find that your opinions are ignored or you are insulted. Both of these conditions happen everyday (sometimes in the same newsgroup at different times!) on UseNet.

N O T E Microsoft has recently moved their support forums from CompuServe to UseNet. This is a great move because it opens up support forums to folks who don't subscribe to CompuServe such as AOL and Prodigy members, not to mention pure Internet users. You can expect many other organizations to follow suit by moving their support forums to UseNet. I wonder how CompuServe feels about all this? ▉

File Transfers—Downloading with FTP

One of the first developed Internet services allows users to move files from one place to another—the file transfer protocol (FTP) service. This service is designed to enable you to connect to a computer on the Internet (using an FTP program on your local machine), browse through the list of files that are available on the remote computer, and retrieve files. FTP lets you transfer any type of files—programs, text, pictures, sound, or any other file format.

▶ **See** "What Is FTP?" **p. 808**

N O T E FTP also allows you to upload files to a remote host, as long as you are allowed to write to that host. If you are connected to your personal account on the remote host, this should be no problem. If you are connected to an anonymous FTP site, many of these sites provide an incoming directory to allow you to contribute to the collection on the server. ▉

What Are FTP Servers?

FTP is an example of a client/server system. In this kind of system, you use a program on your local computer (called a *client*) to talk to a program on a remote computer (called a *server*). (Fig. 1.5 shows an example of a graphical FTP client.) In the case of FTP, the server on the remote computer is designed to let you download and upload files. Many other client/server services are available on the Internet. Some of these services, such as Gopher and Archie, are discussed later in this chapter.

TIP Windows 95 comes with a basic command-line FTP client.

FIG. 1.5

WS_FTP allows you to easily view directories on your local machine and a remote Internet host and to transfer files between the two machines.

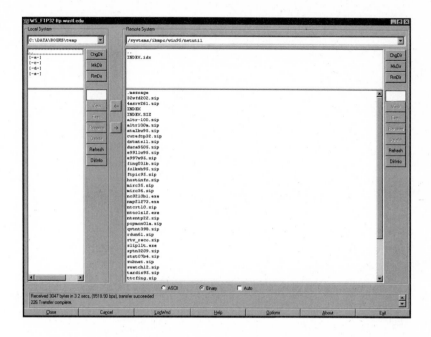

To connect to a computer system using an FTP program, the remote system must have an FTP server running on it. This server must be set up by the administrators of the machine, and the administrators decide which files and information are made available through the FTP server.

At one time, using FTP involved entering cryptic commands to a UNIX command line. Now that more PCs and Macintoshes are connected directly to the Internet, new graphical interfaces have been developed to make FTP easier to use. Many of the Windows-based FTP programs provide interactive browsers that allow you to quickly change directories and select the files that you want to transfer on your local machine and on the remote machine.

When you connect to a remote machine using FTP, you must log in to an account on the remote machine. If you have an account on the machine, you can use FTP to log in to your account and upload and download files between your local machine and your account on the remote machine. This allows you to easily move files between one Internet host and another.

What Are Anonymous FTP Servers?

One common type of FTP server is an anonymous FTP server. This server connects to a remote host and downloads files without having an account on the machine. You still need to log in when you connect to a machine that has an anonymous FTP server. However, you use the special username "anonymous" when you connect. This anonymous username lets you log in by providing any password you want.

Anonymous FTP servers are one of the major means of distributing software and information across the Internet. There is a large amount of software available on anonymous FTP servers. Much of the software is shareware, which means that you can try the software for free and pay the author if you decide to keep it. Some of the software is freeware—the author provides the software for anyone to use free of charge. Software is available for many different types of computer systems, such as UNIX, IBM PC, and Macintosh systems. You can find a wide assortment of programs, including games, communications software, and system utilities. You can also find a lot of other files, containing recipes, movie reviews, pictures—almost anything you can think of.

Locating Files at FTP Sites   One of the most frustrating problems with the Internet is the difficulty of finding information such as the location of FTP sites, host resources, sources of information, and so on. Imagine going into your local public library and finding books in piles on the floor rather than arranged on shelves according to a book-classification scheme. And instead of a central card catalog, there might only be notes placed on some of the piles stating what people had found in that pile. Well, this is how the Internet has been for most of its existence; there are many resources, but no easy way to classify and locate them.

Most FTP sites do not have a listing of all their available files. Sometimes the only way to locate a file or find interesting files is to click the folders to show the contents of the directories, and then look through them.

Because the format of the file and directory names depends on the machine that is being used as the FTP server, what you see depends on the type of system you connect to. If the server is running on a UNIX system, for example, the file names appear with any combination of upper-case or lowercase letters, and can be of any length.

If, on the other hand, the system you connect to is a VMS system (from Digital Equipment Corporation), the file names will be only uppercase. Other systems, such as PCs and Macintoshes, display files and directory names in their standard formats.

On some machines (especially the very large archive sites), the site maintainers keep an index of available files with brief descriptions of what the files contain. This is very helpful, and makes finding useful files much easier. When you enter a directory, you should look for a file called INDEX (either in uppercase or lowercase). You also should look for a file called README (or perhaps readme, or read.me). These README files are descriptions of the contents of the directories or information about the server system.

If you have a question about an FTP server, or about the contents of the files there, you can send an e-mail message to the "postmaster" of the FTP machine. For example, if you connected to the machine **rs.internic.net**, you should send e-mail to the address **postmaster@rs.internic.net**. Some FTP servers have a different person to contact; in this case, the name of the contact person is displayed when you connect to the machine, or is in a README file in the first directory you see when you connect.

Locating Files Using Archie   Information retrieval systems are being explored as a way to locate information resources on the Internet. Even though a complete central list of all the resources on the Internet does not exist, the various information retrieval systems go a long way towards making a resource easy to find.

▶ **See** "Archie," **p. 886**

Archie was the first of the information retrieval systems developed on the Internet. The purpose of Archie is simple—to create a central index of files that are available on anonymous FTP sites around the Internet. To do this, the Archie servers periodically connect to anonymous FTP sites that participate and download lists of all the files that are on these sites. These lists of files are merged into a database, which then can be searched by users.

To use Archie, you must either have an Archie client program such as WSArchie shown in Figure 1.6 running on your local machine, or use Telnet to connect to one of the Archie servers and search the database there.

FIG. 1.6

WSArchie provides a graphical interface that you can use to search the Archie databases for files.

When you have connected to one of the Archie database machines, you can search the database for a program or file. Because the database only knows the names of the files, you must know at least part of the file name for which you are looking. For example, if you are looking for a program that compresses files (makes them smaller), you would search the database for the word *compress*. The Archie program returns the location of all the files that are named "compress."

Now, this search only returns those files exactly named "compress," so it wouldn't return the location of a file named "uncompress" (which undoes the work of the compress program).

Archie, though, lets you search for a string of characters that is anywhere in the file name. If you tell the Archie program that you want to do a *substring search*, it looks for files that have your search string anywhere in the file name. Similarly, you can tell the Archie program to match the file name even if it has different capitalization than your search string.

The Archie server provides the machine name and location of the files that match the string for which you are searching. You can use the FTP program to connect to the machine and download the file to your local machine. The main limitation of Archie is that you have to know at least something about the name of the file to search for it; if you don't have any idea what the file is called (for example, you want a program that searches for viruses on your machine and don't know that it is called scanv), you may have to try several searches using different strings before you find something that looks useful.

Another limitation of Archie is that not all sites on the Internet that have anonymous FTP servers participate in the Archie database. There may be a file that fits your specifications at a non-participating site, but Archie cannot find it because it is not in the database. Despite these limitations, however, Archie is a very useful tool for locating files to download through FTP.

N O T E As the World Wide Web has grown over the last few years, people have put together Web pages that link to large collections of software and collections of files related to particular topics. You can use one of the Web search engines discussed in Chapter 34, "Searching for Information on the Internet," to look for software and files in these collections. One of the advantages of Web search engines is that you can often search for topic words, not just file names, because the Web pages often have comments about the files and these comments are also searched. ■

Retrieving Information Using Gopher

Gopher is another information distribution service within the Internet. Sites on the Internet that distribute information through the Gopher system set up and run Gopher servers to enable people with Gopher clients to display and download files and directories. Gopher provides a menu-based interface to the resources available from the Gopher server, eliminating the need to enter cryptic commands to move between directories and retrieve files.

▶ **See** "What Is Gopher?" **p. 834**

N O T E You can use Archie through Gopher. Connect to **gopher.unl.edu** and select Archie from the Internet Resources menu for a simple interface to Archie. ■

The functionality of Gopher is similar to FTP, but Gopher can connect you to other Internet services in addition to displaying and retrieving directories and files. Displaying or downloading a file is as easy as selecting an item from a menu (see Fig. 1.7). This ease of use, plus the ability to put descriptive titles on the menu items, makes Gopher a much easier method of browsing files than simply using FTP.

FIG. 1.7
WSGopher is a client program that provides a GUI that you can use to connect to Gopher servers.

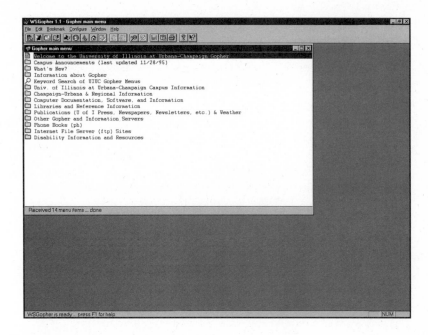

▶ **See** "Why Use Gopher?" **p. 834**

One of the big advantages of the Gopher system is that you can include menu items on a server that, when selected, move the user to other Gopher servers on the Internet. For example, one menu item on machine A's Gopher server may say `Connect to Machine B Gopher`. When that menu item is selected, your Gopher client connects to machine B's Gopher server, just as if you had connected to it when you ran your Gopher client.

What Is Gopherspace?

This ability to link Gopher sites together makes it easy to examine the files available at one site and then move on to other interesting Gopher sites. All Gopher servers are at some point interconnected—this network of Gopher servers is known as Gopherspace. When a new Gopher site becomes available on the Internet, the administrators send an e-mail message to the maintainers of the Gopher software (at the University of Minnesota) to have their sites included in the master list of all Gopher sites worldwide. Many organizations run Gopher servers: universities and colleges, companies, and government agencies all have information available through Gopher.

On the CD

The Gopher maintainers run a Gopher server (located at the address **gopher.tc.umn.edu**) that lists all the known Gopher servers and lets you connect to them. This gives you a good starting place to browse through all the Gopher servers and discover the wealth of information available on the Internet. Some of the top Gopher servers are included on the NetCD, but the main Gopher server at **gopher.tc.umn.edu** is the best place to begin exploring the information on Gopher because you can get to every Gopher server that exists from there.

Locating Files Using Veronica

With all the Gopher sites available, though, it may be hard to locate a site that carries the information and files you want. You probably want to search the Gopher sites for a document you want. A service, called Veronica, is available to do this.

▶ **See** "Searching Gopherspace with Veronica," **p. 851**

Just as Archie is a service that searches file names and directories on anonymous FTP servers, Veronica searches menu items on Gopher servers. To use Veronica, you have to be connected to a Gopher server that gives you access to a Veronica server. The Veronica database is built by scanning the Gopher menus on servers around the world, and can be searched by selecting Search Gopherspace using Veronica, which is found on the Other Gopher and Information Servers menu of the Gopher site **gopher.tc.umn.edu**.

Because Gopher menu items can be descriptive phrases (more than just file names), it can be easier to find information of interest through Veronica than it is through Archie. The entries in a Gopher menu can say something relevant about the contents of a file or directory (Topographical Maps, for example), rather than just listing the exact name of a file or directory. Veronica may find a file at an FTP site that Archie wouldn't because you can use Veronica to search for information on topics (maps, for example), rather than just searching for file names.

When Veronica has finished searching Gopherspace, it builds a Gopher menu that contains all of the items it has found to match your search. You can then examine those items by selecting them, just as you would from any Gopher menu.

Locating Documents Using WAIS

Whereas Gopher is a good system to use for exploring the files and systems available on the Internet, suppose you want to find all documents available on a particular subject. The *WAIS (Wide Area Information Server)* is a system that searches for your subject through documents on servers all over the world. WAIS (pronounced "ways") searches a set of databases that has been indexed with keywords, and returns addresses where you can locate documents that would be of interest to you.

The heart of the WAIS system is the use of client software running on your local computer that lets you ask for information in simple English. The client takes your question and sends it off to the WAIS server you select. The server takes your question and searches all the documents it knows for the information you want. If it finds documents that match your question, it returns indexes to these documents, which you can then use to download the documents and display them on your local system.

One of the key features of the WAIS system is the ability of a WAIS server to have indexes that actually point to other WAIS servers. A central site on the Internet maintains indexes to all known WAIS servers on the Internet; you can use this central site as a starting point for your searches. For example, say you want to find out all the times that President Clinton mentioned the city of Atlanta, Georgia, in his speeches.

You can set your search database to be directory-of-servers, which is located on the machine **quake.think.com**. As a quick example of how WAIS works, using this database, you search for President Clinton, and it returns (among others) a database resource marked "clinton-speeches." You can now use this database to search for Atlanta Georgia. This search returns some number of documents, and the first ones are the ones that best match your question. These speeches, when retrieved, are the ones that mention Atlanta, Georgia.

▶ **See** "Using WinWAIS," **p. 860**

Interactive Internet Communications

In the early days of the Internet, communication speeds were relatively slow, compared to today's modem speeds. This limited how information was exchanged to physically moving files from one computer to another. With today's lightning fast communications speeds, real-time transfer of audio data is very practical, and real-time video is quickly becoming practical. These two capabilities open the door to many types of applications that benefit from live communications.

▶ **See** "The Basics of IRC," **p. 898**

Internet Relay Chat

Internet Relay Chat (IRC) is a service that was originally developed, as a replacement for the UNIX talk program in the late 1980s. IRC enables multiple people to "talk" simultaneously (by typing, of course). Like many other Internet services, IRC is a client/server application. People who want to talk with each other must be running an IRC client (see Fig. 1.8), and they must connect to an IRC server. Once on the server, they select the channel on which they want to talk (channels often are named for the topic they discuss, if they restrict themselves to a particular topic). For example, the hot-tub channel is supposed to simulate conversations that would occur between occupants of a hot tub.

When you are involved in an IRC channel, you can type to the other participants from your terminal while you see what others are typing on theirs. This is an interesting way of having a real-time conference, but the speed of communication is rather slow, since typing something is much slower than speaking. It does, however, allow everyone to participate equally, preventing any one person from taking over the conversation by "shouting" or "talking" continually.

Live Video Conferencing

As research into expanding the amount of information that can be carried on our data highways continues, people are developing hardware and programs that will allow live video to be broadcast from one computer to another. At this time, good quality live video is not commonplace because of the communication speeds needed to transfer the huge amount of information involved. But as the bandwidth increases, it should be possible to hold remote meetings and attend classes electronically.

▶ **See** "Video Conferencing on the Net," **p. 955**

FIG. 1.8

mIRC lets you chat in real-time with people around the world.

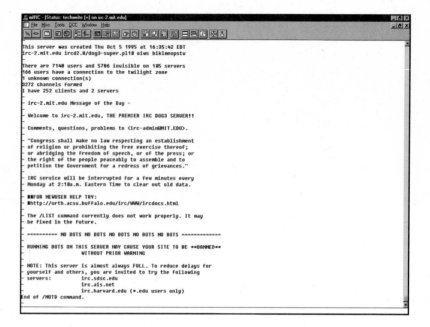

Interactive Games

There are a number of servers on the Net that allow you to participate live in multi-player games. Games known as MUDs, MOOs, and MUSHes have been developed over the last few years to allow people from all over the world to have some live recreational interaction. In addition, the designers of a number of the popular graphical games developed for PCs in the last few years are planning to add Internet access abilities to the games so that these commercial games can be played interactively over the Net.

▶ **See** "The Beginnings of Internet Games," **p. 970**

N O T E   Microsoft has recently announced a new technology called DirectPlay. DirectPlay lets game designers create action packed, multiplayer games for the Internet. ▪

Live Voice

Carrying audio over the Internet is a lot simpler than carrying video, since there isn't as much information involved. In the past year or so, several services have sprung up that let Internet users have live conversations.

▶ **See** "Using the Internet as a (Phone,)" **p. 928**

Phone by Net

When real-time audio became practical on the Net, someone figured out that it would be just as easy (and a lot cheaper) to talk to someone using the Internet instead of your long distance phone company. Although it's not quite the same as talking to someone on the phone, there are a lot of advantages to conversing over the Internet.

Connecting to Host Resources Using Telnet

Just as a host can run an FTP server to allow you to transfer files, a computer on the Internet can be set up to run any program automatically when you connect to that computer. There are numerous hosts providing this type of service (also called host resources) on the Internet with information about everything from agriculture to space research. Some of these host resources are similar to bulletin board systems, with which you may be familiar. But instead of dialing into one of these systems using a telephone line and modem, you can connect to these systems over the Internet using a program called Telnet. Other host resources are programs that run automatically when Telnet connects to the host. For example, some host resources let you get weather forecasts, find out team schedules for different sports, or play a game of chess.

▶ **See** "What Is Telnet?" **p. 792**

 T I P Windows 95 comes with a Telnet application.

Although Telnet does let you access host resources quickly, the primary use of Telnet is much more basic. Telnet is a method used to connect two computers together; it provides a terminal connection to the remote machine. This connection enables you to type commands to the remote machine, just as if you had a terminal hooked into it. You are probably already familiar with the idea of a terminal program; if you have a modem connected to a personal computer that you use to dial into computer systems, you use a terminal program to talk to the modem and remote system.

Just as you use a local FTP program to connect to an FTP server on another machine on the Internet, you use a Telnet program on your local machine to talk to the Telnet server on another machine anywhere on the Internet. The main difference between FTP and Telnet is that when you connect to the remote machine with FTP, the FTP server only lets you do things related to transferring files. When you connect to a machine using Telnet, what you see really depends on what the host resource provides. You may see a bulletin board menu system, or a simple command-line interface, or you may just receive some output without typing anything. It all depends on what the particular resource provides.

Commercial Online Services

Although not originally part of the Internet, the commercial online services have all connected to the Internet in the past two years. Most online services now provide a real IP connection to the Internet. They don't always provide a convenient news or mail server, however, so you still have to use the software provided by the service for news and e-mail.

Microsoft now has its own online service, Microsoft Network (MSN). MSN has gone through some significant changes since it was introduced with Windows 95. The strategy is to make MSN more of an Internet content provider rather than a self-contained online service. MSN's evolution illustrates Microsoft's belief that control of the Internet's content is vital to their success. ●

Your Cyber Rights and Responsibilities: Law and Etiquette

by Ralph Losey

You have important legal rights and responsibilities in cyberspace, just like anywhere else. Contrary to popular opinion, the Internet is not some kind of Wild West frontier beyond the laws of any country. There is no place in cyberspace—or anywhere else for that matter—where laws somehow magically end.

Rest assured—or if you're planning criminal activities on the Internet, be worried—the long arm of the law does stretch into cyberspace. Just about everyone connecting to the Internet from a computer located in the United States is subject to U.S. law. These laws apply throughout the U.S., even if you are sitting at your keyboard and talking to someone in Timbuktu.

Foreign citizens outside the U.S. are subject to the laws of their own country. (That's another story that we won't get into.)

For the most part, the application of U.S. laws to our space should be cause for comfort, not alarm. Under U.S. law, we enjoy legal rights and freedoms that people in many other countries only dream about. The laws of the Internet are not as complicated as you might think;

Free speech and association on the Internet
Your rights and responsibilities on the Internet.

The slander and libel limitation
Your protection from "flames" that burn.

The important distinction between Internet publisher and distributor
Should a computer network be treated as an information distributor or an information publisher?

Obscenity limitations
The risks of selling porn on the Net.

Privacy, copyright, and fair trade on the Internet
Learn your rights and responsibilities.

Protect yourself from crime on the Internet
See a state-by-state list of the computer crime laws now in effect across the country. New laws can also be found on the Net.

they are the same laws that apply to the rest of your life. You are probably already familiar with most of them.

So relax, enjoy your time in space; you have rights here, just like anywhere else. Outside of cyberspace, you don't break the law without knowing it (except perhaps that time you spit on the sidewalk!). You are as unlikely to break the law by mistake on the Internet as you are in real life.

With a few spitting-on-the-sidewalk type exceptions that I'll point out to you, the commonsense notions of right and wrong, legal and illegal, apply on the Internet just like anywhere else.

Follow these and the basic legal principles, tips, and pointers in this chapter and you can stay within the law and observe Netiquette. ■

Law on the Internet

With a few important exceptions that I'll spell out later, you have the right to say and write just about anything you want on the Internet. You also have the right to go anywhere on the Net and join almost any group that you want.

Most of these rights are commonplace and assumed in our country, and are the same kind of rights you enjoy when not on the computer. These rights all spring from the First Amendment to the United States Constitution.

 For the full text of our Constitution, see my Web site at **http://seamless.com/rcl/const.html**.

 For a good listing of over 1,000 law-related Web sites on the Internet, see the Seamless Web site's directory of links at **http://seamless.com/road.html**. For a good example of a law-related Web site, take a look at mine at **http:/seamless.com/rcl**.

First Amendment

Thanks to the First Amendment and a strong legal culture in the United States, you now have more rights and personal liberties than at any time in written history. Under the First Amendment's right of free speech, you can believe and think whatever you want, and you can publicly say or write just about anything.

Free speech means freedom of expression in any form—speech, writings, art, music, dance, movies, and so on. Some governmental limitations on free expression are permitted, but they are on the far fringes where your speech constitutes fighting words, plots a crime, incites a riot, or is "obscene."

We'll discuss some of these limitations as applied to the Internet later. But before we get to the few exceptions to free speech, it helps to understand the strength and importance of the general rule guaranteeing your free speech. As a U.S. citizen on the Internet, you are free to express yourself in just about any way you want without fear of government retaliation.

For over two centuries, the First Amendment has fulfilled its original purpose to give the press and all citizens the freedom to report abuses of power by public officials, to hear news critical of the government, and to exchange information and opinions without interference by government officials.

In our culture, the lack of government censorship has always been considered vital to our pursuit of happiness and our search for truth, justice, and knowledge. We have always believed that freedom from governmental supervision makes possible and facilitates our search for self fulfillment through art, religion, literature, and music, as well as public debate.

Under the First Amendment, you are also guaranteed the right to associate with anyone you please, to peacefully assemble in public groups, and to form and belong to any groups that you want.

On the Internet this means you can freely assemble in online communities without government interference. Both of the fundamental First Amendment liberties of free speech and free association come into play every day to protect your activities on the Internet.

 For a good introduction to these issues, check out the First Amendment Cyber-Tribune at **http://w3.trib.com/FACT/**.

Within the last 75 years, the First Amendment has been the subject of tens of thousands of lawsuits, and judges and lawyers have written hundreds of thousands of pages of legal opinions about it. But the First Amendment of the United States Constitution itself is short:

> Congress shall make no law respecting an establishment of religion, or prohibiting the free exercise thereof; or abridging the freedom of speech, or of the press, or the right of the people peaceably to assemble, and to petition the Government for a redress of grievance.

Since World War I and especially since around 1960, the courts have created a vast body of written case law that interprets and applies these few words. The appellate decisions interpreting the Constitution make up the legal precedent that courts today, even the Supreme Court, are obliged to follow.

There are literally tens of thousands of U.S. Supreme Court and other lower court cases pertaining to the First Amendment and other provisions of the Constitution.

 To find some of the important First Amendment cases online, see **http://www.law.cornell.edu/topics/first_amendment.html**. Check out the collection put together by the Congressional cyber-librarians at **http://www.pls.com:8001/his/93.htm**.

The case law interpreting the First Amendment has slowly evolved so that today it provides us with a host of rights and liberties. This legal precedent now serves as a bulwark of protection from misguided legislatures and judges, demagogues, and would-be despots of all persuasions. That is because statutes enacted by any legislature, even the U.S. Congress and Senate, which violate the Constitution, are illegal, void, and can be declared invalid and unenforceable by the courts.

 TIP If you're thinking right about now that all lawyers take themselves and the law too seriously, see the Law Jokes Web site at **http://gnn.com/gnn/bus/nolo/jokes.html**.

As we will see, a bill enacted by Congress in February 1996, the "Computer Decency Act," which tried to regulate speech on the Internet, was recently struck down by the courts as unconstitutional. This is a normal and natural process in our country. Technologies change, but human nature remains the same.

New technologies create new areas of culture, and someone in government tries to chill the exercise of First Amendment rights there. The process has gone on for centuries. Time and again the law, lawyers, judges, and individual citizens rise to the challenge, and foil the attempts of a few misguided government officials.

First the courts adapted to the new technologies of the railroads and telegraphs, then the automobiles and telephones, then radio, television, and videotape recorders. Now the challenge is from computers and the Internet. Society, the courts, and the law will once again adapt to the new technologies. It is critically important to us, and to all future generations, that the legal adaptations continue our traditions of freedom and human rights.

 TIP For a good collection of human-rights-related Web sites, see **http://www.iwc.com/entropy/marks/hr.html**.

A Few Commonsense Limitations on Free Speech

The right to free expression on the Internet, like anywhere else, is subject to some restrictions and commonsense guidelines. For instance, this right doesn't protect perjury, a threat, or a fraud. You are always at risk if you lie or if you incite people to riot or criminal activities.

For instance, there is the famous example given by Supreme Court Justice Oliver Wendell Holmes of the person who knowingly lies and shouts, "FIRE!" in a crowded theater. If a panic ensues and people are hurt, that person can be arrested.

Depending on how badly people are hurt by the panic, the person is subject to various degrees of criminal and civil liability. However, if that person shouted an obscenity in the same crowded room, he might get everyone annoyed and some quite angry, but the person shouldn't be arrested for the speech alone.

The government can't punish a speaker for inflammatory speech unless it can show that the speech "is directed to inciting or producing imminent lawless action, and is likely to incite or produce such action." This is an almost impossible legal standard for the government prosecutors to satisfy.

For that reason, your speech, no matter how offensive or inflammatory, is hard for the government to prohibit. You are pretty much free to say what you want and express whatever crazy ideas you may have, so long as you are not plotting a crime or selling pornography (an important exception for the Internet that we'll get into later).

In spite of the clear laws, there always seem to be a few public officials around who want to try and punish speech that is offensive to voters.

 TIP For a good Web site resource on censorship, see **http://fileroom.aaup.uic.edu/FileRoom/ documents/TofCont.html**.

For instance, a University of Michigan student recently posted a sick story on the Internet newsgroup alt.sex.stories, which graphically described torture, rape, and murder. Nothing that unusual so far, but this guy went one step further and gave the fictional victim the real name of one of his female classmates.

Then he went still further and started e-mailing messages to a friend that the fantasies no longer did the trick for him and now he wanted to do it for real. They started exchanging e-mail about the possibility of attacking 13- and 14-year old girls in his neighborhood.

They were turned in, and the government arrested the student with the sick story. He spent 29 days in jail as a danger to the community while undergoing psychological evaluation. The evaluation showed there was no evidence that he was a danger to himself or the community.

The court threw out the indictment and questioned the prosecutor's good judgment in bringing the case in the first place. The violent fantasies of the student were simply too far removed from an imminent lawless action to justify his arrest.

Amazingly, the government again indicted the student, this time for a different violation: transmitting a threat in interstate commerce. Again the court threw it out, based on the First Amendment, with harsh words for the prosecutor for so unwisely pursuing what the judge thought was a school disciplinary matter. (The student was expelled from school.) For the full, convoluted story of this case, see **http://www.eff.org/pub/Legal/Cases/ Baker_UMich_case/**).

The First Amendment prevents all governments—federal, state, and local—and the police and prosecutors of these governments from prohibiting or restraining your speech based on its content. The fact that your speech offends people, or even disrupts civil order and disturbs the peace, doesn't mean the speaker can be restrained by the government.

You can't punish a speaker because listeners become violent. Indeed, in one famous U.S. Supreme Court case, Terminiello v. Chicago in 1949, the Court noted that free speech may best serve its purpose when it "induces a condition of unrest, creates dissatisfaction with conditions as they are, or even stirs people to anger."

N O T E Remember that the First Amendment only prohibits governmental restraints. Your speech may still be legally restrained by nongovernmental sources, such as in a commercial setting by contract. For example, a computer network can require you to agree to its rules of censorship as a condition of membership. You don't have to agree, of course, and you can take your business elsewhere. But, if the agreement requires you to abide by certain speech restrictions, such as no profanities, then the network provider can legally censor your messages that violate the agreement. The provider can even terminate your membership or otherwise exercise its rights under the subscription agreement if you break it. There are certain legal risks to the network provider in trying to control the content, which we will get into later, but it has the legal right to try and do so.

Although you can pretty much say what you want on the Internet, even if it's unpopular or outrageous, there is still need for some commonsense restraints and courtesy. The basic moral persuasions, albeit not legal rules, that normally limit what you can or should say in the real world, apply with equal force on the Internet. Common mutual respect, human decency, and politeness are as needed on the Internet as anywhere else.

 T I P Familiarize yourself with Netiquette and don't do things in cyberspace that you wouldn't do in person. For a good list of Netiquette rules, see **http://www.in.on.ca/tutorial/netiquette.html**.

The Slander and Libel Limitation

Although there is no good Internet equivalent to inciting cyberpanic by shouting, "FIRE" in a theater, typing **VIRUS** in all caps in a crowded chat room might alarm a few of the knobbiest. Still, even if it results in an immediate Net split in which everyone leaves a chat room, no one's life would be endangered to justify making it illegal and it's unlikely that even the most uptight prosecutor could be persuaded to indict the villain.

But, before you go around shouting, "VIRUS" because it's the kind of speech that can't be outlawed, remember that you could still be subject to civil lawsuits and damages for your loud lie. For example, if you lied and said a sysop or Webmaster had files in his cyberspace with lots of nasty viruses and worms, that could be libelous. If people believed you, it could damage a good reputation or hurt someone's business.

If you write lies about a person or his or her business, that's *libel*; if you say it, it's *slander*. (Lies about a business are called *trade libel*.) If the libel damages the business—for instance, if people stop buying that business's software for fear of viruses—you could be sued and forced to pay the damages such as the lost profits from lost sales. The law protects the truth, but not a lie.

N O T E If you write, say, in a mailing list or chat room, that another person is a software thief or her computer files are contaminated with viruses, and it's true, then it's protected free speech. It's only libel or slander if it's not true.

You can call someone a crook, if it's true. But, you'd better be prepared to prove the truth of your assertions in court if the person sues you! If it's not true, then you are at risk—your flame outburst could end up busting you financially. ■

A major exception to this libel rule involves public figures who can be either elected officials or celebrities. For libel of a person who is a public figure such as an elected government official like the President, it has to be proven that the disparaging remarks were false and were made with malice or a reckless disregard for the truth. Sometimes the public figure might be able to prove that the statement was false—for instance, prove that she is not a crook. But, malice or recklessness are very hard to prove.

If, for instance, you called your mayor a cocaine user and she responded by suing you for libel, the mayor would not only have to prove that it was not true but she would have to prove that you made the statement out of malice or with reckless disregard for whether it was true or not.

The law requires public figures to put up with a lot of verbal abuse. But without this rule, a publisher could be held liable for the mere reporting of false facts about public officials. The press would be chilled from reporting the news for fear of being swamped by libel suits by news figures upset by unfavorable stories.

This happened in the past and led The Supreme Court to make this rule in the famous case of *The New York Times* v. Sullivan (**http://www.eff.org/pub/Legal/Cases/ nytvsullivanlibelpubfigures.notes**).

 TIP For more on libel, public figures, and the Net, see **http://www.eff.org/pub/Legal/**.

Are Computer Networks Information Distributors or Publishers?

The question of libel and flaming in cyberspace has already hit the courts. For instance, Cubby, Inc. v. CompuServe, Inc., 776 F.Supp. 135 (S.D.N.Y. 1991) involved a flame in the Journalism forum on CompuServe by a cyberpublication called Rumorville. (For a complete copy of the court's opinion, see my Web site at **http://seamless.com/rcl/compu.html**.)

Cubby v. CompuServe is a New York federal district court case. In the context of a libel dispute, this case raises a legal question that is very important to the Internet.

It's the question of whether a computer network should be treated as an information distributor or an information publisher. The Cubby v. CompuServe case shows how the consequences of this legal distinction can have far-reaching effects on our life in cyberspace.

The Rumorville publication on CompuServe provided daily cyberreports about broadcast journalism and journalists. Believe it or not, Rumorville had an electronic newsletter competitor somewhere else in cyberspace that also provided such reports called Skuttlebut.

Rumorville is alleged to have made defamatory remarks about Skuttlebut and Skuttlebut's owner. Rumorville supposedly said, among other things, that Skuttlebut was a "new startup scam" and its owner had been "bounced" from his last job in broadcast journalism.

Skuttlebut, under its corporate name of Cubby, Inc., then sued Rumorville, its individual proprietor, and also CompuServe, all for libel, trade libel, and unfair business practices. The fact that Skuttlebut also sued CompuServe is what makes this case so interesting.

CompuServe defended itself by saying that even if it was true that Rumorville illegally disparaged Skuttlebut, CompuServe could not be held liable for what went on in its forum as a matter of law because it neither knew nor had reason to know of the statements; it was just a distributor. Cubby argued to the contrary that CompuServe was a publisher and should be held responsible for what it published on its forums.

Under the law, a person who publishes, or who repeats or otherwise republishes defamatory statements is subject to liability as if he had originally said it. Cubby also argued that the forum leader was a CompuServe agent and so CompuServe was vicariously liable for the actions of its agent.

The court agreed with CompuServe and held that it was acting as a vendor or distributor of information/speech, not a publisher, and that the forum leaders were not CompuServe agents.

A publisher such as a newspaper is responsible for what it publishes. If the contents of a story in a newspaper are libelous, the publisher can be found liable along with the author.

On the other hand, information vendors, such as bookstores, newsstands, or libraries, have long been protected from liability for defamation in the materials they distribute unless they knew or had reason to know of the defamation. They are considered to be passive conduits of information and so are screened from liability unless they are somehow at fault.

Any alternative would be disastrous. In the words of the Supreme Court in Auvil v. CBS 60 Minutes, it would force distributors to set up

> ...full time editorial boards...throughout the country which possess sufficient knowledge, legal acumen and access to experts to continually monitor incoming... (materials) ...at every turn. That is not realistic. More than unrealistic in economic terms, it is difficult to imagine a scenario more chilling on the media's right of expression and the public's right to know.

CompuServe Decision

Guided by such Supreme Court decisions, the federal trial judge who decided the CompuServe case considered the difference between publishers and distributors. His ruling is now important legal precedent for the Internet. Read for yourself what the judge had to say:

> CompuServe's CIS product is essentially an electronic, for-profit library that carries a vast number of publications and collects usage and membership fees from its subscribers in return for access to the publications.

> CompuServe and companies like it are at the forefront of the information industry revolution....While CompuServe may decline to carry a given publication altogether, in reality,

once it does decide to carry a publication, it will have little or no editorial control over that publication's contents....

CompuServe has no more editorial control over such a publication than does a public library, bookstore, or newsstand, and it would be no more feasible for CompuServe to examine every publication it carries for potentially defamatory statements than it would be for any other distributor to do so.

...Obviously, the national distributor of hundreds of periodicals has no duty to monitor each issue of every periodical it distributes. Such a rule would be an impermissible burden on the First Amendment....

Technology is rapidly transforming the information industry. A computerized database is the functional equivalent of a more traditional news vendor, and the inconsistent application of a lower standard of liability to an electronic news distributor such as CompuServe than that which is applied to a public library, bookstore, or newsstand would impose an undue burden on the free flow of information.

Given the relevant First Amendment considerations, the appropriate standard of liability to be applied to CompuServe is whether it knew or had reason to know of the allegedly defamatory Rumorville statements.

The court went on to hold that CompuServe neither knew nor had reason to know of the statements on its forums, and so granted a summary judgment in CompuServe's favor on all counts. The case went on between Rumorville and Skuttlebut, but nobody much cares about that petty dispute!

We can hope that the Cubby v. CompuServe case will be followed by other courts around the country and that computer networks will be classified for First Amendment purposes as distributors, not publishers.

But, in a case involving a different network, Prodigy, at least one court has already gone the other way and treated a network as a publisher. (Stratton Oakmont, Inc. v. Prodigy Services Company, a Partnership of IBM Corp. and Sears-Roebuck & Co.)

A complete copy of the court's decision can be found on my Web site at **http://seamless. com/rcl/prodigy.html**. The New York state court judge in the Prodigy case was well aware of the CompuServe and CBS *60 Minutes* decisions. In fact, he quoted extensively from both of these cases and used them to support his decision. The judge did so by distinguishing the facts of these different cases.

Stratton Oakmont v. Prodigy involves an alleged libelous statement made by an anonymous user in the Money Talks forum on Prodigy. The unknown cyberposter said, among other things, that Stratton Oakmont, a securities investment banking firm, was a "cult of brokers who either lie for a living or get fired" and that the owner was a "soon to be proven criminal."

Stratton Oakmont then sued Prodigy and John Doe, the unknown villain, for libel, claiming the remarks were untrue, causing severe damages. Stratton claimed that Prodigy was a publisher and that the moderator of the Money Talk forum was Prodigy's agent. So far it sounds a lot like the CompuServe case, so why did the judge reach the opposite result?

The answer lies in Prodigy's own statements to the public and the manner in which it tried to run the network as a "family place" where all offensive material was screened out. The court considered such facts as Prodigy's advertising, its promulgation of "content guidelines" for all of its users, its use of a software screening program that could supposedly prescreen all bulletin board postings for offensive language, and its use of Board Leaders hired, among other things, to police its boards and delete offensive speech.

Prodigy protested to the contrary that it had changed its policy or it didn't really mean what it said, and couldn't possibly police the more than 60,000 messages a day that go through its cyberspace. The judge was unconvinced. He found it was undisputed that Prodigy had set itself up as a private censor that could control the content of everything posted to its network.

That is essentially why he found Prodigy to be a publisher whereas CompuServe was not. It's kind of like "live by the sword, die by the sword."

Prodigy Decision

Here is what the judge said when he ruled against Prodigy and found it could be liable for libelous remarks posted in its forums (Stratton Oakmont v. Prodigy):

> Prodigy has uniquely arrogated to itself the role of determining what is proper for its members to post and read on its bulletin boards. Based on the foregoing, this Court is compelled to conclude that...Prodigy is a publisher rather than a distributor.

> Prodigy has virtually created an editorial staff of Board Leaders who have the ability to continually monitor incoming transmissions and in fact do spend time censoring notes. Indeed, it could be said that Prodigy's current system of automatic scanning, Guidelines, and Board Leaders may have a chilling effect on freedom of communication in cyberspace, and it appears that this chilling effect is exactly what Prodigy wants, but for the legal liability that attaches to such censorship.

> Let it be clear that this Court is in full agreement with Cubby v. CompuServe and Auvil v. CBS 60 Minutes. Computer bulletin boards should generally be regarded in the same context as bookstores, libraries, and network affiliates.

> (Citations omitted) It is Prodigy's own policies, technology and staffing decisions which have altered the scenario and mandated a finding that it is a publisher. Prodigy's conscious choice, to gain the benefits of editorial control, has opened it up to greater liability than CompuServe and other network providers that make no such choice.

The consequences of classifying Prodigy as a publisher, not a distributor, are to increase the network's exposure and liability for the contents of everything posted on its forums. Beyond Prodigy, it means that if any cybernetwork exercises editorial control over content or even if it just claims it is going to do so, then it may be held legally responsible for all the information supposedly under its control.

Obviously, this was a bad decision for Prodigy and network providers in general. After the ruling, which was not a final order, Prodigy settled with Stratton and Stratton dropped its case against Prodigy. The parties then went back to court together and in a very unusual legal maneuver, asked the judge to please withdraw his opinion! He refused, noting the importance of the legal precedent involved.

Many contend that unless the Prodigy opinion is reversed, or neutralized by legislation, it will have a chilling effect on the entire Internet and impose unrealistic duties on all networks. But, it might just have the opposite effect.

The networks may be forced by fear of liability to back off of all censorship. They may be forced to stop any monitoring or editorial control, and start acting more like the telephone company. If you are offended or libeled in such a free network, you'll have to turn to the particular publisher who libeled you. You won't be able to also sue the electronic library that brought you the offending material.

Part
I

Ch

2

If someone slanders you over the telephone, you would sue the slanderer. You wouldn't even think of suing the telephone company. Networks that try to go the other way and promise clean, inoffensive Disney-esque content as Prodigy once did will have to act with such strong controls that its expenses and charges will go sky-high. Few users are likely to pay the price for such censored, clean networks.

Prodigy got itself into the current legal mess it is now in by holding itself out to the public as a controller of the content of its network. The CompuServe and Prodigy cases read together provide a clear message to all information networks that they are better off not "knowing or having reason to know" the contents of the information in their cyberspace. If they do, they may be treated as the publishers, or republishers, of the information and be liable for what they publish.

Congress has recently enacted legislation to try and neutralize some of the burdensome effects of the Prodigy opinion. It is contained in the mammoth "Telecommunications Reform Bill." This legislation is infamous on the Internet for also including the "Communications Decency Act," which will be discussed later at length. Many overlook that the bill also included new statutes designed to shield networks like Prodigy from liability for libelous statements made by its users. It requires the courts to treat networks like distributors, not publishers, for purposes of libel only. It does not address other areas where a network might be liable for the actions of its users, such as copyright violations or trademark infringement. Although the new law lessens the problem, it still remains a thorny legal issue that the courts will have to address in the future.

Obscenity Limitations on Free Expression

It's legal to read or look at anything you want in the privacy of your own home, even the most obscene pornography anyone can imagine. But, some forms of adult sexual content are considered so offensive, so obscene, that even though it may be legal to possess it in your own home, it's illegal for anyone to sell it to you or to publicly display it.

Obscene expressions can be legally prohibited from public sale and exhibition. The trouble is, people can't agree on what obscene means.

The Supreme Court has struggled with this issue for years. One person's obscenity might be another's art. Tastes and personal values differ so much in this large and multicultural country. Some Supreme Court justices claimed to "know it when they see it," but they still couldn't put a workable legal definition on obscenity.

Finally, in 1974, the Supreme Court came up with a flexible, compromise-type of illegal obscenity test in Miller v. California. Materials are considered legally obscene and thus outside of First Amendment protection if:

- The average person applying contemporary community standards would find that the materials, taken as a whole, appeal to the prurient interest.
- The materials show or describe, in an obviously offensive way, sexual conduct specifically prohibited under state law.
- The work, taken as a whole, lacks serious literary, artistic, political, or scientific value.

Under this test, "community standards" became the key.

The Miller test allowed for cultural diversity, recognizing the fact that what is shocking and offensive to an ordinary person in a small town, might be ho hum in Las Vegas or New York City. The Miller community standards test avoided what the Supreme Court saw as the evil of the "absolutism of imposed uniformity," which would strangle the diversity of different attitudes and tastes of people in different communities.

Under this interpretation of the First Amendment, a movie can be legally sold and displayed in one community, but banned and illegal as pornography in another. The Supreme Court dodged the impossible question of "What is obscenity?" by letting the local communities decide, subject of course to certain general parameters.

Further, the Court has consistently held that the private possession and viewing of obscene materials remain protected by the First Amendment, no matter where you live.

Under the Miller test of pornography, if you live in that proverbial conservative small town, you might not be able to buy the particularly dirty book you want in any adult bookstore in your town. But, you can still travel to the big city, buy the book there, and then bring it home and secretly look at it without fear of arrest and imprisonment.

A compromise was reached that seemed to work. Then along came the Internet and threw the whole question of "community" into doubt.

NOTE   Many of the places you visit on the Internet really have no physical location. Where is a newsgroup located, a Web site, a discussion group, a chat room? Is it the particular geographical locale in which the computer temporarily hosting the cyber connections is located? What if there are several such host computers located in different communities? Alternatively, is it the local community of each individual participant in the online community? If so, how can that possibly work when most online communities now have members from all over the place, from both the big city and the small town?

The participants in most electronic groups on the Internet are probably from all over the world, not just the U.S. So, what community standards should govern the virtual communities of the Internet? They simply don't follow the normal limitations of space and time. When you log on to the Internet, you log on to a new kind of space, a computer space that really has no geographical location. ▪

The creation of virtual communities raises the next big obscenity legal issue of our times. It is just now starting to hit the courts and it will probably take years before the issue is settled. The Miller test definitely has to be rethought because the geographically based community standards don't apply to transmissions over a global network.

Today, computer networks allow the formation of virtual communities globally, without any significant impact on local, territorial communities. Eventually the law will catch up with the new technologies and cyberculture.

The courts will begin to recognize virtual communities as having their own independent existence, their own rights to define what is and is not acceptable to the community of computer users who voluntarily choose to come together in cyberspace. The First Amendment right to free association demands this.

But to a judge and prosecutor who have never used a computer, much less logged on to the Internet, the notion of virtual communities must seem like "pie in the sky" gibberish. The first case to apply the Miller community test in cyberspace seems to have run into just this kind of techno-gap problem.

U.S. v. Robert and Carleen Thomas

The case of U.S. v. Robert and Carleen Thomas shows just how messed up things can get in the law when police and judges first try to deal with new technologies they don't understand. Mr. and Mrs. Thomas, residents of San Francisco, were indicted by a federal grand jury in Memphis, Tennessee (a place they had never even visited), for transporting obscene materials over the Internet.

In the words of the government press report that announced their arrest in San Francisco on February 3, 1994: "The Thomases operated a computer bulletin board service specializing in pornographic material enabling other computer users throughout the country to receive pornographic material via their computer."

They were subsequently found guilty by a jury in Memphis, and convicted of 11 counts of transmitting obscenity through interstate phone lines via their bulletin board. Each count carries up to five years in prison and a $250,000 fine.

The decision was affirmed on appeal, and a second appeal is now pending before the U.S. Supreme Court. The high court is expected to hear this case and have the final word on it. Watch for this opinion as it could have a big impact on the availability of "adult materials" on the Net.

A full copy of the decision of the first appellate court is on my web at **http://seamless.com/rcl/thomas.html**.

Most commentators criticize this appellate court opinion as being based on several fallacious assumptions. The Court assumed the Thomases should have known where each of their subscribers was physically located, whether these communities would find each computer file downloaded by these subscribers to be pornographic, and, if so, should have been able to prevent them from doing so. (For more commentary and analysis of the decision, see **http:// www.eff.org/pub/Legal/Cases/AABBS_Thomases_Memphis/**).

The facts of the case are important to understand the potential negative consequences to the Internet of this decision and why many legal experts expect (hope) the Supreme Court will reverse it on appeal.

The saga began when a postal inspector in Tennessee, acting on the complaint of an unknown computer user in western Tennessee, logged on to the Thomases' "adult only" bulletin board. The Thomases ran their BBS from a computer in their home in San Francisco. The BBS had a sign-on warning that it contained adult materials and you needed a password to access it. The password was only issued to adults after application and payment of a modest membership fee.

The postal inspector applied for membership under a fake name, paid his fee, and began his detailed inspection of the in-excess-of 20,000 GIFs and other images on the BBS. Our tireless government worker then selected the worst, kinkiest junk he could find on the board and downloaded it onto his computer in Memphis.

The inspector had caused the Thomases to commit a crime in Tennessee without their even knowing about it! He also ordered the nastiest videos he could find and had them sent to him in the mail. Another crime committed by the Thomases.

N O T E I've read some of the original materials in the court file. The postal inspector's search warrant affidavit includes a description of the stuff he selected, all of which he carefully viewed, of course.

I couldn't even finish reading the descriptions! Bestiality, rape, torture—perverse, vile, and sick by most people's standards.

Make no mistake about it, the board had some very hard-core stuff on it, and apparently the Thomases were making a lot of money off this junk. I can't help but think this influenced the trial and appellate judges in Tennessee who were assigned to decide this case. ■

The Thomases knew very well what was on their board. Their name was on every item, every GIF. They even answered some of the "undercover" postal inspector's questions about the junk. Apparently there is a market for this, and they made money on the downloads and video sales.

Based on the postal inspector's descriptions of some of the videos he ordered, it's easy to understand how a jury in western Tennessee would decide it was all pornography, even the computer GIFs. The question is, should the standards and values of a jury in western Tennessee be imposed on the rest of the country?

Should the local standards of the most conservative communities in the country control and decide what everyone else in cyberspace is allowed to see? Should we force all virtual communities to limit their speech to conform to the most restrictive communities in the physical world?

Back to the facts. Even though the Thomases had never advertised in Tennessee, had no contacts with the state whatsoever, and it was the law enforcement officer in Tennessee, not the Thomases, who took all the actions to gain access to the materials and be transported to Tennessee, the Thomases woke up to a knock on their door one day to find themselves under arrest for an indictment in Tennessee.

The federal officers had a search warrant and they seized all of the Thomases' computers and software, including the private messages of their 3,500 BBS members. Even their backup tapes were taken.

This was not the first time police had seized the Thomases' equipment and stopped their BBS. In 1992, all the Thomases' computer equipment was seized by the San Jose Police Department. After inspecting all of the materials on their BBS, the police returned the equipment and did not press charges.

The police found no adult or child pornography, and determined that the materials were not pornographic by the standards of their community—the San Francisco Bay area. Similar materials could be found in hundreds of adult bookstores throughout that community.

N O T E After the arrest and seizure by federal agents from Tennessee, the Thomases were released on bail, but it took them months to get all their computer equipment back. An excerpt from the motion filed by the Thomases' attorney in federal court in San Francisco to try and force the return of their computer equipment gives some flavor as to what this case is about:

It is hard to determine the reasons the Western District of Tennessee has reached out in an attempt to impose its standards on the Northern District of California. Perhaps it is the simple desire to obtain tens of thousands of dollars' worth of computer equipment. Had it applied for a warrant to search an adult book store in San Francisco, it would have been laughed out of court.

Is an electronic version of an adult book store that different? ▪

The Thomases were later tried and convicted in Memphis. As mentioned, it was affirmed on appeal, but there is a second appeal now pending before the Supreme Court.

The conviction and affirmance have outraged many in the Internet community. They are concerned that this decision may allow one local geographic community to dictate the standards for the entire cybercommunity.

This is just the kind of "absolutism of imposed uniformity" that the Miller case was designed to avoid. The Thomas decision allows censorship even though adults could easily have avoided the unwanted materials, and prevented their children from accessing them.

It will be interesting to see what the Supreme Court does. You'll no doubt be reading about this case on the Internet.

Child Pornography Limitations

We all want to try to protect our children from unwanted influences on the Net. The question is how to go about doing that without infringing on everyone's First Amendment rights.

To begin with, the First Amendment does not protect child pornography or child pornographers. That is not the question. As a society, we have already decided that it is a crime, and we have many laws against it. Unlike obscene materials, the mere possession of child pornography may be a crime, even in the privacy of a home.

Under federal law, child pornography is any "visual material" that depicts a child either engaging in explicit sexual acts or posing in a "lewd and lascivious" manner, when the manufacture of such material involves the actual use of a real child (18 U.S.C. '2251, et seq.; Sexual Exploitation and Other Abuse of Children Act).

This is material that is illegal regardless of whether it is obscene. That means you don't have to ask any questions about "community standards."

N O T E Child pornography laws are really completely separate from adult obscenity laws. Obscenity laws are aimed at forbidding expression. They assume that some things are socially harmful by virtue of being expressed or shown.

Child pornography laws, in contrast, are not aimed at "expression" at all. They are instead designed to try and protect children from abuse. They try to destroy a market for materials that cannot be produced without sexually abusing children.

In fact, if the child in a child-porn movie is a computer animation and no real child was used in the production, the movie would not violate the child pornography laws (although it would probably still violate the obscenity laws under most community standards).

Also, child pornography laws do not apply to any written works at all since they do not involve the use of children. They're aimed at videos and pictures, and designed to protect the innocent child actors and models.

We have other laws on the books, mostly state laws, that prohibit an adult from engaging in sex with a minor, exposing themselves, and so on. Sexual abuse and seduction of children have long been illegal in our country. Child pornographers and pedophiles who use the Net to try and lure children for their perverse crimes are being arrested every day under the existing laws.

For instance, in September 1995, the Justice Department in one fell swoop searched 125 homes across the country and arrested dozens of people, culminating a two-year investigation of child pornographers and pedophiles on America Online (AOL).

AOL had started the investigation when it discovered child pornography on its network and notified the FBI. Still, there are real dangers to children cruising unsupervised on the Net, just as there are real dangers to children left alone in their own neighborhoods. We would all like to make the world a safer place for our children.

The question is: Do we need additional laws directed at the Net to stop this problem? Many people think not, especially with the development of new software and other technologies that allow parents to keep adult areas of the Internet off limits to their children. For a description of some of this new technology, see the report to Senator Leahy at **http://www.cdt.org/iwg/ part2.html**.

Let the users police themselves, many say—the problem of children on the Net is a nonproblem that has been blown way out of proportion by a sensationalizing press, poor research, and vote-hunting politicians. (See the critique at **http://www2000.ogsm. vanderbilt.edu/cyberporn.debate.cgi**).

We'll address this question further when we consider the Communications Decency Act passed by Congress and quickly declared unconstitutional by the courts.

To Inspect or Not to Inspect?

Existing law already presents a troubling question for information providers on the Internet. What happens if someone posts a file to his or her BBS, Web site, or user group that contains either child pornography or obscene materials?

If you know about it and it's clearly illegal, the answer is easy. Get rid of it, fast. But, should you be on the lookout for it? Should you monitor and inspect the GIFs and other media uploaded onto your turf to keep it clean?

If you do monitor, how do you decide if it's obscene or not? How do you determine if a person shown nude or in a sex act is a minor (under 18) or not? Maybe it's better not to look at all?

As far as disparaging comments go and the possible liability for republishing libel, we've already seen that under current law (Prodigy), it's probably better not to know, not to inspect, not to act like an editor who prescreens publications.

You should have clearly posted policies and agreements that prohibit such speech, but at the same time you should announce to all users that you do not prescreen, edit, or in any other way act as a publisher. But, does that also hold true for child pornography or obscenity?

Do you say it's prohibited, will not be tolerated, and will be removed if found and brought to the attention of law enforcement? Then do you also say that no effort will be made to prescreen? Do you warn users to beware of illegal postings because you have not inspected the postings, and cannot do so or lose your legal status as a distributor?

This question is still very much in doubt, especially as applied to child pornography. My best guess right now is that it's probably better not to inspect and to warn every user of that. For if you do inspect, you may once again be found to be a republisher and held criminally liable for all the materials in your cyberspace.

Under criminal law, including criminal obscenity statutes, the government must prove "scienter" (essentially, "guilty knowledge" on the defendant's part) before a defendant can be found guilty. So, if the government can't prove beyond a reasonable doubt that a system operator (sysop) knew or should have known that there was obscene material on her system, the operator should not be found guilty of an obscenity crime.

But, if the sysop had a policy of inspection and missed one, or wrongly guessed if something was obscene or someone was under 18, then she might be found guilty under the "should have known" standard. If she did not have an inspection policy and clearly advised users of this fact, that it wasn't policed by her and they should proceed at their own risk, it would be much harder to prove "should have known."

The question of child pornography is harder because the mere possession may be a crime. If there is a child-porn GIF in a sysop's computer and she doesn't know it, the sysop might still be criminally guilty for possession alone.

Again, no one knows for sure now. We can hope that there would be no criminal liability for unknowing possession of child pornography because there would be no criminal intent, no scienter.

If a sysop is held criminally liable even though she didn't know or have reason to know, then all sysops will be forced to inspect, and to inspect carefully, or else shut down. The law can't go in that direction, at least not for long, without changing around a lot of other legal rules.

If fear of child pornography forces everyone to inspect, then under current law everyone will in turn be opened to civil liability under defamation and the like. There will be no more computer networks, everyone in cyberspace will be a publisher, like it or not. That would cause quite a negative First Amendment chill on the Net!

The legal situation is a little clearer when a sysop somehow knows that there is illegal material in his space, say, by accidental perusal or someone telling him. The sysop then has a duty to delete the obscenity or child pornography, and perhaps even the libel (especially if the sysop knows it to be libel).

The sysop may even then have the additional duty to suspend or revoke the privileges of the user who posted the materials. The severity of the sysop's response would depend on the seriousness of the offense.

If it's clearly child pornography, as in the AOL case, the sysop probably also has a duty to alert the police. If the sysop becomes aware of the illegal materials and does nothing about it, or responds inadequately, that may create the necessary scienter for criminal prosecution. So even if you don't inspect, if you happen to see it or are told about it, delete it and punish the poster.

CAUTION

As a final legal-type disclaimer, remember that all of cyberlaw is a murky area of very tricky legal waters where the only constant is change. By the time you read this, new laws may have been enacted or court cases decided, that change everything. This is especially true of obscenity and child pornography issues.

This book does not provide legal advice. When in doubt, consult an attorney. If you are a cybernetwork, a sysop, forum leader, newsgroup moderator, Webmaster, or an electronic publisher of any kind, you should have an attorney and ask her for legal advice on your particular situation.

Even if you are just a user who likes to post (upload) "adult materials" on the Internet, you should probably have the advice of an attorney, too, or else you may run the risk finding out later that you were a publisher of pornography and didn't even know it.

The uploading of files may constitute publication. Depending upon the community in which you live or the community in which the courts eventually decide applies to your cyberactivities, you may be surprised to discover that what you thought was cool and socially acceptable, your community finds obscene and criminal.

Part
I
Ch
2

Communications Decency Act

On February 1, 1996, Congress enacted the Communications Decency Act, "CDA" for short, and President Bill Clinton signed it into law. The CDA was part of the Telecommunications Reform Bill, which further deregulated the phone industry, and as mentioned, gave some protection from libel suits to network providers.

A copy of the CDA can be found on my Web site at **http://seamless.com/rcl/cda.html**. The full Telecommunications Reform Bill can be found at **http://www.senate.gov/~leahy/s652.html**.

The CDA purports to prohibit the use of "indecent" or "patently offensive" language or pictures in front of minors on the Net.

Pointers to extensive commentary and other information on the act can be found at **http://www.eff.org/pub/Legal/Cases/EFF_ACLU_v_DoJ/**.

Indecency is something far less than obscenity and includes such things as comedian George Carlin's "seven dirty words." Because no one knows what "pornography" is and it varies from community to community, the meaning of "indecent" or "patently offensive" is really a mystery.

By outlawing "indecency," Congress was basically trying to extend to the Internet the government regulation we now allow over television. But, the unique governmental rationale for broadcast television censorship by the FCC just does not apply to cyberspace.

The Internet is not a limited resource like television. There are millions of Webs on the Net, not just a few local television stations, and the Webs are not being broadcast into your home. You have to find them, call them up, and link up to them. For this and many other reasons, most commentators agree that the Internet should not be treated like television or regulated by the FCC. For a detailed discussion of these issues, see **http://www.cdt.org/iwg/IWGrept.html**.

The problems we've discussed with obscenity and child pornography for networks and information providers are magnified a million times when extended to indecent speech. For example, under this new law, if someone posts a note on your Web site with certain four-letter words or uploads a GIF that someone somewhere in the U.S. considers indecent and a kid looks at it, you could conceivably be held criminally liable, fined up to $50,000, or jailed for six months.

TIP For a list of adult Web sites that might be considered indecent and illegal by prosecutors if the courts allowed the CDA to be enforced, see http://thehugelist.com/malaise.html and go to the adult-only section. The warnings and disclaimer language, which attempt to comply with the CDA, is very interesting. For instance, if you're from a conservative state like Tennessee or Florida, you're not supposed to even enter this hot-list of adult sites. For a list of more mainstream sites that could be banned by the CDA, including such places as the Sistine Chapel and other museums wherein nude art can be found or such potentially offensive books online as The Adventures of Huckleberry Finn, see **http://www.eff.org/BlueRibbon/sites.html**.

The Internet community and companies with business interests connected with the Net such as Microsoft, Netscape, AOL, CompuServe, and the like, had all lobbied hard against the CDA. Alternative bills were introduced in Congress to try to protect children without threatening free speech.

A half-hearted opposition and protest against the proposed legislation had been organized on the Internet itself, led by the Electronic Frontier Foundation and others. See **http://www.eff.org/pub/Censorship/Exon_bill/**.

But, there was a complacency in the Internet community about the CDA. Few seemed to be very concerned about it. Everyone seemed overconfident and blindly pleased with themselves.

See, for instance, the Web site at **http://www.cdt.org/net_protest.html** that touts the "great success" in December 1995 of "net.citizens" in opposing the then proposed CDA legislation.

The CDA seemed so obviously unconstitutional that most believed Congress would never enact it. Even House Speaker Newt Gingrich went on record as saying the proposed legislation was probably unconstitutional.

This complacency was naive. It was an election year. A vote to protect children is a popular thing even if it violates the Constitution. Few in Congress understand the Internet, much less the potential negative impact of the CDA on free speech rights.

The first major test of the political clout of the Internet community by us so-called "net.citizens" proved to be a major disaster. The CDA passed by a huge majority in Congress, with both Republicans and Democrats voting and with little or no publicity in the media.

Most people didn't know that this bill was potentially devastating to the Internet. The burden then fell entirely to the courts to try to protect your rights to free speech in cyberspace.

The same day the CDA was signed into law by President Clinton, February 8, 1996, the ACLU (**http://www.aclu.org/**) sued the federal government (as represented by Janet Reno, head of the Justice Department) in federal court to challenge its constitutionality. Other suits were filed soon thereafter by numerous groups.

Individual net.citizens were even allowed to join in the cases as class plaintiffs over the Internet and over 40,000 people did so. The cases were all consolidated into one big lawsuit in Philadelphia: ACLU v. Reno, and assigned to a special three-judge federal panel.

The passage of the CDA finally awoke the Internet community. The complacency and indifference to the law and politics were replaced by shock and outrage. A Citizens Internet Empowerment Association was formed and a mass Internet protest was organized. See **http://www. cdt.org/ciec/**.

Part
I
Ch
2

Thousands of Webs changed their background color to black for 48 hours to publicize and protest the enactment of the CDA. Some Webs still have a black background for that reason. See, for instance, **http://www.surfwatch.com/surfwatch/censorship.html**.

A "blue ribbon" campaign to support free speech and oppose the CDA was started. See **http:// www.eff.org/blueribbon.html**. You will still see these blue ribbons all over the Web. For example, see **http://seamless.com/rcl/infolaw.html**.

The Internet community protested vigorously, albeit too late to do much good, because they realized how disruptive the CDA could be to the Internet. It could make the entire Internet a child-safe "happy Net" where all children could frolic unsupervised by their parents. A place where Big Brother would be in charge, censoring every Web site for what Big Brother considers offensive, a place where the young—supposedly ever so fragile techno-nerds—could never be offended or find inappropriate materials.

The CDA could, in effect, take the world's largest library and screen out or burn all of the books except for the ones in the children's department! Your right to say something on the Net that might be considered offensive would be threatened by the CDA. The proud American tradition of free expression would be in jeopardy.

It is at times like this that the importance of the First Amendment and constitutional government really strikes home. The idea of legislating morality on the Internet was too appealing for most politicians, especially in an election year. There was now no stopping them outside of the courtroom.

Fortunately, inherent in our constitutional form of government is the courts' ability to review and declare unconstitutional legislation to be null and void—to make a "law" you must obey on penalty of incarceration into a non-law that no one has to comply with.

This is exactly what has happened. On February 15, 1996, just a few days after the CDA's enactment, the court hearing the case issued a temporary restraining order (TRO) forbidding the federal government from enforcing the "indecency provisions" of the CDA. It did so even before hearing any evidence in the case because it appeared obvious that this portion of the law, at least, was unconstitutional.

This TRO was followed by an injunction against investigations of any CDA violations. The injunction was prompted by an FBI investigation of CompuServe's possible violation of the

CDA. The trial of this case was concluded in May 1996 before a special three-judge appellate panel.

All the testimony of witnesses and the arguments of lawyers in the trial can be found on the Internet, along with commentary, at several locations. See **http://www.aclu.org/issues/ cyber/trial.htm?146,116** or see **http://www.epic.org/free_speech/censorship/ lawsuit/**.

The judges decided the case on June 11, 1996, and issued their judgment holding that the CDA violated the First Amendment of the Constitution of the United States. A complete copy of this important 100-page opinion is found on my Web site at **http://seamless.rcl/ freespeech.html**. The court held that speech on the Internet is entitled to the highest degree of protection from censorship. The CDA's prohibition of indecent speech was held to be too vague and unnecessary. The court found that less restrictive means of protecting children were available, such as software screening programs. The court's lengthy decision also makes some very interesting factual findings about the Internet, how it works, and how it is different from all other types of communication. For instance, it finds that the Internet is more akin to tele- phone communication than to broadcasting. This finding may be followed by other courts. If so, it will help protect networks from liability as publishers held responsible for the content of everything written by its users.

ACLU v. Reno

Here is a some of what each of the three judges on the panel had to say when they ruled against the government and held the Communications Decency Act to be unconstitutional (ACLU v. Reno):

Judge Sloviter:

I believe that "indecent" and "patently offensive" are inherently vague, particularly in light of the government's inability to identify the relevant community by whose standards the material will be judged...

When Congress decided that material unsuitable for minors was available on the Internet, it could have chosen to assist and support the development of technology that would enable parents, schools, and libraries to screen such material from their end. It did not do so, and thus did not follow the example available in the print media where non-obscene but indecent and patently offensive books and magazines abound. Those responsible for minors under- take the primary obligation to prevent their exposure to such material. Instead, in the CDA Congress chose to place on the speakers the obligation of screening the material that would possibly offend some communities. Whether Congress' decision was a wise one is not at issue here. It was unquestionably a decision that placed the CDA in serious conflict with our most cherished protection—the right to choose the material to which we would have access.

Judge Buckwalter:

This statute, all parties agree, deals with protected speech, the preservation of which has been extolled by court after court in case after case as the keystone, the bulwark, the very heart of our democracy. What is more, the CDA attempts to regulate protected speech through criminal sanctions, thus implicating not only the First but also the Fifth Amendment of our Constitution. The concept of due process is every bit as important to our form of government as is free speech. If free speech is at the heart of our democracy, then surely due process is the very lifeblood of our body politic; for without it, democracy could not survive. Distilled to its essence, due process is, of course, nothing more and nothing less than fair play. If our citizens cannot rely on fair play in their relationship with their government, the stature of our government as a shining example of democracy would be greatly diminished. I believe that an exacting or strict scrutiny of a statute which attempts to criminalize protected speech requires a word by word look at that statute to be sure that it clearly sets forth as precisely as possible what constitutes a violation of the statute. The reason for such an examination is obvious. If the Government is going to intrude upon the sacred ground of the First Amendment and tell its citizens that their exercise of protected speech could land them in jail, the law imposing such a penalty must clearly define the prohibited speech not only for the potential offender but also for the potential enforcer.

Judge Dalzell:

Any content-based regulation of the Internet, no matter how benign the purpose, could burn the global village to roast the pig...

Cutting through the acronyms and argot that littered the hearing testimony, the Internet may fairly be regarded as a never-ending worldwide conversation. The Government may not, through the CDA, interrupt that conversation. As the most participatory form of mass speech yet developed, the Internet deserves the highest protection from governmental intrusion. True it is that many find some of the speech on the Internet to be offensive, and amid the din of cyberspace many hear discordant voices that they regard as indecent. The absence of governmental regulation of Internet content has unquestionably produced a kind of chaos, but as one of plaintiffs' experts put it with such resonance at the hearing:

'What achieved success was the very chaos that the Internet is. The strength of the Internet is that chaos.'

Just as the strength of the Internet is chaos, so the strength of our liberty depends upon the chaos and cacophony of the unfettered speech the First Amendment protects. For these reasons, I without hesitation hold that the CDA is unconstitutional on its face."

Because the CDA has been declared unconstitutional, the law is void. So, even though the CDA was "passed into law" by an overwhelming majority of Congress and the Senate, it is not now "law" because the court has determined that it violates the supreme law of our country, the Constitution.

This means that no one has to try to follow the CDA, and the government can't try to enforce it. It is as if the law were never enacted.

In our constitutional form of government, the judiciary has power over the legislative and executive branches of government as necessary to protect the people from laws that violate the Constitution. If the court decides that a law, such as the CDA, violates our Constitution, then that "law" is not a law, because our Constitution is supreme.

So, for the moment, the CDA is not a valid law because a panel of three federal judges has decided the CDA violates the Constitution. But, the danger of the CDA to the Internet is not over. The government has appealed to the Supreme Court. The Supreme Court will have the last word on the subject, unless Congress repeals the act.

(Senator Patrick Leahy, **http://www.senate.gov/~leahy/**, has introduced a bill to repeal the CDA, but it does not yet have much support in Congress. See **http://epic.org/free_speech/ censorship/repeal.html**.)

If the Supreme Court reverses the decision, the law could go back into effect. It could become valid again and could be enforced by the police. The high court's opinion could affect your rights on the Internet for years to come.

So, too, could any other law that Congress may enact to try to police the Internet. It is folly to continue to rely on the wisdom of the judiciary alone to protect our rights on the Internet.

We can hope that all of us, even politicians, will become better informed about the Internet and so will come to understand that we need the same rights and freedom in cyberspace that we enjoy and take for granted everywhere else. The protection of our constitutional rights is everybody's concern and business, not just the business of lawyers and the courts.

N O T E For an update on the CDA case, and other cases and legislation affecting the Internet, check out the Web site of the Electronic Frontier Foundation at **http://www.eff.org/**. The EFF keeps abreast of all legal issues affecting the Internet. You'll not only find the latest news, but a wide range of intelligent commentary by Internet leaders and lawyers.

Also see the ACLU Web site at **http://www.aclu.org/**, the Web site of the Center For Democracy & Technology at **http://www.cdt.org/**, and the Electronic Privacy Information Center's Web site at **http:/ /www.epic.org/**. ▪

Your Rights and Responsibilities for Privacy on the Internet

Although the Fourth Amendment prohibits unreasonable searches and seizures by the government, there is no place in the Constitution that explicitly says you have a right to privacy. Still, in the last century, the courts have found a fundamental right to privacy implied in the Constitution.

Legal decisions, and state and federal legislation have set up legal protections to try to guarantee us the right to privacy, to be left alone, and to be secure in our communications. As U.S. citizens, these rights are again carried with us when we enter the Internet.

E-mail Privacy—Who Else Can Read Your E-mail?

E-mail is one of the biggest uses of the Internet. How secure and private is it? Aside from the intended recipients, who else, if anyone, can legally read your mail? E-mail is not legally the same as the U.S. mail and not entitled to the same protections.

If a network provider wanted to, it could make a condition of network use that you agree to allow it to read your e-mail at any time for any reason. You in turn could agree to disagree and take your business elsewhere!

Most Internet providers and networks don't have such an agreement. They keep your e-mail private and don't peek unless required to do so by warrant or subpoena, as we'll discuss later.

The situation is very different in the workplace with company networks. Management can and usually does make it a condition of use of the company's computer network that the employees *do not* have a right to privacy of their e-mail.

The justification is that you are only supposed to be using the company computers and e-mail systems for company business. Management has a right to inspect its employee's work. It's the employer's computer system and so the employer can put whatever restrictions it wants on the system.

So far, in the few cases that have hit the courts in this area, when an employer reads an employee's e-mail and some terrible, embarrassing thing is revealed, hurting the employee, who subsequently sues, the employer's practice has been upheld as legal.

Absent new legislation in this area, e-mail and other computer privacy will probably not be needed in the workplace. So, don't assume your e-mail at work is private and confidential unless the employer has a policy that expressly makes it private.

For a list of cases indirectly related to email privacy, see **http://www.eff.org/pub/Legal/ Intellectual_property/Legal/email_privacy.citations**.

Outside of the workplace, read the subscription or user agreement with your networks. You should have a right to the privacy of your e-mail unless the agreement specifically provides to the contrary. Two federal laws apply to keep it private, discussed next.

Federal Computer Privacy Laws

Congress has enacted and revised two laws so that they apply to e-mail and other computer telecommunications: the Electronic Communications Privacy Act, 18 U.S.C. §2501, et seq., and the Stored Wire and Electronic Communications and Transactional Records Act, 18 U.S.C. §2701, et seq.

Copies of both of these laws are included on the CD that accompanies this book. Many other states have their own computer laws and privacy laws that might apply to you. Some are listed later in this chapter.

Part I
Ch 2

The Electronic Communications Privacy Act is the federal wiretap law. It was amended in 1986 to clarify its application to computer transmissions. No one can intercept your communications without your authorization—for instance, no one can secretly wiretap your telephone or your computer data line—except the government.

The government can only do it if it first gets a warrant from a judge. The judge, in turn, is only supposed to issue a wiretap warrant under the very limited circumstances spelled out in the law.

The wiretap law applies only to electronic data, be it voice or data, that is in transit. Once the data arrives somewhere and is stored in a computer, for example, this law no longer applies. (See Steve Jackson Games, Inc. v. United States Secret Service at **http://www.io.com/SS/ appeal-opinion.html**.)

TIP For more information on these laws and the intriguing case of the Secret Service's illegal raid on the Steve Jackson Games bulletin board, see the Web sites at **http://www.io.com/SS/** and **http:// www.eff.org/pub/Legal/Cases/SJG/**.

That is where the other law kicks in, the Electronic Communications and Transactional Records Act. This law protects data such as e-mail that is stored somewhere and is no longer in transit.

An example is e-mail stored in your Internet provider's computer before you access and download it onto your computer. E-mail that has arrived at your provider's computer is no longer in transit, even if it hasn't reached its final destination, namely your computer.

Both laws have hefty criminal and civil penalties for their violation. The Electronic Communications and Transactional Records Act has several provisions to protect a sysop or other network provider from substantial liability for inadvertent or necessary interceptions of the private transmissions of its users.

A provider is shielded from liability if the interception, disclosure, or use of the communication was done "in the normal course of his employment while engaged in any activity which is a necessary incident to the rendition of his service or to the protection of the rights or property of the provider of that service."

The idea behind this exception is that the provider might inadvertently see your e-mail while working on a technical problem, just as the mailman might see a postcard to you. Other circumstances are spelled out in the law in which a provider can access a communication to or from a user, but the provider is prohibited from divulging the contents of the communication to anyone.

The only exceptions to the nondisclosure rule are in court-ordered disclosure by warrant or subpoena. Again, the law spells out the circumstances and complex requirements for the government to obtain such court orders.

An important arbitrary distinction is made in the law for messages that have been stored by the provider for more than 180 days. The law is complicated and you are urged to read it for yourself to understand the details, but simply put, messages or files stored for fewer than 180 days are much harder for the government to get to. After 180 days the government can require a provider to produce communications with just a subpoena, a court document far easier for a prosecutor to obtain than a warrant.

 TIP Never leave your messages with an e-mail server for more than 180 days. Download and delete with the server/provider.

Cryptology, Secret Codes, and the Clipper Chip

Another highly controversial Internet privacy law issue concerns the federal laws limiting the use and transmission of coded messages. Certain cryptology software is illegal to use and very illegal to send out of the country. It is even illegal to publish certain technical data about encryption theory without first getting a license from the government.

If you wonder why the government has such extreme paranoia on this subject, just remember World War II. Many believe our greatest secret weapon in the war was not the atom bomb but our ability to crack the German and Japanese codes, and our contra ability (thanks primarily to Native American languages) to send impenetrable codes.

We could read their secret messages; they couldn't read ours. It provided a tremendous military advantage. This is why codes have always been top secret, classified military stuff. Today, codes are primarily a matter of computer science, not esoteric languages. For this reason, the federal government classifies certain cryptology software as military weapons. The software can't be exported without a weapons permit!

A lot of people on the Internet think that the government should stop treating cryptology, the science and study of secret writing, like a dangerous tool that only the military should have. They contend that we have a First Amendment right to freely discuss and use secret codes, and that we need to do so to preserve our privacy.

They cite the dangers of Big Brother having a computer record of everything you do and buy, of hackers and criminals reading your e-mail, stealing your credit card numbers, and the like. Perhaps most important, they contend that the government's laws on this subject are hindering the development of a private, secure Internet, one not so vulnerable to attack by hackers, criminals, con men, and the like.

See, for instance, the EFF files at **http://www.eff.org/pub/Privacy/**. Also see the Electronic Privacy Information Center Web site at **http://epic.org/** and the Internet Privacy Coalition Web site at **http://www.privacy.org/ipc/**, which promote a "Golden Key Campaign" to support and preserve the right to communicate privately.

You'll see many Webs around the Net with a "Golden Key" logo, which means they support the Internet Privacy Coalition and the right to use secret codes. For more information on the Golden Key privacy initiative, see **http://www.eff.org/goldkey.html**.

One of the rallying cases in this area has been the government's prosecution of a cryptologist, Phil Zimmerman, who invented a software encryption program called Pretty Good Privacy or

PGP. Zimmerman posted his software on the Internet, free for the taking by anyone who wanted to keep his or her communications secure. See **http://www.eff.org/pub/Net_info/ Tools/Crypto/PGP/**.

The problem is, PGP is good, so good that some think even the super secret National Security Agency can't crack it. Naturally, there are many in the government who don't want hostile governments or criminals to have such a "weapon." Even though the cold war is over, they want to be able to eavesdrop and crack any codes necessary for "national security purposes" or to fight the never ending "war on crime."

That's why the government is instead promoting, and may require by law, the use of the so-called "Clipper Chip" for encoding. Right now that's the government's solution for how to make the Internet and other cyberspace more secure from criminals and hackers.

With the Clipper Chip, the government always has the key to encode any encryption. For more information on the Clipper Chip see **http://www.eff.org/pub/Privacy/Clipper/**.

Needless to say, there are problems with this idea. For one, foreign governments won't buy into a worldwide computer network where the U.S. government always has the keys in its pocket to all encrypted messages. A lot of honest U.S. citizens are also concerned about that.

The likes of Zimmerman's PGP code loose on the Internet, a cyberspace without national boundaries, is perceived by some as a threat. His posting of PGP on the Internet may well have violated several federal laws, a possibility Zimmerman knew about when he posted it. Zimmerman was under federal grand jury investigation for this reason, but reacting to political pressure, the prosecutors in early 1996 decided to drop the case.

Still, the legal battles in this area go on. Two other cryptologists in separate lawsuits recently challenged the federal government's right to regulate cryptology and computer codes as a military weapon.

The suit by mathematician Daniel Bernstein in a California court was a big success. The court held that his cryptology software called "Snuffle" was equivalent to speech, not conduct, and so entitled to the full First Amendment protection. See the favorable ruling at **http:// www.eff.org/pub/Legal/Cases/Bernstein_v_DoS/Legal/960415.decision**.

But, the very similar suit by another mathematician, Philip Karn, in a federal District of Columbia court, was a failure. The court upheld the Department of State decision that Karn's software containing encryption code was a "munition" subject to regulation under the Arms Export Control Act. See the decision at **http://www.qualcomm.com/people/pkarn/export/ decision.html**.

With mixed results so far in court, the battle over your right to use secret code continues on the political front. Opposing bills are now pending in Congress.

President Clinton has introduced a bill to mandate the use of the Clipper Chip. See **http:// www.eff.org/pub/Privacy/Clipper/Clipper_III/**.

Several other opposing bills have been introduced to deregulate cryptology. See **http:// www.eff.org/pub/Privacy/Clipper/Clipper_III/Crypto_bills_1996/**.

Keep your eye on this legislative battle at the EFF Web and elsewhere (**http://www.eff.org/ pub/Alerts/**). It will once again be an interesting test of whether the Internet community has developed any political clout and acumen.

Your Rights and Responsibilities for Copyright on the Internet

Copyright is the place in cyberspace law where you're most likely to inadvertently break the law. For instance, any time you reply and copy a person's previous message on a newsgroup or mailing list, you may technically be violating copyright law.

It's a spitting-on-the-sidewalk kind of offense and no one is likely to complain—but still you copied someone's writing without first asking and receiving permission. It violates copyright law to copy anybody's writing, even their public postings on a newsgroup, unless you have consent.

The same holds true when you forward someone's e-mail without their permission. It is also a copyright violation to scan someone else's photos, say, from a magazine and post the GIF on the Internet—even if no one pays you anything for it. The same holds true for copying an audio recording or a video.

With a few limited exceptions, which we will talk about later, copyright law prohibits the copying of another person's work (writings, GIFs, audios, movies, whatever) without that person's permission. If you copy another person's electronic message, then you have violated that person's copyright unless his posting expressly states that you have that person's consent to copy it.

The fact that it's electronic, not paper, or doesn't have a copyright claim or notice on it, has nothing to do with it. It's protected by copyright law whether it is electronic or paper form, with or without copyright notice.

Some copyright violations are of the trivial, spitting-on-the-sidewalk kind, such as recopying another person's note in full when you reply to it in a newsgroup. If that kind of violation ever went to court it would probably be thrown out based on an implied grant of permission to copy for the limited purpose of reply.

You may also have a right to copy a previous posting under the so-called "fair use" exception to copyright, which we'll talk about later. The implied consent would be found from the common practice of the virtual community. People do it all the time, so by participating, you implicitly consent to having your message copied, at least to all participants in that group.

But, what if someone took your newsgroup message and posted it to a thousand other groups? This frequently happens on the Net. Usually it's obvious that the writer wants to have her message published as far and wide as possible.

But, what if she didn't? What if it was hardcopied and sold on the street? In that case, the technical spitting-on-the-sidewalk type of copyright violation might become a lawsuit, especially if the writer who owns the copyright of her work is somehow damaged by the unauthorized copying.

What if the copied message libeled someone? What if it caused the author to lose a job? What if the message was, for instance, a short story and another person claimed it as his own? What if someone else made money by selling the story to a movie producer?

To be safe, better ask for permission before you transmit a copy outside the confines of the virtual community in which it was posted. In the context of e-mail, also, it's good practice not to forward a letter to others unless the original author of the e-mail knows and consents.

That's not only required by technical copyright law, but is also common courtesy and Netiquette, especially if the material is somehow sensitive or you don't know the sender that well.

TIP   Never claim another's work as your own, or publish or revise that work without permission. When in doubt—ask for permission.

There is also the question of copying on the Web. As a practical necessity, there is an implied grant of permission to copy Web materials onto your own computer, at least into its memory. How else can you see it? Web browsing, like many other Internet uses, is based on copying from one computer to another.

When you access a Web site, a copy of the materials on the sender's computer is transmitted to your computer. The Web is based on such copying, so a grant is necessarily implicit; but, that implied consent to copy is not without limits. It may only extend from RAM onto your hard drive.

Absent a specific notice to the contrary on the Web site, the consent to copy Web materials probably does not extend beyond your own computer. For instance, it would be a copyright violation to send a copy to someone else's computer, or to print hard copies and give them away, or worse, sell copies to others.

When you sell copies of the material, you have almost certainly crossed the line of an author's implied consent to copy materials he posts on the Web.

N O T E   The line of implied consent on the Web, as elsewhere on the Internet, is an ill-defined area of the law. To avoid being a defendant in one of the cases that will surely come along to define that line and as good Netiquette, always ask for permission from the Webmaster or other information provider before you distribute copies of any of their work.

Usually the writer will be pleased to consent, so long as you provide proper credit to her, leave any copyright notices intact, and don't change it. ▰

Legally, you do not have to ask permission before you put a hyperlink in your own Web site to someone else's Web site. A link doesn't involve copying. It's just a citation. Still, people frequently ask each other for permission to do so and it never hurts to ask.

In fact, it's good Netiquette and Net politics to do so because it frequently results in reciprocal links back to your Web site. Although the hyperlink itself needs no permission under copyright law, the description you put on the link might run afoul of other laws, such as negligence, fraud, or libel.

Be careful not to make an incorrect description of the linked Web site. That might damage the other Web site. If for any reason the other Webmaster doesn't want to be linked to your Web site, then don't do it—not as a matter of law, but as Netiquette.

Why should you link to someone who doesn't want you to? It's not exactly cyber rape, but it's offensive nonetheless. For more information on Web-law-type questions, see the FAQ at **http://www.patents.com/weblaw.sht**.

 For more information on Web copyright, see **http://www.benedict.com/webiss.htm#can**.

The ABCs of Copyright Law

To help "stay legal" in the little-known waters of copyright law, it helps to have a handle on the basic rules. These rules can guide you when you encounter a new situation and are unsure of your rights and responsibilities.

Also, for a Web-based primer on copyright law, see **http://www.ilt.columbia.edu/projects/copyright/index.html**.

Still, remember the old but true sayings: "a little bit of knowledge is a dangerous thing," and "only a fool has himself for a lawyer." Copyright law can get very complicated and very involved, particularly in the area of emerging technologies.

 Ask a lawyer when confused about copyrights, particularly when a commercial transaction is involved. The lawyers who should know about copyrights are called *intellectual property* lawyers.

Basically, copyright law provides that the "author" of any "original work" has the "exclusive rights" to it, including the sole right to copy the work. *Author* is a copyright term that is broadly applied to mean the creator of any original work, be it a book, a play, a movie, a song, a picture, a computer program, and so on.

Works are in turn very broadly defined to include all kinds of original expressions, including software and electronic media of all types. Courts have held that the amount of originality needed for a work to be original, and so qualify for copyright protection, is very low.

For works created after 1978, the protection is limited to the duration of the author's life, plus 50 years after the author dies. The duration of copyright for works created before 1978 under an earlier version of the law is somewhat different, but the old rules that govern pre-1978 works are too complex to try to explain here.

Part

I

Ch

2

The exclusive rights granted to authors include much more than just the right to copy. They include the exclusive right to make modified versions of the work (called *derivative works*), to distribute the work, transmit it, perform it, or run it on a computer.

Copyright law is derived from a short passage in the U.S. Constitution and from lengthy federal legislation that implements that passage. It is governed exclusively by federal law, which means that no state can pass its own copyright laws.

Article I, Section 8 of the U.S. Constitution gives Congress (and Congress alone) the power "To promote the progress of science and useful arts, by securing for limited times to authors and inventors the exclusive right to their respective rights and discoveries." Based on that constitutional passage, Congress has enacted numerous patent and copyright laws.

 TIP A copy of the complete text of U.S. copyright law can be found on my Information Law Web site at **http://seamless.com/rcl/things.html#statutes**.

N O T E   Government works lie outside of copyright law. Thus, for instance, all federal laws are not subject to copyright and can be freely copied by anyone. The laws lie in the public domain because the author is the government and the government is owned by us, "we the people." The same holds true for government pamphlets, reports, photographs, charts, and the like. ■

It helps to have a general understanding of the distinction between copyright law and patent law. Patents cover innovative inventions that implement ideas. Copyrights cover original works that express ideas. Neither cover the ideas themselves.

Thus, you can't patent the idea of a car, only a particular car that embodies that idea. Similarly, you can't copyright an idea, say, the idea of icon-based software interfaces. You can only copyright a particular original expression of the idea.

The line between idea and expression can sometimes become blurry in copyright law—judges have written thousands of pages on it, especially in the area of computer software—but the general idea of the distinction is clear enough in most cases.

The only way to keep an idea to yourself, and keep anyone else from copying the idea, is to keep it secret. Companies sometimes try to do that with trade secrets and agreements, but it is generally impractical. Once the idea has been expressed, someone else is free to express the same idea, so long as they don't copy your particular expression of the idea.

You can't copyright (or patent, for that matter) a fact or a law of nature. The fact of exception to copyright was recently greatly strengthened by a decision of the Supreme Court Feist Publications, Inc. v. Rural Telephone Service. (For more information, see **http://seamless.com/rcl/feist.html**.)

The Feist decision has enormous ramifications for the Internet and for computer databases in general. Feist permits the free copying of facts gathered by others, so long as you don't copy any original selection or arrangement of the facts, and your copying doesn't extend beyond plain facts to include original creative content.

N O T E For a full discussion of this fascinating area of the law—fascinating to me, anyway—see my article, "The Practical and Legal Protection of Computer Databases," in the Information Law Web site at **http://seamless.com/rcl/article.html**. That article contains a full discussion of Feist. ■

Government works are not the only ones that are in the public domain and outside copyright protection. All works whose copyright time has expired fall into the public domain—Shakespeare, for instance—as do particular works that the authors have intentionally dedicated to the public domain.

Anyone can decide to relinquish all or part of their exclusive rights. Under previous copyright law, it was even possible to unintentionally waive your copyright by publishing a work without a copyright notice.

 For a Web site with information about works that are supposedly in the public domain, see **http://northcoast.com/savetz/pd/pd.html**.

Many people think you have to apply for a copyright. Wrong! You don't apply for a copyright. You have one automatically by law as soon as you create something.

You can elect to register your copyright with the Copyright Office in Washington, D.C., but registration has never been a prerequisite of copyright protection. Still, it's a good idea to register your copyright if your work is valuable and you may need to take legal action to protect it.

 For copyright registration forms, instructions on how to register, and other good information on copyrights, see the Copyright Web site at **http://www.benedict.com/register.htm#register**.

You can't file suit to enforce your copyright unless and until you register it. Also, you are not eligible for statutory damages, awards, or attorney fee awards for infringements that occur before registration.

Many people also think that you have to put a copyright notice on a work for it to be protected by copyright law. Wrong again! That used to be the law, but now U.S. law follows international copyright treaty and the copyright notice is not necessary.

You automatically have a full copyright even if you don't state a claim to one on the work itself. If you say nothing, a full claim to copyright is implied. Still, a notice is a good idea, particularly if your work goes out of the country.

N O T E A copyright notice should state the name of the author, the date the work was published, and the word copyright or its abbreviations, copr. or ©. For instance, a notice would read name, date, ©, all together on one line—as in, Ralph Losey © 1995. It also doesn't hurt to add "All Rights Reserved," especially if your work may end up in South America. ■

If you want to dedicate your work to the public domain or otherwise relinquish some of your exclusive rights, then you need to say so on the work itself. This reverse kind of copyright notice is starting to be known as a *copyless notice*. If you don't see a copyless notice, then you should assume that the author claims full copyright. When in doubt, contact the author.

 There are companies that specialize in obtaining copyright clearances, such as Total Clearance, Inc. at **totalclear@aol.com**. Also try the Copyright Clearance Center's Web site at **http:// www.copyright.com/**.

In addition to the general misconceptions about copyright law just discussed, there are some Internet-specific myths. Quite a few people in cyberspace seem to think that copyright somehow does not apply on the Internet. They believe that copyright law is now an archaic vestige of the past.

Some tell you that anything on the Internet has been dedicated to the public domain and can be freely copied. Another version of the myth is that copyrights don't apply to computer files in general and the Internet in particular under some sort of "fair use" exception or another.

These notions are not true. They are myths from an earlier era of the Internet when it was the exclusive home of scientists and academics. They are perpetuated by many who just don't like the idea of copyright in general and think everything should be freely copied. See for instance the Anti-Copyright Web site at **http://www.mayhem.net/copyright.html**. The Internet is just like anywhere else—you can't take a person's intellectual property or creative works without his permission. Property rights are alive and well on the Internet, and ignorance or misconception of the law is no defense.

 For a good discussion of Internet-specific copyright law, see the Copyright Web site at **http:// www.benedict.com/intnet.htm#intnet.**

N O T E To add to the confusion, legislation is now pending in Congress called the National Information Infrastructure Copyright Protection Act (NII), which could substantially change copyright law on the Internet.

For a detailed critique of NII and how it could adversely affect the Internet, see the Digital Future Coalition Web at **http://www.ari.net/dfc/info/Copyright**. The EFF is strongly opposed to this legislation and has a policy statement against it at **http://www.eff.org/pub/Alerts/ hr2441_051495.alert**. █

A legal exception to copyright that is often misunderstood is the fair use exception. It is a much smaller loophole than most people realize. It allows you to take small quotes of another author's work and put them into your work.

For instance, you may use short quotes in a book of literary criticism, a short film clip in a movie review, or you may copy an article for classroom discussion. The criteria for the test varies from case to case but, generally, to qualify you must meet the following five criteria:

- You have to take very little of the copyrighted work.
- The quoted portions have to be a small part of your own work.
- Your quoting can't interfere with sales of the original copyrighted work.
- Your sales don't depend on the copied materials.
- Your use of the copied materials promotes a public objective like education or commentary. Your work doesn't have to be nonprofit to qualify, but it helps.

In several Internet copyright cases that have gone to court, the defendant tried to use the fair use doctrine. It didn't work.

 TIP For more about the fair use doctrine, see **http://www.benedict.com/fair.htm#fair** and **http://www.eff.org/pub/Legal/fair_use_and_copyright.excerpt**. For a recent case in which the fair use doctrine defense was successfully used outside the Internet, see Princeton University Press v. Michigan Document Services, Inc. found on my Web site at **http://seamless.com/rcl/fairuse.html**.

As the Internet gets bigger and bigger, and cyberspace becomes an integral part of commerce, more claims of copyright infringement are hitting the courts. Copyright infringement that doesn't have a significant impact on someone's pocketbook is frequently tolerated by the owner of the copyright. But, when the damages start to hurt, the tolerance of most authors lessens accordingly.

That is what is happening now on the Internet and is likely to continue for the next several years. We'll see more Internet copyright infringement suits until the myth of the copyright-free Internet is finally laid to rest. In this chapter, we look at two of these cases, one brought by *Playboy* magazine and the other by the Church of Scientology.

Make no mistake about it, the damages that can flow from a copyright infringement can be substantial, even if the infringement was not intentional.

The civil remedies include an injunction, seizure, and impounding of all illegal copies—which can include seizure of your computers if that is where the copies are stored—an attorney fee award, an award of actual damages or alternatively of statutory damages of between $500 and $20,000 per infringement at the discretion of the judge, or up to $50,000 per infringement if the violation was intentional.

Intentional copyright infringement for profit is also a criminal violation; as anyone who watches home videotapes well knows, violation can subject you to imprisonment or fines. But, in an important Internet case, a court recently held that it's not criminal to intentionally copy and distribute software programs for free over the Internet. See U.S. v. LaMacchia on my Web site at **http://seamless.com/rcl/criminal.html**.

Because there was no personal benefit to the infringer, there was no criminal act. The infringer could be sued civilly for damages for copyright infringement by the companies whose software she copied, but she couldn't be prosecuted by the government for a criminal violation.

Any other result could have led to the widespread criminialization of the commonplace occurrence of people sharing programs with each other. This is still a civil violation, but it's not criminal and you can't go to jail for doing it unless you make money on the exchange.

Playboy Enterprises, Inc. v. Frena

Many people have discovered just how easy it is to scan a picture and put it on their computer screen. With super VGA monitors the quality is remarkable. Many have also learned how to upload their favorite pictures into cyberspace. There they can be viewed by other graphics connoisseurs around the world.

Tens of thousands or more of such computer graphics are exchanged between computers all the time. Many of the human beings who sit in front of these computers like to see provocative pixels of naked people—naked women, usually.

By now, you probably realize that unless you took the pictures or have the permission of the photographer, scanning and copying the pictures is a copyright violation. You also probably suspect that this is all a spitting-on-the-sidewalk-type infringement that the owner of the photograph's copyright wouldn't care about. Indeed, it has been tolerated for years, but one copyright owner, *Playboy* magazine, finally had enough.

To be sure, *Playboy* has been a favorite target of computer hobbyists who like naked GIFs. It's so easy to scan their centerfolds and make impressive digital pictures. The practice is widespread and almost commonplace on thousands of BBSs around the country.

Somebody at *Playboy* must have figured this was having an adverse impact on their bottom line. So, they picked a blatant BBS infringer to make an example of, and sued for copyright and trademark infringement, and unfair competition.

Playboy won the lawsuit and defendant George Frena, the small BBS owner, ended up with a $500,000 judgment against him (see the Playboy Enterprises, Inc. v. Frena decision located at **http://seamless.com/rcl/playb.html**).

Frena, the sysop owner, claimed that he didn't know there were *Playboy* copyrighted GIFs on his board. He said they were all uploaded by subscribers and he had no knowledge of this activity. *Playboy* didn't contest that the original copies had come from subscribers and not Frena, but it argued that he knew about it, permitted, even encouraged it, and therefore was a republisher.

There are several credibility problems with Frena's "ignorance defense." It was undisputed that he had over 170 *Playboy* files on his not-too-big board. In many of the GIFs, the *Playboy* text had been removed and replaced with ads for Frena's BBS. Last, he had used the *Playboy* trademark to identify and name the files.

It is clear from Judge Schlesinger's opinion that the judge didn't believe Frena when Frena claimed that he didn't know the *Playboy* photos were on his board. Still, to avoid the credibility issue, the judge ruled that Frena violated copyright law and was liable even if he was an innocent infringer.

Judge Schlesinger noted that intent to infringe is not needed to find copyright infringement. Intention is only a necessary element of criminal copyright infringement. In civil cases, the only relevance of knowledge and intent is in the judge's equitable determination of the amount of statutory damages to impose.

Frena also tried to defend using the fair use exception to copyright. This defense failed primarily because the judge found that Frena's public display and transmission of the *Playboy* pictures was for a "clearly commercial" use. The BBS was a for-profit enterprise in which users paid $25 a month to access his board.

Judge Schlesinger also found that *Playboy* was injured by the copying—deprived of lost revenues from magazine sales by the easy availability of *Playboy* pictures in cyberspace. The judge did not determine the amount of damages. Before that issue was finally decided, the parties reached a $500,000 settlement agreement.

It is interesting to note that *Playboy* has since gone on the Net with its own Web pages. (See **http://www.playboy.com/**.) Yes, it includes the ability to download files of naked playmates!

Scientology v. NETCOM (and Just About Everyone Else)

Another new copyright case that these days is getting a lot of attention by legal Net watchers is one of the many lawsuits brought by the Church of Scientology (**http://www.scientology.org/**). This one is against a well-known Internet provider, NETCOM: Religious Technology Center v. NETCOM On-Line Communication Services, Inc. For the full background on this interesting case, see **http://www.cybercom.net/~rnewman/scientology/erlich/home.html**.

This case may be important to the Internet community because it attempts to hold a provider liable for copyright infringement from the mere transmission of infringing materials through its network. Scientology sought an injunction against NETCOM prohibiting its transmission of any materials it claimed violated its copyrights.

NETCOM claimed that this was not only an illegal request, but an impossible one. If granted, NETCOM said the request would effectively shut down its services and make anyone on the Internet a potential copyright infringer. Scientology has taken action against other people on the Net, trying to prevent public distribution of its secret and copyrighted religious writings.

See, for instance, **http://www.eff.org/pub/Censorship/Scientology_cases/** and **http://www.cybercom.net/~rnewman/scientology/home.html**.

The underlying dispute in the Netcom case is between Scientology and one of its former leaders, Dennis Erlich. Erlich left the church and is now a leader of the opposition against Scientology. He uses Scientology's own secret publications to expose Scientology and support his contention that it is a fraud.

He sent several internal Scientology documents to a UseNet news group on the Internet (**alt.religion.scientology**). Also see **http://www.yahoo.com/Society_and_Culture/Religion/Scientology/**. NETCOM was the Internet provider that was used by Erlich to post the allegedly infringing materials to the newsgroup. (There was a BBS intermediary who was also sued.)

Part
I

Ch
2

There is a question about whether the Scientology works were really infringed or not, and whether the fair use doctrine might apply to Erlich's noncommercial activities. But, aside from these questions, NETCOM claims that it cannot be liable because it is a passive distributor of information, not a publisher.

This is essentially the same distinction we've seen before in the area of libel and pornography. NETCOM is opposing the well-funded Scientology action against it by arguing that copyright liability should not be extended to passive information conduits like NETCOM that merely transmit data, much as a telephone company does.

The Playboy case does, however, pose problems for NETCOM because it held that the BBS was liable even if its copyright infringement was innocent. NETCOM argues that it is physically impossible for it to control the content of the information it carries (over 150,000,000 key-strokes of information per day). Scientology argues to the contrary that technical means exist for NETCOM to screen out Scientology materials. NETCOM denies this.

This case is ongoing, but there has already been one important ruling in favor of NETCOM. It can be found at **http://www.eff.org/pub/Legal/Cases/CoS_v_the_Net/ whyte_netcom_112195.order**. Here the court distinguishes the Playboy case and refuses to impose liability on an Internet provider for innocent participation in infringement.

The court correctly notes that this would put an impossible burden on the Internet community and decides that it's better to treat providers like a phone company, not like a publisher. The case against NETCOM still continues, however, on a legal theory of contributory infringement liability.

A trial will be necessary to determine if NETCOM participated in the infringement by not deleting the files after notice. Here the issue of NETCOM's claimed inability to control the flow of information over its network will be determined by the court.

Look for the latest on this and other Scientology censorship cases on the EFF Web at **http:// www.eff.org/pub/Legal/Cases/CoS_v_the_Net/**.

Fair Trade on the Internet

When the government first started the Net and paid for it, there was an "acceptable use policy," which among other things banned all commercial activity on the Net. For better or for worse, these early days of the Internet as an ivory tower are over. Not only is commercial activity tolerated, the Net is fast becoming a booming center of commerce.

As you do business on the Internet, just remember its Netiquette and noncommercial history. The soft sell is definitely the best approach—so, too, is the provision of bona fide information, such as an infomercial, and free services along with the trade. Pure commercial speech is still frowned on by most Net users.

The freedom to engage in commercial speech, to own property, and to contract are basic con-stitutional rights that are all carried over onto the Internet. Under the law, these freedoms carry the responsibilities of honesty, good faith, and fair dealing. The old legal principle of *caveat emptor*, let the buyer beware, has been long abandoned by most courts and will not be resurrected again for the Internet.

Fraud, pyramid schemes, bait and switch, misleading advertising, simple negligence, gross negligence, defective products, unconscionable contracts, breach of contract, theft, conspiring to fix prices, unfair trade, trade libel, usury, sale of unregistered securities, unlawful discrimination, and so on—these are all just as illegal on the Net as anywhere else. Any business practices not allowed in your hometown would probably also be illegal on the Net.

There is one unfair business practice spawned on the Net that is new and unique to the Net. It's the foul art of spamming. *Spamming*—the practice of sending out unsolicited e-mail and news postings to large groups of users—is an anathema to everyone.

It is junk mail on a grand scale. It wastes Internet resources and even costs some recipients of the junk mail who are charged by the item by their providers. It may be legal but if you do it, your reputation on the Net is dead.

The users themselves will quickly retaliate and put you out of business. Don't believe the bogus get-rich-quick-on-the-Internet schemes you may read about. The spam scams won't work.

When Is a Deal a Deal?

Most contracts or agreements are enforceable as soon as there is a meeting of the minds on the essential terms of a deal. Contrary to popular opinion, most verbal agreements are legally enforceable even though they are often hard to enforce because the unwritten terms are disputed.

To be sure, some agreements must be in writing to be enforceable like an agreement to sell real property or to pay the debts of another. The rule is commonly called the Statute of Frauds.

Still, in most states, even for those kinds of agreements, there are many exceptions to the Statute of Frauds as, for instance, when there is partial performance of the agreement, or there is a later writing consistent with the agreement.

So, if you make a deal on the Internet, don't assume it's not enforceable just because you've never signed your name to a piece of paper. If you make a deal with someone over the Net, plan to stick by it and expect the other person to also.

Having said that verbal agreements are frequently enforceable, it's still recommended that you always confirm your deals in writing. If nothing else, that is the best way for all concerned to know what duties and obligations they have assumed. Otherwise, there is likely to be an argument later about exactly what was agreed to.

When things go bad later, you will be amazed at how widely recollections can vary of a deal you made on IRC last month. If your deal involves a new business undertaking or a substantial amount of money, you should probably see a lawyer before the deal is made.

It's better to spend a few bucks for assistance up front instead of waiting till later when things go bad and you have to spend all you've got. A "legal stitch in time can save nine." I've seen it happen a million times. Trust me, I'm a lawyer.

N O T E Whenever you make an agreement on the Net and everyone involved is not a resident of the same state, it's important to decide in advance which state law will govern. The same goes double if a person or company from another country is involved.

You should also decide in advance the forum for any dispute resolution, be it mediation, arbitration, or litigation. If you have to go to court to enforce the deal—say, to get your money—what court will that be and whose law will govern?

These are very important questions when things go sour. Right now, the law has few answers in the context of cyberspace, so you had better decide for yourself in advance. If you don't, you could be unpleasantly surprised later when a judge throws out your case and tells you that you have to go to a court in Timbuktu.

So, when is a deal confirmed in writing? Does e-mail suffice? It might if a signature is not needed by the law of the state or foreign country that governs the agreement. Sometimes e-mail might not be good enough even if there is no Statute of Frauds or its foreign country equivalent. E-mail can become an evidentiary problem of later proving that there was a bona fide meeting of the minds.

One person to the agreement could try to wiggle out of it later and claim it was not his or her letter, that he or she never agreed to it. E-mail can be easily forged or altered. It might be hard to prove the authenticity of the e-mail and thus of the agreement.

Courts are used to dealing with letters and the U.S. mail in which it is presumed that a letter posted to someone is received by them and they have to prove the contrary. Also, a written document with a person's signature is presumed to be authentic.

Most e-mail today does not have a signature that can be verified by an expert. Lawyers are concerned about the evidentiary problems still inherent in proving e-mail and other electronic deals. That's why most lawyers still recommend that a written document be prepared and signed by the parties.

That may well change in the future as laws change, electronic signatures become foolproof, and the authenticity of electronic documents is easier to confirm by experts. Three states—Florida, California, and Utah—have already addressed the problem with legislation concerning electronic signatures.

In Florida, the new law that went into effect on May 31, 1996, is called the "Electronic Signature Act of 1996." It provides for the authentication of electronic documents, but does not spell out exactly how the electronic signature verification process works.

These and other new laws should facilitate trade in cyberspace by taking some of the uncertainty out of e-mail and other electronic signatures. This area of the law is rapidly changing. Look for news from your friendly cyber lawyer on this issue because it could have a big impact on what you say and do in e-mail.

For more information on forgery-proof electronic signatures and how you can get one, see **http://www.verisign.com/**, and generally on this subject, see **http://www.eff.org/pub/ Privacy/Digital_signature/**.

 TIP Until the law in this area is clarified and becomes more certain, be sure to confirm any important agreements you make on the Net with U.S. snail mail and ink-on-paper signatures.

Network-Use Agreements

Most networks and Internet providers require their subscribers and users to agree to their standard form agreement as a condition of use. These agreements usually spell out the provider's acceptable use policy, which are the basic rules of conduct, and set forth terms of payment. Some providers later confirm the agreement with paper and a signature.

These agreements are probably enforceable even if they are just electronic, and never confirmed with paper and ink. Still, some of their specific terms may be unenforceable if a court finds them to be unconscionable—that is, totally unfair and unreasonable.

One court has already done this to the term in CompuServe's agreement that purports to allow CompuServe to sue any of its subscribers in Ohio, instead of the subscriber's home state, for any violation of the contract. See **http://www.eff.org/pub/Legal/Cases/ cis_v_patterson.notes**.

A network or other provider has the right to cancel your subscription and terminate your service if you don't comply with its rules even if its rules violate free speech. Remember that the First Amendment protects you from the government, not a private company.

Competition and the forces of a free economy are supposed to protect you from oppressive contractual requirements that suppress free speech. Right now there appear to be enough providers to keep this from being a problem. There are tens of thousands of Internet providers and more coming each day.

The competition should continue to protect us from overreaching providers. The network agreements, on the other hand, should protect us from the rude spammers and flamers, and allow the networks to screen them out.

 TIP Read your provider's agreement. If there is something in there you don't like, tell them about it!

Newsgroups and Web sites are also information providers. Most on the Net are now free, but this is likely to change. I suspect that more and more will add premium areas that can only be accessed with a password, for a charge.

Some already have agreements as a condition of admittance. More will probably do so in the future, especially if any files are transferred or if there is any kind of charge to users. These agreements can try to protect the operators from liability from the actions of their users.

Written agreements should also be prepared for all the advertisements now being sold on the Web, but today this is often not done. Instead, the parties have an ill-defined verbal agreement.

If you are spending money for a Web site or an ad on somebody else's Web site, then you have the right to have the full terms of your agreement spelled out in writing. Confirm it by e-mail or fax, and if enough money is involved, get the ink signature on paper.

Software License Agreements

There is a lot of confusion about all the different kinds of software agreements out there—shareware, freeware, free trials with expiration dates, beta tests, licenses in perpetuity, site licenses, license per user, license per computer, software sales, shrink-wraps, contracts of adhesion, look and feel.

This is a complex subject, and the confusion extends to most lawyers and judges now being called on to decide these new questions.

I can only touch on the surface of this law, but for those who want more detailed information on software licensing and related intellectual law issues, many good articles can be found at the EFF Web site **http://www.eff.org/pub/Legal/Intellectual_property/** and also at the International Federation of Library Associations Web site at **http://www.nlc-bnc.ca/ifla/II/cpyright.htm**.

For information on a software developer trying to protect her work, see **http://www.island.com/LegalCare/welcome.html**. For some of the latest cases on this and related issues, see **http://www.eff.org/pub/Legal/Intellectual_property/Legal/Cases/**.

One recent case you may have heard about is Lotus v. Borland (**http://www.eff.org/pub/Legal/Intellectual_property/Legal/Cases/Lotus_cases/**), in which the appellate court recently in effect held that the user interface, the lotus menu, could not be copyrighted. A copy of the *Lotus v. Borland* case can be found on my Web site at **http://seamless.com/rcl/lotus.html**.

The shrink-wrap kind of agreement is now in widespread use for software. Shrink-wrap is a license in which there is a sticker on the outside of the package that warns you that if you break the seal, you agree to the license inside. The license may also say that if you don't agree to all the terms, then return the software immediately for a full refund.

Online equivalents of the shrink-wrap have now become commonplace. You come to a screen where an arcane license or other agreement is presented to you and you are asked to indicate, yes or no, whether you agree to all the terms.

If you say yes, you go on. If you say no, you're out. Windows 95 has such a screen as part of the installation process. You can expect more of the same from everyone else.

Are these kinds of agreements enforceable? Probably yes. But, enforcement against individual consumers is rare and the law is still unsettled. Again, it is largely an evidentiary problem.

What if your minor child opened the shrink wrap for you or entered into the domain for you? A minor can't enter into a legally enforceable contract. If you never saw the agreement, how could you have agreed to it? There would be no meeting of the minds necessary for contract formation.

Beyond proof of intent, there is the issue of unconscionability. There is no negotiation over the terms of these agreements. You either accept the form deal or not. Also, the parties have unequal bargaining strength.

Legally, these form agreements are called *contracts of adhesion*. The courts will not enforce a term in a contract of adhesion that they feel is very unfair or overreaching to the consumer. So, if you've inadvertently pledged your firstborn in one of those form computer agreements that no one reads, don't worry about it, it's not enforceable.

Software on trial for a limited time is now a commonplace marketing device on the Net. Give the software away at first. People will come to depend on it—get hooked on it—and then they will want the updates and improvements as they come out. They will even be willing to pay for the next version!

Eudora and Netscape have used this strategy successfully. It's kind of like shareware. If you end up using a shareware program you try out, then go ahead and pay for it. Send in the few bucks for the shareware—pay for the upgrade. The law requires it. You agreed to do so when you received the software.

Sure, you'll never be caught if you don't follow the agreement, but you should do it because it's the right thing to do. It pays someone for his or her honest labor and efforts, and keeps his or her in business to develop yet a better version of him or her product for your computing pleasure. More so than almost any other industry, software developers depend on the honesty and fairness of the consumers to keep afloat.

Trademarks and Internet Domain Names

A *trademark* is a name or design used by a business to identify its product. A *service mark* does the same thing for a service. Trademarks and service marks are protected by state and federal laws. The basic rule of these laws is to protect the first user of a name from latecomers who try to use the same name to identify their products or services.

If the use of a same or similar mark is likely to cause confusion to consumers, then the law will prohibit the use of the mark by the latecomer. Trademarks can be registered in the Patent and Trademark Office in Washington. This allows people to determine whether a name is available for use or not. For more information on trademark laws, see **http://www.law.cornell.edu/topics/trademark.html**.

TIP For more information on Internet domain names and the law, see my Internet Law Page at **http://seamless.com/rcl/iplaw/**.

Internet domain names are a form of trademark. They frequently identify a commercial service or product. If you have a domain name that is important to you, then you'd better try to protect that name from use outside the Net by a trademark registration.

For information on the registration process and forms, see **http://www.naming.com/naming/trademark.html**. We can hope that you won't be unpleasantly surprised to find that someone else already has the rights to your name on a similar product or service. If they do, you could be infringing their trademark, and they could sue you and force you to stop using their name.

Internet domain names and trademark law have become a very hot area in Internet law lately. For more information on this, see **http://www.law.georgetown.edu/lc/internic/domain1.html**. Many lawsuits are now underway concerning trademark infringements on the Internet or against computer companies.

We've already seen how *Playboy* sued the BBS for both copyright infringement and for violation of its trademark. Singer Bob Dylan has sued Apple Computer for naming a computer language Dylan. It was supposedly an abbreviation for Dynamic Language.

Astronomer Carl Sagan also complained to Apple when it starting using Sagan as the internal code name of a computer that became the Macintosh 7100. Apple stopped using his name, but instead started calling it the BHA.

Sagan sued Apple anyway for trademark infringement, defamation, and invasion of privacy, claiming that it was well known that Apple used BHA as an acronym for Butt-Head Astronomer. The judge reportedly threw out Sagan's case.

Network Solutions, Inc., is the company now responsible for the assignment of domain names on the Internet. It has been caught up in disputes between holders of domain names on the Internet and holders of preexisting trademarks of the same name.

For example, ex-video jockey Adam Curry uses the domain name of MTV and his former employer doesn't like it. MTV has sued him for trademark infringement. Curry claims it gave him permission to do so, that it said it was not interested in the Internet. (For a copy of Adam Curry's public statement about the case, see **http://www.eff.org/pub/Legal/Cases/curry_v_mtv.announce**.)

Assuming that MTV did give him permission, it was obviously before it understood the Internet, and the potential value and importance of a domain name. Adam Curry's MTV Web site is now visited by an average of 35,000 people a day.

There are other cases where a competitor has deliberately reserved the use of its competitor's name as a domain name to try and lock them out. (It didn't work!) Some people even suggest you do this as a moneymaker. Apparently, a few people have made money reserving, then selling, a good domain name—but look out, you could end up in a lawsuit if someone else's trademark is involved.

See, for instance, the case in which Hasbro, the makers of the famous kiddies board game "Candy Land," sued the owners of the domain with the same name (**http://**

www.candyland.com). Candyland on the Internet was an "adults-only" type of Web of dubious "decency."

The toy maker sued and guess who the court is ruling for so far in this case? If you guessed the wholesome toy maker and not the suspicious adult Web owner, then you're right! The court ordered the Web owner to remove all content from that address and stop using the domain name. The once-active address of www.candyland.com is now empty pending a final ruling by the court.

A good article on this interesting case can be found at **http://www.cyberlaw.com/ cylw0296.html**.

Network Solutions now recognizes the problem of trademark rights and domain names. For that reason, in May 1995, it instituted a policy wherein it will suspend the use of a domain name if the person using the name does not voluntarily relinquish it after demand from a company that owns a federal trademark to the name.

Later, in August 1995, Network Solutions announced a new policy by which any company that registers a domain name is required to indemnify it for any expenses it may incur from a lawsuit by someone claiming federal trademark rights on the same name.

The next month, Network Solutions announced that it was going to start charging users a fee of $50 per year to maintain their domain names. This outraged many small, longtime domain users who were used to a free ride.

Trademark Searches

Before you get an Internet domain name, or before you begin to use any new name to identify your company's product or service, check to see if the name is available. At present, Trademark Office registrations are not computerized and you have to pay a service in Washington to do a manual search for you. It costs $150 or more depending on the scope of the search you order.

The search service I use is Government Liaison Services at 1-800-642-6564. If the search report shows that the name you wanted is already taken, you may be disappointed, but you've saved yourself from a big mess later. You should go back to the drawing board to come up with a new name.

Once you find a name that is clear, go ahead and register that name in Washington so that someone else won't use it. State registrations are probably useless for any Net-related business because they only apply for protection in that state.

Also, don't assume that you have the right to use your own name or company name to identify your product; you don't if the name is already a registered mark.

TIP Never use a product or service name until you check to see if the name is already registered.

In March 1996, a lawsuit was filed by a domain owner disgruntled by Network's policy. The plaintiff, Roadrunner Computer Systems, Inc., an Internet provider in New Mexico (**http://www.roadrunner.com/**), challenges the legality of Network's registration policy and seeks an injunction against Network to keep its domain name. (A copy of the complaint filed can be found at **http://www.patents.com/nsicpt1.sht**.)

Network had threatened to take away Roadrunner's domain name, roadrunner.com, because of a complaint by Time-Warner Entertainment Company. Time-Warner owns the U.S. trademark on "Roadrunner" identifying the well-known cartoon and related toy goods.

So far, Network is defending on technical grounds, claiming that its policy and decisions should be treated as government action because it claims to act for the National Science Foundation. If accepted, this would make it harder to challenge Network's actions as the domain-name king.

At the time of this writing, there have not yet been any rulings by the federal court in Virginia hearing this case. For the latest on this interesting case, see **http://www.patents.com/nsi.sht**.

Protection from Crime on the Internet

What kind of crime are you at risk of on the Internet? There are the commercial crimes like intentional copyright infringement, sale of computer counterfeit goods, and good old-fashioned fraud—in which con men promise you a deal too good to be true.

The Internet has unscrupulous people just like anywhere else. But, even more dangerous than the consumer crimes are the more traditional criminal dangers of stalking, burglary, breaking and entering, theft, and vandalism. Cyberburglary happens all the time on the Net.

People who do that—who get into your computers without your permission—are called *crackers* or sometimes *hackers*. These crackers enjoy finding ways to break into your computer system. Some are harmless—they don't do much once they get inside beyond leave you a cyber equivalent of "Kilroy was here."

Some people look up to these benevolent hackers as technical gurus. But, a few hackers are malicious and dangerous indeed. Once inside they may steal and use valuable information like credit card numbers or, if they get into a bank, they may transfer funds.

They may also engage in acts of vandalism like erasing all your files or planting viruses, worms, bombs, and the like that will make your computer malfunction in many strange and sometimes undetectable ways.

One famous hacker, Vladimir Levin, a 24-year-old mathematician in St. Petersburg, Russia, reportedly hacked his way into Citibank in New York. He is alleged to have made unauthorized transfers of $40,000,000 and withdrawals of $400,000.

U.S. authorities finally caught and arrested him in September 1995 at Heathrow Airport in England. He'll be extradited to New York and stand trial for theft, computer misuse, forgery, and false accounting.

Another famous hacker, Kevin Mitnick, was also finally caught in 1995 after successfully eluding the police for years as a fugitive. Many think he is a benevolent type of hacker and should not go to jail. He was indicted on 23 counts of fraud involving the hacking of computers.

Mitnick allegedly stole information worth more than a million dollars, including 20,000 credit card numbers, but he never used any of the information, or the credit cards numbers. He claims to have done it just for the challenge, not financial gain. He hacked into the computers of highly regarded computer security experts who then later helped police track him down.

A few popular books have been written about this recently. See the Web site at **http://www.takedown.com/** on one of those books, *Take Down,* written by Tsutomu Shimomura, the young computer scientist who finally tracked him down.

When cyberspace was first born, the police were easily confused by cyber crimes and by hackers. They didn't understand the technologies well enough to understand the crimes or to catch the criminals. Prosecutors sometimes found that the existing laws were inadequate and didn't clearly apply to allow them to get a conviction.

Those days appear to be over. Now almost every state in the country has enacted computer crime laws and the federal government has one, too. Some detectives are now streetwise to the Net, and more and more of them are patrolling the cyber streets undercover. The FBI and many urban police forces now have special squads that specialize in computer crime. The easy early days for computer criminals are definitely over.

TIP For a good list of Web sites concerning security, see **http://www.cs.purdue.edu/homes/spaf/hotlists/csec.html**.

Table 2.1 is a state-by-state list of the computer crime laws now in effect across the country. New laws are being enacted every year. Most of these laws can be found on the Net. Try looking at the Web site of a university or lawyer in your state.

For a detailed discussion of the various state computer crime laws see **http://www.eff.org/pub/Legal/prosecuting_computer_criminals.article**.

In addition to clearly criminalizing the unauthorized access, use, or interference with a computer, some states are also enacting special laws prohibiting computer stalking. That's where someone follows you around in cyberspace and harasses you. Of course, there are already many laws on the books, as previously mentioned, to prohibit pedophiles, sexual predators, and child pornographers.

Table 2.1   State Computer Laws

AL	Computer Crime Act, Code of Alabama, Sections 13A—8—100 to 13A—8—103
AK	Statutes, Sections 11.46.200(a)(3), 11.46.484(a)(5), 11.46.740, 11.46.985, 11.46.990
AZ	Revised Statues Annotated, Sections 13—2301(E), 13—2316
CA	Penal Code, Section 502
CO	Revised Statutes, Sections 18—5.5—101, 18—5.5—102
CT	General Statutes, Sections 53a—250 to 53a—261, 52—570b
DE	Code Annotated, Title 11, Sections 931—938
FL	Computer Crimes Act, Florida Statutes Annotated, Sections 815.01 to 815.07
GA	Computer Systems Protection Act, Georgia Codes Annotated, Sections 16—9—90 to 16—9—95
HI	Revised Statutes, Sections 708—890 to 780—896
ID	Code, Title 18, Chapter 22, Sections 18—2201, 18—2202
IL	Annotated Statutes (Criminal Code), Sections 15—1, 16—9
IN	Code, Sections 35—43—1—4, 35—43—2—3
IO	Statutes, Sections 716A.1 to 716A.16
KS	Statutes Annotated, Section 21—3755
KY	Revised Statutes, Sections 434.840 to 434.860
LA	Revised Statutes, Title 14, Subpart D. Computer Related Crimes, Sections 73.1 to 73.5
ME	Revised Statutes Annotated, Chapter 15, Title 17—A, Section 357
MD	Annotated Code, Article 27, Sections 45A and 146
MA	General Laws, Chapter 266, Section 30
MI	Statutes Annotated, Section 28.529(1)—(7)
MN	Statutes (Criminal Code), Sections 609.87 to 609.89
MI	Code Annotated, Sections 97—45—1 to 97—45—13
MS	Revised Statutes, Sections 569.093 to 569.099
MT	Code Annotated, Sections 45—2—101, 45—6—310, 45—6—311
NE	Revised Statutes, Article 13(p) Computers, Sections 28—1343 to 28—1348
NV	Revised Statutes, Sections 205.473 to 205.477
NH	Revised Statutes Annotated, Sections 638:16 to 638:19

Table 2.1 State Computer Laws

NJ	Statutes, Title 2C, Chapter 20, Sections 2C:20—1, 2C:20—23 to 2C:20—34, and Title 2A, Sections 2A:38A—1 to 2A:38A—3
NM	Statutes Annotated, Criminal Offenses, Computer Crimes Act, Sections 30—16A—1 to 30—16A—4
NY	Penal Law, Sections 155.00, 156.00 to 156.50, 165.15 subdiv. 10, 170.00, 175.00
NC	General Statutes, Sections 14—453 to 14—457
ND	Century Code, Sections 12.1—06.1—01 subsection 3, 12.1—06.1—08
OH	Revised Code Annotated, Sections 2901.01, 2913.01, 2913.04, 2913.81
OK	Computer Crimes Act, Oklahoma Session Laws, Title 21, Sections 1951—1956
OR	Revised Statutes, Sections 164.125, 164.377
PA	Consolidated Statutes Annotated, Section 3933
RI	General Laws (Criminal Offenses), Sections 11—52—1 to 11—52—5
SC	Code of Laws, Sections 16—16—10 to 16—16—40
SD	Codified Laws, Sections 43—43B—1 to 43—43B—8
TN	Code Annotated, Computer Crimes Act, Sections 39—3—1401 to 39—3—1406
TX	Codes Annotated, Title 7, Chapter 33, Sections 33.01 to 33.05
UT	Computer Fraud Act, Utah Code Annotated, Sections 76—6—701 to 76—6—704
VA	Computer Crime Act, Code of Virginia, Sections 18.2—152.1 to 18.2—152.14
WA	Revised Code Annotated, Sections 9A.48.100, 9A.52.010, 9A.52.110 to 9A.52.130
WI	Statutes Annotated, Section 943.70
WY	Statutes, Sections 6—3—501 to 6—3—505

Part

I

Ch

2

In addition to these state laws, there is a federal law called the Computer Fraud and Abuse Act—18 U.S.C. §1030. (This federal law is found on the CD accompanying this book.) This law, coupled with the federal wiretap laws previously discussed, provides federal agents with powerful legal weapons to fight crime on the Net.

The Computer Fraud and Abuse Act makes it illegal to access a computer without proper authorization, or even to exceed your authorized access level, and imposes criminal and civil penalties. The penalties are most severe for unauthorized access of a federal computer or a computer of a financial institution: up to 10 years imprisonment per offense.

The law also makes it a crime to send a computer virus or other harmful program code into another person's computer, to steal a password, or to traffic in passwords. The Secret Service is charged with enforcement.

There have already been many prosecutions and convictions under this law, some of them controversial for the zeal shown by the Secret Service. One case previously mentioned, Steve Jackson Games, Inc. v. United States Secret Service (see **http://www.io.com/SS/appeal-opinion.html**), involved an illegal seizure of computers and arrest. The Secret Service didn't properly follow the law and ended up paying damages to Steve Jackson in the civil suit that followed.

Another more successful suit by the Secret Service involved its prosecution of Robert Morris, the infamous perpetrator of the Internet worm. United States v. Morris, 928 F.2d 504 (2nd Cir. 1991). (For more information, see **http://seamless.com/rcl/worm.html**.)

Morris was in a Ph.D. program in computer science at Cornell University. (His father happens to be a famous computer security expert.) As a part of his academic studies, young Morris started work on a kind of computer virus that later became known as the *Internet worm.*

The new virus he created exploited flaws in Internet e-mail design so as to infiltrate computer systems and spread to other systems. His goal was to show the inadequacies of security measures on the Internet.

He crossed the legal line when he decided to test his code by surreptitiously releasing it onto the Internet on November 2, 1988, from a computer at MIT. His new baby was supposed to be harmless, just to get in and spread, but not hurt anything. Nobody was supposed to even know it was in his computer.

Morris just wanted to prove a point. But alas, his baby turned into a Frankenstein. It had unexpected side effects. The Internet worm started reproducing itself and spreading far faster than he expected. Before he knew it, computers around the country were starting to crash or become catatonic.

Morris tried to fix things by sending out an anonymous message, this time from a computer at Harvard, explaining how to kill the worm. But, the Internet was already so clogged by the worm that people didn't get his message in time.

Computer systems all over the place were shut down, including systems at leading universities, military sites, and medical research facilities. Millions of dollars of damage was done in the form of lost time to deal with the worm.

Morris was discovered, arrested, and found guilty of violation of the Computer Fraud and Abuse Act. He appealed on the basis that he lacked criminal intent, it was all just a horrible accident, a science experiment gone bad.

His conviction was upheld by the appellate court. It found that the statute only required intent for unauthorized access of a computer, not intent to damage. He was clearly guilty of unauthorized access.

Another interesting prosecution under both the federal Computer Fraud statute and the Wire Fraud statute (18 U.S.C. '1343) involves a well-known hacker, Robert Riggs, known by his computer handle as the "Prophet."

The case was United States v. Riggs. 743 FedSupp 556 (E.D. Ill. 1990). (For more information, see **http://www.eff.org/pub/Legal/Cases/Phrack_Neidorf_Riggs/**.)

The Prophet was charged with devising and implementing a scheme to defraud using computers. Here is the language of the actual amended indictment that describes the scheme:

> To fraudulently obtain and steal private property in the form of computerized files by gaining unauthorized access to other individuals' and corporations' computers, copying the sensitive computerized files in those computers, and then publishing the information from the computerized files in a hacker publication for dissemination to other computer hackers.

This scheme was supposedly known to a secret cabal in the Internet hacker community as the Phoenix Project. The overall purpose of the scheme was to disseminate information that would help other hackers to break into computers and elude law enforcement.

The only thing the prosecutors could nail them on, however, was the theft of a supposedly secret file on the 911 telephone system from a Southern Bell computer (as it turned out it wasn't secret at all). In a convoluted story involving issues of trade secrets, most of the defendants eventually pled guilty and the Prophet went to jail. (See **http://www.eff.org/pub/Legal/Cases/Phrack_Neidorf_Riggs/phrack_riggs_neidorf_godwin.article**.)

 For inside information on hackers and their interesting above-the-law, "all information should be free" philosophy, see Phrack's home page at **http://freeside.com/phrack.html** and a hypertext version of the well-known book on the subject, *The Hacker Crackdown*, at **http://www.eecs.nwu.edu/hacker_crackdown/**. Another interesting and related Web can be found at **http://ww.paranoia.com/**.

The Growing Problem of Computer Viruses

Something as bad as the Internet worm of 1988 hasn't hit since that time, but plenty of other smaller incidents have occurred. This is a growing problem that is not likely to go away any time soon.

Essentially, a computer virus is an act of vandalism and under federal law it's a crime to use a virus to infect another person's computer even if no harm is intended. The problem is, it's very hard to know where a virus came from when you detect it on your computer. Sometimes it's even hard to know your computer is infected.

A personal story will help illustrate the problem and possible solutions to the problem. My law firm's computers were infected for nine months in 1995 before I happened to detect the virus when I bought a new, improved virus-detection program. The old virus-detection program supposedly guarding all our computers had failed to detect the virus.

The virus I found goes by the glamorous name of the stealth_boot.B virus. It just hung out in high memory, looking for a chance to infect the boot sectors of any floppies it could find. Once on a floppy, it would spread to any other hard drives the floppy was put into.

Before we knew it, all our computers and thousands of diskettes were infected with the little stealth bugger. The effect of having the hidden program in high memory was not great: just occasional, seemingly random errors of the kind computer users are all too familiar with. We never suspected a virus!

Once found, the stealth virus was relatively easy to kill, but very time-consuming. There were 18 computers to clean and thousands of diskettes. I knew it would cost thousands of dollars in overtime to cure our disease, so I took a look at our insurance policy, just for the hell of it. Nothing in there about computer viruses, but I went ahead and made a claim anyway.

At first the insurance company was going to deny the claim. This was the first time anyone in the state had ever even made such a claim. But, then it checked with the national underwriters. They decided to pay the claims under the vandalism provision of the policy. The expenses incurred to repair the acts of vandalism were covered.

 TIP   If you get hit with a virus that causes you damages, submit a claim with your insurance company and ask for coverage under the vandalism clause.

My mistake that allowed this virus to get through was low vigilance. I had a false sense of complacency because we had never been infected before, and I didn't bother to upgrade and keep my existing virus checking software current. (Good programs are updated quarterly.)

Now we have the latest software and a strict policy requiring all employees to check any disk before it's run on any of our computers. We treat any new program, even factory issue right out of the shrink-wrap, as potentially bugged.

You can receive software that is infected and the sender has absolutely no idea it's infected. I'm sure that's what happened in our case. As additional protection, whenever a new version of our software virus protection program comes out, we'll be among the first to buy it. It's a good investment. Further, all our computers are now fully inoculated, and forced virus checking is built into the autoexec.bat files.

N O T E   Remember that even the most elaborate virus-detection systems can't protect you from a new and devilish virus. Back up often to prepare for a crash. Also, try and ensure against all kinds of catastrophic computer failure—viruses, lightning strike, theft, fire.

Ask your insurer exactly what is covered in advance of trouble and find out what it will do if your system fails. If you are not covered, look for another company that will insure you. Depending on your business and what the virus or other unexpected loss does to you, the damages could be overwhelming. ■

TIP Assume every new disk or program is infected and don't run it until you've checked for viruses.

There are many good anti-virus Web sites on the Internet that can provide you with a wealth of information. Make time to visit a few of them soon.

For instance, see Symantec's anti-virus Web site at **http://www.symantec.com/avcenter/**, McAfee's Web site at **http://www.mcafee.com/**, IBM's at **http://www.brs.ibm.com/ ibmav.html**, Joe's (it's good, really) at **http://www.valleynet.com/~joe/**, or the Web site of the National Computer Security Association at **http://www.ncsa.com/**. ●

Part
I

Ch
2

Getting Connected

The Various Ways to Connect: Which One Is Right for You?

by Jerry Honeycutt and James Bryce

So you want to get online with the Internet. How should you do it? Which of the methods to access the Internet is right for you? Which will give you the best access to the services you need? Which has the most reasonable cost? This chapter helps you decide how to connect to the Internet by explaining the options and by giving you a set of guidelines you can follow to determine the best access method for your needs.

The next few chapters cover each of the access methods in more detail, but it's worth taking time to consider the alternatives before reading more. That way you'll know which chapters are more relevant to your needs. You also can make sure the details fit within your anticipated requirements.

You'll seldom choose your access method on the basis of cost alone. The services you want to access must be provided and readily available—a simple issue that's often overlooked by newcomers to the Internet. Factors other than cost and services provided may also be important. For example, you should carefully consider the line speeds needed to support the traffic you anticipate, as well as the size and overall purpose of the Internet access.

Learn about the different ways to connection

You'll find a variety of ways to connect to the Internet. You'll learn about each in this chapter.

Compare each method

This chapter compares the advantages and disadvantages of each method so you can make an informed decision.

Add up the costs of each method

You'll learn about the costs of each method.

Learn about other important considerations

There are many other things to think about when choosing a method to connect to the Internet.

In the next few pages I'll discuss the available alternatives, noting the important advantages and disadvantages of each. There are several factors to consider. By the end of this chapter you should be able to narrow the choices down considerably and choose the best method for your needs. ■

Considerations on How to Connect

An overwhelming number of companies offer Internet access or services; all try hard to get your money. Full-page advertisements by online services seem to promise everything you could want, but a careful shop-around shows the promises don't always meet your needs.

You also can run into many strange terms, such as PPP, SLIP, dialup-access, and IP routers. All of these terms are explained in this and following chapters.

Luckily for newcomers to the Internet, there are really only five ways to connect, as follows:

- *Your own direct gateway*—This method uses a dedicated machine (a gateway) to connect into the Internet backbone. This gives you full access to all services but is expensive to set up and maintain. It's really only for large corporations.

- *Internet Service Provider*— These are usually called ISPs. They're direct providers of connection to the Internet. Your machine accesses the ISP's gateway that provides limited or full access to Internet services. These companies are not the same as online services; ISPs only act as gateways to the Internet; online services provide other services and interpose control and filtering between you and the Internet. ISPs often offer dialup and dedicated telephone connections. All offer analog service; many are starting to offer ISDN service. Both ISDN and dedicated services can potentially provide higher data rates and more flexible services. Examples of a direct service provider at the national level include UUNET Technologies and PSI. Local and regional ISPs have sprung up throughout the United States, Canada, and many other countries.

- *Online Services*— This category is designed for the "classic" online services such as CompuServe, Prodigy, and America Online. These are indirect service providers because they interpose their computers between you and the Internet, controlling the interface and possibilities for exchange of information far more than the ISP environment. This control is convenient, as it makes connection easy, but it adds considerably to your costs and may remove functions and access you want. Online service Internet connection is chosen by many individuals who are already using an online service. But not all online services offer all Internet features. And the costs associated with this type of connection can be relatively high when compared to ISPs.

- *Access through your company's system*—This may be available for your personal use as more and more companies are recognizing the benefits of having their staff on the Internet and experienced in Internet use.

- *Free use of someone else's direct gateway*—This usually involves getting permission to use someone else's gateway for full access to all services. This is a handy method for students whose Internet access is usually bundled with their general student fees; those out of school may be out of luck when it comes to finding someone willing to let them use their gateway.

Choosing the connection method that's right for you isn't difficult. Your answers to the following questions will lead you to the most sensible alternative:

- Are you accessing the Internet for your company or for yourself?
- What services do you need?
- How much time will you spend using the system each month?
- How much are you willing to pay?
- What data rate do you want?

If the access is for you, then adding your own gateway doesn't make economic sense. If the access is for your company as a whole, then using online services is too restrictive.

Company Access

If you want company-wide access, online services seldom are able to provide the level of performance or function needed to support company e-mail, FTP, and other Internet services. Online services don't have the throughput larger corporations require, and maintaining a large number of user accounts on someone else's system is not a wise move from a systems administration point of view. In addition, setting up a large number of accounts with online services usually costs considerably more than setting up similar numbers of accounts through a company owned direct gateway or an Internet service provider.

Most companies should obtain their own domain name, for example supercorporation.com. This provides a professional aspect for their e-mail, Web, and other corporate communications. Equally important, a domain name is the property of its owner. As a result it stays with the owner regardless of the means of connecting to the Internet. Contrast this with the user who does not own a domain name. Then the user or firm must use the domain supplied by the service provider. When providers are changed the domain name changes and the electronic mail address changes, and the Web URL changes, and so on. What a mess! We'll cover more on domain names later in this chapter.

CAUTION

Not all Internet service providers provide domain name service and none of the large online services provide it. So this rules out the online services for any serious business right away. Using an online service (or anyone else but yourself) for your domain identity is like getting married—easy to get into, hard to get out of.

The list of alternatives can be narrowed more. It's rare to find a company that can "borrow" another company's gateway. Unless the second company is willing to share the costs of the gateway, most companies that have a gateway are reluctant to let outsiders (or competitors) use their system.

A company is left with the choice of either using a direct gateway to the Internet or using an Internet service provider. The choice between these two options usually comes down to an issue of the size of the company and a comparison of the cost to connect for each method. Setting up a gateway is expensive, but may be cheaper than arranging accounts with a service provider if the volume of traffic is high.

Personal Access

If you want access for yourself, or for a very small company, it's unreasonable to have your own dedicated gateway. Not only is the cost high, but the investment will not pay for itself and will require continual administration. For all but the most affluent, the choice for connecting to the Internet is between borrowing someone's gateway, using a service provider, or using an online service.

Finding a gateway you can use is difficult. Give it a shot, if you like; just call up the local businesses and educational institutions and ask for free access to their Internet gateway —who knows, chutzpah has gotten much bigger things. Usually this type of access is available only if you know someone who can vouch for your reliability. If you're well-connected in the human sense, go for it; you'll get full Internet access at no cost. What have you got to lose? They can only say, "No," and they might say, "Yes."

Setting up an account with an Internet service provider and then making the connection work used to involve a big time startup curve filled with the esoterica of TCP/IP, C, and UNIX. Those days are gone. Any ISP expecting that of its clients is either out of business or soon will be. ISPs either supply users with pre-configured software kits from the free/shareware available on the Internet or sell or support commercial packages.

Most service providers offer a flat-fee rate that provides a certain number of hours free, with a connect-time surcharge after the free hours are used up. This is a cut-throat business and it pays to shop around. It's hard to tell how long we'll be seeing an ISP on every corner. Expect these guys to be gobbled up like mom and pop banks at a meeting of the National Bankers Association.

N O T E The near certainty that you'll be changing ISPs either due to the ISP going out of business, being eaten alive by another ISP, or your finding a better deal, drives home the near absolute requirement that you obtain your own domain name. With that name in hand, your bargaining position is substantially better (you're no longer married to the ISP's name) and your printing costs (for your new cards, et al.) are drastically lower. ■

The last alternative, online services, would seem to be the choice for most individuals. But the proliferation of ISPs both locally and nationally has seriously cut into the online services' market share. Though online services are loath to admit it, it's a little hard for someone who has discovered the full range of resources available on the Internet to take the online services seriously. Let's face it folks, CompuServe, America Online, Prodigy, and Bill's new Microsoft Network are in trouble. They have to come up with some reason for you to use them. If all they're going to do is act as gateways to the Internet, they'd better be ready to compete on price, and they aren't doing that now. If they claim to be providing more than Internet access, you'd better check to see what, if anything, it's worth to you.

Online services certainly are a good way to start until you're better able to decide exactly what your Internet requirements really are. But most such services don't offer full access to all Internet capabilities. And the expense of using an online service for even a few hours a week can become alarmingly high.

Domain Names

A *domain name* is a unique identifier for your company that's used, for example, when mail is addressed to you. Domain names provide two pieces of information separated by a period: your company's online identification, or name, and the type of company or organization you are. For example, Que is an imprint of the publishing corporation, Macmillan Computer Publishing. The domain name for the corporation is mcp.com; the com indicates it's a commercial enterprise. An editor's mail address might be aeinstein@que.mcp.com (Que strives to have well-qualified editors.) The que is the name of a sub-domain; usually this is a division, as with Que, or a specific server. In any case, this part is assigned by the corporation. But the mcp.com is assigned by the InterNIC, the part of the Internet in charge of domain names; in late 1995, the actual administration of naming was contracted to a private company.

You apply to InterNIC for the name; they issue and propagate your name throughout the Internet to name servers that advise other servers looking for you or your company. These servers translate the name to the IP address that is programmed into a particular device on your network. The whole thing is called the Domain Name System (DNS).

N O T E Names mean something to people. It's far easier to remember an address using DNS than it is to recall 198.45.6.32 or whatever IP address is associated with a given domain name. Besides, you can have several names pointing to a single IP address. This technique allows you to have a single machine with a given IP address handling the business of a number of different domains. And any one of those names may move to another IP address without disrupting the others—lots of flexibility. ■

▶ **See** "An Introduction to TCP/IP," **p. 108**

The end part of the domain name, called the *domain identifier*, comes after the period. There are six domain identifiers associated with different types of organizations:

.com	Commercial company
.edu	Educational institution
.gov	A governmental body of the United States of America
.mil	Military of the United States of America
.net	An Internet access provider or other network support type organization
.org	Anything that doesn't fall into one of the other categories; this usually includes charitable and trade associations

These identifiers are used by organizations throughout the world, but notice that the .gov and .mil identifiers are generally restricted to the United States. (OK, since you asked, **socks@whitehouse.gov** or **president@whitehouse.gov**). However, there is another category of domain names arranged by geographic location. Here in Austin, Texas, the city has the domain ci.austin.tx.us. To send e-mail to the mayor you use the address **mayor@ci.austin.tx.us**.

ON THE WEB

Point your browser to **http://www.internic.net** for more on the domain name system.

N O T E This use of the domain name carries over to services other than e-mail: **http://www.mcp.com** and **http://www.ci.austin.tx.us**. Or, in my case, **http://www.bryce.com/~bryce**. All of these are World Wide Web addresses. In the last one, my home page, the /~bryce tells your browser to look in my home directory on the Web server. Actually, this server is under the domain name of my Internet service provider, but through the magic of alias redirection, my domain service, mail servi1ce, and Web service are handled on the ISP's server. ▩

Services You Need

While deciding which method to use to access the Internet, you need to consider the types of services you want from the Internet. If all you need is e-mail, then any kind of access will provide it, but some can be ridiculously expensive.

The Internet offers many types of services; each is explained in depth in other chapters. As a starting point, decide which of the following services are necessary and which ones are less important. Remember,you may want to wait to answer these questions until after you've read the relevant chapters:

- ▪ *Electronic mail (e-mail)*—Sending mail to and from other Internet users
- ▪ *Telnet*—Remote logins to other machines on the Internet that allow you to work on the remote system or try software
- ▪ *FTP*—File transfers between machines that allow you to download software, graphics, and other files
- ▪ *World Wide Web (WWW) access*—An interlinked and usually graphical information service
- ▪ *UseNet newsgroups*—A set of bulletin boards for conversations on many different subjects
- ▪ *Gopher*—An information search and retrieval system
- ▪ *Archie*—A method for finding files to transfer
- ▪ *Internet Relay Chat (IRC)*—A text conversation system much like a CB
- ▪ *Video over the Internet*—This includes multimedia and video conferencing options of all kinds

- *RealAudio*—A newly developing product that can exchange quality audio over the Internet
- *Internet telephone technology*—Allows you to make full duplex phone calls anywhere in the world over the Internet

ON THE WEB

Listen for RealAudio at **http://www.realaudio.com** and ring up Internet phones at **http:// www.itelco.com**. See a plethora of video at **http://www.yahoo.com/Computers_and_Internet/ Video** and **http://www.yahoo.com/Computers_and_Internet/Videoconferencing**.

Any system directly connected to the Internet through a gateway (your company's or a borrowed gateway) can provide complete access to all the services listed above (unless the system administrator blocks them for some reason).

Online services provide e-mail; most are adding the other services slowly. Not all the services are available with all online providers, though, so check with a representative to see what services they offer. You don't want to be frustrated by lack of support for a service you need.

If you intend to use e-mail frequently, it may be worth finding out if any mail you write is sent immediately (the usual case) or batched for transmission at a later time. Batching is used by some services to cut costs because the Internet link needs to be connected only for a few minutes at regular intervals. However, your e-mail delivery is slowed with a batch system.

N O T E In my experience, batching of mail is a major drawback. When I'm working on a project, I'm frequently talking on the phone, faxing, and e-mailing all at once. If the e-mail is delayed at either end, it substantially slows the work. I've noticed batching delay often happens when the classic online services are used. ■

T I P If your service provider batches your e-mail, you can use someone else's SMTP mail server to send your e-mail. I won't print a specific address here for fear of flooding some poor, unsuspecting mail server with messages, but you can easily find public SMTP mail servers on the Internet. You can try combining `smtp.`, `mail.`, or `mailhost.` with the domain name of a popular Internet service, such as **mailhost.domain.net**.

Direct Connection Through a Gateway

A direct connection (often called a *dedicated connection*) is one in which you or your company attach to the Internet backbone through a dedicated machine called a *gateway* or *IP router*. The connection is over a dedicated telephone line capable of high-speed transfers. The gateway becomes part of the Internet architecture and must remain online at all times. You can then use a computer on the gateway's network to access the Internet services.

Part

II

Ch

3

N O T E   The term "dedicated" is used in various ways. In this case I am referring to a device actually attached to the Internet. Sometimes "dedicated" simply means the Internet service provider has a modem set aside for your use; this arrangement does not stipulate a machine always reserved for your connection. ■

Typically, dedicated connections imply high volumes of traffic and require systems with multi-megabit data rates. This type of connection usually is used by a large corporation to provide Internet access to employees. It's unlikely that an individual or small company would have direct gateway access primarily because of the high cost of installation and maintenance.

To create a direct access system, you must work with the Internet Network Information Center (InterNIC) to establish a domain name and IP addresses for your company. Then you must install gateways on the Internet backbone. The capital expense of such a system is high, both for initial hardware and software and for continuing support. Considerable costs may also be involved for dedicated telephone lines capable of supporting high data rates.

Obtain a copy of the Internet RFC (Request for Comment) 1359, "Connecting to the Internet," to see what steps you should follow. This document was developed specifically to help companies attach to the Internet.

N O T E   You can obtain a copy of this or any other RFC by pointing your Web browser to **http://ds.internic.net**. I also suggest you check out **http://www.ietf.org** to see what the Internet Engineering Task Force is up to; they write the RFCs.

To obtain a printed copy of the RFC, call the Internet Network Information Center at 800-235-3155, have the RFC number at hand. ■

Connecting Through Another Gateway

An alternative method of connecting to the Internet through a gateway relies on using a "friendly" machine or network. In such a system, a corporation or educational institution that has an Internet gateway may allow you to access the Internet through their system, usually through an attached modem. Because this type of access gives you freedom on their networks, many organizations now refuse this type of piggy-back access.

If you're lucky enough to find a company or school that will let you use their network, you simply call into a communications port on the network or gateway, then route through the gateway to the Internet. In many ways, it's as though you are a machine on the provider's network. Typically, you have unlimited access to the Internet's services, though some companies do set restrictions.

This type of access is usually readily available for students. Most universities have dedicated gateways to the Internet and allow registered students to dial in to the systems for full access. Usually, the Computer Sciences or the Information Technology department has information about access.

N O T E If you're a student, connecting through your school's Internet gateway is the most economical and least limiting option. If you've graduated, check out the alumni association, credit union, or other university- affiliated organizations to see if your continued membership includes Internet access. If they don't know what you're talking about, ask to see their PR people and executive director and suggest Internet access be added as a perk to encourage membership. ■

Using an Internet Service Provider

Internet service providers are companies with an Internet gateway shared among many organizations and individuals. ISPs can be local, regional, national, or international in scope. An ISP offers you options in three distinct categories: telephone line, protocol, and service.

Telephone Line Options

Telephone line options include various ways for you to connect with the ISP over the telephone system. There are more ways than you might think:

- Dialup connection through the telephone system
- Dedicated connection through the telephone system
- Plain Old Telephone Service (POTS, analog)
- Integrated Service Digital Network (ISDN)

A *dialup connection* is established only when you dial the provider and connect. Notice that the most emphasis is on your dialing the provider. But some providers also have the capability to dial you up. This would be useful if you want to have the provider connect when new mail is received, when an FTP transfer is requested, or a Web request is made of a server at your location.

A *dedicated connection* is a telephone line that is attached from your location to the provider and is always connected. There's sort of a middle ground of a "quasi-dedicated" connection that uses a dialup line that is never hung up. This sort of line is useful when you don't want to have the delay for connection or you want greater data rates than a standard telephone line can carry. Dedicated connections can be very expensive.

POTS is plain old telephone service, or, more formally, analog telephone technology. It's been with us for over 100 years. It's the line attached to your phone—that one sitting next to you right now. To use it with your computer, you attach a modem and call up the ISP.

ISDN is the new kid on the block. It's a totally digital technology. As a result, it offers the potential for much greater data rates than POTS. It also is able to set up and tear down connections in a fraction of a second; as a result when your equipment dials up your ISP, you're connected in less than a second—the same for disconnection. ISDN effectively destroys any advantage a dedicated line used to have. More and more ISPs are offering ISDN. Many providers are charging slightly more for ISDN than for POTS. Often the ISP has equipment that is totally ISDN and simply "spoofs" POTS calls that use modems, therefore, POTS calls use the same telephone numbers for analog service as ISDN calls.

Part
II

Ch
3

N O T E You'll hear some horror stories about difficulties getting ISDN service from your phone company. Most of these stories are dated. ISDN is invading so rapidly now, you'll probably have little difficulty finding competent help from your "local exchange carrier," telespeak for the phone company. True, you might have to go through two or three people to find someone trained in ISDN, but you should be successful with persistence. ■

▶ **See** "Setting Up an ISDN Connection," **p. 173**

Protocol Options

Your ISP may offer you several protocol options that affect what you can do with your Internet connection and how fast you can do it. Now just what do I mean by protocol options? Protocol options are the rules and standards the ISP's computers use to talk to your computers:

- Shell
- Serial Line Internet Protocol (SLIP)
- Point to Point Protocol (PPP)

A *shell protocol* provides a way for your computer to act as a terminal: by looking into the programs actually running on the computers of your ISP. So if you ask for a file transfer from some computer out on the Internet using FTP, the file will be transferred not to your computer, but to the computer of your ISP; you're simply seated at a dumb terminal connected to the ISP's computer. Then you'll have to go through another step to have the ISP's computer transfer the file to you. If you want to use the World Wide Web, you'll probably be limited to a character-based browser, such as Lynx, which is unable to convey the graphic nature of the Web and often can't handle complex interactions such as interactive forms. In other words, you don't want a shell protocol connection! Well, the only reason you would want one is that the equipment you have is not powerful enough to run some of the Internet applications or maybe your ISP doesn't offer anything but a shell account. But wait a minute! This is a book about using the Internet with Windows; your equipment is powerful enough. If your service provider doesn't offer a connection that lets you browse the Internet with graphical tools, get rid of the service provider. The only real reason for a shell account now is isolation of your system from the Internet. Since you're only running as a terminal, the bad guys out there can't get into your computer.

A *SLIP* connection lets your computer become a real node on the Internet. Now you can execute FTP and really get the file. SLIP allows you to connect your computer over a serial link, such as a telephone line. SLIP also allows your computer to send and receive IP packets using the TCP/IP protocol. But SLIP is an older remote access standard that is typically used by UNIX remote access servers. Use SLIP only if your ISP's site has a UNIX system configured as a SLIP server for Internet connections. The remote access server must be running TCP/IP. SLIP is not in great use today as PPP is taking over. SLIP lets you use the Web and have all the graphics and interactive forms. SLIP is a desirable protocol, but it's getting a little old and never was formally adopted as an official Internet protocol, so let's move on to PPP.

A *PPP* connection is the most advanced standardized connection you can get. It's a developing protocol and offers better performance and additional features over SLIP. Current work on PPP includes elements for aggregating multiple communication channels and compression. You want a PPP protocol connection! (But you can settle for SLIP if that's all you can get for a while.)

PPP has become the standard for remote access. Microsoft recommends that you use PPP because of its flexibility and its role as an industry standard and for future flexibility with client and server hardware and software. If a dial-up client is running PPP, it can connect to a network running IPX, TCP/IP, or NetBEUI protocols. PPP is the default protocol for the Microsoft Windows 95 Dial-Up adapter. In short, PPP has the following advantages involving standard protocols:

- PPP supports a standard way of encapsulating datagrams over serial links. This uses the ISO standard protocol High Level Data Link Control (HDLC). Since this is a standard that is nearly universal, IBM's mainframe communications use a relative of HDLC; it provides great flexibility for heterogeneous interconnection.

- PPP uses Link Control Protocol (LCP) that checks the integrity of the connection. It sets up such things as compression and various security protocols including Password Authentication Protocol (PAP) and Challenge Handshake Authentication Protocol (CHAP) that are standard throughout data communications.

- PPP supports a broad spectrum of network control protocols including NetBIOS Frames Control Protocol (NBF CP), Internet Protocol Control Protocol (IPCP), and Internet Packet Exchange Control Protocol (IPXCP) that works with the NetWare IPX protocol family.

ON THE WEB

For the minutia, all Internet standards tune into **http://www.ietf.org** and then to **http://ds.internic.net/rfc/rfc1880.txt**.

Since we're most concerned with Windows you'll probably be hearing about something called *WinSock*, short for *Windows Sockets*. Many people mistake this for a particular implementation called Trumpet WinSock, but that's an error. WinSock is a well-defined application program interface (API) that has become the de facto standard for Windows-based, communications-capable applications. Many software products incorporate the WinSock standard; Microsoft uses it in Windows 95 and Windows NT. Trumpet WinSock is just another implementation of the WinSock standard, albeit a widely used and excellent one. Microsoft was a founding member of thirty companies, the WinSock Group that was launched in 1991. Microsoft's Windows Open Systems Architecture (WOSA) includes WinSock. Version 2 of WinSock supports

- TCP/IP (and thus PPP)
- IPX/SPX (NetWare)
- AppleTalk
- OSI

ON THE WEB

See **http://www.stardust.com** for the latest on WinSock; you can also blow your horn at **ftp.trumpet.com.au**.

Service Options

Now for the good parts.

Your ISP can supply you with Internet services that actually do something for you. Look for an ISP that provides the following services:

- Electronic mail
- Name
- World Wide Web
- News
- Firewall

You already know what electronic mail is. Your provider should have an e-mail server on the Internet at all times. It should send out all messages you send within a few seconds of your request; that is, it should not batch e-mail for any appreciable period of time. It should be able to deal with all attachments and electronic mail.

▶ **See** "Files," **p. 231**
▶ **See** "Sending E-mail to Online Service Users," **p. 238**

Name service is vital to you. Your ISP should provide a service that allows you to have your own domain name and have it serviced on the ISP's machines. This way you can be sure the world knows who and where you are. The ISP will have to help you apply for a domain name and participate in periodic renewals. Once you receive the name, the ISP will make sure all Internet traffic addressed to that domain is directed to your mailbox, Web server, or other receiving location and protected from invasion or corruption by other users.

World Wide Web service means the ISP has a program running on a server that can store hypertext documents you prepare for your own home page. You should be able to change the contents of your own directory and home page at any time and as often as you like. World Wide Web service can include additions such as the ability to read and insert in a database responses to forms you've placed on the Web (Common Gateway Interface, CGI scripts).

▶ **See** " Getting Started: Basic Decisions," **p. 460**
▶ **See** " A Brief Look at *cgi-bin*," **p. 532**

News service is provided to receive newsfeeds from the newsgroups on the Internet. There are thousands of such groups. Every day a provider must download additions to the newsgroups, delete old items, and add new items. This takes a considerable amount of disk space. In many cases, a provider will choose not to take all the possible newsfeeds; some feeds will be chopped due to anticipated lack of interest, others for concern over possibly offensive content, and so on. If your ISP doesn't have a newsgroup you want, ask for it; usually the ISP can establish a connection. And should you want to establish a newsgroup, the ISP can help with that as well.

TIP I wouldn't subscribe to any independent service provider that doesn't give you access to the Clarinet newsgroups. These are regular newsfeeds about hundreds of topics such as business, national, and world news. It also has industry specific newsfeeds such as computers, travel, or insurance.

TIP You don't have to use only the news through your ISP; other sites are available over the Internet; just enter the site's URL as your news location.

Firewall service is security maintained by your ISP to block hackers from you and your information. This protects you from virus attacks, theft, and destruction of information. An elaborate collection of techniques is used to provide firewalls. In some cases *proxy servers* are set up to monitor Internet traffic into and out of your network. These servers are application specific—that is, they work only with a particular database or whatever you are seeking to protect. As a result, they can have much more protection built in than a router that must deal with generic forms of network traffic.

ON THE WEB

Get your firewall plans from **http://www.iwi.com/pubs/faq.htm**.

As you might suspect, not all, or even most, ISPs provide all these options. But now you have some idea of the range. Of course, the more you get the more you pay. But you'll be pleasantly surprised by the competitive marketplace.

Frontdoors and Backdoors

Let's take another perspective on these services. Telephone line options and protocol options fall into a category I call the frontdoor. Frontdoor options get you into the Internet. You have to have a frontdoor to reach the Internet or nothing will happen. Think of this in a physical way: a frontdoor is the connection of your computer through the phone lines to the Internet service provider's modem or ISDN terminal adapter bank.

On the other hand, backdoor options are the services that are provided once you're on the Internet. These services include mail service, Web service, domain name service. Since these services are provided through the Internet there's some magic possible. Here's the trick: You can have different providers for your frontdoor and backdoor options; in fact you can have a number of backdoor providers, all at the same time! Many people think their mail service must be provided by the same provider they dial into, which is wrong. The same goes for the Web and domain services and any number of other services that might appear on the Internet.

Everything Is Connected to Everything Else

Got it? Because on the Internet everything is connected to everything else, the physical location of a service is irrelevant once you're on. You don't care that someone else's Web page you're reading is on a server on the other side of the planet. Why should you care that the server that receives and stores your e-mail is also far away?

Why do you care? In shopping around you might find a provider that can give you a great deal on the frontdoor, but either doesn't have what you want in backdoor options or charges too much for them. For example, you might want to use a national provider like PSI for your frontdoor because they have points of presence in most major cities of the United States and can handle both POTS and ISDN with a single phone number. On the other hand, they may require you to use their domain name or charge too much for domain service. Fine. Use PSI for your frontdoor. Now shop around and find other providers that will cut you a good rate for domain name service, mail service, and all the other backdoor options. You might find you'll need one for domain name and e-mail and another for Web service. The Internet can handle all this: Simply configure your software to point to the appropriate location for the service. This book's already saved you its price.

If a provider won't sell you a backdoor service without selling the frontdoor, point out the great reduction in their costs your deal will make; they don't need a line for you, or a modem, and so on. These are really the big costs to an ISP. If they still don't bite, go somewhere else. And remember, unlike frontdoor options, you don't have to get your backdoor services locally; literally anyone in the world can provide them to you!

TIP   Remember, the incremental cost of providing many of these options is minor to an ISP; use this knowledge to get a lot for your money as I've just described, by shopping around.

N O T E   The setup procedure for using direct service providers is much easier than it was as the Internet took off with commercial use. Now Windows-based packages are available directly aimed at providing access through these providers. Often the providers have a listing and built-in configuration already in the software; you simply select your provider and enter your name. Internet Chameleon from NetManage, Internet in a Box from Spry/CompuServe, and SuperTCP from Frontier are examples of such programs.   ▧

Online Services

Online services like CompuServe, America Online, and Prodigy were popular before they offered Internet access. They provided a place for conversation, file transfer, and experimentation with new software. Now online services are rushing to connect to the Internet in an effort to attract new users and avoid mass defection of current ones.

Online (or indirect) service providers have expanded their Internet content dramatically in response to user demands. All online services have e-mail capabilities to and from the Internet; most offer or are in the process of developing UseNet access, FTP capabilities, and World Wide Web facilities. Now the largest providers have these classic Internet services.

Online services are a good choice for the casual Internet user who expects to be on the Internet less than two or three hours a month. If you occasionally want to send e-mail or browse newsgroups, and you don't anticipate spending a lot of time each day on the system, the online services are probably your best alternative. They charge users a basic fee as well as a connect-time rate, so low-volume users are not facing too large a monthly bill.

> **CAUTION**
>
> Beware: the Internet is addictive, and your plan to spend only half an hour a day can quickly change as you scan the UseNet newsgroups and especially the Web! Some services such as CompuServe, America Online, and Prodigy can add a hefty surcharge as your use grows. Check out the marketplace; charges change over time in response to demand and competition.
>
> When considering an online service, ask if there's a charge for each message (e-mail or newsgroup article) you send or receive. These charges can quickly add up! If there are charges other than a flat-amount connect time fee, find out if the additional charges are based on characters or messages sent and received. If you plan to download graphics, sound files, or binaries, character-based fees can add up at an alarming rate.

If you want to make use of some of the service's other features, the online service may be your best choice. Some of the other features offered are

- Large file download areas and technical support (a strength of CompuServe)
- Graphics-based multi-player games and general news (features of Prodigy)
- Online access to magazines and search databases (a good feature of America Online)

For any extensive use of the Internet, without use of the other features, online services have not been a good buy.

Connecting to an online service provider is easy. All you really need is a modem and a communications software package from the service or some software designed for the service from a third party. Unless you've been in deep space for the last ten years, you've probably gotten hundreds of online software disks in the mail and with hardware and software you've bought or been given.

Most online services have access numbers in large urban centers, so long-distance telephone bills are not an issue unless you live in the country or out of the immediate toll-free calling area. Check the availability of a dial-in port; some services may have too few lines (which may mean a lengthy wait to get access, or force you to use inconvenient hours). All major online services have 800 telephone numbers that provide this kind of information, as well as local access telephone numbers.

> **CAUTION**
>
> Make sure the online service you choose has a local number. Long-distance numbers add to your costs. Some systems that have 800 numbers add their cost to your bill when you use them. Also, some services require you to access the system through a packet-switched network (such as Tymnet, Datapac, and SprintNet), that adds its own connect charges. Make sure that you understand exactly how much access is going to cost you.

Part
II

Ch
3

Most online services now offer UseNet newsgroups, although some services filter the newsgroups received. They usually restrict newsgroups both to reduce the overall volume (approximately 90M per day) and to act as a censor to prevent "questionable" material from being available through their family-oriented services. For example, some services restrict any newsgroup with the word *sex* in the title. When asking about these services, find out if a full UseNet feed is available.

The major online services have graphical interfaces for Internet services. Some smaller ones rely on character-based systems, which may not be what you want. Character-based systems also limit the Internet facilities you can access. Use of the World Wide Web is severely hampered by a character-only interface.

 TIP Character-based browsers are available. The most popular is Lynx available at **ftp2.cc.ukans.edu/ pub/WWW/DosLynx/DLX0_A.EXE**.

There is a snobbishness within the Internet's e-mail and UseNet newsgroups; this is directed against those who used online services for access. These users are identified by their user names, which have the online service domain names attached (such as aol.com or compuserve.com). Users who accessed through online services were not considered to be really a part of the Internet community, but more like users sneaking in through a backdoor. Most of the folks who expressed such negative sentiments have been put out to some distant pasture where they belong. If you come in through an online service, you should and will be treated with all the respect you show others. Anyone who acts otherwise toward you is not worthy of your concern; ignore them.

 TIP You'll even run into some who feel that Windows, DOS, and Mac users shouldn't be on the Internet and that the Internet should be reserved for the UNIX, C, and TCP/IP elite.

Other Ways to Connect

There are some connection alternatives that haven't been mentioned so far, primarily because they are difficult to find and usually available only through the good graces of a user.

One of the Internet access methods is through a traditional bulletin board system (BBS). Some BBSs have now added limited Internet access to their services. The most commonly added feature is Internet e-mail capabilities, although a few BBSs also provide some UseNet newsgroup downloads and limited FTP or WWW features. The Internet capabilities tend to be more common on subscriber-based BBSs (where you pay either a flat fee or a connect-time fee) rather than the free-service BBS. To find a BBS that has these services in your area, check with local user groups, other bulletin board systems, or one of the magazines that caters to the BBS market.

Another alternative is to gain access through a professional society or organization that has user services. Some groups have BBS or online systems dedicated to member support, with a wide variety of capabilities available. A few groups have started to offer limited Internet services, especially e-mail that ties in with their professional e-mail service. If you belong to a national or international professional group, you should inquire about their membership services. Also, local organizations, ranging from yachting clubs to bowling teams, offer members access to their computer systems. Check with any groups you may belong to about Internet access.

For the very casual user, there's another choice that is becoming trendy—online bars and cafes. These places let you use a terminal to Net surf while you sip your favorite beverage (using a computer-generated username or one chosen by you as your login). Although the number of online establishments of this nature is still quite small, the popularity should ensure their spread to many cities.

Libraries and service-oriented businesses such as copy shops are starting to offer Internet access. Libraries often provide at least some limited use for no charge, but they may crack down when you spend ten hours playing Internet games.

Important Considerations

Here are the important points to bear in mind when choosing a service provider. There are numerous stories of users who selected a service provider before carefully considering all the factors and found themselves either severely limited in what they could access or faced with costs far out of proportion to what was expected. It's better to be safe and consider these points carefully again!

Services

Make sure the service you're considering supports the Internet features you want. After you decide what features you want from your Internet access (e-mail, FTP, UseNet newsgroups, WWW, name, and so on) ask your intended service provider if the services are fully supported. Many providers have a habit of telling you they are supported when in fact they only offer a subset or restrict some services in some way. Be direct and ask about limitations.

Some systems restrict access to Internet games such as multiuser dungeons (MUDs) to cut down on heavy Internet usage. If you're planning on using someone else's gateway, ask whether they object to your accessing this type of service.

Ask if the service limits the UseNet newsgroups. Is FTP service fully supported to any machine on the Internet? Is anonymous FTP supported? Does the system support World Wide Web? Are Gopher and Archie available? You get the idea. Decide what you want; then don't accept anything less.

 TIP Remember, through splitting between backdoor and frontdoor options, you can use more than one provider to get the right mix of cost and services.

Availability

If you're choosing an access method for a company or organization, you have to decide if the system should be available 24 hours a day. If so, and you don't want to have any delays in sending or receiving information through the Internet, a direct connection or direct service provider is necessary. Decide how often you want to check the Internet for traffic to you.

The same consideration applies to an individual. Do you want to check the Internet every hour for mail, or is once a day adequate? If you're using an online service and dialing in every hour, the expenses become very high. If you must have frequent access, an online service provider is a poor choice.

Cost

For many users, cost is a primary item in selecting a service. The most economical solution is to find a gateway you're allowed to access free of charge. This is relatively easy for university students but much more difficult for others. Therefore, you must carefully weigh the costs involved with other services.

Ask your service provider for a detailed fee schedule. Sometimes the charge depends on the services you access and the amount of time you spend on the service. Almost all services have a flat-fee monthly rate; many have a connect fee based on time beyond the flat-fee.

Make sure you know how you'll be billed for Internet access: is it time-, character-, or message-based? Is there a packet-switching network fee on top? If you're using an online service, ask if the Internet service is a "premium" service with additional fees over the usual service fee.

Don't assume high prices are related to better service; conversely, low prices may not mean the best deal. Make a list of the services you need and estimate your average and highest weekly usage; then shop around for the service that gives you all the services you need at the best price. Remember, some services include more than Internet access in their price: Will you be using those additional services?

Access

The access issue ties in with costs to some extent, especially if there is no local number for the service you want to use. Long distance bills add up, especially when you're spending several hours a week reading UseNet newsgroups or navigating the Web. An 800 number is no guarantee of free access. Most online services have a surcharge for use of an 800 line, since the line is considered a convenience for the user.

Several of the national providers have *points of presence* (*POP*) in all the major cites in the United States and Canada and often in Europe and Asia. If you need such coverage, they're worth a careful look.

ON THE WEB

Check out **http://www.cybertoday.com/isps** for listings of ISPs and references to other ISP lists throughout the world.

Ask about the number of lines an online service offers. Having a local access number is not a benefit to you if you can't access it when you want. Some online services keep only a few modems available in small population centers; it's worth finding out how easy it will be for you to access the system. It's not good to have to wait until the wee hours of the morning to connect!

Check the speeds supported by the access lines. Currently the fastest generally used modems on POTS lines operate at 28.8 kilobits per second (Kbps); your provider should offer this rate for most lines, and you should buy a 28.8 Kbps modem to enjoy the full advantage of the service. ISDN is becoming widely available and offers data rates in multiples of 64 Kbps with fraction of a second set up/tear down times; ask if the provider has ISDN.

▶ **See** "The Advantages of ISDN," **p. 177**

Some systems shut down for a couple of hours late at night for system backups, or are shut down part of some day during the week. Ask your service provider if they have round-the-clock access, limited access during certain hours, or no access at some periods.

Part

II

Ch

3

Software

If you're using an online service, there may be a special software package needed to access the system. Although these software applications are usually free, you still have to find a copy and learn how to use it. Also, some systems don't work well with some communications packages. Check with the service provider to find out if your favorite communications software will work, or whether you should use their own interface.

As a general rule the online services provide the software you need to connect. Now that software is almost always Windows-based and new versions are available taking advantage of Windows 95's power. The major online services, CompuServe, America Online, and Prodigy, all incorporate Internet software in these packages.

Security

Security is important to protect your activities on the system. You don't want someone else to be able to access your e-mail mailbox or see what newsgroups you're reading. Ask the intended service provider how they manage security and whether they support any kind of encryption for sensitive mail messages. This broaches the issue of firewall services.

Many online systems make it clear in their user agreements that you have no rights to privacy if you use their system. Read your agreement carefully. It may look like mumbo-jumbo, but you could be giving up some important rights to privacy.

Technical Support

Technical support is usually an issue for the individual user. Although most corporations have knowledgeable people on staff to handle gateways and routers, the ins and outs of making everything connect up may make it necessary to use service help from a provider even for the largest of users. It's good to know how much (if any) support you can expect from a service. Beware of promises. One popular online provider touted their help lines as being fully staffed by professionals 24 hours a day; often there was at least a two-hour wait for someone to answer a call; then another long wait for a call back from them with the answer!

Even though you may be an experienced computer user, you'll still need technical support. Many services have a lot of protocol behavior that's transparent to the user, but which can cause anomalous behavior. Having someone to ask about the problem is not only handy but vital to the functioning of your communications systems. ●

Connecting Through a LAN with Windows 95 and Windows NT

by Craig Zacker

While the 16-bit Windows operating systems (Windows 3.1 and Windows for Workgroups) have some rudimentary support for networking, they both require third party software to allow them to connect to the Internet. Their 32-bit counterparts, however, Windows 95 and Windows NT, ship with all of the software you need to connect to almost any local area network. They have also fully integrated the TCP/IP protocols into the operating system, which allows you to use your LAN to connect directly to the Internet. If your company has a high-speed network connection to the Internet, you will achieve performance levels through the network that might make you want to throw away your modem.

Both Windows 95 and Windows NT Workstation 4.0 include support for many different Ethernet and Token Ring network interface cards, a TCP/IP protocol stack that includes a WinSock library, and a collection of the standard TCP/IP applications, such as PING, FTP (File Transfer Protocol), and Telnet. This chapter explains the process of installing and configuring the software modules needed to connect both Windows 95 and Windows NT PCs to the Internet through a LAN.

Some basic information about TCP/IP networks

TCP/IP is the native protocol suite used on the Internet and is becoming an increasingly popular choice for local area networks as well.

Types of Internet connections found on LANs

The way in which your LAN is connected to the Internet will determine the services that you can use, the performance level, and the security of your network.

How to install TCP/IP support in Windows 95 and Windows NT

The TCP/IP stack, although it ships with the operating system, is not installed in Windows 95 by default. Windows NT users who elected not to install TCP/IP during the operating system installation, may do so later.

How to configure the TCP/IP protocol

Correct configuration of the TCP/IP operating parameters is crucial to a successful network connection.

How to test and troubleshoot your TCP/IP connection

Both Windows 95 and Windows NT include a collection of diagnostic utilities for the TCP/IP protocols.

N O T E If your computer is not directly connected to a LAN (with an Ethernet card, for example), or if your LAN is not directly connected to the Internet and you use a modem connection instead, see Chapter 5, "Connecting to a PPP or SLIP Account with Windows 95." ▪

This chapter assumes that your computer is already physically connected to the LAN and that your network interface card is already installed and operating with other network protocols (such as those used with the Novell NetWare or Microsoft Windows Network clients). ▪

An Introduction to TCP/IP

TCP/IP (Transfer Control Protocol/Internet Protocol) is the name given to a collection of protocols that were designed in the 1970s for use on the large-scale, mixed-platform, packet-switched network that eventually became known as the Internet. The motivating force behind their creation was to design a set of protocols that would operate independently from any particular hardware platform or operating system. The Internet is composed of many different kinds of computers, from PCs to mainframes, all of which run TCP/IP.

Although Windows 95 and Windows NT support other communications protocols (such as IPX/SPX to communicate with Novell NetWare servers and NetBEUI to communicate with Windows NT servers), your system requires TCP/IP to talk to other computers on the Internet. Programs such as FTP, Telnet, and World Wide Web (WWW) browsers are all based on the TCP/IP protocol.

N O T E Many administrators of heterogeneous networks have come to adopt TCP/IP as their sole networking protocol. It can be used with all of the major network operating systems, and can increase network efficiency by reducing traffic levels and simplifying administration. ▪

The TCP/IP Protocols

TCP/IP is named for its two most commonly used protocols, but it is actually a suite composed of dozens of different protocols. Many of these operate invisibly to the average user, however, addressing the enormous problems of network access and internetwork routing that affect a network as large and diversified as the Internet.

The TCP/IP protocols can be said to operate on four levels:

- ▪ Network Access
- ▪ Network
- ▪ Transfer
- ▪ Application

The Application protocols function closest to the user interface of the two communicating systems, while the Network Access protocols function closest to the network medium itself. The following sections examine these four types of protocols individually, but they all work together on each TCP/IP-equipped computer.

Network Access Protocols   Network Access protocols are used to facilitate the transmission of IP packets over all kinds of network types. Some, like the Address Resolution Protocol (ARP), allow TCP/IP to be used with a specific type of network interface adapter. ARP, for example, is used to translate IP addresses (the unique identifiers by which networked computers are known to TCP/IP protocols) to the MAC addresses hardcoded into Ethernet adapters.

Other Network Access protocols are devoted to the routing of packets between networks. In TCP/IP parlance, a device that is connected to two or more networks and exchanges data packets between them is called a gateway. When you connect to a remote site over the Internet, your packets may wend their way through dozens of different gateways during the trip. Protocols like GGP, the Gateway to Gateway Protocol, allow these gateway systems to exchange information amongst themselves. In this way, they can advertise their capabilities and make more efficient routing decisions as a result.

N O T E   The function of a gateway on a TCP/IP network should not be confused with the definition of the term in the general networking vocabulary. Standard networking usage defines a gateway as a device that translates between different protocols. A TCP/IP gateway fulfills the functions that are more traditionally associated with the term router.

Network Protocols   The primary Network protocol is the Internet Protocol (IP). IP functions as the delivery service for all of the other TCP/IP protocols, which are carried within IP packets. The packets transmitted by IP are known as *datagrams*. An IP datagram contains all of the information it needs to reach its ultimate destination: the IP address of the receiving system and the Transport protocol on that system to which it should be delivered.

IP is what is known as a *connectionless, unreliable* protocol. Far from describing the protocol's efficiency, these are technical terms that define its capabilities. A connectionless protocol is one that transmits packets without ascertaining whether the destination machine is able to receive them, and without receiving any acknowledgment in return. An unreliable protocol is one that contains no inherent mechanism for detecting and correcting errors. The reason for the omission of these vital networking services in IP is that they are provided by higher level protocols when they are needed. Providing these services for every IP packet would greatly increase overall network traffic unnecessarily.

Transfer Protocols   There are two protocols that function at the Transfer level, both of which use IP as their carrier. These are TCP, the Transfer Control Protocol and UDP, the User Datagram Protocol. TCP is by far the more commonly used of the two, forming the combination with IP for which the entire suite is named. All of the Internet connections that you will make to FTP and World Wide Web sites will use TCP and IP.

TCP is a *reliable, connection-oriented* protocol. This means that before any user data is transmitted, a series of handshake packets are exchanged between the source and destination computers. This ensures that the destination system is ready to receive data and establishes a logical connection between the two machines that will be maintained during the entire transmission. Each file that is sent to your computer during an FTP or HTTP (World Wide Web) session is transmitted using a separate TCP sequence. Each sequence is composed of multiple TCP segments corresponding to the individual IP datagrams.

Part
II

Ch
4

The reliability of TCP is provided by a checksum that is computed for each segment at the source. Upon reaching the destination system, the checksum is recomputed and the results compared with the value included in the segment. If the two values match, then the transmission is deemed successful and an acknowledgment is returned to the sender. If the values do not match, the segment is discarded. Unacknowledged segments are then automatically re-transmitted by the source. This process is known as positive re-acknowledgment with re-transmission.

These and other control mechanisms in a TCP transmission add significantly to the amount of traffic that is passed over the network. For that reason, TCP is only used when guaranteed delivery of data is required, such as when transferring data files. For less critical tasks, the User Datagram Protocol is employed. Like IP, UDP provides no acknowledgment of delivery or error correction. It is often used in cases where reliability is provided at a higher level, or when packets are so small that a complete retransmission affords less traffic than the inclusion of TCP's control overhead. UDP is typically used for logons, browsing, name resolution, and broadcast transmissions.

Application Protocols   The TCP/IP suite also includes protocols that provide services directly to applications, or indeed are applications in themselves. FTP and Telnet are examples of these, providing file transfer and terminal emulation services directly to the user through a standard interface, regardless of the platform on which they are run. Other, less visible Application protocols are the Domain Name Service (DNS), the Routing Information Protocol (RIP), and the Simple Mail Transfer Protocol (SMTP).

IP Addressing

One of the basic requirements for any network is a means to identify each of the individual computers so that a transmission can be sent from a node to any other node. This posed a particularly complex problem for the designers of TCP/IP, who had to devise an addressing system that could accommodate the computers on the thousands of different networks that make up the Internet.

The result of their efforts is a 32-bit IP address that uniquely identifies every network and host on the Internet. (A *host* is defined as the TCP/IP network interface within the computer, not the computer itself. A PC with two network interface cards is said to have two hosts, each of which must have its own IP address.)

This IP address is nearly always written in decimal form as four numbers (called *octets*), each ranging from 0 to 255, separated by periods (for example, 192.58.107.230). Each octet represents 8 bits (or 1 byte) of the 32-bit address. The IP addresses identify both the network on which the host is located, and the host itself. The network is always identified first in the IP address, but the number of octets used to represent the network can vary, depending on the class of the IP address assigned to your network.

Since every IP address on the Internet must be unique, there must be a clearing-house where addresses are registered to prevent duplication. The InterNIC (Internet Network Information Center) Registration Services Center, currently operated by Network Solutions, Inc. of

Herndon Virginia, performs this function. InterNIC registers the networks of businesses and other organizations based on the number of hosts they require. Three address classes exist, as shown below:

- Class A—The first bit of a class A address is always 0, meaning that the first octet of the address can have a value between 1 and 126. Only the first octet is used to represent the network, leaving the final three octets to identify 16,777,214 possible hosts. The subnet mask for a class A address would typically be 255.0.0.0.

- Class B—The first two bits of a class B network are always 1 and 0, meaning that the first octet can have a value between 128 and 191. The first two octets are used to identify 16,384 possible networks, leaving the final two octets to identify 65,534 possible hosts. The subnet mask would typically be 255.255.0.0.

- Class C—The first three bits of a class C network are always 1, 1, and 0, meaning that the first octet can have a value between 192 and 223. The first three octets are used to identify 2,097,151 possible networks, leaving the final octet to identify 254 possible hosts. The subnet mask would typically be 255.255.255.0.

InterNIC registers only networks, not individual hosts. It is the responsibility of the network administrator to assign host addresses in such a way as to avoid duplication.

N O T E The IP addresses used on your network will depend on the arrangement made with your Internet service provider (ISP). You may have an entire network address (of any class) registered to your organization, or you may lease a range of host addresses from the ISP's network. ▪

If your LAN is large (or divided into multiple network segments), your network administrator might choose to divide the network address assigned by InterNIC into *subnets*. A subnet is simply a logical subdivision of IP addresses that is used only within an organization's network. That is, subnet information is not transmitted out to the Internet.

A subnet is created by taking some of the bits of the IP address that identify the host and using them to identify a network address instead. The function of the *subnet mask* value required as part of every TCP/IP configuration is to identify which bits of the IP address represent the network and which the host. Viewing the address as a binary value, ones represent network bits and zeroes host bits.

For example, your company may operate a large internetwork that is composed of many network segments. If they were to register a class B network address, then a subnet mask of 255.255.0.0 would normally be applied. Since the decimal number 255 is equivalent to the binary number 11111111, this means that the first two octets of each IP address identify the network and the last two octets identify the host. Your network administrator may find it easier, however, to break up those 65,534 possible host addresses into 256 subnet addresses of 256 hosts each, for organizational reasons. To do this, a subnet mask of 255.255.255.0 is applied at each workstation, and the third octet now can be used to identify a logical subnet. Routing functions within the boundaries of the class B network can utilize the subnet information, but on the Internet, the third octet is seen as part of the host address.

IP addresses can be manually assigned and tracked by network administrators, but there are also server modules that dynamically assign IP addresses to workstations, as needed. These modules are defined by an Internet standard that was developed by Microsoft (in conjunction with several other organizations) and is called the Dynamic Host Configuration Protocol (DHCP). The Windows NT Server product ships with a DHCP service, and several third-party products provide the service as well.

Host Name Resolution

Along with the unique IP address, each computer on the Internet has a unique *host name* assigned to it. The host name is provided as a convenience to the user, who can more readily remember a name than a sequence of numbers. A host name usually consists of three or more groups of characters separated by periods and organized from right to left. The *domain name* part of the host name is assigned when your organization registers its network with InterNIC. This domain name is the equivalent of your network address and is found at the rightmost part of the host name; for example, all computers at International Business Machines (IBM) have a domain name of ibm.com.

Domains in the United States are registered using one of the accepted Internet domain types, which represent the activities of the network being registered. Among these are .com, for commercial enterprises, .gov, for government networks, .mil, for military networks, .edu, for educational institutions, and .org, for non-commercial organizations. Outside the United States domains usually reflect only the country in which the network is located: .fr for France, .uk for the United Kingdom, etc. As with IP addresses, only the domain name is registered with InterNIC. The network's administrator is responsible for maintaining the individual host names.

N O T E Many ISPs are able to register your domain for you, as part of their service. However, InterNIC can be contacted directly: by phone at (800) 444-4345 in the U.S., (619) 455-4600 in Canada, or by electronic mail at **info@internic.net**. Requests for Internet registration can be sent to hostmaster@internic.net. More information about the registration process is available from their anonymous FTP server, is.internic.net, in the /internic/faq directory, or on the World Wide Web at **http://rs.internic.net**. ▓

Host names can be assigned in any manner desired. Small organizations might add only one segment to the domain to make up the complete host name (for example, host1.ibm.com). Larger organizations might add several other segments (for example, server1.marketing.eastcoast.ibm.com) to designate the network, department, or workgroup in which the host is located. However long the host name is, it always corresponds to a unique IP address. By default, the host name of a Windows 95 or Windows NT machine is the computer's machine name with the domain name appended to it.

As stated earlier, host names are provided as a convenience for users. One of the first steps in any TCP/IP communications process is to replace host names with IP addresses, after which only the IP addresses are used to identify the computers involved. Since host names and IP addresses are both assigned by the network administrator and are not registered with InterNIC, there must be a mechanism located on the network that converts the host names into IP addresses, and vice versa. This process is called *name resolution*.

TIP One of the most common causes of failures to connect to an Internet site is a name resolution problem. When this occurs, try substituting the site's IP address for the host name, and a connection can often be established.

The HOSTS Table   Name resolution can be performed in several different ways. The simplest is for a conversion table to be stored on each computer. This is traditionally known as a HOSTS file. HOSTS is a simple ASCII text file listing IP addresses and their corresponding host names, in the following format:

```
127.0.0.1          localhost
102.54.94.97       rhino.acme.com        # source server
38.25.63.10        x.acme.com            # x client host
```

The IP addresses must be separated from the host names by at least one space, and all of the text following the pound sign ("#") is treated as a comment. Whenever a host name is used in one of the operating system's TCP/IP utilities, its IP address is looked up in the local HOSTS file and substituted for the host name.

N O T E Notice the first entry in the sample HOSTS file above, specifying localhost as the host name for the address 127.0.0.1. The 127 network address is always reserved for what is known as loopback services. It allows a machine to address itself, for testing purposes.

The HOSTS file is a static table. It is not changed except through manual editing. If a host name is not found in the HOSTS file, the system then turns to the network for name resolution. Placing the names and addresses of frequently accessed machines into your HOSTS file can therefore speed up the name resolution process and conserve network bandwidth.

The Domain Name Service   The main disadvantage of having the HOSTS table on the local machine is that it must be individually updated on each system whenever a new site is accessed. This why name resolution is usually performed at the server level instead. A domain name service (DNS) is the tool most often used for this purpose. A DNS is a static table like a HOSTS file, except that it is accessed from a server by many different users. When a new machine is added to the local network, the DNS table must still be manually updated, but only once for all of the users on the network.

A DNS that is connected to the Internet also works with other DNSs to resolve any host name that a user might specify. When you register a domain name with InterNIC, you specify two DNS servers for your domain, a primary and a backup. These servers become the authoritative sources for DNS information regarding your domain.

When a user at a remote site uses a host name to contact a system in your domain for the first time, his computer will fail to find the name in its own DNS. That DNS will then query another DNS on the other side of its Internet gateway for the host name. This DNS, too, will fail to find a valid entry, and the request will be passed upstream eventually to one of the *core* servers that are updated from the InterNIC databases. Your network's DNS server will be specified as the source for information about your registered domain, and all of the DNSs down the line will be updated with the requested host name and its IP address taken from your DNS.

Part
II

Ch
4

This way, information about your network has a means of propagating itself throughout the Internet, but it is only accessed on demand. No single DNS maintains information about every system on the Internet, a task that would be impossibly huge. Each DNS only maintains entries for the remote systems actually accessed by its users.

The Windows Internet Name Service A DNS is an effective means of name resolution for many networks, but it is still no more than a lookup table, a static list that must be manually updated by the network administrator. Services that automate the process of IP address assignment like Windows NT's DHCP can thwart traditional DNSs. It becomes impossible to maintain a DNS with IP addresses that change dynamically according to use. Windows NT therefore includes a name resolution mechanism called WINS (the Windows Internet Name Service) that runs over NetBIOS and is automatically updated as new addresses are assigned by DHCP. A single Windows NT server running WINS and DHCP can provide dozens or hundreds of Windows workstations with all of their TCP/IP configuration data.

N O T E Just as HOSTS is a lookup table on a local machine that is used to resolve host names into IP addresses, you can also use a static table stored in a file called LMHOSTS that performs the same function for NetBIOS names and is structured in much the same way. LMHOSTS is a carry-over from LAN Manager 2.x that provides a degree of interoperability between the two sets of software. LMHOSTS files also allow you to use keywords to perform more advanced name resolution functions, such as preloading the cache and specifying a domain controller. ▪

Connecting LANs to the Internet

There are many different ways for a LAN to be connected to the Internet. The type of connection can depend on the number of LAN users and their specific Internet needs as well as budgetary concerns. The types of links most often used by corporate networks are covered in Chapter 9, "Setting Up a High-Speed Internet Connection."

The type of Internet link used can also affect a computer's TCP/IP configuration. Simply setting up an open gateway to the Internet and assigning users public IP addresses opens up the local network to all manner of abuse from outside the network. Remember, network traffic can run in both directions.

Internet security should therefore be a major concern to a LAN administrator. A significant segment of the growing Internet industry is devoted to firewalls and other security products. A *firewall* is a filter that is placed between the LAN and the Internet. The filter can be configured to allow only certain kinds of Internet traffic (in either direction) to reach specific computers.

You may, for example, be permitted to access World Wide Web sites on the Internet but be prevented from hosting your own Web server on your machine. In other words, HTTP traffic is allowed in from the Internet, but not out to it.

Your computer may not even be assigned an IP address that is registered on the Internet at all. It is not necessary or economical, for example, to use a registered IP address for a machine that requires Internet access for only short periods each day. Many sites allow users to access the Internet from the internal network using a router that is configured with a range of external addresses. Each user's unique internal IP address is mapped to a dynamically assigned Internet address when access is requested. This way, a single 256-user Class C address can actually service 1000 or more occasional Internet users.

It is never a good idea to guess at the type of Internet service being used on your local network. No matter how knowledgeable you are, every network is unique, and there are likely to be factors of which you are not aware. Misconfiguring your workstation's TCP/IP configuration can at the least inconvenience other users, and at most cripple the entire network. Always check with a network administrator before changing any of the TCP/IP parameters discussed in the upcoming sections.

Installing TCP/IP Support in Windows 95

If your computer system already has an Ethernet or Token Ring adapter (or any other type of network card for that matter) installed and operational, then installing the TCP/IP protocol in Windows 95 is easy.

To install the Windows 95 TCP/IP protocol, open the Network control panel (by choosing Start, Settings, Control Panel, Network). The Configuration page, shown in Figure 4.1, lists all of the network components already installed on your computer. If the control panel already lists TCP/IP, then the Windows 95 TCP/IP protocol is already installed and you need not install it again (you can proceed to the section "Configuring the Windows 95 TCP/IP Protocol").

Part

II

Ch

4

FIG. 4.1
The Network control panel lists all available network components.

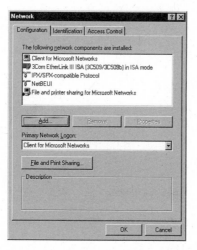

To install the Windows 95 TCP/IP protocol, click the Add button, which displays the Select Network Component Type dialog box. Select Protocol and then click Add. You then see the Select Network Protocol dialog box, shown in Figure 4.2. In this dialog box, select the manufacturer (in this case Microsoft) and the exact network protocol (in this case TCP/IP).

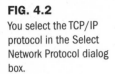

FIG. 4.2

You select the TCP/IP protocol in the Select Network Protocol dialog box.

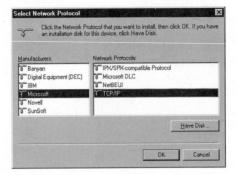

After selecting the TCP/IP protocol from the Network Protocols list, click OK to confirm your selections in each of the dialog boxes. When you click OK on the Network control panel, Windows 95 installs the TCP/IP protocol support from your installation media. At this point, you might be prompted to insert your Windows distribution CD-ROM or floppy disk.

N O T E Most TCP/IP programs that run under Windows (including Windows 95) use a library called WINSOCK.DLL (for Windows Sockets, an implementation of the TCP/IP socket library for Windows-based computers). This library enables applications to set up TCP/IP connections to other computers easily and to communicate with applications on the other computer. Earlier versions of Windows did not include a WinSock library, but Windows 95 includes the library as part of the TCP/IP package.

If your network application (such as a WWW browser) is WinSock-compatible, it should work fine with Windows 95's built-in WinSock library. Be sure not to let any other applications that you may install overwrite this file. Some programs (CompuServe's WinCIM, for example) ship with their own WINSOCK.DLL, which is substantially different from the file included in Windows 95. It is a good idea to keep a backup copy of this file whenever you install any Internet connectivity products. ▪

Configuring the Windows 95 TCP/IP Protocol

After installing the Windows 95 TCP/IP protocol driver, you must configure the TCP/IP protocol so that it matches the configuration requirements of your local area network and your Internet service provider. Although you must be sure to restart Windows 95 when the configuration is complete, you can configure the protocol without rebooting the system after the TCP/IP driver installation by answering No when you are prompted to restart Windows. To configure the TCP/IP protocol, open the Network control panel and then select the TCP/IP protocol from the list of installed network components. Click Properties to view (and change) the TCP/IP settings. Figure 4.3 shows the first page of the TCP/IP Properties dialog box, called IP Address.

CAUTION

You should ask your LAN administrator to provide the correct TCP/IP configuration settings for your workstation. Using incorrect TCP/IP configuration settings can cause serious problems on your LAN, so you should check first before setting or changing anything.

FIG. 4.3

The TCP/IP Properties dialog box enables you to configure the protocol settings.

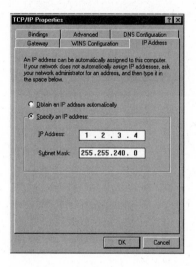

Part

II

Ch

4

The Windows 95 IP Address Page

The IP Address page provides two ways to specify an IP address for your computer. To enter an address manually, you click the Specify an IP address option and then type the numeric IP address in the boxes provided. Alternatively, you can click the Obtain an IP address automatically radio button to have an address assigned by a DHCP server on your network when Windows loads.

If your computer has a fixed IP address (one that is permanently assigned to the computer), you should enter that IP address into the page's IP Address field. To enter the IP address, type the four sets of digits in the field's four boxes. If you type a three-digit number (such as 128), the cursor automatically moves to the next box. To move to the next box manually, you can click the next box or type a period.

You must also enter the proper subnet mask (for example, 255.255.255.0) into the Subnet Mask field, to designate which bits of the IP address define the network and which define the host (see "IP Addressing" earlier in this chapter). You enter the subnet mask just as you entered the IP address.

N O T E DHCP is supplied as an optional service in the Windows NT Server product. Do not assume that it is active, unless you are directed to use this option by your LAN administrator. DHCP can also be configured to automatically assign values for virtually any of the other TCP/IP parameters covered in this section, so be sure that you know exactly which parameters are being assigned when you use it. ■

CAUTION

Resist the temptation to randomly select an IP address on the correct network and use it if it works. Always check with your network administrator to ensure that you enter the correct value for the IP address and subnet mask so that a record of your address can be maintained. If you mistakenly enter the same address as another machine, then neither system will function properly.

The Windows 95 Gateway Page

The TCP/IP Properties dialog box's Gateway page (shown in Fig. 4.4) allows you to specify the default gateway system that connects your LAN to the rest of the Internet. Your network administrator can tell you the proper address to use.

As stated earlier, a gateway is a TCP/IP system that is connected to two or more networks, routing traffic between the two. You may have more than one gateway system on your local network, in which case multiple addresses can be specified on this page. The secondary gateways will only be accessed, however, if the primary gateway cannot be contacted.

FIG. 4.4

The Gateway page enables you to set your default gateway address.

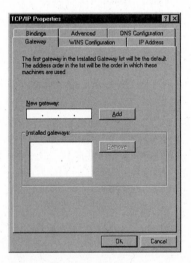

To set your default gateway address, type your gateway's IP address into the New Gateway field and then click the Add button. This adds the new gateway to the Installed Gateways list. This list can include more than one gateway address. To remove a gateway address from the list, select that address and then click the Remove button.

N O T E If you can use TCP/IP programs (such as Telnet or FTP) to connect to computers on your LAN but cannot connect to computers outside of your LAN, your Gateway address is probably configured incorrectly or missing. ■

The Windows 95 DNS Configuration Page

By clicking the DNS Configuration tab on the TCP/IP Properties dialog box, you display the DNS Configuration page (shown in Fig. 4.5). In this page, you can specify the addresses of the DNS (Domain Name Service) systems that you wish to use. As with most of the TCP/IP settings, you should talk to your network administrator to ensure that you enter the correct values.

FIG. 4.5

Specify your DNS servers in the DNS Configuration page.

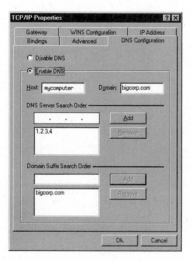

If your network uses DNS to translate from host names to IP addresses, you should select the Enable DNS option and configure the rest of the settings on this page.

In the Host text box, you enter the specific host name for your computer. In the Domain text box, you enter your network's domain name. For example, if your computer's full host name is mycomputer.bigcorp.com, you enter **mycomputer** in the Host text box and **bigcorp.com** in the Domain text box.

In the DNS Server Search Order field, you enter the first server's IP address. Then click the Add button to add the DNS server to the list of servers. If your network has multiple DNS servers, you can enter the IP addresses one at a time and then click Add to add them to the list. If you want to remove an entry from the list of DNS servers, select that entry and then click the Remove button.

N O T E Unlike gateways, additional DNS servers specified on this page will be accessed in order if no entry for the requested host name is found in the HOSTS file or the first DNS address. ■

Part

II

Ch

4

At the bottom of the DNS Configuration page, you can create a list of domains to search when you try to access just a host name. For example, if you enter the domain bigcorp.com (by typing **bigcorp.com** into the Domain Suffix Search Order text box and then clicking A<u>d</u>d) and then try to connect to a computer called *server*, your computer would first try to look up the name *server* in the Domain Name System and then try to look up the name server.bigcorp.com.

You can remove an entry from the list of domains to search by selecting the entry and then, clicking the Re<u>m</u>ove button.

TIP If you can connect to computers by typing their IP addresses but not by using their host names, you probably have not set up your DNS server addresses correctly. Also, if your computer takes more than 30 seconds to connect to another computer, check to see if one of your DNS server entries is incorrect. Such delays can be caused by your computer trying the first entry in the list of DNS servers and, if the entry is incorrect (or the DNS server is unavailable), waiting for that server to respond. Eventually, your computer gives up and moves on to the next DNS server—which results in a significant delay while your computer connects to another machine.

N O T E If you access a particular site frequently, you should add its domain name into your domain suffix search order. Then you can connect to that host simply by typing only its specific host name rather than its full Internet name.

For example, if you often connect to computers at another.corp.com, add that domain name to the search order; then you can connect to a machine called server.another.corp.com simply by typing the name **server**.

The Windows 95 WINS Configuration Page

When you select the TCP/IP Properties dialog box's WINS Configuration tab, you see the WINS Configuration page shown in Figure 4.6. WINS is another method, like DNS, for translating host names into IP addresses (see "The Windows Internet Name Service," earlier in this chapter for more information). Computers usually are set up to use a Domain Name Service to translate host names to IP addresses, but your administrator might prefer that you use WINS instead of, or in addition to, DNS.

If your LAN administrator has set up a WINS server on your network, you can set your computer to use the WINS server by selecting the <u>E</u>nable WINS Resolution check box. You must enter the IP address for your network's primary WINS server, and you might also have to enter the secondary WINS server.

You use the S<u>c</u>ope ID text box to specify which computers can receive your network traffic. Only computers with the same S<u>c</u>ope ID setting as your computer receive your network traffic; likewise, your computer receives messages only from other computers with the same S<u>c</u>ope ID setting. Unless your network administrator tells you otherwise, you should leave this infrequently used setting blank.

FIG. 4.6
Configuring a WINS
server for the TCP/IP
protocol.

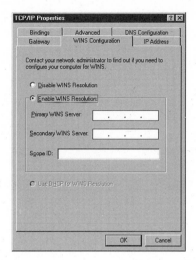

If your network has a DHCP server set up, that server might automatically provide addresses for the WINS servers. Check with your network administrator to see whether this feature is available; if it is, you can select the Use DHCP for WINS Resolution option at the bottom of the page.

Part

II

Ch

4

The Advanced and Bindings Pages

The last two pages, Advanced and Bindings, are quite simple. The only setting that the Advanced page offers is to specify that TCP/IP be the default protocol. In most cases, you can safely leave this setting unselected.

In the Bindings page, you can configure which network clients (such as the client for Microsoft Networks) use the TCP/IP protocol. By default, the installation of TCP/IP binds the protocol to all of the network clients that can utilize it. If you have the Microsoft Client for NetWare Networks installed, you may notice that it is not listed here. This is because Microsoft's TCP/IP stack cannot be used with IP-enabled NetWare servers unless a Novell client is installed. You can safely select all available clients to enable each to use the TCP/IP protocol.

Installing TCP/IP Support in Windows NT 4.0

Although the dialog boxes look a bit different, the process of installing TCP/IP support in Windows NT Workstation 4.0 is fundamentally the same as that for Windows 95.

To begin the TCP/IP installation, load the Network control panel and select the Protocol tab. Click the Add button to display the Select Network Protocol dialog box, as shown in Figure 4.7. Select TCP/IP from the list of protocols and click OK.

You will then be prompted to specify whether or not you wish to use DHCP to obtain your TCP/IP configuration settings. If your network administrator has configured a DHCP server to deliver all of the necessary settings, then responding Yes to this query will complete all of the configuration tasks covered in the next section automatically.

FIG. 4.7

The TCP/IP installation process in Windows NT is as simple as that of Windows 95.

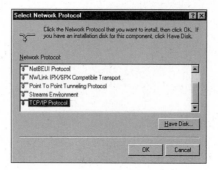

Windows NT will now copy files, prompting you to insert your installation CD-ROM, if necessary. When this process is complete, TCP/IP will be added to the listing on the Protocol page of the Network dialog box. You can then proceed directly to the next section, and configure the protocol, if necessary. Once you have completed the configuration tasks, click the Close button and restart your computer.

Configuring the Windows NT TCP/IP Protocol

If you do not have a DHCP server on your network, then you must configure the TCP/IP protocol manually. To do this, select TCP/IP in the Protocol page of the Network dialog box and click the Properties button. The Microsoft TCP/IP Properties dialog box appears. Configure each of the pages with the appropriate settings, as shown in the following sections.

N O T E   Be aware that any specific values entered into the TCP/IP configuration screens override the values supplied by a DHCP server. If you have a functioning TCP/IP configuration and your LAN administrator later implements DHCP, be sure to remove the settings from the Properties dialog box that will be assigned by the DHCP server. ∎

The Windows NT IP Address Page

The IP Address page of the TCP/IP Properties dialog box in Windows NT (shown in Fig. 4.8) is very similar to that of Windows 95. You enter the values for your IP address and Subnet Mask just as explained in "The Windows 95 IP Address Page" earlier in this chapter.

The IP Address page in Windows NT differs from that of Windows 95 in two ways. First, the Default Gateway address is entered here, instead of in a page of its own. The value is entered just as previously described in "The Windows 95 Gateway Page," except that the capability to specify additional gateway addresses is found by clicking the Advanced button in Windows NT.

FIG. 4.8

The Windows NT IP Address page includes the Default Gateway setting and the ability to configure settings for multiple network adapters.

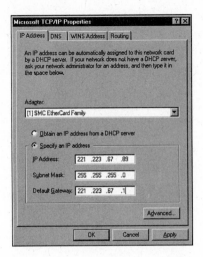

Second, the IP Address and WINS pages in Windows NT both allow you to specify different values for each network adapter installed in your system. You would need to do this if your machine is connected to two different local networks (in which case it could function as a gateway), or if you simultaneously used a network interface card to connect to your local TCP/IP network and a dial-up connection to an Internet service provider. Be sure that the correct adapter is displayed when specifying your IP Address settings.

Part

II

Ch

4

The Windows NT DNS Page

In Windows NT, you elect to use DNS host name lookups for your TCP/IP connections by checking the Enable DNS for Windows Resolution box on the WINS Address page. Apart from this, the DNS page in Windows NT appears and functions exactly like its Windows 95 counterpart (see "The Windows 95 DNS Configuration Page," earlier in this chapter).

The Windows NT WINS Address Page

The WINS Address page (see Fig. 4.9) contains controls for all three of the mechanisms covered in the "Name Resolution" section, earlier in this chapter. You can specify the addresses of your primary and secondary WINS servers and enable the use of DNSs and an LMHOSTS file by checking the appropriate boxes. You can also import an LMHOSTS file from another machine by clicking the Import LMHOSTS button and browsing the network for the file.

N O T E   Windows NT can use any combination of WINS, DNS, and LMHOSTS resources for name resolution. You select which mechanisms you will use on the WINS Address page, and then use the DNS page and/or manually edit the LMHOSTS file to configure the other services. ∎

FIG. 4.9
In the Windows NT WINS
Address page, you
select the name
resolution mechanisms
that you wish to use for
each network adapter
on your system.

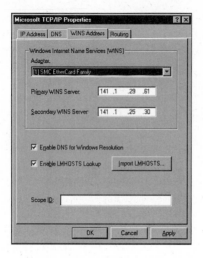

The Windows NT Routing Page

The final tab in the TCP/IP Properties dialog box displays a page with only a single option. When more than one network adapter is installed in a Windows NT machine (creating what is known as a *multi-homed* system), the routing of IP datagrams is disabled by default. If you want your computer to route TCP/IP traffic between the two networks (thereby causing the machine to function as a gateway), you must click the Enable IP Forwarding box on the Routing page.

Testing Your TCP/IP Connection

After configuring your TCP/IP protocol settings in either Windows 95 or Windows NT (and reviewing them a couple of times to make sure that they are correct), reboot your system and logon to the network. You should then test your TCP/IP connection to ensure that it works correctly.

If your network card already works with other protocols (which you can check by opening your Network Neighborhood from the desktop and seeing whether any other computers are visible), you can check your TCP/IP connection by using the program PING.EXE, which is in your Windows folder.

PING is a DOS program that sends a special IP packet to another computer. This *echo request* packet should cause the remote computer to return an *echo reply* packet to your computer. The PING program sends the packet and waits for the echo to return.

From the command line of an MS-DOS Prompt window, type the command **ping** followed by the IP address of another computer on your LAN. For example, if your network administrator tells you that one of your local DNS servers has the address 192.44.55.66, you can enter the command **ping 192.44.55.66**. The PING program then sends a series of packets to the remote computer and reports whether it receives replies. If the computers send and receive the packets correctly, your TCP/IP connection is working correctly.

If the PING command fails, check whether your TCP/IP settings are correct. If you cannot get the TCP/IP connections to work correctly, check with your network administrator.

You can check your name resolution servers by using the PING program with a host name rather than an IP address. For example, enter the command **ping *hostname*** (substituting *hostname* with a valid host name on your LAN). If the command completes correctly, your system can translate the host name into an Internet address and contact the remote machine.

Now you can check whether your connection to the Internet as a whole works correctly by using the PING program with a host name outside of your LAN. Pick a computer at a large site that should be available most of the time; for example, you might use the host **ftp.microsoft.com** (which is the FTP server at Microsoft Corporation).

If the PING command fails the first time, don't be too concerned; the remote server might be unavailable when you try it. Try other hosts. If you cannot contact any hosts outside of your LAN, check your gateway configuration. ●

Part

II

Ch

4

Connecting to a PPP or SLIP Account with Windows 95

by Mike O'Mara

In addition to the built-in capability to connect to the Internet through a local area network (as described in Chapter 4, "Connecting Through a LAN with Windows 95 and Windows NT"), Windows 95 and Windows NT both include built-in software that allows your computer to connect to the Internet using a modem. You don't need additional software to connect your system to the Internet via an Internet Service Provider (ISP) so you can use Internet applications such as Web browsers. However, you can still use Trumpet Winsock and other Internet dialer software if you insist. This chapter will cover setting up Windows 95 to access the Internet via a modem connection. The next chapter will cover configuring the corresponding features in Windows NT.

In order to connect to the Internet using the Windows 95 dialing software, you will need to set up your modem as a network interface. In addition, you will configure the network software to dial your Internet service provider and connect your computer to their network.

The Windows 95 dial-up networking supports most of the connection protocols required by Internet service providers, including the Serial Line Internet Protocol (SLIP), SLIP with compression, the Point to Point Protocol (PPP), the Password Authentication Protocol (PAP) variation of

Installing support for dial-up networks

Learn how to install network protocols and Windows 95's built-in dialer for connecting to dial-up networks.

Configuring your dial-up connection

A successful dial-up connection to your Internet service provider (ISP) requires the correct configuration settings for the TCP/IP protocol and other options.

Connect to your Internet service provider

Learn about the process of making connection to the Internet by logging onto your ISP.

Use the Dial-Up Scripting tool to automate your connection

You can automate those entries you normally type into a terminal screen each time you log onto the Internet.

Troubleshoot common dial-up problems

Discover the solutions to some common dial-up networking problems.

PPP, NetWare connect, and the Windows NT Remote Access Protocol (RAS). In addition, the Windows 95 dialing software has the ability to automate the connection process using dialing scripts. ■

Installing Dial-Up Networking Support

If your computer had a modem installed in it when you installed Windows 95, the Dial-Up Adapter (software which functions as a virtual network device working over your modem) and the Dial-Up Networking support should already be installed on your system. Before you can use your modem to connect to the Internet, you need both the Dial-Up Networking software and a Dial-Up Adapter installed on your system.

You can check to see if the Dial-Up Networking support is installed on your system by opening the Add/Remove Programs control panel (Start, Settings, Control Panel, Add/Remove Programs). Select the Windows Setup tab and click the Communications item in the list of components. Click the Details button to list all of the communications components that are available.

In the list of communications components (as shown in Fig. 5.1), the Dial-Up Networking component is shown as already installed (the check box is checked). If the box is not checked, click the check box and click OK to install the Dial-Up Networking software. You may be prompted to insert your distribution CD or floppy during the installation process.

FIG. 5.1
Installing the Dial-Up Networking support is done through the Add/Remove Programs control panel.

You can check to see if the Dial-Up Adapter is installed on your system by opening the Network control panel (Start, Settings, Control Panel, Network). The Dial-Up Adapter should appear in the list of installed network components on the Configuration tab.

If the Dial-Up Adapter is not already installed, you can install it from the Network control panel. Click the Add button to open the Select Network Component Type dialog box, which lists all the different types of network components you can install.

Click the Adapter item in the list, and click the Add button. This brings up the Select Network Adapters dialog box. This dialog box lists all the types of network adapters supported by Windows 95. On the left side of the dialog box is a list of manufacturers and on the right side is a list of adapters from that manufacturer.

To install the Dial-Up Adapter, scroll down the list of manufacturers until you find Microsoft. Click the Microsoft entry and the Dial-Up Adapter item will be displayed in the list of Network Adapters. Select the Dial-Up Adapter from the list and click OK. Selecting the Dial-Up Adapter is shown in Figure 5.2.

FIG. 5.2

Install the Microsoft Dial-Up Adapter from the Network control panel.

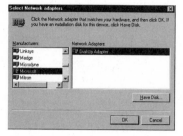

Installing Network Protocols

Once you have dial-up networking support installed, you must install support for the protocols that your Internet connection will require. Since all Internet applications work with the TCP/IP protocol, you should first install the Windows 95 TCP/IP network support.

Installing the TCP/IP support in Windows 95 is similar to installing the Dial-Up Adapter support described previously. Open the Network control panel (Start, Settings, Control Panel, Network) to the default, Configuration tab. Click the Add button to bring up a dialog box listing the network components to install. Select the Protocol component and click Add.

This brings up the Select Network Protocol dialog box, shown in Figure 5.3. Select Microsoft from the list of manufacturers and TCP/IP from the list of network protocols available. Click OK to install the TCP/IP protocol support. You may be asked for your installation CD or floppies during the installation process.

Part

II

Ch

5

FIG. 5.3

Installing the TCP/IP support from the Network control panel.

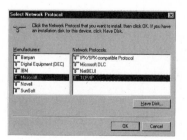

Now that the TCP/IP protocol is installed on your system, you must tell the Dial-Up Adapter that you will be using the TCP/IP protocol on connections through that adapter. Open the properties for the Dial-Up Adapter by selecting Dial-Up Adapter from the list of network components on the Configuration tab of the Network control panel and clicking Properties.

Click on the Bindings tab of the Dial-Up Adapter properties sheet, and make sure that the check box next to the TCP/IP protocol is checked. This allows the Dial-Up Adapter to use the TCP/IP protocol.

Installing SLIP and Scripting Support

When you configure your dial-up connection, you must tell the connection software what type of dial-up server you are connecting to. By default, Windows 95 supports connections using the Point to Point Protocol (PPP), Remote Access Service (RAS) and Netware Connect. If your ISP is still using the older Serial Line Internet Protocol, you may have to install support for SLIP before using your dial-up connection.

 TIP Many Internet service providers support both SLIP and PPP connections. Since PPP offers error correction and data compression, you should use it if possible. Check with your Internet service provider to see if PPP is available to you before installing SLIP support in Windows 95.

Support for SLIP and dial-up scripting is provided in a separate software package that is included on the Windows 95 CD-ROM distribution in the directory /admin/apptools/slip.

NOTE If you have the floppy disk distribution of Windows 95, you can get the SLIP and scripting support from the Microsoft FTP site (**ftp.microsoft.com**/softlib/MSLFILES/) in the file dscrpt.exe. This is a self-extracting file; download the file into a temporary directory and run the file there to unpack the files. ▓

To install the SLIP and dial-up scripting support, start the Add/Remove Programs control panel (Start, Settings, Control Panel, Add/Remove Programs). Select the Windows Setup tab and click the Have disk button. Enter the directory where the SLIP and dial-up scripting files are located (either on the Windows 95 CD-ROM or your local disk). Select the installation file RNAPLUS.INF and click OK to install the support files.

After you have installed the support for SLIP and dial-up scripting, you can remove this feature at any time by opening the Install/Uninstall tab from the Add/Remove Programs control panel. Select the SLIP and Scripting for Dial-Up Networking entry from the list of software that can be uninstalled and click the Add/Remove button to delete the software from your Windows 95 setup.

Setting Up a Dial-Up Networking Connection

After you have installed the Dial-Up Networking support in Windows 95, you are ready to set up your networking connection to your Internet service provider. In order to set up your connection, you should obtain the following information from your service provider:

- The type of connection supported (SLIP, PPP, RAS, etc.)
- The telephone number to dial

- Your IP address (if it is permanently assigned)
- Your full Internet domain name
- The IP addresses of all DNS servers
- The IP address of the service providers' gateway machine
- Your login name and password

Generally, your Internet service provider is experienced in helping you set up your dial-up connection; your provider should be able to quickly provide you with the information you need.

To set up a dial-up connection, open the Dial-Up Networking folder found in the My Computer folder on your desktop. This folder (shown in Fig. 5.4) contains the Make New Connection wizard, which leads you through the steps necessary to create a new dial-up connection.

FIG. 5.4

The Make New Connection wizard is found in the Dial-Up Networking folder.

Start the Make New Connection wizard by double-clicking on the wizard. This brings up the first page of the wizard, shown in Figure 5.5. On this page, you can name your dial-up connection (which makes it easier to remember which system you are connecting to if you have several different systems you use regularly) and specify the modem you will be using to connect.

FIG. 5.5

Setting up your connection with the Make New Connection wizard.

Part

II

Ch

5

On this page, you can also configure your modem settings for this connection by clicking on the Configure button. This brings up the Properties dialog box for your modem. On the General tab (shown in Fig. 5.6) you can set the volume of the speaker on the modem and the maximum speed that your modem will support. Pick the highest speed from the list that your modem supports (if your modem speed is not listed exactly, such as 14,400 baud, you can safely pick the next highest speed; for example if you have a 14,400 baud modem, pick 19,200 baud). If your modem supports it, you also have the option to force your connection to be made at a particular speed (by checking the Only connect at this speed box).

FIG. 5.6

Setting the general
modem properties.

The Connection tab on the modem properties (shown in Fig. 5.7) allows you to set up options such as the number of data bits, parity, and stop bits for the modem. Unless your Internet service provider tells you otherwise, or you encounter problems with your connection, you can simply leave these settings at their default values.

FIG. 5.7

Setting the connection
modem properties.

The settings listed under Call preferences are useful, however. You should generally leave the Wait for Dial Tone before dialing box set, but if you have a very long telephone number to dial (for example, you use a calling card or long distance service) or your service provider takes a particularly long time to answer, you may need to change the Cancel the Call if not connected within settings. Either lengthen the time limit or uncheck this option to entirely disable this feature.

The final option on this page allows you to automatically disconnect your dial-up connection if the connection is idle for a period of time. This is useful to prevent running up long telephone bills if you forget to terminate your connection.

On the Options tab (shown in Fig. 5.8) you can set up your connection to bring up a terminal window either before or after the phone number is dialed (or both). Bringing up the terminal window before the number is dialed is useful if you need to set special options in your modem before you connect.

FIG. 5.8
Setting connection
options for your
modem.

Bringing up the terminal window after dialing allows you to manually type the commands necessary to log in to your ISP and start your connection. This option will be discussed further in the section, "Connecting to your Internet Service Provider."

Another option on this page allows you to specify manual or operator assisted calling. This feature is useful if you have to go through an operator to make your call; choosing the option causes the system to wait for you to click the "connect" button before continuing your call.

The final option allows you to display the modem status indicator on your taskbar. This indicator shows up as a small modem with status lights that blink when sending or receiving data.

Now that the configuration options on the modem have been set, you can continue to set up your dial-up connection. Click the Next button to go on to the next page of the Make New Connection wizard, shown in Figure 5.9.

FIG. 5.9
The second page of the
Make New Connection
wizard.

This page allows you to set the area code, telephone number, and country code for this connection. This is fairly self-explanatory; fill in the full telephone number for your Internet service provider (the number in the figure is just an example). Click the Next button to continue.

The final page of the wizard confirms that your connection is set up with the name you gave it. Click Finish to complete the setup process.

Your new connection appears in the Dial-Up Networking folder, as shown in Figure 5.10.

FIG. 5.10

The newly configured connection in the Dial-Up Networking folder.

> **N O T E** Note that some general modem settings are changed from the Modem control panel. Options such as disabling call waiting, using a calling card, pulse or tone dialing, and others are configured from this control panel. ■

Configuring Your Dial-Up Connection

After doing the initial setup of your connection, you will have to set several options to specify the type of connection you are making with your Internet service provider. This configuration is done through the property sheet for your dial-up connection. Bring up the properties sheet by right-clicking the icon for your connection in the Dial-Up Networking folder and choosing Properties. This property sheet is shown in Figure 5.11.

FIG. 5.11

Setting the properties for your dial-up connection.

The property sheet lists the important options for your connection on the main page, including the telephone number, area code, and the modem to use. Clicking on the Configure button brings up the modem configuration sheets described previously.

Clicking the Server Type button brings up the Server Type's dialog box, as shown in Figure 5.12. This dialog box allows you to set up the type of server you are connecting to, the network protocols that will be used over this connection and several advanced options.

The types of servers that are available to select from are

■ CSLIP: UNIX Connection with IP Header Compression (this option is only available if you install SLIP support)

■ NRN: NetWare Connect

■ PPP: Windows 95, Windows NT 3.5, Internet

FIG. 5.12

Setting up options on the Server Types page.

- SLIP: UNIX Connection (this option is only available if you install SLIP support)
- Windows for Workgroups and Windows NT 3.1

Pick the appropriate connection for your Internet service provider. Most of the time you will pick either PPP or SLIP.

Depending on the server type you select, you will be able to set different advanced options. Checking the Log On to Network option tells Windows 95 to try to log onto the network when you connect, using the user name and password provided in the connection page.

Selecting Enable Software Compression allows Windows 95 to compress the data going through your modem, which allows more information to flow through the connection. This option will only work if your modem and the remote modem support compression.

Selecting Require Encrypted Password ensures that your computer will only send out passwords that are encrypted when logging in to remote computers or services. This option only works when the remote computer or service supports encrypted passwords, but using this option decreases the chance that someone may intercept your password.

Under the Allowed network protocols, you should select only those protocols that you will use over this connection. Most of the time, you can select just the TCP/IP protocol to use Internet applications. If you are going to be using any of the other protocols, you should select their options.

Clicking the TCP/IP Settings button brings up the dialog box shown in Figure 5.13. This dialog box allows you to specify your IP address, DNS servers, and WINS servers if your ISP assigns static IP addresses for your machine or these servers. For most connections, you can select the Server assigned options, which means that your Internet service provider's software will send these values to you when you connect.

If your Internet service provider supplies specific settings for your IP address, DNS servers, or WINS servers, enter them on this page.

Part

II

Ch

5

FIG. 5.13
Setting up your
connection's TCP/IP
settings.

Connecting to Your Internet Service Provider

Once you have your connection set up, you can test your connection to your service provider. How the connection proceeds depends on the type of computer or service you are connecting to. This section provides you with some notes on connecting to different types of computers.

Start the process of connecting to your ISP by double-clicking the icon you created in the Dial-Up Networking folder. The Connect To dialog box appears as shown in Figure 5.14. When the dialog box first appears, Windows 95 enters your default username. You'll need to change the User Name to the User ID you need to use to log onto your ISP's computer. Also enter your Password (which will appear as asterisks for security). If you're not concerned about the security risk of recording your password, you can check the Save password option to instruct Windows 95 to record the User name and Password entries so you won't have to re-enter them each time you connect. Click Connect to dial the remote computer.

FIG. 5.14
Enter your User name
and Password into this
dialog box.

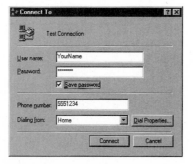

When you connect to a remote computer, your system first dials the number you specified in the connection properties. When the remote computer answers, your modem first establishes settings (such as connection speed and error correction) with the remote modem.

Next, your computer's software attempts to talk to the remote software to log on and establish the connection protocol (such as PPP, SLIP, or NetWare Connect). How this connection is established depends on the type of remote computer and the protocol.

ISPs rarely use NetWare Connect. If your service provider uses this protocol, the system administrator will instruct you on the required log in procedure.

Using the PPP protocol, Windows 95 can automatically negotiate the connection to the remote computer and log on using the User name and Password you supply in the Connect To dialog box. You'll see status messages as Windows 95 verifies your ID and password and establishes the connection. Then, a message appears confirming the successful connection and showing what speed the modems are operating at.

N O T E When connecting with the PPP protocol, there are two options for passing your password to the PPP server. These two options are PAP (Password Authentication Protocol) and CHAP (Challenge Authentication Protocol). If you have selected the Use Encrypted Password option for your connection, it will force the use of the CHAP protocol.

If your service provider requires CHAP, but you have not selected this option, you will be asked to confirm the use of the encrypted password when you connect. ▓

Some Internet service providers use systems to provide SLIP and PPP access that require you to type a login name and password at a terminal screen before allowing access to their system. After you are logged in, you often type a command (such as "slip") to start the protocol your connection needs. After these commands are processed, your protocol is established and you can use the connection.

When using this type of connection, you can use the option to bring up a terminal window after dialing (as specified on the Options tab of the modem properties). The terminal window allows you to see prompts from the remote system and manually type in your username, password, and the command to start your connection.

At this point, the service provider may display a message giving you the IP address assigned to your computer for this session. You should write this address down, because you may need it in a minute. After the protocol is established, you can click the Continue button (F7) to start using the protocol. You may see a dialog box asking you for the IP address assigned to you; if so, type in the number you just wrote down.

N O T E After you have made sure your connection works correctly, you can automate the connection process by using dial-up scripting. Using a dial-up script allows you to automatically enter your username, password, and any commands. Dial-up scripting is discussed later in this chapter. ▓

If you are connecting to a Windows NT server (using the Remote Access Service, for example), you won't need to perform any manual input in order to establish your connection. The Dial-Up Networking software automatically passes along your username and password and establishes the protocol for you.

Part

II

Ch

5

Using Dial-Up Scripting

If your connection requires that you type some information in order to connect (such as your username and password), you can automate this process by using Dial-Up Scripting. Dial-Up Scripting support is provided in the Microsoft Plus! for Windows 95 package, but is also available (in a somewhat limited version) in the standard Windows 95 package.

N O T E The Dial-Up Scripting software provided at no charge on the standard Windows 95 disk or from the Microsoft Web server is not the full package, but it supports the most commonly used commands. Unfortunately, there is no documentation on exactly the differences between the free version and the Plus! pack version. ▪

Getting the Dial-Up Scripting Software

If you have Microsoft Plus! for Windows 95, the Dial-Up Scripting software is installed as part of the installation of the Plus! software.

If you do not have the Microsoft Plus! package, but you have the CD-ROM version of Windows 95, you can find the Dial-Up Scripting utility under the Admin directory of the CD-ROM. Follow the instructions on how to install the support using the Add/Remove Programs control panel.

If you do not have the CD-ROM version of Windows 95, you can get the Dial-Up Scripting software from the Microsoft Web page (**http://www.microsoft.com**). The name of the self-extracting archive file is Dscrpt.exe. Put this file into a temporary directory and run it to automatically unpack the component files. Then, you can install the software using the Add/Remove Programs control panel.

Setting Up a Script for an Internet Connection

Once you have the Dial-Up Scripting software installed, you can add a script to one of your existing Internet connections by running the scripting tool (which is found under Start, Programs, Accessories, Dial-Up Scripting tool).

The Dial-Up Scripting tool lets you assign a script to a particular connection. The Dial-Up Scripting software includes some sample script files that you can copy and modify to suit your needs. To assign a script to one of your dial-up connections, select the connection you want the script assigned to, and then type the name of the script file in the File Name box. You can edit the script by clicking the Edit button.

Using the Scripting Language

The basic idea of the Dial-Up Scripting language is to wait for the remote system (the one you are connecting to) to prompt for certain information, and then to automatically provide this information. While there are quite a few advanced commands in the scripting language, the basic ones (the ones you will use frequently) are

- ■ `proc`—Start a script procedure or program
- ■ `waitfor`—Wait for the remote computer to output a string
- ■ `transmit`—Send a string of characters to the remote computer
- ■ `delay`—Wait for a specified amount of time
- ■ `getip`—Set your Internet address from the remote system
- ■ `endproc`—End a script procedure or program

For an example of using a script, let's assume that the procedure for connecting to your Internet service provider is as follows:

- ■ The remote computer prompts you with `name:`, and you type in your login name.
- ■ The remote computer prompts you with `password:`, and you type in your password.
- ■ The remote computer prompts you with `command:`, and you type in the command `PPP` to start up the connection.

So, in your script you would use Waitfor commands to wait for the remote computer to output each string, and then use transmit commands to send the right information. The scripting language provides several variables that make sending information easier—these variables hold the information you entered on the dial-up connection properties page:

- ■ `$USERID`—Holds the user name specified in the connection dialog box
- ■ `$PASSWORD`—Holds the password specified in the connection dialog box

An example script that automates the above procedure might look like this:

```
proc main
waitfor "name:"
transmit $USERID + "^M"
waitfor "password:"
transmit $PASSWORD + "^M"
waitfor "command:"
transmit "PPP^M"
endproc
```

N O T E In the above example, the `"^M"` characters simulate pressing the Enter key to send each line. ■

This example script is sufficient (with minor changes depending on the prompts that your service provider gives you) to log into most Internet service providers. More information about the scripting tool and all the commands it implements is provided with the tool itself.

Since the release of the Windows 95 operating system, several third-party packages have become available that replace or augment the standard Windows 95 dial-up software. The two main packages that are available currently are the 32-bit version of the popular Trumpet Winsock package and the RoboDUN dialup package.

Connecting with Trumpet WinSock

Trumpet WinSock was one of the most popular programs used to connect to the Internet with Windows 3.1. Trumpet was distributed as shareware on the Internet so it was easily available, it was inexpensive to register, and most every service provider had experience with it and recommended it for their customers. For all of those reasons, many people who used this with Windows 3.1 have been hesitant to abandon the familiarity of Trumpet WinSock in favor of the built-in Internet connectivity features in Windows 95.

N O T E   Some earlier versions did not have a strict way to enforce the 30-day trial on the unregistered shareware. If you are using an unregistered version, be aware that you will need to register to continue using it beyond 30 days. ■

However, using the existing versions of Trumpet that were written for Windows 3.1 meant sacrificing some functionality in Windows 95. Although Trumpet 2.0 and 2.1 will run with Windows 95, you can't use any 32-bit applications such as the 32-bit versions of Netscape 2.0 or WinVN with 3.1 versions of Trumpet.

Trumpet has now released some upgrade files that enable current users of Trumpet to continue using Trumpet with Windows 95 and 32-bit applications. Why would you want to do this? If you have been using Trumpet, several reasons could include:

- Old Trumpet login scripts still work with the upgrade so you don't have to create new login scripts as you would with Windows 95 dial-up networking.
- Your service provider *still* won't provide support for Windows 95.
- You have had problems getting Windows 95's Internet connection to start automatically when you start an Internet application. If this is an important convenience to you, Trumpet may handle this better.
- You are an advanced user and need the use of Trumpet's many diagnostic features,

So, if you need to use Trumpet for those reasons or any others, here is how you do it. You need to get the 32-bit Trumpet files from NetCD95 or some other source. On NetCD95, they are in the \netutils\trump95 directory. You can also find this at most any major FTP site or WWW software site including TUCOWS. The home Web site for Trumpet is at **http://www.trumpet.com.au**. However, since this site is in Australia, if you are in the U.S., try the mirror site at **http://www.trumpet.com** or try to find a local copy of the program before fetching it from the home site.

CAUTION

If you do not have Trumpet currently installed and are attempting to set up your first Internet connection, it is recommended that you use Windows 95 built-in Internet connection rather than Trumpet.

Upgrading to Windows 95 Version of Trumpet

Upgrading to the Windows 95 version of Trumpet involves renaming some Windows files and copying the new Trumpet versions:

 T I P This is a simple procedure and the chances of anything going wrong are small. But, to be safe and prevent any possible disasters, make a backup copy of everything in your Trumpet directory before proceding.

1. Rename the two Windows 95 internetworking files. The two files you need to rename are

   c:\windows\winsock.dll

   c:\windows\system\wsock32.dll

   Change the extension on both of these files from .dll to something else, such as .MS (to remind you that these are the Microsoft versions of the winsock files).

2. Extract the following files from the Trumpet for Windows 95 ZIP file (or copy these files from NetCD95):

   tcpman.exe

   Winsock.dll

   twsk16.dll

   wsock32.dll

3. Move these files to your Trumpet directory. You will be prompted to replace existing versions. Confirm all replacements.

4. Verify that your Trumpet directory is in your Path statement in autoexec.bat. If you have been using Trumpet and it works, this is already there. If not, add it. If you make any changes, you will need to restart Windows before using Trumpet.

That completes the installation process and you are now ready to run the new version and connect to the Internet.

N O T E If you ever decide to stop using Trumpet as your WinSock and want to use Windows 95's built-in WinSock, rename the two files from step one back to their original names and remove the trumpet entry from your path statement. Then see the directions earlier in this chapter for configuring dial-up Windows 95 internet connectivity. ▪

Using Trumpet WinSock

If you are familar with the Windows 3.1 versions of Trumpet, you already know how to use this version. As a quick refresher, you can start Trumpet and connect to the internet by:

- Starting any Internet application such as Netscape or WS_FTP
- Starting Tcpman.exe, which is the executable part of the Trumpet package

Part

II

Ch

5

Doing either of these will result in Trumpet dialing your ISP and logging you in (if you have automatic login enabled in the Trumpet options). This results in the familiar Trumpet screen shown in Figure 5.15.

FIG. 5.15

The main Trumpet Window shows a log of all activity such as dialing and login, as well as the results of your login scripts including your IP address.

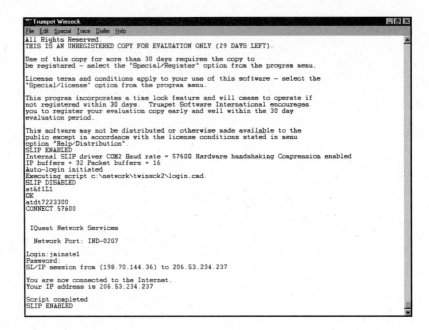

After this, you should be able to use Trumpet and connect to the Internet just as you always have in the past.

The RoboDUN Dialing Software

The RoboDUN package is a replacement for the Windows 95 dial-up scripting tool. It provides functionality similar to the standard dial-up scripting, but has a somewhat more sophisticated scripting language, and includes a dialing package.

RoboDUN is available freely through many Windows 95 shareware sites (**http:// www.windows95.com** is a good source; look for the file rdun61.zip) and was written by Mark Gamber (**markga@epix.net**).

Once you have the RoboDUN archive file, installing the software is as easy as extracting the files from the archive into a folder on your system. The package includes two programs, RDUN32 (which is the software to manage your connections) and ROBODUN (which handles the dialing and scripting support).

To enable the RoboDUN package, run the manager software and click the Start RoboDUN button to start the support software. Select one of the available connections and click Edit to start editing the dial-up script for that connection.

N O T E Examples of dial-up scripts are provided in the RoboDUN Help file. Most of the commands provided with RoboDUN are similar to those provided with the Windows 95 scripting language. ■

After you have set up a script, it will be used whenever your connection is started.

Troubleshooting Your Dial-Up Connection

Dial-up connections are harder to troubleshoot than connections through a local area network, because there are more things that can go wrong with the connection. A problem with your modem, telephone line, Internet service provider, or connection setup can all cause your connection to fail or work poorly. This section gives you some things to check if your connection is not working correctly.

If Your Modem Does Not Dial

If your modem does not dial at all when you try to connect to your Internet service provider, you should first check to make sure that you have the correct modem configured for your system. Open the Modems control panel and verify that the modem type and COMM port connection reported is the same as the actual modem installed. When you installed the modem, the wrong modem may have been detected; reinstall the modem support with the correct type of modem.

Once you have confirmed that the modem is the correct type, check that the modem is working with the system correctly. Open the System control panel, select the Device Manager tab and select the modem under the Modems item. Click Properties to open the properties sheet for the modem. Make sure that the sheet indicates the modem is working correctly. If the sheet indicates a problem, check your modem and communications port settings.

If the modem is reported as working correctly, check your phone connection to make sure the modem is connected to the phone line. You can also try dialing your modem manually using the Phone dialer application found in under Start, Programs, Accessories on your Start Bar.

Your Modem Dials, But the Other Modem Doesn't Answer

First, try the connection a second (or third) time to make sure that the problem wasn't only a temporary one. Make sure that you are dialing the correct number for this connection. Verify the area code and any access codes that may be added to the phone number are correct, also. Depending on phone conditions (for example, if the phone system is particularly busy), you might need to add extra time after getting an outside line. Most modems allow you to add a pause by putting a comma (,) into the telephone number.

If the telephone number is correct, check with someone at the remote site to make sure their system is on and the modem is working correctly.

Part
II

Ch
5

The Other Modem Answers, But the Connection Fails

This is one of the most difficult situations to diagnose, and this is where most problems with dial-up connections happen. The first step is to verify that all your connection and modem settings are correct, especially the settings for the remote server type. Most Internet service providers have information packets for users of Windows 95 systems that list all the correct settings for connections to their systems. Matching these settings is critical! Small details such as selecting hardware or software flow control in the Modem's Advanced Connection Settings dialog box can cause problems, even if you've successfully connected using those settings before.

If the settings are correct, turn on the option to display a terminal window after dialing the modem (This option is found under the properties for the dial-up connection). This terminal window allows you to see what is happening after the modems connect; any error messages or problems will usually be immediately obvious (such as an invalid user name, password, or server type).

Internet Applications Don't Work

If your connection starts up, but your Internet applications (such as a WWW browser or FTP program) don't work, you should first check your TCP/IP settings to make sure that they are correct.

An easy way to check your TCP/IP settings is to run the program "winipcfg" (found in the Windows directory). This program displays all the information about your current TCP/IP setup, including your IP address, DNS servers, and other network settings. You can easily verify that your TCP/IP settings are correct.

If you cannot connect at all to any Internet service, make sure your IP address is set correctly. This is often a problem when you have to enter the IP address manually during the connection process. If your service provider automatically sets up your IP address when you connect, make sure that your TCP/IP settings for your connection are set up to automatically set your IP address (and DNS servers if applicable).

If you can connect to an Internet service using an IP address but not by using an Internet host name, your DNS servers are set up incorrectly. Check with your service provider for the addresses of their DNS servers so you can manually set them up in your TCP/IP settings.

If you can connect to some Internet services (in particular, ones that are local to your service provider) but not to Internet hosts outside of your local service provider, your gateway address is probably incorrect. Check with your service provider for the address of their Internet gateway machine so you can enter it into your configuration. ●

Connecting to a PPP or SLIP Account with Windows NT

by Mike O'Mara

Like Windows 95, Windows NT can connect to the Internet through a modem link to an Internet service provider (ISP) and connect to the Internet through a local area network (LAN), as described in Chapter 4, "Connecting Through a LAN with Windows 95 and Windows NT." This chapter concerns itself with an Internet connection through an ISP, although it's also possible to get Internet access indirectly by connecting to a LAN that is connected to the Internet.

Windows NT Workstation 4.0 includes built-in software that allows your computer to dial up your ISP and make a connection to the Internet. This enables you to use Internet applications such as a Web browser.

Windows NT's Remote Access Service (RAS) software provides the means to dial your ISP and make a connection to the Internet. To use this kind of connection, you must configure RAS to handle the Internet's TCP/IP network protocol to dial your ISP and connect your system to their network. And, of course, you'll need a properly installed and configured modem.

Windows NT supports the standard connection protocols needed by ISPs, including the Serial Line Internet Protocol (SLIP), the Point to Point Protocol (PPP), and the

Installing RAS support for dial-up networks

Windows NT's Remote Access Service software provides the means to make a dial-up connection to an Internet service provider (ISP).

Configuring your dial-up network connection

Proper configuration is an essential step in establishing a successful dial-up Internet connection.

Connecting to your ISP

Learn what to expect during a typical logon process for an ISP.

Using scripts to automate your connection

Scripts can automate the tedious process of responding to logon prompts each time you connect to your ISP.

Troubleshooting common dial-up problems

We offer possible solutions to some of the most common problems with dial-up Internet connections.

Password Authentication Protocol (PAP) variation of PPP. In addition, Windows NT can automate the connection process using dialing scripts. ▪

Installing RAS

RAS is the built-in Windows NT component that handles dialing and answering calls, and making network connections via modem (or direct cable). The software can do more than just make a connection to an ISP. However, since this chapter is devoted to making a dial-up Internet connection, we'll limit our discussion to that aspect of RAS.

RAS is part of the normal Windows NT installation. Typically, you won't need to do anything to add the software to your system. You do, however, need to configure RAS to use the TCP/IP network protocol and set it up to connect to your ISP.

You can confirm that RAS is installed on your system by opening the Network control panel (Start, Settings, Control Panel, Network) and clicking the Services tab. RAS should be listed along with the rest of the network services, as shown in Figure 6.1.

FIG. 6.1
The Network dialog box showing RAS already installed.

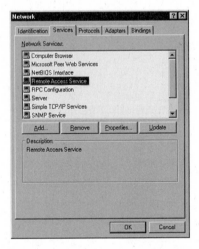

If RAS is not already installed, you can click the Add button to open the Select Network Service dialog box shown in Figure 6.2. Click the Remote Access Service item in the list and click the OK button to install the software. NT may ask you to supply the system CD or floppy disks.

Back in the Network dialog box, select Remote Access Service and click the Properties button to open the Remote Access Setup dialog box shown in Figure 6.3. (If you've just installed RAS, this dialog box opens automatically.)

The list should show RAS attached to your modem. If not, you can click Add and then click Install Modem to start the modem installation wizard to complete that portion of the setup task.

FIG. 6.2

Installing Remote
Access Service.

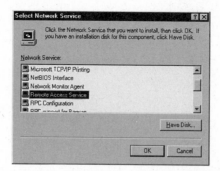

FIG. 6.3

The buttons allow you
to configure Remote
Access Service.

Click the Configure button to open the Configure Port Usage dialog box shown in Figure 6.4.
You can configure RAS to make calls, receive calls, or both. For normal Internet access, you
can choose the Dial Out Only option. (If you have needs other than Internet access that require
receiving calls as well, choose Dial Out and Receive Calls.) Click OK to return to the Remote
Access Setup dialog box.

FIG. 6.4

For calling your ISP,
choose Dial Out Only.

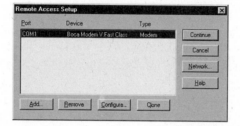

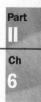

Part

II

Ch

6

Next, click the Network button to open the Network Configuration dialog box shown in Figure
6.5. (The figure shows the dialog box as it appears if you elect to use RAS for dial out only.
Additional options appear in the dialog box if you chose to configure RAS to receive calls also.)
Here you can specify which network protocols RAS can use.

For normal Internet access, choose only the TCP/IP option. (Check other options only if you
have specific needs for the other protocols.) Click OK to close the Network Configuration
dialog box and then click Continue to close the Remote Access Setup dialog box.

FIG. 6.5
You need to choose only TCP/IP for Internet access.

Installing Network Protocols

Having RAS installed to make the connection between your computer and the Internet won't do much good if your system can't speak TCP/IP—the language of Internet. So you'll need to make sure the TCP/IP network protocol is installed on your system.

Open the Network control panel (Start, Settings, Control Panel, Network) and click the Protocols tab to view the list of network protocols installed on your system (see Fig. 6.6). If the TCP/IP protocol doesn't appear in the list, click Add to open the Select Network Protocol dialog box. Select TCP/IP from the list and then click OK. Supply the system CD or floppy disks when NT requests them.

FIG. 6.6
If you plan to use the Internet, you'll need to have the TCP/IP protocol installed.

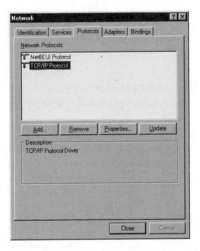

Don't be concerned about configuring TCP/IP properties such as IP address, DNS server settings, and such. Later, when you define a Dial-Up Networking phonebook entry for your ISP, you'll have the opportunity to enter those settings for each phonebook entry.

A network protocol must be linked to an adapter or service for it to be used with that adapter or service. These links are called *bindings*. When you install a network protocol, NT automatically links the new protocol to all available adapters and services. But you can disable some bindings to restrict the flow of data through your system.

You need to make sure the TCP/IP protocol is available to the RAS. To confirm the status of the bindings for the TCP/IP protocol, click the Bindings tab in the Network control panel dialog box. NT displays status messages as it checks the bindings between protocols, adapters, and services on your system and displays them in the list in the Bindings tab (see Fig. 6.7).

Select All protocols from the Show bindings for list box, then expand the TCP/IP entries (TCP/IP Protocol and WINS Client). Make sure the Remote Access WAN Wrapper option is enabled under each one. If you don't plan to use TCP/IP with your other network adapters, you can disable those options. In fact, for security and performance purposes, it's a good idea to do so.

If you're knowledgeable about network configuration, you can enable and disable other bindings to fine tune the configuration and then click OK. Windows NT stores your bindings and prompts you to restart your computer so your changes can take effect.

FIG. 6.7
Make sure the bindings link Remote Access Service to the TCP/IP protocol.

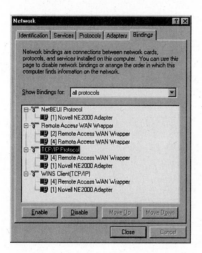

Setting Up a Dial-Up Networking Connection

Once you have RAS and the TCP/IP protocol installed, the preliminaries are out of the way and you can get on with setting up a dial-up connection to your ISP. But first, you'll need to obtain the following information:

- The type of connection supported (SLIP, PPP, or PPP with password authentication)
- The phone number to dial
- Your IP address (if it is permanently assigned)
- Your full Internet domain name
- The IP addresses of all DNS servers
- The IP address of the service providers' gateway machine or router
- Your login name and password
- Modem configuration details

Part
II

Ch
6

ISPs are in the business of helping users set up dial-up connections and should be able to provide all the information you need. Even if the ISP isn't experienced with configuring Windows NT 4.0, you shouldn't have any problem getting the needed information since it is the same as that needed to configure dial-up access with Windows 95 and other operating systems.

Dial-Up Networking is the name of the utility that handles your outgoing RAS calls and network connections. Dial-Up Networking keeps all the details about the way you connect to your ISP (or other dial-up connection) in a phonebook. Then, to make a dial-up connection, you can simply select a phonebook entry and click a button.

To create a Dial-Up Networking phonebook entry for your ISP, begin by double-clicking on the Dial-Up Networking icon in the My Computer window. If this is the first time you've accessed Dial-Up Networking, a small message box appears noting that you have no phonebook entries.

Clicking OK launches the New Phonebook Entry Wizard shown in Figure 6.8. (If the Dial-Up Networking dialog box appears, you can launch the wizard by clicking the New button.) Enter a name for your phonebook entry and click Next.

FIG. 6.8

The New Phonebook Entry Wizard automates the process of setting up a connection for your ISP.

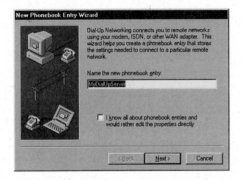

On the next page of the wizard (shown in Fig. 6.9), check the I am calling the Internet option. If your ISP supports Password Authentication Protocol (PAP) logons, check the second option as well. If, however, your ISP needs a manual logon or assigns static IP addresses, check the third option. Click Next to proceed.

FIG. 6.9.

Answer the general questions first.

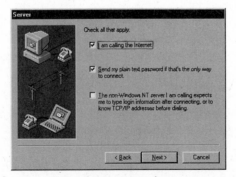

The Phone Number page is where you enter the phone number you want your modem to dial. If you check the Use Telephony Dialing Properties option as shown in Figure 6.10, Windows NT compares the number to your current dialing location at the time of the call and automatically adds long distance codes and outside line access numbers as needed. After entering the phone number, click Next.

FIG. 6.10
Enter the phone number Dial-Up Networking should dial.

Depending on the choices you made on the Server page, the wizard may prompt you for more information, such as choosing the SLIP or PPP protocol and whether to use a script or terminal window for log in. Enter the information as requested. Then, when you reach the final page of the wizard, click Finish to add the newly defined entry to your Dial-Up Networking phonebook. Upon completion of the wizard, you return to the Dial-Up Networking dialog box, as shown in Figure 6.11.

FIG. 6.11
The starting point for Dial-Up Networking.

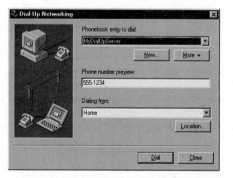

Part

II

Ch

6

Customizing Your Dial-Up Connection

The information you enter when using the New Phonebook Entry Wizard may be all that's needed to get you connected to your ISP. However, you may need to fine-tune the configuration settings for an entry to make a successful connection or to get better performance.

To edit the connection settings, choose the phonebook entry in the Dial-Up Networking dialog box, click More, and choose Edit entry and modem properties. This opens the Edit Phonebook Entry dialog box shown in Figure 6.12.

FIG. 6.12
Customizing the phonebook entry.

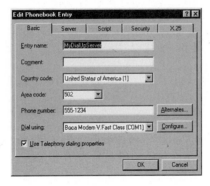

Configuring the Basic Settings

The settings on the Basic tab allow you to edit the entry name, phone number, and so on. If your ISP has more than one phone number available, you can click Alternates to open a dialog box where you can enter alternate phone numbers.

If Dial-Up Networking can't connect to the main phone number, the software automatically attempts to call the other numbers on the list. Near the bottom of the dialog box, you can choose a modem from the Dial Using drop-down list box.

Click Configure to open the Modem Configuration dialog box shown in Figure 6.13. Here you can adjust modem settings for use with this connection. If you have trouble with connections to your ISP, the ISP's technical support staff may suggest changing some of these settings for compatibility with their modems.

FIG. 6.13
These modem settings apply when using the selected Dial-Up Networking phonebook entry.

N O T E Note that some general modem settings are changed from the Modem control panel. Options such as disabling call waiting, using a calling card, pulse or tone dialing, and others are configured from this control panel. ■

Specifying the Server Type

Click the Server tab to bring up the page shown in Figure 6.14. The first option on this page is the Dial-Up server type. The default is PPP: Windows NT, Windows 95 Plus, Internet. This is the setting you should use for most dial-up Internet connections.

It handles connections to PPP accounts needing manual logons as well as accounts with automatic password authentication (PAP or CHAP). Your other choices are SLIP: Internet and an option for connecting to older Windows systems.

FIG. 6.14

Tell Dial-Up Networking about the server you want to connect to.

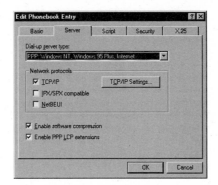

  Many ISPs support both SLIP and PPP connections. Since PPP offers error correction and data compression, you should use it if possible. Check with your ISP to see if PPP is available to you before settling for SLIP as the server type.

In the Network protocols section of the Server page, make sure the TCP/IP option is checked. Normally, for an Internet connection, that is the only protocol that should be active. You should disable the IPX/SPX Compatible and NetBEUI protocol options.

The All-Important TCP/IP Settings

To configure the TCP/IP settings for this connection, click the TCP/IP Settings button. This opens the PPP TCP/IP Settings dialog box shown in Figure 6.15.

Typically, an ISP automatically assigns an IP address to your computer when you log on. The address is temporary—good only for the duration of your connection and returned to the ISP's pool of available IP addresses when you log off.

Choose the Server Assigned IP Address option to configure your connection to accept dynamic addresses. On the other hand, if your ISP has assigned your system a permanent IP address, you should choose Specify an IP address and enter the address into the space provided.

Most ISPs maintain one or more name servers. By default, Dial-Up Networking is configured to get the address of the name servers from the server when you connect. However, if your ISP provides you with the specific addresses of its name servers, you can choose Specify Name

Server Addresses and type in the addresses. (Although most ISPs have DNS servers, few have WINS servers as well. Consequently, you will normally leave the WINS settings blank.)

FIG. 6.15

If your ISP assigns you a permanent IP address, enter it here.

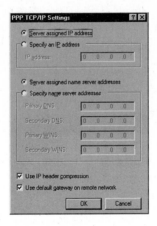

The last two options in the dialog box—Use IP Header Compression and Use Default Gateway on Remote Network—can usually remain in their default (checked) state. Change them if instructed to do so by your ISP.

If you have trouble connecting, you might want to try deactivating the Use IP Header Compression option. When you are through editing the TCP/IP settings, click OK to close the PPP TCP/IP Settings dialog box and return to the Server tab of the Edit Phonebook Entry dialog box.

Back on the Server page, you'll find two more options—Enable Software Compression and Enable PPP LCP Extensions. You can usually leave both options enabled unless instructed by your ISP to make changes. You might also try disabling one or both options if you have trouble connecting to your ISP.

Setting the Logon Options

If your ISP requires you to manually log on to their system activating your SLIP or PPP connection, you'll need to tell Dial-Up Networking how to handle the logon procedure. Click the Script tab to display the page shown in Fig. 6.16.

To start with, you'll want to choose the Pop Up a Terminal Window option. This causes Dial-Up Networking to open a terminal window immediately after making a modem connection to the remote computer. You can use the terminal window to log onto the remote computer, then close it once your SLIP or PPP connection is completed.

Later, after you verify that your connection is operating properly with a manual logon, you can automate the process with a script. (Scripts are covered later in this chapter.) If you need to send commands to your modem before dialing, click the Before Dialing button to open a dialog box where you can elect to open a terminal window or edit scripts for that purpose.

FIG. 6.16
This page allows you to specify how to handle manual logon procedures.

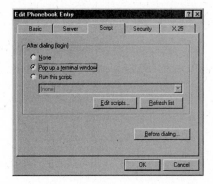

If your PPP account at your ISP supports password authentication, click the Security tab to display the page shown in Figure 6.17. Here you can specify the level of security applied to your password.

For normal Password Authentication Protocol (PAP) accounts, choose the first option (Accept Any Authentication Including Clear Text). If your account supports Challenge-Handshake Authentication Protocol (CHAP) and you want to ensure that your password is always sent in encrypted form, choose Accept Only Encrypted Authentication. The third option, Accept Only Microsoft Encrypted Authentication, doesn't apply to normal Internet access accounts.

FIG. 6.17
You can enable encrypted passwords for a CHAP account.

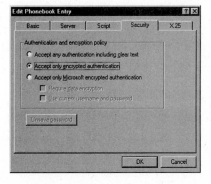

After adjusting the settings, click OK to close the Edit Phonebook Entry dialog box.

Connecting to Your ISP

After you've set up and configured a Dial-Up Networking phonebook entry for your ISP, you're ready to test the connection. To call your ISP, open the Dial-Up Networking dialog box (double-click Dial-Up Networking in the My Computer window), choose the appropriate entry in the Phonebook entry to dial list box, and choose your dialing location from the Dialing From list box. (Click Location to create or edit the location if necessary. For instance, you might need to

Part

II

Ch

6

edit the Location setting if you need to specify dialing codes for outside line access or long distance calls.) Click Dial to start the call.

The first time you try to call a phonebook entry, Dial-Up Networking opens a dialog box (see Fig. 6.18) for you to enter the username and password needed to gain access to your account. Dial-Up Networking automatically enters the username you entered when you installed or logged onto Windows NT. You'll need to replace it with the user ID for your account with your ISP.

 T I P If you start a 32-bit Internet application, such as a Web browser, without first establishing an Internet connection, Windows NT will attempt to establish a dial-up connection for you using the default phonebook entry. The dialog box shown in Figure 6.18 will appear automatically.

When you type your password, NT displays asterisks to hide the password from prying eyes. For an Internet connection, you'll probably leave the Domain box blank. It's normally used only for connections to Windows NT networks via RAS servers.

If you want Windows NT to save your user name and password, check the Save Password option. If you do (and the connection is successful), this dialog box does not appear the next time you dial this phonebook entry—Dial-Up Networking uses the saved user name and password instead. Click OK to proceed with the connection.

FIG. 6.18
Enter your user ID and
password here.

Once your username and password are entered, Dial-Up Networking displays a status message as it initializes your modem and dials the remote computer. When the remote computer answers, your modem negotiates settings (such as connection speed and error correction) with the remote modem.

Next, your computer's software attempts to talk to the remote software to establish the connection protocol (PPP or SLIP). How this connection is made depends on the type of remote computer and the protocol.

N O T E When you connect with the PPP protocol, there are two options for passing your password to the PPP server. These two options are PAP (Password Authentication Protocol) and CHAP (Challenge Authentication Protocol). If you have selected the Use Encrypted Password option for your connection, it forces the use of the CHAP protocol.

If your service provider requires CHAP but you have not selected this option, you are asked to confirm the use of the encrypted password when you connect. ▣

If you have a PPP account that supports password authentication, Dial-Up Networking attempts to log on automatically using the username and password you entered in the previous dialog box (or saved in your password file). On the other hand, if your ISP requires you to log on manually (and you configured Dial-Up Networking to open a terminal window as described in the previous section), the software opens a terminal window, such as the one in Figure 6.19.

In this window, you can receive prompts from the remote system and respond by typing commands to log on to the remote system. If you must complete a manual log on, it usually consists of entering your username and password, and perhaps typing a command, such as SLIP or PPP, to start the connection protocol. Once the manual logon is complete, click <u>D</u>one to close the terminal window.

FIG. 6.19
A terminal window allows you to log on to the remote computer manually.

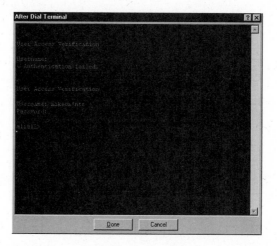

N O T E   After you have made sure your connection works correctly, you can automate the connection process by using dial-up scripting. Using a dial-up script allows you to automatically enter your username, password, and any commands. Dial-up scripting is discussed in the section "Using Dial-Up Networking Scripts," later in this chapter. ▣

Dial-Up Networking displays status messages as it negotiates the connection protocol and makes the Internet connection to the remote computer. Once the connection is completed, the message shown in Figure 6.20 appears.

Click OK to close the message box. Now your computer is connected to the Internet and you can use your Web browser, any of Windows NT's Internet tools, or other Internet applications.

FIG. 6.20
Success! Your
connection to the
Internet is complete.

When you're ready to end your connection to the Internet, right-click the Dial-Up Networking button on the taskbar, point to Hang Up Connection on the menu that appears, and then choose the connection you want to end. Confirm your desire to disconnect by clicking Yes in the message box that appears.

Using Dial-Up Networking Scripts

If your connection requires that you type some information (such as your username, password, or protocol) in response to on-screen prompts before you can connect to your ISP's system), you can automate this process by using Dial-Up Networking's scripting capability. Unlike Windows 95 in which dial-up scripting is provided in the Microsoft Plus! for Windows 95 package, basic scripting is included in Windows NT's Dial-Up Networking software.

N O T E Scripts aren't necessary for most PPP connections. Dial-Up Networking can automatically log onto a remote system that supports password authentication. Scripts are needed only to replace the manual logon that is required of SLIP accounts and some older-style PPP accounts. ■

Setting Up a Script for an Internet Connection

The key to successfully automating the logon process with a script is carefully noting the exact procedure needed to log on manually. You must know what prompts appear on-screen and how you must reply to log on. Exact spelling and capitalization is critical!

Then you can create a script that waits for significant prompts and enters the appropriate text in response. You'll need to log on manually a number of times to determine exactly what prompts and responses should be included in the script.

To automate your logon with a script, start by opening the Dial-Up Networking dialog box (My Computer, Dial-Up Networking), selecting the phonebook entry you want to automate, and opening the Edit Phonebook Entry dialog box to the Script tab (More, Edit entry and modem properties, Script). Choose the Run This Script option and then select a script from the drop-down list box.

Initially, the Run This Script list box contains only a single item: Generic Login. This is a sample script that looks for prompts containing the strings "ogin" and "assword," and responds with the user name and password from the Connect To dialog box. While this script may suffice for some connections, you'll probably need to create or modify scripts for your specific needs.

To create or modify a script, click Edit Scripts. This opens the Dial-Up Networking script file (Switch.inf) in Notepad (see Fig. 6.21). The file itself contains instructions for its use.

In addition to the Generic Login script, the file contains a couple of other sample scripts that you can activate and use or modify. To create or modify scripts, simply edit the script file and save it.

FIG. 6.21
The Dial-Up Networking script file.

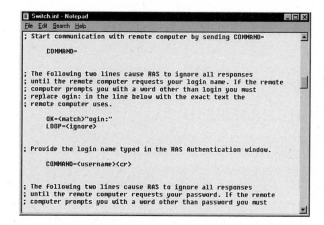

Each script is identified by a heading: a name enclosed in square brackets. The heading is followed by commands, one to a line, to wait for certain prompts and enter responses. Any line that begins with a semicolon is a comment line and is ignored by the program.

The instructions appear in the file as comments and the sample scripts are disabled the same way. To enable a sample script, delete the comment character (the semicolon) at the beginning of each command line in the script.

Learning Dial-Up Scripting

The best way to learn how to use Dial-Up Networking scripts is to look at a couple of examples. The sample scripts in the Switch.inf file are hard to read because of all the comments surrounding the commands. So we have reproduced them here without the distracting comments:

```
[Generic login]
COMMAND=
OK=<match>"ogin:"
LOOP=<ignore>
COMMAND=<username><cr>
OK=<match>"assword:"
LOOP=<ignore>
COMMAND=<password><cr>
OK=<ignore>
```

```
[Login for YourLoginHere]
COMMAND=
OK=<match>"ogin:"
LOOP=<ignore>
COMMAND=YourLoginHere<cr>
OK=<match>"assword:"
LOOP=<ignore>
COMMAND=YourPasswordHere<cr>
OK=<ignore>

[Sample SLIP login]
COMMAND=
OK=<match>"ogin:"
LOOP=<ignore>
COMMAND=YourLoginHere<cr>
OK=<match>"assword:"
LOOP=<ignore>
COMMAND=YourPasswordHere<cr>
COMMAND=<cr>
COMMAND=<cr>
COMMAND=<cr>
COMMAND=<cr>
COMMAND=
OK=<match>"Home"
LOOP=<ignore>
COMMAND=SLIP<cr>
```

The [Generic login] script uses variables (<username> and <password>) to insert the username and password you enter in the Connect To dialog box into the script output. The other two scripts simply record your user name and password in plain text in the script.

To use these scripts, you replace YourLoginHere and YourPasswordHere with your own login name and password. You may also need to replace the text appearing in quotes following the <match> statements with the text of the prompts from your login procedure.

After editing the script file, save it and close the Notepad window. Then click the Refresh list button to force Dial-Up Networking to reread the file and add the scripts it contains to the Run this script list box.

TIP There's more information on scripting in the RAS Help file. To display the Help file, Start, Run, then type Rasphone.hlp in the Run dialog box and click OK.

Once you specify a script, click OK to close the Edit Phonebook Entry dialog box. The next time you dial the Dial-Up Networking phonebook entry, the terminal window does not appear. Instead, Dial-Up Networking runs the script to perform the logon.

Troubleshooting Your Dial-Up Connection

A number of factors can contribute to problems with your Dial-Up Networking connection. A problem with your modem, phone line, ISP, or connection setup can all cause your connection to fail or work poorly. Even the smallest configuration detail can cause a mismatch between your system and your ISP.

One thing that can help you troubleshoot Dial-Up Networking connections is the information available in the Dial-Up Networking Monitor dialog box shown in Figure 6.22. To open the dialog box, right-click the Dial-Up Networking button on the taskbar and choose Open Dial-Up Monitor. The dialog box appears on top of the other open windows so you can monitor activity over your dial-up connection.

FIG. 6.22
The Dial-Up Networking Monitor dialog box provides a wealth of troubleshooting information.

Besides monitoring activity in the Dial-Up Networking Monitor dialog box, you can try the following solutions if your Dial-Up Networking connection isn't working properly.

If Your Modem Does Not Dial

If your modem does not dial at all when you try to connect to your ISP, first check to make sure you have the correct modem configured for your system. Open the Modems control panel and verify that the modem type reported is the same as the actual modem installed and that it's installed on the correct COM port. When you installed the modem, the wrong modem may have been detected; reinstall the modem with the correct type of modem.

If the modem is properly configured, check your phone connection to make sure the modem is connected to the phone line. You can also try dialing your modem manually using HyperTerminal or the Phone dialer application found under Programs, Accessories on your Start menu.

Your Modem Dials But the Other Modem Doesn't Answer

First, try the connection a second time to make sure that the problem wasn't only a temporary one. Make sure that you are dialing the right number for this connection. Verify the area code and any access codes that may be added to the phone number.

Part
II

Ch
6

Depending on phone conditions (for example, if the phone system is particularly busy), you might need to add extra time after getting an outside line. Most modems allow you to add a pause by putting a comma (,) into the phone number.

If the phone number is correct, check with someone at the remote site to make sure their system is on and the modem is working correctly.

The Other Modem Answers But the Connection Fails

This is one of the hardest situations to diagnose and this is where most problems with dial-up connections happen. The first step is to verify that all your connection and modem settings are right, especially the settings for the remote server type.

Most ISPs have information packets for users listing all the correct settings for connections to their systems. Make sure you match these settings exactly.

If everything else checks out, the problem might be that the ISP does not allow LCP extensions. To disable LCP extension requests, select the phonebook entry in the Dial-Up Networking dialog box and open the Edit Phonebook Entry dialog box (More, Edit entry and modem properties). Click the Server tab and clear the Enable PPP LCP extensions option. Click OK to close the dialog box and try the connection again.

Internet Applications Don't Work

If your connection starts up but your Internet applications (such as a WWW browser or FTP program) don't work, first check your TCP/IP settings to make sure that they are right.

Again, select the phonebook entry in the Dial-Up Networking dialog box and open the Edit Phonebook Entry dialog box (More, Edit entry and modem properties). Click the Server tab and click TCP/IP Settings to open the PPP TCP/IP Settings dialog box.

Make sure the IP address and name server addresses are correct. If you still have trouble connecting despite having the correct addresses entered, try disabling the Use IP Header Compression option. Make sure the Use Default Gateway on Remote Server option is checked unless you have specific instructions to the contrary from your ISP. ●

Connecting with Windows 3.1 and Trumpet WinSock

by Jerry Honeycutt and Tim Parker

While the best way to connect to the Internet is when your computer is connected directly to a computer network (that is in turn connected to the Internet), there are many cases where this is not possible. If you do not work at a company that has a computer network connected to the Internet, or your school is not connected, you will probably not have direct access to the Internet from your computer.

Although you can use many of the Internet services through other types of accesses (such as CompuServe or one of the other types of Internet service providers discussed in this section), the ideal method of accessing Internet services is by having your computer send and receive information directly with Internet hosts.

So if your computer is not directly connected to the Internet or a local network (perhaps you do not even have any hardware to connect to a network in your system), how can you connect your computer directly to the Internet? The answer is by using an SLIP or PPP package to connect to an Internet service provider through a modem. ■

Learn about SLIP and PPP

If you're connecting via a phone line, you need to know about SLIP and PPP.

Understand the SLIP/PPP requirements

You don't need any exotic hardware or software to use SLIP or PPP. You'll learn what the hardware and software requirements are in this chapter, though.

Get SLIP/PPP software for your computer

You learn where you can get the software that you need to connect to the Internet via the phone.

Install and configure trumpet WinSock

Trumpet WinSock is the most popular SLIP/PPP software on the Internet. Learn where to get it and how to install it.

Fix those pesky problems

Dial-up connections come with their own set of problems. This chapter helps you fix them.

N O T E   The version of trumpet WinSock that you read about in this chapter is for Windows 3.1. You can't install it in Windows 95 or Windows NT and expect 32-bit Internet programs to work. Windows 95 and Windows NT come with a free dialer, anyway (see Chapters 5, "Connecting to a PPP or SLIP Account with Windows 95" and 6, "Connecting to a PPP or SLIP Account with Windows NT"). ■

Introduction to SLIP/PPP

Before we can talk about the details of obtaining and setting up your computer to use the SLIP or PPP packages, we need to talk a little about what these packages are and how they allow your computer to talk to the Internet. We also briefly review what the *TCP/IP protocols* are and how they relate to SLIP/PPP.

What Is SLIP/PPP?

SLIP stands for the Serial Line Internet Protocol, and as its name implies, it allows your computer to use the Internet Protocol over a serial link, such as a telephone line. When your system is connected to a SLIP service provider (which connects your machine to the Internet or some other network), your computer can send and receive IP packets just as if it were directly connected to the network. This means that any software on your computer that uses the TCP/IP protocol (such as Telnet or your Web browser) will work properly.

PPP stands for the Point to Point Protocol, which also connects your computer system to a network over a serial line. The PPP protocol is different from SLIP, however, in that it does not provide the Internet Protocol to your system (you must obtain a separate piece of software to perform this function). PPP basically gives your computer system a network device, which can be used with TCP/IP protocol software (sometimes called a *protocol stack*) to transmit packets to a network.

As you can see, SLIP is somewhat more convenient than PPP because SLIP provides the Internet Protocol software as part of the package; whereas PPP is usually more efficient, because it has to deal with only the low-level job of moving packets over a serial link. PPP also is better at correcting errors caused by noisy telephone lines and generally provides a more robust connection than SLIP. For these reasons, some network service providers offer only PPP connections.

N O T E   If you have a choice between PPP or SLIP, choose PPP every time. PPP is a faster connection protocol that is much easier to configure than SLIP. ■

There are several freely available PPP and SLIP packages for IBM-compatible systems. Also, many mini-computers today, such as computers from Sun Microsystems, come with SLIP and/or PPP software built in, which allows them to easily act as SLIP/PPP service providers.

▶ **See** "An Introduction to TCP/IP," **p. 108**

What Is TCP/IP?

TCP/IP stands for the Transmission Control Protocol/Internet Protocol, and it is the communications standard between hosts on the Internet. Defining the basic format of the data packets on the Internet, TCP/IP allows programs to exchange information with any other host on the Internet. In fact, the Internet can be defined as all of the connected computers that use the TCP/IP protocol standard to communicate.

Requirements to Use SLIP/PPP

While most computers today are capable of running SLIP/PPP software, there are several things you should consider before trying to run this software on your system. This section outlines the hardware and software requirements for running SLIP/PPP.

Although SLIP and PPP do not require as many system resources as direct network connections require, SLIP and PPP do have some specific system requirements. There also are some system configurations that allow much better network performance. This section discusses these system requirements.

Most of the requirements to run SLIP or PPP software on your system are the same as for running any large application such as Microsoft Windows. To get the best network performance, you need a relatively fast computer with a high-speed modem. In addition, you should check into the quality of your telephone line in order to ensure that you get good data transmission.

▶ **See** "Important Considerations," **p. 103**

▶ **See** "Why a High-Speed Connection?" **p. 208**

Main System Requirements

In order to get good network performance through an SLIP or PPP connection with a 28.8 Kbps modem, you should have at least a 80386 25MHz processor, with at least 4M of free main memory after the operating system has started. Because most SLIP and PPP software add several device drivers to your system, and running network applications can take up a lot of system resources, the more memory you have, the better your network applications will run.

Most network applications (such as Mosaic or Gopher) are designed to run with Microsoft Windows, so you should make sure that your system has Microsoft Windows version 3.1 or later. If your system runs Windows well, it also will probably run network applications reasonably well, allowing you to transfer information quickly.

Modem Requirements

In addition to your main computer system, you must have a modem to use SLIP/PPP. While almost any modem allows you to use SLIP/PPP, the faster the modem you have, the better network performance you have. At the minimum, you should have a 9600 baud modem; while this will have relatively slow performance, this is adequate for occasional use.

Part

II

Ch

7

N O T E If you intended to browse the Web, you'll want to invest in a high-quality 28.8 Kbps modem. The Web contains too much graphics, sounds, and other multimedia content for a 9600 baud modem. ▨

For best network performance, you should use a 28.8 Kbps modem with data compression, if possible. This will allow you to comfortably use network programs that require a high data-transfer rate (such as Mosaic) with good performance. Modem speeds and capabilities are increasing constantly—some network providers are installing ISDN (Integrated Services Digital Network) for even better network access.

Of course, having a high-speed modem (or one with error correction or compression) will not do you much good if the modem you are connecting to does not have similar capabilities. This is an important point to consider when choosing a network service provider. See the section "Finding SLIP/PPP Service Providers," for more such considerations.

T I P If you haven't already purchased your modem, contact your service provider and ask them for a suggestion. Often, they can cut you a great deal on a modem. They also can suggest a modem that works well with the modems that they use. Pairing up modems assures you that you'll get the best performance possible, with as few errors as possible.

Telephone Line Requirements

Because the telephone line connects your local computer system to the remote network provider, you should make sure that it provides good-quality service before using it for SLIP/PPP access. A noisy or low-quality telephone line can cause problems with your network connection, such as the following:

- Slower transmission speeds than would normally be possible with your modem
- Transmission errors or retransmitted network packets
- Dropped connections or pauses in transmission

Unfortunately, one of the last things considered when setting up an SLIP/PPP connection is the telephone line characteristics. It is only when serious problems develop (such as transmission errors or dropped connections) that the telephone line is checked. PPP is less sensitive to telephone line problems than SLIP, so a telephone line that works with PPP may have problems if you switch to SLIP.

You should ensure that your telephone line does not have static or other noise on it. If the line you use for your network connection is different from the regular telephone line you use for voice communications, you should put a telephone on the network line to listen for good-quality connections. While this test is not conclusive—a telephone line that sounds fine can still cause problems with a modem—a noisy line definitely causes transmission problems with either SLIP or PPP.

If you expect to use a telephone line for critical network connections, you should contact your telephone company to arrange for a data-quality line or ISDN connection. Have the company ensure that your line is capable of handling high-speed data communications. Note that a data-quality line often costs significantly more than a regular telephone line—before you switch, you should check with your telephone company for its rates.

Finding SLIP/PPP Software

Some of SLIP/PPP packages are provided by commercial vendors, and some are either shareware or are demonstration versions of a commercial package. You should be able to easily find an SLIP/PPP package that connects your computer system to your Internet service provider.

In order to find an SLIP/PPP package, first check with your Internet service provider. Your provider may provide a package for connecting to its service; if it does provide a package (or can recommend one), you should use that package in order to ensure compatibility with your provider's services. Most Internet service providers either provide software or can recommend a package to you.

▶ **See** "What Is FTP?" **p. 808**

If your Internet service provider does not supply a package, or you haven't picked a service provider yet, you can pick from several packages available at no charge. Several packages are available through anonymous FTP on the Internet, but because you probably don't have access to the Internet yet, this route may not be available to you.

The CD-ROM (NetCD) included with this book provides several SLIP/PPP packages; the NetManage Chameleon 4.1 package with Instant Internet (which is a fully functional demonstration version of a commercial package available from NetManage), trumpet WinSock, the Crynwr SLIP and Packet drivers, Slipper, CSlipper, and GoSLIP packages.

You should check the documentation for these packages to find one that meets your needs; for example, some of the packages are oriented toward Windows applications, while others are DOS oriented. One of the packages provided on NetCD will certainly meet your needs.

Finding SLIP/PPP Service Providers

Many Internet service providers have a wide variety of services available. Many have both *shell accounts*, where you dial into one of the service provider's computers and use Internet services from there, and SLIP/PPP accounts, where you connect to the service provider's computer or terminal server using SLIP or PPP and then are directly connected to the Internet.

When you contact an Internet service provider for information about its services, you should ask about its SLIP/PPP services. Here's some information that is important to find:

■ What speed and type of modems does the provider have available? Make sure that it has high-speed modems and ones that support hardware compression and error correction.

Part

II

Ch

7

This lets you make sure that your modem works correctly to make a good SLIP/PPP connection.

- How many SLIP/PPP lines does the provider have available, and what is its ratio of lines per SLIP/PPP hours of connection? This gives you an indication of how difficult it is to connect to the provider.

- Does the service provider make SLIP or PPP software (and any auxiliary software) available to users? If not, will any of the publicly available software work correctly with the provider's system?

- Will the service provider give you a permanently allocated Internet address (as opposed to giving you a different number each time you connect)? If you get a permanently allocated address, you can publish your address for people to contact your machine when it is connected.

- What are the rate structures for SLIP/PPP access? How many hours of connect time are you allowed each month (or week)? You should decide what your usage will be; if you want to be connected all the time, many service providers will charge you differently than if you connect for only a few hours a week.

- Does the service provider have any package deals or special agreements with the telephone company to provide ISDN to its customers?

- What other services, such as mail forwarding and file storage, will be provided?

Naturally, you should decide what level of SLIP/PPP service you need before you make your decision on a service provider. Your decision on a service provider should reflect both your current and future needs—look for a provider that can not only give you good service now, but can also grow with your needs in the future.

 All of the Internet service provider lists tell you if the service providers have SLIP or PPP access, and should give you an indication of their rate structures. For example, the InterNIC Provider List and the PDIAL List provided on NetCD have this information.

Setting Up Trumpet WinSock SLIP Software on Your System

 You can find several good programs with which you can connect to the Internet. trumpet WinSock is by far the most popular, however. trumpet WinSock is a program that provides SLIP and PPP capabilities. This package is shareware and is available on NetCD, the CD-ROM included with this book, or through an anonymous FTP on the site **ftp.trumpet.com**.

You install the software and configure it to work with your Internet provider. The next sections describe how to install and configure the trumpet WinSock package.

Installing the Trumpet WinSock Package

Installing the trumpet WinSock package is simply a matter of copying the files that make up the software into a directory on your computer system.

If you received the trumpet WinSock package through FTP, you received it as a ZIP archive. Unzip this archive into a directory on your system, such as C:\TRUMPET. If you use the version of trumpet WinSock from NetCD, you simply copy the files into a directory on your system.

After you copy the trumpet WinSock files into a directory on your system, add this directory to your PATH by editing your AUTOEXEC.BAT file. For example, the new PATH statement may look like this:

```
PATH C:\TRUMPET;C:\DOS;C:\WINDOWS;
```

The file INSTALL.DOC (which is in Word for Windows format—you can use the file INSTALL.TXT if you do not have this software) gives complete instructions for installing and configuring the trumpet WinSock package for various systems.

Configuring the Trumpet WinSock Package

To configure the trumpet WinSock package, you must run the program TCPMAN.EXE from the trumpet WinSock package. You either can run this program from the Windows File Manager or, in the Program Manager, you can open the File menu and choose Run.

The first time you run the TCPMAN.EXE program, it displays the window shown in Figure 7.1. This figure shows the various fields that you must set to use the trumpet WinSock package.

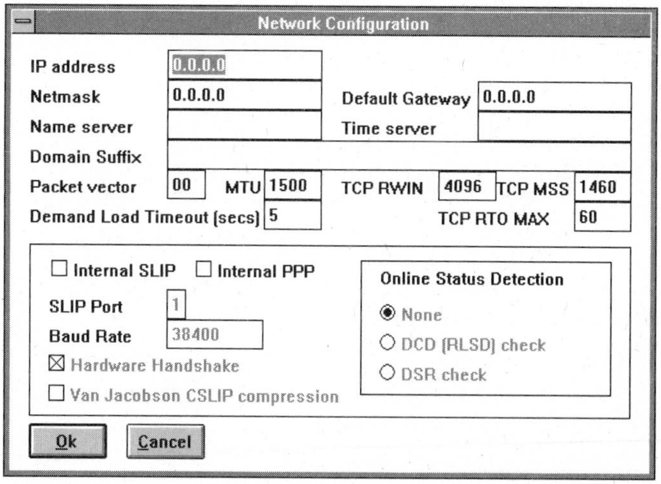

FIG. 7.1
Configuring the trumpet WinSock package—these are the basic configuration options.

Network Configuration	
IP address	0.0.0.0
Netmask	0.0.0.0 Default Gateway 0.0.0.0
Name server	Time server
Domain Suffix	
Packet vector 00 MTU 1500 TCP RWIN 4096 TCP MSS 1460	
Demand Load Timeout (secs) 5 TCP RTO MAX 60	

☐ Internal SLIP   ☐ Internal PPP

SLIP Port   1
Baud Rate   38400
☒ Hardware Handshake
☐ Van Jacobson CSLIP compression

Online Status Detection
◉ None
○ DCD (RLSD) check
○ DSR check

[Ok] [Cancel]

Part
II

Ch
7

Configuring the trumpet WinSock package is somewhat similar to the NetManage Chameleon package. The following are the basic steps:

1. Select either Internal SLIP or Internal PPP, depending on the type of service from your Internet provider.

2. Fill in the IP address, netmask, gateway address, name server, and domain suffix as provided by your Internet service provider.

3. Fill in the *communications port* (the port your modem is on) and the baud rate that your modem supports. You can usually determine these settings from your modem documentation.

After you fill in these basic options, the trumpet WinSock program displays the window shown in Figure 7.2, which shows the status of your connection.

FIG. 7.2

The trumpet WinSock status and operation window.

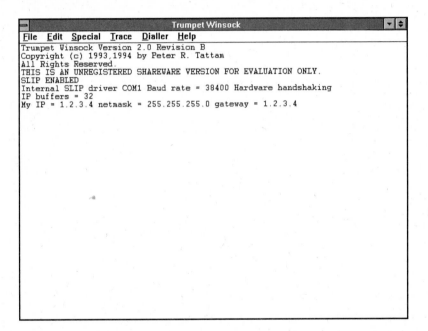

After the basic configuration is done, open the Dialer menu and choose Manual Login to manually connect to your service provider. This allows you to test your connection and run network software.

After you test your connection to your service provider, you can edit the dialing scripts by opening the Dialer menu and choosing Edit Scripts. Full instructions on what you need to do when editing these scripts is provided in the trumpet WinSock documentation.

Diagnosing Common SLIP/PPP Software Problems

As with any communications program, SLIP and PPP software is sensitive to problems with telephone lines and with the host you are connecting to. While each SLIP/PPP package may provide error messages and other information to help with diagnosing communications problems, this section gives some general information that can help you pinpoint the cause of some common problems.

Failure to Connect to Service Provider

The most common reason your SLIP/PPP software fails to connect to your Internet service provider is that all the lines for the provider will be busy. Most SLIP/PPP packages will tell you that the line was busy, but some will not. To diagnose this problem, you can try to dial the telephone number on a regular telephone to see if you get a busy signal or a modem carrier (that loud noise you hear when the other modem answers).

Other causes of a failure to connect are a noisy telephone line (you can try a different line or try again later) or a hardware problem at your service provider (in which case, the remote modem never answers). Again, you can either listen on a regular phone while your software tries to connect to the service provider, or you can enable the speaker on your modem if it has one. If you have an external modem (one that has a front panel with indicator lights), you often can monitor the progress of your connection by watching these lights.

You shouldn't overlook the obvious problems, by the way. Make sure that you've plugged the phone line into the correct plug on the backside of the modem. Most modems have two plugs: one for the wall and one for a phone. Also, make sure that you've correctly configured your serial port's IRQ and I/O address. See your computer or modem's manual if you need help configuring your serial port.

Your SLIP/PPP Connection Hangs

Often, the only indication that your connection has *hung* (your application stops responding to your input) is that you stop getting data. If your SLIP/PPP software is well written, it allows you to close your connection down gracefully, but often your applications will be hung and you will have to either kill them or reboot your machine.

One common cause of a connection hang is that your telephone line has either hung up (for example, someone may have picked up another extension of the telephone line you were using) or the line may have gotten noisy enough for your modem to hang up the line.

Once again, enabling the speaker on your modem (at a low volume level) can help you notice if your connection has hung up. You can also watch the OH (on hook) light on your modem to see if it goes out, indicating that it hung up. If your telephone line is often noisy or you get random service interruptions on your line, you should contact your telephone company to have them check your line.

Part
II

Ch
7

N O T E   Some telephone companies are hesitant to debug problems when a computer is used on regular (voice-grade) lines. You may have to be persistent, telling them that you often have audible noise on the line. ▬

Slow Network Response

The most common reason for slow network response is that your service provider is over-loaded. This occurs when so many people are connected that the service provider can't keep up with the demand. You have a few solutions for this problem. You can connect during off-peak hours when other folks aren't as likely to connect. You can call your service provider and let them know of your plight in an effort to increase their capabilities. Last, you can move to a service provider that can better handle the load.

Slow network response (or slow transmission speeds) is often caused by a noisy telephone line, which causes modems to work at a slower baud rate than their top speed because the modem has to correct for data errors. You can close your connection and try again to get a better line, or if you experience this condition often you can contact your telephone company to have them check your telephone line.

In some cases, your Internet service provider may have several different speeds of modems available, with the highest speed modems being the first available. If all of the high-speed modems are in use, you may receive a slower speed modem. Often your SLIP/PPP software will indicate the connection speed when your Internet connection is established. For example, the NetManage Chameleon package has an option to display the modem dialog when the connection is established—this will tell you the real speed that your modem is connected at.

If the high-speed modems connected to your Internet provider are often in use and you are not able to get a high-speed connection, you should ask the provider to add more modems. You may have to change to a different Internet service provider to find one with more high-speed modems. ●

Setting Up an ISDN Connection

*by Jerry Honeycutt and
James Bryce*

ISDN is the acronym for Integrated Services Digital Network, not that that tells you very much. ISDN really boils down to a telephone technology that delivers digital signals to your house or business. Plain Old Telephone Service (POTS) is the regular telephone connection you have now; it uses analog signaling. What this means and why it's important to you is the subject of this chapter.

The information in this chapter is condensed from several chapters in *Special Edition Using ISDN* by James Y. Bryce; this book, published by Que, covers these and many more ISDN topics in detail. ∎

Learn the difference between digital and analog

What's the difference between digital and analog signaling and why should you care?

Learn about ISDN

This chapter describes what ISDN is and where it came from.

Set up ISDN service

You'll learn how to set up ISDN service with your phone company. It's easy.

Wire your home or business for ISDN

Setting up your home or office for ISDN is easy. You'll learn how to wire your connection in this chapter.

Learn about the hardware you need for ISDN

You really don't need a lot of hardware to enjoy an ISDN connection.

N O T E You can save yourself a lot of headaches if you look for a package deal. Many independent service providers will sell you a complete ISDN package that includes the telephone company setup charges, ISDN terminal adapter, and ISDN service. They'll even coordinate the whole bit for you. ■

Digital and Analog

The meanings and distinctions between digital and analog are fundamental to an understanding of just what is going on in most of computing and telecommunication.

An analog signal is created and handled in electronic circuits as if one or more of its characteristics, for example strength (amplitude) or pitch (frequency), can be increased or decreased in amounts that are as large or as small as we want. There is *no quantum of quantity in the quality* we are describing as analog.

Okay, that's a little too much alliteration. I'll try again. There is no smallest unit into which we can divide our information. A recording of music would, until very recently, use equipment designed to convert sounds received acoustically into variations in electrical frequency, phase, and amplitude tracking; these parallel and continuous variations in the air are what your ears perceive as sound. If you had sense organs that could detect electrical variations, you could read those variations directly. You would not need any code, protocol conventions, or higher math to turn the received electrical impulses into what you perceive as sound. These electrical signals would assume an unlimited number of amplitude levels, phase relationships, and frequencies. An analog transducer such as a microphone creates an analog stream of information in the new medium (electricity) and conveys a continuous replica of the information in electronic form.

A digital signal presumes there is a *quantum of quantity in the quality* you are describing as digital. Translation: there is a smallest unit into which you can divide your information. In its most frequent use with computers, "digital logic," it implies only two states of electrical signals are recognized: one and zero. Regardless of some variations in the electrical signals in a computer or digital transmission line due to faulty components, noise, or whatever, all are resolved into ones and zeros. In many instances, this makes a digital system less prone to malfunction than an analog system. As strange as it seems, it is possible to create all of mathematics from this simple "two-valued logic."

It's possible to encode sounds, pictures, and other information into a stream of ones and zeros. The whole trick of encoding otherwise analog material such as sound is the fineness of the sampling of that material: the smaller the unit of sampling, the more closely digital encoding can subsequently be decoded to reproduce the original analog information. Let's say you want to encode analog sounds into digital information. You build a device that looks at the analog signal and samples it at various times. The more samples taken, the more exactly the digital pulses can carry details of the original analog information.

This seems like a lot of effort to, in effect, actually lose information. The only way you can get an exact replica of the analog signal is by sampling it an unlimited number of times, and this would probably cost you an unlimited amount of money. Why not just stick with the analog form in the first place? Why go through all of this? You will probably decide to use the digital form because it solves two very troublesome problems: noise and attenuation.

In broad perspective, a telephone system consists of two functions: transmission and switching. *Transmission* involves the cables, microwave, and so on that are used to get information from one point to another. *Switching* involves the equipment the transmission elements are hooked to that direct signals among desired sources and destinations. The larger an analog system becomes, the more expensive and complex the transmission and switching problems become. Digital techniques approach transmission and switching in a very different way that results in considerably less cost and complexity for telephone systems of the size you need—global. Let's look at the major problems in an analog system and see how digital approaches them more efficiently and economically.

Noise

Noise is anything that does not make up the desired communication; the desired communication is called the *signal*. Noise is like the marble that a sculptor chips away to release the hidden form within a work of art. An analog system is by its nature noisy. The first telephone systems were simple analog designs; they were very limited in the distances from which they could transmit sounds; these limits were defined in large measure by the noise floor of the system. The *noise floor* is the very least noise that exists in your system after you've removed everything else. Your signal must be at a higher volume or frequency than this floor or you lose it in the noise. As the wires of those systems grew longer, more and more noise began to be heard, which could come from the following sources:

- Random motion of the molecules making up the wire (heat)
- Electrical disturbances such as lightning
- Other signals flowing in parallel wires being induced onto your wires (crosstalk)
- Electrical power from adjacent equipment

On a short run, a mile or so, these items tended to stay in the background and were not noticed by, or at least were not of concern to, telephone users. But as the wires became longer, the noise level began to approach that of the signal (signal to noise ratio) and could no longer be ignored.

A number of techniques were adopted to overcome various types of noise: loading coils, noise-canceling circuits that reversed the phase of the noise, shielded and twisted cables, and coaxial cables. Through it all, noise gradually increased and avoidance and cancellation of noise became the bulk of the cost in long distance transmission.

Attenuation

Worse, as the noise became stronger, the signal became weaker, attenuated, while going through the system. As electrical energy travels through a conductor, it encounters resistance to its flow determined by the physical properties of the conductor. This resistance turns some of the electrical energy into heat and random molecular motion, therefore adding to the noise.

Scientists and engineers seek to reduce this resistance by selection of materials that have low resistance. Silver has the least resistance of any generally available conductor; copper has a higher resistance but is much cheaper and is the usual choice for cables.

The attenuation that results from the resistance affects different parts of the signal in different ways. The low frequency components are diminished a little, but the high frequency components are severely diminished. This *frequency selective attenuation* ultimately results in voices that lack most of their highs. The high ranges contain a good deal of the information needed to understand speech. As transmission lines become longer and longer, you might hear someone's now overly bass voice sounds at the distant end but be unable to understand the words spoken.

The remedy for a weak, selectively attenuated signal in an analog circuit is the addition of an amplifier that takes the received signal and increases its amplitude. The amplifier must increase the amplitude of the received high frequencies much more than that of the low frequencies to make the voice intelligible. (*Slope equalization* is the buzz word.) At the same time your amplifier increases the amplitude of the signal, it increases the amplitude of the noise. Enter ever more elaborate and expensive techniques to cancel noise and to restore naturalness to the signal. Long distance and international carriers worked diligently perfecting ways to make an analog signal travel great distances with low distortion and favorable signal to noise ratio. But their efforts always resulted in very expensive and complicated equipment. The industry needed a technological advance to send analog voice by digital means.

Sample your voice signal several times each second, then for each sample, assign a number representing the characteristics of the analog signal at that instant. The more times you sample, the more numbers you get per second and your approximation of the original, analog signal will be most accurate. Then express these numbers in binary form and transmit these binary numbers as strings of ones and zeros over your transmission system. It's a miracle, because most of your transmission problems disappear. Why?

N O T E The general rule is the sampling must be at a rate twice that of the highest frequency you want to transmit. For ordinary speech the highest frequency needed for comfortable intelligibility and fidelity is considered to be 4 kHz (4,000 cycles per a second). The sampling rate is then 8,000 (8,000 times a second). ▨

Let's start with noise. Now that you know there are only two possible elements making up your digital signal, ones and zeros, you can design electronic circuits that look for only the unique electrical waveform that represents a one or a zero. This design process can become quite complicated, but is at least limited to isolating only two waveforms. Contrast this with the analog environment, which must consider everything received as signal unless complex circuits such as noise cancellers give it other information to the contrary.

The same rules regarding attenuation and distortion apply to the digital signal, but you can tolerate a lot of distortion when you are looking for only two states. You can determine an item is a one; it may have been severely distorted and attenuated, but you know for certain it is a one. Rather than amplifying what you received, that is, increasing its strength and thereby retaining and increasing the distortion, you regenerate it. Usually the device used for this is called a repeater. Since you know what a perfect one is specified to be given the standard protocols in your system, you can identify this thing you received, though distorted, because it still falls within the parameters for a one. Thus, you can create a perfect one and send it on its way to the next leg of the transmission system. *Presto*, all the distortion is gone from the signal. *Change-o*, the noise disappears, because it never gave rise to either a one or a zero in your regeneration device.

Amplifier, Regenerator, Repeater

These terms often are mixed in text or conversation.

An *amplifier* is an analog device that increases the amplitude of a received signal and to a greater or lesser extent, depending on the sophistication of its design, and sends it on, noise, distortion and all.

A *regenerator* is a digital device that determines when a digital one or zero is received, creates a new one or zero, retimes the bit stream, and sends it on its way. Now it gets confusing because sometimes a manual or company will call a box that is a digital regenerator an amplifier.

Repeaters are even more confusing. Most of the time the term repeater refers to a regenerator; in fact, repeater is the prevalent term used to describe what is actually an analog amplifier. When in doubt, figure out what the box is actually doing and don't rely on the often arbitrary nomenclature.

A digital signal seeks to render information to be conveyed by analysis of the information into a collection of discrete electrical signals, each either a one or a zero. Even if you had sense organs that could detect variations of electrical signals, you would not be able to perceive the message being sent because the digital signal is by definition not an analog of the original phenomenon. All you could determine would be that a string of marks and spaces, ones and zeros, frequency x and frequency y, phase 90 degrees and phase 270 degrees, was going by.

In and of itself, this stream would make no sense. You must have an agreed-upon means of taking the ones and zeros and transforming them into something meaningful to you. You must have a protocol that tells you that 1000001 is to be interpreted as "A" (in the ASCII code set, your protocol). And you must be more sophisticated. You must know when to start counting ones and zeros and when to stop, and what constitutes a package of information. Timing, synchronization, packets, and frames enter the picture. All of this is a part of the standards that make up your communications system. Now let's look at ISDN as it uses these concepts to improve your computer and telephone connections.

The Advantages of ISDN

ISDN, Integrated Services Digital Network, uses these methods of digital technology to give you:

- A faster data rate when you connect your computer to other systems over the phone system
- Faster set up and tear down when you place a data call
- More information about a call in progress

You've probably already heard about the increased data rate ISDN provides (see Fig. 8.1). But have you though about improvements that result from faster set up and tear down? Think how long it takes a modem to sync up with another modem: remember all the squawks and buzzes? None of this happens with ISDN. The connection is made in a fraction of a second (see Fig. 8.2). This can cut down greatly on your connection time. It means you can be cruising the Web, clicking a hyperlink, calling up your Internet service provider, downloading the information, and disconnecting. The next link you click duplicates the process. There's no reason to be connected while you're reading the page! ISDN is much more efficient in its use of the telephone connection and its demands on the Internet service provider for lines and equipment.

FIG. 8.1

The higher the data rate, the better it is for your use of the connection. ISDN provides 64 Kbs B channels for communication. Two B channels can be combined.

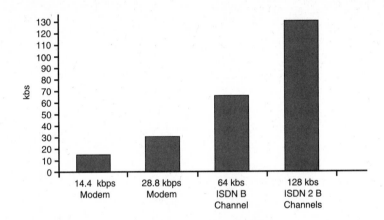

FIG. 8.2

The shorter the time, the better it is for you.

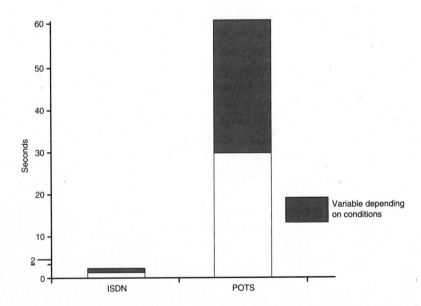

Telephone Systems

As I mentioned earlier, telephone systems are composed of two major parts:

- Transmission
- Switching

Each is essential to telephone communication and each plays a big role in the current importance of ISDN to you.

Transmission

Transmission gets a signal from point A to point B. In particular transmission is concerned with issues surrounding transmission media. Media used in telephony come in four flavors:

- Twisted pair cable
- Coaxial cable
- Fiber optic cable
- Radio

Because of noise and attenuation characteristics, fiber optic cables carry the most information the greatest distance and twisted pair copper cables carry the least information the shortest distance. Coax falls somewhere in between. Radio is frequently restricted, due to the need to share spectrum space with others.

Prior to the wide use of fiber optics, long distance carriers relied on coaxial cable supplemented with microwave radio, using analog radio technology to carry signals. Fiber and digital technology have proven more economical and capable of carrying vast amounts of information; therefore, microwave and coax are being phased out.

Today, virtually all of the telephone system is based on fiber optic cables carrying digital signals; cities are connected by interexchange carriers also using fiber. Central offices within cities are connected to each other using fiber optics. The only place you'll find any copper twisted pair running analog signals today is the *local loop*, the cable from the central office to your office or house. It is the local loop that is the determining factor in the data rate, noise, and errors associated with your use of the telephone system. The local loop is the weak link.

Long ago the local exchange carriers and the interchange carriers (long distance carriers) decided it was in their best interests to use fiber optics for telephone exchange to telephone exchange communication. This decision saved them a lot of money. Ensuring that the signals going down those cables were digital, since your whole electronic technology has concentrated on perfecting digital transmission for nearly 40 years.

However, you're faced with a twisted pair to the telco (tech talk for telephone company) switch. And that twisted pair places a severe limit on the data rate that can be delivered to you. ISDN helps get the last gasp of use out of that twisted pair because it delivers a digital, rather than analog signal. Soon you'll have to go to fiber, coax, or wireless methods. Twisted pair is the best most of us have, so let's get the most out of it. You can anticipate development of a competitive market for improvement in media. Suddenly, capital that was written down over 20 to 40 years by traditional telephone companies will be depreciated out in five, and you'll get far more for far less.

Switching

The first automated exchanges were collections of magnetically operated rotary switches that stepped through each pulse sent from the dial. A connection was made to an identical switch that stepped to the next digit and so on: hence the name of the equipment, *step by step*. Following this design a more elaborate and flexible, but still electromechanical, design called a *cross-bar switch* began to take over.

As we moved into the 1960s, the earliest electronic switching technologies were based on analog technology then still used in the telephone. The 1970s saw the development of the first digital switches, concurrent with the flow of digital information on the transmission side of the equation. Now there was every economic reason to keep information in digital form throughout the system. Conversion back and forth through switches was expensive. With rare exception, it was to the operating companies' advantage to use both digital switches and digital transmission lines. Figure 8.3 shows how we're currently hooked up.

FIG. 8.3

Notice the digital connections among telephone switches along with the fiber optic cables. Now look at the copper twisted pair that carries analog signals to you.

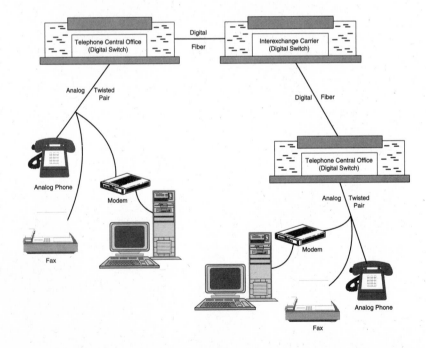

At the very end this wonderful digital information system was converted to analog for that last mile or two down the twisted pair copper loop. This conversion was not cheap; it needed codec devices and electronic gear to convert digital to analog and back, but it was deemed cheaper than rewiring the loop or going to a digital technique and placing new digital equipment at the subscriber's location or at the least making the digital to analog conversion there.

Today ISDN finishes the job. It delivers digital information to the subscriber. The subscriber decides whether or not the equipment he connects is digital or analog and supplies the connection devices to make it work.

N O T E Although it may seem that just about anything can be connected to an ISDN system, be aware that it takes special electronics to use ISDN. If you attempt to call an analog modem with your ISDN equipment, it won't connect. If someone with an analog modem attempts to call your ISDN equipment, nothing happens. Although there are some ISDN devices that embed analog modems for such instances and some that go so far as to be able to detect the difference and automatically switch, other equipment is not so agile. In short, moving to ISDN provides no backward compatibility with POTS; don't throw your modems out yet. Figure 8.4 assumes use of ISDN electronics that enables connection of analog gear to use one or more of the digital B channels of ISDN. ■

FIG. 8.4
With ISDN, the telephone signal is digital all the way to your house or business. You can use your existing analog equipment on ISDN only with appropriate adapters in your ISDN electronics.

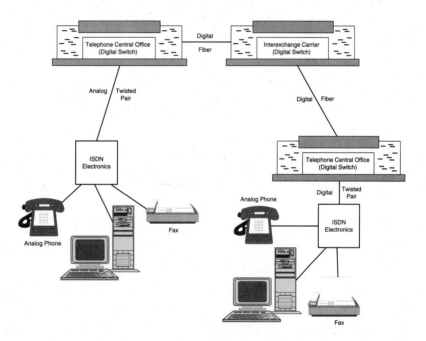

Here are the factors that play into your efforts to make ISDN work for you:

- You must have a local exchange carrier that has ISDN available to your area.
- The carrier may have a digital switch, but that switch may not be ISDN compliant; or it may not be compliant with the new National ISDN standards for the equipment you buy.
- The local exchange carrier may be able to get ISDN to a switch for you but still be unable to supply a cable adequate to carry the digital information from the switch to you.

- All of this may be technically possible, but there may not be a tariff filed with the appropriate government regulatory authority allowing the carrier to connect ISDN to you.

- And, finally, although the switch may be right, the wires may work, and the tariff may be available, the price to you is horrendous.

Narrowband ISDN

You're concerned with "narrowband ISDN" that carries data rates of a few hundred to a few million bits per second. On the horizon is "wideband ISDN" delivering tens and hundreds of megabits; that area is outside the scope of this discussion and not yet widely available. Narrowband ISDN comes in two forms:

- Basic Rate Interface (BRI)
- Primary Rate Interface (PRI)

If you're a larger business or an Internet service provider, you may be interested in PRI; it delivers about 1.5 megabits per second service. However, the big emphasis in this book is on BRI; it delivers two B channels of 64 kilobits per second and one D channel at 16 Kbps. "What is all this B and D stuff," you say? Glad you asked. Here's the word.

> **N O T E** A new family of protocols and hardware has the potential to dramatically increase the data rates delivered on the local loop—we're talking megabits, folks. Check out the *DSL technologies (ADSL, HDSL, and SDSL) briefly described under "The Internet on Cable TV, Dishes, Power Lines, and Pipes?" in Chapter 8. And look at these Web sites: **http://www.sbexpos.com/sbexpos/ association/adsl/home.html**, **http://www.alumni.caltech./~dank/isdn** and **http:// www.bryce.com/~bryce**.

ISDN uses the basic rate interface (BRI) to deliver two channels of 64 Kbps each. These "B channels" are designed to carry the information the subscriber wants to transmit across the network. There is a third channel running at 16 Kbps. This "D channel" is used primarily to control the flow of information through the network. It provides call set up and tear down, network monitoring, and other overhead functions. As the D channel is separate from the B channels, the signaling is called "common channel." This is a form of out of band signaling since it is, by definition, not in the same band as the data bearer channel.

The D channel is common to the B channels controlled. In other services, such as your plain old telephone service (POTS), information for telephone network control is carried within the same channel as that of the subscriber using a technique called "in band signaling." You'll see later in this chapter how this influences your actual usage of the circuit.

Once a call is set up, the D channel is not fully utilized and may be made available for user packet traffic. Call control always takes priority over user packets, but the capacity of the D channel is ideal for such things as credit card identification and simple terminal-to-host sessions.

Basic rate interface ISDN delivers three separate channels for your use: 64 Kbps, 64 Kbps, 16 Kbps (this combination is often called *2B+D*). This is transmitted over the same pair of wires that carried only one channel of comparatively small capacity analog information with POTS.

Basic Rate Interface D Channel   Let's start with the D channel, the most radical departure from the analog world. In a way, the two most important things ISDN brings to the table are its inherently digital nature and the D channel.

In the analog world, a telephone call is controlled in band. When you pick up the phone, an "off hook" signal is sent to the central office switch which detects the condition and connects you to a dial tone indicating you may proceed to use the system. You enter various tones using the "dual tone multiple frequency" (DTMF) in band signaling available from the buttons on the phone. If you have a rotary phone, you make and break the line rapidly creating pulses that are counted at the exchange switch. In the earlier mechanical switches, the pulses actuated stepper relays that selected each successive number. In modern electronic switches the pulses are counted and converted to DTMF signals. In fact, there is a whole mini-industry manufacturing devices to convert the pulses to tones since a great deal of the world is still tied to the rotary dial.

It makes you wonder. Why does it take more equipment to translate the dial pulses than to directly accept the DTMF tones, but many local exchange carriers continue to charge extra for DTMF service? It's sort of like the question of why ISDN often costs more than POTS when it is the POTS analog signal that must be converted to digital for carriage through the otherwise digital switch and telephone network. No one ever said telephone system pricing made sense outside the never-never land of rate regulation, antiquated telephone accounting methods, and the monopoly marketplace.

Anyway, one way or another, the pulses or tones set up a path to the phone you are calling. Then a ringing current is placed on the line of the called phone. This is really a strange beast. Suddenly you go from a low voltage direct current line to ninety volts of alternating current to ring the bell. If you happen to be holding on to the line when it is rung, you'll ring too. Take note. This could be dangerous.

> **CAUTION**
>
> When working on your telephone wiring, be sure it is disconnected from the line coming into your house or office. Ringer current is not as dangerous as the electric power running through your building, but under the wrong conditions, especially your particular physical condition, it could seriously harm or even kill you.
>
> The picture of a movie star taking a bath while using a phone is an invitation to tragedy. Perhaps wireless phones are safe in such circumstances; wired phones never are. Even without ringer current, as is the case with ISDN, transient electrical spikes of hundreds or even thousands of volts may appear on the line from accidental contact with power wiring or lightning strokes. Play it safe.

When the ringer current appears at the called phone, circuitry in the phone directs it to the bell or other attention-getting device and the phone rings. Now at the calling party's end you hear the buzz, buzz you have learned to associate with a ringing phone. There is no direct correlation between the "ringing" you hear in the handset and the actual ringing of the bell on the called phone. This is why you frequently encounter a phone being answered "before it has rung." The physical phone rang at the called party end, but the buzz you as the calling party associate with ringing had not been initiated by the central office switch on your end. Now you know the secret; it's all smoke and mirrors. Since the system is really digital and you're using analog devices at both ends, the digital switches fake what you've come to associate with analog calls. When the called party answers, his phone goes "off hook," signaling his central office switch that the call has been answered and turning off the ringing current. Your call can now proceed.

You both talk for a while when suddenly you hear a tone in the earpiece of your phone. At the called party's end there is a momentary click, click and loss of a syllable or two you were speaking at the time. You explain you must take another call and depress the switchhook; this sends a momentary off condition to your central office switch which has been programmed to interpret this as a signal to place your original called party on hold and transfer you to the new "call waiting" party. You may now switch back and forth between the two by using the switch hook to signal the central office switch.

I've just outlined the current technology of analog in band signaling. Any time you want to make a change in the call setup, you must interrupt your ongoing call to advise the central office switch of your desires. The same is true for the switch; to advise you it must signal in band, interrupting your call in progress. Your actions in dialing with a rotary dial, DTMF tones, or switchhook manipulation create analog signals that must be interpreted into digital instructions for the switch. These are complex, expensive, roundabout ways of adapting the analog local loop to an otherwise digital telephone system.

ISDN does away with this. The D channel becomes the vehicle for signaling. This signaling is common channel. Your calls are never interrupted because the signal that a call is waiting, for example, is sent over the D channel. When such a signal arrives at your ISDN phone, you have determined what will happen. Perhaps a screen on the phone blinks with the number or name of the calling party. Perhaps your computer monitor detects the call and switches you to a data base entry associated with the calling party. In any case there is no need for signaling in the same channel as you are using for talking. In fact, there is no way for signaling to take place in the B channel. All signaling takes place in the D channel:

- When you pick up the handset of an ISDN phone, that phone sends a "setup" message on the D channel to the central office switch.
- The switch acknowledges receipt of the message on the D channel and turns on the dial tone for the selected B channel.
- When you dial the phone, it sends each digit to the switch on the D channel.
- After the first digit is dialed, the switch turns off the dial tone on the B channel.
- When the switch has received enough digits to complete the call, it sends a "call proceeding" message to your phone on the D channel.
- The switch then sends a "setup" message to the phone you are calling on that phone's D channel.

- The called phone sends an acknowledgment to the switch.

- When the called phone handset is removed, that phone sends a "setup" message to the switch on the D channel.

- It is expected that the phone will be a multi-button type so the answering party will now select the button for your call; this sends a "connect" message to the switch on the D channel.

- Now the switch sends a "connect" message to your phone on the D channel and connects your selected B channel with that of the called party.

- Now you talk.

During the call you notice a flash on your phone's viewing panel and hear a beep from the phone; you look at your computer monitor and find it showing an incoming call and offering to retrieve the party's records from your database. Neither you nor the party to whom you are currently speaking is interrupted by tones or clicks; all the signaling for the call waiting is done over the separate D channel while your call proceeds on a B channel. You may elect to place your current party on hold by pressing buttons on your phone or making selections on your connected computer. You never use the switchhook. You may leap back and forth between the parties or several other call waiting parties or engage selected ones in conference calling. All this is possible due to the flexibility of D channel signaling.

Notice mention of the connected computer. Although much of the D channel signaling may take place with a fancy ISDN phone, a simple phone, even an old POTS phone, with an appropriate terminal adapter and a PC, used in conjunction with ISDN, can give even more flexibility. This is the beauty of ISDN. In the past all of the tricks of telephones were contained in the switch or your PBX. Now with ISDN and D channel signaling, a great deal of processing may take place in the equipment on your desk as it is working in what is essentially a peer relationship with the switch.

With ISDN the telephone industry is making the same sort of transition as the computer industry did in moving from terminal to host networks to peer to peer and client/server local area networks. More intelligence is being placed nearer the user with the user in control. You can expect this evolution to continue. With network packet protocols taking on more functions that replace historic switch functions, expect to see simpler central office switches, more complex network protocols and richer user equipment and choices. All of this results from the move to digital information in the local loop and D channel common channel signaling; these are all elements of ISDN.

OK, so now aren't you ready for the B channels, the real carriers of your information? Not so fast. Remember the D channel is used for signaling and most of that signaling takes place during call set up and tear down. Are you going to waste a 16,000 bit per second channel during the remainder of the time? Not at all. You may use the unused capacity of the D channel to transmit packet switched information.

If you live in an area where a special set of standards, called Signaling System #7, has not been implemented, you may find your ISDN is limited to two B channels, each with only 56 Kbps capacity. In this case the remaining 8 Kbps of each channel have been "robbed" to do signaling duty normally handled by Signaling System #7. This limitation applied to a substantial amount of Pacific Bell's California ISDN system when first implemented; over time the system will be fully compliant and all its B channels will be 64 Kbps without bit robbing.

The Interface Between You and the Phone Company   Figure 8.5 shows several terms you need to know to be conversant with ISDN. First notice the box called "NT-1." This is electronic gear that you must have to make ISDN work for you. Often this is a separate device that is connected on one side to the telephone company's single twisted pair cable. The other side has two twisted pair lines that connect to your equipment. The line from the telephone company provides a "U interface." This is converted to an "S/T interface" for connection to your equipment.

FIG. 8.5
The U interface comes from the telephone company. The S/T interface is required for your equipment.

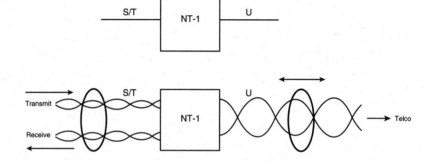

Something happens in the NT-1 device when it's converting a one pair signal from the telephone company into two pairs for distribution to your equipment. It is more economical for the telco to use only one pair rather than two, but from your viewpoint there is a major disadvantage. On the one pair U side you may only connect one NT-1 device. So if you have half a dozen devices to tie onto your ISDN line, you don't want them to require a U interface; you want an S/T interface because the S/T side allows you to connect a number of additional devices.

Basically the U interface side carries full duplex information on the single pair. This means information travels in both directions simultaneously. Engineering constraints prevent such an arrangement from allowing multidrop connections of the sort you probably want for several devices. Consequently, conversion to the S/T interface breaks the signal into two paths, one transmit, one receive. Which is which depends on whether you are looking from the point of view of the NT-1 or a piece of terminal equipment; what is transmission for one is reception for the other. Each signal is now carried on a separate pair, and you are allowed to connect multiple devices. The rules of connection for ISDN are quite different from a POTS installation, but flexibility in the long run is much greater.

A third or even a fourth pair may also be connected to the NT-1; each of these additional pairs is used for powering other equipment in your system. In many cases, especially those involving computers, this powering feature is not needed.

One thing becomes clear from the U versus S/T design: equipment that incorporates the NT-1 functions internally with no S/T interface connection limits to your use of an ISDN line. You'll see this arrangement in computer boards that connect directly to the BRI U interface. Often this arrangement reduces costs; however, flexibility for use of other equipment on your ISDN line is sacrificed. You'll explore a number of practical options later.

N O T E Frequently you'll find devices marked with an R interface; usually this is understood to be for connection to analog telephone equipment, phones, modem, and faxes. You can see the advantage of this; with such a connection you can use your existing analog equipment on the ISDN line. But the R interface is not limited to the analog telephone specification. It could be a connection to totally different equipment so long as that equipment is not ISDN compliant. ■

The B Channel   Now that you've covered the D channel and the interfaces, you'll look at the B channels, the ones that will do most of your work.

A BRI provides two B channels of 64 Kbps each. This is like having two independent telephone lines. Each has a different telephone number. The proper term here is "directory number" (DN). In fact you may have several directory numbers for each B channel. This would enable you to have several devices on the S/T multidrop side of your NT-1; each device would have a different directory number. For example, you could have a fax machine, a telephone, and a computer all using one B channel, but each with a different directory number. This works through the D channel signaling with each device. Of course these must be ISDN-type devices that can communicate with the D channel and make it happen.

N O T E Watch out. We are now entering the world of ISDN numbers. There are two kinds you must remember. I've already mentioned the directory number (DN). Since you're familiar with that from the POTS world, the only thing new to remember is the ability to have different directory numbers for each device using a B channel. But there is more to it. Your equipment is identified with a terminal endpoint identifier (TEI). This in turn is wrapped up with the service profile identifier (SPID). It is here that things get sticky. How the TEI and SPID numbers are assigned and what they mean can vary from telco to telco and switch to switch. You will need to enter the DN and SPID when you configure your equipment. It is very important to get this information from the telephone company so your configuration goes smoothly. ■

Ordering ISDN Service

Why a section on ordering telephone service? If you asked this question, the chances are you've not yet attempted to order ISDN, or when you ordered it you were very lucky. It's not as simple as POTS. It's not simple at all. Very strange things have been reported by those attempting this task. Upon reaching one telephone company a caller was told he couldn't have ISDN. He asked why; the response was, "It's illegal." Be prepared for anything.

Ordering is a word we all understand. If you want something, you order it. So, if you want ISDN, you order it. But what is provisioning? Provisioning is the telephone company's side.

A telephone switch must be "provisioned" to supply services. In the case of ISDN, the switch must be designed for ISDN and then must be provisioned to provide such ISDN services as the company wants to supply, has tariff approval to supply and that can be supplied by the switch hardware and software. We've come a long way from the "number please" manual switchboard. There are so many options and possibilities inherent in ISDN generally, and far more when combinations are assembled, that making it all work and explaining what it is and how to use it becomes overwhelming.

When you call up for ISDN service, the order person may fill your order promptly and efficiently; the installer may connect you perfectly and test the line to insure it talks to the switch; your equipment supplier may provide excellent software and hardware, but you may find that nothing works. Why? The order was accepted based upon what your telephone company considered "generic" ISDN, but you needed some features or capabilities that are not in that "generic" package. Now comes the hard part; what do you need that you did not get, and what exactly did you get?

This involves us in a litany of standards. In the beginning it was in the interest of switch manufactures to provide features and capabilities unique to their switch and unavailable or inaccessible to their competitors' switches. This was fine as long as all your ISDN went through only that manufacturer's switch and needed nothing that this manufacturer lacked. This placed the onus of making a particular piece of customer-provided equipment work on your back and the back of the manufacturer of the customer-provided equipment (CPE) maker. It also made it hard to call other ISDN installations if they didn't have the same configuration and equipment as your local exchange carrier. This led to a period of ISDN stagnation that persisted until 1988, when the North American ISDN Users' Group, the National Institute of Standards and Technology, and Bellcore decided to team up and develop the National ISDN series of specifications starting with National ISDN 1 (NI-1), finalized in 1991. This was followed by NI-2, which was released in 1994; NI-3 was released in December of 1995.

ON THE WEB

You'll find these standards at **http://www.bellcore.com/ISDN/ISDN.html** and **http://www.ocn.com/ocn/niuf_top.html**.

Each NI-x provides specific descriptions of what a telephone switch is to provide. Now both you and the makers of customer premises equipment (CPE) can be assured that the hardware and software you have will work with any switch meeting a given NI-x standard, if the elements of that standard contain everything needed for your particular applications.

Look at what this really says. It brings the switch makers to the table with various sets of least common denominator features and functions. It says if that collection of features and functions includes all you need, it is technically possible for your equipment to work with the switch. But it doesn't answer the following questions:

- Given that the switch can technically be provisioned to supply what I need, how do I ask for the particular collection of features and functions that make my device work?

- What if the switch supports NI-x, but I need something that is not in NI-x?
- Even if I know how to order the right stuff, and the switch can be provisioned for it, what if there is no tariff for it?

N O T E Microsoft has made it a lot easier to order ISDN service. They provide a Web site that helps you determine which telephone companies in your area offer ISDN; whether or not they can install the appropriate equipment in your area; whether or not they can sell you service; and if there are any package deals in your area. Microsoft goes much further by letting you actually order your ISDN service online and specify how the phone company should configure your ISDN line. Check it out at **http://www.microsoft.com/windows/getisdn**. ■

ISDN Ordering Codes   The complexity of ordering became so great that industry specialists designed a collection of "ISDN Ordering Codes." These codes are designated by letters of the alphabet and are designed to cover virtually all the combinations of needs commonly encountered by users of ISDN. Most manufacturers of ISDN equipment now advise buyers of the appropriate codes to use for their equipment. This standardization has simplified the process considerably.

Limited Options   In reality, most of the complexity of ISDN ordering comes not from computer data users, but from voice users. If you're going to use your ISDN connection for data and, at most, simple voice communications, you can probably get by with the limited options approach.

And here are your selections from one of the big local exchange carriers:

0B+D	(packet and signaling on D)
1B+D	(only signaling on D)
1B+D	(packet and signaling on D)
2B+D	(only signaling on D)
2B+D	(packet and signaling on D)

You get voice or data on demand; this means your customer provided equipment (CPE) requests one or the other through the D channel.

So that's it. What do about 95 percent plus of the ISDN subscribers take? Just exactly what you want: 2B+D (only signaling on D). The cost differences among the selections between one and two B channels are several dollars per month, but not so great as to make most users opt for only one B.

Wiring for ISDN

Wiring? Do you have to consider wiring to use ISDN? Yes. ISDN is designed to deal with much higher data rates than those of POTS. As a result the specifications for wiring are stricter. This applies not only to wiring of the telephone company; it also applies to the wiring in your house or business.

Remember the discussion of noise and attenuation? The greater the distance a signal travels down a cable, the more it is weakened (attenuated) and the more non-signal interference (noise) adds up to confuse or obscure your desired communications. This distorts the digital information reducing the usable data rate and eventually making it impossible to operate within ISDN specifications.

Cautions When Wiring

Now I'm starting to talk about the wiring at your house or business. I expect you may examine it during this discussion. So please read and heed the following warnings:

CAUTION

Read and heed the cautions in the text. If you don't know how to handle wires and electricity, hire someone who does.

Do not work on your telephone wiring at all if you wear a pacemaker. Telephone lines carry electrical current. To avoid contact with electrical current:

- Never install telephone wiring during a lightning storm.
- Never install telephone jacks in wet locations unless the jack is specially designed for wet locations.
- Use caution when installing or modifying telephone lines.
- Use a screwdriver and other tools with insulated handles.
- You and those around you should wear safety glasses or goggles.
- Be sure that your inside wire is not connected to the access line while you are working on your telephone wiring. If you cannot do this, take the handset of one of your telephones off the hook. This will keep the phone from ringing and reduce, but not eliminate, the possibility of your contacting electricity.
- Do not place telephone wiring or connections in any conduit, outlet or junction box containing electrical wiring.
- Installation of inside wire may bring you close to electrical wire, conduit, terminals, and other electrical facilities. EXTREME CAUTION must be used to avoid electrical shock from such facilities. You must avoid contact with all such facilities.
- Telephone wire must be at least six feet from bare power wiring or lightning rods and associated wires, and at least six inches from other wire (antenna wires, doorbell wires, wires from transformers to neon signs), steam or hot water pipes and heating ducts.
- Before working with existing inside wiring, check all electrical outlets for a square telephone dial light transformer and unplug it from the electrical outlet. Failure to unplug all telephone transformers can cause electrical shock.
- Do not place a jack where it would allow a person to use the telephone while in a bathtub, shower, swimming pool, or similar hazardous location.

■ Protectors and grounding wire placed by the service provider must not be connected to, removed, or modified by the customer.

This list or warnings is from the North American ISDN Users' Forum (NIUF) as stated in their excellent and detailed "ISDN Wiring and Powering Guidelines (Residence and Small Business)." Your local building codes, ordinances, and other laws govern over the suggestions made here and throughout this book. Please use common sense when working around electricity. This list and the book provide several suggestions to help you, but they cannot cover all possibilities or dangers. If you really don't have a general knowledge of electricity and methods for working around it, have a professional do the job for you.

It's often possible to run ISDN over the existing wiring in your house or business. However, if possible, it is best to install new wiring to insure maximum performance and future upgradability. You should use Category 3 cable at a minimum; it is best to use Category 5. These categories of twisted pair cable have been developed to carry high data rate digital signals. The details of wiring are too extensive for coverage in this book. In the event you plan to install cabling or modify your existing cabling; refer to the NIUF book *ISDN Wiring and Powering Guidelines (Residence and Small Business)* mentioned earlier, and to *Special Edition Using ISDN* by James Y. Bryce (Que 1995, ISBN 0-7897-0405-6).

ISDN Hardware

This is the part you've probably been waiting for. Here are some ideas about the actual hardware you can use to connect to ISDN; in ISDN terminology these devices are called *terminal adapters*. There are three types of such devices:

■ External terminal adapters

■ Internal card terminal adapters

■ Routers with built-in terminal adapters

I'll go through a detailed configuration for the Motorola BitSURFR, an external terminal adapter that connects through the serial port. The BitSURFR is aimed at the general computer user and is available from many computer "superstores" at prices comparable to higher end modems. The discussion of its configuration gives a flavor of the details you'll need to set up most ISDN terminal adapters. The serial port equipment is fairly similar in its setup. The internal cards differ considerably within breed. By the time you get to routers, the setup is so varied and frequently complex, no brief treatment such as this is possible.

N O T E The information included about products is subject to very rapid change in this exploding market; check suppliers for the latest details and check out Dan Kegel's ISDN web site, **http://www.alumni.edu/~dank/isdn** and mine, **http://www.bryce.com/~bryce**, for additional information and ideas.

Also, the inclusion of a product or the exclusion of some other product is in no way a commendation or condemnation. Choices were made to represent types and concepts. Many products left unmentioned are well worthy of your consideration. ■

External Terminal Adapters

I'm calling this first category of ISDN hardware "external ISDN terminal adapters." You'll find terms like "ISDN modem" and simply "terminal adapter" also used for these boxes. The distinguishing characteristics are:

- Stand-alone box with its own power supply
- Connection to your computer through the serial port (although closely related equipment using the parallel port is available)
- Use of the AT command set so the device will work with your existing modem programs

Serial Port Issues   As you'll see, this equipment provides a straightforward solution to using ISDN. But, as always, there are drawbacks. The primary drawback is the serial port itself. These ports are limited in their data rate performance. If you're using Windows 3.x, the native drivers with Windows limit your serial port speeds to considerably less than those supported by ISDN. Your solution is to install a third-party serial port driver. Three very popular programs that perform this function are TurboCom, CyberCom, and KingCom. These are usually supplied as a part of external ISDN adapter software.

These software programs will do you no good if you have an older serial port. It's mandatory that you have a 16550A UART on the serial port you're using for ISDN. Otherwise, you'll be unable to realize the data rate gains of ISDN. If you're using a recently manufactured PC you probably have a 16550A. Older machines don't have them. You can buy a board with one or more 16550A serial ports for less than $50.

If you've moved to Windows 95, you'll be glad to know there's no need for special software drivers for your serial ports. Assuming you have 16550As for serial hardware, Windows 95 comes with support for data rates clear up to and including 921,600 bits per second, as shown in Figure 8.6.

Windows 95 also brings UNIMODEM to the world of modem-type devices. It provides a single, universal modem driver. This means you will no longer be selecting a modem type within your applications—Windows 95 takes care of that for you. It's much the same as the move from needing applications to contain drivers for every printer under DOS to being able to write solely to the Windows printer software as it became possible with Windows 3.x. Now, applications that use modems, or ISDN terminal adapters that are addressed as modems, one need only write to UNIMODEM. It's easier for the writers, and it's easier for the users.

Windows 95 also provides Windows Telephony API (TAPI) as a part of the Windows Open Services Architecture (WOSA). This greatly simplifies communication and control of telephone interconnection. In particular, the added control available through use of D channel signaling is recognized in versions of Windows 95 that followed the initial release.

FIG. 8.6
Notice the range of
date rates extends up
to 921,600 bps, far
more than the 57,600
bps of Windows 3.x.

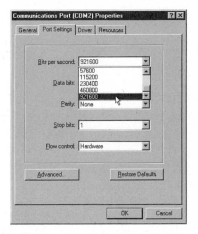

Windows 95 also supports the Universal Serial Bus (USB). USB revolutionizes the connection of devices to your computer. It operates at 12 megabits per second and supports up to 63 devices with isochronous and asynchronous data communications. Your keyboard, mouse, modems, ISDN devices, and lots more will use USB. It's here; Windows 95 has it. Check it out at **http://www.teleport.com/~USB**.

 A number of ISDN features were not available in the first release of Windows 95. You can check the version by right-clicking on My Computer and choosing Properties. Be sure to get the most recent release to take full advantage of ISDN. Check **http://www.microsoft.com**. USB (Universal Serial Bus)

AT Command Set   A central characteristic of serial port terminal adapters is use of the AT command set originally developed by Hayes. This makes it easy to run modem applications. But watch out for variations. For example, the usual tone dialing command is "ATDT," but some equipment with combination ISDN/analog modem functions reserves "ATDT" for calling with the analog modem and uses "ATD" for calls with the ISDN functions.

N O T E   A good example of this ATD/ATDT difference is the 3Com Impact; ATD enables ISDN calling; ATDT enables analog modem calling. On the other hand, a similar product from U.S. Robotics, the I Modem, uses ATDT to dial and determines whether to use an analog modem or ISDN from the response sent back from the far end device. ■

The advantage of the AT command set will diminish over time as development of ISDN specific drivers continues. But for now these developments are just starting, so the AT commands are quite a help. A number of excellent serial port devices are available. I'll use the Motorola BitSURFR as an example.

Motorola BitSURFR   The Motorola BitSURFR was designed to be a plug and play device taking full advantage of such features in Windows 95. Figure 8.7 shows the BitSURFR as detected by Windows 95 during hardware installation. All you have to do is connect the

BitSURFR to an available serial port and run the Windows 95 hardware installation from the Windows 95 Control Panel. Click Start, click Settings, click Control Panel, and double-click Add New Hardware. Then choose Next and allow Windows 95 to find the plug and play (PnP) BitSURFR for you. All of the settings will be done automatically.

FIG. 8.7
Windows 95 with Plug and Play detected the Motorola BitSURFR.

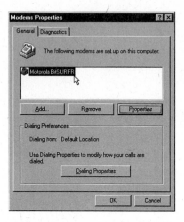

Your next step is to install the BitSURFR configuration software supplied by Motorola. Insert the disk provided and again go to the Control Panel. This time select the Add/Remove Program icon and let Windows 95 find the disk and setup program for you. Then go to START, choose PROGRAMS, and then select the Motorola group; double-click the program icon created for the Motorola BitSURFR software.

From the initial screen (see Fig. 8.8), open the Access menu and choose Define Adapter. In the Define Adapter dialog box, Figure 8.9, click the Model drop-down arrow list, click BitSURFR, and then click OK.

Go to the main screen ribbon and choose File, New. You'll have a screen like Figure 8.10 showing a number of selection tabs. You're on the right one to start "ISDN Provisioning." Fill in the SPIDs, directory numbers, and switch type supplied you by your telephone company. If you have no other information to the contrary from the telco or other sources, leave the TEI entries as "automatic."

> **CAUTION**
>
> Do not insert dashes or spaces in the SPIDs or directory numbers. Often these characters will cause your configuration to fail.

Choose the Protocols tab (see Fig. 8.11). Choose V.120 if you're connecting to an async serial device at your Internet provider. Often, providers use Adtran equipment for V.120; if this is the case, change the frame sizes to 253. If you're connecting to a synchronous device—that usually means a router—choose "PPP." BONDING is a method used to aggregate multiple B channels; chances are you'll have a recent version of the software with a selection for MP, indicating

"Multilink PPP" also. If you have the ability to use more than one B channel through your Internet provider agreement, the provider will tell you what should be entered here.

FIG. 8.8

This is the Motorola BitSURFR Configuration Manager Main Screen. You'll first select the BitSURFR under Access, then choose New under File.

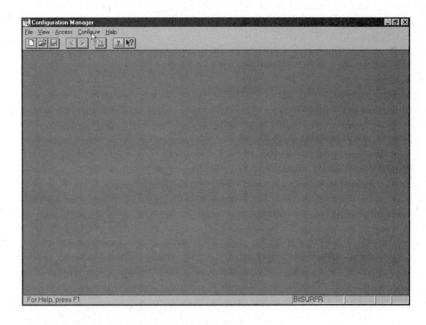

FIG. 8.9

Motorola BitSURFR Define Adapter selection provides a way to choose among Motorola's ISDN devices. The photograph at the right is the BitSURFR.

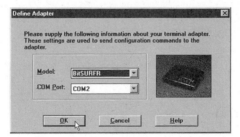

As a start I suggest in the "Call Establishment" part you set the channel speed to 56 Kbps or 64 Kbps depending on what is available from your switch. Leave Speech for the Originate Voice Calls As setting, and Data for the Originate Data Calls As setting.

In the "DTR" screen start with "Ignore." If your line doesn't hang up, try "Hang Up" or "Reset." Set "Asynchronous" if you're calling another serial device. Set "Synchronous 1" if you're calling a router; if that doesn't work, you may also need to try "Synchronous 2."

Select the next tab, Operations. I suggest you check the Extended Response box to receive more extensive messages, as shown in Figure 8.14. With this selection you'll receive more extensive messages while the BitSURFR is placing calls or encountering errors; these will help you diagnose or avoid problems. Enabling local character echo puts the characters you type on your screen, escape sequence guard keeps brief glitches from bringing the device down, and the dial response messages give you an indication of what's going on much the same as the responses from a modem like CONNECT or BUSY.

FIG. 8.10

BitSURFR ISDN Provisioning selections are reflected on the table labeled ISDN. Insert SPIDs, directory numbers, and switch type.

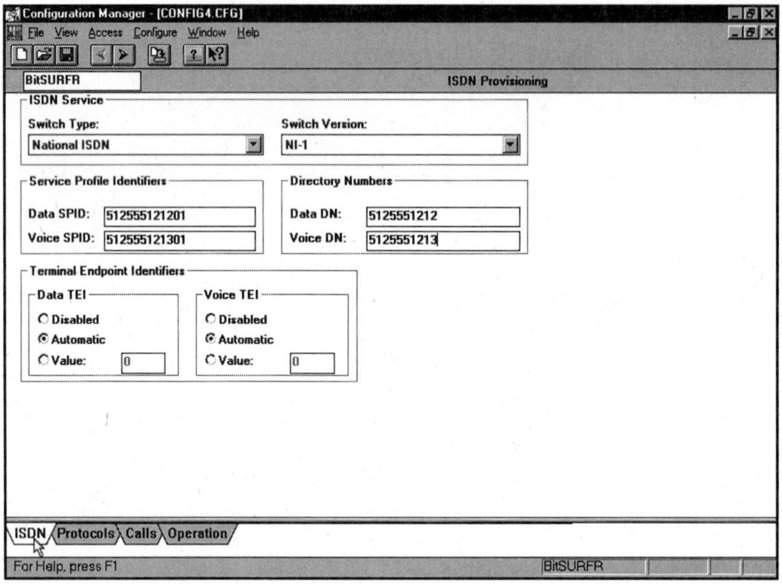

FIG. 8.11

The BitSURFR Protocols tab selection allows you to select from among V.120, clear channel (64 Kbps), PPP async to sync and BONDING.

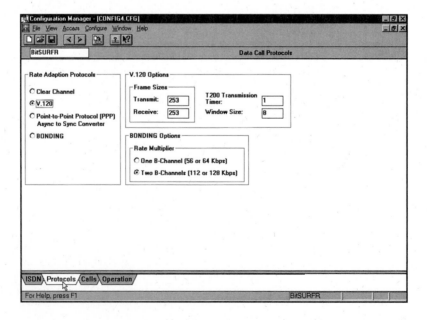

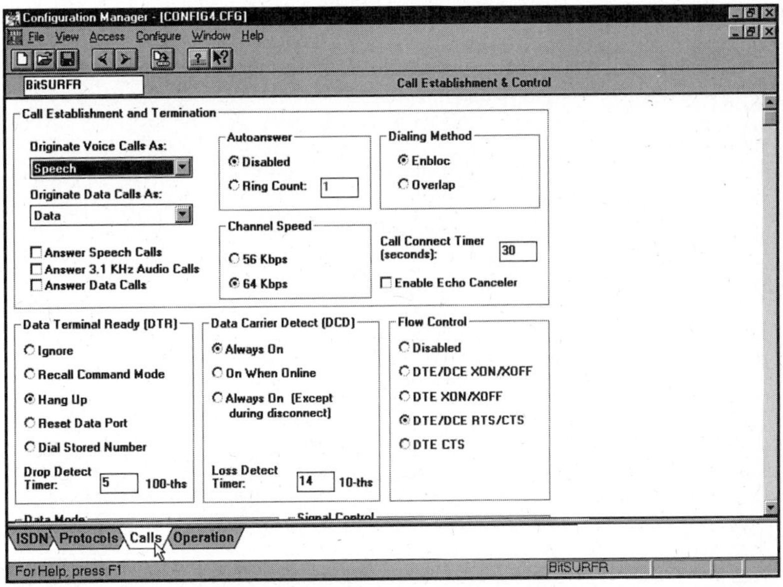

FIG. 8.12

The top half of the BitSURFR Calls tab has a large number of selections for establishing and terminating connections.

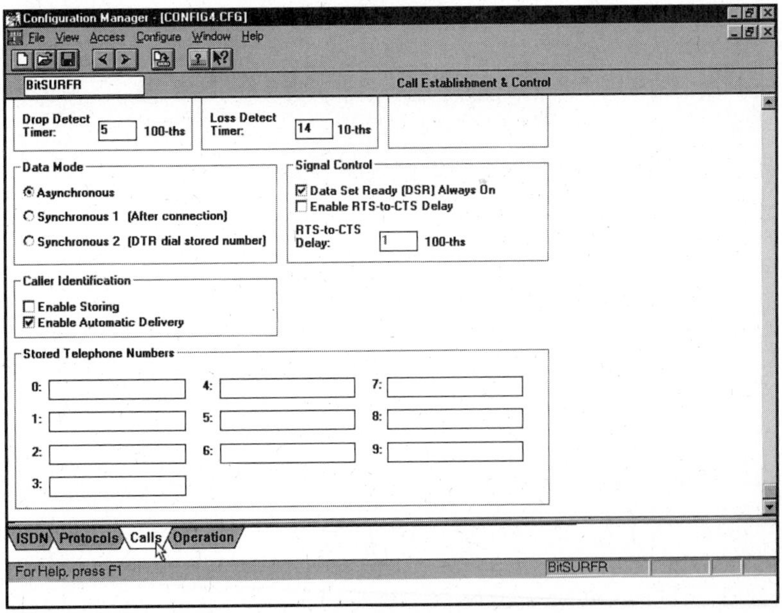

FIG. 8.13

The bottom half of the BitSURFR Calls tab provides a number of selections including caller identification and stored numbers.

The little button on the ribbon that is all alone, third from the right, is the Update button. Click it and you'll get a window asking if you want to update the device's configuration with the new material. Choose Save and Restart. This does just what it says and brings up a percentage complete meter (see Fig. 8.15). If you fail to save you've accomplished nothing. If you want to be able to restore this particular configuration after you've made other changes, save your configuration to a file. Choose File, Save As, and give this configuration a file name. If you attempt to exit the program without saving it should stop you, but just be sure.

FIG. 8.14
The BitSURFR Operations tab sets up the AT command operations.

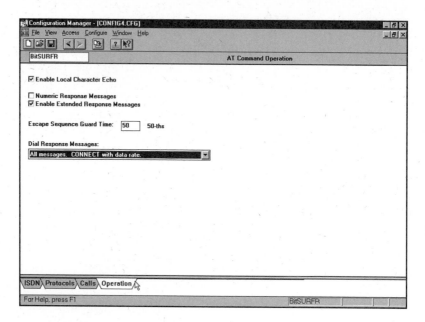

FIG. 8.15
The BitSURFR Update in the midst of loading a new configuration.

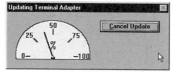

Motorola has provided several options to preconfigure so you don't really have to do anything but enter your switch type and numbers. Choose Configure, Quick Setup (see Fig. 8.16). One of the four choices for async and sync operation will probably take care of you. Then you might do a little customization such as disabling auto answer, but it's a lot better than trying to figure out what all of the obtuse technical possibilities actually mean and then what to do with each one.

Other External Terminal Adapters   The Motorola BitSURFR is not the only member of this breed. 3Com has the Impact that may have the easiest setup on the market. Adtran offers the ISU Express. US Robotics has a serial port version of the I Modem (it's also available in an internal card version). And Zycel provides a similar unit that takes advantage of the much faster operation of the parallel port. I expect all of these companies and many more to offer Universal Serial Bus products as that standard catches on.

FIG. 8.16

The BitSURFR Quick Setup selection does most of your setup work. Check it out; then customize as needed.

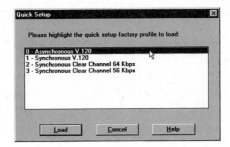

Options Available   All of the external products I've mentioned and many of the other types either come with or have options for inclusion of several, possibly important to you, features:

- Analog port: This allows you to connect a regular phone, modem or FAX to the device and use a B channel for analog phone calls. Some of these create "ringer current" and can ring a phone or make a modem or FAX answer; some do not have ringer current and can't. Most give preference to the voice call. So if you're using 2 B channels for data and pick up the phone, the device will drop one data channel to allow you to make the call.

- Support for multilink PPP (MP). This is a very important feature. It means you can put two B channels together and get twice the data rate of one. This only works if your Internet provider supports MP.

- Internal NT1 support is often available. This means you don't have to buy an external NT1; you have a U interface right on the box. But it also means you can only use the ISDN device itself. You can't connect anything else to your ISDN line. An external NT1 allows you to connect other equipment; in this case you should get the S/T interface on your unit.

- Built in analog fax/modems so you don't have to have another analog device. Some devices require you to issue the proper command to tell the device you want a modem or digital call. Others are able to sense the device calling or being called and switch automatically.

Internal Card Terminal Adapters

These internal card products are computer cards designed to plug into the internal bus of your computer. Such cards are made for the Industry Standard Architecture (ISA), MicroChannel (MCA), or Peripheral Component Interconnect (PCI). For now the ISA bus is so prevalent, I'll limit this discussion to it for simplicity. The ideas expressed carry over to most of the other bus structures.

You've already seen some of the details of configuration so in this section you'll see some more ideas of how a product can use the fancy interfaces available with Windows 95.

You'll need Microsoft' ISDN Accelerator Pack if you're using an internal terminal adapter. You can download it from **http://www.microsoft.com/windows/software/isdn.htm**.

US Robotics Sportster ISDN 128K   You plug this into an ISA bus machine and run through a configuration similar to the one previously described. It does not support V.120 but does support PPP and multilink PPP so you can use both B channels. It has a connection for analog phones, faxes and modems, but it does not provide ringer current. However, US Robotics has an optional device that will produce ringer current when attached to the card. Now for the good part—the user interface using Windows 95. Take a look at Figure 8.17.

FIG. 8.17

The US Robotics ISDN 128K Main Application Window showing the initial connection ISDN has over the D channel in a graphical format. The tool buttons and menu selection bar provide controls.

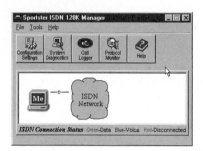

It's too bad you can't see this all in color. The lines representing connections are red and green and blue in various states. In any case, figure 8.16 indicates your ISDN connection is functioning properly. The D channel is always up, regardless of whether or not you're engaged in a call.

Now look at Figure 8.18. This shows an ISDN data connection using two B channels. Notice the clear, graphical representation. And then look at Figure 8.19 for a data call on one B channel and a voice call on the other. Wow!

FIG. 8.18

An ISDN data connection using two B channels. Data transmission over the B channels is shown in blue.

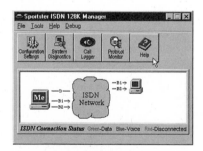

FIG. 8.19

An ISDN voice connection on one B channel is represented by a green line; the remaining B channel in blue carries data.

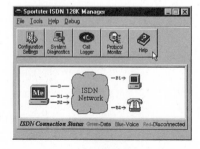

Digi International DataFire   Digi International produces the DataFire ISDN board. This board, the USR Sportster ISDN 128K, and other boards are supported by Microsoft's ISDN additions to Windows 95. These additions make installation and configuration of supported products very easy.

N O T E   Initially, there was some concern over the complexity of configuration and impenetrability of Digi International's documentation. The DataFire was a "Not Ready for Prime Time" rating as a result. Microsoft has ridden to Digi International's rescue with ISDN support for the DataFire built into Windows 95. This frees manufacturers such as Digi from problems surrounding creation of user interfaces and allows them to concentrate on making better products. As long as they write to Microsoft's interfaces, this will work for them, for Microsoft, and for you. ▪

Here's all there is to installing the DataFire. First, take a look at the I/O addresses available for the card. Digi gives you the following options:

- ▪ 110h
- ▪ 140h
- ▪ 150h
- ▪ 300h
- ▪ 310h
- ▪ 340h
- ▪ 350h

TIP   An "H" or "h" after a number means the number is hexadecimal—base 16. You can use the Windows calculator, in the scientific view, to convert between hexadecimal and decimal numbers.

Open the computer and plug the card in. The card's not really Plug and Play or software configurable. In other words, you have to do the work. If you've made a list of the I/O locations used on the machine, pick one for the DataFire that's not used elsewhere and set the card switch as described in the manual; the switch is on the top edge of the card and made for viewing and changing while the card is in place. Don't throw the switches while the juice is on.

You don't have a listing of the I/O locations already used? Go into Control Panel, select System, and then Device Manager and go through the various devices checking the Resources tab on each to see if any of the I/O addressing conflicts.

If this is too tedious, skip it and pick one of the DataFire selections. If you've got a conflict, it'll show up on the Device Manager as an exclamation point in yellow over the DataFire card icon; then you can change the I/O on the DataFire Resources screen until you find one that works. Then turn off the computer and reset the switches on the card.

Go to Control Panel. Choose the Network icon (see Fig. 8.20) to display the Network tabbed dialog box.

FIG. 8.20

Select the Network icon to start the process of installing the DataFire.

In the Network tabbed dialog box, choose the Configuration tab and then select Adapter. The Select Network Component Type dialog box appears; choose Add. The Select Network Adapters dialog box appears (see Fig. 8.21). Choose Digi International and the type of card from the list.

FIG. 8.21

The Select Network Adapter dialog box is where you select the DataFire adapter.

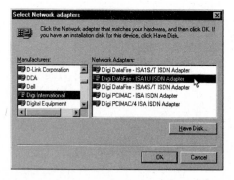

Close the various other dialog boxes and return to the Network tabbed dialog box where you can double-click the DigiDataFire to display the Properties sheet. Choose Resources and enter the I/O you set on the card. Then you'll be sent to the ISDN Configuration dialog box (see Fig. 8.22). Here you can select Next and begin the process of switch selection (see Fig. 8.23).

You'll finish with dialog boxes asking for directory numbers and SPIDs much like that shown in the Motorola BitSURFR example earlier. Then you simply go to the My Computer icon your desktop, double-click the My Computer icon, choose Dial-Up Networking, and the icon for the

FIG. 8.22
This is the ISDN Configuration dialog box; choose Next to continue.

FIG. 8.23
Here are the ISDN switch types. Notice that switches for North America, Europe, and Japan are included.

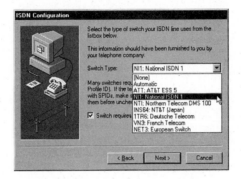

DataFire card. Enter your login name and password and click Connect; then you're on your way (see Fig. 8.24).

FIG. 8.24
Connecting to the DataFire: Open My Computer, select Dial-Up Networking, DataFire, and then enter your login name and password and hit Connect.

Other ISDN Cards   Many ISDN cards are available. US Robotics also makes its I modem in a card version. IBM offers the WaveRunner in ISA, Microchannel, and PCMCIA form; both of these cards have chips on board that can be reprogrammed with software to completely change the card's personality. They both can handle V.120, PPP, MP, and function as analog fax and modem devices. ISDN*Tek makes several cards from the very simple and inexpensive "Commuter Card" with a single B channel up through complex multi-channel cards.

Routers for ISDN

While it may seem far afield to discuss LAN equipment in a book devoted to the general user of Internet and ISDN, it's really not. Think about a LAN connection for a minute. Ethernet offers a data rate of 10 megabits. That's quite a lot more than what is available through the serial or even the parallel port. And an Ethernet card today can be as cheap as $50.00 or less!

Therefore, use a router to make your connection. There's little doubt this will give you a fast, if not the fastest, connection possible. However, routers currently cost anywhere from half to twice as much as the other ways you may connect to ISDN. Those prices are dropping now, however.

Just what is a router? In a few words, it's a device that senses traffic on a network and, when it sees traffic bound for a location other than your LAN, routes that traffic to the appropriate place over a wide area connection—ISDN. It's fast because you've already configured it to know what the network addresses are on your network and what the addresses are on the other network(s) your want to connect with. When it sees those other addresses, it dials the number of the foreign network and passes the traffic.

Now here's where the magic of ISDN comes into play. Since ISDN has such a rapid set up and tear down, you don't need to be connected all the time if you have a fast router. It can connect, pass traffic, and disconnect so quickly you won't even know the line's not up all the time! Of course this requires careful configuration and coordination with your Internet service provider.

Although routers are becoming easier to set up, they're still more daunting by far than external devices or cards. Here are the names of several product and companies that offer routers appropriate for your consideration:

- Cisco offers the 1003; this is a small router built to the specifications and configuration options of Cisco's larger routers. It's no picnic to configure, but if your company uses Cisco, it's certainly a major contender.

- Ascend provides the Pipeline 25 and 50; Ascend has the lion's share of the Internet service provider market for ISDN equipment. The small routers are fairly easy to set up and, in some versions, include features such as analog ports.

- Combinet offers several models such as the 2060; the most recent versions have software that configures through the Windows interface and finally brings ease of set up to the world of routers.

- 3Com offers some routers for small office and home use in its NetBuilder Line.

- Gandalf has the LANLine 5242I that sets up with DTMF (TouchTone) signals and Windows.

Which Is Best?

"Which is best?" you ask. After all you bought this book looking for THE answer. The answer is all types are good and will get you connected through ISDN. The serial port equipment is simple and inexpensive. The cards are more difficult to set up, but comparably priced. The routers are more expensive and difficult to set up, but often give the best performance. It's time to jump in. You already know that in this industry, what you buy this year is seriously obsolete in a couple of years. The real question is: Can it help me do what I want to do now and save or make enough money to pay for itself before I replace it? I suggest the answer is always yes for all these items. ●

Setting Up a High-Speed Internet Connection

by James Bryce

Now that you're sure you want to hop onto the Internet, you'll want to ensure that you do it in the fastest way possible. After all, you'll never reach superhighway speeds if you're stuck at a traffic light. Fortunately, there are a lot of practical ways to get from here to there, for both you and your company.

Getting up to speed on the Internet can be as simple as installing a 28.8 Kbps modem; this will double your Internet access speed, if you've been using a standard 14.4 Kbps modem. But there are ways to pump up your Internet performance even further. *Integrated Services Digital Network (ISDN)* technology was discussed in Chapter 8 and is the most likely choice for many individual and organizational environments. In this chapter I'll cover high speed methods other than ISDN; these include digital high-speed dedicated lines, such as T1 and T3 connections. The phone and cable companies are constantly improving the current technology and thinking about the future of telecommunications systems; all these developments have a direct influence on your Internet performance. ■

Faster Internet access is available

In this chapter, you'll learn about what the phone companies are doing to speed-up Internet access.

High-speed access doesn't cost a fortune

This chapter describes low-cost ways to give your company high-speed Internet access.

High-speed access for large organizations

You'll learn about implementations for large organizations.

The future of the Internet

You'll learn about the information superhighway's future.

TIP   Use a 28.8 Kbps modem if you can. 14.4 Kbps works pretty well. 9.6 Kbps really makes you wait, and 2.4 Kbps gives you time for lunch.

Why a High-Speed Connection?

On the CD

Once you've surfed on the Internet, you realize that there's a lot of information out there. If browsing is the fun part, then downloading demands extreme patience. But that's not the worst problem. If you're connected at too slow a speed, you won't even be able to use the best Internet utilities out there, including some on the CD-ROM included with this book.

> **CAUTION**
>
> If you have less than a 14.4 Kbps modem, you'll be disappointed when you use graphical browsers to access the Internet. These utilities—some of which are listed below—demand higher speed connections to handle the constant data transfers necessary to make them work.
>
>   WinWeb
>
>   Mosaic
>
>   Netscape
>
>   Cello
>
>   NETCOM NetCruiser
>
>   Pipeline

TIP   Virtually all graphical browsers offer an option that turns off downloading of graphics. If you're using slower connections, and often even if you have a fast connection, you'll find turning graphics off helps you find what you want more quickly.

You'll be more productive and have more fun if you have a high-speed connection. Face it; all the really cool stuff for the Internet is only accessible through graphical front ends. Ask any computer pros, and they'll tell you not to run anything with the word graphical in it when connected to a slow modem. Don't misunderstand though; there are some graphical interfaces out there that are designed to connect at 14.4 Kbps and that work splendidly, but if you want to cruise in style, you'll need a high-speed connection.

> **N O T E**   Keep these limited data rate issues in mind when you design hypertext for use over the World Wide Web. It's a good idea to provide a Text Only option button that users can select. It's also helpful to include a text description of images that will appear when viewers have graphics turned off or use text only browsers. Whatever you do, be sure that both the meaning of your message and the users' selections are visible in a text-only browser. ■

▶**See** "Planning Your Own WWW Home Page," **p. 459**

Graphical Internet browsers like Mosaic allow you to see images on-screen, play videos, and listen to sounds. But those images, sounds, and videos are all located somewhere out on the

Net, not on your computer. This means that to play these sounds and watch these videos, you must first transfer them to your computer, a sometimes time-consuming process.

Say you want to see an image of the Mona Lisa. When you click a button that says "View Mona Lisa," the image in digital format is crammed through your tiny phone lines until it's recreated on your desktop screen. You've swapped time to load for image detail.

 T I P   You'll actually save money—if your time is worth anything—with a higher speed modem, ISDN, or the methods in this chapter. How long it takes to recoup your investment depends on how much you use the connection.

That image can be fairly large. You could be waiting several minutes before you see it if you use a 14.4 Kbps modem. Just think of driving onto the ramp of an interstate highway and stepping on the accelerator; you want quick acceleration to highway speed, but your five horsepower car is so underpowered it takes two minutes to get up to speed. That's the feeling you'll have if you try to view the Mona Lisa with an underpowered connection. Some interesting technology allows an image to be compressed on the host end and blasted to you faster, but it could still be annoying waiting for the image to appear.

Video presents a greater problem, as the image is constantly changing. To run full screen, full motion video takes several megabits of data rate. Currently available compression and other techniques can achieve pretty good results with a single ISDN PRI. If you are willing to settle for some jerkiness, 3 BRI lines do a passable job. When you get down to a single BRI, the image is really only acceptable for desktop use. On the desktop, an image is scaled down to a tiny window on-screen and runs at a flickering rate of 10–15 frames per second. Even at this smaller scale, analog transmission is almost useless as a carrier.

To lessen the effect of delays and to enable an image to run at all in some cases, programs now compress the image file at the host end, download the file to your local hard disk, and then use your computer's processor to play it back. You're in for a delay, but at least you can do it. But why bother? If you really want performance, there are higher speed options.

When ISDN Basic Rate Interface Isn't Enough

Most small organizations in typical fields will probably be satisfied with the 128 Kbps of an ISDN BRI line. If more capacity is needed, additional BRIs can be installed. Up to a point this is an excellent strategy. Is there a point where adding BRIs isn't the best route? I'm glad you asked, but I don't have a firm answer. It all depends on the pricing for alternatives in your area. The two most logical alternatives are ISDN primary rate interface (PRI) and T carrier service.

ISDN Primary Rate Interface (PRI)

Chapter 8 dealt mostly with ISDN's basic rate interface, as that is the cheapest method of buying ISDN service. ISDN is also available in the form called primary rate interface (PRI). With

PRI instead of the two B channels and one D channel of BRI, you get 23 B channels and an expanded 64 Kbps D channel. Do the math and you get 23×64 Kbps or nearly 1.5 megabits per second bandwidth. That's nearly as fast as expensive dedicated T1 speeds, and it can be a lot cheaper. Once you have a PRI installed, the next PRI you install at your location can have 24 B channels and no D channel; the D channel on your first PRI can control several additional PRIs—exactly how many lies with your local exchange carrier, tariffs, and switching equipment.

CAUTION

Well, it seems any time you go to a need for several B channels you should get a PRI. Not so fast. Ironically the pricing of PRI service is sometimes such that it pays you to install multiple BRIs rather than a PRI! Check costs carefully.

The Hitch in Switched-56

Two common technologies for wide-area internetworking are *Switched-56* and *Dedicated-56*. Switched-56 gets its name from its circuit switching technology and its 56 Kbps speed.

Switched-56 is a good choice when you want a low-cost, moderate-speed connection that you don't need running all the time. Figure 9.1 shows the layout of a Switched-56 system. That's because Switched-56 is a dial-up service. You only pay for what you use, and this is important as we move up the bandwidth scale to T1 and T3 connections discussed in a later section.

FIG. 9.1

A typical Switched-56 connection.

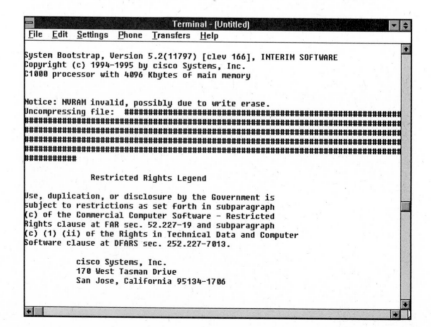

Dedicated-56 is the same as Switched-56, but it's not switched—it's dedicated. A dedicated line is always connected from one point to another. Both have the same startup costs of between $700 and $900 for the phone company hook up, about $1,000 for the CSU/DSU (Channel Service Unit/Data Service Unit), and well over $1,000 for a router for LAN connection. The price scale of routers varies widely depending on the functions needed.

Switched-56 and Dedicated-56 have limited bandwidth and should be used only if your requirements for the connection are light. If you spend more than two or three hours per day on a 56 Kbps line, it's time to move up to ISDN.

> **CAUTION**
>
> In reality Switched/Dedicated-56 is a dying technology—it's rapidly being killed by ISDN. Most of the time you'll find no economic reason to use Switched/Dedicated-56; in almost every case you'll find the costs several times the cost of an ISDN BRI, and offers less than half the data rate and none of the sophistication of D channel control.

Switched/Dedicated-56 also has another problem. It relies on analog/digital switches that are becoming archaic, making it generally more expensive than ISDN. The phone company plans on phasing out this technology in favor of ISDN. Of course the income per line will be less, but the number of ISDN lines will be many times that of switched/dedicated-56. ISDN will retain compatibility with 56 Kbps connections, albeit at the slower 56 Kbps rate.

Like all high-speed connections, to set up a Switched-56 or a Dedicated-56 connection, you must contract with your phone company or your Internet provider. Internet providers typically charge around $125 per month for dial-up service and $400 a month for dedicated service. Initial hook-up rates are around $1,200 if you already have the router and CSU, and $3,400 if you don't.

Frame Relay

Frame relay is based on a good deal of the work that went into ISDN, yet frame relay is expanding wildly outside the auspices of ISDN development.

Recent reports show frame relay use jumping from about 1500 sites to over 5000 from the early 1994 to the beginning of 1995; later reports support a similar upward trend. This is a huge leap and shows the value of frame relay in providing a way to take existing communications needs and merge them into a more economical form.

Frame Relay and X.25

So what's frame relay? In a few words, it's a major improvement in the way packet switching has been done under X.25 (an interfacing protocol). The difference becomes clear when you realize frame relay is packet switching with most of the overhead removed.

ON THE WEB

Frame your questions and set up a relay to **http://cell-relay.indiana.edu** to find out about the Frame Relay Forum.

First off, frame relay eliminates a whole layer of the ISO OSI model (The International Standards Organization's definition for each networking layer). That'll save you tons of cost and time sending your packets around. Take a look at Figure 9.2. This shows the three layers required by X.25.

FIG. 9.2
X.25 layers.

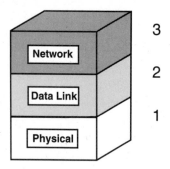

X.25

Now look at Figure 9.3. There are only two layers used in the frame relay structure, Physical and Data Link. This means that considerably less processing is used along the way from frame handler to frame handler throughout the network. This means reduced time and cost.

FIG. 9.3
Frame relay layers.

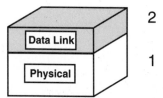

Frame Relay

How Frame Relay Works

How can frame relay throw away a whole layer and still take care of the job? To answer that, let's look at what goes on with X.25. In layer three the protocol handles a number of questions:

- Is this a data packet?
- Is the connection active?

- Have I received a valid layer three acknowledgment?
- What is the next expected sequence number, and does the packet I just received have that number?

If all of these questions are answered yes, an acknowledgment is sent back. If any are answered no, error recovery is undertaken. Here's what happens at layer two:

- Is this a valid frame?
- Is this an information frame?
- Have I received a valid acknowledgment?
- Move window to accommodate information.
- Are all frames acknowledged? If no, restart timer and see if window fits. If yes, request retransmission. If no, recover from error.
- Send acknowledgment of layer two.

If the answer to any of these is no, another error is created at layer two.

TIP Don't spend your day trying to figure out all of what is going on here. Just notice that there are acknowledgments, connections, and sequence numbers passing through the process.

Here's what goes on in frame relay (see Fig. 9.3). Since there is no layer three, "all" of this is at layer two:

- Is this a valid frame?
- Does it use a known data link connection identifier?

That's it. While X.25 requires at least 10 frame processing steps across two separate layers, frame relay does the job in two steps within a single layer. Moreover, it works without acknowledgments or sequence numbers. Frame relay recognizes that its transport will most likely be through a reliable digital network and risks problems that were expected to be remedied by acknowledgments and sequence numbers in X.25.

NOTE Is there a risk in using frame relay since it seems to do away with all the protections built into X.25? Not really. Any higher layer protocol you might be using with frame relay will catch what frame relay misses. The real problem might be a substantially diminished performance, contrasted with X.25 in the case of truly poor or noisy conditions. But then our assumptions are that you'll be using frame relay over clean digital circuits.

As a general rule, frame relay runs at from 56/64 Kbps up to 512 Kbps. It's capable of running at much higher data rates. The data field size is dependent on vendor; the maximum is 4096 bytes. Since frame relay has a variable data field contrasted with the fixed field of 48 bytes in ATM, as I'll describe next, it has a low overhead compared to ATM.

Frame Relay doesn't compete with Switched-56 or Dedicated-56, nor does it replace high-speed leased lines in general. Instead, frame relay is a protocol that is typically used over high-speed

Part II

Ch 9

lines; it replaces the older standard, X.25. It allows the large bandwidth of a leased line to be split up into dynamic channels. With dynamic channels, frame relay is able to use all of the bandwidth available from the entire frame relay connection. With the old technology, expensive multiplexers are used to split up the bandwidth into fixed channels. Fixed channels only guarantee that you'll have the bandwidth from one available channel at a time.

Mulitplexers aren't suitable for current technologies such as video conferencing. Frame relay allows the entire bandwidth to be split up into whatever is needed at the moment. This is especially important when Internet connections, video conferencing, and other technologies are used simultaneously. Because frame relay only gives each channel what it needs, it's an elegant, cost-effective solution.

The older X.25 standard was used for remote terminal access. The standard doesn't operate well in the high-speed Internet world because X.25 doesn't support the Internet protocol (TCP/IP) well over wide-area networks. Frame relay, on the other hand, is far more intelligent when it comes to purely digital data. Frame relay routers assume that there are no errors in the transmission, and blasts them along to their proper destination. There's no worrying about the possibility that a blip in an analog transmission might slip by.

Connecting with frame relay gives larger organizations a scalable solution to Internet access. Once again, you connect to the Internet by going through a service provider, such as NETCOM On-Line Communication services.

To implement frame relay, your organization will have to replace its current set of routers and bridges with frame relay-compatible equipment. Frame relay is an excellent solution to the growing problem of not enough bandwidth. It's a significant investment—consult your Internet provider, your information systems department, and the phone company before making this leap.

TIP Many hardware suppliers are making their equipment modular so you change among frame relay, ISDN, analog, X.25, etc., with minimum expense, while retaining most of your investment. This modularity is worth it to you.

Ironically, as telephone companies install ATM to carry more and more traffic, frame relay will be carried over ATM. The two methods do not conflict; they're complimentary.

T Carrier Connections

As the telephone system evolved into digital transmission, the industry developed a system of multiplexing information called *T carrier.* The "T" designations correspond to digital signal (DS) nomenclature as shown in Table 9.1.

Table 9.1 T Carrier System

T Carrier	DS Level	Data Rate	Voice Channels
T1	DS 1	1.544 Mbps	24
T1C	DS 2	3.152 Mbps	48
T2	DS 2	6.312 Mbps	96
T3	DS 3	44.736 Mbps	672
T4	DS 4	274.176 Mbps	4032

Part
II

Ch
9

The T1 and T3 lines are generally available to organizations. T1s and T3s handle all kinds of transmissions—voice, fax, video, or data. These lines are also the most costly of the available connections.

Basically, T1 is the all-digital backbone of the telephone infrastructure. It was originally meant to carry voice transmissions from central office to central office, or to connect the phone company's many central offices (COs). T1s are used for connection of telephone customer sites and for high-speed Internet connections.

T1s use *Time Division Multiplexing (TDM)* and Pulse Code Modulation. Based on the research and mathematics developed by H. Nyquist, TDM allows the capacity of the T1 line to be divided up into 64 channels. The Nyquist rule states that it is possible to recreate analog signals—voice, for example—on a digital line. It requires that the sampling rate of the analog signal be twice the highest analog frequency. For voice transmission, the highest frequency carried is 4000 Hertz; therefore, 8000 samples per second are taken. There are 24-total channels on a T1, and each is multiplexed—or divided up—so that each channel carries one sample at any one time.

Pulse Code Modulation is the method used to convert analog samples into digital format. PCM calls for the sample size to be exactly 8 bits. PCM and TDM work together to provide 64,000 bits of bandwidth to each channel, or 8 bits multiplied by 8,000 samples per second equals 64,000 bits per second. Taken together, each T1 connection can have 1.544 megabits per second (Mbps) of bandwidth. Like ISDN, however, some signaling packets are used, bringing the overall transmission bandwidth down to 1.536 Mbps. This true bandwidth is known as the DS-1, or Digital Signal 1.

T1s are commonly used as the backbone technology in large organization's WANs. The T1 line is a physical connection, meaning that the phone company has to come in and physically provide you with the service. The phone company typically connects the T1 directly to your organization's PBX. This is accomplished through a network interface unit connected to the T1, the channel service unit (CSU), the channel bank, and the PBX.

To create an Internet connection, you must arrange all of the details of your connection with a service provider. Most providers will furnish you with all the equipment you need, such as a router and a digital service unit (DSU). Some routers have DSUs built in. This allows the

Internet connection to feed directly into your local-area network. In most cases, Internet providers make all the arrangements for you, and you never have to deal with the phone company directly.

 Choose routers that have built-in, modular DSUs. They are more manageable, and it's easier to get support on one unit from a single company; and you can change them as your needs change.

▶ **See** "An Introduction to TCP/IP," **p. 108**

What this means to you is that you'll have the highest-speed Internet connection available. You'll have plenty of bandwidth so that your organization's Internet server won't tax your T1. All that's necessary now is to load the software to allow transport to take place.

The Highest of High Speed Connections

High speed doesn't end with T1. In fact, the T-carrier system extends to T3 and beyond. As you move higher in number up the T-carrier chain, you get faster speeds. For example, T3 lines can pump your data at a rate of about 44.8 Mbps—the capacity of 28 T1 lines.

The main difference between T1 and T3 is that T3 lines require higher bandwidth lines to transport the data at nearly 44.8 Mbps. While T1 typically uses twisted-pair wires, T3 uses fiber optical cables, digital microwaves, and coaxial cables.

The Internet on Cable TV, Dishes, Power Lines, and Pipes?

The future of Internet high-speed connections is not clear. For the first time, the telephone companies face a challenge from a totally different kind of competitor—cable TV. The telephone companies themselves have been trying to purchase large stakes in the big cable companies. Cable has a lot to offer, including huge penetration into residential areas. The cable itself can handle throughput of about 500 Mbps —that's significantly greater than the twisted pair wires currently coming into your home through phone lines.

The fact that the same cable that brings Showtime into your home may also be your telephone wire is all part of the convergence of computer and telephone technology, *computer telephony integration (CTI)*. Sooner or later your notebook computer, your TV, and your telephone will be tethered by the same cord. Currently, various cable hookup technologies are being tested for Internet access. This is part of the development of a set-top box that is expected to broker communications to your home and business in competition with the telephone company.

Other developments promise more competition. This means more function, higher data rates, and lower prices for you. Look for wireless delivery methods including cellular, microwave, and satellite. And don't be surprised if your electric power company, gas company, and water company offer Internet and other communications links using their rights of way, cables and pipes.

And now for something completely different. AT&T, Motorola, and others have perfected and are beginning to deliver the following acronyms:

- ADSL
- HDSL
- SDSL

This industry is really about selling alphabet soup, but I'll clue you in on what this all means. *Asymmetric digital subscriber line* (*ADSL*), *high bit-rate digital subscriber line* (*HDSL*), and *symmetric digital subscriber line* (*SDSL*) all refer to a new technology that delivers data rates of as much as 8 Mbps over a single twisted pair to your house or business. Wow! What this technology does to ISDN, we don't know yet, but it could be a boon for using existing twisted pair to deliver multi-megabit data rates almost anywhere.

ADSL is asymmetric in providing much higher data rate from the upstream location (the Internet, for the purpose of our discussion) to you than you deliver back. Since most of the time, you're downloading files or Web pages, this may be your best bet. SDSL provides the same data rate in both directions and can co-exist with ISDN on the same pair. HDSL takes two pair and gives T1 (or E1) without repeaters over distances that have required repeaters in the past.

ON THE WEB

For more info on *DSL, see **http://www.sbexpos.com/sbexpos/association/adsl/home.html**, **http://www.alumni.caltech.edu/~dank/isdn**, and **http://www.bryce.com/~bryce**

SONET and ATM

If the telephone companies don't buy into cable TV, or if the regulators don't let them, they've got some interesting alternatives. As it becomes clear that the T-carrier system cannot provide the bandwidth necessary for today's Internet infrastructure, the phone company is grooming SONET as the replacement for the nation's telecommunications backbone.

SONET stands for *Synchronous Optical Network*. It's just a fancy term for an all fiber-optic transport that once and for all rids the nation of slow copper-wire links. Besides super-fast speeds, SONET has the claim to fame that it can run almost all of the current and planned network capabilities, such as broadband ISDN, Asynchronous Transfer Mode (ATM), Switched Multimegabit data services (SMDS) and Fiber distributed data interface (FDDI).

ATM seems like it will be the choice protocol to run over SONET. ATM is a cell relay protocol that uses extremely small 53-byte cells to transport data. Small cells are important as they better handle the bursts and flows that are common in wide-area networks. ATM is probably the only protocol that will allow entire gigabit cinema movies to be transported over the nation's wires. But that's a completely different story.

SONET comes in several implementations, like the T-carrier system. The first is called OC-1 (optical carrier). It can deliver speeds of up to 51.84 Mbps, or 28 DS-1 links. Most of the interest today is in OC-3, which can deliver 155.52 Mbps, the equivalent of 84 T1 connections. That's a lot of bandwidth. But it doesn't stop there. SONET has capabilities that extend it well into the billion-bit-per-second range—or gigabits per second. Figure 9.4 shows how all these technologies fit together.

While there are no plans to sell this technology directly to organizations, it has a large impact on wide-area networking and the Internet.

FIG. 9.4
The Big Picture of everything packed into ATM and then into SONET. From *Special Edition, Using ISDN* by James Y. Bryce (QUE 1995).

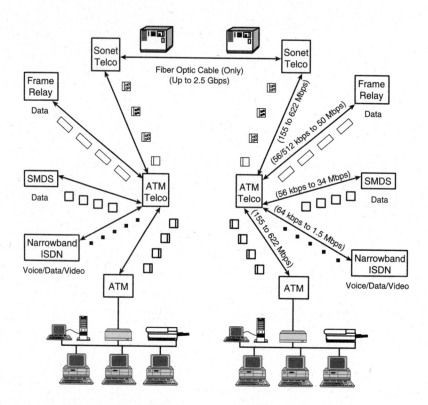

Digital Dilemmas: Which Type Do I Need?

You know all about the various possible connections to the Internet; now you need to know which one is right for you. Unfortunately, there's no easy answer. It depends largely on how much you're willing to spend. If you're a small accounting firm that wants to use the Internet for e-mail, you certainly don't want to waste money on a T1 connection. You'll never recoup the investment. But if you're thinking about whether to go with ISDN or Switched-56, that's a much tougher question. See Table 9.2 for some suggestions here.

Table 9.2 Choosing Your Connection Technology

Hours Used per Person per Day	Number of Users	Connections to Consider	Best Bet
0–1	1	BRI, 14.4/28.8 modem	Modem
1–2	1–2	BRI, 14.4/28.8 modem	BRI
2–3	2–10	BRI, Switched-56	BRI
3–5	10–15	BRI, Dedicated-56	BRI
3–5	15–40	PRI, T1, Frame Relay	PRI, FR
3–5	40+	PRI, T1, Frame Relay	PRI, FR
3–5+	100+	PRIs, T1s, T3	T3 (PRI, FR?)

N O T E   Your mileage will vary, so be careful when choosing an Internet provider. Think about growth in your Internet usage. The wrong investment in hardware can set you back thousands of dollars; consider modular equipment that can be incrementally upgraded. Plan carefully, and consult your Internet provider. ■

Part
II
Ch
9

The Cost of Being on the Internet

Your Internet connection doesn't always end with getting your organization on the Internet. You'll often want to let others access your network. This could involve setting up FTP or Telnet access, or creating your own World Wide Web (WWW) home page. If you want your organization to have a presence on the Internet, you'll need to consider how that affects your bandwidth. Each user who accesses your network is going to nibble away at your available bandwidth.

If you think estimating your own bandwidth need is tough, just imagine estimating everyone else's needs. There will be people accessing your data for business use, personal use, or even by accident. There's no mathematical formula for estimating the connection space that these people will take up—you'll have to make educated guesses and play it by ear. ●

Using Internet E-mail

How Internet E-mail Works

by John Jung

Electronic mail (e-mail) is one of the most widely used services on the Internet. E-mail is easy to send, read, reply to, and manage, and it is fast and convenient. For these reasons, it has grown from a simple service offered to researchers for communicating ideas and results to a complex, talented messaging system. This chapter looks at e-mail and its role on the Internet.

E-mail has many advantages over regular communications methods such as postal services or fax technology. It is much easier to write an e-mail message than to write a formal paper letter or note, for example. Many studies have shown that recipients are much more likely to reply to an e-mail message than a written request, primarily because of the ease of formulating the response.

E-mail can be read and written at any time, independent of time zones and business hours. This makes it easy for busy people to keep in touch with others on a daily basis, whenever they find some spare time. The ability to carefully formulate replies at leisure also helps prevent hasty comments. E-mail is also global, allowing messages to pass from Japan to the U.S. in minutes, regardless of the time they were sent.

E-mail is also economical and very fast. It is much cheaper to send an e-mail message than a letter, or to make a long

Internet e-mail protocol

Learn about the protocols that make it possible to send and receive Internet e-mail.

Finding e-mail addresses

Need to find someone's e-mail address? This chapter shows you how to look it up online.

Handling large files

This chapter shows you how to send and receive large files using Internet e-mail.

Guidelines for using e-mail (etiquette)

Besides legal issues involving e-mail, you'll learn about guidelines for conducting yourself on e-mail.

Learn how to send mail to online service users

Everyone who can receive Internet e-mail is not actually on the Internet. Here, you'll learn how to address your messages to them.

distance telephone call. Typically, e-mail messages can be delivered to a recipient within minutes of being sent, while replies are just as fast. E-mail doesn't require paper (ecologically sound), and it is easy to dispose of (no landfill problems). E-mail is simply an excellent choice for communications, solving many problems without imposing many new ones.

In this chapter, we will look at several different aspects of e-mail, both in general and as they apply to the Internet. By the end of this chapter you should know enough about e-mail to use the Internet for sending and receiving e-mail. You'll also learn about transferring files through e-mail and the generally accepted rules of behavior. ■

Simple Mail Transfer Protocol (SMTP)

The Internet uses a TCP/IP-family protocol called the Simple Mail Transfer Protocol (SMTP) as the standard method for transferring electronic mail over the Internet system. SMTP is also used in many local-area and wide-area networks, although there are many other competing e-mail protocols available for LANs. In many ways SMTP is similar to FTP. It is a simple protocol with basic operational capabilities.

▶ **See** "An Introduction to TCP/IP," **p. 108**

SMTP is accessed by a system's electronic mail routing program. UNIX systems, for example, use a program called sendmail, which receives requests for e-mail transfers from the user's mail applications (such as the UNIX mail program, Lotus Notes, and so on). The actual source application of the mail doesn't matter, as long as it can communicate with the sendmail system (or equivalent routing program on other systems).

The sendmail utility implements SMTP and several other mail protocols simultaneously. Usually, this type of mail program runs all the time, especially in multi-user systems that support background processes. (Background programs that run all the time are called *daemons* in the UNIX vocabulary.) On smaller systems, such as PCs, the mailing program must be run either as a Terminate-and-Stay-Resident (TSR) program (and can be activated by a trigger of some sort) or the mail program must be started up each time you want to transfer mail.

Companies that have large mail systems let the sendmail program run continuously so it can keep a constant watch for incoming and outgoing mail messages. System administrators set the program to check the Internet for incoming messages on a regular basis (usually at least hourly, often more frequently). The system's users do not interact with the sendmail program directly, instead using a front-end mail program (such as cc:Mail, Microsoft Mail, Eudora, or Lotus Notes) for the composition and reading of mail messages.

SMTP handles messages in *queues* (also called spools). When a message is sent from a mail application to SMTP, it places it in an outgoing queue. SMTP attempts to forward the message from the queue whenever it connects to remote machines. If the targeted mail host can't find the user to which the message is addressed, it returns the message immediately. Otherwise, if SMTP cannot forward the message within a predetermined amount of time (usually a day or two), the message is returned to the sender with an error message or removed from the system.

When a connection is established between two computers that use SMTP, the two systems exchange authentication codes. After verifying each machine's status, one system sends a command to the other to identify the first mail message's sender and provides basic information about the message. The receiving SMTP system will return an acknowledgment, after which the message itself is transmitted. SMTP uses TCP/IP to handle the messages.

SMTP is smart enough to handle multiple destinations for the same message in an efficient manner. If more than one recipient of the same message is identified, the message is transmitted only once, but the receiving system will then make copies to each of the recipients. This reduces the amount of traffic between machines.

The sender and recipient address fields of an SMTP message use standard Internet formats, involving the username and domain name. The technical details of SMTP are beyond the scope of this book and are unlikely to be pleasant reading for even the most technical person.

Store and Forward

Internet E-mail and the U.S. Postal Service (snail mail) have a lot of differences (speed, cost, temperament), but they both get messages to their destinations in roughly the same manner: *store and forward*. For example, a parcel you send from Dallas to Denver may take a path like this:

1. Your postal carrier picks up the letter in Dallas and takes it to the Post Office, where it's sorted and placed on a truck.

2. The truck delivers it to another post office, where it's sorted and placed on another truck.

3. Step 2 is repeated over and over until your mail eventually reaches the Post Office in Denver. A postal carrier then delivers your letter to the recipient.

Internet e-mail works in much the same way. Your e-mail program puts your message in a mail-header (the envelope) and places it on the network using SMTP. Then, your e-mail is passed from network to network (the Post Offices) using mail gateways (the trucks). After your e-mail arrives at the correct network, it's delivered to the recipient's mail box by a mail agent (the postal carrier).

X.400 and X.500

The original dream for electronic mail was quite simple. Each message would have a standard header section with information about the sender, recipient, subject, and some status codes. The definition of the mail message format was agreed upon by the CCITT (International Consultative Committee on Telephones and Telegraphs), a United Nations sanctioned standards body. They called the mail standard X.400 (pronounced "X dot four hundred").

X.400 couldn't be used alone because some method of determining the routing to the recipient of each message was necessary. Enter another standard called X.500, which provides a mechanism for a master database of e-mail addresses. X.400 would create the package containing the message and X.500 would figure out who it was going to and how to get it there.

X.400 and X.500 are used by some systems but have not achieved standard usage across all networks. The most common mail transfer method still remains SMTP.

Finding Someone's E-mail Address

When you want to send mail to someone, you need the person's address (in this case, his or her e-mail address consisting of the username and machine being used). There are several utilities available for determining someone's e-mail address, such as Finger, WHOIS, and Netfind.

These utilities do not guarantee being able to find e-mail addresses, since the majority of users are not on systems that allow these utilities to access their user lists (or they want to remain private). Current estimates are that only one or two percent of all Internet users can be located with one of these methods.

N O T E   Some large corporations and universities allow you to search for a user on their system. Some provide this search mechanism by Finger and others by home pages. If you're having problems looking someone up at a particularly large institution with the tools in this chapter, you can also ask for help. Don't be afraid to send e-mail asking for help to the "postmaster" or "webmaster" of the site of the person you're trying to find. They might be able to point you to some special facility they have to help you find the person you're looking for. ▪

N O T E   Web users can take advantage of two particularly good home pages to find other users. One is the Four11 information service, which can be accessed by going to **http://www.four11.com/**. You must join their database of users to be able to use it. But once you've signed on, you can search for anybody else in the Four11 listings. A good general directory of White Pages can be found at **http://home.netscape.com/home/internet-white-pages.html**. Netscape users can simply select the White Pages menu item under the Directory menu heading. Simply follow the link of the particular White Pages you'd like to use. ▪

In the near future, a global X.500 directory will exist that contains addresses for all users who want to be found (much like the telephone directory contains all numbers except those that have been specifically requested to remain unlisted). Such white pages are being created by various companies, but none of them have come close to building a complete directory.

There are several direct methods of determining e-mail addresses, ranging from telephoning a person and asking to examine e-mail messages from a person for his or her address. Some people, though, rely on a set of standard utilities, covered in brief in the following sections.

T I P   Eudora provides a feature you can use to find people's mail addresses. See Chapter 13, "Using Eudora," for more information.

Finger

Finger is a standard utility supplied with the TCP/IP protocol family that lets you determine who is a valid system user and who is logged into a system you have access to. It can be used to find out a person's username and if a mail recipient is logged in on the destination machine (if you are allowed to query the system). Not all sites will allow you to do a Finger, depending on how the system administrator has set up the system.

To determine if a user is on a machine, issue a command on the UNIX command line as follows:

```
finger username@domain.name
```

where "username" is the user's login name and "domain.name" is the machine's domain. You must have the complete username and domain name. For example, the command

```
finger president@whitehouse.gov
```

would tell you if the President was a valid user and logged into the White House's network. It can also show other information about the user, if he has supplied it for general distribution. (This particular example won't actually work because of security restrictions at the White House, but you get the idea.)

If you happen to know the domain name of where a friend is located, but you don't know his username, you can also use Finger. You can see everybody who's currently logged into a particular system by simply specifying the "@domain.name". For example, the command:

```
finger @whitehouse.gov
```

would tell you who's currently using the computer *whitehouse.gov*. You see the person's username in the left hand column and his real name next to it.

> **N O T E** There are a number of graphics-based finger programs for Windows 95. Each of them presents the same finger information, but formats it differently. You'll find WS-Finger and Finger at **http://www.cwsapps.com/ftp.html**, for example. You can also use Eudora to finger people.

Finger can be used for purposes other than determining usernames and addresses. By Fingering some sites, you can get access to information such as Nielson television ratings, Billboard Magazine music charts, and details about recent earthquakes. Lists of Finger sites are available through UseNet. Here are a few Finger addresses for you to try:

Earthquakes: **quake@geophys.washington.edu**

Baseball scores: **jtchern@ocf.berkeley.edu**

NASA press releases: **nasanews@space.mit.edu**

Carnegie-Mellon Computer Science Coke Machine: **coke@l.gp.cs.cmu.edu**

Tropical Storm forecasts: **forecast@typhoon.atmos.colostate.edu**

To use these addresses, simply specify them in the Finger command. For the latest NASA press release, for example, you would issue the command:

```
finger nasanews@space.mit.edu
```

and you will get a message returned with the information you need. You cannot use Finger through electronic mail, though, which poses a limitation for users with access to the Internet by e-mail only. For those users, one of the other search utilities must be used.

WHOIS

The *WHOIS* program and its accompanying database is maintained by Network Solutions Inc. and AT&T. Contrary to popular belief, this isn't meant to be a complete database of all Internet users. The *WHOIS* database is a complete repository of everybody who is in charge of a part of the Internet. That is, the systems and network administrators for companies and organizations.

To use the WHOIS system, enter all or part of the proper name of the person you are trying to locate on a command line. If the WHOIS database has anything that matches the name, it is displayed or e-mailed to you.

There are several ways to use the WHOIS service. For most users who have full Internet access, the easiest way to use the WHOIS service is to Telnet into a WHOIS server and access the database directly. Alternatively (and for those without full Internet access), you can send an e-mail request to the WHOIS server and let it perform the search and mail back the results (a process that is not as time-consuming as it sounds). Users more comfortable with Gopher can also access WHOIS servers. Web users aren't left out; InterNIC has provided a home page for searching the WHOIS database.

▶ **See** "Anonymous FTP," **p. 808**

Most users rely on the primary InterNIC server as their WHOIS site. A list of all WHOIS servers can be obtained through anonymous FTP to **sipb.mit.edu** as the file whois-servers list in the pub/whois directory. Using an alternative server may reduce response time.

Most UNIX systems, as well as some online services like Delphi, allow WHOIS commands to be entered directly on your command line. The syntax of the UNIX version of WHOIS (which is the same for most other versions) is

```
whois [-h hostname] username
```

with the hostname optional. If a hostname is supplied, it needs to be preceded with a -h option to prevent the WHOIS server from thinking you are asking for a username. Examples of valid WHOIS queries are

```
whois -h tpci.com tparker
whois "doe, john"
```

When the WHOIS command displays its results, it will show all names that match with the corresponding NIC handle, a unique identification number, the e-mail address, and sometimes a telephone number if supplied by the user. Even more information can be displayed by querying with the NIC handle only. For example, if you queried for the name "John Doe" and found three matches, use the number of the user you want more complete details on, such as

whois NT123

where "NT123" was the unique number shown in the reply from the WHOIS server.

You can access the WHOIS system through e-mail, too. Address the message to one of the WHOIS servers (such as **mailserv@ds.internic.net**) with no subject specified. The body of the message should be the same as a WHOIS UNIX command, such as:

whois tparker

One variant of the command that is commonly supported is to put a period in front of the person's username to identify to the WHOIS server that you are specifying a username and not an organization name (instead of relying on the -h option to show a host name). This would change the message body to:

whois .tparker

The problem with the WHOIS service is that it covers only a small percentage of the Internet's users (currently only about 80,000 of the over 20,000,000 Internet users). But then, that's not the intent of the database. The best use of WHOIS service is to find out e-mail addresses for network administrators in companies or organizations. If you receive junk e-mail from someone, you can simply use WHOIS to find the network administrator for that user. You can then e-mail the offending user's network administrator and complain about the junk letter.

N O T E You can use the InterNIC (the Network Solutions Inc. database of addresses) system by Telneting to **ds.internic.net**, logging on as "guest", and selecting the option titled InterNIC Directory Services ("White Pages"). The software is still under development, but you will be able to see its capabilities. You can have information about InterNIC automatically sent to you by sending e-mail to **info@internic.net**. Gopher users can access Internic by going to **rs.internic.net**. Web users can directly search the WHOIS server by pointing their browsers to **gopher://rs.internic.net/ 7waissrc%3A/rs/whois.src**. ■

Netfind

Netfind is a still-experimental service that approaches username location in a different manner than WHOIS. Instead of maintaining a database of users, Netfind goes out to different network gateways and queries them for the usernames. Ideally, Netfind will be given an approximate geographical location to narrow its search.

When run, Netfind prompts you for two pieces of information (if you have them): the user's first and last names or a login name (only one of the two can be used), and a location for the user (which can be narrow, such as a specific site, or more general, such as a city or state).

You can access Netfind by logging into a Netfind server and querying it for information. Unfortunately, it doesn't do a complete search as some systems will not allow queries of their user lists. Therefore, Netfind isn't much more comprehensive than Finger.

Part
III

Ch
10

If you want to experiment with Netfind, Telnet to **bruno.cs.colorado.edu** and log in as "netfind". The master Netfind system will prompt you for your actions. There are several other Netfind servers available, mostly at universities and colleges. You can also Telnet to **pascal.sjsu.edu**, **ra.oc.com**, **ds.internic.net**. In each case, log in as "netfind."

N O T E People with Web browsers have the added advantage of using some WHOIS home pages. Simply point your browser to **http://www.nova.edu/Inter-Links/netfind.html** and enter your Netfind keys. ■

Knowbot Information Service

The Knowbot Information Service (KIS) is an experimental service that tries to automate the address-finding process. KIS doesn't maintain its own database but instead queries other address databases it knows about, including those mentioned previously. KIS uses, for example, the WHOIS server, the Finger utility, the X.500 directory, MCI Mail's directory, and several machine and country specific services.

By providing a front end to several different addressing services, KIS lets you enter the search information only once, instead of having to retype names for each different service. It also lets you use a standard format, negating the need to keep track of syntax for three or four different address location utilities. Any information retrieved by KIS is reformatted and presented in a standard format, regardless of its origin.

You can use KIS by either Telneting to a KIS server or by addressing e-mail to the KIS server. There are several KIS servers available, which must be accessed through a specific port (usually port 185). If you have telnet access, you can try the KIS system using this KIS server:

> telnet nri.reston.va.us 185

N O T E There are a number of home pages that have KIS search forms. One such Web page is at **http://info.cnri.reston.va.us/kis.html**. Simply enter the person's name that you're trying to find, select the information sources to search, and submit the query. ■

Other KIS servers are available. A current list is available from the **nri.reston.va.us** server. Note that the use of port 185 is mandatory and must be specified on the telnet command line.

E-mail requests for searches must follow a specific format. Response time from the KIS servers is usually very good. To send e-mail to the KIS server, address your query to

> netaddress@nri.reston.va.us

The body of the message should have one or more of the following keywords in it, followed by the data to be used by the server:

■ service specifies any particular service you want to add to the default search list. Unless you have a lot of experience with KIS, don't use this parameter the first few times.

- org is the organization to which the user belongs, usually specified as a full or partial domain name.

- identifier uses the appended information for the search instead of a username. This is used when specifying a user ID number instead of a name (necessary for services like MCI Mail and CompuServe).

- query is followed by the username you wish to locate.

An example of an e-mail query sent to the KIS server would have a message body of

```
org tpci
query tparker
```

which would try to find the user tparker on any organization that has the letters tpci in the domain name.

UseNet User List

Users of UseNet unwittingly contribute to a user list (see Chapter 27, "How UseNet Works"). As each newsgroup message passes through the Massachusetts Institute of Technology's servers, a program gathers all the usernames and builds a database of UseNet users and their addresses.

You can query this list by e-mail, although few users seem to use it on a regular basis. To send a query to the UseNet User List, address a message to

mail-server@pit-manager.mit.edu

No subject is required for the e-mail, but the contents of the message should be in the following format:

send *usenet-addresses/username*

For example, the following query will try to locate a UseNet user with the last name parker:

send *usenet-addresses/*parker

The response will include a list of the usernames that match your specified string, their full names (if it is supplied in the newsgroup postings), and the dates of their last postings.

N O T E If you want to make it easy for other users to track you down, send a couple of postings to a UseNet newsgroup so that you appear on the MIT list. ■

Files

Most E-mail systems do not impose limitations on the types of files that can be sent, as long as the network protocol can handle the characters. However, getting files into the proper format can require running the file through a utility. It is also common practice to compress large files for transmission.

Part
III

Ch
10

ASCII Format Only

Most of the Internet relies on 7-bit ASCII characters, which are ideal for most text-based messages. Problems can occur with binary files and more complex icon-based languages (such as Chinese and Japanese), but there are solutions available for these files, too.

The Internet e-mail system handles binary files by converting them to 7-bit ASCII characters, using one of several different character-conversion programs. The most popular conversion utilities are UUEncode and UUDecode (see Chapter 15, "Encoding and Decoding Files").

UUEncode converts 8-bit characters into a 7-bit representation that can be converted back to its original format with the UUDecode program. In some cases, UUEncoded files are tagged with the file extension .UU or .UUE, although this is not a widely used convention.

> **CAUTION**
>
> If your message is not 7-bit ASCII characters, it must be converted before being sent or the contents will be corrupted. Use UUEncode and UUDecode for binary files.

The Internet system is generally unable to handle binaries in their native form. Anything sent in this manner will be truncated to 7-bit ASCII, making it virtually impossible to reconstruct the original message. UseNet news and e-mail in particular face this restriction, so be sure to convert binary files to ASCII before sending.

Having issued that warning, the Internet doesn't care about the contents of the files you send. Assuming they have been properly converted to allow transmissions, you can send sound files, graphics, multimedia movies, and any other kind of application you wish. The Internet ignores the contents of messages, concentrating only on the information in the message headers that are added by TCP/IP.

E-mail has a distinct advantage over the Internet when it comes to transferring files from a user application, because it allows disk formats to be completely ignored. A file written in Microsoft Word for Macintosh can be sent (UUEncoded, of course, but you seldom have to worry about that) to a user on a PC. The PC version of Microsoft Word will recognize the file's format as Word for Macintosh and offer to perform a conversion for you. This type of conversion applies to most popular application formats, also making e-mail an efficient way to distribute files. This may not work well with graphics and sound files unless they are in a standard format (such as JPEG or MIDI).

N O T E A new 8-bit to 7-bit converter that's gaining rapid use is the **MIME** encoding scheme. This method overcomes some of the technical shortcomings of UUEncode and UUDecode, and is well integrated into many newer programs. Its major shortcoming is that it's not as widely available for UNIX machines as UUEncode and UUDecode. Additionally, MIME is being incorporated into more and more newer applications, especially e-mail programs. ■

N O T E The Macintosh has its own standard method of converting 8-bit files to 7-bit files, known as BinHex. BinHex essentially does everything that MIME and UUEncode/UUDecode do, but is Macintosh specific. There are a number of Windows 95 and UNIX programs available that will un-BinHex files. See Chapter 15, "Encoding and Decoding Files," for more information about BinHex. ■

File Compression

Large files are usually not transferred as they are but are compressed by a utility to save on transmission time. There are several compression and expansion utilities in use, most of which are incompatible with each other.

DOS-based systems usually use one of two popular types of compression and expansion utilities, both from PKWare. PKZIP and PKARC are the utilities that compress files, enabling several files to be assembled into a single, larger library file for transmission. This is very useful when sending several small files to a single user. PKZIP and PKARC will create the archive file, then compress it to a smaller size than the original files. When the compressed archive file is received, the same utility can be used to expand the file and then extract the contents.

These utilities are usually recognized by their file extensions in a DOS system. Files that have been compressed with PKZIP have the extension .zip, while PKARC files have the extension .arc. ZIPped and ARCed files are not compatible because they use different algorithms. An .arc file cannot be uncompressed with PKZIP.

N O T E Windows users can simplify the handling of ZIP files with a utility called WinZip. WinZip is a graphical front-end to PKZIP that offers some of the same functionality built in. You can get WinZip from anonymous FTP at **ftp.winzip.com**. The self-extracting executable can be found at winzip/winzip95.exe or winzip/wz16v61.exe for Windows 3.1 users. ■

Macintosh users commonly use a compression utility called StuffIt, which produces files ending with .sit. As with DOS utilities, StuffIt can handle multiple files and compresses all types of contents.

UNIX systems take a two-step approach to PKZIP and StuffIt by using different programs for different aspects. To collect several files into one large file, it's common to use the tar utility (tape archive). Tar accepts a number of command line options for what operation to perform, the file to use, and which files to access. The most common syntax for it is:

```
tar -cvf filename.tar files
```

N O T E On some versions of UNIX, each command line option must be specified separately. So instead of

```
tar -cvf ...
```

you would need to type in

tar -c -v -f ... ■

Another method in UNIX for collecting a lot of files together into one large file is *cpio* (copy in and out). It is a bit more complex to use than tar, so cpio is not generally used by casual users. Also cpio requires a file that contains a list of files to be collected and then the use of various file redirecting gymnastics. The most common syntax for using cpio is:

```
cpio -covB < [file with list] > filename.cpio
```

N O T E   When sending binaries or large files, first use a compression utility and then UUEncode the file. ■

Once a library file has been created, it can be compressed with a standard UNIX utility. Most UNIX systems support the commands `compress` and `uncompress`. A compressed file has the file extension .z. Fortunately for Windows 95 users WinZip 6.0, a graphical front-end to PKZIP, can read in and extract compressed files.

N O T E   There is a much older set of UNIX compression and uncompression programs called *pack* and *unpack*. These programs are no longer used and are being phased out by all major UNIX operating systems manufacturers. ■

It is not unusual to receive files that have been put into a library, compressed, and then UUEncoded. File extensions are not usually sent through electronic mail when using UNIX, so make sure you clearly indicate in the Subject field of the message which utilities have been run on the file. For example, the subjects:

> Chapter 4 of Book (MS Word, ZIPped)
>
> Graphics files (.arc)
>
> Draft proposal (compressed)

tell the recipient how to treat the file when it is received. By putting the details of the program used in parentheses, you save the recipient the trouble of trying to figure out which compression or conversion utilities you have employed. It is sometimes impossible to know which utility to use by looking at the ASCII characters in the file.

 T I P   Chapter 15, "Encoding and Decoding Files," describes how you can determine what type of encoding scheme was used on a file just by looking at the text.

Legal Issues and E-mail

There are three aspects of electronic mail that involve legal issues: copyright, libel, and privacy.

Take care to avoid copyright issues when transferring files. It is illegal to distribute copyrighted information by any means, electronic or physical. This is not restricted to transferring binary versions of an application, although this is a primary source of litigation. Copyright regulations extend to cover published material, too. It is quite common to find graphics that have been scanned by a user for personal use distributed through the Internet. This is illegal, since the copyright owner has not granted the right to disseminate the material.

Some material is prohibited by federal laws (primarily certain types of pornography), and although e-mail may seem a simple way to send and receive this type of material, traffic monitoring and tracing is not a complicated matter. Even descriptions of some material may be illegal, depending on the country you are sending e-mail to or from. If you are sending mail out of the country, you may be placing your recipient in trouble.

Libel is as applicable within e-mail messages and newsgroups as in a published book. There have recently been several well-publicized cases of an Internet user suing another user for comments made in private correspondence and generally-accessible messages in UseNet newsgroups. Again, prudence is important, as the legal definitions of libel may differ from country to country.

The right to privacy is not assured with electronic mail. Unlike mail sent through the postal service, there is no requirement for a company not to read your incoming and outgoing messages. This is especially applicable if you use your employer's equipment. In many cases, policies are not established for e-mail privacy, so assume all your e-mail is subject to scrutiny. Even on the networks, anyone with a gateway can read messages passing through. It has been suggested many times that several intelligence-gathering organizations routinely scan the high volumes of Internet traffic for items of interest.

Even though e-mail may be deleted from your mailbox, do not assume it has been completely destroyed. Backups are regularly made of system drives, especially in larger organizations. Company policies usually require regular backups that include incoming and outgoing mail messages. Subpoenas can be issued for your e-mail records.

NOTE Another legal issue to deal with here in the United States: A couple of high-profile cases recently have involved someone sending threatening e-mail, in these cases to the President. The senders were arrested and are awaiting trial on federal charges. Penalties can include several years in prison and large fines. The general lesson to be learned from this is that behavior that is illegal in other forms (a threatening phone call or letter, for example) may be illegal in e-mail too, depending on your local or national laws. ▪

Encryption

If you want to send a message with a degree of protection, you can use *encryption*. Encryption is not a guarantee that your message won't be read (anyone with the sophistication to tap an Internet gateway won't be bothered by a simple encryption scheme), but it may prevent casual browsing. Some compression software packages include a simple encryption process that can be turned on with a command line option.

NOTE WinZip provides a means of password protecting ZIP archives. Before adding any files to an archive, select the Password menu selection under the Options menu heading. Type the password you want to use to encrypt your files and add as many files you want. ▪

CAUTION

While WinZip does allow you to put in a password for ZIP files, it can't do it alone. To use this feature, you must have the DOS-based version of PKZIP that WinZip can use.

There are many encryption schemes available, some commercial and some public domain. One of the most secure systems currently available uses the Data Encryption Standard (DES) public-key method. These systems are still breakable, but usually involve massive computer resources to be penetrated.

A popular DOS package for encrypting messages is PC-CODE, which performs a character transposition followed by a substitution, a process called *super encipherment*. This type of system requires the recipient to know a code word to decode messages.

One of the easiest code schemes available on many systems is called *ROT13*. The name derives from code wheels that had two sets of alphabets close together. One wheel was rotated to align with the second at some point in the alphabet, and the letters would be read from the two wheels. A ROT13, scheme would "rot"ate the wheels "13" positions a part (hence ROT13), so that the letter "A" would be "M". This provides a simple code scheme.

Many mail systems and UseNet news readers have ROT13 built in, both for encryption and decryption. Consult your mail and news reader documentation or help files for information on how to use this feature. This type of system is crude, but it doesn't require your recipient to have any secret codewords to break the message. In most cases, ROT13 is not used for security to protect from simple browsing. If a user sees a message that has ROT13 applied, he may be too lazy to decode it.

N O T E   ROT13 won't protect your messages from prying eyes. That's not the intent. It is intended to put the responsibility for viewing a potentially offending message with the recipient—not the sender. It's similar to those license agreements found on sealed diskette envelopes: opening this package (decoding this message) means that you'll abide by certain terms and conditions (you won't hold me responsible). ▨

E-mail Etiquette

The UseNet is governed by a code of conduct called *netiquette*. E-mail has a set of proposed rules for etiquette, both to protect the sender and recipient (see the earlier section "Legal Issues and E-Mail"), and to ensure proper behavior in electronic messages. Here are some of the more important guidelines:

- *Read your mail!* Many users let their e-mail back up, intending to read all the old messages when they have time. This is rude to the senders and may result in your missing something important. Keep it current. Also, if you find you are getting mail you shouldn't, inform senders that you should be taken off their distribution lists.

- *Specify a subject.* Always use a subject heading that identifies your message. This is necessary to allow the recipient to prioritize messages.

- *Clearly identify yourself.* Don't assume that your recipient knows who you are or can figure it out from the header information attached to your message. Give your name and any contact information that you want the recipient to have. To make this easy, copy a standard, short identification file into your messages.

- *Know and respect your recipient.* Even if you do not know the recipient, respect him. Do not use sarcasm or questionable humor unless you know the recipient will not take it personally. Also avoid the syndrome of assuming that e-mail is anonymous and hence allows you to say anything you want. E-mail can be easily traced back to the sender.

- *Avoid outbursts.* Do not get angry in your e-mail. It may come back to haunt you. Again, many users perceive e-mail as less formal than a written letter and hence they feel freer to say what they wish. If you want to blast someone, write your message offline and carefully consider the contents before sending it. Your e-mail may be printed out and used against you in the future.

- *Use proper English.* E-mail messages should be properly spelled, punctuated, and grammatically correct. A poorly written and misspelled letter reflects very badly on you.

- *Be brief.* There is a tendency to ramble when writing e-mail messages, as they often follow your train of thought. As with spelling and grammar, the succinctness with which you present your message reflects on you. Long, rambling messages with little real content tend to be ignored before the recipient has read the entire message.

- *Avoid copying messages to others.* For some reason, e-mail inspires users to send copies of a message to long lists of users, many of whom are uninterested in the contents. Only send copies to those who really should receive a copy; otherwise, it can reflect badly on you.

- *Don't request replies or receipts unless necessary.* As with copies to many users, e-mail also inspires the "please reply" and "please confirm receipt" syndromes. A reply may not be appropriate, while confirmation notes can be a waste of time for the recipient. Use these requests only when absolutely necessary-

- *Avoid using Priority or Urgent tags.* Some mail systems let you tag the message as very important. Use these only when necessary, or your judgment may be questioned. It's the old "cry wolf" story.

- *If replying to a request, fully identify the original question.* Receiving e-mail with the sole contents "yes" or "no" without any indication of what was originally asked can be frustrating. It is sometimes best to copy portions of the original message into the reply.

- *Never assume your mail is private.* As mentioned earlier in this chapter, assume your mail is not private and can be read by others. If in doubt, carefully consider whether you want your e-mail contents to be made available to others to read.

Handling Unwanted E-mail

Like it or not, eventually your e-mail address will be distributed to people you don't want to have it. In theory, e-mail addresses are private, but it is difficult to keep addresses this way unless you send mail only to a few discreet people. Your e-mail address will undoubtedly end up on a distribution list for someone who sends out junk e-mail. Junk mail includes get-rich-quick schemes, unsolicited business opportunities, requests for donations, newsletters that you never requested, and other types of promotional literature. How do you handle this type of mail?

Because the Internet is relatively unpoliced, there are only a few things you can do about unwanted mail. The most obvious is to simply delete the mail, which at times may not be prudent. However, downloading messages, scanning their contents, then deciding you don't want them can be both costly and time-consuming. Also, some users find themselves getting many messages of this type a day, so the simple weeding-out process of junk from important material can be tiresome.

Sometimes the direct approach will work. Send e-mail back to the originator (if they are identified) and request that your name be removed from the distribution list. In many cases, though, the sender uses an anonymous user ID or hides behind other user's names, especially with illegal or immoral schemes.

You can send a message to the sender's system postmaster, informing him of the problem and requesting action be taken. To address mail to a postmaster, you need to know the originating domain. This is harder to hide in a message, so it can be usually determined by reading the e-mail header. Send your request to "postmaster@domain.name". The postmaster login is a special system administrator login. Usually, they can help control the offending user. If the postmaster of the system doesn't help, try the system administrator.

N O T E While sending e-mail to the postmaster or system administrator is reasonable, they don't always read their e-mail. Why? Because the postmaster and system administrator's login names are used for other activities relating to their jobs. The system administrator gets e-mail about daily backups that are completed, system problems, and the like. The postmaster receives similarly automated messages about e-mail and UseNet. If you really need to contact somebody in charge of a domain, use WHOIS to find the contact e-mail address. ■

Finally, if you receive harassing or threatening mail, you should consider calling a law enforcement organization. Getting threats on e-mail is the same as getting them by postal service mail or over the telephone, which is illegal. Unfortunately, not many law enforcement agencies have experience with electronic media, so be patient and explain the problem. Keep copies of all the mail messages.

Sending E-mail to Online Service Users

You've learned about how the Internet handles electronic mail. Not everyone is directly connected to the Internet, but instead relies on an online service provider such as CompuServe,

America Online, or The Microsoft Network online service (MSN). Before sending e-mail to an online service user, you need to understand what types of message each user can receive. You also need to understand how to address your message to them and possibly how they need to address messages to the Internet. You'll learn about both issues in the remainder of this section.

UUNET

Users of UUNET Technologies service do not need special handling except when machine-specific addresses are not properly set. In some cases (notably, when the recipient of a message does not have his or her own registered domain name) it is necessary to specify the UUNET domain name as part of the address. This is usually only necessary if your mail is returned as undelivered and you know the destination is a UUNET user.

If the full address must be used, the domain name is written as UUNET.UU.NET. There is no regular domain name specified as part of the address (the .NET is actually the domain type specifier). The syntax for routing mail with this type of address is

Part
III

Ch

10

username.domainname@UUNET.UU.NET

If there is a submachine that the message must be sent through, it, too, is specified as part of the address:

username%machine.domainname@UUNET.UU.NET

For example, the address

tparker%beast%merlin.tpci@UUNET.UU.NET

would send mail to the primary machine, tpci, on the UUNET network, through the machines merlin and beast, to the user tparker. This type of addressing is usually needed when the hardware network is not properly set up to identify users and machines. Luckily, most systems don't need this type of addressing anymore, unless they use the UUCP mail system exclusively.

Notice that the format of this type of addressing requires the domain name to be separated by a period and not the "@" sign as usual.

America Online

To send mail from within America Online's e-mail system to the Internet, there is no special addressing required. The mail system can figure out where the mail is to go from the format of username@domain.name, so for example,

rmaclean@mig.com

is a valid entry for the Send To: field in the mail system. The rest of the mail message requires no special codes or identifiers.

Sending mail from the Internet to an America Online user requires the user's AOL user name and the domain name "aol.com". For example, mail addressed to userID@aol.com

would find the person with the specified user ID. The domain name should be all lowercase.

N O T E   If you mail a message to a member of America Online, you may receive a message back
stating that the AOL users mailbox is full. America Online mailboxes cannot hold more than
550 pieces of mail from any source. You may have to wait a day and resend the message, or contact
that individual in some other fashion.

America Online has recently added the ability to send MIME-encoded files to anyone, anywhere on the Internet. Of course the recipient must also be using a service and mail reader
that support the MIME format. They have also changed the way that they send messages.
When you are sending long messages, either to other America Online members or to other
Internet addresses the first 2K of each messages will be sent as standard text. The rest of the
message is sent as a MIME attachment.

> **CAUTION**
>
> America Online can only process one file attachment at a time. If someone mails an AOL user a message or
> an AOL member sends a file to an Internet user with multiple files attached, AOL's MIME encoder will encode
> all the files into one attachment. If this happens, you will have to have a third party MIME decoder to
> separate the single attachment back into its original parts.

CompuServe

CompuServe has a limit of approximately 2,000,000 ASCII seven-bit characters in a message.
The system automatically converts eight-bit text to seven-bit. CompuServe's mail system automatically UUEncodes messages that you send to the Internet. It also automatically UUDecodes
messages it receives from the Internet.

For a CompuServe user to send e-mail out to the Internet is relatively simple. The message is
composed in the same manner as internal e-mail, but the address of the recipient is modified to
provide the word "Internet" as part of the Send To line. For example:

internet:president@whitehouse.gov

and

INTERNET: jerry@honeycutt.com

are valid e-mail addresses for sending mail outside the CompuServe system. Case is unimpor-
tant for the "internet" portion of the address. A space may follow the colon, or the address may
follow immediately (the mail system will ignore any spaces that directly follow the colon).

To send mail to a user on CompuServe, you must know his or her CompuServe ID number,
which usually is five numbers, a separator (which must be a period—commas are not supported, despite their frequent use in CompuServe ID numbers), and then three or four more
numbers. The CompuServe domain name is compuserve.com.

> **CAUTION**
>
> When sending to a CompuServe user, make sure the user ID has a period, not a comma.

Addressing mail to a CompuServe user takes the usual Internet format. For example,

> 12345.678@compuserve.com

is a valid address (assuming the CompuServe ID is correct). If the CompuServe ID is invalid, the e-mail should be returned with an error message. Mistyping the CompuServe ID number is a common error, so it is worthwhile to ask for a confirmation of receipt message.

Delphi

There is no Delphi-imposed limitation on message length. And no additional charges are imposed for Internet e-mail. Delphi members can send mail out to the Internet with a special format of address at the Send To: prompt. The format is

> internet"username@host.name"

where the normal Internet address is placed in quotation marks and is preceded with "internet". For example, to send mail to the President from within the Delphi mail system, use the Send To: address:

> internet"president@whitehouse.gov"

Without the quotation marks, the Delphi system cannot properly parse the address, and the mail will not be delivered properly.

To send mail to a Delphi user, the domain name delphi.com is used. The format uses the Delphi username as part of the address:

> username@delphi.com

which is the usual Internet format.

GEnie

To send mail to an Internet user from within the GEnie mail system, you must use a special address format. At the Send To: prompt, use the syntax

> username@host.name@INET#

Without appending the INET#, the mail parser will not direct the mail properly.

To send mail to a GEnie user, the domain name "genie.geis.com" must be used. For example, the address:

> username@genie.geis.com

would be correct, assuming the username is valid.

MCI Mail

Sending mail to an Internet user from within MCI Mail requires specifying several portions of the mail system's prompts in a special manner. When sending mail through MCI Mail, you will be asked for the recipient's name in the TO: field. Use the recipient's real name (not the Internet addressee's username) followed by (EMS). The (EMS) designation informs MCI that you are sending mail to an external mail system. MCI Mail then asks for the EMS:; specify "internet." Finally, when the system asks for the MBX: give the full Internet address. To send mail to Santa Claus (using a mythical domain name) the process would be:

TO: Santa Claus (EMS)

EMS: internet

MBX: sclause@northpole.com

Sending mail to an MCI Mail user is complicated somewhat by the naming scheme used by MCI. A user can have a user ID generally composed of either a 7 or 10 digit phone number, a username made up of their first initial and full last name (such as tparker), or a full username made up of their complete first and last names (such as tim_parker). The complication is that MCI Mail does not require unique usernames of either form, so there may be more than one person with the names "tparker" or "tim_parker" on the system. The only unique identifier is the user ID number.

This lets you address mail to an MCI Mail user in one of three different ways:

userIDnumber@mcimail.com

shortname@mcimail.com

fullname@mcimail.com

Only the first format is guaranteed to reach the user you really want. Of course, the usernames are much easier to use, so if you are going to send mail to an MCI Mail user frequently, you may want to check whether either of the name formats is unique. You can sometimes do this with test messages if the recipients are cooperative.

MCI Mail also offers group addresses to companies in the form of Remote Email System accounts. Addressing for Remote Email Systems works by including the name of the company in the address in the following format:

username%REMS ID@mcimail.com

The REMS ID field lets MCI Mail know which company should receive the message. The company's mail system then reads the username to decide which specific individual in their company should receive that piece of mail.

For an example, if you wanted to send a message to Santa Clause at his toy factory with the MCI Mail ID number 9876543210, you would address the message to:

sclause%9876543210@mcimail.com

N O T E If you do not know the MCI Mail user ID for the company, you can substitute the company's full name in the REM ID field. Remember to replace any spaces in the company's name with underscores.

Prodigy

Prodigy is simple to use as far as Internet access is concerned. A recent revision to the Prodigy mail system has expanded the mail service considerably, supporting all standard file types and addresses.

To send mail from within Prodigy to a user on the Internet, use the standard format of the recipient's address:

username@host.name

The mail system will parse the To: entry and recognize it as an Internet address, routing it through Prodigy's gateway.

To send mail to a Prodigy user, use the domain name "prodigy.com" with the user's user ID on the system. For example,

TSR45AB@prodigy.com

would reach the user with the user ID TSR45AB. Prodigy imposes no limits on the size of messages.

Part

III

Ch

10

The Microsoft Network

The Microsoft Network, or MSN as it is commonly referred to, is the new kid on the block as far as service providers go. This service was introduced with the release of the Windows 95 operating system. Since it has been available, The Microsoft Network has subscribed hundreds of thousands of users and is quickly becoming one of the most popular new services to purchase Internet access from.

Users of The Microsoft Network must use Microsoft Exchange when sending and receiving messages. When MSN account holders need to send mail to other users across the Internet, they use the following standard addressing system:

username@domain.name

So if an MSN user wanted to send mail to Santa Claus, he would still enter sclaus@northpole.com in the To: field of the Exchange mail form.

CAUTION

At some times you may experience problems sending messages to a single address for no apparent reason. When this happens, change the address in the To: field of the mail form to:

[SMTP:usernam@domain.name]

Assuming that the username and domain name are correct, this will improve your chances of getting the message to its destination.

When sending mail to an MSN customer, you simply need to address the message to:

MSNCustomerID@msn.com.

The Microsoft Network uses a series of numbers and letters for each individual's member ID. Since each member ID must be unique, you do not have to worry about sending information to the wrong person. Generally, an MSN member ID number is going to be some combination of a user's name or nickname, or a reference to his favorite hobby.

List of Services

Table 10.1 presents a summary of the formats for addressing e-mail in and out of the most popular service providers. This table is based on the "Internet Mailing Guide" maintained by Ajay Shekhawat of the State University of New York, Buffalo. The complete guide may be obtained by anonymous FTP from **ftp.msstate.edu** in the directory /pub/docs. It is also available through some UseNet newsgroups. If you cannot find a copy of the Internet Mailing Guide, post a message to the newsgroup **news.answers** requesting a mailed version of directions to its location.

As a rule, each online service has its own domain name. Certainly the most popular services examined in this chapter do, although a few exceptions are shown in the following table.

Table 10.1   How to Send Mail to and Receive Mail from Popular Services

Online Service	To Send Mail	To Receive Mail
America Online	username@aol.com	username@host.name
AppleLink	username@ applelink.apple.com	username@host@ internet#
AT&T Mail	username@attmail.com	internet!host! username
BITNET	username%site. bitnet@gateway or username@site.bitnet *Note:* Gateway must be both an Internet and BITNET gateway.	username@host@gateway username@domain.name *Note*: Varies between sites. Check with system administrator.
BIX	username@dcibix.das.net	

Part

III

Ch

10

Online Service	To Send Mail	To Receive Mail
CGNET	username%CGNET@ Intermail.ISI.edu	Address mail to "intermail". The header of the message must have "Forward: Internet" on the first line, "To: username@host.name" on the second, and a blank third line.
CompuServe	nnnnn.nnn@ compuserve.com	internet:username@ host.name
Delphi	username@delphi.com	internet"username@ host.name"
EasyLink	username@eln.attmail.com	
EASYnet	VMS using NMAIL: nm%DECWRL:: \"username@host\"	
	Ultrix: username@host.name	
	IP: \"username%host.name \"@decwrl.dec.com	
	DECNET: DECWRL:: \"username%host\"	
	Envoy (Canada)	att!attmail!mhs! envoy!username@ UUNET.UU.NET
	or	
	/C=CA/ADMD=TELECOM.CANADA /O=ENVOY/DD.ID =username@SPRINT.COM [RFC-822=\"username(a)host.name\"] INTERNET/TELEMAIL/US	
FidoNet	firstname.lastname@ nnn.nnn.nnn.nnn.fidonet.org *Note:* Replace four sets of nnn with FidoNet point, node, network, and zone numbers, respectively. Routes through UUCP.	First line of message is addressed: username@ host.name
Genie	username@ genie.geis.com	username@host.name@ INET#

continues

Table 10.1 Continued

Online Service	To Send Mail	To Receive Mail
MCI Mail	username@mcimail.com *Note:* Users mail has more than one non-unique name (see MCI Mail above). Specify the recipient's name followed by (EMS) in the "To" section of the mail prompts, "internet" in the "EMS" section, and the full Internet address in the "MBX" prompt. See above for details.	
Microsoft Network (MSN)	usename@msn.com	username@host.name
NASA Mail	username@ nasamail.nasa.gov	Send mail to "POSTMAN" with the first line of the message set to "To: username@host.name"
NSI-DECNET (Span)	username@host. SPAN.NASA.gov	AMES::\"username@ host.name\"
SInet	username@ node.SINet.SLB.COM or username%node@ node1.SINet.SLB.COM	M_MAILNOW::M_ INTERNET::"username@ host.name"
SprintMail	/G=firstname/S=lastname /O=organization/ADMD=	(C:USA,A:TELEMAIL,P: INTERNET,"RFC-822":<user
THEnet	username%host.decnet@ utadnx.cc.utexas.edu	UTADNX::WINS% "username@host.name"

Using Microsoft Exchange

by Jerry Honeycutt

Most Internet services are actually two cooperating programs: a *server program* on the host computer and a *client program* on your computer. The server sits quietly in the background, moving around bits of information and talking to the client. The client is the program that you actually experience. That is, it presents you the information that it gets from the server.

Internet mail is no exception. You must have access to a *mail server,* which your online service provides. The *mail client* is your problem, however. It moves your messages from the mail server to your computer so that you can view them. Likewise, it moves new messages from your computer to the mail server so that the mail server can forward them to their destination.

If you're using Windows 95 or Windows NT (both referred to as *Windows 95*, from here on out), you don't have to look very far for a good Internet mail client. Windows comes with the most versatile client available: Microsoft Exchange. Exchange, in combination with Internet Mail service, lets you move messages to and from the Internet. In this chapter, you'll learn how to install and use Exchange for Internet mail. You'll also learn how to use Exchange's more advanced features to personalize how you use Internet mail.

Learn what Microsoft Exchange can do for you

Exchange is easily the most versatile mail package available for Windows 95. This chapter shows you why you should use it.

Install Microsoft Exchange

You'll learn how to install Exchange with Internet Mail service (and how to get it right the first time).

Learn about Exchange's main window

Exchange's main window is easy to use. This chapter shows you each part of Exchange's main window: the toolbar, folder pane, and message pane.

Work with Internet Mail

You'll learn how to send and receive mail, use the Address Book to simplify addressing, and neatly organize your mail into folders.

Customize Exchange just the way you want it

This chapter shows you how to change a variety of Exchange's settings. It also shows you a great add-in for Internet mail called Internet Idioms.

N O T E Exchange is a beast when it comes to memory and disk usage. You need a minimum of 8M of memory to run Exchange, but I recommend that you have at least 12M. Exchange also uses approximately 15M of disk space for the program and temporary files. But that's not the most astonishing part. My mail folders use over 100M. These files contain about six months of messages with attachments. Your mileage may vary. ▓

▶ **See** "Electronic Mail (E-mail)," **p. 12**

Understanding Exchange's Special Features

Should you use Exchange for Internet mail? Well, that depends. You'll be able to better answer that question after you understand Exchange's special features and how they differ from other Internet mail clients such as Microsoft Internet Mail and Eudora.

Most Internet mail clients are very simple programs. They do only Internet mail. They don't do rich text formatting (RTF), and they certainly don't do embedded OLE (object linking and embedding) objects across the Internet. They send and receive Internet mail messages and attachments. That's all. But that may be all you really need. In fact, most people don't use clients that support RTF or OLE. These clients load fast, use little memory, and have fewer options to confuse the user.

On the other hand, Exchange is the most flexible mail client available. You can use it to check mail from a variety of sources. You can send rich formatted messages. You can even embed OLE objects into a mail message. The sections that follow describe some of these special Exchange features. If you like or possibly even require these features, you should use Exchange.

▶ **See** "Using Microsoft Internet Mail," **p. 281**

▶ **See** "Using Eudora," **p. 303**

Open Architecture

The most exciting aspect of Exchange is that it doesn't do very much on its own. It's an empty shell that knows how to talk to components called *MAPI (Mail API) service providers* (service providers or services for short). These service providers perform very specific tasks such as exchanging mail with a server or storing messages in a folder. You make a service available by "plugging" it into Exchange. Try this analogy: Exchange is similar to the motherboard in your computer. The computer doesn't do anything until you plug video and sound cards into it. Likewise, Exchange doesn't do anything until you plug mail and folder service providers into it.

Thus, the actual heart of Exchange isn't Exchange itself. The heart of Exchange is the service providers that you use with it. Do you want to exchange mail through CompuServe? Plug in the CompuServe mail service. Do you want to send and receive faxes using Exchange? Plug in the Fax service. Likewise for Microsoft Mail, The Microsoft Network, and the Internet. You get the idea. Mail services are only a portion of the story. Here's a list of the types of service providers that Exchange supports:

▓ *Mail Services.* Exchange comes with a handful of mail services that let you move messages to and from a mail server. These include Exchange Server, Microsoft Mail,

The Microsoft Network, the Internet, CompuServe, and Fax. Many more service providers are available from third-party vendors.

■ *Personal Folders.* The Personal Folder service lets you store and organize all of your messages in a hierarchical group of folders. These folders are known as the *Universal Inbox*, because you can receive mail from a variety of mail services into the same folders. Get it?

■ *Personal Address Book.* The Personal Address Book service lets you store common e-mail addresses for different mail services, all in one place. You can store Microsoft Mail, Internet, and Microsoft Network addresses all in the same address book, for example.

So what does all this mean? It means that you have the flexibility to set up your mail client to fit your needs almost exactly. If you're like me, you receive mail from a variety of sources. I get mail from CompuServe, The Microsoft Network, the Internet, and Microsoft Mail. I don't want to have to use four different mail clients to keep track of all my messages. I can set up Exchange to deliver mail from all four mail services into the same mail folder.

I also like to have multiple groups of mail folders. I have a small set of folders that I can quickly copy to my notebook computer and take on the road. I also have a larger set of folders in which I archive mail, but I never copy them to my notebook computer. If I had to copy all of my messages to my notebook computer every time I hit the road, I'd spend a lot of time at the coffee machine.

Part
III

Ch
11

Three Mail Clients in One

Exchange lets you work with mail in a way that best suits what you're trying to do. You can work with mail in your folders, for example, or you can also work with mail that you've received from a particular person. Here are three ways that Exchange lets you work with your mail:

■ *Inbox*—You'll normally use the Exchange Inbox to work with your mail. This lets you see each of your mail folders and the contents of the currently selected mail folder. You can use this view to send and receive mail and to organize your mail in folders.

■ *Find*—Exchange has a powerful search feature that lets you find messages using any combination of the sender, recipient, subject, and message body fields. It also has a more advanced feature that lets you search for messages based upon attributes such as file size and age. After you've searched your mail folders for a particular group of messages, you can work them in the Find window just like you do in the Inbox. This lets you reply to the messages you found, delete the messages you don't want, or move them into different folders.

■ *Personal Address Book*—It seems odd to consider the Address Book as a place to work with messages. Imagine that you have a list of folks to whom you want to send a message, however. You can pop up the Address Book, highlight each person's name, and click on the New Message button to create a new message that's already addressed.

▶ **See** "Searching for Mail in Your Mail Folders," **p. 275**

▶ **See** "Using the Address Book," **p. 271**

Rich Text Formatting

You don't have to settle for mail messages that look like they come straight off the teletype. RTF lets you use character formatting, bulleted lists, and paragraph alignment to format your message. You can create a very attractive mail message that looks similar to a word-processed document.

RTF doesn't work well if the recipient doesn't have a mail client that understands rich formatting, however. Microsoft Mail users are okay. But other mail clients may not display the special formatting or paragraph alignments. The result is usually poorly formatted text that contains no special character formatting.

Sending Rich Messages to Mailing Lists

Most mail list servers can't deal with rich formatted mail messages. The result is usually a message posted to the mailing list that contains poorly formatted text and attachments—not a good thing to do to a mailing list. The actual text of the message is usually okay, but the text formatting gets a bit messed up.

Sending a rich formatted message to a mailing list is an invitation to get flamed by the other subscribers. They consider it rude to post these types of messages to the list. Fortunately, you can disable rich messages for a particular mail address so that you don't accidentally send one to a mailing list. For more information, see the Troubleshooting guide in "Sending Internet Mail," later in this chapter.

Embedded Objects

You know that new technology has come of age when you don't even know that you're using it. OLE (object linking and embedding) is an example. You use OLE every day with Windows 95 and don't even know it. It's a key part of the desktop and desktop extensions. Internet Explorer uses OLE to host Web pages within its window. MAPI service providers have OLE interfaces. You're also familiar with embedding OLE objects inside of documents. You can embed an Excel spreadsheet inside of a Word document, for example. When you insert a picture in a document, you're actually using object embedding.

Exchange lets you embed OLE objects inside of mail messages, too. You can fire off a message to your relatives that contains a picture of yourself. You can send a message to your boss that contains the latest widget sales forecast. Better yet, you can insert in your mail message a "letter head" that you created with Micrografx Designer. The possibilities are endless. The only catch is that the recipient's mail client has to support OLE embedded objects, too.

So what's the difference between attaching a file to a message and embedding an OLE object in a message? When you attach a file to a message, you see the icon in the message. The recipient actually has to open the attachment and save it as a file. You actually see the contents of an embedded object in your message, however. If you insert a graph from an Excel spreadsheet in a mail message, for example, you'll see the actual graph in the message—not an icon. Figure 11.1 is a clear example of both an embedded object and an attached file.

FIG. 11.1

You see icons for file attachments and the actual contents of an embedded file.

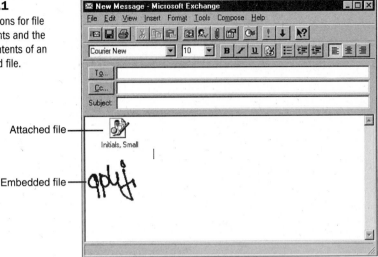

Attached file ——

Embedded file ——

TIP To learn more about how Windows 95 uses OLE, see *Platinum Edition Using Windows 95* (0-7897-0797-7), by Que.

Getting Ready to Use Exchange for Internet Mail

Do you already have Exchange installed? You probably know the answer to this off the top of your head. Just in case you're not sure, however, use the following steps to determine if you do have Exchange installed:

1. Look for the Inbox icon on your desktop. If you don't see it, you don't have Exchange installed on your computer.

2. If you do see the Inbox icon, right-click on it and choose Properties. If you see the dialog box shown in Figure 11.2, you don't have Exchange installed on your computer.

If you don't have Exchange installed, follow the instructions in the next section, "Installing Exchange." If you do have Exchange installed, skip the next section and move on to "Setting Up Internet Mail Service."

N O T E If you're an experienced Windows 95 and Internet user, you can skip the rest of this section and strike out on your own. Internet Mail service is available from Microsoft's FTP site at **ftp.microsoft.com/Softlib/MSLFILES/INETMAIL.EXE**. Download and run this file and follow the instructions that it installs in the Start menu under Programs, Accessories, Internet Tools. ■

FIG. 11.2
The instructions in this chapter use the Add/Remove Programs Control Panel applet because double-clicking on the Inbox icon, as instructed in this dialog box, produces inconsistent results.

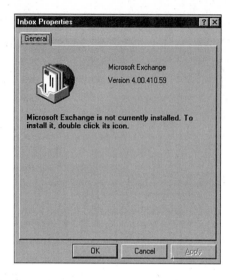

Installing Exchange

You can double-click on the Inbox icon to install Exchange. This produces different results, however, depending on how your computer is configured. Therefore, these instructions use the Add/Remove Programs Control Panel applet, which is more reliable. You'll need your Windows 95 CD-ROM or diskettes to install Exchange. Here's how:

1. Double-click on the Add/Remove Programs icon in the Control Panel, and Windows 95 displays the Add/Remove Programs property sheet.

2. Click on the Windows Setup tab. The tab should look similar to Figure 11.3.

FIG. 11.3
Note that if Microsoft Exchange has a check mark beside it, you have already installed Exchange.

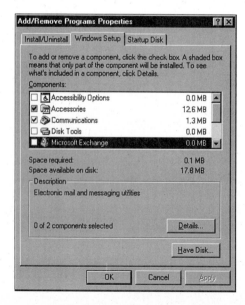

3. Select Microsoft Exchange by clicking on the box to its left until you see a check mark in the box.

4. Click on OK, and Windows 95 asks you for either the Windows 95 CD-ROM or disk number 6.

5. Insert the appropriate disk in the drive. Click on OK, and follow Windows 95's instructions. It shows you its progress as it copies Exchange's required files to your computer. Then it starts the Inbox Setup Wizard.

6. Click on Cancel when you see the Inbox Setup Wizard. Why? You don't want to configure your services until you've installed Internet Mail service in the next section. When the wizard asks you if you're sure, click on Yes.

> **N O T E** In some cases, you may already have Internet Mail service installed on your computer. In particular, most OEM computers (Compaq or Hewlett-Packard) have Internet Mail service preinstalled. You'll also have Internet Mail installed on your computer if you've installed Internet Explorer, as described in Chapter 17, "Using Microsoft Internet Explorer." If this is the case, don't click on Cancel. Instead, go directly to step 2 of "Configuring Exchange for the First Time," later in this chapter. ▓

Setting Up Internet Mail Service

Before configuring Exchange for Internet mail, you need to get Internet Mail service from Microsoft's FTP site. The following steps use the Windows 95 built-in FTP client. You don't need to understand how FTP works to use these steps, however (see Chapter 31, "Using FTP and Popular FTP Programs"):

1. Choose Run from the Start menu, type **ftp**, and press Enter. You'll see a window that looks similar to an MS-DOS window except that it displays the ftp> prompt.

2. Type **open ftp.microsoft.com** and press Enter. If you're using Dial-Up Networking and not already connected to the Internet, click Connect when you see the Connect To dialog box.

3. Type **anonymous** and press Enter when FTP prompts you for the user name. Then type your full mail address when FTP prompts you for your password. **jerry@honeycutt.com**, for example.

4. Type **cd /Softlib/MSLFILES** and press Enter when you see ftp> again. Note that Microsoft's FTP site isn't case-sensitive.

5. Type **get inetmail.exe** and press Enter. FTP copies Internet Mail service to your Windows 95 desktop.

6. Type **bye** and press Enter to log off of the FTP server and close the FTP window.

   ▶ **See** "Using FTP from the Command Line," **p. 809**

Part

III

Ch

11

Now that you've downloaded Internet Mail service from Microsoft's FTP site, you're ready to install it. Here's how:

1. On your desktop, double-click on Inetmail.exe. You don't need to copy this file into its own temporary folder because it expands its contents into Windows' temporary folder.

2. Click on Yes to confirm that you want to install Internet Mail service, and then Setup displays a license agreement.

3. Click on Yes to confirm that you accept the terms of the license agreement. Setup extracts the Internet Mail service files into Windows' temporary folder and installs them.

4. Click on OK to close Setup. Then restart your computer.

> **CAUTION**
>
> You must restart your computer before trying to configure Internet Mail service in Exchange.

Where do you go from here? If you've followed the steps in the previous section, you should have all of Exchange's required files installed on your computer, but you haven't yet configured Exchange. You should also see the Inbox icon on your desktop. You'll need to follow the steps in the next section, "Configuring Exchange for the First Time."

If you skipped the previous section, however, Exchange should be completely installed and configured to work with other mail services. You'll need to add Internet Mail service to your current profile, though. In this case, skip the next section and use the steps in "Adding Internet Mail Service to Exchange."

N O T E   Make sure that you have a working Internet connection before you try to configure Exchange for Internet mail. See Chapter 4, "Connecting Through a LAN with Windows 95 and Windows NT," to learn how to connect to the Internet via a network. See Chapter 5, "Connecting to a PPP or SLIP Account with Windows 95," to learn how to connect to the Internet via Dial-Up Networking. ▪

Configuring Exchange for the First Time   You've installed Exchange and Internet Mail service; you have a working Internet connection; and you've restarted your computer, right? Now you're ready to use the Inbox Setup Wizard to configure Exchange for the first time. Here's how:

1. Double-click on the Inbox icon on your desktop to start the Inbox Setup Wizard as shown in Figure 11.4.

2. Select Internet Mail service by clicking on the box next to it until you see a check mark. Make sure that any other services you find in this list are not selected so that you can follow these instructions closely. Then click on Next, to configure Internet Mail. The Inbox Setup Wizard asks you to select how you're connecting to the Internet.

3. Select Modem if you're using Dial-Up Networking to connect to your Internet service provider; otherwise, select Network. Click on Next. If you're using the Internet through a network, the wizard skips step 4.

4. Choose from the list the Dial-Up Networking connection that you use to connect to the Internet. You can also click on New, to create a new connection. Click on Next to continue, and you'll see the dialog box shown in Figure 11.5.

FIG. 11.4
This list shows all the mail service providers available on your computer. (Your list may be different from the one you see in this figure.)

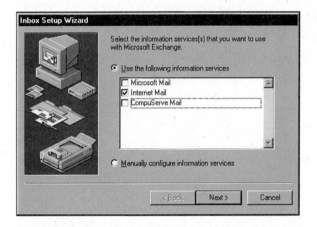

FIG. 11.5
If you're using different SMTP and POP3 mail servers, you can specify a different SMTP server after you've completed the Inbox Setup Wizard.

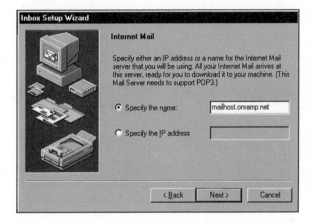

5. Select Specify the Name and then type the domain name of your Internet mail server. Alternatively, you can select Specify the IP Address and then type the IP address of your Internet mail server. Click on Next to continue.

6. Select Off-line to manually check your messages, or select Automatic to let Exchange automatically check your messages. Note that if you intend to use Microsoft Fax, I recommend that you manually check your messages because of an annoying bug in Exchange that causes Internet mail and Fax to compete for the modem every time you start Exchange. Click on Next to continue, and you'll see the dialog box shown in Figure 11.6.

7. Type your mail address and full name in the spaces provided. Your mail address includes your account name and mail server name. **jerry@honeycutt.com**, for example. Click on Next to continue.

FIG. 11.6
The name you type in Your Full Name is the name that recipients of your mail messages actually see.

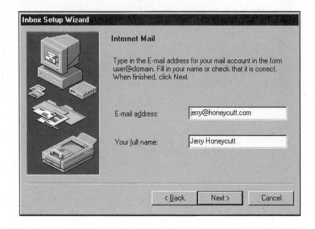

8. Type your account name and password in the spaces provided. Note that your account name and password are probably case-sensitive. Click on Next to continue.

9. Accept the default file name for your address book, or select a different file. If the file doesn't exist, the Inbox Setup Wizard creates it for you. Click on Next to continue.

10. Accept the default file name for your mail folders, or select a different file. If the file doesn't exist, the Inbox Setup Wizard creates it for you. Click on Next to continue.

11. You're finished! The Inbox Setup Wizard reports the services that you've configured, as shown in Figure 11.7. Click on Finish to close the wizard and load Exchange.

FIG. 11.7
This list reports only the mail services that you've installed. You also installed the Personal Address Book service and the Personal Folders service.

Adding Internet Mail Service to Exchange If you've already installed and configured Exchange, you can't use the Inbox Setup Wizard to install Internet Mail service. You'll use the Inbox property sheet, instead. Here's how:

1. Right-click on the Inbox icon that you'll find on your desktop and then choose Properties. Windows 95 displays the MS Exchange Settings tab, as shown in Figure 11.8.

FIG. 11.8

If you see Internet Mail in this list, select it and click on Properties, to configure Internet Mail service. You can skip steps 2 and 3.

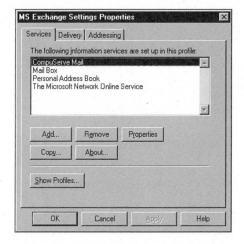

2. Click on Add to add a new mail service to your configuration. Windows 95 displays the Add Service to Profile dialog box.

3. Select Internet Mail from the list and then click on OK. Windows 95 displays the Internet Mail tab shown in Figure 11.9.

Part

III

Ch

11

FIG. 11.9

Click on Advanced Options if you're using different SMTP and POP3 mail servers, type the name of your SMTP server, and click on OK.

4. Type your full name, mail address, mail server, account name, and password in the spaces provided. Then click on the Connection tab to specify how you're going to connect to the Internet, as shown in Figure 11.10.

FIG. 11.10

If you're using Dial-Up Networking and you haven't created your connection yet, click on Add Entry to create it.

5. If you're using Dial-Up Networking to connect to the Internet, select Connect Using the Modem. Then select a Dial-Up Networking connection from the list, click on Login As, type your PPP user name and password, and click on OK. Otherwise—if you're connecting to the Internet via your network—select Connect Using the Network.

6. Click OK to save your changes to the Internet Mail Connection tab.

7. Click on OK to save your changes to the profile.

Getting Acquainted with Exchange

Using Exchange to send and receive Internet mail is just as easy as using any other Internet mail client. Even though Exchange may seem to have an overwhelming number of features, you really need only a few of them to send Internet mail.

This section shows you how to start and stop Exchange. It also shows you Exchange's main window, including its toolbar, folder pane, and message pane. You'll learn how to send and receive Internet mail messages, as well as other advanced tasks such as organizing your mail, in the sections that follow.

Starting and Stopping Exchange

You need to open Exchange before getting started. You can use either the Inbox icon or the Start menu, as shown here:

- Double-click on the Inbox icon that you'll find on your desktop, or
- Choose Programs, Microsoft Exchange from the Start menu.

Do you think two ways to start Exchange is more than enough? Well, you'll find three ways to close Exchange:

- Choose File, Exit from Exchange's main menu to close Exchange and leave your other messaging applications running, or
- Choose File, Exit and Log Off from Exchange's main menu to close Exchange and any other messaging applications such as Schedule+, or
- Click on the Close button in Exchange's caption bar. This is a quicker way to close Exchange. It's the same as choosing File, Exit from Exchange's main menu.

TROUBLESHOOTING

If Exchange crashes (which seldom happens; wink, wink), I can't restart it without restarting Windows 95. When Exchange crashes, it frequently leaves a task running called Mapisp32. Open the task manager by pressing Ctrl+Alt+Del. Be careful that you press this key combination only once, because the next time you press it your computer will reboot. End the task called Mapisp32 by selecting it and clicking on End Task. Another window will open asking you to confirm the deed, so click on End Task again. If a task called Inbox - Microsoft Exchange is running, end that task, too. You can now restart Microsoft Exchange.

Understanding the Main Window

If you've successfully installed and started Exchange, you'll see Exchange's main window as shown in Figure 11.11. Along the top of the window, you'll notice Exchange's menu and toolbar. The status bar is at the bottom of the window. The body of the window contains two panes. The left-hand pane shows all of your mail folders and the right-hand pane shows all of the messages contained in the currently selected mail folder.

N O T E   Exchange presents a lot of information in its window. If your computer limits you to a small monitor (laptop computers and such), you can see more information about each message if you hide the folder pane. Click on the Show/Hide Folder List button in Exchange's toolbar until all you see is the message pane. You can still change to a sub-folder by double-clicking on it in the message list. You can also change to a folder's parent folder by clicking on the Up One Level button.

Toolbar   You can do almost everything you'll want to do with Exchange by using its toolbar. Table 11.1 shows you the picture, name, and purpose of each button on the main window's toolbar. You can also customize this toolbar as described in "Customizing the Toolbars," later in this chapter.

FIG. 11.11

Exchange's main window is similar to Explorer's: folders in the left-hand pane and the contents of the selected folder in the right-hand pane.

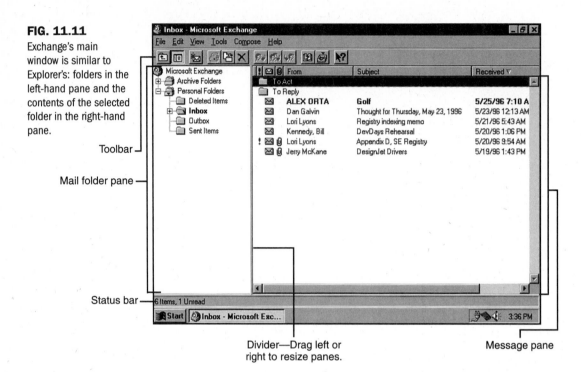

Toolbar

Mail folder pane

Status bar

Divider—Drag left or right to resize panes.

Message pane

Table 11.1 Exchange's Main Toolbar Buttons

Button	Name	Description
	Up One Level	Changes folder to the parent of the selected folder.
	Show/Hide Folder List	Toggles whether the mail folders are visible or not.
	New Message	Creates a new message.
	Print	Prints the selected message.
	Move Item	Selects a folder into which you want to move the selected message.
	Delete	Deletes the selected message.
	Reply to Sender	Replies to a message's sender.
	Reply to All	Replies to all addresses in To, From, and Cc fields of the selected message.

Button	Name	Description
	Forward	Forwards a message.
	Address Book	Opens the Address Book.
	Inbox	Changes folder to the Inbox.
	Help	Click select an object about which you want help.

T I P   You can see the name of each button by holding the mouse pointer over it for a few seconds until a *tooltip* pops up.

▶ **See** "Customizing the Toolbars," **p. 279**

Folder Pane   The folder pane contains all of Exchange's mail folders, as shown in Figure 11.12. At the very top of the pane, you see Microsoft Exchange, which contains all of the Personal Folders services (folder services) that you installed in Exchange. In this case, it contains services that I've named Archive Folders and Personal Folders. Exchange installs Personal Folders by default. I've added Archive Folders (to learn how to add folder services, see "Configuring Exchange," later in this chapter).

Part
III

Ch
11

FIG. 11.12

The folder pane uses a tree view just like Explorer. Click on a plus sign (+) to expand a branch or click on a minus sign (-) to close a branch.

Personal Folders services

Special purpose mail folders

Additional mail folders

Bold folder names indicate unread messages.

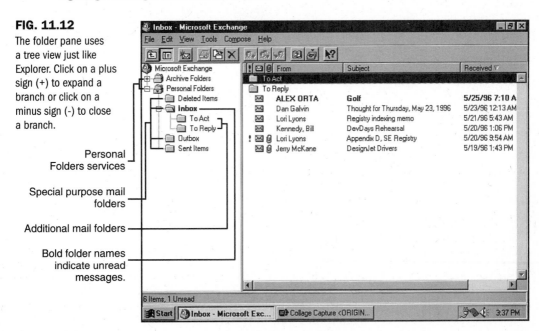

Each folder service contains any number of folders in which you can store mail messages. Only one of the folder services can contain the special-purpose mail folders, however. These include Deleted Items, Inbox, Outbox, and Sent Items. The service that contains these folders has an icon that's different from the others. Its icon contains the little down arrow. Here's the purpose of each special folder:

Deleted Items	The Deleted Items folder contains all of the messages you've deleted.
Inbox	The Inbox folder contains all of your incoming mail messages.
Outbox	The Outbox folder contains any new mail you've created, but not sent.
Sent Items	The Sent Items folder contains any messages that you've actually sent.

Message Pane   The message pane contains the contents of the selected mail folder, as shown in Figure 11.13. It can contain both sub-folders and message headers. Double-click on a sub-folder to display the contents of that folder. Double-click on a message header to see the contents of that message.

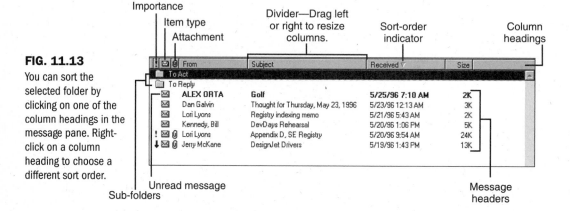

FIG. 11.13
You can sort the selected folder by clicking on one of the column headings in the message pane. Right-click on a column heading to choose a different sort order.

Did you notice that Exchange set one of the message headers in bold characters? If Exchange bolds a message's header, you haven't read the message. Likewise, if Exchange bolds a sub-folder's name, the sub-folder contains unread messages. This is Exchange's way of relentlessly reminding you to read your messages.

 TIP   Choose Edit, Mark as Read to mark a selected message (or messages) as read without actually opening the message.

Each folder has a number of columns (see Table 11.2). By default, the Inbox and any folders that you create have the following columns. The only difference between the Outbox and Sent Items folders and the other folders is that Sent Items folder substitutes the To column for the From column and the Sent column for the Received column.

Table 11.2   Column Headings and Their Descriptions

Icon	Name	Description
❗⬇	Importance	Indicates how important the sender thought his or her message was to you. You'll see an exclamation point for very important messages, a down arrow for unimportant messages, and nothing for normal messages.
	Item Type	Indicates the type of the item by displaying the icon associated with the document.
📎	Attachment	Indicates that the message has a file attachment, by displaying a paper clip in the column.
	From/To	Contains the display name, not the mail address, of the person who sent you the message or to whom you're sending the message.
	Subject	Contains the subject of the message.
	Received/Sent	Contains the date and time that you received the message in your Inbox or put the message in your Outbox.
	Size	Contains the total size of the message, including any attachments.

The *sort-order indicator* (the little arrow next to a column name) indicates that Exchange is sorting the folder by that column. If the arrow points down, the most recent messages are at the top of the list. If the arrow points up, the most recent messages are at the bottom of the list. See "Customizing a Mail Folder," later in this chapter, to learn how to sort a folder.

Part

III

Ch

11

Organize Documents in Exchange

Exchange is a great place to organize all of your important documents. You can put anything in a mail folder—not just a message. For example, you can store Word documents and .BMP files in mail folders. Then you can organize the documents and files just like you organize your mail messages. Figure 11.14 shows what the manuscript and artwork for this chapter look like when they're organized in a mail folder.

When you drag and drop a document into a mail folder, you see the document's icon in the Item Type column. The Subject column contains the actual file name (minus the extension) of the document. When you're ready to edit a document, you don't have to drag it back out of the mail folder. Just double-click on the document in the folder, and it'll open in the associated program. When you save the document, you're actually saving it back into the mail folder.

FIG. 11.14

You can customize the headings for folders in which you're storing documents, so that they make more sense for documents. See "Customizing a Mail Folder," later in the chapter.

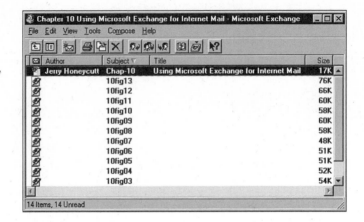

Working with Internet Mail

Internet mail is pretty straightforward. You'll send and receive mail messages. You'll also want to use an address book to keep all those nasty Internet mail addresses straight. And last, you'll want to organize your mail messages into folders so that you can easily find what you're looking for.

This section explores each of these activities in detail. It also contains a number of Troubleshooting guides that that help you solve many common problems with Exchange. If you're having a problem with Internet mail, see if the guides help you fix your problem before giving up and calling the support line.

Sending Internet Mail

 Sending a new mail message is easy. Click on the New Message button in Exchange's toolbar. As a result, you'll see the New Message window shown in Figure 11.15. Table 11.3 shows you what each toolbar button does. Note that the title of this window is initially "New Message," but Exchange changes the window's title after you type text in the subject line and move the cursor to a different field.

 TIP You can quickly send a file via the Internet. Right-click on the file in Explorer and choose Send To, Mail Recipient. Windows 95 opens the New Message window described in this section, with the file already attached to the message. Cool, huh?

FIG. 11.15
Mail messages that have signatures or other decorations look better when you use a fixed-width font such as Courier New. See "Using Internet Idioms to Add Internet Features," later in this chapter, for more information.

Send button ——

Carbon-copy addresses

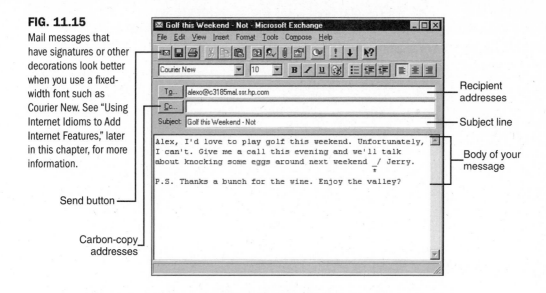

Recipient addresses

Subject line

Body of your message

Table 11.3   New Message Toolbar Buttons

Button	Name	Description
✉	Send	Puts the message in the Outbox folder to be transmitted later.
💾	Save	Saves the message in the current folder—don't send.
🖨	Print	Prints the message.
✂	Cut	Cuts the current selection to the Clipboard.
📋	Copy	Copies the current selection to the Clipboard.
📋	Paste	Pastes contents of the Clipboard at current cursor position.
📖	Address Book	Opens the Address Book.
👤	Check Names	Looks up partial addresses in the Address Book.
📎	Insert File	Inserts a file at the current cursor position.

continues

Part
III

Ch
11

Table 11.3   Continued

Button	Name	Description
	Properties	Opens property sheet for message.
	Read Receipt	Requests a read receipt.
	Importance: High	Sets or removes high importance.
	Importance: Low	Sets or removes low importance.
	Help	Clicks and select an object about which you want help.

Once the New Message window is open on your desktop, you need to fill in all the details. Use these steps:

1. Type in the To field the Internet mail addresses to which you want to send your message. Separate each address with a semicolon (;). Alternatively, you can click on the To button and then choose one or more addresses from the Address Book. See "Using the Address Book," later in this chapter, to learn how to use the Address Book.

2. Type in the Cc field the Internet mail addresses to which you want to send a carbon copy. Separate each address with a semicolon (;). Alternatively, you can click on the Cc button and then choose one or more addresses from the Address Book.

3. In the Subject field, type a brief description of the contents of your mail message. Your mail messages are more reader-friendly if you don't leave the Subject field blank, and you type an accurate description of the message's content.

4. Type the complete body of your message in the space provided. If you have Microsoft Word installed, consider spell-checking your message before sending. To do so, choose Tools, Spelling from the message's menu.

> **CAUTION**
>
> Even though you can rich format Internet mail with Exchange, don't do it—unless you know that the recipient is using a mail client that understands RTF. Most other mail clients don't know how to handle rich formatting. This can make it difficult for the recipient to read your message.

5. Click the Send button to place your message in Exchange's Outbox. Note that Exchange hasn't transmitted your message yet. It's queued up with the rest of your outgoing mail, waiting for you to connect to the mail server and to transmit.

Each time you create a new mail message, Exchange places the message in the Outbox folder. It doesn't transmit it to the mail server. You can accumulate a number of messages and then, when you're ready, transmit them all at once. Choose Tools, Deliver Now if Internet Mail is the only mail service you've installed in Exchange. Otherwise, choose Tools, Deliver Now Using, Internet Mail if you've installed multiple mail services such as CompuServe or Microsoft Mail. As a result, Exchange sends all the Internet mail messages that it finds in your Outbox folder to the mail server. It also retrieves to your Inbox all of the mail messages that it finds on the mail server —the subject of the next section, "Receiving Internet Mail."

▶ **See** "E-mail Privacy—Who Else Can Read Your E-mail?" **p. 55**

▶ **See** "Sending Encoded Files Using Microsoft Exchange," **p. 349**

TROUBLESHOOTING

I can receive mail from the server just fine, but why can't I send any? Did your service provider give you a different server for SMTP than for POP3? If so, select Tools, Services from Exchange's main menu. Then select Internet Mail from the list and click on Properties. In the Internet Mail property sheet, click on Advanced Options. Type the name of the SMTP server and click on OK. Click on OK to save your changes to your Internet Mail settings and then click on OK again to return to Exchange's main window.

A recipient of my mail messages reports that the messages have equal signs (=) at the end of each line. This is a common complaint when posting a message to a mailing list. There are two ways to fix this. First, make sure that you disable RTF for the recipient by disabling Always Send Message in Microsoft Exchange Rich Text Format in the recipient's Address Book entry. Second, choose Tools, Services from Exchange's main menu; select Internet Mail from the list and click on Properties; click on Message Format on the General tab; click on Character Set; change the character set to US ASCII; and then click on OK four times to save your changes and close all the open dialog boxes.

Part

III

Ch

11

Receiving Internet Mail

Receiving your Internet mail is easier than creating and sending it. Each time Exchange transmits your mail, it also retrieves your new mail, so you'll use the same steps that you learned in the previous section. Choose Tools, Deliver Now if Internet Mail is the only mail service you've installed in Exchange. Otherwise— if you've installed multiple mail services—choose Tools, Deliver Now Using, Internet Mail. As a result, Exchange sends to the mail server all the Internet mail messages it finds in your Outbox folder. It also retrieves all of the mail messages it finds on the mail server to your Inbox.

Exchange stores your new messages in the Inbox folder. In addition, Exchange sets in bold characters the message header of any message that you haven't read. Makes them kind of hard to miss, eh? Exchange also puts the New Mail icon in the taskbar. Double-click on a message header to open the message in its own window, as shown in Figure 11.16. Table 11.4 shows you what each button in the message's toolbar does. When you're finished reading the message, click on the window's close button to close it.

T I P Are you tired of getting messages with inaccurate subject lines? Change a new message's subject to fit its content. When you close the message, Exchange asks you if you want to save the changes. Click on Yes.

Date/time sent   Close—Click to close message.

FIG. 11.16
Except for the subject line, you can't change any of the header information for a message you've received.

Carbon-copy addresses

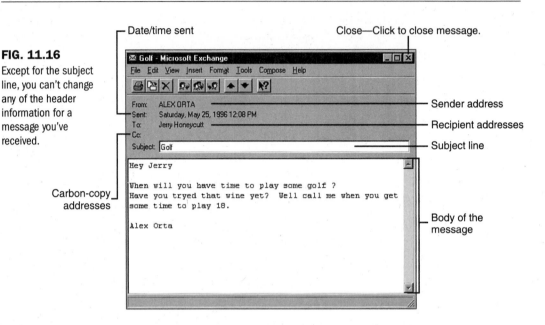

Sender address

Recipient addresses

Subject line

Body of the message

Table 11.4 New Message Toolbar Buttons

Button	Name	Description
	Print	Prints the message.
	Move Item	Selects a folder into which you want to move the selected message.
	Delete	Deletes the message.
	Reply to Sender	Replies to the message's sender.
	Reply to All	Replies to all addresses in the To, From, and Cc fields.
	Forward	Forwards the message.
	Previous	Opens previous message in list.

Button	Name	Description
▼	Next	Opens next message in list.
▶?	Help	Click and select an object about which you want help.

There's a lot more to do than just look at your new message all day long. You can print, organize, and reply to it, among other things. You can also navigate to other messages in the folder, without actually closing the message window. That is, you don't have to close the current message before viewing another. Table 11.5 lists the more common activities that you'll do from a message window.

Table 11.5   Message Window Toolbar Buttons

Icon	Name	Description
🖨	Print	Click on the Print button to print the message to the current printer. Note that Exchange doesn't prompt you for the printer.
📂	Move	Click on the Move Item button to open the Move dialog box, as shown in Figure 11.17. Select the target folder from the list and then click on OK. Exchange moves the message from its current folder into the folder you selected.
✕	Delete	Click on the Delete button to delete the message and move to the previous or next message, depending on your settings in the Read tab of the Options property sheet (for more information, see "Configuring Exchange"). Note that when you delete a message, you're actually moving it to the Deleted Items folder. If you regret deleting a message, you can drag it back out of the Deleted Items folder to any other folder.
↩	Reply	Click on the Reply to Sender button to reply to only the person who sent the message. Alternatively, click on the Reply to All button to reply to every address in the Sent, To, and Cc fields. As a result, Exchange opens a New Message window with the contents of the original message indented and the To and Cc addresses prefilled. Clicking on the Forward button is similar to clicking on the Reply button, except that it leaves the addresses blank so that you can forward the message to a different address.
▲ ▼	Navigate	Click on the Previous button to open the previous message in the current window, or click on the Next button to open the next message in the current window. The message window closes when you reach the beginning or end of the list.

Part

III

Ch

11

FIG. 11.17
Don't double-click on a folder that contains sub-folders in order to expand the branch. The OK button is the default button on this dialog box. Thus, double-clicking will cause the message to immediately move to the folder you selected.

 TIP

When you reply to a mail message, delete as much of the original message as you can while still leaving enough so that the recipient knows what you're replying to. This makes the message easier for the recipient to read, because that person doesn't have to wade through a bunch of stuff he or she doesn't care about anymore. Besides that, it's just a thoughtful thing to do.

▶ **See** "Handling Unwanted E-mail," **p. 238**

TROUBLESHOOTING

I can send a message to other people. They can send a message to me, too. But when they reply to a message I send them, I don't get anything back. Select Tools, Services from the Exchange main menu. Then select Internet Mail in the list and click on Properties. Look at the E-mail Address field—is it correct? This is the address that other people will use when they reply to your message. Click on OK to save any changes that you make. Click on OK again to return to Exchange's main window.

I choose Save Password when Exchange asks for my password. Regardless, every time I check my Internet mail, Exchange asks me for my password again. Windows 95 keeps all your passwords tidy by storing them in a password list (those PWL files in your Windows folder). You gain access to this password list by typing your name and password when you first log onto Windows 95. If you bypass the logon prompt by pressing Esc, then Exchange can't find your password list. Thus, it prompts you for your password again. Also, if you didn't type a password when you first installed Windows 95, Windows 95 won't maintain a password list for you. Look for a file in your Windows folder with the PWL extension whose name is the same as your logon name. Delete this file and then restart Windows 95. This time, type a password when Windows 95 asks.

Exchange hangs up while checking my mailbox, or it tells me that the mail server "timed out." When you check your mailbox on the mail server, the mail server runs a special program called a *POP*. If your computer crashes while you're checking your mail, this program will continue running—even if you're not connected. The next time that you try to check your mail, the mail server won't respond to Exchange; this is called *timing out*. This problem is frequently called *pop-lock*. The only thing that you can do about it is call your service provider and have it kill the running POP. You can also just wait patiently, as most providers have a process that detects these renegade POPs and removes them.

Using the Address Book

Remember the address from the previous sections? **alexo@c3185mal.ssr.hp.com**. You definitely don't want to have to remember and type that every time you send a message to Alex. Even my mail address, **jerry@honeycutt.com**, is too much to type every time. That's why Exchange comes with the Personal Address Book service. With the Address Book, you can store your frequently used addresses by name. You can store my mail address as Jerry Honeycutt, for example. Likewise, I can store Alex's mail address as Alex Orta. An added bonus is that you're less likely to incorrectly type a mail address—thus, you'll have fewer returned messages.

 To open the Address Book, click on the Address Book button in Exchange's main toolbar. You'll see the Address Book window shown in Figure 11.18. Table 11.6 shows what each toolbar button does.

FIG. 11.18

You can do an incremental search of the Address Book by typing the first few characters of a name in Type Name or Select from List. Exchange highlights the closest matching entry after each character.

Incremental search

Available mail addresses by name

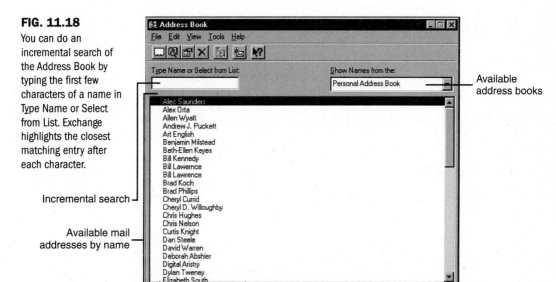

Available address books

Part
III

Ch
11

Table 11.6   New Message Toolbar Buttons

Button	Name	Description
	New Entry	Creates a new Address Book entry.
	Find	Searches the Address Book for entries containing a string.
	Properties	Enables you to view and change properties for the selected Address Book entry.

continues

Table 11.6   Continued

Button	Name	Description
	Delete	Deletes the current Address Book entry.
	Add to Personal Address Book	Adds an address from a different address book to the Personal Address Book.
	New Message	Composes a new message that is preaddressed to the selected addresses.
	Help	Enables you to select an object about which you want help.

▶ **See** "Sending E-mail to Online Service Users," **p. 238**

Adding New Internet Mail Addresses   Like most things you do in Exchange, you'll find an easy and a hard way to add an entry to the Address Book. First, the easy way: right-click on an address in a message and then choose <u>A</u>dd to Personal Address Book. That's all there is to it. Now, the hard way:

1. Click on the New Entry button in the Address Book. Exchange displays a dialog box that lets you pick which kind of address you're adding.
2. Select Internet Mail Address from the list and then click on OK. Exchange displays the New Internet Mail Address Properties dialog box shown in Figure 11.19.

FIG. 11.19
Don't select Always Send Messages in Microsoft Exchange Rich Text Format unless you're absolutely sure that the recipient's mail client can handle RTF.

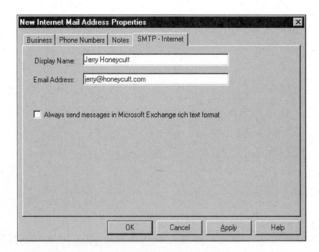

3. Type the person's real name in Display Name, and his or her Internet mail address in Email Address.
4. To save your new mail address, click on OK.

Using a Mail Address from the Book   Remember those T<u>o</u> and <u>C</u>c buttons in the New Message window? When you click on one of these buttons, Exchange opens an Address Book window (see Fig. 11.20) that lets you select the address you want to use in your mail message. You can click on either button to select names for both T<u>o</u> and <u>C</u>c. Select an address from the list and then click on T<u>o</u>-> to add it to the To address list. You can also add names to the Cc address list by selecting an address from the list and then clicking on <u>C</u>c->. When you're finished selecting mail addresses, click on OK.

FIG. 11.20

You can add new entries on the fly by clicking on <u>N</u>ew. You can change existing entries by selecting them and then clicking on P<u>r</u>operties.

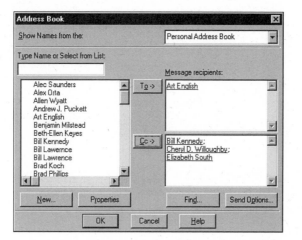

 T I P   Exchange provides a much quicker way to add addresses to your mail message. Type a portion of the name, the first three or so characters, and then press Alt+K. Exchange looks for the closest match in the Address Book and substitutes it for the partial name you provided. If I type **Jerry** and press Alt+K, for example, Exchange substitutes Jerry Honeycutt in the address field. Even better, if I type **Cheryl W** and press Alt+K, Exchange finds Cheryl D. Willoughby in the Address Book. If Exchange finds more than one address that matches, it pops up a dialog box that contains all the matches it found. Choose one from the list.

Working from the Address Book   Believe it or not, you can use the Address Book for your mail client. Why? Imagine that you're on a mail rampage. You have a list of 20 people to whom you want to send messages. In some cases, you want to address a single message to five or more individuals. You can do this all from Exchange's main window, but you can do it faster from the Address Book. Here's how:

1. Open the Address Book.

2. Select each name that you want to include in your mail message's address by holding down the Ctrl key while clicking on each name.

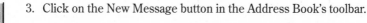 3. Click on the New Message button in the Address Book's toolbar.

Part

III

Ch

11

Exchange opens a New Message window that's preaddressed with the names that you selected in step 2. Type the subject and body of your message and then click on the message's Send button.

 TIP You can open the Address Book directly from Windows 95, bypassing Exchange's main window, by creating a shortcut to Exchng32,exe and adding **/a** to the end of the command line.

Organizing Your Mail

By default, Exchange installs a single folder service called Personal Folders that contains the Deleted Items, Inbox, Outbox, and Sent Items folders. Imagine receiving a few hundred messages—all of them stored in your Inbox folder because you don't have anywhere else to stash them. Yep, things will get out of hand pretty quick.

Exchange lets you create as many folders as you like so that you can store all those mail messages. You can also *nest* folders as deep as you like. That is, you can create a folder inside of another folder. By creating nested folders, you can organize your mail messages by category, company, subscription, or whatever. It largely depends on your own taste and needs.

Adding and Using Mail Folders   Creating a new folder is easy. In the folder pane, select the folder under which you want to create a new folder. Then choose File, New Folder from Exchange's main menu. Type the name of the folder in the New Folder dialog box and then click on OK. When you're ready to copy a mail message into a folder, select the folder that contains the message you want to copy. Then drag the message from the message pane onto the target folder and drop it.

Here are some more suggestions for using mail folders in Exchange:

■ Create a folder called Subscriptions that has a single sub-folder for each mailing list and newsletter subscription you receive. Save the original reply to your subscription in Subscriptions, and save each mailing from the list or newsletter in the appropriate sub-folder.

■ Create a folder for a company that you work with. Then create a sub-folder for each project you're working on. Put general company mail in the company's main folder and put mail for each project in that project's folder.

■ Create two folders under the Inbox folder called To Act and To Reply. When you receive a message that requires an action or a reply that you can't get to immediately, stash the incoming message in either folder. These messages will nag you forever or until you take action—whichever comes first. When you're ready to act or reply to a message, move it to a different folder.

▶ **See** "What Are Internet Mailing Lists?" **p. 330**

Customizing a Mail Folder   Each and every mail folder keeps track of its own settings. You can change a mail folder's sort order, for example, and it'll remember it apart from the sort order of other mail folders. You can also change the actual columns that each folder displays. Changing a folder's sort order is easy. Right-click on the column by which you want to sort and then choose either Sort Ascending or Sort Descending. You'll see a little arrow next to the column you're sorting by.

Changing the columns that a folder uses is more complicated, but doable. Here's how:

1. In the folder pane, select the folder you want to change.

2. From Exchange's main menu, choose View, Columns. Exchange displays the Columns dialog box shown in Figure 11.21.

FIG. 11.21
If things get a bit out of hand, you can restore the folder's default columns by clicking on Reset.

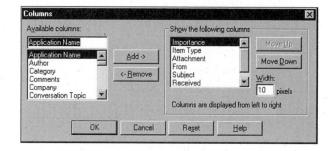

3. Add any columns you want to display for this folder by selecting each column in Available Columns and then clicking on Add->. The column name moves from the left-hand box to the right-hand box.

4. Remove any columns you don't want to display for this folder by selecting each column in Show the Following Columns and then clicking on <-Remove. The column moves from the right-hand box to the left-hand box.

5. Change the order of the folder's columns by selecting each column you want to arrange in Show the Following Columns, and then clicking on Move Up to move the folder up in the list or Move Down to move the folder down in the list.

6. Click on OK to save your changes.

Searching for Mail in Your Folders

After you've accumulated a few hundred messages (it happens), finding a message you need in a hurry can be quite frustrating. You open up this folder and that folder—looking at the long list of messages and trying to identify the one you want by its subject line. We both know how useful subject lines frequently are, right?

Thankfully, you can use Exchange's Find to locate a message. You can use it to search by any combination of the From, To, and Subject fields, as well by as any text in the body of the message. Here's how:

1. In Exchange's folder pane, select the folder in which you want to search.

2. From Exchange's main menu, choose Tools, Find. Exchange displays the Find window, as shown in Figure 11.22.

Part
III

Ch
11

FIG. 11.22
You can stop a search before it's finished by clicking on Sto**p**.

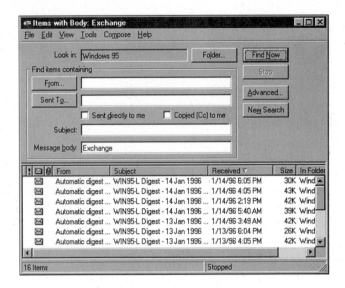

3. Fill in any combination of the F**r**om, Sent T**o**, Subject, and Message **B**ody fields. In addition, to find only those messages that are addressed to you as opposed to copied to you, you can check Sent **D**irectly to Me; to find only those messages that are copied to you, you can check Cop**i**ed (Cc) to Me.

4. To start your search, click on Find **N**ow. Find displays the results (refer to Fig. 11.22). You can do almost anything you'd like to each message, such as replying to it or moving it to another folder, by right-clicking on it.

 You can open the Find window directly from Windows 95, by-passing Exchange's main window, by creating a shortcut to EXxchng32.exe and adding **/s** to the end of the command line.

Customizing Exchange

Exchange is easily the most customizable Internet mail client you'll find. It's incredible. You can use third-party add-ons to enhance it. You can change a plethora of settings that affect how you send and receive messages. You can even customize each toolbar in Exchange. And you've already learned how to customize folders.

This section shows you how to do the most popular Exchange customizations. It doesn't give you step-by-step instructions, however, because customizing Exchange has far too many possibilities. Experiment and enjoy.

Using Internet Idioms to Add Internet Features

Internet Idioms is an add-on for Exchange that makes Exchange a bit more Internet-friendly. It adds a tab to the Options property sheet (**T**ools, **O**ptions) that lets you change the font used for incoming messages, append a signature to the end of each outgoing message, and indent replies using a specific character. You can get your own copy of Internet Idioms at **www. halcyon.com/goetter/inetxidm.htm**. If you're unfamiliar with how to download a file from a Web page, see Chapter 17, "Using Microsoft Internet Explorer," or Chapter 18, "Using Netscape 3." Download Inetxidm.zip by clicking on the Intel link that you'll find halfway down the Web page. Here's how to install it:

1. Unzip Inetxidm.zip into a temporary folder so that you can easily clean up these files.

2. Copy Inetxidm.dill to C:\Windows\System. Don't forget to view hidden files in Explorer by choosing View, Options. Then select Show All Files and click on OK. Otherwise, you won't see Inetxidm.dill.

3. Double-click on Inetxidm.reg to merge its changes into the Registry.

Figure 11.23 shows the Internet Idioms tab on the Options property sheet.

FIG. 11.23
Internet Idioms makes Exchange behave more like traditional Internet mail clients.

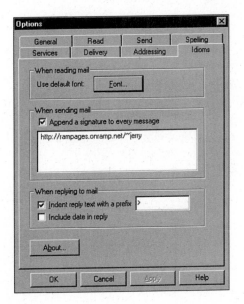

Part
III

Ch
11

Here's what you can do on the Internet Idioms tab:

- Click on Font to choose which font you want to use for incoming Internet messages. The best font for Internet mail is Courier New. Many folks who use mail signatures rely on a fixed-width font, such as Courier New, to format those interesting ASCII artworks such as this one:

```
                         -                        Jerry Honeycutt
             (o o)         http://rampages.onramp.net/~jerry
   —ooO—(_)—Ooo- - - - - - - - - - - - - - - - - - - - - - - - - -
```

- Click on Append a Signature to Every Message, and Internet Idioms will attach the signature you type in the space provided to each mail message you send.

- Select Indent Reply Text with a Prefix to indent the original contents of a message to which you're replying with the characters you type in the space provided.

- Select Include Date in Reply to include the date of the original message to which you're replying.

▶ See "Signatures," p. 723

Configuring Exchange

Exchange has an amazing variety of options that you can use to customize how Exchange works. Rather than describe each and every option, I'll describe what you'll find on each tab of the Options property sheet. Click Tools, Options to get to it. Here's what you'll find on each tab:

General	Contains options that determine what Exchange does when you receive a new message, what Exchange does when you delete a message, and what profile you'll use with Exchange.
Read	Contains options that determine what Exchange does when you delete a message that you're viewing and how Exchange handles the original message in a reply.
Send	Contains options that determine the default attributes of a new mail message, including its font; whether or not you want a receipt; its sensitivity; and its importance.
Spelling	Contains options that determine how the spell checker works. The spell checker is available only if you've also installed Microsoft Word.
Services	Contains each MAPI service provider that you've installed in Exchange. You can add additional services, including new folder services, by clicking on the Add button.
Delivery	Determines which folder service receives incoming mail messages. The chosen folder is the one that has the little down arrow in its icon and contains the Deleted Items, Inbox, Outbox, and Sent Items mail folders. It also determines the order in which each mail service is used to process an outgoing message.
Addressing	Determines which address book service Exchange uses. It also determines the order in which address books are searched for matching names when you press Alt+K.

TROUBLESHOOTING

I have a second Exchange mail file (files with the PST extension) that I want to merge into my current Exchange mail file. Exchange doesn't have an option to merge mail files, though. Sure it does. It's just very subtle. Add a second Personal Folders service to your configuration that points to your second Exchange mail file. Then you'll see both sets of mail folders in the Exchange window. Copy the messages and mail folders you're merging from the second set of mail folders to your first set of mail folders. Then remove the second folder service from your configuration.

I created a new Internet mail message and then transmitted all my mail. The message is still in the Outbox. It won't budge. Choose Tools, Options from Exchange's main menu and then click on the Delivery tab. Make sure that Internet Mail is at the top of the list, by selecting it and clicking repeatedly on the up arrow. This list determines the order in which mail services process a message. If you're (1), sending Internet mail; (2), have the Microsoft Network mail service installed; and (3), the Microsoft Network mail service appears before Internet Mail in this list, then Exchange waits to process Internet mail addresses with the Microsoft Network mail service because it knows how to handle Internet mail addresses, too. Thus, the Internet Mail service never gets a crack at your Internet Mail messages.

Customizing the Toolbars

Each and every window in Exchange has its own toolbar. You can change the toolbar for Exchange's main window, the New Mail window, the Find window, and the Address Book, for example. Here's how:

1. Choose Tools, Customize Toolbar from the window's main menu. You'll see the Customize Toolbar window shown in Figure 11.24.

2. Add any buttons you want to display on the toolbar by selecting each button in Available

FIG. 11.24

Keep in mind that each window's toolbar looks a bit different than Exchange's main toolbar.

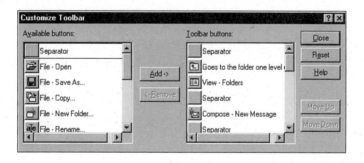

Buttons and then clicking on Add->. The button moves from the left-hand box to the right-hand box.

3. Remove any buttons you don't want to display for this folder by selecting each button in Toolbar Buttons and then clicking on <-Remove. The button moves from the right-hand box to the left-hand box.

4. Change the order of the buttons by selecting each button you want to arrange in Toolbar Buttons and then clicking on Move Up to move the button up in the list or Move Down to move the folder down in the list.

5. Click on Close to save your changes.

Using Microsoft Internet Mail

by Jerry Honeycutt

So, how did you end up here? Did you decide that you don't want to mess around with Microsoft Exchange's multiple mail services and profiles? Are you looking for a fast, lightweight, Internet-only mail client? Or are you just shopping around before you decide which Internet mail client you'll use? Doesn't matter. You've come to the right chapter. It shows you how to get a hold of and install one of the sleekest Internet mail clients available: Microsoft Internet Mail.

There are two schools of thought regarding software these days. First, many organizations believe that you have to stuff every possible feature into a program and make it so open that you can plug a square peg into a round hole. Second, others have come to realize that single-minded programs that do one job, and do it better than all the rest, are the way to go. Microsoft Internet Mail (Internet Mail) fits into the second category. It does only one thing. It sends and receives Internet Mail. It doesn't do faxes. It doesn't do CompuServe Mail and Microsoft Mail. It does Internet mail better than most other mail clients available, however. ∎

Download and install Microsoft Internet Mail

This chapter shows you how to download Microsoft Internet Mail and News. Installing it is easy, too.

Explore the Microsoft Internet Mail window

Most of Microsoft Internet Mail's features are available in its main window through the message pane, preview pane, toolbar, and icon bar.

Work with Microsoft Internet Mail

Sending and receiving Internet mail is easy. You'll learn more advanced tasks, too, such as organizing your mail into folders and using an address book.

N O T E If you buy into Microsoft's strategy for integrating the Internet into the Windows 95 desktop, and you don't need the additional features that Exchange offers, Internet Mail is a "must have." It's the first wave of Internet clients from Microsoft that will completely integrate into the Windows 95 desktop. Internet Mail already lets you view your mail messages through Windows 95's Explorer, for example. Other examples include Microsoft Internet Explorer (described in Chapter 17, "Using Microsoft Internet Explorer") and Microsoft Internet News (described in Chapter 28, "Using Microsoft News"). ■

▶ **See** "Using Microsoft Internet Explorer," **p. 379**

▶ **See** "Getting Ready to Use Microsoft Internet News," **p. 738**

Getting Ready to Use Microsoft Internet Mail

Internet Mail and Internet News come together in one file called Internet Mail and News (Mailnews95.exe or MailnewsNT.exe). If you've already installed the Internet Mail portion as described in Chapter 28, "Using Microsoft Internet News," you'll see the Internet Mail icon in My Computer, and possibly the Internet Mail shortcut on your desktop. If you have already installed Internet Mail, go directly to "Configuring Internet Mail," later in this chapter.

The Internet Mail and News file isn't on the NetCD (Microsoft is funny that way), so you'll have to download it from Microsoft's Web or FTP sites. Downloading it from Microsoft's Web site is the easiest of all. Point your Web browser at **http://www.microsoft.com/ie/iedl.htm**. Then click on the Download Software link and follow the instructions you see on the Web page to download Mailnews95.exe for Windows 95 or MailnewsNT.exe for Windows NT. You can save this file into any folder you like, because it expands its contents into Windows' temporary folder.

The next best thing is to download the file from Microsoft's FTP site. You need a working Internet connection to use the following steps, but you don't need to understand how FTP works (see Chapter 31, "Using FTP and Popular FTP Programs"):

1. Choose Run from the Start menu, type **ftp**, and press Enter. You'll see a window that looks similar to an MS-DOS window, except that it displays the ftp> prompt.

2. Type **open ftp.microsoft.com** and press Enter. If you're using Dial-Up Networking and are not already connected to the Internet, click Connect when you see the Connect To dialog box.

3. Type **anonymous** and press Enter when FTP prompts you for the username. Then type your full mail address when FTP prompts you for your password: **jerry@honeycutt.com**, for example.

4. Type **cd /Softlib/MSLFILES** and press Enter when you see ftp> again. Note that Microsoft's FTP site isn't case-sensitive, so you don't have to worry much about capitalization.

5. Type **get Mailnews95.EXE** and press Enter to download the Windows 95 version, or type **get MailnewsNT.EXE** and press Enter to download the Windows NT version. FTP copies Internet Mail service to your Windows desktop.

6. Type **bye** and press Enter to log off of the FTP server and close the FTP window.

▶ **See** "Using FTP from the Command Line," **p. 809**

N O T E Microsoft hasn't developed a Windows 3.1 version of Internet Mail and News. The company
has announced its intention to do so, however. When the Windows 3.1 version is available,
you can expect Microsoft to name the file something like Mailnews31.exe. Substitute this file name in
the instructions just given to download it. ▪

Installing Internet Mail

Internet Mail is so easy to install, it's almost vulgar. Internet Mail comes in a self-extracting,
self-installing file. You don't have to unzip the file, run the setup program, and clean up the
garbage it leaves behind. Here's how to install it:

1. Download Mailnews95.exe, as described in the previous section, if you haven't already.
2. Double-click on Mailnews95.exe to start the extractor, and it displays a license agreement for you to read. If you've just finished downloading the file, refresh the folder into which you downloaded it by pressing F5 to see the correct icon.
3. Click Yes to accept the license agreement. The extractor copies its files into Windows' temporary folder and runs the Internet Mail and News Setup Wizard.
4. Type your name and organization in the spaces provided. The Setup Wizard pre-fills these fields with the information you provided when you installed Windows. Click Next.
5. Click Next, again, to confirm your name and organization. The Setup Wizard displays the dialog box shown in Figure 12.1. This gives you the choice between installing Internet Mail, Internet News, or both.

FIG. 12.1
Internet Mail and
News works well with
Microsoft Exchange, so
you can safely install
both if you use
Exchange.

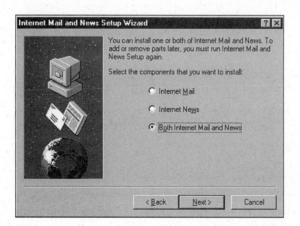

6. Select Internet Mail, Internet News, or Both Internet Mail and News. Then click Next to continue.
7. Click Next to install Internet Mail and News in the default folder. Otherwise, click Change Folder to install Internet Mail and News into a different folder; then, click Next.

8. Click Finish. The setup wizard installs the appropriate files onto your computer. It also copies some files into your C:\Windows\System folder.

9. Click OK once the setup wizard indicates that it's finished. Click Yes to restart your computer. You must restart your computer for the changes to take effect.

Configuring Internet Mail

Configuring Internet Mail is almost as easy as installing it. You need to know the name of your mail server, account name, and password. That's about it. After you answer a few well-thought-out questions, Internet Mail will pop up on your desktop for the first time. Use these steps to configure Internet Mail:

1. Double-click the Internet Mail shortcut that you'll find on your desktop. If you've already removed the shortcut from your desktop, you can choose Programs, Internet Mail from the Start menu. The Internet Mail Configuration wizard pops up, telling you that your Internet service provider gave you all the information you needed to configure the program. Click Next to continue, and you'll see the window shown in Figure 12.2.

FIG. 12.2

The name that you type in Name is the display name that recipients of your mail messages will see. The mail address you type in Email Address is the address to which those same recipients will reply.

2. Type your full name in Name and your mail address in Email Address. The mail address includes your account name and mail server name. Click Next to continue, and you'll see the window shown in Figure 12.3.

N O T E If you've registered your own mail domain, use that mail address in step 2. This ensures that folks replying to your mail are actually seeing your personal mail domain. For example, my actual mail address is **jerry@onramp.net**. I've registered my mail domain as **honeycutt.com**, however, so I type **jerry@honeycutt.com** in step 2.

FIG. 12.3

Usually, you'll use the same mail server for both POP3 and SMTP. Unless your Internet service provider explicitly gives you different server names, type the same name in both fields.

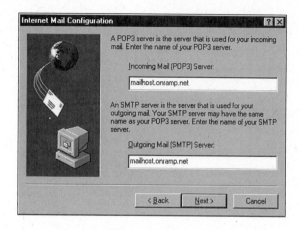

3. Type the name of your POP3 mail server in Incoming Mail (POP3) Server. Type the name of your SMTP server in Outgoing Mail (SMTP) Server. Click Next to continue, and you'll see the window shown in Figure 12.4.

FIG. 12.4

Your mail account is the name you use to log on to your mail server. It's not the name you use to log on to your PPP account. In many cases, both accounts use the same name.

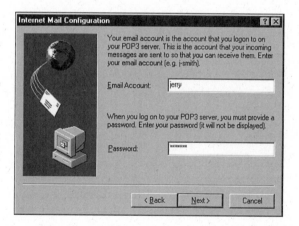

Part
III

Ch
12

4. Type your mail account name in Email Account, and type your password in Password. Click Next to continue, and setup displays a window that asks you about your connection.

5. Select I Use a LAN Connection if you connect to the Internet via your network, choose I Connect Manually if you connect to the Internet manually, or choose I Use a Modem to Access My E-mail and choose a connection from the list if you connect using Dial-Up Networking. Click Next to continue.

6. Click Finish to save your settings.

Getting to Know Microsoft Internet Mail

Internet Mail is a very straightforward mail client. Pretty much everything that you want to do is right there in its main window. You can perform various actions such as creating a message or checking your mail by clicking on the toolbar or icon bar. You can change folders and preview message headers in the message pane. You can even preview messages in the preview pane without opening the messages in their own window.

This section shows you how to start and stop Internet Mail. It also shows you Internet Mail's main window, including its toolbar and icon bar, message pane, and preview pane. In the sections that follow, you'll learn how to send and receive Internet Mail messages, as well as how to perform other advanced tasks such as organizing your mail into folders or maintaining your address book.

Starting and Stopping Internet Mail

You've already started Internet Mail once—to configure it. You may have even left it running on your desktop. You need to know about the different ways to start Internet Mail, however, so that you can choose the one that's right for you. Take a look:

- Double-click the Internet Mail shortcut that you'll find on your desktop. Internet Mail opens in its own window.

- Choose Programs, Internet Mail from the Start menu. Likewise, Internet Mail opens in its own window.

- Double-click the Internet Mail icon that you'll find in My Computer. If you've configured My Computer to browse folders in a separate window, Internet Mail opens in its own window. On the other hand, if you've configured My Computer to browser folders using a single window, Internet Mail opens in the current window.

- Open Windows 95 Explorer and select Internet Mail from the folder pane. Internet mail opens in the right-hand pane of Explorer, as shown in Figure 12.5.

> **TIP** In Figure 12.5, you're getting a glimpse of the famed "Nashville" Windows 95 update, which Microsoft intends to release later in 96. Nashville integrates the Internet into the desktop (more specifically, into the Explorer shell) using OLE technology.

Internet Mail certainly has a lot of options for getting at it. It has almost as many ways to shut it down, too:

- Choose File, Close from Internet Mail's main menu if Internet Mail is running in its own window. Alternatively, you can click the window's Close button (the one in the caption bar).

- Select a different folder in Windows 95 Explorer if Internet Mail is running inside of Explorer.

FIG. 12.5

You can also view UseNet newsgroups in Windows 95 Explorer by selecting Internet News in the folder pane.

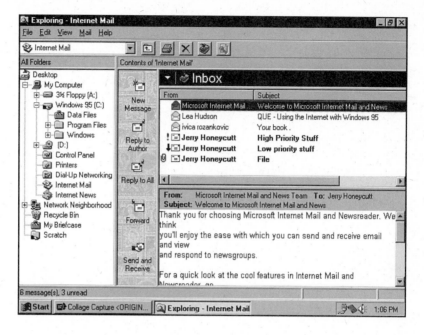

N O T E Make sure that you have a working Internet connection before you try to use Internet Mail. See Chapter 4, "Connecting Through a LAN with Windows 95 and Windows NT," to learn how to connect to the Internet via a network. See Chapter 5, "Connecting to a PPP or SLIP Account with Windows 95," to learn how to connect to the Internet via Dial-Up Networking. ■

Exploring the Main Window

Start Internet Mail now if you didn't leave it running on your desktop after installing it. Make sure that you open it in its own window so that you can better follow this chapter. You should see a window that looks similar to Figure 12.6. Along the top of the window, you see Internet Mail's menu and toolbar. Right under the toolbar, you see Internet Mail's icon bar. Internet Mail divides the rest of the window between the message pane on the top and the preview pane on the bottom.

The Toolbar Why does Internet Mail have a toolbar and an icon bar? Good question. There is a distinction between the two, however. The icon bar provides bigger actions—create a message or transmit mail to the server, for example. The toolbar provides smaller actions that apply to what you see in the window. Print or delete the current message, for example. Table 12.1 shows you the picture, name, and purpose of each button on the toolbar. You'll learn about the icon bar next.

Part III

Ch 12

FIG. 12.6

You can send and receive mail, organize mail in folders, and preview your messages from the main window.

Toolbar

Icon bar

Message pane

Divider—Drag to resize message and preview panes.

Preview pane

Status bar

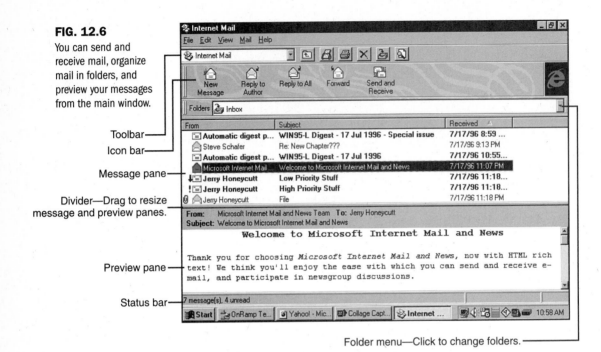

Folder menu—Click to change folders.

Table 12.1   Internet Mail Toolbar Buttons

Button	Name	Description
	Up One Level	Changes folders to the parent folder of the current folder.
	Print	Prints the selected message to the default printer without prompting.
	Delete	Deletes the selected message.
	Go to Inbox	Changes to the Inbox mail folder.
	Find	Searches for a message in the folder.

TIP You can see the name of each button by holding the mouse pointer over it for a few seconds until a *tooltip* pops up.

Did you notice the drop-down list box on the left-hand side of the toolbar? This lets you change back and forth between Internet Mail and Internet News, as shown in Figure 12.7.

FIG. 12.7
You can alternate between Internet Mail and Internet News—all in the same window.

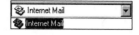

The Icon Bar   Whereas the toolbar performs very specific actions on a selected message or folder, the icon bar performs bigger actions such as sending a message or transmitting your mail to the mail server. You'll find five icons in the icon bar. Table 12.2 shows you each icon's picture, gives you its name, and tells you what it does.

Table 12.2   Internet Mail's Icon Bar

Icon	Name	Description
 New Message	New Message	Opens a new message window.
 Reply to Author	Reply to Author	Replies to the selected message.
 Reply to All	Reply to All	Replies to all the addresses in the selected message.
 Forward	Forward	Forwards the selected message.
 Send and Receive	Send and Receive	Exchanges mail messages with the mail server.

Part
III

Ch
12

User Interface Innovations?

Icon bars are Microsoft's latest and greatest user-interface innovation. Microsoft has demonstrated icon bars for a long time, but we're just now seeing them in products such as Internet Mail, Internet News, and Internet Explorer. If the icon bar bugs you (it does take up a lot of space), you can hide it by choosing View, Icon Bar until you don't see a check mark next to the Icon Bar menu item.

Alternatively, you can move the icon bar to a different part of the screen by putting your mouse pointer in the icon bar so that it's not on top of an icon. Your mouse pointer will change to an awkward-looking hand. Click and drag the icon bar to the top, bottom, left, or right side of the window.

The Folder List   Just like most Internet mail clients, Internet Mail lets you organize your mail messages into folders. The folder list (just above all your message headers) displays the icon and name of the current folder. You change folders by clicking anywhere on the folder list and then selecting a folder from the drop-down list, as shown in Figure 12.8.

FIG. 12.8

One of Internet Mail's weakest parts is that you can't nest folders in Internet Mail. So any folder that you add appears at the end of this list.

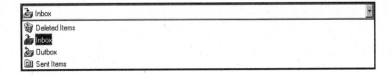

By default, Internet Mail uses four special-purpose folders: Deleted Items, Inbox, Outbox, and Sent Items. Here's what you'll find in each one:

Deleted Items	The Deleted Items folder contains all of the messages you've deleted.
Inbox	The Inbox folder contains all of your incoming mail messages.
Outbox	The Outbox folder contains any new mail you've created, but not sent.
Sent Items	The Sent Items folder contains any messages that you've actually sent.

The Message Pane   The message pane, shown in Figure 12.9, is the heart of Internet Mail. It contains all of the messages that are in the current folder. Double-click a message header to open the message in its own window. Better yet: select a message by clicking it once, and you'll see its contents in the preview pane. This way, you can quickly read each mail message by starting from the top and then tapping the down-arrow key to move the next message.

FIG. 12.9

You can sort the current folder by clicking one of the column headings in the message pane. Right-click a column heading to choose a different sort order.

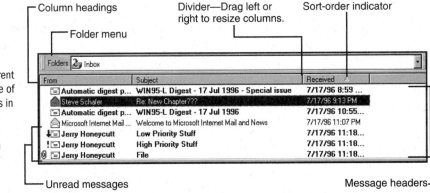

Internet Mail uses some special icons to indicate the contents, priority, and status of each mail message. Table 12.3 shows you what each icon represents.

Table 12.3   Icons in a Message Header

Icon	Name	Description
	Attachment	The message contains an attachment.
↓	Low Priority	The message is a low priority.
!	High Priority	The message is a high priority.
▢=	Envelope	You haven't read this message.
✉	Open Envelope	You have read (opened) this message.

> **T I P**   In addition to using the closed envelope to indicate that you haven't read a message, Internet Mail sets the message header in bold characters so that you can't miss it.

The Message Preview Pane   The preview pane displays the contents of the selected message so that you can quickly read a message or determine if you want to open a message in its own window. The top portion of the preview pane shows you the mail header (To, From, and Subject), as shown in Figure 12.10. You scroll the preview pane up and down to see the rest of your message.

FIG. 12.10

If you don't like the preview pane, you can get rid of it by choosing View, Preview Pane, None from Internet Mail's main menu.

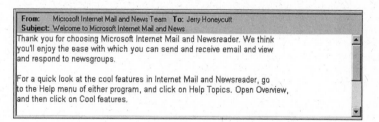

> **T I P**   You can hide the mail message's header information by choosing View, Preview Pane, Header Information until you don't see the check mark. Note that you'll have to open a message in its own window to extract its attachments if you hide the message header.

Working with Internet Mail

Using Internet Mail to send mail is easier than writing a letter to your mother. You address, write, and send the message just like a letter. You don't get hand cramps, though, and you don't pay any postage. You're out of excuses. Receiving Internet mail is even easier—you don't have to walk out to the mailbox.

The best part about Internet Mail is that it isn't prone to as many problems as the more complex Internet mail clients such as Exchange. It's a very straightforward program. This section shows you how to send and receive mail, send file attachments, use a signature with your mail, use the Address Book, and organize your mail into folders.

Sending Internet Mail

 With Internet Mail open on your desktop, click on the New Message icon in the icon bar. As a result, you'll see the New Message window shown in Figure 12.11. The title of the window changes as you type in the subject line.

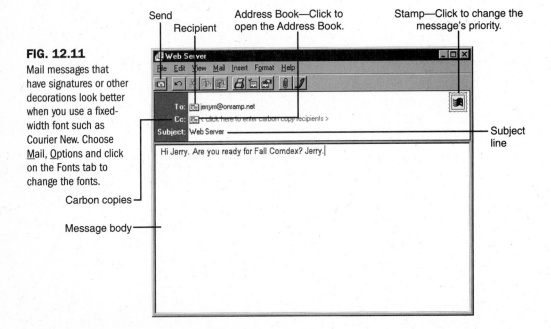

FIG. 12.11

Mail messages that have signatures or other decorations look better when you use a fixed-width font such as Courier New. Choose Mail, Options and click on the Fonts tab to change the fonts.

 If you're using a large desktop (800×600, for example), shrink the New Message window to about a quarter of your display's width. This makes sure that each line in your message breaks at a reasonable place, so that people with smaller desktops don't have to read a zig-zaggy message like this:

This is a sample of a message that is
sent from
a message window that is wider than the

recipient's
message window. It's harder to read,
huh?

The New Message window's toolbar contains a handful of useful buttons. Table 12.4 shows you the picture, name, and description of each button.

Table 12.4   New Message Window's Toolbar

Icon	Name	Description
	Send	Puts the message in the Outbox folder to be sent later.
	Undo	Undoes the last edit.
	Cut	Cuts the current selection to the Clipboard.
	Copy	Copies the current selection to the Clipboard.
	Paste	Pastes the contents of the Clipboard at the current location.
	Check Names	Looks up partial addresses in the Address Book.
	Pick Recipients	Opens the Address Book to pick addresses for To and Cc.
	Insert File	Attaches a file to this message.
	Insert Signature	Inserts your ASCII signature.

Once the New Message window is open on your desktop, you need to fill in all the details. Use these steps:

1. Type in the To field the Internet mail addresses to which you want to send your message. Separate each address with a semicolon (;). Alternatively, you can click the Pick Recipients button to select names from the Address Book. See "Using the Address Book," later in this chapter.

2. Type in the Cc field the Internet mail addresses to which you want to send a carbon copy. Separate each address with a semicolon (;). Alternatively, you can click the Pick Recipients button to select names from the Address Book.

3. Type in the Subject field a brief description of the contents of your mail message. Your mail messages are more reader-friendly if you don't leave the subject line blank, and you type an accurate description of the message's content.

4. Type the complete body of your message in the space provided. If you have Microsoft Word installed, consider spell-checking your message before sending. To do so, choose Mail, Check Spelling.

5. Click the Send button to place your message in Internet Mail's Outbox. You haven't transmitted your message yet. It's queued up with the rest of your outgoing mail, waiting for you to connect to the mail server and transmit.

N O T E The first time that you send a mail message, Internet Mail pops up an annoying reminder that you haven't yet transmitted your mail. Click Don't Show Me This Message Again to make sure it goes away forever. ▓

As you've read, each time you create a new mail message, Internet Mail places the message in the Outbox folder. The message waits there until you actually connect to the mail server and transmit your messages. Click the Send and Receive icon in Internet Mail's icon bar to do just that. As a result, Internet Mail sends all the messages it finds in your Outbox folder to the mail server. It also retrieves to your Inbox all the messages it finds on the mail server.

▶ **See** "E-mail Privacy—Who Else Can Read Your E-mail?," **p. 55**

▶ **See** "Using the Address Book," **p. 300**

▶ **See** "Sending Encoded Files Using Microsoft Exchange," **p. 349**

◆

TROUBLESHOOTING

I can receive mail from the server just fine, but why can't I send any? Did your service provider give you a different server for SMTP than for POP3? If so, select Mail, Options from Internet Mail's main menu and then click the Server tab. Type the name of your SMTP mail server in Outgoing Mail (SMTP), and click OK to save your changes.

Setting a Message's Priority   A mail message's priority tells the recipients how important you thought your message was to you or them. You can set a message's priority to low, normal, or high. Normal is the default. Click the stamp icon and then choose the priority of your message, as shown in Figure 12.12.

Attaching a File   Internet mail has a great advantage over other forms of communication. Besides being able to quickly fire off a message to anyone in the world, you can also send files to anyone in the world. Recipients usually get the files pretty quickly, too.

FIG. 12.12

Use High Priority
sparingly. If you send
too many high-priority
messages, other folks
will start to ignore your
pleas.

 Internet Mail supports both MIME and UUENCODE for file attachments. You don't have to
worry about those nasty details, however, because Internet Mail takes care of it all. Create a
message as described in the previous section. Before you send it, however, click the Insert File
button on Internet Mail's toolbar. Pick your file from the Insert Attachment dialog box, and
click Attach. The New Mail window will now show you your attachments in the attachment
pane, as shown in Figure 12.13. You can attach as many files as you like, too.

FIG. 12.13

You can use smaller
icons, or even a list
view, to show your
attachments. Right-
click anywhere in the
attachment pane and
then choose View,
Small Icons, or List.

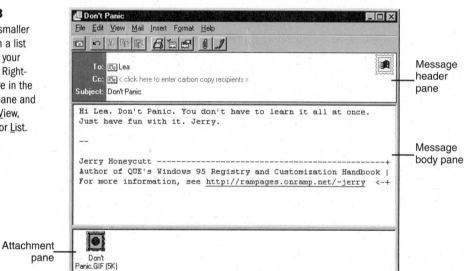

Message
header
pane

Message
body pane

Attachment
pane

▶ **See** "What Are File Encoding and Decoding, and Why Are They Needed?," **p. 348**

Adding a Signature to Your Message   Mail signatures are somewhat unique to Internet mail
and newsgroups. They express something interesting about yourself, such as a favorite quotation or hobby. Many people put the URL of their home page in their signature. Others use
fancy ASCII artwork for their signature. Here's what my mail signature looks like:

```
Jerry Honeycutt --------------------------------------------------+
Author of QUE's Windows 95 Registry and Customization Handbook ¦
For more information, see http://rampages.onramp.net/~jerry  <-+
```

Part

III

Ch

12

You can have Internet Mail automatically add a signature to every outgoing message, or you can insert it only when you feel that it's appropriate. Regardless, you have to configure Internet Mail so that it knows about your signature. Here's how:

1. Choose Mail, Options from Internet Mail's main menu. Internet Mail displays the Options property sheet.
2. Click the Signature tab.
3. Select Text and then, if you want to type your signature right there in the property sheet, type your signature in the space provided. Otherwise, select File and then click Browse to select a text file containing your signature.

 TIP Prevent frustration! Keep your signatures small—no more than three lines of text with, perhaps, a border.

4. Deselect Add Signature to the End of All Outgoing Messages if you want to manually choose when to use a signature.
5. Click OK to save your changes.

> **CAUTION**
>
> Unless you know exactly who is going to read your mail, I don't recommend putting your home address or telephone number in your signature. You don't want unexpected guests or strange telephone calls, do you?

 Now that you've configured Internet Mail, you're ready to start using your signature. If you told Internet Mail to automatically insert your signature at the end of every outgoing mail message, you don't have to do anything special. On the other hand, if you told Internet Mail not to automatically insert your signature, you have to click the Insert Signature button on the New Message's toolbar to insert your signature at the current cursor position.

What's in a Signature?

You'll encounter a variety of signatures on the Internet, particularly on UseNet newsgroups. Here are a few ideas for ASCII artwork to get you started, however:

```
 /\/\
(oo)
 \@

.oooO
  (   )   Oooo.
   \ (   (   )
    \_)   ) /
         (_/
        -
       (o o)
-oOo--(_)--Ooo--------------------+ jerry@honeycutt.com
                         +-------------------->
```
                                            Jerry Honeycutt

If you're looking for an even more raucous signature, check out the **alt.fan.warlord** newsgroup. The name is misleading. You can find the biggest and gaudiest signature on the Internet in this newsgroup. You'll pick up a few ideas, however.

More frequently, you'll come across very simple signatures that contain a favorite quotation or exalt some principle about which the author feels strongly. For example, you can see that some signatures are not beyond shameless self-promotion:

```
+----- ----- ----  ----  ---  ---  --   --   -    -         -+
¦ Jerry Honeycutt/jerry@honeycutt.com — — —+                  ¦
¦                                          v                  ¦
¦                        Buy Special Edition Using the Internet NOW ¦
+----- ----- ----  ----  ---  ---  --   --   -    -         -+
```

Receiving Internet Mail

Receiving Internet mail is easier than creating and sending it. Each time Internet Mail transmits your mail, it also retrieves your incoming mail. To send and receive mail, click the Send and Receive icon in Internet Mail's icon bar. As a result, Internet Mail sends to the mail server all the messages it finds in your Outbox folder. It also retrieves to your Inbox all the messages it finds on the mail server.

Internet Mail stores your new messages in the Inbox folder. In addition, you'll see the closed envelope icon next to each unread Internet mail message. Internet Mail also sets each unread mail message's header in bold characters. Double-click on a mail header to open the message in its own window, as shown in Figure 12.14. Table 12.5 shows you each button on the message's toolbar, including its picture, name, and purpose in life. When you're finished with the message, click the window's Close button to close it.

FIG. 12.14

Internet Mail doesn't let you change the message's mail header or contents. The message is read-only.

Recipient addresses

Subject line

Message body

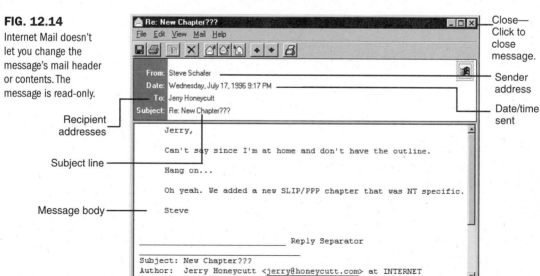

Close—
Click to close message.

Sender address

Date/time sent

Table 12.5 New Message Toolbar Buttons

Button	Name	Description
	Save	Saves the message as a text file.
	Print	Prints the message.
	Copy	Copies the message to the Clipboard.
	Delete	Deletes the message.
	Reply	Replies to the message's sender.
	Reply All	Replies to all addresses in the To, From, and Cc fields.
	Forward	Forwards the message.
	Previous	Opens previous message in list.
	Next	Opens next message in list.

 TIP First, look at a message in the preview pane. If it's a short message, you don't need to open it in its own window. In addition, you may find that you don't want to read the message at all (message screening?).

As you can see from the message's toolbar, Internet Mail provides a lot of actions you can do from the message window. You can print, organize, and reply to a message. You can also navigate to other messages in the current folder without actually closing the message window. Here are some of the more common activities that you'll do in message window:

Icon	Name	Description
	Print	Click the Print button to print the message to the current printer. Note that Internet Mail doesn't prompt you for the printer.
	Delete	Click the Delete button to delete the message and move to the next message. Note that when you delete a message, you're actually moving it to the Deleted Items folder. If you regret deleting a message, you can move it back out of the Deleted Items folder to any other folder.

Icon	Name	Description
	Reply	Click the Reply to Sender button to reply to only the person who sent the message. Alternatively, Click the Reply to All button to reply to every address in the Sent, To, and Cc fields. As a result, Internet Mail opens a New Message window with the contents of the original message indented and the To and Cc addresses prefilled. Clicking the Forward button is similar to clicking the Reply button, except that clicking the Forward button leaves the addresses blank so that you can forward the message to a different address.
	Navigate	Click the Previous button to open the previous message in the current window, or click the Next button to open the next message in the current window. The message window closes when you reach the beginning or end of the list.

▶ **See** "Handling Unwanted E-mail," **p. 238**

TROUBLESHOOTING

Internet Mail hangs up while checking my mailbox, or it tells me that the mail server "timed out."
When you check your mailbox on the mail server, the mail server runs a special program called a *POP.*
If your computer crashes while you're checking your mail, this program will continue running—even if
you're not connected. The next time that you try to check your mail, the mail server won't respond to
Internet Mail; this is called *timing out.* This problem is frequently called *pop-lock.* The only thing that
you can do about it is call your server provider and have it kill the running POP. You can also just wait
patiently, as most providers have a process that detects these renegade POPs and removes them.

Saving Attachments   You can handle messages containing file attachments two different
ways. You can immediately launch an attachment by clicking the paper clip icon and choosing
one of the attachments. Figure 12.15 shows you an example. Internet Mail executes the file by
loading it in the associated program. It launches a .bmp file in Microsoft Paint, for example.

If you want to save the attachment to your disk, open the message containing the attachments
in its own window. Remember, double-click the messages header in Internet Mail's message
pane. Internet Mail divides the message window into three panes, instead of two: message
header, message body, and attachment. Right-click one of the attachments, as shown in Figure
12.16, and choose Save As to save the attachment to your disk.

FIG. 12.15
If you've hidden the mail header, you won't be able to launch attachments this way. Choose View, Preview Pane, Header Information until you see the check mark.

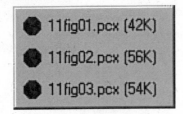

FIG. 12.16
You can save only one attachment at a time. You can open all the attachments, however, by selecting them all, right-clicking one of them, and choosing Open.

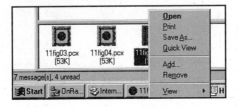

Using the Address Book

Internet mail addresses are cumbersome. That's just the way it is. Trying to remember that Widgy's address is **cwidgy@srr.iz.widget.com** is asking too much. You don't have to remember addresses like this when you send a mail message, however. Typing **Jerry** is definitely easier than typing **jerry@honeycutt.com** every time you want to send me a message, isn't it? Well, Internet Mail comes with an Address Book that lets you associate real names you can remember with Internet mail addresses (*aliases*). Just as in the previous example, you don't have to type as much, and you're less likely to have mail returned to you because you're not going to be as prone to making typos.

Choose File, Address Book from Internet Mail's main menu. There isn't a corresponding toolbar button.

Adding New Internet Mail Addresses   You'll find two ways to add addresses to Internet Mail's Address Book. First, right-click a mail address within a message window and then choose Add to Address Book. Internet Mail adds the address you selected using its current display name (the name you see in the message) and its underlying Internet mail address. You can also add addresses manually, which you'll want to do when you first set up Internet Mail, so that your favorite mail addresses are immediately available. Here's how:

1. Choose File, Address Book from Internet Mail's main menu to open the Address Book.
2. Click the New Contact button to open the Properties dialog box.
3. Type the person's first name and last name in the spaces provided. Then, type the person's mail address in E-Mail Address, and click Add.
4. Click OK to save your new mail address.
5. Choose File, Close from Address Book's main menu to close the Address Book.

Using a Mail Address from the Book   It's far better to use an entry from your address book than it is to type the address in by hand. With a New Message window open on your desktop, click the Pick Recipients button on the message's toolbar. Internet Mail pops open the Select Recipients window, shown in Figure 12.17. You can add names to both your To or Cc lists. Select an address from the list and then click To-> to add it to the To address list. You can also add names to the Cc address list by selecting an address from the list and then clicking on Cc>. Click OK when you finish selecting mail addresses.

FIG. 12.17
You can add new entries on the fly by clicking New Contact. You can change existing entries by selecting them and then clicking Properties.

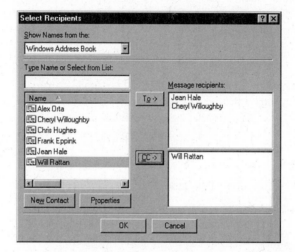

 TIP   Internet Mail provides a much quicker way to add addresses to your mail message. Type a portion of the name, the first three or so characters, and then press Alt+K. Internet Mail looks for the closest match in the Address Book and substitutes it for the partial name you provided. If I type **Jerry** and press Alt+K, for example, Internet Mail substitutes Jerry Honeycutt in the address field. Even better, if I type **Cheryl W** and press Alt+K, Internet Mail finds Cheryl D. Willoughby in the Address Book. If Internet Mail finds more than one address that matches, it pops up a dialog box that contains all the matches it found. Choose one from the list.

Part
III

Ch
12

Organizing Your Mail

When you first installed Internet Mail, it set up four mail folders for free (say that one real fast): Deleted Items, Inbox, Outbox, and Sent Items. You didn't have to create these special-purpose folders.

These folders aren't enough, however. If you get a handful of messages a day, your Inbox is going to get pretty ugly. Internet Mail lets you create additional mail folders, however, so that you can stash the mail that you want to save. As for the rest: I recommend deleting them.

Adding and Using Mail Folders   Internet Mail lets you create as many folders as you like. You can't nest mail folders, however. This makes true organization a bit of a pain. To create a new mail folder, choose File, Folder, Create from Internet Mail's main menu. Then type the name of your folder and click OK. You'll see your new folder in the folder list in the message pane.

When you're ready to move a mail message into a folder, right-click the message that you want to move, choose Move To, and then select the target folder from the sub-menu. Alternatively, you can copy a message by choosing Copy To. Internet Mail doesn't provide a way to drag and drop mail messages into folders.

Customizing a Mail Folder   Each and every mail folder keeps track of its own settings. You can change a mail folder's sort order, for example, and it'll remember that sort order apart from the sort order of other mail folders.

Changing a folder's sort order is easy. Right-click the column by which you want to sort and then choose either Sort Ascending or Sort Descending. The *sort-order indicator* (the little arrow next to a column name) indicates that Internet Mail is sorting the folder by that column. If the arrow points down, the most recent messages are at the top of the list. If the arrow points up, the most recent messages are at the bottom of the list.

You can also change the actual columns that each folder displays. Here's how:

1. Select the folder you want to change from the folder menu.

2. Choose View, Columns from Internet Mail's main menu. Internet Mail displays the Columns dialog box, shown in Figure 12.18.

FIG. 12.18
If things get a bit out of hand, you can restore the folder's default columns by clicking Reset.

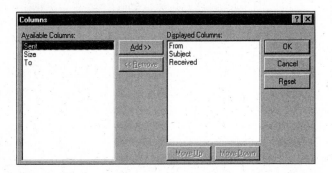

3. Add any columns you want to display for this folder by selecting each column in Available Columns and then clicking Add. The column name moves from the left-hand box to the right-hand box.

4. Remove any columns you don't want to display for this folder by selecting each column in Displayed Columns and then clicking Remove. The column moves from the right-hand box to the left-hand box.

5. Change the order of the folder's columns by selecting each column you want to arrange in Displayed Columns and then clicking Move Up to move the folder up in the list or Move Down to move the folder down in the list.

6. Click OK to save your changes.

Using Eudora

by James O'Donnell

Eudora is one of the most widely used e-mail programs on the Internet, partly because it's so good, and partly because it runs on multiple platforms. It's easy to set up, use, and is intuitive. That is, most commands make sense and are linked in a logical way. For example, the Mailbox menu selection gives you the choice of In, Out, Trash, New, and a list of mailbox names. That sounds easy enough, doesn't it?

With Eudora, you can send mail, retrieve mail, file mail, resend mail, and save and edit mail—and not only text mail and binary mail, but video and audio mail as well. Eudora comes in two versions, a freeware version known as Eudora Light, and its commercial counterpart, Eudora Pro. This chapter discusses the capabilities of the freeware Eudora Light, and then lists what other things you can do if you choose to upgrade to the commercial version. ■

What is Eudora?

In this chapter, you are introduced to Eudora Light and Eudora Pro, full-featured freeware and commercial e-mail clients that run under Windows and the Macintosh.

How do I install and configure Eudora Light?

Installation and configuration guidelines are discussed for setting up Eudora Light as your e-mail client.

How do I manage my e-mail tasks with Eudora Light?

Learn how to perform all of your normal e-mail tasks, such as sending and receiving e-mail, sending replies, sorting and organizing incoming e-mail.

How do I attach binary files with Eudora Light?

Learn about Eudora Light's support for automatically encoding and decoding binary attachments to be sent along with e-mail messages.

What additional capabilities can I get with Eudora Pro?

Find out what additional capabilities you can use if you purchase the commercial version of Eudora, Eudora Pro, such as message filtering, spell checking, MAPI support, and support for the UUEncode binary file encoding method.

Downloading and Installing Eudora Light for Windows

Eudora was originally written as a progra m for the Macintosh, and has since been ported to Windows. Qualcomm, the makers of Eudora, maintain two versions, the freeware version, Eudora Light, and a commercial version known as Eudora Pro. In this chapter, you'll find out how to download and install Eudora Light, and learn how to use its many features. Then, you'll find out what additional capabilities are available with Eudora Pro.

Downloading Eudora Light

The most recent version of Eudora Light available at the time of this writing is Eudora Light 1.5.4, which is included on the CD that came with this book. Also, the most recent version of the Eudora Light program can also be downloaded from Qualcomm's FTP or WWW site.

Getting Eudora Light from the CD   Retrieving Eudora Light from the CD-ROM, which comes with this book, is a simple matter of going through the HTML front-end the CD-ROM uses and then copying the file Eudor154.exe from the CD-ROM to a temporary directory on your hard disk. While you're at it, copy the documentation files, 152word.exe and 152pdf.exe, which are self-extracting files that contain documentation for Eudora Light in either Microsoft Word or Adobe Acrobat Portable Document Format.

> **N O T E**   The documentation files contain the most recent user's manual for Eudora Light, current as of version 1.5.2. There are release notes in the Eudora Light 1.5.4 archive to update the documentation from version 1.5.2 to 1.5.4. ■

Getting Eudora Light via FTP   The most recent version of Eudora Light, along with lots of other goodies from Qualcomm, is always available for anonymous FTP from Qualcomm's FTP site. To obtain it, connect via anonymous FTP to ftp.qualcomm.com. The executable file, Eudor154.exe is available in the directory /quest/windows/eudora/1.5. The documentation files are available in /quest/windows/eudora/documentation.

Getting Eudora Light via the World Wide Web   As you might expect, Qualcomm also makes the most recent versions of Eudora Light available through its Eudora Web site (see Fig. 13.1), located at **http://www.qualcomm.com/quest**. By clicking on the "Eudora Light Freeware" button, you can access and download both the program and documentation archives for Eudora Light.

T I P   If you want to stay informed of the most current version of Eudora, add the Qualcomm Eudora Web site to your list of Favorite Places (or bookmark it) and refer to it periodically.

FIG. 13.1

Qualcomm's Eudora Web site gives you access to their freeware e-mail client, as well as support and information for the commercial version.

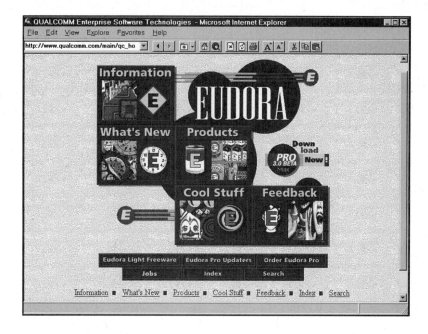

Installing Eudora Light

Once you have Eudor154.exe downloaded and in a temporary directory on your hard disk, you are ready to install it. If you have a different version of Eudora Light, the installation instructions may be the same—check out the instructions that came with it to be sure. The installation process is fairly straightforward and follows these steps.

1. Execute the self-extracting file—this creates a number of files in the temporary directory.

2. Execute the program Setup.exe. This starts up a Windows Installation Wizard, as shown in Figure 13.2.

FIG. 13.2

Eudora Light uses an Installation Wizard to guide you through the installation process.

Part
III

Ch
13

3. Follow the Installation Wizard through the installation process, selecting the 16- or 32-bit version of Eudora Light, and the installation directory.

 T I P If you're using Windows 95 with a 16-bit WinSock, you'll need to use the 16-bit version of Eudora Light. Or better yet, change over to Microsoft's 32-bit WinSock.

▶ **See** "The Various Ways to Connect: Which One Is Right or You?," **p. 87**

4. When the installation is complete, you see the alert box shown in Figure 13.3, which gives you the opportunity to read the README file that came with your copy of Eudora Light. It's always a good idea to read this, as it may contain last-minute tips and information about using this release of the program. The README for Eudora Light v1.5.4 is shown in Figure 13.4.

At this point, Eudora Light is installed and ready to run. You can find a shortcut to it under the Start, Programs menu.

FIG. 13.3

After a successful installation, you can read the README file for your release of Eudora Light.

FIG. 13.4

The README file contains last-minute information about the current release that didn't make it into the manual. It's a good idea to take a look at it.

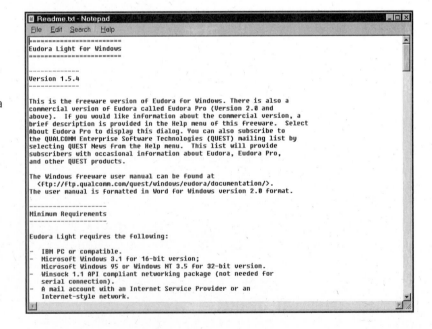

N O T E This chapter tells you all you need to get Eudora Light configured and running, but you might want to take a look at the manual using the Adobe Acrobat Reader (see Fig. 13.5). The manual is also avaliable in Microsoft Word format. ■

FIG. 13.5
While Eudora Light is not supported, it does have an excellent manual available for it that can be read on-screen using the Adobe Acrobat Reader.

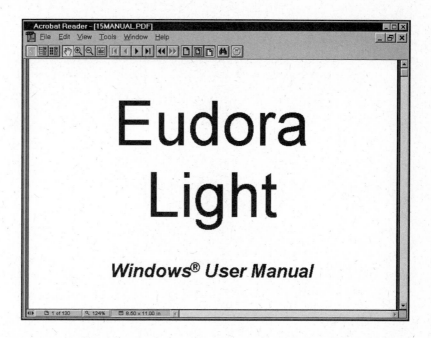

If you are upgrading an older version of Eudora Light, simply follow the same steps above, and the newer version will be installed in place of the current version you are running.

 T I P You might find it easier to keep the icons for Trumpet WinSock, Eudora, Telnet, FTP, and WS-FTP in the same Start button program group. This will help you from fumbling around different directory windows while you're online. This is especially important if your access provider is a toll call.

Adapting Eudora for Several Users

If more than one person is using Eudora on the same PC, you can create as many versions as you want so that each is password-protected.

To create another Eudora folder, do the following:

1. Open the Start menu and choose Settings, Taskbar. The Taskbar properties sheet appears.

2. Select the Start Menu Programs tab.

3. Click the Advanced button.

Part
III

Ch
13

4. Choose File, New, Folder. Type in the name of the new Eudora folder and then select it.

5. Choose File, New, Shortcut.

6. Click the Browse button to find the Eudora executable.

Entering a Password

The first time you start Eudora, you'll be asked for a password, which defaults to the POP server password (either the one your access provider gave you or what you changed it to). Once you've entered the password, you won't have to enter it again. If you happen to change the password on your POP account, you'll have to update your Eudora password. To do this, select the Special menu and choose Forget Password. The next time Eudora checks for mail, it will again ask you for your password.

To change the password, perform the following steps:

1. Choose Special, Change Password.

2. Enter the current password and click OK.

3. Enter the new password and click OK.

N O T E   If you're the only person using the program, you don't have to worry about your password being saved. If several people are going to use the same program, and security is an issue, choose Eudora Forget Password every time you exit it. ■

Configuring Eudora

No Internet client program will work out of the box without some help from the user. At a minimum, you have to supply information about your Internet service provider and the various servers available through your account.

As you might expect, therefore, the first time you open Eudora Light you have things to do. You must provide the address of your Internet provider's POP server and the system that handles and holds your incoming e-mail. You may also have to provide the address of an SMTP server, which handles outgoing traffic.

Open Eudora Light's Options dialog box by choosing Tools, Options, then follow these steps:

1. In the Getting Started option category, type the name of your e-mail account in the POP Account box. In all likelihood, you'll use your regular e-mail address. Also, type your Real name and select your Connection Method (see Fig. 13.6).

CAUTION

In some cases—especially if your account is on a large system that uses aliasing to route e-mail to and through different servers—your POP Account's name may differ slightly from your regular address. Be sure you enter the correct name in the POP Account text box by getting it from your Internet provider. This information in this text box has to be correct or Eudora Light can't access your incoming e-mail.

FIG. 13.6
The Getting Started option category allows you to enter your POP Account and Real Name, as well as your Connection Method.

2. Under Personal Information, as shown in Figure 13.7, you can also add an alternate Return Address if you wish. Note that the POP Account and Real Name text boxes are the same as in the Getting Started category, and don't need to be reentered.

FIG. 13.7
You can use a different Return Address for outgoing e-mail.

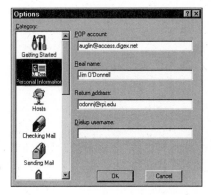

3. The Hosts option in the Category list box allows you to specify the SMTP host used for outgoing e-mail (see Fig. 13.8), if it's different from the one used for the POP Account.

FIG. 13.8
If your host for outgoing e-mail is different than that for incoming, enter that information here.

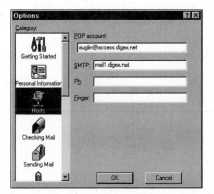

4. The final set of options you should set to get started are under the Checking Mail category. Choosing this category allows you to specify how often Eudora Light will check for your e-mail, and gives you some other options for downloading mail messages (see Fig. 13.9).

FIG. 13.9
You can configure
Eudora Light to check
for your incoming e-mail
at regular intervals.

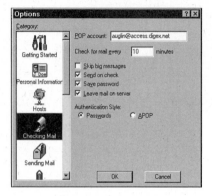

5. Click OK to accept your new configuration data.

There are other configuration options that you can take a look at, though the ones discussed in this section are the most important for getting up and running. The other options categories are

- Sending Mail—Allows you to set various formatting and delivery options for outgoing e-mail.

- Attachments—Sets the binary file encoding type and default attachment directory on your local hard drive for receiving attachments. An *attachment* is usually a binary file, such as a word processing, graphic, sound, executable, or zip file, that is sent along with a text message. It needs to be encoded so that it can be sent along with an e-mail message. You should select an encoding method that you know that the recipient of your e-mail message possesses (so if your recipient is also using Eudora Light, you can select any method).

- Fonts & Display—Gives you the capability to select the font used for screen and printer display, as well as allowing you to set other display options.

 It's usually a good idea to use a monospace font, such as the default Courier. This is because e-mail messages are frequently formatted with a monospaced font in mind.

- Getting Attention—Gives you options for how Eudora Light should inform you when you have e-mail.

- Replying—Sets the options that control to whom a reply will go, either to just the original sender, or also to all of the other recipients of the message.

■ Dialup—Allows you to set up the dialing parameters so that Eudora Light can automatically establish a connection and retrieve your e-mail over a dial-up, as opposed to PPP or direct network, connection.

■ Miscellaneous—Gives you access to various miscellaneous options, such as what key commands enable you to go from message to message, and whether to delete the Eudora Light Trash folder upon exit..

■ Advanced Network—Contains several advanced network options that you will usually not need to worry about. One parameter you may need to set if you are having problems with your network connection is to increase the network timeout value. If you have a slow mail server, you can cut down on timeouts by increasing this value from the default of 60 seconds to 90 or 120 seconds.

Creating and Sending E-mail Messages

With Eudora Light, it's easy to send Internet e-mail. Open the Message menu and click New Message. A blank mail form pops up on your screen. Follow these steps to write and send a message:

1. Type the e-mail address of the person, group, or company you're trying to reach in the To field (see Fig. 13.10). Note that you can include more than one name in the To field. Press the Tab key to go to the next line.

FIG. 13.10

Eudora Light's mail form. Note the gray line separating the message header from the text.

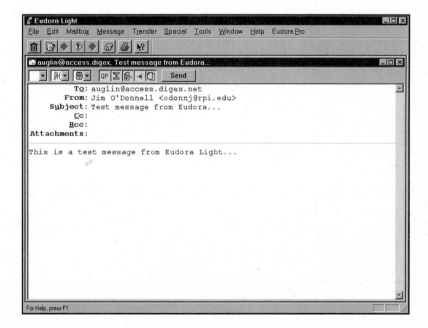

Part

III

Ch

13

2. In the Subject field, type a two- or three-word summary of your message. Press Tab again.

TIP   Keep your Subject summaries short but descriptive. A good subject description is like a newspaper headline: It'll make your messages stand out in a crowded In box on the receiving end of your correspondence.

3. You may want to send copies of your message to more than one person. If so, type the e-mail addresses of the additional recipients (separating them with commas) in the Cc field. Press Tab when you're done.

4. The Bcc field gives you a chance to send a "blind carbon copy" of your message to other people. If you want, enter the e-mail addresses for the copies (separated by commas) and press Tab when you're done.

TIP   Bcc works almost exactly like Cc, except that the recipient listed in the To field gets no notice from your mail server that the added copies went out.

5. Now you're ready to type the text of your message. The cursor should now rest in Eudora Light's message window, just below the gray line crossing the screen. You can go ahead and type your message.

6. When you're done, click the button on the extreme right of Eudora Light's toolbar. Depending on your Tools, Options, Sending Mail, Immediate Send settings, this button is captioned Send or Queue. Click it to send your new message directly to your mail server or to your outgoing message queue for later delivery. If you wish to send a message when you are set up for queuing, or vice versa, simply hold down the Shift key while you click on the button.

7. If you're connected to the Internet, clicking the Send button will bring up a status indicator panel almost immediately. It has a button on it that you can click to cancel the outgoing message if you change your mind.

8. To send messages stored on disk once you're logged on, open the File menu and click Send Queued Messages. A status indicator pops up to let you watch the progress of your mailing.

Addressing Your Mail with Nicknames

The new message procedure works fine if you're e-mailing a new or infrequent correspondent. But for people you keep in touch with every day, it's a little cumbersome.

You can use two Eudora Light features, Nicknames and Quick Recipients, to create and maintain a personal address book (see Fig. 13.11). Open your Nicknames list by opening the Tools menu and clicking Nicknames.

FIG. 13.11

Eudora Light's Nicknames and Quick Recipients features speed the process of addressing e-mail to your most frequent correspondents.

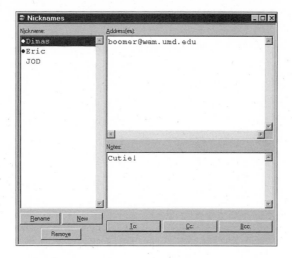

Creating a new nickname is simple. With the Nicknames window open, follow these steps:

1. Click the New button.
2. A dialog box called New Nickname pops up (see Fig. 13.12). Type the name of the person or group in the What Do You Wish to Call It? text box.

FIG. 13.12

Type the name of your correspondent in the box provided in the New Nickname dialog box.

3. Check the Put It On the Recipient List box if you want to create a Eudora Light menu shortcut to the new nickname. Such shortcuts are called Quick Recipients. We'll discuss them in a moment.
4. Click OK. You'll see the new nickname highlighted on the Nickname list.
5. Highlight any text appearing in the Address(es) box and change it so it reflects the correct e-mail address for this person. You can also make notes about each nickname, to help you remember things about them or your relationship with them.

TIP There is an even quicker way to create a nickname. Within any open message, click the Special menu and select Make Nickname. Eudora Light asks you to supply a name as before. You should immediately open the Nicknames window and edit the Address(es) field. You'll find that Eudora Light copies both the Sender and Reply-To addresses to this field when you select Make Nickname; chances are you want to keep only one of them.

The Nicknames window controls input to a disk file that holds your address book. It stays open until you choose Close from the File menu or until you click the Close box. You can switch in and out of the Nicknames window at your convenience, using commands on the Window or Mailbox menus, while you work on your messages. If you change your Nicknames file in any way, however, Eudora Light won't let you close the window until you confirm or discard the modifications (see Fig. 13.13).

FIG. 13.13

Eudora Light gives you the choice of saving or throwing away changes to your Nickname list.

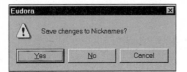

Addressing Your E-mail with Quick Recipients

Once your address book is fairly well settled, you won't want to open the Nicknames window every time you create a new piece of e-mail. Eudora Light lets you avoid that detour by letting you add your most useful addresses directly to its menus.

You got a hint of this capability when you created your first nickname. When Eudora Light asked you for the name, it also gave you a chance to put it on the Quick Recipients list. Try it now by creating a new nickname. Before you're done, check the Put It On the Recipient List box, just below the line where you enter the name (refer to Fig. 13.12). You can add an existing nickname to the Quick Recipients list by right-clicking the name in the Nicknames window and selecting Add to Recipient List, as shown in Figure 13.14. Once you click OK, go to Eudora Light's menus and click Message, followed by New Message To (see Fig. 13.15).

FIG. 13.14

You can add existing nicknames to the Quick Recipients list by right-clicking on them in the Nicknames window.

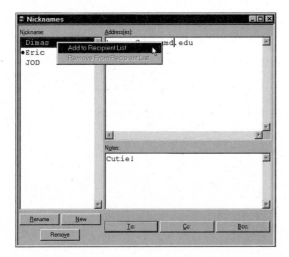

FIG. 13.15
Your Quick Recipients actually appear in Eudora Light's menus!

The Quick Recipients list gives you the ability to perform every basic Nickname function without ever opening the Nicknames window, which is a tremendous convenience. Eudora Light unfortunately hides this capability by scattering its various Quick Recipients commands among three different menu headings. Table 13.1 lists the commands now available to you.

Table 13.1 Eudora Light Menu Commands Using the Quick Recipients List

Command	Menu	Action
New Message To	Message	Creates a new message addressed to the Quick Recipient.
Reply To	Message	Creates a new mailing to the Quick Recipient that quotes an existing message.
Forward To	Message	Sends a copy of an existing message to the indicated Quick Recipient.
Redirect To	Message	Sends a copy of a message you've gotten to the indicated Quick Recipient, without changing the message's From field.
Insert Recipient	Edit	Adds a Quick Recipient to any of an outgoing message's address fields. Use the mouse to point to To, Cc, or Bcc first.
Add as Recipient	Special	Adds a highlighted e-mail address to the Quick Recipients list only. It will not add the address to the Nickname list.
Remove Recipient	Special	Deletes a name from the Quick Recipients list only. It does not alter the Nickname list.

Part
III

Ch
13

CAUTION

You'll probably want to use the Quick Recipients feature for only your dozen or so most frequent correspondents. Beyond that, the menus get a bit unwieldy.

Signing Your Mail

Eudora Light is capable of automatically adding what Internet users call a signature file, or sig file for short, to the end of your outgoing messages.

E-mail sigs—in their simplest form—offer readers more information about a message's sender, such as a corporate affiliation and a phone number. They've become part of Internet lore because there's a certain breed of Nethead who won't settle for simplicity. To these people, no sig is complete unless it includes a bit of elaborate ASCII (consisting of regular text characters) artwork. For instance, the sig file I sometimes use is the following, with my initials rendered using ASCII art:

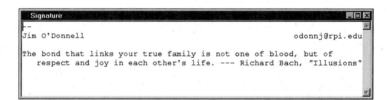

Eudora Light's Tools, Options, Sending Mail, Use signature setting defaults to include a signature file at the end of your posts. You open the signature file by choosing Tools, Signature. The file is blank when you start Eudora Light for the first time; it's up to you to create your own sig (see Fig. 13.16). Type what you want. Store it by choosing Save from the File menu, or from the dialog box that pops up when you click the Close box (see Fig. 13.17).

FIG. 13.16

Eudora Light allows you to create a sig file that can be attached to all of your outgoing messages.

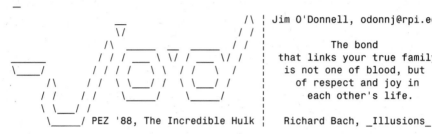

FIG. 13.17

If you've made changes to your sig file, you need to save them before they can be used.

You can choose to leave a sig off any given message. Near the middle of the message toolbar, you see a box with the script letters "JH" (which stands for the most famous signature—John Hancock). Click on it and a drop-down box opens to let you cancel the sig.

N O T E Keep your sig simple: Name, address (via e-mail and/or snail mail), affiliation, and phone numbers suffice for most professionals. Artwork isn't essential, but it won't hurt anything as long it doesn't add to the length of your sig. Don't let it get more than about five lines deep; more than that and you're costing your readers connection time and, possibly, additional fees. The one I showed previously is a little long for common use—a shorter version I usually use is

```
—
Jim O'Donnell                                        odonnj@rpi.edu

The bond that links your true family is not one of blood, but of
    respect and joy in each other's life. — Richard Bach, "Illusions"
```

Also note that Eudora Light stores your sig file in the Eudora Light directory in the file signatur.pce. So, if you want to use the same file as the sig file for other programs, you can by specifying that file. ∎

Reading and Managing E-mail Messages

Eudora Light's handling of incoming message traffic is probably one of the strongest parts of the entire package. Filing and keeping track of your old e-mail is a cinch because the program lets you create a hierarchical set of mailboxes and transfer messages between them. Each mailbox has a "table of contents" that gives you a full rundown of the messages stored inside. And, if need be, you can save, print, and copy your messages just as you would with any other Windows 95 program.

When you're online, picking up your e-mail with Eudora Light takes two clicks of the mouse. Choose File, Check Mail or press Ctrl+M and Eudora Light logs on to your mail server and downloads every message that waits for you there.

 TIP If you've left the Sending Mail option category's Send on Check option on, Eudora Light sends any outgoing message queued on your disk as soon as it's done picking up new e-mail.

Eudora Light deposits new messages in a database called the In box. When you have new e-mail, you can read it by choosing the Mailbox menu and selecting In.

Understanding Eudora Light's Mailboxes

The In box is just one of three boxes Eudora Light uses by default. There's an Out box for e-mail you've sent or that is waiting in queue, and there's a Trash box for messages you've deleted. You can create additional mailboxes of your own.

No matter which mailbox you open—and they're all accessible from the Mailbox menu—Eudora Light will present some basic data about the messages it contains. The format is standard for every mailbox (see Fig. 13.18).

Part

III

Ch

13

FIG. 13.18

Eudora Light Mailbox windows offer summary information about the messages they hold.

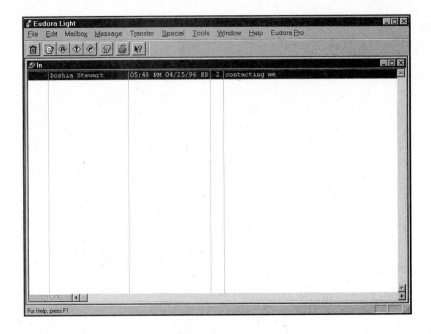

Most of the fields in the Mailbox window are self-explanatory. Each line represents one message. There's a box that lists the address or Eudora Light nickname of the person who sent or received the message involved. There's another that indicates when it was sent and a small one that says how big it is. The largest field, the one on the right, reports on its subject.

The leftmost box is a bit more mysterious at first glance. In it you'll find, depending on the mailbox that's open, a series of one-letter codes that tell you the message's status. These codes are the most important:

- A bullet next to a message in the In box window says you haven't read it yet.
- An R next to an In box listing means that you've posted a reply to the original sender.
- An S beside an Out box item means that the message has been sent.
- A Q seen beside an Out box listing means you haven't posted that message yet.

Aside from these, you may see a D or an F next to an In box item. They mean, respectively, that you've redirected a message sent to you by mistake or forwarded a copy to a third party.

Opening and Replying to Messages

You can open any message by double-clicking its mailbox listing. Alternatively, you can use the cursor keys to scroll through the listing and press Enter to open a message window.

With a message open or highlighted, create a return mailing by choosing Message, Reply or pressing Ctrl+R. Eudora Light opens a new message and pastes into it the text of the post you're answering. Use Windows cut, copy, and paste commands to reorganize and trim this quotation, and then type your reply.

On the Message menu you also see commands that let you forward copies of a given piece of e-mail to anyone you want, or redirect e-mail that came to your address by mistake. Clicking those options pastes the text into a new message; you have only to fill in the address and click the Send or Queue button.

Storing Old Mail

There's nothing wrong with keeping old e-mail in the In and Out boxes and sending messages to the Trash box as they become obsolete. That works fine if you're a low-volume e-mail user.

But if you're not—say you get dozens or even hundreds of messages each week, some business-related, some personal, others from a mailing list or two—you'll want to customize your mailbox setup.

Creating New Mailboxes   Create new mailboxes by choosing New from the Mailbox menu. Eudora Light responds by opening the New Mailbox dialog box (see Fig. 13.19).

FIG. 13.19
Eudora Light allows you to very easily create new mailboxes, and to create folders in which to nest mailboxes.

Enter a name in the text box provided. Clicking OK creates the mailbox. You'll find the newly created mailbox toward the bottom of the Mailbox menu.

You can also nest menus under the Mailbox selector—which creates subcategories for different posts—by checking the Make It a Folder box. Click OK, and you have another Mailbox menu item that can hold new mailboxes and folders of its own.

N O T E   Custom mailboxes do for your messages what the Start menu does for your programs. But you have to think about how you want to organize your message traffic. You also have to set up a mailbox structure that makes your most important messages the easiest ones to reach. Don't go crazy nesting folders and mailboxes. After they pile up more than about three deep, it's easy to lose track of things. ■

Transferring Messages Between Boxes   The Transfer menu lets you shuffle messages between mailboxes. With one exception, it will mirror the look of your Mailbox menu. To move a message from one mailbox to another, follow these steps:

1. Open or select the message you want to move.
2. Open the Transfer menu and scroll through your mailbox hierarchy until you find the box you want to send the message to, and then click it.

The one thing you can't do with Transfer is move a message to the Out box. Eudora Light reserves the Out box for messages it has sent or is waiting to send.

Part
III

Ch
13

Otherwise, the Transfer menu is quite flexible. You'll notice that it has a New command; it lets you create new folders and mailboxes on the fly as you're moving your e-mail around.

If you need to reorganize the folders and mailboxes themselves, then choose Tools, Mailboxes. The window that opens lets you move them around (see Fig. 13.20). It works like the Windows 95 Explorer: Click the folder icons on one side of the window until you find the mailbox you want to move, and then do the same on the other side until you've highlighted the destination. Click the Move button that points to where you want the mailbox to go.

FIG. 13.20

The Mailboxes window lets you rearrange your mailbox and folders hierarchy.

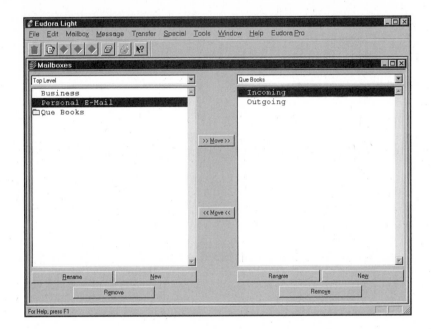

Deleting Mail

Eudora Light gives the user several ways to get rid of old messages, but they all involve sending them to the Trash box first. Eudora Light continues to store messages there unless you tell it to clear the Trash box when you quit the program.

You can send a message to the Trash by any of the following:

- Pressing the Delete key
- Pressing Ctrl+D
- Clicking the toolbar's delete/trash icon
- Choosing Transfer, Trash

All of these functions work from within a message or from a mailbox window; they also work with groups of messages that you select from a mailbox window using the mouse with the Shift and Ctrl keys, just as you do when you're working with files in Explorer.

Clean out the Trash box by opening Eudora Light's Special menu, and then choosing Empty Trash. Bear in mind that you're actually deleting files here; this operation is exactly the same as emptying Recycle Bin in Windows 95, and it is just as permanent.

You can set Eudora Light to empty the Trash by itself. Open the Tools, Options, Miscellaneous dialog box from the Special menu, and click to place a check mark in the Empty Trash when exiting.

Working with Attachments to Mail Messages

Work-at-home types will be glad to know that they can send and receive complex binary files like spreadsheets or word processor documents via the Internet's e-mail service. It is, however, a feat that demands a bit of wizardry on both ends of the transaction. But Eudora Light handles it automatically.

Internet e-mail can't deal with binary files directly; the computer on the sending end has to convert them to ASCII text before putting them on the wire. The machine on the receiving end has to change them back. Eudora Light has built-in software that does this automatically.

Encoding Options

With Eudora Light you can attach a binary file to any outgoing message. Depending on your orders, the program will convert it to ASCII using one of two popular encoding protocols—BinHex or MIME.

BinHex was originally developed within the Macintosh community where it is still extensively used. It's more than adequate for transferring text files, but it's not completely reliable for complex files like images and other multimedia.

Programmers developed the MIME protocol to answer this problem. Thanks to extensive support through the industry, MIME encoding is now virtually a standard. Almost all major messaging software packages—Microsoft Exchange and Lotus cc:Mail—support it.

Unfortunately, Eudora Light doesn't support another major protocol, UUEncoding, that's popular on UseNet's binaries newsgroups. Qualcomm supports this capability only in its commercial e-mail package, Eudora Pro (see the UUENCODE support section, later in this chapter).

Attaching Files

You'll need only a couple of mouse clicks to attach a file to an outgoing message. With a new message open, follow these steps:

1. Choose Attach File from the Message menu.

2. Eudora Light displays a standard Windows file selection dialog box—you can't just type the file name into the Attachment field. Work through your directory structure until you see the file you want, and then highlight it.

3. Click OK. The file's name and path should appear in your message's Attachment's field (see Fig. 13.21).

Part
III

Ch
13

FIG. 13.21

Eudora Light allows you to attach multiple binary files to a single message.

Click this drop-down list box to select an encoding protocol.

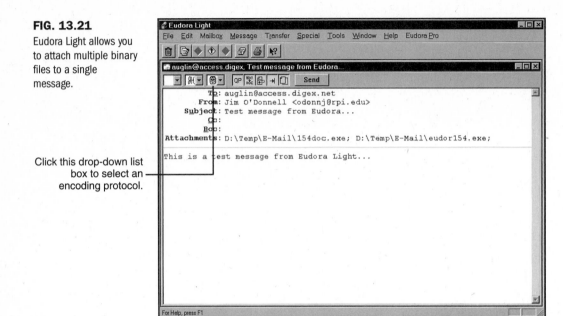

4. Choose an encoding protocol by clicking the drop-down box in the middle of Eudora Light's toolbar.

Post your message in the ordinary manner. Eudora Light will encode and send the file after it's done sending the actual text.

Eudora Light requires almost no help from you to deal with incoming file attachments, as long as they're MIME- or BinHex-encoded. They're decoded automatically and stored in the directory you've specified in the Options dialog box (refer to Fig. 13.6).

Incoming file attachments that are UUEncoded need special handling. You'll have no trouble picking them out of your ordinary message traffic because they'll contain ASCII gibberish unreadable by humans. Save them to disk by choosing File, Save As, and then run them through a separate UUDecoding program like WinCode. If the file was large enough that it got split up into multiple pieces, you will need to rejoin the pieces by hand before you decode them.

Mail Sorting and Message Handling

Keeping up with a heavy message load is a tough job. Mailboxes and folders help matters considerably, but they're not enough by themselves.

You would not, however, see them as a blessing if you had to pick through a half dozen mailboxes and a few hundred old mailings, just to find the post that told you how many people your boss was bringing to lunch.

Eudora Light fortunately has powerful sort and search features that make traffic control a manageable problem.

Sort Options

You can ask Eudora Light to sort a mailbox's message display in any of five ways by opening the Edit menu and choosing Sort. Most people find the first four of these methods useful:

- Sort by Status classifies messages by the entry in the mailbox's Status/Priority box.
- Sort by Sender groups them by the address of the author or recipient.
- Sort by Date arranges them in chronological order, earliest to latest.
- Sort by Subject alphabetizes them according to the first letters in each message's subject field.
- The fifth sort option, Sort by Priority, isn't all that important unless you work in a large organization and use e-mail to communicate with your coworkers. Eudora Light gives you the option to assign a priority level to each outgoing message (accessible via a drop-down box on the extreme left of the toolbar). Most Internet users, however, don't bother with this feature.

Finding a Message

Eudora Light also gives you the ability to search for a message that contains a specific phrase or word. Just open the Edit menu, choose the Find submenu, and then select Find (see Fig. 13.22).

FIG. 13.22
Eudora Light's Find feature lets you search message headers or text for a specific word or phrase.

The Find dialog box has a text box to enter the text you want to find. Checking the Match Case box tells Eudora Light to locate exact matches; leaving it blank tells it to report any instance of the word or phrase you're looking for.

The Summaries Only box gives you the option of telling Eudora Light to only search message headers. Leaving this box unchecked tells Eudora Light to ignore the headers in favor of searching the full text of each message.

You can repeat any search by opening the Edit menu and selecting Find Again from the Sort submenu.

Rerouting Mail

Eudora is pretty flexible when it comes to sending a message to other people, replying to a message, or forwarding a message you received. Table 13.2 provides you with all the options for rerouting mail.

Table 13.2	Rerouting Mail
When You Want to...	**Do This**
Reply to a message	Open the Message menu and choose Reply, or press Ctrl+R, or click the Reply button. This puts the text of the original message into so-called quotations, creates a new message to the person you're replying to, and keeps the same subject.
Forward a message	Open the Message menu and choose Forward, or click the Forward button. This puts the text into quotations, keeps the subject the same, and leaves a blank space for the recipient.
Redirect a message	Open the Message menu and choose Redirect, or click the Redirect button. This puts the text in quotations, leaves the recipient blank and indicates the route that message has taken on the From line.
Send again	Open the Message menu and choose Send Again. The message will be sent to everyone it was sent to the first time and to the person who originated it.

Eudora Pro

In addition to the capabilities discussed earlier for Eudora Light, Qualcomm's commercial version of the software, Eudora Pro, adds additional features and capabilities. With Eudora, Qualcomm uses a more common method of promoting and marketing Internet programs: creating and distributing freeware versions of their software, and then selling versions that have greater capabilities. Eudora Light is by no means a crippled version of Eudora Pro. It is a fully functional program in its own right. However, Eudora Pro adds additional capabilities that are very useful to someone with above-average e-mail needs.

Message Labels

By choosing Tools, Options, Labels, Eudora Pro allows you to create seven different color coded labels. These labels are assigned in incoming mail, either by you manually, or automatically using message filters (see the next section on message filters). When a message is labeled, the entire summary line of the message in its mailbox changes color to the color of the label. In this way, you can easily find messages that you have assigned to a given label.

Message Filtering

One of the most important additional capabilities of Eudora Pro is its message-filtering functions. Using message filtering, you can automatically scan incoming or outgoing messages for certain strings, and then perform functions on that message accordingly. Filters are set up as shown in Figure 13.23.

FIG. 13.23

Eudora's Message Filters can greatly ease the task of sorting through large amounts of incoming e-mail.

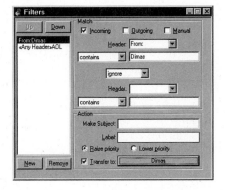

Message filters can be set up to match various parts of incoming or outgoing messages. The search criteria for the filters that you can control are the following:

- You can set them up to scan any of the standard message headers (To, From, Subject, Cc, and Reply-To), all headers, or body text.

- The selection criteria can be if the field searched contains, doesn't contain, is, is not, starts with, or ends with a given string, or if the header field appears at all.

- A second filter can be applied and a match can be made if both of the filters apply, one or the other applies, or the first applies but not the second.

If the filter is satisfied, the following actions can be taken with the message:

- *Change the subject of the message to a given string.* Instead of replacing the subject of the message, you can add to the existing subject by including an ampersand (&), which expands to the original subject.

  Example: If you are on an Internet mailing list and receive all such mail from one account, you can set up a filter to look for e-mail from that account and flag it by changing the subject to "MAILING LIST: &". This flags it as an item from a mailing list and preserves the original subject.

- *Attach a label to a message.*

  Example: You can set up filters to look for mail from the members of your workgroup and attach a "WORK GROUP" label to these messages. Then all of these messages will be labeled accordingly and displayed in their mailbox with the same color.

Part
III

Ch

■ *Raise or lower priority.*

Example: If you receive lots of e-mail and like to prioritize it so that you can read the higher priority messages first, you can use message filters to automatically raise or lower the priority of messages from different people.

■ *Transfer messages to one of your mailboxes.*

Example: This is probably one of Eudora Pro's most useful capabilities. If you receive a lot of e-mail from mailing lists, other people, or from any other venue, you can set up filters to automatically direct this mail into an appropriate mailbox. In this way, you can organize your e-mail even before you read it, and read the mail you are most concerned with first. Figure 13.23 shows a filter I have set up to automatically transfer incoming mail from Dimas into a Dimas mailbox.

Spell Checking

Eudora Pro includes a built-in spell checker that you can use to check the spelling of your outgoing mail messages. To do so, follow these steps:

1. While in the message window, right click and select Check Spelling (see Fig. 13.24)
2. Choose Edit, Check Spelling, or press Ctrl+6.

FIG. 13.24
Eudora Pro allows you to
spell check mail
messages at the touch
of a mouse button.

If Eudora Pro thinks it finds a misspelling, it gives you the Check Spelling dialog box shown in Figure 13.25. From here, you can fix the word (either by typing in the correct spelling or accepting one of the suggested spellings), or ignore the warning if the word is, in fact, spelled correctly. If it is a word that you are likely to use again, you can add it to your own dictionary by clicking the Add button. After that, the word will no longer be flagged as misspelled.

FIG. 13.25
If Eudora Pro thinks you
have misspelled a word,
it gives you a chance to
correct it—it even
suggests possible
corrections!

MAPI Support

MAPI (Messaging Application Program Interface) is a protocol that lets you send e-mail messages from any MAPI-compatible application—this may include your word processor, spreadsheet, graphics program, or other application. When sending such an e-mail message through a MAPI-compatible mail system, the message is automatically encoded and sent to its destination. If the recipient of the message is also using a MAPI-compatible mail program, it will be automatically decoded upon receipt.

UUEncode Support

In addition to the MIME and BinHex encoding schemes available in Eudora Light, Eudora Pro also allows you to use UUEncode. In general, when sending e-mail to other users of Eudora, Light or Pro, you will usually want to use MIME or BinHex, because they are more commonly supported. However, UUEncoding is widely used on UseNet newsgroups and Internet mailing lists. So, Eudora Pro's support for UUEncoding and UUDecoding makes it very useful if you frequently get messages from these mailing lists. ●

Part
III

Ch

13

Using Internet Mailing Lists

by James O'Donnell

Once you have an e-mail account connected to the Internet, a wide range of activities opens up to you. Some are what you might expect, such as the capability to exchange messages with anyone in the world similarly connected. As you've seen earlier in this part of the book, you can exchange complex messages through the use of e-mail programs such as Eudora and Microsoft Exchange.

▶ **See** "Installing Exchange," **p. 252**

▶ **See** "Installing Internet Mail," **p. 283**

The Internet has a wide range of services and resources that require varying levels of connection. Internet e-mail is usually the first level, and the most common level of access. There are many activities that you can access simply with an e-mail account.

In this chapter, you will learn how to subscribe to and use Internet mailing lists to access, well, just about anything you can imagine! ■

Subscribe to Internet mailing lists

This chapter shows you how to join and quit the two most popular types of mailing lists: LISTSERV and Majordomo.

Find just the right mailing list

Learn how to get descriptions of thousands of LISTSERV mailing lists.

Subscribe to a LISTSERV mailing list

It's easy to subscribe to a mailing list. This chapter shows you how.

Get files from mailing lists

Both LISTSERV and Majordomo mailing lists let you retrieve files.

Learn about Netiquette

This chapter shows you how to properly behave when using a mailing list.

What Are Internet Mailing Lists?

Every time I sign on to my e-mail account, I have a message waiting for me like the one shown in Figure 14.1.

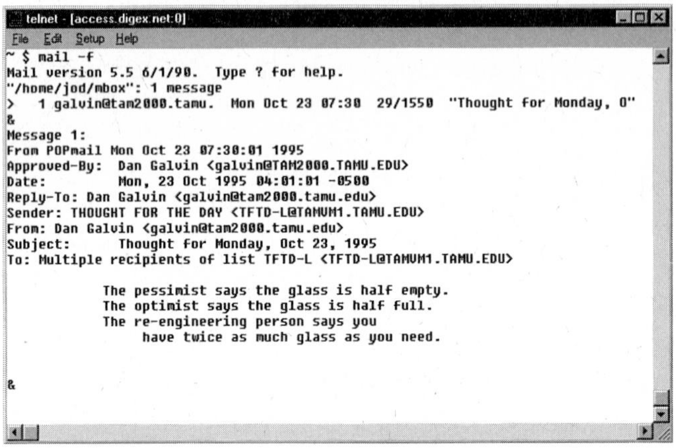

FIG. 14.1

My daily message from TFTD-L.

```
telnet - [access.digex.net:0]                                              _ □ ×
File  Edit  Setup  Help
~ $ mail -f
Mail version 5.5 6/1/90.  Type ? for help.
"/home/jod/mbox": 1 message
>   1 galvin@tam2000.tamu.  Mon Oct 23 07:30  29/1550  "Thought for Monday, 0"
&
Message 1:
From POPmail Mon Oct 23 07:30:01 1995
Approved-By:  Dan Galvin <galvin@TAM2000.TAMU.EDU>
Date:         Mon, 23 Oct 1995 04:01:01 -0500
Reply-To: Dan Galvin <galvin@tam2000.tamu.edu>
Sender: THOUGHT FOR THE DAY <TFTD-L@TAMU1.TAMU.EDU>
From: Dan Galvin <galvin@tam2000.tamu.edu>
Subject:       Thought for Monday, Oct 23, 1995
To: Multiple recipients of list TFTD-L <TFTD-L@TAMUM1.TAMU.EDU>

              The pessimist says the glass is half empty.
              The optimist says the glass is half full.
              The re-engineering person says you
                    have twice as much glass as you need.


&
```

I get this message—well, a different one each weekday—because I have subscribed to an Internet mailing list called TFTD-L. ("TFTD" is an acronym for "Thought for the Day.")

There are several different varieties of Internet mailing lists available—you'll get an idea of just how many in a bit. Some are like TFTD-L, which has a specific, limited function. It's essentially one-way, from the originator of the list to the recipients (although with TFTD-L, you can send comments and suggestions to the person who runs the list).

Other mailing lists function like magazines, periodically sending out long messages, each consisting of one or more articles concerning the list topic. Usually, these lists allow—even welcome and depend on—submissions from people like you who are members of the list. One of the more common types of lists, however, is one that functions as an e-mail *exploder.* Whenever anyone sends a message to the mailing list, a copy of the message is then sent out to each person on the list.

Internet mailing lists can serve a number of different activities, including the following:

- The list administrator can use it to deliver information to the list subscribers.
- Subscribers to the list can send out information to all the other subscribers.
- You can post files to the list, or retrieve files of interest that other subscribers have posted.
  - ▶ **See** "ASCII Format Only," **p. 232**
  - ▶ **See** "Attaching Files," **p. 321**
  - ▶ **See** "Encoding and Decoding Files from Windows," **p. 354**

Because of the restrictions the Internet puts on files that are sent through e-mail—mainly that they must be ASCII files—binary files such as picture files, executables, and compressed file archives must be encoded into ASCII first. This is discussed in Chapter 15, "Encoding and Decoding Files."

Regardless of how the list functions, however, each one has its own set of rules, set by the list administrator. The following section discusses some of these rules and some other distinctions about list types. You also learn how to use mailing lists—including how to find what lists are out there and how to subscribe to a list.

Mastering a Mailing List

Using a mailing list is easy, and it might be best to simply show you the steps needed to join one. To join TFTD-L, just send an e-mail message to the e-mail address

LISTSERV@TAMVM1.TAMU.EDU

You can leave the Subject line blank, because it'll be ignored. The first line of the body of the message has to be

SUBSCRIBE TFTD-L *Your Name*

For example, I'd use the following:

SUBSCRIBE TFTD-L Jim O'Donnell

▶ **See** "Simple Mail Transfer Protocol," **p. 224**

(For step-by-step instructions on sending commands, see "Working with LISTSERV Mailing Lists" and "Using Majordomo Mailing Lists," later in this chapter.) You should get a response to that message in a couple of minutes, so here's a little bit of background in the meantime. How to join and use any given Internet mailing list is a function of how the list is administered. The list may be as simple as someone doing everything manually, including adding people to the list of recipients, reading all of the incoming messages, and then using an alias list to send the message to everyone on the list.

Usually, however, public mailing lists run automatically through software systems on the host computer. There are several common list managers, the biggest of which is LISTSERV. There is also a system called Majordomo, and countless other less common or private systems. LISTSERV, and Majordomo and other systems will all perform the same basic function. However, each mailing list program runs a little differently, and has different features, advantages, and disadvantages. Next are some specific guidelines on subscribing to these systems.

Working with LISTSERV Mailing Lists

You already know a little bit about LISTSERV lists. You probably guessed that TFTD-L is one of them. LISTSERV is flexible and can perform many mailing-list options. It can be intimidating, especially because it tends to use very cryptic list names and commands. However, LISTSERV makes it easy to join and quit mailing lists, and to send messages to them.

Part

III

Ch

14

There are two basic categories of actions you'll take with LISTSERV mailing lists. The first is sending commands, such as those to join or quit a list. The second is sending messages to the list itself. Since you have to join the list before you can use it, we'll discuss sending commands first.

Each time you wish to send LISTSERV a command or commands, you must remember the following:

- Commands are sent to LISTSERV through e-mail messages and the first part of the e-mail address—the part before the "@"—will always be "LISTSERV."
- LISTSERV ignores the Subject line, so you can leave it blank.
- LISTSERV doesn't care whether the commands are in uppercase, lowercase, or even mixed case.

With that information in mind, follow these steps to send one or more commands to a LISTSERV mailing list:

1. Use your Internet mail program to create a new mail message and send it to the LISTSERV address. The one for TFTD-L is **LISTSERV@TAMVM1.TAMU.EDU**. Depending on your mail program, you may type this address at the command line with the `mail` command:

   mail LISTSERV@TAMVM1.TAMU.EDU

   Or you may type **LISTSERV@TAMVM1.TAMU.EDU** on the To line of the e-mail message.

2. Leave the Subject line blank.
3. In the text area of the message, enter LISTSERV commands, one per line.
4. Send the e-mail message. The reply will usually come in a few minutes.

Subscribing to and Unsubscribing from LISTSERV Mailing Lists

By now, you should have received a reply from your subscription request. If you followed the example earlier in this chapter. It normally takes a few minutes, but when dealing with the Internet, your individual results may vary. When you subscribe to a LISTSERV list, you actually get two responses. The first shows the output of the commands you sent (in this case, only one command, the subscription request, was sent). It looks something like Figure 14.2.

The second message, usually resulting from a subscription command, is a welcoming message providing essential information about the list. Part of the welcome message from TFTD-L appears in Figure 14.3.

The important parts of the message are worth noting. As the welcoming message states in the first paragraph, it's a good idea to save a copy of it for future reference.

Probably the most important information is in the second paragraph, which is the difference between the list address, **TFTD-L@TAMVM1.TAMU.EDU**, and the corresponding LISTSERV address, **LISTSERV@TAMVM1.TAMU.EDU**. The first address is called the *mail exploder* *address;* anything sent to that address is (usually) sent to everybody on the list. The second address, as mentioned earlier, is the address to send commands.

FIG. 14.2

The output message from the LISTSERV SUBSCRIBE command.

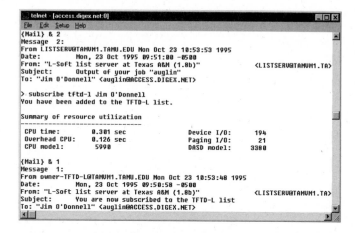

FIG. 14.3

The welcome message from TFTD-L.

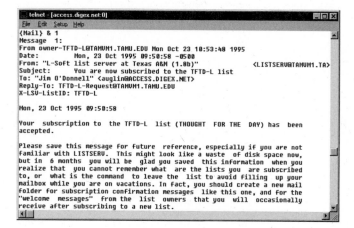

T I P To distinguish between LISTSERV addresses, remember that LISTSERV commands should go to the "LISTSERV" address and messages to a specific list, such as TFTD-L, should go to the "TFTD-L" address.

You're liable to feel a little foolish (and if you don't, a whole bunch of other people will probably send you e-mail to try to make you feel foolish) if you send a LISTSERV command to subscribe to the list to the wrong address.

Not only won't you be signed off, but a copy of your message is sent to everybody on the list! Fortunately, LISTSERV will sometimes recognize this mistake and save you some embarrassment by bouncing back your command with an explanation, as shown in Figure 14.4.

Part

III

Ch

14

FIG. 14.4

Oops! I used the wrong LISTSERV address!

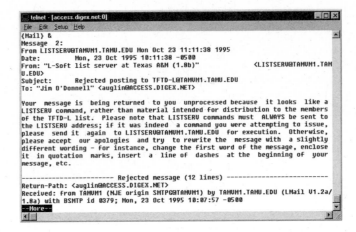

Similar to subscribing to a LISTSERV list, unsubscribing (or "signing off" to use the same terminology LISTSERV uses) is very straightforward. To unsubscribe, follow these steps:

1. Create an e-mail message to be sent to, for example

   LISTSERV@TAMVM1.TAMU.EDU

2. Leave the Subject line blank.

3. In the message body, type the command

   SIGNOFF TFTD-L

4. Send the e-mail message.

Available Lists

Well, you know how to join TFTD-L now, but what other lists are available? Hopefully, LISTSERV can help. To get some help from LISTSERV, e-mail a command to the "LISTSERV" address, with the HELP command typed in the body text of the message. A few minutes after sending the help message, LISTSERV returns something like the reply shown in Figure 14.5.

FIG. 14.5

The LISTSERV Help message.

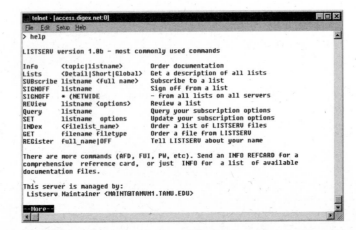

If you examine Figure 14.5, you'll see a LIST command. Send an e-mail message to LISTSERV with this command

LIST

Sending this command returns a list with the name and a short description of all of the LISTSERV mailing lists that are administered at this computer (**TAMVM1.TAMU.EDU**, at Texas A&M). The beginning of the list looks like Figure 14.6. Not all of the entries are shown (there are 113), but LISTSERV will send you the whole list. You can scroll through or treat it as any other e-mail message to view it.

FIG. 14.6

Local mailing lists at Texas A&M.

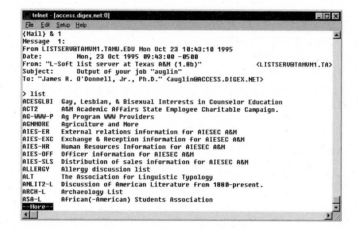

You might find something of interest to you in these 113 groups. It's also possible that you might not. One of the nice things about LISTSERV, however, is that not only does LISTSERV handle its own mailing lists, but a given LISTSERV site (at Texas A&M, for example) also knows about all (or many) of the other LISTSERV sites. To get this more complete listing, you need to issue a command to see the global list.

To display a global list, send an e-mail message to LISTSERV with the following command:

LIST GLOBAL

Figure 14.7 shows the reply after you request the global listing.

Again, most of the entries are not shown, but LISTSERV will send you an e-mail message with all of them. With well over 7,000 entries from which to choose, you should be able to find something to your liking.

N O T E The fact that many LISTSERV systems are interconnected in this way allows you to send your commands to just about any of them, and LISTSERV will forward the command to the appropriate place. For example, even though the TFTD-L list resides on the LISTSERV at Texas A&M, I could subscribe to it by sending the SUBSCRIBE command to LISTSERV@UM.MARIST.EDU. The LISTSERV at Marist College will forward my request automatically to the one at Texas A&M, and I will be subscribed to the list.

Part

III

Ch

14

FIG. 14.7

Global mailing lists from Texas A&M.

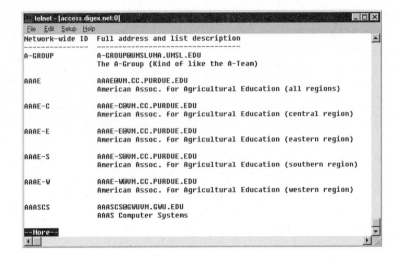

If you want to narrow the search a little (or don't have the room on your computer or e-mail account to get the full global list; it's well over 100K long!), you can include search keywords in your command. For example, I'm a big hockey fan, so I might send the following e-mail message to LISTSERV:

```
LIST GLOBAL HOCKEY
```

Figure 14.8 shows the reply, which includes only lists dealing with hockey as a topic.

FIG. 14.8

Hockey-related lists that the Texas A&M LISTSERV knows about.

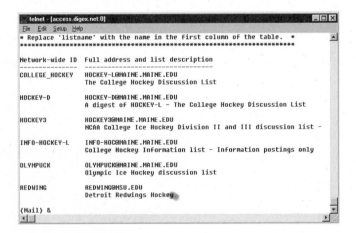

Notice in the global lists that the full address of each mailing list appears in the listing. If you want to join one of these lists, however, you can simply send your subscription request to the Texas A&M LISTSERV host, or to any others that you know about. Unless the name of the list is not unique (unlikely), the LISTSERV forwards the request appropriately. If the name isn't unique, LISTSERV is kind enough to send you a message to that effect, and to tell you what your options are.

▶ **See** "Anonymous FTP," **p. 808**

N O T E   Probably the best way to find mailing lists that might be of interest to you is to request the global list and use your favorite editor to search through that list. You can also check out the list of lists on NetCD (the CD-ROM included with this book), under \docs\lists. Stephanie da Silva maintains this list of publicly available mailing lists; you can get a current copy this list using anonymous FTP from **rtfm.mit.edu** in the directory /pub/usenet-by-group/news.lists. The list will be in 14 parts, named like

`Publicly_Accessible_Mailing_Lists,_Part_??_14`

As you might have guessed, this is also posted to the newgroup **news.lists** on a monthly basis, around the 19th of each month. ▦

Using Other LISTSERV Commands

You now know everything you need to get started with LISTSERV, and, in fact, probably know everything you'll ever need to know. As you saw from the previous help message in Figure 14.5, however, there are other things you can do in addition to subscribing, signing off, and requesting lists.

One of the things you had to do when subscribing was to list your name along with the subscription request. LISTSERV needs to have your full name (preferably your real one, although there usually isn't any way to verify this) before it will process subscription requests.

N O T E   One way to avoid having to specify your name each time you subscribe to a new mailing list is to register with the LISTSERV, using the REGISTER command:

`REGISTER James R. O'Donnell, Jr., Ph.D.`

This registers your name and e-mail address with this LISTSERV, so that you don't have to include your name on subscription requests. ▦

After you send an e-mail message with this command, LISTSERV sends you a reply message similar to the one shown in Figure 14.9.

N O T E   The LISTSERV REVIEW command allows anyone to find out who the subscribers are on a given list. If you'd rather people not be able to tell if you are on a LISTSERV mailing list, you can do this with the LISTSERV REGISTER command. Send an e-mail message to LISTSERV with the command REGISTER OFF in the body of the message. Then, you won't be reported as a subscriber to any mailing lists that reside on that particular LISTSERV system. ▦

Part
III

Ch
14

If you want to learn more about LISTSERV, or about some of the less commonly used commands, you can send a message with the simple command, INFO, as the body of the message.

FIG. 14.9

LISTSERV response to the REGISTER command.

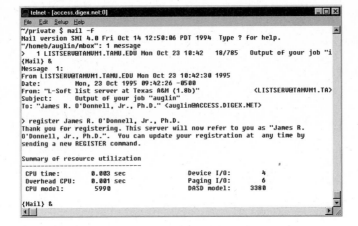

LISTSERV will send a reply message explaining what types of information it has available, as shown in Figure 14.10.

FIG. 14.10

LISTSERV information files.

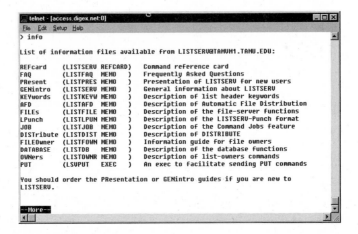

The last topic of general interest is how to retrieve files from LISTSERV. For example, each of the information files listed in Figure 14.10 can be retrieved either through an INFO command, or by getting the appropriate file. So, to get the command reference card file REFcard (the first one on the list in Fig. 14.10), you can either e-mail the command INFO REFCARD or GET LISTSERV REFCARD.

In addition to the information files shown in Figure 14.10, there are other files that a given LISTSERV will have. In order to get a list of those files, send the INDEX command to the LISTSERV server.

In response to the INDEX command, the Texas A&M LISTSERV sends you a list of files that looks something like the one shown in Figure 14.11 (it's kind of messy, but, unfortunately, that's how it looks coming from the LISTSERV program).

FIG. 14.11
LISTSERV file index.

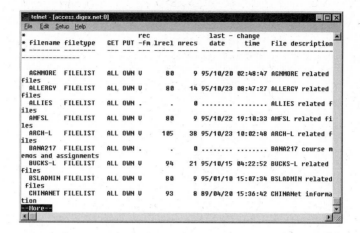

To get one of these files, send LISTSERV the GET command, followed by the file name and file type of the desired file, as in:

```
GET LISTSERV FILELIST
```

Sending Messages to a LISTSERV Mailing List

Once you are on a mailing list, depending on the nature of the list, you may want to send messages to the list, which will then get sent out to all the list subscribers. This process is very similar to sending a LISTSERV command, except that you use the list address, not LISTSERV. Follow these steps to send a message to the mailing list:

1. Use your Internet mail program to create a new mail message and send it to the mailing list address. For example, if I wanted to post a comment to HOCKEY-L, I'd send a message to HOCKEY-L@TAMVM1.TAMU.EDU. (HOCKEY-L doesn't reside at Texas A&M, but remember that my request will get forwarded to the correct LISTSERV system.)

2. Put a meaningful subject in the Subject line. This is different than with LISTSERV commands, where the subject is ignored. When sending out a message to everyone on a list, you should make your subject as specific as possible so the other subscribers can tell at a glance whether or not they want to read your message.

3. Enter your message in the text area. You can post files to the mailing list by encoding the file and including it in your message.

4. Send the e-mail message. You will usually receive a copy of your message back from the mailing list in a few minutes.

▶ **See** "Attaching Files," **p. 321**

▶ **See** "File Encoding and Decoding with Microsoft Exchange and Eudora," **p. 349**

Part
III

Ch
14

LISTSERV Miscellany

Although all of the procedures described so far have included only one command, you can place as many commands as you like in each message to LISTSERV. For example, if you want to change the name under which you are registered, subscribe to the HOCKEY3 mailing list, sign off the TFTD-L mailing list, and get the command reference card, you can send one message to:

LISTSERV@VM.MARIST.EDU

with the message body of

```
SUBSCRIBE HOCKEY3 Jim O'Donnell

REGISTER James R. O'Donnell, Jr.

SIGNOFF TFTD-L

info refcard
```

And everything you want will get done. To review what took place in this example, I first sent this message to a different LISTSERV site, this one at Marist College. As I mentioned, the list requests are forwarded; in the case of HOCKEY3, to the University of Maine, and TFTD-L to Texas A&M. My name at the University of Maine will be "Jim O'Donnell," since that is what I included on the command line where I subscribed to HOCKEY3, but the Marist LISTSERV will register me as "James R. O'Donnell, Jr.". The last thing I wanted to again point out in this example is that you don't need to put all of your commands in capital letters; LISTSERV can't tell the difference.

Using Majordomo Mailing Lists

Another type of program that you sometimes find running Internet mailing lists is a program called Majordomo. Majordomo tends to be used for smaller lists, and doesn't have the great connection of LISTSERV. A given Majordomo site is aware of the lists that it is running, but no others.

Sending Majordomo Commands

The procedure for sending commands to a Majordomo system is almost identical to that for LISTSERV commands, except the address is a little different.

1. Use your Internet mail program to create a new mail message and send it to the Majordomo address. The one I use is at **MAJORDOMO@VECTOR.CASTI.COM**. Depending on your mail program, you may type this address in at the command line with the `mail` command

   mail MAJORDOMO@VECTOR.CASTI.COM

   Or you can type **MAJORDOMO@VECTOR.CASTI.COM** on the To line of the e-mail message.

2. Leave the Subject line blank.

3. In the text area of the message, enter Majordomo commands, one per line, in uppercase, lowercase, or mixed case.

4. Send the e-mail message. The reply will usually come in a few minutes.

Getting Majordomo Help

Take a look at the Majordomo help message to get the lay of the land. Just as LISTSERV expects its command to be sent to the LISTSERV address, Majordomo expects commands to be sent to **Majordomo@VECTOR.CASTI.COM**. Send an e-mail message to the Majordomo address with the command in the body text of

HELP

(Majordomo, like LISTSERV, also doesn't care about the letters being upper- or lowercase.) The response to a HELP command will look something like Figure 14.12.

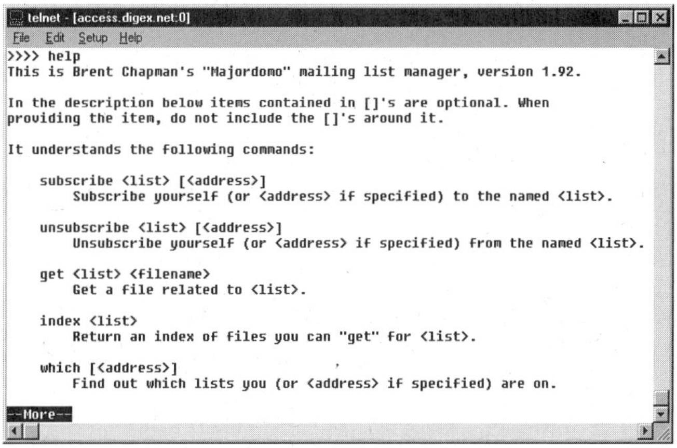

FIG. 14.12

A Majordomo help message.

```
telnet - [access.digex.net:0]
File  Edit  Setup  Help
>>>> help
This is Brent Chapman's "Majordomo" mailing list manager, version 1.92.

In the description below items contained in []'s are optional. When
providing the item, do not include the []'s around it.

It understands the following commands:

    subscribe <list> [<address>]
        Subscribe yourself (or <address> if specified) to the named <list>.

    unsubscribe <list> [<address>]
        Unsubscribe yourself (or <address> if specified) from the named <list>.

    get <list> <filename>
        Get a file related to <list>.

    index <list>
        Return an index of files you can "get" for <list>.

    which [<address>]
        Find out which lists you (or <address> if specified) are on.

--More--
```

Subscribing to and Unsubscribing from Majordomo Lists

Subscribing to and unsubscribing from a Majordomo list is similar to the same operations for LISTSERV lists. In the case of Majordomo, however, UNSUBSCRIBE is used (rather than SIGNOFF) to quit a list. With Majordomo, you don't need to specify your name with the SUBSCRIBE command. The Majordomo server automatically recognizes the e-mail address and name from which you're sending the message.

N O T E One feature of Majordomo that isn't in LISTSERV is that in the SUBSCRIBE or UNSUBSCRIBE command, you can optionally specify a different e-mail address. This is handy if you temporarily don't have access to the e-mail account you normally use, but want to issue a command as if it came from that address. Another time this comes in handy is if you need to unsubscribe from a list because the e-mail address from which you originally subscribed is no longer active. ▪

Part
III

Ch
14

Finding Majordomo Lists

In order to find out what mailing lists a given Majordomo supports, simply send an e-mail message to the Majordomo list with the LISTS command in the body of the message.

You receive a message like the one shown in Figure 14.13.

FIG. 14.13

Majordomo lists message.

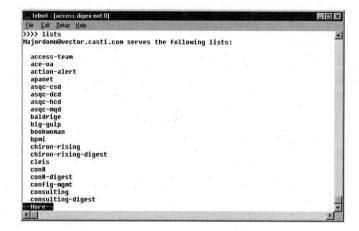

Majordomo Miscellany

Like LISTSERV, Majordomo allows multiple commands per e-mail message sent. And, you still have to be careful of where to send your messages. Commands are sent to

> **MAJORDOMO@VECTOR.CASTI.COM**

If you want to send a message to all of the subscribers on the list, send the message to, for example:

> **DC-MOTSS@VECTOR.CASTI.COM**

Like LISTSERV, Majordomo has the INDEX and GET commands for requesting an index of files, and retrieving one of those files, respectively. One convenient option that Majordomo has is the WHICH command; it tells you which lists you are a member of.

Accessing Private or Other Mailing Lists

It is likely, in your travels throughout the Internet, that you will run across other mailing lists that aren't LISTSERV or Majordomo lists. Not to worry, however. In almost all cases—except for truly private lists—these lists are run by people who welcome your participation, and they normally make it easy to figure out how to join, quit, and contribute to the list.

Understanding Different Mailing List Types

In addition to what software (or person) administers a mailing list, and what topic or topics the list covers, there are a few other distinctions between mailing lists that are important to understand.

Working with Moderated and Unmoderated Lists

A *moderated list* is one in which a person or persons reviews and approves all messages before they are posted to the list. These lists tend to have more formal discussions, and also, as you might expect, tend to stay on topic. In this type of list, all messages posted to the list first go to the list moderator for review. This type of list tends to be fairly informative, but usually has little *traffic* (messages flowing back and forth).

Most lists are *unmoderated*. If you want to reply or post a message to a list, you send it to the mailing list address and, after some small delay, your message is posted. These types of lists are more free-flowing than moderated lists, sometimes on topic, sometimes off. Quite often, several different discussions, or *threads*, are taking place at once. Usually, these different threads are distinguished by informative subject lines, although this isn't always the case. Traffic on an unmoderated list can be very heavy. Sometimes, however, the signal-to-noise ratio is low, and the possibility of a flame war always exists (see the "Using Netiquette" section).

Working with Digestified and Undigestified Lists

Sometimes, high traffic mailing lists are sent out as digests, rather than as individual messages. A *digest* is a collection of messages that the mailing list program or administrator accumulates and then sends out after a certain amount of time, or after a certain length is reached.

The advantage of a mailing list digest is that you are not receiving e-mail messages every couple of minutes. Having your computer beep or flash every time you get a message can be distracting. However, when you receive messages as a digest, it becomes harder to follow different conversation threads, because you can't identify a message by the subject line.

Using Netiquette

If you spend any amount of time on Internet mailing lists, in UseNet newsgroups, or on IRC (see Chapter 35, "How Internet Relay Chat Works" and Chapter 36, "Using mIRC, Netscape Chat, and Comic Chat"), you quickly become familiar with *Netiquette,* the term used to describe the proper way of behaving on the Net.

As a newcomer, some of the people who have been around for a while may cut you some slack, but they are just as likely to get annoyed for any Netiquette breaches on your part. There is certainly no enforcement mechanism on much of the Internet, but still, you don't want to get a bad reputation. On Internet mailing lists that are directly administered by someone, it is possible to get yourself thrown off the list.

Part
III

Ch
14

But, as in most cases, good etiquette on the Internet is mostly a matter of common sense. If you keep a few things in mind, you shouldn't have any problems.

Understanding Bandwidth or Signal-to-Noise Ratio

Two terms that come up often in Internet discussions, of which mailing lists are an example, are *bandwidth* and *signal-to-noise ratio*.

Bandwidth refers to how much information can be transmitted over a mailing list (or whatever), whereas signal-to-noise ratio measures how relevant the discussion actually taking place is to the supposed topic of the discussion. There are quite a few ways that the relevant discussion (the signal) can be obscured by the irrelevant discussion (the noise). There are two more common ways to avoid noise: by reading the FAQ and by avoiding test messages.

Reading the FAQ!　Most Internet mailing lists that have been around for a while have a list of "Frequently Asked Questions," commonly referred to as a FAQ. This list of questions (and answers!) is usually posted frequently. Before you ask your own question on the list, it is usually a good idea to look through the FAQ to see whether the question has already been addressed.

If you have a hard time locating a FAQ, you might want to use the LISTSERV or Majodomo INDEX command to see whether you can retrieve the FAQ. If not, you can safely post a short little message asking whether there is a FAQ for this list.

Avoiding Test Messages　A common habit of people new to Internet mailing lists is the desire to send out a test message, "to see if it works." These messages usually have a subject of "Test message: do not read," and something like "This is a test, please ignore" in the body of the message.

Even with the "do not read" warning, this sort of message is liable to annoy a lot of people. Most of these mailing lists have been up and running a long time, and it's normally a safe bet to assume that they work as advertised. And in any case, sending a message to 10, 20, hundreds, or even thousands of people for a test is not good use of Internet bandwidth.

Replying to Questions　Many mailing lists exist to provide support for computer software or products from other users. In these sorts of lists, people frequently ask questions about how to perform a certain action, or ask for help fixing a problem that they might have. If you are able to help them with their problem, your first impulse might be to whip out a quick reply and post it to the list. That's not always the best way to do it.

Because of the way mailing lists work, being posted from a central machine far and wide across the Internet, there might be considerable delay between when a given message reaches different users. If the question asked was a relatively simple one, four or five or ten people might read it, solve it, and post a solution, before any of them have seen what other people have written.

If it's a fairly simple problem, it might be a better idea to e-mail your solution to the person who posted the original question, rather than to the whole list. Then, if it turns out that there is a lot of interest on the list in that topic, the original sender can summarize the solutions received and post the summary.

Avoiding Flame Wars

A fairly pernicious waste of Internet bandwidth deserves its own discussion, and that is the flame war. A *flame war* is what happens when someone (no blame here!) either gets a little too personal in a reply to someone else, or takes a comment from someone else a little too personally. Before you know it, the original topic of discussion is lost as the list becomes filled with passionate messages insulting different people. Very often, well-meaning souls who try to step in and moderate between two people are drawn in as well.

The best way to react if someone insults you—flames you—on an Internet mailing list is to take some time and decide whether it is really worth responding. Did you misread the intention of the mail? Are you taking it too personally? If you decide that you really need to respond, do everyone else on the list a favor, and take the discussion to private e-mail between you and the offending party. This will leave the mailing list open for the discussion it is intended for.

Changing Your E-mail Address or Going on Vacation

One problem you might have after you have joined a mailing list is that you receive a lot more e-mail than you counted on. Even though TFTD-L sends out only one message a day (not including weekends), there are other lists that have much more traffic. Hopefully, you'll be able to check your e-mail often enough so that this isn't a problem, but what happens if your e-mail address changes or if you go on vacation?

When your e-mail address changes, that means your old account has probably gone away. But, the mailing list is still sending you e-mail. Even if your account has completely gone away, the computer system that the account was on still has to deal with all of the messages the mailing list is sending out, probably by flagging them as undeliverable and sending them back. The computer that hosts the mailing list still has to send you out the message and deal with the undeliverable messages that get sent back.

Eventually, the mailing list will figure out that you have gone away, but you can save a lot of Internet bandwidth and resources by conscientiously quitting lists when your e-mail account changes.

A similar problem can happen when you are temporarily unable to access your e-mail account, usually when you go on vacation. In this case, your mailing lists continue to send you e-mail. If you belong to one or more high traffic mailing lists, you can potentially receive a huge amount of e-mail while you're on vacation. It is possible that the number of messages received might exceed the storage capabilities of your computer account or system. If this might be a problem, it's probably a good idea to temporarily quit your high traffic lists until you return.

To summarize, you can save yourself, the mailing list administrators of the lists to which you belong, the system administrators of your computer and the mailing list computer, and the whole Internet, a lot of time, effort, and otherwise wasted resources by doing the following:

Part
III

Ch

14

■ Quit all mailing lists when the e-mail address to which they are sent changes or is discontinued. If you forget to do this until after the address goes away, and thus can no longer use it to issue a command to quit, you must use a different address to send a message to the mailing list administrator asking him or her to remove your old address from the list.

■ If you're going on vacation, or your e-mail will not be accessible for an extended period of time for some other reason, consider temporarily quitting any high volume mailing lists to which you belong. You probably won't be able to read all the messages you get while you're gone anyway, and so the messages are just going to tie up resources on the Internet and on your computer.

Anonymous Mailing Services

If you would like to be on a mailing list that is discussing a sensitive topic, you can usually subscribe with a reasonable assurance that you can maintain your anonymity. Most mailing list administrators respect the potential desire of their subscribers to remain anonymous.

Internet Mailing Lists and UseNet

There are many similarities between Internet mailing lists and UseNet (see Chapter 27, "How UseNet Works"). Both allow many people with similar interests to have discussions and share information over the Internet. As we have seen, Internet mailing lists occur completely over e-mail; UseNet newsgroups use a different mechanism, and require a news reader at your computer. Because of this, Internet mailing lists are more widely available. In fact, there are some mailing lists that echo UseNet discussions, so that people who don't have access to a news reader can participate.

Regardless, the two share many of the same characteristics and limitations. Both are limited to ASCII information only, so binary files must be encoded before they can be sent. The same rules of netiquette apply to discussions. One advantage of UseNet, if you have access to a news reader on your computer, is that you don't have to worry about lots of messages piling up in your mailbox if you are away for an extended period of time. ●

Encoding and Decoding Files

by Jerry Honeycutt and James O'Donnell

In Chapter 16, "How the World Wide Web Works," you learn about the hottest new way of using the Internet, the World Wide Web (WWW). As you've probably heard, the WWW allows you to easily surf around the Internet, viewing text, graphics, sounds, and movies—information in many different forms.

Long before the existence of the WWW, however, people were exchanging non-text information—graphics, sounds, and binary files such as executables and zip archives—using other methods. Internet applications such as FTP (see Chapter 31, "Using FTP and Popular FTP Programs") and Gopher (see Chapter 32, "Using Gopher and Popular Gopher Programs") allow this binary information to be accessed and retrieved directly over the Internet. However, it's also possible to send and receive binary information through means that are normally restricted to text only, such as Internet e-mail and UseNet, by encoding and decoding files containing such information. ■

Learn how to attach files to your e-mail

You'll learn how to use Microsoft Exchange and Eudora to send encoded files through e-mail.

Visually recognize different encoding schemes

Sometimes you need to be able to see what encoding scheme was used by looking at it. Here, you'll learn to recognize MIME encoding and UUEncoding.

Install and use Wincode

Wincode is a popular program for encoding and decoding binary files. In this chapter, you'll learn how to install and use it.

Learn about BinHex

BinHex is the encoding scheme most used on Mac computers. You'll learn how to recognize it.

What Are File Encoding and Decoding, and Why Are They Needed?

Suppose that someone—finally!—takes a decent picture of me playing hockey (as opposed to the pictures of me falling down, which I usually get), and I want to send a copy of the picture home to my father. This being the computer age—and me being cheap—I decide to scan the picture and send a copy of the graphics file to my father through e-mail. How do I send that graphics picture through e-mail? (see Fig. 15.1.).

FIG. 15.1

Look, Dad! I really can play hockey!

File encoding takes files with binary information, such as this graphics file, executable programs, or compressed file archives, and converts them to ASCII text files. *Decoding* converts the files back. After a binary file has been encoded into an ASCII text file, it isn't in a very useful form. If it's a program, it can't be run, and if it's a picture, it can't be viewed. To be usable, the file must be decoded back into its original binary form.

As you probably figured out from the introduction to this chapter, there's a very important use for an encoded file: Unlike the binary file from which it is made, an encoded file can be more easily transmitted over the Internet. The original networks were never set up to carry anything but text, which generally uses only seven bits of information per byte. Because binary information uses all eight bits, the networks were not able to transmit it. There are ways of transmitting binary files over the Internet, particularly FTP and the World Wide Web (WWW), but some Internet services are still limited to text. Internet services limited to text are primarily Internet e-mail, including Internet mailing lists, and UseNet.

▶ **See** "ASCII Format Only," **p. 232**

On the CD

The process of encoding involves taking a binary file, in which eight bits per byte are used, and converting it into a text file that uses seven bits per byte. As you might guess, the encoded file is going to be bigger than the original file. It's common to compress a file before encoding it. Files meant to be used on a PC will generally be zipped (and can be unzipped using PKZIP and WinZip, both of which you'll find on the NetCD).

▶ **See** "ASCII Format Only," **p. 232**

▶ **See** "What Are Internet Mailing Lists?," **p. 330**

▶ **See** "What is FTP?," **p. 808**

Part
III

Ch
15

What Types of Encoding and Decoding Are There?

The two most common types of encoding are MIME and UUENCODE. MIME, which stands for Multipurpose Internet Mail Extensions, was developed to provide a standard means of exchanging various types of binary information through the Internet. UUENCODE is an older "standard," originally developed for UNIX systems. Not all versions of UUENCODE/ UUDECODE are compatible with one another, so when you have a choice, it's usually better to use MIME.

N O T E You may be wondering why it's called UUENCODE and UUDECODE. In the fine tradition of many programs and commands that come from UNIX ("grep," "awk," "ls," and so on), the meaning of the command isn't immediately obvious. The clue comes from "UUCP," which comes from "UNIX-UNIX CoPy." So, UUENCODE and UUDECODE were originally meant to facilitate the transfer of binary files from one UNIX system to another UNIX system. ■

There is another kind of file encoding that's very popular in the Macintosh world; it's called *BinHex*. Later in this chapter, you'll see how to recognize files encoded with BinHex, but because it's not likely that you'll find any files encoded that way (unless you communicate with MAC users), this chapter doesn't spend much time on BinHex.

File Encoding and Decoding with Microsoft Exchange and Eudora

As discussed in their respective chapters (see Chapter 11, "Using Microsoft Exchange," and Chapter 13, "Using Eudora"), both Microsoft Exchange and Eudora are e-mail programs that run under Windows and allow you to attach binary files to e-mail messages.

Sending Encoded Files Using Microsoft Exchange

Microsoft Exchange allows you to send encoded files using either MIME or UUENCODE. To select between these two methods, follow these steps:

1. Start Microsoft Exchange by double-clicking the Inbox icon on your desktop, and then open the Tools menu and choose the Services item.

2. Highlight the Internet Mail service entry and then click the Properties button.

3. Click the Message Format button.

4. Select the Use MIME When Sending Messages check box to use MIME encoding and then clear the check box to use UUENCODE (see Fig. 15.2).

FIG. 15.2

This check box in the Message Format dialog box controls whether Exchange uses MIME or UUENCODE encoding.

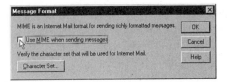

After you select the type of encoding, including an encoded file is fairly straightforward. From the Compose menu, choose the New Message item. This gives you the e-mail message composition window shown in Figure 15.3, in which I composed a quick message and am now ready to attach the binary graphics file.

FIG. 15.3

When you want to send e-mail using Microsoft Exchange, it gives you this window in which to compose your message.

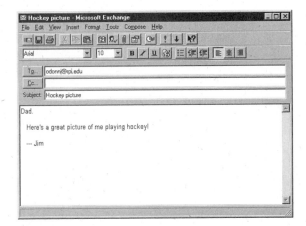

Figure 15.4 shows the menu bar in the composition window. Files are attached to the message using the Insert File button (Paperclip).

FIG. 15.4

Click the Insert File button of the menu bar to attach a file to your message.

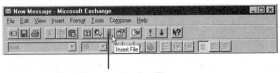

Click here to attach a file.

In response to clicking the Insert File button, the window shown in Figure 15.5 appears. From here, you can select the file to be attached. If this is a binary file, such as the graphics file I am sending, make sure that you click the radio button to insert the file as An Attachment. After you have made this selection, the composition window will appear (see Fig. 15.6). From here, you can send the message normally, and the file that you attached will be encoded according to the method you selected.

FIG. 15.5
Select the file to attach to this e-mail message. If it's a binary file, make sure to click the radio button to insert it as An Attachment.

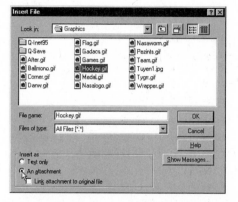

FIG. 15.6
After you have attached the file, it appears in the composition window, as shown. The message is ready to be sent!

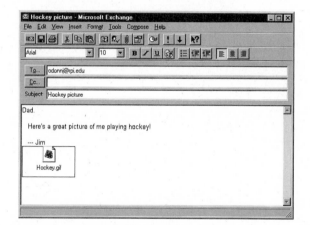

Sending Encoded Files Using Eudora

Eudora allows you to send encoded files using either MIME or BinHex. In the composition window for sending e-mail with Eudora, you can select between these two methods right from the menu bar, as shown in Figure 15.7. Because you are using Windows 95, you will almost always want to choose MIME, unless you are sending the message to someone who is using a Mac. (Note that if both you and the recipient of the message are using Eudora, you can choose either method, because Eudora automatically detects the type of encoding. In general, however, unless the recipient is using a Mac, you will always want to use MIME.)

To attach a binary file to an e-mail message in Eudora, compose the message normally and then choose the Attach File item from the Message menu (or press Ctrl+H), as shown in Figure 15.8. You will be given a standard Windows file-selection dialog box from which you can select the file to include. Once that is done, the file name—or names, as more than one file can be attached—appear in the Attachments section of the message.

FIG. 15.7

Eudora allows you to select the encoding method right from the menu bar of each message; in general, you will want to use MIME encoding.

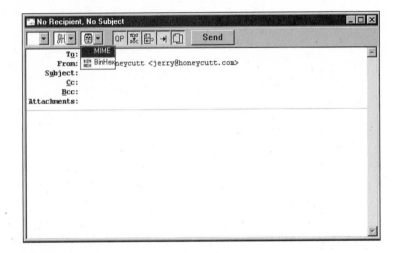

FIG. 15.8

Attach a file in Eudora either by selecting this menu item or by pressing Ctrl+H.

Recognizing Different Encoding Schemes

If you're using an e-mail program such as Microsoft Exchange or Eudora, the encoding and decoding method used will be pretty irrelevant. These programs encode outgoing files and decode incoming files automatically, and you'll never need to know exactly how. However, if you don't use these e-mail programs, or if you obtain an encoded file through some other means, it's important to know how to recognize what the encoded files look like—this makes it a lot easier to figure out how to decode them.

Figures 15.9 and 15.10 show the resulting e-mail messages with the attached hockey picture, using MIME encoding (from Eudora) and UUENCODE encoding (from Microsoft Exchange).

FIG. 15.9
The top of an e-mail message including an attached graphics file encoded using MIME.

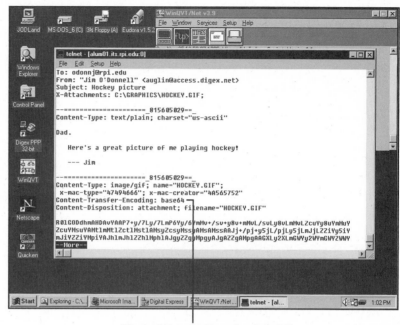

"Content-Transfer-Encoding: base64"

"Encoding: 6 TEXT, 2393 UUENCODE"

FIG. 15.10
The top of an e-mail message including an attached graphics file encoded using UUENCODE.

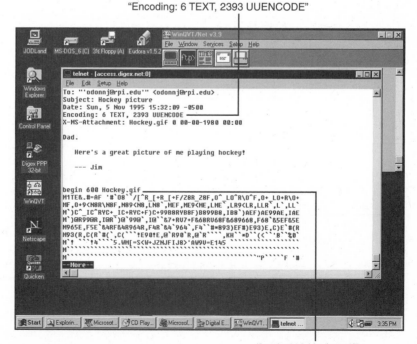

"begin 600 Hockey.gif"

It's fairly easy to distinguish between files encoded with MIME and those encoded with UUENCODE:

- MIME-encoded files include a line, such as that shown in Figure 15.9, that reads `Content-Transfer-Encoding: base64`.

- UUENCODEd files begin with a line such as `begin 600 Hockey.gif` (the `600` is a UNIX file permission code that you don't really need to worry about), as shown in Figure 15.10.

- UUENCODEd files end with a line that reads `end` (not seen in Figure 15.10 because the file is longer than the screen).

At the end of this chapter, you'll take a look at what BinHex-encoded files look like.

> **CAUTION**
>
> Whenever you look at an encoded file, either MIME or UUENCODE encoding—by viewing it with an editor, for instance—be very careful not to change any of the characters inside the encoded file. If the file is a graphics or sound file, changing it can cause the decoded file to be distorted. If the encoded file is a zip file or executable program, changing any characters can render the decoded file useless.

Encoding and Decoding Files from Windows

As mentioned earlier, if the only encoded files you deal with go through Microsoft Exchange, Eudora, or some other e-mail program or UseNet newsreader that automatically encodes and decodes the files, there really isn't anything else you need to know. However, it is likely that every once in a while you will run into an encoded file that hasn't gone through your mailer, or you might need to encode a file that you aren't mailing right away. To do that, you need a program that allows you to encode and decode files from Windows. Wincode is such a program.

NOTE The current version of Wincode, v2.7.1, is not a Windows 95, 32-bit application; it was written for Windows 3.1 and Windows for Workgroups. Thus, it references Windows 3.1 elements, such as the Program Manager. However, the program does work the same under Windows 95. ■

Installing Wincode

Assuming you're starting with a zip file containing the Wincode files (I started with wncod271.zip), install Wincode as follows:

1. Unzip the file, preferably into its own subdirectory, such as c:\temp. Alternatively, you can install this directly from NetCD, which accompanies this book.

2. From the Start button on the taskbar or from Windows Explorer, run c:\temp\install.exe. (If you're running the installation from a different directory or from NetCD, change the drive and/or directory as needed to match your system.)

The installer displays a dialog box like the one in Figure 15.11, which shows the amount of space it requires. You might also take a look at the license agreement. Then click on Accept to continue.

FIG. 15.11

The Wincode installer shows you how much space on your hard disk it needs (at the bottom of the license window).

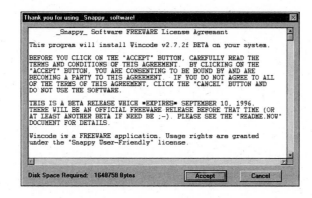

This information allows you to answer the installer's next question of where to install Wincode, shown in Figure 15.12.

FIG. 15.12

The Wincode installer gives you the option of selecting the Destination Directory in which to install the program.

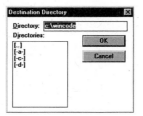

3. Click on OK to select the default directory or enter another directory in the place of the default, c:\wincode.

4. After you've chosen the destination for the installation of the program, you'll get the screen shown in Figure 15.13, which gives you one more chance to review your options and continue with the installation (or decide not to). Note that unless you're still using the Program Manager, you should deselect the Add/Create Program Manager Group check box. Click Install to continue or click Cancel to quit.

If you click Install at this point, the installation will commence and quickly finish (it's not that big of a program, really). You'll get a few other dialog boxes, mentioning that an installation log file was created and giving you an opportunity to view the Readme.txt file (which tells you how, for a small fee, you can get full documentation for the program).

FIG. 15.13

The Wincode installer screen when it's ready to commence with the installation. (Review the options shown on this screen and then click Install or Cancel.)

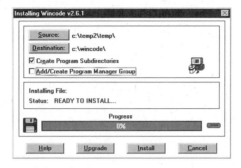

5. Because Wincode was written for Windows 3.1 and Windows for Workgroups, the installation process puts neither an entry for the program in the Start menu nor a shortcut on the desktop. To give myself easy access to the program, I created a standard Windows 95 shortcut to the program and put it on the desktop (see Fig. 15.14). Note that, as will be shown later, Wincode supports drag-and-drop encoding and decoding of files.

FIG. 15.14

This shows a shortcut to the Wincode program on my Windows 95 desktop.

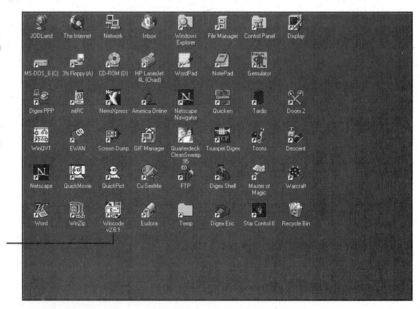

Wincode icon ——

Using Wincode to Encode a File

If you read through the Readme.txt file for Wincode, you'll see that the author has an unusual method of marketing his program. The program itself is *freeware*; this means that the program is free, but it is copyrighted, and is, therefore, not public domain. The author charges $5 to send the Help file for the program. This $5 also entitles you to upgrades of the program and technical support via e-mail.

As the author states, however, using the program without the HELP file is relatively simple; you learn how to do that in the following sections. For the sophisticated parts of the program, however, and to support the author for producing a useful program, you might want to send him the $5 for the Help file.

N O T E You might be tempted to use the program without sending the author the $5 fee for the Help file, especially if you don't need its more sophisticated features. Or you might just never get around to sending in the money. As the author states, that's okay. If you get good use out of Wincode, however, you might want to send in the $5. It's a very reasonable price for such a slick program, and by sending in the money, you can support the author's further development of this and other Windows utilities. ■

When you start Wincode, you see the screen shown in Figure 15.15.

FIG. 15.15

You can access Wincode's commands through the menus or by using the buttons along the top.

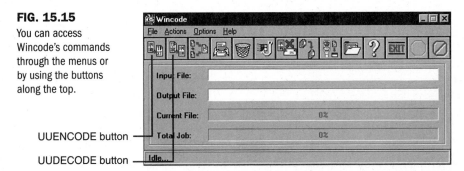

UUENCODE button

UUDECODE button

The first step is to select which encoding method you would like to use. This is done by choosing the Encode item from the Options menu, which results in the dialog box shown in Figure 15.16. The encoding methods are shown in the Code Type drop-down list to the right; the two selections you are interested in are UUE (UUEncoding) and BASE64 (MIME encoding). Once you select one of these, you will be given the choice of a header type, as shown in Figure 15.17. It's safe to select whatever the default value is here.

To encode a file, either choose the Encode item from the File menu, click the Encode button—the first button from the left in the toolbar on the top of the window—or simply drag a file from the Windows Explorer onto the Wincode shortcut icon on the desktop. In the first two cases, you'll get the dialog box shown in Figure 15.18, in which you select the file(s) you'd like to decode.

As the file is encoded, the name of the input and output file appears in the appropriate places in the Wincode window, and the status bars will move from left to right as the encoding occurs. If the process occurs without a problem, a dialog box appears telling you that the operation was a success.

FIG. 15.16

Select either UUE for UUEncoding or BASE64 for MIME encoding.

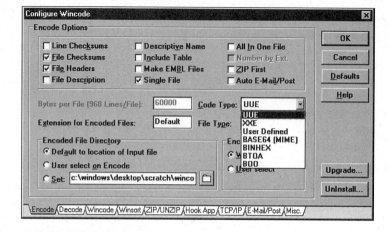

FIG. 15.17

You can go ahead and accept the default value of header type for your encoding selection.

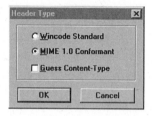

FIG. 15.18

This dialog box allows you to select file(s) to encode.

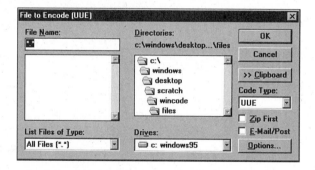

 TIP If you encode a file and can't find the encoded file, you may need to check the Encoded File Directory section of the Encode Options dialog box (refer to Fig. 15.16). You can select for the encoded file to be placed where the input file is, select a dedicated directory for encoded files (the default is c:\wincode\encode), or have Wincode ask you each time. There is also a similar section in the Decode Options and ZIP/UNZIP Options dialog boxes.

Using Wincode to Decode a File

Using Wincode to decode a file is as easy as using it to encode one. You simply choose the Decode item from the File menu, click the Decode button—the second button from the left—or drag the encoded file onto the Wincode desktop icon. For the first two methods a dialog box appears, allowing you to select the file to decode.

N O T E You may be wondering how Wincode knows when to encode and when to decode a file if it is dragged and dropped onto the Wincode desktop icon. Because Wincode is a Windows 3.1/Windows for Workgroups application, it uses the file extension to detect encoded files and will attempt to decode them. All other files are encoded. The Decode Extensions area in the Decode Options dialog box menu (see Fig. 15.19) allows you to enter a list of extensions for Wincode to use to recognize encoded files. ■

FIG. 15.19
The Decode Options dialog box allows the selection of various decoding options.

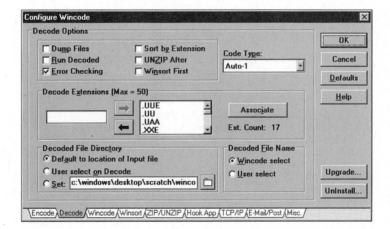

Other Features of Wincode

There are a couple more features of Wincode that I want to mention—a few of the more sophisticated features you can learn about by registering your copy of the program with the author and receiving the Help file. Obviously, I've discussed only UUEncoding and UUDecoding one file. Wincode allows you to do much more. You can automatically concatenate split encoded files in an order that you specify, in order to join and then decode them. A very sophisticated feature is the ability to "hook" Wincode into a program like Eudora, which allows you to use Wincode's features directly from that other application.

One thing you can do is set up Wincode to automatically zip a file or group of files before encoding or unzip a zipped file archive after decoding. These options are enabled in the encode and decode dialog boxes. To set this up, you need to click on the ZIP/UNZIP tab on the decode dialog box. The ZIP/UNZIP Options dialog box appears, as shown in Figure 15.20. The most important options you need to set are the locations of the zip and unzip program. After these are set, selecting the ZIP or UNZIP button in the encode or decode file selection dialog boxes allows this function to be done automatically.

▶ **See** "Using Eudora," **p. 303**

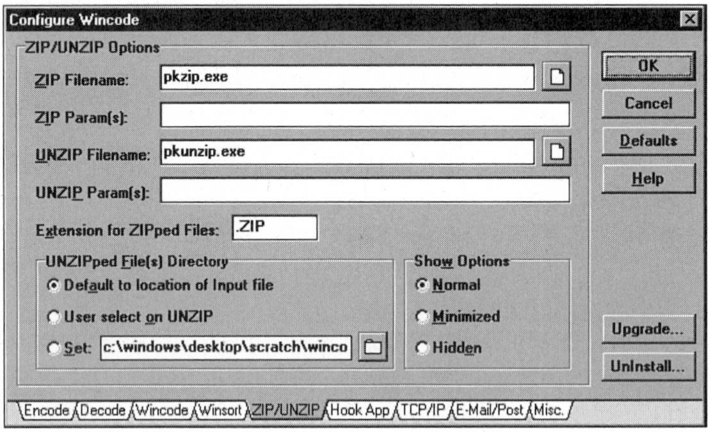

FIG. 15.20

Here you can tell Wincode where to find the programs you use for zipping and unzipping files; it can then do it for you automatically.

File Encoding and Decoding on UseNet

As mentioned earlier, UseNet is similar to Internet e-mail in that only text information can be exchanged. As will be discussed in later chapters, UseNet is the Internet equivalent of the office bulletin board; in addition to text messages that get posted, there is also the desire to post pictures and other non-text information. Thus, the same need exists to be able to encode binary information, and the same methods can be used. Currently, the standard on UseNet groups is that BinHex is used in the Mac-specific groups, while UUEncoding is used in most other cases. Just as with e-mail, if your newsreader does not automatically decode such files, you'll need a program like Wincode to do it.

▶ **See** "How UseNet Works," **p. 715**

Recognizing Macintosh BinHex

Sometimes on UseNet, or elsewhere on the Internet, you'll run into files that have been encoded with something other than UUENCODE or MIME encoding. Probably the most common of these files will be those encoded using the Macintosh BinHex program; a sample is shown in Figure 15.21.

FIG. 15.21

This file looks a little like a MIME-encoded file, but it's a Macintosh BinHex file.

The World Wide Web

How the World Wide Web Works

by Mary Ann Pike

The World Wide Web (WWW or Web) is one of the newest Internet services. The WWW allows you to combine text, audio, graphics, and even animation to make a document a learning experience. Links within WWW documents can take you quickly to other related documents. And the speed of the Internet makes it as easy to view a WWW document from halfway around the world as it is to view one from your hometown.

The various WWW browsers allow you to explore WWW Internet sites, giving you quick access to hypermedia documents provided at those sites. Not only does the WWW provide quick graphical access to hypermedia documents, it also allows you to use the same GUI to interface to other Internet services, such as FTP, Gopher, and UseNet newsgroups. The WWW is the closest the Internet has come to a comprehensive, user-friendly interface. ∎

Learn about the history of the WWW

The Web hasn't been around very long. You'll learn about its brief history in this chapter.

Understand concepts important to the WWW

You don't need to understand how the Web works to use it, but learning some basic concepts will enhance your experience.

Understand the future of the WWW

Most of the Internet's evolution such as VRML and multimedia is happening on the Web.

Find more information about the WWW

This chapter shows you where you can find more information about the Web.

History of the WWW

The history of the WWW is fairly short. In 1989, some researchers at CERN (the European Laboratory for Particle Physics) wanted to develop a better way to give widely dispersed research groups access to shared information. Because research was conducted between distant sites, performing any simple activity (reading a document or viewing an image) often required finding the location of the desired item, making a remote connection to the machine where it resided, and then retrieving it to a local machine. In addition, each activity required running a number of different applications (such as Telnet, FTP, and an image viewer). What the researchers wanted was a system that would enable them to quickly access all types of information with a common interface, removing the need to execute many steps to achieve the final goal.

Over the course of a year, the proposal for this project was refined, and work began on the implementation. By the end of 1990, the researchers at CERN had a text-mode (non-graphical) browser and a graphical browser for the NeXT computer. During 1991, the WWW was released for general usage at CERN. Initially, access was restricted to hypertext and UseNet news articles. As the project advanced, interfaces to other Internet services were added (WAIS, anonymous FTP, Telnet, and Gopher).

During 1992, CERN began publicizing the WWW project. People saw what a great idea it was, and began creating their own WWW servers to make their information available to the Internet. A few people also began working on WWW clients, designing easy-to-use interfaces to the WWW. By the end of 1993, browsers had been developed for many different computer systems, including X Windows, Apple Macintosh, and PC/Windows. By the summer of 1994, WWW had become one of the most popular ways to access Internet resources.

Important WWW Concepts

Like the word "Internet," which seems to imply a well-defined entity (which, of course, it isn't), "World Wide Web" seems to imply a fixed (or at least defined) set of sites that you can go to for information. In reality, the WWW is constantly changing as Internet sites add or delete access to their information. Learning about some of the basic concepts of the WWW will help you understand the nature of the Web.

Browsers

To access the WWW, it is necessary that you run a WWW browser on your computer. A browser is an application that knows how to interpret and display documents that it finds on the WWW. Documents on the WWW are hypertext documents (see the next section, "Hypertext (and Hypermedia)," for more information about hypertext). Hypertext documents are not plain text. They contain commands that structure the text by item (different headings, body paragraphs, and so on). This allows your browser to format each text type to best display it on-screen.

For example, if you connect to the Internet using a simple VT-100 compatible terminal, you have to run a text-based WWW browser, such as Lynx. This browser formats any documents that you receive so that they can be displayed in the fonts available on a terminal, and enables you to move between keywords in the document by using the arrow keys. Lynx, however, will not display any graphic or multimedia objects in a Web document because it is designed to run on a text-only terminal that cannot display these objects. The graphics and multimedia objects cannot be displayed regardless of whether you are running Lynx on a terminal or in a terminal Window on your PC.

If you have a more sophisticated terminal like an X terminal, you can use a graphics-based browser like the X version of Mosaic. If you are running on a PC or Macintosh, you can use the PC or Macintosh version of the Mosaic browser, or one of the other WWW browsers that have been developed for these computers. These browsers are GUI applications that take advantage of the graphic capabilities of these terminals and computers, allowing you to use different sizes, fonts, and formatting for different text types.

In addition to displaying nicely formatted text, browsers can also give you the ability to access documents that contain other media besides text. For example, if you have a sound card in your PC, or a driver (a program that controls a piece of hardware) for your PC speaker, you can hear sound clips that are included in WWW documents. Some other media that can be accessed in WWW documents are images and animation. Your browser may need helper applications to display different media files.

▶ **See** "Read, Listen, Watch, and Interact: Multimedia Is Here," **p. 437**

Not only can you access different media in WWW documents, but some browsers can be set up so that appropriate applications will be started to display a document of a particular type. For example, if a WWW document contains a reference to a document that is in Microsoft Word for Windows format, you can set up your browser so that it automatically starts up Word for Windows to display that document when it is retrieved.

Some browsers also give you access to other Internet services. For example, you can access anonymous FTP servers, Gopher servers, WAIS servers, and UseNet news servers from many browsers. Many browsers also let you do remote logins using the Telnet protocol, although a helper application is usually required for this.

Hypertext (and Hypermedia)

When you use the WWW, the documents that you find will be hypertext documents. Hypertext is text that contains links to other text. This allows you to quickly access other related text from the text you are currently reading. The linked text might be within the document that you are currently reading, or it might be somewhere halfway around the world.

In addition to text, many of the documents you retrieve may contain pictures, graphs, sounds, or even animations. Documents that contain more than just text are called hypermedia documents, because they contain multiple media.

HTML

When you retrieve a document from the WWW, the text that you read on-screen is nicely formatted text. To do this, the documents that you read on the WWW cannot be plain text, or even text with specific formatting information in it (because the person who places a document on a WWW server doesn't know what type of computer or terminal is being used by the person reading the document).

To ensure that everyone sees documents displayed correctly on-screen, it was necessary to come up with a way to describe documents so that they are displayed in the best format for the viewing terminal or computer. The solution to this problem turned out to be HTML.

HTML (hypertext markup language) is used when writing a document that is to be displayed through the WWW. HTML is a fairly simple set of commands that describes how a document is structured. This type of markup language allows you to define the parts of the document, but not the formatting, so that whatever browser that is being used can format it to best suit that browser's display.

▶ **See** "HTML Basics," **p. 494**

HTML commands (called *tags*) are inserted around blocks of text in a document to describe what the text is. So, for example, within a document you have text that is marked as the various heading levels, simple paragraphs, page headings and footers, bulleted items, and so on. There are also commands that let you import other media (images, sounds, animations), and commands that let you specify the links to other documents (or text within the same document). When your browser retrieves the document and interprets the HTML commands, it formats each structure in the document (headings, bullets, plain paragraphs, and so on) in a way that looks best on your display. Figures 16.1 and 16.2 show the HTML code for Microsoft's home page and the corresponding file displayed in Internet Explorer.

▶ **See** "HTML Elements," **p. 502**

N O T E   It's easy to learn HTML formatting commands. If you want to learn about them and create your own Web documents, see Chapters 20 through 23. ▪

Links

One of the defining features of any hypertext document is the *link* (also known as a *hyperlink*). Links are simply references to other documents. But they aren't just stated references like "see page two for more information." They are actual live links, where you can activate the link (usually by clicking it) and cause whatever it references to appear on screen. When someone writes a hypertext document, he or she can insert links to other documents that contain information relevant to the text in the document.

WWW documents are all hypertext documents. Besides its document description commands, HTML contains commands that allow links in a document. Many of them are hypermedia documents, containing links to pictures, sounds, or animations, in addition to document links.

FIG. 16.1
The HTML code for Microsoft's home page.

FIG. 16.2
The same Web page as it is displayed by Internet Explorer.

You can link a Web page to any type of file you can create. Here are some of the types of documents to which a Web page can link:

Web pages

Sound files

Picture files

Mail addresses

FTP sites

Gopher sites

Newsgroups

Telnet hosts

There are two parts to a hypertext link. One part is the reference to the related item (be it a document, picture, movie, or sound). In the case of the WWW, the item being referenced could be within the current document, or it could be anywhere on the Internet. This is called the *URL reference*.

The second part of a hypertext link is the *anchor*. An anchor is the actual representation of the link on the Web page. The author of a document can define the anchor to be a word, a group of words, a picture, or any area of the reader's display. The reader may activate the anchor by pointing to it and clicking with a mouse (for a graphical-based browser) or by selecting it with arrow keys and pressing Enter (for a text-based browser).

N O T E   You'll learn about HTML in Chapter 21, "Using HTML to Build Your Home Page." If you're curious about what a link looks like in HTML, however, here's a sample:

<A HREF="http://www.yahoo.com/">Yahoo</A>

The first part of this link, the bit between the left (<) and right (>) brackets, is the URL reference. The word *Yahoo* is the text anchor that the browser underlines on the Web page. And the last part ends the link. ▨

 T I P   One way of identifying a link on a graphical WWW interface is to watch the cursor. Your cursor may change to another shape when it passes over a link. For example, the cursor changes to a pointing hand in Internet Explorer.

The anchor is indicated in different ways depending on the type of display you are using. If it is a color display, anchor words may be a special color, and anchor graphics may be surrounded by a colored box. If you have a black-and-white display, anchor words may be underlined, and anchor graphics may have a border drawn around them. On a simple terminal, anchor words may be in reverse video (and, of course, there would be no graphics!). See Figure 16.3 for examples of anchors.

When you click on the anchor, your browser fetches the item referenced by the link's URL reference. This may involve reading a document from your local disk, or going out on the Internet and requesting that a document be sent from a distant computer to yours. The reference indicates what type of item is being retrieved (HTML document, sound file, and so on), and your browser tries to present the material to you in the appropriate format.

FIG. 16.3

An example of hypertext anchors in Internet Explorer. (Anchor words are blue and underlined on-screen.)

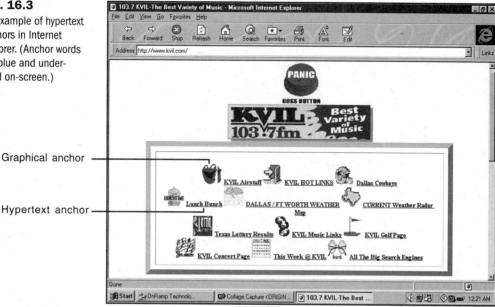

Graphical anchor ——

Hypertext anchor ——

> **N O T E**   If you do not have the correct helper application for the type of item that is retrieved (a driver for sound files, for example), the item is still retrieved by your browser. Most browsers will offer you the option of saving the file to disk or defining a helper application for the file when you try to load a file of an unknown type. ▪

URLs

One of the goals of the World Wide Web project was to have a standard way of referencing an item, no matter what the item's type (a document, sound file, and so on). To achieve this goal, a Uniform Resource Locator (URL) was developed.

A URL is the location of the item that you want to retrieve. The location of the item can range from a file on your local disk to a file on an Internet site halfway around the world.

A URL reference can be set up to be absolute or relative. An absolute reference contains the complete address of the document that is being referenced, including the host name, directory path, and file name. For example, **http://www.bigcompany.com/stuff/page.html**. A relative reference assumes that the previous machine and directory path are being used, and just the file name (or possibly a subdirectory and file name) are specified.

> **N O T E**   If you save a document to your local disk, you should check to see if the references in the document are absolute or relative. If the document references other documents with relative addresses, you will not be able to view those documents unless you copy them to your local disk and set them up with the same directory structure as they had at the original site. Absolute references will always work unless your Internet connection fails or the referenced documents are moved. ▪

The URL is not limited to describing the location of WWW files. Many browsers (including Mosaic) can access a number of different Internet services, including anonymous FTP, Gopher, WAIS, UseNet news, and Telnet.

A typical URL would look like this:

> **http://www.eit.com/web/www.guide**

N O T E The document **http://www.eit.com/web/www.guide** is an overview of the WWW. ■

T I P Even if you are retrieving files from a server that is running on a PC, you must use a slash (/) to indicate a subdirectory, not a backslash (\).

The initial item in the URL (the part that ends with a colon) is the protocol that is being used to retrieve the item. A protocol is a set of instructions that defines how to use that particular Internet service. In this example, the protocol is HTTP, the Hypertext Transfer Protocol developed for the WWW project. The two slashes after the colon indicate that what follows is a valid Internet host address or symbolic location. It can be either the text as shown previously, or the actual IP address of the site. In this URL, you want to find a file on that machine; what follows after the host name is a UNIX-style path for the file you want to retrieve.

The URL in the prior example tells a WWW browser to retrieve the file www.guide from the /web directory on the Internet host www.eit.com, using the HTTP protocol.

Other protocols that WWW browsers can use to retrieve documents are listed in the following table:

Protocol	Use
gopher	Starts a Gopher session.
ftp	Starts an FTP session.
file	Gets a file on your local disk if followed by ///c|; or, equivalent to FTP if followed by //. Any local disk may be specified, and it must be followed by the bar character rather than a colon, because the colon has a special significance in a URL.
wais	Accesses a WAIS server.
news	Reads UseNet newsgroups. Newsgroup names don't use the //. For example, **news:alt.fan.enya.**
telnet	Starts a Telnet session.

HTTP

Another of the goals of the WWW project was to have documents that were easy to retrieve, no matter where they resided. After it was decided to use hypertext as the standard format for WWW documents, a protocol that allowed these hypertext documents to be retrieved quickly was developed. This protocol is HTTP, the Hypertext Transport Protocol. HTTP is a fairly simple communications protocol that takes advantage of the fact that the documents it retrieves contain information about future links the user may reference (unlike FTP or Gopher, where information about the next possible links must be transmitted via the protocol).

N O T E http://www.w3.org/hypertext/WWW/Protocols/HTTP/HTTP2.html and http://www.ietf.cnri.reston.va.us/ids.by.wg/http.html contain IETF (Internet Engineering Task Force) drafts that discuss the HTTP specification. ▨

Home Pages

All WWW users can set up their own home pages to link to sites they use frequently. Home pages can also be developed for groups who use the same resources. For example, a project may need to set up a home page that gives links to all project-related items that exist.

N O T E Many people refer to the primary welcome page of a site as the home page for that site. This is not really a home page because it is for general use and does not organize information that is of interest to one specific person or group. ▨

Clients and Servers

Two terms heard frequently when the WWW is discussed are client and server. A WWW client is an account on an Internet site that requests a document from the WWW. The WWW servers are the programs that provide access to collections of WWW documents at different sites on the Internet.

Client software is a program (like Netscape or Internet Explorer) that you use to view WWW documents. Server software is a program that manages a particular collection of WWW documents on an Internet host.

Future Developments on the Web

As good as it currently is, people are working to make the WWW even better. Over the next few years, new developments will allow for display of more complicated documents and the addition of live communications in documents. Chapter 26, "The Future of the Web: VRML, SGML, and Web Chat," discusses some of these emerging technologies in more detail.

VRML

In an effort to add another dimension to the Web, VRML (Virtual Reality Modeling Language) has been developed. VRML allows three-dimensional images to be displayed from the Web. This new capability will eventually allow for things like walk-throughs of buildings and environments, virtual examination of three-dimensional objects, etc.

▶ **See** "VRML: The WWW in Three Dimensions," **p. 700**

Live Communications

You can currently display audio and video on the Web, but you are limited to playing back previously created files. The next development will be incorporating live audio and video in Web documents. One of the products currently being developed will allow multiple users to connect to a Web sight and talk to each other (as if they were in a room together). WebChat, discussed in Chapter 26, is such a product.

▶ **See** "Audio Applications on the Web," **p. 708**

Built-In Multimedia

Sun Microsystems has developed Java, a language based on C++ that enables you to load an object in a document without needing a special viewer for that object (the viewer is built in to the object, essentially). Not only does it eliminate the need for viewers, it also allows you to customize your viewer application by creating applets you distribute with your Web page. More information and demos of the HotJava browser can be found at **http://java.sun.com**. Netscape is also supporting the inclusion of Java objects in Web documents.

In addition to supporting Java, Netscape has developed a way to incorporate live objects directly into Web documents. Netscape has agreements with the developers of some helper applications to allow functions of the applications to be imported directly into Netscape. Instead of having to start a helper application in a separate window when you encounter a multimedia file, the relative pieces of the application appear directly in your document. The multimedia file is then played within the document.

Learning More About WWW

The WWW, like the Internet, changes constantly. New servers become available and old ones go away. Eventually, new protocols for accessing new Internet services will be available. New browsers will be written, and old ones will get new features. There is so much information changing rapidly that anything in hard print (like this book) will become out of date quickly. (Only somewhat out of date, though! Most of the information will be current.)

There are a number of ways that you can find out more information about what is current on the WWW. This section gives you pointers to some of the most useful sources of information.

UseNet Newsgroups

If you have access to UseNet newsgroups, a number of them are directly related to the WWW. The following table gives descriptions of them:

UseNet Newsgroup	Description
comp.infosystems.www.advocacy	Comments and arguments over the best and worst

UseNet Newsgroup	Description
comp.infosystems.www.announce	World-Wide Web announcements. (Moderated)
comp.infosystems.www.authoring.cgi	Writing CGI scripts for the Web
comp.infosystems.www.authoring.html	Writing HTML for the Web
comp.infosystems.www.authoring.images	Using images, imagemaps on the Web
comp.infosystems.www.authoring.misc	Miscellaneous Web authoring issues
comp.infosystems.www.browsers.mac	Web browsers for the Macintosh platform
comp.infosystems.www.browsers.misc	Web browsers for other platforms
comp.infosystems.www.browsers.ms-windows	Web browsers for MS Windows
comp.infosystems.www.browsers.x	Web browsers for the X-Window system
comp.infosystems.www.misc	Miscellaneous World Wide Web discussion
comp.infosystems.www.servers.mac	Web servers for the Macintosh platform
comp.infosystems.www.servers.misc	Web servers for other platforms
comp.infosystems.www.servers.ms-windows	Web servers for MS Windows and NT
comp.infosystems.www.servers.unix	Web servers for UNIX platforms
comp.os.os2.networking.www	World Wide Web (WWW) apps/utils under OS/2

Part
IV

Ch
16

Electronic Mailing Lists

There are several electronic mailing lists that are dedicated to the WWW. A number of them are run by the WWW Consortium (the following sections that contain no other subscribing information fall under this category). To subscribe to one of these groups, send e-mail to the address **listserv@w3.org** with the line:

subscribe *mailing_list_name your_name*

(Insert the name of the mailing list you want to join in place of *mailing_list_name* and your first and last name in place of *your_name*.)

TIP These mailing lists tend to be of a more technical or administrative nature. (Post in newsgroups to ask questions about how to do something or where to find something on the WWW.)

www-lib   This mailing list contains discussions about architecture and new features, exchange of diffs, bug reports etc., for the W3C Reference Library. There is also a nice hypertext archive.

www-style   This mailing list contains a discussion of HTML style sheets to support standardization and implementations.

www–html   This mailing list is a technical discussion of the design and extension of the HTML language.

www–talk   This mailing list is for technical discussions among people who are interested in the development of WWW software.

www-security   This list discusses all aspects of security on the World Wide Web.

To subscribe to the www-security mailing list, send an e-mail message to **www-security-request@nsmx.rutgers.edu** with the message body:

subscribe www-security

This will subscribe the address that is in the mail header From field to the mailing list.

www-sites   This mailing list is for discussing issues of concern to commercial sites using World Wide Web technology.

To subscribe, send an e-mail message to **majordomo@qiclab.scn.rain.com** with the message body:

subscribe www-sites Name *your_e-mail_address*

www_marketing   This list offers a discussion on how to use the Web for sales and marketing.

To subscribe, send an e-mail message to **majordomo@xmission.com** with the message body:

Subscribe www_marketing *your_e-mail_address*
end

WWW Interactive Talk

WWW Interactive Talk (WIT) is a new type of discussion group that has been formed for the WWW. In some ways it is similar to UseNet newsgroups. The creators of this forum, however, have tried to overcome some of the limitations of the UseNet groups by structuring the discussion of a particular topic. Each topic is presented on a form that shows the topic and proposals for discussion about the topic. Under the proposals there are arguments for and against each proposal.

N O T E The designers of WIT hope that this format allows readers to see if the topic has been adequately discussed before they submit their own comments. As a comparison, often in UseNet newsgroups, a point will be made over and over again, because readers respond before they see if someone else has already brought up the same point. ■

This is a new and somewhat experimental discussion format. Currently, there is a WIT discussion area set up at **http://www.w3.org/wit/hypertext/WWW**. This area is not limited to WWW discussions (any topic can be introduced), but it is a place where you are likely to find some people to talk to you about the WWW.

The WWW Itself

Of course, one of the best places to find information about the WWW is on the WWW itself. Here are a few URLs that will take you places where you can find out more about the WWW and what can be found.

N O T E When you view a document on the WWW, you are actually retrieving it from a computer somewhere on the Internet. When you do this, you are making demands on the Internet host that is providing the information, and also on the network itself. Please try to keep your document viewing to things that are of interest to you so that you don't make unnecessary demands on the network or individual Internet hosts. ■

World Wide Web Consortium The following URL takes you to the World Wide Web Consortium:

> **http://www.w3.org/hypertext/WWW/TheProject.html**

This document gives you pointers to WWW information. Some of the information you can find here includes: available client and server software; lists of WWW servers grouped by subject, by country, and by service; technical information about the WWW; and other background information.

NCSA Mosaic Demo Document Follow this URL (**http://www.ncsa.uiuc.edu/demoweb/ demo.html**) to the NCSA Mosaic Demo Document. This document gives a brief description of Mosaic. Its main attraction, however, is a large list of interesting documents that can be found on the WWW.

InterNIC The following URL takes you to the InterNIC directory of directories, at the main Internet Network Information Center:

> **http://ds.internic.net/cgi-bin/tochtml/0intro.dirofdirs/**

This resource is intended to help people locate information on specific topics. There are links from this document to many different lists of Internet resources. Many of these resources are in WWW format, or are accessible by one of the other Internet services (FTP, Gopher, and so on).

Entering the World Wide Web: A Guide to Cyberspace The following URL takes you to the document "Entering the World Wide Web: A Guide to Cyberspace:"

http://www.eit.com/web/www.guide

This document gives you a good overview of the World Wide Web, and points you to some interesting information repositories on the WWW.

Books

A number of books have been published recently to help you better understand and effectively use the WWW. Two books that you should reference are *Using the World Wide Web* (0-7897-0645-8) and *Special Edition Using HTML* (0-7897-0236-3), both published by Que. *Special Edition Using HTML* gives you in-depth information on building exciting Web pages. *Using the World Wide Web* helps you understand what the WWW is and how to find the information you need most. ●

Using Microsoft Internet Explorer

by Jerry Honeycutt

A recent C|NET article calls the latest go-round of Microsoft's Internet Explorer a "white-hot Navigator-killer." Could it be true? Possibly. Internet Explorer now matches Netscape feature for feature. Frames, multimedia, Java, and other important innovations are all there. It even supports Netscape Plug-ins (or is that Microsoft plug-ins now?). Internet Explorer goes a bit further, however, by adding capabilities such as VBScript and ActiveX technology.

You may have missed it—I did at first because it's quite subtle, but very important: Microsoft doesn't simply refer to Internet Explorer as a Web browser. They refer to it as a "Web Platform." An architecture. An operating environment. The implications are astounding. Calling it a platform implies that Internet Explorer is the basis upon which Microsoft and other organizations will build bigger and more important applications.

Here, ActiveX is the center of attention. The scope of this book doesn't allow me to delve into Internet Explorer from a developer perspective, but you can find more information about ActiveX technology in Microsoft's Internet Development Toolbox. Point your browser to **http://www.microsoft.com/intdev/default.htm** for more information. ■

Download, install, and configure Internet Explorer

Throw out your Microsoft Plus! CD-ROM and get rid of your last Internet Explorer download. You see how to download and install the latest version of Internet Explorer.

Tour Internet Explorer

Take this quick tour of Internet Explorer and its main window. You'll also get the low-down on that new graphical wonder-bar that replaced the toolbar.

Surf the Web like a pro

This chapter shows you how to use all the new features to get around the Web like never before.

Move your Favorites folder to the Start menu

This chapter shows you a Registry hack you can use to move the Favorites folder to the Start menu so your favorite Web sites are in both places.

Optimize Internet Explorer for slow connections

This chapter shows you how to load Web pages faster, so you don't have to wait as long.

Protect yourself while surfing

Internet Explorer offers security, too, so that you can pay for things online, run distributed programs safely, and protect your children.

Getting Ready to Use Internet Explorer

Internet Explorer isn't on the NetCD, so you'll need to download it from Microsoft's Web site. Point your Web browser at **http://www.microsoft.com/ie/iedl.htm**. Then, click the Download Software link. Follow the instructions you see on the Web page to download the version of Internet Explorer that is appropriate for your platform and language.

If you don't have a browser yet, you can nab it from Microsoft's FTP site. You need a working Internet connection to use the following steps, but you don't need to understand how FTP works (see Chapter 31, "Using FTP and Popular FTP Programs"):

1. Choose Run from the Start menu, type **ftp**, and press Enter. You'll see a window that looks similar to an MS-DOS window except that it displays the ftp> prompt.

2. Type **open ftp.microsoft.com** and press Enter. If you're using Dial-Up Networking and not already connected to the Internet, click Connect when you see the Connect To dialog box.

3. Type **anonymous** and press Enter when FTP prompts you for the user name. Then, type your full mail address when FTP prompts you for your password; **jerry@honeycutt.com**, for example.

4. Type **cd/Softlib/MSLFILES** and press Enter when you see ftp> again. Note that Microsoft's FTP site isn't case sensitive so you don't have to worry much about capitalization.

5. Type **get msie30.EXE** and press Enter to download the Windows 95 version, or type **get ntie30.EXE** and press Enter to download the Windows NT version. FTP copies Internet Mail service to your Windows desktop.

6. Type **bye** and press Enter to log off of the FTP server and close the FTP window.

▶ **See** "Using FTP from the Command Line," **p. 809**

Microsoft products keep getting easier and easier to install. Internet Explorer is no exception. Its setup program does all the work, and you don't even have to clean up after it. Internet Explorer comes in a self-extracting, self-installing file. Here's how to install it:

1. If you haven't already done so, download Internet Explorer as described earlier. You won't see the correct icon until you press F5 to refresh the folder in which you downloaded the file.

2. Double-click on the appropriate file (msie30.exe, ntie30.exe) to start the setup program.

3. Click Yes when the setup program announces that it will install Internet Explorer, and it will copy the files it needs into Windows' temporary folder.

4. Click I Agree to accept the license agreement, and the setup program installs Internet Explorer on your computer.

5. Click Yes to restart your computer. You must restart your computer for the changes to take effect.

N O T E Make sure that you have a working Internet connection before you try to use Internet Explorer. See Chapter 4, "Connecting Through a LAN with Windows 95 and Windows NT," to learn how to connect to the Internet via a network. See Chapters 5, "Connecting to a PPP or SLIP Account with Windows 95," and 6, "Connecting to a PPP or SLIP Account with Windows NT," to learn how to connect to the Internet via Dial-Up Networking. ∎

What's New in Internet Explorer 3.0?

You'll find a lot of new features in Internet Explorer including the much-awaited frames and Java. To help you get an idea of just how extensive these features are, take a look at this list:

- *Look and Feel*—Internet Explorer sports a whole new look and feel. The most notable change is the new graphical toolbar (affectionately referred to as the wonder-bar).

- *ActiveX Documents*—Internet Explorer is actually just an empty container in which you use ActiveX objects such as an HTML object to view Web pages. That means that you can put a lot more than just a Web page in Internet Explorer. You can put a Word document or any other OLE object in Internet Explorer as shown in Figure 17.1.

Part
IV

Ch
17

FIG. 17.1
Try it out yourself: Choose File, Open; pick a Word DOC file (or any other embeddable file type) on your computer; and click OK to open it in Internet Explorer.

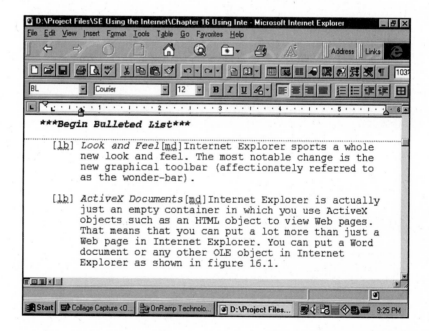

- *ActiveX Controls*—You'll see a whole new wave of dynamic Web pages thanks to ActiveX controls. These controls let a developer distribute applications by embedding them into Web pages.

- *ActiveX Scripting*—ActiveX scripting lets you plug a variety of scripting languages into Internet Explorer. Currently, Microsoft provides VBScript and Java Script.

■ *Security*—Internet Explorer supports the most common security schemes for making transactions over the Internet: SSL and PCT.

■ *Internet Ratings*—You can protect your children from obscenity and violence using Internet Explorer's rating system.

■ *Frames*—Web designers use frames to divide the browser window into smaller chunks. The next time you have a choice between a no-frames version of a Web site and a frames version, you can take the frames version.

Starting and Stopping Explorer

After you installed Internet Explorer, it dumped an icon on your desktop that looks like a globe with a magnifying glass in front of it. Double-clicking this icon is, of course, the easiest way to start Internet Explorer. There are a handful of other ways to get it going, however, such as these:

■ Choose Programs, Internet Explorer from the Start menu, or

■ Choose Run from the Start menu and type a URL such as **http://www.microsoft.com**, or

■ Double-click an Internet shortcut.

When you're ready to close Internet Explorer, click the window's close button, or choose File, Close from the main menu.

  Each time you start Internet Explorer, it loads the same starting page from the Web. You can change the starting page by opening the Web page you want to use. Then, choose View, Options from Internet Explorer's main menu; click the Navigation tab; click Use Current to set your start page to the current page; and click OK. You can also get back to your start page at any time by clicking the Home button.

Looking at Internet Explorer's Window

If you haven't already done so, start Internet Explorer now so that you can follow the examples in this chapter. The first time you start Internet Explorer, you see a window that looks very similar to Figure 17.2 (I've completely expanded the toolbar). All by itself, this window is very simple. That's because the Web pages and applications that you load in Internet Explorer define the function and appearance of its window.

Table 17.1 shows you the picture, name, and purpose of each button that you see in the toolbar; Table 17.2 shows the name and purpose of each link.

FIG. 17.2
No, there isn't a bug in Internet Explorer's toolbar. The buttons are normally black and white. Each button changes to color when you move your mouse over it.

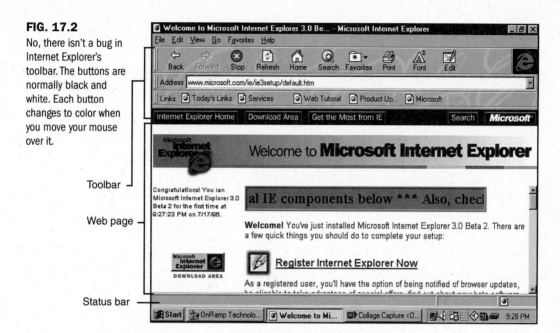

Toolbar ⌐

Web page

Status bar

Table 17.1   Internet Explorer Toolbar Buttons

Button	Name	Description
Back	Back	Opens the previous Web page in Go menu
Forward	Forward	Opens the next Web page in Go menu
Stop	Stop	Stops loading the current Web page
Refresh	Refresh	Reloads the current Web page
Home	Home	Loads your personalized start page
Search	Search	Loads your personalized search page
Favorites	Favorites	Opens the Favorites folder
Print	Print	Prints the current Web page
Font	Font	Changes to the next font in View, Fonts

Table 17.2 Links Section

Link	Description
Today's Links	Opens Microsoft's Web index, which contains new links every week
Services	Opens Microsoft's Services page, which contains business services
Web Tutorial	Opens Microsoft's Web Tutorial page to learn about the Web
Product Updates	Opens Microsoft's product update page to get the latest goodies
Microsoft	Opens Microsoft's home page

N O T E If you didn't get Internet Explorer from Microsoft, the Quick Links section on your toolbar may not contain the same buttons. Computer manufacturers and other companies can customize the Quick Links section before redistributing Internet Explorer. ■

The toolbar (wonder-bar) requires a bit of explaining. You've already gathered that it's not a normal, button-oriented toolbar, haven't you? It has two important characteristics:

- You can collapse and expand it, and
- When two sections of the toolbar overlap, you can slide one right or left to get it out of the way.

This is innovative stuff. Figure 17.3 shows you three possible views for the toolbar.

N O T E Each figure in this chapter shows the toolbar completely expanded so that you can see it all. I don't recommend that you use Internet Explorer this way. Completely collapse the toolbar by dragging the divider as far up as it will go. You'll end up with a thin toolbar, but you'll have more space to view Web pages. You can get to the other sections of the toolbar by clicking on their label as shown in Figure 17.3. If the toolbar completely annoys you, you can hide it by choosing View, Toolbar until you don't see a check mark next to the Toolbar menu item. ■

FIG. 17.3
You can click and drag the divider to change the toolbar's size as shown in this figure, or you can also click and drag inside of the Address or Quick Links section.

Opening a Web Page (or Other URL)

The Web would be useless if it didn't have things to do, places to go, and people to see. As you've learned, however, the Web has millions of pages for you to see.

And Internet Explorer has all sorts of ways to get you there. You can get there via the scenic route, by clicking links to jump from page to page, or you can get there via the direct route. This section shows you the direct route—giving Internet Explorer an exact URL. "Getting Around the Web," later in this chapter, shows you the more roundabout route.

 TIP   When typing a URL such as **http://www.que.com**, you don't have to type the **http://** portion. Internet Explorer automatically adds this for you.

▶ See "Links," **p. 368**

Type an Address in the Address Bar

The quickest way to get to a Web page is to type its URL in the Address section of the toolbar. If your toolbar is collapsed, click the Address label so you can see it. Type an address in the Address section and press Enter. As a result, Internet Explorer opens the Web page at that address.

Part
IV

Ch
17

The Address section remembers the last 15 URLs that you typed in it. Click the down-arrow to open the drop-down list as shown in Figure 17.4. Click a URL, and Internet Explorer opens that Web page.

FIG. 17.4
Here's a trick. Click once in the Address section. Then, use the up and down arrow keys to quickly preview each URL in the list. This works only if you're caching pages.

Click here to drop down the list.

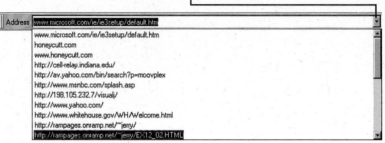

```
Address  www.microsoft.com/ie/ie3setup/default.htm

         www.microsoft.com/ie/ie3setup/default.htm
         honeycutt.com
         www.honeycutt.com
         http://cell-relay.indiana.edu/
         http://av.yahoo.com/bin/search?p=moovplex
         http://www.msnbc.com/splash.asp
         http://198.105.232.7/visuali/
         http://www.yahoo.com/
         http://www.whitehouse.gov/WH/Welcome.html
         http://rampages.onramp.net/~jerry/
         http://rampages.onramp.net/~jerry/EX12_02.HTML
```

▶ See "URLs," p. 371

TROUBLESHOOTING

Why does Internet Explorer tell me that it can't find a URL I typed in the Address section? I'm positive that the Web page exists and that I typed it correctly. Did you use uppercase and lowercase letters where appropriate? URLs are case-sensitive. That is, if you type **www.myserver.com**, when the URL is really **www.MyServer.com**, Internet Explorer won't be able to find it.

Open a Web Page Using the Menu

The next fastest way to open a Web page is to use Internet Explorer's File, Open menu. Choose File, Open from the main menu, type a URL in the Open dialog box, and click OK. Internet Explorer opens that Web page.

You're not limited to opening Web pages from the Internet, incidentally. You'll notice that this dialog box says: "Type the Internet address of a document or folder, and Internet Explorer will open it for you." Documents? Yes, Internet Explorer can open documents on your computer, too. If you have Microsoft Excel installed on your computer, for example, you can open an Excel spreadsheet right there in Internet Explorer.

Folders? Yes to that, too. You can browse your computer's folders right there in Internet Explorer. When you open the Favorites folders, for example, you're actually browsing C:\Windows\Favorites—just like it was a Web page.

TIP You can open a Web page without leaving the page you're currently viewing. Choose File, New Window from the main menu, or press Ctrl+N to open a second copy of Internet Explorer. You can now browse different Web sites in each window.

Use the Favorites Menu

You'll definitely come across quite a few Web pages that you'll want to visit again. I go back repeatedly to the Microsoft Web site to catch the latest news about Windows 95 and Internet Explorer, for example. I also frequent USA Today, Federal Express (to make sure that these chapters make it to Que), and the many search tools described in Chapter 34, "Searching for Information on the Internet."

Fortunately, Internet Explorer lets you keep track of all your favorite Web pages with the Favorites folder. This folder is like any other folder on your hard drive. See it for yourself by opening C:\Windows\Favorites in Windows 95's Explorer. What makes it special, however, is that Internet Explorer displays whatever it finds in this folder on the Favorites menu—subfolders and shortcuts. Figure 17.5 shows what my Favorites menu looks like. Choose Favorites from the main menu, and click one of the Web sites to open it.

Part
IV
Ch
17

FIG. 17.5

You can also put FTP sites, newsgroups, and shortcuts to your computer's folders in the Favorites folder.

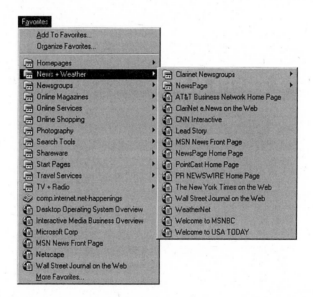

 T I P Have you found a Web page that you just have to share with friends? Choose File, Send To, Mail Recipient. Your hot find will be sent via e-mail. All the recipient has to do to open the Web page is double-click on the shortcut in the mail message.

Adding a Web page to your Favorites folder is easy. First, you need to have Internet Explorer displaying the Web page that you want to add. Then, choose Favorites, Add to Favorites from Internet Explorer's main menu. Internet Explorer displays the Add to Favorites dialog box. Click Create In to expand this dailog box so that you see something similar to Figure 17.6. Then, choose the folder from the list in which you want to save the shortcut, and click OK.

FIG. 17.6
Click the plus sign (+) to expand a folder's contents or click the minus sign (–) to hide a folder's contents.

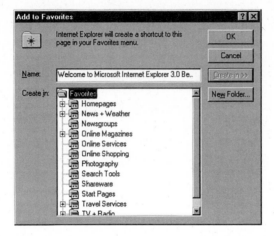

Consider organizing your favorites into subfolders. Stashing all your favorites in one folder is a bad idea because it'll get really ugly, really fast. In the Add to Favorites dialog box, you can create a new folder underneath the current folder by clicking on the Create New Folder button.

 TIP Organize all of your favorite Web sites into subfolders. Then, copy the ones that you use most frequently to the top level of the Favorites folder. Your most useful Web sites will be only two mouse clicks away.

Combine Your Favorites and Start Menu Folders

Have you ever wished that your Favorites and Start Menu folders were one and the same? That is, would you like all of your favorite Web pages to be available in your Start menu, as well as the Favorites menu?

Pssst. Don't tell Microsoft, but you can do it. The following steps involve the Registry, so be very careful. Obviously, you use them at your own risk:

1. Open Notepad and type the following lines very, very carefully. If this is all a bit unnerving, you'll find this on the NetCD in a file called Favorite.reg.

   REGEDIT4

   [HKEY_CURRENT_USER\Software\Microsoft\Windows\CurrentVersion\Explorer\Shell Folders]

   "Favorites"="C:\\WINDOWS\\Start Menu\\Favorites"

   [HKEY_CURRENT_USER\Software\Microsoft\Windows\CurrentVersion\Explorer\User Shell Folders]

   "Favorites"="C:\\WINDOWS\\Start Menu\\Favorites"

2. Save the file to your desktop in a file called Favorite.reg.

3. In Windows 95 Explorer, double-click the Favorite.reg file that you just created. The Registry Editor will merge these changes into the Registry.

4. Move C:\Windows\Favorites to C:\Windows\Start Menu.

Now you can open your Favorites menu from the Start menu as shown in Figure 17.7.

FIG. 17.7
You can get to your
Favorite folder much
faster now. Right-click
on the Start button,
and choose Explorer to
manage your Favorites
folder.

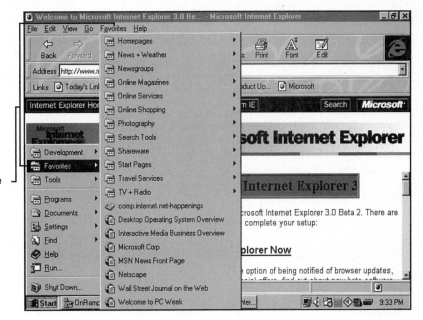

Both open the
same folder.

Use a Shortcut

Internet Explorer makes it really easy to create shortcuts to Web sites. Open the Web page for which you want to create a shortcut, and choose File, Create Shortcut from Internet Explorer's main menu. Internet Explorer displays an annoying dialog box that tells you it's going to put a shortcut to the current page on your desktop. Click OK to get rid of it. Move Internet Explorer out of the way so that you can see your desktop. You'll notice a new shortcut that is named after the title of the Web page.

The next time you want to open this Web page, double-click the shortcut. You can move this shortcut to other places on your computer, too. You can stash it in the Start menu, for instance, so that it's immediately available. You can also keep shortcuts on your desktop.

N O T E   Microsoft provides a great set of tools called PowerToys—free of charge at **http://www. microsoft.com/windows/software/powertoys.htm**. PowerToys contains a tool called Contents which you can use to gain quick access to your shortcuts. Install Contents as described in the PowerToys file. Then, store all of your shortcuts in a folder on your desktop. Right-click the folder and choose Contents, and a submenu will drop-down showing you all of your shortcuts. Pick one from the list to open that Web page in Internet Explorer. ■

Getting Around the Web

If the only way you could meet new friends was to walk up to a total stranger and introduce yourself, you'd probably be a very lonely person. You network with the people you know so that you can meet new and exciting people.

Likewise, if you had to know the URL of a Web page in order to get to it, you'd quickly give up on the Web and return to television. The way you find new and exciting Web pages is by networking on the Web. That is, you follow the links from page to page taking note of what you find along the way.

Most of the Web's features that let you get around are traits found in Web pages—not Internet Explorer. Links, text and graphical, are a Web feature that you can use in any Web browser, for example. Internet Explorer adds features to a Web page's navigation, however, that make it easier to get around. You're not stuck with the mouse, for instance, because you can use the keyboard. You can also keep a history of all the Web pages you've visited so that you can quickly move forward and backward. And Internet Explorer now supports frames!

 Watch the mouse pointer. If it changes from a pointer to a hand, it's over a link. Look at Internet Explorer's status bar to see the URL when the mouse pointer is over a link.

 Do you want a quick synopsis of what links are on a Web page? Print it. When you print a Web page using Internet Explorer, it adds a table at the end that contains the name and URL of every text and graphical link on the page. You can turn this feature off in the Print dialog box by deselecting Print Shortcuts in a table at the end of the document.

Hang Up Your Mouse

Finally. Someone delivers a Web browser that you can use without a mouse. You'd think that everyone is "into" the mouse considering how important it is in Windows. It's a fact of life. Regardless, the world contains a lot of folks who absolutely, militantly refuse to use a mouse.

The Tab and Shift+Tab keys work similarly in Internet Explorer as they do in most dialog boxes. Press Tab to move to the next link on the Web page. Press Shift+Tab to move to the previous link on the Web page. As you're moving from link to link, you'll see a thin border around the current link. All there is to do now is press the Enter key to "click" the link. It doesn't just work with text links either; you can use the Tab key with all of these:

Graphical links

Text links

Images which are not a link

Hotspots within client-side image maps

The Address section of the toolbar

Internet Explorer supports many other keyboard shortcuts (see Table 17.3).

Table 17.2   Internet Explorer Keyboard Shortcuts

Keys	Description
Tab	Selects the next link
Shift+Tab	Selects the previous link
Enter	Activates a link
Shift+F10	Opens the context menu for a link or image
Ctrl+Tab	Moves to the next frame
Shift+Ctrl+Tab	Moves to the previous frame
Alt+Left-arrow	Moves backward in the history
Alt+Right-arrow	Moves forward in the history
F5	Refreshes the current Web page
Esc	Stops downloading the current Web page
Ctrl+0	Opens a new Web page
Ctrl+N	Opens a new Internet Explorer window
Ctrl+P	Prints the current Web page

Part
IV

Ch
17

Go Back Through History

Did you know Internet Explorer collects business cards? Well, kind of. I'm an avid business card collector. Every time I meet someone, I ask for their business card, take it home, and stash it in the drawer with all the rest. Every once in a while, I'll grab one of those cards and give that person a call. Internet Explorer lets you do the same thing on the Web. Rather than toss cards into a drawer, however, it saves a shortcut to all the Web pages that you've recently visited in its history folder (C:\Windows\History).

Internet Explorer displays all of the Web pages that you've visited during the current session in the Go menu (It empties this list each time you start). It displays about seven shortcuts at a time; and, if you've visited more than seven Web pages during the current session, it adds more to the list when you get close to the end. Choose Go from the main menu and you'll see a list similar to the one shown in Figure 17.8.

If you're too darned lazy to open the Go menu, you can use the Back and Forward buttons on the toolbar to accomplish the same thing. Click on the Back button and the check mark shown in Figure 17.8 will move up the list. Click on the Forward button and the check mark will move down the list.

FIG. 17.8
The most recent Web page is at the bottom of the list with the least recent Web page at the top of the list.

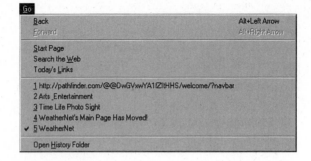

 T I P   Did you forget to put a great Web site in your Favorites folder? Your history folder is a great place to get shortcuts for your Favorites folder. Open C:\Windows\History and C:\Windows\Favorites (C:\Windows\Start Menu\Favorites if you moved it as described earlier), and drag shortcuts from the history folder to the Favorites folder.

Use Frames

Frames have, until now, been a feature specific to Netscape. Not anymore. Internet Explorer does frames. Frames allow the Web page to split the Internet Explorer window into sections. Each frame on the window can point to a different URL. Figure 17.9 shows you an example of a Web page that uses frames to present a navigation bar along the bottom, a title across the top, hot links along the left-hand side, and the main body of the Web page filling the remaining space. While you're visiting this site, the navigation bar will always be there so that you can quickly open a different Web page in the body of the window.

FIG. 17.9
The Forward and Back buttons work just as you expect them to when you're using them with frames. Internet Explorer has removed a lot of confusion regarding these buttons.

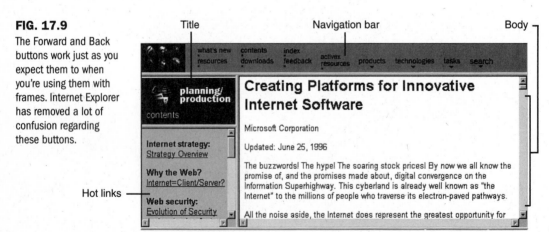

N O T E   You'll run across many Web sites that say *Netscape Enhanced, Best Viewed with Netscape,* or something similar. Hog wash. It doesn't mean anything anymore because you can view those sites just fine with Internet Explorer. ■

Getting Around the Web Faster

Here's a prescription for frustration: take 1 slow modem, add 20 very big Web pages with large images, and mix in 4 or 5 cups of coffee. It's enough to drive the most patient person mad. Fortunately, Internet Explorer provides a few options for speeding things up a bit. As with everything in life, nothing's free. To make Internet Explorer load faster, you'll have to give up something such as fancy pictures. As well as telling you how to speed up Internet Explorer, the sections below will tell you what the trade-offs are.

Stop a Web Page Before It's Finished

Internet Explorer starts painting images on the Web page right away—even before it has downloaded the entire image. That's why the images look really fuzzy or you see the first part of the image when you first go to a Web page. If you've seen enough to know that you want to click on one of the links and move on, go ahead. You don't have to wait for the pictures to finish painting to click on them.

Likewise, you don't have to finish loading a Web page and all its pictures. You can click the Stop button in the toolbar anytime. This will stop Internet Explorer from loading the rest of the page. And because Internet Explorer loads the text of a Web page before it starts loading the pictures, you'll still see most of what you want anyway. Internet Explorer displays as much as it can as shown in Figure 17.10. This can lead to some pretty incomplete-looking Web pages, though.

Cache the Web Pages You Receive

Internet Explorer keeps a cache of all the pages you visit. Normally, Internet Explorer loads each Web page, from the Web, once each session. For example, the first time that you visit **http://www.microsoft.com** during a session, Explorer saves the Web page and all its graphics to the cache. If you go off and visit other pages and come back to **http://www.microsoft.com** later, Internet Explorer loads the Web page from the cache, not the Web.

The trick is to make Internet Explorer load Web pages that you've already visited from the cache instead of from the Web—every time. It takes a fraction of the time to load Web pages that you've already visited from the cache than from the Web. Choose View, Options, from Internet Explorer's main menu, and click the Advanced tab. Click the Settings button, and Internet Explorer displays the Settings dialog box as shown in Figure 17.11. Select Never and click on OK. Click OK again to save your options. Feeling better now? (Have another cup of coffee, then.)

T I P Don't get caught with out-of-date pages (as I have a few times on this book). If you think that a Web page may have changed, press F5 to get a fresh copy from the Web server.

Part
IV

Ch
17

FIG. 17.10

If you stop a Web page from loading, this is what it will look like. This doesn't mean something is wrong, though.

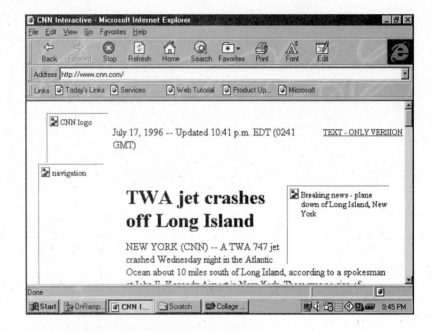

FIG. 17.11

Don't make your cache larger than 20 percent of your drive. You'll waste drive space for Web pages that you'll probably never use again.

Turn Off Images

The option of last resort is to totally disable pictures. Internet Explorer will load just the text of each Web page. This is much faster, but it reduces a lot of your enjoyment because you won't have all those pretty pictures to look at. Choose View, Options from the main menu and click the General tab. Deselect Pictures, Sounds, and Video.

Now you won't have to wait while Internet Explorer downloads a 100K picture or a 700K AVI file. When you disable pictures, Internet Explorer displays the alternate caption for it. In some cases, you can still get an idea of what was in the picture because the caption can be very descriptive.

 TIP Many sites such as Microsoft's put a link somewhere on their page that says Text Only. You'll usually find it at the top or the bottom of the Web page. Click this link to view a text version of the same Web pages that loads much faster.

Protecting You and Your Children

Part
IV
Ch
17

Internet Explorer has a number of new security features designed to protect you and your children while surfing the Internet. It supports SSL (Secure Sockets Layer) and PCT (Private Communication Technology) so that you can make transactions across the Internet safely. That is, you can shop on-line. Internet Explorer also supports *code signing* so that you can run Java programs on the Internet without worrying about someone trashing your machine. Internet Explorer supports Internet Ratings so that you can control what your children see when they look at Web pages.

Secure Transactions

A lot of people are afraid to purchase things on-line because of the hysteria created by the media. In actuality, it's about as safe as using your credit card at 7/11. I've never hesitated to purchase software on-line, for example, because Internet Explorer makes it a lot safer by supporting PCT and SSL. It's automatic, too, so you don't have to worry about forgetting to do something important before you buy those flowers for mom on-line (**http://www. 800flowers.com**). When you connect to a business on the Internet, they're using a secure Web server. The Web server and Internet Explorer work together to make sure that you can make your transaction safely.

When you're shopping at a secure Web site, you'll see an icon in the status bar that looks like a padlock. This lets you know that you can safely make a transaction. You'll also notice that the URL in the Address section of the toolbar is a bit different. Instead of its being **http:// www.business.com**, it's **https://www.business.com**.

> **CAUTION**
> If you're ever given the choice between a secure transfer using Netscape Commerce Server or a standard transfer, choose the secure transfer. Internet Explorer can talk to the Netscape Commerce Server just fine—regardless of what the Web page tells you.

▶ **See** "World Wide Web," **p. 1003**

Safe Content

Internet Explorer supports both VBScript and JavaScript content (applet). These applets are great. They can cause security problems for your computer, however. Internet Explorer is smart enough to recognize an applet that could be a potential problem and warn you about it. You can also configure how belligerent you want Internet Explorer to be about security, too. Here's how:

1. Choose View, Options from Internet Explorer's main menu. Click the Security tab and you'll see the property sheet shown in Figure 17.12.

FIG. 17.12

The Security Tab.

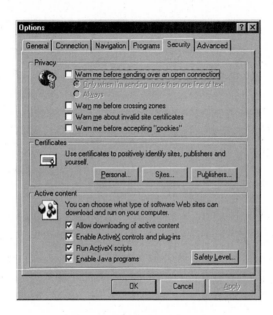

2. Click the Safety Level button, and choose the level of security you want: Expert, Normal, None. Expert security warns you when you're fixing to run an applet that could cause security problems. Normal automatically prevents you from running an applet that could cause security problems. None turns off this security feature. Click OK to save your changes.

3. Click OK to save your changes to the Security tab.

Internet Ratings

The media (some specific print rags, too) have made a very big deal about pornography on the Internet. While it's true that there is pornography on the Internet, it's not quite as common as the media would lead you to believe. It doesn't come looking for you and your children, either. You have to go looking for it, and, in some cases, your children might be just as tempted to look for porn as they are to look up four-letter words in the dictionary.

In those rare cases where you or your child might stumble onto questionable material, Internet Explorer is prepared to step in and help. It supports an Internet Ratings system whereby Web publishers can voluntarily rate their Web site. Then, you can control which ratings you want to allow in Internet Explorer. Here's how to set it up:

1. Choose View, Options from Internet Explorer's main menu, and click the Advanced tab.

2. Click the Enabled Ratings button. The first time that you set up the ratings, Internet Explorer asks you for a password. This is for parental control. Type your password in the spaces provided, and click OK. You'll see the property sheet shown in Figure 17.13.

FIG. 17.13

You can also add additional ratings systems by clicking the General tab, or you can use an online rating bureau by clicking the Ratings tab.

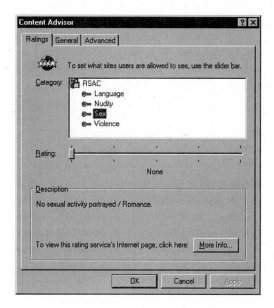

3. Choose the ratings category you want to set from Category: Language, Nudity, Sex, or Violence.

4. Move the slider to the right to allow more explicit material for that category, or move it to the left to prevent explicit material for that category. You'll see a description of what types of material each setting allows.

5. Repeat steps 3 and 4 for each category you want to change, then click OK to save your ratings.

6. Click OK again to save the Security tab.

The next time you open the Internet Ratings property sheet, you'll be asked for your password. No one can change these ratings without the password. You can change your password by clicking the General tab in the Internet Ratings property sheet. Then, click Change Password.

▶ **See** "Are Computer Networks Information Distributors or Publishers?" **p. 37**

T I P   If you really want to see what your child has been looking at, check the history folder. Open
C:\Windows\History in Windows 95's Explorer, and sort the list by date. You can visit each site by
double-clicking the corresponding shortcut.

Using Netscape 3

by Lori Leonardo

Netscape is another popular Web browser that you can pick up on the Net. Although not free, Netscape is no more expensive than many of the commercial games that you might purchase—and it's a great deal more useful. Netscape has many nice features, including background image loading, secure data transmission, multiple document windows, and built-in plug-ins for video viewing, sound, and 3-D presentations. ■

How to find and install Netscape 3

The Install Wizard lets you install Netscape 3 in one easy step.

How to use the Netscape interface

Netscape is a graphically oriented, very powerful application.

How to navigate the Web with Netscape

You can move between WWW documents in several different ways.

How to customize Netscape to your taste

You can change the default appearance and color of the hyperlinks in the documents that Netscape loads.

Getting Netscape Up and Running

Trying the Netscape browser is easy. If you have an FTP program, you can retrieve the browser and evaluate it for 90 days for free (after that, you have to register and pay for it). Before you get the software, however, make sure that your system is properly set up to run Netscape. When you do get the Netscape software, external applications are already built-in to Netscape 3. These external applications allow you to automatically view movies, hear sounds, and experience all the multimedia documents that are available on the Web.

Will Your Computer Run Netscape?

Before you can run Netscape for Windows on your personal computer, you must make sure that your computer system is capable of running the software. Although this requirement may seem to be fairly basic, it is disappointing (not to mention annoying) to spend several hours getting software and setting it up, only to discover that Netscape does not run under your operating system or that your modem is too slow to use Netscape effectively.

First, your computer system must be capable of running Microsoft Windows 95 (there are versions of Netscape for the 16-bit versions of Windows, but in this book, we are focusing on the use of Internet applications with Windows 95). If you do not already have Windows 95, you must purchase and install this software before you can run the 32-bit version of Netscape.

The basic Netscape for Windows configuration requires about 3.5M (megabytes) of disk space for the minimum Netscape software and documentation without the plug-ins and 16M with the standard configuration including the plug-ins. You also need some temporary disk space (about 4M) to hold the compressed Netscape files while you are unpacking them. In addition to this basic disk space requirement, Netscape requires some disk space to hold temporary files while it is running; disk space for documents that you want to store locally; and disk space for any viewers that you need to display movies, image files, sound files, and so on. Netscape also uses additional storage space to cache documents across sessions of the Navigator. Web pages, images, wave files, and tables are cached to your hard drive. The maximum amount of space consumed by the disk cache is controlled from the Cache and Network option of the Preferences dialog box that you will learn more about later in this chapter.

Needless to say, if you want to take full advantage of Netscape and use it to browse the WWW, you need an Internet account. If your PC is not directly connected to the Internet and you are using a SLIP or PPP connection, you need a relatively fast modem (14,400 bps is the minimum recommended speed).

In addition to the system requirements, Netscape for Windows requires a direct connection to the Internet, through a network card in your system or through some kind of modem connection.

Where to Get Netscape

Although the Netscape software is not free, it is available through anonymous FTP. Netscape Communications Incorporated is allowing people to pick up the software from its FTP site, use the software for a 90-day trial period, and then pay for the software (a moderate $39 at the time this book went to press) if they decide to keep it. This section discusses how to get this software.

▶ **See** "What Is FTP?" **p. 808**

N O T E Netscape Communications usually has available a released version of their software that you can purchase with or without documentation, for which they will provide support. They also often make available the next version of their software that is still under development (called a beta version). They do not charge a fee for use of the beta version, but the software does expire (become nonfunctional) after a certain date. ▪

The basic Netscape software is available through anonymous FTP at the machine **ftp.netscape.com**. You can find either the latest released version of the software, or the latest beta version, which is the one that is discussed in this chapter. The beta version can be found at **http://home.netscape.com/comprod/mirror/client_download.html**. This directory has both a 16- and 32-bit version of the Netscape beta; be sure to pick up the 32-bit version to use with Windows 95, located in the file n3230b5s.exe.

N O T E In Windows 95, you store your files in *folders*. Many other operating systems use the term *directory*. Some FTP programs (like WS_FTP) simply show you the names of the directories on the remote host (and on your local machine), not using the iconic folder representation for the directories. For that reason, the term directory has been used when discussing the retrieval of files from FTP servers. If you use a graphical FTP client other than WS_FTP (or if you use a Web browser to retrieve files from the FTP server), you may see the directories represented as folders. ▪

T I P If you have an older version of Netscape (or another Web browser, such as Microsoft Internet Explorer), you can go to the Netscape home page (**http://home.netscape.com**), follow the links to the latest version of Netscape, and download it from there.

If you have a Windows-based FTP program, such as WS_FTP (included on the NetCD that comes with this book), and you want to retrieve the Netscape software from the Internet, use the following procedure:

1. Connect to your Internet provider.
2. Start the FTP program.
3. Click Connect, and enter the address of the site that you are using. Enter **anonymous** as the user ID and your e-mail address as the password.
4. Navigate to the directory that contains the Netscape software on the Remote System.
5. When you reach the correct location, select the files to be transferred and initiate the transfer.
6. After transferring all the files you need, close your FTP connection, then exit FTP.

You may encounter one problem in obtaining the Netscape software; because this software is so popular, the Netscape site often is very busy. A limited number of users can connect to the site at the same time; at busy times, you may not be able to connect. Netscape communications has a number of different anonymous FTP machines available; try adding a number from 2 through 20 after "ftp" in the host name (for example, **ftp://ftp4.netscape.com/pub/ navigator/3.0/3.0b5/windows/standard/n3230b5.exe**) to reach a less-busy machine. Or, there are a number of mirror sites where you can pick up the software:

- Washington University in St. Louis at **http://wuarchive.wusti.edu/packages/www/ Netscape/navigator/3.0/3.0b4/windows/standard/n3230b5s.exe**

- University of Texas at Dallas at **ftp://lassen.utdallas.edu/pub/web/netscape/pub/ navigator/3.0/3.0b4/windows/standard/n3230b5s.exe**

- Central Michigan University/Computer Center at **ftp://ftp.cps.cmich.edu/pub/ netscape/navigator/3.0/3.0b4/windows/standard/n3230b5s.exe**

- University of Texas at Austin, North America at **ftp://ftp.the.net/mirrors/ ftp.netscape.com/pub/navigator/3.0/3.0b4/windows/standard/n3230b5s.exe**

> **CAUTION**
>
> Under Windows 95, if you are currently using any verisons prior to this release, you will get multiple uninstall entries in your Add/Remove program. Do an uninstall to remove your previous Netscape Navigator version before you install version 3.0.

Another thing to keep in mind when you are looking for this software is that just as you move files around on your computer, the system administrators of the FTP sites occasionally move files or rename directories. If you can't find the files that you are looking for, look in another directory because they may be somewhere else.

Obtaining Auxiliary Software for Netscape

Netscape not only directly displays the text and inline graphics from HTML documents, Netscape's built-in plug-ins enable the Navigator to handle pictures, sounds, and animations (movies). For information on helper applications that are not built-in to Netscape, Chapter 19, "Using Helper Applications with Web Browsers," discusses how to get and install other helper applications.

Installing Netscape on Your System

Since this version of Netscape is specifically for Windows 95, use the Programs Wizard to install the software. To set up the software, follow these steps:

1. Move the Netscape self-extracting file you retrieved from the FTP site to a temporary folder on your hard drive (for example, C:\install).

2. Run the self-extracting file by double-clicking it in the Windows Explorer, or by selecting Run from the Start button and typing in the path and name of the file (for example, C:\install\n3230b5s.exe).

A DOS window appears, showing you the files that are being extracted from the self-extracting file. If any of the files being extracted currently exist, you are asked if it is OK to overwrite them. When all the files have been extracted, close the DOS window (if it hasn't closed by itself). The temporary folder now contains the original self-extracting file and several other files.

3. Next, the Install Wizard takes you through the setup process step by step.

4. Click Install.

5. Click Next to install the Nescape files into the default directory /Netscape.

6. Click Browse to select a different directory to install the Netscape files.

7. Select Finish.

8. Follow the instructions in the Setup program. It suggests exiting all Windows programs while the installation is done and performs the installation.

9. You get a dialog box stating that your Netscape setup is complete. Click OK to close this dialog box. You then get a dialog box asking if you want to read the Readme file. Click Yes to read the file or No to exit to Windows.

10. When the setup finishes, it will leave an open window showing the contents of the Netscape/Program/Navigator folder, containing shortcuts to Netscape and its Readme file. Close this window.

11. The setup of the Netscape software is now complete. You can remove the files from the temporary folder; they are no longer needed.

N O T E   You can easily add Netscape to your Start Menu/Programs item. Open the Programs folder that is in the folder where you installed Netscape. Drag the Navigator folder from Program to your desktop. Open the Windows folder, then open the Start Menu folder (if multiple people have profiles on your PC, you'll need to open the Profiles folder under the Windows folder, then open the Start Menu under your personal folder). Drag the Navigator folder from the desktop to the Programs folder under the Start Menu folder.

Now when you open the Start menu and select Programs from the taskbar, you will find an item called Navigator that will allow you to start Netscape Navigator. ▪

Although you can customize the Netscape software to meet your needs, you can run the software without any further work. You will, of course, need to set up your Internet-connection software before using Netscape to access WWW documents.

Using the Netscape Interface

After you have installed all the software that you need to run Netscape, you can connect to your Internet provider and start Netscape. Netscape is a very powerful application, but it is graphically oriented and not difficult to use after you are familiar with all of its features.

Starting Netscape

Before starting Netscape, you will need to be connected to the Internet. If your Internet connection is via your LAN, be sure that you are logged on to your network. If you are connected to the Internet through a modem, start your TCP/IP software, and log in to your account.

After you establish your Internet connection, open the Start menu and select Programs, Navigator, Netscape Navigator. Netscape starts up, and you are ready to explore the Internet with Netscape.

The Netscape Window

When Netscape starts, it loads the document that is specified as the home page in the Preferences dialog box (choose Options, General Preferences). Unless you have specified a personal home page, your window should look like the one shown in Figure 18.1 (which shows the default Netscape Welcome page).

FIG. 18.1

The different parts of the Netscape window are shown here on the default Netscape Communications welcome page.

Title bar—
Menu bar—
Toolbar—
Location field—
Directory buttons—
Content area—
Mail icon—
Progress bar—
Security indicator—
Status bar—

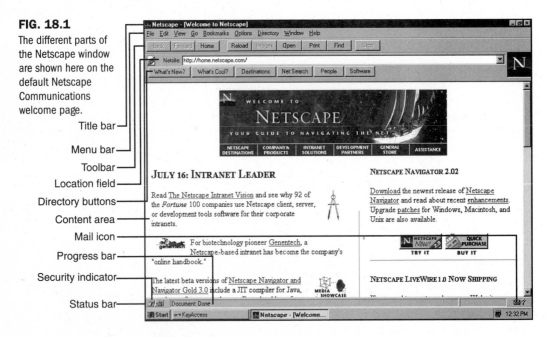

The URL for the default home page is **http://home.netscape.com**.

The following list briefly describes each window part. The remainder of this chapter contains detailed discussion of Netscape's features.

■ The *title bar* contains the usual window-function buttons (Control menu, Maximize, Minimize, and Close buttons), as well as the name of the application (Netscape) and the name of the WWW document you are viewing.

■ The *menu bar* gives you access to all the functions that you need to use Netscape. You can retrieve documents to view, print documents, customize your Netscape window, navigate between documents, annotate documents, save files, and access Netscape's online Help system.

■ The *location field* shows the URL of the current document. When you open a document, its URL is displayed, and the Netscape logo (at the right end of the bar) blinks while the document is being retrieved.

■ The *directory buttons* give you quick access to some items in the Directory menu.

■ The *content area* is the area of the window in which you see the text of a document and any inline images that it may contain.

■ The *status bar* serves two functions. The first is to display host connection and document loading information. While Netscape is loading your document, it shows the progress of the different document elements (text and individual graphics) that are being loaded, using a counter to show the number of bytes loaded compared with the total size of the document or image that is being loaded.

When you are viewing a document, the status bar shows the URL of the hyperlink on which your cursor rests.

■ The *progress bar* to the right of the status bar is a bar graph showing what percentage of the entire document has been loaded.

■ The *security indicator* to the left of the status bar is a key symbol that indicates the security status of your document. If the key is broken, the current document is not secure. If the key is unbroken on a blue background, the document is secure.

■ The *mail icon* to the right of the progress bar opens the Mail window and checks for new messages.

■ The *toolbar* gives you quick access to some of the most-used features in Netscape (see Fig. 18.2). By default, the toolbar contains buttons labeled to describe the actions that they perform. You can configure the toolbar to show pictures that represent the actions or pictures with the descriptions printed below them.

The following list provides basic descriptions of the toolbar buttons:

■ *Back* displays the preceding document in the history list.

■ *Forward* displays the following document in the history list.

■ *Home* goes to the default home page.

■ *Reload* reloads the current document.

■ *Images* loads the images in a document, if you had image loading turned off.

■ *Open* enables you to open a URL.

■ *Print* sends the currently loaded document to your printer.

■ *Find* locates a text string in the current document.

■ *Stop* stops the loading process for the current document.

FIG. 18.2
The buttons in the
toolbar are found at the
top of the screen.

What Is a Home Page?

Your home page (or home document) is the document that you tell Netscape to display when it
starts. This document should contain links to the documents and WWW sites that you use
most frequently. Many people mistakenly use the term "home page" for the welcome page that
you see when you connect to a WWW site. A home page gives you access to the WWW sites or
documents that you use most. Your project or company may have its own home page to give
members easy access to needed information. You can load someone else's home page or design your own.

When you start the Netscape software, it comes with the home page predefined as the
Netscape Communications welcome page. You probably will want to change this page, because
the Netscape page may not be very useful to you. In addition, retrieving a document causes a
load on the machine on which the document is located. If everyone used the Netscape welcome page as his home page, the Netscape WWW server would become considerably slower.

Telling Netscape What Home Page to Load

Netscape allows you to set your home page in its Preferences dialog box. To use the Preferences dialog box, follow these steps:

1. Choose Options, General Preferences. The Preferences dialog box appears and the
   Appearances tab appears (see Fig. 18.3).

FIG. 18.3

The Preferences dialog box lets you configure different Netscape features. You can set what home page to load (if any) on the Appearances tab.

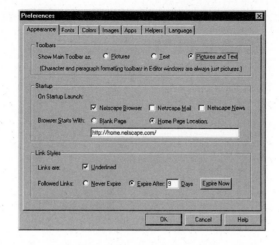

2. If you want a home page to be displayed, choose the Home Page Location radio button. (Choose the Blank Page radio button if you don't want to load a home page.)

3. Click the text box below the Home Page Location radio button.

4. Enter the URL of the document that you want to use as your home page.

5. Choose OK to save your home page setting and exit the Preferences dialog box.

T I P You can click the Home button in the toolbar to reload your home page quickly. (The Home button looks like a house, if you have pictures turned on.)

Your home page can be a document on your computer or any document that you can access at a WWW site. (See Chapter 20, "Planning Your Own World Wide Web Home Page," for details on creating your own home page or turning a file that's saved on your computer into a home page.)

When you start Netscape, the document that you defined as your home page will be displayed in the content area. After the home page loads, the URL for your home page appears in the location bar (if you have the location bar enabled). When your home page is loaded, you can click any of the links on your home page to load the documents that you use frequently.

If you want to return to your home page at any time, open the Go menu and choose Home to reload your home-page document.

Moving Between Documents

After you start Netscape, you can move between WWW documents in several ways; you can click links in the document that you are viewing, or you can use Netscape's Open Location dialog box to enter a URL. You can also type a URL directly into the text box in the location field (press Enter at the end of the URL to load that document).

Part

IV

Ch

18

If you loaded a home page, that page probably includes links to other documents. After all, the purpose of the WWW is to enable you to move between related documents quickly, without having to enter long path names. If a document contains no links, it's not a very useful WWW document. But even if your current document has no links, you can still move between documents by entering the URLs for the documents that you want to view.

N O T E Netscape gives you a few other ways to move between documents. You can use bookmarks that contain items with predefined URLs. Creating and using bookmarks is covered in the section "Creating Lists of Your Favorite URLs," later in this chapter.

In addition, the Directory menu gives you access to some interesting, important Internet documents, and directory buttons enable you to load these documents quickly.

Using Links to Move Between Documents

A *link* can be a word, a group of words, or an image. Netscape can indicate the hypertext links in a document in several different ways. If you have a color monitor, the links can be displayed in one color (maybe blue) and other text in a different color (maybe black). If you have a black-and-white monitor, the links can be underlined (the default).

If you have a color display, Netscape enables you to keep track of the links that you've visited recently. After you load a document, the next time you come across a link to that document, the link is displayed in a different color (magenta) rather than blue. You can set up Netscape so that the memory of your visit to a link expires after a certain period of time (or you can set it so that it never expires). You also can reset the expiration date of all links so that all links start out the same color (blue) again.

When you move your cursor over an area of the screen that contains an active link, your cursor changes from an arrow to a pointing hand. The URL associated with each link that you pass over appears in the status bar (if the status bar is enabled). To activate a link, click it. Netscape loads that document and displays the URL for the document in the location bar (if the location bar is enabled).

Look at the Netscape home page in Figure 18.4. The following phrases are links: reported, high-security 128-bit, Download, Netscape Navigator, enhancements, and patches. When you run Netscape on a color display, you see the links in blue (they are underlined in the figure), which is the default hyperlink color. The URL of the active link, *Netscape Navigator* (with the pointing-hand pointer over it) appears in the status bar.

Customizing the Hyperlink Indicators

You can change the default appearance and color of the hyperlinks in the documents that Netscape loads. To customize Netscape's link attributes, follow these steps:

1. Choose Options, General Preferences. The Appearance sheet should be displayed in the Preferences dialog box.
2. To have links underlined in a document, select the Underlined check box.

3. You can set the number of days after which followed links (URLs that you've previously loaded) expire. Click the box next to the Expire After radio button, and enter the number of days. When the amount of time since you have accessed a link is longer than this time, the link becomes blue again.

   If you click the Never Expire radio button, any link that you follow will be shown in magenta until you clear all links.

4. Click Expire Now to clear the expiration information from all of your links immediately. A confirmation box appears, asking whether you definitely want to mark all of your links as not visited. If you choose Yes, all links will be displayed in blue, whether or not you have accessed them recently (until you access them again). Click Cancel to leave the expiration information on your links as is.

5. When you have the options set to your satisfaction, choose OK.

You can also change the color of your new and followed links. To do so, see the section "Setting Netscape's Color Scheme," later in this chapter.

FIG. 18.4
The Netscape home page shows the hyperlinks underlined.

Cursor over active link

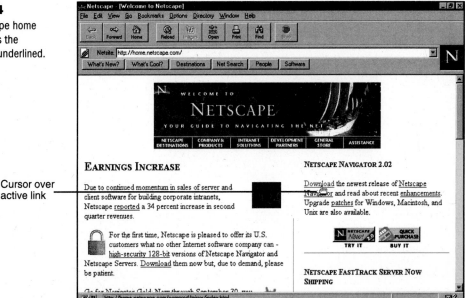

Moving Backward and Forward

Typing long URLs and scrolling through documents to look for the links you want can get rather tedious. If you're jumping between several documents, take advantage of three helpful navigating commands: Back, Forward, and Reload.

Netscape keeps information about what documents you have loaded (see the discussion of the history list in "How to Get Where You Were," later in this chapter) and allows you to move between these documents quickly by using the Back and Forward commands. The Back command takes you to the preceding document that you had open. To go back, choose Go, Back or click the Back button.

The next command is Forward. What you have to remember about Forward is that you can move forward only after moving back. (This concept is rather confusing, but it will make more sense after you read about history lists in "How to Get Where You Were," later in this chapter.) To move forward, choose Go, Forward or click the Forward button.

The last command is Reload. This command redisplays the document that you are currently viewing. To reload the current document, choose Go, View, Reload or just click the Reload button.

Using URLs to Move Between Documents

If you don't want to go to any of the documents for which links are displayed in the current document, or if you did not load a home page (you do not currently have a document displayed), you can load a new document by specifying its URL to Netscape. Refer to Chapter 16, "How the World Wide Web Works," for information on how to correctly format a URL. To enter a URL directly, follow these steps:

1. Choose File, Open Location and the Open Location dialog box appears (see Fig. 18.5).

FIG. 18.5
The Open Location dialog box allows you to directly enter the URL for the next document that you want to view.

2. To open a new document, enter a new URL in the box.

 T I P   To open a document quickly, type a URL into the text box in the location bar and press Enter.

3. Click Open to load the URL that you entered, or click Cancel if you do not want to load that document.

Opening Multiple Documents

A very useful feature of Netscape is its capability to display multiple documents at the same time. To open another document window, choose File, New Web Browser. This window has the same history list as the window from which it was opened, with the displayed document being the oldest document in the history list. You now can view any document you want in any of the open Netscape document windows.

Caching Documents

When you are reading documents, you often move back and forth between one document and others that are linked to that document. To keep from having to load a document every time you view it, Netscape keeps copies of the last few documents that you viewed on your local computer. Keeping copies of previously viewed documents is called *caching*.

Caching keeps Netscape from making unnecessary demands on Internet resources. Caching does take up resources on your own computer, though, so you can cache only a limited number of documents. Netscape enables you to specify the amount of memory and disk that it can use for caching. Follow these steps:

1. Choose Options, Network Preferences. The Cache tab should appear in the Preferences window (see Fig. 18.6).

FIG. 18.6
Set the amount of memory and disk space to as much as you can spare to keep from reloading documents frequently.

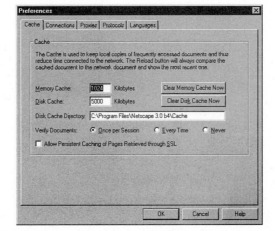

2. The Cache tab allows you to set up the amount of memory and disk space that Netscape can use for caching. The default settings are 600K of memory and 5M (5000K) of disk space. Change them if you want to use more or less of your system resources for cache.

3. You can set the folder that Netscape uses for disk caching. To do so, enter the path in the Disk Cache Directory text box.

4. If you want to clear the current contents of your memory or disk caches, click Clear Memory Cache Now or Clear Disk Cache Now. When you click either of these buttons, a confirmation box asks whether you definitely want to clear that cache. If you click Yes, the cache is cleared immediately. Click No if you decide not to clear the cache.

5. The Allow Persistent Caching of Pages Retrieved through SSL (Security Sockets Layer) check box determines whether the pages you view using SSL security are stored in the cache. The default, unchecked, does not allow SSL pages to be cached.

6. When you have the options set to your satisfaction, choose OK.

Setting Netscape's Color Scheme

You can set color options for parts of the Web pages displayed in Netscape. Some of the things you can set are

- The color that Netscape uses to display unexplored and followed links in a document.
- The colors that Netscape uses for document text and the color or image that is used for the background.
- You can set Netscape so that it always uses your color specifications, regardless of the colors specified in a document.

To set your own color specifications, follow these steps:

1. Choose Options, General Preferences, then select the Colors tab (see Fig. 18.7).

FIG. 18.7
Set up your link color, text color, and document background information from the Colors tab.

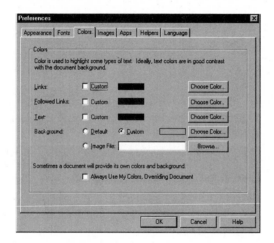

2. Select the color options you want.
3. Choose OK.

What You See When a Document Is Loaded

When you load a document, Netscape gives you a great deal of information about what is happening. Stars streak through the sky of the Netscape icon to the right of the location field, the Stop button in the toolbar turns red, and messages appear in the status area. All these signals help you follow the progress of a document load.

Status Bar Messages   Viewing a WWW document involves many different activities. Netscape needs to contact the server where the document lives, ask the server whether it has the document, and then ask the server to transfer that document to your computer. Through messages in the status area, Netscape tries to tell you what steps have been accomplished and what still needs to be done as it is loading the document. These messages can include the following:

- ▓ Connect: Looking up Host:<hostname>
- ▓ Connect: Contacting Host:<hostname>
- ▓ Connect: Host Contacted: Waiting for reply...
- ▓ Document: Received <nnn> of <nnnn> bytes
- ▓ Transferring data
- ▓ Document: Done

The Netscape icon is a useful indicator of the status of the document load. Stars streaking across the icon with no other activity can be the first (and sometimes, the only) indication that a problem exists—if, for example, your counter stops increasing, even though it hasn't reached the full load size.

It is nice to be able to watch the counter increase (and the bar graph) as the elements of the document are loaded. These features give you an idea of how far along you are and how much longer you can expect to wait before the document is loaded.

Stopping a Document Load   Occasionally, you may want to abort the loading of the current document. Perhaps you clicked a link inadvertently, or perhaps you discovered the document that you wanted to view contains huge graphics that you don't have time to download.

You can stop a document load in two ways. If your toolbar is displayed, click the Stop button to cancel the load. (The Stop button is red while a document is loading.) You also can choose Go, Stop Loading to abort the load.

You will find that if you stop a load, you are likely to get a partial copy of the document that was loading. (A Transfer interrupted! message probably will appear at the end of the partial document.) Choose Go, Back to return to the preceding document, and continue your navigation from there.

Controlling the Loading of Graphics   Loading documents can take a few minutes, especially if the document contains many large graphics and your computer has a relatively slow (less than 9,600 bps) connection to the Internet. One thing you can do to speed the loading of the document is to tell Netscape not to load the inline graphics from the document. To do this Choose Options, Auto Load Images (the option is turned off when there is no check mark next to it).

 T I P   The Images button in your toolbar becomes active when Auto Load Images is turned off.

The next new document that you load will not have any graphics displayed; instead, placeholder icons will be displayed where the graphics should be (see Fig. 18.8). To load the images that the placeholders represent, click the Images button in the toolbar, or choose View, Load Images.

You can also load individual graphics from their placeholder icons. If you want to load a single graphic, right-click its placeholder and select Load this Image from the pop-up menu.

Part

IV

Ch

18

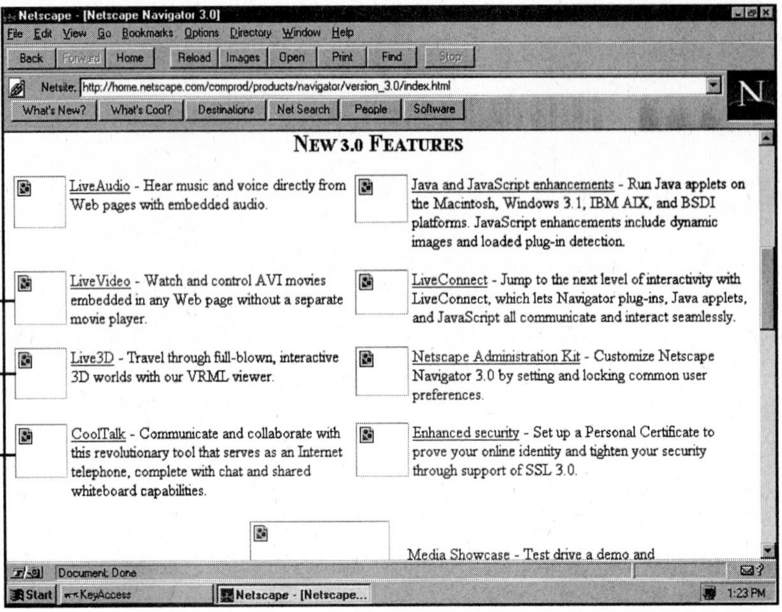

FIG. 18.8
When you tell Netscape not to load inline graphics, it places icons where the graphics would be.

Image placeholders

You can configure the following other image-related features of Netscape:

- By default, Netscape begins to display an image while it loads it. You can set Netscape so that it loads an entire image first and then displays it. This procedure may be faster if you have a good Internet connection.

- You also can set Netscape to dither colors so you can create the closest match to the color that is specified. It takes longer to do this, but it produces more accurate images.

- You can set Netscape so that it displays the palette color closest to the one specified in the graphic. This method loads images faster, but the colors may be slightly off; however, it should be adequate for most graphics that you would be viewing online.

To set Netscape's image options, follow these steps:

1. Choose Options, General Preferences, then select the Images tab. The Images sheet enables you to specify how you want Netscape to load images and display colors (see Fig. 18.9).

2. Select the Display Images options you want.

3. Click OK.

FIG. 18.9

The default image settings are Dither and Display Images While Loading.

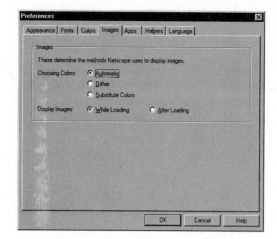

Looking for Information in a Document

If the WWW document that you are reading is short, you can scroll through the document (or press the Page Up and Page Down keys) to find information that interests you. If you have loaded a very long document, though, Netscape provides a quick way to look for information. Follow these steps:

1. Open the Edit menu Find dialog box (see Fig. 18.10).

FIG. 18.10

The Find dialog box enables you to specify the search words and the direction of the search.

2. In the Find What text box, enter the word for which you want to search.

3. To specify the direction of the search, select Up (towards the beginning of the document) or Down (towards the end).

4. Click Match Case if you want Netscape to match the exact capitalization of the word that you entered.

5. Choose Find Next to begin the search. If a match is found, Netscape scrolls the window to the section where the match appears and highlights the matching text. An alert box informs you if no match is found.

Saving Documents

In general, the purpose of the World Wide Web is to provide one copy of a document that many people can view. At times, however, you may want to save a copy of a document to your local computer. Netscape gives you several options for saving documents.

The first way to save a document is to choose File, Save As. The Save As dialog box appears, enabling you to browse through your directories and store the file wherever you want. You can save the file as HTML, text, or the native format of the file.

TIP Shift-click a link to save the document associated with that link to disk instead of displaying it.

You can save the document associated with a URL in your current document directly to disk rather than loading it into Netscape. To do so, right-click the link for that document and select Save this Link as from the pop-up menu that appears.

NOTE When you save an HTML document to your local disk, remember that the document probably contains hyperlinks. These links can be relative or absolute. An *absolute reference* contains the complete address of the document that is being referenced, including the host name, directory path, and file name. A *relative reference* assumes that the preceding machine and directory path are being used; only the file name (or possibly a subdirectory and file name) is specified.

If the document references other documents that have relative addresses, you cannot view those documents unless you copy them to your local disk and set them up with the same directory structure that they had at the original site. You may want to set up a document and its linked documents on your local disk, if you want to be able to view the document without connecting to the Internet. One problem is that if the original document changes, you are not aware that you are viewing an outdated version of the document.

Absolute references always work unless your Internet connection fails or the referenced documents are moved.

Printing Documents

In addition to being able to save documents, you can print documents directly from Netscape. Choose File, Print to send a copy of the current document to your printer or click the Print button.

One of the nice features of Netscape is that you can preview the current document before printing it. Choose File, Print Preview. Netscape creates a preview of the document in a separate window (see Fig. 18.11). This preview window enables you to look at each page of the document, zooming in and out wherever you want. When you are satisfied with the print preview, you can print the document directly from this window.

FIG. 18.11
The print preview window enables you to see what your document will look like before it is printed.

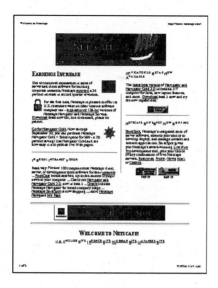

Customizing the Displayed Window Areas

Some of the window elements in Netscape are optional (not, however, the document viewing area; Netscape wouldn't be very useful without that!). The title bar and menu bar cannot be removed, but the toolbar, location field, and directory buttons can be turned off. Turning off these window elements gives you a bigger viewing area, but it also removes some time-saving and informational features. The following list describes how to turn these features off or back on (the feature is turned on if a check mark appears next to it in the menu):

- To turn off the toolbar, choose Options, Show Toolbar.
- To turn off the location field, choose Options, Show Location.
- To turn off the directory buttons, choose Options, Show Directory Buttons.
- To turn off the Java Console, choose Options, Show Java Console.

CAUTION

If you remove either the location field or the directory buttons, the Netscape icon shrinks to a size that is more difficult to see. If you remove both of the areas, the icon disappears, causing you to lose one of the visual clues that gives you information about document loading.

If you remove the toolbar, you lose the ability to cancel document transfers quickly, because the Stop button in the toolbar has been removed from the window. (You can still cancel transfers by choosing Go, Stop Loading.)

Changes now take effect immediately after you select the menu item. Netscape 3 automatically saves the changes as your new default settings.

Working with Local Files

When you think of using Netscape, you think of retrieving documents from WWW servers on the Internet. Netscape can read documents from your local file system, as well as from halfway around the world. If you share documents among members of your organization, many of the documents that you view may be on a local file server or your local computer.

Netscape provides an option that makes loading a local file easy. If you want to load a local file, choose File, Open File. The Open dialog box appears (see Fig. 18.12). This dialog box enables you to browse through all your local disks to find a file.

FIG. 18.12
The Open dialog box enables you to enter a local file name or browse your local file system to find the next document that you want to view.

You also can load a local file in the same manner that you load any URL. Choose File, Open Location to open the Open Location dialog box. To specify a local file, precede the location of the file with **file:///c|** (you can substitute any of your local disks for c). The three slashes tell Netscape that you are looking for a local file; the bar is used instead of a colon because the colon has a specific purpose in a URL. Use slashes between the folder names in the file location that you enter, even though you usually use the backslash to separate folder names in Windows 95. Netscape translates the slashes properly when it retrieves the file.

▶ See "URLs," p. 371

Local URLs can be used anywhere that URLs are used—as bookmarks, links in documents, and so on.

Effective Browsing Techniques

Navigating between WWW documents can be confusing. Documents often connect to documents that you have already read. You can't always remember which of several related documents contains the information that you really need.

Sometimes, you can't tell from the hyperlink whether the document is of interest to you, and loading documents uses valuable time. Often, you waste time loading documents that you dismiss immediately. This section helps you learn to reduce unnecessary document loading and circular navigating.

How to Keep Track of Where You've Been

Keeping track of where you are and where you were is one of the biggest challenges of using the WWW. Suppose that you're reading a document that deals with agriculture, and you click a hyperlink that takes you to Hay Field Seeding Suggestions. The document turns out to be one that you loaded earlier—when you found a hyperlink for Pasture Management Techniques. How can you avoid this frustrating repetition?

One suggestion is to have a home page that provides links to your most-visited WWW pages. This home page is useful, for example, if you work on a group project and frequently use documents with known locations. You can create your own home page, or someone can create a project home page for your group. In this scenario, you probably are already familiar with the servers, if not with the exact documents.

But what if you're navigating in uncharted waters on the WWW? Although it sounds difficult, you probably can learn to recognize the URLs of the sites that keep information that interests you. If the location field is displayed, the URL for the current document appears there. The status bar shows the URL of a hyperlink when you move the cursor over it (see Fig. 18.13). As you move between documents, you begin to remember some of the URLs that you see frequently; when you put your cursor on a hyperlink, you recognize documents that you know.

FIG. 18.13

The status bar displays the URLs of hyperlinks when the cursor is on top of them.

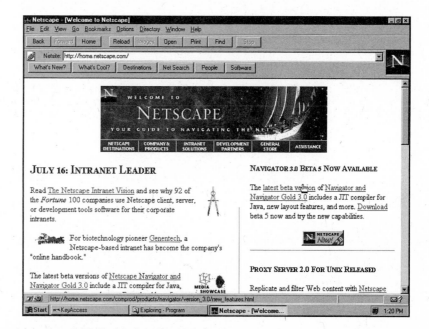

How to Get Where You Were

Trying to navigate back to a document that you viewed in the current Netscape session also can be challenging. In general, to go to the document that you viewed before the current document, choose <u>G</u>o, <u>B</u>ack (or click the Back button in the toolbar). Opening the menu and choosing the G_o, F_orward command (or clicking the Forward button) takes you to the last document that you viewed after the current document. This arrangement sounds rather confusing, but it is understandable if you examine how Netscape determines these links.

 TIP   If the History dialog box is open when you use the Forward and Back commands, you can see the highlighted item move in the list of URLs.

The W_indow menu contains an option called H_istory, which displays a dialog box similar to the one shown in Figure 18.14. Notice that a list of URLs appears in this dialog box; the URL for the current document is highlighted.

FIG. 18.14
The Netscape History dialog box shows a linear list of URLs that you visit.

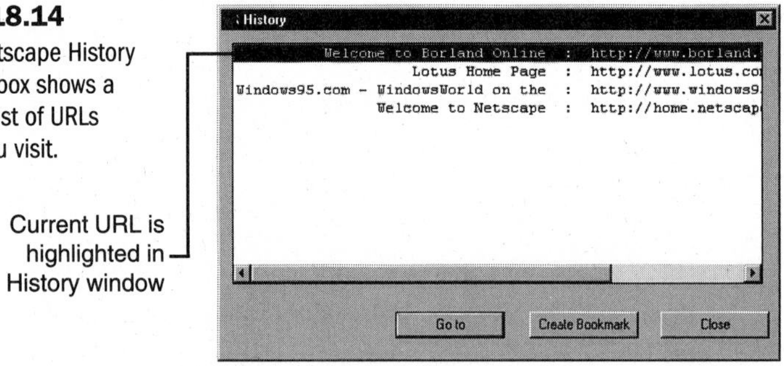

Current URL is
highlighted in
History window

History
Welcome to Borland Online : http://www.borland.
Lotus Home Page : http://www.lotus.co
Windows95.com - WindowsWorld on the : http://www.windows9
Welcome to Netscape : http://home.netscap

Go to   Create Bookmark   Close

The history list shows you the URLs of the document chain that led you to this point, as well as any documents that you visited after the current document. If you use the Back command, you move up in the list; if you use the Forward command, you move down the list. Click any URL in the list and click Go To to jump to that document (and that point in the list).

CAUTION

You can use the Back and Forward commands to move between documents that you have already visited (which are shown in the history list). In previous versions of the navigator, if you jumped to a new document while you were in the middle of the list, you erased the links at the end of the list and could not use the Forward command to return to those documents. In version 3, however, navigation for frames allows you to move Back and Forward through page links frame by frame.

To move quickly between documents that you load, use the history list. If you want to add a new document to the list of documents that you're viewing, make sure that you're at the end of the list before you jump to that document. You don't have to use hyperlinks to add the document you load to the history list. Load the document from the Open Location dialog box (choose F_ile, Open L_ocation, or click the Open toolbar button), and it is added to the list.

You will notice when you open the G_o menu that the last few documents that you visited (a maximum of 15) are displayed at the bottom of the menu (see Fig. 18.15). The documents are shown in the order in which you opened them, with the most recent document appearing at the top of the list. The ten newest documents are numbered so that you can access them quickly without using the mouse. A zero appears to the left of the most recently visited document; the nine documents following it are numbered sequentially.

FIG. 18.15

The Go menu enables you to quickly access the last few documents that you visited.

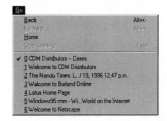

Creating Lists of Your Favorite URLs

If you don't want to create a home page that contains all of your favorite WWW documents, Netscape offers an alternative to keep track of these documents. To quickly access your favorite URLs, you can create bookmark files. You can have any number of bookmark files and can save any number of URLs to each file.

Setting Your Current Bookmark File

The default bookmark file is bookmark.htm. You can have any number of bookmark files, although only one can be set as the current bookmark file. To set your current bookmark file, follow these steps:

1. Choose Bookmarks, Go to Bookmarks or Window, Bookmarks to open the Netscape Bookmarks window (see Fig. 18.16).

FIG. 18.16

The Netscape Bookmarks window lets you load and edit any of your bookmark files.

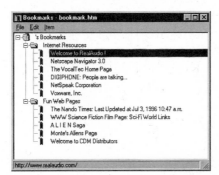

2. Choose File, Open to get the Open Bookmarks File window (see Fig. 18.17).

3. Use the browser to find the folder where you keep your Bookmark files. Click the file that you want to use as the current Bookmark file (the path is entered in the text box automatically when you click the file).

4. Choose Open to make the selections take effect, or click Cancel if you decide not to change the current bookmark file.

FIG. 18.17
The Open Bookmarks File window lets you browse your file system for the Bookmark file you want to load.

Creating and Editing Bookmarks

After you define your current bookmark file, you can create bookmarks in several ways. The simplest way is to choose Bookmarks, Add Bookmark. This command writes the title and URL of the current document as the last item in your bookmark file. You do not need to visit a document, however, to add it to your bookmark file. The Netscape Bookmarks window allows you to add and edit bookmarks in the current bookmark file.

To use the Bookmark List dialog box, follow these steps:

1. Choose Bookmarks, Go to Bookmarks or Window, Bookmarks to open the Netscape Bookmarks window.

2. To search for an item in your Bookmark list, enter the string of characters that you want to search for in the Find text box, and then click Find. Netscape finds all occurrences of the character string (regardless of capitalization), whether the string occurs as part of a word or as an entire word.

   The Find command searches from the current Bookmark down, and will find strings in the URLs associated with entries.

In addition to adding the current document, you can add any document to the list, edit the documents that currently appear in the list, group items onto submenus, and add separators in the lists.

If you want to edit one of the bookmarks in the list, select it, then choose Item, Properties. Information about that bookmark appears in the text boxes labeled Name, Location, Last Visited, Added On, and Description. You can edit the Name, Location, and Description entries. The name is the entry that appears in the bookmark list. The location is the URL of the document. The description appears below the name when you view the bookmark file as a document.

To add a new item to the list, select the item that you want the new item to follow. Then select one of the following from the Items menu:

- Insert Separator causes a line to be added below the selected item. This line appears when the bookmarks are displayed in the Bookmarks menu.

- Insert Folder causes the words New Folder to appear in the Bookmark list and the Name text box in the Bookmark Properties dialog box. Change the Name entry to whatever you want the header to be. Once you've created the folder, you can select current bookmarks and drag them into the folder. The folder appears under your Bookmarks menu item, and bookmarks within the folder appear as a submenu from that menu item.

- Insert Bookmark causes the words New Bookmark to appear in both the bookmarks list and the Name text box in the Bookmark Properties dialog box, and enters the current time and date in the Added On field. Change the Name entry to whatever you want it to be. Then enter the URL of the document you are adding in the Location box. If you want to, you also can add a description of the document in the Description box.

To remove an item from the Bookmarks list, select the item, and then choose Edit, Delete. To copy an item, select it, and then choose Edit, Copy. To paste the item, select the item that you want the copied item to follow and choose Edit, Paste.

Using Bookmarks

Bookmarks enable you to access documents quickly. You simply open the Bookmarks menu and select any of the bookmarks that appear at the end of the menu; Netscape loads the document associated with that bookmark. If the Netscape Bookmarks window is open, you can select any item in the bookmarks list and then choose Item, Go to Bookmark to load that document.

> **N O T E** Netscape has a feature that lets you quickly check to see whether the documents in your bookmarks list have changed recently. Choose Window, Bookmarks to open the Bookmarks window. From the Bookmarks window, select File, What's New. In the dialog box that appears, select either All bookmarks or Selected bookmarks, and then choose Start Checking. Netscape will go out and check the documents that you requested to see if they've changed since the last time you accessed them. When it is finished, you will get a dialog box telling you how many documents were checked, and how many have changed. The changed documents will be highlighted in your bookmarks list. ■

Sharing Bookmarks

Netscape makes it very easy for you to share your bookmarks with other users. If you want to share entire bookmark files, simply give the users a copy of your bookmark files. Those people then can specify any of those files as their current bookmark file, and they will be able to access the same documents that you can.

You also can save the current version of your bookmarks list to a file from the Netscape Bookmarks window. Simply choose File, Save As, and use the Save Bookmarks File dialog box that appears to select the folder and file to which you want to write the bookmarks. You then can give that file to other people.

If you get someone else's bookmark files and you don't want to bother changing files all the time to use them, you can add the bookmarks from those files to your main bookmarks file. Open the bookmarks file that you want to add the new bookmarks to. In the Netscape Bookmarks window, choose File, Import. You get an Import Bookmarks File dialog box that allows you to select the file that you want to import from your file system. When you select the file that you want to import, all the Bookmarks from that file are added to the top of the current Bookmarks list, preserving any menu structure that was in the imported list.

Understanding Netscape's Security Features

Many people seem to feel that because computers are machines, communications between computers are secure (no people are involved). Nothing could be further from the truth.

Communication on the Internet involves data being forwarded from the sending computer to the receiving computer through several intermediate computers. A possibility exists that someone could be looking at the information passing through the intermediate computers. He could even set up another computer to pretend to be the receiving computer, so that everything you send goes to someone who was not intended to see the information.

For this reason, sending sensitive information (such as your credit card number) over the Internet is not a good idea. Any information sent over the Internet is at risk—e-mail messages, file transfers, and particularly information from electronic forms that you may fill out with your WWW browser.

There is, however, a solution to this problem. Netscape Communications has built security features into its Web browser and server. A very secure encryption standard can be used for transmitting information between the Netscape browser and a Netscape server. This encryption prevents anyone who is observing the information at an intermediate point from making any sense of it. The Netscape browser shows the security status of the document that you are viewing in several ways as follows:

- If the key symbol to the left of the status bar is broken, the current document is not secure. If the key is unbroken on a blue background, the document is secure. If the unbroken key has two teeth, the encryption is high-grade; if it has one tooth, the encryption is medium grade. When you are viewing a secure document, a thin blue line will appear above the content area.

- Dialog boxes can warn you when you are entering or leaving a secure WWW server, and also warn you when you are going to submit information with an insecure form.

You can specify whether you want to see the alert dialog boxes for different security conditions. To do so, select Options, Security Preferences and then make sure the General tab is displayed (see Fig. 18.18).

FIG. 18.18

You can specify how Netscape alerts you about the security status of the WWW servers and documents that you visit.

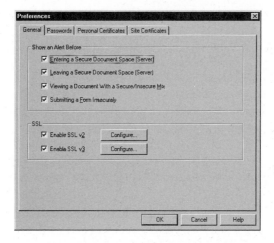

You also can get security information about the document that you are currently viewing from the Document Information dialog box (see Fig. 18.19). Choose View, Document Info to display this dialog box.

FIG. 18.19

The Document Information dialog box tells you the document title and location, and when it was last modified, in addition to information about the security of the document.

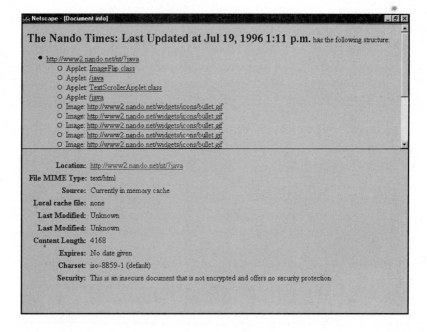

Introducing Netscape 3's Newest Features

The newest release of Netscape Navigator has many significant enhancements that completely integrate audio, video, Internet phone, and VRML 3-D capabilities. What I mean by integrate is that these capabilites are built-in features of Netscape 3. The next section on External Plug-in Applications cover additional popular helper applications that are external to Netscape 3. By external, I mean that they are not built-in to the product.

Here are a few of the new features:

- LiveAudio—Embedded voice and music enhancements can be heard right from Web pages.
- LiveVideo—Any Web pages embedded with AVI movies can be played without the support of additional video viewers.
- LiveConnect—Integrate all live online communications that include plug-ins, Java applets and JavaScript.
- Live3D—Interact with 3-D environments through Netscape's VRML viewer (formerly WebFX).
- CoolTalk—Communicate with Internet chat phone capabilities.
- Java and JavaScript—Run Java applets with enhancements that include dynamic images and loaded plug-in detection.
- Enhanced Security—Set up a Personal Certificate with added security through SSL (Security Sockets Layer) 3.0 support.
- Netscape Administration Kit—Set and lock common user preferences by customizing Netscape 3.

Additional new features include support for new HTML tags including audio/video embedding and table colors. Frame navigation allows you to move through hyperlinks frame by frame. LiveCache allows for the continuation of loading an interrupted file as well as a preloading cache for CD-ROMs. QuickTime also allows for embedded plug-ins to play sound and video models as well as dynamic animations.

For more information on Netscape 3 enhancements, check out **http://home.netscape.com/ comprod/products/navigator/version_3.0/index.html**.

▶ **See** "Understanding Helper Applications and Plug-Ins," **p. 436**

External Plug-In Applications

Before the Internet was commercialized, the standards for all Internet services were defined by the various Internet administrative committees, and all interfaces for a particular service (like FTP or Gopher) had the same features. Now that commercial companies are developing interfaces for the World Wide Web (the newest and least standardized Internet service), they are putting into their Web browsers proprietary features that other browsers do not have, attempting to become the standard rather than to follow it.

One of these proprietary features that Netscape has added is the *plug-in*, which adds the ability to embed pieces of helper applications directly into Web documents. With plug-ins, you don't need to start the helper application in a separate window when loading a multi-media file—you just use the piece of the helper application interface that appears in the document. Netscape has made agreements with a number vendors to incorporate plug-ins for their applications. Some of the popular plug-ins available at the time this book was published were

- Adobe Acrobat 3.0
- Corel CMX Viewer for vector graphics
- Tumbleweed Software Envoy 7 viewer
- Visual Components Formula One/NET Excel-compatible spreadsheet
- Progressive Networks Real Audio live audio player
- Macromedia Shockwave for Director for multimedia presentations
- VDOnet VDOLive for display of video images
- LiveUpdate's Cresendo Plus 2.0 for adding sound to your Web pages
- Vream's Wirl 3D interactive Web browser

To see a list of the current plug-ins available for Netscape, open **http://home.netscape.com/comprod/products/navigator/version_2.0/plugins/index.html**. The remainder of this section discusses some of the more interesting and useful plug-ins.

Part
IV

Ch
18

Real Audio

Progressive Networks has made an agreement with Netscape Communications to develop a plug-in of their Real Audio product. Real Audio lets you listen to live audio broadcast over the Internet. To incorporate the Real Audio plug-in for Netscape, you must first load the Real Audio player onto your PC. To do this:

1. Go to the URL **http://www.realaudio.com/products/ra2.0/**.
2. Scroll down the page and select Real Audio Player 2.0.
3. Fill out the form that appears on this page.
4. Once the form is completed, select Go to download page and download the Real Audio player ra32_201.exe file to a temporary directory on your PC, such as C:\Install.
5. From Windows Explorer, double-click the .exe file you loaded in the temporary directory to install Real Audio.
6. Enter the information requested by the setup program.
7. Choose the Express setup to install Real Audio with default setting.
8. During the installation, you will be asked if you want to install the Netscape plug-in. Click Yes.

After the Real Audio player is installed, the Real Audio will start up and play a message. You are now ready to use Netscape to view documents that include Real Audio plug-ins. You must first exit and restart Netscape after installing Real Audio in order to view Real Audio plug-ins in WWW documents.

For an example of a document that contains a Real Audio plug-in, open **http://www.realaudio.com/products/ra2.0/pn.htm**. Near the bottom of this page, you will see the control panel for the Real Audio player (see Fig. 18.20). Click the Play/Pause button (the left-most button) to hear a message from the Vice President of Software Development at Progressive Networks.

FIG. 18.20
The Real Audio control panel plug-in lets you start, stop and pause the audio, skip forward and back, and set the volume of the audio that is played.

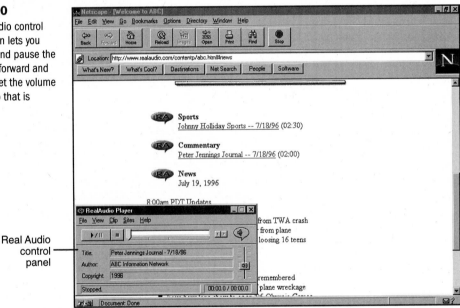

Real Audio control panel

Shockwave

Macromedia has made an agreement with Netscape Communications to develop a plug-in (called Shockwave) of their Director product. Shockwave lets you view multimedia movies within your Web documents. To incorporate the Shockwave plug-in for Netscape, you must first load the Shockwave player onto your PC. To do this:

1. Open the **http://www.macromedia.com/Tools/Shockwave/Plugin/plugin.cgi**.

2. Under the Netscape 2.0 section, click one of Shockwave's easy download instructions for Director version 5.0b1. Choose your platform and application and download the Shockwave n32d50b1.exe file to a temporary directory on your PC, such as C:\Install.

3. From Windows Explorer, double-click the .exe file you loaded in the temporary directory. This unpacks the Shockwave files in a DOS window and runs the setup program.

4. Follow the installation instructions, making sure that the Install Shockwave for Director check box is selected.

5. Choose the directory where you want to keep Shockwave if it is other than the default C:\Netscape\Program.

6. When the installation is complete, close the Shockwave folder that appears open on your desktop.

You are now ready to use Netscape to view documents that include Shockwave plug-ins. You must first exit and restart Netscape after installing Shockwave in order to view Shockwave plug-ins in WWW documents.

For an examples of a documents that contains a Shockwave plug-ins, open **http://www.macromedia.com/Tools/Shockwave/Gallery/shock.html**.

Adobe Acrobat 3.0

Adobe has made an agreement with Netscape Communications to develop a plug-in (formally called Amber) of their Acrobat product. Acrobat 3.0 lets you view Adobe PDF (Portable Document Format) files within your Web documents. To incorporate the plug-in for Netscape you must first load the Acrobat viewer onto your PC. To do this:

Part
IV

Ch
18

1. Open the URL **http://www.adobe.com/acrobat/3beta**.

   If you enter the old Amber URL address at **http://www.adobe.com/Amber/Download.html**, a direct link takes you to the correct /acrobat/3beta Web address and will display this correct URL.

2. Click Download Beta Software button to the Free Acrobat Reader for Windows Now! and download the Acrobat EXE file to a temporary directory on your PC, such as C:\Install.

3. From Windows Explorer, double-click the EXE file you loaded in the temporary directory. This unpacks the Acrobat files in a DOS window.

4. Close the DOS window and double-click the Setup.exe file from Windows Explorer.

5. Follow the installation instructions. Choose the directory where you want to keep Acrobat if it is other than the default C:\Acroweb.

6. When the installation is complete, you can choose to read the readme.txt file or return to Windows 95. Close the Acrobat folder that appears open on your desktop.

You are now ready to use Netscape to view documents that include PDF files. You must first exit and restart Netscape after installing Amber in order to view Amber plug-ins in WWW documents.

To see how the Acrobat plug-in works, open **ftp://ftp.adobe.com/pub/adobe/Acrobat/PDFsamples/2KHENRY6.PDF**. From this page, you can load a number of PDF documents that can be displayed by the Acrobat plug-in (see Fig. 18.21).

FIG. 18.21

The Adobe Acrobat plug-in lets you display PDF documents in your Netscape window, adding a toolbar and status bar that lets you customize how the document is viewed.

Adobe acrobat toolbar

Adobe Acrobat status bar

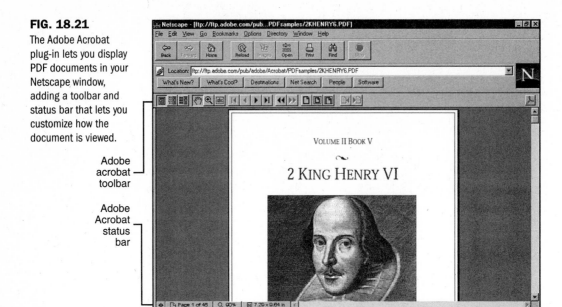

Other Internet-Related Features

The main function of Netscape is to allow you to view documents on the WWW; however, there are a number of other Internet-related services that you can access from Netscape.

Internet E-mail

Netscape contains a complete Internet e-mail interface. You will need to tell Netscape your name, e-mail address, an outgoing mail (SMTP) server (an Internet host that can send e-mail), and an incoming mail (POP) server (an Internet host that collects your mail and holds it until you log in to read it). To set all these options, choose Options, Mail and New Preferences, and fill in the information on the Servers and Identity tabs in the Preferences window (see Figs. 18.22 and 18.23).

 TIP   You can send e-mail quickly by choosing File, New Mail Message from any Netscape document window.

Once Netscape is configured correctly, to read your Internet mail choose Window, Netscape Mail (or click the mail icon to the right of the progress bar at the bottom of the Netscape window). You will be prompted for your Internet account password, and Netscape will log in to your account and transfer any mail that you have to your local disk. From the Netscape Mail window (see Fig. 18.24) you can read your mail, organize your mail into folders, and send mail.

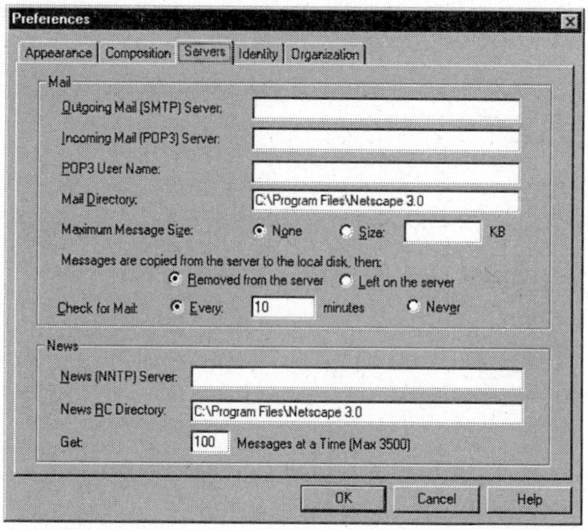

FIG. 18.22
Fill in the incoming and outgoing mail server information, as well as your mail account name and local mail folder on the Servers tab of the Preferences dialog box.

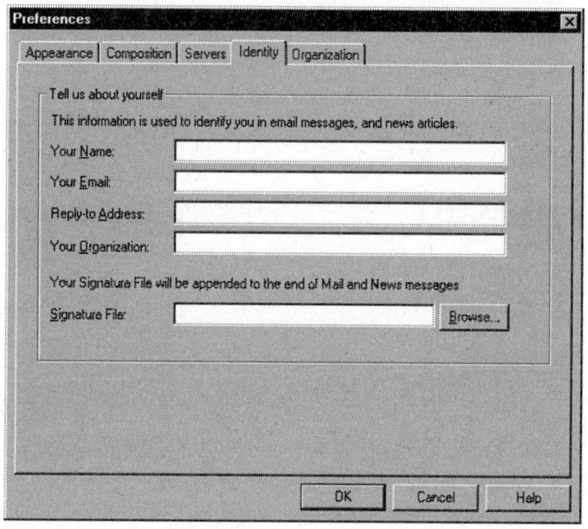

FIG. 18.23
Fill in your name and e-mail address (and any other personal information) on the Identity tab of the Preferences dialog box.

CAUTION
Be sure to choose File, Close when you want to close the Netscape Mail window. If you choose File, Exit, Netscape will exit all of your windows.

Reading UseNet Newsgroups

Netscape also provides an interface that lets you read and post to UseNet newsgroups. In order to do this, you must choose Options, Mail and News Preferences and enter an NNTP server (a machine that lets you read and post to news groups) and the path to your News RC folder in the indicated text boxes on the Servers tab of the Preferences dialog. Once you have entered a valid server, you can open the News window by choosing Window, Netscape News (see Fig. 18.25). From this window you can subscribe to newsgroups, load the messages headers from your subscribed groups, and read articles.

FIG. 18.24
The Netscape Mail window has a toolbar that allows you to quickly read and send mail.

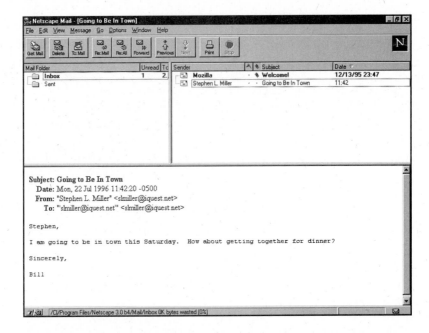

FIG. 18.25
The Netscape News window has a toolbar that lets you quickly read and post articles, reply to articles, and move between articles and newsgroups.

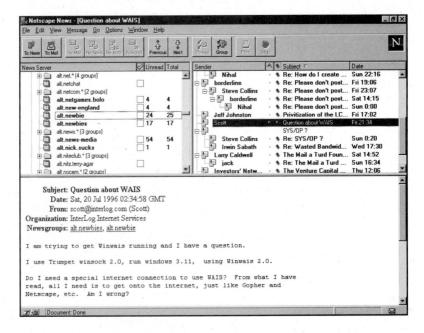

> **CAUTION**
>
> Be sure to choose File, Close when you want to close the Netscape News window. If you choose File, Exit, it will exit all of your Netscape windows.

Click the newsgroup that you want to read. Netscape will load a list of the available articles. Click the article that you want to read and Netscape will load the article. When you read newsgroups, the toolbar in your Netscape News window lets you post new and follow-up articles, send a reply to the author of the article, and move back and forth between articles and newsgroups.

> **CAUTION**
>
> If you try to read a newsgroup that has several thousand unread articles, it could take a long time (over 30 minutes) to load the list of headers if you are connected to news server with a 14.4 or 28.8 modem.

Java Compatibility and JavaScript

In the past year, Sun Microsystems has developed a new programming language based on C++ that allows Web pages to contain more than just pictures, sounds, and movies (which you need browser applications to view). With their Java language, when you download a Web page you can actually load a mini-application (called an *applet*) that can do almost anything the author of the applet wants it to do.

Netscape supports Web pages that contain Java applets. Some of the demo applications that you can find from the Netscape home page show how you can get live updates of information on your Web page, communicate live with other users, do expert graphics generation, and other activities not supported by the basic WWW concepts. These applets are designed to be very secure, with safeguards against viruses and tampering. This technology is supported by many Web browsers. But Netscape is among the leading Web browsers, and the flexibility that Java introduces to Web pages is so powerful that Java has really taken off this year.

To see some examples of what Java can do, load **http://home.netscape.com/comprod/ products/navigator/version_2.0/java_applets/index.html**, page down to the Java Applet Demos section of the document, and load any of the Web pages that are listed there. Following the demos section is the Java Resources section, which contains pointers to the Java home page and to other places where you can find out more about Java.

> **CAUTION**
>
> Java will not work if using a 32-bit Trumpet WinSock. Java must be disabled to use Trumpet WinSock with Navigator 3.0.

Part

IV

Ch

18

Netscape's scripting language, JavaScript, a language similar to Java, can be embedded in Web pages. This scripting language allows you to detect user events (like data input or mouse clicks) from the Web page, and to respond to those inputs immediately, rather than passing the information back to a server and having the server respond. It also lets you manipulate Java objects, giving you greater flexibility in designing your Web page.

The new release of Netscape 3.0 has many Java and JavaScript enhancements. The JIF compiler for Java (for Windows 95 only) is integrated into the Navigator. This compiler makes running Java applets and applications faster from within the Navigator.

JavaScript evaluation enables the creation of more dynamic documents by allowing attributes of one HTML element to depend on information about previously placed elements on the Web page. A JavaScript expression can be used in any HTML tag to specify a value. The size of an image or table can be easily calculated by using JavaScript. For more information, see Chapter 25, "Using JavaScript for Developing Web Applications."

To get more information on JavaScript, open **http://home.netscape.com/comprod/ products/navigator/version_2.0/script/script_info/index.html.**

Using Helper Applications with Web Browsers

by Joe Kraynak and Mary Ann Pike

Everyone has experienced multimedia. On any given day we exercise all our senses to process a variety of information. That information is packaged in different forms: text and pictures in newspapers and magazines, advertisements on highway billboards, reports at work, music and news on the radio, and sound and video on the television set. The WWW offers access to a wealth of information; much of it is stored as multimedia documents.

Most browsers, including Netscape Navigator, Mosaic, and Internet Explorer, require that you download and install *plug-ins* or *helper applications* (often called *viewers* or *players*) to display images or play movies, sounds, presentations, and virtual worlds. These external viewer programs enable you to play files in standard multimedia formats: JPEG image files, WAV audio files, MPEG movie files, VRML files (virtual worlds), Shockwave files (interactive, multimedia files), and a host of other file types. When you have the different viewers installed on your PC, getting them to work with most browsers is a straightforward process.

After you read this chapter you should be able to set up viewers and configure your Web browser to use them. ■

How to choose between a plug-in and a helper application

Understand the differences between plug-ins and helper applications, and determine which is best for you.

What you can expect to find in multimedia documents

The Web offers pictures, recordings, video clips, interactive games and presentations, and much more.

Where to get different viewers

Find most of the helper applications you need by visiting a single Web site.

How to install viewers on your PC

Once you've downloaded the helper application or plug-in you need, you must install it on your hard drive.

How to set up your browser to use the installed viewers

Plug-ins set themselves up, but if you have a helper application, you'll have to configure your Web browser to use it.

Understanding Helper Applications and Plug-Ins

As you know, Web browsers can open and display HTML coded files (Web pages) and text documents (files with the .txt extension). Many Web browsers (including Netscape Navigator, Internet Explorer, and Mosaic) can also display *inline images* (icons and small graphics) and GIF and JPEG images (larger graphics, such as photos, paintings, and illustrations). Some Web browsers can even play audio clips, inline video clips, and Java applets (small programs written specifically for the Web).

However, no Web browser is capable of displaying every file type you will encounter on the Web, in newsgroups, or at FTP file sites. When your Web browser is incapable of displaying a file type that you're trying to play, the browser looks for help. It needs the aid of another application that can handle the file type. These applications are called *helper applications* (helper apps for short) or *plug-ins*. If no helper app or plug-in is available, the browser usually prompts you to specify the application you want to use to play the file, as shown in Figure 19.1.

FIG. 19.1

When your browser can't display a file, it asks you to specify the helper app you want to use to open the file.

You can obtain the helper applications or plug-ins you need by downloading them from the Internet, as you'll learn later in this chapter. Many of the most popular helper applications and plug-ins are included on the NetCD at the back of this book.

If you are using Netscape Navigator or Internet Explorer 3.0, you have a choice to make. Do you want a helper application or a plug-in? A helper application is typically a small, fast-running stand-alone application. It is not part of the browser. When the browser encounters a file type that it cannot itself handle, the browser runs (spawns) the helper app, and the helper app opens the file and plays it. When you install a plug-in, on the other hand, the plug-in becomes a part of the browser, extending the browser's capabilities. Plug-ins are typically smaller than helper apps and they run faster. They are also easier to set up; you simply run the installation program. With helper apps, you must set up file associations that link specific file types to the helper app.

In this chapter, you learn how to get, install, and use both helper apps and plug-ins.

N O T E   In addition to allowing you to use helper applications and plug-ins, Internet Explorer 3.0 allows you to play files using ActiveX controls. ActiveX allows Web developers to place all sorts of files right on their Web pages. As long as you have the required ActiveX control installed, all you have to do is load the Web page, and the ActiveX objects play. To find out more about ActiveX, visit Internet Explorer 3.0's home page at **http://www.microsoft.com/ie**. ▪

N O T E   If you have a full-featured program (such as CorelDRAW!) for viewing or playing multimedia files, you can set it up as a helper app. However, these large programs typically take a long time to start up, making them less desirable for cruising the Internet. ■

Read, Listen, Watch, and Interact: Multimedia Is Here

Web developers have figured out how to transform just about every type of media into a digital form that can be placed on the Web. For years Web pages have included sounds and pictures to stimulate the senses and make Web pages more attractive. More and more Web pages are including short video clips (or links to video clips) that you can play using the right viewer. Recently, Web developers have begun to include games, small programs, presentations, and interactive, three-dimensional worlds that you can explore in virtual space.

The two major Web browsers, Netscape Navigator, and Internet Explorer (both at version 3.0), can play most multimedia files themselves. They can display graphics that are embedded on Web pages, play background audio, and even handle in-line video clips. Both of these browsers also come with their own VRML player, for exploring interactive, three-dimensional worlds. However, no browser is capable of playing all the files you might meet on the Web.

The following sections provide a brief overview of the various file types you'll encounter on the Web, and what you'll need to play them.

Graphics Galore: Images on the Web

If you enjoy thumbing through illustrated books or watching slide shows, you'll love the images on the Web. If you're a history buff, for example, you can take a trip to the University of Georgia's library server to examine a collection of photographs that chronicle the various Works Progress Administration (WPA) projects that were built in Georgia, including streets, airports, and schools.

Two types of images are on the WWW. The first type are images that appear within Web documents. These *inline* images can be viewed in the documents when you open them in your browser. For example, the graphic icon or seal that is included at the top of a home page is an inline image. You can see them, but they're too small to pull up in a graphics program and enhance, crop, or otherwise play with.

Web pages can also include larger graphic images or links to full-fledged graphics that you might want to look at a little more closely, save, print, or enhance in a graphics program. These images are usually stored as GIF (Graphics Interchange Format) and JPEG (Joint Photographic Experts Group) files. GIF and JPEG files are compressed to save space and transmission time. The JPEG format is an industry standard for compressing 24-bit and 8-bit color, and gray-image files. GIF images take up less space than JPEG images, but they represent only 8-bit images and 256 colors, whereas JPEG supports 24-bit images and 16.7 million colors.

Most Web browsers can display GIF and JPG files themselves. Netscape Navigator, Internet Explorer, and Mosaic are all capable of displaying these file types. If all you want to do is view GIF and JPEG (or JPG) files, you don't need a plug-in or helper application to do it; just use your browser. However, you can't use your Web browser to edit an image, change its colors or contrast, brighten it, crop it, or manipulate it in any other way. You have to open the file in a graphics program or a graphics helper application or plug-in.

Another limitation of Web browsers is that they cannot handle a wide range of graphic file formats. GIF and JPEG are usually the only two they can display. If you encounter a graphic created in Paintbrush or CorelDRAW!, you're out of luck. Table 19.1 lists some of the most common graphic file formats you encounter on the Web. Keep in mind that 90 percent of the images you meet are GIF or JPEG files.

Table 19.1   Some Graphic File Formats

File Type	Description
BMP	Bit-mapped file format
CDR	CorelDRAW!
EPS	Encapsulated PostScript
GIF	Graphics Interchange Format (bit-mapped)
JPEG	Joint Photographic Experts Group
PCD	Kodak Photo CD
PCX	Paintbrush file
PDF	Acrobat Portable Document File
PIC	Macintosh Graphic
PS	Postscript
RAS	Sun Microsystems RAS files
TARGA	TrueVision
TIFF	Tagged Image File Format
WMF	WordPerfect Meta File
XBM (X Windows Bitmap)	UNIX bitmap image

On the CD

If you encounter a graphic file type that your browser cannot display, you must install a plug-in or helper app that can handle that file type. Table 19.2 lists some popular and powerful graphics viewers. Public-domain and shareware viewers, such as LViewPro for Windows 95, are available on the Net (and on the CD that accompanies this book). Commercial browsers, such as Internet In A Box, are bundled with viewers. You learn more about these graphics viewers later in this chapter, including how to install them and set them up to work with your browser.

Table 19.2   Shareware and Freeware Image Viewers

Medium Type	Viewer
GIF/JPEG/TIFF/BMP	LViewPro, Paint Shop Pro, VuePrint, Thumbs Plus, WebImage, ACDSee
BMP, TGA	Paint Shop Pro, LView Pro, Thumbs Plus
PCD	Paint Shop Pro, Thumbs Plus, ACDSee
PCX	ACDSee, Paint Shop Pro
PIC	Paint Shop Pro
PS Postscript files	GhostScript
Adobe PDF	Adobe Acrobat Reader

Let's Hear It—How to Enable Sound

To hear the sounds of the Web, you really should have a sound card. Sound cards enable you to play, record, or generate sounds of any kind, including speech, music, and sound effects. With a good sound card and the appropriate drivers (which usually come with the sound card), you can travel through the Web and listen to a jazz session, a volcanic eruption, or a debate on taxes.

Some Web browsers, such as Netscape Navigator 2.0 and later, are capable of playing most audio file types, including WAV, AU, and AIF. Internet Explorer 3.0 can even play real-time audio (RA) files. Some Web pages have embedded audio files. If you have a browser that supports background sounds (and your speakers are turned on), as soon as you connect to the page, the background audio starts playing. On most Web pages, however, you must click on a link to an audio file to start playing it.

You may encounter some less common audio file types on the Web, such as RA, VMF, MID, or VOC, or you may have a Web browser that can't play audio clips. In such a case, you need to install a helper app or plug-in that can handle the audio file type. Table 19.3 lists the common audio file formats you encounter on the Web. Table 19.4 lists some popular (shareware) audio players that you can use to play these file types. You learn more about these audio players later in this chapter, including how to download and install them, and set up your browser to use them.

Table 19.3   Common Audio Formats

File Type	Description
AIFF/AIF	Audio Image File Format
AU	UNIX audio file
MIDI	MIDI file

continues

Part

IV

Ch

19

Table 19.3 Continued

File Type	Description
RA	Real Audio file
SND	Sun/NeXT sound files
VMF	Internet Wave files
VOC	Creative Voice
WAV	Waveform audio

Table 19.4 Shareware and Freeware Audio Players

Medium Type	Player
AIFF/AIF	Netscape Audio, WHAM
AU	WPlny, WHAM, Netscape Audio
MIDI	Midi Gate, Crescendo
RA	Real Audio
SND	WPlny
VMF	Internet Wave
VOC	WHAM, WPlny
WAV	Media Player, WHAM, TrueSpeech WAV, WPlny

Real-Time Audio With most sound files, your browser downloads the file completely before it starts to play it. The latest developments in audio technology enable you to play real-time audio. With real-time audio (typically RA files), the audio player starts playing the recording as soon as it starts to receive the file. This creates the impression that you're listening to a live broadcast. These "broadcasts," however, are not necessarily "live." There is a delay of at least the time it takes to record the sound and store it in a file.

One of the most popular real-time audio players on the Web is RealAudio, which you learn about later in this chapter.

MIDI Files for Synthesized Tunes Unlike most sound files that are actually recordings of music or voice, MIDI (Musical Instrument Digital Interface) files are sort of like sheet music. Your sound card can read the MIDI file and determine how to play all of the instruments. Because your sound card does much of the work, MIDI files are typically small; they cannot store voice recordings. MIDI files are generally used for synthesized instrumentals of classical or popular songs.

Most audio players cannot play MIDI files. You need a special MIDI player, such as Crescendo, described later in this chapter.

Lights, Camera, Action—How to Enable Movies

In the 1930s and 1940s, audiences could watch the latest news events in movie theaters that played newsreels. In the 1950s, 1960s, and 1970s, television crews traveled all over the world to capture current events. In the 1980s, with the invention and wide distribution of video camcorders, individuals who captured interesting and newsworthy events could get their footage broadcast. Now, at the turn of the century, the Internet opens a vast avenue for video (news, entertainment, commercials, and so on) that individuals and companies record and place on the WWW.

By bypassing the traditional outlets for video—broadcast and cable companies—the Web promises to deliver a tremendous amount of specialized video information that we otherwise would not be able to access. In addition, because Web video is "on-demand," we can watch when our own schedule permits. One example of WWW video is a QuickTime movie that shows people hang-gliding from ridges and mountains in California (the video is on a server at Stanford University). Table 19.5 shows some of the video file formats that you may come across.

Table 19.5   Video Formats

Format	Description
AVI	Video for Windows
MOV/QT	Apple's QuickTime movies
MPEG/MPG	(Motion Picture Experts Group)
VDO	VDO Live (real-time video)

You can get digital movies through WWW browsers using MPEG (Motion Picture Experts Group) and QuickTime file formats. Download time, however, may be excessive if you are using a modem. For example, with a 14.4 Kbps modem, it may take you five minutes to download a 10 second clip. These frustrating time factors are likely to become less of a problem as larger bandwidths and faster modems become available. Table 19.6 lists some of the video viewers that are available.

Table 19.6   Some Freeware and Shareware Video Viewers

Medium Type	Player
AVI	Media Player, NET TOOB
MPEG movies	MPEGPLAY, VMPEG Lite, NET TOOB
MOV	QuickTime Video, NET TOOB
VDO	VDO Live

Part
IV

Ch
19

N O T E Don't expect TV/VCR-quality visuals from the movie clips you download. Video clips typically are played in a window that's about two square inches, they're jerky, and the sound quality (if you're lucky enough to get a clip with sound) is usually muffled. Until the Internet develops better compression standards and faster transfer rates, video on the Internet will remain less than dazzling. ▨

Real-Time Video   AVI movie clips are usually huge (three to four megabytes for a 30-second clip). MPG (MPEG) files are slightly smaller. The trouble with these file types is that your movie viewer must completely download the file before it can start playing the clip. If you have a modem connection, you may have to wait 15 to 20 minutes before you can start viewing the clip—hardly the "video on demand" you expected.

To help, companies are developing real-time video players, such as StreamWorks and VDO Live that can start playing a video clip as soon as it is received. In this way, you can immediately cancel the download if the video clip is not what you expected. You learn more about real-time video players later in this chapter.

Windows 95 Media Player   Windows 95 comes with its own multimedia player that can play MIDI and AVI files. The player should be in the main Windows 95 directory under the file name mplayer.exe. However, Media Player isn't the most robust video player around. It doesn't even offer a File/Save command for saving the clip to your disk after you watch it.

Interactive Shockwave Presentations

The players and viewers you've encountered so far in this section enable you to passively view multimedia files on the Web. A company called Macromedia is helping to make Web sites more interactive by enabling developers to create and post interactive multimedia presentations, tutorials, and games on the Web.

Macromedia offers several products for creating interactive CDs. You've probably used many of the CDs that Macromedia's tools have been used to create. Recently, developers have used these tools to create Web versions of their presentations. Macromedia has developed a Shockwave player that you can use with Netscape Navigator or Internet Explorer 3.0 to play these interactive Shockwave presentations and games.

N O T E The latest release of Internet Explorer, version 3.0, is designed to work with plug-ins designed for Netscape Navigator. ▨

Exploring Virtual Worlds

Another way that developers are working to make the Web more interactive is by creating interactive, three-dimensional worlds with VRML. VRML (pronounced "vermal") stands for Virtual Reality Modeling Language, a programming tool used to create these virtual worlds.

To explore a virtual world, you need a VRML browser. There are several VRML browsers out there, including Live3D (for Netscape Navigator), Microsoft's VRML viewer (an add-in for Internet Explorer), WIRL (a helper app), and many more. Later on in this chapter, you find a list of the most popular VRML browsers. Once you've installed the browser, just click on a link to play the virtual world. Figure 19.2 shows a sample world displayed in Live3D.

FIG. 19.2
VRML promises to transform the Web from two-dimensional pages into three-dimensional worlds.

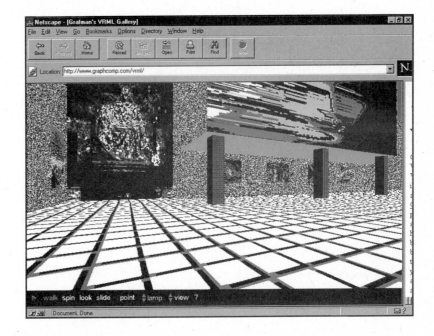

NOTE Like Java files, VRML files contain code that the VRML browser interprets and plays. Unlike a Java applet, each of which comes with its own set of controls, VRML worlds rely on the browser for controls. ■

Microsoft Document Viewers

In its attempt to be more active on the Internet, Microsoft has developed a set of viewers that enable people who do not have Word, Excel, or PowerPoint to view Word documents, Excel spreadsheets, and PowerPoint presentations. You can pick up any of these viewers for free at Microsoft's Web site: **http://www.microsoft.com**.

Popular Multimedia Viewers

Every day, some company somewhere develops a new helper application or plug-in and places it on the Web for interested users to download. Finding your way through this slough of browser add-ons can be confusing. To help you select the right helper app or plug-in for you, this section provides a list of the most popular and useful helper apps on the Web, including a brief description of each.

Later in this chapter, you learn where to look on the Web to find lists of helper applications and plug-ins. If you just can't wait, open your favorite Web search tool (Yahoo, WebCrawler, Alta Vista), and search for the helper app or plug-in by name.

Graphic Image Viewers

Although most Web browsers can display JPG and GIF pictures, you might need a graphic image viewer to display less common graphic files or to modify and enhance the images you find. The following sections introduce some common viewers.

Paint Shop Pro   Paint Shop Pro can display nearly all graphics file formats you encounter on the Web, including common JPG and GIF files, and rare CorelDRAW!, TARGA, and PIC files. It can even display Kodak PhotoCD images. Paint Shop Pro is more of a full-featured graphics program than a simple image viewer, and provides you with all of the tools you need to crop, enhance, and manipulate the dimensions of the images you download. You can use Paint Shop Pro for 30 days for free. After that, you are legally (and morally) obligated to register the prod-uct for $69. If you have to pick only one image viewer, Paint Shop Pro is it.

LViewPro   LView Pro is the 32-bit version of one of the most popular image viewers on the Web. LView Pro can handle a wide range of graphic file formats, including JPG, GIF, and TIFF, and it includes advanced graphics tools that enable you to adjust the color, contrast, brightness, and dimensions of displayed images. LView Pro is shareware that requires a $30 registration fee, if you decide to continue using it. When you register, you get a beefed-up version of the program that can handle more file types.

Thumbs Plus   Thumbs Plus excels in two respects. First, it is ideal for managing folders packed with images and video clips. Thumbs Plus acts as a high-powered File Manager or Windows Explorer. When you start Thumbs Plus, a list of folders appears on the left, repre-senting the directories on your hard drive. When you select a folder that contains graphics files, Thumbs Plus displays the contents of that directory, showing a thumbnail version of each image.

Thumbs Plus also excels in the number of file types it can display, including not only GIF and JPG images, but also AVI and MOV video clips, WAV sound files, and UUEncoded files (which are common in newsgroups).

VuePrint   Like Thumbs Plus, VuePrint supports not only image file types, but also audio and video clips. It also provides thumbnail views of supported file types, making it easier for you to manage your gallery of downloads. If you're serious about your multimedia, VuePrint is a must have. After downloading and installing VuePrint, you have 15 days to use it for free. After that, you should register the program for a mere $40, well worth the price for such a full-featured viewer.

ACDSee   Although not the most powerful of the lot, ACDSee is the fastest and cleanest image viewer around. It can handle the standard JPEG and GIF images, as well as less common Kodak Photo CD, TGA, TIFF, and PCX files.

Audio Players

Netscape Navigator and Internet Explorer can play most types of audio files, including WAV, AU, and AIF files. However, you're browser might need help playing less popular formats. Read the following sections to determine which audio player you need.

RealAudio   RealAudio is the most popular of the new audio players and can handle real-time audio (RA) files. With RealAudio, you can connect to sites, such as ABC and NPR, and listen to "live" broadcasts (see Fig. 19.3). After downloading the Real Audio player, fill out the form for requesting a password at **http://www1.realaudio.com/get_password.html**. This gives you access to sites at **http://www.realaudio.com**, where you can try out your new player. Right after you complete the installation, the Real Audio player starts, and plays a message thanking you for installing the software. Make sure your speakers are turned on.

FIG. 19.3
With RealAudio, you can listen to "live" broadcasts.

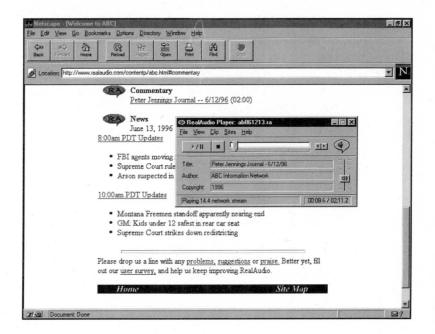

Part
IV

Ch
19

WHAM   WHAM (short for Waveform Hold And Modify) is a good basic audio player, but many of the new Web browsers can play most of the file types that WHAM can handle, including WAV, AU, and AIF files. However, if you have an older Web browser that you just can't part with, WHAM is a useful addition.

WPlny   WPlny (short for Windows Play Any file) is an alternative to WHAM. As with WHAM, WPlny can play most common audio clips, including WAV, AU, and SND files. If your Web browser can already play these file types, you don't need WPlny. However, the program is free.

Crescendo   Crescendo is one of the best helper apps for playing MIDI (synthesized music files). After you install Crescendo, and set up your Web browser to use it (as explained later), go to the MIDI Jukebox at **http://www.pensacola.com/~sunstar/jukebox.html**, where you'll find scads of synthesized versions of your favorite oldies.

Midi Gate   One of the few helper apps that can play MIDI files, Midi Gate is useful for playing synthesized music clips. However, that's about all that Midi Gate is useful for. It can't handle other audio file types, and it doesn't offer many tools for editing MIDI files.

Video Players

Internet Explorer 3.0 is one of the first Web browsers to support video. Most browsers require a special video player. Some of the more popular players are listed in the following sections.

NET TOOB NET TOOB can handle a wide variety of video file types, including MPEG, AVI, and MOV. When you download NET TOOB, be sure to download the additional drivers for playing AVI and MOV files. NET TOOB also comes with a cool screen saver utility that plays a King Kong video clip. Although NET TOOB does not currently support real-time video, plans are in the works.

VDO Live VDO Live is a small, quick video player that plays real-time video. Currently VDO Live can play VDO files, which are not all that common on the Web. However, as VDO Live catches on, you'll find more VDO files. After downloading and installing VDO Live, check out some VDO files at **http://www.vdo.net/products/vdolive/gallery/**.

VMPEG Lite If you want to play only MPEG clips, VMPEG Lite is the best of the lot. It's small, it's fast, and it can handle any MPEG/MPG file you'll bump into, whether it's a sound clip or movie clip. After installing it, check out the Internet Movie Archive at **http://www.eeb.ele.tue.nl/mpeg/**.

MPEGPlay MPEGPlay is good for playing MPEG video clips, but it can't handle other video file types. In addition, the shareware version is limited to playing video clips that are one megabyte or smaller, which rules out a large portion of the MPEG video clips you find on the Web. For a $25 registration fee, you can get the full version, which enables you to play larger files.

QuickTime for Windows One of the highest quality video file types on the Web are MOV files, and you need Apple's QuickTime to play them. You can find a bunch of MOV video clips at **http://www.hollywood.com**. If you have a modem connection (even a fast one), you might become a little frustrated playing MOV files. They're huge!

Interactive Multimedia and VRML Browsers

Shockwave and VRML are breathing new life into the Web, giving pages a third dimension, and making the Web more interactive with games, presentations, and self-directed tutorials. To play these worlds, your browser might need the help of one of the helper apps or plug-ins described in the following sections.

Shockwave If you want to play Macromedia Director, Freehand, or Authorware files, the only game in town is Shockwave. Most of the Macromedia files you encounter are Director "movies," which are interactive games, presentations, and tutorials. They're cool, and they're compressed, so they play fairly quickly. When you go to Macromedia (**http://www.macromedia.com**), you're given the choice to download individual players (for example, Shockwave for Director) or all the players. Each player has its own installation procedure (see Fig. 19.4.).

FIG. 19.4

You can play a Shocked version of Concentration at Disney's Toy Story site.

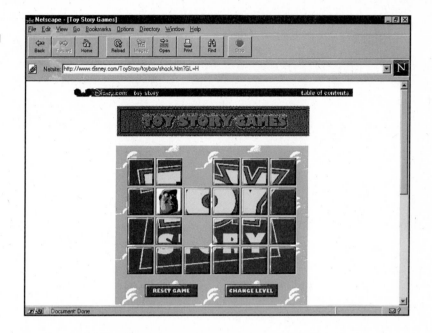

Live3D   Live3D is a Netscape Navigator plug-in for playing VRML files. It's a good, basic VRML viewer that lets you explore virtual worlds by flying, walking, or changing the perspective. As with all VRML viewers, you'll find a set of controls at the bottom of the screen for moving through or spinning the world in 3-D. You can also right-click inside a world to view a pop-up menu with additional options.

During the Netscape Navigator 2.0 era, Live3D was offered as a plug-in. With version 3.0, Netscape bundled Live3D with the full version of Netscape Navigator, making Live3D an integral part of the browser. If you downloaded and installed the full version of Navigator 3.0, you already have Live3D.

Microsoft's VRML Viewer   Microsoft's VRML viewer is currently an add-in (Microsoft's name for a plug-in) that works with Internet Explorer 2.0. This VRML Viewer is very similar to Live3D, offering simple, intuitive controls for exploring virtual worlds.

With the release of Internet Explorer 3.0, Microsoft plans on building the VRML browser right into its Web browser through Direct3D. By the time you read this, Direct3D should be an integral part of Internet Explorer 3.0.

WIRL   WIRL is one of the best VRML viewers on the Web, and it comes with a good collection of demos, including a three-dimensional piano that you can play by clicking on its keys (see Fig. 19.5). After downloading and installing WIRL, check its directory for a list of demos; they play off your hard drive faster than they play off the Web.

Part

IV

Ch

19

FIG. 19.5
WIRL's piano demo lets
you play a 3-D piano.

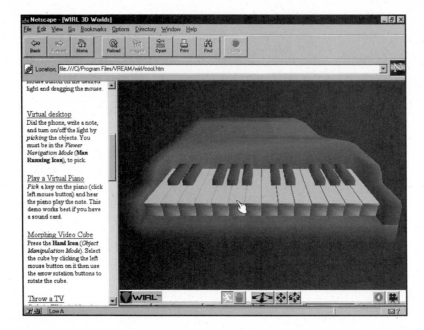

Pioneer   If you're interested in creating your own virtual worlds, consider Pioneer. Not only is it a masterpiece in the market of VRML browsers, but it also includes tools for creating your own worlds. The shareware version is trimmed down, and if you get serious about creating worlds, it'll cost you about $500 for the full version. Yet, Pioneer is worth checking out.

Finding and Installing Multimedia Viewers

Before you can use a helper app or plug-in to play multimedia files and explore three-dimensional, virtual worlds, you must download and install the helper app or plug-in you need. With helper apps, you must also configure your Web browser to use the helper app.

In the following sections, you learn where to go to download the most popular helper apps and plug-ins, how to install them on your hard drive, and how to configure your Web browser to use them.

N O T E   It's easier to configure your Web browser to use a plug-in rather than a helper app. With a plug-in, you run the installation program, and it sets up the Web browser to use that plug-in by default. With helper apps, you must fiddle with file associations. ■

Retrieving Helper Apps and Plug-Ins

A number of the helper apps discussed in this chapter can be found on NetCD. If the helper app you want is not on the CD (or, if you want to check to see if there is a more recent version), you may be able to pick it up from one of the many software archives on the Internet. Mosaic (**http://www.ncsa.uiuc.edu/SDG/Software/WinMosaic/viewers.htm**), Netscape (**http://home.netscape.com/assist/helper_apps/**), and Microsoft (**http://www.microsoft.com/ie**) have collections of helper applications and plug-ins at their sites. (Keep in mind that Microsoft is planning on redesigning Internet Explorer, so that it can use Netscape Navigator plug-ins.)

Another great place to look for helper apps and plug-ins is Stroud's Consummate Winsock Applications list at **http://www.stroud.com**. After you connect to Stroud's, click on the graphic at the top of the page to view the Main Menu. As shown in Figure 19.6, you'll find links to several categories of helper apps and plug-ins. Another great place to try is Tucows at **http://www.tucows.com**.

FIG. 19.6

Stroud's Consummate Winsock Applications list contains links for all of the helper apps and plug-ins you need.

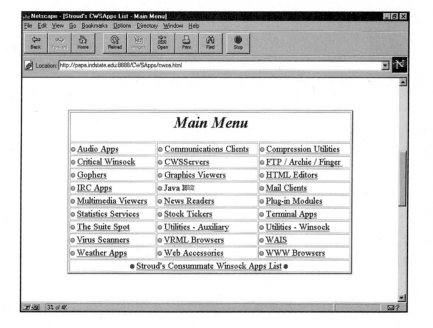

Part IV

Ch 19

N O T E Stroud's Web page is pretty busy. If you can't connect, go to Yahoo at **http://www.yahoo.com** and search for **stroud**. This displays a list of mirror sites. Click on a site that's close to where you live. Also, check the date at the site to make sure it has been updated recently. Some mirror sites update their list more frequently than others. ■

In the past, you could usually download a viewer simply by clicking on its link (Stroud's list has several links to FTP sites from which you can download the helper app or plug-in). Recently, however, many companies request that you enter your name and e-mail address before down-loading the file. Alternately, you may have to use a form to specify which version of the viewer you want (plug-in or viewer) and the platform you use (Windows 95, Windows 3.1, Mac/OS). The point is, that if the download link does not work, go to the company's Web page, and follow the trail of links to find the form you have to fill out.

In most Web browsers, when you click on a link to download a viewer file, the browser displays a dialog box saying that it cannot open the file, and asks if you want to save it to a disk. When you say yes, you can fill in the information about where you want to put the file in the Save As dialog box that appears, and then choose OK. The viewer is then copied to your disk, and you are ready to install it.

Installing Multimedia Viewers

After you've found a viewer that you want to use and have downloaded the viewer file to your PC, you will probably need to install the viewer. This may be as simple as unzipping the file you've retrieved, or it may involve going through a Windows setup procedure. In general, to install a multimedia viewer, do one of the following:

- To install a viewer from the CD at the back of this book, follow the installation instructions in Appendix A, "What's on the CD." (Remember that the software included with the CD is shareware and must be registered and paid for if you use it.)

- If the viewer comes as a .zip file, install WinZip (you can find a link for it at Stroud's or Tucows or on the NetCD). WinZip can extract the file. Once the files are extracted, look for a README file, open it in your text editor, and follow the installation instructions.

- If the viewer comes as a self-extracting archive (.exe) file, place the file in its own directory, and run it from Windows Explorer or File Manager. Most .exe files extract themselves and then automatically run the installation utility. However, some files require that you run a Setup or Install file to do the installation. Run the Setup program, and follow the on-screen instructions.

- If you just installed a plug-in while your Web browser was running, you must restart your Web browser to enable it to identify and activate the new plug-in.

If you install a plug-in, your job is done. The plug-in becomes a part of your Web browser, and your browser uses it when it encounters file types that the plug-in is designated to play. If you installed a helper application, you must set up your Web browser to use it, as explained next.

N O T E   If you install Netscape Navigator plug-ins, you can get information about the plug-ins by opening the Help menu and selecting *About Plug-ins.* Navigator displays a page showing the names and locations of all of the plug-ins you've installed. ▮

Configuring Your Browser to Use Helper Applications

Installing a helper application doesn't necessarily enable your Web browser to use it. In most cases, you must set up a file association that links a particular file type (say a MOV or AVI file) with a specific helper app (for instance, QuickTime for Windows). Once you've specified a file association for your Web browser, it "knows" which helper app to use to play a file of a particular type.

The following sections explain how to set up file associations in the three most popular Web browsers: Internet Explorer, Netscape Navigator, and Mosaic.

A Word About MIME Types

Multimedia files are transferred across the Internet using a technology called MIME (Multipurpose Internet Mail Extensions). MIME was developed to extend the Internet e-mail standard to allow any type of data (not just text) to be sent via e-mail. The WWW browsers use this same standard for identifying the type of multimedia files. If the browser cannot determine which helper app to use by looking at the MIME type, it uses the specified file extension.

When you're creating file associations, you'll be asked to specify a mime and submime type; for example, the mime type might be video, and the submime type might be avi (video/avi).

Most Web browsers have a list of standard MIME types/subtypes in their helper application configuration section. Usually, you can add your own MIME types to these lists. In many cases, you can check the helper app's README file to determine this information. If you're not sure, pick the closest mime/submime type, or create a new one, and then be sure to specify the extension of the multimedia file type you want to play.

Setting File Associations in Internet Explorer

The easiest way to set file associations in Internet Explorer is to click on a link to play a file. Internet Explorer displays a dialog box asking if you want to open the file; click on the Open button. If you luck out and a file association has already been created, Internet Explorer downloads the file, and starts the helper app, which plays the file. If no association has been created, Internet Explorer displays the Open With dialog box, which shows a list of applications on your hard drive.

You can type a description of the file type in the text box at the top to help you remember it later (for when you edit your file associations). Click on the application you want to use for this file. If the helper app you want to use is not in the list, click on the Other button, and use the Open With dialog box to select the helper app.

If you want Internet Explorer 3.0 to always use the selected application to open files of this type, click on Always Use This Program to open this file. Click OK. Now, whenever you click on a link for this file type, Internet Explorer 3.0 automatically runs the associated helper app and uses it to play the file.

You can also set file associations manually. If you worked with file associations in File Manager or in Windows Explorer, you already know how to set file associations in Internet Explorer. Take the following steps:

Part
IV

Ch
19

1. Open the View menu, select Options, click the Programs tab, and click on the File Types button. The File Types tab appears, as shown in Figure 19.7, displaying a list of currently associated files.

FIG. 19.7

You can set file associations manually.

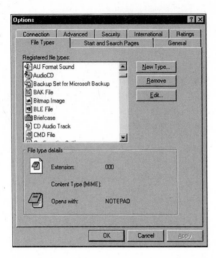

2. Click on the New Type button. The Add New File Type dialog box appears (see Fig. 19.8).

FIG. 19.8

The Add New File Type dialog box.

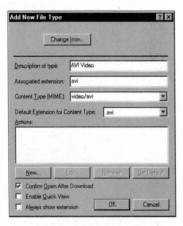

3. Click inside the Description of Type text box, and type a description (for example, **AVI video**).

4. Click inside the Associated Extension text box, and type the extension for this file type (for example, **avi**). Windows uses this extension to assign an icon to the file type.

5. If you know the file's MIME type, open the Content Type (MIME) drop-down list, and choose the MIME type for this file. (If it isn't listed, you can type a new MIME type in the text box; for example, type **video/avi**.)

6. If the Default Extension for Content Type drop-down list is available, open it and select the extension you want to use as the default for the specified MIME type. (Some MIME types have multiple file name extensions associated to them.)

7. Under Actions, click on the New button. The New Action dialog box appears.

8. In the Action text box, type **open**.

9. Click on the Browse button, and use the Open With dialog box to select the helper app you want to use to open the new file type. Click on the Open button. The New Action dialog box displays the **open** command in the Actions list.

10. Click OK. This returns you to the New File Type dialog box.

11. Click the Close button. The new file association is created.

You can set up only one application to handle any given file type. If you try to associate two applications to the same file type, an error message appears, indicating that an application is already using that file type. You have two options. You can delete the file association that's causing the conflict, or you can edit it to assign the desired application to the file type.

Configuring Viewers in Netscape Navigator

As with Internet Explorer, the easiest way to set up helper apps in Navigator is to click on a link for the file type that you want to play. If no helper app or plug-in is assigned to play the selected type of file, Navigator displays a dialog box, prompting you to select the application in which you want to open the file. Once you select the application, Navigator creates the file association for you.

> **CAUTION**
>
> Be careful if you configure a viewer from the Unknown File Type dialog box. Netscape may not choose an appropriate MIME type for the file type you've selected, and you may end up launching the application you've picked for other file types that it can't handle.

The other option is to set up file associations in advance (before you try playing files of a particular type). To set up file associations in Navigator, take the following steps:

1. Choose Options/General Preferences and select the Helpers tab (see Fig. 19.9).

2. Scroll through the list of file types and associated files extensions until you find the file type that your viewer can handle, and select that file type.

3. If you need to add a new file extension to the list of extensions associated with that file type, enter them in the File Extensions field, separated by commas. Do not include the dot at the beginning of the file extension.

4. In the Action area, choose the radio button that describes what you want Netscape to do when it loads files associated with this MIME type.

Part
IV

Ch
19

FIG. 19.9

The Helpers tab enables you to associate MIME types with helper applications, and to add new MIME types.

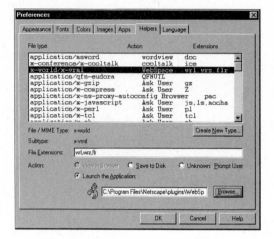

- Choose Save to Disk if you want to save the files directly to disk.

- Choose View in Browser if you want Navigator to try to load and display the file itself. Navigator can only handle files that contain information formatted as text, HTML, JPEG, GIF, or XBM information.

- Choose Launch the Application if you want to launch a viewer with the file loaded into it; enter the path to the application in the text box below the radio button. You can click Browse to bring up the Select An Appropriate Viewer dialog box in which you can look through your directories to find the viewer. Select the viewer in the dialog box and its path will be automatically entered in the text box.

- You can also click the Unknown: Prompt User radio button if you want Navigator to bring up a dialog box that asks what you want to do with the file when it finds a file of that MIME type.

5. When all the information is entered correctly, click OK to close the Preferences dialog box and save the viewer information.

If the list of MIME types does not include the type of file you want to assign to a helper application, you can create a new MIME type. Click on the Create New Type button, and use the Configure New Mime type dialog box to type in a Mime and Mime SubType. Then, perform the steps above to assign a helper application to the new type. When creating a new MIME type, keep these tips in mind:

- If you don't know the MIME type, enter **application** in the Mime Type text box.

- In the Mime SubType text box, type a word that describes the subtype. For example, if you want to start Word when you load a .DOC file, you could make the subtype x-word (an x is usually put in front of a user-defined subtype).

- Once you create a MIME type, there's no option for deleting it, so make sure you enter the information correctly.

You can change the file associations at any time. For example, if you want to download a bunch of movie files to your disk to play later, you can click on the Save to Disk option for that file type. Navigator then saves selected media files to your disk rather than playing them in the helper app.

Setting Up Helper Apps in Mosaic

Once you have installed viewers on your PC, you need to configure Mosaic to use these viewers. Older versions of Mosaic required you to edit the MOSIAC.INI. However, there is now a sheet in the Preferences dialog box you can specify which viewers you have and which file types they can handle. To configure Mosaic:

1. Choose Options/Preferences. In the Preferences dialog box, select the Viewers tab to customize Mosaic to use viewers (see Fig. 19.10).

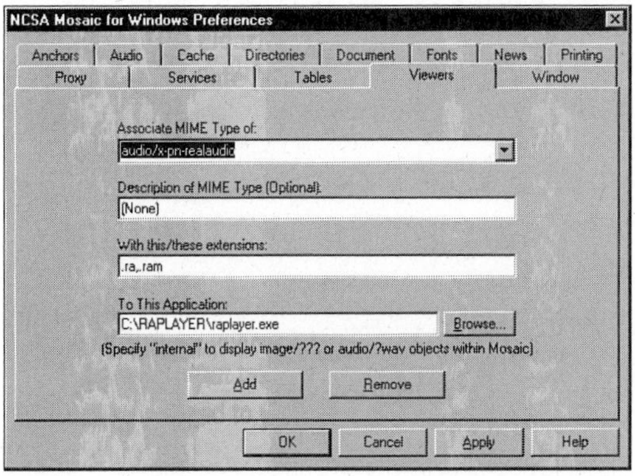

FIG. 19.10

With the Viewers tab in the Mosaic Preferences dialog box you can associate helper applications with any MIME type.

2. Click the arrow to the right of the Associate MIME Type Of: text box. Scroll through the list until you find the MIME type for the viewer you are installing.

3. Enter a description of the MIME type in the indicated text box (this is optional).

4. Enter the file extension(s) that are associated with this MIME type in the With this/ these extensions text box. If you have multiple file extensions, separate them with a comma. Be sure to include the dot at the beginning of the file extension.

5. In the To This Application text box, enter the path to the viewer. You can click Browse to bring up a Browse dialog box to let you look through your directories to find the viewer. If you click the viewer in the Browse dialog box, its path is automatically entered in the text box.

6. Once all the information on this sheet is entered correctly, click OK to close the Preferences dialog and save the viewer information.

If the MIME type you're looking for is not listed, you can create a new MIME type. On the Viewers tab, click Add, and use the Add Viewer dialog box to define a new MIME type. You can then assign a helper app to the new MIME type, as explained in the previous steps. You can edit these file associations at any time.

Testing Helper Apps and Plug-Ins

Once you've installed your helper apps or plug-ins, you should test them out to make sure they are installed correctly. To test a helper app or plug-in, you can connect to a Web page that contains the file types you want to try out, and then click on a link. Or, you can go to a special helper app test page on the Web that contains links to small files of various types (see Fig. 19.11). You can find these test sites using the following URLs:

http://www-dsed.llnl.gov/documents/WWWtest.html

http://ned_lerc.lerc.nasa.gov/test/viewtest.htm

http://www.uky.edu/Transgenic/TestPage.html

http://www.astro.ku.dk/~milvang/multi_color.html

http://www.mit.edu:8001/afs/athena.mit.edu/astaff/project/wwwdev/www/helper.html

http://www.swin.edu.au/csit/viewers.html

FIG. 19.11

The Web has several viewer test pages.

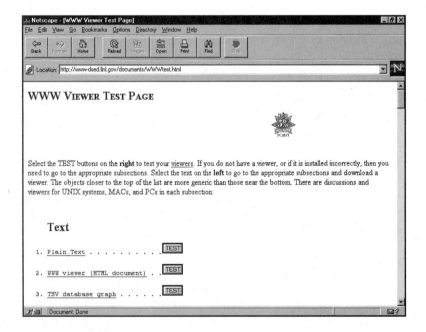

If you get an error message saying that your browser cannot find the helper app for this file type, there's something wrong with the file associations in your Web browser. Go back and edit the associations to point the file extension to the correct helper app. Most error helper app errors can be avoided or corrected by editing a file association.

If you installed the helper application correctly and the file association is correct, there could be a problem with your Internet service provider's server. If you're trying to play a rare file type, the service provider's server may not be set up to handle it. If you can't correct the problem on your end, contact your service provider.

TROUBLESHOOTING

I downloaded a picture and it opened correctly in LView (or any other multimedia viewer). But I went back to view the picture later, and the file wasn't there. What happened? The problem isn't with LView or any of the viewers. When your browser downloads multimedia files for viewing, it creates a temporary file, and that is what you view. If you want to save multimedia files that you download for later use, save them before you exit the viewer application—or save them to your local disk and then view them. If you decide that you'd like to keep a file after you exit the viewer, you may still be able to find the file in your browser's temporary directory.

Using Viewers

Once you have installed, configured, and tested your viewers, you can take them out on the open road. If you're viewing a document that contains links to multimedia files, or if you're browsing an FTP or Gopher site, all you need to do is click the link to the multimedia file. Your browser loads the document, automatically starting the viewer that you defined for displaying that type of multimedia file.

Note that because the media file is loaded in an external application, you can continue to use your browser window while the helper application loads and displays the image, although this might slow down the download process. ●

Part

IV

Ch

19

Planning Your Own World Wide Web Home Page

by Bill Brandon and Joe Schepis

This chapter introduces you to concepts you will need to consider as you plan and develop your WWW home page. Some will be basic layout considerations as used in the print media. Other decisions, such as where you house your WWW home page, will be more complicated.

While following chapters discuss how to create and enhance your pages, this chapter concentrates on how to plan your pages. Factors such as picking your audience, laying out your pages, finding a place to host your pages, and keeping your visitors coming back for more are considered. The pricing structures used by WWW providers when charging you for your WWW pages are also examined. ■

Designing a good home page

A good home page requires more than just HTML code. It takes planning and a clear vision of the results you want.

Deciding where to store your home page

You have many options for housing your home page; in particular, cost is a major factor. Learn about the common charges for using someone else's system to store your pages.

Choosing between HTTP and FTP for online file storage

There are two ways to store online files, which offer you flexibility, economical pricing opportunities, and better access.

Generating interest in your home page

If you build it, will they come? Not if they can't find it! Use the many services of the Web and the Internet to let people know where you are and why they should be interested.

Choosing HTML editors and filters

Like any other construction project, building a Web site is easier with the right tools.

Getting Started: Basic Decisions

Now that you've gotten an idea from the previous chapters of all the different things you can do on the World Wide Web, you are probably excited about putting up your own WWW home page.

Before you start planning your own home page, it might prove useful to look at who already has home pages. Figures 20.1 through 20.6 show some of the interesting people and organizations who have home pages.

FIG. 20.1

This figure shows the NASA Goddard Space Flight Center home page (**http://www.gsfc.nasa.gov/gsfc_homepage.html**).

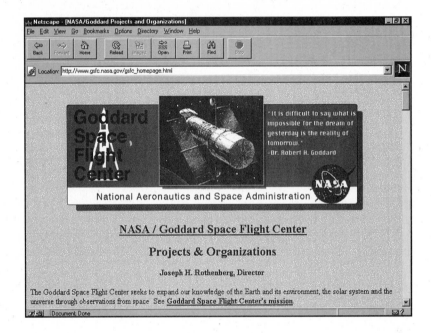

FIG. 20.2

This is Senator Kay Bailey Hutchison's home page (**http://www.senate.gov/~hutchison**).

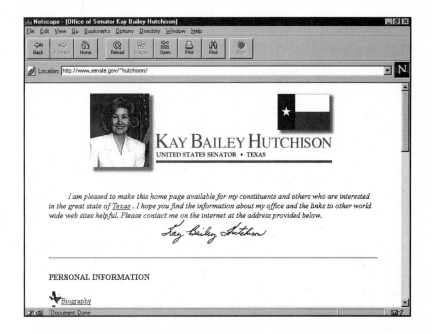

FIG. 20.3

The African Global Network offers a Web page for the African and African-American communities (**http://www.GlobalDrum.com/**).

FIG. 20.4

The Pawws Financial Services home page allows you to view delayed stock quotes (**http://pawws.com/**).

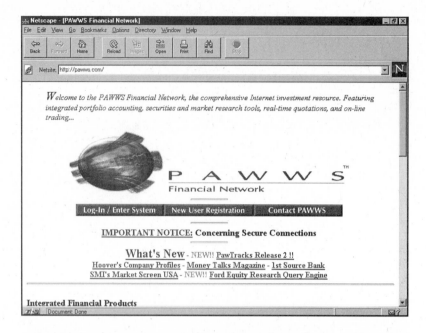

FIG. 20.5

This figure shows the USA Today home page which is updated daily (**http:// www.usatoday.com/**).

FIG. 20.6
Try the Cowboy Poets on the Internet for a little of the culture of the West, including the voices of the poets (**http://www.westfolk.org/**).

There are many reasons to have a home page, but they really narrow down to the following key points:

- You can reach an amazing number of people.
- It is relatively inexpensive compared to traditional advertising and information distribution methods.

Anyone who wants a presence on the World Wide Web can have one by simply creating his or her home page and posting it at a WWW site. If you can use a word processor, you can design an HTML document. Putting a home page on the WWW can be fun and rewarding.

If you want your page to rise above the rest and to get noticed, the simple creation process should be preceded by some planning. There are two major questions you need to answer. First, who is your audience? The answer to this question helps you make many important decisions about the appearance and layout of your page, and the kinds of content you place on it. Knowing your audience also helps you decide whether you should build your page to be viewed with the latest and greatest Web browsers, or if you should be more generic in your approach. The second major question is about your objective for the page. Does your page support your business, or is it a reflection of your avocation? Knowing this helps you decide which capabilities to give your home page and determine the best methods for generating and keeping interest in it.

The next three chapters will get you started on your way to establishing your presence on the World Wide Web.

Planning for Your Audience

With the release of many new network software products, such as Windows 95 and the America Online and CompuServe browsers, we know that many more people will have access to the WWW than ever before. However, getting these millions of people to visit your home page is unlikely. This is mainly because of two factors. First, there are so many places to go and things to do on the Web, that people pick and choose where they spend their electronic time with some care. Secondly, unlike traditional advertising, which comes to the user, the Internet user must find your advertisement.

Your home page then should be targeted for a certain audience and should be designed to encourage them to visit your page. Who do you envision visiting your home page? Business people? Casual users looking for something new and exciting? Special interest groups like a local Girl Scout troop or the Lion's Club? The wording of your home page, the graphics you decide to use, and where you decide to post announcements for your home page should all hinge on your anticipated audience. For instance, if a law firm were advertising its services, its choice of words and graphics would be conservative and would lend an air of professionalism (see Fig. 20.7).

FIG. 20.7

The Nolo Press Self-Help Law Center.

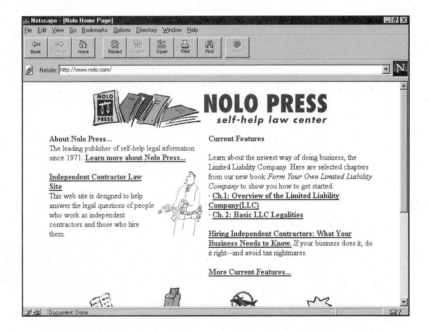

However, a rock band could use wording and graphics that were more experimental, reflecting its style and statement (see Fig. 20.8).

FIG. 20.8

The Def Leppard home page reflects the style of its latest tour while allowing the user to listen to audio selections and order merchandise.

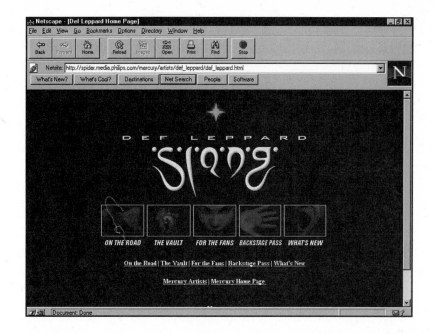

The law firm may wish to describe its company profile, its staff of dedicated employees, its hard-won cases, and happy clients. The rock band may give users information about upcoming concerts, and allow them to hear a cut from one of the group's CDs and order it right from their computer.

Remember, your home page, like your business card or resume, says a lot about you. It is a reflection of the person or organization who created the page. A messy and hard to read page will not be as popular because it is not simple and engaging. Likewise, pages with huge quantities of text and many links often become tedious to users. Care must be made in creating a page that expresses all you want to say, while remaining desirable for users to access.

In many cases, repeat visitations are desirable. This is the case for anyone using the Web to market and/or sell a product or service. These types of pages especially must allow for ease of access and use.

The first W in WWW stands for World. This is important to keep in mind as you design and plan your pages. Whether or not you are interested in having a presence to the world when you put your page on the WWW, you *will* have a presence to the world. If your page has general access to one person on the Internet, it will have access to *all* persons on the Internet. This means you will get visits from people in other countries and other cultures. When designing your pages you may wish to keep this in mind. Slang or street phrases, which in one culture may be apparent, can be confusing for those to whom English is a second language. Likewise, content may be an issue as cultural, social, and political codes differ from country to country.

Even though the world has access to your pages, you need to be conscious of local laws and government guidelines. Just because a site in one country can offer encryption software for

Part

IV

Ch

20

downloading does not mean that you can. Creating such a site in the United States is against the law.

This caution extends even to your page's content. For example, it may be completely legal for someone to post pornographic material to a site in one country, but completely illegal for you to do so in your country or city. The rule of thumb is to always go by the laws of the place you live in.

The bottom line with the Web is that it has been mostly unregulated and open territory. It is similar to the old West: anything and everything goes, and the laws are just beginning to be written. Indeed, this is one of its major attractions and one of the primary reasons that the Web is so popular—it offers something for everyone. How long this "wide-open" state will continue remains to be seen. Governments, from the United States to Germany to China, are making a considerable effort to control access and content, with varying degrees of success.

As the Web and Internet grow and mature you can expect to see more changes in what is allowed and what is illegal. You should try to keep abreast of WWW developments. One method to do this is to keep current with the many Internet and Web magazines that are beginning to appear. Magazines such as *Boardwatch, Netguide, Wired, Mondo 2000,* and *Internet World* offer the latest breaking information on the politics of the Web and Internet.

Housing Your Home Page

One of the first questions you need to answer is, "Where am I going to store my home page?"

▶ **See** "Using FTP and Popular FTP Programs," **p. 807**

If your Internet provider allows users from the outside to FTP in, or is running a WWW server, you may be able to store your pages locally on your provider's computer.

If your provider does not allow FTP access from the outside and is not running a WWW server, you may need to find somewhere else to place your pages. For more information on FTP, see Chapter 31, "Using FTP and Popular FTP Programs."

▶ **See** "America Online," **p. 239**

▶ **See** "CompuServe," **p. 240**

▶ **See** "Prodigy," **p. 243**

> **N O T E** Many companies that have Internet access allow their employees to create and maintain a personal Web page. Of course, this is a courtesy, but you can speak to your network administrator for company policies and to set up an account. Also, Internet access providers, like America Online and CompuServe, are now offering home page services. ▨

Many commercial WWW providers exist. Finding them is a matter of reading the various Net newsgroups that discuss them. Some good newsgroups to read include the following:

> **comp.infosystem**
>
> **comp.infosystems.www**
>
> **comp.infosystems.www.announce**

Another good source are the What's New pages on the many popular search engines. The following WWW URLs give you access to lists that allow you to see what's new on the WWW as well as search for information such as WWW providers and authors:

http://webcrawler.com/select/nunu.new.htm

http://cuiwww.unige.ch/

http://www.lycos.com/lycosinc/index.html

NOTE If you have a networked computer, that is to say if your computer has a registered IP address and node name within a domain, you may wish to investigate whether you can provide your own Web site. By simply adding Web server software to your computer, you can make your computer a Web site.

There are Web server applications available for all operating systems on PCs, Macs, and UNIX platforms. They enable your computer to serve HTML documents back to requesting clients. If you choose to go this route, you can save quite a bit in provider costs and easily maintain your Web page. Table 20.1 shows some of the more important Web server applications. More information about these servers can be found at **http://www.webcompare.com/**.

One disadvantage may be that if your page becomes popular or is used to transmit large amounts of data, your local network traffic may increase and therefore decrease the throughput available for the rest of your networking needs. Electronic security and forms processing, cgi-bin, may be other issues to consider before moving to your own Web server. But if you have the necessary computer resources available—that is, the minimum processor and memory required by the server software and a network card—then you can experiment with this approach until higher throughput capability or greater network security become necessary. ▦

Table 20.1 HTTPD Server Programs by Platform

Platform	Server
Macintosh	CL-HTTP, EasyServe, ExpressO HTTP Server, FTPd, httpd4Mac, InterServer Publisher, Jigsaw, MacHTTP, NetPresenz, NovaServer, Power MachTen, Web Server 4D, WebSTAR
UNIX	Apache, Apache-SSL, CL-HTTP, ExpressO HTTP Server, FTP Web Server, GN, IBM Internet Connection Secure Server, INTRAnet Jazz ServerNCSA HTTPd, Netscape Enterprise, Netscape FastTrack Server, Open Market Secure WS, Open Market WebServer, Oracle WebServer, , SCO OpenServer, Sioux, Spinner, SU/httpd, TECWebServer, thttpdWN, Zeus Server
Windows 3.1	Quarterdeck
MS-DOS	HypeIt

Part
IV

Ch
20

continues

Table 20.1 Continued	
Platform	**Server**
Windows 95	Alibaba, Commerce Builder, FolkWeb, Purveyor, Quarterdeck WebServer, SAIC-HTTP, WebQuest, WebSite
Windows NT	Alibaba, Commerce Builder, FolkWeb, Microsoft's Internet Information Server, Netscape Enterprise, Netscape FastTrack, Purveyor, Quarterdeck, SafetyWEB NT, SAIC-HTTP, Spry Web NT, WebQuest, WebSite

What Will It Cost?

There are many Internet providers, and each has its own set of charges ranging from impossibly inexpensive to outrageously expensive. Services offered vary, but in general, price does not always mean quality. Many affordably priced services are very stable and have all the options you will need. Be wary of providers that have too many users and not enough hardware, as these systems are often so clogged that people cannot readily access your pages because of excess traffic.

Determining whether or not a particular provider can give you stable and quick service is not always easy. A good measure is to ask for a one or two week trial period. During that week, try out the service during different times of the day. Weekdays are busier than weekends with most of the local usage occurring in the morning (when people log in to start their day and read their e-mail), around dinner (just before leaving the office, or after classes) and throughout the evening (a free-for-all). If the system you are trying is sluggish more than 30 percent of the time, it is probably not meeting its users' demands. All systems display periods of sluggishness, as various high-priority programs and users do important transactions. But sustained sluggishness is a good indication of a weak system. If you find a performance problem, contact the sysop or administrator of the system and ask him about the problem. See what their immediate plans are for growth. If the sysop does not address your needs adequately, move on to a different provider.

N O T E Many people who are used to free Internet access do not understand charging money for WWW services. There are many good reasons for charging for WWW space. But the most compelling is the amount of resources it takes. Consider a Web server site getting several hundred requests per second for huge pictures, audio files, movies, and documents. The load requires large machines with the proper capabilities. By charging for the use of these machines, wasted bandwidth is kept to a minimum. Furthermore, as the Net increases in the number of users and the level of sophistication, more and more capable servers are required. Charging for service allows providers to meet the needs of the changing WWW population and technology. ▪

If your access is free, you're lucky. Most people will need to pay for housing their WWW home page information. You will probably be charged either a simple monthly fixed fee, or by the amount of storage and throughput that your pages use on the Web server. If you are charged a fixed fee, the payment structure is simply like a cable TV charge. If you are charged by the amount you use, there are two charges:/storage and throughput. In this respect, the WWW is kind of like a cellular phone, where you pay a basic fee every month to have the service *and* a variable fee depending on how much it is used. As with any other communication service, it pays to shop around. Some Internet Service Providers offer substantial amounts of storage or large throughput in their basic fee. Due to competitive pressures, fees are dropping all the time, but use some caution when selecting a provider based on cost. Will the provider who undercuts everyone else by 25% be around in six months? The following sections outline the storage and throughput charges in more detail.

Storage Charge

A *storage charge* is a monthly charge taken against the amount of disk space your pages and other data take to store. Rates go throughout the spectrum, but you can expect to pay between $1 and $10 dollars per megabyte. A normal page, with 50 or so lines of text and a nice, but conservative, graphic takes about 20,000 bytes, and the charges are very inexpensive (on the order of pennies a month).

 TIP To avoid large monthly storage fees, limit the storage of large images, huge databases, and sound or movie libraries on services that charge fees. Store these items, instead, on anonymous FTP sites and place a link to them on your home page.

To calculate a monthly storage charge, simply take your total bytes used, divided by the number of megabytes per unit your provider is charging you, and take the result times the dollar amount it is charging you.

For example, if you are being charged $5 per megabyte, and you have a picture that is 17,285 bytes and a text file that is 4,892 bytes, your storage charge will be approximately 11 cents. The following detail the formula and steps that produce the result:

The formula:

Your_Cost = (Total_bytes_used / Unit_amount) * Cost_per_unit

The variables:

Total_bytes_used: 22,177 (17,285 + 4892)

Unit_amount: 1,048,576 bytes

Cost_per_unit: $5

Doing the calculation:

Your_Cost = (22,177 /1,048,576) * 5.00

Your_Cost = (0.021149635) * 5.00 Your_Cost = 0.1057—or rounded up, 11 cents a month.

Part

IV

Ch

20

N O T E　Because of the cost of maintenance and user tracking, many providers ask for a minimum
amount per month. For example, bills less than $25 might be rounded up to $25 to handle
the administration of the account. ▓

Throughput Charge

In many cases, you will be charged for the number of bytes transmitted to all the users visiting
your pages. This is called a *throughput charge*. Prices again range from below one dollar per
megabyte to many dollars per megabyte. In general, take the size of your pages times the number of times they are accessed to figure out throughput charge. Most providers offer some type
of logging capability to allow you to monitor your charges and some can even limit the number
of users allowed to visit your site in order to keep charges at bay until you have a good idea of
the popularity of your pages.

 T I P　When choosing an Internet provider that imposes throughput charges, carefully consider the use of
multiple, large graphic images within your page. Each time a user requests to visit your page through
the Web server, all of the data from your page and its embedded inline graphics are transmitted over
the network.

Other Charges and Freebies

Some Internet service providers bundle a certain amount of Web page design services with
each account. Some provide simple CGI-scripts to handle simple forms processing. Others
charge you for everything. It's worth asking about exactly what additional services, if any, you
get in the basic charge.

Do you want to have files available for download via FTP (file transfer protocol)? Some Internet
Service Providers support this, and others don't. The prices vary, as well, so you should ask up
front about the storage capabilities outlined later in the section "Storing Pages and Associated
Documents."

Do you want people to be able to pay for your products and services online? If so, the ISP
needs to be able to support credit card transactions. Not all Service Providers are able to do
this, and the fees for credit card processing vary with each Provider. This is another area in
which it pays to shop around.

As automated page features supported by JavaScript and Visual Basic Script become more
popular, you might want to add them to your page. You should investigate whether your ISP
can, or plans to, support these features and others listed in the sections following titled "Automation" and "Custom Options." Does the Provider have someone on staff who can write
applets for you? What is the fee, and is it competitive?

If your Internet service provider includes page design in the basic setup fee, ask to see some of
the pages that were designed by the Provider or the Provider's contractor. Being able to code
HTML competently and being able to design an attractive, effective Web page are two different
talents. If the "free" pages don't meet your standards, you need to consider having your page

designed by your own staff or a professional. Remember that you want your Web site to stand out from millions of other Web sites. This aim sometimes costs a little money to achieve.

Storing Pages and Associated Documents

A typical Web site offers information to users in the form of a "page," but it can also provide users with other kinds of documents and files as well. For example, a business might want customers to be able to obtain a price list for its products. One way to do this would be to put the price list on the home page as a table. Another way would be to make a link from the home page to another HTML document (another page, in other words) containing the price list. In another example, a researcher might want to make studies and other papers available to colleagues. If she makes each paper a page, these documents could take a long time to load, and there might be information that could not be included this way. So she could place the documents on a server to be downloaded by others.

There are two mechanisms for storing HTML documents: the FTP anonymous mechanism and HTTP. The previously mentioned price list is an example of a document stored using HTTP. The research papers are an example of the use of FTP anonymous.

Documents stored using the FTP anonymous method may be retrieved by using an ftp:// WWW prefix in the URL address. This method does not need a WWW server, as the browsers (such as Mosaic and Netscape Navigator) know intrinsically how to do an FTP. In this case, the user's browser contacts the machine containing your document via anonymous FTP, retrieves the document and its related information, and then displays it to the user. This method offers you the simplest way to create a Web page because so many sites offer inexpensive anonymous FTP.

The second mechanism for storage of WWW pages involves sites that run WWW servers (known as HTTP, or HTTPD servers). These sites offer the ability to have the server retrieve and transmit documents when requested by the user's browser. These types of documents may be retrieved by using an http:// prefix in the URL address.

There are basic differences in the capabilities between HTTP and FTP methods. Basically, HTTP does everything FTP does and more. The FTP method retrieves any document and satisfies links to other documents, images, and sounds. However, FTP does not allow you to access databases, forms, or participate in any kind of truly interactive activities. For these mechanisms, you need the capabilities of an HTTP server.

It is possible to house your pages at an FTP site while still making use of a Web server. A WWW browser can load and view an HTML document stored locally or at a remote site. The remote site can be an FTP or an HTTP server. The same goes for files linked to the HTML document. That is, you can embed links to the files on the FTP server in your HTML document. The files may be all on one server in one location, or they may be on many different servers in many different places.

However, for advanced capabilities such as forms processing, you must at least point the form to an HTTP server. This capability allows you to place documents on an FTP system, but have them point to a Web server for any complex needs you may have. This may save you money by allowing you to avoid bandwidth and storage costs on a commercial Web server.

Accommodating Different Browsers

The question of how sophisticated you can get in designing your pages is complicated by the fact that not all users have the same browser with equal capabilities to access your information. Because some users are still using text-only browsers, such as Lynx, and others are on full graphic browsers, like Mosaic or Netscape Navigator, each views your information differently. Furthermore, there are many different versions of both text-only and graphic/text browsers and each version has its own flaws and strengths. Table 20.2 shows some of the more popular browsers for the various platforms; additional information is available in the World Wide Web Frequently Asked Questions (FAQ) list at **http://www.boutell.com/faq/** or **http://www.shu.edu/about/WWWFaq/**. Because of this diversity, designing your pages to fit all people presents a problem.

Table 20.2 Popular Web Browsers

Platform	Browser	Comments
Macintosh	Enhanced Mosaic	From Spyglass. Multi-platform commercial versions of NCSA Mosaic can only be licensed by OEMs. Home page at **http://www.spyglass.com**.
	NCSA Mosaic	Multi-platform and free. FTP from **ftp.ncsa.uiuc.edu/Mosaic/Mac**.
	Netscape Navigator	Tables, HTML extensions. Free to nonprofit and educational institutions; free evaluation period for individuals. Home page at **http://www.netscape.com/info/how-to-get-it.html**. FTP from **ftp.netscape.com/pub/navigator/**.
MS/DOS	DOSLynx	Can view GIFs, but not in-line. FTP from **ftp2.cc.ukans.edu/pub/WWW/DosLynx**.
	Minuet	Both text-mode and graphics-mode display. FTP from minuet. **micro.umn.edu/pub/minuet/latest**.
Text-Mode	UNIX/VMS	EMACS w3-mode. For dumb terminals. FTP w3.tar.gz from **ftp.cs.Indiana.edu/pub/elisp/w3**.
	Line Mode	FTP from **www.w3.org/pub/www/**.
	Lynx	**www.nyu.edu/pages/wsu/subir/lynx.html** for FTP sites.

Platform	Browser	Comments
	PERLWWW	FTP from **archive.cis.ohio-state.edu/ pub/w3browser/w3browser-0.1.shar**.
	VMS	By Dudu Rashty. FTP from **vms.huji.ac.il/ www/vms_client**.
Windows 3.1/ NT/95	Cello	From Cornell. Outdated. FTP from **ftp.law.cornell. edu/pub/LII/cello**.
	Enhanced Mosaic I-COMM	From Spyglass. Operates without a TCP/IP connection. Requires UNIX or VMS shell account. Home page at **http://www.best. com/~icomm/icomm.htm**.
	Internet Explorer	From Microsoft. Many HTML extensions. Home page at **http://www.microsoft.com**.
	Netscape Navigator	See previous listing under Macintosh.
	SlipKnot	Operates without SLIP or PPP connection. Requires UNIX shell account. FTP from **ftp://ftp.coast.net/SimTel/win3/internet**. Home page at **http://www.interport.net/ slipknot/slipknot.html**.
	UdiWWW	Supports most of proposed HTML 3.0 plus Netscape extensions. Home page at **http:// www.uni-ulm.de/~richter/udiwww/ index.htm**.
	WinMosaic	From NCSA. FTP from **ftp.ncsa.uiuc.edu/ PC/Windows/Mosaic**. Home page at **http://www.w3.org/hypertext/WWW/ MosaicForWindows/Status.html**.

Part
IV
Ch
20

One solution is to design multiple pages, and at the top of each page give the user the choice to switch to the other page, which supports a different type of browser. For example, at the top of the graphic page it could say:

Click here to go to the text version of this page.

Likewise, at the top of the text page it could say:

Click here to go to the graphic version of this page.

The obvious problem with this method is that it requires two or more versions of the same information. Furthermore, this does not fix the problem of some browsers' lack of support for certain HTML features.

The general solution is that while you design your pages to the audience you are trying to reach, try not to embody too much functionality in pictures. This way, if a user on a text-only system sees your page, it is still useful to him or her.

In general, feel free to include graphics in your documents, but realize that the more meaning you place in the graphics, the less text-only users will be able to glean from your page. You will see in Chapter 21, "Using HTML to Build Your Home Page," that there is a way to provide an identifying tag in each place where an image will appear to those using a graphical browser. That way, the text-only user won't miss as much. As the Web progresses, you will see fewer and fewer text-only browsers being used; but for now, you must keep these users in mind.

Home Page Options

Chapter 21 details many of the formatting options available in home page design. However, before you begin to create your page, it is a good idea to review the kinds of data that can be incorporated into WWW documents.

Simple Text

Text for HTML documents can be entered through the use of any simple text editor, like Notepad, or a word processor. Simple commands embedded into the text instruct the browser how to format that text. Web pages are always simple ASCII documents. Notepad automatically saves your file as ASCII text. Specifically instructing your word processor to store the text in ASCII format is all it takes to create WWW pages.

Because most of the content of a page is usually text, formatting options are given that allow you to display the text in a pleasing manner. It is important to remember that each browser is different in that it is potentially running on different platforms. This means that each user may be seeing your page in a different size window, with different fonts and different color capability. The WWW browser takes care of making your information fit the user's window. To accomplish this, the browser changes the number of words on a line to fit the particular view. Because you may not always wish the browser to do this, special formatting commands exist that make it possible to override the browsers reformatting.

In addition to allowing you to control how text flows, the browser allows you to specify how text looks. This includes size, emphasis, and use of white space (areas with no text).

The following formatting command concepts can help you create effective home pages by allowing you to break text into more readable sections and to apply highlighting and emphasis to important words:

- *Variable font sizes* allows you to create titles and headings that enable the user to find information quickly.
- *Bulleting* allows lists to be made, and WWW browsers support multiple levels of bullets as well as numbered lists. Support for bulleting in your pages is made even easier by simple indentation commands, allowing bulleted items with multiple lines of text to flow and wrap correctly.

■ *Horizontal rules* allow you to break areas by placing lines that stretch from left to right across the document.

Use of these simple formatting capabilities adds surprising life and professionalism to a document. It can often be the difference between a normal ho-hum page and an outstanding page.

Links

Linking is what the Web is all about. Creating links, also known as *hyperlinks*, allows you to have objects on one page point to other pages. For example, a word, phrase, or picture in one document, when chosen by the user, can cause another document, sound, or picture to be retrieved. Even movies and binary files may be retrieved using links.

You can link any object to any document on your system or any other system on the Web. This capability allows you to have links in your document that take people to other locations.

You should place at least one link in each document. That link brings the user up a level in your document hierarchy. This is not mandatory, but is at least polite because it gives the user somewhere to go from your page.

The simplest use of linking is to subdivide a long document into several small documents and use linking to move between them.

 Don't place too many links on one page. An excessive number of links means the user won't be able to jump to them all and just makes extra work for you.

WWW browsers allow you to link to a tremendous number of services and capabilities. You can link to an anonymous FTP, a WWW (HTTP) server, a Net news server, a mail handler, a Telnet session, or a Gopher service. Because of this, clicking on any hyperlinked object can cause any of a number of exciting things to happen, from retrieving binary files to logging into remote machines.

Inline Images

An inline image is a black-and-white, or limited color picture that is inserted directly into a document at the point the HTML command is issued. Color pictures may contain up to 256 colors, and may be dithered to simulate full color pictures. The capability to use inline images allows you to create documents that include pictures. Text can be made to flow in and around the picture, with certain restrictions, much like a magazine layout.

WWW systems inherently know how to place GIF and XBM images inline with text. Depending on your browser, other image types may be externally viewed in a pop-up window, but may not be viewed inline in the browser.

▶ **See** "Graphics Galore: Images on the Web," **p. 437**

Inline images can be used for the following reasons:

■ To make a page appear more readable or entertaining

■ To simulate a button that may be pushed

Part
IV

Ch

20

- To express information
- To create a map that may be pushed

The simplest use of inline images is just to increase the readability of a page. Inline images can be used to make fancy bullets, company logos, section separators, gothic lettering for paragraph starts, and other graphic elements. All the figures in this chapter show pages that use inline images to help communicate their messages. As you look at the various figures, you can see how each designer used the same inline image capability to produce a different look and feel.

One of the most interesting aspects of inline images is their ability to create custom buttons. In other words, by using the linking capability of the HTML document, you may create any type of graphic button and cause that button, when pushed, to access or hyperlink to other graphic images, sounds, or documents. This allows you to create very beautiful and creative interfaces and to add life to otherwise dull text pages. This *hyperlinking* is one of the reasons the WWW is so popular—simple point-and-click navigation (see Fig. 20.9).

FIG. 20.9
The Yahoo page combines hyperlinked text and forms. Selecting either the text or entering a search string brings you to the associated page.

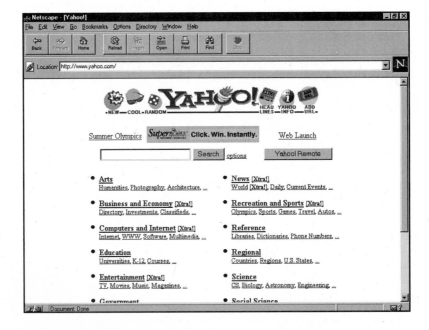

Inline images may be used to impart information that may be awkward in text format. Graphs, charts, formulas, scientific visualization, and statistical viewing are just some of the ways inline images can be used to express data.

It is also possible to create a picture where elements in the picture can be chosen. For example, a picture could show a scene of a desk, and touching different items on the desk with the mouse would cause different documents to be retrieved. This ISMAP capability offers many exciting design possibilities. ISMAP merely stands for "IS MAPped," indicating that the image is subdivided, or mapped, into multiple regions. Maps were formerly costly to implement in storage and throughput. It was necessary to have a program running on the server to handle the task of identifying the location the user selected and then translating this into a file name. Recent advances in Netscape have made it much easier and cheaper to do maps; Netscape allows you to put the map and all the programming on the browser's side of things. This is discussed briefly in the later section "Custom Options."

Figure 20.10, the Softbank Exposition and Conference page, uses a map. Each of the individual logos can be selected, and when picked brings you to information about that choice.

FIG. 20.10
The Softbank Exposition and Conference page makes excellent use of a graphical map to guide the user.

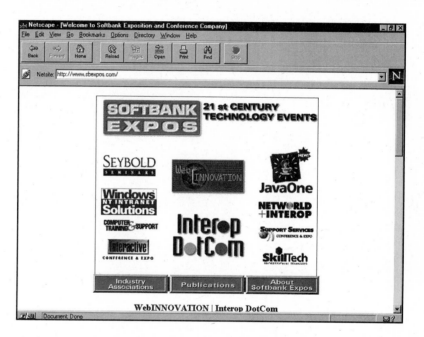

NOTE ISMAP capability and the equivalent Netscape technology are not discussed in this book, but information may be found online. ▪

 You don't need to store your inline images on the same system as your HTML documents. They may be pulled from anywhere in the world on-the-fly, and inserted in your document. However, be advised that the user will most likely have to wait longer while the server that houses the image to be inserted is contacted and the image is downloaded.

An important idea to remember is that the overuse of images leads to pages that are slow for modem users to retrieve and display. This also makes pages large and can increase your Web costs—something to consider if you are paying for your throughput. One advantage to WWW browsers is their ability to cache images. This means that if an image is used on more than one page, it only needs to be loaded once. This fact makes using images cheaper if you simply remember to reuse the same image file, as a page header, for instance, throughout your pages.

Sound

Sound may be linked in your documents and stored anywhere. Because sound files may be large (absolutely mammoth in fact) you may want to store them where the price is cheapest and not on the same machine as your pages. Sounds are usually stored either in WAVE or AU format and require a *player* to be heard. Although most browsers support playing sounds using an external viewer, it is not a good idea to embody critical information in a sound format. Another option is the use of the RealAudio player and sound stored in RA format; in this case, the sound is played back by RealAudio, which is available as a plug-in for Netscape. You can see (and hear) an example of all three audio formats on the Atlantic Records page, **http://www.atlantic-records.com/DigitalArena/**.

Unless you have unlimited free access, and storage and throughput, you are not going to offer a lot of sounds unless you are getting large commercial benefits from them. Because of their size, sounds have high storage and throughput costs. Although it should also be kept in mind that sounds also tend to be popular because there is a (surprisingly) large audience of users who have fast Internet access, and thus do not have to wait for a long download.

Creating sounds to place in your pages involves playing the sound from an external source and recording a sample of that sound onto your computer. Many commercial and shareware programs exist that provide this capability for most of the popular platforms, including Windows 95. However, to input quality sound, most people end up investing in sound hardware for their computers. Most of the popular sound software supports WAVE or AU type format most commonly found on the WWW. In many cases, it is less expensive to engage the services of an audio production company than to buy all the equipment and record your own. A professional audio production also sounds much better than anything most people are likely to produce on their own.

With the latest multimedia capabilities available on both home and office computers, providing pre-recorded sounds for a page has become much simpler. Most computers with CD-ROMs are provided with software to play music CDs and have the capability to *record* audio segments to disk. Once on disk, the sound recording can be precisely edited and special effects can be added. As in the case of commercial and shareware clip art, there are many places on the Internet that are repositories of sound clips. Also, there are more and more sound clip and special effects CDs available at a nominal cost.

Forms

Forms capabilities have opened up the Internet for major commercial possibilities. The use of form handling allows you to design documents that can accept information and decisions from the user. The form is then submitted to a Web server and a response is sent to the user. The response may be anything, from another form to a document, a sound, or an image.

The use of forms requires that you have access to a Web server (HTTP). The document that contains the form may be housed anywhere, but the information submitted by the user *must* be sent to a Web server for processing. However, a single document may have many forms and each form may be sent to a different server if desired.

Forms may contain many different elements. Radio buttons allow you to pick one choice from many. Check boxes allow you to select many options from a list of choices. Text input lines and areas allow the user to enter free-form text. List and Option choosing allow users to select items from a list of choices. All of these may be combined to create useful forms for polling user input, gathering statistics, processing sales orders, controlling games and entertainment, or any other situation where user input is necessary or helpful.

Tables

You are probably familiar with tables and what they can do to dress up a document from your experience with word processors. You can format your Web document to use tables in much the same way. You can even do math in tables on your Web document. Tables can be incredibly useful as part of many page designs.

An important contribution of tables is that they enable you to organize the content of your Web page, and to mix text and images in ways that you can't using any other means.

Figure 20.11 gives a simple example of a table, with and without the use of borders. Figure 20.12 shows how a borderless table can put text to the right of an image.

FIG. 20.11
This is a simple example of how a table can organize information.

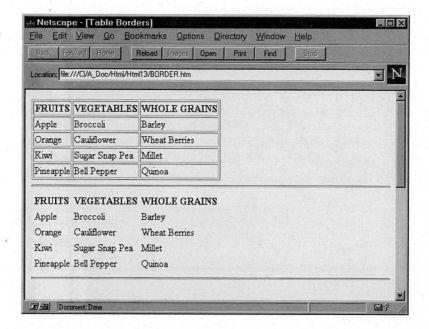

Part
IV

Ch
20

FIG. 20.12
Using tables, you can display graphics alongside text.

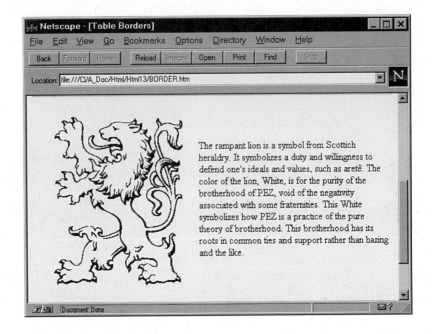

There are plenty of users whose browsers don't support tables. If some of these need to access your page, you should consider using one of several alternatives, such as a list or preformatted text. You could also simply capture a screen shot of the table, as created with your word processor, and place the resulting image in the document. Tables are demonstrated in Chapter 21, "Using HTML to Build Your Home Page."

Frames

If your audience uses, primarily, the latest version of Netscape, you can really improve the appearance of your pages by using frames. A frame is something like a table, except that tables only organize a display. Frames create windows that tile together to make a page easier to work with and better-looking. Each window can be changed separately from the others. In some cases, a window can be scrolled independently of the other windows.

Figure 20.13 illustrates how frames are used on a real estate home page.

A major consideration in planning your page is whether your typical users will be able to see features, such as frames. Frames are supported by Netscape 2.0 and later, but not necessarily by other browsers, including earlier and popular versions of Netscape. As you will see in Chapter 20, Netscape does provide a way for users without frame-capable browsers to see an alternative page.

There is one other thing to consider when using frames. That is, users cannot navigate through frames the same way they navigate through other sites. The Back button doesn't back you out of a frame; it takes you to the previous frame. If a user is in a window with frames and moves to a window without frames, the frames disappear. Finally, to bookmark a frame, it is necessary to right-click inside the frame. Users may not know this and get frustrated trying to get out of the frames, or to another feature.

FIG. 20.13
The Aspin Estates & Cottages home page demonstrates the use of frames to break up and organize the display. Note that two windows scroll.

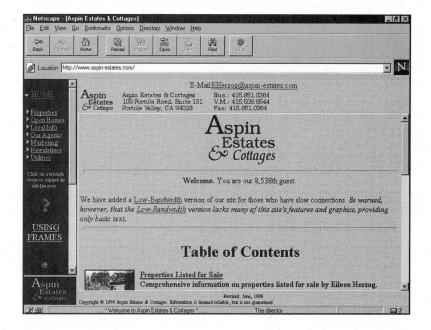

Pictures, Movies, and Binaries

Besides allowing you to insert a GIF image inline in a document, the Web also allows you to retrieve, or download, GIF or JPEG images, MPEG movies, and other binaries and compressed files. In fact, support for many types of images and formats is possible. Most capable browsers will support GIF and JPEG, at least.

Any unknown file type encountered by a browser can be saved to the user's local disk as a binary file. Most browsers have a dialog window that pops up and asks the user what to do with the unknown file type just transferred. Netscape, for example, allows you to configure an external viewer or save the file to disk. This allows any data in any format to be transferred. Viewers exist that allow many formats to be viewed. Shareware and commercial postscript viewers, MPEG movie viewers, and TIFF viewers, just to name a few, can be found on the Internet.

In general, if you offer a nonstandard format, you should also offer the user the ability to download the viewer, or at least provide a link to the appropriate viewer.

Interactivity

You see a lot of information in the popular press and on the Web about the more futuristic possibilities of Web use. Nearly all of these possibilities have to do with Web pages that interact with the user. Virtual reality and the Virtual Reality Markup Language (VRML), Web

Part
IV

Ch
20

conferencing and Web Chat, and modular enhancements (applets) are all coming and you may want to plan for them on your home page. Chapter 26, "The Future of the Web: VRML, SGML, and Web Chat," discusses these in detail. Most of these, however, are not yet practical for most Web sites. The exceptions are ShockWave, Java, and VBScript.

These methods have been developed by Sun Microsystems and Microsoft to make Web pages dynamic and interactive. Both methods are script languages, but there are fundamental differences between the two approaches.

Sun's Java is a C-like language used to create programs, which are compiled and run just like any other application. But the important difference between C applications and Java applications is that the latter runs on almost any 32-bit system. If the resulting compiled Java program can be embedded into a WWW page, it is called an *applet*.

Applets are served with the Web page in which they are embedded (along with necessary data files). They run only on the client system. No special server software is necessary, so your ISP's current Web server is completely capable of handling these applets. To embed an applet on a Web page, you enclose its name and some necessary attributes within a pair of APPLET container tags.

A properly written Java applet runs on any 32-bit platform that has a Java-capable browser, such as HotJava or Netscape 2.0, installed on it. In other words, the same application runs on Macs under System 7, Windows NT and 95, and UNIX. If a browser can't display Java applets, it won't display anything when it sees APPLET tags. The exception is when those APPLET tags also have some HTML code included between them to inform the user that the browser is unable to load Java applets.

N O T E   A 16-bit implementation of Java is reported to be in development. Whether it will be compatible with the 32-bit variety, or even whether it will ever be released, are matters for speculation at the time of this writing. ▓

Most of the time, Java applets are used to deliver multimedia—sound, animations, and graphics, as well as text. However, they can do much more. For an example of an outstanding applet, try the nuclear power plant simulation on the Web at **http://www.ida.liu.se/~her/npp/ demo.html**. You may also enjoy The Impressionist, at **http://reality.sgi.com/grafica/ impression/**. Development of Java applets is beyond the scope of this book.

There is another way to deliver multimedia to browsers, and that is with JavaScript, a joint development by Netscape and Sun. You can write a program with JavaScript and embed the program code directly in the HTML of a page. Like Java applets, the program code is enclosed between tags, only they are <SCRIPT> tags. Unlike applets, JavaScript programs are not compiled. At this time, JavaScript only runs on 32-bit systems under Netscape 2.0.

With JavaScript, the application runs on the client. This means that the JavaScript program replaces forms and CGI scripts for some applications and relieves the burden on the server. See Chapter 25, "Using JavaScript for Developing Web Applications," for details and to learn how to write your own JavaScript.

You should be aware that there are security concerns regarding the use of Java. While there are plenty of safeguards built into Java, it is theoretically possible to get around these, and a number of actual "holes" have been found. The debate over Java's safety rages. Sun is working to come up with safe ways to run untrusted applets in a trusted environment, but the rumors and misunderstandings continue. Some people and some organizations, as a matter of policy, disable Netscape's ability to use Java applets and JavaScript. A few nervous ISPs reportedly refuse to allow any Java applets to reside on their servers. You may want to consider this before you plan to use Java for any critical features of your page.

Microsoft has announced (but not released at the time of this writing) its own entry in the HTML extension category, Visual Basic Script. This combination of Visual Basic and Microsoft's OLE Scripting service goes beyond JavaScript in its capabilities. Visual Basic Script can be used to create applications on the client side and on the server side. In addition, it is upwardly compatible with Visual Basic for Applications (VBA), which means that a programmer can link the functionality of Microsoft Office applications and Visual Basic 4.0 to applications located on a Web site. This is generally consistent with Microsoft's vision of the future of documents and systems.

Visual Basic Script supports the same platforms as VBA and MS Office 7.0: 32-bit Macintosh and Windows. Initial plans were to give away licenses and source code for Visual Basic Script. This probably means someone will port it to UNIX sooner or later.

Like JavaScript, Visual Basic Script for client side applications is embedded into HTML documents and interpreted by the browser. Currently the only browser that responds to Visual Basic Script is Internet Explorer 3.0, but this should change once the language is finally released. On the server side, Visual Basic for Applications works much like the Binary Gateway Interface (BGI), so forms and other applications can be developed. For full functionality, some server-side programming will require the use of Visual Basic 4.0 and Visual C++.

All of this means that Visual Basic Script may become a standard for corporate use on "intranets," more than for general use on the World Wide Web. Still, it is an area worth watching for future developments. You can learn how to make basic use of Visual Basic Script in Chapter 24, "VBScript and ActiveX for Developing Web Applications."

Automation

Another capability brought to Web pages by Netscape 2.0 is automatic update of Web pages. The techniques that support this are called *server push* and *client pull*. You can use these to create automated slide shows, "teaser" pages, which display for a few seconds and then disappear, and to automatically advance viewers to another page or even another site. Microsoft's Internet Explorer now supports these features as well.

Server push is used for data-driven applications. One example might be automation of icons; Java applets also do this, but they run on the client system. To use server push, a CGI program is run on the server. This script keeps the connection from the server to the client open and "pushes" a stream of data at the browser. (Usually the connection to the client is closed as soon as the latest page is sent from the server.)

Part
IV

Ch
20

Client pull does not require a CGI script or any special programming on the server side. Instead, a special tag, <META>, is placed in the HEAD section of the Web page and Netscape takes it from there. Here is an example:

```
<HTML>
<HEAD>
<META HTTP-EQUIV="Refresh" CONTENT="30; URL=newpage.htm">
</HEAD>
<BODY>
Please wait 30 seconds for the next page
</BODY>
</HTML>
```

This displays the message: Please wait 30 seconds for the next page. Netscape then waits 30 seconds and loads newpage.htm.

Custom Options

One of the Web's most useful capabilities is that it can be modified to fit almost any need or application. Custom programs may be designed, using either a scripting language or a programming language, that can accept special links and forms, and produce a variety of interactive output.

Games, user tracking, session management, cash transaction processing, and order entry are just some of the applications for custom server code. Chapter 21, "Using HTML to Build Your Home Page," gives a brief overview of this custom code capability (called *cgi-bin*). This cgi-bin programming is usually written in C or PERL scripting languages, and is used to process incoming information from a form and perform some manipulation on that data. One difficulty with using cgi-bin code is getting it designed. cgi-bin programming requires a bit of understanding and devotion to learn how it works. Furthermore, it requires access to a server to test your program. However, if you lack the time or expertise, many organizations exist that will gladly custom design solutions to fit your needs. These companies can be found throughout the Web. Also offered on the Web are many sites that have pre-written cgi-bin software. This software can be used as a model, or as is often the case, as the solution itself, for custom capabilities.

Fortunately, it is becoming less necessary to use CGI programming for many features, as browsers become more feature-rich and advances in the HTML standard continue. You have already learned about some of these advances in preceding sections, but there are others. For example, it is now possible to create clickable imagemaps that are implemented on the client side. An image map is an image on which the user may click in different areas to select URLs. Of course, the user must be running Netscape 2.0 or a compliant browser. This is addressed in Chapter 21.

In planning for the use of client-side features implemented through Netscape extensions, remember that not everyone will be using Netscape Navigator 2.0 to look at your page. Plan to provide either an alternate menu or an additional cgi-bin reference in your HTML (a single imagemap can be defined to work both client-side and server-side). With the latter option, a browser that understands the Netscape extension uses the imagemap. A browser that does not understand the extension will cause the cgi-bin program to run on the server.

What Goes into a Good Home Page

Even the most sophisticated computer user can be overwhelmed by an onslaught of data. And many of your users may not be all that savvy. You should make every effort—in the design of your home page—to keep it simple and to present your information in a logical way that leads the user in an orderly progression through your material.

Many new, or occasional, Web page designers pay most attention to the HTML source code for their pages. After all, if the Web page doesn't make sense to Web browsers, or if the page doesn't work right, people won't buy and they won't come back. However, using valid HTML is only one of several factors needed to create a quality Web page. What makes a great page is valid HTML plus outstanding content, attractive presentation, elegant layout and style, and a certain *je ne sais quoi*.

One way to make your information more accessible is to include ample *white space*. This is space that doesn't contain pictures or text. A full page of unparagraphed text will be intimidating to anyone. Try to present your information in lists or tables so that key points are easily identified. Also, don't put picture after picture. Try to frame them in the page, leaving some space around them. Use of white space (empty areas in your page) is important because it allows the components of your document to appear less crowded.

You should strive to present your information in easily assimilated portions. Pay attention to paragraph lengths. If they become too long, try to break them up into two or three shorter paragraphs. Try to make sure each link stands by itself and does not crowd the other choices.

If your document is very long, you might want to consider links that allow the user to jump around in the document. Or, instead of having one document that is five pages long, you might want to make a single page presenting key themes with links to other pages that describe in more detail the specific information the user might be interested in.

The use of graphics can add interest to your page. Even the most conservative page could use an inline picture in the title of the home page. Your choice of graphics depends on the type of image you are trying to present. The law firm used as an example earlier might use a simple square of granite or marble. The rock band might have a graffiti wall or some of its cover art.

TIP If you are planning links to other pages from your home page, you might consider using the same graphic at the top of each page to create a sense of grouping or unity. As pointed out in the text, this also has the benefit of loading faster, as browsers cache images.

If you don't have pre-formatted graphics and textures in your computer, they are available for little or no cost at various sites around the Internet. Or you might try your local computer software stores for CD-ROM libraries of clip art and pre-created graphics.

Part
IV

Ch
20

Where can you learn to do all of this? There aren't many formal schools in Web page design, after all. One way to learn is to look at what others have done to create outstanding Web pages. And the easiest way to find these great pages is to use the various recognition services—the organizations that give awards for quality design.

For examples of aesthetic excellence, take a look at the High Five award winners. You will find a new one each week at **http://www.highfive.com**, sponsored by typographer David Siegel. Siegel also offers two essays on Web page design for your consideration: "Severe Tire Damage" and "The Balkanization of the Web." Check them out, along with Siegel's Tips for Writers and Designers, at **http://www.dsiegel.com**.

To see the winners for content, presentation, and quality of experience, look at pages that have been given the Point Top Five award. These are chosen for being among the best, smartest, and most entertaining sites around, and are listed at Point's home page, **http://www.pointcom.com/**.

You can learn by talking to other Web developers, too. Contact them by using any of the mailing lists or newsgroups that focus on Web page design.

Newsgroups

> **alt.fan.mozilla**
>
> **alt.Hypertext**
>
> **comp.infosystems.www.authoring.cgi**
>
> **comp.infosystems.www.authoring.html**
>
> **comp.infosystems.www.authoring.images**
>
> **comp.text.sgml**

Mailing Lists

> HTML Authoring Mailing List (see **http://www.netcentral.net/lists/html-list.html**)
>
> NETTRAIN Mailing List

Finally, here are two pages that give you good advice about page design, at least in terms of things to avoid:

> The HTML Bad-Style Page (**http://www.earth.com/bad-style**)
>
> Top Ten Ways to Tell If You Have a Sucky Home Page (**http://www.winternet.com/~jmg/topten.html**)

It's not hard to create attractive and dynamic HTML home pages, but you should put some effort into the design to make sure that it has the suitable look and feel for your products and services.

Generating and Keeping Interest

There are a number of ways to attract people to your Web site. Some of these work best when you are just starting, and others work better once you are established.

The best way to create initial interest in your new home page is to post it to the myriad of What's New lists on the Internet. If you've already been navigating on the Web, you probably have your favorite. Many people check their favorite What's New service weekly.

Some of these services display a new site for many weeks, and some for just a few hours. Some have rules about acceptability of listings, and you should check to be sure your site conforms to these rules before you submit it. The method for posting to a list may be different for each list. If you have the URL for a list you would like to post to, go to it. Most lists contain the information for posting to it somewhere within the document. Posting to lists is generally very easy, requiring you to enter data into clearly labeled areas. Once you've created your HTML home page, you go to the lists appropriate for your field, and list your home page.

N O T E   Some What's New lists take a very long time to post additions. Sometimes these tend to be at universities, and if you post your notice during a break, there might not be anyone there to update the file. ▪

N O T E   To get the best duration of promotion for your home page, post to pages that update immediately, and to lists that take a while. Then when the steam generated from the first list is waning, new users will be directed to you from the later posting lists. ▪

The result of posting to these lists can be phenomenal. An art gallery that went online had *thousands* of people "walk through its virtual gallery" in the first week. You should also be aware that the traffic generated by What's New lists tends to be casual browsers rather than people with a strong interest in your product or service.

On a longer-term basis, you need to continue to attract new viewers. There are four ways to do this.

You can advertise or promote your page on the Web, using sponsorships, indexes, and links from other home pages. Some of these methods cost actual money and may not be suited for a page that supports your avocation. Low-cost, or no-cost, methods of promotion include getting links to your page placed on other pages. If you have money to spend, many commercial Web pages sell advertising space. To know where to advertise and how much to spend on promotion, consider the following four questions:

- ▪ How much traffic must you get to visit your Web page?
- ▪ Is your Web page one that appeals to many people, or only to a select few?
- ▪ How much time and money do you have to support advertising?
- ▪ Must your site be well-known in order to contribute to the success of your business?

Part

IV

Ch

20

You can register your Web site with the Web search servers, such as Lycos, Alta Vista, Infoseek, Inktomi, Webcrawler, or Yahoo. Most people find what they need on the Web by using one of these services. There may also be a specialized index page that covers your exact area of interest. These span the range of human interests from art (**http://www.artplanet.com/index.html**) to big dogs (**http://is.dal.ca/~dcodding/dane.html**), from pediatrics (**http://www.med.jhu.edu/peds/neonatology/poi.html**) to special needs education (**http://schoolnet2.carleton.ca/~kwellar/snewww.html**), and from trucks (**http://www.truck.net**) to fashion (**http://www.fashion.net**). Nearly all of the search servers have a page that offers a form with which you can add your site to their index. If this is more work than you care to undertake, you can use a submission service to register your site. Some of these services charge a fee. Others, such as Submit-It (**http://www.submit.com**) are free.

You can set up your Web page so that it attracts the attention of *Web crawlers* (also known as *spiders*, *robots*, *walkers*, *worms*, and *wombats*). A Web crawler is an autonomous program that travels from one page to another via the links between pages. As it goes, it records the pages it finds and the contents of those pages are entered in a database. Some of the Web crawlers are accessible to the general population (e.g., Webcrawler at **http://webcrawler.com**). The commercial services use crawlers, too. The easiest way to get listed by any of these crawlers is to go to the home page and submit your page for listing. To attract other crawlers, it is essential that links to your page be present on other pages; otherwise a crawler has no way of getting to your page. In addition to establishing the links, you must give the crawler the information it needs in order to index your page with all the others it finds. While some crawlers use page titles, headings, or the frequency of words in the text, to generate index entries, most look for a <META> tag in the HTML. If you assign a keyword list to the META field, the crawler uses those keywords for the index.

Finally, you can post a notice about your new Web site on the Internet newsgroups. A newsgroup is much like a public bulletin board or forum, although each newsgroup has its own set of rules and customs. Some newsgroups are moderated; somebody enforces the rules and customs and can block any posting that violates them. The best newsgroups to use for promoting your Web site are the announcement groups, dedicated to the purpose of broadcasting messages dealing with new sites and services. The leading example of these groups is **comp.infosystems.www.announce**, which accepts nearly all announcements sent to it. You may also want to consider announcing in **comp.internet.net.happenings**, and in **misc.entrepreneurs**, both of which specialize in business sites. You can post in other newsgroups that involve topics covered by your site, but be sure to check a site out for a while first and conform to the other users' expectations for commercial posts, before you submit any information to the group. This lessens the chances that you will be seen as violating "Netiquette."

Unless you have a service or product that everyone just has to have, you need to figure out how you are going to get people back to your home page after their first visit. To keep interest in your home page, like anything else, you have to keep it in front of your audience. You can just repost it to your favorite lists, but when people get to your page and find the same old stuff, they won't stay around. But if you are offering new features, then people have a reason to visit you again. Offering new features allows you to repost your announcement, each time talking about your newest addition. This helps to guide in the people who missed your advertising the first time around.

For example, the law firm might mention the addition of a new partner and invite users to check out the new partner's profile. The rock band can stagger its audio selections, changing it from time to time and announce the new selection in the appropriate lists. Individuals can put the URL in their e-mail signatures.

 TIP When you plan your home page, also plan your future additions. An HTML home page can be a powerful sales and marketing tool. Use it to its full advantage!

Another way to get people to return again and again to your site is to offer free entertainment or information. Features such as the joke of the week will draw people to your site to see your "free service." Law firms and accountants can provide legal or tax tips that are updated on a periodic basis. Some sites have cartoonists who offer a daily or weekly chuckle.

Grouping yourself with other vendors in a Virtual Mall can help draw customers, just as malls in the real world do. But in general, a visible storefront in an online mall does not guarantee you any more business than simply advertising your wares on the popular lists. Paying extra for "prestigious" mall space is not always what it is worth.

Finally, consider offering your viewers a way to be notified automatically any time your page changes. This is possible through a service called "URL-Minder" and it is free to you and to your viewers. You do this by embedding a form on your page that readers can use to request notification of changes to your page. You can have URL-Minder send a generic notice or a tailored message. Information and the HTML needed to create the form are to be found at **http://www.netmind.com/URL-minder/example.html**.

HTML Editors and Filters

The general method of building HTML pages is to create them in a standard text editor or word processor. This, however, requires that you become quite familiar with the HTML language. While HTML, in general, is fairly simple, if becoming an HTML guru is not on your agenda, you may wish to investigate Editors and Filters. These systems allow you to create and view HTML pages in time-saving ways.

Editors

HTML editors are programs specially designed to allow you to create HTML documents interactively. These are usually point-and-click programs with nice user interfaces. These programs allow you to start with simple ASCII documents and create links, text formatting, and place images. There are many popular editors, including the following:

Part
IV

Ch
20

For Windows

Cool Edit

Emacs HTML Mode

HotDog (Standard and Professional)

HoTMetaL

HTML Assistant

HTMLed

HTML Writer

Live Markup

Microsoft Internet Assistant

Netscape Gold (Win95 only)

Quarterdeck WebAuthor

WebEdit

For Mac

Arachnid

Emacs HTML Mode

Microsoft Internet Assistant

World Wide Web Weaver

HTML.edit

For UNIX

AsWedit

Emacs HTML Mode

Each of these editors has different features, strengths, and weaknesses. Each also has different restrictions for use, and you should make sure to read any licensing or other agreements that come with the editor before using it.

Filters

Filters offer yet another method for creating HTML documents. By using a filter with your favorite text editor or word processor, you can extend its capabilities and allow it to create HTML documents. This is often very useful because most popular editors already have bold and italic capability, and extending these to produce HTML code is generally easy.

Popular filters are available for the following software packages:

BibTeX

DECwrite

Framemaker

Interleaf

LaTex

MS Word

nroff

PowerPoint

QuarkXPress

Scribe

Texinfo

troff

VAXDocument

Word for Windows 2.0

Word for Windows 6.0

WordPerfect

Filters work by translating word-processor formats directly into HTML. Often, filters include extensions to the word processor that add the capability to create HTML links and drop inline images.

Where to Find Editors

HTML editors may be found on the CD that is a part of this book. In addition, HTML editors may be found all over the Internet. Using WebCrawler to search for some of the editors produces many sites that provide the software. The Web has many sites that offer the editors, but most of the tools are concentrated on the following site that allows you to learn about many of them:

http://www.w3.org/hypertext/WWW/Tools/

Filters are also spread all over the Internet, but again, can be found concentrated in the following WWW site:

http://www.w3.org/hypertext/WWW/Tools/Word_proc_filters.html

Download the software or filter and examine both the online documentation as well as any text files, readmes, or manuals that are included in the archive. Help can often be found in the WWW newsgroups as well as the IRC #www channel.

Pros and Cons

HTML editors and filters can provide a quick method for creating HTML documents. They are especially useful for the designer who lacks the time to handcraft HTML pages. Editors and filters are also useful for learning HTML. By using an editor or filter to create a page, and then looking at the resulting HTML document, you can learn how to create your own pages.

Nonetheless, there are numerous problems with using filters and editors. First is the fact that they are often limited or simply behind the times. This means that new capabilities in new browsers are often not found in the filter and editor. Secondly, filters and editors often produce messy HTML, code that is difficult to read and edit, and is generally less efficient than HTML produced by hand.

By this I mean wasting bytes. Often, there are many ways to do the same thing in HTML, and sometimes editors often pick a less efficient method of producing a document. This results in an accumulation of unnecessary bytes in the document, which, while small in themselves, can compound into many dollars worth of data when downloaded thousands of times a month.

The bottom line on editors and filters is, pick one that works for you and that you are happy with. Use it only if you find that it is truly a time-saving system. ●

Using HTML to Build Your Home Page

by Bill Brandon and Joe Schepis

This chapter familiarizes you with the HyperText Markup Language (HTML) and teaches you how to build your own WWW Home page using HTML. You will also learn how to add form handling capabilities and other advanced features to your page. Anyone who can use a word processor should have no trouble mastering the techniques necessary to construct innovative and exciting WWW Home Pages.

While HTML contains many commands and capabilities, this chapter will focus on the commands most used to make effective pages. In cases where more than one command will produce a similar output, this chapter will cover only the most popular command. Four of the newer or more advanced features of HTML are addressed near the end of the chapter: forms, tables, frames, and client-side image maps.

HTML is undergoing constant change. Standardization of the language is the job of the World Wide Web Consortium (W3C) at the MIT Laboratory for Computer Science. This group standardizes the syntax for widely deployed features such as tables, applets, and text flow around images, while providing backwards-compatibility with previous standards. This means that there are always ways to write a version of your home page that can be read by any and all Web browsers.

How to program in HTML

HTML is a simple system of tags that turn a plain text file into a Web document and enhance it with features that communicate your ideas more powerfully.

URL naming conventions

Understanding URL addresses is critical to successfully providing information to other users.

How to create and use HTML forms

Forms are the basic interactive mechanism on the Web; they allow users to respond to questions and surveys and to provide you with information about themselves.

How to use tables and frames

Tables are very valuable in ordinary documents to help readers understand relationships. In a Web document, tables offer the same advantage; frames give you even more flexibility in laying out your Web page.

How to use client-side imagemaps

Go beyond text menus and hyperlinks in connecting the user to your content with imagemaps.

HTML 2.0 and HTML 3.2 are the current and pending HTML standards, respectively. Both extend the capabilities of the original HyperText Markup Language. HTML 2.0 provides what is for now the common core of HTML. It is recognized by the overwhelming majority of Web browsers in daily use. Therefore, this chapter is based on the HTML 2.0 standard. Extensions to the 2.0 standard added by Netscape and Microsoft and features of the 3.2 standard are identified as such when they are presented.

Keep in mind that this chapter focuses on the techniques to create Web pages. To use the HTML codes presented in this chapter, you need to place them in a text file to be accessed by your Web provider's HTTP server. The next two chapters introduce you to a few methods of inputting the HTML elements. ■

▶ **See** "Using Internet Assistant," **p. xxx**. (Ch 27)

▶ **See** "Using Netscape Navigator Gold and HotDog to Create Web Pages," **p. xxx**. (Ch 28)

HTML Basics

This section introduces you to the concepts necessary to understand how to create your own WWW pages. Included in this section are an overview of HTML functionality and a description of HTML formatting rules.

How HTML Works: An Overview

HTML is a system that allows users to embed simple markup elements within standard ASCII text documents to provide an integrated visual display. In other words, a document created in any word processor and stored in normal ASCII format can become a Web page with the addition of the appropriate HTML elements. The Web page author can perform tasks such as the following:

- Specify relative text size and flow in a document
- Integrate inline pictures with text
- Create links to other online documents
- Integrate audio and external pictures into documents
- Create interactive forms

HTML supports many other features, including tables, frames, and animation. What makes this exciting is that these features can be used by computers of all kinds, around the world. Someone with a Mac or an Amiga can enjoy Web pages that were created on a PC and stored on a UNIX server. The key to this flexibility is learning how to use HTML elements.

The HTML Element

An HTML command is termed an *element*. HTML elements allow you to modify how a normal text document appears to the user when viewing it in a WWW browser. HTML elements are embedded within the ASCII document and provide instructions to browsers concerning formatting and inclusion of outside elements such as pictures and audio.

An HTML element always appears as a word or phrase placed between less-than and greater-than characters. For example, the following list shows some basic HTML elements:

```
<pre> allows preformatted text to preserve layout
<a> ...  </a> defines hypertext links and targets
<b> ...  </b> makes text bold
<img src="picture.gif"> inserts an image
```

Each of the elements in the preceding list share a common format in that they always begin with the less-than character (<) and always end with the greater-than character (>). The content between the two characters is a command. HTML browsers regard anything contained between < and > as a command.

HTML browsers will ignore any element that does not make sense. That is, any element that doesn't contain something that the browser regards as a valid command, is skipped by the browser. This capability ensures that HTML documents can be understood by even the simplest of browsers by allowing them to skip over elements that they may not be able to handle. If a browser understands an element, it will display text, graphics, and media in predictable and consistent ways, no matter what computer platform the browser happens to be running on.

Elements come in two basic types, non-empty and empty. To explain these two mechanisms, we need to examine how an HTML element is used to handle the problem of displaying text.

Some text needs to be handled as a block. For example, if you wish to make a word or phrase bold, you need to specify both the START and END of the block of text that needs to be bold. In order to do this, an HTML element is placed at the BEGINNING of the word or phrase, and another HTML element is placed at the END of the word or phrase. The text that appears between the two elements is affected by the elements. This is known as a non-empty element.

Empty elements do not require an ending element to complete the command. Empty elements stand by themselves as complete commands. For example, if you wish to insert a picture into a text document, you only need specify a single element to do this. The concept of ending the picture does not make logical sense, thus no ending element is required.

Several elements exist that could be thought of as working as either empty or non-empty. For example, an element that specifies the beginning or ending of a paragraph could stand by itself as an empty element. There is no real necessity for marking both the start and end of a paragraph, only the start. However, a paragraph is a logical block, and thus, could be thought of as non-empty. In order to combat this problem, new releases of HTML support both empty and non-empty versions of some commands (in these cases, this chapter will fall back to the simplest use of the commands, the empty use).

When using non-empty elements, the decision of what to place for the ending element is simple. When a particular element is chosen for the beginning element, the SAME element is chosen for the ending element. The two elements are simply written slightly differently by causing the ending element to have a leading slash character (/) just before the element name. The following example shows this:

<b> **This text will be bold** </b>

In this example, we desire to make text bold. The <b> element does this. Because we need to specify the SIZE of the area to be bold, this is obviously a non-empty element and will require a terminator. Because we choose the <b> element, the terminator for this element is always </b>. This is a universal law in HTML. Elements that terminate a block will be the same element that started the block, with the inclusion of the leading slash.

Elements are case-independent, meaning that elements may be expressed in either uppercase, lowercase, or even mixed-case.

TIP Making all your element commands uppercase can often save time when creating a document by allowing you to quickly separate commands from the text itself.

Many elements contain parameters that help describe what function the command is to perform. For example, an element that specifies that an image be placed inline in the document must specify the NAME of the image. This is considered a *parameter*, or argument. The following example shows just such a command:

<IMG SRC="flowers.gif">

This is an image (<IMG>) element and specifies that an image should be placed in the document. The SRC= portion of the element describes the name of the picture to be loaded. This is a parameter to the <IMG> element.

Parameters are always listed after the element name, and commands with more than one parameter may have the parameters listed in any order.

Notice that the data portion of the parameter (as in "flowers.gif" in the previous example) is placed in double quotes. In most cases HTML will honor data with or without quotes. However, use of quotes is required if you are embedding special characters or spaces within the data.

TIP In general, the best rule to follow is to always place the data portion of any parameter within quotation marks to ensure compatibility with all browsers.

How HTML Deals with Spaces and Carriage Returns

When you enter a document in your word processor, you may have added extra carriage returns and consecutive spaces for formatting purposes. However HTML ignores extra carriage returns and spaces, so when that document is displayed using HTML, carriage returns and consecutive spaces will not appear. This enables the browsers to make appropriate decisions as to how to display the document based on the user's window size and font size. You will undoubtedly find this to be a blessing because it decreases the amount of formatting you are required to do within your document. At the same time, you will find this to be an inconvenience because it is often difficult to get specific formatting that you do wish.

The rules for space and carriage return are simple. More than one consecutive space is simply treated as a single space. Carriage returns are simply removed.

Though these rules are simple, the Web page author needs a way to control horizontal and vertical spacing of text and graphics. In order to overcome the limitations imposed by automatic formatting, HTML provides several elements for specialized formatting, such as <PRE>, <P>, and <BR>. These are described in the next section.

Reserved Words in HTML

Because of the use of the < and > characters to delimit an element, you may begin to suspect that using these characters inside your document may be a problem. In fact, the < and the & characters, are characters that are reserved within HTML. As we already know, < is used to signify the start of an element. The & character is used to access characters that are not available on the keyboard (such as characters with accent marks, and so on). In order to correctly represent the <, >, and & symbols in a document, when you do not intend for them to be interpreted as HTML commands, you must replace them with alternate characters. The following is a partial list of the more frequently used special characters:

Special Character	Description
&lt	Replaces < (less-than sign)
&gt	Replaces > (greater-than sign)
&amp	Replaces & (ampersand) by itself
&quot	Replaces " (double quote)

For example, say you have the following text you need to place in HTML form:

```
The "A & B" new price is <$10.99>
```

The HTML version of this would be:

```
The &quot A &amp B &quot new price is &lt $10.99 &gt
```

While this seems awkward, this solves the problem of using the special characters without confusion and is not too difficult to remember or implement.

> **N O T E** Not all browsers support the entire set of special characters. Additionally, some browsers ignore the first space after a special character. If you experience trouble using a special character, revert to the original character and check the results. To fix spacing problems try adding additional spaces around your special characters. ■

Many other special & strings exist for characters like Ñ and Ü. Table 21.1 is a list of most of the special characters you can display using &.

Part
IV
Ch
21

Table 21.1 Codes for Special Characters

Code	Character
&AElig	Æ
&Aacute	Á
&Acirc	Â
&Agrave	À
&Auml	Ä
&Ccedil	Ç
&Eacute	É
&Ecirc	Ê
&Egrave	È
&Euml	Ë
&Iacute	Í
&Icirc	Î
&Igrave	Ì
&Iuml	Ï
&Ntilde	Ñ
&Oacute	Ó
&Ocirc	Ô
&Ograve	Ò
&Ouml	Ö
&Otilde	Õ
&Oslash	Ø
&Uacture	Ú
&Ucirc	Û
&Ugrave	Ù
&Uuml	Ü

For lowercase letters, substitute the lowercase letter in the &string for the uppercase letter. For example, Ñ is displayed with &ntilde.

File Extensions and HTML

HTML automatically recognizes many types of files by their extension. The following is a list of extensions and their meanings to HTML. Extensions that are more than three letters should have the last letter removed (as in htm versus html) or should use the shortened version (as in .jpg versus .jpeg) when using them on platforms that do not allow longer extensions, such as DOS.

Extension	Description
.html	An HTML document with text and elements
.gif	A .gif formatted color image
.xbm	An X formatted black-and-white image
.xpm	An X formatted color image
.txt	A text file, no changes are made
.text	Same as .txt
.jpeg	A .jpeg compressed color image
.jpg	Same as .jpeg
.mpeg	An .mpeg compressed series of images
.mpg	Same as .mpeg
.au	An .aiff compressed audio file
.wav	A .wave compressed audio file

In addition to these formats, compression schemes such as .z and .gz extensions are supported. In some cases, files encountered with formats unknown to the Web browser are treated as .text files, and shown to the user without modification. Recently released browsers, however, prompt the user to save unrecognized formatted files to disk (for later use) or to configure a viewer on the fly. To get an idea of the file types and extensions recognized by Netscape Navigator 2.0, for example, choose Options, General Preferences and select the Helpers tab. This displays a scrollable window of known file types and what action Netscape will take upon encountering each file you download.

URL Naming Convention

URL (often pronounced Earl) stands for Uniform Resource Locator, and is the mechanism used by the WWW to find a particular page, image, or sound. Basically, you can think of a URL as the address by which you find a page.

There are two types of URLs. The first is an *absolute URL*. This URL is a complete address, and nothing more is needed to find the information. The second type of URL is a *relative URL*. A relative URL is one that only contains the necessary address to find what you want from where you currently are.

Part
IV
Ch
21

For example, your street address might be:

> 1700 S. Stadium Dr.
>
> Bontia, CT 47052

This would be an absolute address, as it is all that is necessary to find you. However, once I'm standing in your front lawn, the relative address of:

> 1800

would be all that is necessary for me to find a house on the next block. I no longer need the street, city, or state because I am already there.

HTML uses a similar mechanism when specifying addresses of where to find documents.

A typical absolute URL consists of the following items:

> service://host:port/path/file.ext

"service://" indicates how the document is being accessed. Some of the more frequently used services include:

Service	Description
file://	Uses FTP to retrieve a local file
ftp://	Uses FTP to retrieve the file
http://	Uses a WWW server to retrieve the file
gopher://	Uses a gopher mechanism
telnet://	Uses Telnet to access a remote machine
news:	Reads remote news

Notice that "news:" differs from the rest of the services in that it does not include the // characters. The // characters are not required on all the services, only on the ones shown with it.

"host" indicates in what machine the information you wish to get resides (for example, your host might be www.somewhere.com).

":port" is optional, and need only be included if the information is not available using the default port specified by the service, like in the case of a proxy server (for example, Gopher uses a default port of 70, HTTP uses 80).

"path" indicates the route from the URL home directory to the desired information (for example, the path to your home directory on machine www.somewhere.com might be usr/people/me).

"file.ext" indicates the actual name of the file you wish to retrieve.

While creating or editing your Web page, you should check it often to make sure of the accuracy of your HTML elements and that your text and graphics are positioned properly. One way to do this is to save your page, launch your Web browser, and use the file:// URL method to specify your page. Your browser will then display a preview of your page.

In many situations, an URL need not have the path and file.ext. In these cases, a default document will be provided from the requested system.

An example of an absolute URL would be

http://www.iquest.net/cw/cookware.html

This accesses the file cookware.html, which exists in the directory cw on the host www.iquest.net. The file will be accessed using the host's WWW server, as indicated by http://.

Relative URLs include only a piece of the full address. Relative URLs are only used inside an HTML document to find other information relative to that document and also stored on the same machine. For example, if the cookware.html file requires a p1.gif picture, the URL can be done one of two ways:

ABSOLUTE:	<img src="**http://www.iquest.net/cw/new.gif**">
RELATIVE:	<img src="new.gif">

The first syntax we understand, as it is absolute. The second relative syntax is a little more confusing. Because we had already retrieved the cookware.html file from the cw directory, the system will then look in the cw directory to satisfy any relative requests.

TROUBLESHOOTING

My URL command isn't working. It refuses to connect to the proper document. Check the URL to see if any / separator characters were accidentally entered as \ characters. Users who are familiar with DOS frequently enter the incorrect slash out of habit.

Why do some of my URLs not work correctly with anchors? Depending on your browser, you may find that relative URLs may not work correctly when using them with anchors (<A>). This may especially be true when using HTML files local to your computer. In cases where a relative URL fails, replace it with an absolute URL to fix the problem.

HTML Document Organization

The HTML standard specifies that a good HTML document should have elements that divide the document into descriptive and functional areas. The functional area is the part that tells the browser how to display the HTML document. The descriptive area is intended for the browser, to assist it in correctly parsing the HTML. In actual practice, however, many people choose to leave these elements out, or misuse the elements. They can get away with this because browsers are forgiving enough to be able to function without all of the formatting information. It is not a good idea to leave out the elements that are there for the browser, since some are intelligent enough to make good use of the information.

The basic format for an HTML document is as follows:

Format	Description
`<DOCTYPE>`	Tells browsers, validation tools, and other software what version of HTML follows; most browsers don't care if this tag is missing
`<HTML>`	Identifies a document as an HTML document rather than a plain text document; most browsers don't care if this is missing
`<HEAD>`	Begins the document head, the primary descriptive area; this tag can be omitted
`<TITLE>`	Defines the document title and is always required
`</TITLE>`	Closes the document title and is always required
`</HEAD>`	Closes the document head; if `<HEAD>` is omitted, this tag can be left out as well
`<BODY>`	Begins the document body, the functional area; not required, and in some cases (when using Frames) it must be left out
`</BODY>`	Closes `<BODY>`
`</HTML>`	Closes the document

The actual commands `<HEAD>` and `<BODY>` will be described in the next section. However, the information placed between `<HEAD>` and `</HEAD>` is used to describe the document to the browser, and does not directly impact the user (usually). The information between the `<BODY>` and `</BODY>` elements includes your actual document information, and all formatting elements used to describe and display that information.

In Chapter 20, "Planning Your Own World Wide Web Home Page," I mentioned that you may want to include a `<META>` tag with a list of keywords so that Web crawlers can index your site. The `<META>` tag goes in the document head. Some Web crawlers look for keywords, others for a description. Here is an example of both:

```
<HEAD>
<META NAME="Keywords" CONTENT="Progressive,Fusion,Bluegrass,Rap">
<META NAME="Description" CONTENT="This page features new releases from
BoyzInDaBoonDoks, the hot new Progressive Fusion Bluegrass Rap group.">
</HEAD>
```

HTML Elements

This section describes the most frequently used HTML elements. These are the elements you will need to create any basic home pages.

Elements that Affect Text Size

The HTML creator has some control over the font size of the text that is displayed to the user. Obviously, this is highly browser-dependent. Most browsers honor these commands, but some (mostly text-only) browsers ignore or change them.

The use of text size commands is for situations where you want to create titles that are larger than the rest of the text. This is used to call attention to, or delineate, text.

The text size commands are all non-empty, meaning that they require terminating elements. The basic format of the element is as follows:

<H?> The text to display </H?>

Where ? is a number one-through-six. <H1> specifies the largest heading size available, <H2> the second largest, and so forth, to <H6>, which is the smallest size (see Fig. 21.1). The actual size of the font is dependent on user's browser. For example, a title and subtitle with regular text might appear like this:

<H1> The title </H1>

<H2> The sub-title </H2>

This is normal text that appears after the subtitle.

FIG. 21.1

This figure shows several different text sizes.

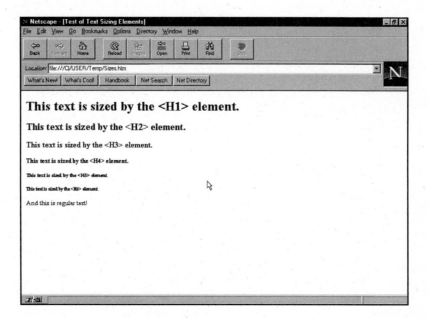

Notice that no text size was needed for the normal text, as the termination element </H6> simply changed the text size back to the default, normal, text size.

Elements that Affect Text Positioning

HTML tends to reorganize the positioning of text in your document, removing all carriage returns and extra spaces. If you want these extra carriage returns and spaces left in your document, how do you achieve it? Better yet, how do you keep HTML from playing with your document's format in the first place?

To achieve this capability, elements exist that force carriage returns and paragraph starts. In addition, formatting commands exist that instruct the HTML system not to modify the text in any way, allowing it to appear exactly as specified. The most common text formatting commands follow.

Break Text Line The <BR> command allows you to force a break (<BR>) into your document at the point of the <BR> command. This is a forced carriage return and will be absolutely honored by the browser. Because <BR> is an empty command, no terminating </BR> is required.

Example:

HTML:	This is an example
Result:	This is
	an example

Paragraph Break The <P> command instructs the browser to begin a new paragraph. This is identical to the <BR> command with the exception that it places two carriage returns in the text. In general, all paragraphs should have a <P> at the beginning or end. This command is an empty command, with no </P> required. However, because paragraphs can be thought of as logical blocks, most HTML systems will honor </P> at the end of a paragraph for consistency.

Example:

HTML:	This is<P>an example
Result:	This is
	an example

Preformatted Text The <PRE> command is useful when you want text to look exactly as you have it specified in the file. <PRE> is a non-empty element that requires a </PRE> to conclude the formatting of the text block. All text appearing between the <PRE> and </PRE> elements is displayed as is, including paragraphs, carriage returns, and spacing. This is the primary recommended method for forcing formatting to be exactly as you desire. However, when you use <PRE>, the text within the <PRE> is displayed in a non-proportional font and is restricted in sizing options.

For example:

HTML:	This is
	some text
	<PRE>

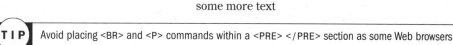

<table>
<tr><td></td><td>This   is
some more text
</PRE></td></tr>
<tr><td>Result:</td><td>This is some text
This   is
some more text</td></tr>
</table>

TIP   Avoid placing <BR> and <P> commands within a <PRE> </PRE> section as some Web browsers ignore them.

Horizontal Line   The <HR> command allows you to place a horizontal ruling across the page. On most browsers, this is accompanied by a blank line above and below the ruling. The <HR> command is useful for delineating sections of text from each other (see Fig. 21.2).

FIG. 21.2
This figure shows elements that affect text formatting.

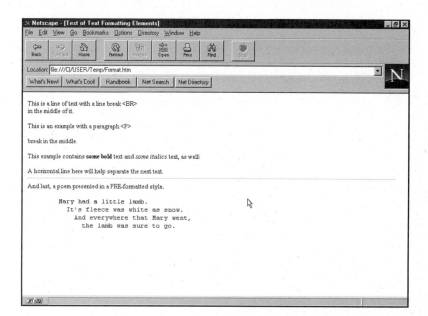

Elements that Affect Text Emphasis

Often, it is desirable to emphasize text by using **bold** or *italic* text. The following physical style elements help create these types of effects.

Bold Text   The <B> command allows you to specify text that is bold. To use this, simply put a <B> in front of the text you wish bold, and a </B> terminator after the text you wish bold. The text between the <B> and </B> will appear bold in the final display. There is an equivalent "logical style" tag pair, <STRONG> and </STRONG>, that usually results in the text being shown bold.

Part
IV

Ch
21

Example:

HTML: This is <B>very bold</B> text

Result: This is **very bold** text

Italicized Text   The <I> command allows you to specify text that is italic. To use this, simply put a <I> in front of the text you wish to be italic, and a </I> terminator after the text you wish to be italic. The text between the <I> and </I> will appear italic in the final display. The equivalent logical style tag pair is <EM> and </EM>.

Example:

HTML: This is <I>some italic</I> text

Result: This is *some italic* text

Underlined Text   The <U> command allows you to specify text that is underlined. This is treated exactly as <B> and <I> are. However, only some of the browsers currently available honor this element. Some translate the element into bold or italic, while others simply ignore the element entirely.

Example:

HTML: This is <U>underlined</U> text

Result: This is underlined text

Elements that Insert Inline Images

One of the advantages of HTML is its ability to place images right into the document itself. This gives HTML documents a magazine look and feel, and greatly enhances the readability and enjoyment of a page.

The <IMG> command allows you to insert an image directly into the document at the point you issue the command. <IMG> is an empty command, and requires no closing </IMG> element.

The general form of the <IMG> command is as follows:

<IMG SRC="filename">

For example, <IMG SRC="flower.gif"> would retrieve the image flower.gif from the CURRENT directory (because it is a relative URL) and will display it in the document. The SRC parameter is not optional, and should specify either an absolute or relative URL.

The <IMG> command has optional parameters that may be used to specify how the image is integrated with the document:

ALIGN

The ALIGN parameter specifies how the image is lined up with neighboring text on the left and right of the image. The three choices are: ALIGN=TOP, ALIGN=MIDDLE, and ALIGN=BOTTOM. Choosing one of these will cause the text to be aligned accordingly.

ALT

The ALT parameter specifies alternate text to be used to replace the image, in the event that the user's browser cannot display images. This is a useful and important parameter because it solves the problem of creating a graphic page that can be used with a non-graphic browser.

Figure 21.3 shows the IMG command, and how various parameters affect the display of the information.

FIG. 21.3

This figure shows the IMG command with ALIGN set to TOP, MIDDLE, and BOTTOM.

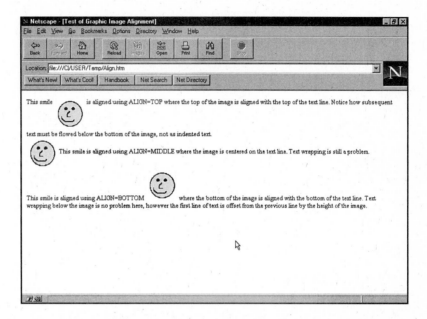

You may display inline images with the .gif, .xbm, and .xpm extensions. Current versions of the browsers do not allow .jpeg or .mpeg files to be displayed as inline images. (For information on other image formats, see the "Elements that Are Anchors and Links" section later in this chapter.)

Elements that Insert Lists and Indentation

HTML provides many mechanisms for achieving lists and indentation. However, the <UL> and <OL> elements are so useful that we will ignore the other methods and stick to these two.

The <UL> and <OL> elements, by themselves, provide indentation. When used with the <LI> element, they provide bulleted or numbered lists.

Indented Lists   The <UL> element specifies that all text beneath the <UL> element is to be moved to the right by one column. You may nest <UL> elements to make further indentations. Each </UL> restores the last section one column to the left. Using <LI> in conjunction with <UL> causes bulleted lists to be created. Figure 21.4 shows a few ways multiple indenting and listing can be used effectively.

Part

IV

Ch

21

Example:

    This is an example of UL

    <UL>This is indented one column

    Same with this line

    <UL>This is indented two columns

    Same with this line

    </UL>Now back to one column

    </UL>Now back to no columns.

There is no difference between <UL> and <OL> when used in this manner.

FIG. 21.4
This figure shows the multiple use of <OL> and <UL> list elements.

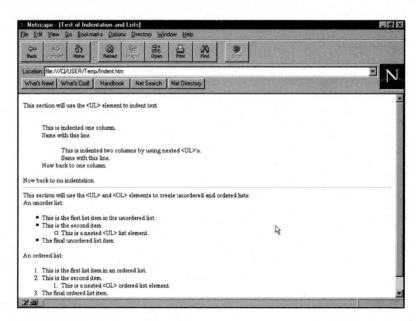

Bulleted and Numbered Lists   Use the list item element, <LI>, to create bulleted lists with <UL> and to create numbered lists with <OL>. To use <LI>, place an <LI> at the beginning of each line to be bulleted or numbered.

Example:

    This is a list of points

    <UL>

    <LI> This is the first point

    <LI> This is the second point

If we are using <OL> instead, our example becomes:

Example:

This is a list of points

<OL>

<LI> This is the first point

<LI> This is the second point

</OL>That's all folks!

The automatic numbering includes the period and a space as part of the formatting.

The HTML system will automatically handle nesting the <UL> and <OL> elements, and will change the bullet style for each nested section (depending on the browser). Furthermore, if a particular indented line runs past the width of the screen, it will automatically be wrapped correctly, and will appear properly indented as it flows to the next line.

Elements that Are Anchors and Links

One of the most important aspects of HTML is its ability to point to other documents and pictures. This is termed an *anchor* by the HTML standard, but also is commonly called a link or hyperlink.

The basic concept of an anchor is to specify a reference to another object. HTML supports references to the following types of items:

- Any other HTML document
- Any non-HTML document (pictures, binary files, text, and so on)
- Any point within the current HTML document

The <A> and </A> anchor elements are used to create a link to another file or position within the current file.

To create an anchor, the <A> and </A> are placed around the item to be anchored. Either text or inline images may be anchored. For example, if the elements are placed around a text string, the string becomes a link. Then, by selecting that string, the link occurs. Likewise, if the anchor is placed around an image, touching the image causes the link to occur. If the link is to another document, the document is immediately retrieved and displayed. If the link is to a position within the current document, that portion of the document is jumped to and displayed. If the link is to a non-HTML file, the file is retrieved and displayed using the browser's external viewer capabilities or stored on the user's drive (as in linking to an executable).

There are no limits to the number of links, nor to where an anchor may be placed. Links may not be nested, of course, but beyond that, links may appear anywhere and point to anything.

To create a link to another document or file, you use the HREF parameter in the <A> command as follows:

```
<A HREF="file.html"> This text is linked </A>
```

In this example, the text, "This text is linked," would appear chooseable to the user. Selecting it will cause the referenced file, file.html, to be retrieved and displayed to the user. In this case, the HTML parameter points to either an absolute or relative URL specifying the document to retrieve. By using an absolute URL, you can point to a local file in another directory on your server.

Another example of an anchor is as follows:

```
<A HREF="http://web.com/p.exe"><IMG SRC="p.gif"></A>
```

In this example, the image p.gif is anchored and selectable by the user. Upon the user selecting the image, the file p.exe is retrieved from the site web.com via that site's http:// web server. In this case, because the file is not an HTML file, it will be sent to the user as a binary file to be stored on its local drive.

You also may anchor into a position within a document. This type of anchor is useful if you have a lengthy page that is broken into distinct text areas or subjects. The anchor essentially acts as an index to the document, allowing you to jump directly to any section that interests you.

To anchor a position, you start by specifying a label. The document you anchor to may be either the current document or any other document on any machine. To set up such a link, specify your anchor as follows:

```
<A HREF="#label1"> Select here to go there </A>
```

Now, to specify the place to jump to when the user selects the preceding string, go to that place in the document and insert a line like this:

```
<A NAME="label1"> This is the section to go to </A>
```

The #label1 in the HREF is used as a label within the current document. The word "label1" may be anything, with the # character specifying the label function (for example, #hello, #ok, and so on, are valid as labels). The NAME= parameter specifies the label itself, which is given without the leading # sign. When the user selects the "Select here to go there" text, he will instantly be placed at the NAME= area of the document, which in this case would be "This is the section to go to." This capability allows you to create a table of contents and other indexes to use for jumping around within a document.

TROUBLESHOOTING

My label isn't working right. How can I fix it? Make sure that you have spelled both the reference to the label, and the label itself, correctly. Since labels are case-sensitive, make sure that capital and lowercase letters appear in the same places for all occurrences of the label.

To better illustrate this capability, here is a more concrete example:

```
<UL>
<LI> Pick <A HREF="#l1">here</A> for the News
```

```
<LI> Pick <A HREF="#12">here</A> for the Weather
</UL>
     .
     .
     .
<A NAME="11">The News</A><P>
Today's news is brought to you by those who care.<P>
Peace is everywhere, there is no news.<P>
     .
     .
     .
<A NAME="12">The Weather</A><P>
```

If you lived in Hawaii, you would know what the weather was!<P>

In this example, a table of contents at the top allows the user to select "here" for News and Weather. The News and Weather items appear further in the file. Note that HREF is used at the source and NAME is used at the destination. The label you use should only appear once in the document, but may be referenced from as many locations as you want.

You may create links to anchors within OTHER documents, by specifying the anchors as follows:

```
<A HREF="file.html#L1">Pick here</A>
```

In this example, the file file.html will be retrieved relative to the current URL, and the label L1 will be immediately jumped to within that document.

Browser Control Elements

Some of the elements exist to give the browser an easier time of understanding your HTML. We list these last because they are not necessary to make HTML work, but should be provided to adhere to the HTML standard.

Header Element   The <HEAD> element specifies the header of your document. This is used to place all items that are not part of the actual document contents. This includes the title and other descriptive items. You may completely ignore using <HEAD> elements, as they are not necessary to produce usable HTML. However, a good HTML programmer will include these. The <HEAD> element is always terminated with the </HEAD> element.

It is important to note that plain text that appears inside a <HEAD> </HEAD> element will appear in your document just as if the header elements were not present.

Title Element   The <TITLE> element is required. Most browsers have an area that shows the title of the current document to the user. Whatever you surround with the <TITLE> element will show up in that area. The proper use of this element is to embed it within a <HEAD> </HEAD> section, as shown in the following:

Example:

<HEAD> <TITLE> Debi's Home Page </TITLE> </HEAD>

Body Element   The <BODY> element specifies the content of your document. This is the meat and potatoes of your page and contains the actual text itself, along with all formatting elements. The <BODY> element is always terminated with the </BODY> element.

Here is an example of a simple, full HTML document.<HEAD><TITLE>My first Page</TITLE></HEAD>

<BODY>

<H1>This is my first page</H1>

<HR>

Hello World!

</BODY>

Combining Elements

Most of the HTML elements may be used together and in combinations. However, some combinations will not necessarily produce the expected result. Furthermore, in some situations, a result obtained in one browser may differ from the result obtained in another browser. The following list of items gives areas to be aware of in creating HTML pages and combining elements:

- In general, browsers will not allow you to have text that is both bold and italic at the same time. Usually the innermost set of elements is the one used for the effect. For example, <B><I>Hi</I></B> will produce an italic "Hi" instead of bold, or bold italic.

- Multiple <P> or <BR> in a row are often treated as carriage returns, with duplicates ignored.

- You may put text next to an image, with the ALIGN parameter allowing you to position the text. However, if the text runs past the end of the screen, it will wrap around to the next line, and will not lay nicely next to the image. Remember that people are using browsers in windows of different sizes. Often, a more effective way is to place the image in one cell of a table and the text in an adjacent cell. The latest versions of most browsers, including Netscape, Internet Explorer, and Mosaic, can handle tables.

- You may put pictures next to pictures. To make the pictures have extra spacing between them, put a <PRE> and </PRE> around the entire set of pictures with the spacing you desire between each picture. Again, a table is often a better way to handle this requirement.

- Pictures next to pictures may not necessarily look the same on all browsers. Some browsers will not load pictures larger than the screen. Other browsers will not honor <PRE> command before images, and will cause multiple images on a line to wrap to the next line if they extend past the end of the line. To avoid this situation it is a good idea to plan images so that they stand little chance of wrapping, or look good if they do wrap.

- Placing large <H1> or other sized text next to a picture is possible if you include the picture within the element. For example, to put <H1> sized text next to a flower picture, use this syntax:

```
<H1><IMG SRC="flower.gif"> Flowers!</H1>
```

If you do not do this, the text will appear on the next line as <H?> elements, which imply blank lines before and after the element.

Creating a Simple Home Page

Now that you have the background and basic tools for creating HTML pages, it's time to write your own page. This section gives an example home page to use as a framework for creating your own page. A personal page has been chosen for this example, but it can easily be transformed into a commercial, educational, or entertainment page just by modifying the content and links.

The following listing shows the page in its entirety. Note that it uses pictures (.gif) and links. You will obviously want to change the pictures to be your own (or omit them if you don't have pictures). The same applies to the links. Use your favorite text editor to enter the page. Then use the Open Local (or Load Local, or Open URL) feature of your particular browser to view your page (see Fig. 21.5).

```
<HEAD><TITLE>My Home Page</TITLE></HEAD>

<BODY>

<H1><IMG SRC="p1.gif" ALIGN=MIDDLE>Welcome to my home page</H1><P>

<HR>

Welcome to my personal home page. This page is an example of a simple but powerful
HTML document.<P>

Please pick one of the following choices:<P>

<UL>

<LI> <A HREF="#bio">A <b>brief</b> biography</A><BR>

<LI> <A HREF="me.gif">A picture of me</A><BR>

<LI> <A HREF="http://web.nexor.co.uk/susi/susi.html">My favorite searcher</A>
   <BR>

<LI> <A HREF="http://www.iquest.net/">My providers homepage</A><BR>

<LI> <A HREF="file://martian.com/">Where I work</A><BR>

</UL>

<HR><HR>

<H2><A NAME="bio">My Biography</A></H2><P>
```

The following is a brief biography/resume. I currently work as a mission specialist for Martian Travel. Please feel free to contact me if you have use for an astro-engineer.<p>

<PRE>

Name: Webster Webmaster   Age: 36

Occupation: Engineer   Edu: PhD

Email: web001@webmaster.web

</PRE>

<hr>

webmastered by web001@webmaster.web

</BODY>

FIG. 21.5

An example of a complete WWW page.

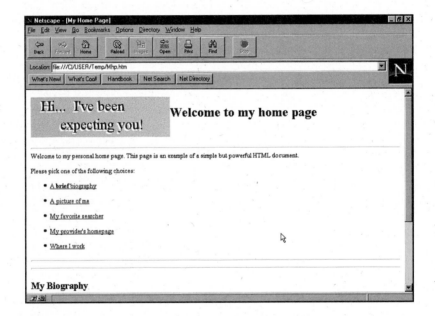

  By studying the HTML used to create "My Home Page," you can see there are many opportunities for typographical errors. Fixing typos, tuning and adjusting your page layout is done using a technique developed well before HTML... trial and error!

Notice that in designing the page, the general design concepts of not crowding too much information on the page and breaking up the information into easily handled sections have been used. Experiment with various formatting techniques until you find the one that best fits your needs and style. For a thorough description of planning a home page, including planning the page's design, see Chapter 20, "Planning Your Own World Wide Web Home Page."

TIP As you explore the WWW, you will see some interesting layouts and techniques on personal and commercial home pages. If you want to know the HTML codes used to produce the effects you see, take a look at the source code! Most graphic Web browsers allow you to "View Source," which opens your default text editor with the Web page's HTML text file shown.

Enhancing Your Page by Creating Interactive Forms

HTML's capability to handle forms allows interaction with the users in ways that simple links cannot manage. The following list offers just a few of the ways to use forms:

- User surveys and polls
- Search criteria for database retrieval
- Button and check box mechanisms for option selection
- Order entry
- Interactive message and newsgroup handling
- Game mechanisms

There are two basic steps to setting up a form system. The first involves creating your form in your HTML document. The second step is to determine the mechanism for retrieving the information. For this step, you can write the mechanism yourself, find an existing method, or have someone write it for you. In this chapter we will explore how to create the form in HTML.

How Forms Are Processed

Before you explore the elements used in the construction of forms, you need to have a basic understanding of how forms are processed.

Forms require the use of a World Wide Web server known as an HTTP daemon. HTTP (HyperText Transfer Protocol) is often referred to as HTTPD because it is a daemon (a background running process). The purpose of the HTTP server is to handle your form when it is submitted. Consider this—once a user has filled in a form, he or she submits it. To *whom* is it submitted? What *happens* to the information? And, *what* type of HTML response is returned to the user?

These questions indicate that there must be some intelligence handling the form information. This intelligence must be able to determine the type of form, be able to handle the incoming data, and produce some type of response for the user.

This is handled by a program or script running on an HTTP server. After a form is filled out, it is submitted to the server indicated in the form's URL. By analyzing the URL, the server hands the form to the appropriate program or script that deals with that form.

Basically, this all means that while forms are extremely useful, they cannot be used unless accompanied by software running on an HTTP server to process that form.

Part
IV

Ch
21

As you learn how to create forms, you will discover the mechanisms by which the server knows how to deal with a form and what options are available. You will also see what options exist for form builders who lack the expertise or time to create their own form handling systems.

The Basic Form Element

As previously discussed, a form is the mechanism for getting information back from a user. A document may contain more than one form, but forms never appear inside other forms. A form contains many elements that describe different aspects of the form. HTML form elements are:

- Radio buttons
- Check boxes
- Lists
- Text-entry areas

A form contains one or more of these elements. There are no limits on the number of elements that may be used. However, there will certainly be a limit to the number of form elements a user will pay attention to, so plan your form with care.

The <FORM> element defines the beginning of a form. Because a form encompasses a block of other elements, the <FORM> element is obviously a non-empty element. Use </FORM> to define the end of the form.

The <FORM> element contains two parameters: the ACTION parameter and the METHOD parameter. An example of a <FORM> element is as follows:

```
<FORM ACTION="url" METHOD="technique">
```

The ACTION parameter specifies a valid relative or absolute URL. The form will be transmitted to the URL specified by ACTION when the form is submitted.

The METHOD specifies the technique used by the server to send the form data to the program specified by the ACTION. There are two basic types of METHODS—GET and POST.

The GET method is the oldest. It is also the default. If you do not specify a method, GET will be used automatically. When a form using the GET method is received by an HTTP server, the form elements are converted into a command line statement and are passed to the program or script specified by the ACTION.

The POST method is newer and more powerful than GET. Because of the limitations of GET, it is recommended to use POST. In fact, most HTML documentation recommends that you change existing GETs into POSTs to remain compatible with future versions of the HTML language and HTTP servers. Instead of passing the form information to the ACTION via the command line, POST submits the form information via standard input (STDIN) on the HTTP server. While this may appear confusing, it does not need to be a crucial decision by you, the form designer. The software you are interfacing to will dictate whether or not the POST or the GET method should be used.

Look now at an example FORM element:

```
<FORM ACTION="http://www.com/cgi-bin/top" METHOD="POST">
```

In this FORM element, you can see that the form data will be sent to the ACTION specified as a server (http://) named www.com. The server will access the program or script named top, which appears in the server's cgi-bin directory. The METHOD indicates that the form will be submitted to the top program using the POST method.

Knowing what to use for an ACTION or METHOD consists of either talking to the staff at your server site or reading the documentation that accompanies your server's form handling software.

The *INPUT* Element

The <INPUT> element is the most-often-used form command because it lets you create many types of controls that allow the user to make choices. Controls include two types of buttons the user may turn on and off, as well as windows into which text can be typed. The <INPUT> element is an empty element, requiring no termination.

The <INPUT> element has many parameters. The most important one is TYPE. The TYPE parameter specifies what kind of control to create, and may be assigned any of the following values:

Value for *TYPE*	Description
"checkbox"	Implements a button that may be toggled either on or off.
"radio"	Allows you to implement a group of buttons where only one of the group may be turned on at any one time.
"text"	Allows the user to enter a line of text.
"password"	Same as Text, but the characters entered by the user are shown as asterisks (or similar, concealing characters).
"reset"	Causes a button to appear that, when selected, resets all the other form elements to their default values.
"submit"	Causes a button to appear that will transmit the form to the URL (Action) when selected.

If no TYPE is specified in the <INPUT> element, TYPE = "text" is assumed by default.

Here is an example of a simple <INPUT> command that implements a check box style button (the NAME parameter is shown for completeness and is discussed next). Remember that this command may only appear between <FORM> and </FORM> elements:

```
<INPUT TYPE="checkbox" NAME="test">
```

Each of the TYPE elements has its own parameters to help further define the element. The next sections show examples of each of the TYPE elements and explains their parameters. Almost all the elements discussed utilize the NAME parameter; therefore, these sections will begin by discussing the NAME parameter first.

Part

IV

Ch

21

Submit and Reset are the only two FORM elements that do not use the NAME parameter.

The *NAME* Parameter   NAME is a required parameter to all INPUT elements except the SUBMIT and RESET elements. Basically, the NAME parameter creates a label that will be associated with the user response. This allows the server that interprets the form to determine which response from the user goes to which form element.

The word you equate to NAME can be any word and never appears to the user in any form. Examples of the NAME parameter and some possible arguments or labels include the following:

```
NAME="user_text"
NAME="variable1"
NAME="variable2"
NAME="their_email_address"
NAME="a"
```

You will see NAME used in the examples of most of the other <INPUT> parameters. Please refer to these as working examples of the NAME parameter.

 It's better to use names that are short but descriptive, as this reduces the amount of data transmitted. Descriptive names aid in locating the name when you need to modify the form.

Creating Checkbox *TYPE* Input Elements   The check box TYPE allows you to create a button that the user can turn on or off. It is like a toggle switch. This allows you to ask a simple question for which you get one of two possible responses. You may have any number of check boxes in your document. Each is independent of all the others. When a form is submitted, only the boxes that are checked by the user are actually submitted. The server always assumes all the other boxes are unchecked. If you want to have a check box checked by default (so that when the user initially sees it, it is already checked), place the parameter CHECKED in the element. The CHECKED parameter functions like a switch and requires no data or argument following the parameter.

```
<INPUT TYPE="checkbox" NAME="name" VALUE="value" CHECKED>
```

Checkbox elements may also contain a VALUE parameter. This allows you to set a string that is sent for the *on* state. If no VALUE parameter appears, the default of on is selected. VALUE is used in conjunction with NAME, which is set to a symbolic label equated to the VALUE. For example, if NAME = "setting" and VALUE = "on", then when the user selects that check box, the server will be sent "setting = on".

If more than one check box uses the same NAME, each one selected by the user will be sent to the server. For example, if one check box has NAME = "pet" and VALUE = "dog" and another check box has NAME = "pet" and VALUE = "cat" and both have been selected, both "pet = dog" and "pet = cat" will be sent to the server.

The following are some examples of check boxes (remember, this must appear within a <FORM> and </FORM> element). See "Creating a Complete Form," later in this chapter.

```
<INPUT TYPE="CHECKBOX" NAME="brochure" VALUE="yes" CHECKED> Would you like a
   brochure?
```

This example will place a check box next to the string "Would you like a brochure?".

By default, the check box will be checked (CHECKED). When the information is sent to the server, it will be sent "brochure = yes" (because of NAME and VALUE).

The following is a more complex example:

```
Select the type of pet you have:<P>
<INPUT TYPE="checkbox" NAME="pet" VALUE="dog" > Dog<P>
<INPUT TYPE="checkbox" NAME="pet" VALUE="cat" > Cat<P>
<INPUT TYPE="checkbox" NAME="pet" VALUE="fish" > Fish<P>
<INPUT TYPE="checkbox" NAME="pet" VALUE="horse" > Horse<P>
<INPUT TYPE="checkbox" NAME="pet" VALUE="bird" > Bird<P>
<INPUT TYPE="checkbox" NAME="pet" VALUE="snake" > Snake<P>
```

This set would produce output as shown in Figure 21.6.

FIG. 21.6

Any or all of these check boxes may be checked by the user at once.

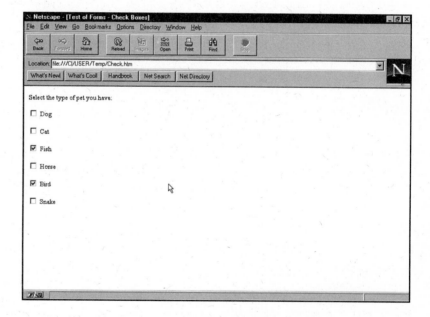

As you can see, following the text "Select the type of pet you have:," six check boxes are displayed. Each box is labeled by a type of pet, allowing users to indicate whether or not they have that type of pet. Any of the boxes may be marked by a user. For each box that is marked, a string consisting of the NAME and the VALUE will be sent to the server. For example, if the user selected Dog and Horse, "pet = dog" and "pet = horse" will be sent to the server.

Because each check box is unique, you should never have two check boxes with the same NAME and VALUE parameter. It is okay to have check boxes with the same NAME and different VALUEs, or the same VALUE and different NAMEs.

Creating Radio *TYPE* Input Elements   The radio TYPE allows you to create a button that acts just like check box in that you can turn it on and off. However, radio buttons differ in that, within a group of buttons, only one may be selected at a given time. Selecting a button in a group will deselect the button that is currently picked and turn on the newly selected button. This is useful when you want the user to select only one choice from a series of choices.

```
<INPUT TYPE="radio" NAME="name" VALUE="value" CHECKED>
```

N O T E   To allow the user to make more than one selection from a group of choices, use "checkbox" as the argument for the TYPE parameter. To force the user to only select one option, use "radio" as the argument. ■

Like check boxes, radio buttons have a NAME parameter that allows you to label the box for the server. Each radio button that has the same NAME is in the same group. Out of that group, only one button may be activated at any time.

The VALUE parameter acts just as it does for CHECKBOX and specifies a unique word that is sent with the form when that particular button is activated.

If one of the buttons in a group has the CHECKED parameter, it is automatically depressed when the form is first displayed to the user. This allows you to select a default button in a group.

The following are examples of radio buttons (this must appear within a <FORM> and </FORM> element).

```
What type of credit card are you using?<P>
<INPUT TYPE="radio" NAME="credit" VALUE="visa" CHECKED> Visa<P>
<INPUT TYPE="radio" NAME="credit" VALUE="mc" > Mastercard<P>
<INPUT TYPE="radio" NAME="credit" VALUE="discover" > Discover<P>
<INPUT TYPE="radio" NAME="credit" VALUE="diners" > Diners Club<P>
<INPUT TYPE="radio" NAME="credit" VALUE="ae" > American Express<P>
```

This set would produce output as shown in Figure 21.7.

This example will display five radio buttons below the string "What type of credit card are you using?" Each of the radio buttons belongs to the group "credit."

The first button, Visa, is selected by default (CHECKED). If the user were to select the Discover choice, as an example, when the form is submitted the server will receive "credit = discover" (NAME = VALUE) for this group of buttons.

 TIP   Radio buttons that are in the same group do not necessarily need to be grouped together on the screen as well.

Creating Text *TYPE* Input Elements   It is frequently useful to accept single lines of free-form input from a user. This can be used to take e-mail addresses, phone numbers, credit card numbers, comments, or any other simple typed information.

FIG. 21.7
An example of HTML radio buttons. Only one radio button may be selected at any time.

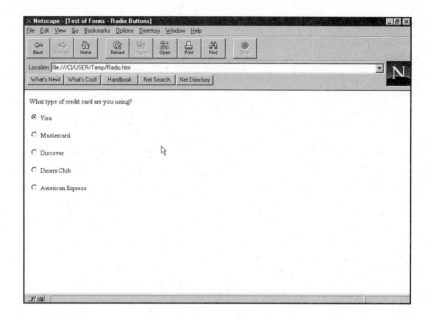

```
<INPUT TYPE="type" NAME="name" VALUE="value" SIZE=40 MAXLENGTH=100>
```

Like most of the other <INPUT> parameters, the text TYPE is associated with a NAME field that allows you to label it for the server. Place a symbolic name for this text box in the NAME parameter. For example, setting NAME="email" will send the server "email =", followed by whatever text the user enters in that field.

The VALUE parameter will set a default string to appear in the box when it is first displayed. If no VALUE parameter is encountered, the box will be empty when first displayed.

A SIZE parameter allows you to set the size of the displayed text box. Setting SIZE="40", for example, will set a text window 40 characters wide. If text is typed that is longer than 40 characters, it will scroll correctly. Many browsers support multiple lines of text and allow you to set SIZE = width, height to specify more than one line. For example, setting SIZE = "40,10" sets a text window 40 characters wide by 10 lines high. Because HTML also supports a multiple line TEXTAREA command, it is recommended that you do not use the height feature of SIZE within text itself.

If you do not include the SIZE parameter, the text window will automatically be set to 20 characters.

 T I P
Only the physical size of the window on-screen is affected by SIZE, not the amount of text that can be typed into the window by the user.

Part
IV

Ch
21

TROUBLESHOOTING

I created a text area of a specific *SIZE*, but my characters don't fit. Different browsers handle SIZE differently. Some equate it to number of characters, others to different width rules. As a good practice, do not make SIZE too large as it may not fit on all users' screens. A normal size of between 10 and 40 characters will work fine in most cases.

A MAXLENGTH parameter is included to set a maximum number of characters that may be entered for text fields. If no MAXLENGTH parameter appears, the text field is of an unlimited length. For example, if MAXLENGTH = "100", only 100 characters may be typed into the text window.

The following are some examples of text windows. (As mentioned in "Creating a Complete Form," later in this chapter, this must appear within a <FORM> and </FORM> element.)

```
Please enter your E-MAIL address: <INPUT TYPE="text" NAME="email">
```

This line will place a text entry window next to the string "Please enter your E-MAIL address:."

Whatever the user enters will be transmitted to the server as "email=" followed by his or her typed text.

For example, if the user types debi@high.tech.com, the server will receive "email=debi@high.tech.com."

The following is another example:

```
Enter your first name: <INPUT TYPE="text" NAME="first" MAXLENGTH=20> <P>
Enter your last name: <INPUT TYPE="text" NAME="last" MAXLENGTH=20><P>
Enter your address: <INPUT TYPE="text" NAME="address" SIZE=80><P>
Comments: <INPUT TYPE="text" NAME="comments" VALUE="Please send info"_
SIZE=80><P>
```

This set would produce output as shown in Figure 21.8.

This example displays four lines. The first line allows the user to enter his or her first name. The first name is limited to 20 characters of typed text (MAXLENGTH). When the user submits the form, "first=" will be sent to the server immediately followed by the information he or she typed.

The second line repeats the actions of the first line, but for the last name of the user. Again, the user is limited to entering a maximum of 20 characters.

The third line allows the user to enter an address. The address window is 80 characters wide (SIZE=80), but the user may type unlimited amounts of information into that window (by the lack of a MAXLENGTH statement).

The final line allows the user to enter a comment. The size of the window is again set to 80 (SIZE=80). The window will initially display to the user with the string "Please send info" already in it as a default string (VALUE=). The user may change the string by typing in the window.

FIG. 21.8

A single line text area in an HTML form can be typed into by the user.

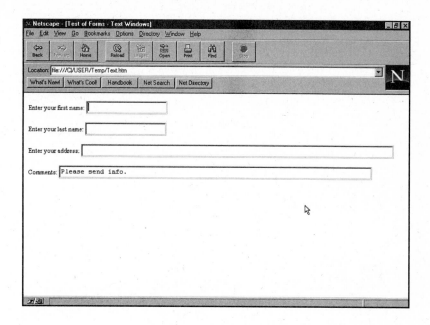

TIP MAXLENGTH is useful when using forms with databases, to ensure that the information typed by the user is not longer than the maximum size allowed by your particular database.

Creating Password *TYPE* Input Elements You may want to accept information from a user, but not have it appear on the user's screen. This allows you to collect passwords, credit-card numbers, and other personal data while keeping the user assured that prying eyes will not see what is entered. The PASSWORD type allows this action. While it does not encrypt the data in any way, it does keep the data from appearing physically on the user's screen as it is typed.

```
<INPUT TYPE="password" NAME="name" VALUE="value" SIZE=40 MAXLENGTH=100>
```

The NAME, VALUE, SIZE, and MAXLENGTH parameters all work exactly as they do for text.

The following is an example of a password window (it must appear within a <FORM> and </FORM> element).

```
Please enter your account password: <INPUT TYPE="password" NAME="pass"_
    SIZE=10>
```

This line will display a text window after the string "Please enter your account password."

The window will be sized to display only 10 characters (SIZE=10), but will accept any length string entered (by the lack of a MAXLENGTH statement). When the typed information is sent to the server, "pass = " is transmitted followed by the user's typed text (NAME =). The user will only see asterisks, or a similar character (depending on the browser) regardless of what they type.

Part

IV

Ch

21

Creating a Button to Reset a Form   HTML has the capability to define a single button that can reset a form. The form is reset to all its default values as specified by the various parameters of each of the form's elements.

```
<INPUT TYPE="reset" VALUE="value">
```

The RESET type button does not have a corresponding NAME= parameter, because it is never transmitted to the server. RESET is handled in the user's browser, automatically, as the user depresses the button.

The only parameter used by RESET is the VALUE= parameter. Whatever you set VALUE= to will be used as the label for that button.

The following is an example of the RESET button (this must appear within a <FORM> and </FORM> element).

```
<INPUT TYPE="reset" VALUE=" Push here to reset this form ">
```

This line will result in a button being created that has the string "Push here to reset this form" in it. When the user pushes the button, all text fields will be set to their default values. Text fields with no default value specified will be cleared. Check boxes and radio buttons with CHECKED set in their definitions will be automatically turned on, with the non-CHECKED definitions automatically turned off. TEXT and PASSWORD areas with VALUE= statements will be set to the string specified by VALUE=, or will be blanked if no VALUE= statement appears.

Creating a Button to Send a Form   The INPUT element TYPE="submit" is used to create the button that submits the form to the server.

```
<INPUT TYPE="submit" VALUE="value">
```

N O T E   Every form you create must have a SUBMIT button definition or the data will never be processed! ■

When this button is selected, the form and its current contents will be sent to the server specified by the ACTION of the <FORM> line, using the <FORM> line's METHOD.

The SUBMIT type button does not have a corresponding NAME= parameter, because the button itself is never transmitted to the server. Instead, SUBMIT causes the entire form to be transmitted when the user depresses the button.

The only parameter used by SUBMIT is the VALUE= parameter. Whatever you set VALUE= to will be used as the label for that button.

The following is an example of the SUBMIT button (it must appear within a <FORM> and </FORM> element as mentioned in "Creating a Complete Form" later in this chapter):

```
<INPUT TYPE="submit" VALUE=" Push here to send this form ">
```

This line will result in a button being created that has the string "Push here to send this form" in it. When the user pushes the button, all filled in fields will be sent to the server specified in the <FORM> statement. Fields and buttons that are not set to anything will not be transmitted.

Using the *TEXTAREA* Element

Often, it is useful to be able to accept a block of text from the user. Having this ability allows users to cut and paste entire documents into HTML pages. This, in turn, allows large quantities of information to be passed back and forth. It can save both HTML-page room, as well as database room, by combining what would be many TEXT elements into a single TEXTAREA.

```
<TEXTAREA NAME="NAME" ROWS=10 COLS=40> </TEXTAREA>
```

The TEXTAREA element is not a type of the <INPUT> command, but instead it is its own element just as <INPUT> is.

Like the <INPUT> types, <TEXTAREA> is associated with a NAME field that allows you to label it for the server. Place a symbolic name for this text box in the NAME parameter. For example, setting NAME = "body" will send the server "body = " followed by whatever the user types in for that TEXTAREA.

The <TEXTAREA> element also has ROWS and COLS parameters. These are used to specify the size of the TEXTAREA window that is displayed to the user. This does not limit the user in how much he or she can type, but merely limits the size of the window displayed to the user. As the user types and overfills the window, the window should automatically grow sliders to aid in moving the view for the user.

To use ROWS and COLS, simply set them equal to the number of rows and columns you want in your TEXTAREA. For example, setting ROWS=10 and COLUMNS=80 sets a field 10 characters high and 80 lines wide.

The TEXTAREA element is a non-empty element. This means that it must have a </TEXTAREA> terminator. Anything between the <TEXTAREA> and </TEXTAREA> elements will appear as default information inside the text area. If nothing appears between the two elements, no default information will be placed in the text area when it appears to the user.

The following is an example of the TEXTAREA element (remember, this must appear within a <FORM> and </FORM> element; see "Creating a Complete Form," later in this chapter):

```
<TEXTAREA NAME="resume" ROWS=8 COLS=80></TEXTAREA>
```

In this example, a text area is created that is eight lines high by 80 characters wide. The user may type any amount of information into this area. The area contains no default information.

The following is another example:

```
Please enter any special instructions:<P>
<TEXTAREA NAME="instructions" ROWS=5 COLS=40>No special instructions</TEXTAREA>
```

This set would produce output as shown in Figure 21.9.

FIG. 21.9
As shown here, the
TEXTAREA form
element accepts more
than one line of typed
text.

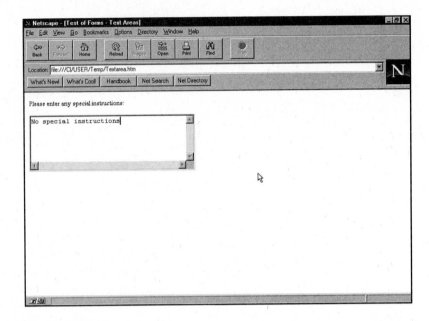

TROUBLESHOOTING

**Some browsers will not deal with the default text specified between the <TEXTAREA> and
</TEXTAREA> elements. When displayed by these browsers, the text will appear outside of the
text area.** One solution is to try the VALUE= parameter within the <TEXTAREA> element. Some
browsers recognize this as an alternative mechanism for specification of default text. It is possible that
your browser may not accept either mechanism, in which case there is no way to have default text.

This example places a text window five lines high by 40 characters wide. It is named "instructions" and will be passed to the server as "instructions=" followed by whatever text the user
enters. The first time the field is presented to the user, it has the default contents of "No special
instructions."

Using the *SELECT* Element to Create a List

HTML form handling allows you to create several types of lists. Each list presents one or more
items to the user and may have a single item or several items selected from the list.

```
<SELECT NAME="LIST">    </SELECT>
```

When lists are displayed, they appear either in an inset window, or in a pop-up window. Inset windows that contain a list larger than the window itself will have a slider on the side that allows you to access other items in the list. Where check boxes are useful for small lists, the <SELECT> element allows lists of any size to be created.

Lists are bounded by the <SELECT> and </SELECT> elements. Only two things may appear between these two elements. The first is any free-form text; and the second is the <OPTION> element. No other HTML elements may appear between the <SELECT> and </SELECT> elements.

The <SELECT> element starts a list. The NAME parameter must be associated with the <SELECT> element and allows you to label the list for the server. Place a symbolic name for this text box in the NAME parameter. For example, setting <SELECT NAME="list1"> will send the server "list1=" followed by the name, for each item selected in the list. For example, if the list contains "Dog," "Cat" and "Mouse," and "Dog" and "Cat" are selected, both "list=Dog" and "list=Cat" will be sent to the server. The specification of "Dog," "Cat," and "Mouse" are done using the <OPTION> element that is discussed later in this section.

The <SELECT> element has an optional SIZE parameter. If the SIZE parameter is missing, it is assumed to be equated to the value 1. When size is set to 1, the list is as a pop-up window where you may select only one of the items in the list. This use is similar to radio-buttons, where only one of a group may be selected.

When the SIZE parameter is larger than 1, it is presented as an inset window containing a list of selectable items. The number that is assigned to SIZE sets the maximum number of items that are in the inset window at one time. For example, if the list is set to SIZE=5, 5 items from the list are visible at one time. Items not visible in the list may be accessed by using the slider that appears to the right of the list.

Another optional parameter of the <SELECT> element is the MULTIPLE parameter. MULTIPLE has no value associated with it. Using MULTIPLE forces the list to be displayed in an inset, scrollable window. Additionally, when MULTIPLE is present, the user may select more than one item from the list. This is done by holding down the Ctrl key while selecting additional items in the list.

The <OPTION> element appears between the <SELECT> and </SELECT> elements. There is one <OPTION> for every item that may be picked in the list. <OPTION> has one parameter associated with it—SELECTED.

If SELECTED is set, the item associated with that <OPTION> is automatically selected by default. If MULTIPLE is specified in the <SELECT> element, more than one SELECTED parameter may appear.

The following is an example of the SELECT element (this must appear within a <FORM> and </FORM> element):

```
Please select your favorite ice cream toppings:<P>
<SELECT NAME="list1" SIZE=3 MULTIPLE>
<OPTION SELECTED> Chocolate
<OPTION> Fruit Preserves
<OPTION> Nuts
<OPTION> Butterscotch
<OPTION> Candy sprinkles
</SELECT>
```

Part
IV

Ch
21

This set would produce output as shown in Figure 21.10.

FIG. 21.10
The inset list window shows three items; the slider allows the user to select the options that are hidden.

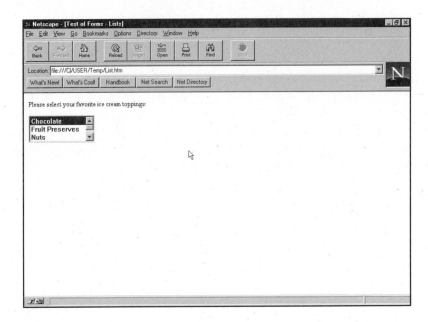

In this example, a select box is created that is large enough for three items. The rest of the items will be accessible by scrolling (SIZE = 3). The select area will allow the user to select more than one item (MULTIPLE), and each item selected will be transmitted to the server using "list1 = " followed by the item that was selected. The select box in this example has five items in it that may be chosen by the user.

Chocolate is selected by default (as almost everybody loves chocolate), but may be de-selected by the user if desired.

N O T E Remember that no HTML element should appear between the <SELECT> and </SELECT> elements except the <OPTION> element.

Creating a Complete Form

Now that you have examined the fundamental elements necessary to complete a form, let's put them all together and see how a form actually looks.

For this example, you will create an order form that allows the user to purchase a new car (see Fig. 21.11). The order form will begin by accepting free format text from the user, for a name, phone number, and address. The form displays a series of radio buttons that allow the user to pick the color of the car. Beneath the radio buttons is an inset list of options for the car.

The user may pick one option from the list, or hold down the CTRL key while picking from the list to select multiple options. After the inset box, a series of check boxes allows the user to select how they want to be responded to. Finally, the SUBMIT button is displayed, which allows the user to actually send the form to the HTTP server.

```
<FORM ACTION="http://www.car.com/cgi-bin/sellcar" METHOD=POST>
Enter your name:  <INPUT TYPE="text" NAME="name" SIZE=40> and phone:  <INPUT
    TYPE="text" NAME="phone" SIZE=20><P>
Enter your address: <TEXTAREA NAME="address" ROWS=5 COLS=50>Put your address
    here</TEXTAREA><P>
Choose a color for your car<P>
<INPUT TYPE="radio" NAME="color" VALUE="red" CHECKED> Red
<INPUT TYPE="radio" NAME="color" VALUE="white" > White
<INPUT TYPE="radio" NAME="color" VALUE="blue" > Blue
<INPUT TYPE="radio" NAME="color" VALUE="black" > Black
<INPUT TYPE="radio" NAME="color" VALUE="cream" > Cream<P>
Select your car options:
<SELECT NAME="options" MULTIPLE SIZE=4>
<OPTION> Bucket Seats
<OPTION> Sport Styling
<OPTION> AM/FM Radio
<OPTION> CD Player
<OPTION> Turbo charged engine
<OPTION> Tinted Windows
</SELECT> <P>
Select what you want us to do now:<P>
<INPUT TYPE="checkbox" NAME="dispose" VALUE="mail"> Send information about my
    choices<BR>
<INPUT TYPE="checkbox" NAME="dispose" VALUE="sale"> Have a salesperson call<BR>
<INPUT TYPE="checkbox" NAME="dispose" VALUE="make"> Make me a car and call me
    when it's done<P>
<INPUT TYPE="submit" VALUE=" Press this button to submit your form ">
</FORM>
```

TROUBLESHOOTING

I created my forms, but everything appears to be a text area, even my radio buttons and check boxes. Some browsers are not case-independent in the button type. Therefore, make sure to use "radio," "checkbox," and "text" when defining these buttons. Use of uppercase may not work in many browsers for these words.

This example begins by opening the form with a <FORM> statement. In this statement, you specify that the form is to use the POST method of transferring data and that it is to send any filled out form to the URL **http://www.car.com/cgi-bin/sell car** as specified by the ACTION statement.

Next, you accept the user's name, address, and phone number using TEXT windows. The address is entered into a multiple-line TEXTAREA, while the phone numbers and user's name are each single-line text windows.

FIG. 21.11

The new car order form combines most of the FORM elements.

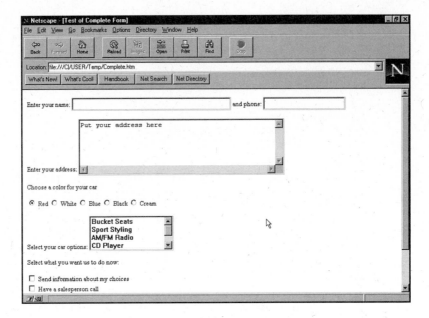

Next, the user is allowed to select the color of his or her car as one of five possible choices. Note that you have defaulted the color to Red, and that only one color can be picked from the list because it is a RADIO type group of buttons.

Beneath the car color choices is a select box with various options for the car. The user may select any number of these options because the <SELECT> element has the MULTIPLE parameter within it.

Toward the end of the form, the user can select up to three METHODs of follow-up. They may check any or all of the three CHECKBOX elements.

Finally, the last button allows the user to send the form to the server specified (car.com) by the ACTION parameter of the <FORM> element.

Understanding How Forms Are Submitted

Anybody can design a form. The resulting form will be usable, in that it can be filled out and submitted. However, at this point you must ask, "submitted where?" For a form to be useful, it must be submitted to some place that will know what to do with the data in the form. Because each and every form is different, this often requires custom solutions.

There are two problems associated with determining how a form is handled. The first problem is where to send the form data. In other words, what to set the ACTION parameter of the <FORM> element to.

Second, you must determine what you want to do with the data. You may want the data to be e-mailed to you. Or, you may want the data appended to a file or integrated into a database. The database can be designed to provide instant feedback to the user so that immediately after the user submits the form, the entire HTML system is modified to incorporate the user's information. There are an infinite number of things you can do with form data depending on your needs.

Interestingly enough, both of these problems have the same solutions. If you can write a shell script, in PERL perhaps, or a fairly simple program in C or similar language, you probably have enough skill to write your own form-handling software. For people who do not have the programming or script skills, or simply lack the time, off-the-shelf solutions already exist for many form needs.

Before you see how a solution can be implemented, you need a better understanding of exactly how a server deals with a form. To do this, let's examine a simple example. In this example, you will play the role of the user. You have just filled out a form and you hit the SUBMIT button. At that moment, the user's browser software accumulates the information contained in the form and transmits it to the URL pointed to by the ACTION parameter of the <FORM> element.

So far so good. Your information is somewhere between you and the server that is going to handle it. When the information reaches the server, it is examined by the server. The URL must direct the server where to find a program that will handle your form data. For example, the following may have been your ACTION URL:

```
<FORM ACTION="http://www.com/cgi-bin/remailer?bob@www.com" METHOD="POST">
```

In this FORM element, you see a valid URL for the ACTION that points to a server (http://) named www.com. The server finds a program named remailer in the cgi-bin directory (more on cgi-bin later). The METHOD is POST so the server will communicate with the remailer program using that method. If there is information to be passed to the remailer program on the command line, it is separated by the question mark character (?) from the program name itself.

So, back to your data. As your data enters the server (www.com), the server examines the URL information and (in this example) invokes the remailer program. It hands the string bob@www.com on the command line to the remailer program and also transmits the contents of your filled-out form to the remailer program. The transmission occurs on the command line for GET methods and through standard input for POST methods.

The server's software (remailer, in this case) examines and handles the form information and formats a response for you, the user. The response is sent back to you via the server and arrives on your screen.

So, we can again see the two basic problems. First, where do you send your data? Second, what to do with it?

The simplest way to handle a form is to have all the submitted forms e-mailed to a single destination where they can be examined at will. This is known as *form remailing*, and many server sites already provide some type of form remailing services. Commercial form remailers typically involve a small monthly charge to pay for the service of forwarding your e-mailed forms. Form remailers require you to provide a single e-mail address to send the contents of all forms. Remailers then take all incoming forms, format them into readable responses, and send the forms to you. This method is easiest because it is usable even if you don't have access to a server site. This means that you can run pages out of a directory using file://, and still take advantage of form-handling capabilities.

If you have access to a server site and can design your own software or scripts, you can easily implement your own form-handling program. It is beyond the scope of this chapter to provide details on how to construct server form-handling software, as that subject would be a book in itself. However, the methods are simple enough that anyone with about a moderate level of experience in writing scripts should be able to implement simple form-handling programs.

Another solution involves finding archives of existing software. Many form-handling systems have been placed in the public domain on the Internet. These often may be used outright or modified slightly to accommodate any special needs. However, use of preexisting software again requires that you have access to a server on which to implement it.

Finally, many consultants and service bureaus exist that are more than happy to implement custom-designed form solutions. These groups will write your software as well as help you find a cost-effective server site on which to place it.

A Brief Look at *cgi-bin*

At the end of the last section, you saw an example of the use of cgi-bin in what appeared to be a path. Here is the line again, for your reference:

```
<FORM ACTION="http://www.com/cgi-bin/remailer?bob@www.com" METHOD="POST">
```

While the cgi-bin looks like a path, in effect it is a special word recognized by the server (in this example, www.com). CGI (Common Gateway Interface) is a special mechanism for interfacing Web servers with programs, allowing them to handle form and other input. cgi-bin programs may be pointed to from any link or form. Links pass all information to the form on the command line, as if a GET were issued. Forms pass information by GET or POST METHOD.

When a server sees an URL coming across that contains the cgi-bin directory, it knows to call the program referenced by the URL and hand it the data in the URL and form (if a form is present). It also knows to expect a response from the cgi-bin program that it sends back to the user.

Anytime a browser submits a form to a server, it expects a valid HTML response from the server. If no response is received in a reasonable period of time (two to three minutes in most browsers), the browser returns an error. All `cgi-bin` programs must return some form of HTML response to the user via the server. This is accomplished by the `cgi-bin` program's writing the desired response, as valid HTML, to standard output (STDOUT). The server receives the output and sends it back to the user's browser (in the form of valid HTML).

Enhancing Your Pages with Tables

If you've used a word processor, you know how much tables can do to improve the appearance, organization, and readability of a document. One of the first improvements made by Netscape that attracted widespread attention was the addition of tables to documents on the Web.

Tables in HTML are incredibly useful. Of course, the most basic use is simply creating tabular layouts of material on a page. But you can also solve the problem of keeping images and text side by side with a table. You can group data, format information, and solve many other presentation problems.

The HTML 2.0 standard did not include table elements; these were at first a Netscape enhancement. Eventually other browsers (Internet Explorer, NCSA Mosaic) also added tables to their repertoire. Tables are now part of the HTML 3.2 standard. Current plans of the W3C are to add the ability to do math within tables to HTML 4.0.

As you read through this section and plan your own Web pages, remember the millions of Web surfers who will not be able to see your tables. Their percentage of the total market may be small, but they still represent a huge number of potential customers. Plan an alternate page for them, on which you provide the same information using lists or preformatted text. Place a link to this page on the page with your table. A nice touch would be a caption such as, "Can't see the table? Click here for alternate page."

In this section, you'll learn how to put together an attractive table for basic purposes, how to spiff it up with heading styles and color, and how to put tables and images within tables.

Creating a Basic Table

Figure 21.12 is a basic, if not terribly impressive, table. The HTML source for this table is in Listing 21.1. After you learn how this little table was created, using just four HTML elements, we'll go on to improve it substantially.

You can see that the source code has a simple structure to it. Each row of the table is enclosed between a pair of <TR> tags, and each cell in each row is defined by a pair of <TD> tags. Read on to learn the rest!

Part
IV
Ch
21

FIG. 21.12

This table shows the starting point for creating tabular layouts on the Web.

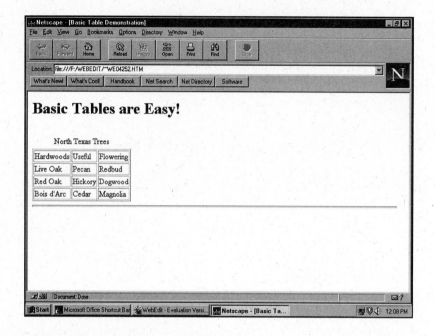

Listing 21.1   Source Code for Figure 21.12

```
<!DOCTYPE HTML PUBLIC "-//W3C//DTD HTML 3.0//EN">
<!TABLDEM1.HTM>
<HTML>
<HEAD>
<TITLE>Basic Table Demonstration</TITLE>
</HEAD>
<BODY>
<H1>Basic Tables are Easy!</H1>
<BR>
<TABLE BORDER=1>
<CAPTION ALIGN=top>
North Texas Trees</CAPTION>
     <TR>
          <TD> Hardwoods</TD>
               <TD> Useful</TD>
               <TD> Flowering</TD>
     </TR>
     <TR>
          <TD> Live Oak</TD>
          <TD> Pecan</TD>
          <TD> Redbud</TD>
     </TR>
     <TR>
          <TD>Red Oak</TD>
          <TD>Hickory</TD>
          <TD>Dogwood</TD>
     </TR>
     <TR>
```

```
                    <TD>Bois d'Arc</TD>
                    <TD>Cedar</TD>
                    <TD>Magnolia</TD>
         </TR>
  </TABLE>
  <HR>
  </BODY>
  </HTML>
```

The *TABLE* Element　　The first tag in building a table is the `<TABLE>` tag. This is a non-empty tag, or container, with several attributes that may be set to better format the resulting table.

`<TABLE BORDER=1> </TABLE>`

In the case of our simple table, we used only the BORDER attribute, to place a border around the table and around the individual cells. The number ("=1") can be set as desired to make the table look more or less substantial. You can set `BORDER=0` to eliminate the border lines, but the results are unpredictable. If you want a table without borders, just leave out the BORDER attribute.

BORDER is in the HTML 3.2 standard. However, only Netscape supports the numerical setting at this time. Internet Explorer 2.0 will turn borders on or off but sets its own width. NCSA Mosaic does not support BORDER or any other attributes for TABLE.

The *CAPTION* Element　　This is an optional element, used simply to tell people what the content of the table might be. A table works fine without it.

　　`<CAPTION ALIGN=top>` North Texas Trees `</CAPTION>`

`<CAPTION>` is another container and has just one attribute, ALIGN. You can use the attribute to place the caption at either the top or at the bottom of the table. The default is to place the caption at the top of the table, so if ALIGN had not been specified here, the result would have been exactly the same. On the other hand, if you leave CAPTION out, there is no caption.

The *TR* and *TD* Elements　　These are the heart of what makes tables work. Each row of the table is "built" from data elements, which are what fill the cells. You can have as many rows as you like, but each row must have the same number of cells. If you don't define enough in a row, or if you define more in one row than in the others, the browser will adjust by adding cells to keep things all square.

```
<TR>
<TD> Hardwoods</TD>
<TD> Useful</TD>
<TD> Flowering</TD>
</TR>
```

Both `<TR>` ("Table Row") and `<TD>` ("Table Data") are containers. They do have attributes that can be set, but none were used for this example.

Every cell in this table is filled. If you leave a cell empty, most browsers will cause that cell to look "different" from the rest. You can put a non-breaking space in a cell to prevent this by typing ` ` in the TD container, like this: `<TD> </TD>`.

Creating a Better Basic Table

There are quite a few things wrong with our basic table. The cells are very cramped, mainly. It would be nice to spread things out a bit. Another problem is that the column headings are hard to distinguish from the rest of the cells.

Figure 21.13 shows how much the appearance of our table can be improved with just a few simple changes. The table is wider, and there is more white space inside each cell. The column heads have been emphasized, and the entries have been centered within their cells. Listing 21.2 gives you the entire source code for this page.

FIG. 21.13

A few simple additions to the basic table source code make for a much more attractive result.

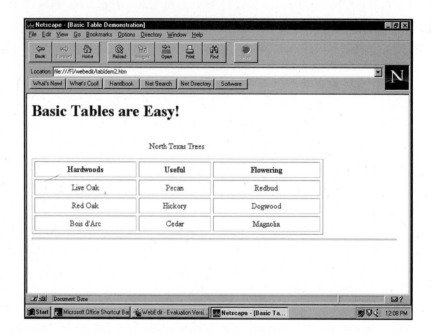

Listing 21.2   Source Code for the Table in Figure 21.13

```
<!DOCTYPE HTML PUBLIC "-//W3C//DTD HTML 3.0//EN">
<!TABLDEM2.HTM>
<HTML>
<HEAD>
<!-- created: 6/12/96 8:57:56 PM -->
<TITLE>Basic Table Demonstration</TITLE>
</HEAD>
<BODY>
<H1>Basic Tables are Easy!</H1>
<BR>
<TABLE ALIGN=center WIDTH=80% BORDER=1 CELLSPACING=5 CELLPADDING=5>
<CAPTION ALIGN=top>
```

```
North Texas Trees</CAPTION>
     <TR>
          <TH> Hardwoods</TH>
          <TH> Useful</TH>
          <TH> Flowering</TH>
     </TR>
     <TR>
          <TD ALIGN=CENTER> Live Oak</TD>
          <TD ALIGN=CENTER> Pecan</TD>
          <TD ALIGN=CENTER> Redbud</TD>
     </TR>
     <TR>
          <TD ALIGN=CENTER>Red Oak</TD>
          <TD ALIGN=CENTER>Hickory</TD>
          <TD ALIGN=CENTER>Dogwood</TD>
     </TR>
     <TR>
          <TD ALIGN=CENTER>Bois d'Arc</TD>
          <TD ALIGN=CENTER>Cedar</TD>
          <TD ALIGN=CENTER>Magnolia</TD>
     </TR>
</TABLE>
<HR>
</BODY>
</HTML>
```

More Attributes for *TABLE*   Much of the improved appearance in the table is due to the use of three TABLE attributes: WIDTH, CELLSPACING, and CELLPADDING.

`<TABLE ALIGN=center WIDTH=80% BORDER=1 CELLSPACING=5 CELLPADDING=5>`

The WIDTH attribute causes the table to stretch until it takes up the specified percentage of the width of the browser window. A percentage is used because you can't predict how the viewer will have her browser set up.

CELLSPACING and CELLPADDING are Netscape enhancements that include extra space within each cell and between cells in the table. If your table is borderless, the two attributes are equivalent. Internet Explorer 2.0 supports both of these attributes, but NCSA Mosaic does not.

The *TH* Element   In the first row of the table, we changed the TD elements to TH, or table headers.

```
<TR>
<TH> Hardwoods</TH>
<TH> Useful</TH>
<TH> Flowering</TH>
</TR>
```

By default, the TH element causes the text between the tags to be bold and centered. You can use the ALIGN attribute to move the text to the left or right. For example, `<TH ALIGN=left>`. Also, by default the header is centered vertically in the cell. The VALIGN attribute permits you

Part
IV

Ch
21

to move the header to the TOP, MIDDLE, or BOTTOM of the cell. That is, <TH ALIGN=right VALIGN=bottom> would put the entry in the lower right corner of the cell. You can also set VALIGN in the TR element to put all text in the row on a common baseline (<TR VALIGN=BASELINE>)

Using *ALIGN* Within *TD* Elements In a similar fashion, you can use the ALIGN attribute in the TD elements. By default, data in table cells other than headers is aligned to the left of the cell. The TD elements shown in the next bit of code center the cell contents.

```
<TR>
<TD ALIGN=CENTER> Live Oak</TD>
<TD ALIGN=CENTER> Pecan</TD>
<TD ALIGN=CENTER> Redbud</TD>
</TR>
```

You can also use VALIGN in these cells, as described above for TH.

Using Advanced Table Elements

You can probably handle about three-quarters of all the Web page tables you will ever have to create with the elements and attributes introduced in the first two examples. However, the time will come when you need to create a table along the lines of the one shown in Figures 21.14 and 21.15. Listing 21.3 is the source code for both of these figures; the difference in their appearance is the result of using two different browsers.

FIG. 21.14

This table has heads that span more than one row or column.

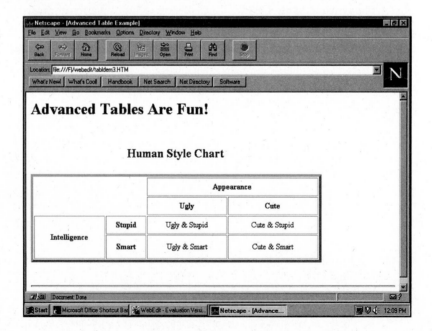

FIG. 21.15
This borderless table uses background colors in the cells, but you can only see the colors with Internet Explorer 2.0.

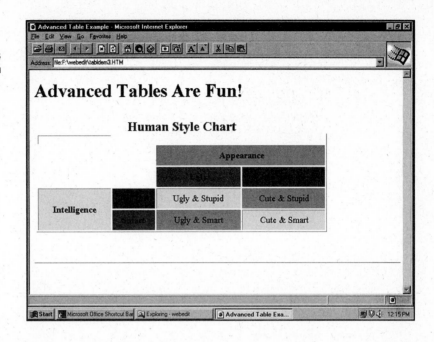

Listing 21.3 Source Code for Both Figures 21.14 and 21.15

```
<!DOCTYPE HTML PUBLIC "-//W3C//DTD HTML 3.0//EN">
<!TABLDEM3.HTM>
<HTML>
<HEAD>
<TITLE>Advanced Table Example</TITLE>
</HEAD>
<BODY>
<H1 ALIGN=left>Advanced Tables Are Fun!</H1>
<BR>
<TABLE BORDER = 5 WIDTH=80% HEIGHT=50%>
<CAPTION><H2>Human Style Chart</H2></CAPTION>
<BR>
    <TR>
        <TD></TD>
        <TD></TD>
        <TH COLSPAN=2 BGCOLOR=LIME>Appearance</TH>
    </TR>
    <TR>
        <TD></TD>
        <TD></TD>
        <TH BGCOLOR=RED>Ugly</TH>
        <TH BGCOLOR=BLUE>Cute</TH>
    </TR>
    <TR>
        <TH ROWSPAN=2 BGCOLOR=YELLOW>Intelligence</TH>
        <TH BGCOLOR=BLUE>Stupid</TH>
```

continues

Part
IV

Ch

21

Listing 21.3 Continued

```
                <TD ALIGN=CENTER VALIGN=CENTER BGCOLOR=YELLOW>Ugly & Stupid</TD>
                <TD ALIGN=CENTER VALIGN=CENTER BGCOLOR=LIME>Cute & Stupid</TD>
        </TR>
        <TR>
                <TH BGCOLOR=RED>Smart</TH>
                <TD ALIGN=CENTER VALIGN=CENTER BGCOLOR=LIME>Ugly & Smart</TD>
                <TD ALIGN=CENTER VALIGN=CENTER BGCOLOR=YELLOW>Cute & Smart</TD>
        </TR>
</TABLE>
<BR>
<BR>
<HR>
</BODY>
</HTML>
```

Figures 21.14 and 21.15 illustrate part of the problem with using advanced elements. Although they were created from the same source code, the tables appear substantially different when viewed with Netscape Navigator and with Internet Explorer. Navigator can't use the color information. As a result, the empty cells in the upper left part of the table look a little odd. Being able to use color to differentiate cells allows the Internet Explorer browser to make that group "invisible."

The *HEIGHT* Attribute for *TABLE*   Netscape and Microsoft Internet Explorer allow the use of the HEIGHT attribute. This works in a manner similar to WIDTH. You set a percentage here to control how much of the vertical space in the browser window is taken up by the table. This is another way to add white space and to improve the overall appearance of your table.

```
<TABLE BORDER = 5 WIDTH=80% HEIGHT=50%>
```

Other browsers, such as NCSA Mosaic, do not support the use of HEIGHT.

Using Heading Styles Inside Elements   In this example, we used a text size container to emphasize the table caption. You can do this with TH and TD elements, too.

```
<CAPTION><H2>Human Style Chart</H2></CAPTION>
```

Any of the physical (<B>, <I>) or logical (<STRONG>, <EM>) containers can be used as well. Any browser that can do tables will have no trouble handling this trick.

Spanning Columns and Rows   One of the most useful additions for many purposes is the ability to have a heading that spans more than one column or more than one row, up to the full width or height of the table. The result groups columns and rows, and makes it possible to place a large graphic or image next to several cells full of information. This capability is provided by the COLSPAN and ROWSPAN attributes, now part of HTML 3.2.

The use of both attributes is illustrated in this example:

```
<TR>
<TD></TD>
<TD></TD>
<TH COLSPAN=2 BGCOLOR=LIME>Appearance</TH>
```

```
</TR>
<TR>
<TH ROWSPAN=2 BGCOLOR=YELLOW>Intelligence</TH>
<TH BGCOLOR=BLUE>Stupid</TH>
<TD ALIGN=CENTER VALIGN=CENTER BGCOLOR=YELLOW>Ugly & Stupid</TD>
<TD ALIGN=CENTER VALIGN=CENTER BGCOLOR=LIME>Cute & Stupid</TD>
<TR>
</TR>
<TH BGCOLOR=RED>Smart</TH>
<TD ALIGN=CENTER VALIGN=CENTER BGCOLOR=LIME>Ugly & Smart</TD>
<TD ALIGN=CENTER VALIGN=CENTER BGCOLOR=YELLOW>Cute & Smart</TD>
</TR>
```

Notice that when COLSPAN is used, it is not necessary to define the cell elements included in the span. Likewise, when ROWSPAN is used, the first cell of the rows included in the span do not have to be defined. In the example, COLSPAN and ROWSPAN were used inside the TH element, but they can be used with TD as well.

Anytime you span rows and columns, take a look at the results with your browser before you put the document up on the Web. It is easy to overlap rows and columns, making a terrific mess of your carefully planned table. If you plan to do much work with tables, it is worth it to invest in a tool like Ken Nesbitt's WebEdit that has dialogs and Wizards to build the table source code for you.

Internet Explorer Enhancement: *BGCOLO*   Netscape doesn't handle empty cells especially well. You can group the empty cells and fill them with some kind of caption or graphic. Or you can put non-breaking spaces ( ) in them and so create a visual distraction for the viewer who is using Netscape. Another solution is to just leave them empty and accept the odd 3-D result. You can also simply turn off the borders if this will provide acceptable results for viewers.

You can do something different for your viewers who use Internet Explorer, though. You can turn off the borders and put a background color in the cells you are using. This provides a rather sophisticated, finished look to tables, as you saw in Figure 21.15. With the borders off, users of other viewers won't know that they're missing a thing. (Netscape does support background colors, but not in individual table cells. You have to make the whole page background one color.)

```
<TH BGCOLOR=RED>Smart</TH>
```

You may use one of sixteen commonly understood color words with the attribute; these describe the standard 16-color VGA palette. The acceptable words are BLACK, WHITE, GRAY, RED, GREEN, BLUE, YELLOW, FUSCHIA, MAROON, PURPLE, NAVY, OLIVE, SILVER, TEAL, LIME, and AQUA. You can also use a six-character hexadecimal value to specify any of over 16 million colors. The hexadecimal value is preceded by the # sign, and consists of three pairs of characters, each representing the amount of red, green, and blue in the color specified. Discussion of this topic is beyond the scope of this chapter. Most intermediate to advanced-level programming books provide an indepth explanation of hexadecimal color values. One particularly good explanation will be found in Chapter 5, "Graphics and Palettes," of Que's *Building Multimedia Applications with Visual Basic 4*, for example.

Useful Table Tricks

From time to time you come up against a layout need that you just can't seem to satisfy. Page designs often need a table in the middle of a lot of text that wraps around the table. Normally, HTML just stops displaying text, displays the table, and then starts displaying the text again. Other page designs call for a picture or graphic in a certain relationship to other images or to some text. These two layouts are impossible (or at least difficult) to do without tables, and here are two tricks that you can perform from time to time to amaze your viewers and confuse your competitors.

The result of these tricks is shown in Figure 21.16. Listing 21.4 gives the details. The easiest trick is the use of right alignment and <BR> tags within a cell to format text. This is so straightforward that it isn't discussed below. But placing a table within a table, and putting an image (a .gif image is used here, but .jpg will work as well) inside a cell take a little more description.

FIG. 21.16

This table contains another table and an image.

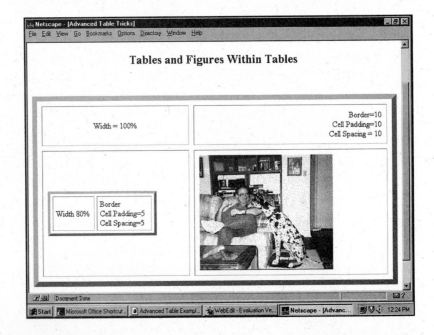

Listing 21.4 Source Code for the Table-Within-a-Table and for Using Graphics Inside Tables

```
<!DOCTYPE HTML PUBLIC "-//W3C//DTD HTML 3.0//EN">
<!TABLDEM4.HTM>
<HTML>
<HEAD>
<TITLE>Advanced Table Tricks</TITLE>
</HEAD>
<BODY>
<H1 ALIGN=left>Some Nifty Table Tricks</H1>
```

```
<BR>
<TABLE BORDER = 10 CELLPADDING=10 CELLSPACING=10 WIDTH=100% HEIGHT=50%>
<CAPTION><H2>Tables and Figures Within Tables</H2></CAPTION>
<BR>
     <TR>
          <TD ALIGN=CENTER VALIGN=CENTER>Width = 100%</TD>
          <TD ALIGN=RIGHT VALIGN=CENTER>Border=10<BR>Cell Padding=10<BR>Cell
          Spacing = 10</TD>
     </TR>
     <TR>
          <TD>
             <TABLE BORDER=5 CELLPADDING=5 CELLSPACING=5 WIDTH=80%>
                       <TR><TD>Width 80%</TD><TD>Border<BR>Cell
                       Padding=5<BR>Cell Spacing=5</TD>
                  </TR>
          </TABLE>
          </TD>
          <TD><IMG SRC="DOG1A.GIF"></TD>
     </TR>
</TABLE>
<BR>
<BR>
<HR>
</BODY>
</HTML>
```

Table Within a Table   All the excitement happens in the first cell of the second row of the table. This is a good illustration of the principle that TD containers can hold nearly any kind of source code that you require.

```
<TD>
    <TABLE BORDER=5 CELLPADDING=5 CELLSPACING=5 WIDTH=80%>
              <TR><TD>Width 80%</TD><TD>Border<BR>Cell
              Padding=5<BR>Cell Spacing=5</TD>
         </TR>
</TABLE>
</TD>
```

Other than being inside a pair of tags in a table, the table code in this illustration is perfectly ordinary. You might want to notice how the table data elements are all on a single line. This is legal and makes the source code a little easier to follow.

However, some browsers cannot handle the nested source code and lose all the information in the "inside" tables. Netscape Navigator 2.0 and Internet Explorer 2.0 have no problem with the source code above, but Mosaic trashes the table. As a result, if you need to use this feature, think about how you can present an alternative view of your information to the approximately one-half of viewers with other browsers.

One method worth considering instead of a table-within-a-table is to put your data in an unordered or an ordered list within a cell of the main table. All table-capable browsers can handle this arrangement.

Images Within Tables   The final trick is very easy. All that is necessary to incorporate an image in a table is to place the IMG tag in the desired cell.

```
<TD><IMG SRC="DOG1A.GIF"></TD>
```

The cell (and the row) will size automatically to accommodate the image. If this would cause alignment problems with text in adjoining cells, simply span the number of rows or columns necessary and place the graphic in the space created. If you turn the border off, you can create very effective image and text combinations.

Improving Your Home Page with Frames

While tables do a lot to help you organize data on your page, tables won't organize your entire browser display window. That's what frames are intended to do. By adding frames, you create "panes" within the browser window. Each of these frames is independent of the others. That is, each frame can display a different HTML document, can be scrolled independently of the other frames, and can be resized by the user.

Frames are supported by Netscape Navigator 2.0 and later. You can expect to see them supported in coming versions of Internet Explorer and other major browsers. You should note, however, that HTML 3.2 does not include frames, and it is possible that the HTML 4.0 standard will not, either. You can include in your HTML a simple line that will provide a message to users of browsers that are not frame-capable. This message looks like the one in Figure 21.17; the method for producing it is explained in the section below on the <NOFRAMES> element.

FIG. 21.17
When you use frames, be sure to let the viewer using a browser that can't show frames know what is going on.

Some people love frames and others love to hate them. However, frames are really no different from any other set of Web page features. When well-used, they can contribute to an effective Web site. When badly used, frames annoy the HTML purist and confuse the unwary Web surfer. These are matters entirely within your control.

Basic Frame Creation

In their most basic form, frames are easy to set up and use. Figure 21.18 illustrates one possible layout in which the main browser window is broken up into four frames. As you can see in Listing 21.5, the content of each frame actually comes from a different HTML document.

FIG. 21.18
This browser window contains four independent frames.

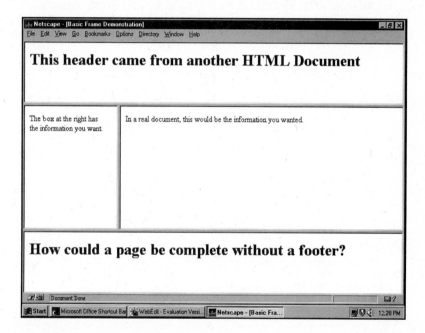

Listing 21.5 Source Code that Takes Content from Four Files and Places It into Four Independent Frames

```
<!DOCTYPE HTML PUBLIC "-//W3C//DTD HTML 3.0//EN">
<!FRAMDEM1.HTM>
<HTML>
<HEAD>
<TITLE>Basic Frame Demonstration</TITLE>
</HEAD>
<FRAMESET ROWS="25%,50%,25%">
    <FRAME SRC="header.htm">
    <FRAMESET COLS="25%,75%">
        <FRAME SRC="label.htm">
        <FRAME SRC="info.htm">
    </FRAMESET>
```

continues

Part
IV

Ch
21

Listing 21.5   Continued

```
    <FRAME SRC="footer.htm">
</FRAMESET>
<NOFRAMES>
If you can see this, your browser can't display frames.
</NOFRAMES>
<BR>
<HR>
</HTML>
```

The `<FRAMESET>` Container   The code to establish and control frames in the browser window is placed inside the `<FRAMESET>` container. In this case, the ROWS attribute is used to set up three rows of frames, occupying one-fourth, one-half, and one-fourth of the vertical space of the browser window.

```
<FRAMESET ROWS="25%,50%,25%"> </FRAMESET>
```

Each of the individual frames must be defined individually, between the two tags. On one row, we will have two frames, and so another FRAMESET container is used with the COLS attribute. In this case, one frame will take up one-fourth of the browser window's width and the other will occupy the remaining three-fourths.

```
<FRAMESET COLS="25%,75%"> </FRAMESET>
```

Again, each of the frames on this row will have to be defined between the two tags.

The `<FRAME>` Element   Frames are defined by using the `<FRAME>` tag. There are several attributes that can be specified for this tag, but here we have only used the most basic one, SRC. This identifies the file which provides the content of the frame. You could specify an image or another Web site if necessary.

```
<FRAME SRC="header.htm">
```

In this case, the referenced file must exist on the same server as the HTML document containing our home page. Notice that `<FRAME>` is an empty element. You don't need a `</FRAME>` tag.

The `<NOFRAMES>` Element   What about the millions of people using browsers that don't understand frames? You can give them an explanation of what's going on with your page by using the `<NOFRAMES>` container.

```
<NOFRAMES>
If you can see this, your browser can't display frames.
</NOFRAMES>
```

This is how the message shown in Figure 21.17 was produced. You could place a link to a page with an alternate view inside this container, too. That would be a much better way to handle this situation than to just tell the viewer that he is out of luck.

Scrolling Frames   Our basic example only put a little text into each of these frames. What if there was so much information that it wouldn't fit into the space available?

Figure 21.19 shows how Netscape automatically adds a scroll bar to the right side of a frame that displays a file too large to fit. You don't have to add any code to get this to happen. The next section on More Advanced Frame Features shows you what to do if you do not want scroll bars.

FIG. 21.19

When there is more text or other content than a frame can hold, Netscape automatically provides a scroll bar.

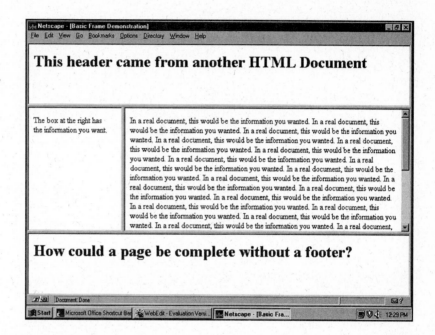

More Advanced Frame Features

Having a feature as flexible as frames presents the page designer with some fundamental problems. Suppose you design your frames to "fit" a browser window of a certain size in a certain way. Small things the user does (displaying the toolbar for example) will adversely affect the layout. A frame that was just the right size may sprout a scroll bar, even though all the text or the image in the frame is still fully visible. If the user resizes a frame, the results may negate the organization you had in mind when you built the frames in the first place. And finally, there is the question of controlling layout—when you never know what size browser window your page will be displayed in.

Figure 21.20 shows a rather ugly page with a number of frames on it. Each of these frames illustrates the methods Netscape provides to deal with these problems. If you run the source code shown in Listing 21.6, you will see that some of these frames can be resized, while others cannot be. The comments in the source code (`<!This is a comment.>`) identify the effect of certain lines, but they will not show up when the source code is run.

FIG. 21.20

This page employs a number of Netscape features that give the designer some control over the flexibility of frames.

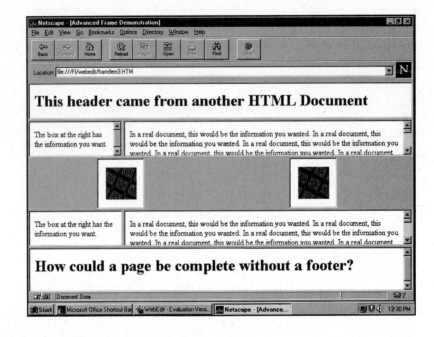

Listing 21.6 Illustrates Some Control Features for Frames

```
<!DOCTYPE HTML PUBLIC "-//W3C//DTD HTML 3.0//EN">
<!FRAMDEM3.HTM>
<HTML>
<HEAD>
<TITLE>Advanced Frame Demonstration</TITLE>
</HEAD>
<!In the next line, one frame row is 108 pixels high, others get 25% of what's left.>
<FRAMESET ROWS="25%,25%,108,25%,25%">
<!Scrolling turned off in next line to make sure those pesky scrollbars never show up.>
    <FRAME SRC="header.htm" SCROLLING=NO>
    <FRAMESET COLS="25%,75%">
<!Notice that because scrolling was not disabled, you get those scrollbars here.>
        <FRAME SRC="label.htm">
        <FRAME SRC="info1.htm">
    </FRAMESET>
<!Next line makes two frames 108 pixels wide and spaces them proportionally across the screen.>
    <FRAMESET COLS="*,108,2*,108,*">
<!Inserting empty frames here as spacers.>
        <FRAME>
<!Making sure graphic displays without scroll bars, centered in frame, can't be monkeyed with.>
        <FRAME SRC="yokai.gif" SCROLLING=NO MARGINWIDTH=16 MARGINHEIGHT=16 NORESIZE>
        <FRAME>
        <FRAME SRC="yokai.gif" SCROLLING=NO MARGINWIDTH=16 MARGINHEIGHT=16 NORESIZE>
    </FRAMESET>
    <FRAMESET COLS="25%,75%">
        <FRAME SRC="label.htm" SCROLLING=NO>
        <FRAME SRC="info1.htm">
    </FRAMESET>
```

```
    <FRAME SRC="footer.htm">
</FRAMESET>
<NOFRAMES>
If you can see this, your browser can't display frames.
</NOFRAMES>
<BR>
<HR>
</HTML>
```

Scrolling Control   In Figure 21.20, you can see that, although the "header" and "footer" frames are the same size, the header has no scroll bar while the footer has one. Similarly, the label in the first frame on the second row has a scroll bar, while its mate in the fourth row does not.

These scroll bars are visual distractions only; they are not needed but Netscape adds them automatically. In fact, if you simply change the options for the taskbar to enable Autohide, the scrollbars cited will automatically disappear.

You can prevent scroll bars from being added to a frame by using the SCROLLING attribute of the <FRAME> tag. This was done in the example to protect the "header", the small frame on the fourth row, and the frames in which both of the graphics are displayed.

```
<FRAME SRC="header.htm" SCROLLING=NO>
```

If you load a large document into a frame that is too small to show it all but has SCROLLING set to No, the user will not be able to scroll down to see the rest of the document.

Absolute and Proportional Spacing   The example in Figure 21.20 uses three different methods to support spacing of frames. One of these, the percentage method, is already familiar to you. The other two methods, setting an absolute size and setting sizes as proportions, are new to you.

The percentage method uses a very straightforward approach: <FRAMESET COLS="25%,75%">. This just gives the frame the specified percentage of the frame's width or height. But how to handle cases like the frames in the third row, where we have placed graphics of a certain size?

You can set the absolute dimensions of a frame in pixels if you need to. Of course, the dimensions will stay the same as the browser window size varies, and the result may be a truncated frame (ow!). To use absolute dimensions, just enter a number representing the frame dimension in pixels.

```
<FRAMESET ROWS="25%,25%,108,25%,25%">
```

In this line of code from the example, the height of the third row of frames has been set to 108 pixels. Since the graphic in the frames on this row is 64 pixels square, this allows 22 pixels above and below the graphics to accommodate margins and the width of the actual row itself.

```
<FRAME SRC="yokai.gif" SCROLLING=NO MARGINWIDTH=16 MARGINHEIGHT=16>
```

Normally, Netscape will place a graphic in the upper left corner of a frame, with a small margin. In order to center these graphics in the frame, we specified an additional 16 pixel margin all the way around by using MARGINWIDTH and MARGINHEIGHT. Sometimes a bit of experimentation is required to get these quantities just right. However, they are always specified in absolute terms, and Netscape will honor those dimensions as long as the browser window is large enough to accommodate them.

This brings us to the third method for setting spacing in frames. This is known as proportional spacing and it allows setting spacings that relate to each other as well as to the browser window dimensions. To get the graphics in the third line spaced just right, so they would always bear a certain relationship to each other, we couldn't simply use percentages. Therefore, proportional spacing was used.

```
<FRAMESET COLS="*,108,2*,108,*">
```

In this line, the frames that actually contain the graphics were made 108 pixels wide to match their height. This is the absolute method. But we wanted to surround and separate the graphics with empty frames in the proportion of 1:2:1. That is where the asterisks are used. If the method isn't obvious, add up the number of asterisks indicated (1+(2 times 1)+1 = 4). Use this total as the denominator of a fraction. For each frame set with this method, the numerator is the number of asterisks. So in this case, the two empty frames on the ends of the row are one-fourth of the total browser window less the 216 pixels used for the frames with graphics in them. The empty frame in the middle is given half the total browser window less the same 216 pixels.

But what if the user resizes the frames with the graphics in them?

Resize Control   By default, frames can be resized by the person viewing them. When the mouse cursor moves over the boundary of a frame, the cursor becomes the familiar double-headed arrow that you have seen in tables in word processors. All the user has to do is click and drag the boundary to change the frame size to the desired dimensions.

You may, for many good reasons of your own, want to keep some or all of your frames just a certain size. To do that, add the NORESIZE attribute to your frame definitions.

```
<FRAME SRC="yokai.gif" SCROLLING=NO MARGINWIDTH=16 MARGINHEIGHT=16 NORESIZE>
```

With this attribute invoked, the mouse cursor no longer changes to a double-headed arrow. The user cannot resize the frame at all, and your layout is protected.

Using Client-Side Image Maps

In your travels around the World Wide Web, you have probably seen links to other pages or sites that were set up as clickable images. That is, when you click on the image map, or on certain parts of the image, you jump to another place on the Web just as if you had clicked on a regular highlighted word link.

Until recently, it took quite a bit of effort to perform this feat. Mainly you had to have a CGI script running on your server that would figure out where the user had clicked and would then do the appropriate linking. This was a hard system to live with, especially if your page resided on somebody else's server.

However, you can now write HTML that will implement clickable image maps right on your page, as it runs in the browsers of people viewing your page. The old system ran totally on the server. The new system runs totally on the client, so you don't need a CGI script at all. For now, Netscape Navigator 2.0 and Internet Explorer 2.0 run these maps; you will have to come up with another solution (regular menu, lists, etc.) for users of the other browsers.

Figure 21.21 is a homely example of such a client-side image map. The graphic was created from five .gifs on the companion CD, using a paint program to assemble them. If the user clicks on one of the arrows, she will be sent to one of four direction-related files. If she clicks on the center, she will get a message (actually in another file) encouraging her to make up her mind and pick an arrow. Listing 21.7 gives the details. In fact, most of the listing just sets up a simple borderless table and places the directional tags in the cells. It takes only eight lines to do the work of the clickable image map. (These eight lines are embedded inside the center cell of the three by three table.)

FIG. 21.21

Each of the arrows in this clickable image map conceals a hyperlink to a different file.

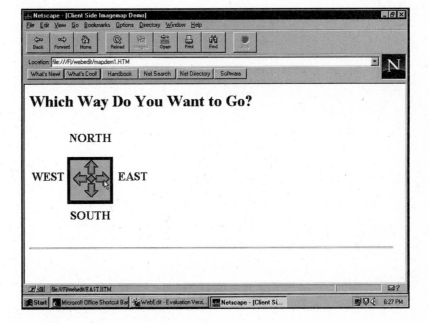

Listing 21.7   Sets Up a Clickable Image Map by Defining Hot Zones on the Graphic and Associating These with Destinations

```
<!DOCTYPE HTML PUBLIC "-//W3C//DTD HTML 3.0//EN">
<!MAPDEM1.HTM>
<HTML>
<HEAD>
<TITLE>Client Side Imagemap Demo</TITLE>
</HEAD>
<BODY>
<H1>Which Way Do You Want to Go?</H1>
<BR>
<TABLE ALIGN=center>
    <TR>
        <TD>
        <TH><H2>NORTH</H2> </TH>
        <TD>
    </TR>
    <TR>
        <TH><H2>WEST</H2></TH>
        <TD>
            <MAP NAME="4WAY">
            <AREA SHAPE="RECT" COORDS="35,0,55,35" HREF="NORTH.HTM">
            <AREA SHAPE="RECT" COORDS="35,55,55,90" HREF="SOUTH.HTM">
            <AREA SHAPE="RECT" COORDS="0,35,35,55" HREF="WEST.HTM">
            <AREA SHAPE="RECT" COORDS="55,35,90,55" HREF="EAST.HTM">
            <AREA SHAPE="RECT" COORDS="35,35,55,55" HREF="UNSURE.HTM">
            </MAP>
            <IMG SRC="4WAY.GIF" USEMAP="#4WAY">
        </TD>
        <TH><H2>EAST</H2></TH>
    </TR>
    <TR>
        <TD>
        <TH><H2>SOUTH</H2></TH>
        <TD>
    </TR>
</TABLE>
<BR>
<HR>
</BODY>
</HTML>
```

Setting Up the Map

Setting up a clickable client-side image map is extremely simple. You need a graphic to use for the map, to begin with. In the example, the graphic is a .gif file that is 90 pixels on a side. It was put together using a simple paint program and five .gif graphics from the companion CD-ROM for this book. The arrows are approximately centered in the 90×90 area.

There are really only two steps: defining the hot zones where the links will be placed and identifying which graphic contains the hot zones. The first of these jobs is done with the <MAP> container, and the second is done with an <IMG> tag.

<MAP> Container   The <MAP> container has one attribute; it simply gives a name to the map. Naming the map is important since you may have more than one image map on any given page.

```
<MAP NAME="4WAY"> </MAP>
```

The space within this container is where the <AREA> tags go.

<AREA> Tag   The <AREA> tag sets up the links from the different areas of the map. Within each area tag, a hot zone is defined on the map graphic, and the browser is told what HTML file is linked to this hot zone:

```
<AREA SHAPE="RECT" COORDS="35,0,55,35" HREF="NORTH.HTM">
<AREA SHAPE="RECT" COORDS="35,55,55,90" HREF="SOUTH.HTM">
<AREA SHAPE="RECT" COORDS="0,35,35,55" HREF="WEST.HTM">
<AREA SHAPE="RECT" COORDS="55,35,90,55" HREF="EAST.HTM">
<AREA SHAPE="RECT" COORDS="35,35,55,55" HREF="UNSURE.HTM">
```

The <AREA> tag has three attributes. First is SHAPE, which tells the browser whether the hot zone is rectangular (RECT), circular (CIRCLE), or polygonal (POLY). To make the entire graphic the hot zone, SHAPE=DEFAULT. If SHAPE is not defined, then a rectangular hot zone is assumed.

The second attribute is COORDS, the coordinates the browser uses to locate the hot zone. All coordinates use pixels as units, and base locations on the simple X,Y system, beginning with 0,0 in the upper left corner of the bitmap. For a rectangular zone, all that is needed are the coordinates of the upper left and lower right corners of the rectangle. For a circle, three numbers are included in the quote marks: the X and Y coordinates of the center of the circle, and the length of the radius of the circle in pixels. For a polygonal area, the X and Y coordinates of each vertex of the area are given.

In the case of our graphic, we know that the tip end of each arrow is in the center of one of the sides of the 90×90 box. We estimate that a rectangle, centered on the arrow and about 20 pixels wide by 35 pixels long, would make a satisfactory hot zone. A little math gives us the coordinates of the two required corners. A fifth hot zone is defined in the dead center of the graphic, to help the undecided.

The third attribute for AREA is the old familiar HREF, or the target for the hyperlink. In the example, we used five local HTML files but we could have used any URL that was required. In the event that we had an area that we wanted to make unclickable, we could have replaced HREF= with NOHREF. This sometimes comes in handy.

Providing the Image   The final line causes the map to reference the correct graphic.

```
<IMG SRC="4WAY.GIF" USEMAP="#4WAY">
```

The IMG tag does what it always does: it loads the image. For the sake of providing the desired layout, <IMG> loads the image into the center cell of the table. The USEMAP attribute is what actually makes the client-side image map work. It references the name defined for the image map at the start of the MAP container (<MAP NAME="4WAY">). In this case, the reference goes to "#4WAY" because the MAP definition is in the same document as the reference to it. But the MAP definition and the SRC image can be anywhere. In these cases, just place a valid URL as the value in the USEMAP=" " reference.

To help out viewers who aren't using Netscape Navigator or Internet Explorer, there are two things you can do. One, if you can set up the CGI program to support a server-side image map, is to combine the definitions in a single line.

```
<A HREF="cgi.bin/binfile"><IMG SRC="map.gif" USEMAP="#map" ISMAP></A>
```

If the viewer's browser supports client-side bitmaps, the map in the USEMAP definition is used. Otherwise, the ISMAP attribute causes the CGI program binfile to run on the server and provides the clickable image that way.

The other method is to create a link to a page that contains a regular text menu. Netscape and Internet Explorer users will still get the client-side image map.

```
<A HREF="textmenu.htm"><IMG SRC="4WAY.GIF" USEMAP="#4WAY"></A>
```

Where to Get More Help

If, while designing your page, you run into questions not answered in this chapter, feel free to make use of the experts who abound on the Internet. WWW help is available 24-hours a day from live people via the #WWW group on IRC (Internet Relay Chat). Likewise, non-real-time help may be found on the Net News group **comp.infosystems.www**. Finally, many documents exist on the Internet and WWW concerning the WWW and authoring your own pages. Use WebCrawler to search for HTML, WWW, and HTTP for starters. ●

CHAPTER 22

Using Navigator Gold to Create Web Pages

by Scott Walter

Publishing on the Web is suprisingly easy, and creating your own home page is probably the best first step. It's a great way to get a feel for how HTML works, and you'll produce something you can use, too. How do you go about producing a home page? Well, you can use any of several freeware, shareware, and commercial HTML authoring tools. But in this chapter, you're going to learn about one in particular: Netscape Navigator Gold. ■

Working with Navigator Gold

How the program works and what all its buttons, menus, and dialog boxes do.

Pictures, lines, and tables

Easily incorporate graphics, tables, or divider lines into your pages.

Publishing your work

Now that you've designed your pages, it's time to load them onto the Web.

Formatting, formatting, and more formatting

A whirlwind tour through page, text, character, and other advanced formatting goodies.

Working with Navigator Gold

Netscape Navigator Gold contains everything that Netscape Navigator contains, plus some great authoring and editing tools that help you create a Web page from scratch or take a Web page that you like and modify it. In this chapter we've assumed that you are working with Navigator Gold. You can download it from the same place you retrieved the plain vanilla version of Navigator, Netscape's home page at **http://home.netscape.com/**.

How Do You Open the Editor?

Navigator Gold has a special Editor window. There are two (or more) ways to open this window:

- To edit a copy of the document you are currently viewing, choose File, Edit Document or click the Edit toolbar button. You'll see a dialog box (which we'll look at in detail in a moment). Click the Save button and the browser window closes and is replaced by the Editor window, displaying the document. (You can reopen the browser window by choosing File, Browse Document, or by clicking the Browser button.)

- To create a new document from scratch from the browser window, choose File, New Document and then choose Blank, From Template, or From Wizard. If you choose Blank, the browser window closes and is replaced by a blank Editor window. The From Template and From Wizard choices only work if you're connected to the Web—they take you to pages at Netscape's Web site that feature pre-built Web page templates and a step-by-step Web page creation, Wizard, respectively.

- To edit a copy of a document on your hard disk—a home page that you've created, for instance—choose File, Open File in Editor and then select a file on the Open dialog box. The Editor window opens, displaying the file you chose (the browser window remains open).

> **N O T E** If you have both the Editor and Browser windows open, you can close one and the other will stick around. You can always open the other again by using the Browser button from the Editor, and vice versa. ▪

Why whould you want to edit an existing document? Eventually, you'll want to modify documents you created earlier, of course. But editing an existing document is also a great way to create your first Web document. Find a document that you think looks good—one that you'd like to copy—and edit that document, replacing the original headings with your headings, keeping the images and links you need, and so on. Then save the modified document on your hard disk.

> **N O T E** If you open a document that contains HTML code that Netscape Gold doesn't understand—for example, Frames—that portion of the page will be displayed as straight HTML code surrounded by "broken tag" icons. ▪

What happens when you open a document in the Editor window? If you opened a file that's stored on your hard disk, the Editor opens and displays the document. If you chose File, Edit Document (or just clicked on the Edit toolbar button), though, you'll see the dialog box shown in Figure 22.1.

FIG. 22.1

When you open a document from the Web, you have to tell Navigator Gold what to do with the links and graphics.

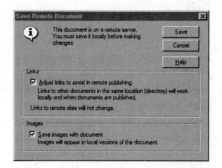

If you change your mind, simply click the Cancel button. But if you want to continue and modify the document that is currently displayed in the browser, you must decide what to do with the links and graphics in the document. Netscape is going to copy the document to your hard disk, and you need to tell it how. Here are your options:

Images—Save Images with Documents Make sure this check box is checked if you want to use the images in the document you are copying. Netscape will copy the HTML document from the Web as well as the embedded images. If you know that you don't want the pictures, clear the check box.

Links—Adjust Links to Assist in Remote Publishing If you choose this check box, Netscape will convert the links in the files to absolute links. For instance, say you are copying a file that contains an HTML link like this:

```
<A HREF="book.htm">Book Titles</A>
```

This link points to a file called book.htm—it's what's called a *relative link*, because it doesn't give the full URL to that document. In effect, the link says, "Get book.htm, which is in the same directory as the current document." But once the document is on your hard disk, book.htm is no longer in the same directory, so the link won't work. If you chose this option, though, Netscape converts the link to something like this, for instance:

```
<A HREF="http://www.bigweb.com/books/book.htm">Book Titles</A>
```

Now the link contains the full URL to book.htm, so it continues to work.

When you click the Save button, you'll see a dialog box like the one shown in Figure 22.2. This is simply a reminder that you *don't own stuff you find on the Web!* You can click the check box to tell Netscape not to display the message next time, then click OK. Then you'll see a Save As dialog box. Find the directory in which you want to save the copied document, type a filename, then click Save.

> **CAUTION**
>
> You should understand that you don't own something you "borrow" from the Web. If you borrow something from the Web and simply keep it for your own use, there's no problem. But if you publish Web pages using pictures and text you grabbed from another Web site, you may be guilty of copyright infringement. If you use the borrowed stuff as a template, though, replacing everything in the page with your own stuff, there's no problem in most cases (though it's possible for a particular design to be copyrighted, too).

FIG. 22.2

Netscape warns you that the things you find on the Web don't belong to you!

The Editor Window

Once you've opened the Editor window, you'll see something like Figure 22.3. This shows the current Netscape home page inside the Editor.

The Paragraph Format toolbar

The Character Format toolbar

FIG. 22.3

The Editor window provides the tools you need to create or modify a Web page.

The File/Edit toolbar

The red bar indicates that you are in edit mode.

Notice that the mouse pointer hasn't changed to a hand because in edit mode you can't navigate via the links.

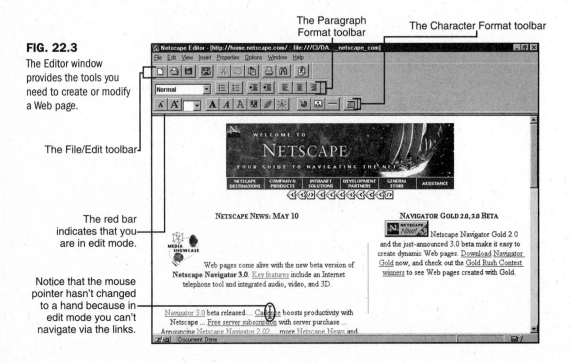

Here's a quick summary of what each button does.

- New Document—Click this button to open a new blank Editor window so you can begin a new document, or choose to use a Template or the Page Wizard.
- Open File to Edit—Click this button to open a file on your hard disk.
- Save—This button saves the document on your hard disk.
- View in Browser—Click this button to change back to the browser window.
- Cut—Highlight text in the document and click this button to remove the text, placing it in the Windows Clipboard.
- Copy—This button copies highlighted text to the Clipboard.
- Paste—Click this button to paste text from the Clipboard to the document.
- Print—Prints the document.
- Find—Opens the Find dialog box so you can search the document.
- Publish—Transfers your Web page and associated files to the Internet using HTTP or FTP protocol.
- Paragraph Style—The Editor uses a system of styles, much like most good word processors. You can click text and modify it by selecting a style.
- Bullet list—This button lets you create a bulleted list.
- Numbered list—Clicking this button creates a numbered list in the document.
- Decrease indent—Moves indented text back to the left.
- Increase indent—Indents text to the right.
- Align left—If a paragraph is centered or aligned to the right (right-justified), click here to change it to left alignment.
- Center—Centers the selected paragraph.
- Align right—Right-justifies the selected paragraph.
- Decrease Font Size—Highlight text and click here to decrease the size one level. (There are seven font sizes, from -2 to +4, with 0 being the default size. These are relative sizes, not directly related to point size.)
- Increase Font Size—Highlight text and click here to increase the size one level.
- Font Size—Highlight text and then choose a font size setting to make the text larger or smaller than the default for that text style.
- Bold—Highlight text and click this button to make it bold (or to remove bold, if the text is already bold).
- Italic—Highlight text and click this button to make it italic.
- Fixed Width—Highlight text and click this button to change the text to a fixed width (monospace) font, a font in which all characters take up the same space.
- Font Color—Highlight text and click this button to change the text color.
- Make Link—Inserts a link in the document.

- Clear All Styles—Highlight text and click this button to remove all the text styles, changing the text back to the default font for the paragraph style.

- Insert Target (Named Anchor)—Inserts a target name for frames and links to jump to inside a page.

- Insert Image—Opens the Insert Image dialog box, which helps you insert a picture into your document.

- Insert Horizontal Line—Inserts a horizontal line across the document.

- Object Properties—When you click certain objects in your document (images, links, and horizontal lines) and then click this button, the appropriate properties dialog box opens. Highlight text and then click the button to modify general document characteristics (title, colors, and so on).

Entering Your Text

As an example of how to work with the Editor, let's try creating your own home page—a page that opens when you open the Netscape browser, containing all the links you need. Type the following into a new, blank Editor window (you can see an example in Fig. 22.4):

```
My Home Page
This is my very own home page
Really Important Stuff
These are WWW pages I use a lot.

Not So Important Stuff
These are WWW pages I use now and again.

Not Important At All Stuff
These are WWW pages I use to waste time.
```

Right now all you have is basic text; look in the Paragraph Style drop-down list box (the list box on the left side of the Paragraph Format toolbar) and you'll see it shows Normal.

You can quickly change the paragraph styles. For instance, try the following:

1. Click the My Home Page text, then select Heading 1 from the Paragraph Style drop-down list box.
2. Click the Center toolbar button.
3. Click the This is my very own home page text, then click the Center toolbar button.
4. Click the Really Important Stuff text, then select Heading 2 from the Paragraph Style drop-down list box.
5. Click the Not So Important Stuff text, then select Heading 2 from the Paragraph Style drop-down list box.
6. Click the Not Important At All Stuff text, then select Heading 2 from the Paragraph Style drop-down list box.

FIG. 22.4
Start typing the headings into the Editor; you'll find it's just like working with a word processor.

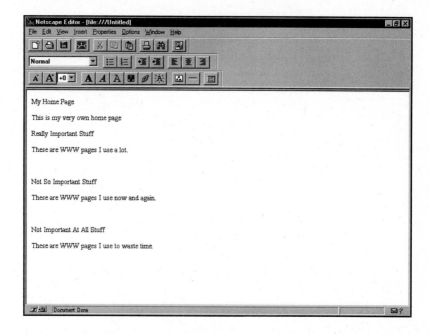

Now what have you got? Your page should look something like that in Figure 22.5.

FIG. 22.5
A few mouse clicks, and you've formatted the document.

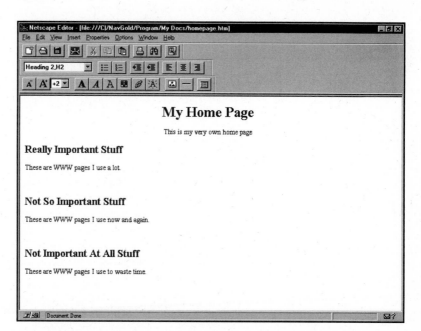

Before you go on, save what you've done: Click the Save button, type a name (homepage, if you wish), then click the Save button. The Editor will save the file with an .htm extension.

 TIP Want to see what you've just done? Choose View, Document Source, and you'll see the HTML source document that the Editor has created for you. If you're not an HTML purist and want to "tweak" your HTML code by hand, choose View, Edit Document Source instead.

Where Did My Line Breaks Go?

Did you create multiple line breaks in your document by pressing Enter? If so, when you finally view your document in the browser window, those line breaks will be gone; the Editor doesn't like multple line breaks.

For example, try this: Place the cursor at the end of a paragraph (a paragraph that is followed by another paragraph, not the last one in the document) and press Enter several times. Several blank lines appear. Save the document, then press Ctrl+R to reload the document from the hard disk into the Editor. You'll see that the blank lines have gone!

Why? Well, this seems to be a holdover from creating a Web document by entering the HTML codes. Web browsers ignore blank lines in the HTML document. Rather, they only move text down a line when they see a special tag: the <P> or <BR> tag. Of course, there's no reason that the Navigator Gold Editor should do the same; if you entered a blank line, you probably want it there. Nonetheless, that's the way it is.

 TIP If you've made changes to your document, but want to go back to the way it was the last time you saved it, simply press Ctrl+R or choose View, Reload.

However, there is a way to add a blank line. Place the cursor at the end of a line and choose Insert, New Line Break (or simply press Shift+Enter). A blank line appears. This time, if you save the document and then reload it, the blank line remains.

How About Links?

Now you're going to get fancy by adding an *anchor*, a link to another document. For example, you may want to add a link to the Netscape home page (on the other hand, you may not; you can always choose Directory, Netscape's Home to get there, even if you are using your own home page). Or, perhaps you'd like a link to a favorite site.

N O T E   The HTML tags used to create links are often known as *anchors* because many people refer to links themselves in the Web documents as anchors. ■

Click the blank line below These are WWW Pages I use a lot, then click the Link button or choose Insert, Link. You'll see the dialog box shown in Figure 22.6.

FIG. 22.6
Enter the text you want
to see and the URL you
want to link to; you can
choose named targets,
too.

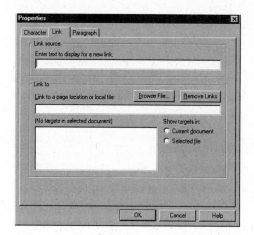

In the first text box, type the text that you want to appear in the document: the words that you
will be clicking to use that link. In the second box, type the URL of the page you want to link to.
The radio buttons let you list named Targets in either the Current document or a Select file.
To pick one as your link, just click it and it will appear in the second box.

You create a Target by highlighting text or placing your cursor where you want a target to
appear, then clicking the Insert Target (Named Anchor) button on the bottom toolbar. You'll
get a dialog that asks you for a target name. Links that jump to this target from the same page
will have a destination of "#name," while links that jump in from another page will have a destination of "thispage.htm#name."

N O T E   You can find URLs in a number of places. You might press Alt+Tab to switch back to the
browser window, then use the browser to go to the page you want and copy the URL from
the Location bar. Rember also that you can right-click a link in a Web document and choose Copy
This Link Location. You can also copy URLs from desktop shortcuts: Right-click the shortcut,
choose Properties, click the Internet Shortcut tab, and then press Ctrl+C to copy the URL.

You can also get links from another document or elsewhere in the same document: Right-click a link in
the Editor and choose Copy Link to Clipboard. ■

Notice the Browse File button; this lets you enter the URL of a file on your hard disk, which is
very handy if you are creating a series of linked pages. And there's a Remove Links button, too.
This is only active if you click inside a link in your document and then open this dialog box.
Clicking the button removes the URL so you can enter a new one, or so that you can retain the
document text but remove the link from it.

 Here's another way to create a link: Hightlight text that you typed into the document earlier and
then click the Link button (or right-click the highlighted text and choose Create Link Using Selected).
The highlighted text will appear in the dialog box. All you need to do is enter the URL and click OK.

More Nifty Link Tricks

You can also create links by copying them from the browser window. Position the windows so that both are visible. Then click a link in the browser window, but hold the mouse button down. You'll notice the link turn red. Now, with the mouse button still held down, drag the link from the browser window over to the Editor window (as shown in Fig. 22.7), move the pointer to the position you want to place the link, and release the mouse button.

FIG. 22.7

You can drag links from the "What's Cool?" page (or any other Web document) into the Editor.

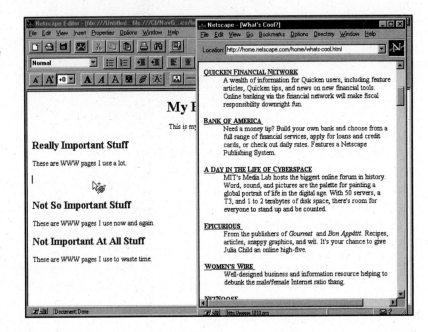

Finally, why not grab links from your bookmarks? You've probably already created bookmarks to your favorite sites, and you can quickly create links from them. Choose Window, Bookmarks to open the Bookmarks window.

Now you can drag bookmarks from the Bookmarks window onto your document in the Editor. As long as you don't click anywhere in the document—simply drag and release where you want the new link—the Bookmarks window remains above the Editor window.

 TIP   To open a browser window containing the document you are editing so that you can test the document you've created, choose File, Browse Document.

What About Pictures?

No self-respecting Web page would be complete without a picture or two, would it? Luckily, the Editor provides a way for you to insert pictures.

Place the cursor where you want the picture, then choose Insert, Image, or click the Insert Image button. You'll see the dialog box shown in Figure 22.8.

FIG. 22.8

The Insert Image dialog box helps you place the image in just the correct manner.

Start by clicking the Browse button right at the top of the dialog box, and select the image you want to use (or, you may type a URL into this text box, and the Editor will go out onto the Web and grab the specified file). If you wish, you can also enter an alternative image in the second text box. This is the image that should be used if the first image isn't available. And you can enter the alternative Text, too, into the third text box. This is the text that is shown if the browser viewing your page is not displaying inline images.

 The alternative image option doesn't work well for all browsers. If the primary image is not available, some browsers will not be able to display the alternative image, as this is a Netscape feature that has not yet been adopted by all other browser publishers. Also, if you define an alternative image, other browsers viewing your page with inline images turned off may not be able to view the alternative text. The alternative-image information in the HTML file "confuses" them and stops them from reading the text.

The Copy Image to the Document's Location check box in the lower left corner of the dialog box tells the Editor to copy the picture from its original location to the directory in which the document is stored.

Now take a look at the Alignment box. This is where you define how text on the same line as the image should be wrapped around the image. Each button shows a visual sample of what the image will look like with its designated alignment.

You can now tell the Editor how much space to leave around the image—or whether you want a border around it. The three text boxes under the Space Around Image heading allow you to enter a size, in pixels, between the left and right sides of the image and the text, and between the top and bottom of the image and the text. You can also define the size of a border around the text.

The text boxes under the Dimensions heading let you set the <u>H</u>eight and <u>W</u>idth of the displayed image. Values of 0 mean "original size," which you can also reset by clicking the Original Size button.

The <u>E</u>dit Image button lets you (logically enough) edit the image you've chosen. If you haven't already configured an image editor through the <u>O</u>ptions, <u>E</u>ditor Preferences menu selection, you'll be given a chance to do so automatically.

Finally, how about turning the image into a link to another document? If you want the reader to be able to click the image to view another document, click the Link tab and you can create a link for the image.

When you've finished, simply click OK and the image is inserted into the document. How can you modify the image later? Many ways: double-click the image, click the picture then click either the Object Properties or Insert Image toolbar button; or right-click and select Image <u>P</u>roperties from the pop-up menu.

TIP Do you want to find some icons you can use in your documents? Go to an icon server: a Web site from which you can download icons or even link your documents across the Web to a particular icon. Try the following sites:

- ▓ **http://www.bsdi.com/icons/**
- ▓ **http://www-ns.rutgers.edu/doc-images/**
- ▓ **http://www.dl.unipi.it/iconbrowser/icons.html**
- ▓ **http://www.cit.gu.edu.au/~anthony/icons/**

Where are you going to get pictures for your documents? You can create them yourself using a graphics program that you can save in a .jpg or .gif format (many can these days). You can also grab them from the Web, remember! Find a picture you want, right-click it, and choose Save This Image As.

TIP There's a special command that makes sure that the text placed after an image appears below the image, not "wrapped" around it. Let's say you've aligned the picture so that the text following it appears on the right side of the picture. You can now place the cursor in the text at the point that you want to move it down below the image, then choose <u>I</u>nsert, <u>B</u>reak below Image(s). The text that appears after the cursor is now moved down, below the image.

Adding Horizontal Lines

Horizontal lines are handy. You can use them to underline headers, as dividers between blocks of text, to underline important information, and so on. And the Editor allows you to create a number of different types of lines, as you can see in Figure 22.9.

FIG. 22.9

This dialog box helps you create a line; you can see examples in the Editor.

To place a line across the page, place the cursor on a blank line or in a line of text after which you wish to place the line, and click the Insert Horizontal Line button (or choose Insert, Horizontal Line). A line is placed across the page. But what if you don't want a line all the way across the page, or if you want a different style or thickness? You'll have to modify the line.

Select the line; with the cursor at the end of the line, simply press Shift+Left Arrow (or simply click directly on the line). The line will appear to change color or size—it will be highlighted. Now click the Object Properties button to open the Horizontal Line Properties dialog box, which you can see in Figure 22.9. Double-clicking the line, or right-clicking and selecting Horizontal Line properties from the pop-up menu will also bring up this dialog box.

There are a variety of controls in this dialog box. First, you can tell the Editor where you want the line: aligned against the Left, in the Center, or aligned against the Right. Notice, however, that by default, the line has a width of 100 percent (that is, it's 100 percent of the width of the document's window). The alignment settings have no effect until you modify the width setting. (If a line is 100 percent, how can you center it after all?)

There are actually two ways that you can adjust the line's width: by Percent or by Pixels. Both are selected from the drop-down list to the right of the Width text box. The Percent setting refers to the width of the document (when the window is maximized). So a line that has a width of 50 percent will stretch across half of the document's window.

The Pixel setting is harder to predict, though. A pixel is the smallest unit that your computer monitor can display. For instance, in VGA mode a monitor displays 640 columns and 480 rows of pixels. So if you create a line that's 60 pixels wide, it will be about 10 percent of the width of the document—in VGA mode. But what if the person viewing the document is using a different resolution—1024 by 768, for example? In such a case, the line that was 10 percent of the width in VGA is now about five percent of the width. Of course, this doesn't matter if you are creating a home page for your own use, but bear it in mind if you are creating documents that you plan to put out on the Web.

There are two more settings: the Height, which is measured in pixels, and 3-D Shading. The 3-D effect is created by using four different lines to create a "box"—the left and top lines are dark gray, and the bottom and right lines are white. Clear the 3-D check box, and your horizontal line will be a single, dark, gray line.

Creating Tables

Navigator Gold now lets you easily create tables. Select Insert, Table from the menu and you'll get the dialog box shown in Figure 22.10.

FIG. 22.10

Netscape Gold's table creating dialog box makes it easy to define all aspects of a table.

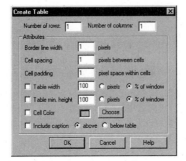

Number of rows and Number of columns each default to 1, but that doesn't make much of a table; set these to the values you want. This is all you really need to define to create a table, but the Create Table dialog also lets you set Border line width, Cell spacing (the number of pixels between cells), Cell padding (pixels of white space inside of cells), Table width, Table minimum height (these too in pixels or as a percentage of window width), and Cell Color. You can also check the Include Caption check box to put a caption above or below the table.

Once a blank table is created, you enter information into the cells by clicking in them and typing (of course, you can also insert images or links into table cells). You move from cell to cell using the arrow keys.

You can create "nested" tables by moving the cursor into an empty cell and creating a new table there.

Once created, you can modify a table using the menus. From the Insert menu, you can insert a new Table, Row, Column, or Cell at the cursor position. The Properties menu lets you change the properies for a Table, Row, or Cell. The Row and Cell (see Fig. 22.11) selections bring up dialog boxes that let you define text alignment and cell color (both) and column span (cell only). You can also choose Delete Table, Delete Row, Delete Column, or Delete Cell from the Properties menu.

FIG. 22.11
The Cell Properties
dialog box lets you
customize individual
table cells.

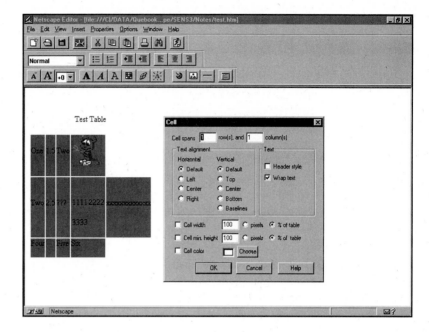

Publishing Your Work

Once you've created an HTML page, you'll probably want to publish it on the Web or on an intranet. With Gold, this is now a one-step process. Just click the Publish button on the toolbar, or choose File, Publish from the menu. You'll get the dialog box shown in Figure 22.12.

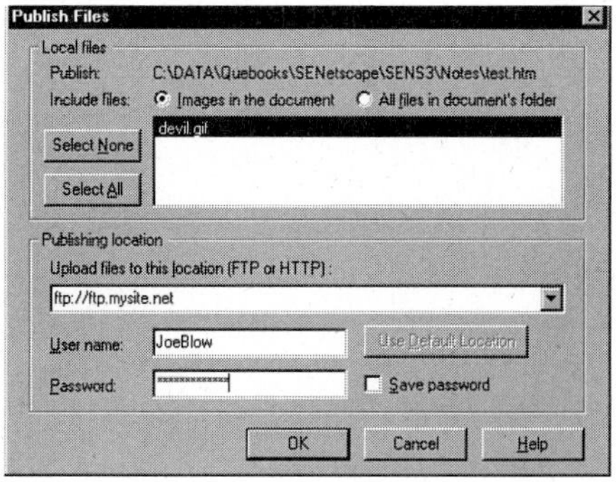

FIG. 22.12
The Publish dialog box
lets you publish your
page on the Web.

From this dialog box, radio buttons in the Local files area let you choose to include in your upload only the Images in the Document, or All Files in Document's Folder. A file list lets you choose individual files to include, or you can Select None or Select All using buttons.

The Publishing Location box includes fields for the URL of your upload destination, as well as your User Name and Password. When these have been set, a single click on OK uploads your page to its destination.

Creating Multiple Documents

You may want to create a hierarchy of documents. Create a home page, a page that appears when you open Netscape, with a table of contents linked to several other documents. In each of those documents, you could then have links related to a particular subject: one for business, one for music, one for your kids, and so on.

This is very simple to do. Create and save several documents in the Editor (probably putting them all in one directory for simplicity). Each time you finish one, choose File, New Document to clear the screen so you can create the next one. When you have all your documents completed, open your home page document again (click the Open File button or choose File, Open File), and enter links to each page, using the method previously described.

How Can I Use My Home Page?

You've created a home page; now how do you use it? Complete the following procedure:

1. Click the Open Browser button, or choose File, Browse Document. The Netscape browser opens and displays your document.
2. Click the Location text box, highlighting the URL.
3. Press Ctrl+C to copy the URL.
4. Choose Options, General Preferences, and click the Appearance tab.
5. Click the Home Page Location option button (in the Startup area).
6. Click inside the text box below this option button.
7. Press Ctrl+V to paste the URL into the text box.
8. Click OK.

Now, the next time you start your browser, you'll see your very own home page.

Here's a Good One—Let's Change It

Navigator Gold provides a wonderful way to quickly create Web pages—by "borrowing" them from the Web and modifying them to your requirements. If you see a page you like—one that has many links that you'll need in your home page, for instance, or one that uses a particularly attractive format—you can open that page and make changes to it and then save it on your hard disk.

You can work in the document in the same way that you would with documents you created yourself. You can delete text and replace it with your own and change text using the formatting tools.

How do you highlight text? The Editor window works like a word processor. Simply click in the text to place the cursor, then use the arrow keys to move around in the text. You can also hold down the Shift key while you press the arrow keys to highlight text. Ctrl+Shift+Left Arrow and Ctrl+Shift+Right Arrow work (selecting an entire word at a time, though you can't do the same with the Up and Down arrow keys). Also, you can use the mouse cursor to select text: Hold down the mose button while you drag the pointer across text to highlight it or double-click a word to select it.

 TIP As with a word processor, you don't need to highlight text in order to modify paragraph formats. If you want to change the paragraph style, indentation, or alignment, simply click once in the paragraph and then make your change.

When you've made the changes you need, click the Save button or choose File, Save and you'll be able to save the document on your hard disk. (No, you can't save it to the original location even if you own that location!)

Lots More Formatting

There are a number of formatting tools we haven't looked at yet. You can format a paragraph in many different ways by setting up indents and alignment as well as by choosing a paragraph style. And you can modify particular words or individual characters, too, by changing colors and type styles.

The Other Paragraph Styles

You've only seen a couple of paragraph styles so far, so let's take a look at the others. In Figure 22.13, you can see examples of all the different Heading levels as well as Normal text, the Address style, and the Formatted style.

FIG. 22.13
The headers, formatted, and address styles.

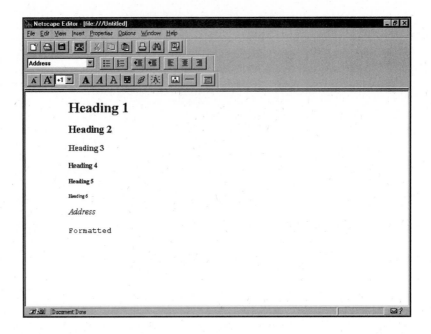

You can apply any of these styles by placing the cursor inside the paragraph you want to modify and then selecting the style from the drop-down list box (or by picking the style form the Properties, Paragraph cascading menu). Note that what you see depends on how you've set up Netscape; other browsers may display these styles in a different way.

N O T E Browsers normally remove blank lines and multiple spaces when viewing a document. The Formatted style tells the browser to keep the text format as it appears in the HTML document. In fact, unless you are using the Formatted style, the Editor won't let you type multiple spaces into a document. Also, long lines of Formatted text will run off the side of the window—the text will not wrap to the next line.

However, note that Navigator Gold currently doesn't allow you to enter multiple blank lines, even if you've selected the Formatted style. ■

How About Creating Lists?

You can also use the Paragraph Styles drop-down list box and a couple of the toolbar buttons to create lists. You can create bulleted lists, numbered lists, and definition lists.

The quickest way to create a bulleted list is to place the cursor on a blank line and then click the Bulleted List button. You'll see a bullet (a black circle) appear at the beginning of the line. Type the first entry, press Enter, type the next entry, press Enter, and so on. When you get to the last entry press Enter and then select Normal from the Paragraph Style drop-down list box. You can see an example in Figure 22.14.

FIG. 22.14

You can create lists using the paragraph styles.

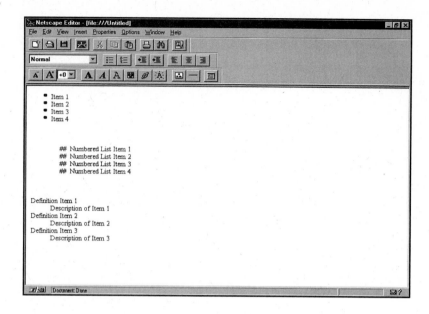

Part

IV

Ch

22

You can create a numbered list in the same way by using the Numbered List button.

Another form of list is the definition list, which you can create by alternating lines between the Description Title and Description Text styles.

There's another way to work with lists—and other paragraph formats. Here's how to use it. Place the cursor on a blank line and then click the right mouse button. Choose Paragraph/List properties from the pop-up menu. You'll see the dialog box shown in Figure 22.15.

FIG. 22.15

The dialog box allows you to format a variety of paragraph and list styles.

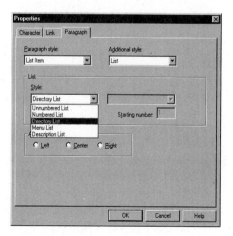

Select the paragraph or list type you want to create in the Paragraph Style drop-down list on the left. If you've selected a List item, pick the Style from the second drop-down list. Finally, select the number or bullet type from the list on the right. Pick Left, Center, or Right alignment, then click OK and the first line is correctly formatted.

This dialog box creates not only numbered and unnumbered lists, but also several other unusual paragraph styles: Block Quotes, Directory Lists, Menu Lists, and Description Lists. Other styles may be added later, too.

Positioning Paragraphs

Now let's see how to move paragraphs around the page. You can use the five toolbar buttons on the right side of the Paragraph Format toolbar to indent paragraphs, align them to the left, center them, or align them to the right. You can combine alignment settings and indentations as well, as shown in Figure 22.16.

FIG. 22.16
You can position paragraphs in a variety of ways.

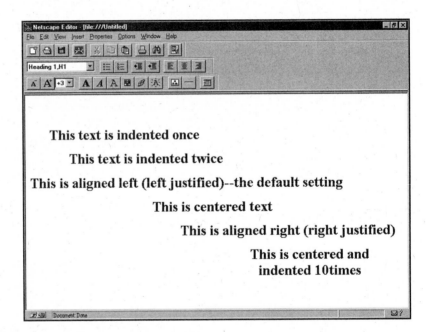

How Can I Modify Character Formats?

You have quite a bit of control over individual characters. In effect, you are telling your document to override the way in which the browser that opens your document displays the characters. A browser, for example, may have a default text color set, but you can override that color and define your own. Figure 22.17 shows a variety of character formats.

FIG. 22.17
Highlight text and click the appropriate button to modify it.

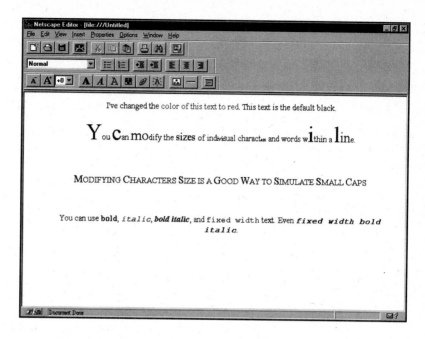

Simply highlight the characters you want to modify, then click the appropriate button (or choose the appropriate entry from the Properties, Character submenu), as follows:

■ Font Size—Change a character's size, ranging from -2 to +4. That is, from two "units" below the normal style size, to four "units" above. These are not absolute measurements—it's not 2 points to 4 points, for instance. Rather, they are relative sizes; the browser displaying the document simply decreases or increases the text a certain amount below or above the normal size for that paragraph style.

■ Decrease Font Size—Click here to decrease the size one unit.

■ Increase Font Size—Click here to increase the size one unit.

■ Bold—This changes the character to bold (or removes bolding, if the text is already). You can combine this with italic to create "bold italic" text.

■ Italic—Click here to change the text to italic (or to remove italic).

■ Fixed Width—This changes the text to a fixed width (monospace) font, a font in which all characters take up the same amount of space.

■ Font Color—You'll see a dialog box from which you can choose a color.

■ Clear Styles—Click here to remove all the text styles, changing the text back to the default font for the paragraph style.

Here's an example of how to use these tools. Take a look at Figure 22.14, then follow this procedure:

1. In a blank document, type all the text you see in Figure 22.17. Don't worry about the different formats, simply type all the text starting at I've changed the color all the way to fixed width bold italic at the bottom.

2. Now, highlight a few words of the first line, then click the Font Color button. Click the red, then choose OK. The text will change color.

3. Select a letter or several letters on the second line. Then select a size from the Font Size drop-down list box, or click the Increase Font Size or Decrease Font Size buttons. Try several letters and different sizes.

4. You should have typed all of line three in capitals. Select the first letter of the first word, and increase its size. Modify all the first letters that you want to "capitalize" and increase their size the same amount, so simulate a "small caps" font.

5. Highlight the word bold on the last line and click the Bold button.

6. Highlight the word italic on the last line and click the Italic button.

7. Highlight the words bold italic on the last line and click the Italic button and then the Bold button.

8. Highlight the words fixed width on the last line and click the Fixed Width button.

9. Highlight the words fixed width bold italic on the last line and click the Fixed Width button, then the Italic button, and finally the Bold button.

Nonbreaking Spaces   Here's one more character format we haven't looked at yet: You can choose Insert, Nonbreaking Space to create a special space between words. This space is treated as part of the two words it divides. When you change the size of the Editor window (or when the person viewing the document changes the size of the Browser window), text has to be wrapped down onto the next line. Now, words are never split in two when Netscape does this wrapping; the text is always broken at a space. But the text won't be broken at one of the nonbreaking spaces—instead Netscape has to break the text at the first normal space that appears before the nonbreaking space.

JavaScript   There are two more character-format types that you may have noticed in the Properties, Character submenu: the JavaScript (Client) and JavaScript (Server) formats.

JavaScript is a special scripting language. It lets you use some of the power of C or C++ without knowing either programming language. You'll learn more about JavaScript in Chapter 25, but for now, all you need to know is that you can enter JavaScript commands into your documents by choosing Properties, Character, JavaScript (Server) or Properties, Character, JavaScript (Client) formats (depending on which type of command you are entering) and then typing the command. The server commands will appear as blue text, the client commands as red.

Document Properties—General

Web documents have a variety of properties related not to any particular paragraph or character, but to the document overall. You can modify this by choosing Properties, Document. Click the General tab and you'll see the information in Figure 22.18.

FIG. 22.18

The Document
Properties box lets
you set colors, the
document title, author
name, and more.

These are the things you can modify here:

Document Property	What It Modifies
Title	The title of the document. This is displayed in the browser's title bar, in history lists, bookmark lists, and so on.
Author	This places the <meta name="Author" content= "author's name"> tag into your document. It's one of the META variables that can be located in the Head of the document.
Description	A brief description of the contents of your document. This information can be helpful to readers searching for a specific topic.
Other Attributes	Keywords and Classification that you want, searching services such as Yahoo to help users locate your document on the Web. Use category names you think best apply to your document.

Appearance

Click the Appearance tab to see a pane. You have to option buttons at the top. You can choose to either Use Custom Colors (you'll be able to define custom colors and background for this particular document) or Use Browsers Colors (the document will use whatever colors and background are defined by the browser viewing it).

Just below the option buttons you'll see the Color Schemes drop-down list box. From this you can choose from predefined color schemes; currently, you can choose about a dozen different color schemes. Future versions will also allow you to create and save your own schemes.

Now you can select the text colors you want to use. You can modify the color of Normal Text, Link Text, Active Link Text (this is the color of a link when you point at it and hold down the mouse button), and Followed Link Text (the color of links that lead to documents you've already visited). Clicking one of these buttons opens the Color dialog box.

Finally, you can modify the background. Either choose a Solid Color (click the Choose Color button to select that color), or an Image File—click the Browse button to find a file you want to use as the background image.

N O T E   The way it stands right now you can only set all or nothing. In other words, you can't define a special color for the background, yet keep the browser defaults for everything else. If you change one item, all the other items are also defined as overridden parameters.

You can choose colors that are the same as the default colors for Netscape. For instance, these colors will override a reader's settings if they are different from the defaults. ▨

Advanced Settings

Power HTML users will appreciate the settings available under the Advanced tab (as shown in Fig. 22.19).

FIG. 22.19
The Advanced tab lets you set system and user variables.

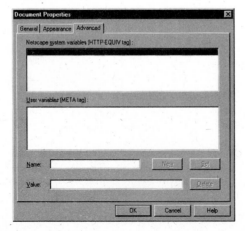

Here's what you can set in this dialog box:

Document Property	What It Modifies
Netscape System Variables	This is information that is sent in a "response (HTTP-EQUIV) header" from a server. A response header is information sent to a browser or other program when it request information about the document. The information is contained in the HEAD of the document, and may include an expiration date and keywords, for instance. You add this information by clicking in the System Variables box to select it, then typing a value into the Name and Value fields at the bottom of the dialog box, and clicking the Add button.
User Variables (META)	The META variables are placed in the HEAD of the document, and are used to identify the document to servers and browsers allowing them to index and catalog the document.
Name	Type a new user variable name here.
Value	Type the user value here, then click the Set button.

You can add more user variables. In fact you can add variables that a server may want to include in its response header. For instance, you might type Expires in the Name field, then Tue, 24 Dec 1997 into the Value field. When you click Set, the Editor adds this tag to the Head of the document:

```
<META HTTP-EQUIV="Expires" CONTENT="Tue, 24 Dec 1997">
```

This then becomes the Expires date shown in the Document Info when you select View, Document Info in the Netscape Browser.

You can also use this feature to add keywords to your document (so the document can be indexed and cataloged) and a reply-to address, to create tags such as these:

```
<META HTTP-EQUIV="Keywords" CONTENT="Art, Sculpture">
<META HTTP-EQUIV="Reply-to" CONTENT="robin@sherwood.com (Robin Hood)">
```

Editor Options

You can set default options for the Editor. Choose Options, Editor Preferences to see the Editor Preferences dialog box. Click the Appearance tab to see the same area that we looked at a moment ago; you can use this to define the colors used by new documents you create.

Click the General tab to see the area shown in Figure 22.20. This is where you define the default Author name, HTML source and Image editor, and the URL of the HTML document you'll use as a source for your templates (this defaults to a location on Netscape's Web server).

FIG. 22.20

The Editor Preferences dialog box tells the Editor how to set up new documents.

Click the Publish tab to set your Links and Images defaults. You can select the Keep Images With Document check box to tell the Editor that, when you insert an image, you want to move it to the same directory as the document into which it is being inserted. You can also tell the Editor to Maintain Links. Your choice here defines the status of the option buttons in the Save As dialog box that appears when you are opening the editor with a document you have found on the Web.

The Default Publishing Location box is where you enter information about the site where you Publish (upload) your finished pages. Enter the site address, your username, and password information (only check the Save password box if you're sure no one else has access to your system!).

More to Come?

You can expect to see many more features added over the next few versions of Navigator Gold. You may find tools that help you create forms, frames, and JavaScripts. You'll also probably be able to create imagemaps—pictures with hotspots on them that lead to other Web documents—special characters, and add sounds and multimedia.

 The latest version of Netscape Navigator Gold can be downloaded for evaluation from Netscape's home site at **http://home.netscape.com/**. Just follow the links to the download section.

CHAPTER 23

Using Microsoft FrontPage

by Neil Randall and Dennis Jones

Microsoft FrontPage lets you design and administer World Wide Web sites. Not just Web pages, which any number of excellent programs let you do, but entire Web sites, collections of linked pages. In fact, once you've acquired FrontPage, there's nothing standing between you and putting your site live on the Web. ■

Install Microsoft FrontPage

FrontPage is easy to install. Learn how to here.

Learn about all the parts of FrontPage

FrontPage has three parts: FrontPage Explorer, FrontPage Editor, and Personal Web Server. This chapter shows you how they all work together.

Let WebBots make your job easier

WebBots are innovative tools that you drop onto a Web page to automatically handle mundane chores or eliminate the need to write complicated scripts.

FrontPage contains the following three major components:

- FrontPage Explorer lets you create Web sites from scratch and even gives you wizards and templates to take you from no site at all to a site with a solid basis, in only a few minutes. If you already have a Web, Explorer gives you a visual view of it and lets you carry it further.

- FrontPage Editor allows you to create individual pages or edit those pages you've created earlier in a what-you-see-is-what-you-get (WYSIWYG) editing environment.

- FrontPage Personal Web Server lets you test all aspects of your Web and even allows you to serve your Web to the Internet.

Put all these components together and you have what amounts to a complete Web site publishing environment. To make your Web complete, you'll want to mount it on a computer that's connected to the Internet over a fast connection 24 hours a day; but even with a basic modem, you can serve up a part-time site to get started. It's almost all here.

 This chapter is strictly an overview of FrontPage. To completely learn how to use FrontPage to build a Web site requires a whole book, such as *Special Edition Using Microsoft FrontPage* by Que.

Installing FrontPage

As of this writing, FrontPage was available for Microsoft Windows 95 and NT only. They haven't developed a Windows 3.1 version, and probably won't.

If you've downloaded a beta version of the program, it arrives as an executable, self-extracting file. Run the file and then look for the install or setup utility common to your operating system. In Windows this is the Setup.exe file. Run that utility and the installation will be more or less automated.

Once the installation process begins, your first choice is to decide on typical installation or custom installation. Typical installation includes all three of FrontPage's components; the client software (FrontPage itself), the Personal Web Server (a small program that lets you test Webs when you create them), and the server extensions (files that let FrontPage work with existing Web servers). Through Custom installation, you can elect to exclude any of these components or, if you chose not to install portions before, you can do so at this time. Normally, on first receiving the product, you should install the entire set of features.

Like all programs, FrontPage offers self-installation into a default directory, which can be changed if you want. Likewise, FrontPage requires a separate directory for the Personal Web Server and for any Webs you create. This is also given a default location, and your next step is to confirm or change that directory. Next, you'll be asked for the folder or program group in which to place the FrontPage icons, and you'll be given a screen showing all the directories you've chosen.

At this point, FrontPage takes itself through the rest of the installation. When it's finished, you'll be asked if you want to start FrontPage Explorer. Since you'll want to spend the next few weeks of your life learning how to use the full suite of capabilities in this package, why not say "yes" and get started! When FrontPage Explorer has loaded, find the Microsoft FrontPage folder and load the Personal Web Server as well. Now go back to Explorer, choose File, New Web and start your Web creation career.

Part

IV

Ch

23

If You Already Have a Web Server Running

You're not forced to use the Personal Web Server that ships with FrontPage. If Web server software is already running on your computer, there is a reasonable chance FrontPage will work just fine with it. However, because FrontPage must interact directly with your server to perform its magic, you'll need to install the FrontPage extensions for your server. FrontPage offers extensions for the most popular servers on UNIX and Windows, but does not for all available servers. If you're not sure, use the Personal Web Server because FrontPage installs extensions for it right out of the box.

The Parts of FrontPage

FrontPage consists of several major components, all of which fit together to make a complete Web site publishing package. The integration of the programs is covered in depth later in this chapter. The following short descriptions serve only as a means to start you thinking about the package's many possibilities.

FrontPage Explorer

The heart of the entire package, FrontPage Explorer is designed to let you see the Web you have created. Explorer provides three main views of your Web:

- *Outline View* lets you see the hierarchical relationships and links among pages, and resembles the outliner in a word processor.
- *Link View* gives you a clear graphical picture of how pages in your Web are linked together, as well as how they link to Web documents outside your site.
- *Summary View* shows you technical details about each of the files in your Web.

Together, the three views let you see how your Web is constructed and, in the process, helps you determine what else needs to be done to perfect that Web. Broken links are shown clearly, and links can be updated to automatically change references. In addition, Explorer automatically creates and maintains a To Do List of tasks still to be completed, and you can assign these tasks to anyone on your team of coworkers.

Most important, Explorer lets you create Webs. You can build Webs that are entirely empty, into which you must insert all your documents from scratch or, more significantly, Explorer's wizards and templates will build entire Webs and set them in place. Once they exist, your task is to customize them and add to them. However, having something to start with always makes the overall task easier.

Finally, Explorer lets you set options for your Webs to help you manage them. You can determine who will have access to the Web sites at various levels: everyone from administrators to Web authors and even end users. If you want to restrict access to your Webs to people within your own company, you can do so. If you want users to register before entering your site, you can do that as well. And if you want coworkers to be able to author pages in the Web, but not change the administrative options, it's as easy as a few entries in a dialog box.

FrontPage Editor

There's no lack of good packages out there that let you author Web documents. Typically they're called HTML editors because Web pages are written primarily in *HyperText Markup Language*. However, in the case of Microsoft FrontPage, you really don't have to know HTML to generate some first-rate pages. Like your word processor, which doesn't show you the formatting codes unless you specifically ask to see them, FrontPage Editor operates on the principle that you want to see the results of your design decisions rather than the codes and tags necessary for their implementation. In other words, FrontPage Editor is a WYSIWYG program, and while it's not the first such program to hit the market, it's the most complete to date.

FrontPage Editor supports advanced HTML features such as tables, forms, and frames. It also lets you set the color and formatting of your pages through a series of dialog boxes, thereby making it easier to standardize the way your Web looks to others. In the case of forms and frames, in fact, it goes a step further, offering wizards to help you build these relatively complex elements. And FrontPage also offers automation tools called *Bots*, which are explained as follows.

If you've ever tried to get a form on your Web to actually do anything, you know how difficult it can be. Designing the form itself is relatively easy; programming the scripts to allow it to interact with the server, so that clicking the Submit button sends the data somewhere useful, is another beast entirely. The Bots in FrontPage's forms remove much of this difficulty, as well as the need to learn the interface scripting process known as CGI. You can't do all complex CGI-like interactions with these Bots, at least not in the early versions, but FrontPage makes it possible for even Web authoring novices to offer full interaction in their Web sites.

▶ **See** "HTML Editors and Filters," **p. 489**

▶ **See** "HTML Basics," **p. 494**

Personal Web Server and Web Server Extensions

If you want to host your own Web site, you need a piece of software called *Web server software*. This software, when on a computer that's connected to the Internet, lets you make your Web site accessible to users on the World Wide Web. To be effective, a Web server machine should be connected to the Internet 24 hours per day at a much higher speed than even the fastest modem allows. But, if you want, you can use the Personal Web Server to offer even part-time connections at slower speeds.

However this isn't really the main function of the Personal Web Server. Instead, it's designed as a way for you to test your Webs as you develop them. Once you've created some pages, you'll want to see what they look like in your favorite Web browser (Netscape, Internet Explorer, Mosaic, and so on). To do so, all you need do is start the Personal Web Server, set it for "local" mode, and then load your browser and see if everything works. As long as you're connected to the Internet at the time, you can test internal and external links alike, and you can ensure that your Web pages look exactly as you want them to.

> **N O T E** When you use the Personal Web Server with your favorite Web browser, you open Web pages in the browser through the Web server. That is, you don't open Web pages as files from the disk, you open them using HTTP and the Personal Web Server. ▪

Server Administrator   FrontPage comes with a Server Administrator, which functions primarily as a way to install and keep track of server extensions and to set restrictions on author access. Most access issues are already part of FrontPage Explorer, but here you can set base-level access restrictions. This server administrator isn't nearly as powerful as the administration tools that come with full-featured Web server software, except for the installation of server extensions.

Server Extensions   The most important concession made by the FrontPage package is that people will want to use its Web creation tools but not necessarily its included server. In fact, there's no way a professional Web server site will be willing to change from its well-established server software, so the only way to make FrontPage widely useful is to include support for existing servers. FrontPage does this through *server extensions*, which install files and directories into the existing server software to let the server work with all of FrontPage's features.

Getting data from forms is just one example (albeit an important one) of what the extensions accomplish. As explained briefly earlier, FrontPage takes the programming sting out of making forms return the data that users provide. But because FrontPage does this in a non-standard way (in fact, almost all servers handle this differently), something has to tell the server software what the FrontPage form is trying to do. That something is the server extension. Essentially, the server extensions add functionality to the server software to allow it to work with FrontPage as well as with the software it already supports.

FrontPage offers server extensions for many of the most popular servers. Some of these are included in the package, while others are downloadable from the FrontPage Web site at **http://207.68.137.35/frontpage/freestuff/agreement.htm**.

▶ **See** "Running a Web Server on Windows 95," **p. 1049**

Starting Your Web with FrontPage Explorer

To create a Web, you must be running a Web server. If you have a server in place, you can use Explorer to create a Web for it only if a FrontPage server extension exists for that particular server. As shipped, FrontPage supports several popular Web servers, including the Netscape Commerce and Communications servers and O'Reilly's WebSite server. As they become available, extensions for most servers will be made available on Microsoft's Web site, at **http:// 207.68.137.35/frontpage/freestuff/agreement.htm**.

As you'd expect, it also supports the Personal Web Server that comes with the FrontPage package.

If you're running a Web server that isn't supported by a FrontPage extension, you can still make use of FrontPage. Using a machine other than your Web server machine (always a good idea anyway), connect to the Internet and load the FrontPage Personal Web Server, and then create your Web. Once it's completed, you can export it to the Web server machine.

Starting a New Web Site

To build a Web site, open your Web server (Personal Web Server is fine) and then open FrontPage Explorer. Choose File, New Web. The New Web dialog box appears, which you can see in Figure 23.1.

FIG. 23.1
The choices shown in the New Web dialog box let you begin a new Web easily.

This dialog box gives you several choices, ranging from Empty Web through Corporate Presence Wizard. The difference lies in the relative simplicity or complexity of the possibilities. Here are some of the templates and wizards you'll find in this dialog box:

- The Normal Web creates a Web with a single blank page, which will be the Web's home page.
- The Corporate Presence Wizard walks you through the process of creating an organization-style Web.
- The Customer Support Web provides you with a framework for developing customer support services.

- The Discussion Web is excellent for setting up a discussion site; creating one from scratch is a time-consuming business.
- The Empty Web is just that; it creates a Web structure without even one page in it. You use this if you've already prepared a home page and need an empty Web to install it into.
- The Learning FrontPage Web is a brief but useful tutorial Web for the software package.
- The Personal Web sets up a single home page for you, with a selection of possible hyperlink destinations you can delete or customize as you like.
- The Project Web establishes a Web you can use to manage and track a project.

An empty Web is exactly what its name suggests; you get a Web, but there's nothing in it. Selecting the Corporate Presence Wizard, on the other hand, launches a wizard (a software automation tool) that takes you step-by-step through the initiation of a Web site fully populated by page templates designed specifically for establishing a corporate presence. The choice is yours: start with nothing or start with a sophisticated template.

Why would anybody forego the templates and start with an empty Web? The answer lies very much in your confidence and creativity, as well as your experience in Web design. If you've put together a number of Webs and you know exactly how you want to start and what you want to include, a template might very well be a detriment rather than a benefit. But, if you're about to begin your first site or you know very well that you could use a good assistant, by all means start with a template.

Loading a Web into Explorer

Once you have one or more Webs created, you can load them into Explorer by choosing File, Open Web or by clicking the Open icon on Explorer's toolbar. The Open Web dialog box appears (see Fig. 23.2).

FIG. 23.2
At this stage, the Open Web dialog box has no Webs to load.

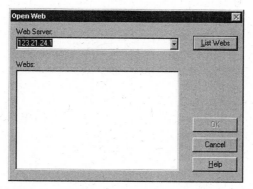

Your first task is to choose the Web server where the Web resides. First, load the Personal Web Server into memory and then return to the Open Web dialog box and open the Web Server drop-down list box. This reveals all servers you've worked with so far; if you've dealt only with the localhost IP number, that is the only IP that appears in this field.

With the desired Web server showing in the Web Server drop-down list box, click the List Webs button. In the Webs list box, you now see the names of the Webs you have created in the selected Web server (see Fig. 23.3). If you're opening a Web from a server on a remote computer, and especially if you're using a modem connection (even 28.8 Kbps), getting a list of the Webs can take several minutes. Eventually, however, it appears.

FIG. 23.3

To avoid frustrating yourself with unnecessary load times, be sure to choose the correct Web.

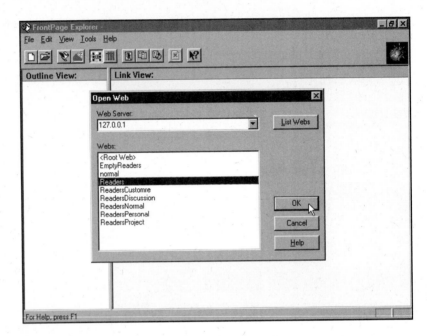

Click the Web you want to work with and then click the OK button. When you click Open, a dialog box appears and requires a username and password for author permissions, and those elements you established earlier. Once the Readers Web is loaded, for example, you see the Explorer window shown in Figure 23.4.

Working with Explorer's Views

By default, the Explorer window shows two views—*Outline View* and *Link View*. These are the two views you'll work with most, although *Summary View* exists to help you keep detailed control over all elements of your Web. The Outline and Link views are shown on either side of the vertical separator in Figure 23.4.

Outline View   Figure 23.5 shows Outline View expanded by sliding the vertical separator fully to the right edge of the screen. This figure shows clearly why it's called Outline View; like the outline view of a word processor, it shows the various headings and subheadings distinguished by indentation. In this figure, all (except the last) headings are fully open, as indicated by the minus signs beside the main topic headings. For example, Readers Home Page, at the top of the view, has been opened to reveal the remainder of the topics. By clicking the minus sign, you can close the Readers Home Page topic, and by doing so you'll close all other headings in Outline View as well. All headings in this Web stem from the home page; therefore all pages are subordinate to that page.

FIG. 23.4
The Readers Web is now loaded and ready to edit.

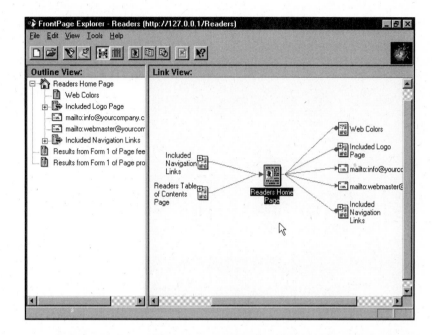

FIG. 23.5
These are the cascaded headings of Explorer's Outline View.

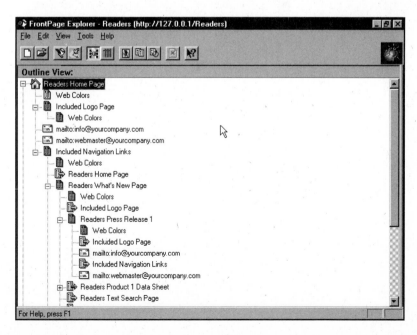

In fact, however, the division is not topic and sub-topic. Instead, Outline View shows links among pages. Main links lead to sub-links, and sub-links to further sub-links, and so forth. These links appear even more clearly in Link View, but they're helpfully presented in Outline View as well.

Link View   Explorer's Link View is, in fact, where you'll do the bulk of your work on your Web, except of course for the actual task of constructing HTML pages, for which you'll use FrontPage Editor. Link View shows the Web from the perspective of the currently selected page in Outline View, but you can maneuver around the Web by using Link View alone. Like Outline View, Link View shows the Web as a series of pages with or without additional links leading from them, and you can expand or contract the links to see a larger portion of that particular part of the Web.

To show how Link View changes as you open an increasing number of pages, examine the following series of figures. Figure 23.6 shows Link View of the Readers Web from the perspective of only the home page and its direct links. In this case, the Links to Images toggle in the View menu has been marked, which is why the right side of the window now shows the image links in addition to the normal document links. Note the plus signs on several of the pages; as in Outline View, these pages can be expanded to reveal their links.

FIG. 23.6

In this figure, you can see the basic Link View from the Readers home page.

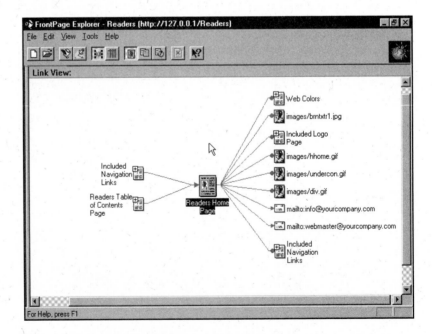

In Figure 23.7, the plus sign on the Readers Table of Contents page has been clicked, and the result is the appearance of another collapsed page icon to the far left of the screen. Figure 23.8 shows what happens when that page is expanded: a wide variety of new page icons appear.

FIG. 23.7
A single new icon appears in the Web after expanding the TOC page.

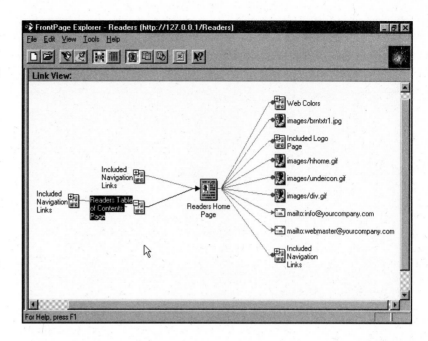

FIG. 23.8
Link View expands even further to show the navigation links.

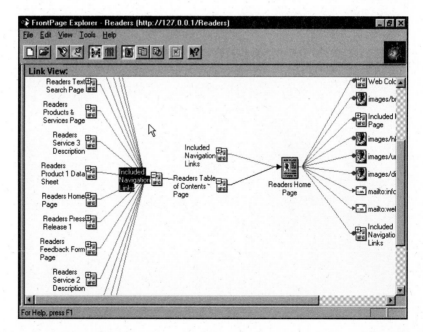

Finally, in Figure 23.9, you can see what happens by clicking the Readers Product 1 Data Sheet icon. This is another collapsed page icon, and it leads to a series of three more collapsed page icons. By clicking these, the Web can be expanded until there is nothing more to see.

FIG. 23.9

The Web expands further, revealing links to previously viewed pages.

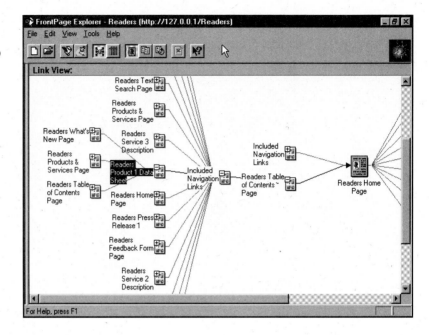

Working with Individual Pages

Once you reach a page you want to work with, you can work with it by clicking it. At this point, you have several choices. Double-clicking opens that page in FrontPage Editor, where you can edit it and save it directly back to the Web (even if you're editing it on a remote computer). Right-clicking the icon reveals a pop-up menu with the following five options:

- *Move to Center*   Centers Link View on that page's icon.
- *Open*   Loads the page into the editor you have specified for that file (see the section "FrontPage Explorer Menus" later in this chapter for more details).
- *Open With*   Loads the page into an editor you select from the resulting Open With dialog box.
- *Delete*   Lets you erase the page from the Web and simultaneously erases links to other pages.
- *Properties*   Opens the Properties dialog box (see the section "FrontPage Explorer Menus" later in this chapter for more details).

Beyond that, any work you do on individual pages occurs through FrontPage Editor, not Explorer. The point of Explorer is to let you see your Web and keep track of it, not to alter and edit individual pages.

Editing a Web Page in FrontPage Editor

Fortunately, with FrontPage Editor, you don't have to be intimately acquainted with the HTML tags that control the appearance of your pages. The editing tools do this work for you. All you need to keep in mind, for now, is that the body section of every Web page is made up of combinations of the following three basic elements:

- Text
- Images
- Hyperlinks

Part

IV

Ch

23

Text is just that: headings (not to be confused with the head), paragraphs, lists, and so on. Images are graphics you use to give your pages variety and impact. Hyperlinks are the most important part of any Web page because they connect users to related pages and sites.

▶ **See** "HTML Elements," **p. 502**

Adding Text to a Page

You can use several different methods to put text onto your page. The simplest kinds of text are the heading and the paragraph.

Using the Insert Menu to Add Headings You use headings to mark off major divisions and subdivisions of meaning within a page. FrontPage Editor offers the six levels of headings that are standard with HTML. To place one on a page, use the following steps:

1. Position the blinking text cursor where you want the heading to appear.
2. Choose Insert, Heading. The Heading submenu, with six possible selections, appears.
3. Select 1 (Largest). The blinking text cursor enlarges.
4. Type some text. You see the largest heading style. Press Enter.
5. Choose Insert, Heading, 2 (Large). Type some text. The next level of heading appears. Press Enter.
6. Repeat steps 4 and 5 until you've seen as many of the different heading styles as you want.

Applying Text Styles with the Change Style Box A faster and more convenient way to change heading levels is with the Change Style drop-down list box, which actually lets you choose from all the heading levels and text styles available. (If you've used styles in Microsoft Word, the technique is immediately familiar.) To see the styles, click the arrow button at the right of the Change Style drop-down list box (see Fig. 23.10).

FIG. 23.10

You can apply styles easily by selecting from the list in the Change Styles box.

To use this method to change a text style, use the following steps:

1. Select the text you want to modify by clicking anywhere inside it.
2. Click the arrow button at the right of the Change Style drop-down list box. The list of styles appears.
3. Click the style you want. The selected text takes on the new style.

As you've already guessed, this method works for all text, not just for headings. In some cases you might want to compose most of the text of your page in the Normal style (the default) and then use the Change Style drop-down list box to modify sections of it.

 TIP Don't overuse the larger heading styles on a single screen. If you do, a visitor to your site may feel as if she's being shouted at. Think of headings as signaling divisions and subdivisions of content, rather than as a method of emphasis.

Adding Ordinary Text In FrontPage Editor, you produce ordinary, default text with the Normal style. This style's font is set to Times New Roman, and you can't change it. Actually, there wouldn't be much point in doing so, because many browsers can be set to display text in a font of the viewer's choice. So even if you could use many different fonts, and took a lot of trouble with your typography, there'd be no guarantee that a visitor to your site would see it the way you do.

If you've used other Web authoring tools, you likely already suspect that FrontPage Editor's Normal style produces what the others call paragraphs. This is absolutely correct. Unfortunately, there is an ongoing debate over exactly what "paragraph" means in Web authoring. In fact, FrontPage Editor's Insert menu distinguishes four styles of paragraphs: Normal, Formatted, Address, and Heading. In this chapter, we're restricting ourselves to working with the Heading and Normal paragraphs.

N O T E In HTML, a paragraph isn't just a stream of characters followed by a carriage return/ linefeed pair. It is a strictly defined page element and it begins and ends with tags. For the Normal paragraph in FrontPage Editor, these tags are <p> and </p>. FrontPage Editor inserts them for you, of course. ▪

To write ordinary text, use the following steps:

1. Place the cursor where you want the text to begin.

2. Choose Insert, Paragraph, Normal. Normal appears in the Change Style box.

3. Start typing. When you reach the end of a paragraph, press Enter, as you usually do. This starts a new paragraph, with the proper HTML paragraphing tags. Continue typing until you've said what you want to.

You can see an example of Normal text in Figure 23.11. When a browser displays this, it automatically inserts a blank line before the start of each paragraph. You can't change this behavior.

FIG. 23.11

You use the Normal style to generate paragraphs of ordinary text.

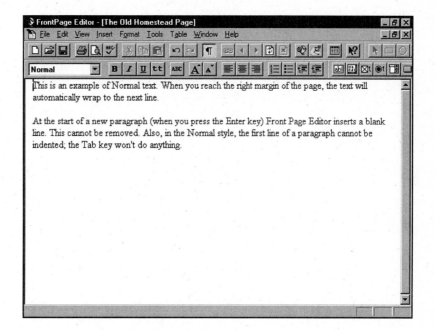

But what if you want extra whitespace between paragraphs? Well, if you've used other Web page editors, you'll know that you can't put in blank lines by merely pressing the Enter key. The whitespace shows up in the editing window just fine, but browsers ignore it.

But with FrontPage Editor, the blank lines you get by pressing the Enter key do appear in some recent browsers. FrontPage Editor achieves this by inserting an , which is an escape sequence between the paragraph tags when the Enter key is pressed. Browsers that recognize this extension (including Netscape 2.0, NCSA Mosaic 2.1, and Microsoft Internet Explorer 2.0) don't "crunch" the whitespace; they let it show up. You'll find this word processor-like feature to be a great improvement over earlier Web page editors, which demand that you insert a line break element to generate whitespace between paragraphs.

Part
IV

Ch
23

Laying Out Text Effectively

Just getting words onto the page isn't enough. Good text layout affects a page's attractiveness and readability. FrontPage Editor has several tools to help you enhance the appearance of your pages: horizontal lines, centering, block indentation, and character formatting.

N O T E If you've made a complicated edit that didn't work out and you want to discard the changes before you go on, you can use FrontPage Editor's Reload command. Choose Tools, Reload (or the Reload button on the toolbar) and FrontPage Editor reloads the file as it was before the edit. You'll be asked if you want to save the changes you did make; assuming you don't, answer No. ▪

Using Line Breaks to Control Text Formatting It's convenient that FrontPage Editor has simplified using whitespace between paragraphs, but what about the opposite problem? That is, if you need short lines of text kept all together (quoting poetry, for example) how do you keep FrontPage Editor from putting blank lines between these one-line paragraphs? If you try pressing Enter where you want the text to break, you'll always get a blank line. The solution is to insert line breaks. The line break orders a browser to jump to the very next line of its window and then deal with whatever comes after the break.

The procedure is simple: to keep short lines of text together, you press Shift+Enter when you reach the end of each line. This inserts a
 (line break) tag into the text stream, which orders a browser not to leave a blank line before the start of the next line of text. If you've turned on Format Marks (either with the View menu or the Show/Hide Format Marks toolbar button) you'll see a line break symbol in the FrontPage Editor workspace. These symbols, of course, don't show up in a browser.

N O T E Choosing Insert, Line Break provides specialized line breaks, as well as the basic one you get with Shift+Enter. ▪

Aligning Text Horizontally You'll often want headings or other text to be somewhere else than at the left margin. To do so, use the following steps:

1. Click anywhere in the text you want to align.
2. Choose Format, Paragraph. The Paragraph Format box appears.
3. Click the arrow button at the right of the Paragraph Alignment drop-down list box. The alignment options list appears.
4. Select the alignment you want, and choose OK.

These alignments are Netscape extensions, not part of standard HTML 2.0.

N O T E The Left alignment and the Default alignment both put text against the left margin. The difference is in the HTML code generated; Left puts a <p align=left> instruction immediately before the image source code. Default doesn't put in anything, but for all practical purposes, they do the same thing. ▪

T I P A quick way to align text is to use the Align Left, Center, and Align Right buttons on the formatting toolbar.

Applying Character Styles   A confusing aspect of character styles is the difference between the physical and logical styles. What it boils down to is this: If a browser sees the HTML tags for italic or bold characters (physical styles), it puts italic or bold on the screen, no matter how the browser preferences are set. But if it sees the emphasis or strong HTML tags (logical styles), it checks its preference settings to see how its user wants emphasized or strong text to appear. The default for the browser usually displays this text as italic and bold, respectively. However, if the user changed her emphasized preference setting to 14-point Caslon, the browser dutifully displays Caslon instead of italic. In short, logical styles are flexible at the browser end and physical ones are not.

When it comes to the mechanics of applying character styles, FrontPage Editor again resembles a word processor. To apply a style to text, you select that text and then choose Format, Characters. The Character Styles dialog box appears (see Fig. 23.12). Tables 23.1 and 23.2 specify how Web browsers display these styles.

Part IV

Ch 23

FIG. 23.12
You use the Character Styles dialog box to modify the appearance of selected text.

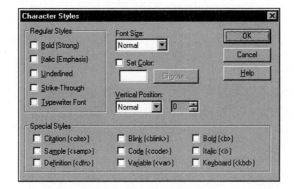

T I P You can also click the toolbar buttons to get bold, italic, underlined, or typewriter characters. However, the bold and italic buttons force logical styles, not physical styles.

Table 23.1   Physical Character Styles in FrontPage Editor

Style	Effect
Bold	Forces browser to display bold
Italic	Forces browser to display italic
Underlined	Forces underlining
Typewriter font	Forces monospaced font, default Courier

Table 23.2 Logical Character Styles in FrontPage Editor

Style	Effect
Strong	Bold unless changed by browser options
Emphasis	Italic unless changed by browser options
Strike-through	Strike-through characters
Citation	Italic for citing references
Sample	Output sample (resembles typewriter font)
Definition	Italic for definitions
Blink	Blinks text
Code	HTML code (resembles typewriter font)
Variable	Usually italic for defining a variable
Keyboard	Indicates user-supplied text (resembles typewriter font)

You can also change the size of the displayed text. Choose the size for the Font Size drop-down list box (see Fig. 23.13).

FIG. 23.13
Using the Font Size drop-down list box to select a new size for the text.

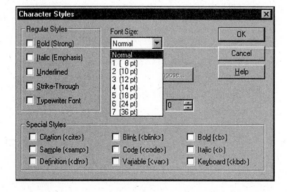

This sizing is actually keyed to Netscape's font size extension, so it won't work with browsers that don't support this particular extension.

 TIP To quickly format some characters, select the text, right-click it to open the shortcut menu, and click either Properties or Format Characters. Whichever you do, the Format Characters dialog box appears.

Putting an Image onto a Page

FrontPage, at its default settings, stores your Web in an appropriately named folder inside the C:\FrontPage Webs\Content folder. Within your Web's folder are several more folders, and one of these is the images folder. This is the most convenient place to keep the graphics for your Web, since FrontPage automatically displays the images folder's content when you choose Insert, Image. Of course, having all your images in one place also makes it easier to stay organized.

Once you've added a graphic to the images folder, use the following steps to insert it into your page:

1. Place the cursor where you want the image to appear.
2. Choose Insert, Image. The Insert Image dialog box appears with a list of image files (see Fig. 23.14). If no Web is open, this list is empty.

FIG. 23.14
Using the Insert Image dialog box to select an image from the list displayed. (The From URL and From File buttons let you reach graphics in other locations.)

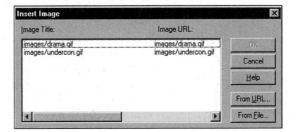

3. Select the image file you want by clicking its name in the list.
4. Choose OK. FrontPage Editor inserts the image into the page.

> **CAUTION**
> Be careful of using really wide graphics. If your visitor is running her browser at less than full screen, or her hardware only supports VGA (640×480) resolution, the image may be lopped off at the side. Keep the image width to less than five or six inches and test.

Aligning and "Floating" Images Centering or right-aligning an image is simple. You select the image and then choose Format, Paragraph. Then you open the Paragraph Alignment drop-down list box and pick the alignment you want. When you choose OK, the image is repositioned.

Often you'll want to get text to wrap around an image. FrontPage Editor supports two Netscape extensions that let you "float" an image so that this happens. These extensions use the align left and align right values, which FrontPage Editor inserts into the generated HTML code for you. To make an image float against the left or right margin so that existing or future text wraps around it, use the following steps:

1. Select the image.

2. Choose Edit, Properties. The Image Properties dialog box appears.

T I P A quick way to the Image Properties dialog box is to right-click the image, without selecting it. Click Properties in the shortcut menu, and the Image Properties dialog box appears.

3. Click the arrow button beside the Alignment drop-down list box to open the list of alignment options (see Fig. 23.15).

4. Select the Left or Right option.

5. Choose OK. The image moves to the appropriate margin and any text present flows around it.

FIG. 23.15

You use the Image Properties dialog box to position an image.

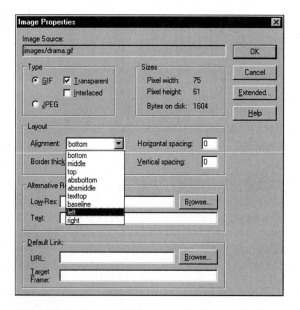

Deleting a Floating Image   If you carefully inspect the text near the image, you'll see a small black rectangle the height of the line. Depending on how you assembled the text and image, the rectangle may not be adjacent to the image but embedded in the text nearby. This actually marks the spot where the align HTML code has been inserted into the paragraph. This handle is important because you need it if you want to delete the image. Selecting the image and pressing the Delete key doesn't remove the image and neither does selecting it and choosing Edit, Clear. You can right-click on the image and choose Cut to remove the image, however.

To delete the image, position the cursor immediately to the right of the small rectangle and press the Backspace key or put the cursor immediately to the left of the rectangle and press the Del key. The image vanishes and any wrapped text moves in to fill the hole.

TROUBLESHOOTING

I used the Right alignment option from the Paragraph Format dialog box to position an image at the right margin. But my text isn't wrapping around it. What's wrong? You may understandably think that the Left and Right alignment options in the Paragraph Format dialog box are the same as the Left and Right alignment options in the Image Properties dialog box. They aren't, although they use exactly the same wording. The difference is that the paragraph alignments don't allow text wrapping; they merely position the image. Incidentally, don't apply mixed Image Properties alignments and Paragraph Format alignments to the same image. A graphic with a Right paragraph alignment and a Right Image Properties alignment may behave unpredictably. There's no practical reason to mix the alignment types, anyway.

Making Transparent Images You want to give your pages a unified and harmonious appearance, and you achieve this through your choice of images, text, and layout. You can add to this sense of unity by using transparent GIF images (only GIFs support this option; it doesn't work with JPEGs). A transparent image lets the page background appear through parts of the graphic, as though the picture were painted on acetate instead of paper. This embeds the image into its surroundings and gives a sense of integration. You can see the difference in effect in Figure 23.16.

FIG. 23.16
The transparent GIF is better harmonized with its surroundings than the one below it, which is opaque.

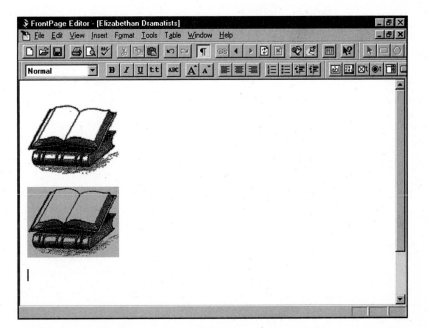

To achieve this effect, select the image and then choose Edit, Properties to open the Image Properties dialog box. Mark the Transparent check box in the Type section. Choose OK.

If you feel that a graphic looks better if a particular color in it is transparent, you can get this effect with the Make Transparent tool from the Image toolbar. To make a particular color invisible, use the following steps:

1. Select the graphic and click the Make Transparent button.
2. Put the cursor (it looks like the eraser end of a pencil) on the color you want to do away with, and click. All instances of that color in the graphic become transparent.

TIP When you first look at the image properties for some graphics, the Transparent check box is grayed out because the graphic contains no transparent colors. To establish a transparent color, use the Make Transparent tool.

Providing Alternative Text   This is important. You have to tell people who are running their browsers with images turned off or who are using a text-only browser that there's an image in the page. Even if they have images turned off, they might like to see your graphic, but they have to know it's there.

You add alternative text by using the Image Properties dialog box. In the Alternative Representations section, use the Text box to type the word or phrase that stands in for the graphic. Choose OK. (Remember to test the results!) Do not try to give an elaborate description of the picture. A few well-chosen words are plenty. This feature, incidentally, is part of standard HTML.

Linking Your Pages

As stated earlier, hyperlinks are the key elements of the Web and its most powerful tool. From any location in any Web page, you can link to:

- Another location in the same page
- Another page in the same Web
- A page in another Web on the same host machine
- A resource anywhere in the Web or the Internet (pages at other Web sites, FTP sites, Gopher sites, and so on)

Using Bookmarks to Link Locations in the Current Page   As with all links, you need two things to link locations in the current page through the use of bookmarks: the hyperlink itself, and the destination it takes the viewer to. In this case, our destination is a specific place on the current page. Since it models itself on a word processor, FrontPage Editor refers to this destination as a *bookmark*, which is a common tool in major Windows word processors. This makes sense, since we're working with pages, anyway.

You can link to a bookmark from any page in your Web, and you can establish bookmarks in any page that you have permission to modify. Incidentally, the formal HTML term for a bookmark is *named anchor*.

N O T E The term "bookmark" is also used in Netscape to mean an entry in a quick-access list of Web or Internet sites. FrontPage Editor uses "bookmark" differently, to mean a page location, rather than a site address. ▪

To set up the bookmark, which is the destination of the link, use the following steps:

1. Select an appropriate word or phrase, anywhere in the page, to be the bookmark (you can't choose an image to be a bookmark).
2. Choose Edit, Bookmark. The Bookmark dialog box appears (see Fig. 23.17).

FIG. 23.17
You use the Bookmark dialog box to define the destination of a hyperlink.

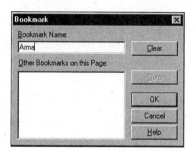

3. The selected text shows up in the Bookmark Name text box. You can accept this or type something else.
4. Choose OK. A dashed underline appears under the bookmarked text (this underlining does not appear in a browser).

 T I P To clear a bookmark, click anywhere in the marked text, and choose Edit, Bookmark, Clear. The Bookmark vanishes.

With the bookmark defined, you next set up the hyperlink itself. First make the origin page active and then use the following steps:

1. Select the image or text you want to make into the hyperlink.
2. Choose Edit, Link or click the Create or Edit Link button on the toolbar. The Create Link dialog box appears (see Fig. 23.18).
3. If the Open Pages sheet isn't the active one, click the Open Pages tab to make it so.
4. In the Open Pages sheet, select the name of the current page (the page that is to contain both the hyperlink and the bookmark).
5. In the Bookmark box, use the arrow button to display the Bookmark list.

6. Select the bookmark you assigned to the destination. When you do, its name appears in the Bookmark text box.

7. Choose OK.

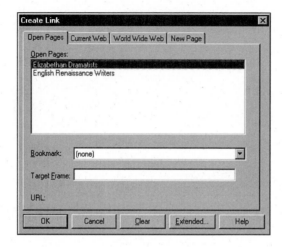

If you used text as the hyperlink, you'll see that it's now highlighted and underlined with the default link color. If you used an image, there's no visible change to it. This is why it's important to have a redundant text label for image-based hyperlinks.

Now save the page and test it by viewing it in your browser. Clicking the hyperlink brings the destination into view in the browser window.

 When you put the cursor on top of a link, FrontPage Editor's status bar displays the name of the Bookmark that is the link destination. In the status bar, the bookmark name is preceded by a pound sign (#). This is the HTML code that indicates a named anchor.

Linking to an Open Page in the Current Web Hyperlinks give you tremendous flexibility in structuring your Web. For instance, you could keep a table of contents on a single page and set up links to other pages that hold the information itself. In general, hyperlinks make it unnecessary to produce monster pages. This has at least two advantages: shorter pages are easier to maintain, and it's easier to keep navigational aids handy for the reader. Also, most readers start to lose their orientation if they have to keep scrolling through screen after screen of information.

FrontPage Editor's linking tools let you set up your connections with a minimum of difficulty. To establish a link to an already open page in the current Web, use the following steps:

1. If you don't want a bookmark in the destination page, go directly to step 2. If you do, make the destination page active, define the bookmark, and return to the original page.

2. Select the image or text you want to use for the link.

3. Choose Edit, Link or click the Create or Edit Link button on the toolbar. The Create Link dialog box appears.

4. Click the Open Pages tab to view the Open Pages sheet. Select the destination page from the list.

5. If you defined a bookmark, choose it from the Bookmark list box.

6. Choose OK.

Test the link in your browser. If you defined a bookmark as the destination, the link takes you directly to it. If you didn't, the link takes you to the top of the destination page.

Linking to Closed Pages This is really more of a shortcut than a feature. It simply lets you make a link within the current Web without bothering to open the destination page. To do so follow these steps:

1. Select the text or image for the link and then choose Edit, Link.

2. When the Create Link dialog box appears, click the Current Web tab (see Fig. 23.19).

3. Use the Browse button to insert the destination page name into the Page box, or type the name in. You can type in a bookmark, if one has been defined (and if you can remember it). Then choose OK to establish the link.

FIG. 23.19

Use the Current Web sheet for quick linking to another page.

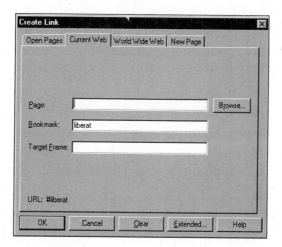

Linking to the World Wide Web You will now get a real sense of the power of hyperlinks. Local hyperlinks are useful tools, but connecting your pages to the Web puts vast resources at your disposal. Remember, though, that it's your visitors who count here. They will use the resources you've selected, so you have a lot of responsibility to them.

Links to the Web are set up through the World Wide Web sheet in the Create Link dialog box (see Fig. 23.20). The Protocol box lets you select which protocol the link uses, and the URL box is where you put the address of the resource. If you don't find the protocol you want to use in the Protocol box, select (other), and type the protocol in the URL box. When you've filled it in, choose OK.

FIG. 23.20

Use the World Wide Web
tab to connect your
pages to the resources
of the Web and the
Internet.

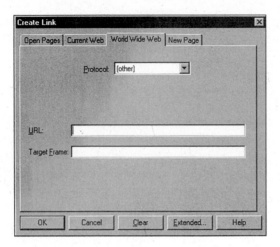

 TIP   To avoid typing a long URL, you can use Edit, Copy to copy it from your browser's Location text box and
then paste it where you need it with Ctrl+V.

It's that simple. To test the link, save the page, open your PPP or SLIP connection, and try it
out in your browser. To make sure you get valid results, clear your browser's cache before
testing.

Your links to the World Wide Web work the same way as the links within your own Web. If a
visitor to your page clicks a link that references a page somewhere else in the Web, she'll go
there. If she clicks a link to an image file that resides on another server, her browser displays
that image in a window all by itself.

Testing and Editing Links   Like FrontPage Explorer, FrontPage Editor has a Follow Link
command. To use it, click the link and choose Tools, Follow Link. If the link is to the current
page, the page scrolls to that location. If it's to another page, the other page is opened. If the
link references a page on another server, FrontPage Editor tries to find that page and open it.
In this case, if the server isn't responding, nothing happens for a long time. If you suspect this
has happened, choose Tools, Stop to end the linking attempt. Then it's time to figure out what
went wrong and fix it. Often it's a typographical error in the URL; sometimes it's a problem at
the server end.

Editing a link is simplicity itself. Click anywhere in the link text, or select the link image, and
choose Edit, Link. The Edit Link dialog box appears, but the four sheets in it are exactly the
same as those in the Create Link dialog box. Make any changes you want, and choose OK.

Using Tables for Better Content Organization

Like lists, tables are common in our lives, especially in business and science. In Web pages,
they can contain text and images, just as printed tables do. You can use them to arrange text in

parallel columns or to set an explanatory block of text beside the image that resides in the adjacent cell. You can insert lists into cells, and you can even insert tables into other tables. All this gives you tremendous flexibility in arranging data and images (see Fig. 23.21).

FIG. 23.21
An image is in the left cell of the table's top row and a bulleted list in the right. Table borders are shown for clarity; they're optional.

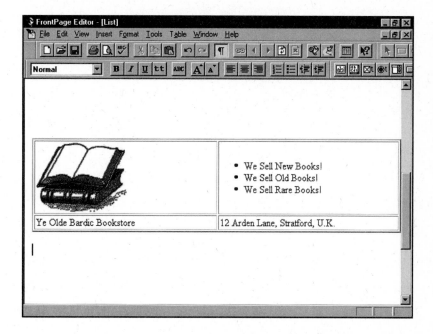

Tables can also contain hyperlinks to other resources, which gives them a whole new dimension. You can make a table containing thumbnails of images and link these to the larger versions. In another example, each entry in a periodic table of the elements can be linked to a resource that gives detailed information about that element. Additionally, you can insert forms or a WebBot into a cell, which makes a table almost an interactive tool in itself.

At the present writing, tables are supported by Netscape 2.0, Internet Explorer 2.0, and NCSA Mosaic 2.1, so you shouldn't feel too wary about including them in your pages. Each browser treats visible cell borders differently, though, so check to see what the borders look like in each browser before you settle on using them. Also, borders may look peculiar if they're enclosing empty cells, so it's best to test.

Setting Up a Table FrontPage Editor gives you a lot of options for table appearance. In this, it's much like a high-end word processor. But don't begin a complicated table by plunging right into FrontPage Editor. Begin by planning it, even if only by roughing it out on paper. You'll save yourself a lot of time and revision.

Once you've worked out the table's content and organization, use the following steps:

1. Choose Table, Insert Table. The Insert Table dialog box appears (see Fig. 23.22).

FIG. 23.22
You set up a table and specify size, width, and layout parameters in the Insert Table dialog box.

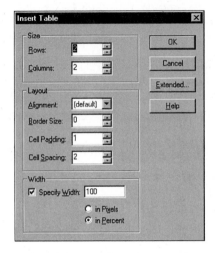

2. In the Rows and Columns spin boxes, specify the number of rows and columns.
3. In the Alignment drop-down list box, specify whether you want the table against the left margin, centered, or against the right margin.
4. In the Border Size spin box, specify how many pixels thick the cell and table borders are to be. A value of zero specifies no borders.
5. In the Cell Padding spin box, specify how many pixels of space you want between the cell contents and the inside edge of the cell boundary.
6. In the Cell Spacing spin box, specify how many pixels of space you want between cells.
7. In the Specify Width text box, specify how wide you want the table to be, either in pixels or as a percentage of the browser window.
8. When you are done, choose OK. The table appears. If you chose a Border Size of zero, the cells are outlined in dotted lines (see Fig. 23.23) These dotted cell boundaries don't appear in a browser.

Actually putting content into a cell is straightforward. Click in the cell and, if it's text you want, just start typing. The text wraps when it reaches the cell margin, pushing the bottom of the whole row down so that you can keep going. To insert images, other tables, lists, or any other page element, click in the cell and use the appropriate menus to insert the component. The cells resize to suit the content.

Modifying the Properties of an Existing Table As you work on a table, you may discover that you need to change some of its characteristics. To do this, click anywhere in the table, and choose Table, Table Properties. The Table Properties dialog box appears (see Fig. 23.24).

FIG. 23.23

Two empty tables: the upper table has a border size of zero and a width of 75%; the lower table has a border width of 2 and a width of 50%.

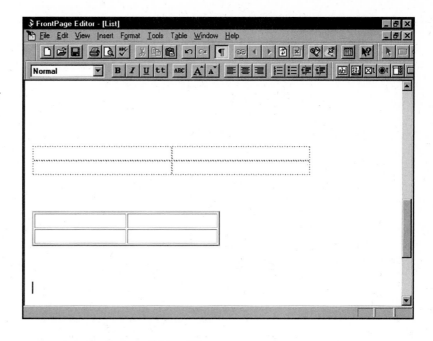

FIG. 23.24

Change the settings for an existing table with the Table Properties dialog box.

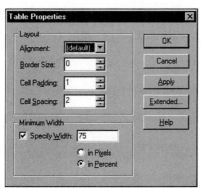

The Table Properties dialog box duplicates part of the Insert Table dialog box. You can modify the table layout and the width of the table using the same procedures.

 TIP To get to the Table Properties dialog box quickly, right-click anywhere in the table and select Table Properties from the shortcut menu.

Adding Rows or Columns Even with the best planning, you sometimes discover a class of information you didn't allow for, and you need a new row or column for it. To add either one, select the existing row or column that will be adjacent to the new one. Choose Table, Insert

Rows or Columns. The Insert Rows or Columns dialog box appears (see Fig. 23.25). Fill in the data for the number of rows or columns to insert, and where they should go relative to the selection you made. Then choose OK.

FIG. 23.25

Use the Insert Rows or Columns dialog box to add data space to your tables.

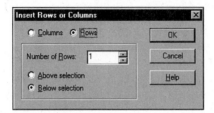

Inserting a Cell   If you deleted a cell and decide you want its real estate back, you can insert a new cell by using the Table, Insert Cell. Where the new cell appears is governed by the following:

- If the cursor is in an empty cell, the new cell is added immediately to the left of the current cell.
- If the cursor is at the left end of any data in a cell, the new cell is added on the left of the current cell.
- If the cursor is at the right end of any data in a cell, the new cell is added on the right of the current cell.

Inserting a brand new cell can be a bit quirky. The table's width isn't fully dynamic; that is, FrontPage Editor doesn't resize the column width consistently as you add cells to a row. This can give you unpredictable results in browsers. For this reason, plan ahead to avoid having to insert a lot of new cells.

Inserting a Table into an Existing Table   You can get interesting effects by putting a table inside a cell of another table. To do this, click the cell where you want the sub-table to appear, and choose Table, Insert Table. Set up the sub-table properties as you like and then choose OK. You can see an example of a table in another table's cell in Figure 23.26.

Splitting and Merging Cells   A perfectly regular grid of cells may not exactly match the way your data needs to be laid out. To change the cell patterns so that they serve your purposes better, you can split or merge them. To split a cell, click in it, and then choose Table, Split Cells. The Split Cells dialog box appears (see Fig. 23.27).

Now you have a choice of dividing the cell into columns or rows. Set up whichever you want, and choose OK. Splitting the cells leaves the data intact in the left cell (row split) or the upper cell (column split). In Figure 23.28 you can see a table with both row-split and column-split cells.

FIG. 23.26
Placing a table within the cell of another table gives a "subdivided" effect. Both tables have captions.

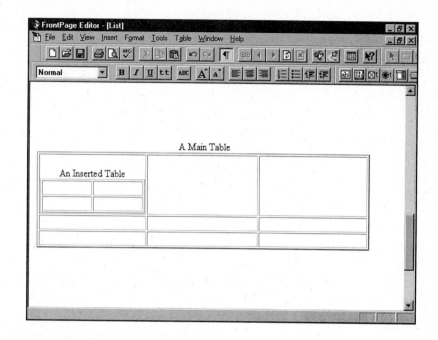

FIG. 23.27
You can change a table's cell subdivisions by splitting cells.

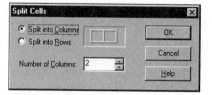

To put cells together, select them, and then choose Table, Merge Cells. The data will flow across the merged cells, though you may have to do some reformatting.

Making Cells Span Rows and Columns Another way of modifying your table's grid is to make a cell bigger or smaller. This is called spanning, and you change a cell's span by using the Cell Properties dialog box. Select the cell and choose Edit, Properties. In the Cell Span section, enter the number of rows or columns you want the cell to stretch across and choose OK. The ultimate effect of this can be very similar to merging or splitting cells. However, it is different in that, when you span a cell, the cells it spans across are "pushed" down or sideways, as if you had inserted cells. You can delete these extra cells, of course. In the example in Figure 23.29, the large center cell was produced by setting its span at 2 rows and 2 columns. The cells that were pushed out to the right and downward by this were then deleted.

FIG. 23.28

The top right cell has been split into two rows and the bottom left cell into three columns.

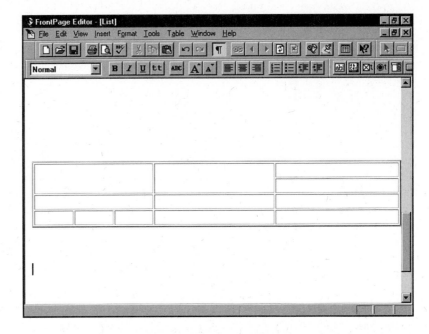

FIG. 23.29

Using cell spanning lets you customize your table's appearance.

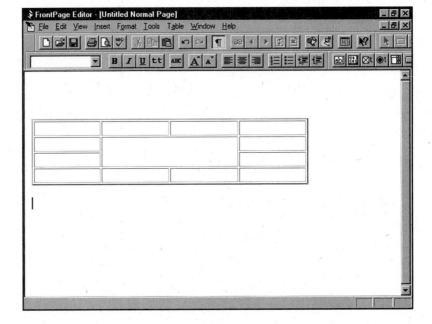

Aligning the Content of a Cell   Depending on your cell content, you may want it positioned in different places. An image, for example, usually looks better if it's centered within the cell borders. Again, you get these effects by using the Cell Properties dialog box. In the Layout section, you can specify horizontal and vertical text alignment with the drop-down list boxes. Figure 23.30 shows an image with the Horizontal Alignment set to Center and Vertical Alignment set to Middle.

FIG. 23.30
Centering text in cells improves its appearance.

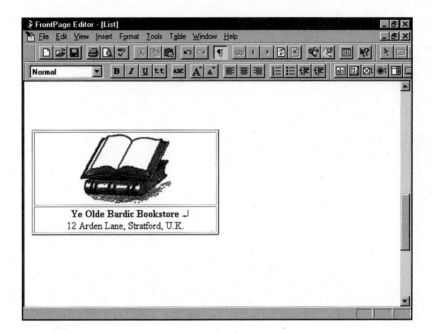

Understanding WebBots

WebBots (or *Bots*) are a key part of FrontPage because they automate certain procedures that other Web authoring tools require you to hand-code in HTML or in a scripting language like Perl. FrontPage puts several different kinds of Bots at your disposal.

But what's a Bot? Well, simply put, a Bot represents a chunk of programming that gets embedded into the HTML code of a page when you insert the Bot. Depending on the type of Bot, the program it represents executes when

- The author saves the page.
- A visitor to the site accesses the page.
- The visitor clicks on an interactive portion of the page, such as the Submit button for a form.

Some WebBots are used only with forms; others are called "utility" Bots because they carry out useful, routine tasks that streamline page and site creation. A few Bots are almost invisible; they execute automatically when you tell FrontPage Editor to do something and show up neither in FrontPage Editor nor in a browser. An example of the last type is the image map Bot. If you inspect the HTML code for an image map, you'll see the word "Bot" tucked away in it. That's as close as you ever get to this particular WebBot.

You use the Insert menu to put any of the "visible" Bots into a page. We'll look at some of the simple utility Bots, just to get acquainted with Bot behavior.

Using the HTML Markup Bot to Insert Unsupported HTML

While FrontPage Editor supports many extensions to HTML 2.0, there are a few it doesn't provide support for. If you want unsupported HTML code in your page, you could, of course, edit this into the page directly, using a text editor or a specialized HTML editor.

 You can edit an HTML file directly using a text editor. In FrontPage Explorer, right-click on a Web page and choose Open With. Choose Text Editor from the list and click on OK. Make any changes you wish to the HTML file using the text editor and save them. Then, from FrontPage Explorer, choose File, Import; and click on Import Now to import your changes back into the Web. You can also import other Web pages into your Web in this manner.

But there's an easier way. The HTML Markup Bot lets you insert whatever HTML code you want into your Web page. For example, suppose that you need to use the Netscape bullet extensions with a bulleted list. FrontPage Editor doesn't support these bullets, so you turn to the HTML Markup Bot. Choose Insert, Bot. From the Insert Bot dialog box, select HTML Markup Bot. Then choose OK. The HTML Markup dialog box appears.

Now you write the code for the bulleted list. When you finish, choose OK. FrontPage Editor displays a small yellow icon, with a <?> in it, at the insertion point. This is actually a container for the code you inserted. All you have to do to get rid of the code is delete the yellow container. If you want to modify the code, select the container and choose Edit, Properties. The HTML Markup dialog box with the existing code will appear.

Include Bot

The Include Bot inserts the contents of a file into a page. You use this if you have several pages in a Web that need identical formatting for one or more elements, such as a standard heading at the top of each page. By using the Include Bot, you can include this heading on as many pages as you like. Furthermore, if you need to change it (a new logo, for example) you can make the change in only one file, instead of editing every page where the element appears. Each page using the Include Bot is updated automatically when the included file changes.

To use the Include Bot, select it from the Insert Bot dialog box and choose OK. The Include Bot Properties dialog box appears (see Fig. 23.31).

FIG. 23.31
You specify the included file with the Include Bot Properties dialog box.

Enter the URL of the file to be included, either by typing it or by selecting Browse to search the current Web. Note that you can only enter page URLs, not image URLs.

Scheduled Image Bot

The Scheduled Image Bot inserts a graphic file from the Web and displays it for a specified period of time. If the time period has not arrived or has elapsed, one of the following happens:

- A message such as Expired Scheduled Image appears in FrontPage Editor. When the page is viewed from a browser, nothing appears.

- A specified alternate image appears in both FrontPage Editor and Web browser.

The Scheduled Image Bot is particularly useful for advertising or displays that only run for a period of time. With the Scheduled Image Bot you can, for example, insert a client's advertisement for a day or week and, after the time expires, replace it with a specified alternative.

To put a scheduled image into your page, select that Bot from the Insert Bot dialog box. The Scheduled Image Bot Properties dialog box appears (see Fig. 23.32).

FIG. 23.32
Use the Scheduled Image Bot Properties dialog box to specify how long an image will be included on your page.

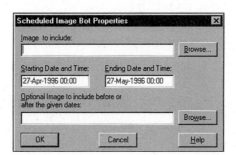

Then use the following steps:

1. Use the browse button to select an image from the Web, or type in the URL of the image.

2. Specify the starting and ending date and time for the image to appear. The defaults are today's date for the starting date and one month later for the ending date.

3. Optionally, specify an image to be displayed before or after the dates given in step 2. If this field is left empty, a brief message appears in Editor telling you that the image is not being displayed, and nothing shows up when viewing the page via a Web browser.

A scheduled image has the following behaviors:

■ Although the image looks like a normal one, you can't select it and edit the image properties, such as borders, image type, or alignment. If you do select it, and choose Edit, Properties, the Scheduled Image Bot Properties dialog box appears instead. In other words, the object on the page is really a Bot, not an image.

■ If the computer's system date falls outside the range given by the start and end dates you specified in the Bot, the message Expired Scheduled Image appears in FrontPage Editor in place of the image. Neither the image nor this message appears in a browser.

■ Placing the cursor over a scheduled image doesn't make it turn into the Bot cursor. The Bot cursor does appear if the Expired Scheduled Image message is showing.

■ You can link or unlink the image using Edit, Link (or Unlink) and the usual linking methods.

Using the Search Bot

When you insert a search Bot, a simple form appears allowing a reader to search all pages in the current Web, or a discussion group, for a string of words. When you insert a Search Bot, you get the Search Bot Properties dialog box (see Fig. 23.33).

FIG. 23.33
Using the Search Bot Properties dialog box to establish the parameters of a search.

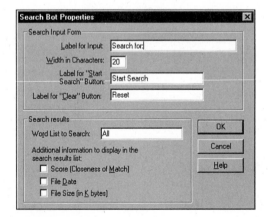

N O T E   The Search Bot searches only the current Web. It isn't intended as a search engine for locations beyond that Web. ■

You can modify the Bot's properties in the following ways:

■ Put your own text, such as "Search My Web For:" in the Label for Input text box.
■ Set the field width for the search string.
■ Customize the Clear and Start button labels.

- Specify the Word List to Search, to set the search range. "All" searches all the Web pages of the current Web. If you've set up a discussion group, you can enter its directory name here, and the Bot searches all entries in that discussion group directory. If you want to exclude some pages from a search, you must store these in a hidden directory.

- Use the check boxes to specify whether to display the closeness of the match, the last update of a matched page, and the matched page's size in kilobytes.

When a visitor to your site submits words to search for, the Search Bot returns a list of pages on which the words appear. If your Web is complex or large, your visitors will thank you for including an easily accessible Search Bot.

Table of Contents Bot

This Bot creates a table of contents for your Web site. To use it, select the Bot from the Insert Bot dialog box. The Table of Contents Bot Properties dialog box appears (see Fig. 23.34).

FIG. 23.34
Setting the Table of Contents Bot Properties lets you customize this essential part of a Web.

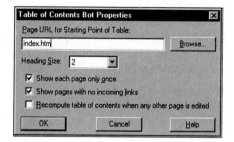

With this Bot, you can

- Select the page that is the starting point of the TOC. On execution, the Bot follows all links from this page. If you want a list of all pages on your Web, assign the home page as the starting point.

- Choose the heading size for the table of contents. The TOC heading is taken from the Page Title of the starting page.

- Mark the Show Each Page Only Once check box to keep the same page from appearing over and over in the TOC. Without this box selected, you'll get a TOC entry for the page for each link to it.

- Mark the Show Pages with No Incoming Links check box to include all pages on the site, even orphan pages with no links to them.

- Mark the Recompute Table of Contents When Any Other Page Is Edited check box to update the TOC every time you edit a page in the Web. Large Web sites can take a long time to update, so mark this box only if you can wait. To "manually" update a table of contents, open the page containing the table of contents Bot and re-save it.

TROUBLESHOOTING

**I inserted a TOC Bot, but it's not showing the TOC in the FrontPage Editor workspace, just three
dummy entries. And I can't edit the dummy entries. What have I done wrong?** You haven't done
anything wrong. You don't see the real TOC except in a browser. Admittedly, this makes page layout a
little more difficult, since you can't see directly what the page is going to look like. The best way to deal
with this is to load your browser, with the caching turned off, and use the browser display to evaluate
your work as you go. Remember, however, that this TOC page will inevitably be fluid because it will
change as your site gains and loses pages. So be sure not to use a design that depends on rigid
positioning of page elements for its effect.

Timestamp Bot

The Timestamp Bot automatically inserts the last date the page was saved or updated. Optionally, it can also include the time of either of these events.

It's a simple Bot. Use its properties dialog box to select whether it gives the date of the last edit
or the date the page was updated. An update is either the last edit or when the page's URL was
regenerated because of a change in the structure of the Web. ●

CHAPTER 24

VBScript and ActiveX for Developing Web Applications

by Jerry Honeycutt

Visual Basic Scripting Edition (VBScript from now on) is a very simple language from Microsoft that lets you add exciting, active content to your Web pages. You can connect scripts to a form, for example, so that you can do form processing right there on the client-side instead of relying on server-side processing. You can add games to a Web page. The possibilities are staggering. Take a look at Microsoft's VBScript examples for a taste of what's possible. The URL is **http://www.microsoft.com/vbscript**.

If that's not enough, you also can add ActiveX objects to your Web pages. ActiveX objects are OLE objects that you can distribute with your Web page. You insert them into a page with a special <OBJECT> tag, and optionally control those objects with VBScript code.

This chapter provides information about creating great Web pages with VBScript and ActiveX objects. It isn't a Visual Basic language tutorial, however. In fact, I don't cover the VBScript keywords in this chapter at all. You will find a resource on the CD-ROM that fully describes the VBScript language (see Appendix A, "What's on the CD," for more information). If you're familiar with Visual Basic or any other variant of Basic, you'll have few problems picking up VBScript. ■

Learn how to work with and manage VBScript projects

In this chapter, you'll learn about the tools you need for using VBScript and how to manage a VBScript project.

Add VBScript code to your Web page

VBScript is a very simple language. You'll learn how to add code to your HTML files, how to organize the scripts in your HTML files, and how to work with event handlers.

Link Visual Basic code to your forms

The most important usage for visual Basic Script is handling events in your HTML forms. Learn how here.

Use the ActiveX control pad to add objects

You can distribute ActiveX objects with your Web page so that you can add new capabilities to it. You use the Control Pad to insert those objects.

N O T E To learn everything you need to know about VBScript and ActiveX objects, you would need a whole book, and have I got the book for you—Que's *Visual Basic Script by Example*, written by yours truly. This book contains everything you need to know in order to master VBScript and ActiveX objects. It's loaded with examples that you can use in your own Web pages. ■

Understanding VBScript

VBScript really is a simple language. If you're a bit familiar with Visual Basic or Visual Basic for Applications, and you understand how to create Web pages using HTML, you'll pick up VBScript in no time. Even if you don't know a lot about Visual Basic, you can probably still cobble scripts together by using the examples in this chapter.

There are some things you need to know about VBScript, however, because you have to do everything yourself—unlike Visual Basic. You won't find a VBScript development environment, so you have to settle for a text editor, the ActiveX Control Pad, and Internet Explorer. Organizing scripts is a bit more difficult, too, because you don't have an integrated editor like Visual Basic 4.0 that keeps it all tidy for you. Visual Basic 4.0 also handles naming event procedures for you—VBScript doesn't. So, you have to learn VBScripts conventions for connecting forms to scripts. You will find more information about all of these topics in the remainder of this section.

 T I P You can download Microsoft's complete VBScript documentation from its Web site. Point your browser at **http://www.microsoft.com/vbscript**.

What You Need to Develop with VBScript

All you need for viewing Web pages that use VBScript is a script-enabled browser such as Internet Explorer 3.0 (or greater). Chapter 17, "Using Microsoft Internet Explorer," shows you how to download and install Internet Explorer. You don't have to install any other special software, and you don't have to download and install a bunch of ActiveX objects in advance because the most popular ActiveX objects already come with Internet Explorer.

Internet Explorer is the first (of course) of many Web browsers to support VBScript. As the standards' bodies (W3C) accept ActiveX and VBScript, you can count on other browsers such as Netscape Navigator to support both technologies. It's a put-up or shut-up kind of deal. In the mean time, clever vendors such as NCompass Labs, Inc. have created plug-ins that you can use with Netscape to support VBScript and ActiveX objects. Need more information? Point your Web browser at **http://www.ncompasslabs.com**, or install the demo version you find on the CD-ROM.

N O T E On the Internet, the availability of technology across all platforms is a key to that technology's success. As a Web developer, it doesn't make sense for you to rely on technology that is only available for the Mac, does it? Likewise, Microsoft knows that if UNIX and Mac users don't have support for VBScript and ActiveX objects, no one will develop Web pages with it because they can't reach the largest possible audience; all those UNIX and Mac users will be left out in the cold. Thus, Microsoft makes the VBScript source code available to anyone wanting to port VBScript to an unsupported platform. Due to this unprecedented move, you can expect to see VBScript running in a variety of environments before too long. Yes, VBScript will proliferate the Internet. ▪

Understanding What You Need to Know   If you already know how to write programs with Visual Basic, you're way ahead of the game. HTML is a lot easier to learn than writing good Visual Basic programs. Chapter 21, "Using HTML to Build Your Home Page," contains a crash course on HTML language. Learning HTML is a different story from learning how to create great Web pages, however. In practice, the only way to learn to create Web pages that please the eye and don't try the user's patience is to look for examples that work. Then, mimic those.

If you know HTML, on the other hand, but don't know the least bit about Visual Basic, don't panic. The CD-ROM contains a VBScript language tutorial that will get you up to speed quickly. Alternatively, you can check out Microsoft's Web site to learn more about the VBScript language features. Point your browser at **http://www.microsoft.com/vbscript**.

Using Text and HTML Editors   As a developer, you don't get much more than what the user already has: Internet Explorer or a VBScript-enabled Web browser. You don't get a full-blown development environment like Visual Basic. No form editor. No debugger. The exception is the ActiveX Control Pad, a tool you'll learn about later. So, what do you use to edit scripts? I'm not sure that you're going to like the answer, but here it goes: Notepad. You can use any text editor, but I used Notepad for most of the examples in this chapter. If it makes you feel any better, you can refer to it as "Microsoft Visual Notepad."

It's senseless to lay out Web pages by hand these days. You'll want to use an HTML editor to create the layout of your Web pages. The best I've seen is Microsoft FrontPage, which you learn about in Chapter 23, "Using Microsoft FrontPage." You can buy it from the computer store now, or you can wait until it ships with Microsoft Office 7.0. Either way, FrontPage is a WYSIWYG (What-You-See-Is-What-You-Get) HTML editor with an interface very similar to Microsoft Word.

T I P   Don't be surprised to see VBScript support built into future versions of Microsoft FrontPage. This lets you attach scripts to forms and objects while you're visually editing a Web page.

Nabbing ActiveX Objects   VBScript is certainly useful to glue forms together. You can validate a form before sending it to the server. You can pre-fill data in a form. You also can make elements within a form interact with each other.

After a while, forms get kind of dull—especially considering all those cool ActiveX objects just sitting there waiting for you to insert them into your Web page. You can add all sorts of fancy labels to your page. You can insert a timer object so that you can update the Web page periodically. You can use a vertically scrolling marquee that continuously scrolls a Web page or image before the user's eyes. The list goes on and on.

Internet Explorer comes with a variety of controls already. That is, these controls don't have to be downloaded from the Web server because the user already has them. Here's what they are:

Animated Button	A button that can contain an AVI animation similar to those annoying flying sheets of paper when you copy a file in Windows 95.
Chart	A chart control that lets you display numerical data in line, pie, bar, and a variety of other charts. You have complete control of the display.
Gradient Control	A cool control that lets you display a swipe of color across an area of the Web page. The color gradually grows lighter or darker depending on the settings you use.
Label	A text label that gives you complete control over color, font, size, rotation, and so on. You also can use a label as a click target.
New Item	A control that displays a "new" symbol for a certain period of time. You can use it to point out new content on your Web page.
Popup Menu	A control that lets you create a pop-up menu just like in Windows 95. You can put anything you want in the menu. Try using it instead of a toolbar or combobox sometime.
Preloader	An object that downloads and stores a file in the user's cache so that it's ready and waiting for the user. You can use it to start downloading a Web page in advance of the user actually clicking on the link—making your Web site really soar.
Stock Ticker	An object that displays information from a URL in a horizontally scrolling area. It continuously updates the information from the URL.
Timer	An object that fires an event at every clock tick. You can use it to update your Web page at certain intervals.

N O T E   The objects that ship with Internet Explorer are freely available and distributable. Many third-party controls require that you purchase a developer license to create Web pages with them, however. In particular, you won't be able to use the ActiveX Control Pad, described in the following section, to insert tags for these controls into a Web page without a proper license. ■

Using the ActiveX Control Pad   The ActiveX Control Pad is the closest thing to a VBScript development environment that you're going to find right now. It does two things. First, it lets you insert objects in HTML files without worrying about the format of those nasty <OBJECT> and <PARAM> tags. Second, it lets you use a special ActiveX control called the Layout control to place an object anywhere on a Web page you like. You have total two-dimensional control over the object's placement. The nice thing about using the Control Pad (many folks refer to it as the Xpad) is that it's visual. You're not staring at HTML tags. You're actually looking at the objects in the Layout control as they'll appear on the Web page.

You also can set an object's properties using a property sheet, much like you can in Visual Basic. Figure 24.1 shows an example of a layout control with a few objects in it. Notice the property sheet.

FIG. 24.1
The ActiveX Control Pad smacks a bit of Visual Basic's form editor. You can't visually edit all objects you put in a Web page, however—only the Layout control.

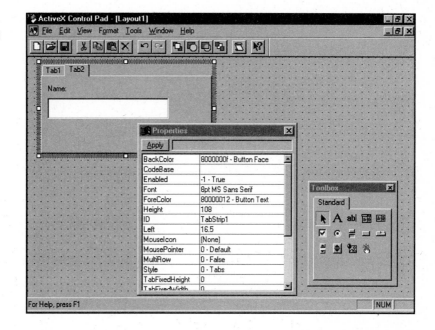

The Control Pad also comes with additional controls you can use in your Web pages—beyond what Internet Explorer comes with. These controls should be used within a Layout Control, however. You'll recognize most of the following controls from Windows 95:

Option button	Enables the user to choose between a variety of options by clicking the box next to the option.
Tab strip	Creates a set of tabs. The user can click each tab to bring the contents of that tab forward.
Scrollbar	Puts a scroll bar on the Web page.
Spinner	Lets the user increment or decrement a value by clicking the up or down arrow.
Label	Puts a classic label on your Web page.
Image	Contains an image.
Hot spot	Defines an area on the Web page which, when clicked, causes an event to fire.
Textbox	Puts a classic text box on the Web page.
Listbox	Puts a classic list box on the Web page.
Combobox	Puts a classic combobox on the Web page.

Checkbox	Puts a check box that enables the user to turn an option on or off.
Command Button	Puts a button on the Web page.
Toggle Button	Puts a button that toggles on or off each time the user clicks on it.

HTML Browser Control lets you display Web pages within your Web page. Neat, huh?

Here's How VBScript Works

Before moving on to other parts of this book, there are a few basic things you need to know about ActiveX Scripting and VBScript. First of all, they're not the same thing (see Table 24.1).

Table 24.1 Scripting Parts

When You See This	It Means This
ActiveX Scripting	The technology that makes it possible for a program such as Internet Explorer to host scripting engines like VBScript or JavaScript.
VBScript Engine	The technology that actually interprets, compiles, and runs VBScripts from a Web page.

ActiveX Scripting is like Donahue reuniting old friends: a middle-man. Internet Explorer uses ActiveX Scripting to talk with the VBScript engine. By sitting in the middle as it does, it frees the browser from having to know too much about the particular scripting engine. The benefit? You can plug a variety of scripting engines (VBScript, JavaScript, and maybe even CobolScript one day) into the browser. It also lets the browser developers focus on what they do best, building browsers, instead of twiddling around with scripting languages.

Embedding Scripts in Your Web Pages You embed scripts in an HTML file using tags, much like any other content you put in a Web page. Scripts are put between the <SCRIPT> and </SCRIPT> tags (see Listing 24.1).

Listing 24.1 What the Browser Does at Parse Time

```
<SCRIPT LANGUAGE="VBSCRIPT">
<!--
    Alert "Howdy from Texas" ' Evaluated & executed when the page is loaded

    Sub Pause ' Evaluated and stashed away for later use
        MsgBox "Click on OK to Continue"
    End Sub
-->
</SCRIPT>
```

What all this means isn't important right now, What is important is what your browser does with the script. When your browser loads a Web page that includes scripts (*parse time*), it immediately evaluates each <SCRIPT> block it encounters. It grabs everything in this block and passes it off to the scripting engine.

The scripting engine takes a look at the script block that the browser gave it and looks for any sub-procedures and variables outside of a sub-procedure (global variables). It compiles these and stashes their names in an internal table for later use. If you had a sub-procedure called DisplayName, for example, the scripting engine compiles that sub-procedure's code, saves it, and puts the name of the sub-procedure in a table. Later, when you call the sub-procedure called DisplayName, the scripting engine looks up that procedure in the table and executes the code associated with it.

You may have noticed in Listing 24.1 that you can include statements outside of a sub-procedure. The scripting engine executes statements it finds outside of a sub-procedure—immediately. This is called *immediate execution*. Microsoft also refers to scripts that the browser executes immediately as *inline scripts*.

Just remember that VBScript executes inline scripts as it loads the Web page. It saves variables and sub-procedures in a symbol table for later use, however.

Part
IV

Ch
24

N O T E You should follow Microsoft's coding conventions when you write scripts. These coding conventions are guidelines for how you name variables and procedures. They are also guidelines for how you format your scripts in HTML and where you put scripts. You can learn more about Microsoft's coding conventions at **http://www.microsoft.com/vbscript/us/vbstutor/ vbscodingconventions.htm**.

Understanding VBScript's Limitations
VBScript isn't without its limitations. Here's a brief look at some of the most notable:

- Everyone in the world can see your code. There are few secrets on the Internet. If you've written a nifty bit of script, there isn't anything stopping other folks from ripping off your code. Likewise, there's nothing stopping you from lifting someone else's code, either.

- VBScript is just a scripting language. By itself, you're limited to working within the Web page. You also have a limited set of keywords and runtime functions. You can get around a lot of VBScript's limited feature set by creating your own ActiveX objects, however.

- Microsoft has removed just about every keyword that could cause a security problem for your computer. You don't have to worry about viewing a Web page that uses VBScript. The worst thing that could happen is that a poorly written script could cause the browser to crash. On the other hand, ActiveX objects could be a problem. For example, Microsoft removed CreateObject from VBScript due to security concerns. It didn't take long for some clever programmer to develop an ActiveX object that simulates the CreateObject keyword, however.

Organizing the Scripts Within an HTML File
Microsoft's coding conventions don't say quite enough about organizing scripts within your HTML files. I'll make up for that here with some

suggestions for how you can better organize your scripts by placing them at the appropriate places within the HTML file.

Each of the sections that follow suggest where to put different types of scripts in your HTML files. These are only suggestions; you're free to bend them any way you want. In "Putting Scripts in the <HEAD> Block," I make a very strong suggestion that you should follow, however: Put helper procedures in the <HEAD> block of your HTML file. Your scripts may not work properly if you don't organize them the way I've indicated.

Using Inline Scripts   You'll add a lot of inline scripts in your Web pages. Inline scripts are blocks of statements that you write outside of a normal procedure. The browser executes them in the order it encounters them as it opens the Web page. This is a great way to do work as the browser opens the Web page or even to change the contents of the HTML file itself.

Put an inline script anywhere in an HTML file where you feel it's appropriate. If you want to dynamically add content to the HTML file, for example, put a script in the exact location where you want to add the content. Listing 24.2 is an example of such a script. It prompts you for your name and adds a greeting to the HTML file as the browser opens it.

Listing 24.2   Organizing Inline Scripts in an HTML File

```
<HTML>
This is static content on the Web page.<BR>

<SCRIPT LANGUAGE="VBScript">
<!--
 strName = InputBox( "What is your name?" )
 Document.Write "Howdy " & strName &
   ". This is dynamic content on the Web page.<BR>"
-->
</SCRIPT>

This is more static content on the Web page.
</HTML>
```

Figure 24.2 shows you what this HTML file looks like in Internet Explorer.

Putting Scripts in the <HEAD> Block   Many scripts you create contain procedures that have a supporting role. If you're creating a Web page that displays the average sale for each of four territories, for example, you'll probably create a function called `GetAverageSale` and then invoke it once for each territory's numbers. Also, if you have a handful of statements that you can use in many different places, you'll put those in a procedure and invoke it by name from each place.

You should put most of your scripts containing procedures in the <HEAD> block of your HTML file. Why? Two reasons. First, organizing most of your scripts at the beginning of your HTML file separates the scripts from the content of your page. You can find scripts faster this way.

FIG. 24.2

The first and last lines of text are static text contained in the HTML file. The middle line is dynamic text created by a script.

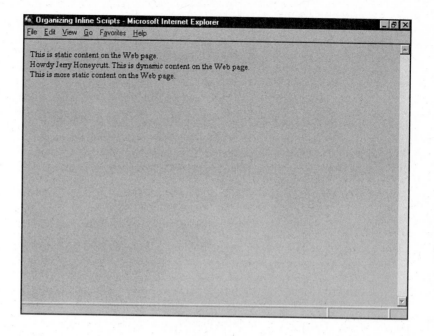

Second, scripts are evaluated as the browser loads the Web page—top to bottom. VBScript doesn't actually stash away a procedure's name until the browser sees the <SCRIPT> block and passes it to the scripting engine. Thus, if you reference a procedure's name in an inline script that isn't defined until later in the HTML file, your script may not work properly. The easiest way to get around this problem is to make sure all of your general procedures are defined before any of your inline scripts.

Take a look at Listing 24.3. Notice that I defined the function called GetAverageSale in the <HEAD> tag of the HTML file. Because I defined it before I tried to use it, its name is available to the inline script later in the file. If I defined it after I tried to use it in the inline script, I'd get an error as the browser loads the Web page. Also note that I defined the global variable sstrUserName in the <HEAD> section, too. This assures me that the global variable is available in every inline script I create.

Listing 24.3 Organizing Procedures in an HTML File

```
<HTML>
<HEAD>

<SCRIPT LANGUAGE="VBScript">
<!--
  Dim sstrUserName

  Function GetAverageSale( sngTotalSales, intSalesQty )
      GetAverageSale = sngTotalSales / intSalesQty
```

continues

Part

IV

Ch

24

Listing 24.3 Continued

```
 End Function
 -->
 </SCRIPT>

 </HEAD>

 <BODY>

 <SCRIPT LANGUAGE="VBScript">
 <!--
  MsgBox "Hello " & sstrUserName
  MsgBox "Average sale is " & GetAverageSale( 1000, 20 )
 -->
 </SCRIPT>

 </BODY>
 </HTML>
```

Organizing Event-Procedures   If you followed the arguments in the previous section, you'd put event-procedures for forms in the <HEAD> section of your HTML file. In fact, you might put all of a form's event-procedures inside of a single <SCRIPT> block so that they're all together as one big blob of script.

You can make life easier on yourself if you don't, however. Put event-procedures within the <FORM> block for two reasons:

■ You'll have an easier time maintaining a form's event-procedures if you organize them near the actual form. You don't want to have to flip back and forth between the form and the top of the HTML file.

■ Putting a form's event-procedures inside of the <FORM> block prevents you from having to specify the form's name when accessing an element's properties and methods. Normally, you access the value of a text box element with a statement such as *form.element. value*. If you put the scripts inside the <FORM> block, however, you can access the value of the same text box with a statement like *element.value*. It cuts down on the typing.

Listing 24.4 shows you an example of an HTML file that contains a form. You'll notice a script that contains an event-procedure for the Hello button within the <FORM> block. Not only does this example show you the merits of keeping your event-procedures near the forms they service, it shows you that you don't have to use a form's name to access its elements.

Listing 24.4 Organizing Event-Procedures for a Form

```
 <HTML>
 <FORM NAME="Myform">
 Name:
 <INPUT NAME="MyName" TYPE="TEXT" >
 <INPUT NAME="Hello" TYPE="BUTTON" VALUE="Hello">
```

```
<SCRIPT LANGUAGE="VBScript">
<!--
 Sub Hello_OnClick
     MsgBox "Hello " & MyName.Value
 End Sub
-->
</SCRIPT>
</FORM>
</HTML>
```

Organizing Scripts Within Frames   As you've learned, you can divide the browser window into smaller sections called frames. The entire browser window contains a single HTML file, and each frame contains yet another HTML file. Consider this HTML file, for example:

```
<HTML>
<FRAMESET COLS="10%,90%">
    <FRAME NAME="Left" SRC="left.html">
    <FRAME NAME="Right" SRC="right.html">
</FRAMESET>
</HTML>
```

This example is a Web page that contains two frames. The left-hand frame contains the HTML file called left.html, and the right-hand frame contains the HTML file called right.html. So, in this arrangement, where do you put your scripts? It depends. The important considerations are that (1) the top-level HTML file is always available, and (2) the HTML files in each frame may or may not always be available.

Thus, if you want to have access to a script (procedures or global variables) all the time, from any frame, you should put them in your top-level HTML file, like this:

```
<HTML>
<SCRIPT LANGUAGE="VBScript">
<!--
 Dim strYourName
 Sub DisplayName
     MsgBox strYourName
 End Sub
-->
</SCRIPT>
<FRAMESET COLS="10%,90%">
    <FRAME NAME="Left" SRC="left.html">
    <FRAME NAME="Right" SRC="right.html">
</FRAMESET>
</HTML>
```

In this case, you can get access to the global variable strYourName from any frame's HTML file. You also can invoke DisplayName from any frame's HTML file. You do such by prefixing each name with top. to indicate to VBScript that you're referring to the top-level HTML file. Here's an example of setting strYourName to Jerry from left.html:

```
top.strYourName = "Jerry"
```

On the other hand, put scripts that you only need to access from within a frame inside of the HTML file that you display in that frame. You don't need to do anything differently to access the script because it's already within the scope of that HTML file.

Hosting Your ActiveX Web Pages

Beyond the actual tools you need to create Web pages with VBScript, you need a place to host your Web pages. Yes, you can create VBScript pages for your own entertainment, but what's the use? You want to show off to the world, right? You need to have access to a Web server on which you can put your Web pages and any ActiveX controls you use in those Web pages.

Many Internet service providers give you a little Web space free with your subscription. If it's less than 1M, however, you may need to get a bit more space. By the time you cram all your pages, images, and controls on the server, 1M may not be enough.

How Events Work on a Web Page (VBScript)

Windows sends messages to an object to let it know that you've done something horrible such as clicked it with the mouse. In VBScript, you don't have any way to receive messages, however. Even if you could receive messages, the object would get the message before you ever got a crack at it. So, how is your script going to know that something has happened to the object?

In VBScript, an object causes events in response to the messages the object receives. When you click inside of an object, Windows sends a message to the object telling it that you clicked the mouse. In turn, the object causes a click event, and the browser looks for a special VBScript procedure called an event-procedure to handle that event.

How does the browser know which event-procedure is the right one? It looks for a procedure whose name begins with the name of the object, followed by an underscore (_), and ending with the name of the event—Button_OnClick, for example. You specify the name of each object in your HTML file, and each type of object has a predefined set of event names that you'll learn about later in this chapter.

 In VBScript, triggering an event also is known as firing an event. A button fires the OnClick event, for example. This is the convention I'll use from here.

Demonstrating an Event-Procedure

Take a look at Listing 24.5. The <SCRIPT> tag in the head contains a procedure called btnButton_onClick. Based upon the naming convention you learned earlier, you gather that this is an event-procedure for an object called Button that handles the OnClick event. All it does is display Ouch! You clicked me. in a message box. Take a look at the form in the body of the HTML file. It contains a single element I've named—Button—using the <INPUT> tag's NAME attribute. The combination of this name and the name of the event is how the browser knows to execute the event-procedure called `btnButton_OnClick` each time you click the button.

Listing 24.5—Demonstrating an Event-Procedure

```
<HTML>
<SCRIPT LANGUAGE="VBScript">
<!--
 Sub btnButton_onClick
     MsgBox "Ouch! You clicked on me."
 End Sub
-->
</SCRIPT>

<FORM><INPUT NAME="btnButton" TYPE="BUTTON" VALUE="Click Me"></FORM>
</HTML>
```

Using an Inline Event-Handler

VBScript is very flexible. You just learned how to handle an event using an event-procedure. You can handle events in other ways, too. For example, you don't have to create a separate procedure for an event at all. You can handle it as an attribute in the element's tag as shown in Listing 24.6.

Listing 24.6—Using an Inline Event-Handler

```
<HTML>
<FORM>
<INPUT NAME="btnButton" TYPE="BUTTON" VALUE="Click Me"
   OnClick='MsgBox "Ouch! You clicked on me."' LANGUAGE="VBScript">
</FORM>
</HTML>
```

Notice that this example doesn't have a `<SCRIPT>` tag anywhere in it. Look at the `<INPUT>` tag closely, though. It contains an attribute that is a script. Its name is the name of the `OnClick` event. When the button fires the `OnClick` event, it executes everything between the single quotes ('). Take note here as this is one of those exceptions. The value of an event's attribute is surrounded by single quotes, unlike other attributes that use double quotes ("). You can put multiple statements in the event's attribute by separating them with colons (:) like this:

```
OnClick='MsgBox "Hello World" : MsgBox "Hello Again"'
```

The LANGUAGE attribute specifies which language you're using for the inline script. You could just as easily use JavaScript as VBScript. If you don't specify a language anywhere in your HTML file, the browser defaults to JavaScript.

Part
IV

Ch
24

Some events pass arguments to the event-handlers. How do you handle arguments when you're handling the event inline? Like this:

```
MouseMove(shift, button, x, y)='window.status="The mouse is at " & x & "," & y'
```

Using the *FOR/EVENT* Attributes

Yes, VBScript provides one more way to handle events. If you don't want to use an event-procedure and you don't want to use an inline event-handler, you can use the <SCRIPT> tag itself. This involves using the FOR and EVENT attributes of the <SCRIPT> tag. These attributes let you associate a script with any named object in the HTML file and any event for that object. Take a look at Listing 24.7.

Listing 24.7—Using the *FOR/EVENT* Attributes

```
<HTML>
<SCRIPT LANGUAGE="VBScript" FOR="btnButton" EVENT="OnClick">
<!--
 MsgBox "Ouch! You clicked on me."
-->
</SCRIPT>
<FORM><INPUT NAME="btnButton" TYPE="BUTTON" VALUE="Click Me"></FORM>
</HTML>
```

This file defines the button just as in Listing 24.7. The difference is that you won't find an event-procedure in this HTML file. Take a look at the <SCRIPT> tag, though. It contains the FOR and EVENT attributes that define the object and event associated with that script. FOR="btnButton" EVENT="OnClick" says that when an object named Button fires the OnClick event, execute every statement in this script.

Some events pass arguments to the event-handlers. How do you handle arguments when you're handling the event using the FOR/EVENT syntax? Like this:

```
<SCRIPT LANGUAGE="VBScript" FOR="btnButton"
  EVENT="MouseMove(shift, button, x, y)">
```

The enclosed script then can use any of the parameters passed to it by the MouseMove event.

Handling Common Events

If you're a Visual Basic programmer, you'll be surprised by the limited number of events available for each object you'll find on a Web page. You just don't need to handle events such as DblClick, DragDrop, DragOver, MouseDown, MouseUp, and so on. They don't make sense in this context. That leaves you with a handful of events such as OnClick, mouseMove, onMouseOver, and so forth. Note that you won't find any keyboard events at all.

Each and every intrinsic or ActiveX object defines its own events. You'll have to look at that object's documentation to find information about the exact events it provides. I describe many of these objects in this book, however. Also, many of the browser's objects such as the Window or Document object support events such as onLoad. Look at those objects' documentation for more information about the events they fire.

Mouse Events   Almost all objects you put on a Web page fire a few mouse events. Here are the common ones:

MouseMove	Fires as the mouse moves over an object. This event reports the mouse's position as it moves. You can use it to implement fly-over help.
OnMouseOver	Fires each time the mouse moves over an object. The difference between this event and MouseMove is that it only fires once each time the mouse crosses the object and it doesn't report its position.
OnClick	Fires each time you click the left mouse button over an object. You can use this event to implement your own image maps or validate a form before you submit it to the server.

State Events   Many elements such as a text box or buttons support events that tell you when their state changes. This includes when they get or lose focus, when their data changes, and when the user selects something from a list:

OnBlur	Fires when an object loses the keyboard focus. You can use this event to validate the contents of a text box before the user moves on to another object.
OnFocus	Fires when an object gets keyboard focus. An object has focus when what you type or do with the keyboard affects that object. You can change focus by pressing the Tab key or clicking on another object with the mouse.
OnChange	Fires each time the user changes data in the object. For example, each time the user types a character in a text box, the text box fires this event.
OnSelect	Fires each time the user selects an item in a list or combo box.

Part
IV

Ch
24

CAUTION

Be careful not to create cascading events. This occurs when your event-procedure causes the same event to fire over and over again. If your event-handler for the OnChange event changes the contents of the text box, for example, the OnChange event fires again. This eventually will cause your script to crash.

The Scripting Object Model

Microsoft's scripting object model (model, from now on) exposes a variety of Web-related objects to your scripts. You can manipulate the Web browser and Web page, for example. Microsoft's model is compatible with the model used in JavaScript. The only difference is that any ActiveX scripting language can use the model in Microsoft's Internet Explorer, including JavaScript and VBScript. Just leave it to Microsoft to do things bigger and better, eh?

This section gives you a brief overview of the scripting object model as shown in Figure 24.3. It describes the objects you see in the model, the relationship between each object, and how to access the properties, methods, and events in each object.

FIG. 24.3
A shaded box indicates that one or more of that particular object can exist. You can have multiple frames in a window, for example.

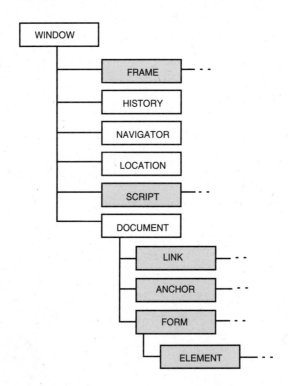

Window

A window object is always at the top level. This is easier to understand if you relate the model to what you actually see on your desktop. You see the browser window first. Then, you see a document inside of the browser window, forms inside a document, and so on. A window object contains a variety of properties, methods, and events. Table 24.2 gives you a brief overview, however.

Table 24.2 Window Properties, Methods, and Events

Properties	Methods	Events
name	alert	onLoad
parent	confirm	onUnload
self	prompt	
top	open	
location	close	
defaultStatus	setTimeout	
status	clearTimeout	
frames	navigator	
history		
navigator		
document		

Every window contains a handful of other objects, including a history, a navigator, a location, scripts, and a document. A window also can contain one or more frames. You access each of these objects using the corresponding properties as shown in Table 24.3.

Table 24.3 Accessing A Window's Objects

To Access This	Use This Property
Frame	frames
History	history
Navigator	navigator
Location	location
Script	procedure
Document	document

As a general rule, you access properties that have plural names, such as `frames`, using an array. You can tell how many objects are in the array using the `length` property, like this:

```
window.frames.length
```

Each element of that array represents a single object of that type. To access the second frame in a window, for example, use the following syntax (start counting from 0):

```
window.frames(1)
```

Frame   A window optionally can contain one or more frames. It depends on whether or not you use the <FRAMESET> tag in your Web page. If you do use it, the frame's array contains an element for each frame you define—starting from 0. The following bit of scripting gets the name of each frame in the window, for example:

```
For intI = 0 to frames.length - 1
    strName = frames(intI).name
Next
```

You also can use a frame by name if you give it a name in the <FRAME> tag. Consider this frame:

```
<FRAME NAME="Body" SRC="http://www.myserver.com/body.html">
```

You can access it using its name, like this:

```
strName = Body.name
```

The frame object doesn't introduce any new properties, methods, or events. That's because each frame object is really just a window object. You use the same properties, methods, and events that you see in Table 24.2 in the previous section.

The important thing to note here is how you get around frames. That is, if you define a frame called Body, that contains a frame called TopBody inside it, that also contains a frame called ReallySmallFrame, you can access the properties of ReallySmallFrame like this:

```
Top.Body.TopBody.ReallySmallFrame.name
```

What's going on here? Think of a frame as a window for a moment, and it should become clear. You have a window called Top, that contains a window called Body, that contains a window called TopBody, that contains a window called ReallySmallFrame.

You also can access each frame using the frames array of each window (frame). Assuming that each of the frames you saw earlier is the first frame defined in each HTML file, you can access them like this:

```
Top.frames(0).frames(0).frames(0).name
```

If ReallSmallFrame was actually the second frame in TopBody, you'd access it like this, instead:

```
Top.frames(0).frames(0).frames(1).name
```

History   Each window contains a history object that contains the window's history. That is, it contains a list of every Web page it has displayed in that window. Table 24.4 shows you its properties.

Table 24.4   History Properties and Methods

Properties	Methods
length	forward
	back
	go

Navigator   Each window contains a navigator object that contains information about the Web browser. Table 24.5 shows you its properties.

Table 24.5   Location Properties

appCodeName
appName
AppVersion
userAgent

Location   Each window contains a location object that defines the URL of the Web page it contains. Table 24.6 shows you its properties.

Table 24.6   Location Properties

href
protocol
host
hostname
pathname
port
search
hash

Script   Scripts live within the window object. Never mind the fact that you define scripts within the document object. The model stores them under the window object. Each scripting object is actually the name of a procedure: sub-procedure or function.

If you're working with scripts inside of frames, you can get quick and easy access to a window's procedures by using the window's name in conjunction with the procedure's name. For example, if you're writing a script in a deeply embedded frame, you can access a script in the top level window like this:

```
top.MyProcedure()
```

You can access scripts within other frames by using the frame name or the parent keyword, instead. To access a script in the second frame below the current window, use this statement:

```
frame(1).MyProcedure()
```

To access a script in the parent frame, use this statement:

```
parent.MyProcedure()
```

Document

The next major object in the model is the document object. This represents the actual Web page that you see in the window, including the text, links, forms, etc. that you see on the page. A document object contains a variety of properties and methods. Table 24.7 gives you a brief overview.

Table 24.7 Document Properties and Methods

Properties	Methods
linkColor	write
aLinkColor	writeLn
vLinkColor	close
bgColor	clear
fgColor	open
anchors	
links	
forms	
location	
lastModified	
title	
cookie	
referrer	

Every document contains a handful of other objects, including links, anchors, and forms. You access each of these objects using the corresponding properties as shown in Table 24.8.

Table 24.8 Accessing a Document's Objects

To Access This	Use This Property
Link	links
Anchor	anchors
Form	forms

As you've learned, you access properties that have plural names, such as forms, using an array. You can tell how many objects are in the array using the length property, like this:

```
document.forms.length
```

Each element of that array represents a single object of that type. To access the first link in a document, for example, use the following syntax (start counting from 0):

```
document.forms(0)
```

Because scripts are in the window's scope, not in the document's scope, you have to reference a document's properties and methods by name, like this:

```
document.name
```

You can't drop off the document. portion like you can drop off the window. portion of a window object's properties and methods. You can access forms and objects without using document., though.

Link   The document's links property is a read-only array of link objects; you know, links on the Web page that you define with the <A HREF=URL> and </A> tags. You access it like other object arrays, except that you can't refer to a link by name. The following example is the third link on the document.

```
document.links(2)
```

Table 24.9 lists the link object's properties and events.

Table 24.9 Link Properties and Events

Properties	Events
href	mouseMove
protocol	onMouseOver
host	onClick
hostname	
port	
pathname	

continues

Table 24.9 Continued

Properties	Events
search	
hash	
target	

Anchor The document's `anchors` property is a read-only array of anchor objects. You create anchors on the Web page using the `<A NAME="NAME">` and `</A>` tags. You access it like other object arrays, except that you can't refer to an anchor by name. The following example is the third anchor on the document.

```
document.anchors(2)
```

Table 24.10 names the anchor object's properties.

Table 24.10 Anchor Properties

name

Form A document object can contain one or more form objects. It depends on whether or not you've used the `<FORM>` tag in your Web page. If you've used forms in your Web page, `document.forms.length` indicates the number of forms on the page. The following script gets the name of each form in the window.

```
For intI = 0 to document.forms.length - 1
    strName = frames(intI).name
Next
```

You also can use a form by name if you give it a name in the `<FORM>` tag. Consider this form:

```
<FORM NAME="MyForm">
```

You can access it using its name, like this:

```
strName = document.MyForm.name
```

Table 24.11 describes the form object's properties, methods, and events.

Table 24.11 Form Properties, Methods, and Events

Properties	Methods	Events
action	submit	onSubmit
encoding		
method		
target		
elements		
hidden		

The form object contains one additional object: the element object. You access it using the `elements` array.

You have to explicitly use the `document.form` way to access a form because the form and document objects aren't in the same scope. Remember that scripts belong to the window and forms belong to the document.

You can put scripts inside of a form object, however. In that case, you don't have to use the `document.` method for accessing the form in your script. You can just use the form name. Here's an example of a script embedded inside of a form object:

```
<FORM NAME="MyForm">
<INPUT NAME="txtName" TYPE="TEXT" SIZE="40">
<INPUT NAME="btnFill" TYPE="BUTTON" VALUE="Fill">
<SCRIPT FOR="btnFill" EVENT="onClick">
<!--
 txtName.value = "Jerry"
-->
</SCRIPT>
```

If you want to access a form's elements outside of the `<FORM>` tag, you have to fully qualify the property, like this:

```
document.MyForm.txtName.value
```

Element   A form contains one or more elements, or controls as you probably know them. These include buttons, text boxes, and list boxes. You access each element using the `elements` array. The following script gets the name of each element in a form.

```
For intI = 0 to document.MyForm.elements.length - 1
    strName = document.MyForm.elements(intI)
Next
```

You also can get at an element using its name if you give it a name in the `<INPUT>` tag. Consider this frame:

```
<INPUT NAME="btnDone" TYPE="BUTTON" VALUE="Done">
```

You can access its current value using its name, like this:

```
strCaption = document.MyForm.btnDone.value
```

Table 24.12 describes the element object's properties, methods, and events.

Table 24.12   Element Properties, Methods, and Events

Properties	Methods	Events
form	click	onClick
name	focus	onFocus
value	blur	onBlur
defaultValue	select	onChange
checked	removeItem	onSelect
defaultChecked	addItem	
enabled	clear	
listCount		
multiSelect		
listIndex		
length		
options		
selectedIndex		

Handling a Form's Events

Earlier, you learned that objects on the Web page fire events when they need your attention. A button fires the onClick event when the user clicks on the button. A text box fires the onChange event when the user changes the contents of the text box.

Most, if not all, of the scripts you write are attached to events. They're event-handlers. Events are pretty much the only way your scripts get a chance to run after the Web page loads. They're the only way you can interact with the objects on a page, including a form's elements.

Handling the *onClick* Event

Most of the elements you can add to a form support the onClick event. These include the button, check box, and text fields. An element fires the onClick event anytime the user clicks the mouse on the element. In some cases, notably the select element, an element fires the onClick event when the user selects an item in a list.

Listing 24.8 contains a form that displays the contents of txtName when the user clicks on the button btnDisplay. I named the event-procedure btnDisplay_onClick because I'm handling the onClick event for the object named btnDisplay.

This example also shows you how to read the value of an element. btnDisplay_onClick reads the value from the text field called txtName. Did you notice the .value bit? You have to explicitly use the property name containing the value. If you're a Visual Basic programmer, this may take a bit getting used to (it did for me) because you're used to using an object's default property, which is usually the value.

Listing 24.8 Handling the *onClick* Event

```
<HTML>
<SCRIPT LANGUAGE="VBScript">
<!--
 Sub btnDisplay_onClick
     alert "Hi " & MyForm.txtName.value
 End Sub
-->
</SCRIPT>
<FORM NAME="MyForm">
    <INPUT TYPE=TEXT VALUE="Jerry" SIZE=40 NAME="txtName">
    <INPUT TYPE=BUTTON VALUE="Display" NAME="btnDisplay">
 </FORM>
 </HTML>
```

Handling the *onFocus* Event

Listing 24.9 shows you how to handle the onFocus event for an element. An element fires the onFocus event any time the user gives focus to a control. The user can give focus to a control by pressing the Tab key until it becomes the current control or by clicking on the control with the mouse.

Listing 24.9 Handling the *onFocus* Event

```
<HTML>
<TITLE>Howdy</TITLE>
<SCRIPT LANGUAGE="VBScript">
<!--
 Sub txtName_onFocus
     status = "Type your first name in this field"
 End Sub
-->
</SCRIPT>

<FORM NAME="MyForm">
    <INPUT TYPE=TEXT VALUE="Jerry" SIZE=40 NAME="txtName">
    <INPUT TYPE=BUTTON VALUE="Display" NAME="btnDisplay" onClick="alert 'Hi ' &
```

continues

Part
IV

Ch
24

Listing 24.9 Continued

```
txtName.value">
</FORM>
</HTML>
```

Handling the *onBlur* Event

An element fires the onBlur event when the element loses focus. An element can lose focus because the user pressed the Tab key to select a different element, or the user clicked on a different element with the mouse.

Listing 24.10 shows you an example of handling the onBlur event. This example just clears the status line. You can use the onBlur event to do any last minute processing before the element loses focus, though.

Listing 24.10 Handling the *onBlur* Event

```
<HTML>
<SCRIPT LANGUAGE="VBScript">
<!--
 Sub txtName_onFocus
     status = "Type your first name in this field"
 End Sub

 Sub txtName_onBlur
     status = ""
 End Sub
-->
</SCRIPT>

<FORM NAME="MyForm">
    <INPUT TYPE=TEXT VALUE="Jerry" SIZE=40 NAME="txtName">
    <INPUT TYPE=BUTTON VALUE="Display" NAME="btnDisplay" onClick="alert 'Hi ' &
txtName.value">
 </FORM>
 </HTML>
```

Handling the *onChange* Event

Listing 24.11 shows you how to handle the onChange event. An element fires this event when the user changes the contents of the element.

Listing 24.11 Handling the *onChange* Event

```
<HTML>
<SCRIPT LANGUAGE="VBScript">
<!--
 Sub txtName_onChange
```

```
        alert "You changed the field"
   End Sub
   -->
   </SCRIPT>

   <FORM NAME="MyForm">
          <INPUT TYPE=TEXT VALUE="Jerry" SIZE=40 NAME="txtName">
          <INPUT TYPE=BUTTON VALUE="Display" NAME="btnDisplay" onClick="alert 'Hi '
     &              txtName.value">
       </FORM>
     </HTML>
```

Setting and Getting an Element's Value

What good is a form if you can't get and set the values of the elements on it, huh? You read the value of most elements using the element's value property, like this:

```
alert MyForm.txtName.Value
```

You also can set the value of an element by assigning a string to the element's value, like this:

```
MyForm.txtName.value = "jerry"
```

The examples in this section show you how to get at the values of other types of elements, including list boxes. This section also shows you how to do other things with fields such as how to disable them.

Adding ActiveX Objects with the ActiveX Control Pad

In the previous section, you learned how to interact with forms and elements using VBScript. You saw examples of connecting a script to a button's click event, for example. You also saw how to get and set the values of different types of elements in your event-handlers. You can use these skills to put together great Web pages that use forms for user input.

For real user interaction, however, you need to turn to ActiveX objects (I use the terms control and object interchangeably). Don't get me wrong; forms are fine. They add even more to a Web page now that you can interact with them using VBScript. ActiveX objects bring more to the party, though, because they're totally flexible, and you'll find a wide variety of objects available.

Adding an Object the Hard Way (by Hand)

You can do things the hard way or you can do things the easy way. The best way to learn about ActiveX objects is to add them to your HTML file the hard way, though.

That's exactly what you're going to do in this section. You'll learn how to put ActiveX objects on your Web page and how to set an object's properties using HTML tags.

Objects in HTML   ActiveX objects act like and quack like the elements on a form. That is, you interact with each ActiveX object properties, methods, and events in exactly the same way that you interact with an element. You get and set the object's properties, you call an object's methods, and you handle an object's events when the object needs attention.

The <OBJECT> Tag You use the <INPUT> tag to put controls in forms. It tells the browser that you're inserting a control in that location, and it gives the browser enough information about the control you're using so that the browser can initialize and display the correct control. For example, you can tell the browser that you want to use a button control with a tag like this:

```
<INPUT NAME="btnButton" TYPE="BUTTON" VALUE="Click Me">
```

The <OBJECT> tag does the same thing. It provides the browser with information about the object you want to put on the Web page, such as the type of object you want to display, its name, and its size. Here's what an <OBJECT> tag looks like:

```
<OBJECT CLASSID="clsid:Number" ID=Label WIDTH=Width HEIGHT=Number>
```

The <OBJECT> is a bit more difficult to understand than the <INPUT> tag, though. First, it doesn't have a TYPE attribute that you set to the type of control you're using. You set a CLASSID attribute, instead, which is the way your computer identifies ActiveX objects on your computer. An object's *classID* is a strange looking, 16-byte, hexadecimal number, like this one:

```
FE3A6742-0214-0617-1019-001044830612
```

 TIP To learn more about classIDs and the Registry, see *Special Edition Using the Windows 95 Registry* by Que. This book shows you how objects organize their settings in the Registry, and it gives you a detailed description of classIDs.

The <OBJECT> tag also has an ID attribute, which works just like the element tag's NAME attribute. It gives that particular instance of the object a name that you can use in your scripts. You can optionally use the <OBJECT>, WIDTH, and HEIGHT tags to specify the exact size of the object on the Web page.

Here's what a complete <OBJECT> tag looks like:

```
<OBJECT CLASSID="clsid:FE3A6742-0214-0617-1019-001044830612" ID=MyControl
WIDTH=250 HEIGHT=100>
```

The <PARAM> Tag You use the <PARAM> tag to set each individual property for your ActiveX object. In Visual Basic, you can use a control's property sheet. If you're adding an object to your HTML file by hand, however, you have to use the <PARAM> tag. This tag's format is simple:

```
<PARAM NAME=PropertyName VALUE=PropertyValue>
```

The NAME attribute is the name of the property you're setting. The VALUE attribute is the actual string value to which you want to set the property. You can set a property called Enabled to False like this:

```
<PARAM NAME="Enabled" VALUE=<False">
```

Using Labels on Your Web Page In Visual Basic programs, you use labels to add text to the program's forms. You already can put text in an HTML file, though, so why in the world do you need a label control? Flexibility. The only thing you can do with text in an HTML file is control its size, font, and in some cases, its position. You have complete control over an ActiveX label, though, including its rotation, color, and more.

To add an ActiveX Label object to your HTML file, insert the following tags in the file at the point you want to display the label:

```
<HTML>
<OBJECT ID="lblMyLabel" CLASSID="clsid:99B42120-6EC7-11CF-A6C7-00AA00A47DD2"
    WIDTH="250" HEIGHT="100">
<PARAM NAME="Caption" VALUE="This is my label.">
<PARAM NAME="Angle" VALUE="0">
<PARAM NAME="Alignment" VALUE="4">
</OBJECT>
</HTML>
```

Feel free to change the <OBJECT> tag's ID, HEIGHT, and WIDTH attributes to suit your needs. You must type the CLASSID attribute exactly as I've shown you here.

Each of the <PARAM> tags sets one of the object's properties. These set the Caption, Angle, and Alignment properties. The label object has many other properties you can change, but these are the basics.

Listing 24.12 shows you a complete example of an HTML file with the ActiveX label object you saw earlier. It sets the label's properties to the basics, but you can use the Rotate and Align buttons to reorient the label on the page as shown in Figure 24.4.

Listing 24.12   Placing a Label on a Web Page

```
<HTML>
<OBJECT ID="lblMyLabel" CLASSID="clsid:99B42120-6EC7-11CF-A6C7-00AA00A47DD2"
    WIDTH="500" HEIGHT="250">
<PARAM NAME="Caption" VALUE="This is my label.">
<PARAM NAME="Angle" VALUE="0">
<PARAM NAME="Alignment" VALUE="4">
</OBJECT>

<FORM NAME="MyForm">
<INPUT NAME="btnRotate" TYPE="BUTTON" VALUE="Rotate">
<INPUT NAME="btnMove" TYPE="BUTTON" VALUE="Move">
<SCRIPT LANGUAGE="VBScript">
<!--
 Sub btnRotate_onClick
     lblMyLabel.Angle = (lblMyLabel.Angle + -5) Mod 360
 End Sub

 Sub btnMove_onClick
     lblMyLabel.Alignment = (lblMyLabel.Alignment + 1) Mod 9
     lblMyLabel.Caption = "This is my Label (" & lblMyLabel.Alignment & ")."
 End Sub
-->
 </SCRIPT>
 </FORM>
 </HTML>
```

FIG. 24.4

Click on the Move
button to see where
each alignment number
puts the label.

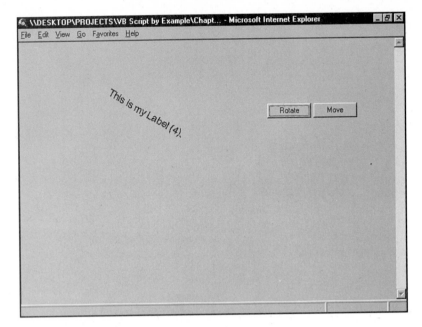

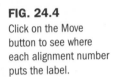

FIG. 24.4

Click on the Move
button to see where
each alignment number
puts the label.

Popping Up a Menu on Your Web Page   Have you ever seen a menu pop up right there in the middle of a Web page? I don't mean Internet Explorer's right-click menu. I'm talking about a menu that the Web page actually creates. You can do just that with the ActiveX PopUp Menu object.

Listing 24.13 shows you what a PopUp Menu object looks like in an HTML file. The <OBJECT> tag for this control sets its ID attribute to mnuPopup, so that is how you name the event-procedures as shown later in the script. Notice that I've set the WIDTH and HEIGHT attributes to zero. I do this so that the actual control doesn't take up any space on the Web page. You only want to see the control when you pop up the menu, right?

You add each menu item using the <PARAM> tag. As always, you name the property you're setting with the NAME attribute. You set the property's value using the VALUE attribute. The menu's items have properties that start with Menuitem[0], Menuitem[1], ..., Menuitem[N]. You must add menu items in sequence; otherwise the PopUp Menu object gets confused. If you remove a menu item, don't forget to renumber the property names.

Listing 24.13   Popping Up a Menu on the Web Page

```
<HTML>
<OBJECT ID="mnuPopup" WIDTH=0 HEIGHT=0 CLASSID="CLSID:7823A620-9DD9-11CF-A662-
    00AA00C066D2">
<PARAM NAME="Menuitem[0]" VALUE="First Item">
<PARAM NAME="Menuitem[1]" VALUE="Second Item">
<PARAM NAME="Menuitem[2]" VALUE="Third Item">
<PARAM NAME="Menuitem[3]" VALUE="Fourth Item">
```

```
<PARAM NAME="Menuitem[4]" VALUE="Fifth Item">
<PARAM NAME="Menuitem[5]" VALUE="Sixth Item">
</OBJECT>

<SCRIPT LANGUAGE="VBScript">
<!--
 Sub mnuPopup_Click( intItem )
     alert "You clicked on item #" & intItem
 End Sub
 Sub btn_onClick
     mnuPopup.PopUp
 End Sub
-->
</SCRIPT>
<INPUT NAME="btn" TYPE="BUTTON" VALUE="Click me">
</HTML>
```

The script at the bottom of the listing shows you how to display the menu and handle its `Click` event. You have to somehow tell the PopUp Menu object to display the menu. That's what the event-procedure for the button control does. It calls the PopUp Menu's `PopUp` method to display the menu at the current mouse position. Figure 24.5 shows you what the menu looks like. The menu fires the `Click` event any time the user makes a selection from the menu. The only argument your event-procedure accepts is the number of the menu item that the user picked, starting from one.

FIG. 24.5

You also can give the PopUp method the x and y arguments to specify an exact location for the menu.

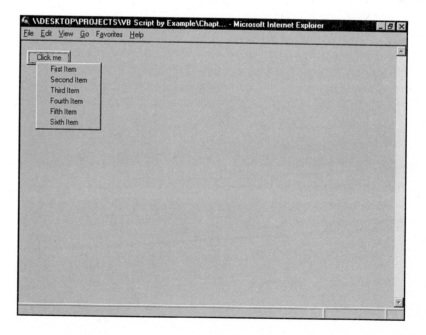

Adding an Object the Easy Way (ActiveX Control Pad)

You've learned the hard way, and I promise you that once you see how easy adding objects with the ActiveX Control Pad is, you'll never go back. All you have to do is point at the place you want to insert an object, tell the Control Pad to insert the object, and fill in the object's property sheet. It doesn't get any easier. In fact, Visual Basic programmers will like doing business this way because they're already familiar with it.s

> **N O T E** You need to install the Control Pad before you can use it. You can get it from Microsoft's Web site at **http://www.microsoft.com/intdev/author/cpad/download.htm**. ■

The Control Pad has three primary features for VBScript developers. Here's what they are:

- The Control Pad lets you easily insert ActiveX objects into your HTML files using a graphical user interface. This means that you don't have to fool around with those <OBJECT> tags at all.

- The Control Pad provides the Script Wizard, which lets you create event-handlers by associating events with actions. You make these associations using a graphical user interface, too. That means that you can avoid as many of those <SCRIPT> tags as possible, but you still need to write them when working on more complicated scripts.

- The Control Pad lets you graphically edit Layout Controls. You can actually place and edit controls just like the form editor in Visual Basic.

T I P The ActiveX Control Pad contains the complete VBScript reference and a complete HTML reference. Choose Help from the Control Pad's main menu. Choose either VB Script Reference or HTML Reference.

Getting Acquainted with the Control Pad Figure 24.6 shows you the Control Pad window with an HTML file in it. You can open many HTML files in Control Pad because it's an MDI application. You switch between each open HTML file using the Window menu.

The top of the HTML file contains an object. You can see the <OBJECT> tag in the file. You also can see the object icon in the margin of the editor window. Click on this icon to change the object next to it in the editor window. Just below the object, you see a script. You also can see the script icon in the margin of the editor window. You can edit the script using the Script Wizard by clicking on this button.

You can type any text you like in the editor window. You can add forms to the file, for example. You also can add everyday text and tags such as headings, lists, etc. If you're really into punishment, you can add objects to your HTML by typing them in the editor window. Considering the features you learn in the next section, however, I strongly discourage you from doing that.

Placing Objects into Your HTML File Inserting an object into an HTML file is easy. Position your mouse pointer at the point at which you want to insert an object, and right-click. Choose Insert ActiveX Control, and you'll see a dialog box similar to the one shown in Figure 24.7. This dialog box lets you pick one of the many controls that are available on your computer.

FIG. 24.6

The editor window shows you the contents of your HTML. Open the HTML file in your Web browser to preview what the Web page looks like.

Script icon —

Object icon   Script Wizard button

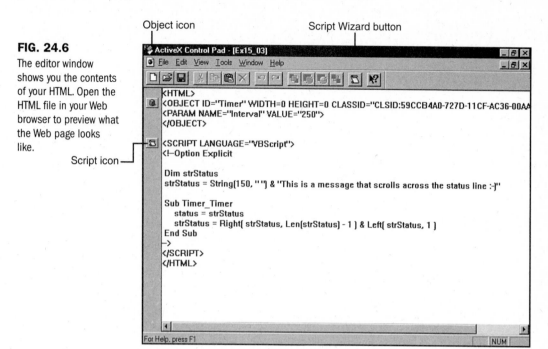

```
<HTML>
<OBJECT ID="Timer" WIDTH=0 HEIGHT=0 CLASSID="CLSID:59CCB4A0-727D-11CF-AC36-00AA
<PARAM NAME="Interval" VALUE="250">
</OBJECT>

<SCRIPT LANGUAGE="VBScript">
<!--Option Explicit

Dim strStatus
strStatus = String(150, " ") & "This is a message that scrolls across the status line :-}"

Sub Timer_Timer
    status = strStatus
    strStatus = Right( strStatus, Len(strStatus) - 1 ) & Left( strStatus, 1 )
End Sub
-->
</SCRIPT>
</HTML>
```

For Help, press F1   NUM

Part
IV

Ch
24

FIG. 24.7

The usable ActiveX controls are called things like `Microsoft ActiveX` *something* or `Forms 2.0` *Something*. Don't use the objects whose names end with `Ctl`.

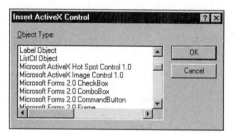

Select one of the controls, such as the `Label Object` and click on OK. The Control Pad opens up the Object Editor and property sheet for the control as shown in Figure 24.8. You can change each of the control's properties using the property sheet shown in the figure. You also can adjust the size of the control by grabbing one of its handles in the Object Editor and dragging it.

Using a control in this manner is called using it at *design time*. You're designing how the control is going to look on your Web page. The user uses the control at *run time*, however, because all she is doing is using a page built with that control. Many controls require that you have a license to use it in design time. The controls you see in this chapter don't require a license, however, because they all come with Internet Explorer.

FIG. 24.8
Select a property and
change it at the top of
the property sheet.

Change its value here. ──────

Select a property here. ──────

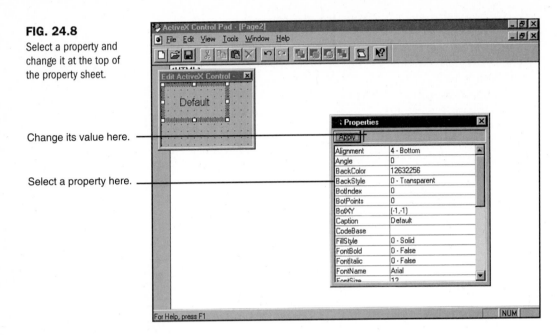

After you've made your changes to the control's property sheet, close both windows by clicking on the graphical editor's close button (the button with the X). After you close both windows, the Control Pad inserts the <OBJECT> and <PARAM> tags into your HTML file that match
how you filled in the property sheet.

You can change the properties in the HTML using the Control Pad's text editor. The next time
you open that control's property sheet, the property sheet will reflect any changes you made.

 The Control Pad has its own annoying way to format the <OBJECT> and <PARAM> tags. You might as
well make all of your tags consistent with the way the Control Pad formats them so that your scripts will
be easier to read.

Editing Scripts Using the Control Pad's Script Wizard   Do you miss the Visual Basic integrated development environment? I do. Even if you've never used Visual Basic before, you
have to wonder if there isn't a better way to do this stuff.

Yes, there is. The Control Pad's Script Wizard. To call it a wizard is a bit misleading because it
doesn't act or quack like other wizards in Windows 95. It does give you a smooth interface for
editing the events of each object in your HTML file, though. In fact, it lets you edit an object's
events two different ways:

   ■ The list view lets you associate an event with a list of actions. You give arguments for
     those actions by answering questions in the Script Wizard.

   ■ The code view is more of a traditional programming approach. You select an object's
     event and edit the code in the window.

The following sections show you how to use both methods for editing event-handlers in your HTML file. You can't use the Script Wizard to edit other types of scripts, though, such as support functions and sub-procedures. That is, you can't use the Script Wizard to edit a sub-procedure that's not an event-handler. You can create event-handlers that call your sub-procedures and functions, however.

TIP Are you not sure which properties, methods, and events a particular object in your HTML file supports? Click on the Script Wizard button in the toolbar, and select that object in the left-hand pane to see its events. Select that object in the right-hand pane to see its properties and methods.

List View   Script Wizard's list view lets you edit an event-handler with the simplest of ease. Click on the Script Wizard button in the toolbar to open the Script Wizard. Then, click on the List View button at the bottom of the window. You see the window shown in Figure 24.9.

Part

IV

Ch

24

FIG. 24.9
In most cases, the list view is all you ever need to create exciting Web pages.

Events

Properties and Methods

Actions associated with the selected event

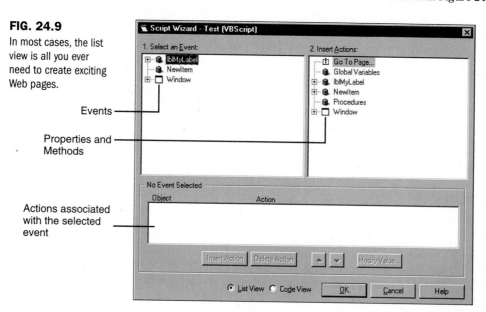

Here's how it works. You associate an object's event with another object's methods and properties, like this:

1. Expose the events for an object in the left-hand pane by clicking on the plus-sign (+) next to the object. Select an event that you want to handle. You can select the window object's onLoad event, for example.

2. Expose the methods and properties for an object in the right-hand pane by clicking on the plus-sign (+) next to the object. Select a method or property that you want to associate with the event you selected in the left-hand pane.

3. Click on the Insert Action button below the bottom pane. If you selected a property, Control Pad prompts you for the value you want to assign to that property in the

event-handler. If you picked a method that has arguments, Control Pad prompts you for the arguments you want to use. If you picked a method that doesn't have arguments, Control Pad doesn't prompt you for anything at all. After you've answer any questions that Control Pad asks, it inserts the association in the bottom pane.

4. You can rearrange the order of the actions in the bottom pane by selecting an action and clicking on the up- and down-arrow buttons to move it around in the list. You also can remove an action by selecting it and clicking on the Delete Action button.

5. When you're happy with the way you're handling that particular event, you can move on to another object and another event or close the Script Wizard by clicking on OK.

Code View   If you're more comfortable with the traditional programmer view of life (optimistic about everything), you can use the Script Wizard's code view. This works just like the list view, except that you don't see a list of associated events and actions in the bottom pane. You see the actual code the Script Wizard creates, instead.

Click on the Script Wizard button in the toolbar to open the Script Wizard. Then, click on the Code View button at the bottom of the window. You see the window shown in Figure 24.10.

FIG. 24.10

You have to use the code view if you want to use statements such as If...Then ... Else in your event-handler.

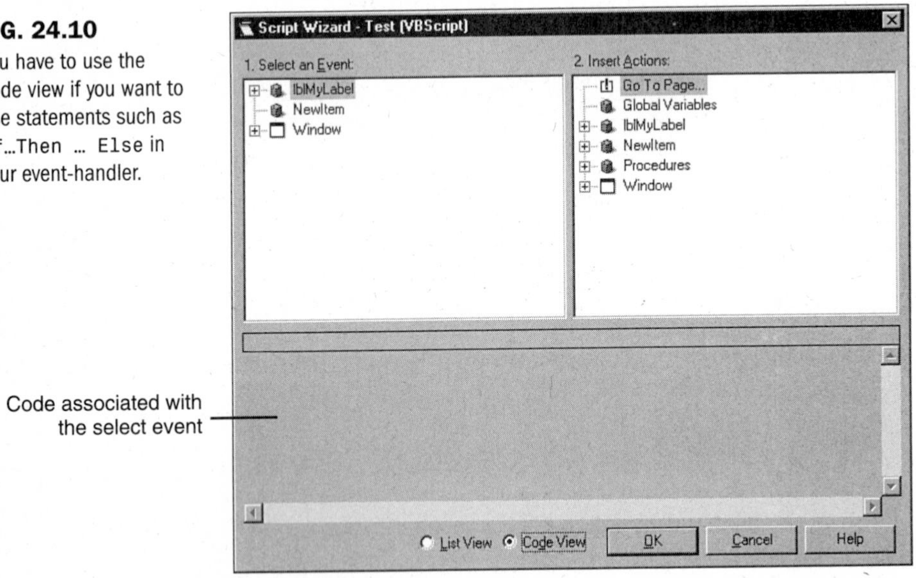

Code associated with the select event

You can insert actions into the bottom pane of the code view just like you do in the list view. That is, you select an event in the left-hand pane and select an action in the right-hand pane. This view doesn't have an Insert Action button, however, so you double-click on the action in the right-hand pane to add it to the bottom pane.

After you've added a few actions to the event-handler by double-clicking on them in the right-hand pane, you can edit the code any way you like. You can add or change the arguments for each method you use. You can add conditional and looping statements. You can do whatever you want.

When you're happy with the way you're handling that particular event, you can move on to another event, or close the Script Wizard by clicking on OK.

 Keep your Web browser running with the Web page you're working on open. Then, you can flip to the browser and refresh the Web page to see your changes while you're working in Control Pad.

Part

IV

Ch

24

CHAPTER 25

Using JavaScript for Developing Web Applications

by David Gunter and Scott J. Walter

You already know that Web pages are written using the HyperText Markup Language, or HTML. You may also know that Netscape introduced a number of HTML extensions in the 1.*x* releases of Netscape Navigator. With the release of Navigator 2.0, Netscape has added a powerful new capability: JavaScript, a language that lets you write programs that Navigator executes when users load or browse your pages. This chapter teaches you how to use JavaScript to power up your Web pages. ■

Introduction to JavaScript

JavaScript allows you to embed commands in an HTML page; when a Navigator user downloads the page, your JavaScript commands will be evaluated. These commands can be triggered when the user clicks on page items, manipulates gadgets and fields in an HTML form, or moves through the page history list.

N O T E   You've probably heard JavaScript called by its earlier-version name: *LiveScript*; at the time of this writing most of JavaScript's capabilities are based on the functionality of LiveScript. As more and more HTML page designers and enterprise application developers create scripts that define the behavior of objects to run on both clients and servers, you'll continue to see improvements and changes for the better in JavaScript. Just as Java (and any other software, for that matter) becomes better in response to its programmers' and developers' imaginations, so will JavaScript. If you're interested in following up on the latest revisions and additions, keep Netscape's home page (**http://home.netscape.com/**) at the top of your bookmarks list. ■

Some computer languages are compiled; you run your program through a compiler, which performs a one-time translation of the human-readable program into a binary language that the computer can execute. JavaScript is an interpreted language; the computer must evaluate the program every time it's run. You embed your JavaScript commands within an HTML page, and any browser that supports JavaScript can interpret the commands and act on them.

Don't let all these programming terms frighten you off—JavaScript is powerful and simple. If you've ever programmed in dBASE or Visual Basic, you'll find JavaScript easy to pick up. If not, don't worry; this chapter will have you JavaScripting in no time!

N O T E   Java offers a number of C++-like capabilities that were purposefully omitted from JavaScript. For example, you can only access the limited set of objects defined by the browser and its Java applets, and you can't extend those objects yourself. For more details on Java, see Chapter 28, "Using Microsoft Internet News," and Chapter 29, "Using the Agent Newsreaders." ■

Why Use a Scripting Language?

HTML provides a good deal of flexibility to page authors, but HTML by itself is static; once written, HTML documents can't interact with the user other than by presenting hyperlinks. Creative use of CGI scripts (which run on Web servers) has made it possible to create more interesting and effective interactive sites, but some applications really demand client-side scripting.

JavaScript was developed to provide page authors a way to write small scripts that would execute on the users' browsers instead of on the server. For example, an application that collects data from a form then POSTs it to the server can validate the data for completeness and correctness before sending it to the server. This can greatly improve the performance of the browsing session, since users don't have to send data to the server until it has been verified as correct. The following are some other potential applications for JavaScript:

■ JavaScript can verify forms for completeness, like a mailing list registration form that checks to make sure the user has entered a name and e-mail address before the form is posted.

■ Pages can display content derived from information stored on the user's computer—without sending the data to the server. For example, a bank can embed JavaScript commands in its pages that look up account data from a Quicken file and display it as part of the bank's page.

■ Because JavaScript can modify settings for applets written in Java, page authors can control the size, appearance, and behavior of Navigator plug-ins, as well as other Java applets. A page that contains an embedded Director animation might use a JavaScript to set the Director plug-in's window size and position before triggering the animation.

What Can JavaScript Do?

JavaScript provides a rich set of built-in functions and commands. Your JavaScripts can display HTML in the browser, do math calculations (like figuring the sales tax or shipping for an order form), play sounds, open new URLs, and even click buttons in forms.

 TIP A function is just a small program that does something, and a method is a function that belongs to an object. For more lingo, see Chapter 28, "Using Microsoft Internet News."

Part
IV

Ch
25

Code to perform these actions can be embedded in a page and executed when the page is loaded; you can also write methods that contain code that's triggered by events you specify. For example, you can write a JavaScript method that is called when the user clicks the Submit button of a form, or one that is activated when the user clicks a hyperlink on the active page.

JavaScript can also set the attributes, or properties, of Java applets running in the browser. This makes it easy for you to change the behavior of plug-ins or other objects without having to delve into their innards. For example, your JavaScript code could automatically start playing an embedded QuickTime or .AVI file when the user clicks a button.

What Does JavaScript Look Like?

JavaScript commands are embedded in your HTML documents, either directly or via a URL that tells the browser which scripts to load. Embedding JavaScript in your pages only requires one new HTML element: <SCRIPT>...</SCRIPT>.

The <SCRIPT> element takes two attributes: LANGUAGE, which specifies the scripting language to use when evaluating the scripts, and SRC, which specifies a URL from which the script can be loaded. The LANGUAGE attribute is always required, unless the SRC attribute's URL specifies a language. LANGUAGE and SRC can both be used, too. Here are some examples:

```
<SCRIPT LANGAUGE="JavaScript">...</SCRIPT>

<SCRIPT SRC="http://www.fairgate.com/scripts/common.js">

...

</SCRIPT>
```

NOTE For security reasons, the SRC attribute was never implemented in the earlier releases of Navigator. As of Navigator 3.0 beta 5, it is now available (but is not yet supported by Internet Explorer). Keep in mind, however, that if you implement the SRC attribute, your site will only work for those people using Navigator 3.0 beta 5 or greater. ■

JavaScript itself resembles many other computer languages; if you're familiar with C, C++, Pascal, HyperTalk, Visual Basic, or dBASE, you'll recognize the similarities. If not, don't worry; the following are some simple rules that will help you understand how the language is structured:

- JavaScript treats all letters as lowercase (except for quoted strings), so document.write() and DOCUMENT.WRITE() are the same.

- JavaScript is pretty flexible about statements. A single statement can cover multiple lines, and you can put multiple short statements on a single line—just make sure to add a semicolon (;) at the end of each statement.

- Curly braces ({}) group statements into *blocks*; a block may be the body of a function or a section of code that gets executed in a loop or as part of a conditional test.

Figure 25.1 shows a small piece of JavaScript code embedded in an HTML page; the frontmost window shows the original HTML file, and the Navigator window shows its output.

FIG. 25.1
The foremost window shows a small piece of JavaScript code embedded in a simple HTML file; the Navigator window shows the result of loading that page (which executes the JavaScript).

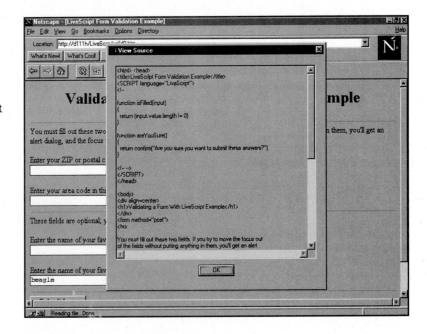

JavaScript Programming Conventions

Even though JavaScript is a simple language, it's quite expressive. In this section we'll cover a small number of simple rules and conventions that will ease your learning process and speed your JavaScripting.

Hiding Your Scripts   You'll probably be designing pages that may be seen by browsers that don't support JavaScript. To keep those browsers from interpreting your JavaScript commands as HTML—and displaying them—wrap your scripts as demonstrated in Listing 25.1.

Listing 25.1   Hiding Your Scripts from Non-JavaScript Browsers

```
<SCRIPT LANGUAGE="JavaScript">
<!-- this line opens an HTML comment
document.write("You can see this script's output, " +
               "but not its source.");
// this line closes the HTML comment -->
</SCRIPT>
```

The opening `<!--` comment causes browsers to disregard all text they encounter until they find a matching `-->`, so they won't display your script. You do have to be careful with the `<SCRIPT>` tag, though; if you put your `<SCRIPT>...</SCRIPT>` block inside the comments, even Navigator will ignore it (and all your JavaScript code as well)!

N O T E   You may notice that the closing comment line in Listing 25.1 starts with a double slash (`//`), the JavaScript comment identifier. This is necessary, because once JavaScript starts processing lines within a `<SCRIPT>` tag, it assumes that *all* lines are JavaScript code until the closing `</SCRIPT>` tag. The double slash effectively hides the closing comment tag from JavaScript, which would otherwise try to evaluate the line. ■

Comments   It's usually good practice to include comments in your programs to explain what they do; JavaScript is no exception. The JavaScript interpreter will ignore any text marked as a comment, so don't be shy about including them. There are two types of comments: *single-line* and *multiple-line*.

Single-line comments start with two slashes (`//`) and are limited to one line. *Multiple-line* comments start with `/*` on the first line, and end with `*/` on the last line. Listing 25.2 demonstrates several examples.

Listing 25.2   Examples of JavaScript Comments

```
// this is a legal comment
/ illegal -- comments start with two slashes
/* multiple-line comments can
be spread across more than one line, as long as
they end. */
/* illegal -- this comment doesn't have an end!
// this is OK...as extra slashes are ignored //
```

The JavaScript Language

JavaScript was designed to resemble Java, which in turn looks much like C and C++. The difference is that Java was built as a general-purpose object language, while JavaScript is intended to provide a quicker and simpler language for enhancing Web pages and servers. In this section, you learn the building blocks of JavaScript and how to combine them into legal JavaScript programs.

Using Identifiers

An identifier is just a unique name that JavaScript uses to identify a variable, method, or object in your program. As with other programming languages, JavaScript imposes some rules on what names you can use. All JavaScript names must start with a letter or the underscore character (_), and they can contain both upper- and lowercase letters and the digits 0–9. (Remember, JavaScript doesn't distinguish between cases, so UserName, userName, and USERNAME all refer to the same thing in a JavaScript program.)

JavaScript supports two different ways for you to represent values in your scripts: literals and variables. As their names imply, literals are fixed values that don't change while the script is executing, while variables hold data that can change at any time.

Literals and variables have several different types; the type is determined by the kind of data that the literal or variable contains. The following is a list of the types supported in JavaScript:

- *Integers*, or whole numbers—Integer literals are made up of a sequence of digits only; integer variables can contain any whole number value from 0 to more than 2 billion.

- *Floating-point*, or decimal numbers—10 is an integer, but 10.5 is a floating-point number. Floating-point literals can be positive or negative, and they can contain either positive or negative exponents (which are indicated by an *e* in the number). For example, 3.14159265 is a floating-point literal, as is 6.02E24 (6.02 x 10^{24}, or Avogadro's Number).

- *Strings*, or sequences of characters—Strings can represent words, phrases, or data, and they're set off by either double (") or single (') quotes. If you start a string with one type of quote, you must close it with the *same* type.

- *Booleans*, or true/false values—Boolean literals can only have the values of either true or false; other statements in the JavaScript language can return Boolean values.

Using Functions, Objects, and Properties

Before we go any further, let's talk about functions, objects, and properties. A *function* is just a piece of code that does something; it might play a sound, calculate an equation, or send a piece of e-mail. An *object* is a collection of data and functions that have been grouped together. The object's functions are called *methods*, and its data values are called *properties*. The JavaScript programs you write will have properties and methods, which will interact with objects provided by the browser and its plug-ins (as well as any other Java applets you may supply to your users).

TIP A simple guideline: an object's properties are things it knows, and its methods are things it can do.

Using Built-In Objects and Functions   Individual JavaScript elements are *objects*; for example, string literals are `string` objects, and they have methods that you can use to do things like change their case. JavaScript also provides a set of useful objects to represent the browser, the currently displayed page, and other elements of the browsing session.

You access objects by specifying their names. For example, the active document object is named `document`. To use document's properties or methods, you add a period and the name of the method or property you want. For example, `document.title` is the `title` property of the ¦document object, and `"Navigator".length` would access the `length` property of the `string` object named `Navigator` (remember literals are objects, too!).

Using Properties   Every object has properties—even literals. To access a property, just use the object name followed by a period and the property name. To get the length of a string object named address, you can write:

```
address.length
```

and you'll get back an integer that equals the number of characters in the string. If the object you're using has properties that can be modified, you can change them in the same way. To set the `bgColor` (background color) property of a `document` object, just write:

```
document.bgColor = "blue";
```

You can also add new properties to an object just by naming them. For example, let's say you define an object called `customer` for one of your pages. You can add new properties to the `customer` object like this:

```
customer.name = "Scott Walter";
customer.address = "Somewhere out there";
customer.zip = "55122";
```

Finally, it's important to know that an object's methods are just properties, so you can easily add new properties to an object by writing your own function and creating a new object property using your own function name. If you wanted to add a `Bill()` method to your `customer` object, you could do so by writing a function named `BillCustomer()` and setting the object's property like this:

```
customer.Bill = BillCustomer;
```

To call the new method, you'd just write:

```
customer.Bill();
```

Array and Object Properties   JavaScript objects store their properties in an internal table that you can access in two ways. You've already seen the first method—just use the properties' name. The second method, *arrays*, allows you to access all of an object's properties in sequence. The function shown in Listing 25.3 prints out all the properties of the specified object.

Listing 25.3 Displaying an Object's Properties

```
function DumpProperties(obj, objName) {
    var result = "";
    for (i in obj) {
        result += objName + "." + i + " = " + obj[i] + "\n";
    }

    return result;
}
```

N O T E You'll see this code again in the "Sample JavaScript Code" section, and we'll explain in detail what it does. For now, it's enough to know that there are two different, but related, ways to access an object's properties. ■

HTML Elements Have Properties, Too JavaScript provides objects for accessing HTML forms and form fields, and is especially valuable for writing scripts that check or change data in forms. JavaScript's properties allow you to get and set the form elements' data, as well as specify actions to be taken when something happens to the form element (as when the user clicks in a text field, or moves to another field).

N O T E For more details on using HTML object properties, see the section "HTML Objects and Events." ■

JavaScript and the Browser

Now that you understand how JavaScript works, let's talk about how the browser supports JavaScript.

When Scripts Get Executed

When you put JavaScript code in a page, the JavaScript interpreter built into the browser evaluates the code as soon as it's encountered. As the interpreter evaluates the code, it converts it into a more efficient internal format so it can be executed later. When you think about it, this is similar to how HTML is processed; browsers parse and display HTML as they encounter it in the page, not all at once.

However, functions don't get executed when they're evaluated; they just get stored for later use. You still have to explicitly call functions to make them work. Some functions are attached to objects, like buttons or text fields on forms, and they are called when some event happens on the button or field. You might also have functions that you want to execute during page evaluation; you can do this by putting a call to the function at the appropriate place in the page, like this:

```
<SCRIPT LANGUAGE="JavaScript">
<!--
myFunction();
// -->
</SCRIPT>
```

Where to Put Your Scripts

You can put scripts anywhere within your HTML page, as long as they're surrounded with the <SCRIPT>...</SCRIPT> tag pair. Many JavaScript programmers choose to put functions that will be executed more than once into the <HEAD> element of their pages; this provides a convenient storage place. Since the <HEAD> element is at the beginning of the file, functions and JavaScript code that you put there will be evaluated before the rest of the document is loaded.

Sometimes, though, you have code that shouldn't be evaluated or executed until after all of the page's HTML has been parsed and displayed. An example is the DumpURL() function described later in this chapter; it prints out all the URLs referenced in the page. If the function is evaluated before all the HTML on the page has been loaded, it'll miss some URLs, so the call to the function should come at the page's end.

N O T E For more information on the DumpURL() function, see the section, "Building a Link Table." ◼

Objects and Events

In addition to recognizing JavaScript when it's embedded inside a <SCRIPT>...</SCRIPT> tag, the browser also exposes some objects (and their methods and properties) that you can use in your JavaScript programs. Also, methods can be triggered when the user takes certain actions in the browser (called *events*).

The *location* Object   The location object holds the current URL, including the hostname, path, CGI script arguments, and even the protocol. Table 25.1 shows the properties and methods of the location object:

Table 25.1 Properties of the *location* Object

Property/ Method	Type	What It Does
href	String	Contains the entire URL, including all the subparts; for example, **http://home.netscape.com:80/index.html**.
protocol	String	Contains the protocol field of the URL, including the first colon; for example, **http:**.
hostname	String	Contains only the domain name; for example, **home.netscape.com**.

continues

Table 25.1 Continued

Property/Method	Type	What It Does
port	String	Contains the port (if specified), such as **80**. If no port is specified, this property is empty.
host	String	Contains the hostname and port number; for example **home.netscape.com:80**.
path	String	Contains the (directory) path to the actual document; for example, / for the root directory.
hash	String	Contains any CGI arguments after the first # in the URL.
search	String	Contains any CGI arguments after the first ? in the URL.
toString()	Method	Returns the location.href; you can use this function to easily get the entire URL.
assign()	Method	Sets location.href to the value you specify.

The *document* Object   The document object, as you might expect, exposes useful properties and methods of the active document. Table 25.2 shows documents, properties, and methods.

Table 25.2   Properties of the *document* Object

Property/Method	Type	What It Does
title	String	Contains the title of the current page (from the HTML <TITLE> tag), or Untitled if there's no title.
location	String	A location object that identifies the location of the current page.
lastModified	String	Contains the date the page was last modified (changed).
forms[]	Array	Contains all the FORMs in the current page.
links[]	Array	Contains all hyperlinks in the current page.
write()	Method	Writes HTML to the current document, in the order in which the script occurs on the page.

The *history* Object   The list of pages you've visited since starting the browser is called the *history list*, and is accessible via the history object. Your JavaScript programs can move through pages in the list using the properties and functions shown in Table 25.3.

Property/ Method	Type	What It Does
back()	Method	Contains the URL of the previous history stack entry (that is, the one before the active page).
forward()	Method	Contains the URL of the next history stack entry (that is, the one after the active page) or is empty if the current page is at the top of the stack.
go(x)	Method	Moves x entries forward (if x > 0) or backward (if x < 0) in the history stack.

Table 25.3   The *history* Object

The *window* Object   The window object is associated with the window in which a document is displayed. Think of the window object as an actual Windows or Macintosh window, and the document object as the content that appears in the window. JavaScript provides the following methods for doing things in the window:

- alert(*strMessage*)—puts up an alert dialog box and displays the message specified by *strMessage*. Users must dismiss the dialog box by clicking the OK button before they can do anything else (within the browser).

- confirm(*strMessage*)—puts up a confirmation dialog box with two buttons (OK and Cancel) and displays the message specified by *strMessage*. Users may dismiss the dialog box by clicking Cancel or OK; the confirm() function returns true when users click OK and false when they click Cancel.

- prompt(*strMessage*)—puts up an input dialog box with a text entry field and two buttons (OK and Cancel) and displays the message specified by *strMessage*. Users may dismiss the dialog box by clicking either button, and can type data into the field that (if the dialog is closed by clicking OK) can be passed back to JavaScript for processing (such as entry into a form).

- open(...)—allows you to open a second complete browser window and load a document into it. You can also control whether the new window has menus, a statusBar, a toolBar, and other gadgets (for creating your own custom dialogs).

- close()—allows you to close a particular window (that you created earlier with open()), or to shut down the browser itself.

Part
IV

Ch
25

HTML Objects and Events

JavaScript also provides access to individual HTML elements as objects, each with its own properties and methods. You can use these objects to customize your pages' behavior.

Properties Common to All Objects   The methods and properties in this section apply to several HTML tags; note that there are other methods and properties, discussed after the following table, for anchors and form elements. Table 25.4 shows the features that these generic HTML objects provide.

Table 25.4   Properties and Methods Common to Most HTML-Oriented JavaScript Objects

Property/ Method	Type	What It Does
onFocus	Event	Called when the user moves the input focus to the field, either via the Tab key or a mouse click.
onBlur	Event	Called when the user moves the input focus out of this field.
onSelect	Event	Called when the user selects text in the field.
onChange	Event	Called only when the field loses focus and the user has modified the data held within; use this function to trigger a validation test.
onSubmit	Event	Called when the user clicks the Submit button of a form.
onClick	Event	Called when a button (on a form) is clicked.
focus()	Method	Moves the input focus to the associated object.
blur()	Method	Moves the input focus away from the associated object (and onto the next object in sequence).
select()	Method	Selects the specified object.
click()	Method	Simulates the pressing of the associated button.
enable()	Method	Enables (un-grays) the associated object.
disable()	Method	Disables (grays) the associated object.

N O T E   Note that the focus(), blur(), select(), click(), enable(), and disable() functions are object methods; to call them, use the name of the object you want to affect. For example, to turn off the button named Search, you'd use:

```
form.search.disable();
```

Anchor Objects   Hypertext anchors don't have all the properties just listed; they only have the onFocus, onBlur, and onClick methods. You modify and set these methods just like others. Remember that no matter what code you attach, Navigator's still going to follow the clicked link—after executing your code.

N O T E   With the release of Navigator 3.0, the onClick event can now be told *not* to activate the hyperlink that was just clicked (by returning a value of false). For example, if you defined a link as follows:

```
<A HREF="http://home.netscape.com/"
   ONCLICK="return confirm('Are you sure?');">
```

Clicking the link will display a confirmation dialog box and, if the user clicks the No button, the link won't be followed.

This is currently only available from Navigator 3.0.

Form Objects   Table 25.5 lists the properties associated with HTML FORM objects; the later section "HTML Events" also presents several methods that you can override to call JavaScript routines when something happens to an object on the page.

Table 25.5   Form Object Properties

Property/Method	Type	What It Does
name	String	Contains the value of the form's NAME attribute.
length	Integer	Contains the number of elements in the form (and, therefore, in the elements[] array).
method	Integer	Contains the value of the form's METHOD attribute (0 for GET, 1 for POST).
action	String	Contains the value of the form's ACTION attribute.
encoding	String	Contains the value of the form's ENCTYPE attribute.
target	Window	Window targeted after submit for form response.
elements[]	Array	Contains all the objects that make up the form.
onSubmit	Event	Called when the user clicks the Submit button of a form. If a value of false is returned from this event, form submission is stopped.
submit()	Method	Forces the submission of the associated form.

Objects in a Form   One of the best places to use JavaScript is in forms, since you can write scripts that process, check, and perform calculations with the data the user enters. JavaScript provides a useful set of properties and methods for text INPUT elements and buttons.

You use INPUT elements in a form to let the user enter text data; JavaScript provides properties to get string objects that hold the element's contents, as well as methods for doing something when the user moves into or out of a field. Table 25.6 shows the properties and methods that are defined for text INPUT elements.

Table 25.6   HTML INPUT Object Properties

Property/Method	Type	What It Does
name	String	Contains the value of the field's NAME attribute.
value	String	Contains the field's contents.
default	String	Contains the initial contents of the field (as specified by the VALUE attribute).

continues

Table 25.6 Continued

Property/ Method	Type	What It Does
onFocus	Event	Called when the user moves the input focus to the field, either via the Tab key or a mouse click.
onBlur	Event	Called when the user moves the input focus out of this field.
onSelect	Event	Called when the user selects text in the field.
onChange	Event	Called only when the field loses focus and the user has modified the data held within; use this function to trigger a validation test.

Individual buttons and check boxes have properties, too; JavaScript provides properties to get string objects containing the buttons' data, as well as methods for doing something when the user selects or deselects a particular button. Table 25.7 shows the properties and methods that are defined for button elements.

Table 25.7 Button Object Properties

Property/ Method	Type	What It Does
name	String	Contains the value of the button's NAME attribute.
value	String	Contains the button's VALUE attribute.
onClick	Event	Called when the user clicks the associated button.
click()	Method	Simulates the user clicking the associated button.

Radio buttons are groups so that only one button in a group can be selected at a time. Because all radio buttons in a group have the same name, JavaScript has a special property, index, for use in distinguishing radio buttons. Querying the index property of a radio button object returns a number (starting with 0 for the first button), indicating which button in the group was triggered.

For example, you might want to automatically put the user's cursor into the first text field in a form, instead of making the user manually click the field. If your first text field is named UserName, you can put this

```
form.UserName.focus()
```

in your document's script to get the desired behavior.

Programming with JavaScript

As you've seen in the preceding sections, JavaScript has a lot to offer page authors. It's not as flexible as C or C++, but it's quick and simple. Most important, it's easily embedded in your Web pages, so you can maximize their impact with a little JavaScript seasoning. This section covers the gritty details of JavaScript programming, including a detailed explanation of the language's features.

Expressions

An *expression* is anything that can be evaluated to get a single value. Expressions can contain string or numeric literals, variables, operators, and other expressions, and they can range from simple to quite complex. For example,

```
x = 7;
```

is an expression that uses the assignment operator (more on operators in the next section) to assign the result 7 to the variable x. By contrast,

```
(quitFlag == true) && (formComplete == false)
```

is a more complex expression whose final value (a Boolean) depends on the values of the quitFlag and formComplete variables.

Operators

Operators do just what their name implies: they operate on variables and literals. The items that an operator acts on are called its operands. Operators come in the following types:

- *Binary operators*—which need two operands. The four math operators you learned in elementary school (+ for addition, - for subtraction, * for multiplication, and / for division) are all binary operators, as is the assignment operator (=) seen earlier.

- *Unary operators*—which only require one operand. The operator can come before or after the operand. the --operator, which subtracts one from the operand, is a good example. Either count-- or --count will subtract 1 from the variable count.

Assignment Operators   *Assignment operators* take the result of an expression and assign it to a variable (you can't assign the result of an expression to a literal). One feature that JavaScript has that most other programming languages don't is the ability to change a variable's type "on-the-fly," as demonstrated in Listing 25.4.

Listing 25.4   Changing a Variable's Type

```
function TypeDemo() {
    // first, pi is a floating-point
    var pi = 3.1415926;
    document.write("Pi is " + pi + "\n");
```

continues

Listing 25.4 Continued

```
// now, pi is changed to a Boolean
pi = false;
document.write("Pi is now " + pi + "\n");
}
```

This short function first prints the value of `pi`. In most other languages, though, trying to set a floating-point variable to a Boolean value would either generate a compiler error or a runtime error (with the exception of C, which will valiantly try to set the variable to *some* value...though not necessarily what you want). JavaScript happily accepts the change and prints `pi`'s new value: `false`.

The most common assignment operator, =, simply assigns the value of an expression's right side to its left side. In Listing 25.4, the variable `pi` got the floating-point value `3.1415926` after the first expression was evaluated. For convenience, JavaScript also defines some other operators that combine common math operations with assignment (listed in Table 25.8).

Table 25.8 JavaScript Shorthand Operators

Operator	Example...	...is Equivalent to...
+=	x += y	x = x + y
-=	x -= y	x = x - y
*=	x *= y	x = x * y
/=	x /= y	x = x / y
++	x++	x = x + 1
--	x--	x = x - 1

Math Operators The previous sections gave you a sneak preview of the math operators that JavaScript furnishes. You can either combine math operations with assignments, as shown in Table 25.8, or use them individually. As you'd expect, the standard four math functions (addition, subtraction, multiplication, and division) work just as they do on an ordinary calculator.

The negation operator (-) is a unary operator that negates the sign of its operand. To use the negation operator, you must place it before the operand.

JavaScript also adds two useful unary operators: -- and ++, called (respectively) the *decrement* and *increment* operators. These two operators do two things; they modify the value of their operand and return the new value. They also share a unique property: they can be used either before or after their operand. If you put the operator after the operand, JavaScript will return the operand's value, *then* modify it. If the operator is placed before the operand, JavaScript will modify the operand *first*, then return the modified value. The following short example might help clarify this seemingly odd behavior:

```
x = 7;      // x set to 7
a = --x;    // x set to 6, THEN a set to 6
b = a++;    // b set to 6, THEN a set to 7
x++;        // x set to 7
```

Comparison Operators   It's often necessary to compare the value of two expressions to see whether one is larger, smaller, or equal to another. JavaScript supplies several comparison operators that take two operands and return true if the comparison's true, and false if it's not. (Remember, you can use literals, variables, or expressions with operators that require expressions.) Table 25.9 shows the JavaScript comparison operators.

Table 25.9   Comparison Operators

Operator	Returns TRUE When:
==	The two operands are equal
!=	The two operands are not equal
<	The left operand is less than the right operand
<=	The left operand is less than or equal to the right operand
>	The left operand is greater than the right operand
>=	The left operand is greater than or equal to the right operand

TIP The comparison operators can be used on strings, too; the results depend on standard lexicographic ordering.

It may be helpful to think of the comparison operators as questions; when you write

```
(x >= 10)
```

you're really saying, "Is the value of variable x greater than or equal to 10?"

Logical Operators   Comparison operators compare quantity or content for numeric and string expressions, but sometimes you need to test a logical value—like whether a comparison operator returned true or false. JavaScript's logical operators allow you to compare expressions that return logical values. The following are JavaScript's logical operators:

- ■ && (read as "and"). A binary operator, && returns true only if both operands are true. If the first operand evaluates to false, && returns false immediately (without evaluating the second operand).
- ■ ¦¦ (read as "or"). A binary operator, ¦¦ returns true if either operand is true.
- ■ ! (read as "not"). A unary operator, ! returns true if its operand is false and vice versa.

N O T E Note that && and ¦¦ won't evaluate the second operand if the first operand provides enough information for the operator to return a value. This process, called *short-circuit evaluation*, can be significant when the second operand is a function call. For example:

```
keepGoing = userQuit && theForm.Submit();
```

If userQuit is false, the second operand—which submits the active form—won't be evaluated (meaning the method won't be executed, in this case). ■

Controlling Your JavaScripts

Some scripts you write will be simple; they'll execute the same way every time, once per page. For example, if you add a JavaScript to play a sound when users visit your home page, it won't need to evaluate any conditions or do anything more than once. More sophisticated scripts might require that you take different actions under different circumstances; you might also want to repeat the execution of a block of code—perhaps by a set number of times, or as long as some condition is true. JavaScript provides constructs for controlling the execution flow of your script based on conditions, as well as repeating a sequence of operations.

Testing Conditions   JavaScript provides a single type of control statement for making decisions: the if...else statement. To make a decision, you supply an expression that evaluates to true or false; which code is executed depends on what your expression evaluates to.

The simplest form of if...else uses only the if part. If the specified condition is true, the code following the condition is executed; if not, it's skipped. For example, in this code fragment:

```
if(document.lastModified.year < 1995)
    document.write("Danger!  This is a mighty old document.");
```

The message will only appear if the condition (that the document's lastModified property says it was modified before 1995) is true. You can use any expression as the condition; since expressions can be nested and combined with the logical operators, your tests can be pretty sophisticated:

```
if((document.lastModified.year == 1996) &&
    (document.lastModified.month >= 10)) {
    document.write("This document is reasonably current.");
}
```

The else clause allows you to specify a set of statements to execute when the condition is false.

Repeating Actions   If you want to repeat an action more than once, you're in luck! JavaScript provides two different loop constructs that you can use to repeat a set of operations.

The first, called a for loop, will execute a set of statements some number of times. You specify three expressions: an initial expression that set the values of any variables you need to use, a condition that tells the loop how to determine when it's done, and an increment expression that modifies any variables that need it. Here's a simple example:

```
for(count=0; count<100; count++
    document.write("Count is " + count);
```

This loop will execute 100 times and print out a number each time. The initial expression sets our counter, count, to zero; the condition tests to see whether count is less than 100, and the increment expression increments count.

You can use several statements for any of these expressions, like this:

```
for (i=0, numFound=0; (i<100 && (numFound<3); i++) {
    if(someObject.found())
        numFound++;
}
```

This loop will either loop 100 times or as many times as it takes to "find" three items—the loop condition terminates when i >= 100 or when numFound >= 3.

The second form of loop is the while loop. It executes statements as long as its condition is true. For example, you could rewrite the first for loop about like this:

```
count = 0;
while(count < 100) {
    document.write("Count is " + count);
    count++;
}
```

Which form you prefer depends on what you're doing; for loops are useful when you want to perform an action a set number of times (and you know how many times you wish to loop), and while loops are best when you want to keep doing something as long as a particular condition remains true.

JavaScript Reserved Words

JavaScript reserves some keywords for its own use. You may not define your own methods or properties with the same name as any of these keywords; if you do, the JavaScript interpreter will complain. Table 25.10 lists the current reserved words.

Table 25.10   JavaScript Reserved Words

abstract	extends	int	super
boolean	false	interface	switch
break	final	long	synchronized
byte	finally	native	this
case	float	new	throw
catch	for	null	throws
char	function	package	transient

continues

Table 25.10   Continued

class	goto	private	true
const	if	protected	try
continue	implements	public	var
default	import	return	void
do	in	short	while
double	instanceof	\static	with
else			

 TIP Some of these keywords are reserved for future use (hint: think Java!). JavaScript might allow you to use them, but your scripts may break in the future if you do so.

Command Reference

This section provides a quick reference to the JavaScript commands that are implemented as of Navigator 3.0 and Internet Explorer 3.0. The commands are listed in alphabetical order; many have examples. Before we dive in, here's what the formatting of these entries means:

- All JavaScript keywords are in `monospaced` font.
- Words in *italics* represent user-defined names or statements.
- Any portions enclosed in square brackets ([]) are optional
- *{statements}* indicates a block of statements, which can consist of a single statement or multiple statements enclosed by curly braces ({})

break   The `break` statement terminates the current `while` or `for` loop and transfers program control to the statement following the terminated loop.

Syntax

```
break
```

Example

The following function scans the list of URLs in the current document and stops when it has seen all URLs or when it finds a URL that matches the input parameter *searchName*.

```
function findURL(searchName) {
   var i=0;

   for(i=0; i<document.links.length; i++) {
      if(document.links[i] == searchName)
         break;
   }
```

```
    if(i < document.links.length) {
        alert("Found " + searchName + " in position " + i);
    } else {
        alert("" + searchName + " not found!");
    }
}
```

continue   The `continue` statement stops executing the statements in a `while` or `for` loop, and skips to the next iteration of the loop. It doesn't stop the loop altogether like the `break` statement; instead, in a `while` loop it jumps back to the condition, and in a `for` loop it jumps to the update expression.

Syntax

```
continue
```

Example

The following function prints the odd numbers between 1 and x; it has a `continue` statement that goes to the next iteration when i is even.

```
function printOddNumbers(x) {
    var i=0;

    while(i < x) {
        if((++i % 2) == 0)
            continue;
        else
            document.write("" + i + "\n");
    }
}
```

for   A `for` loop consists of three optional expressions, enclosed in parentheses and separated by semicolons, followed by a block of statements executed in the loop. These parts do the following:

- The starting expression, *initialExpr*, is evaluated before the loop starts. It's most often used to initialize loop counter variables, and you're free to use the `var` keyword here to declare new variables.

- A *condition* is evaluated on each pass through the loop. If the condition evaluates to `true`, the statements in the loop body are executed. You can leave the condition out, and it will always evaluate to `true`. If you do this, make sure to use `break` in your loop when it's time to exit.

- An update expression, *updateExpr*, is usually used to update or increment the counter variable or other variables used in the *condition*. This expression is optional; you can update variables as needed within the body of the loop if you prefer.

- A block of statements is executed as long as the *condition* is `true`. This block can have one or multiple statements in it.

Syntax

```
for ([initialExpr ;] [condition ;] [updateExpr]) {
    statements
}
```

Example

This simple statement prints out the numbers from 0 to 9. It starts by declaring a loop counter variable, *i*, and initializing it to zero. As long as *i* is less than 10, the update expression will increment *i*, and the statements in the loop body will be executed.

```
for (var i=0; i<10; i++) {
    document.write("" + i + "\n");
}
```

for...in   This is a special form of the `for` loop that iterates the variable *variableName* over all the properties of the object *objectName*. For each distinct property, it executes the statements in the loop body.

Syntax

```
for (variableName in objectName) {
    statements
}
```

Example

The following function takes as its arguments an object and the object's name. It then uses the `for...in` loop to iterate through all the object's properties; when done, it returns a string that lists the property names and their values.

```
function dumpProps(obj, objName) {
    var result = "";

    for (i in obj) {
        results += objName + "." + i + " = " + obj[i] + "\n";

    return result;
}
```

function   The `function` statement declares a JavaScript function; the function may optionally accept one or more parameters. To return a value, the function must have a return statement that specifies the value to return. All parameters are passed to functions by value—the function gets the value of the parameter, but cannot change the original value in the caller.

Syntax

```
function name([param] [, param [..., param]]) {
    statements
}
```

Example

```
// This function returns true if the active document has the title
// specified in the theString parameter and false otherwise
//
function PageNameMatches(theString) {
   return (document.title == theString);
}
```

if...else The if...else statement is a conditional statement that executes the statements in *statementsBlock1* if *condition* is true. In the option else clause, it executes the statements in *statementsBlock2* if *condition* is false. The blocks of statements may contain any JavaScript statements, including further nested if...else statements.

Syntax

```
if (condition) {
   statementsBlock1
} [else {
   statementsBlock2
}]
```

Example

```
if (Message.IsEncrypted()) {
   Message.Decrypt (SecretKey);
   else {
   Message.Display();
}
```

return The return statement specifies the value to be returned by a function.

Syntax

```
return expression;
```

Example

The following simple function returns the square of its argument, *x*, where *x* is any number.

```
function square(x) {
   return x * x;
}
```

this Use this to access methods or properties of an object from within that object's methods. The special word this always refers to the current object.

Syntax

```
this.property
```

Example

If setSize() is a method of the document object, then this refers to the specific object whose setSize() method is called.

```
function setSize(x, y) {
   this.horzSize = x;
   this.vertSize  = y;
}
```

This method will set the size for an object when called as follows:

```
document.setSize(640, 480);
```

var   The var statement declares a variable *varName*, optionally initializing it to have a value *val*. The variable name *varName* can be any JavaScript identifier, and *val* can be any legal expression (including literals).

Syntax

```
var varName [= val] [, varName [= val] [..., varName [= val]]];
```

Example

```
var numHits = 0, custName = "Scotty";
```

while   The while statement contains a condition and a block of statements. If *condition* is true, the body is executed; then the condition is reevaluated and the body is executed again (if *condition* is true). This process repeats until *condition* evaluates to false, at which time program execution continues with the next statement after the loop.

Syntax

```
while (condition) {
   statements
}
```

Example

The following simple while loop iterates until it finds a form in the current document object whose name is OrderForm, or until it runs out of forms in the document.

```
var x = 0;
while ((x < document.forms.length) &&
       (document.forms[x].name != "OrderForm")) {
   x++;
}
```

with   The with statement establishes *object* as the default object for the statements in the block. Any property references without an object explicitly identified are assumed to be associated to *object*.

Syntax

```
with (object) {
   statements
}
```

Example

```
with (document) {
   write("Inside a with block, you don't need to " +
```

```
            "specify the object.");
    bgColor = "gray";
}
```

Sample JavaScript Code

It can be difficult to pick up a new programming language from scratch—even for experienced programmers. To make it easy for you to master JavaScript, this section presents some examples of JavaScript code and functions that you can use in your own pages. Each of them demonstrates a practical concept.

Dumping an Object's Properties

In the earlier section, "Array and Object Properties," you saw a small function, DumpProperties(), that sets all the property names and their values. Let's look at that function again now to see it in light of what you've learned.

```
function DumpProperties(obj, objName) {
    var result = ""; // set the result string to blank

    for (i in obj)
        result += objName + "." + i + " = " + obj[i] + "\n";

    return result;
}
```

As all JavaScript functions should, this one starts by defining its variables using the var keyword; it supplies it an initial value, too, which is a good habit to start. The meat of the function is the for...in loop, which iterates over all the properties of the specified object. For each property, the loop body collects the object name, the property name (provided by the loop counter in the for...in loop), and the property's value. We access the properties as an indexed array instead of by name, so we can get them all.

Note that this function doesn't print anything out. If you want to see its output, put it in a page (remember to surround it with <SCRIPT>...</SCRIPT>!), then at the page's bottom, use

```
document.writeln(DumpProperties(obj, objName));
```

where obj is the object of interest and objName is its name.

Building a Link Table

You might want to have a way to automatically generate a list of all the links in a page, perhaps to display them in a separate section at the end of the page, as shown in Figure 25.2. DumpURL(), shown in Listing 25.5, does just that; it prints out a nicely formatted numbered list showing the hostname of each link in the page.

FIG. 25.2

The DumpURL()
function adds a
numbered list of all the
links in a page at the
end of the page.

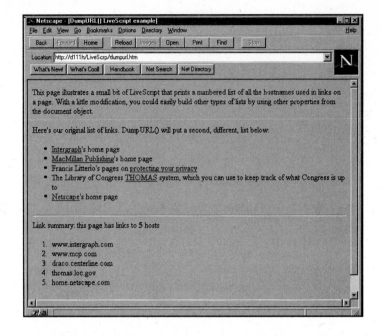

Listing 25.5 *DumpURL()* Displays a Numbered List of All the URLs on a Page

```
function DumpURL() {
    // declare the variables we'll use
    var linkCount = document.links.length;
    var result = "";

    // build our summary line
    result = "<hr>\nLink summary: this page has links to <b>" +
            linkCount + "</b> hosts<br>\n";

    result += "<ol>\n";

    // for each link in the document, print a list item with it's hostmane
    for(var i=0; i<linkCount; i++)
        result += "<li> " + document.links[i].hostname + "\n";

    // add thye closing HTML for our list
    result += "</ol><hr>\n";

    return result;
}
```

This function starts by declaring the variables used in the function. JavaScript requires that you
declare most variables before using them, and good programming practice dictates doing so
even when JavaScript doesn't require it. Next, you build the summary line for your table by
assigning a string literal full of HTML to the result variable. You use a for loop to iterate
through all the links in the current document and add a list item for each to the result variable.
When you finish, add the closing HTML for your list to result and return it.

Updating Data in Form Fields

There have been several mentions of the benefits of using JavaScript to check and modify data in HTML forms. Let's look at an example that dynamically updates the value of a text field based on the user's selection from one of several buttons.

To make this work, you need two pieces; the first is a simple bit of JavaScript that updates the value property of an object to whatever you pass in. Here's what it looks like:

```
function change(input, newValue) {
    input.value = newValue;
}
```

Then, each button you want to include needs to have its onClick method changed so that it calls your change() function. Here's a sample button definition:

```
<input type=button value="Mac"
       onClick="change(this.form.display, 'Macintosh')">
```

When the button is clicked, JavaScript calls the onClick method, which happens to point to your function. The this.form.display object points to a text field named display; this refers to the active document, form refers to the form in the active document, and display refers to the form field named display.

Of course, this requires that you have a form INPUT gadget named display!

Validating Data in Form Fields

Often when you create a form to get data from the user, you need to check that data to see if it's correct and complete before sending mail, or making a database entry, or whatever you collected the data for. Without JavaScript, you have to POST the data and let a CGI script on the server decide if all the fields were correctly filled out. You can do better, though, by writing JavaScript functions that check the data in your form on the client; by the time the data gets posted, you know it's correct.

For this example, let's require that the user fill out two fields on our form: zipcode and area code. We'll also present some other fields that are optional. First, you need a function that will return true if there's something in a field, and false if it's empty:

```
function isFilled(input) {
    return (input.value.length != 0);
}
```

For each field you want to make the user complete, you'll hook to its onBlur event handler. onBlur is triggered when the user moves the focus out of the specified field. Here's what your buttons look like:

```
<input name="zipcode" value=""
       onBlur="if(!isFilled(form.zipcode)) {
                   alert('You must put your zipcode here!');
                   form.zipcode.focus();
               }">
```

When the user tries to move the focus out of the zipcode field, the code attached to the onBlur event is called. That code in turn checks to see if the field is complete; if not, it nags the user and puts the focus back into the zipcode field.

Of course, you could also implement a more gentle validation scheme by attaching a JavaScript to the form's Submit button, like this:

```
<script langage="JavaScript">
<!--
function areYouSure() {
    return confirm("Are you sure you want to submit " +
                    "these answers?");
}
// -->
</script>
...
<form method=post action="..." onSubmit="return areYouSure();">
```

A Pseudo-Scientific Calculator

If you ask any engineer under a certain age what kind of calculator he or she used in college, the answer is likely to be "a Hewlett Packard." HP calculators are somewhat different from the ordinary calculators; you use *reverse Polish notation*, or *RPN*, to do calculations (see Fig. 25.3).

FIG. 25.3
The fields on this page are tied to JavaScript functions that keep the user from moving the input focus until the user supplies a value.

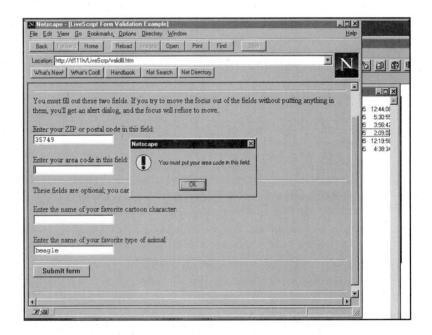

With a regular calculator, you put the operator in between operands. To add 3 and 7, you push 3, then the + key, then 7, and finally = to print the answer. With an RPN calculator, you put the operator *after* both operands. To add 3 and 7 on an HP-15C, you have to push 3, then Enter (which puts the first operand on the internal stack), then 7, then +, at which time you would see the correct answer. This oddity takes a bit of getting used to, but it makes complex calculations go much faster, since intermediate results get saved on the stack (for quick use as operands in further calculations).

Here's a simple RPN example. To compute

$$((1024 * 768) / 3.14159)^2$$

you'd enter:

```
1024, Enter, 768, *, 3.14159, /, x²
```

to get the correct answer: 6.266475×10^{10}, or about 6.3 billion.

Netscape provides an RPN calculator as an example of JavaScript's expressive power. Let's take a detailed look at how it works. Listing 25.2 shows the JavaScript itself (note that these are really in the same file; we've just split them for convenience). Figure 25.4 shows the calculator as it's displayed in Navigator.

FIG. 25.4

Navigator displays the RPN calculator as a table of buttons, with the accumulator (the answer) and the stack at the top.

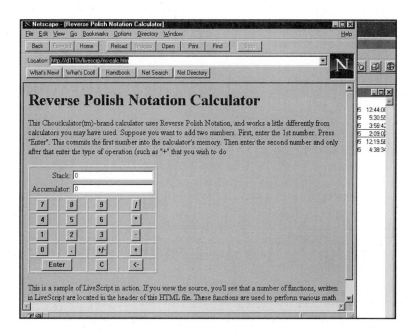

The HTML Page   Listing 25.6 shows the HTML for our calculator's page. For precise alignment, all the buttons are grouped into a table; the accumulator (where the answer's displayed) and the stack (where operands can be stored) are at the top.

Listing 25.6   The HTML Definition of the RPN Calculator Example

```html
<form method="post">
<table border=1 align=center>
   <tr align=center>
   <td colspan=4>

      <table border=0>
         <tr>
            <td align=right>Stack:</td>
            <td><input name="stack" value="0"></td>
         </tr>
         <tr>
            <td align=right>Acc:</td>
            <td><input name="display" value="0"></td>
         </tr>
      </table>

   </td>
   </tr>

   <tr align=center>
      <td>
         <input type="button" value=" 7 "
            onClick="addChar(this.form.display, '7')">
      </td>
      <td>
         <input type="button" value=" 8 "
            onClick="addChar(this.form.display, '8')">
      </td>
      <td>
         <input type="button" value=" 9 "
            onClick="addChar(this.form.display, '9')">
      </td>
      <td>
         <input type="button" value=" / "
            onClick="divide(this.form)">
      </td>
   </tr>

   <tr align=center>
      <td>
         <input type="button" value=" 4 "
            onClick="addChar(this.form.display, '4')">
      </td>
      <td>
         <input type="button" value=" 5 "
            onClick="addChar(this.form.display, '5')">
      </td>
      <td>
         <input type="button" value=" 6 "
            onClick="addChar(this.form.display, '6')">
      </td>
      <td>
         <input type="button" value=" * "
            onClick="multiply(this.form)">
      </td>
```

```
    </tr>

    <tr align=center>
       <td>
          <input type="button" value=" 1 "
             onClick="addChar(this.form.display, '1')">
       </td>
       <td>
          <input type="button" value=" 2 "
             onClick="addChar(this.form.display, '2')">
       </td>
       <td>
          <input type="button" value=" 3 "
             onClick="addChar(this.form.display, '3')">
       </td>
       <td>
          <input type="button" value=" - "
             onClick="subtract(this.form)">
       </td>
    </tr>

    <tr align=center>
       <td>
          <input type="button" value=" 0 "
             onClick="addChar(this.form.display, '0')">
       </td>
       <td>
          <input type="button" value=" . "
             onClick="addChar(this.form.display, '.')">
       </td>
       <td>
          <input type="button" value="+/-"
             onClick="changeSign(this.form.display)">
       </td>
       <td>
          <input type="button" value=" + "
             onClick="add(this.form)">
       </td>
    </tr>

    <tr align=center>
       <td colspan="2">
          <input type="button" value=" Enter " name="enter"
             onClick="pushStack(this.form)">
       </td>
       <td>
          <input type="button" value=" C "
             onClick="this.form.display.value = 0 ">
       </td>
       <td>
          <input type="button" value=" <- "
             onClick="deleteChar(this.form.display)">
       </td>
    </tr>

</table>
</form>
```

Part
IV

Ch
25

Notice that each button has an onClick event handler associated with it. The digits 0 through 9 all call the addChar() JavaScript function; the editing buttons (C for *clear* and < - for *backspace*) call functions that change the value of the accumulator. The Enter button stores the current value on the stack, and the +/- button changes the accumulator's sign.

Of course, the operators themselves call JavaScript functions too; for example, the * button's definition calls the Multiply() function. The definitions aren't functions themselves; they include function calls (as in the digit buttons) or individual statements (as in the *clear* button).

The JavaScript   All the onClick events shown in the previous section need to have JavaScript routines to call. Listing 25.7 shows the JavaScript functions that implement the actual calculator.

Listing 25.7   The JavaScript Code that Makes Up the RPN Calculator

```
<script language="JavaScript">
<!-- hide from non-JavaScript browsers

// keep track of whether we just computed display.value
//
var computed = false

// push the the accumulator (display) onto the stack
//
function pushStack(form) {
   form.stack.value   = form.display.value;
   form.display.value = 0;
}

// add a new character to the display
//
function addChar(input, character) {
   // auto-push the stack if the last value was computed
   //
   if(computed) {
      pushStack(input.form);
      computed = false;
   }

   // make sure input.value is a string
   //
   if(input.value == null || input.value == "0")
      input.value = character;
   else
      input.value += character;
}

function deleteChar(input) {
   input.value = input.value.substring(0,
                input.value.length - 1);
}

function add(form) {
```

```
      form.display.value = parseFloat(form.stack.value)
                      + parseFloat(form.display.value);
      computed = true;
}

function subtract(form) {
    form.display.value = form.stack.value
                    - form.display.value;
    computed = true;
}

function multiply(form) {
    form.display.value = form.stack.value
                    * form.display.value;
    computed = true;
}

function divide(form) {
    var divisor = parseFloat(form.display.value);

    if(divisor == 0) {
        alert("Don't divide by zero, pal...");
        return;
    }

    form.display.value = form.stack.value / divisor;
    computed = true;
}

function changeSign(input) {
    if(input.value.substring(0, 1) == "-")
        input.value = input.value.substring(1, input.value.length)
    else
        input.value = "-" + input.value
}

// done hiding from old browsers -->
</script>
```

As you saw in the preceding HTML listing, every button is connected to some function. The addChar() and deleteChar() functions directly modify the contents of the form field named display—the accumulator—as do the operators (add(), subtract(), multiply(), and divide()).

This code shows off some subtle but cool benefits of JavaScript that would be difficult or impossible to do with CGI scripts (or, if possible, at least incredibly slow—each update of the form would have to be sent *to* the server for processing, and a new form sent *back* to the browser). First, notice that the divide() function checks for division by zero and presents a warning dialog box to the user.

More important, in this example, all the processing is done on the client—imagine an application like an interactive tax form, where all the calculations are done on the browser and only the completed, verified data gets POSTed to the server. ●

Part
IV

Ch
25

CHAPTER 26

The Future of the Web: VRML, SGML, and Web Chat

by Lori Leonardo

Four years ago, almost no one had heard of the World Wide Web. UseNet, e-mail and Internet mailing lists, Telnet, and FTP were the tools of choice for exchanging ideas and information through the Internet. The establishment of the World Wide Web and the release of browsers for "surfing the Web" allowed people to view and exchange text, graphics, and other information interactively for the first time. The use of hypertext links allowed related information throughout the world to be linked together.

Just as the development of the World Wide Web has been faster than anyone could have imagined two years ago, the new developments appearing on the horizon will extend the capabilities of the Internet and the World Wide Web in ways that can scarcely be imagined today. In addition to the text, graphics, sound, and other information currently available on the Web, new developments will add increased capabilities, three-dimensional graphics, real-time audio and video, and who knows what else!

In this chapter, we look at the developments on the horizon that give us a glimpse into the future of the World Wide Web. ∎

SGML—Standard Generalized Markup Language

A means of producing documents for multiple uses, including HTML.

Java applets

Modular enhancements to Web browsers available by sending applets in real-time with WWW documents.

VRML—Virtual Reality Modeling Language

A way to develop three-dimensional VRML worlds on the Web.

Multimedia video and audio applications for the Web

Additional capabilities for specialized multimedia features have been provided by built-in viewers or helper applications.

Some hints on how you can keep up with new WWW developments

Stay on top of the cutting edge of technology where significant changes occur rapidly.

SGML on the Web

Information is transmitted on the World Wide Web through documents using markup tags that identify the structure and type of information content in a standard way—these standards allow others to write software (Web browsers) to present the information. Separating the process of identifying the information structure from the way it will be presented gives Web publishers the ability to take advantage of technological advances to display captured information content in increasingly new and fresh ways without always having to go back and revise the source text.

What Are SGML and HTML?

Standard Generalized Markup Language (*SGML*) is an international standard designed to facilitate the exchange of information across systems, devices, languages, and applications. *HTML* is *HyperText Markup Language*, an implementation of SGML markup for distributing knowledge on the World Wide Web. The use of disciplined markup added to content enables authors all over the world to prepare information for Internet distribution, knowing that people using Web browser software on various platforms will be able to view it.

Although the development of HTML and SGML proceeded on separate paths, the paths have converged with the standardization of HTML 2.0 and HTML 3.0 as conforming to SGML. While SGML purists would assert that HTML, in particular early HTML, does not rigorously implement all of the SGML principles—for example, hierarchical structure and elimination of presentation-specific markup from a document instance—documents that conform to the HTML 2.0 and 3.0 DTD (Document Type Definition) rules now meet the SGML criteria.

SGML and HTML were created to solve a problem: people using different computer systems and document processing tools had difficulty passing information to one another. Although the difficulty of passing information between proprietary applications has improved somewhat with import filters, it is still a problem for those who pass documents between more than one proprietary application. The benefits of using standard markup designed to cross proprietary boundaries is well illustrated by the growth of the Web and successful SGML implementations. The problems that can occur when proprietary extensions are added to some but not all browsers are also illustrated by the current dilemmas that Web publishers encounter.

SGML defines a way to write and implement markup rules. The markup rules are called a *Document Type Definition* (*DTD*). The HTML DTD is one set of SGML rules.

What Is a DTD?

An SGML Document Type Definition (DTD) is the specification of the rules for a set or class of documents with the same structure. The rules specification includes the definition of what elements can appear, the name or tag that will be used to identify them, where the elements can be used (you might not want to allow a list to appear in a footnote), what attributes can be used to provide additional information (for example, security level), and external entities that may be used in conjunction with the content to provide components stored elsewhere (for example, graphic image files).

HTML is defined by its DTD, a definite set of markup rules for a particular, widely applicable type of hyperlinked information that includes several levels of headings, paragraphs, lists, and so on—most of the early information distributed via the World Wide Web.

The Benefits of SGML

The major benefits of using full SGML as well as HTML are as follows:

- The ability to define your own markup rules to fit special needs that HTML alone does not handle well.

- A Style Editor that allows the publisher to set Paragraph Styles (font family, size, color), Content Formatting (justification, indentation, spacing), before or after text (and style), and miscellaneous features such as table formatting, background color, or page breaks for a print style sheet.

- A Navigator feature that generates an expanding Table of Contents when the publisher right-clicks an element type and then selects the Add button. Additional Navigators for figures or experts can also be provided.

- The use of entities, which allow a safe, easy way to include boiler plate components in an SGML document.

SGML Viewer: Panorama FREE and Panorama Pro

SoftQuad's Panorama is the first SGML viewer (helper application) to enter the Web scene that can display SGML information from any set of rules (any DTD) without first converting it to HTML. Because Panorama is already available, we have used it to illustrate points in this section and will tell you how to obtain and use it. SoftQuad Panorama, developed for SoftQuad by Synex Information AB in Sweden, is available in two versions: a freeware version commonly called Panorama FREE and the commercial, supported version, Panorama Pro. When just the term Panorama is used, I am referring to generic capabilities available in both versions.

Panorama and Panorama Pro are viewer/helper applications. They work in conjunction with a compatible Web browser such as NCSA Mosaic, Netscape Navigator, and most browsers based on Spyglass Mosaic. The browser sends the request to download the information and delivers it to Panorama for display. Both versions of Panorama allow you the same, full capabilities to access and view SGML files on the Web. You may select between Styles and choose any Navigator (expanding Table of Contents) that the information provider makes available. For the curious, the ability to show tags and navigate the SGML tree are also available.

However, some features are available only in Panorama Pro that may make it more desirable, even mandatory, and worth the $195 suggested retail price. Features available in Panorama Pro include the following:

- The ability to Print, Save, and Open (local) files
- The ability to create your own Styles and Navigators

- The ability to create and manage Webs (a new facility for creating your own links among documents, bookmarks, and annotations)
- Technical support (the freeware version has none)

 TIP Some users may need the capabilities that the additional features provide; others may purchase it just because the features are fun to use. If you are preparing SGML information for the Web, you will need the Pro version to prepare the style sheets and the Netscape Navigator to deliver your information.

The fact that the less full-featured version is freeware makes the need to decide painless. You can try the free version first, then upgrade later.

Installing Panorama FREE

If you already have Netscape Navigator installed, the configuration step for SoftQuad's Panorama FREE is easy because the Panorama setup includes configuration of the browser(s) to use Panorama as a helper application for SGML documents. To install Panorama FREE, perform the following steps:

1. Download the file panofr10.exe from SoftQuad's Web site at **http://www.sq.com/ products/panorama/pan-free.htm** into a temporary folder on your hard drive.

2. Execute panofr10.exe, which is a self-extracting compressed file, in Windows or DOS. For example, from the Windows 95 Explorer, double-click the panofr10.exe file name in the temporary folder.

3. Run the program setup.exe, and answer the questions it gives you. It is safe to accept the default selections for most questions.

   You will be asked if you would like to configure the Netscape Navigator browser to work with Panorama FREE. If you answer yes to this question, the browser will be set up to use Panorama FREE as a helper application for SGML documents.

N O T E If Panorama FREE does not give you the option of being installed with one of your browsers—this will happen with some versions of Netscape Navigator—or if you add a browser after Panorama FREE is installed—you can perform this step manually. In your browser, choose Options, General and select the Helpers tab. Add a helper application for MIME types text/sgml and text/x-sgml using the following information, which is the same for both except for the MIME subtype:

```
MIME type: text
MIME Subtype: sgml for one, x-sgml for the other
Suffixes (or extensions): .sgml, .sgm
Program: xxx/panorama.exe (where xxx is the path to the folder where you
installed Panorama)
```

4. You will then be asked which of the compatible browsers to set up for the initial execution from Panorama FREE. Select your favorite browser. You can change this selection through the Options menu in Panorama FREE.

5. When the Setup program completes, you are ready to access SGML files on the Web. Connect to the Internet, bring up Netscape, and look for "SGML on the Web" resources.

That's it. You're ready to go. Access NCSA/SoftQuad SGML on the Web at the URL:

http://www.ncsa.uiuc.edu/SDG/Software/Mosaic/ WebSGML.sgml

to find SGML information on the Web. As you access an SGML file, your browser will recognize the SGML MIME type and automatically bring up Panorama to display it.

SGML Example versus HTML Example

Let's take a look at a site that has both SGML and HTML versions to try to get some idea of how they differ. You won't see any dramatic differences between these two for this site, but there are some important differences that we will discuss.

First, take a look at Figure 26.1 and Figure 26.2. They show some information from the Jet Propulsion Laboratory on Magellan Image Data. Figure 26.1 located:

http://stardust.jpl.nasa.gov/mgddf/chap2/ chap2.htm

shows the hypertext link (Figure 2.1 on Web page) that allows you to view Figure 26.2. To navigate through the chapter, you need to scroll up and down through the document.

FIG. 26.1

The HTML version of JPL's Magellan Image Data document.

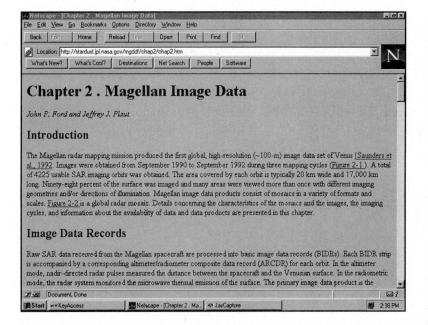

Part

IV

Ch

26

Figures 26.3 and 26.4 show the same document in their SGML versions. Notice the URL address. The only difference is the .SGML extension. The information is the same, but the presentation is dramatically different. The important differences are the following:

■ The SGML Navigator shown at the left of the browser window allows easy navigation throughout the document. It's possible to use tags to accomplish a similar effect in HTML, but SGML does this automatically from the SGML source.

■ Incorporating graphics information naturally within the document is easier with SGML.

■ A greater variety of presentation styles are available with SGML documents.

FIG. 26.2

You can view the document's figures by clicking hypertext links—Figure 2.1 on Web page.

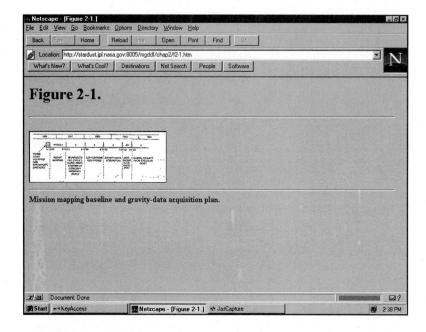

FIG. 26.3

The SGML version of the Magellan Image Data document includes a Navigator to allow easy movement through the document.

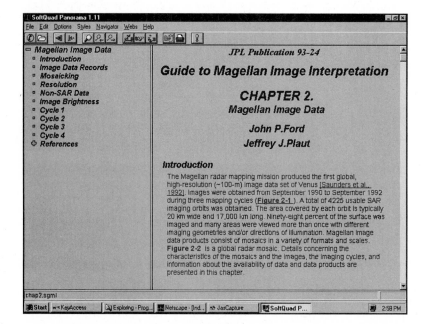

FIG. 26.4

Graphics can be easily incorporated into SGML documents—Figure 2.1 on Web page.

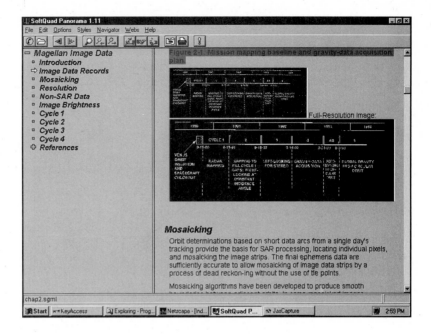

Other SGML Applications

"An add-on that will handle any SGML DTD?"—yes, it appears to be here. The University of Waterloo's MetaClient prototype allows for direct viewing of SGML files. It uses Java to bootstrap itself and handles arbitrary language semantics including, of course, SGML. Waterloo's MetaClient is an example of the overlapping nature of new Web technologies. SGML and Java are combined in an applied generic Modular approach to provide an SGML plug-in mega-applet.

The goals of the MetaMedia Project at the University of Waterloo, found at **http:// www.cgl.uwaterloo.ca/~mmccool/Meta/index.html,** are "the creation and analysis of *structured networked executable media.* Rather than monolithic downloadable applications, we are building a system which will support the dynamic definition of the syntax and semantics of arbitrary *executable content languages.*" In simpler terms, their project is to produce a MetaClient that can understand arbitrary SGML. This approach is intended to produce not single-purpose plug-in applications, but rather a mega-applet approach that can receive language syntax rules with the content and deliver the information in an appropriate fashion. Language includes but is not limited to SGML. The grammar-driven frontend is designed to handle not only arbitrary SGML markup but also any arbitrary grammar-driven language. I'm speculating that sooner or later this approach could handle dynamic translations between English, French, German, Russian, Chinese, and the like.

Part
IV

Ch
26

Enhancing Your Web Browser On-the-Fly

By design, Web browsers have provided basic capabilities to view text and, in the case of GUI browsers, simple graphics. Additional capabilities for specialized multimedia features have been provided by viewers or helper applications. Although new versions and new browsers continuously deliver enhanced functionality, there is a limit to what they can incorporate and still be practical.

Sun's Java and JavaScript languages have begun an exciting new wave of plug-in techniques for adding functionality to the Web. Hyper-G applies this modular approach to the handling of Internet information.

What Is Java?

In the spring of 1995, news of Java, a new language Sun had been researching for several years, began to come out—a language to deliver applets, small programs along with content, to the client machine. By delivering these applications with the information, it's possible to add unlimited functionality to Web browsers that support it.

The Java approach includes the following characteristics:

- Object-oriented—Modular components, safe, reusable.
- Simplicity—Designed to be easy to use.
- Distributed programs and processing—Automatic update of just the components you need that execute on the user's machine.
- Architectural neutrality and portability—Interoperable code that runs on any platform without additional steps to prepare it.
- Interactivity with users and other components—Plug-and-play components to isolate and add functions.

We will show an example of a Java document using Netscape Navigator 3.0, which includes Java support. There are other browsers with Java support—including Microsoft's Internet Explorer, and, of course, Sun's own HotJava browser.

HotJava is a WWW browser developed by Sun that is written in Java. HotJava was created to demonstrate the use of the language rather than to be, at this point, a full featured browser. It supports downloaded Java applets, and is available in versions for SPARC/Solaris and for 32-bit Windows (NT and 95).

To obtain the HotJava browser, go to The HotJava Browser at the URL **http://java.sun.com/hotjava.html**.

A Java Example

The central site for well-organized Java information with easy-to-follow links is Java—Programming for the Internet at the URL **http://java.sun.com/**.

There are also many Java applets that can be obtained from the URL at **http://www.gamelan.com/.**

It is through URL using Netscape Navigator 3.0 that I found and loaded a simple game of hangman, called "Hang Duke at the URL" at **http://www.javasoft.com/java.sun.com/applets/applets/Hangman/index.html.**

This game allows you to try to save Duke from an unfortunate fate by guessing the word represented by the line of dashes. Correct guesses, entered by hitting the letter you want to guess, result in the letters being filled in (and also give appropriate audio feedback). Incorrect guesses result in the incorrect letter being displayed, a piece of Duke being shown on the gallows, and an unfortunate scream. If you get the word, as shown in Figure 26.5, Duke is set free and dances a little jig for you. If you fail, as shown in Figure 26.6, poor Duke…

FIG. 26.5

Save poor Duke by guessing the word. If you get it, a grateful Duke will dance a little jig for you.

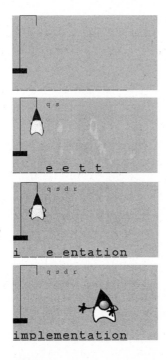

Part

IV

Ch

26

FIG. 26.6

If you can't get the word…poor Duke.

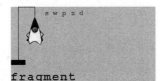

This may seem like a silly little example, but by being able to deliver small applications to your browser, its functionality can be infinitely increased, when necessary. Ticker tapes and animations, interactive forms, data checking, revolving chemical components that educate, games for relaxation—these are just a few of the current uses.

What Is HyperWave?

HyperWave (formerly codename Hyper-G), with client browsers Amadeus for Windows and Harmony for UNIX, offers a "modular" approach to the storage and delivery of Internet information, especially with hyperlinks, which it stores in a separate database. The technology is being developed by IICM, the Institute for Information Processing and Computer Supported New Media at Graz University of Technology, Austria. From what I read about the technology, this "real hypermedia" technology guarantees automatic hyperlink consistency that would solve the problem of broken links and provide other benefits.

The volume of information is increasing so fast both within sites and across the Web that managing content files and links becomes increasingly difficult, much less the task of reworking information to take advantage of new improvements. The HyperWave is designed to address this problem. HyperWave is a server technology, designed to support most if not all of the current methods of delivering Web information, including Gopher, HTML, FTP, and HyperWave.

For more information on HyperWave and links to instructions for downloading the software, see IICM at the URL:

http://fiicmpc21.tu-graz.ac.at/hyperwave/

VRML: The WWW in Three Dimensions

Virtual reality and 3-D technology developments have brought excitement to our lives—to game players with Doom, to remodelers designing improvements to homes, to forensic scientists, researchers, and to anyone who can benefit from information presented in three dimensions. VRML brings this technology to the Web by allowing the creation and viewing of 3-D VRML worlds.

What Is VRML?

VRML, the Virtual Reality Modeling Language, is an authoring standard currently defined at version 1.0, for creating 3-D documents on the Web. These documents create VRML worlds that a user can navigate in and around using the capabilities of a VRML compatible browser. The current standard is file-based, involving the transfer of 3-D scenes to the local computer—VRML source files usually have a WRL extension—after which all navigating through the scene is done there. Like HTML documents, VRML worlds can contain links to other documents, graphics, text, HTML documents, or other VRML worlds.

VRML has its roots in the OpenInventor 3-D standard developed by Silicon Graphics, which is still very active in developing VRML and tools for its use. The VRML standard is currently at version 1.0, with a committee of VRML users and developers continuing its development. Freeware, shareware, and commercial VRML tools are becoming widely available. In the next section there are VRML examples using Live3D, a VRML plug-in that comes with Netscape Navigator 3.0.

Installing Live3D, a VRML Plug-In for Netscape

To get a little better feel for what using a VRML browser is like, we will install and try out one of them: Live3D (formerly WebFX by Paper Software). The latest version of Live3D used here is designed to work as a plug-in module for Netscape Navigator 2.0 and later, although it is included as a built-in plug-in with Navigator 3.0. Some of the same individuals at Paper Software who were involved in the development of WebFX are also part of the development team for Live3D. The instructions for installation are as follows:

1. If you have the minimum version of Netscape 3.0 that does not include the Live3D plug-in, you can download the program 3dns32d.exe by going to the URL **http://home.netscape.com/ comprod/products/navigator/live3d/download_live3d.html**, and following the steps shown there, and putting the program into a temporary directory on your hard drive.

2. Run 3dns32d.exe—this is a self-extracting file that will unpack itself into the temporary directory.

3. Run setup.exe. If you installed Netscape Navigator 3.0 in the default location and wish to do the same for Live3D, you may select the defaults for the Live3D setup process.

4. After runing the Setup program, double-click on the Live3D icon. This opens Netscape 3.0 and loads Live3D. From now on Live3D is installed as a Netscape Navigator built-in plug-in module and will automatically run when you encounter a VRML source file when using Netscape.

Configuring Live3D

Live3D allows you to customize its behavior in several different ways. This customization is achieved using a pop-up menu and submenus that first appear by a right-click.

Each of the six entries shown in the main pop-up window gives you different options for customizing Live3D. The most important submenus are as follows, but feel free to experiment with these and the others to get a feeling for what you can do with Live3D:

- *ViewPoints*—Its pretty easy to get lost in a VRML world, especially when you're just learning your way around. The Entry View selection in this submenu allows you to quickly move back to the point at which you entered the VRML world.

- *Detail*—Once a VRML world has been downloaded to your computer, the navigation through that world is handled locally. Because VRML worlds can be quite complex, this process can be slow, particularly on older computers. If you find this to be the case on your computer, you can adjust the level of detail by use of this submenu. By switching from Solid to Wireframe or Point Cloud, you decrease the complexity of the image and may improve the response time.

- *Heads Up Display*—The entries in this submenu dictate what information is shown on the Live3D heads up display when it is enabled.

Live3D makes it quick and easy to navigate in VRML worlds, through the use of navigational tools such as Walk, Spin, Look, Slide, Point, Lamp, and View (see Table 26.1). With viewpoints and optional gravity, 3-D worlds have a realistic quality.

Table 26.1   Live3D's Navigational Controls

Navigation Tool	Description
Walk	Activates a link at any distance if Point is not selected.
Spin	Clicks and drags on objects to spin or rotate.
Look	Moves closer into an object if Point is not selected, similar to Walk.
Slide	Lets you fly over and under objects.
Point	Toggles switch to zoom in on an object without activating the link.
Lamp	Changes the lighting of the 3-D world.
View	Resets the 3-D view to the original view.
?	Toggles Help to display above commands.

If you find yourself walking into walls in your VRML world, click on the scene with your *Right* mouse button (short cuts), select Navigator and make sure Collision Detection is checked.

For more information of Live3D, including sample VRML demos, check out this site: **http:// home.netscape.com/comprod/ products/ navigator/live3d/index.html**.

Example VRML World on the World Wide Web

Here is an example VRML world that gives a good example of what can be achieved with VRML worlds that might not be as effective with a standard HTML Web page. It also demonstrates how these two types of documents and ways of presenting information can be very effectively used in tandem.

Using Netscape Navigator 3.0 with the Live3D plug-in installed, connect to the URL:

http://esewww.essex.ac.uk/campus-model.wrl

Note the WRL extension denoting a VRML world source document. After the connection is made by Netscape, the Live3D plug-in is called, the VRML world source is downloaded, and the image shown in Figure 26.7 is shown. While it isn't readily obvious, this the University of Essex campus, as seen from a long way off.

To get a closer look, put Live3D in fly mode and fly in toward the VRML world. Give yourself a little bit of height to be able to see more of the campus buildings. As you get closer, you will see the campus layout shown in Figure 26.8.

FIG. 26.7
The entry point to the
University of Essex
VRML world.

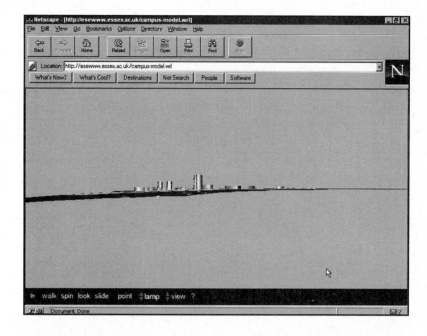

FIG. 26.8
Using the Slide
command, fly in closer
to the university and
see a view of the
campus.

As we learned earlier, VRML worlds and HTML documents can call one another interchangeably. The University of Essex site uses this ability to not only convey the three-dimensional
layout of their campus, but to allow visitors to learn more about the different campus facilities.
In Figure 26.9, a cursor has been placed over a building which has a hypertext link, indicated

by the presence of the hand cursor and the URL label in the upper left-hand corner of the screen. This building is the library. By double-clicking, an HTML Web page is called that gives information about the library (see Fig. 26.10). More VRML examples can be found at **http://www.sdsc.edu/SDSC/Partners/vrml/examples.html**.

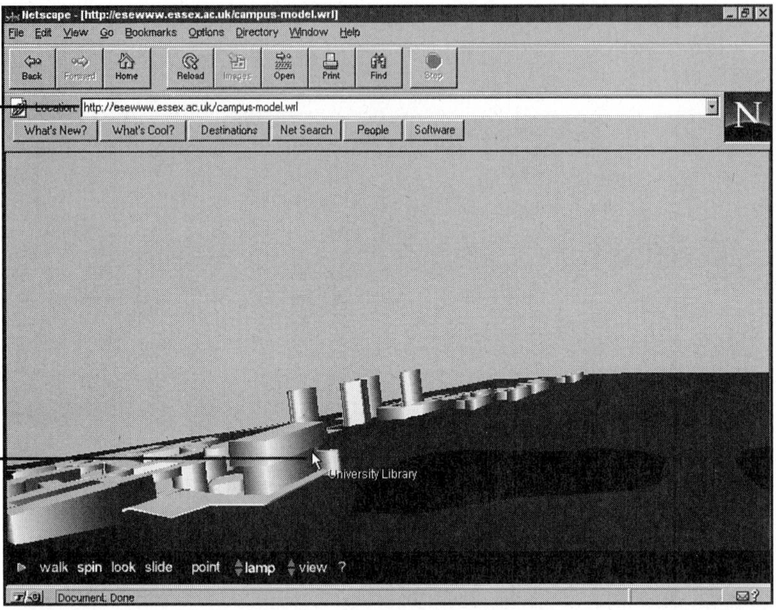

FIG. 26.9
By placing the pointer over a given building and double-clicking...

URL label

Hand pointer

FIG. 26.10
...you can jump to an HTML document with information about it.

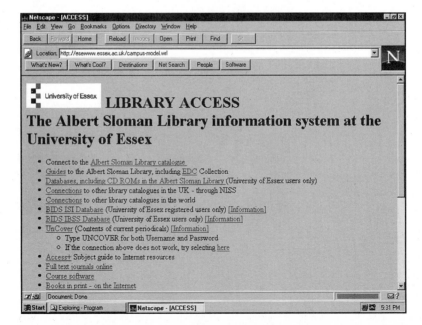

Because the VRML world is a 3-D model, you can look at it from any angle, including from below (which isn't very helpful) and from above, as shown in Figure 26.11—giving you a useful map of the University of Essex campus!

FIG. 26.11
We can even fly (Slide) up high enough and look down to get an aerial map of the campus.

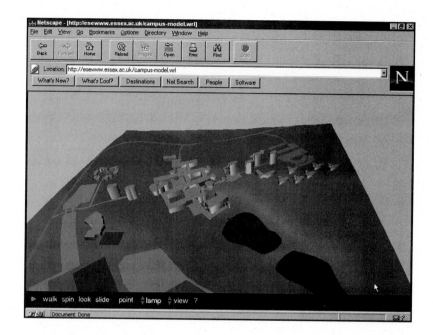

VRML Resources on the Internet

Once you have your system setup to view VRML documents, you'll want to start cruising the Internet and the Web to see what VRML resources and worlds are there. The list is growing every day. Following are a few of the bigger sites that will direct you to many other VRML resources—browsers, authoring tools, worlds, and object libraries:

- Netscape maintains a directory of many VRML worlds located at **http://home.netscape.com/comprod/products/navigator/live3d/cool_worlds.html**.

- A group called Mesh Mart maintains a Web site of many VRML resources, including browsing and authoring tools and VRML worlds at **http://cedar.cic.net/~rtilmann/mm/vrml.htm**.

- NCSA, the authors of NCSA Mosaic, have a VRML Web page at **http://www.ncsa.uiuc.edu/General/VRML/VRMLHome.html** (VRML at NCSA).

- A repository of VRML information is maintained at **http://rosebud.sdsc.edu/vrml/**.

- Wired has a VRML Forum at **http://vrml.wired.com/**.

- As discussed previously, Silicon Graphics is very active in VRML development. A site with information about their WebSpace products is located at: **http://webspace.sgi.com/**.

Video Applications on the Web

In addition to the text, graphics, and simple sounds that are accessible through the World Wide Web, there are continuing efforts to enhance the multimedia capabilities of the Web. Several video applications are being introduced that give you this ability—two examples are StreamWorks, by Xing Technology Corporation, and Shockwave, by Macromedia. We will use Shockwave as an example to demonstrate some of these capabilities. You can get more information about StreamWorks from the Xing Technology at the following URL:

http://www.xingtech.com/streams/index.html.

Soon Netscape is coming out with Live3-D API (Application Programming Interface). Live3D API will extend Netscape's plug-in, Java and JavaScript, with interfaces that will support 3-D applications. With Live3D API, multimedia 3-D applications like online 3-D presentations, 3-D geography, 3-D chat rooms and of course 3-D multiuser games will be the standard.

Installing Shockwave

The Macromedia Shockwave for Director plug-in application is a cross-platform integration tool for multimedia designers to combine animation, sound, digital video, along with graphics, text, and who knows what else to create truly dynamic presentations of information on the Web. This product will make the popular Macromedia Director technology available on the Web, and from reports it is a robust plug-in implementation that is available now. Partnerships with Sun, Microsoft, Netscape, Silicon Graphics, Navisort, and others are quickly bringing technology integrated with popular browsers to the Web that provide the ability to produce interactive media content such as product demos and press kits for the entertainment and advertising industries.

The words—integrated, cross-platform, compressed, and interactive—associated with the implementation of this popular software on the Web make it a likely candidate to increase even further the power of the Web.

Information about Shockwave begins at the Welcome to Macromedia! page at URL **http://www.macromedia.com/**.

You can choose to read information, or if you want to obtain and install the plug-in, you can do the following:

1. Click the hotspot, Get the Shockwave Plug-In Now, which takes you to Shockwave: Plug-In Center at URL **http://www.macromedia.com/Tools/Shockwave/Plugin/plugin.cgi**

2. Choose the link to obtain the Shockwave plug-in for the platform you desire, for example, Shockwave for Windows 95 at URL **http://www.macromedia.com/Tools/Shockwave/sdc/ Plugin/Win95Plg.htm**. Choose the platform and application, Director 5.0 (Beta), and click Find Plug-ins.

3. Select one of the ftp sites that corresponds to the version for your browser, and click to download the plug-in.

4. Download n32d50b2.exe into an temporary directory.

5. Double-click n32d50b2.exe. It will unzip and launch the setup program. Follow the instructions that appear on the screen.

6. Double-click setup.exe to install the Shockwave plug-in.

You are now ready to run Shockwave examples!

Using Shockwave

Links to examples demonstrating the software may be found Macromedia Shockwave Vanguard at URL **http://www.macromedia.com/Tools/ Shockwave/Gallery/shock.html**.

> **CAUTION**
>
> As you might imagine, the size of video information can get quite large. Keep this in mind, and keep an eye on the status bar of your browser when you download Shockwave examples, especially if you have a slow connection to the Internet.

Other examples can be found through **http://www.teleport.com/~arcana/shockwave/**.

This above site, in particular, features many video animation links to other Shockwave sites and can show you more of what Shockwave can do. This site also demonstrates an animated Shockwave banner, as shown in Figure 26.12.

FIG. 26.12
The Shockwave Web Sites list includes a video animation of their welcome banner.

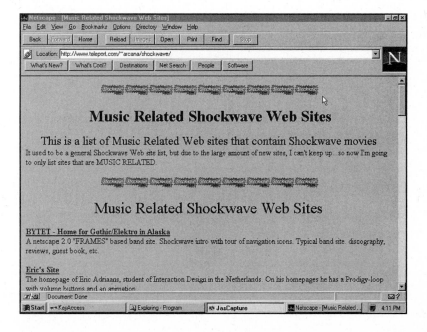

Part IV
Ch 26

Audio Applications on the Web

In addition to the video multimedia Web applications discussed in the previous section, there are dedicated audio applications also becoming available. Some of these, such as WebPhone, by the Internet Telephone Company, specialize in point-to-point uses—in essence, offering low-cost telephony over the Internet. Other applications such as TrueSpeech by the DSP Group, Inc., and RealAudio by Progressive Networks, are a bit more general; they offer live, point-to-point capability, as well as on-demand audio from stored sources.

The RealAudio application will be used to demonstrate some of the audio capabilities you can get through the Net. To find out more about WebPhone, see the Internet Telephone Company at URL **http://www.itelco.com/**.

For more information about TrueSpeech, see the DSP Group, Inc., at URL **http://www.dspg.com/**.

Installing RealAudio

You can listen to other audio with the RealAudio add-in from Progressive Networks. The RealAudio home page is at URL **http://www.realaudio.com/**.

N O T E A version of the RealAudio software is already built into Microsoft's Internet Explorer. ■

1. Copy the file ra32_201.exe from the NetCD into a temporary folder on your hard drive.
2. Execute ra32_201.exe, which is a self-extracting compressed file, in Windows or DOS. For example, from the Windows 95 Explorer, double-click the ra32_201.exe filename in the temporary folder. After extracting its files, the RealAudio setup program will automatically be executed.
3. It is safe to accept the default selections for the RealAudio questions. RealAudio will configure itself as a plug-in application for Netscape Navigator 3.0. For other browsers, you may need to manually set it up as a helper app. In your browser, choose Options, General and select the Helpers tab. Add a helper application for MIME types text/sgml and text/x-sgml using the following information, which is the same for both except for the MIME subtype:

```
MIME type: audio
MIME Subtype: x-pn-realaudio for the other
Suffixes (or extensions): .ra, .ram
Program: xxx/raplayer.exe (where xxx is the path to the folder where you
installed RealAudio)
```

That's it. You're ready to go.

Using RealAudio

A list of RealAudio locations is kept at URL **http://www.prognet.com/contentp/hotcoolnew.html** (see Fig. 26.13).

FIG. 26.13

You can access an extensive list of RealAudio sites at this URL.

You can jump to a virtual radio station, directly located at **http://www.theflash.com/**, and can choose from a playlist of selections as shown in Figure 26.14.

FIG. 26.14

The playlist at **http://www.theflash.com/**.

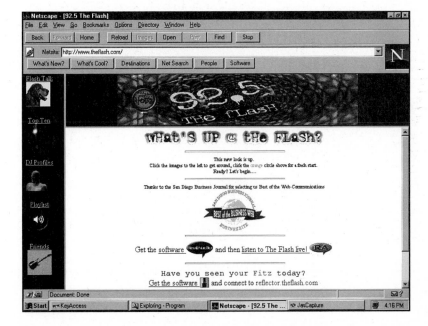

Part

IV

Ch

26

FIG. 26.14

CONTINUED.

The playlist at **http://www.theflash.com/**.

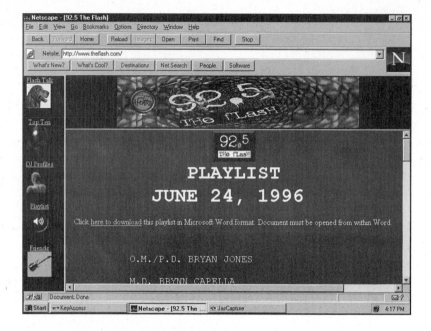

Keeping Up with New Technology

When you talk about the future of the Web, you are talking about the cutting edge of technology, where significant changes occur rapidly. If you want to keep up with the latest and greatest you need to check major sites every week to see if there are new versions and products. Web sites that provide primary information about a new technology one week tend to be reorganized relatively frequently so you need to be flexible and persistent to find good information.

Those who work with Web futures work with pre-release beta software that sometimes has many bugs still in it. The software changes rapidly; last week's bugs may be fixed, but new features may completely change how one accesses a feature—for example, bookmark management—and new problems may occur with features that worked fine before. Accessing the latest and greatest on the Web is not a venture for the faint of heart. It's hairy but also fun to see what's coming.

 TIP While it's always a good idea to make frequent backups of your computer files, it's particularly a good idea if you're going to be spending a lot of time working with beta-release software.

These factors make it difficult to provide correct information in a book such as this one. The information will change before the publication process can be completed; this is true about the Internet in general, and it is even more true when you are talking about new technologies. However, we can tell you some good ways to keep up with new developments. In general, if you want to stay out on the cutting edge, try to do the following:

- Keep your eyes and ears open. Keep your notepad handy. Record addresses wherever they appear.

- Use the search sites to see if the Web indexes list the new sites where information can be found. If you do not already have a couple of good search sites such as Lycos, Infoseek, OpenText, or WebCrawler in your bookmark list, click the Net Search button in Netscape or go to W3 Search Engines at URL **http://cuiwww.unige.ch/meta-index.html**, which contains pointers to a variety of search sites.

- Go to the sites found in your search and read the information. Pay attention to license and hardware requirements. You'll need sufficient disk space and sometimes special hardware, such as a sound card, to experiment with some of the new technologies.

- You will usually find information about downloading the latest software needed to access a feature. You may need to follow a few links to find it. Follow the instructions that are provided. This is likely to be the best and latest information and, in general, it will tell you what you need to know.

- For most of the latest software, you are instructed to download the software into a temporary folder (sometimes stated as a directory) and execute the self-extracting compressed file. In Windows 95, the Save to Disk dialog box allows you to set up a new folder before you download the file, and I recommend that you do so.

- You can execute the self-extracting file in several ways. I usually double-click it in the Explorer; sometimes I click Start on the taskbar, then choose Run, Browse to locate the file, and then Okay to execute it.

- Next, check for a readme file to look for the installation instructions. Sometimes these are located on the Web, on or near the page where you downloaded the software. Sometimes the instructions will have another name with a .txt or a .doc extension. Use Word Pad or your favorite editor to read them. Frequently they contain important information, so do read them.

- Usually, after any special instructions, they will tell you to run setup.exe or install.exe. Before you actually do this, decide what you want to name the folder you will install the components in. This is especially important when you want to run more than one program. Then run the setup or installation program.

- Follow any instructions to configure the software.

- Test away and let the developers know if you encounter problems. You'll normally find the address on the same page you find the download link.

Frequently, beta versions are freely available for testing. However, unless you have the patience to put up with a few problems and the time to inform the developers when you find them, you might be better off to wait until the software is stable. ●

Part
IV

Ch
26

P A R T

V

UseNet Newsgroups

CHAPTER 27

How UseNet Works

by James O'Donnell

For many users, UseNet is the Internet. Even with the explosive growth of the World Wide Web, UseNet is still one of the most popular parts of the Internet's many services, with millions of users accessing it daily. Like all Internet services, no special hardware is required to access UseNet.

The term UseNet refers to a mechanism that supports discussion groups—called *newsgroups* in the UseNet vocabulary—that allow users from anywhere on the Internet to participate. Originally conceived for the exchange of technical information, the UseNet soon became much more. Newsgroups were developed for non-technical subjects such as hobbies, news items, and social subjects.

With UseNet, you can access anywhere from 8,000 to over 15,000 newsgroups (depending on the capabilities of your news server) covering an incredible variety of subjects. Looking for details on programming with the latest C++ language compiler for Microsoft? There's a newsgroup for it. Your aquarium has a growth of brown algae on the glass? Check the aquaria newsgroups. You're trying to decide which suspension fork to add to your mountain bike? The thousands of enthusiastic cyclists in newsgroups specializing in bikes can help. You want a sound clip of a shuttle take-off to rattle your PC's new

What is UseNet

UseNet is like a bulletin board that you can use to share information with others all around the world.

How UseNet is organized

UseNet's hierarchical organization makes it easy for you to find the type of information you want.

How you can best use UseNet

This chapter is full of tips that you can use to get the most out of UseNet.

Surfing and lurking—terms you will encounter

Like other parts of the Internet, UseNet has its own jargon that you need to learn.

How to use news filtering and search services

Search services such as DejaNews make it easy to find UseNet postings that you're looking for.

Netiquette: Your behavior on UseNet

Before posting a message to UseNet, make sure that you understand UseNet's standards for behavior.

sound card and speakers? There are many places to look. Any subject you can think of probably has a newsgroup for support.

This chapter discusses general UseNet information, most of which will apply to every operating system, including Windows 3.1, Windows 95, and Windows NT (Apple, too). In the following chapters, you'll learn about using Microsoft News and Forte's Agent newsreaders. ■

What Is UseNet?

UseNet is not a network, but a service carried over the Internet. In many ways, you can think of UseNet as an organized electronic mail (e-mail) system, except there is no single user that mail is sent to. Instead, the messages you and everyone else using UseNet write are sent to a newsgroup section, available for anyone who accesses that newsgroup.

Some e-mail terminology applies to UseNet. You write something that you want to let others read—a message or article—and send it (post it) to the newsgroup. You can use a special piece of software called a *reader* to look at newsgroup contents. Also, just about all Web browsers can also read news.

▶ **See** "Getting Ready to Use Microsoft Internet News," **p. 738**

The sending and receiving of UseNet newsgroups is handled by software that knows how to download the articles, as well as how to post them to the network. In addition to the capabilities available through your Web browser (if you have one), a wide variety of public domain, shareware, and commercial software exists that gives you access to UseNet newsgroups. An excellent freeware program called Free Agent is discussed in Chapter 29, "Using the Agent Newsreaders." Microsoft News is another freebie that you'll learn about in Chapter 28.

The UseNet is not managed or controlled by anyone specifically, but is more a matter of communal control. Once a newsgroup has been created, anything can be sent to the newsgroup and made accessible to everyone else on the Internet (unless a group is specifically created to prevent this, as you will see shortly in the section "Moderated Newsgroups").

There are no formal rules about the language you can use in an article, or about your behavior on UseNet. There are generally accepted principles that have been adopted by the UseNet community as a whole, but there is no real enforcement other than other users' force of opinion (which can be quite formidable). If you are accessing UseNet through a company or organization, the system administrators may impose some rules on you, but these are locally decided and not set by UseNet.

A Very Brief History of UseNet

The origins of the UseNet lie with the UNIX operating system in a release called V7. V7 offered a program called UUCP (UNIX to UNIX Copy), which allowed two machines to transfer files easily. In 1979, UUCP was used by two Duke University graduate students, Jim Ellis and Tom Truscott, to exchange messages between their two servers.

Other users got in on the act and used UUCP to provide messaging between their machines. University of North Carolina's Steve Bellovin went as far as writing a set of shell scripts to provide simple news software between UNC and Duke. These routines transferred and managed messages and news between the two sites. In 1980, the system was described to a wide audience at the annual Usenix conference. (Usenix is a UNIX user group.)

The shell scripts led to a version written in the C programming language, which was widely distributed and led to many new machines joining the informal news network. This software was modified several times more with many new features added at each step, resulting in the main routines for handling uploading and downloading newsgroups, and managing the articles with news readers.

Apart from the software for handling the articles within a newsgroup, several news readers have been developed over the years to allow users to access the newsgroups through a friendly front-end. Naturally, all the news readers were developed with different features and capabilities. Most of the popular newsreaders are freeware or shareware, and are readily accessible to anyone who wants them. There are newsreaders available for just about every operating system.

UseNet Behavior

What limits are there on your behavior on UseNet? As mentioned earlier, UseNet doesn't have formal rules. Instead, the network users and your local system administrator impose limits, although in some cases they cannot be enforced.

This has one of two outcomes. If someone complains about your behavior on a UseNet newsgroup (or newsgroups) to your system administrator and he or she agrees, you may get warned about your network access or have your account taken away. If the system administrator doesn't care (or you don't have one), then there is nothing the UseNet community can do other than continue to post articles against you. That's one of the double-edged swords of UseNet. In theory, you can say anything you want, regardless of how many people you hurt or insult. On the other hand, as a newsgroup reader, you also have to put up with this behavior. Luckily, there are some steps you can take to eliminate this type of posting.

There are a few individuals who continue their personal attacks using the UseNet, unhindered by system administrators or coworkers. On the whole, though, UseNet users are a well-behaved group who follow a set of mutually agreed-upon guidelines for network behavior, often called *Netiquette*. You learn about it later in this chapter in the section called "Netiquette." These are good guidelines to follow anytime you're online, including when you're using mail or online services such as CompuServe.

Part
V

Ch
27

Newsgroup Names

With thousands of newsgroups available, a naming system is necessary to enable you to find the groups that are of interest to you. The UseNet user community tries to create newsgroups that are tightly focused on a subject, so you don't get messages about a car for sale in the middle of a newsgroup devoted to automotive technical advice.

To help differentiate groups, there are several levels of newsgroup names used. The first level of hierarchy is a generic identifier that lets you know whether the newsgroup is technical, social, recreational, or some other general category. There are a few such identifiers in use:

Identifier	Category
biz	Business
comp	Computers
news	General news and topical items
rec	Recreational (hobbies and arts)
sci	Scientific
soc	Social
talk	Debate-oriented
misc	Newsgroups that don't readily fall into one of the other categories

These groups are usually circulated world-wide. There is another group category called "alt" (for alternative) that, while very popular, is not as widely distributed and tends to be less formal than the other groups. The alt groups are usually where stronger language and behavior is tolerated, almost like an underground newspaper tends to be more radical than mainstream versions.

NOTE Some system administrators don't subscribe to the alt groups, both to cut down the amount of material that must be transferred and to filter out some of the more adult-oriented material that is in the alt newsgroups at times. Given the looser nature of the alt groups as far as behavior is concerned, though, the alt groups can be the source of some interesting conversations and information.

After the main newsgroup identifier, the next level tends to give the primary subject area. For example, **rec.audio** and its subgroups discuss audio systems, **sci.biology** is biology-oriented, and **alt.tasteless** has some very bizarre material in it. In most cases, there is a further division below this level, breaking the subject into even more specialized areas. These third-level areas are usually used when a newsgroup gets too many messages covering a wide variety of subjects to sustain a casual reader.

For example, **rec.autos.driving** is about the driving experience and how to better handle a car. The newsgroup **rec.autos.antique** is for aficionados of older cars. The **rec.autos.tech** group is where discussions of manifolds, gasoline, and rack-and-pinion steering are found. In many cases, there can be a half dozen special classes underneath the general category. That's not always the case, of course, as less popular newsgroups may have only one title.

N O T E You may find some variety in sites and what they carry. For example, some sites don't carry certain groups, while some newsgroups seem to show up with different names depending on where you access them from. ■

There can be even further specification of a newsgroup name, although this is unusual. A common place to find long newsgroup names is the computer section. For example, there is a newsgroup called comp.os.ms-windows.apps.word-proc, which is about word processors for the Windows operating system. Newsgroups with five or six name layers are the exception in all but the comp and sci groups.

The names are similar in the alt newsgroups. In many cases there are identical groups, differing only in the first part of the name. For example, there is both a **rec.autos.antique** and **alt.autos.antique** newsgroup. The same subjects are discussed in both, although the alt groups are not as widely distributed. This duplication can happen when the readership of an alt group grows large enough to justify the creation of a group in an "established" hierarchy. So, **alt.autos.antique** might "graduate" to become **rec.autos.antique**; however, the original alt group will often continue on, with a gradually decreasing readership as people move over to the rec version.

Often, though, alt newsgroups have no equivalent main-stream group because of the contentious issues involved or because of the smaller circulation of the newsgroup. For example, a newsgroup devoted to the highlights of the social season in Kansas City will be of little interest to a reader in Australia, so an alt group with limited distribution is ideal.

New and Bogus Newsgroups

New newsgroups are usually created by popular assent, with enough users wanting the group to sustain its continued use. However, it is possible for anyone to create a new newsgroup if they know the procedure. Unfortunately, new newsgroups that are created as a joke—known as *bogus newsgroups*—are common, usually to be removed a day or two later when no traffic is experienced in the newsgroup. The adding and removing of bogus newsgroups can take a bit of time as well as annoy users. An example of a bogus newsgroup is **swedish.chef.bork.bork.bork**, based on a character from Jim Henson's *Muppet Show*.

New newsgroups are often proposed in a special newsgroup called **news.announce. new-users** where support for the new group is determined, a process called a "call for votes" or CFV. New groups can be created unilaterally by an existing group, but netiquette demands a call for votes first in all but the alt hierarchy.

Moderated Newsgroups

Not all newsgroups are open and free for any type of posting. There is the moderated newsgroup, in which one or more users determine whether each message posted to the group is sent for distribution or deleted. The moderator is usually a volunteer who tries to ensure the newsgroup remains on-topic and cuts out any obnoxious or overly insulting articles. He or she also can edit articles to keep users from rambling too much.

Moderated newsgroups are not widespread, but most are popular because they deal specifically with a single subject. For example, the moderated newsgroup **rec.audio.high-end** is devoted to discussions and information about the high-end audio market, meaning the best in sound reproduction possible. By having the newsgroup moderated, readers can avoid the "I need a $100 amplifier" type of message.

Moderating a newsgroup is a lot of work and tends to be thankless. It is not unusual for the role of moderator to change as the load in the group becomes overwhelming for a single person. In some cases, newsgroups can revert from moderated status to open, allowing any posting. One problem with moderated newsgroups is that postings tend to take longer to appear as they must first be screened by the moderator.

When posting to a moderated newsgroup, you don't have to do anything special. The UseNet software will route the message to the moderator's e-mail address automatically.

A list of moderated newsgroups and the moderator's name and e-mail address is available from the newsgroup **news.announce.newuser**. The header of articles in a moderated newsgroup usually makes it clear that the group is moderated and by whom.

Threads

Usually an article will inspire replies. These replies build themselves into a series. This is called a *thread*. Some newsreaders are designed to allow you to follow threads conveniently, keying on the subject of all articles in the thread.

Unfortunately for users who like to follow threads, the subject tends to change in the space of a posting or two, without the subject title changing. This results in a posting in **rec.bicycles.tech** starting out dealing with brake pads and ending up with more than half the postings talking about hair-raising falls down a steep cliff when brakes failed. Threads, for this reason, should be treated as a guideline only.

One advantage to threads is that it allows a user to collect all articles about a particular subject and post them for others to access in a convenient manner. For example, **rec.pets.cats** may have a thread about combing long-haired pets that can grow to several hundreds of articles. These may be gathered and edited by a newsgroup reader and reposted as a summary of the subject.

What Do I Need to Know?

When you first get involved with UseNet, it can be overwhelming. There is a little intimidation about the number of people your postings can get to, as well as an overwhelming sense from the sheer amount of information you have access to. Just finding out how to use UseNet properly can be confusing. For that reason, a number of files have been created to help get you get started, and there is a newsgroup dedicated to helping first-timers, who are called *newbies* in the UseNet lexicon. A friendly word of advice, don't leap into UseNet and start posting articles without knowing what the rules are. You don't want to incur the wrath of thousands of users!

Most newsgroups that you will want to investigate as a first-time user have the word "newuser" in the newsgroup title. Most newsreaders can scan newsgroup titles, so this is an easy way to get started.

The best newsgroup to try is one we've mentioned already, called **news.announce.newusers**. This is where proposals for new newsgroups are posted. Part of the **news.announce.newusers** newsgroup is the regular posting of a set of articles on UseNet, netiquette, and postings. When you find an article that contains valuable information for new users, use your news reader to save the article to a file so you can read it at your leisure.

Five of the important articles that appear on **news.announce.newusers** are

- Rules for Posting to UseNet
- A Primer on How to Work with the UseNet Community
- Answers to Frequently Asked Questions about UseNet
- Emily Postnews Answers Your Questions on Netiquette
- Hints for Writing Style for UseNet

N O T E If you check the **news.announce.newusers** newsgroup and can't find the guides mentioned, wait a few days. They are usually posted weekly or bimonthly, and your news service may have deleted them if the postings are older than the system's pre-set expire time. ▪

The **news.announce.newusers** newsgroup also has a complete list of all active newsgroups and their general subject, a list of moderated newsgroups, and guides to information about each newsgroup.

Another important newsgroup for new users is **news.answers**, which as its name implies, gets you answers to your questions (specifically about UseNet). This group has many veteran users who try to help new users as much as possible, all in the spirit of the UseNet community.

The **news.answers** newsgroup has one other important role. When any newsgroup has a list of Frequently Asked Questions (FAQ) that explain the basics about the newsgroups' subject, it is usually cross-posted to **news.answers**. *Cross posting* means it is posted to two or more newsgroups at the same time.

Getting Started in a Newsgroup

When you first start reading a newsgroup, it is advisable to avoid posting unless you are really determined to let your opinion be heard. Monitor the newsgroup for a little while to find out who the regulars are, what the overall tone of the newsgroup is (is it light-hearted or serious, academic or sarcastic), and whether your messages are worth posting.

T I P It's a good idea to monitor newsgroups for a while until you feel confident about your own postings.

Part V

Ch 27

Before you start asking questions that are considered basic and silly, look for a FAQ (frequently asked questions) file. These are usually posted on a regular basis varying from every couple of weeks to monthly, depending on the newsgroup. Alternatively, check in the **news.answers** newsgroup. The reason for this advice is simple. Nothing is more annoying for frequent users of, say, **rec.aquaria** to receive a posting asking how big of a fish tank should be bought. Usually, the basic information questions are fully answered in the FAQ. Asking this kind of trivial question will either get you a polite note to check the FAQ or a roughly worded reprimand for wasting the newsgroup's time.

Posting Articles

When you read through a newsgroup, there are bound to be many things you want to comment on. That's what the UseNet is all about—inspiring and supporting communications between users. You may notice the most effective postings are well-reasoned, logical, properly laid out, have good grammar and spelling, and don't ramble. Try to follow the same pattern.

Many users have to pay a fee (either through a service provider or download time charges) to receive their newsgroups and nothing will annoy them more than receiving long and pointless postings. Keep this simple fact in mind when you write. Some subjects need many lines to fully explain your ideas, but don't use up valuable space for nothing.

Good grammar and spelling are sometimes difficult to maintain when typing quickly, but do try your best to keep your sentences properly constructed. The odd spelling mistake is easily tolerated, but a message full of them will invite disdain. When you are first getting started with posting messages, it is advisable to write your replies offline and make sure they are properly structured before sending them over the network. A few minutes effort will enhance your status in the newsgroup considerably. Also avoid long, rambling paragraphs. Some users don't seem to know when a paragraph break should be made. Many UseNet users will delete an article immediately if they don't see some structure to the posting.

 TIP If you are using a Windows news reader and it doesn't have a spelling checker (and most don't), use a word processor to compose and check your article then copy and paste it into the news reader.

Not everyone has a fancy message reader that reformats messages to fit on-screen. When you write a message, make sure you use a reasonable line length. UseNet newsgroups are ASCII-based with no formatting characters embedded. Use a 60-65 character line length, and don't forget to remove any special codes your word processor may add (i.e., save as a text file).

Another important no-no: Avoid uploading sizable files such as graphics to a newsgroup that is text-based. A typical graphics file will take up hundreds of kilobytes of space. If you're paying by the line, downloading this file can cost a considerable amount and then it will be something you probably won't want. There are dedicated newsgroups for graphics, or post a message asking if anyone wants your long file first.

N O T E If you post a long file, be considerate and put the phrase "(long)" in the subject area to warn other users. A better alternative is to check for a dedicated subgroup for binaries, pictures, or music files. They exist for many of the newsgroups that regularly involve these lengthy items.

When you gather enough courage to participate in the newsgroups by posting your own articles, there are a few things you have to take care of. First (and most important) is making sure your postings get to their target newsgroup and are not returned to you as undeliverable. Many newbies try sending a message to their favorite newsgroup reading something like this: "This is a test. Don't read it!" When they see the message in the newsgroup, they know they are okay. Unfortunately, millions of other users have downloaded the message (costing money and time) and thousands have probably read it (wasting their time). The normal newsgroups are not the place to test your postings!

There is an easy way to test that your postings are going to the newsgroups properly: Use one of the newsgroups specifically designed for testing. The most commonly used newsgroups for this purpose are **misc.test** and **alt.test**. When they receive a posting from a user, they send an automatic reply to indicate success (this kind of automatic reply is called a "robot" in the UseNet lexicon). You don't have to read the test newsgroups directly, as the reply signifies success. Still, many users like to scan the test newsgroups to see their first posting online.

Signatures

The other important aspect of sending articles is to design your own signature file. Most new users expect to sign their articles with a simple name and sometimes an e-mail address. That's not the way it's usually done on UseNet. Instead, most postings have a several-line block at the end of the article that has the poster's name, e-mail address, and a saying of some sort. Sometimes, there is an ASCII character-based doodle of some sort. Having a witty or clever signature block is a source of prestige on the network.

T I P Keep your signature blocks short! Few things are more annoying than scrolling through pages of fancy signature files when the message was not worth the effort.

Part
V
Ch
27

It would be awkward to have to type in the entire signature block every time you post, so most newsreaders have a feature that allows you to read a file from the hard disk and tack it on at the end of your article. These are called *sig* files. The name of the file varies with the operating system and newsreader.

It is easy to create a sig file. Use a text editor and restrict yourself to the primary ASCII characters. Design a three or four line block that gives all the information about contacting you that you want to send to the newsgroups. Some users put their address and telephone number, while others prefer not to. At a minimum, the signature should have your name and your e-mail address. Phony names are strongly discouraged. You can usually tell young UseNet users by their "Dr. Avenger" or "MegaDeath" name types. Reprobations usually follow, or the user's postings are ignored.

A good signature file is brief. Having a 10 line signature block may look really fancy, but most readers hate wasting the download time. Forget about having huge graphics of your Firebird's Screaming Eagle, or an eight line representation of your favorite rock band's logo. Stick with the minimum, preferably avoiding graphics entirely until you are much more proficient and respected on the UseNet.

A common addition to a signature block is a quotation or saying that you like. These tend to be short and most often humorous. They are fine in signature blocks, as long as they are not obnoxious or too lengthy, as they add a little individualism to your postings. If you scan a few newsgroups for a while, you will see some excellent examples of good signature blocks.

An archive of good and very bad signature blocks is maintained in the newsgroup **alt.fan.warlord**. If you receive the alt newsgroups, it may be worth a few minutes to look at some of the examples. The sig file I use for my e-mail is shown in Figure 27.1. However, since it is a little long, I use the abbreviated version shown in Figure 27.2 for my postings to UseNet.

FIG. 27.1

The normal sig file I use for my e-mail—this is a little long for UseNet postings.

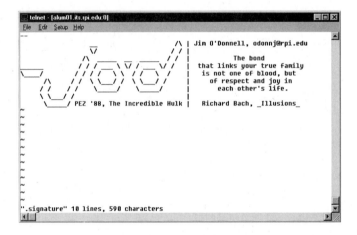

FIG. 27.2

This is the abbreviated version that I use for UseNet.

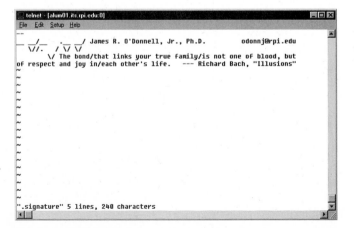

T I P Did you notice that the first line of the sig files shown in both Figures 27.1 and 27.2 consists of a line containing two dashes? Many newsreaders and e-mail programs recognize that this denotes that the rest of the message is a signature block; it's a good idea to start your sig file off this way, too.

N O T E Want to see what a bad signature file looks like? Check out **alt.fan.warlord**. ▨

Anonymous postings are not welcome on the UseNet and since most newsreaders put your Internet address in the header block anyway, they aren't really anonymous. Make sure you sign your messages. If you don't want to use a signature block, at least add a line with your name.

Anonymous Postings

Some service providers allow you to post articles to newsgroups anonymously. On many newsgroups, this is considered very bad behavior: if you don't have the honesty to sign your name, you shouldn't be posting. Many veteran UseNet users set up their system to automatically remove any anonymous postings.

As a general rule, if you have the ability to post anonymously, don't. You may feel you can say things anonymously that you wouldn't say if your name was attached to it, but those sentiments are probably best left unsaid. Besides, many "anonymous" services aren't really anonymous as they maintain a record of who posted what article. These records can, in theory, be used against you.

Note that there are some newsgroups, particularly some of those in the alt hierarchy, in which anonymous postings are considered acceptable. You should be extra careful, if posting anonymously to such a newsgroup, not to abuse the privilege. Also, note that no communication on the Internet is completely secure or anonymous, so be careful not to say or post anything that might come back to haunt you.

N O T E To find out more about one anonymous posting service, send an e-mail message (it doesn't matter what you include in the message) to **anon@anon.penet.fi**. The service will assign you an anonymous mail ID (used for e-mail going through that service only) and send you some information about what you need to do to use the service. You can also get this information by sending e-mail (again, it doesn't matter what) to **help@anon.penet.fi**. ▨

Cross-Posting

Occasionally, you will see a message that is posted on more than one newsgroup. This is called cross-posting and is discouraged. It is also called *spamming* in UseNet jargon. The only time cross-posting is really approved is when the subject fits properly into more than one newsgroup. An example may be about a plant that is toxic to dogs. Cross postings to the pets and plants newsgroups would be appropriate.

Part
V

Ch
27

If you want to cross-post, make sure the article belongs in the newsgroups you choose. A common problem is a new user listing 10 or more newsgroups; some of which are hardly applicable, but they happen to be the user's favorites. If you are replying to an article that is cross-posted, make sure the reply belongs in all the groups, too.

If a posting should be in a subgroup of a large newsgroup, you may want to post a note to the main group informing readers of the more detailed posting in the subgroup. For example, if you have a binary you want to upload to a programming group, place it in the binaries subgroup with a note to the readers of the parent newsgroup that you have placed the binary on the system. This avoids having to page through the binary in both places.

A common and hated example of cross-posting is the "get rich quick" or pyramid scheme article, which inevitably appears many times a year in dozens of newsgroups simultaneously, all thanks to a single user who didn't use common sense. Not only is this kind of message inappropriate in the first place, cross-posting makes it even more annoying. If you see such a post, rather than posting an angry reply yourself—thus creating even more of a waste—you should either ignore it, or jot off a quick e-mail note to the postmaster of the offender letting him know that there is a user abusing Internet privileges.

 TIP To send a note to the postmaster of a user such as **johndoe@internet.domain.name**, you can usually use the address **postmaster@internet.domain.name**.

Who Gets Your Article?—Distribution

It doesn't make much sense to have a UseNet user in Japan read your query about good restaurants in Paris. One of the things you have to think of when posting an article on UseNet is who gets to read it. The article's distribution is an important aspect of your postings.

Most news programs let you specify the distribution with a single word. In most cases, you want the entire UseNet to read your message so you use the "world" setting, which means everywhere on the Internet. In many cases, this is the default value for a posting, but you should get into the habit of checking this regularly to make sure it applies.

Other settings that may be available to your news program include your organization only, your geographic area (city, state, province, etc.), or your country or continent.

If you do post a local-oriented message to the inappropriate distribution ("There's a great Chinese food restaurant next to Algonquin Park" doesn't have much meaning to anyone who doesn't live in the area), you should expect some nasty notes, and rightly so. Don't waste other people's time and money with posts that they can't use.

Replying to an Article

All news readers let you reply to a posted article with a simple command. Replying is the same as composing a new message, except the heading information is pre-filled for you (taken from the original message). There are two kinds of replies, usually. The first is an e-mail reply to the original poster. The second is to post another article to the same newsgroup. In general, you should reply through e-mail if your reply will only be of interest to the original poster. If it will be of general interest to the whole newsgroup, then reply through a follow-up post.

Most news readers will let you choose to include the message you are replying to in your article, sometimes indented. It's fine to include relevant portions of the original, but if you are replying back to the newsgroup, don't keep the entire message unless it is short. Judiciously cut the original down to the salient parts that your reply is addressing. This saves not only download time but also other users' reading time.

Copyrights

Don't post something to the network that is protected by copyright. This includes text, graphics, music, and many other forms of electronic files. Some users adopt an "I don't care. What can they do?" attitude. It's dangerous, as many users have found out when they wound up charged with a copyright violation. Be careful about posting material other than your own words. If in doubt, don't.

The same warning applies for items you capture off UseNet. Just because someone posted a file, don't assume it's free of copyright. There have been several highly-publicized cases of pictures scanned into a file and distributed on UseNet that have led to copyright violation charges against the user who unknowingly downloaded and used them. Again the same warning applies: if you're not sure the file is free of copyright, don't use it.

TIP If you want to post copyrighted material, very often you can send a quick e-mail message to the copyright holder and get his or her permission. You should probably save your request and the reply, and if you get permission, you can go ahead and post the material.

Posting Files

You know how to write articles and how to reply to them, but how do you upload the binary, graphics, or other large files you have on your system's hard drive? UseNet, like all of the Internet, is based on 7-bit ASCII characters, and hence it won't handle 8-bit binaries. Instead, they will be converted to 7-bit, ruining their contents.

A couple of utilities are available for loading binary files onto the UseNet. UUEncode and UUDecode are the most popular. See Chapter 15, "Encoding and Decoding Files," for more information.

N O T E You can't send binary files to UseNet newsgroups. They must be converted to 7-bit format first. ■

Filtering and Searching for News

A common problem for many users is the sheer volume of articles that are interesting and should be read on a daily basis. Another common problem occurs when you are looking for articles on a particular subject. It can take a considerable amount of time to page through the subject lists alone of the newsgroups that deal with programming, for example, to find information you need. Even with threaded news readers that help a little, finding articles on a specific subject can be difficult because the "subject" line of the article doesn't always reflect the contents.

The structure of UseNet doesn't enable you to perform search functions through all the newsgroups unless you do a full newsgroup download and run a utility over each article for some keywords. That process can take hours alone. Luckily, there is a solution—news filtering and searching systems.

News Filtering

The most popular news filtering service is provided by the Database Group or Stanford University's Department of Computer Science. You can send a profile of the articles you are interested in to the service, which will return news articles to you on a regular basis that pertain exactly to your profile. The summaries provide the first 15 lines of the article, along with the date, posting person, and subject lines. All communication with the filtering service is through e-mail.

To use the news filtering service, compose an e-mail message to **netnews@db.stanford.edu** with the following two lines in the message:

    subscribe <keywords>

    period <frequency>

where the keywords are the subjects you are interested in the filter finding for you and the period is how often you want the summaries e-mailed to you. The subject line of the message you send to the service is ignored. Each line in the message must have no leading whitespace characters (spaces or tabs). Case doesn't matter with the keywords. For example, the message:

    subscribe pascal programming

    period 2

will result in you receiving mail every two days with all the articles that have to do with Pascal programming.

The filtering service scans your keywords and uses them to assess the relevance of each article. It does this by assigning a score from 0 to 100 for the article's relevance to your keyword list. You can tell the service to send only articles that have a high correlation by using the keyword THRESHOLD in a message:

    subscribe guppies breeding aquaria

    period 5

    threshold 80

This will return any articles that meet the minimum score of 80 when the service matches articles. The default value for the threshold (unless you specify otherwise) is 60.

You can set a time limit for the filtering service, if you want. Suppose you are writing a term paper on the Bill of Rights and want the filtering service to perform for the next 30 days. You add the keyword "expire" and the number of days the search is to be active:

> subscribe bill of rights
>
> period 1
>
> threshold 80
>
> expire 30

which will give you daily updates on all articles on your subject (with a score of 80 or higher on the matching scale) for the next 30 days only. After the timer has expired, your searches are deleted from the filtering service's database.

There are more features available through the Stanford News Filtering Service, but you should contact the group for a copy of their information sheet. You can get a copy from the **news.answers** newsgroup or from many of the online services.

News Searching

A relatively new service on the World Wide Web is now available for searching for topics through UseNet called *DejaNews*. Its URL is **http://www.dejanews.com**, and its home page is shown in Figure 27.3.

FIG. 27.3
The DejaNews Research Service allows you to search throughout the UseNet hierarchy for topics of interest.

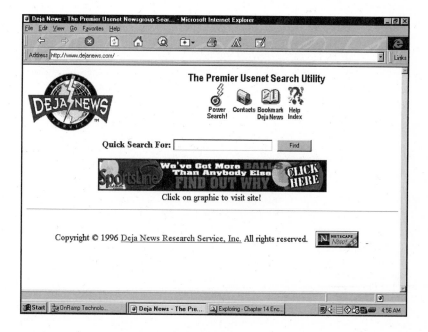

Part

V

Ch

27

You can search for articles throughout the UseNet heirarchy on whatever topic interests you. DejaNews is not all inclusive, as it doesn't cover any of the alt.*, soc.*, talk.*, or *.binaries newsgroups. That still leaves plenty of ground that it does cover. I did my best to stump DejaNews by looking for articles about the Pittsburgh Condors, a basketball team that I vaguely remember used to play in Pittsburgh when I was growing up. As shown in Figure 27.4, I perform this search by asking for a search on Pittsburgh & Condors—the ampersand indicates that you want articles that contain both words, otherwise if will find articles containing one or the other.

FIG. 27.4

Hmmm... Can I find anything on the Pittsburgh Condors?

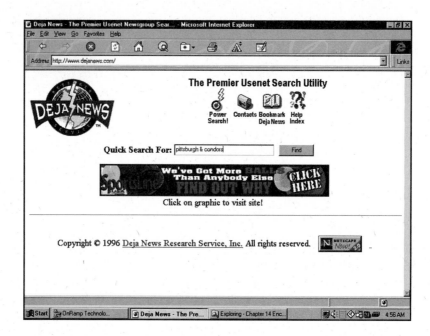

As a result of this search, DejaNews was able to find three articles. Lo and behold, there was some information about the old Pittsburgh Condors (see Fig. 27.5). Of course, things weren't perfect, I got a couple articles which weren't quite what I had in mind. (I could have eliminated those articles by searching for "Pittsburgh Condors," with the quotes, which would have looked for articles with that phrase, rather than just the individual words.)

FIG. 27.5
DejaNews was able to find some truly obscure information for me by scouring the UseNet hierarchy.

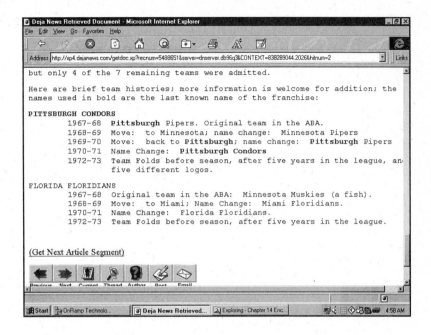

Netiquette

As mentioned earlier, users of the UseNet are expected to follow a set of guidelines for their behavior called *Netiquette*. The complete guide to netiquette is available for you to read in the newsgroup **news.announce.newusers**. It is called "Emily Postnews Answers Your Questions on Netiquette." Before you write your first posting, capture this article and read it thoroughly.

One overwhelming rule on the UseNet is that insulting, degrading, or racist comments are totally out (unless you are in one of the wackier newsgroups like **alt.tasteless**). Reputations are widespread on the UseNet and if you continue with your silly comments, other users will automatically exclude any posting you send.

It has been mentioned before, but it's important to keep your postings clear and succinct. Edit long articles to make them more readable. Repeat posters of long, wordy articles tend to be ignored. If you are excerpting or quoting someone else's article in yours (a common practice), keep the excerpt short and directly relevant. Don't copy the entire message.

Avoid personal messages. UseNet is not a private e-mail service for small groups to communicate; use e-mail for that function. Millions of systems will download your comments (at considerable cost in some cases), so don't be cavalier with their time and money.

Finally, the big one. Despite what the newspapers and some PR companies say, UseNet is not for business items, advertisements, get-rich-quick schemes, or similar postings. Blatant postings to many newsgroups to solicit customers have been tried several times with universal condemnation. It's okay to mention a service you provide, a local store that did good work, or a company that handled something properly for you when it is in context with the rest of the articles in a newsgroup, but direct soliciting should be considered forbidden. One exception to this rule is that there are groups where bartering, swapping, and selling personal items is permissible. For instance, many of the comp.sys groups allow folks to use the newsgroup to sell computer hardware and software they no longer need. If you're in doubt as to whether or not this is acceptable in a given newsgroup, read the newsgroup FAQ or ask the group first.

Pyramid schemes, form letters, and the poor child who is trying to get the world's largest collection of stamps, business cards, credit cards, and so on are either bogus, illegal, or a major breach of Netiquette. The user groups may not have control over what you post (unless they convince your system administrator), but the network is very quick to condemn this kind of behavior.

Abbreviations

To save typing time and make postings shorter, many users employ a set of abbreviations that are commonly known to represent phrases. These are usually typed in capital letters.

Common abbreviations are "IMHO" (in my humble opinion), "BTW" (by the way), and "OTOH" (on the other hand). You will encounter some abbreviations that you can't figure out quickly, as they are used by small groups of users or veterans who are reluctant to type out phrases. One, for example, which had many UseNet users scratching their heads for a while is "ROTFL," which was eventually disclosed as standing for "rolling on the floor laughing." After that, it began showing up all over the place.

Not all abbreviations actually represent a phrase. For example, you will see "<G>" or "<g>" often used. This means "grin" and is meant as a moderator of the tone of the sentence, or to show the poster was making a point with tongue in cheek.

N O T E   It's a good idea to use abbreviations sparingly, as they make some postings difficult to read. Excessive use of abbreviations also is a hallmark of a newbie. ■

Flames

You won't be reading messages on the UseNet long before you see the word *flame*. This has nothing to do with fire, at least in the literal sense. It has its origins in the aeronautical term "flame out" which means to either have your engines quit or your plane catch fire. UseNet uses the term to mean a sharp retort or criticism—sometimes even an insult. There are even newsgroups devoted to flaming.

A user will flame someone when he or she gets mad, by sending a sarcastic or insulting rejoinder to the person who posted the offending article. Usually, flames are inspired by a particularly stupid comment, a stupid response to another article, or a major breach of netiquette.

For the most part, new users are recognized as such and are treated with a little more tolerance than veteran users, although there are some users with no patience at all. You will often see the comment "Don't flame me" in a message, obviously from a user who knows the article may inspire a reply (called *flame-bait*) or who is trying to plead innocence or newbie status.

It is not unusual for a newsgroup to degenerate into a flame war or flame fest for a little while. In such a case, one flame leads to another until a good percentage of the newsgroups' articles are flames. While this can be moderately amusing for a while, it can wear thin quickly. Still, the UseNet community as a whole admires a well thought out and presented flame. The best flames don't appear outright insulting, with subtlety a characteristic of a real flame master.

Shouting

The UseNet is based on simple characters typed on a screen, so there must be some mechanism to emphasize certain words in a message. Users have developed several methods to accomplish this. For example, light emphasis is usually indicated by an underline character before and after a word, as in "this is a _very_ important point," or asterisks in the same manner, such as "make *sure* you save the file first."

The extreme is shouting, which is indicated with uppercase letters, such as "this is a VERY important point." The trick with emphasis is to use it subtly and not to excess. Typing long sentences or paragraphs in uppercase is considered bad manners. Make sure you don't use the Shift-lock key on your keyboard when typing. Excessive shouting is sure to get you flamed.

If you are prone to swearing, get used to typing random characters to replace the offensive (to some) words. For example, "the @#$*&^ company lost the &%^@# key to the car" is a lot less offensive and manages to get the point across. Leave the filling in to the reader. Because some words have different meanings in other countries, this is probably the best way to communicate the feelings.

Surfing and Lurking

The UseNet has many terms that you will encounter as you spend more time in the newsgroups. A couple of terms you will eventually see are *lurking* and *surfing.*

Lurkers are users who read newsgroups but don't post. There's nothing wrong with being a lurker (and no one will know you are doing it), but many UseNet veterans feel that lurkers miss out on the really interesting parts of the UseNet—interaction and participation. That doesn't mean you have to post all the time, but you should post when you feel you have something to say.

Lurking is useful when you want to watch how a discussion on a newsgroup proceeds before committing yourself to it, or when you want to check out a newsgroup for general interest. Most UseNet veterans will advise newcomers to the network to lurk for at least six months before posting, as this gives time to assimilate the overall behavior of the UseNet and the tone of each newsgroup.

Surfers are people who cover a lot of newsgroups, essentially moving from one to the other in the way a wave surfer covers water. Again, there's nothing derogatory about surfing, and it is a term you will see often. In some ways, frequent UseNet users are slightly envious of those with the time to spend surfing across many newsgroups.

Smileys

Smileys (sometimes called *emoticons*) are those little symbols in a message that are made up of a few characters meant to be viewed sideways. The most famous smiley is :), which when viewed from the side has a smiling mouth under two eyes. This is a very simple smiley. There are now entire books devoted to the different and wonderfully complex smileys.

When using smileys in your postings, use them with moderation. Excessive smiley use tends to make your article look silly. A smiley can be very effectively used to modify the tone of a posting, such as "that was really dumb :)" which is intended to mean you are grinning as you say it, essentially having a smile over the subject.

Some of the more popular smileys are:

Smiley	Meaning
:-) or :)	happy
:-(	sad
:-< or :-c	mad or really sad
:-o	wow! or surprise
:-@	screaming or yelling
:-}	grin
'-) or ;-)	wink

Writing Postings: A Checklist

After all the information and rules mentioned in this chapter, you may be feeling a little overwhelmed (and perhaps leery) about posting. You shouldn't. On the whole, the UseNet is populated with considerate, interesting users who tolerate a few goofs along the way. However, a few guidelines will help cut down on the number of flames headed your way:

- *Use the proper newsgroup.* Don't waste users' time by sending the message to the wrong place. Also, avoid cross-posting unless your article is very relevant to the other groups.
- *Make sure the distribution is correct.* Sending a local message to a group who can't use it is inviting a sharp response.
- *Make sure your posting has something to say.* Sending a reply that reads "I agree" is a waste. Only post if you have something to add to the discussion.
- *Don't ramble.* Keep your postings to the point. Remember many users pay to download your messages and resent getting and reading a 100-line article that is a waste of their time.
- *Proper presentation is important.* Try to use proper grammar and spelling at all times.
- *Use a short, inoffensive signature block.* Consider the user who has to pay to download your wonderful 45-line picture of the Mona Lisa rendered with "@" characters.

■ *Use sarcasm and insults carefully.* You may look like a fool if you don't. It's more fun to send than receive and your inappropriate comments are sure to get you blasted.

■ *Unless you are really sure of yourself and ready to receive double the amount back, don't flame anyone.* A gentle comment is better. If you do flame with abandon, make sure you wear your asbestos underwear. ●

CHAPTER 28

Using Microsoft Internet News

by Jerry Honeycutt

Many UseNet newsreaders make a big deal out of all their whizbang features, such as offline reading, kill lists,and so on. These are wonderful features and wonderful programs, but they aren't always easy to use. Either their user interfaces aren't intuitive or, in the case of some of the freeware/shareware newsreaders, they have enough anomalies (bugs) to make them hard to use.

Microsoft Internet News ("Internet News" from now on) is a very simple program that does just about anything any other newsreader does, such as offline reading, binary file decoding, etc. But, Internet News either does these functions automatically or is so intuitive that using it is obvious. For these reasons and more, give Internet News a try—even if you're not using Microsoft Internet Mail. ■

Download and install Microsoft Internet News

Microsoft Internet News is part of Microsoft Internet Mail and News. You'll learn how to install this self-extracting file in this chapter.

Navigate the Microsoft Internet News window

You'll learn how to get around the Microsoft Internet News main window. This chapter shows you the toolbars, message list, and message preview area.

Subscribe to as many newsgroups as you like

Add newsgroups to a list of favorites so that you can quickly view them. Microsoft Internet News also caches your favorites so that they display faster.

Browse a newsgroup; post and read messages

Microsoft Internet News makes newsgroups as intuitively easy to use as Internet Mail.

Work with file attachments

The days that required you to manually download and decode binary attachments are gone. Newsgroup attachments are almost as easy as mail attachments.

N O T E If you buy into Microsoft's strategy for integrating the Internet into the Windows 95 desktop, Internet News is a "must have." It's the first wave of Internet clients from Microsoft that will completely integrate into the Windows 95 desktop. Internet News already lets you view newsgroups through Windows 95's Explorer, for example. Other examples include Microsoft Internet Explorer (described in Chapter 17, "Using Microsoft Internet Explorer") and Microsoft Internet Mail (described in Chapter 12, "Using Microsoft Internet Mail"). ■

▶ **See** "Getting Ready to Use Microsoft Internet Mail," **p. 282**

▶ **See** "Getting Ready to Use Internet Explorer," **p. 380**

Getting Ready to Use Microsoft Internet News

Internet Mail and Internet News come together in one file called Internet Mail and News (Mailnews95.exe or MailnewsNT.exe). If you've already installed the Internet News portion as described in Chapter 12, "Using Microsoft Internet Mail," you'll see the Internet News icon in My Computer and possibly the Internet News shortcut on your desktop. If you already have installed Internet News, go directly to "Configuring Internet News" later in this chapter.

The Internet Mail and News file isn't on the NetCD (Microsoft is funny that way), so you'll have to download it from Microsoft's Web or FTP sites. Downloading it from Microsoft's Web site is the easiest of all. Point your Web browser at **http://www.microsoft.com/ie/iedl.htm**. Then click on the Download Software link and follow the instructions you see on the Web page to download Mailnews95.exe for Windows 95 or MailnewsNT.exe for Windows NT. You can save this file into any folder you like because it expands its contents into Windows temporary folder.

The next best thing is to download it from Microsoft's FTP site. You need a working Internet connection to use the steps that follow, but you don't need to understand how FTP works (see Chapter 31, "Using FTP and Popular FTP Programs").

To download the file Mailnews95.exe, use these steps:

1. Choose Run from the Start menu, type **ftp**, and press Enter. You'll see a window that looks like an MS-DOS window except that it displays the ftp> prompt.

2. Type **open ftp.microsoft.com** and press Enter. If you're using Dial-Up Networking and you're not already connected to the Internet, click Connect when you see the Connect To dialog box.

3. Type **anonymous** and press Enter when FTP prompts you for the user name. Then type your full mail address when FTP prompts you for your password: **jerry@honeycutt.com**, for example.

4. Type **cd /Softlib/MSLFILES** and press Enter when you see ftp> again. Note that Microsoft's FTP site isn't case-sensitive, so you don't have to worry much about capitalization.

5. Type **get Mailnews95.EXE** and press Enter to download the Windows 95 version, or type **get MailnewsNT.EXE** and press Enter to download the Windows NT version. FTP copies Internet Mail service to your Windows desktop.

6. Type **bye** and press Enter to log off of the FTP server and close the FTP window.

   ▶ **See** "Using FTP from the Command Line," **p. 809**

N O T E Microsoft hasn't developed a Windows 3.1 version of Internet Mail and News. It has announced its intention to do so, however. When the Windows 3.1 version is available, you can expect Microsoft to name the file something like Mailnews31.exe. Substitute this file name in the instructions above to download it. ■

Installing Internet News

Internet News is very easy to install. No muss, no fuss. You don't have to unzip the file and you don't have to clean up after it, either. Internet Mail comes in a self-extracting, self-installing file.

Here's how to install Internet News:

1. If you haven't already done so, download Mailnews95.exe as described in the previous section. You won't see the correct icon until you refresh the folder in which you downloaded the file by pressing F5.

2. Double-click on Mailnews95.exe to start the extractor. This displays a license agreement for you to read.

3. Click on Yes to accept the license agreement. The extractor copies its files into the Windows temporary folder and runs the Internet Mail and News Setup Wizard.

4. Type your name and organization in the spaces provided. The setup wizard prefills these fields with the information you provided when you first installed Windows. Click on Next.

5. Click on Next again to confirm your name and organization. The setup wizard displays the dialog box shown in Figure 28.1. This gives you the choice of installing Internet Mail, Internet News, or both.

6. Select Internet Mail, Internet News, or Both Internet Mail and News. Click on Next to continue and the setup wizard displays a dialog box that asks you to pick a folder for your data files.

7. Click on Change Folder to choose a different folder or click on Next to continue. By default, the folder name is a combination of C:\Program Files\Internet Mail and News and your username.

8. Click on Finish. The setup wizard installs the appropriate files into the path you specified. It also copies some files (DLLs and such) into your C:\Windows\System folder.

9. Click on Yes to restart your computer. You must restart your computer for the changes to take effect.

Part
V

Ch
28

FIG. 28.1

If you're using Microsoft Exchange, consider using Microsoft Internet Mail if you don't rely on multiple news services such as CompuServe and Internet Mail.

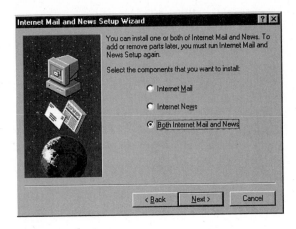

Configuring Internet News

Configuring Internet News is much easier than configuring Internet Mail. You need to know only the name of your news server and your mail address. After you answer a few questions, Internet News pops up on your desktop for the first time. Use these steps to configure it:

1. Double-click on the Internet News shortcut that you'll find on your desktop. If you've already removed the shortcut from your desktop, you can choose Programs, Internet News from the Start menu. The Internet News Configuration wizard pops up telling you that your Internet service provider gave you all the information you need to configure it. Click on Next to continue, and you'll see the window shown in Figure 28.2.

FIG. 28.2

The name you type in Name is the name that people see when they read your newsgroup article (called "message" in Internet News terms). The mail address you provide is the address to which people reply if they reply via mail.

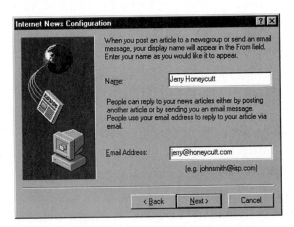

2. Type your full name in Name and your mail address in Email Address. The mail address includes your account name and mail server name. Click on Next to continue and you'll see the window shown in Figure 28.3.

NOTE If you've registered your own mail domain, use that mail address in step 2. This ensures that folks replying to your mail are actually seeing your personal mail domain. For example, my actual mail address is **jerry@onramp.net**. I've registered my mail domain as **honeycutt.com**, however, so I type **jerry@honeycutt.com** in step 2. ■

FIG. 28.3
If you don't recall the name of your news server, try adding **news.** to the beginning of your Internet service provider's mail domain. **onramp.net** becomes **news.onramp.net**, for example.

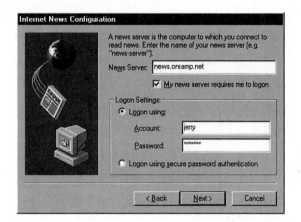

3. Type the name of your news server in Ne_w_s Server. If your news server requires you to log on to the server, select _M_y News Server Requires Me to Logon. Then, select Lo_g_on using, and type your user name in _A_ccount and your password in _P_assword. Alternatively, select Logon Using _S_ecure Password Authentication if your news server supports it. Click on Next to continue.

4. Select I Use a LAN Connection if you connect to the Internet via your network, choose I Connect Manually if you connect to the Internet manually, or choose I Use a Modem to Access my Email and choose a connection from the list if you connect using Dial-Up Networking. Click on _N_ext to continue.

5. Click on Finish to save your settings.

After you've configured Internet News, the first thing it wants to do is jump online and get a list of newsgroups from your news server. It does this so that you have a list of available newsgroups from which to subscribe. It'll connect to your news server and download the name and description of each newsgroup. This can take a long time (several minutes) if you're using a 28.8K connection. It only lasts a few minutes with a 128K ISDN connection, however. While it's downloading the list of newsgroups, it displays status information in a window, as shown in Figure 28.4.

▶ **See** "What Do I Need to Know?," **p. 720**

NOTE Each news server carries a different selection of newsgroups. My provider carries 12,000 newsgroups, for example, while your server may only carry 11,000. This depends largely on the tastes of your Internet service provider. Some providers may not choose to carry the sexually oriented newsgroups. Regardless, most providers do carry the bulk of the socially acceptable newsgroups, such as **comp.os.ms-windows**. ■

FIG. 28.4
Internet News uses two
passes to download the
newsgroups. It down-
loads the newsgroup
names first, then it
downloads the news-
group descriptions.

Starting and Stopping Internet News

You probably left Internet News running on your desktop after you configured it. I'm going to
show you a few ways to start it anyway so that you'll understand all your options.

Here are a few of the ways to start Internet Mail. Do one of the following:

- Double-click on the Internet News shortcut that you'll find on your desktop. Internet
  News opens in its own window.

- Choose Programs, Internet News from the Start menu. Likewise, Internet News opens in
  its own window.

- Double-click on the Internet News icon that you'll find in My Computer. If you've
  configured My Computer to browse folders in a separate window, Internet News opens
  in its own window. On the other hand, if you've configured My Computer to browse
  folders using a single window, Internet News opens in the current window.

- Open Windows 95 Explorer and select Internet News from the folder pane. Internet
  News opens in the right-hand pane of Explorer, as shown in Figure 28.5.

FIG. 28.5
If you've also installed
Microsoft Internet Mail,
you can switch from
Internet News to
Internet Mail by
selecting Internet Mail
in the folder pane.

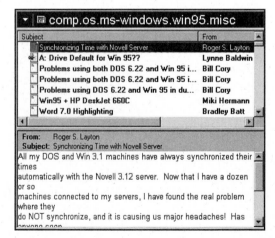

> **N O T E**   You're getting a glimpse at the famed "Nashville" Windows 95 update, which Microsoft intends to release later in 96. Nashville integrates the Internet into the desktop (more specifically into the Explorer shell) using OLE technology. ▪

Internet News certainly has a lot of options for getting at it. It has almost as many ways to shut it down, too. Do one of the following:

- If Internet News is running in its own window, Choose File, Close from the Internet News main menu. Alternatively, you can click on the window's close button (the one in the caption bar).

- If Internet News is running inside Explorer, select a different folder in Windows 95 Explorer.

> **N O T E**   Make sure that you have a working Internet connection before you try to use Internet News. See Chapter 4, "Connecting Through a LAN with Windows 95 and Windows NT," to learn how to connect to the Internet via a network. See Chapter 5, "Connecting to a PPP or SLIP Account with Windows 95," and Chapter 6, "Connecting to a PPP or SLIP Account with Windows NT," to learn how to connect to the Internet via Dial-Up Networking. ▪

Checking Out the Main Window

If you didn't leave Internet News running on your desktop, start it now. Make sure that you open it in its own window so that you can better follow this chapter. You should see a window that looks similar to Figure 28.6.

You see the Internet News menu and toolbar along the top of the window. You also see the Internet News icon bar just below the toolbar. Internet News divides the rest of the window between the message pane on the top and the preview pane on the bottom.

The Toolbar and the Icon Bar

Why does Internet News have a toolbar and an icon bar? Good question. There is a distinction between the two, however. The icon bar provides bigger actions. Post a new message or choose a newsgroup, for example.

The toolbar provides smaller actions that apply to what you see in the window. Mark the current message as read, for example. Table 28.1 shows you the picture, name, and purpose of each button on the toolbar. You'll learn about the icon bar next.

Part
V

Ch
28

FIG. 28.6
You can choose one of your favorite newsgroups, read a newsgroup's message, post your own message, and preview a message from the main window.

Icon bar

Divider—Drag to resize message and preview panes.

Status bar

Toolbar

Newsgroups—Click to change newsgroups.

Message pane

Preview pane

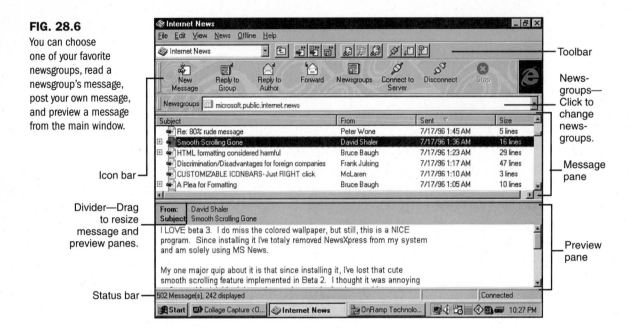

Table 28.1 Internet News Toolbar Buttons

Button	Name	Description
	Up One Level	Moves to the parent newsgroup.
	Next Unread Message	Selects the next unread message.
	Next Unread Thread	Selects the next unread thread, skipping the remaining messages in the current thread.
	Next Unread Newsgroup	Opens the next unread newsgroup, skipping the remaining messages in the current newsgroup.
	Mark Message Read	Marks the selected message as read.
	Mark Thread as Read	Marks all the messages in the thread as read.
	Mark Everything as Read	Marks all the messages in the newsgroup as read.

Button	Name	Description
	Connect to Server	Connects or disconnects from the server.
	Mark Message for Download	Marks a message for download.
	Mark Thread for Download	Marks all the messages in a thread for download.

TIP You can see the name of each button by holding the mouse pointer over it for a few seconds until a *tooltip* pops up.

Did you notice the drop-down list box on the left-hand side of the toolbar? This lets you change back and forth between Internet Mail and Internet News.

The icon bar works exactly like a toolbar except that the icons don't look like buttons (they're bigger), and they don't depress when you click on them. The icon bar contains five icons. Table 28.2 shows you each icon's picture, gives you its name, and tells you what it does.

Table 28.2 The Internet News Icon Bar

Icon	Name	Description
	New message	Opens a new message window.
	Reply to Group	Posts a reply to the newsgroup.
	Reply to Author	Mails a reply to the author.
	Forward	Mails the message to someone else.
	Newsgroups	Opens the Newsgroups window.
	Connect to Server	Connects to the news server.
	Disconnect	Disconnects from the news server.
	Stop	Stops downloading or uploading.

Part

V

Ch

28

T I P If the icon bar annoys you, you can hide it by choosing View, Icon Bar until you don't see a check mark next to the Icon Bar menu item. Alternatively, you can move it to a different part of the screen by putting your mouse pointer in the icon bar so that it's not on top of an icon. Your mouse pointer will change to an awkward-looking hand. Click and drag the icon bar to the top, bottom, left, or right side of the window.

Newsgroups List

Most newsreaders let you subscribe to your favorite newsgroups so that you can open them quickly. That is, you can pick out a handful of newsgroups and stash them in a special list so that you don't have to wade through 10,000 newsgroup names every time you want to open **alt.fan.enya**.

Internet News is no exception. Click anywhere in the Newsgroups list and you'll see a menu similar to Figure 28.7. Pick a newsgroup from the list, and Internet News reads the current message headers from the news server and displays them in the message pane.

FIG. 28.7
If you're using multiple news servers (a cool Internet News feature), newsgroups are indented under each news server.

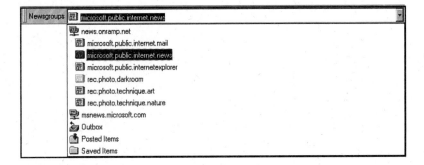

▶ **See** "Subscribing to a Favorite Newsgroup," **p. 750**

▶ **See** "Using Multiple News Servers," **p. 762**

The Message Pane   The message pane shown in Figure 28.8 is the center of attention in Internet News. It displays all the unread messages in the current newsgroup—unless you've configured Internet News to display read messages, too.

Double-click on a message header to open the message in its own window. Even better: You can select a message by clicking on it once, and you'll see its contents in the preview pane.

Did you notice the message headers that contain a little plus-sign (+) next to the subject? This indicates that the message is part of a *thread*. A thread is a group of messages that are related by their subject line. If someone posts a message, for example, and another person replies to that message, both messages constitute a thread.

Click on the plus sign to expand the thread so you can see all its levels. You'll also notice that each level (each level contains replies to the previous level) in a thread is indented so that you can keep track of who's replied to whom.

FIG. 28.8
You can sort the selected folder by clicking on one of the column headings in the message pane. Right-click on a column heading to choose a different sort order.

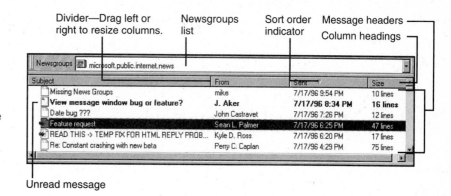

Divider—Drag left or right to resize columns.

Newsgroups list

Sort order indicator

Message headers

Column headings

Unread message

Internet News uses other special icons to indicate the status of a message and its contents. Table 28.3 shows you what each icon represents.

Table 28.3   Icons in a Message Header

Icon	Name	Description
	Read Message	Indicates that you've already retrieved and read the message
	Unread Message	Indicates that you haven't retrieved the message
	Retrieved	Indicates that you've retrieved the message but not read it
	Expand Thread	Indicates that you can click on the plus sign to expand the thread
	Close Thread	Indicates that you can click on the minus sign to close the thread

TIP   Here's a keyboard shortcut. Press the right arrow to expand a thread or press the left arrow to close a thread.

▶ See "Threads," p. 720

The Preview Pane   The preview pane displays the contents of the selected message so that you can quickly read it or determine if you want to open it in its own window. The top portion of the preview pane shows you the UseNet header (from and subject), as shown in Figure 28.9. Use the scrollbar to scroll the preview pane up and down if you want to see the rest of the message.

Part
V

Ch
28

FIG. 28.9

If you don't like the preview pane, you can get rid of it by choosing View, Preview Pane, None from Internet News's main menu.

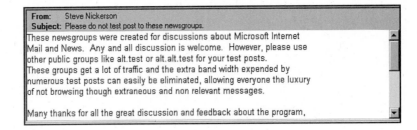

From: Steve Nickerson
Subject: Please do not test post to these newsgroups.

These newsgroups were created for discussions about Microsoft Internet Mail and News. Any and all discussion is welcome. However, please use other public groups like alt.test or alt.alt.test for your test posts. These groups get a lot of traffic and the extra band width expended by numerous test posts can easily be eliminated, allowing everyone the luxury of not browsing though extraneous and non relevant messages.

Many thanks for all the great discussion and feedback about the program,

---

T I P   If you don't like the preview pane, you can get rid of it by choosing View, Preview Pane, None from Internet News's main menu. You can also hide the message's header information by choosing View, Preview Pane, Header Information until you don't see the check mark. Note that if you hide the message header, you'll have to open a message in its own window to extract its attachments.

Getting a Grip on Newsgroups

Internet News provides a user-friendly way to manage your newsgroups: the Newsgroups window. This window lets you keep track of all your subscribed newsgroups, available newsgroups, and new newsgroups (recent additions to the news server).

You can also keep track of multiple news servers using the Newsgroups window. Click on the Newsgroups icon in the icon bar to display the window shown in Figure 28.10.

T I P   If you don't like how Internet News organizes the newsgroups to which you subscribe, create Windows 95 shortcuts to your favorite newsgroups and stash them in a folder. You can organize them any way you like.

Here's how to create a shortcut to a newsgroup: Right-click in a folder, choose New, Shortcut, type the URL for your newsgroup such as **news:alt.tv.simpsons** (don't forget to prefix the newsgroup name with "news:"), and click on Next. Then, type a plain English name for your shortcut and click on Finish.

If Internet News doesn't start automatically when you double-click on the shortcut, choose View, Options from the Internet News main menu, click the Read tab, and select Make Microsoft Internet News as your default news reader.

The Newsgroup dialog box lets you look at your newsgroups in three different ways. You can look at all the available newsgroups by clicking on the All tab. You can look at just the newsgroups to which you've subscribed by clicking on the Subscribed tab. You can also look at any new newsgroups that have been added to the server since the last time you logged on to it by clicking on the New tab. Regardless of which view you're looking at, Internet News displays the subscribed icon next to any newsgroup to which you subscribed.

FIG. 28.10

If you're using only one news server, you won't see the news servers on the left-hand side of this window, as shown here.

Available news servers

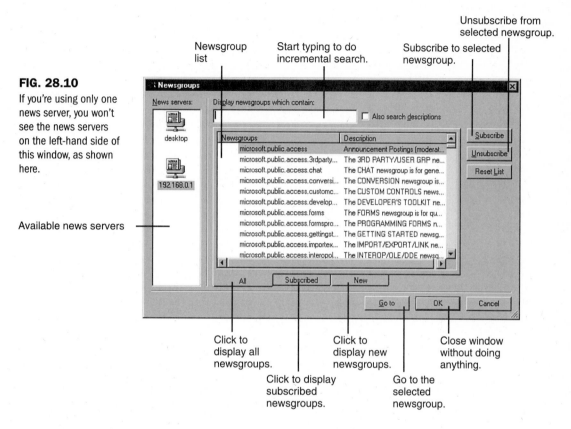

Newsgroup list

Start typing to do incremental search.

Subscribe to selected newsgroup.

Unsubscribe from selected newsgroup.

Click to display all newsgroups.

Click to display subscribed newsgroups.

Click to display new newsgroups.

Go to the selected newsgroup.

Close window without doing anything.

Choosing a News Server

If you've configured Internet News to work with multiple news servers (see "Using Multiple News Servers" later in this chapter), it displays each news server along the left side of the window. Click on one of the icons representing a news server, and Internet News opens that server's list of newsgroups and displays them. If it hasn't loaded any newsgroups from that server, it starts downloading them immediately.

> **N O T E** Tracking multiple news servers is now an absolute requirement for any serious newsreader. Bold statement, huh? Microsoft has recently moved its support forums from CompuServe to UseNet. It has done so by creating its own news server (**msnews.microsoft.com**). Other companies are likely to follow suit as this idea takes off, and each will likely have their own news server. You don't want to have to change your server configuration and download a new batch of newsgroups every time you want to get support from your favorite company. ■

Finding a Newsgroup

Your news server probably has so many newsgroups that it's hard to find the right newsgroup. Internet Mail lets you do an *incremental search* (the search narrows in after each character you type) to limit the list to those newsgroups that match the search string you've typed in the search field.

For example, if you start to type **win95** in the search field, Internet News displays all the newsgroups that contain that string of characters. You can also use multiple keywords in the search field. If you type **win95** and **setup** separated by a space, for example, Internet News limits the list to those newsgroups that contain both words.

> **T I P** Type **alt.** in the search field to limit the list to just the **alt** newsgroups. Likewise, type **comp.**, **rec.**, or **clari.** to limit the list to those newsgroup hierarchies.

▶ **See** "Newsgroup Names" **p. 717**

Test Driving a Newsgroup

You don't have to subscribe to a newsgroup to use it. You can choose a newsgroup from the list of available newsgroups and open that newsgroup in the Internet News message pane. After Internet News updates the message headers from the news server, you can look at all the message headers, read a variety of messages, and post your own messages.

Here's how to go to a specific newsgroup:

1. Click on the Newsgroups icon in the icon bar.
2. Click on the All tab and choose a newsgroup from the list. You can type a string in Display Newsgroups Which Contain to narrow the list.
3. Click on Go To. Internet News opens the newsgroup in the message pane and loads any new message headers from the news server.

After you've lurked around enough to know that you want to come back, you can subscribe to the newsgroup. Choose News, Subscribe to this Group from the Internet News main menu. If you forget to subscribe to an interesting newsgroup before changing to a different one, Internet News thoughtfully asks you if you want to subscribe. Click either Yes or No.

▶ **See** "Surfing and Lurking," **p. 733**

> **T I P** You don't need to wait for Internet News to finish retrieving the latest message headers before you can start reading messages. Internet News is multithreaded. That is, it can read message headers in the background while you're retrieving messages in the foreground.

Subscribing to a Favorite Newsgroup

The term *subscribing* is a bit misleading. You don't actually subscribe to anything. You don't pay for a subscription, and nothing is delivered to your mailbox. Subscribing to a newsgroup simply means that you want to add that newsgroup to a special, smaller list so that you can get at it quicker.

One other significant benefit of subscribing to a newsgroup is that Internet News caches subscribed newsgroups to your hard disk so that you can read messages offline. It also doesn't take as long to read the message headers the next time you log on to the news server. Here's how to subscribe to a newsgroup:

1. Click on the Newsgroups icon in the icon bar to open the Newsgroups window.

2. Click on the All tab.

3. Select the newsgroup to which you want to subscribe and click on Subscribe until you see the Subscribe icon next to it. Repeat this step for each newsgroup to which you want to subscribe.

4. Click on OK to close the Newsgroups window.

Once you've subscribed to a newsgroup, Internet News provides a couple of ways to open it. The quickest is to click on the Newsgroups list right above the message pane and select one of the subscribed newsgroups from the list.

If you're using multiple news servers, pick the news server first, then pick the subscribed newsgroup from the cascading menu. Internet News opens the newsgroup you selected in the message pane and updates its headers from the news server.

Popping up the Newsgroup dialog box isn't as quick, but it gives you a more complete view of the news servers you're using and the newsgroups to which you subscribe. Click on the Newsgroups button in the icon bar, and the Newsgroups dialog box opens on your desktop. Click on the Subscribed tab, select a subscribed newsgroup, and click on Go To. Internet News opens that newsgroup in the message pane and updates the message headers from the news server.

Watching the New Newsgroups

Your news server receives new newsgroups almost every day. Internet News is able to detect these new newsgroups, too, and it gives you the chance to subscribe to them before they disappear forever in the big list.

Internet News checks for new newsgroups each time you connect to a news server. If it finds any, it pops up a dialog box telling you that it found new newsgroups. Click on Yes and Internet News opens the New tab of the Newsgroups window for you.

N O T E Internet News only checks for new newsgroups when it's connecting to a news server. If you're using two news servers, you won't hear about new newsgroups on the second news server until you actually select a newsgroup on that server from the Newsgroups list or you select that news server in the Newsgroups window. ■

Part
V

Ch
28

Unsubscribing from a Newsgroup

OK. You've subscribed to too many newsgroups. It happens to everyone. Now it's time to scale back. Unsubscribing from a newsgroup is similar to subscribing to one.

Here's how to unsubscribe from a newsgroup:

1. Click on the Newsgroups icon in the icon bar to open the Newsgroups window.
2. Click on the Subscribed tab and choose the newsgroup to which you no longer want to subscribe.
3. Click on <u>U</u>nsubscribe. The subscribed icon goes away, but the newsgroup remains in the list until the next time you open the Newsgroups window.
4. Click on OK to close the Newsgroups window.

After you've unsubscribed from a newsgroup, that newsgroup no longer appears in your Newsgroups list, and Internet News no longer caches its messages to your disk.

Posting a New Message

Posting a newsgroup message with Internet News is just like posting a mail message with Internet Mail. That's probably why Microsoft has gone against UseNet convention and used the term *messages* instead of *articles*. The only difference between sending a mail message with Internet Mail and posting a message with Internet News is that you don't address it to a mail address—you address it to a newsgroup name instead.

TIP If you feel an overwhelming need to post a test message to try out these instructions, post it to **alt.test**. This is the only UseNet newsgroup in which posting test messages is acceptable.

Here's how to post a message to a newsgroup:

1. Click on the New Message icon in the icon bar. You'll see the New Message window shown in Figure 28.11.
2. Type the name of each newsgroup to which you want to post your message, separated by a comma. Note that posting a message to more than one newsgroup is called *cross-posting* and is generally frowned upon by the UseNet community.
3. Type mail addresses of each individual that you want to copy via Internet mail, separated by a semicolon in the Cc list.
4. Type the contents of your message in the message body. If you've installed Office 95, you can spell check your message by pressing F7 or choosing <u>N</u>ews, Check Spe<u>l</u>ling.

5. Click on the Post Message button in the toolbar to post your message to the newsgroup. Internet News immediately sends your message to the news server. It may take as long as a few days for your message to reach other servers on the Internet, however.

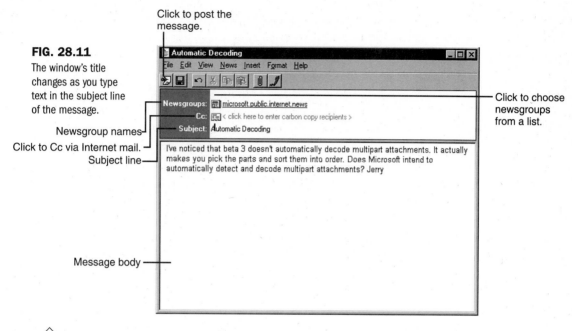

Click to post the
message.

FIG. 28.11
The window's title
changes as you type
text in the subject line
of the message.

Newsgroup names
Click to Cc via Internet mail.
Subject line

Message body

Click to choose
newsgroups
from a list.

I've noticed that beta 3 doesn't automatically decode multipart attachments. It actually makes you pick the parts and sort them into order. Does Microsoft intend to automatically detect and decode multipart attachments? Jerry

TROUBLESHOOTING

Internet News crashed while I was posting a message to a newsgroup. Later, I noticed two copies of my message in the newsgroup. If Internet News crashes while you're posting a message to a newsgroup, avoid the temptation to re-post your message. You'll probably just repeat yourself because in all likelihood your message made it to the server OK. Note that even though Internet News crashes, your information is more than likely safe—just restart Internet News.

▶ **See** "Netiquette," **p. 731**
▶ **See** "Writing Postings: A Checklist," **p. 734**

Attaching a File

 Attaching a file to a newsgroup message works just like attaching a file to a mail message with Internet Mail. Create a newsgroup message as you learned in the previous section. Before you send it, however, click on the Insert File button in the toolbar, pick a file in the Insert Attachment dialog box, and click on Attach. Message windows that contain attachments are split into three panes, as shown in Figure 28.12: message header pane, message body pane, and attachment pane.

Part
V

Ch
28

FIG. 28.12

You can use smaller icons or even a list view to show your attachments. Right-click anywhere in the attachment pane and choose View, Small Icons, or List.

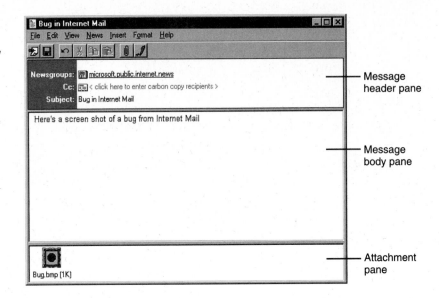

Message header pane

Message body pane

Attachment pane

T I P You can also drag and drop a file into a New Message window.

▶ **See** "File Encoding and Decoding on UseNet," **p. 360**

▶ **See** "Posting Files," **p. 727**

Adding a Signature

Signatures are bits of plain text that you add to the end of every message you send. They're a substitute for your real signature in that they allow you to personalize your message.

Signatures express something interesting about you such as a favorite quotation or hobby. Many people put the URL of their home page in their signature. Others use fancy ASCII artwork for their signature. Here's what my mail signature looks like:

```
Jerry Honeycutt --------------------------------------------------+
Author of QUE's Windows 95 Registry and Customization Handbook ¦
For more information, see http://rampages.onramp.net/~jerry  <-+
```

You can have Internet News automatically add a signature to every outgoing message, or you can choose to insert it only when you feel that it's appropriate. Regardless, you have to configure Internet News so that it knows about your signature.

Here's how to add a signature to your newsgroup messages:

1. Choose News, Options from Internet News main menu. Internet News displays the Options property sheet.

2. Click on the Signature tab.

3. If you want to type your signature right there in the property sheet, select Text, and type your signature in the space provided. Otherwise, select File, and click on Browse to select a text file containing your signature.

 TIP Prevent frustration! Keep your signatures small—no more than three lines of text with perhaps a border.

4. If you want to manually choose when to use a signature, deselect Add Signature to the End of All Outgoing Message.

5. Click on OK to save your changes.

> **CAUTION**
>
> Unless you know exactly who is going to read your mail, I don't recommend putting your home address or telephone number in your signature. You don't want unexpected guests or strange telephone calls, do you?

 Now that you've configured Internet News, you're ready to start using your signature. If you told Internet News to automatically insert your signature at the end of every outgoing message, you don't have to do anything special.

On the other hand, if you told Internet News not to automatically insert your signature, you have to click on the Insert Signature button on the New Message's toolbar to insert your signature at the current cursor position.

▶ **See** "Signatures," **p. 723**

Viewing UseNet Messages

 Internet Mail automatically updates the message headers each time you open a newsgroup. You'll notice the Unread Message icon next to messages that you haven't retrieved, the Re-trieved icon next to messages that you've retrieved but not read, and the Read Message icon next to messages that you've already read. It also sets the message header of each unread message in bold characters.

 Double-click on a message header to open the message in its own window, as shown in Figure 28.13. Table 28.4 shows you each button on the message's toolbar, including its picture, name, and purpose. When you're finished with the message, click on the window's close button to close it.

FIG. 28.13
Internet News doesn't let you change the message's mail header or contents. It's read-only.

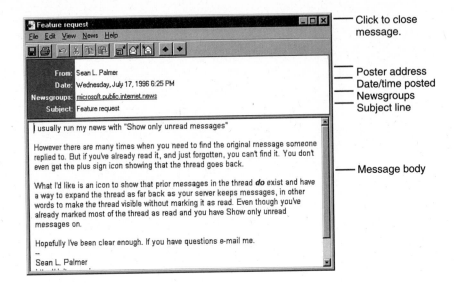

Click to close message.

Poster address
Date/time posted
Newsgroups
Subject line

Message body

Table 28.4 New Message Toolbar Buttons

Button	Name	Description
	Save	Saves the message as a text file
	Print	Prints the message
	Undo	Undoes the last change to the body
	Cut	Cuts selection to the clipboard
	Copy	Copies the message to the clipboard
	Paste	Pastes the contents of the clipboard
	Reply to Group	Posts a reply to the newsgroup
	Reply to Author	Mails a reply to the author
	Forward	Mails the message to someone else
	Previous	Opens previous message in list
	Next	Opens next message in list

As you can see from the message's toolbar, Internet News provides a lot of functions you can do from this window. You can print and reply to a message, for example. You can also navigate to other messages in the newsgroup without actually closing the message window.

Here are some of the more common activities that you'll do in this window:

Icon	Name	Description
	Print	Click on the Print button to print the message to the current printer. Note that Internet News doesn't prompt you for the printer.
	Reply	Click on the Reply to Author button to reply to the author of the posting via mail. Alternatively, click on the Reply to Group button to post a reply to the newsgroup. As a result, Internet News opens a New Message window with the contents of the original message indented. The newsgroup name and subject line are also prefilled.
		Clicking on the Forward button is like clicking on the Reply to Author button, except that it leaves the mail address blank so that you can forward the message to a different address.
	Navigate	Click on the Previous button to open the previous message in the current window or click on the Next button to open the next message in the current window (*next* meaning the message below the current one). The message window closes when you reach the beginning or end of the list.

T I P It's important that you follow the rules on UseNet. One of the biggest no-no's is long quotes, that is, quoting an entire message while adding only a brief comment. Delete most of the original message in your reply, leaving just enough that everyone understands to what you're replying. Keep your quotes under control and you'll make plenty of friends on UseNet.

▶ **See** "Netiquette," **p. 731**
▶ **See** "Writing Postings: A Checklist," **p. 734**

Retrieving a File

In Chapter 27, "How UseNet Works," you learned how file attachments are posted onto a newsgroup using UUENCODE or MIME encoding. Remember that file attachments are encoded into ASCII text and posted as a message. You retrieve the encoded text message and decode it back into its original binary form.

In the not too distant past, this process was painstaking. You had to save the encoded file to your disk and run a special program such as WinCode (see Chapter 15, "Encoding and Decoding Files") to decode the file.

Not anymore. Most modern newsreaders, including Internet News, automatically retrieve and decode file attachments from UseNet. Some do it better than others, however, and Internet News does it better than all of them. Another bold statement, huh? Well, Internet News lets you handle newsgroup file attachments just like Internet mail attachments with little or no difference.

Internet News detects single-part attachments and decodes them automatically. You don't have to do anything special at all. If an attachment has multiple parts (see Chapter 15 if you don't understand multipart attachments), you have to tell Internet News which messages constitute the attachment.

You also have to put the attachments in order (1 of 3, 2 of 3, and 3 of 3) so that Internet News can decode the file correctly. So, how do you do all this?

To decode an attachment divided into several messages, follow these steps:

1. Select all the messages that contain each part of the attachment by pressing Ctrl while you click on each message. These are usually labeled something like this:

    ```
    SUBJECT (0/3)
    SUBJECT (1/3)
    SUBJECT (2/3)
    SUBJECT (3/3)
    ```

TIP In multipart attachments, any part labeled as 0 is usually the text portion of the message that describes the file attachment. You don't have to select this message because it doesn't contain any portion of the file.

2. Choose <u>N</u>ews, Combine and <u>D</u>ecode, and you'll see the dialog box shown in Figure 28.14.

FIG. 28.14

It is most unfortunate that Internet News places messages in this list in the order in which it found them on the Newsgroup because you'll have to re-sort the list every single time.

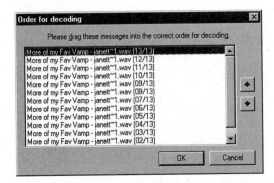

3. Sort the messages into correct order by selecting each file and clicking on the up-arrow and down-arrow buttons. In Figure 28.14, the messages should be ordered from 01/13 to 13/13.

4. Click on OK to retrieve each message, if you haven't retrieved it already, and decode the attachment.

After you've decoded the message, you can treat it like any attachment you would use in Internet Mail. Internet News associates the attachment with the first part or the first message header. If the attachment has four message headers, for example, you can open the attachment, or save it to disk, by opening the first message header, as shown in Figure 28.15—not the second, third, or fourth message headers.

FIG. 28.15
You can save only one attachment at a time. You can open all the attachments, however, by selecting them all, right-clicking on one of them, and choosing Open.

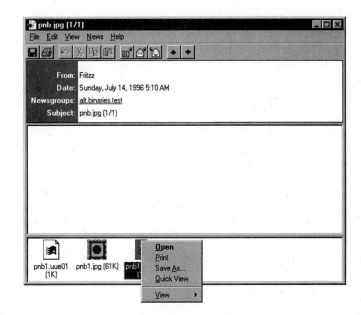

You also can execute the attachment (open it) from the preview pane. You'll see a paper clip in the preview pane's message header. Click on it and choose one of the attachments to execute it. If you choose an MID attachment, for example, the file opens in Media Player.

 T I P If you need a newsreader that automatically detects and sorts each part of a multipart attachment, try out the Agent newsreader. You can learn more about it in Chapter 29, "Using the Agent Newsreaders."

▶ **See** "File Encoding and Decoding on UseNet," **p. 360**
▶ **See** "Posting Files," **p. 727**

Part

V

Ch

28

Replying to a Message

 If your reply only benefits the original author, you should reply via mail instead of posting it to the group. That way you don't use Internet bandwidth and other people's time for information that they don't need or care about. Select the message to which you want to reply in the message pane and click on Reply to Author.

 Alternatively, you can click on the Reply to Author button in the message's window. Internet News pops up the familiar Internet Mail message window. Type your reply in the body of the message and click on the Send button. Internet News stores your reply in Internet Mail's Outbox until you connect to your mail server and transmit your messages.

▶ **See** "Sending Internet Mail," **p. 292**

Posting a Follow-up

 Replying to the newsgroup (following up) posts your reply to the actual newsgroup. Your reply becomes part of a thread. The next time you load the newsgroup, you'll see your message under the message to which you replied—indented one level. In the message pane, select the message to which you want to reply and click on Reply to Group.

 Alternatively, you can click on the Reply to Group button in the message's window. Internet News pops up the familiar new message window that you learned about in "Posting a New Message" earlier in this chapter. Type your reply in the body of the message and click on the Post Message button. Internet News posts your message to the newsgroup immediately.

TIP Some folks really like to cross-post their messages to many, many newsgroups. When replying to a message that's cross-posted, you should consider focusing the reply on one particular newsgroup.

▶ **See** "Posting a New Message," **p. 752**

Customizing the Message Pane

Every newsgroup keeps track of its own settings. You can change a newsgroup's sort order, for example, and it'll remember it apart from the sort order of other newsgroups.

Changing a newsgroup's sort order is easy. Right-click on the column by which you want to sort and choose either Sort Ascending or Sort Descending. The sort order indicator (the little arrow next to a column name) shows that Internet News is sorting the folder by that column. If the arrow points down, the most recent messages are at the top of the list. If the arrow points up, the most recent messages are at the bottom of the list.

You can also change the actual columns that each newsgroup displays. Here's how:

1. Select the newsgroup you want to change from the folder menu.
2. Choose View, Columns from Internet News main menu. Internet Mail displays the Columns dialog box shown in Figure 28.16.

FIG. 28.16
If things get a bit out of hand, you can restore the folder's default columns by clicking on Reset.

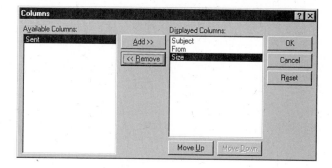

3. Add any columns you want to display for this folder by selecting each column in Available Columns and clicking on Add>>. The column name moves from the left-hand box to the right-hand box.

4. Remove any columns you don't want to display for this folder by selecting each column in Displayed Columns and clicking on <<Remove. The column moves from the right-hand box to the left-hand box.

5. Change the order of the folder's columns by selecting each column you want to arrange in Displayed Columns, and clicking on Move Up to move the folder up in the list or Move Down to move the folder down in the list.

6. Click on OK to save your changes.

Viewing Only Unread Messages

You can view all the messages in a newsgroup by choosing View, All Messages from the Internet News main menu, or you can view only the messages that you haven't read by choosing View, Unread Messages Only. Both have advantages and disadvantages.

If you're viewing only unread messages, you won't see entire threads because the next time you open the newsgroup, the previously read messages don't show up again. In fact, you might not even realize that a message is part of a larger thread because you won't see the plus-sign (+) next to it if the rest of the thread isn't present.

On the other hand, viewing all messages is a bit cumbersome because every message that's been posted shows up in the message pane. New messages will be scattered throughout the list because of time delays between some news feeds.

This is only true if you're sorting by date, by the way. If you're sorting by subject, things really get out of hand because you'll potentially have to look through thousands of message headers to see all the new messages.

Understanding Cached Headers

In a traditional newsreader, all the current message headers are retrieved every time you log on to the news server. A message header may remain on the news server for several days until it finally *scrolls off*.

Part
V

Ch

If you read the message on the first day that it appears, you still have to download it every time you log on to the server—a terrible waste of your time since you've already retrieved it once.

Internet News stores to your disk the message headers it retrieves. It also stores the message bodies of the messages that you've actually read. Then it reads the headers from your disk first and gets the rest of the available headers from the news server.

This makes a radical difference in performance. Instead of downloading 2 or 3 thousand message headers each time you log on to the server, you're downloading 50 or 60 message headers.

N O T E If you find yourself perilously close to running out of disk space, you can purge your cached headers. Choose News, Options from the main menu, and click on the Advanced tab. Click on the Clean Up Now button to open the Local File Clean Up dialog box. Then, click on Compact to compact Internet News's files; click Remove Messages to remove only the cached message bodies (leaving the headers); or click Delete to remove both cached message bodies and headers. ▪

Using Multiple News Servers

As more companies start to offer support groups through UseNet, you'll need to add additional news servers to your configuration. My news server is **news.onramp.net**, for example. I've also configured Internet News to load newsgroups from Microsoft's news server at **msnews.microsoft.com**.

In addition, you may not want to limit yourself to just the news server that your service provider gives you. In Chapter 3, "The Various Ways to Connect: Which One Is Right for You?" you learned about using services from a variety of places on the Internet. These are frequently called *backdoor services,* and backdoor news servers abound on the Internet.

 TIP If your service provider does not carry some of the newsgroups that you want, look for a backdoor service provider whose news server you can use. You might find a public news server that you can use for free. Worst case is that you pay a small nominal fee to use the server.

Here's how you add additional news servers to the Internet News configuration:

1. Choose News, Options from the main menu and click on the Server tab. You'll see the property sheet shown in Figure 28.17.
2. Click on Add to add a server to the list.
3. Type the name of the server in News Server name. If your news server requires you to log on to the server, select My News Server Requires Me to Logon. Then, select Logon using, and type your user name in Account and your password in Password. Alternatively, select Logon Using Secure Password Authentication if your news server supports it.
4. Click on OK to save your changes.

FIG. 28.17

The default server is the one that Internet News uses when you launch a newsgroup from Internet Explorer or from an Internet shortcut.

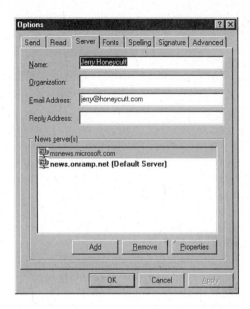

Internet News immediately tries to download a list of the newsgroups that the server carries. ●

CHAPTER 29

Using the Agent Newsreaders

by James O'Donnell

As the number of UseNet newsgroups has increased and the number of articles posted in these groups has sky-rocketed, efficient newsreading software has become a necessity. It is increasingly important for newsreading software to be able to sort groups of articles that relate to the same topic (called threading), to kill (or ignore) articles that are not interesting, and to allow the reader to retrieve only articles that are wanted.

Newsreaders that meet these criteria (and more) are two products from Forté—Free Agent and Agent. Free Agent is a full-featured newsreader that is available at no charge for personal use at home, to students or staff at educational institutions, and to nonprofit organizations.

Agent is a complete newsreading package available commercially that includes all the features of Free Agent, plus e-mail, folders for saving your news articles, and increased article sorting and filtering.

This chapter discusses both the Free Agent and the Agent newsreaders (since some readers may not qualify for the licensing of the Free Agent newsreader). The versions covered in this chapter are Free Agent 1.0 and Agent .99.

Install and configure Free Agent

Free Agent doesn't have an installation program, but it's still very easy to install and configure.

Use Agent for Internet Mail

The commercial version of Agent lets you send and receive Internet mail. Learn how in this chapter.

Subscribe to UseNet newsgroups

All it takes to subscribe to a newsgroup in Free Agent is to double-click your mouse.

Read UseNet articles and retrieve files

Reading articles is easier than subscribing to newsgroups—no need even to double-click.

Post articles to a newsgroup

Posting an article to a UseNet newsgroup is similar to sending Internet mail.

Getting and Installing Agent

Information about obtaining the different Forté products can be found at the World Wide Web (WWW) URL **http://www.forteinc.com/forte**. This site also includes a summary of the features of the two newsreaders, answers to common questions about the readers, and licensing information.

You can download a copy of the Free Agent newsreader from the **ftp.forteinc.com** site through an anonymous FTP. You can find a copy of the Free Agent reader in the /pub/forte/ free_agent directory in the fagent10.zip file (for version 1.0 of Free Agent).

The Agent newsreader can be purchased in several different ways. Probably the easiest is to call Forté using the contact information listed at the end of this chapter. You can order Agent over the phone and download the actual software from **ftp.forteinc.com**. Forté gives you a license key that allows the software to work.

In either case, the software you receive will be a ZIP archive that you should unpack into an installation directory. The files in the zip archive are the entire distribution of the newsreader; no separate setup program is needed.

N O T E Free Agent 1.0 is a 16-bit program written for Windows 3.1. It works quite well in Windows 95, however. Forté sells both 16-bit and 32-bit versions of Agent .99 that offer the same features. ■

Starting and Configuring Agent

When you start Free Agent (by double-clicking the Free Agent icon), the program first asks you to accept the licensing agreement, stating that you are qualified to run the Free Agent reader. If you are not eligible to run the Free Agent reader, you must purchase the Agent newsreader. After the licensing agreement, the Free Agent program prompts you for the configuration information shown in Figure 29.1.

FIG. 29.1
Setting up the initial configuration information for Free Agent.

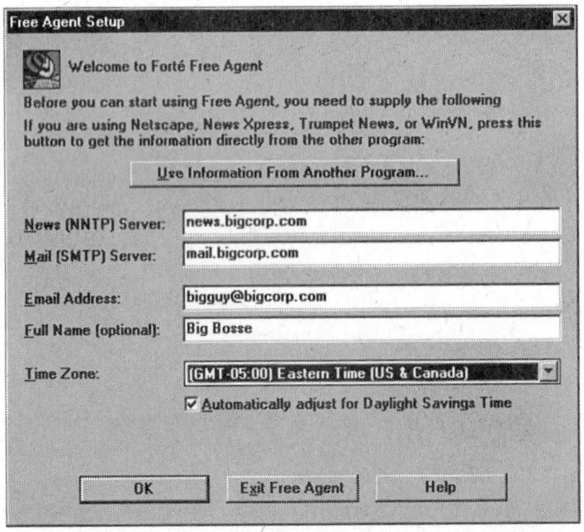

The Configuration page asks you to set up the NNTP server used to read news, the host that acts as your mail server, and your e-mail address and full name (to be used in your posts and outgoing mail). Free Agent also asks you to set the time zone you are in and whether your location observes daylight savings time.

N O T E Note that if you have already set up another newsreader on your system, you may be able to use the information for that reader to configure Free Agent. Click Use information from another program to tell Free Agent what newsreader you have already configured. Free Agent can get information from Netscape, News Xpress, Trumpet News, and WinVN.

In addition to the basic configuration information, Free Agent can import the list of newsgroups you have read from these other programs. ■

Once you have filled in the configuration information, click OK to continue. At this point, Free Agent goes online to your news server to retrieve a list of the newsgroups that are available. If you don't want Free Agent to do this now, click No to abort this step.

N O T E If your news server carries lots of groups or is heavily loaded, downloading the list of newsgroups can take awhile. A server that carries all possible UseNet groups can have well over 10,000 groups available. ■

While Free Agent is downloading the list of available groups, it keeps a running status report of the number of groups it has downloaded in the status bar at the bottom of the screen. Once Free Agent has finished downloading the list of available groups, it allows you to begin subscribing to and reading newsgroups.

If you are installing the Agent newsreader, the program asks for a license key to enable the news program when it first starts up. Enter the license key given to you by Forté. (If you have received the key via e-mail, you can copy it to your clipboard and press Ctrl+V to copy the license key from the clipboard.) Once you have entered your license key, click OK to continue.

After you enter the license key, you see the same configuration screen as in Figure 29.1— except that an additional option to select the spelling dictionary is added. Fill in the requested information as described previously.

Once you have entered the initial configuration information, enter the main program, where you have many additional configuration options. These options are set from the Options menu, which includes several different groups of options for you to set.

Setting Agent Preferences

The Preferences page allows you to set the parameters that Agent uses when retrieving articles, posting articles, and interacting with the user. The first page allows you to set up your User Profile information (see Fig. 29.2).

FIG. 29.2

Information about the user is set on the User Profile page.

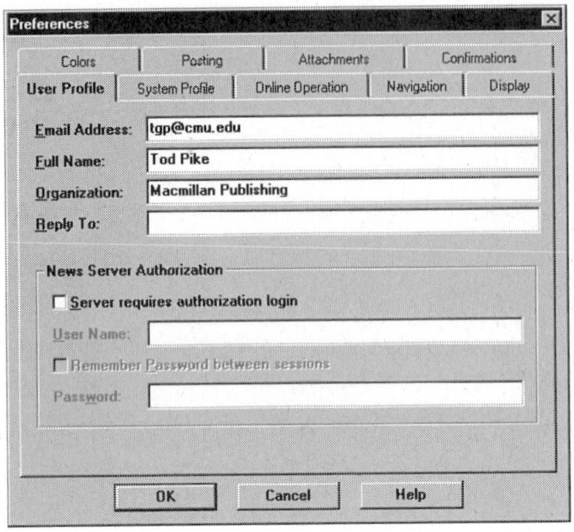

On this page you can set your E-mail Address, Full Name, Organization, and Reply To address (if it is different from your regular e-mail address). These fields are used when you post new articles to groups or reply to a post via e-mail. In addition, if your news server requires you to supply a username and password when you connect, this page allows you to enter this information.

The next Preferences page is the System Profile page, which includes exactly the same information you entered when you first started Agent. If you entered incorrect information at that time, re-enter your news server, e-mail server, and time-zone information here.

The third Preferences page is the Online Operation page that allows you to define how Agent interacts with the news server when it is connected to the server (see Fig. 29.3). The two kinds of operation are online and offline.

You can select the defaults for these modes of operation by clicking the Use Offline Defaults or Use Online Defaults buttons. These buttons set up the common defaults for the two modes of operation.

FIG. 29.3

Online and offline modes are set on this page.

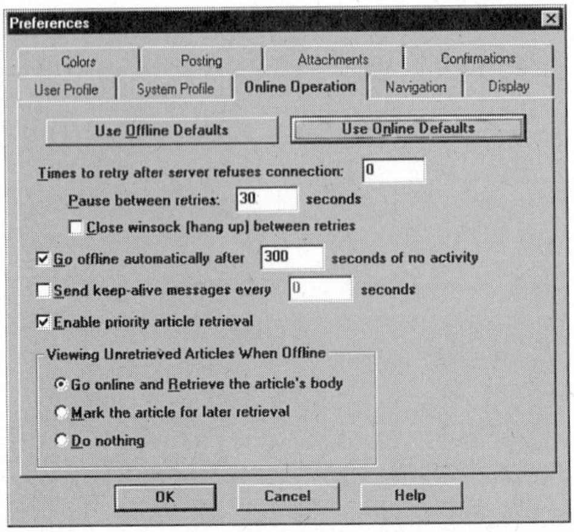

If you pay by the hour for your Internet connection, you should probably pick the offline mode of operation. In this mode, when you ask Agent to retrieve new articles in your subscribed groups, it opens a connection to your news server. Retrieve just the headers for the new articles in your selected groups and then go offline immediately.

This allows you to look through the headers of the articles and select the articles you are interested in reading. Once you have picked the articles, you then ask Agent to retrieve the articles from the server.

Agent again connects to your server, downloads the article bodies you want, and goes offline. You can then read the articles without being connected to your Internet provider (which can save you a significant amount of money).

On the other hand, if you don't pay by the hour for your Internet connection or you are directly connected to the Internet (at work or school, for example), you would probably pick the online mode of operation. In this mode, when you ask Agent to get the new articles in your subscribed groups, it connects to your server and gets the article headers. When you select an article to read, Agent immediately gets the article from your server and presents it to you.

The options that can be set on this page are as follows:

- <u>T</u>imes to Retry After Server Refuses Connection controls how many times Agent tries to connect to your news server if the first connection fails.

- <u>P</u>ause Between Retries controls how long Agent waits between connection attempts. The amount of time is specified in seconds.

- <u>C</u>lose Winsock (Hang Up) Between Retries controls whether Agent hangs up your Internet connection between attempts to contact your news server. You probably don't want to check this unless you set up a significant delay between connection attempts.

- <u>G</u>o Offline automatically allows you to let Agent close the connection to your news server after a period of inactivity. (Activity is defined as sending or retrieving something from the news server, not reading articles or headers on your local computer). The inactivity time is specified in seconds.

- <u>S</u>end Keep-Alive Messages controls whether (and how often) Agent sends a command to your news server to keep the connection active. This is used when dealing with Internet connections that automatically time out when no activity is detected for a period of time. Normally, unless your Internet service provider closes your connection after inactivity, you should not check this option as it needlessly increases your network traffic.

- <u>E</u>nable Priority Article Retrieval allows you to enable a feature of Agent with which you can request that an article be retrieved from the server while Agent is busy downloading other article headers or bodies. In this case, Agent opens a second connection to your news server to try to get the requested article for you immediately.

- The three options under Viewing Unretrieved Articles When Offline allow you to control what Agent does if you double-click an article that has not been retrieved when Agent is not connected to your news server. If you select Go Online and <u>R</u>etrieve Article's Body, Agent does exactly that. If you select <u>M</u>ark the Article for Later Retrieval, Agent does not go online but just marks that article for the next batch of retrievals. _Do nothing_, tells Agent to ignore double-clicks to an article when offline.

The next Preferences page is the Navigation page (see Fig. 29.4). This page allows you to enable or disable different options that control how Agent displays and navigates between articles. These options are self-explanatory, so the information on the page is not duplicated here.

FIG. 29.4

The Navigation page controls how Agent displays articles.

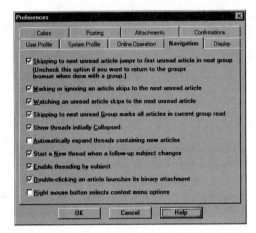

The Display page allows you to control how Agent displays articles (see Fig. 29.5). The first options here let you pick whether the Tool and Status bars are displayed in the main window. The articles settings let you control how many spaces are equivalent to a tab character and what characters are treated as quoting included material when they appear at the beginning of a line.

FIG. 29.5

Many article options are set on the Display page.

TIP It is a usual practice when quoting UseNet articles to put a quote character (typically a right angle bracket >) at the beginning of each line of quoted material. Agent displays these quoted lines in a different color from the regular lines of an article.

The browser's settings allow you to control how much each follow-up line is indented from the original article, the margins allowed when scrolling articles, and the maximum number of levels of follow-up articles that are displayed.

The Colors page allows you to set up the colors to be used when different items are displayed (see Fig. 29.6).

FIG. 29.6

Setting up the colors Agent will use.

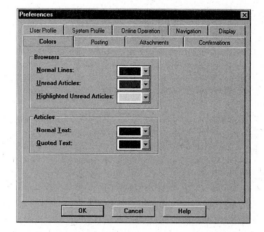

The Posting page sets up the different options used when posting new articles (see Fig. 29.7). The only really nonobvious options are the various "introduction" settings near the bottom of the page. These control what text will be used at the beginning of follow-up articles, e-mail replies, and forwarded e-mail messages. This introductory text helps people remember the article you are referring to.

In the Agent newsreader, there are additional options that allow you to specify introductory text when replying to e-mail since Agent can receive as well as send e-mail.

The Attachments page allows you to control how Agent handles binary file attachments when posting articles (see Fig. 29.8). The first options control whether attachments are sent in one large message or if the attachment is broken up into smaller chunks of a specified number of lines.

TIP Some news servers have a limit on the size of articles they accept. It is probably a good idea to limit the size of your articles to 900 lines or so.

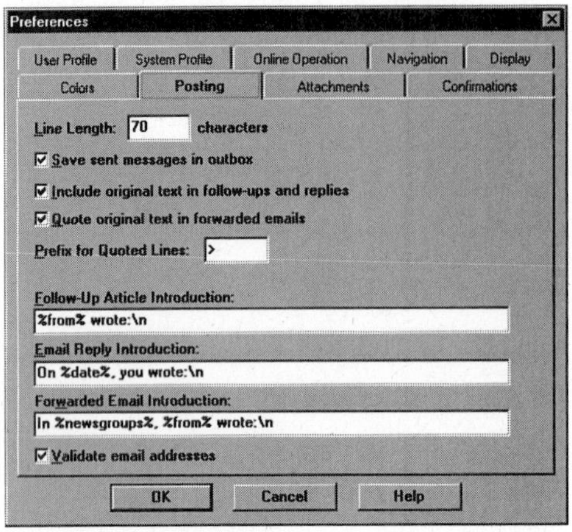

FIG. 29.7

The Posting page controls how Agent posts new articles.

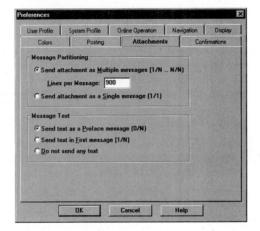

The second set of attachments options controls how the text of an article with an attachment is sent. These options are to send the article text as a separate message (before the attachment is posted), send the text in the same message as the attachment, or not to send text when sending an attachment.

The Confirmations page controls when Agent asks you to confirm an action (see Fig. 29.9). These are pretty much self-explanatory.

The Agent newsreader has an additional Preferences page (see Fig. 29.10). The Spelling page allows you to set up the options that control the built-in spelling checker in Agent (Free Agent does not have the spelling checker option).

Options to control the spelling checker include settings for the default language dictionary and whether the checker always suggests a new spelling when a mistake is discovered. The Agent spelling checker can also detect repeated words in an article.

FIG. 29.8

Setting up options that control attachments.

FIG. 29.9
Choosing when Agent asks for confirmation.

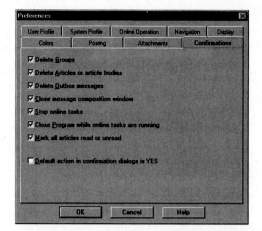

FIG. 29.10
The spelling checker is configured on the Spelling page.

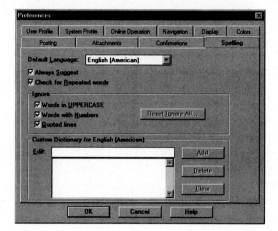

The Agent spelling checker can also be set to ignore words in all uppercase (which are often abbreviations), words in quotes, and words with numbers in them. These settings help to reduce the number of false spelling mistakes that are detected. Finally, you can include a custom dictionary that holds words you often use that are not in the regular dictionary.

Setting Up Signatures in Agent

One thing you will soon notice when reading UseNet news articles is that people often include standard text at the bottom of their articles. This text is called a *signature*, and it usually includes information about the person posting the article (the e-mail address, for example) and sometimes a witty or amusing statement. These signatures should be brief (four lines is customary).

Agent allows you to use the Signatures page found on the Options menu to define signatures that you can add to your postings. The Signatures page, shown in Figure 29.11, lets you set up any number of possible signatures and allows you to specify one of them as the default signature.

When you post an article, you are prompted for the signature to use. You might have one signature for posting to a serious, work-related group and another for a more light-hearted group that you read for fun.

FIG. 29.11

Agent lets you use multiple signatures. Thus, you can use a signature that's appropriate for the newsgroup to which you're posting a message.

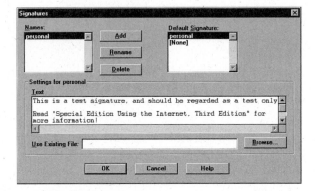

Signature files are controlled from the Signatures page. To add a new signature, click the Add button and type in a name for the new signature ("personal" in the example). Then type in the text for the signature in the Text box.

If you have the text of your signature stored in a file, fill in the file name in the "Use Existing File" box. Click OK to add the signature to the list of available signatures. You can also select one of your signatures to be the default signature. If you have a default signature, it is used automatically whenever you post.

Setting Up Inbound E-mail

The Agent newsreader (as opposed to the Free Agent version) can receive e-mail as well as send it. You can configure the Agent newsreader to receive e-mail by using the Inbound Email menu found under the Options menu.

When you first bring up the Inbound Email menu, Agent asks you to define the folder to be used to receive incoming e-mail messages. Setting up the incoming e-mail folder is done on the New Folder screen (see Fig. 29.12). The default name for this incoming folder is Inbox. Type the name you want to use for the incoming folder into the Folder Name box and click OK to create the folder.

Note that the incoming mail folder shows up in your list of subscribed newsgroups.

Once the incoming mail folder is created, you can configure your e-mail options. The System Profile page, shown in Figure 29.13, allows you to configure how you receive mail. Agent has two methods of receiving mail messages, POP and SMTP.

FIG. 29.12

You must create the incoming e-mail folder before you can receive mail.

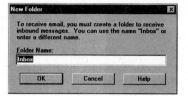

With the POP (Post Office Protocol) method, Agent periodically connects to your POP mail server and retrieves any waiting messages. With the SMTP method, Agent starts an SMTP server on your machine, which can receive incoming mail messages at any time.

FIG. 29.13

Your e-mail options are set on this page.

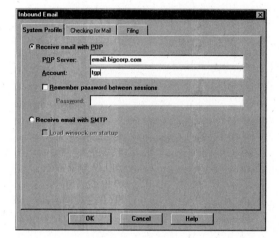

 T I P If you are paying by the hour for your Internet connect time, you should probably use the POP method to receive mail. Agent has your Internet connection open only long enough to receive your e-mail and then closes it, saving you connect time.

If you are using POP, Agent gives you the option to type in your POP account password (along with the POP server and account name information) and to remember the POP password so you don't have to type it in each time. If you are using SMTP, Agent allows you to specify whether your Winsock library is loaded when Agent starts up.

The Checking for Mail page, shown in Figure 29.14, allows you to specify how often Agent checks for mail on your POP server (there are no options for this if you use SMTP, as the SMTP server is always waiting for incoming mail). In addition, you can control whether your mail is deleted from the POP server when you read it and whether large messages should be automatically retrieved.

In addition, you can set up options to display a message and/or play a sound when new mail arrives. You can specify a particular .WAV file for the sound played.

FIG. 29.14
Setting up your mail
retrieval options.

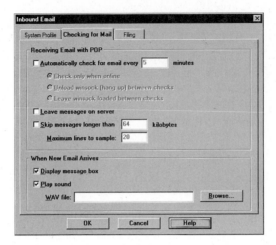

One advanced e-mail feature in Agent is set up with the Filing page. This page allows you to set up mail filters to automatically file a message into a folder if it meets certain criteria. For example, you could set up a filter to refile all messages from "Fred Rogers" into a folder called "neighbors." Mail filters are an advanced (and very powerful) option.

Setting Up Your Fonts

The Fonts pages, found under the Options menu, allow you to set up the fonts used to display groups, folders, and messages (the Browser font). Also, fonts used in message subjects, and fixed and variable text in message bodies, can also be set.

Setting Up Your Window Layout

One of the nicest features of the Agent newsreaders is the ability to change the window layout to suit your needs. By default, the layout has two small windows on the top half of the main display and a large window on the bottom half. The top left window displays the groups available, the top right window shows the articles available, and the bottom window displays messages in the group.

While this layout is OK for many readers, some will want to change it. For example, I prefer to have a narrower (but longer) window for the message text since many articles are long but not wide. Agent allows you to configure your window layout by selecting the Window Layout page from the Options menu. This brings up the configuration page shown in Figure 29.15.

The Window Layout page allows you to configure the layout of the different display windows as well as the contents of those windows. The Layout of Panes option lets you pick the different styles for the three panes. For example, you can have the large window on the left of the screen and the two smaller windows on the right.

FIG. 29.15
Configuring the way
Agent displays your
windows.

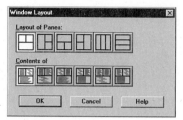

In addition, the Contents of option lets you decide what is displayed in each pane. For this option, the box with the red text in it represents the pane that displays the list of available messages. The box with the black text is for the pane that displays the list of available newsgroups.

The box with the blue text represents the pane where the body of the article or message is displayed. By selecting one of these layouts, you can put the information you want where you want it.

Also, once you have picked a general window layout, you can change the size of each of the panes by dragging one of the borders between the panes to the desired size. Using these controls, you can make the screen look exactly the way you want it.

Once you have decided on a window layout, you can save this configuration as the default by selecting the Save as Default Window Layout item on the Options menu.

Setting Group Options

In addition to the preferences that control Agent's behavior in general, there are options that you can set for each UseNet group. These options control

- When to mark messages as read.
- What messages are eligible to be removed from the local disk.
- When to remove articles from the local disk.
- When to retrieve articles from the news server.
- What fields to include when posting articles.
- Where to store binary attachments to postings when they are extracted.

You can set these options for all groups and also override these settings for individual groups. These options are set through the Default properties and Properties pages found under the Group menu.

Subscribing to and Unsubscribing from Newsgroups

When you first started Agent, the program retrieved a list of the available newsgroups from your news server. This list of all available groups can be displayed by selecting the Show option and All groups and folders suboption found under the Group menu.

To get the list of available newsgroups from the server at any time, select <u>R</u>efresh group list from the <u>O</u>nline menu. To update your list of groups by getting just the newsgroups that have been recently created, select Get new <u>G</u>roups from the <u>O</u>nline menu. You can then display just these newly created groups by selecting the S<u>h</u>ow option and <u>N</u>ew groups found under the <u>G</u>roup menu.

To subscribe to a newsgroup, select the group name and click the Subscribe button (or press Ctrl+S). This marks the group as subscribed. You can display just the groups you subscribe to by selecting the S<u>h</u>ow option and <u>S</u>ubscribed groups and folders found under the <u>G</u>roup menu.

You can unsubscribe from a group by selecting the group name from the list of groups and clicking the Unsubscribe button (or Crtl+S).

 Because some news servers carry thousands of groups, you can use the Find and Find Next buttons to search for a group name that contains a text string.

If you aren't sure what a group is about, you can sample some articles from the group before you subscribe to it. Double-click the group name in the list of available groups and Agent asks you what you want to do: whether to sample a few article headers from the group (50 article headers is the default), get all article headers for the group, or subscribe to the group. Before you subscribe, you might want to get the sample headers and see what topics are being discussed.

To unsubscribe from a newsgroup, click the group name in the list of groups and click the Unsubscribe button on the tool bar (or Ctrl+S). The group will be removed from the list of subscribed groups.

Reading Articles in Newsgroups

Once you have selected the groups that you are interested in, you can begin the actual process of receiving news articles from these groups. There are several ways to retrieve the article headers for your subscribed groups:

- Click the Get Headers in Subscribed Groups button or select Get <u>N</u>ew Headers in Subscribed Groups under the <u>O</u>nline menu. This retrieves all the headers in all of your subscribed groups.

- Select a group (or multiple groups) and click the Get Headers in Selected Group button, or select Get New <u>H</u>eaders in Selected Groups under the <u>O</u>nline menu. This retrieves all the new headers in only the group you selected.

- Select a group (or multiple groups) and select Get <u>A</u>ll Headers in Selected Groups under the <u>O</u>nline menu. This retrieves all headers (even including articles that you have already read or purged from your local disk) for the selected groups.

- Select a group (or multiple groups) and select <u>S</u>ample 50 Headers from Selected Groups from the <u>O</u>nline menu. This retrieves the article headers from the 50 most recently posted articles in the selected groups.

No matter how you retrieve the article headers, you are presented with the screen shown in Figure 29.16. If you are working in offline mode (that is, you have configured Agent to read the article headers only and wait for you to select which articles you want to read), you are presented with the headers for the articles.

The first article in the newsgroup has not been retrieved yet, so Agent tells you that you can press enter to retrieve the article now or type **M** to mark the article for later retrieval.

FIG. 29.16

Selecting articles for retrieval.

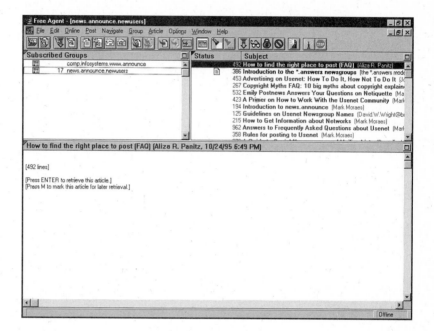

When you mark an article for retrieval, the download icon is shown next to the article (see Fig. 29.17). Also, when an article has been retrieved from the server, there is a text page icon next to the article.

To actually retrieve the article bodies, select Get Marked Article Bodies from the Online menu. You can also select articles with the mouse and select Get Selected Article Bodies from the Online menu without having to go through the steps of marking the articles individually.

Once you have retrieved the articles that are interesting to you, you can begin reading the articles. There are several ways of moving between articles:

- Double-clicking the article header displays that article's body.
- Selecting an article and pressing Enter displays that article.
- Clicking the Next Article button moves to the next retrieved article in the group.
- Using the arrow keys on your keyboard moves between articles and displays them.
- Typing **N** moves to the next article in the group and displays it.

FIG. 29.17

Articles marked for retrieval or already retrieved are marked with special icons.

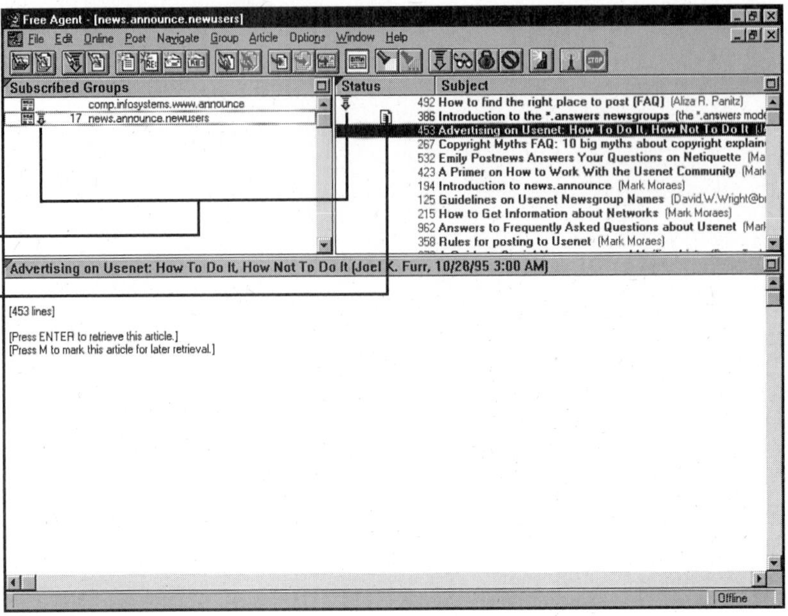

Article marked for retrieval

Article already retrieved

There are also several features that deal with all the articles in the group you are currently reading:

- Click the Skip to Next Unread Group button or select Skip to Next Unread Group from the Navigate menu to mark all the articles in this group as read and move to the next group that contains unread articles. You can also type **S** to do this.

- Mark the current article as read (or unread) or all the articles in the current group as read (or unread) by using the appropriate items under the Article menu.

- Delete the current article or just the article body by selecting the Delete article or Delete article body items under the Article menu.

In Agent and Free Agent there are usually several ways to do common tasks. You can click one of the toolbar buttons, use one of the regular menu commands, or type a keyboard shortcut if you prefer to use the keyboard.

Following Article Threads

When you read a newsgroup that has many different people posting articles about a common subject, using a newsreader that allows you to automatically follow these article *threads* (articles that share a common subject) can make it much easier to read the group. Following article threads allows you to ignore conversations that do not interest you and to keep track of who has said what in a thread.

When you retrieve the article headers for a group, Agent displays the headers in the group window. As shown in Figure 29.18, Agent displays the articles that are responses to an article by indenting these headers below the original article.

FIG. 29.18

The article headers, showing an article thread.

Open/closed icon——

Original article header——

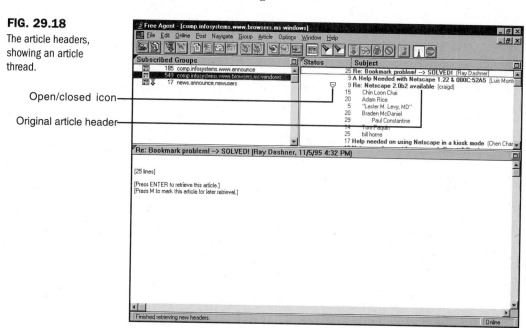

You also see an open/closed indicator to the left of the header for the original article, showing that the thread is displayed either expanded or collapsed. When the thread is displayed expanded, all the articles in the thread are shown.

On the other hand, if you display the thread collapsed, only the first header in the thread is displayed, with an indication of how many articles are in the thread. Switching between expanded and collapsed mode is done by clicking the open/closed icon.

Displaying article threads in collapsed mode allows you to see more article headers in a group. This is especially important in groups where there are only a few threads active at a time; you can easily ignore threads or read the threads you are interested in.

Several Agent commands are used specifically to read articles in threads. These commands are:

- Click View next article in thread or Skip to next article in thread moves to the next article in the thread. If you are at the end of the thread, it moves to the next article in the group.

- Use the analogous commands under the Navigate menu to move to the next article in the thread.

■ Ctrl+T views the next article in the thread.

■ The T command skips to the next article in the thread.

Agent also has several commands to either ignore or automatically retrieve an article thread. You can use the Ignore Thread button to prevent Agent from retrieving or displaying any articles in the current thread.

On a busy newsgroup, this command can significantly reduce the amount of time you spend reading the group. You can also use the Ignore thread item under the Article menu or the I command.

In addition, you can use the Watch Thread button to direct Agent to always retrieve articles in the thread. The Watch Thread item under the Article menu also does this; or you can use the W command from the keyboard.

Posting Articles

Agent allows you to post new articles to newsgroups and to post follow-up articles to articles that you read. You can post a new article to a group by clicking the Post New Article button, selecting New Article from the Post menu, or using the **P** keyboard command. Posting a new article brings up the dialog shown in Figure 29.19.

FIG. 29.19

Posting a new article.

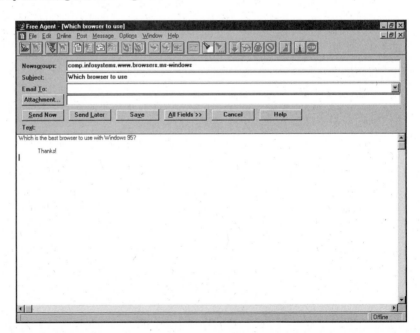

When you post a new article, you should fill in the subject and the text of the article, as well as an optional list of e-mail addresses you want to send copies of the article to.

When you have filled in the fields, select the options to send the article. You can send the article immediately by using the Send Now button, send it later, or save the article into a file.

If you choose to send the article later, you can use the Post Articles and Emails item from the Online menu to actually send the article. This is useful if you want to save up several posts or e-mail messages and send them all at once.

To post a follow-up article to the article you are reading, click the Post follow-up article button, select the Follow Up Article item from the Post menu, or use the **F** keyboard command (type the letter **F**).

Posting a follow-up article fills in the subject of the article for you and inserts a copy of the article you were reading. The inserted article is quoted and inserted at the beginning of each line.

 When you are quoting an article, cut out any unnecessary text from the quoted article, leaving only the text necessary to provide context to your reply.

Extracting Files from Articles

Some articles posted to UseNet groups actually contain binary information that is encoded to allow it to pass through the UseNet news systems. This information is usually encoded either in UNIX UUEncode form or according to the MIME Internet standard. Agent allows you to automatically decode these binary files.

To decode the information in encoded articles, select the article (or multiple articles if the binary attachment is split across articles) and select one of the following options:

- Click the Launch Binary Attachment button (or select Launch Binary Attachments from the File menu). This decodes the attachment in the articles and automatically starts the viewer for the attachment. Agent uses the Windows 95 file associations to determine which viewer to launch to display the attachment.

- Select Save Binary Attachment from the File menu to decode the attachment from the articles and save it into a file on your disk.

- Select Delete Binary Attachment from the File menu to delete the attachment from the articles on your disk.

When you attempt to decode a multipart binary attachment, Agent searches the subject lines of the articles to put the articles in the correct order to decode them properly. If an article in the sequence is missing, the article does not decode properly.

Managing E-mail

As with most newsreaders, Agent and Free Agent can send e-mail messages, both in response to an article or as a new message. In addition, the Agent newsreader can receive e-mail messages and has facilities to manage these messages.

When you set up the e-mail facilities in Agent (as described in the configuration preceding section), you specified the default folder for receiving new mail. This folder was created and appears in your list of subscribed groups. You can also view your mail folders by selecting Show, Folders under the Group menu.

Sending New E-mail Messages

You can send a new e-mail message by clicking the Post New EMail Message button (or by selecting New Email Message from the Post menu). This brings up the window shown in Figure 29.20. On this screen, fill in the e-mail addresses to send the message to, the subject of the message, and the text body of the message.

FIG. 29.20

Sending a new e-mail message with the Agent newsreader.

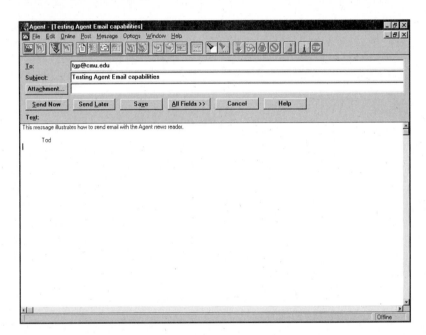

You have the option to attach a file to the message (by clicking the Attachment button) and to send the message now, later, or to save the message in a file on your disk.

To reply to an existing e-mail message, click the Post Reply via Email button (or select Reply via Email from the Post menu). This brings up the window to send the e-mail message, but presets the subject of the message and includes the text of the message you are replying to.

You also have the option to forward an e-mail message to other people: select Forward via Email from the Post menu. This is similar to the Reply via Email option, as it includes the text of the e-mail you are forwarding, but the introductory text at the top of the message is slightly different.

Reading E-mail Messages

The Agent newsreader can receive new e-mail messages (the Free Agent newsreader does not have this feature). While you might not want to use Agent as your primary e-mail reader, it is quite serviceable as a home mail reader (or if you do not receive much e-mail).

Depending on how you configured your e-mail options, you receive e-mail into your Inbox folder at different times when Agent is running. If you configured your Agent reader to use the SMTP mode for receiving e-mail, Agent can receive new e-mail messages any time the reader is in Online mode. If you are using the POP method of receiving e-mail, Agent checks for new e-mail on your POP server periodically.

In either case, when you have received new e-mail, Agent pops up a dialog box letting you know that new e-mail has arrived (see Fig. 29.21). You can configure Agent to display this box, play a sound, or both when new mail shows up. Close the box by clicking OK.

FIG. 29.21

You are notified that new e-mail has arrived with this alert box.

You can read your e-mail messages by clicking the Inbox folder, which displays the mail-reading screen shown in Figure 29.22. This screen is similar to the display used for reading news articles and has the same window layout as the news display.

FIG. 29.22

Reading e-mail messages with Agent.

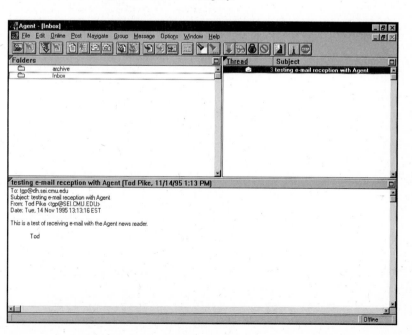

Selecting an e-mail message and typing Enter (or double-clicking the message) displays the e-mail message. Buttons are available, as when you are reading news articles, for skipping to the next message and skipping to the next message in a thread. The same options for collapsing and expanding threads of e-mail messages also exist when you read e-mail, giving you a lot of flexibility in dealing with your e-mail.

Agent also gives you the ability to copy or move your e-mail messages between folders. You can create a new folder by selecting New folder from the Group menu. (You can rename a folder by selecting the folder and selecting Rename folder from the Group menu.) To move a message to a folder, select the message header in the header window and drag the message header to the folder you want the message in.

TIP By default, Agent moves the message to the folder when you drag the message. You can copy the message to a folder by holding down the Ctrl key on your keyboard while dragging the message.

You can also copy or move messages between folders by selecting either Copy to folder or Move to folder from the Message menu. These menu selections bring up a list of available folders: select a folder and click OK to move (or copy) the message.

For people who receive a lot of e-mail or for those who want to automatically organize their mail, Agent offers e-mail filters. These filters allow you to select incoming mail messages according to information in the mail headers (the subject of the message, for example) and automatically file the message into a folder.

For example, if you subscribe to an Internet mailing list on horses, you might file all messages coming from this mailing list into a folder called "horses." This allows you to separate incoming mail into different interests and lets you read important messages faster.

Agent's e-mail filters are maintained through the Filing tab on the Inbound Email options menu shown in Figure 29.23.

FIG. 29.23
Configuring e-mail filters.

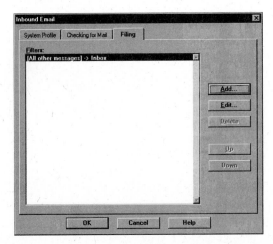

You can add a new filter by clicking the Add button, which brings up the screen shown in Figure 29.24. This screen lets you select the field you are using to control the filter (the From field in this example), the text to search for (horse-list in our example), and the folder to file the message in.

FIG. 29.24

Adding a new e-mail filter.

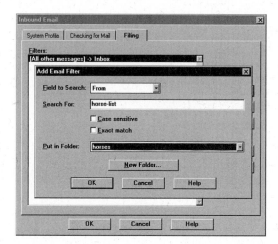

Once you have added a filter, it works automatically until you remove it. You can edit the filter at any time by selecting the filter and clicking the Edit button on the Filing menu.

Since filters are executed from the top of the list down, be careful how your filters are organized. You might, for example, have a filter to file all messages from John Smith into a folder called "smith." You may have a filter to file all messages with a subject of eating into a folder called food. If John Smith sends a message with a subject of eating, it might be filed into either the "smith" or the "food" folder, depending on which is higher on the list. You can change the order of filter execution by clicking the Up or Down buttons.

Locating and Retrieving Information

CHAPTER 30

Using Telnet and Popular Telnet Programs

by Jerry Honeycutt and Tod Pike

Now you've got your connection to the Internet up and running. In Chapter 10, "How Internet E-mail Works," you learned about e-mail and you may have already used the Net to send messages quickly and simply anywhere in the world. I hope you also have had a chance to peek around in a couple of newsgroups on UseNet. By now, you should be getting a feel for the amount of power and potential that's available on the Internet.

Now it's time to broaden your horizons. I hope you've got your bags packed, because we're taking this show on the road! ■

Learn what Telnet is

Telnet turns your $3,000 PC into a dumb terminal. It's pretty cool, though.

Use Telnet to connect to remote computers

This chapter shows you how to connect to thousands of computers all over the world.

Use Telnet with a shell account

This chapter also shows you how to connect to other computers using your Internet shell account.

Learn how to use Windows-based Telnet programs

Windows 95 and Windows NT both come with a basic Telnet client program. Other client programs are available for Windows 3.1.

What Is Telnet?

Telnet is a program that lets you log into a remote computer directly through the Internet. Telnet takes advantage of the way computers are linked on the Net by routing your commands from your computer to the host computer. If you have a direct network connection to the Internet, using Telnet can save you the cost of long-distance bills and also won't tie up phone lines. Even if you have to use a dial-up SLIP or PPP connection to the Internet, telnetting still saves you the long-distance phone call, if your SLIP/PPP number is a local call.

Technically, Telnet is a *protocol*. A protocol is a set of instructions that is used by computers to explain how they'll share information. The proper noun, *Telnet*, is usually meant to describe an application that uses the Telnet protocol. The gerund, *telnetting*, describes using an application that uses the protocol, to connect to a remote computer system, as in, "I telnetted to the MUD."

Protocols work something like this: Let's say you agree to buy a book from a friend in France for 10,000. The value 10,000, while a definite number, means different things depending on whether we're talking about Francs, Dollars, Marks, Pounds, or Lire. When you and your friend agree to negotiate a price in a specific type of currency, you suddenly have a frame of reference from which you can determine value. When two computers agree that they'll share information using a specific protocol, the packages of information that they share with each other suddenly make sense.

You may have heard of protocols if you've ever uploaded or downloaded a file. When uploading or downloading a file, the computer you are connected to will usually give you a list of options for transferring the file that includes names like Xmodem, Zmodem, or Kermit. Xmodem, Zmodem, and Kermit are also protocols—they're sets of standards that tell the receiving computer how the sending computer will be packaging the information that it's sending.

The Telnet protocol does the same sort of thing as an upload or download protocol, only it's telling the remote computer how to transfer commands from the local computer, on which you're working, to another computer in a remote location. This makes it possible for a user in New York to work on a computer in San Francisco (or Berlin, or Alice Springs, or wherever).

▶ **See** "Connecting to Host Resources Using Telnet," **p. 29**
▶ **See** "An Introduction to TCP/IP," **p. 108**

Why Use Telnet?

Let's say you're on a business trip and you'd like to be able to get in touch with your Internet account to pick up your e-mail and read up on the latest UseNet news. Or perhaps you were just talking to friends who said they have programs set up on their computers that perform the type of analysis that your company needs.

In either case, you could use a modem to dial into the remote system and do what you need to do. Depending on where you're located, where the other computer is located, and how long you need to be connected, that could tie up a lot of long-distance time.

Fortunately, you can take advantage of the unique linking of computers through the Internet, which enables you to connect to a remote computer much easier and cheaper than dialing direct. And it's surprisingly easy to use, considering it's a tool that can interact with so many different types of machines to do so many things.

The Telnet protocol is usually contained within a small piece of software that is used while accessing the Internet. Because the Telnet protocol is a standard that is used almost universally throughout the Internet, the mechanics of running Telnet are pretty much the same practically everywhere, regardless of how it's packaged.

Some Quick Background Information

Many people aren't familiar with some of the terminology related to the big computers that comprise quite a bit of the Internet. Some knowledge about how these computers work can help you understand how the Telnet program works and can help explain some of the choices that various Telnet programs offer you.

What's a VT100? Or an ANSI? Or a TTY?

Once upon a time, most of the automated computing in the world was done on big machines—each of which had a huge central processing unit that was often big enough to fill up a whole room. These machines could be used by lots of people, but they couldn't always fit in the same room as the computer (and you probably wouldn't want them all there, anyway).

Users accessed these machines through individual workstations called *terminals*. Terminals are basically keyboards and screens used for entering data. Unlike a PC, a terminal has no processor of its own. It has to be connected to a main computer in order to work.

Manufacturers made terminals fairly standard so they could be used in connection with a variety of computer types. Digital Equipment Corporation (otherwise known as Digital or DEC) manufactured a line of terminals that were fairly common for use with larger computers called the VT series. The VT100 and the VT102 (a slight variation) were probably the most common types of terminal, though you may have also heard of other variations, such as the VT52 or the VT220. (Generally, the higher the number a VT series terminal had, the more sophisticated it was.)

When "regular folks" (not just government scientists or computer science majors) first started using the Internet, most of the big computers on the Net were set up to send and receive information through terminals like the then common VT100. If you wanted to contact one of the big computers through your PC, you needed a program that would "dumb-down" your PC, making it act like a terminal and enabling you to enter and retrieve data from the big machines. Programs like the HyperTerminal program included with Windows 95 are intended to make a PC look like or *emulate* these earlier terminals. For example, HyperTerminal can auto-detect and emulate the VT52 and VT100 terminals, in addition to TTY and ANSI. However, HyperTerminal isn't designed to connect via the Internet; its primary purpose is to connect to systems via an asynchronous serial connection, using a modem, or null-modem cable. Windows 95 comes with a basic Telnet program for use with a WinSock Internet connection. We'll take a close look at it later in the chapter.

Remember, while a PC is hooked up to a remote computer, it acts much like those earlier terminals. The PC is basically being used to display information while the computing actually takes place at a remote machine.

 TIP If you have a choice, choose VT100 or TTY (unless the folks at the computer to which you're trying to connect have specifically told you to use another type of terminal). VT100 is probably the most common terminal type, and TTY is probably the most basic.

Simply put, ANSI and TTY are other standards for entering data and displaying information. Computers that support ANSI terminals can usually display some text in color. TTY is an extremely plain *teletype* style terminal, which probably depends entirely on the remote computer for how the information is displayed on-screen. (A teletype is one of those machines you'd see in newsrooms in old movies that is basically an automated typewriter that types out input from an external source; a TTY terminal is simply an electronic version of the classic news teletype.)

What to Expect When You Connect

If you're used to using a command-line account, you're probably already accustomed to dealing with the Internet through a text-based environment. Telnet doesn't provide a lot of flash; after all, a program has to keep things somewhat simple in order to allow any two random computers to work with each other, despite obvious differences in hardware and software. Telnet will only provide you with command-line access to remote machines.

You may want to go back and read some of the earlier information on interacting with the Internet through a command-line account. Regardless of the service that you access through Telnet (be it an individual account, an automatic BBS on a remote machine, an interactive role-playing game, or a weather server), you will need to follow the same general procedures that are used for accessing a command-line account.

If you're completely unfamiliar with executing commands through a command-line prompt (and are not particularly willing to give it a try), consider using a World Wide Web browser (such as Microsoft Internet Explorer, Mosaic, or Netscape) instead. World Wide Web browsers don't provide you with the same ability to send direct commands to the remote computer that Telnet does, but a browser provides the graphical interface to which you've become accustomed. Even though browsers do connect to a "remote host" (the Web server), it's not designed for direct command-line user input the way a Telnet host is.

▶ **See** "Important WWW Concepts," **p. 366**
▶ **See** "Getting Ready to Use Internet Explorer," **p. 380**
▶ **See** "Getting Netscape Up and Running," **p. 400**

A Brief Word About Addresses

In order to run Telnet, you need to know the address of the computer that you want to reach. The important information is the *host name* of the computer. Telnet uses this host name to contact the remote computer, much like you use telephone numbers to call your friends.

Some corporate network systems may require you to use a *proxy* server to telnet through the local area network security firewall (a *firewall* is the network component that keeps intruders outside your network from getting in). A proxy Telnet server lets you telnet to it, and then it handles the actual transaction to the outside Internet. See your system administrator for specific information if you need to know more about your system's security procedures.

Figuring Out a Host Name from an E-mail Address   In Chapter 10, "How Internet E-mail Works," you learned about addresses for e-mail on the Internet. An e-mail address might look something like the following:

```
bk@access.digex.net
```

bk is the user you want to contact, who is located at access.digex.net.

The phrase access.digex.net points to a specific computer, and is called a *host name*. In order to use Telnet, you must know the host name of the computer that you want to telnet to. If someone wants you to be able to telnet to their system, they'll give you their computer's address in the form of a host name.

> **NOTE** You will come across host names for specific computers in a lot of places as you're surfing the Net. If you use a Gopher server (described later in Chapter 32, "Using Gopher and Popular Gopher Programs") to connect to remote locations, the Gopher will often give you a message stating the name of the host that it's trying to reach. You may want to write this address down, so that you can telnet directly to that site instead of having to cut through the Gopher to get there. ■

If, for some reason, you need to guess what a particular computer's host name is, you can often get it by looking at the e-mail address of someone who works on that system. From the previous example, you could guess that access.digex.net is the remote computer's host name.

But it's not always that simple to determine the e-mail address. If Mary Beth works on her computer at Loyola College, her e-mail address might appear to me as Mary_Beth@grey.loyola.edu. It might also appear as Mary_Beth@green.loyola.edu. But if you tried to telnet either green.loyola.edu or grey.loyola.edu, you would probably get an unknown host error message from your computer.

So what does that mean?

Most likely, the distinction between the green node and the grey node is local. This is important at Loyola, where they've got to direct the mail and generally handle a bunch of users. The Internet doesn't have to worry about such a fine distinction—it just needs to connect to loyola.edu and the local computers handle it from there.

So if you need to guess a node name from an address and the full address doesn't work, try lopping off the first word to the right of the @ symbol, and try again. (In other words, mary_beth@grey.loyola.edu would yield a host name of loyola.edu.) If that doesn't work, call or e-mail the other person and ask her to give you the Telnet address.

Names and Numbers that Mean the Same Thing   In addition to its host name, each computer has a numerical name that means the same thing as its host name. Let's use a fictitious example, say a computer whose host name is hal.jupiter.net with a numerical address of 11.16.19.94 (you'll recognize this set of numbers as an IP address).

When you're using Telnet and you have to enter a computer's address, you can either use its host name (hal.jupiter.net) or its numerical address (11.16.19.94). Sometimes, however, it's helpful to know the number address, even though it may not be quite as easy to remember as its host name.

TIP Some people think words are easier to remember than numbers (but they're sometimes harder to spell). The Net identifies computers by numbers, so try the numerical address if the host name doesn't work.

Think of it this way: If your name is Mary Elizabeth Jones, you may be called Mary, Mary Beth, Mary Elizabeth, MEJ, or any other combination of things. Regardless of your name style, your social security number remains constant.

Likewise, computer operators sometimes change the names of the machines they operate. If a business adds computers or a school reconfigures its system, the system operators may alter names. Generally, the computer retains its numerical name, even though the host name has changed. Knowing the numerical name therefore makes it easier to find the computer that you're trying to reach.

N O T E Sometimes you can reach a computer through its numerical address when you can't reach it through its host name. There are Name Server computers throughout the Internet that turn the host names into their numerical equivalents. Occasionally a Name Server crashes and it becomes difficult—if not impossible—to telnet another computer by using its host name. If, however, you know the numerical address, you don't need the service that the Name Server provides; instead, you can dial direct. ■

Running the Telnet Program from a Command-Line Account

Let's use another fictitious example. Say you're in California and you would like to reach your account at your local service provider in Washington, D.C., at hal.jupiter.net. For now, let's assume that you're borrowing a few minutes on a friend's command-line account in California to access your computer in Washington. Regardless of whether you're using a command-line account or a TCP/IP connection, the basics of telnetting a remote site are roughly the same.

N O T E Experienced users often refer to connecting to a remote computer as telnetting. For example, "I telnetted to my account back at my college to pick up my e-mail." ▪

Part
VI
Ch
30

Connecting to a Remote Computer Using Telnet

If you're connecting to the Internet through a command-line account, you're basically dialing into another computer that holds all of the programs you need in order to access the Internet. One of these programs is Telnet.

Let's say you want to run the Telnet program and connect to your account at hal.jupiter.net. To do this, use the following steps:

1. Log in to the local account.
2. After you've logged in and gotten the command-line prompt, type **telnet hal.jupiter.net.** (Please remember this is only an example address, this system really doesn't exist!)

   The next steps are the same as if you were dialing directly into the service provider that gives you your command-line account.
3. Once Telnet has connected to the remote computer, the Username: prompt appears.
4. Enter your username.
5. After you have entered your username, the remote computer sends a prompt for your password.
6. Type your password.
7. You should now be logged in to your remote account.

Once you type the password, you're logged into your account, and you can use it whether you're at a terminal plugged into the machine itself or logged on through a friend's account on the other side of the country. Telnet disappears, settling into the background where it handles processing your commands to the remote computer. Telnet will automatically close when you log out of the remote account.

TROUBLESHOOTING

When I try to use Telnet, I get a `Trying...` message, but nothing else happens.
What's wrong? If the remote computer that you're trying to call is extremely busy or is down for some reason, Telnet still tries to put you through. The `Trying...` message stays on-screen, but you won't get connected. In this case, you should probably break out of the connection by pressing Ctrl+], which interrupts Telnet and gives you the following prompt:

```
telnet>
```

continues

continued

At this prompt, you can either type a new address that you want to telnet, or you can type **quit** or **q** to go back to your original connection.

If you have tried to telnet a non-existent system (or if you just used the wrong name), Telnet responds with a message that says unknown host. If you get this message, double-check the name of the system that you're trying to reach, and then try again.

N O T E Telnet is almost completely transparent. That means that once it's running, it disappears and you don't even know that it's there.

It's important to remember that when you log onto another computer through Telnet, you're connecting through several other computers. Sometimes, if there's a lot of activity on the Net, the connection may seem sluggish, or it may take a while for the remote computer to respond to your commands.

For those accustomed to using Windows, it may seem like their system has locked up. This phenomenon is generally referred to as *netlag*. It can sometimes be annoying, but it doesn't necessarily mean that there's something wrong with your system.

A Second Way of Starting Telnet from a Command-Line Account

Many of the Internet access providers are actually providing what's called a shell account on a computer that is running the UNIX operating system. If you are telnetting from a computer that's running UNIX, there are several commands you can use to increase the utility of the very simple Telnet program.

Generally, you start Telnet by entering **Telnet** and then the address of a particular computer. In the earlier fictitious example, telnet hal.jupiter.net was entered. This line turns on Telnet and tells it where to connect. Telnet takes it from there.

There is a second way of starting Telnet from a UNIX-based system.

1. At the command prompt, type **telnet**. This prompts the following command line from the Telnet program:

   ```
   telnet>
   ```

2. At the Telnet prompt, type **open** *Hostname*, where *Hostname* is the address of a specific computer. For example, if I wanted to connect to hal.jupiter.net, I would type **open hal.jupiter.net** (some systems may use "connect" instead of "open").

3. When prompted, give your username and password. You should now be connected to the remote computer.

This second method is equivalent to typing telnet hostname, and, frankly, I think it's easier to just type the whole thing as one command. Nevertheless, it's helpful to know about the Telnet prompt because there are a few more commands that can be useful, particularly if you're trying to do a bunch of things at the same time.

Using UNIX to Do Two (or More) Things at Once

Say that you and your friend Juan are working together on a project, and he has written you a note asking you to take some information you've gathered and run it through a program on his account. Telnet makes this easy by letting you directly log on to his account.

Since you know Juan's e-mail address is juanm@hal.jupiter.net, you can guess that the address of the computer to which you're trying to connect is the part of the address to the right of the @, or hal.jupiter.net.

 TIP Remember, for purposes of telnetting, the host name of a computer may include more or less information than the host name on the right side of an e-mail address. Use the e-mail host name only in situations in which you need to guess the host name.

To access Juan's account, you would follow these steps:

1. Type **telnet hal.jupiter.net**. (Again, this is a fictitious example, this system doesn't really exist.)
2. When your computer connects to the remote computer, enter Juan's username and password when prompted.

Let's say that when you tried to do this, you forgot the password that you needed in order to access the account. Fortunately, you knew it was in an e-mail message that Juan had sent to you earlier in the day. If, for some reason, you didn't want to log off Clarknet and try to connect again after getting the password, you could use a few UNIX tricks to keep you logged on the remote computer while you open up your e-mail and get the necessary password. You can keep your Telnet session running, open your mail program (or other application), and return to Telnet by following these steps:

1. Press Ctrl+]. This will bring up the Telnet prompt.
2. Type **z**. This puts Telnet in the background.
3. You should now see a command-line prompt. Enter your mail program (or other application), and get the information that you need.
4. When you're ready to return to Telnet, type **fg**. This brings Telnet back to the foreground.

Using this routine can be helpful if you need to get information from a mail message, check the name of a file, or otherwise use your local host computer to perform some function while logged on to a remote site.

Closing a Connection to a Remote Computer

If you're running Telnet from a command-line account, Telnet usually shuts itself off when you log off of the remote computer.

You may reach a point where the netlag is positively unbearable because another computer bogs down or, for some reason, you need to shut down your Telnet connection to another computer. To shut down, follow these steps:

1. Press Ctrl+] to display the Telnet command-line prompt.
2. Type **close**, which shuts off your remote connection and turns off Telnet.

Running Out of Time

When you log on to a remote computer, that computer often keeps track of how active you are on the system. Telnetting a computer ties up part of its ability to serve other users, and system operators want to ensure their machines are as accessible as possible. Therefore, if you log on to a remote computer and are inactive (not typing anything) for about 15 minutes, the remote computer may log you off. If you send a Telnet connection into the background and forget about it, or if you fail to get back to it in time, the remote computer might log you off, and you will have to log on again.

Connecting to a Telnet Address with a Port

You may see an occasional Telnet address that lists a "port," such as hal.jupiter.net port 2001. Telnetting a particular port enables you to log on to a remote system for a particular purpose, such as a multiuser game or retrieving weather information.

The whole concept of ports goes all the way back to those days when computing was generally done from a large central machine. If you remember the information about terminals from earlier in this chapter, terminals were plugged into ports (actual sockets on the back or side of the machine) on the big machines to serve as input/output devices. On the back of your PC, you probably have a printer port and a serial port, as well as ports for your keyboard and your mouse (and maybe a few others).

Just like your keyboard port is specially designed to get information from a keyboard (or a mouse port from a mouse or mouse-like device), ports on Internet Hosts are set up to do specific functions. Multiuser games (like MUDs, MUSHes, DikuMUDs, and the like) are usually found on port 4201. World Wide Web Servers are normally found on port 80. Telnet access is also provided through a specific port (23), which the Telnet protocol assumes unless you specifically tell it otherwise.

All ports numbered 80 will usually have Web sites (even if not all Web sites are active on port 80); likewise, most port 23s will be used for Telnet, and multiuser games will normally be found on 4201. This is because, believe it or not, there is an Internet organization that actually assigns port numbers to specific Internet uses. These port assignments are, in turn, used in a standard fashion by most hosts throughout the Net. It's possible that specific system administrators may use other ports, but these are the most common ones.

Telnetting a Port

Telnetting a port is remarkably simple. To telnet the previous fictional example, hal.jupiter.net port 2001, you would type the following:

telnet hal.jupiter.net 2001

Telnet automatically logs you on to whatever system is running on port 2001.

Some users with command-line accounts (particularly at colleges and universities) work on a machine called a *VAX*. A VAX is a computer made by DEC, the same company that came up with all those different types of terminals. VAX computers usually don't use UNIX, the operating system used by many machines on the Internet. Consequently, there are occasionally some added steps that you have to take while using a VAX that you don't need when running a machine with UNIX. One of these involves telnetting to a specific port.

If you're operating out of a command-line account on a VAX system, you'll need to use the statement /port= before the port number when you give the Telnet address of the remote computer that you're trying to reach. To telnet to hal.jupiter.net 4201, on a VAX you would type:

telnet hal.jupiter.net /port=4201

Telnetting for Fun

Multi-User Dimensions (MUDs) and their cousins (MOOs, MUSHes, and so on) are multi-player games that work because lots of users can all telnet to the same machine to play at the same time.

Generally, when you telnet to a MUD, you take the part of a character in a game with hundreds, if not thousands of characters. Games are not resolved immediately; rather, the fun is that a plot can develop over months. A premium is placed on originality, inventiveness, and one's ability to stay in character.

As an example, let's say you wanted to telnet to DUNE II, a MUSH loosely based on the universe created by Frank Herbert in his series of Dune Books. At the time of this writing, DUNE II was located at mindport.net, port 4201. To join the fun on DUNE II, you would do the following:

1. At the command-line prompt, type **telnet mindport.net 4201**.

2. When you connect to DUNE II, the credits screen will appear, and you will notice that you have three options. To just take a look around, type **connect guest guest**.

   In this case, you'll be a character named "guest"; the password for this character is also "guest."

3. The game from here is a text-based adventure. Feel free to talk to people (preface your comments with a quotation mark (") to say something to someone else) and wander around. Press buttons. "Read" things. "Look" at things. You'll get the hang of it soon enough. You may want to venture into the Newbie room, where all sorts of helpful stuff will be available.

4. When you decide you want to create a character, telnet to the MUSH, and then type the following:

   create your_new_character's_name your_personal_password

5. From then on, when you want to log on to the MUSH, you'll type the following:

   connect your_character's_name your_password

Using Telnet on a SLIP/PPP Account

The difficult aspect of using Telnet on a SLIP or PPP account involves setting up your TCP/IP connection. After you've got your SLIP or PPP account running, starting a Windows-based Telnet program is just like starting any other Windows Winsock application. (See Chapters 5, "Connecting to a PPP or SLIP Account with Windows 95," and 6, "Connecting to a PPP or SLIP Account with Windows NT," or Chapter 7, "Connecting with Windows 3.1 and Trumpet WinSock," for more information.

Using Windows 95 and Windows NT Telnet

The simplest approach to using Telnet under Windows 95 and Windows NT is to use the version that comes free with each operating system. To keep things simple, I'll discuss using Windows 95 Telnet, because it works the same for both operating systems. Windows 95 Telnet is nothing fancy to look at, but is fairly simple to use and is very reliable.

Setting Up Telnet   You can start using Windows 95 Telnet this easily:

1. Click on the Windows 95 Start button. When the Start menu pops up, select the Run menu item. Windows 95 will display the Run dialog box as shown in Figure 30.1. (If you've used the Run dialog box before, there will be another command already there.)

FIG. 30.1
Running Windows 95
Telnet is very simple.

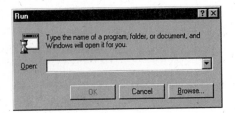

2. Type **telnet**, and click once on the OK button (any previous command will automatically be erased when you start typing). The Telnet window will appear as shown in Figure 30.2.

You can also run the Windows 95 Telnet client from the MS-DOS prompt from within Windows 95 (just like any other Windows application). Telnet can be started from the MS-DOS window command line in this version of Windows.

Adding Telnet to the Start Menu   If you find you're using the Windows 95 Telnet frequently, you may want to set up an icon for it in the Windows 95 Start menu (there's not one by default). To set up an icon, follow these steps:

FIG. 30.2
The Windows 95 Telnet client window is clean and straightforward in design.

1. Right-click an empty space on the Windows 95 taskbar. A pop-up menu will display several items; select Properties with a click of the left mouse button.

2. The Taskbar Properties dialog box will appear. Select the Start Menu Properties tab.

3. Select the Add button. The Create Shortcut dialog box will appear.

4. Click Browse, and choose the Telnet.exe file from your Windows directory. Click on the next button, and the Select Program Folder dialog box will display your group options. Pick the group you want the icon in and click the Next> button.

Windows 95 will display the Select a Title for the Program dialog box. Type the name you want the menu entry to have, and click the Finish button.

 T I P You can also use Windows Explorer to set up an icon quickly. Just use Explorer to view the directory where Telnet is (your Windows 95 directory, usually C:\Windows), click the Telnet.exe file, and drag it to your desktop. Windows 95 will create a shortcut icon automatically.

Connecting with Telnet   Connecting to a remote system with Windows 95 Telnet is also simple. To telnet to a system, make sure that you are connected to the Internet and Telnet is running on your desktop. Then, use these steps:

1. Select the Remote System menu item from the Connect menu. The Connect dialog box shown in Figure 30.3 will appear. (You can select from the history list at the bottom of the pop-up menu if the connection you want is listed.)

Part
VI

Ch
30

FIG. 30.3
Enter the name of the
Telnet host in the Host
Name edit box.

2. Enter the host name you want to connect to, and select the port and terminal emulation you need, if different from the defaults (these settings will probably work for the great majority of hosts).

3. Click the Connect button to complete the connection. The login prompt for the host system will appear in your Telnet screen.

N O T E   You can log on to your complete Telnet session using the Terminal, Start Logging command from the Windows 95 Telnet main menu. This is very useful for capturing commands and other host specific functions to print out later. ■

Using NetTerm for Windows 3.1

Windows 3.1 doesn't come with a Telnet client program (or an Internet dialer for that matter). You need to install a third-party program such as NetTerm—one of the best Telnet clients on the Web. You can get your own copy from the Web at **http://starbase.neosoft.com/ ~zkrr01/ntdl.html**. Click on the nt16290.zip - 16 Bit Version link to download the 16-bit Windows 3.1 version.

 You'll find a 32-bit version of NetTerm at this Web site, too. If you don't want to use the Telnet client program that comes with Windows 95 or Windows NT, replace it with the 32-bit version of NetTerm.

Installing NetTerm is easy. Here's how:

1. Unzip the file you downloaded into a new directory. You can use the 16-bit version of WinZip or Pkzip.

2. Open the File Manager, and click the directory in which you unzipped the file. Double-click SETUP.EXE to start the installation program. You should see NetTerm's Setup program as shown in Figure 30.4.

3. Click Continue to install NetTerm. When the Setup program asks you for the path in which you want to install NetTerm, type a path in the space provided, and click Continue.

4. After the setup program copies NetTerm's files to your computer, it displays a dialog box that tells you it's finished. Click OK to close the Setup program.

FIG. 30.4
Click Continue to install NetTerm, or click Exit to exit the setup program without installing NetTerm.

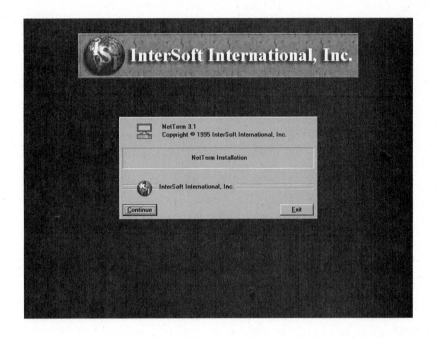

NetTerm's setup program adds its own program group to the Program Manager. Open its program group, and double-click the NetTerm icon to run it. Figure 30.5 shows you what NetTerm looks like.

FIG. 30.5
NetTerm provides a lot more flexibility than Windows 95's Telnet client program. You can stick to the basics if you like, however.

Connect. Click to connect to the currently selected Telnet host.

Phone directory. Click to select a Telnet host or configure a new Telnet host.

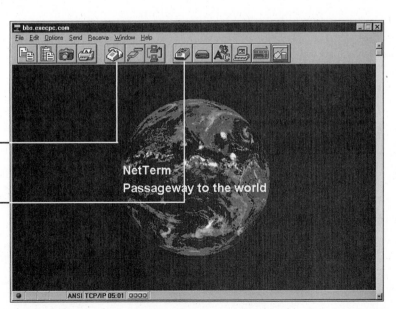

▶ **See** "Setting Up Trumpet WinSock SLIP Software on Your System," **p. 168**

Using Telnet Through a Local Area Network (LAN)

Using Telnet through a Local Area Network depends on the amount of flexibility that the LAN administrators have granted to the users. Generally, LAN administrators will set up access to the Internet through one point on the LAN. The computers connected to the LAN all gain access to the Net through this one point of access. The LAN administrators can then determine how much access the users of the LAN can get from this one source.

On some LANs, individual workstations are set up with their own individual IP address. If you can run TCP/IP at your workstation, then you should be able to run software such as the NCSA WINTel software or the Chameleon Telnet for Windows program the same way as you would through a SLIP or PPP connection.

If TCP/IP isn't available at your individual workstation, your LAN administrator may have created a special mechanism for using Telnet and other Internet utilities. How will you know if TCP is available at your station? You'll probably have to ask your LAN administrator, but if your workstation is set up with programs like Telnet, Mosaic, and FTP, you probably have your own IP address.

If you don't have your own IP address, some Internet access may still be available. Network administrators will sometimes provide access to special versions of Internet utilities that can be used without having to give users their own IP addresses. All Telnet utilities are going to ask for the same types of information, regardless of how they look. Telnet will always require a host name and, when applicable, a relevant port number. If you have this information, you should be able to use Telnet regardless of the way your LAN administrators have packaged it.

Don't Be Afraid to Ask for Help

When you log on to a new system, ask for help if you need it. Most systems that allow Telnet access also have extensive help files for users. These can usually be reached by typing **HELP** at a command-line prompt. (If HELP doesn't work in all capitals, try it in all lowercase, or try entering a question mark. One of them should eventually work. For some systems, the command MAN followed by a command may also produce help on that command although this help is generally limited to help about the operating system, not help files about their services accessible by Telnet.) No one keeps track of whether you've ever read the help files or how many times you went back to check the same thing. If you don't understand something, read the help file and read any other help files that seem like they might have something to do with your problem.

Telnetting to remote systems may sometimes require that you learn the language that those systems use. Remember, these remote systems have a lot of computing power that you can use to your advantage if you take the time to figure out what makes them tick.

 TIP A standard abbreviation among computer users is RTFM—Read the Fine Manual. When connecting to remote computers, be sure to check out their manuals (the system's Help files).

CHAPTER 31

Using FTP and Popular FTP Programs

by Dick Cravens

The Internet and its predecessors were created to facilitate information exchange. The oldest services on the Internet were developed for this purpose. One of these services is FTP. It enables you to examine the files of remote hosts on the Internet and to transfer files between your host and the others.

FTP, similar to many early Internet services, was developed by computer scientists for their own use. Computers were pretty primitive, most lacking the graphics capabilities that are taken for granted today. The people who used the computers expected them to be complicated. The developers, therefore, made no effort to make the interface to the service easy to use. Unless you knew in which place to find the files you wanted, you would never know the information was out there. The reason is that there was no way to search the FTP sites.

Although new Internet services are always being developed, the old services are still useful. Today's Internet users (some of whom are computer scientists who appreciate a good interface) have designed a new look for old services, including FTP. ■

How FTP works

Learn what FTP is, and how you can use it to transfer files to and from other computers on the Internet.

How to use the Windows 95 and NT FTP client

Windows 95 and NT come with a basic FTP client program that you can use. This chapter shows you how to use it.

How to use WS_FTP, a Popular Windows FTP client

WS_FTP is available for Windows 3.1, Windows 95, and Windows NT. It's easy to use, too.

What Is FTP?

You already have seen how you can use e-mail to send a message over the Internet. Now that most e-mail programs support MIME or some type of automatic encoding/decoding mechanism, you can send any type of file through e-mail. There is, however, a limit to the size of the files you can send through e-mail. Suppose that you want to make a collection of files available to anyone who wants to get them. It would be very inconvenient if the people who wanted the files had to contact you to find out what was available. Then, they would have to request that you send them the files they wanted through e-mail. A much better method of making the files available exists—the *file transfer protocol* (*FTP*) service. This service is designed to enable you to connect to a computer on the Internet using an FTP program on your local machine. You can use the service to browse through the files available on that computer, then download or upload files.

N O T E Unlike Internet e-mail, FTP enables you to directly transfer both text and binary files. You can send binary files through e-mail. The mail client must, however, encode them as text first. You must explicitly tell FTP that you are transferring binary files. ▪

What Are Client-Server Services?

The FTP service is an example of a client-server system. In this type of system, you use a program on your local computer (referred to as a client) to request a service from a program on a remote computer (referred to as a server). In the case of FTP, the server on the remote computer is designed to let you download and upload files. Many other services are available on the Internet, though. Some of these, such as Gopher and the World Wide Web (WWW), are discussed in other chapters.

▶ **See** "Important WWW Concepts," **p. 366**

▶ **See** "What Is Gopher?" **p. 834**

To connect to a computer using FTP, the other computer must have an FTP server running on it. The administrators of the server must set up this machine and decide which files and information will be made available on the FTP server.

Anonymous FTP

One common type of FTP server is an anonymous FTP server. With this kind of server, you can connect and download or upload files without having an account on the machine. If the FTP server isn't anonymous, when you connect to it you must provide a username and password, just as though you were logging onto the machine. On an anonymous FTP server, you use the special username *anonymous* when you connect. This term lets you log on by providing any password you want. Often, the server asks you to enter your Internet mailing address as your password.

T I P You can (and in rare cases must) use FTP instead of anonymous to log on to an anonymous FTP server.

N O T E You can retrieve files from a machine that does not have anonymous FTP service. You must, however, have an account on that machine to which you can log on. ▫

Anonymous FTP servers are one of the major means of distributing software and information across the Internet. A large amount of software—often provided free of charge—is available on anonymous FTP servers. Software is available for many different types of computer systems, such as UNIX, IBM PC, and Macintosh.

Using FTP from the Command Line

A number of Windows-based FTP clients are now available. One of them, known as WS_FTP, is described in detail later in this chapter. Originally, FTP was developed to be used from a command-line prompt. The FTP client that comes with Windows 95 and NT is a DOS command-line client.

N O T E To start the Windows 95 FTP client, open the Start menu. Then, select Run and in the Run dialog box, enter **ftp** in the Open text box. Next, click OK. A DOS window running a command-line FTP client appears. ▫

 T I P If you've selected Use AutoDial in your Internet Properties dialog box, the connection to your Internet service provider will start automatically when you try to open a connection to an FTP server.

The exact method you use to connect to an FTP server depends on the software available from your Internet service provider. In general, you use the open command with the name of the machine to which you're connecting. For example, if you want to FTP from the DOS FTP client to the machine **rs.internic.net** (a site that has many documents related to the Internet), use the command **open rs.internic.net**.

When you connect to the FTP server, you are prompted for a login name. If you have an account on the FTP server machine, you can use your account name; if this is an anonymous FTP site, use the login name *anonymous*. After the account name, you are prompted for a password. Naturally, if you logged in using your account name, you use your account's password here. If this is an anonymous FTP site, you can use anything for the password. By convention, however, you should use your e-mail address for the password. This way, the FTP site maintainer can keep track of who has been using the server and contact people who have downloaded files.

Most FTP programs have similar commands. Some of the most useful ones are listed in Table 31.1.

Table 31.1   Commands that Are Part of Most FTP Programs

Command	Purpose
ascii	Changes to text mode
binary	Changes to binary mode
ls	Lists files in the current directory on the FTP server
dir	Lists files, with more information
get *file*	Downloads *file* to your machine
put *file*	Uploads *file* from your machine
cd	Changes directory on the FTP account
lcd	Changes directory on your local computer
mget *files*	Downloads multiple files to your machine
mput *files*	Uploads multiple files from your machine
bye	Logs out from the FTP server
help	Displays a help message showing a list of available commands
binary	Tells the FTP server that you will be downloading a binary file

Your FTP program might have other commands available. Alternatively, your program might use different names for these commands.

Windows-based FTP Clients

On the CD

More and more PCs are being used as Internet hosts; therefore, a number of Windows-based interfaces to standard Internet services have been developed. Most commercial PC TCP/IP packages include interfaces to a number of Internet services, including FTP. The NetCD that comes with this book contains several commercial and shareware FTP interfaces. After your PC is connected to the Internet, you need only install the FTP interfaces to begin your exploration of one of the Internet's oldest and best sources of programs and documents.

Most commercial TCP/IP packages provide an automated setup program to install the different applications. Alternatively, they will at least provide detailed installation instructions. If you get one of the shareware TCP/IP application's packages, such as those included on the NetCD that comes with this book, it is usually just a matter of placing the ZIP file for the application in a directory. Then, you can unpack it. As an example, you learn how to install and use the WS_FTP32 application later in this chapter.

Locating Files

One of the most frustrating problems with the Internet is the difficulty of finding information, such as FTP sites, host resources, and sources of information. Imagine that you went to your local public library and found that the books were not arranged on shelves according to a book classification scheme. Instead, they were in piles all over the floor. Rather than use a central card catalog, the librarians had placed notes on some of the piles stating what people had found in that pile. This scenario describes how the information on the Internet has been arranged for most of its existence. Many resources are available. However, there is no way to easily locate them.

Most FTP sites don't have a listing of all their available files. Some do, however. Generally, the only way to locate a file or find interesting files is to move around in the directories on the FTP server. Then, you must look at the files that are in these directories.

The file listing is in the form that the host machine uses. Therefore, what you see when doing a directory listing varies, depending on the type of system to which you connect. If the server is running on a UNIX system, for example, the file names appear in upper- or lowercase, and can be of any length. If you want to download a file, you must be sure to type the file name exactly as it appears when you do a directory listing.

> **N O T E** It also is important to use the exact case when changing directories while using FTP from the command line. ▪

On some machines, especially the very large archive sites, the site maintainers keep an index of available files with brief descriptions of what they are. These indexes are very helpful, and make finding useful files much easier. When you enter a directory, you should look for a file known as INDEX (in upper- or lowercase letters). You also should look for a file referred to as README (readme, read.me, or something similar). These README files are generally descriptions of the contents of the directories or information about the server system. You should always download the README files and read the contents—the files are put there for a reason. You also might find a file named LS-LR that gives a detailed listing of the directory structure on the site.

If you have a question about either an FTP server or the contents of the files there, send an e-mail message to the postmaster of the FTP machine. For example, if you connect to the machine **rs.internic.net**, send e-mail to the address **postmaster@rs.internic.net**. Some FTP servers have a different person to contact; in this case, the name of the contact person appears when you connect to the machine. The name of this person also can be in a README file in the first directory you see when you connect.

One Internet service known as Archie enables you to search a database containing a list of the files on a number of anonymous FTP servers. The Archie servers connect to registered FTP sites to update the server's database information on a regular basis. For more information about Archie and how to use it, see Chapter 34, "Searching for Information on the Internet."

▶ **See** "Archie," **p. 886**

Downloading and Uploading Files

After you find a file that interests you, you can download it to your service provider account or your local PC if your provider enables you to do so automatically. There are several items that you should be aware of before you download the file. First, use the dir command on the file, or on a long directory listing, if your Windows-based FTP client can do it. You also should make a note of the size of the file you want to download. Make sure that the system to which you are downloading has enough space to store the file; you might have to leave the FTP program and remove some files before you can download the one on which you are working.

Also check whether the file you want to download is a binary file. A *binary file* is one that contains characters that cannot be printed or displayed. Generally, executable programs, picture or sound files, and compressed files are binary data. A *compressed file* is one that is made smaller using a program such as PKZIP or the UNIX compress program. If you want to download a binary file, you must tell the FTP program. Most programs have a binary command to do so. If you aren't sure whether the file is binary, tell your server that it is; in most cases, you can transfer nonbinary files in binary mode without problems.

If the file is very large and the FTP server is slow, or the Internet connection is slow (the machine is in Europe or Asia, for example), transferring the file might take several minutes. If the Internet connection is very slow, the download might stop and you will be logged out; in this case, you should try again. In general, transferring large files after normal work hours is a good idea. The reason is that the system and network loads are lighter.

If you have a Web page on the Internet, you'll need to use FTP to upload your HTML and graphics files to the Web server. Other than that, you probably will not upload many files to Internet FTP sites. You can upload files to some anonymous FTP sites, though. On those anonymous FTP sites that enable uploads, you will see a directory named INCOMING, which is set up as a place in which you should put uploads. If you place a file in the area for uploads, you should upload a short description of what the file is. Alternatively, you can send an e-mail message to the site maintainers to tell them what you uploaded.

TROUBLESHOOTING

I can't execute a binary file that I transferred. If you try to execute a program or to view a graphics file or some other binary file that you have retrieved from an FTP site, and the file appears to be corrupted, check to make sure that you transferred the file using binary mode. If you transfer a binary file in ASCII mode, the file will be corrupted.

Installing WS_FTP

The original version of WS_FTP was a 16-bit application designed to run under Windows 3.1. It is still being maintained. WS_FTP32 is a 32-bit application primarily designed for use with Windows 95 and the Windows NT operating system. The 32-bit application itself is almost exactly the same as the 16-bit version, with only a few minor differences in the appearance of the main window. You will learn about the 32-bit version of WS_FTP in this chapter.

The WS_FTP32 (as well as the 16-bit version known as WS_FTP) program can be found on the NetCD accompanying this book. You must be running Windows 95 or NT to use WS_FTP32. You can install WS_FTP32 by running the NetCD installation as described in Appendix A, "What's on the CD." Alternatively, you can copy the file from NetCD to a directory of your choosing on your hard drive. Then, you can unzip the file into the directory in which you want to keep the application.

If you can't use the CD to load WS_FTP, or you would like to check to see whether a newer version exists, you can use the Windows 95 FTP client discussed earlier in this chapter to get the Ws_ftp32.zip file (currently Ws_ftp32.zip) from **ftp.usma.edu** in the directory **/pub/ msdos/winsock.files**. You also should be able to find Ws_ftp32.zip at **ftp.winsite.com** (formerly **ftp.cica.indiana.edu**) in the directory **/pub/pc/win95/netutil**, or at any of the WinSite mirror sites, including **wuarchive.wustl.edu**, **ftp.cdrom.com**, **ftp.monash.edu.au**, **ftp.uni-stuttgart.de**, **nic.switch.ch**. WinSite gives you a complete list of mirror sites if your connection fails. The reason is that if this happens, all of the anonymous FTP slots are taken. If you download this application instead of using it from NetCD95, you must unzip the files to the directory of your choice.

TIP Once you've unzipped WS_FTP32, you can create a Windows 95 or NT shortcut to it. Simply click on the Ws_ftp32.zip file with the right mouse button. Then, select Create Shortcut. Drag the shortcut that you create to someplace that is easy for you to access—a folder that appears under Programs on your Start menu, for example.

Using WS_FTP

WS_FTP32 (hereafter referred to as WS_FTP) is a 32-bit Windows FTP client. It enables you to connect to hosts on the Internet using the FTP protocol. After you are connected, you can examine the directories on the host. You also can send and receive files to the host, if you have read and write privileges.

Connecting to a Host

When you want to use WS_FTP to retrieve or upload a file, you must first establish your connection to the Internet. (You need to do this if your host is not permanently connected to the Internet.) When your host is on the Internet, follow these steps to connect to the remote host:

1. Open the Start menu. Then, select Programs. You start WS_FTP by selecting it from the Program item in which you originally put it. By default, you get the WS_FTP window and a Session Profile dialog box. (See Fig. 31.1.) You must fill in the information in the Session Profile dialog box to make a connection with a remote host.

N O T E   WS_FTP comes with preconfigured profiles for several of the most popular FTP sites. See "Defining Host Profiles" later in this chapter for more information about selecting preconfigured profiles. ▨

FIG. 31.1

The WS_FTP window and Session Profile dialog box both appear when you start WS_FTP.

2. Click the text box next to Host Name. Then, enter the name of the Internet host to which you want to connect.

3. Unless there is a problem reading the directories on the remote host, leave the Host Type set to Automatic detect.

TROUBLESHOOTING

No remote directories are shown after I connect. If you connect to your FTP server, but no directories or files are shown for the server, perhaps WS_FTP does not know how to handle the directory information that the server is returning. First, check the type of machine to which you are trying to connect. Then, try changing the WS_FTP host type from auto detect to the appropriate type.

4. Click the text box next to User ID. If you intend to connect to an anonymous FTP server, click the Anonymous Login check box. The value is then automatically set to anonymous. If you are going to log in to a personal account on the remote machine, enter your user ID here.

5. Click the text box next to Password. If you have clicked the Anonymous Login check box, and you have previously set up your e-mail address, this address is automatically entered here. If your e-mail address isn't automatically entered, and you are doing an anonymous login, enter your full Internet e-mail address.

   If you are logging in to a personal account, first make sure that the Anonymous Login check box is off. Then, enter the password for your account. This password will not appear on-screen.

6. If you are connecting to a machine that needs an account name as well as a user ID, click the Account box. Then, enter the account name.

7. Click the Remote Host box under Initial Directories. Next, enter the path of the directory you want to examine, if you know it. If you leave this blank with an anonymous logon, the

system shows you the top level directory for the host you specified. Otherwise, if you leave this blank, the system shows you the top level of your home directory.

8. Click the Local PC box under Initial Directories. Then, enter the path on your local file system in which you want to store files that you retrieve.

9. Choose OK to establish the connection.

The Session Profile dialog box disappears. WS_FTP attempts to connect to the account that you specified. You see the actual FTP commands in the log area at the bottom of the WS_FTP window. As long as everything is running smoothly, you don't have to worry about these messages. If a problem occurs, you are notified.

TIP To reopen the Session Profile dialog box after WS_FTP is started, choose Connect from the command buttons at the bottom of the window.

If your connection is successful, your WS_FTP window shows the name of the remote machine in the title bar. (See Fig. 31.2.) The Connect button will change to Close. The left side of the window is entitled Local System; the right side is named Remote System. Both sides contain a split viewing area. The top half of the viewing area shows the directories under the current one; the bottom half shows the files in the current directory.

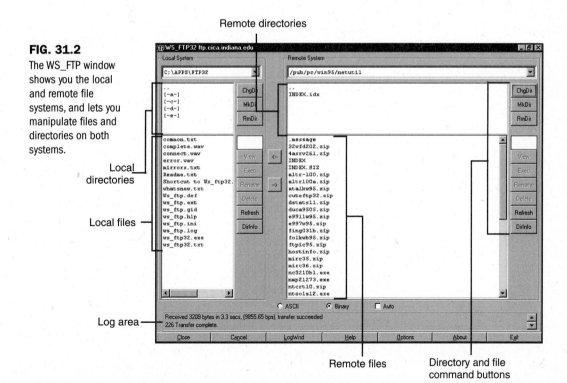

FIG. 31.2
The WS_FTP window shows you the local and remote file systems, and lets you manipulate files and directories on both systems.

TROUBLESHOOTING

I can't connect to the FTP server. You can get one of several different error messages in the log area. One message might indicate that the remote host was not found. This usually means that you entered the name of the server incorrectly. Check the name and try it again.

Another message might indicate that your connection is refused. This usually occurs when a machine is already at its maximum capacity for FTP connections. (Many servers only enable a limited number of anonymous FTP connections.) If you get a `connection refused` message, try to make the connection again. (People are always disconnecting from the FTP servers.) If you attempt a few times, and still cannot connect, try at another time. You also can try another machine that has the same information. A number of sites, referred to as *mirrors*, have copies of the files that are on popular servers. Many popular servers will show you a list of mirror sites if they refuse your connection.

Working in Directories

T I P You can see more of your directory and file lists without maximizing the window. You simply stretch the window so that it goes from the top of the screen to the bottom.

After you establish a connection to your FTP host, you can manipulate the files on both your local and remote machine. You can upload files from your computer to the remote host. You also can download files from the remote host and move between directories. Deleting files and directories (if you have those privileges) are other ways that you can handle data when you connect.

Setting Your Directories   After you establish your FTP connection, the WS_FTP window shows you the local directory that you specified on the left side of the window. You also see the remote directory you specified on the right side of the window. Buttons to the right of each directory area let you manipulate your directories if you have privileges (see Fig. 31.3).

T I P You can double-click a directory to get into it.

To manipulate your directories, follow these steps:

1. If your local and remote directories are not set correctly, use scroll bars in the directory areas to find the one you want. Select the directory. Then, click the ChgDir button to move to that directory. If you click the ChgDir button without selecting a directory, you get the Input dialog box that Figure 31.4 shows.

2. If you want to make a new directory under the current one on either the local or remote file system, click the MkDir button. You see the Input dialog box asking for the name of the directory you want to create. You must have write privileges to be able to create a new directory.

FIG. 31.3

The window shows the directories on the remote and local machines. Buttons to the right of each directory area enable you to change, create, and delete directories, as needed.

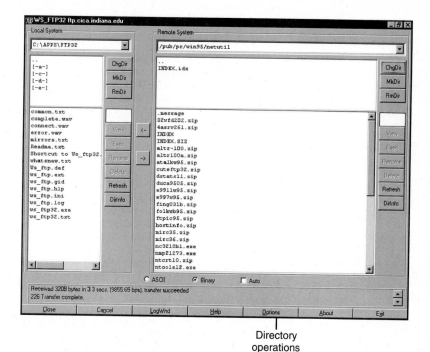

Directory
operations

FIG. 31.4

When you click either of the two buttons, the ChgDir or MkDir, the Input dialog box asks for the name of the directory.

3. If you want to remove a directory, you must first select it. When it is selected, click the RmDir button. You see the Verify Deletion dialog box that Figure 31.5 shows. It asks whether you are sure that you want to delete the directory. Click Yes if you want to delete the directory or No if you don't. You must have write privileges to be able to remove a directory.

FIG. 31.5

WS_FTP prompts you for confirmation before deleting a directory.

4. If you want to see more information about the files in a directory, click the DirInfo button. Notepad is started and shows a long directory listing of the current directory.

The listing includes file modification dates and sizes. (See Fig. 31.6.) You can save this information as you would any Notepad file.

 TIP Some directory listings might be too large to be edited with Notepad. If you want to set a different editor as your default, see "Customizing Your Window" later in this chapter. (WordPad is a good alternative.)

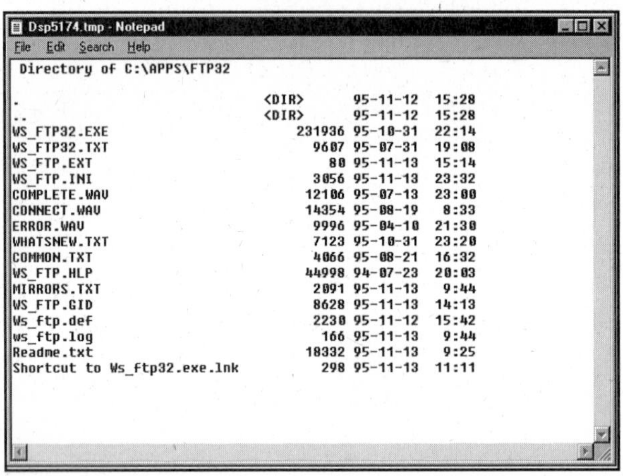

FIG. 31.6

Clicking the DirInfo button brings up Notepad with a file list showing the modification dates and sizes of the files in the current directory.

```
Dsp5174.tmp - Notepad                                    _ □ X
File  Edit  Search  Help
Directory of C:\APPS\FTP32

.                           <DIR>      95-11-12  15:28
..                          <DIR>      95-11-12  15:28
WS_FTP32.EXE               231936  95-10-31  22:14
WS_FTP32.TXT                 9607  95-07-31  19:08
WS_FTP.EXT                     80  95-11-13  15:14
WS_FTP.INI                   3056  95-11-13  23:32
COMPLETE.WAV                12106  95-07-13  23:00
CONNECT.WAV                 14354  95-08-19   8:33
ERROR.WAV                    9996  95-04-10  21:30
WHATSNEW.TXT                 7123  95-10-31  23:20
COMMON.TXT                   4066  95-08-21  16:32
WS_FTP.HLP                  44998  94-07-23  20:03
MIRRORS.TXT                  2091  95-11-13   9:44
WS_FTP.GID                   8628  95-11-13  14:13
Ws_ftp.def                   2230  95-11-12  15:42
ws_ftp.log                    166  95-11-13   9:44
Readme.txt                  18332  95-11-13   9:25
Shortcut to Ws_ftp32.exe.lnk   298  95-11-13  11:11
```

5. If the directory you are examining is changed outside of WS_FTP, this program does not show you the changes, unless you rescan the directory. Click the Refresh button to get the most recent directory information.

Working with Files   The local and remote files for the current directories are shown below the directories. Buttons to the right of each file area let you manipulate your files if you have privileges (see Fig. 31.7).

To manipulate your files, follow these steps:

1. If you want to view one of the text files in the directory, use the scroll bars in the file areas to find the file. Then, select it. Click the View button to view the file. (See Fig. 31.8.) You use the viewer that you set up in the Options dialog box to view the file.

2. If the operating system knows what type of application to run for a particular file extension, WS_FTP lets you automatically open that application with a file loaded. This is similar to the way you can double-click a file in the file manager. WS_FTP calls this executing a file. If you want to execute one of the files in your local or remote directory, use the scroll bars to find the file. Then, select the file. Click the Exec button to execute the file. If the file is on the remote system, WS_FTP first downloads the file to the Windows temporary directory. The program then executes the file.

TIP To associate a file extension with an application, see "Defining Executable File Associations" later in this chapter.

FIG. 31.7

WS_FTP lets you view, execute, rename, and delete files in your local and remote directories. You also can rescan the directory, and edit a copy of the directory listing.

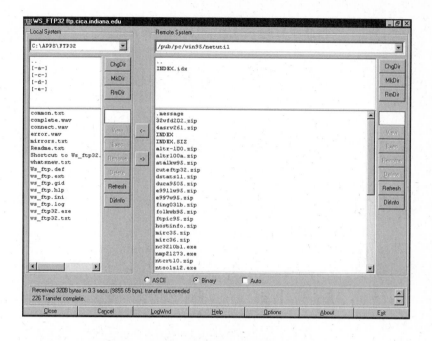

FIG. 31.8

When you view a file, your specified viewer is started with the file loaded. The default is Notepad.

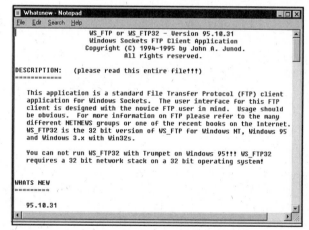

▶ See "Protecting Your Computer," p. 1030

CAUTION

Do not use the Exec button on an executable file, unless you are absolutely sure of what it will do and you are sure you have the file in the right location. You could introduce a virus to your PC by executing a questionable .exe file. It's always a good idea to run a virus checker on files that you get from an anonymous FTP site.

Part

VI

Ch

31

TIP On some file systems, you can use the Rename command to move a file. You do this by specifying the complete path name in the new name.

3. If you want to rename a file on the local or remote directory, use the scroll bars to find the file. Then, select the file. Click the Rename button to change the name of the file. You must have write permission to be able to rename the file.

4. If you want to delete a file on the local or remote directory, use the scroll bars to find the file. Then, select the file. Click Delete to remove the file. You must have write permission to be able to delete the file.

TROUBLESHOOTING

I'm looking for a file on an FTP server. However, it appears in the list of directories.
FTP servers (particularly UNIX-based servers) occasionally have directories that are actually links to other directories. These servers also might have files that are links to other files. The linked directories don't have any files in them. They point, however, to directories that do contain the files. By the same token, linked files do not have anything in them. They point, however, to the actual files.

Unfortunately, you have to choose whether WS_FTP interprets links as connections to files or to directories. (For information on how to do this, see "Setting up Default Session Options" later in the chapter.) If you tell WS_FTP to interpret links as files, it doesn't understand what the linked directories are. The program shows them as files. Then, when you try to examine the linked directory, you get the error Not a plain file. If you tell WS_FTP to interpret links as directories, it shows linked files as directories. Then, you get the error No such file or directory when you double-click one of them.

If you have WS_FTP set to show links as directories, you still can download a linked file. To do so, make sure no files are selected. You can click Refresh to clear any previously selected files. Click the left transfer arrow. Then, enter the name of the file in the input box that appears. Click OK. WS_FTP will begin downloading the file.

Retrieving Files   You probably will use WS_FTP mainly for retrieving files, especially if you are limited to connecting to anonymous FTP sites. After you establish your FTP connection, the WS_FTP window shows you the local directory you specified on the left side of the window. You also see the remote directory you specified on the right side of the window. To retrieve a file from the remote machine, follow these steps:

1. If your local and remote directories are not set correctly, use the directory commands described in the preceding section to navigate to the appropriate ones.

CAUTION
When you transfer a file, the receiving machine might already have one by that name. In this case, the file on the receiving machine will be overwritten, with no warning. To prevent this, see the Send Unique and Receive Unique options described in "Setting Up Default Session Options" later in this chapter.

2. To download a file, select it in the remote file area. Then, click the arrow that's pointing to the local directory. Alternatively, you can double-click the file name if you have double-click set up to do transfers. (For information on setting up the double-click behavior, see "Customizing Your Window," later in this chapter.) The Transfer Status dialog box appears to show you the progress of the transfer (see Fig. 31.9). You can abort the transfer by clicking Cancel in the Transfer Status box. Alternatively, you can choose Cancel from the command buttons at the bottom of the window.

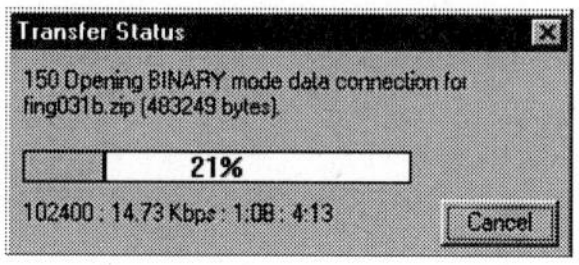

FIG. 31.9

The Transfer Status dialog box shows you what percentage of your file transfer is completed, and lets you abort the transfer.

Part VI
Ch 31

CAUTION

If you abort a download or upload, the receiving machine will have a partial file created. Be sure to delete this partial file.

3. To upload a file, select it in your local directory. Then, click the arrow pointing to the remote directory. Alternatively, you can double-click the file name if you have double-click set up to do transfers. The Transfer Status dialog box appears to show you the progress of the transfer. You can abort the transfer by clicking Cancel in the Transfer Status box. Alternatively, you can choose Cancel from the command buttons at the bottom of the window.

NOTE You can see the actual FTP commands executed for any remote file operation in the log area at the bottom of the WS_FTP window. If you double-click the log area, or if you choose LogWnd from the command buttons at the bottom of the screen, you will get a window that shows a complete history of all the FTP commands WS_FTP has executed in this session. The only time you should need to look at this is if an error occurs while trying to connect to a machine or transfer a file. You also might need to look at it if you are interested in information, such as how long it takes files to transfer, and average transfer rates (which also are kept in the log area). If your connection to an FTP server is refused, the server often will send you a message referring you to mirror sites; you can read that message in the log window.

TROUBLESHOOTING

I can't do anything with the remote directories or files. At times, you might try to do directory or file operations, and WS_FTP seems to be busy for a long time. The program is not doing anything or returns a Send error in your log area. In this case, your connection to the FTP server might have timed out. Most servers will disconnect you after a period of inactivity—if you stop changing directories or transferring files—to free up the connection for others to use. Sometimes, WS_FTP does not seem to recognize that the server has disconnected. The program will stay busy, requiring you to click the Cancel button. Whenever your connection times out, you must click the Close button to reset WS_FTP so that you can make a new connection.

Customizing WS_FTP

You can set up a number of features of WS_FTP to make the application more convenient for you to use. You can define profiles of the sites you use frequently, customize your window, and set default values for some of the transfer options. This section tells you about all the different customizations.

Customizing Your Window   You can change the arrangement of the buttons and viewing areas in your WS_FTP window. To change the layout of the window, follow these steps:

1. Choose Options from the row of buttons at the bottom of the window. You will see the Options dialog box that Figure 31.10 shows.

FIG. 31.10
The Options dialog box enables you to customize the way WS_FTP is set up and how it operates.

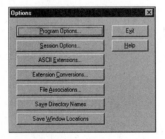

2. Click Program Options to open the Program Options dialog box. Here, you can customize the look of your WS_FTP window (see Fig. 31.11).

3. Click the Alternate Screen Layout check box to reformat the WS_FTP window so that the local directory is on the top, and the remote directory on the bottom. The directory list will be on the left, and the file list on the right (see Fig. 31.12). This places your buttons along the bottom of each directory area.

4. Click the Show Buttons at Top of Screen check box to move the row of command buttons from the bottom of the window to the top (see Fig. 31.13).

5. Click the Show Full Directory Information check box to display any additional file information.

FIG. 31.11

The Program Options dialog box enables you to customize the way WS_FTP appears to the user.

FIG. 31.12

Setting the Alternate Screen Layout puts the local directory information at the top of the window and the remote directory information at the bottom.

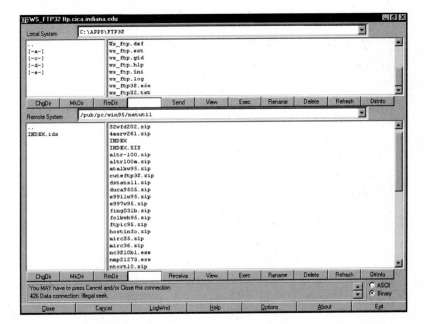

6. Click the Auto Save Host Configurations check box to set the Auto Save Config option in the Session Profile to default to On.

7. Click the Verify Deletions check box if you want to be asked for confirmation when you delete a file. This is the default setting.

8. Click the Show Connect Dialog on Startup check box if you want the Session Profile dialog box to display when you first start WS_FTP. This is the default setting.

FIG. 31.13

The Show Buttons at Top of Screen check box moves the command buttons to the top of the WS_FTP window.

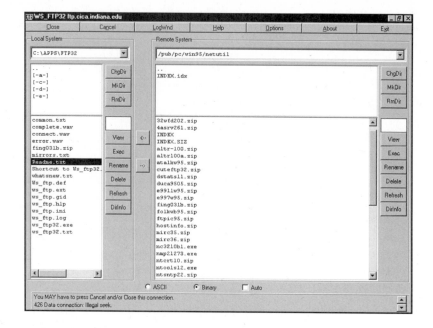

N O T E   There is a Debug Messages option that causes additional debug messages to display in the log area. The author of WS_FTP, however, does not recommend turning this on. The reason is that all valid error messages already will display in the log area. ▪

9.   Click the text box next to Text Viewer to set the default application to be used when you view an ASCII file from one of the directories. (This will default to Notepad.)

10.   Click the text box next to E-Mail Address to set the default e-mail address to be used when logging in to an anonymous FTP server.

11.   Click the Enable Logging check box if you want to create a log file for each file transfer. Enter the name you want to use for the log file in the text box next to Log File Name. A file with that name appears in the same directory as the file you are uploading/downloading.

12.   In the Listbox Font area, click the radio button for the font that you want to use in both the directory and file list areas. If you don't want to use one of the standard fixed or variable width fonts, you can click the Custom Font button. This brings up the Font dialog box that Figure 31.14 shows. This window enables you to scroll through and select one of the fonts available on your system.

13.   Click the Scale Fonts check box to set WS_FTP so that the fonts outside of the directory and file list areas will shrink if the window size is reduced.

14.   Click one of the following radio buttons under the Double Click box. This sets the same action that you would achieve if you double-clicked a file:

FIG. 31.14

The Font dialog box enables you to select the font family, style, and size of the font for the WS_FTP directory and file areas. A sample of the font you select displays.

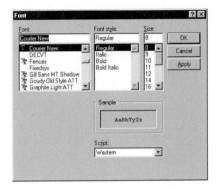

- The Transfer radio button causes the file to be transferred to the other system (uploaded or downloaded) when you double-click it.
- The Execute radio button tries to execute the file in the same manner as the Exec button.
- The Nothing radio button sets this option so that nothing happens when you double-click on a file.

15. In the Rate Display box, click the radio button to set the format used to show your data transfer speed (either bits or bytes per second).

16. Click the text box next to Recv Bytes to set the size of data chunks read during file transfers. (You might try using 4096.)

17. Click the text box next to Send Bytes to set the size of the data packets written during file transfers. If you are directly connected to the Internet, use 4096; otherwise, the value depends on your TCP/IP stack implementation.

18. Choose Save when you have finished setting up the options. (Choose Cancel if you want to abort these changes.)

You also can customize the size and location of your WS_FTP window. To do this, open the Options dialog box. Then, choose Save Window Locations. The next time you start WS_FTP, your window will appear the same size and in the same place as it was when you chose that button.

Defining Host Profiles   If you connect to some Internet hosts on a regular basis, you will probably want to set up automatic connections to those hosts. This saves you the trouble of filling in the box each time you connect. To set up a host profile, follow these steps:

1. Choose Connect from the row of command buttons. You should see the Session Profile dialog box that Figure 31.15 shows.

2. To modify an existing session, select it from the drop-down list next to Profile Name. To clear the fields for a new session, click New.

Part

VI

Ch

31

FIG. 31.15

The Session Profile dialog box enables you to set up the parameters for a connection and save them to use in a later session.

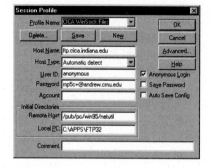

3. In the text box next to Profile Name, enter the name for this session. Good choices might include the name of the site (if it is well known) or the type of files that can be found on the site, such as *PC games.*

4. In the text box next to Host Name, enter the name of the Internet host to which you want to connect.

If your e-mail address is not entered in the Program Options dialog box, you will be prompted for it after you click Anonymous Login.

5. If you are connecting to a personal account, enter the name of the User ID to which you are going to connect. Otherwise, click the Anonymous Login check box. anonymous then appears in this field. Your Internet e-mail address also appears in the Password field. To save the password with the profile, click the Save Password check box.

CAUTION

Do not enter your password and save the session information if you are connecting to a personal account. The reason is that it would be possible for someone to find your password stored on the hard disk and decrypt it. Alternatively, someone also might use the stored password to connect to your personal account and access your files.

Open the Options dialog box. Then, choose Save Directory Names to quickly save the local and remote directory names as the defaults for the profile of the current session.

6. If you want to enter values for the Remote Host and Local PC Initial Directories, fill in these fields.

7. If you want to save this session information, choose Save. Otherwise, choose Cancel to close the window.

You also can configure a number of advanced features for a profile. If you click Advanced, you see the dialog box that Figure 31.16 shows.

FIG. 31.16

The Advanced Profile Parameters dialog box enables you to set up advanced connection features for your profiles.

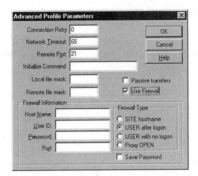

Here's what each of the controls in the Advanced Profile Parameters dialog box does:

- The Connection Retry field lets you specify the number of times a connection will be tried before failing.

- Network Time-out specifies the amount of time (in seconds) that WS_FTP waits for a response from the remote host before failing. Note that your initial connection time-out is set by your WinSock DLL.

- Remote Port is normally set to 21 for FTP transactions. You might need to set the Remote Port to something else if you are going through a firewall (ask your Internet system administrator).

- If you always upload or download the same type of files, enter the mask for those file types in either the Local File Mask or Remote File Mask text box (*.zip, for example). Once WS_FTP has made the connection, click Refresh to activate the mask so that you view only those file types.

- Click the Passive transfers check box if you need to use PASV Transfer Mode. This specifies that the FTP client initiates the data transfer connections rather than the server. This might be needed if your host is behind a firewall.

- Click the Use Firewall check box if your computer is behind a firewall. Check with your system administrator for the type of firewall you are using. Then, click the appropriate radio button under Firewall Type. Fill in the entries under the Firewall Information section. Your system administrator also should be able to tell you what needs to go in these boxes.

Deleting Host Profiles   WS_FTP comes with a number of predefined session profiles that enable you to get to Internet hosts that contain popular programs. You will probably want to delete these entries if you have no need to connect to those hosts. To delete a profile, select it from the drop-down list next to Profile Name in the Session Profile dialog box. Then, choose Delete… Contrary to the ellipses at the end of Delete…, the profile you select will be deleted immediately, with no confirmation.

Setting Up Default Session Options   You can set up the default values for some of the fields in the Connection Session Profile window. To set these defaults, follow these steps:

1. Choose Options from the row of buttons at the bottom of the window.

2. Click Session Options to open the Session Options dialog box (see Fig. 31.17). Here, you can customize your default session settings.

FIG. 31.17

The Session Options dialog box enables you to set defaults for some of the parameters in your Session Profile.

3. If you know the type of host to which you will usually connect, select the host type from the Host Type drop-down list. The default value of Automatic detect will work for most host types.

4. Click the Auto Update Remote Directories check box if you want the remote directory to be refreshed after a file operation. This is the default.

5. Click Show Transfer Dialog if you want WS_FTP to display the Transfer dialog box that shows the percentage of the transfer that is complete. Clicking here also enables you to abort the transfer. Show Transfer Dialog is turned on by default.

6. Click Use PASV Transfer Mode if you need to specify that the FTP client initiates the data transfer connections rather than the server.

N O T E   You might need to use PASV transfer mode if your machine is on a network that has a firewall. ■

7. Click Sort Remote File Listbox if you want the remote file area to be sorted alphabetically. Otherwise, the files are shown in the order transmitted from the remote host.

8. Click Use Firewall if your system is on a network behind a firewall. You must make sure that the firewall information in the Advanced section of the Session Profile window is properly filled out for each connection session.

9. Click Send Unique if you want the remote host to make sure that no conflict in file names exists between the remote and local host. The remote host assigns the name.

10. Click Receive Unique if you want the local host to make sure that no conflict in file names exists between the remote and local host. Any files received that would conflict with an existing file will have the sixth through eighth characters replaced with an incremental number between 000 and 999. The local host assigns the name.

11. Click Prompt for <u>D</u>estination File Names if you want the system to show you the destination file name for every file that is transferred. You can change the destination by entering a full path.

12. Click one of the radio buttons under Sounds to control how WS_FTP indicates events with sound. Your options include the following:

- None eliminates all sound indicators.

- Beeps causes a single beep to be sounded for all events.

- Wave causes the files complete.wav, connect.wav, and error.wav to be used for transfer completions, successful connections, and errors, respectively.

13. Click one of the radio buttons under Transfer <u>M</u>ode to set the default mode that FTP should use to transfer files. The options include the following:

- ASCII transfers the file as text, properly translating the end-of-line character between the remote and local system.

- Binary must be used for any type of executable or encoded file, such as one from a word processor, a graphics file, or a sound file. You can use this option for text files if the remote and local systems are of the same type.

- You must use L8 for VMS nontext file transfers.

- Auto Detect transfers files in binary, unless the file extensions have been pre-defined as ASCII using the Extension setup option described in the next section, "Defining ASCII File <u>E</u>xtensions."

14. Click one of the radio buttons under View Links to specify how you want links to be shown. As Files shows all links as files; As Directories shows all links as directories.

15. When you have completed setting up the session profile defaults, click Save to save these values for the current session. To save them as defaults for all future sessions, click Sa<u>v</u>e as Default.

Defining ASCII File Extensions   If you have your file transfer mode set to Auto Detect, your files will be transferred in binary mode, except for those that have file extensions that you have defined as ASCII. To define ASCII file extensions, follow these steps:

1. Choose <u>O</u>ptions from the row of command buttons at the bottom of the WS_FTP window.

2. Click <u>E</u>xtensions to open the Auto Detect Extensions dialog box. Here, you can define the extensions of ASCII files (see Fig. 31.18).

3. Click in the text field under <u>A</u>SCII mode. Then, enter the file extension. Its length can be up to 10 characters. It also should contain any punctuation that would normally precede it, or be a part of it.

4. Choose <u>A</u>dd to add the extension to the list. Files with this extension will now be transferred in ASCII mode, if the mode is set to Auto Detect.

If you would like to delete an extension from the list, select the extension. Then, choose <u>D</u>elete. The extension will be immediately deleted. Choose Exit to close this window.

Part
VI

Ch
31

FIG. 31.18

The Auto Detect Extensions dialog box enables you to create a list of file extensions that identifies files as ASCII.

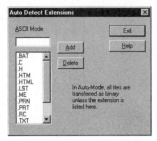

Defining Executable File Associations   You can execute any file in the remote or local directory list. If the file is nonexecutable, you need to specify the application that WS_FTP will start when you launch the file. For example, you might want to start Lview when a .gif file is executed to view the picture in the .gif file. To associate file extensions with applications, follow these steps:

1. Choose Options from the row of command buttons at the bottom of the WS_FTP window.

2. Click Associations to open the Associate window (see Fig. 31.19).

FIG. 31.19

The Associate window enables you to specify the application that should be started when you try to execute a file.

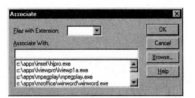

3. Click the box next to Files with Extension and enter the three-letter extension. Do not enter the initial period. If you want to modify an extension, click the arrow to the right of the list. This gives you a drop-down list of the currently defined extensions.

4. Click in the box under Associate With. Then, enter the path to the application you want to start. You can scroll through the list of applications below the box and click the one you want to enter in it. If the application you want is not in that list, you can choose Browse. This gives you a file browser that lets you select the application from your local file system.

5. Choose OK to add the extension to the list.

CAUTION

Any file association that you enter will be saved in the Win.ini file. You also can access the file association from the File Manager. You cannot delete associations that you create in this window without editing your Win.ini file.

Exiting WS_FTP

When you have finished transferring files, close the FTP connection by choosing Close from the command buttons at the bottom of the window. At this point, you can make another FTP connection by choosing Connect from the command buttons. If you are finished using WS_FTP, choose Exit from the command buttons. ●

Part

VI

Ch

31

CHAPTER 32

Using Gopher and Popular Gopher Programs

by Mary Ann Pike

This chapter introduces you to the most popular rodent in Cyberspace: Gopher. In this chapter, you examine the history of the Gopher protocol and how you use it to make information location and retrieval very simple. You also look at several popular Gopher client programs. You learn how to start them quickly and easily. ■

Learn about Gopher

You learn about the Gopher protocol, and how Gopher servers store information.

Set up and use a Gopher client program

HGopher is a great Gopher client program. You learn how to use it to access Gopher servers.

Navigate in Gopherspace

It's easy to get around Gopherspace. This chapter shows you how to locate and retrieve information with Gopher.

Search Gopherspace for something specific

You also learn how to find specific types of information using Veronica to search Gopherspace.

What Is Gopher?

The term *Gopher* refers to a network protocol, a server type, and one of many Gopher client applications used to access information. When you use a Gopher system, you're really using all three entities. The name Gopher comes from the team mascot of the University of Minnesota, where Gopher was developed. The term is also a clever twist on an old saying, "I'm a Gofer: I go fer this; I go fer that!"

As you've seen in earlier chapters, there are many different ways to send and receive information through the Internet. Most of the protocols are for point-to-point connections with servers or systems known in advance, such as File Transfer Protocol or Telnet session; e-mail requires an exact address, and UseNet newsreaders must have a specific server to which to connect.

▶ **See** "What Is Telnet?" **p. 792**

▶ **See** "What Is FTP?" **p. 808**

Gopher is different in design and execution from all of these systems. The Gopher protocol and software enable you to browse information systems. You don't, therefore, necessarily need to know exactly in which place something is stored before you look for it. Although you need to know the address of a Gopher server to get started, after you're there, the Gopher server software presents information in a clear, structured, hierarchical list—similar to a table of contents in a book. This familiar mode of presentation makes even the most complex information easy to access and retrieve. Most Gopher sites have links to others. After you hook up to one site, therefore, it's pretty easy to jump to another.

Many excellent Gopher client programs are available from commercial software vendors. There are also some incredible shareware and freeware Gophers. This chapter discusses a very popular freeware client program, *HGopher*, in detail.

N O T E Most Web browsers also support Gopher very well. Simply use the **gopher://** prefix when composing URLs to Gopher sites in your browser. ▪

The sum total of all Gopher resources on the Internet is known as *Gopherspace*. This term denotes a simple abstraction that describes a constantly growing, always changing system.

Why Use Gopher?

Gopher is incredibly simple to use. If you can use the table of contents in a book or magazine, and click a mouse, you can use Gopher. An incredible amount of information also awaits you in Gopherspace. This information ranges from the latest article in your favorite magazine to the guitar tablature and lyrics for those golden oldies you haven't heard for years.

Gopher is primarily designed as a document retrieval system; however, you can find many types of information on Gopher servers, from simple text to sound and video files.

Although Gopher resources are plentiful and easy to use, there are other excellent reasons to use this system instead of any other. Gopher is a *stateless* protocol. This means that no connection to the remote server site stays open. When you make a request for information using Gopher, the client application on your system connects to the server site. Then, your client application gets the data and closes the connection. Other protocols (FTP, Telnet) tie up a logical port on the host system, preventing other users from getting in. Using Gopher makes you a better *netizen,* or citizen of the net, by maximizing resources.

Understanding Gopher Terminology

Just as with every other Internet technology, Gopher has its own associated jargon. Some of the basics include the following:

- *Item*: A directory, text document, image, or search—basically anything you can retrieve, or any process you can activate—is an item. Items are usually represented by specific icon types.

- *Document*: The actual information associated with an Item is a document. This is usually text. This term, however, refers to almost any form of organized information or media. Similar to items, specific icon types represent documents.

- *Bookmark*: A menu entry linked to a description of how to retrieve an Item is a bookmark.

- *Server*: The system that provides the Gopher menus and stores the documents is a server.

You might encounter other terms specific to particular Gopher clients; however, if you can grasp these terms, you can master navigating Gopherspace without much additional information.

Part
VI

Ch

32

What Is Gopher+?

The original Gopher protocol was a large step toward making network information retrieval easier to do. Even so, it soon became obvious that there were limits to the capabilities of the first generation of Gopher servers. One major limitation was the limited capability to provide detailed information about the resources stored on the server.

Then, along came Gopher+. This set of extensions enables servers to deliver more detailed information about Gopher resources *before* transfer, making Gopher an even more efficient method of distributing information. The user, therefore, can choose to retrieve a simple document in plain ASCII, or a complex one in PostScript.

In addition, this identifies graphics file types. By doing so, Gopher clients can automatically call the proper viewers. Also, Gopher+ servers can provide multiple views of information. The remote user might, for example, select from English or French text. Version information is available for documents at some sites. Information about server administration also is commonly available. If you have a problem, therefore, you can contact the parties in charge through direct mail.

Using HGopher

One of the most popular Gopher client applications for Microsoft Windows is *HGopher*, a public domain version written by Martyn Hampson. Hampson bases HGopher on an earlier program written for UNIX systems. He has, however, elegantly transformed it for the Windows environment. It works well on Windows 3.1, Windows 95, and Windows NT. It is easily the equal of many commercial attempts at a Gopher client.

N O T E HGopher uses external applications for viewer support. You might, therefore, need other applications or utilities to take full advantage of its potential. If you spend any time at all on the Internet, this will not be a major obstacle. You probably have some, if not all, of these programs already. You find them listed in the section "Setting Up Viewers," later in this chapter that explains where to get them. ■

Installing HGopher

When exploring the Internet with Gopher, you first need to get your client software up and running. You can obtain a very good client, HGopher, from most FTP sites. The main FTP site in which to find this is **ftp://ftp.ccs.queensu.ca**. You find Hgoph24.zip in **/pub/msdos/tcpip/winsock/**. You also find HGopher on most of the other major Windows Winsock shareware sites on the World Wide Web.

On the CD

To install HGopher, follow these steps:

1. Create a directory for HGopher, for example, c:\Hgopher.
2. Copy the HGopher ZIP file to the directory created in Step 1.
3. Using an archive utility, such as PKUNZIP or WinZip, decompress the HGopher archive.

N O T E Don't forget to practice safe computing! Please use a virus checker on downloaded files, preferably after decompression. ■

If you want to add an icon for HGopher to the Windows 95 Start menu, follow these steps:

1. To create an icon for HGopher in the Windows Start menu, click an empty space on the Windows 95 task bar using the right mouse button. A pop-up menu displays several items; select Properties by clicking the left mouse button.
2. The Taskbar Properties dialog box appears. Select the Start Menu Programs tab.
3. Select the Add button. The Create Shortcut dialog box appears.
4. Click Browse. Then, choose the hgopher.exe file from the directory in which HGopher was decompressed. Click the Next> button. The Select Program Folder dialog box displays your group options. Pick the group in which you want the icon. Then, click the Next> button.

 T I P You can also use Windows Explorer to set up an icon quickly. Just use Explorer to view the directory in which HGopher was decompressed, click the Hgopher.exe file, and drag it to your desktop. Windows 95 will create a shortcut icon automatically.

N O T E You can use the installer from NetCD to save the time of finding and downloading the HGopher ZIP file. ▪

T I P Niko Mak Computing's WinZip 6.1 is an excellent 32-bit shareware file compression/decompression utility designed specifically for Windows 95. Niko Mak also has a 16-bit version for Windows 3.1. It's available on the NetCD CD-ROM accompanying this book.

To start HGopher, follow these steps:

1. Connect to the Internet through your server or provider.

2. After you're connected, start HGopher by clicking the HGopher icon in your Start menu program group you set up earlier. Alternatively, you can double-click the HGopher icon on your desktop.

3. The HGopher main program window appears with the default bookmarks loaded, as Figure 32.1 shows.

FIG. 32.1

The main HGopher program window shows the default bookmarks.

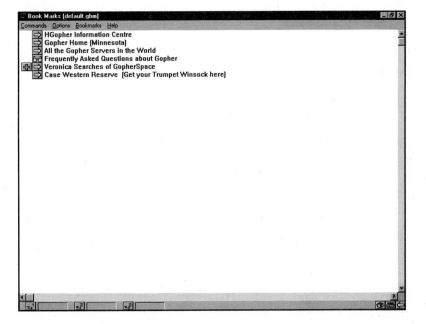

Configuring HGopher

Now that HGopher is on your system and running, you can configure it. HGopher needs some basic information about your network and your computer to function optimally.

To configure HGopher, follow these steps:

1. With HGopher running, choose Options from the HGopher main menu.

2. Choose Gopher SetUp from the menu. The Gopher Set Up Options dialog box appears (see Fig. 32.2).

FIG. 32.2

You can specify your default server in the Gopher Set Up Options dialog box.

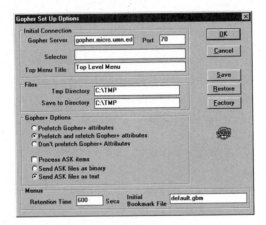

3. If the cursor is not in the Gopher Server field, click this field at the top left in the Initial Connection area of the dialog box. Alternatively, you can move to this area using the Tab key.

4. Type **gopher.micro.umn.edu** in the field. Later, you might want to enter a different Home Gopher server.

5. Click the Tmp Directory field.

6. Enter the complete directory path name for HGopher in which you want to store temporary information. Make sure the directory exists.

7. Click the Save to Directory field.

8. Enter the complete directory path name you want to use for storing information retrieved during your Gopher sessions. Again, make sure the directory exists.

9. Choose Save. This action saves your settings to the hgopher.ini file. HGopher recalls them automatically when you start each session.

10. Choose OK to return to the main HGopher window.

Now you're ready to start exploring new worlds of online information.

Navigating with HGopher

Now that you have completed the installation and basic configuration of HGopher, you can browse whenever you want. Select Go Home from the Commands menu, and your HGopher installation will take you to the home of all Gophers—the University of Minnesota (see Fig. 32.3).

FIG. 32.3

The top page of the University of Minnesota Gopher server is a great place to start your investigation of Gopherspace.

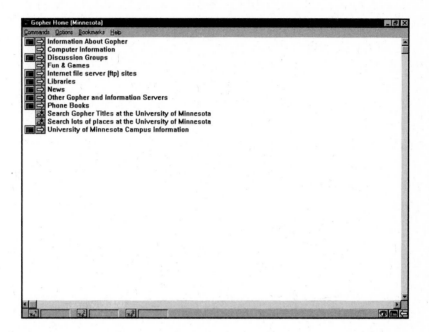

Why arrange the HGopher window this way? It's really quite simple. The HGopher program, in its entirety, is designed to be easy to use and simple to navigate. At the top left, you have the standard Windows application devices. These include the system icon, the window title (HGopher shows the current Book Mark page title), and the window zoom controls. Next is a standard Windows menu, some of which you have already used in setting up HGopher. At the bottom of the window is the status bar. This indicates the status of current connections. It also has several other icon controls. A section later in the chapter discusses these.

The main window displays the menu information during the browsing session. This area shows all Gopher resources. These include different icons representing various data types or different ways to access the information.

What do all of these icons mean? Remember, Gopher information is in a structured hierarchy. Every graphics element of a Gopher menu, therefore, tells us something about that resource. The items on the Gopher menus represent some means of navigating that ordered list. The following are icon descriptions:

■ *Right arrow.* This icon signifies either another directory or additional information at a lower level in the storage order. The information might be contained in many documents. This is functionally the same as a subdirectory in DOS.

■ *Left arrow.* This arrow indicates a directory at a higher level or *back*. This is functionally the same as a parent directory in DOS.

■ *Glasses symbol.* This icon indicates a simple text document.

■ *Binary symbol* (1111). This symbol represents a binary file.

■ *Music symbol.* This icon represents a sound file.

■ *Book symbol.* This symbol represents an index.

■ *Film symbol.* This icon indicates a movie.

■ *Big H.* This icon denotes an HTML hypertext document.

■ *Terminal symbol.* This symbol represents a Telnet resource.

■ *IBM Terminal symbol.* This symbol denotes a TN3270 resource.

■ *Plus symbol.* This symbol is a Gopher+ resource (attributes unknown).

■ *Bullet symbol.* This icon represents a line of information, not a resource.

■ *Red and Blue Screens symbol.* This icon indicates there are multiple views of a resource.

As previously mentioned, there are also a number of icon indicators or controls on the HGopher status line. They include the following:

■ *Lightning symbol.* This indicator tells you the Connection status.

■ *World symbol.* You are informed of a Location status through the World symbol. (You're obviously not at home.) When you click this symbol, the system takes you to the default Book Marks page.

■ *Bookshelf symbol.* You know the Location status when you look at this symbol. (You're on the default Book Marks page.) When you click this control, the system takes you to the current site page.

■ *Eye symbol.* This control tells you the View mode. This icon changes, depending on whether you are copying to a single file or to a directory.

■ *Closed folder symbol.* This icon indicates you are in Copy to File mode; it only appears when you click the eye icon while you are in a file.

■ *Open folder symbol.* This control indicates you are in Copy to Directory mode; it only appears when you click the eye icon while you are in a file.

■ *Right arrow.* This symbol signifies another directory or additional information (perhaps many documents) at a lower level in the storage order. The information might be contained in many documents. This symbol is the same as the one in the main window.

■ *Left arrow.* This symbol indicates a higher level or *back*. It is the same as the one in the main window.

All these controls serve the purpose of making it easier for you to identify the type of information with which you are dealing and to navigate more easily. Even with all this, you might find that you use only two or three controls to find your way around the system.

Use these steps to see how easy it is to navigate using HGopher:

1. When Windows 95 is running and connected to the Internet, click the Start menu button. Then, find the Programs icon you created for HGopher or the icon you created on the desktop.

2. Select HGopher. Open it by clicking the Programs icon. Alternatively, you can double-click the icon on the desktop.

3. After HGopher opens to the University of Minnesota Gopher site page, move the mouse cursor to the Information About Gopher line. Select it by clicking once on the type. HGopher displays the Information About Gopher page (see Fig. 32.4).

FIG. 32.4

You can begin learning about HGopher on the University of Minnesota Information About Gopher page.

N O T E To move to a resource, always double-click the description. Don't click the symbols next to the description line.

4. Move the mouse cursor to the Previous Menu (Top Level Menu) line and double-click. HGopher takes you back to the page you started from.

Transferring Files with HGopher

While HGopher is great for cruising for document retrieval, it can also be useful for obtaining other data formats, as well. In fact, using HGopher is a very easy way to perform FTP transfers.

Follow these steps to transfer a file using HGopher:

1. Return to the University of Minnesota site (see Fig. 32.5). Highlight the Other Gopher and Information Servers entry. Double-click it to travel to it.

FIG. 32.5

The University of Minnesota Gopher server main page contains the link to many other sites.

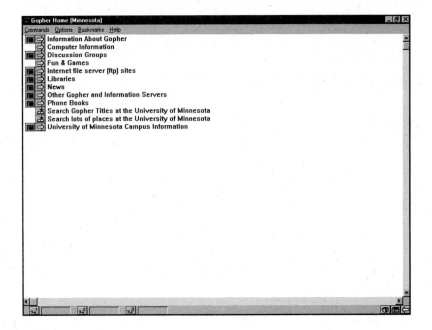

2. Using the techniques you mastered earlier, navigate to the Oakland University OAK Software Repository. When you search, you're usually dealing with hierarchical information. It is best, therefore, to start with the most general information and proceed to narrow the search. In a geographical search, for example, you might start with North America, then USA. Next, you might navigate to California. (See Fig. 32.6.) You might have to scroll down the HGopher display page to find the OAK Repository at the Oakland U. entry.

3. Select the SimTel item. Then, move to that area.

4. Select the Win95 item. Next, move to that area.

5. Select the graphics item, and move to that area. HGopher displays a list of files.

6. Scroll down the page. Then, select a file by double-clicking it. HGopher displays the standard Save As dialog box (see Fig. 32.7).

7. Choose OK to confirm the download directory—the place in which you want the file stored on your local system.

8. Select the Backward button at the lower right corner of the HGopher window. The HGopher display returns to the previous page while the download proceeds. Note that the session progress indicators at the lower left of the HGopher window display the status of both the FTP transfer and the page move (see Fig. 32.8).

FIG. 32.6
The OAK Software
Repository FTP server
menu displays a great
deal of information at
this site.

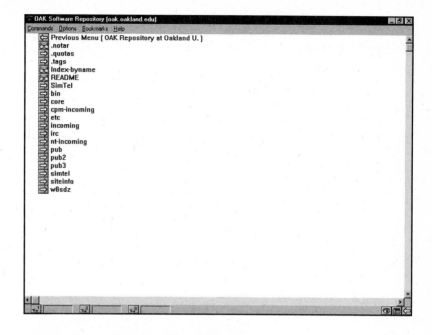

FIG. 32.7
Use the Save As dialog
box to tell HGopher in
which place to save
files on your local drive.

Marking the Gopher Trail with Bookmarks

As you navigate through Gopherspace, you'll probably want to visit certain sites often. Wouldn't it be nice to mark your trail, so that it's easy to return to your favorite spots quickly and easily?

Most Internet programs have a *bookmark* or *hot list* feature to aid in navigation. In this way, you don't have to endlessly retrace your steps. You won't have to memorize or otherwise record endless lists of server addresses. HGopher makes it easy to return to any location by using its Bookmarks feature.

Follow these easy steps to set up an HGopher bookmark:

1. Navigate to the University of Minnesota site again. Highlight the Other Gopher and Information Servers entry. Then, double-click to travel to it.

FIG. 32.8

HGopher uses progress indicators to inform you of the status of your retrieval request.

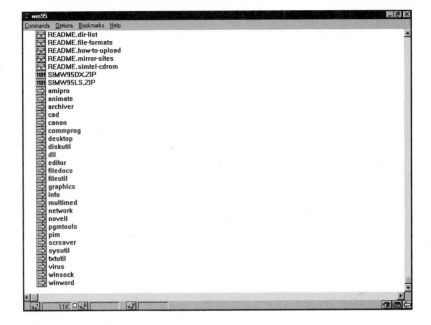

2. Using the techniques you mastered earlier, navigate to the University of Liverpool in the United Kingdom. Again, you begin with the highest level in the hierarchy, for example, Europe. Then, you move "downward" toward your goal. When you arrive, your screen should resemble that in Figure 32.9.

FIG. 32.9

The University of Liverpool server offers many types of information regarding the university, all easily accessible from the Gopher menu.

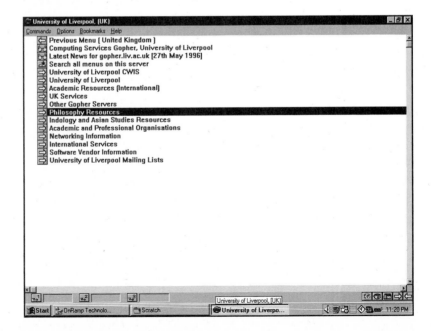

3. Select the Philosophy Resources entry with a single click.

4. Choose <u>B</u>ookmarks from the HGopher main menu. When the menu appears, choose Mark Men<u>u</u>.

5. Choose <u>B</u>ookmarks from the HGopher main menu. When the menu appears, choose Show <u>B</u>ookmarks. Your screen should now resemble that in Figure 32.10.

FIG. 32.10

You can use the Show <u>B</u>ookmarks command to jump to the current Bookmarks menu without losing your current server menu.

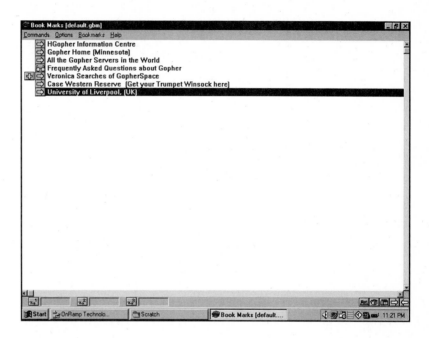

Notice that the University of Liverpool Gopher site now appears in the default bookmark list. Any page marked this way, from any server you visit, will appear there, as well. You can now return to any site on the bookmark list with two simple clicks!

It's important that you save your changes to the HGopher <u>B</u>ookmarks menu. HGopher is a very stable client program; it certainly prompts you to save changes when you exit the program. It's always best, however, to play it safe and save any changes as soon as possible. (Computers do crash unexpectedly for a wide variety of reasons; power fluctuations alone can cause much heartache among computer users.)

To save your HGopher bookmark settings, follow these steps:

1. Choose <u>B</u>ookmarks from the main HGopher menu.

2. You can update the current bookmark list. When the list drops down, choose <u>S</u>ave Bookmarks on the <u>B</u>ookmarks menu. HGopher updates the current bookmark file with your changes.

3. If you want to save a special set of bookmarks, choose Save Bookmarks <u>A</u>s. HGopher displays a standard Save As dialog box, as Figure 32.11 shows.

Part

VI

Ch

32

FIG. 32.11

Use the Save As dialog box to set up a custom Bookmarks file.

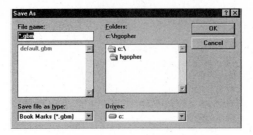

4. Enter the name you want to give the new bookmark file. You can click one of the grayed-out names in the file list. Be aware, however, that you replace that file if you answer yes when HGopher displays the message This file already exists. Do you want to replace it?

5. Choose OK to save your changes.

You can do several things from the HGopher Bookmarks menu. You can correct errors you make when adding bookmarks. You might want to start with the default bookmarks file, then delete some entries made previously. To work from the HGopher Bookmarks menu, Follow these steps:

1. Choose Bookmarks from the main HGopher menu.

2. Choose Show Bookmarks from the Bookmarks menu. HGopher then displays the current Bookmarks menu page.

3. If you want to edit a bookmarks file other than this one, choose Bookmarks from the main HGopher menu again. Then, choose Load Bookmarks. HGopher displays the standard Open dialog box. There, you can select the desired file. Otherwise, proceed to Step 4.

4. Highlight the entry you want to delete by clicking it. Then, choose Bookmarks. Next, choose Remove Bookmark from the main HGopher menu.

5. Save your changes as you learned previously.

You can also edit a bookmark listing's details to change the description and server specification. Other items that you might want to alter include the port setting and data type. To edit these and other details, follow these steps:

1. Choose Bookmarks from the main HGopher menu.

2. Choose Show Bookmarks from the Bookmarks menu. HGopher then displays the current bookmark menu page. (If you're already in this menu, go directly to Step 3.)

3. Click the entry you want to edit. Then, choose Bookmarks. Next, choose Edit Bookmark from the main HGopher menu. HGopher displays the Create/Edit Bookmark dialog box, as Figure 32.12 shows.

FIG. 32.12
Use the Create/Edit Bookmark dialog box to update or alter Bookmarks, if needed.

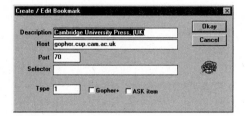

4. Edit the bookmark information, as needed. (Be sure not to alter any information with which you are unfamiliar. If you need assistance, use the HGopher Help system.)

You can also create bookmarks if you have the necessary information. Follow these steps:

1. Choose <u>B</u>ookmarks from the main HGopher menu.

2. Choose Show <u>B</u>ookmarks from the <u>B</u>ookmarks menu. HGopher then displays the current bookmark menu page. (If you're already in this menu, go directly to Step 3.)

3. Choose <u>B</u>ookmarks. Then, choose Crea<u>t</u>e Bookmark from the main HGopher menu. HGopher displays the Create/Edit Bookmark dialog box, as Figure 32.13 shows. Note that there is no information in the dialog box fields; you must provide all necessary information if you create a bookmark entry.

FIG. 32.13
HGopher lets you set up a new bookmark. However, you need to know all the specifics for the bookmark before you begin.

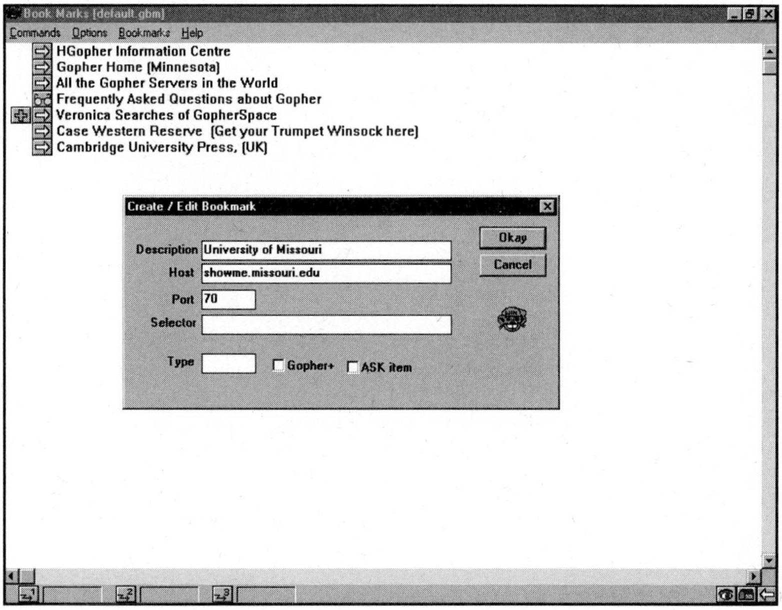

Using Other HGopher Features

Although HGopher is very easy to use, it also has other feature options that can give you a lot of control over how HGopher works. HGopher gives you tremendous control over the *page cache* (the memory and drive space used to store recently displayed pages for quick redisplay), and network setup. The language preferences, fonts, and other program variables in HGopher give the user a tremendous amount of power over the interface and operation of the program.

Resetting HGopher's Page Display Storage   HGopher gives you several levels of menu pages in normal operation. As you travel through Gopherspace, you can easily move forward and backward through the menus, without reloading them every time. The reason is that HGopher stores the menus locally for quick and easy retrieval. Although this is a great idea, it doesn't always work perfectly.

You might at some time find your page cache filled with the same menus. This means that as you click the Forward and Backward symbols at the lower right of the HGopher window you still see the same set of menus as you move. In this event, you can do a cache flush to reset the system. Follow these steps:

1. Choose Options from the main HGopher menu.
2. When the menu list drops down, choose Flush Cache.

Choosing the Copy Mode   You can choose the manner in which HGopher handles information when you retrieve it from a Gopher. Usually you simply want to browse, reading text on your display. However, what if you want the information in a file for later retrieval, distribution, or review? HGopher gives you options for each of these cases.

You can save documents to a specific file in a particular location once. Alternatively, you can tell HGopher to place all documents in a specific directory when you save them. Normally, HGopher places documents in the specified temporary directory. HGopher simply asks you to verify the file name when you save. If you change the Copy Mode setting under the Options menu by choosing Copy to Directory, HGopher lets you specify a new default directory for documents. This can be really useful if you want to save multiple documents organized by location or topic.

Altering the Default Gopher Setup Options   Although you've already performed the basic configurations to get HGopher up and running on your system, you might find that you want to alter some of these later. For example, you might want to alter the default Home Gopher site that HGopher goes to when it first loads.

To alter the default server and other options, follow these steps:

1. With HGopher running, choose Options from the HGopher main menu. Choose Gopher Set Up from the menu. The Gopher Set Up Options dialog box appears (see Fig. 32.14).

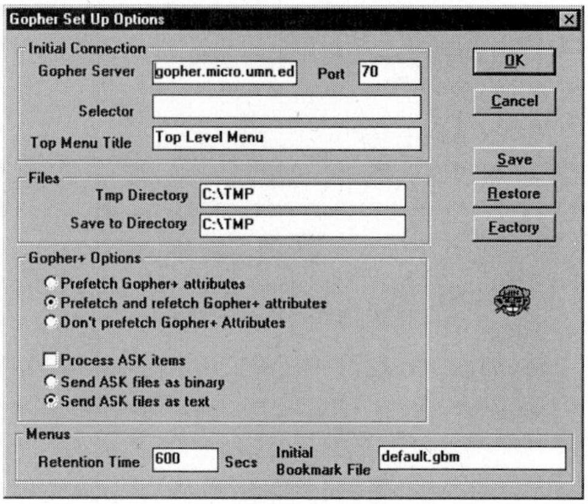

FIG. 32.14

When using the Gopher SetUp Options dialog box, be sure to confirm any information before you enter it here. Otherwise, it can affect your capability to connect to Gopher sites.

In this dialog box, you can edit any of the program defaults, as necessary. Again, don't alter any item you don't understand. You also should not enter any item for which you do not have tested alternative specifications (for more information, see HGopher Help).

Altering Network Setup Options   If you've been able to connect to Gopher sites without fail, you probably don't need to change any of the network specifications. If you find you can connect to most but not all servers and resources, you might need to enter alternative domain name server addresses to correct the problem.

Part VI Ch 32

To change the network settings, follow these steps:

1. Choose Options from the main HGopher menu. Then choose Network SetUp. The Network Setup dialog box appears, as Figure 32.15 shows.

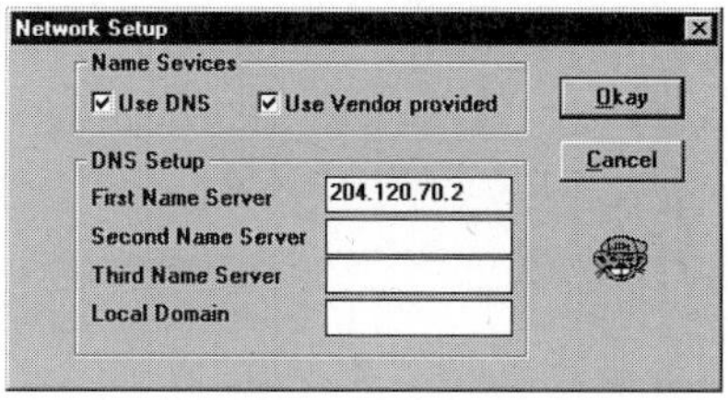

FIG. 32.15

The Network Setup dialog box enables you to specify alternate domain name servers. Be sure to confirm any information before you enter it.

2. The Use Vendor Provided check box should already be selected. If you have had no trouble finding information, don't change this. If you are experiencing trouble, proceed to Step 3.

3. If your service provider, network, or TCP/IP dialup utility doesn't provide reliable domain name search service, you can specify alternate servers. You do this by selecting the Use DNS (Domain Name Service) check box. If you do this, you must have Domain Name Server addresses that have been verified and are ready to be used. Step 4 shows you how to use them.

4. Enter the DNS address in dotted quad (numeric form) in the DNS fields. These must be entered in numeric format, for example, as 128.206.2.252, not dns.ic.ac.uk.

N O T E   Don't make any changes in the Network Setup dialog box that you don't understand, haven't tested, or have not been provided with by qualified personnel. Your computer won't burst into flames if this stuff is wrong, but you won't have much luck doing Gopher searches. ▪

5. The *Local Domain,* your computer, usually is not required; however, you need to enter the name of your local system here, if any entry is made at all. For example, if your machine address is clark.superman.na.earth, for example, you enter **superman.na.earth** in this field.

Setting Up Viewers   HGopher can display almost any type of information found on a Gopher site, as long as you have the proper helper application set up and linked to HGopher's system. For example, if you want to view JPEG-compressed files, you need a compatible viewer. You also need to tell HGopher in which place to find it.

The following includes some example of Windows applications archives:

- ▪ Lviewpro.zip (for JPEG and other images)
- ▪ Mpegv11d.zip (for MPEG movies)
- ▪ Mpegw32H.zip (for MPEG movies)
- ▪ Avipro2.exe (for Video for Windows)
- ▪ Wham131.zip (for audio files)

You can find these viewers at most popular FTP or Web sites, such as the following:

- ▪ **ftp.winsite.com**
- ▪ **gatekeeper.dec.com/pub/micro/msdos/win3/**
- ▪ **ftp.gatekeeper.dec.com/pub/micro/msdos/win3/sounds/**
- ▪ **ftp.papa.indstate.edu/winsock-l/Windows95/**
- ▪ **http://www.tucows.com/**

On the CD

You also can find these and other utilities on the NetCD CD-ROM that accompanies this book. For additional details, see the Viewers section of Appendix A, "What's on the CD." For information on setting up these viewers, see Chapter 19, "Using Helper Applications with Web Browsers."

To set up HGopher for a viewer, follow these steps:

1. Choose Options from the main HGopher menu. Then, choose Viewer SetUp. The Viewers dialog box appears, as Figure 32.16 shows.

TIP   If you don't have viewers for a data type, see the Viewers section of Appendix A. There is also information on this in Chapter 19.

FIG. 32.16

You can specify custom viewers for a wide variety of information formats in the HGopher Viewers dialog box.

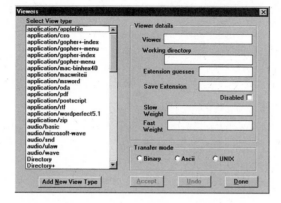

2. Select image/jpeg from the Select View Type scroll list. When you click it, the fields in the right half of the dialog box display the current settings for this data type.

3. Enter the information for your viewer utility in the fields provided. See HGopher Help for detailed information regarding the proper specifications.

> **CAUTION**
>
> Be sure to choose Accept before clicking Done to save your changes for each viewer type. The Viewers dialog box does not save all changes at exit. You should, therefore, Accept all changes for each viewer type as you go.

To test the viewer with an HGopher session, follow these steps:

1. Connect to the Internet through your server or provider.

2. After you're connected, start HGopher by clicking the HGopher icon in your Start menu program group you set up earlier (see Fig. 32.17 for an example). Alternatively, you can double-click the HGopher icon on your desktop.

3. Using the techniques you learned earlier, set up a bookmark for NASA Space Images at the host **gopher.earth.nwu.edu**. Use the selector specification **ftp:explorer.arc.nasa.bov@pub/SPACE/JPEG),** as Figure 32.18 shows.

4. Load the bookmark by selecting Show Bookmarks from the Bookmark menu. Select any of the JPEG files. Then, double-click on the ones you chose to retrieve them. The viewer decodes and displays the image when the transfer is completed.

Searching Gopherspace with Veronica

So far in this chapter, you've looked at the basics of navigating Gopherspace by using two typical Gopher programs, or clients. While this is very simple, there are other tools that you can use to speed up your navigating process. These tools also help you increase your awareness of what a vast resource the Internet can be.

FIG. 32.17
HGopher will open to the University of Minnesota Gopher menu.

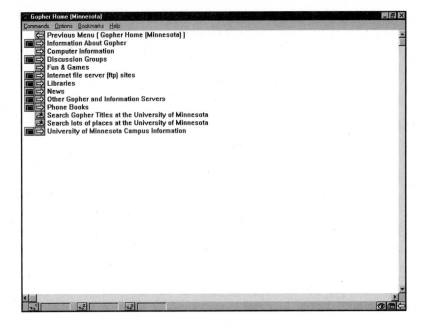

FIG. 32.18
The NASA Space Images archive contains many opportunities to test viewer support with HGopher.

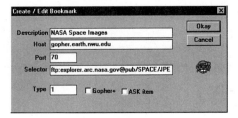

What Is Veronica?

What makes the Net so much fun to surf is that cyberspace can be a display case for humor. Some of the nicest touches are the names given different software packages and services. Who doesn't crack a smile when thinking about "using" a Gopher?

Another classic running joke on the Net is the use of puns on cartoon character names. This trend started with the use of the term "Archie" for server software that searches FTP archives. Not to be outdone, the developers of a search application for Gopherspace concocted the following gem:

Very **E**asy **R**odent-**O**riented **N**et-wide **I**ndex to **C**omputerized **A**rchives

otherwise known as *Veronica*.

Veronica is a service that keeps an index of the titles of all articles in Gopherspace. Veronica searches only for words in directory or document titles. It doesn't do a full-text search of the contents of Gopher resources. A *title* is the name of the Gopher resource, as shown by the server it's on. You can access Veronica through most Gopher clients and servers; in reality, there is no "Veronica client." The result of a Veronica search is a list of Gopher items, displayed in the form of a Gopher menu.

Many Veronica menus display a list of multiple Gopher servers offering Veronica. It theoretically shouldn't matter which server you choose. They should all provide the same information. You might, however, find one to be better than another on a specific topic. (The servers update the index periodically. The schedule, however, is different from one system to another.) You must also consider network traffic, as some servers are more popular than others.

Other Veronica systems simply offer a single menu item. They select the server for you after you enter the search specification.

Using Veronica to Search Gopherspace

If your default Gopher server doesn't offer a Veronica service, you can always fall back to the one at the University of Minnesota. It's available at **gopher.micro.umn.edu**. While the following general example uses HGopher to demonstrate a Veronica search, you can use any Gopher client to do so. Veronica is a service provided by the server, not the client.

To use Veronica with HGopher, follow these steps:

1. Connect to the Internet through your server or provider.
2. Open HGopher by clicking the HGopher icon in the Windows Start menu. Alternatively, you can double-click the HGopher icon on your desktop.
3. After HGopher opens to the University of Minnesota Gopher site page, select the Other Gopher and Information Servers item. After a few seconds, HGopher displays the menu.
4. Select the Search titles in the item named Gopherspace Using Veronica. HGopher displays the menu for that item, as Figure 32.19 shows.
5. Select one of the Search Gopherspace items. Then, double-click it. HGopher displays the Index Search dialog box, as Figure 32.20 shows.
6. Enter the search specification in the Search Strings field.
7. Choose OK. HGopher then displays the menu of items found that relate to that specification.

TIP If you get a message, such as ***Too many connections--Try again soon*** during a Veronica search, don't despair. Pick another server, or try again soon. Many servers are busy. There are certain peak traffic periods for each locality.

Tailoring Your Veronica Queries   How you construct and enter your Veronica query will make as much difference as the server you choose. When entering your queries, follow these guidelines:

■ Use multiword queries to narrow your search more quickly. Veronica supports Boolean operators, such as `and`, `not`, and `or`.

FIG. 32.19

You can select from a wide variety of search types and areas from the Veronica item menu.

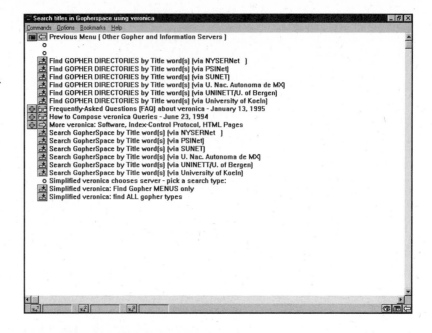

FIG. 32.20

Make your search string as specific as possible.

■ Think creatively about information. There might not be a document or directory titled *Boston Red Sox*. There might, however, be documents containing information on that team under *baseball AND losers*.

■ Use wildcards in your queries. Similar to MS-DOS, Veronica will support the asterisk (*). This support comes, however, only at the end of words.

■ Use the -t flag to narrow your searches for specific document types. The following includes Official Gopher document types, from the Gopher Protocol Document:

0	Text file
1	Directory
2	CSO name server
4	Mac HQX file
5	PC binary
7	Full text index (Gopher menu)
8	Telnet session
9	Binary file

s	Sound
e	Event (not in 2.06)
I	Image (other than GIF)
M	MIME multipart/mixed message
T	TN3270 session
c	Calendar (not in 2.06)
g	GIF image
h	HTML, HyperText Markup Language

What Is Jughead?

One type of Gopherspace directory search is named after yet another cartoon character, Archie and Veronica's friend, Jughead. Developed at the University of Utah by Rhett "Jonzy" Jones, this search tool acronym stands for the following:

Jonzy's Universal Gopher Hierarchy Excavation and Display

Jughead is similar to Veronica in that it offers a means to search Gopherspace. It differs, however, in some ways. Jughead, similar to Veronica, runs as a server on the Gopher site. Jughead also provides a prebuilt table of directory information that can be searched. Unlike Veronica, Jughead is usually implemented for a particular Gopher site. Jughead enables more complete searches of that site versus an overview of the totality of Gopherspace. Think of Veronica as a good general Gopherspace search tool. In contrast, Jughead is the tool of choice for deeper searches of a local system.

Jughead offers Boolean search specifications. This search tool also supports some special commands that you will learn about later in this section.

Searching with Jughead

A good place to start using Jughead is the University of Utah. While this example uses this specific Gopher site and Jughead server, you can use these techniques at any site that supports this server type.

To use the Jughead server at the University of Utah, follow these steps:

1. Connect to the Internet through your server or provider.

2. Open HGopher by clicking the HGopher icon in the Windows Start menu. Alternatively, you can double-click the HGopher icon on your desktop.

3. After your HGopher client opens, move to the University of Utah Gopher site, as Figure 32.21 shows.

Part
VI

Ch
32

FIG. 32.21

The University of Utah Gopher is a great place to start working with Jughead.

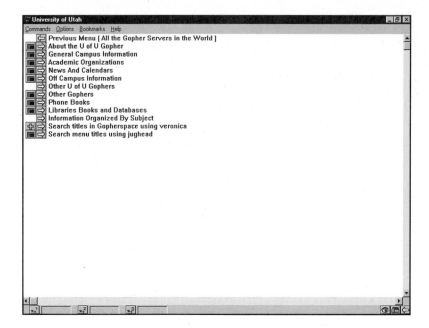

4. Select the Search Menu Titles Using Jughead item. The University of Utah server displays the Jughead menu (see fig. 32.22).

FIG. 32.22

The University of Utah Gopher Jughead menu offers local searching capabilities. It also offers references for other Jughead servers around the world.

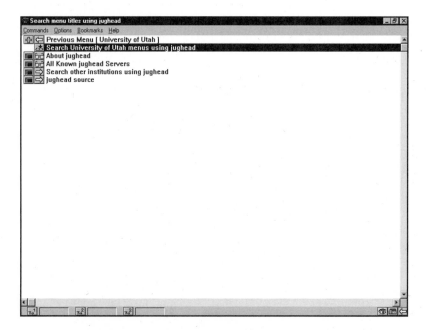

5. Select the Search University of Utah Menus Using Jughead item. The Jughead server will display the Index Search dialog box, as Figure 32.23 shows.

FIG. 32.23

The sparse appearance of the Jughead page hides the power this search tool offers.

6. Using the mouse, place the cursor in the search specification entry field. Click here once. Type your search specification in the field, as Figure 32.24 shows.

FIG. 32.24

Your search string should be as specific as possible. This will shorten the time the search takes.

7. Click Okay. Jughead will display the results of your search, as Figure 32.25 shows.

Part

VI

Ch

32

FIG. 32.25

Jughead shows the results of your search.

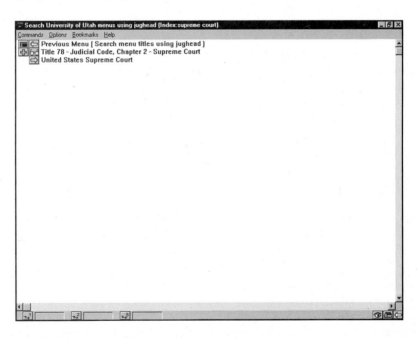

 TIP You can obtain a good list of Jughead servers from the University of Utah Jughead menu. For a great reference, select All Known Jughead Servers. Be sure to make a bookmark!

Tailoring Your Jughead Queries How you construct and enter your Jughead query makes a big difference in the level of success you achieve in your searches. When entering your queries, follow the same general guidelines for Boolean searches as outlined in the previous section about Veronica.

In addition to the common Boolean search techniques, Jughead supports some special commands. The following is the general format for these commands:

```
?command what
```

Each special Jughead command must be prefixed by the question mark. This is followed by the command, then a space. The command search string comes next. Jughead supports the following special commands:

- `?all what`—This returns all matches on search string *what*.
- `?help [what]`—This returns the help document and any optional matches for search string *what*.
- `?limit=n what`—This returns the quantity *n* items matching search string *what*.
- `?range=n1-n2 what`—This returns matches from *n1-n2* for the search string *what*.

While these special commands give you great flexibility in narrowing your searches, you can use only one special command per query. If you happen to make an error with any of these commands, Jughead returns a help document with the type of error included in the document title.

Jughead also reserves special characters for itself. When used in a query, any of the following symbols will be interpreted as a space:

```
!"#$%&'()+,-./:;?@[\]^'{|}~
```

In other words, if you enter *supreme.court*, Jughead will see it as *supreme court*. Under Boolean logic, the latter reads as *supreme AND court*. This might limit your search in ways that you cannot anticipate.

Sites of Interest: The Best of Gopher

Such an incredible variety of information is available through Gopherspace that it's difficult to recommend any specific place to start. For a very good general reference of Gopher sites, begin with the Other Gopher and Information Servers item at the University of Minnesota server. You can proceed from there. ●

CHAPTER 33

Using WAIS and Other Search Tools

by Dick Cravens

W*AIS* stands for *Wide Area Information Servers,* and is pronounced as "ways." WAIS searches for words in documents. To do a WAIS search, you supply a keyword for the information you want. The WAIS servers then search their databases for text or multimedia matches.

Suppose you want to find details about how the NAFTA agreement is affecting your industry. Use a WAIS client, and select the servers. Then, enter the keyword NAFTA, your industry, and any other words to narrow down a search. WAIS comes up with a list of documents ranked according to how many times the keywords are mentioned.

For example, you can find out how the NAFTA agreement affects the apparel industry in Mexico. You search for the keywords NAFTA, Mexico, and apparel. In response, you might get a list of documents detailing the process of the trade talks, and the agreement itself. You might also get lists of companies planning to expand trade with Mexico, and documents about US firms moving operations to this country.

You can then tell WAIS to search for more documents that are similar to the ones that you want. WAIS uses your

Search WAIS servers with WinWAIS and WAIS Manager

You'll learn how to search WAIS servers with the WAIS client programs WinWAIS and WAIS Manager.

Search WAIS servers using HGopher

You can search the WAIS servers with HGopher, too.

Learn how to search WAIS servers using e-mail

You'll learn how to send specially formatted e-mails to WAIS servers, which search for and retrieve documents.

documents as examples. It then tries to find matches based on those documents. This relevance feedback search is one of WAIS' most useful features.

WAIS goes beyond Gopher, FTP, and Archie searches. The reason is that all kinds of information can be indexed on a WAIS server. You'll find still and moving pictures, and sound files and programs, as well as documents.

WAIS was originally developed by Thinking Machines, Apple Computer, Dow Jones, and KPMG Peat Marwick. The freeware WAIS, however, is no longer supported by those companies. CNIDR (Clearinghouse for Networked Information Discovery and Retrieval) now maintains freeware WAIS.

▶ **See** "What is FTP?" **p. 808**

 A *FAQ* (frequently asked questions) list for WAIS can be retrieved using an anonymous FTP at **rtfm.mit.edu** under the directory **/pub/usenet/news.answers/wais-faq**. The document, about eight pages long, also lists some WAIS mailing lists and WAIS client software sites for most platforms.

There are different ways to conduct a WAIS search. Until the Windows-based client software was written, you had to log on to a public WAIS server and use UNIX commands. You still can log on this way, but WAIS software for Windows makes WAISing a breeze. There are also other accessible, but limited, ways to conduct a WAIS search using e-mail and Gopher. ■

Using WinWAIS

 WinWAIS was developed by the Information Systems Division of the United States Geological Survey. This is the reason that WinWAIS includes a map and the capability to use location on earth as a search criteria.

The executable file for WinWAIS is WWAIS24.EXE, available by anonymous FTP from **ridgisd.er.usgs.gov** in the directory /software/wais. You can also obtain it from **http://tucows.com**, an excellent general repository of Winsock software. Version 2.4 contains bug fixes. In the following section, the instructions for loading pertain only to this version. Previous versions need to be set up differently.

Installing WinWAIS

After you retrieve the necessary file to install WinWAIS on your system, you need only extract the program files. Then, you can run the setup program, and create the icons. To create the icons for WinWAIS in Windows 95 and NT, follow these steps:

1. To create a Start menu shortcut icon for WinWAIS, click an empty space on the Windows 95 taskbar using the right mouse button. A pop-up menu displays several items; select Properties by clicking the left mouse button.

2. The Taskbar Properties dialog box appears. Select the Start Menu Properties tab.

3. Select the Add button. The Create Shortcut dialog box appears.

4. Click Browse. Then, choose the wais.exe file from the directory you created for WinWAIS. Click the next button. The Select Program Folder dialog box then displays your group options. Pick the group in which you want the icon. Next, click the Next> button.

> **N O T E** You can also put a shortcut icon for WinWAIS on your desktop very quickly and easily. Just use Windows Explorer to open the directory in which wais.exe is located. There, click once to select it. There, click and hold down the mouse button and drag the file name to the desktop. Windows will automatically create a shortcut icon for you there. ▓

WinWAIS comes with Dialler which is a SLIP communications program. Dialler is correctly spelled this way—the programmer is Australian. You already have a SLIP or PPP dialer that comes with Windows 95. If you're using Windows 3.1, you're probably using Trumpt WinSock to connect you to the Internet. If you want to use the WinWAIS Dialler, you might want to create a Start menu or desktop shortcut icon for it, too. To create the Dialler icon, follow the same basic procedure as in the preceding note. The only difference is that you select the WAISDIAL.EXE file instead of WINWAIS.EXE. If you do choose to use the WinWAIS Dialler, be aware of its shortcomings: It won't support 28.8 modems. Also, it might be difficult to set up.

▶ **See** "Installing Dial-Up Networking Support," **p. 128**

> **N O T E** Ignore the readme.txt file. The sections in the file that deal with installation problems are inaccurate; they haven't been updated to include the latest bug fixes for WinWAIS Version 2.4. ▓

Searching for WAIS Information

After you have WinWAIS installed and set up, you can search for information. First, you have to choose which source to search. WinWAIS comes with two source options, WAIS and ALLSRC. WAIS is the Directory of Sources, a handy place to look if you don't know where to begin. ALLSRC contains hundreds of popular source sites, identified in the list by a descriptive name, such as **Whitehse.src**, a source for White House files.

To set up a search session, follow these steps:

1. With Windows running and an active Internet connection established, open WinWAIS by selecting the WinWAIS 2.4 icon in the Windows 95 Start menu. You can also open the program using the Windows 3.1 Program Manager.

2. Choose File. Then, choose Select Sources.

3. Click the Source Group list box arrow control. Choose either WAIS or ALLSRC.

4. If you choose Directory of Sources, click Done. Alternatively, you can press F3 to return to the search window.

5. If you choose ALLSRC, double-click each source in the list that you want to add. You can also choose Add All, as Figure 33.1 shows. (To remove a source, double-click it.) Click Done to return to the search window.

FIG. 33.1

You can choose the
Directory of Servers to
start your search.

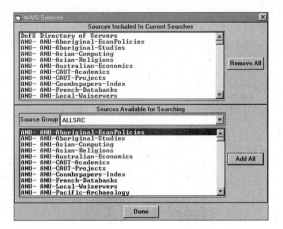

T I P   WinWAIS returns its results faster when you use fewer sources.

---

6. Type the words you want to match in the Tell Me About box.

7. Click Search. The Status line (at the bottom of the screen) should say `Querying Directory-Of-Servers`. An IP address of the server will also be on this line.

T I P   If you get a WinSock Error dialog box, it simply means that WinWAIS couldn't reach that server. If you selected multiple servers, WinWAIS will continue the search with the next server in your list. The search continues after you click the OK button in the error dialog box.

When the search is complete, the Status line will indicate the number of sources found. These will be indexed in the Resulting Documents window on the bottom half of the screen, as Figure 33.2 shows.

WAIS searches are ranked according to how many times the specified words appear in a document. The number of asterisks indicate the frequency with which your search words appear in the document; the higher the number of asterisks, the more times your search words appear in the document.

T I P   Remember, this isn't artificial intelligence. WAIS can only respond to exact word matches. The program bases a rank on the number of citations.

To retrieve a document, follow these steps:

1. Double-click an entry in the Resulting Documents window. WinWAIS will display the document as Figure 33.3 shows.

2. To return to the search window, choose <u>F</u>ile, <u>D</u>one from the main menu (or press F3).

FIG. 33.2

Be patient. It might take a few moments for WinWAIS to check all the servers you've asked it to, especially over a SLIP or PPP connection.

FIG. 33.3

When you double-click a document title, WinWAIS displays it along with complete highlights showing your search reference.

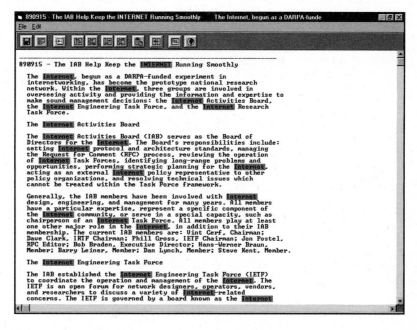

Part

VI

Ch

33

TROUBLESHOOTING

All of a sudden I can't do a search with WinWAIS. I keep getting Connect error messages. Did you add a new TCP/IP stack, or move .DLL files around? Check to make sure you're using the right version of files for the TCP/IP stack program.

Using Relevance Feedback

A WAIS search is powerful. The reason is that it can use what's referred to as *relevance feedback*. This means that it can focus on any resulting document and search for others that are similar to it.

To search using relevance feedback, follow these steps:

1. Perform a search.

2. In the Resulting Documents list, click one or more documents that are most similar to whichever ones are on your selected list.

3. Choose Add Doc. The document appears in the Similar To box as Figure 33.4 shows. Choose Delete Doc to delete it from the same box.

FIG. 33.4

You can perform a relevance feedback search with WinWAIS.

4. Click the Search button (a globe icon) to search for more documents.

Saving Information to the Clipboard

To copy the search information to the Clipboard, follow these steps:

1. Click at the beginning of the text that you want to copy. Then, drag the mouse to the end of the selected text. Next, you can release the button.

2. Open the Edit menu. Then, choose Copy. Alternatively, you can press Shift+F6. You can also click the Clipboard icon.

3. Open Windows Notepad. Then, choose Paste to copy the Clipboard information.

What the WAIS Finds Tell You

WAIS supplies you with a document that tells you details about what information is available at a particular source, and how to obtain it. In many cases, you can get the document itself. Some sites, however, are available only through another retrieval method, such as FTP. The retrieved document will indicate this.

For example, if you query the Directory of Servers for the OSHA Technical Manual, WAIS initially comes up with 46 documents. Double-clicking the OSHA Technical Manual entry retrieves information about the documents. This isn't the document itself, though. It contains information that tells you where to get the document. To retrieve it, you need to use a different tool.

▶ **See** "Using FTP and Popular FTP Programs," **p. 807**

▶ **See** "Searching for Information on the Internet," **p. 871**

TROUBLESHOOTING

The only source I can access is the Directory of Servers. What happened to the other sources?
Make sure the file Allsrc.src is in your WinWAIS directory. If not, copy Allsrc.src from the unzipped file. If you already deleted the unzipped files, retrieve WinWAIS again. Then, put it in a temporary directory, and unzip it. Now, you can copy Allsrc.src to your WinWAIS directory.

Part
VI

Ch
33

Using WAIS Manager 3.1

Overall, WAIS Manager is easier to use than WinWAIS, although neither is very difficult. Earlier versions of WinWAIS were riddled with setup bugs. These problems, however, have been rectified. Now, you need to go through a few more steps to install WAIS Manager.

The simplest way to obtain the latest version of WAIS Manager is to visit the Ultimate Collection of Winsock Software at **http://www.tucows.com/softwais.html** using your favorite Web browser.

Installing WAIS Manager 3.1

You might find it a little difficult to set up WAIS Manager 3.1. The reason is that it was written with a utility known as Toolbook. To unzip and install WAIS Manager 3.1, follow these steps:

1. Extract WAISMAN3.ZIP to a new directory. (You might, for example, want to call it \WAISMAN.) The program will create two directories, \WAISMAN3 and \WAIS_SRC. The file programs are in \WAISMAN3, and the sources are in \WAIS_SRC.

2. To create an icon for WinWAIS, click an empty space on the Windows 95 or NT Taskbar using the right mouse button. A pop-up menu displays several items; select Properties by clicking the left mouse button.

3. The Taskbar Properties dialog box appears. Select the Start Menu Properties tab.

4. Select the Add button. The Create Shortcut dialog box appears.

5. Click Browse. Then, choose the WAISMAN3.TBK file from the directory you created for WAISMAN. Click the Next> button, and the Select Program Folder dialog box displays your group options. Pick the group in which you want to put the icon. Then, click the Next> button.

 TIP Neither Windows 95 nor NT has a file association for .TBK Toolbook files by default. Use Windows Explorer's File Types dialog to set up support for Toolbook applications.

Searching with WAIS Manager 3.1

Although this section comes after the instructions on WinWAIS, perhaps you haven't previously done a WAIS search. If you choose the WAIS Manager 3.1 as your client, you need to know how to do a search.

You first need to define your search terms. WAIS Manager 3.1 is so friendly it even comes with a list of searches. This gives you an idea of what kind of information is available.

To use a predefined search, follow these steps:

1. Using the Windows 95 or NT Start menu button, locate the icon you created for the WAIS Manager. Click the icon to launch the program.

2. Choose Query, Select Query to get the list that Figure 33.5 shows. Alternatively, you can press the large yellow question mark icon.

3. Double-click a query. You will go back to the main menu. The appropriate source will be listed in the Database section. Also, some keywords will be listed under Keywords.

4. If the keywords aren't what you were looking for, you can change them. Alternatively, you can go back and select another query.

5. Specify a maximum number of documents for which WAIS Manager should search.

6. Open the Search menu. Then, choose Search Selection. Alternatively, you can press the icon showing a magnifying glass above a stack of papers.

FIG. 33.5

You can choose a stored query with WAIS Manager 3.1.

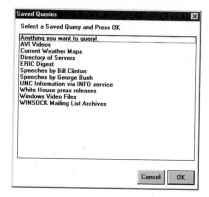

7. WAIS Manager returns a list of possible documents that might fit your search criteria. To retrieve a document, double-click the entry. WAIS Manager displays the document in WordPad.

8. To save the document, choose File, Save As. Then, specify a name.

To create your own search terms, follow these steps:

1. Using the Windows 95 or NT Start menu button, locate the icon you created for WAIS Manager. Click the icon to launch the program.

2. Choose Query, Select Query. Alternatively, you can press the large yellow question mark icon to get a list of sources.

3. Choose one or more sources.

4. Click OK.

5. Choose Keywords. Remember, however, that this is more of a natural language search, not a Boolean search.

6. Choose a maximum number of documents that you want retrieved. The higher the number, the longer the search takes.

7. Open the Search menu. Then, choose Search Selection. Alternatively, you can press the icon displaying a magnifying glass over a globe.

8. WAIS Manager returns a list of possible documents that might fit your search criteria. To retrieve a document, double-click the entry.

TROUBLESHOOTING

No matter what I do, I can't conduct a search. What's the problem? The name server might be down. This means that no one can get through. Perhaps the source server is down. Try FTPing or pinging the server to see whether it is down. If you get no response, it's probably not your fault. You'll probably have to wait until the system is running again.

Part

VI

Ch

33

Using Relevance Feedback

When you use relevance feedback, you show WAIS the kind of documents for which you are searching. WAIS then attempts to get more. To use relevance feedback, conduct a search according to the preceding guidelines. Then, follow these steps:

1. Click the document you want to use as a model for other documents.

2. Click the icon showing a magnifying glass over two connected documents.

You can continue this way for a long time, either narrowing your original search, or getting further away from it—whatever suits your need.

Saving WAIS Information

After you find related documents, you can save the information, and perhaps print it. You can also return to the search results by using one of the following:

- Open the File menu. Then, choose Save As to save the information to a disk file.
- Open the File menu. Then, choose Print. This prints the file.
- Open the File menu. Then, choose Done. Alternatively, you can press F3 to return to the search results menu.

Saving Queries for Future Use

You can save queries that you plan on using again. To save queries, do the following:

1. Choose the Keywords and a source.

2. Open the File menu. Then, choose Save Queries. The query is saved under the keywords. A query to find "Degas paintings," for example, is listed under "Degas paintings" in the saved query list.

The query will be there the next time you look in the list of saved queries.

Using Viewers

WAIS Manager can retrieve nearly any kind of files. However, it needs viewers to show them to you. To see these files, you need to have the program WAIS Manager assigns to a file type. To change assignments, follow these steps:

1. Open the Options menu. Then, choose Default Viewers.

2. Click a type of file to see with what program WAIS Manager can view it. First, you choose WAIS Type. Then, you choose Delete WAIS Type to delete a format. If you want to change the program, choose Edit WAIS Type. Choosing New WAIS Type lets you add a file format.

3. Click OK.

4. Click the entry you just created.

5. Click the View With box. Next, type the name of the viewer file.

6. Choose OK.

WAIS Searches with E-Mail

You also can search WAIS servers with an e-mail request. The advantage of this is that once you've made the request, you can let the software do the work for you. The disadvantage is that the process takes longer. You also can't do relevance feedback.

To do a search with an e-mail request, you can use your regular mail client program. To e-mail a search to WAIS space, you must follow these steps:

- Address the mail to **waismail@quake.think.com**.

- Format the request in exactly the following way, substituting the words in italics with your own parameters:

  search *sourcename keywords*

  The source name is the database you want to search; you are looking for the keywords (see Fig. 33.6).

FIG. 33.6

You can perform a WAIS search with e-mail.

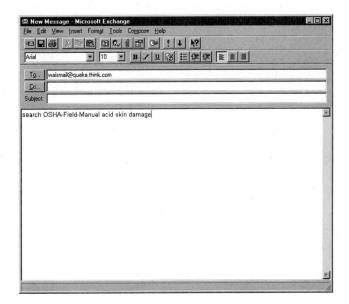

When you get the results, you can choose which documents to retrieve. Again, address e-mail to **waismail@quake.think.com**. Type the word **retrieve,** followed by the DocID (the identification of a document in the search results).

Part

VI

Ch

33

TROUBLESHOOTING

The WAIS Manager sometimes gets hung up on `Retrieving Document from Remote Server,` **for long periods of time. What does this mean?** It can mean that the server is down, and the program won't give up trying to get to it. Alternatively, it can mean the application has quit. Press Ctrl+Alt+Del (all three keys simultaneously) once to see whether you get a message indicating that the application has stopped responding to the system. This will bring up the Close Program dialog box, the user interface for the Windows 95 task manager. Do not press Ctrl+Alt+Del again, or Windows 95 will reboot the computer. If this happens, you'll lose any unsaved work. The Close Program dialog box offers you several choices. You can end the hung task, or shut down. Alternatively, you can cancel, or use Ctrl+Alt+Del to reboot. This is not always the safest choice. At times, however, it's the only way to free up the system.

CHAPTER 34

Searching for Information on the Internet

by Jerry Honeycutt and Dick Cravens

The best way to learn how to search for information on the Internet is to forget what you know about searching for information. There's information, and lots of it. There are software programs, graphics, magazine articles, job postings, government reports, weather maps, and thousands and thousands of documents. The hardest part about searching on the Internet is understanding that the chicken came before the egg, so to speak. That is, the information existed before the programs to find the information did.

Unlike commercial databases, no one planned how everyone was going to access the information. And before the advent of very fast, 486- and Pentium-based PCs, most people didn't have enough raw power to operate more than a bare-bones search tool like Archie or Telnet.

Now, with the World Wide Web, you can apply the easy-to-use browser interface to the task of searching the Net. There is a wide variety of Web sites that specialize in helping you find your way in the maze of Internet information.

▶ **See** "Locating Files," **p. 810**

Learn what you can find

The Internet contains many different kinds of information. In this chapter, you'll learn about what you can find.

Get to know the tools of the trade

The Internet has all sorts of tools to help you find what you're looking for.

Choose the right tool for the job

How do you know which tool to use for which type of search? This chapter shows you how to make that decision.

See sample searches in action

This chapter shows you some samples so that you'll better understand how the search tools work.

Available Information

There is probably every kind of information you can want floating around somewhere on the Internet. If it exists in a computer somewhere, you probably can get to it through the Internet.

Not that you should be able to get anything that exists (some things should remain private—corporate strategy, for example). Internet security will become a bigger issue in the next few years as more people become adept at searching for and retrieving information.

Because you're at the beginning of an Internet information revolution, it's not always easy to find what you want—or even to know how to find it.

While most information is still free on the Internet, commercial services are popping up with "pay for" information. In this chapter, you're going to look at free information (because once somebody wants to sell you something, they will make sure you know how to find them). You'll begin with the simple and go on to the sublime (in Internet terms, anyway).

What Are Search Engines?

The Internet is such a large conglomerate of systems and resources that any attempt to create a comprehensive catalog is doomed to failure. The rate of growth of information currently exceeds any technology's ability to keep pace. Fortunately, the World Wide Web, as a subset of the total Internet, is a bit more manageable in this respect.

The HTTP protocol that drives Webspace offers tools that allow the design of automated search and indexing *engines*, programs that gather data and present it to the Web user in a searchable format. There are several examples of this type of utility on the Web. These programs run on server systems as separate tasks from other server types, perhaps sharing processor resources with the other servers (HTTP, FTP, etc.) in use at that site. Several of the engines have developed from information management research projects in the graduate departments of major universities and have rather beefy hardware to support them; some of these have been developed even further as commercial entities.

Web search engines provide many valuable services:

- Automated search of Webspace for new sites
- Indexing of available sites by URL
- Indexing of site by page titles, text content, quality of content, and "freshness" of content

Early examples of search engines restricted themselves to simple indexes of Web sites by URL and home page title. However, most Web search engines now extend their reach beyond Webspace into UseNet News archives, WAIS, Gopher sites, and even Telnet resources. As the commercialization of Web search engines continues, expect to see not only indexing of content itself but reviews and commentary regarding the indexed sites and material. Competition in this niche service area will only benefit the Web user with a more rich and robust set of tools for research and recreation.

N O T E   Don't mistake a site that simply lists new or interesting sites as a true search engine. The "Pick of the Day" type of site is fun and even useful but rarely has any real software muscle behind it for true searching. ▇

Popular Web Search Engines

Some of the older, venerable Web search sites are still available, and some have been transformed into totally commercial entities (you may even see a spot of advertising here and there, helping pay for some of the processor horsepower needed to keep the indexes current). Table 34.1 lists some of the most popular sites presently available at press time (be aware that the Web changes daily, so don't be surprised if a site moves or disappears altogether).

Table 34.1   Popular Web Sites

Site	Address
555-1212.Com Business Search	**http://www.555-1212.com**
Aliweb	**http://web.nexor.co.uk/public/aliweb/aliweb.html**
City Net	**http://www.city.net/**
Commercial Advertising Server	**http://www.comcomsystems.com/**
CUI World Wide Web Catalog	**http://cuiwww.unige.ch/cgi-bin/w3catalog**
EINet Galaxy	**http://www.einet.net/**
Excite NetSearch	**http://www.excite.com**
Harvest Search	**http://harvest.cs.colorado.edu/harvest/demobrokers.html**
HTML555-1212.Com Area Code Search	**http://www.555-1212.com/ACLOOKUP**
IBM InfoMarket	**http://www.infomkt.ibm.com**
Infoseek	**http://www2.infoseek.com**
Inktomi's Search Engine	**http://inktomi.berkeley.edu/query.html**
Lycos Search	**http://www.lycos.com**
Maple Square-Canada	**http://www.canadas.net/Maple-Square/**
New Riders Yellow Pages	**http://www.mcp.com/nrp/wwwyp**
Nikos Search	**http://www.rns.com/nikos/nikos.html**
Open Market	**http://www.directory.net/**
Open Text Search	**http://www.opentext.com**

Part
VI

Ch
34

continues

Table 34.1 Continued

Site	Address
PointCom Reviews	http://www.pointcom.com/
Power Link Search	http://www.powerlink.com/
Savvy Search	http://rampal.cs.colostate.edu:2000
Tribal Voice Search	http://www.tribal.com
UK WWW Catalogue	http://www.scit.wlv.ac.uk/wwlib
Virtual Yellow Pages	http://www.vyp.com
W3C	http://www.w3.org/
Wandex	http://www.netgen.com/cgi/wandex
WebCrawler Search	http://www.webcrawler.com
What's New Too	http://newtoo.manifest.com
WWW Virtual Library	http://www.w3.org/hypertext/DataSources/bySubject/Overview.html
Yahoo Search	http://www.yahoo.com
Yellow Pages	http://www.yellow.com

That's enough references to provide an idea of the richness and variety of sites available and even to keep you busy for a few minutes, at least. If you want to cut through the crowd and get down to the best of the best, check out the next three sections and see what the most popular engines on the Net have to offer.

Using Lycos

The Lycos search engine was first developed at Carnegie Mellon University and later commercialized by a company incorporated as Lycos Inc. for licensing to other institutions and commercial concerns. The Lycos catalog contains over 10 million pages of Internet content that is available for your perusal (Lycos Inc. claims that this accounts for over 91 percent of the Web).

To use the Lycos catalog:

1. With Windows running and your Internet connection established, open your Web browser (we'll use Microsoft Internet Explorer for this example).

2. Enter **http://www.lycos.com** into your browser's address line to activate the page request. Your browser will display the Lycos home page (see Fig. 34.1).

3. Click once in the Search the Web For: field near the top of the Lycos page. Enter the term you want to search for—for example, **virtual reality** (see Fig. 34.2).

FIG. 34.1

Lycos offers many tools in addition to straight search capabilities.

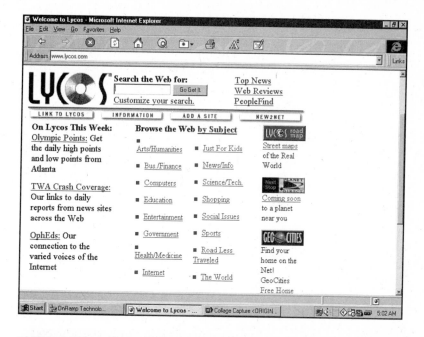

FIG. 34.2

Type your query text and click the Go Get It button to start.

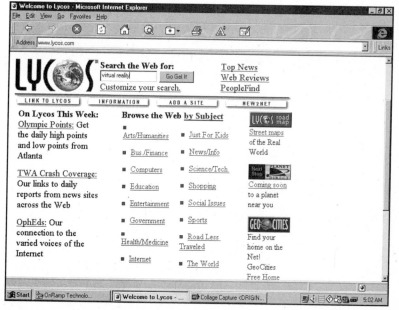

4. Click the Go Get It button, and Lycos will process your search. Note that the URL in the browser's Address field will have changed to reflect your query as well. Don't be surprised if the search takes several seconds (or even minutes), because the Lycos site

is very, very popular. When the search is completed, Lycos will return a page similar to the one shown in Figure 34.3.

FIG. 34.3
Lycos will return a search results page that contains statistical information regarding your query.

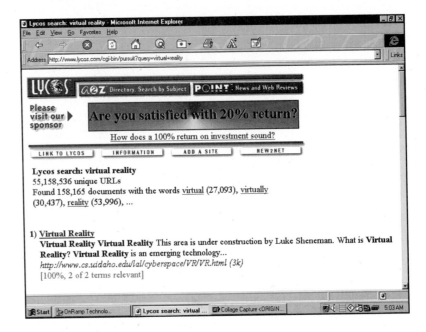

5. This is all fine and dandy, but where's the data? You'll need to page or scroll down to see the actual search results. The Lycos engine will display only the first 10 documents that match your search criteria. Each entry is formatted with a main reference title (actually, a live anchor to the site) and an excerpt from the document. You may want to go directly to the site from this page or simply add the URL to your hotlist directly from here for later reference (see Fig. 34.4).

Beyond such powerful yet rudimentary searches, Lycos offers other rich resources. Lycos provides an index, for example, as shown in Figure 34.5. This appears mid-page on the Lycos home page, but with some systems you may have to scroll down to view it. The index allows you to peruse the catalog by broad topic with greater speed, because the topic areas are pre-indexed.

You can also take advantage of a variety of tools to fine-tune your searches on Lycos. There's a search form that gives you more complete control over the database engine using a simple HTML form that you fill out on-screen. To access the form, simply click the Customize your search link on the Lycos home page. Lycos displays the Lycos search form (see Fig. 34.6).

There are also links that provide help on the Lycos search language and assistance with the Formless interface (a simpler interface for searching).

FIG. 34.4
Many browsers will let you add a link to your hotlist directly from the cursor position. For example, a right-mouse click in Internet Explorer displays a menu for adding to the Favorites list.

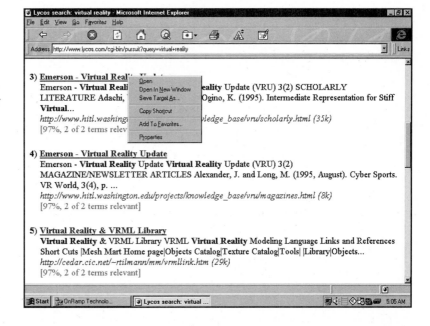

FIG. 34.5
You may have to scroll to view all of the features of the Lycos home page, depending upon the resolution and size of your monitor.

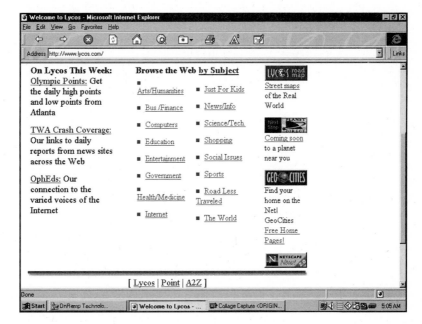

Part
VI

Ch

34

FIG. 34.6

The Lycos search form gives you control over how tight a search to perform and how you want the results displayed.

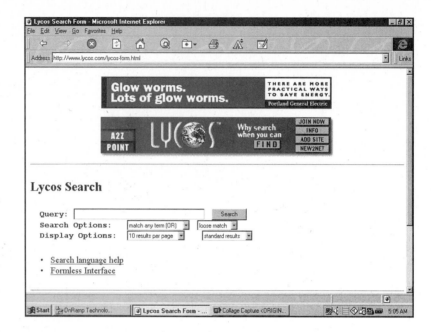

Using WebCrawler

Another search engine is the WebCrawler, now owned by America Online. WebCrawler's a bit flashier than some other sites, but it still delivers a decent search. To use WebCrawler:

1. With Windows running and your Internet connection established, open your Web browser (we'll use Microsoft Internet Explorer again).

2. Enter **http://www.webcrawler.com** into your browser's address line to activate the page request. Your browser will display the WebCrawler home page (see Fig. 34.7).

3. Click once in the field near the top of the WebCrawler page. Enter the term you want to search for. Click the Search button, and WebCrawler processes your search. When it's finished, it displays a list similar to the one shown in Figure 34.8.

4. Since WebCrawler isn't formatting text for each entry, it tends to be pretty fast. You'll also get 25 entries on your first page, with a button at the bottom of the page to return the next 25 (see Fig. 34.9). Don't click the button unless you mean it, because you won't be able to use the Back button in your browser to re-create the first 25 list. (Because the server sees a "next 25" request at this location as updating the same page, moving back will take you back to the initial query page.)

5. Click any link to travel to the page or site referenced.

While WebCrawler attempts to deliver page references in a prioritized list, you may need to adjust your search criteria slightly to narrow your search to get what you need or to add another criteria point (for example, instead of *virtual reality,* try a search on *virtual reality browser*). To do this, return to the main WebCrawler home page and adjust the search criteria as needed, using the controls in the home page form (see Fig. 34.10).

FIG. 34.7
WebCrawler has a very straightforward form interface.

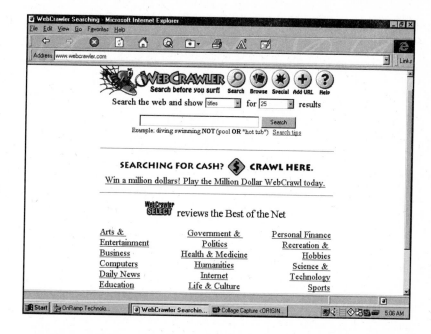

FIG. 34.8
WebCrawler reports results in a straight list format.

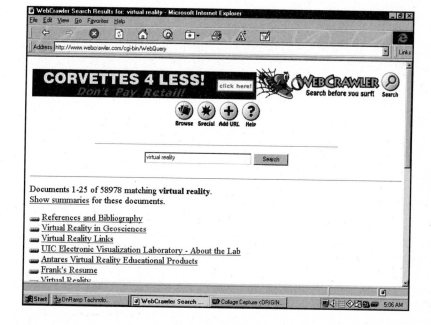

FIG. 34.9
Twenty-five responses
not enough?
WebCrawler has more
ready to go.

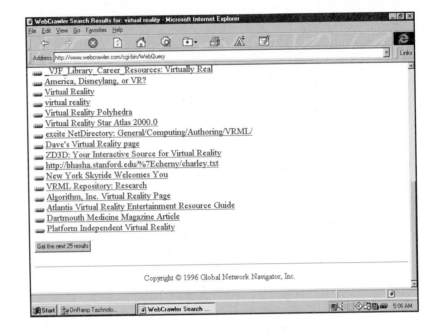

FIG. 34.10
WebCrawler exposes its
search controls on the
main home page,
making it simpler to
refine your search.

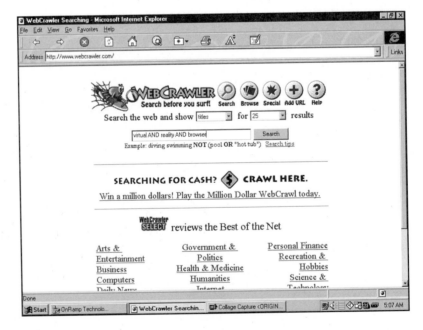

Using Yahoo!

Another great Web search resource is Yahoo!, originally created by David Filo and Jerry Yang while still students in the electrical engineering program at Stanford University. Netscape Communications made this site famous by including a reference to it in the Netscape browser. Simply clicking the Net Search button brought up the Yahoo! home page search form (later versions of Netscape include several other search links as well). It's estimated that over 200,000 users per day visit Yahoo!, totaling over two million search requests per day. The San Jose *Mercury News* has compared Yahoo! to "Linnaeus, the 18th century botanist whose classification system organized the natural world."

Yahoo! is actually a catalog of Internet sites, which Yahoo! gets from users who submit URLs. When you search Yahoo!, you search this catalog. Contrast this to Lycos, which actually scours the Internet and catalogs what it finds. You'll get more hits from Lycos, because it catalogs everything on the Internet. You might get better quality hits from Yahoo!, however, because it depends on user contributions.

To perform a search using Yahoo!, follow these steps:

1. With Windows running and your Internet connection established, open your Web browser.

2. Enter **http://www.yahoo.com** into your browser's address line to activate the page request. Your browser displays the Yahoo! home page (see Fig. 34.11).

FIG. 34.11
Yahoo! offers a clean, well-designed home page with many broad topics organized for rapid display.

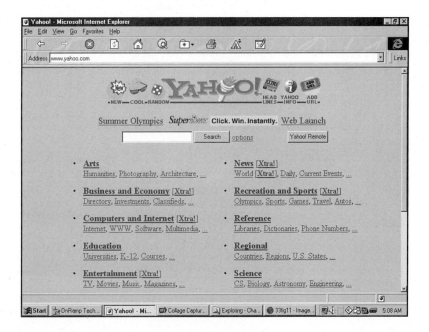

Part
VI

Ch
34

3. Click once in the field near the top of the page. Enter the term you want to search for—for example, **internet phone**. Click the Search button to start your search. Yahoo! returns the results (see Fig. 34.12).

FIG. 34.12
Yahoo! reports your search results, complete with statistics and information about what classification areas your search results were drawn from.

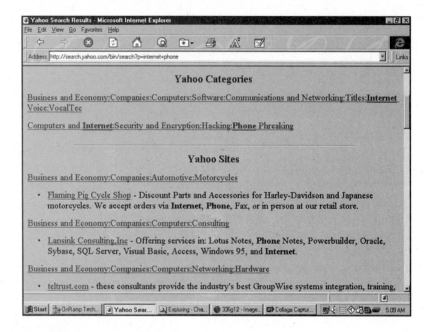

Note that Yahoo! displays a header link for each search hit in addition to the reference itself. This allows you to jump to related information that doesn't necessarily tightly match your search criteria. Sometimes it's useful to have a broader context in which to consider your research—that's part of the charm of the Web that the staff of Yahoo! obviously respects and works to preserve—without letting it interfere with the business of finding specific information.

Yahoo! has added yet another nice touch with the inclusion of the Reuters News Service to the search engine. From the main Yahoo! page, you can directly access the news service with a single click, resulting in the main news page (see Fig. 34.13).

In addition to the Reuters link at the top of the page, many of the main categories on the Yahoo! home page may have the word *Xtra!* in the title link to that area. This indicates additional Reuters news headlines organized by category, available directly from these links.

All the Web's Search Tools

You won't be able to pick a single tool and stick with it for all your searches. You'll need to try your search on one tool, and if you don't get the results you want, go on to another. The following table points you to some of the other search tools you find on the Web.

Tool	URL	Description
Alta Vista	**http://www.altavista.digital.com/**	Indexes the Web and UseNet
Excite	**http://www.excite.com/**	Indexes the Web UseNet; also provides a good catalog with reviews of sites
HotBot	**http://www.hotbot.com/index.html**	Indexes the Web
InfoSeek	**http://www2.infoseek.com/**	Indexes the Web and UseNet; also provides a good catalog
Lycos	**http://www.lycos.com/**	Indexes the Web; provides a small catalog, too
WebCrawler	**http://www.webcrawler.com/**	Indexes the Web; provides a small catalog, too
WWWW	**http://wwww.cs.colorado.edu/wwww**	Indexes the Web
Yahoo	**http://www.yahoo.com/**	Indexes the Web and UseNet; provides an excellent catalog; automatically invokes Alta Vista and DejaVu

FIG. 34.13
Yahoo! offers a rich headline service in addition to the traditional search engine.

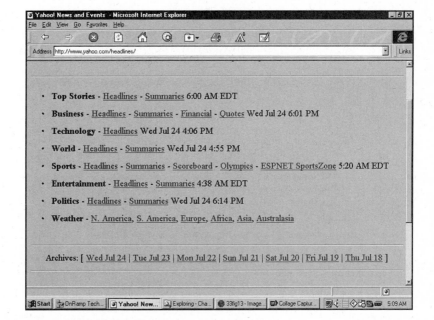

Part
VI

Ch
34

Gathering Information with Telnet

The Internet is a vast ocean of information. What if you're not sure exactly what information exists, but you're certain of the subject you want to find?

Literally hundreds of government agencies, corporations, and universities maintain Telnet sites crammed with current information like magazine articles, consumer warnings, and advisories. Telnet won't search for subjects or anything else, but it's a good way to retrieve files. One of the easiest things you can do on the Internet is telnet to a remote site and tap its resources.

A Telnet program comes with Windows 95 and is very simple to use. It's limited, but sometimes that can be good. When you use Telnet, you know where you're going, even if you don't know what you're going to find. Telneting takes you to a specific place and lets you explore that place only.

You can get a listing of Telnet sites from books and from Internet discussion groups on several of the commercial online services.

Suppose you want to read the Food and Drug Administration's monthly magazine, *FDA Consumer,* but don't feel like going to a major library. You wonder, does the FDA keep a BBS where I can read the magazine online?

You bet it does, and you bet you can. You can find out from an Internet resource listing that the address is **fdabbs.fda.gov** and the login is **bbs** (the password is **bbs**, also). That's all you need to know.

N O T E   Rules and procedures will differ from one Telnet system to another, from host to host. Please expect some differences in procedures as you explore different systems. ■

N O T E   The InterNIC Directory maintains lists of freely available information resources, products, and services. To access InterNIC, use a Gopher client and choose these directories successively:

InterNIC: Internet Network Information Center

Information About the InterNIC

InterNIC Directory and Database Servers

Information About the Directory of Directories or Information on Accessing Our Services ■

Using the Windows 95 Telnet program, log in and register as a new user. Follow the system prompts to get to the Topics list shown in Figure 34.14.

The topic "Consumers" contains the FDA Consumer magazine index and selected articles.

FIG. 34.14

The FDA's BBS is accessible by Telnet.

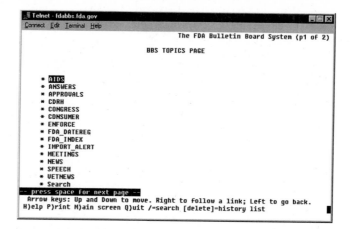

FIG. 34.15

The Lynx help menu in the FDA BBS tells you how to get around.

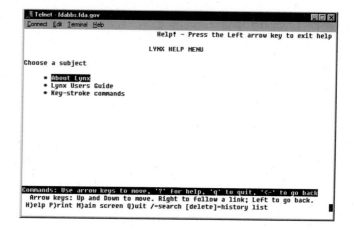

Type **?** to get a listing of commands (see Fig. 34.15).

You'll notice that the FDA BBS is set up using the Lynx interface, a character-only version of an HTTP server—an alternative way to access World Wide Web documents for those without a Web browser (or the equipment to run one). This means you have access to the FDA Web site via Telnet. The only thing you're missing is the graphics; in fact, you're gaining tremendous speed by not having to download them.

Follow the menus at the bottom of the screen for further navigation instructions.

That's all there is to Telneting. Once you know a site you are interested in, come back month after month (or whenever). Telnet isn't fancy, but it's a lot easier than trying to find out where else on the Internet there is an article about new FDA labeling.

Using WSArchie

WSArchie is an Archie client. It enables you to do searches on registered anonymous FTP sites using a simple form to fill in the information you want to search for. The host address and directory paths of the files that are found are returned to you.

Archie

Archie, a derivative of *archive,* lets you search for file names that are stored at public sites. You don't need to know the exact name, just a part of the name.

Archie was the first of the information-retrieval systems developed on the Internet. The purpose of Archie is simple—to create a central index of files available on anonymous FTP sites around the Internet. To do so, the Archie servers connect to anonymous FTP sites that agree to participate and download lists of all the files on these sites. These lists of files are merged into a database, which users can then search.

You can access the Archie databases in several different ways. (For ease of access on the Internet, several different sites have Archie databases; they all contain the same information.) If your host has an Archie client (WSArchie, a Windows-based Archie client, is further discussed later in this chapter), it makes the database search simple. If your host does not have an Archie client, you can use the Telnet program to connect to one of the Archie machines and search the database there. You can also do an Archie search by e-mail, although this can be a little time-consuming. Send e-mail to **archie@archie.internic.net** with the word *help* in the message body for instructions on how to do an e-mail Archie search.

When you have connected to one of the Archie database machines (through a client program or through Telnet), you can search the database for a program or file. Because the database knows only about the names of the files, you must know at least part of the file name you are looking for. For example, if you are looking for a program that *compresses* files (makes them smaller), you can search the database for the word *compress.* You can tell the Archie program to return the location of all the files named *compress,* or that have *compress* as part of their name, by specifying either an exact match or substring search. You can also specify whether the case of the file names has to match the case of your search string.

The Archie server returns to you the machine name and location of the files that match the string you are searching for (if any). This allows you to use the FTP program to connect to the machine and download the file to your local machine. The main limitation of Archie is that you must know at least something about the name of the file to search for it; if you don't have any idea what the file is called (for example, you want a program that searches for viruses on your machine and don't know that it is called scanv), you may have to try several searches using different strings before you find something that looks useful.

> **N O T E** Running an Archie search is a bit like using a spell checker or doing a find-and-replace in your word processor. Bear in mind that the search server programs can work only with what you give them and will try for as exact a match as possible—so be sure to spell carefully. ▪

Another limitation of Archie is that not all sites on the Internet that have anonymous FTP participate in the Archie database. So if there is a file that you would be interested in, but it is at a site that does not participate in the Archie database, you would not be able to find that file with Archie. Even given these limitations, Archie is a very useful tool for locating files for downloading through FTP.

On the CD

The WSArchie program can be found on the NetCD accompanying this book. You can install WSArchie by running the NetCD installation as described in Appendix A, "What's on the CD."

If you can't use the CD to load WSArchie, or you want to check to see if a newer version exists, you can use FTP to get the WSArchie ZIP file (currently, WSARCH08.ZIP) from **ftp.winsite.com** in the directory **/pub/pc/win3/winsock**.

N O T E   If you download WSArchie instead of using it from NetCD, you must unzip the files to the directory of your choice. ▪

Setting Up WSArchie to Work with WS_FTP

WSArchie uses the Internet Archie service to search for files at anonymous FTP sites. If you have WS_FTP installed on your system, you can retrieve the files found directly from WSArchie. First, you must tell WSArchie where to find the WS_FTP program and what parameters it should use. To set up the FTP parameters, follow these steps:

1. Start the WSArchie application. Choose Options, FTP Setup. You see the FTP Setup dialog box shown in Figure 34.16.

FIG. 34.16

You can set up WSArchie to automatically retrieve files resulting from your search using WS_FTP.

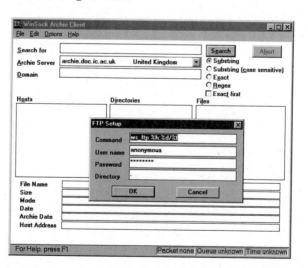

2. Click in the text box next to Command and enter the complete path to the WS_FTP file on your hard disk. Do not delete the `ws_ftp %h:%d/%f`; simply add the path information to the front of it.

3. Click in the text box next to User Name and enter the name of the account you are going to log into. This will default to "anonymous," and you should not change it unless you have a personal account you can log into.

4. Click in the text box next to Password and enter the password you will use to log into the account. Many anonymous accounts allow you to log in with any password; however, many ask that you use your e-mail address, and some require it, so you should enter your Internet e-mail address here (your password will not be displayed on the screen).

5. Click in the box next to Directory and enter the path to the directory where you want the retrieved file to be placed.

6. Choose OK to complete the setup.

Doing a Search

When you want to use WSArchie to look for a file at an anonymous FTP site, the first thing you must do is establish your connection to the Internet (if your host is not permanently connected to the Internet). To use WSArchie to do an Archie search, follow these steps:

1. Double-click the WSArchie icon to open the WinSock Archie Client window (see Fig. 34.17).

FIG. 34.17

Don't be intimidated by all the text fields in the WSArchie interface. It's really quite simple to use.

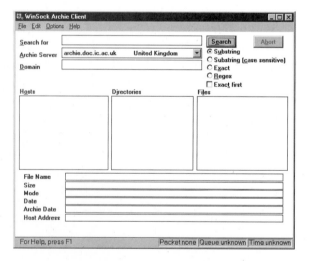

2. Click the radio button next to the type of search you want to do. The following table describes the different types of searches. If you check the Exact First box, WSArchie tries to perform an Exact search first. If it doesn't find a match, it does the search specified by the radio button.

Search Type	Description
Substring	WSArchie returns any files it finds whose names contain the search string (upper- and lowercase letters are ignored).
Substring [case sensitive]	WSArchie returns any files it finds whose names contain the search string with the case of the letters matching exactly.
Exact	WSArchie returns any files it finds whose names exactly match the search string that was entered (including case).
Regex	WSArchie returns any files it finds that match the regular expression specified.

N O T E   A *regular expression* is a way of specifying the possible values for a search string without specifying the exact letters. For each letter position, you can specify ranges of letters to find, ranges of letters to exclude (precede the letters with ^), any number of occurrences of a specific character (follow the character by a *), or any number of characters to ignore (use .*). For example, [0-9] would match any number; [^a-zA-Z] would match any non-letter; [0-9]* would match any number of numbers; win.*[0-9] would match any file name that started with *win* and ended in a digit, with any number of other characters in between. If you want to search for a special character (like a period), you can precede it with a backslash (\). ▪

3. Click in the text box next to Search For and enter the name of the file (or part of the name) that you want to search for.

4. If you want to use a server other than the default one, select a different server from the drop-down list next to the words Archie Server (see Fig. 34.18). You might want to scroll through the list and pick one geographically close to you.

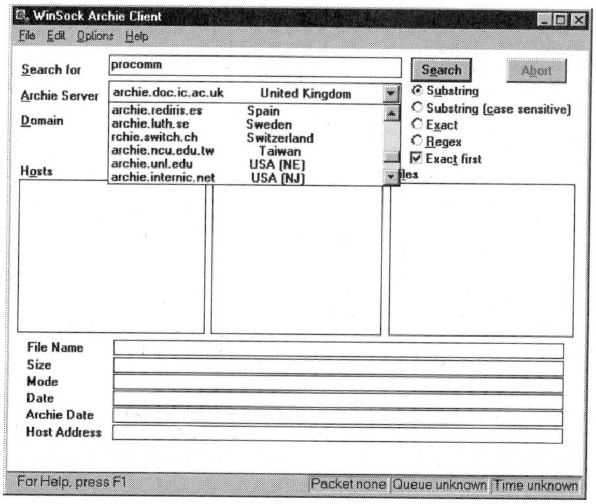

FIG. 34.18

Choosing a server near you may yield quicker response time. If the server is extremely popular, however, it may pay to choose one less geographically close.

Part
VI

Ch
34

N O T E   It's generally considered good "netiquette" to choose the site nearest you when transferring files (this lowers overall network traffic and improves performance for everyone). However, if sites close to you are clogged with traffic, it's okay to visit a geographically remote one—just don't start a bad habit. ▪

5. If you want to limit your search to a specific domain (such as edu for educational hosts), or site (such as umn.edu), or even to a specific machine (ftp.umn.edu), click in the text box next to Domain and enter the information. This can be useful if you know that a file is located at a site but can't remember the location, or if you remember only part of the site name.

6. When you have all the search parameters set, click the Search button. After the search has begun, you can abort it by clicking the Abort button. You might want to do this if you realize that you started an incorrect search, or if the status bar (discussed in the next section, "Getting the Results") indicates that your search will take a very long time to finish.

Getting the Results

WSArchie begins your search by attempting to connect to the Archie server you have specified. Your title bar shows the server you have selected and the *time-out period* for connection attempts. The time-out period specifies how long WSArchie will wait for the server to respond before it decides that the request has failed. WSArchie will try to connect to the Archie server three or four times before it gives up. When WSArchie connects to the Archie server, you will be assigned a place in the server's queue depending on the number of other pending requests.

TROUBLESHOOTING

I can't connect to the Archie server. If you try to do an Archie search and get a message saying that you can't connect to the server you have chosen, the server may be down or may no longer exist. Try selecting a different server and doing the search again.

In the status bar at the bottom of the window, WSArchie gives you information about the progress of your request, including your place in the queue and the number of seconds that WSArchie expects to elapse before your request is serviced. (This information will not be updated after you have been placed in the queue.) When WSArchie makes a connection to the Archie server, it increments the *packet count* (the number of transmitted data units) in the status bar as it receives information from the Archie server.

N O T E   You may see timeout errors in the status bar as the information from the search is returned to WSArchie. This is usually okay, because the communications protocol will try again if the transmission fails occasionally. As long as your packet count is increasing in the status bar, your connection should be okay. If the connections should for some reason be broken (the Archie server goes down, or serious noise develops on the communications line), you should get an alert box informing you of a time-out failure. ▪

If the Archie search was successful, WSArchie shows you the results. In the Hosts area of the window, you see a list of hosts that had files that matched your search string (see Fig. 34.19). The Directories area shows you the directory paths to the files, and the Files area shows you the names of the files that matched in the selected directory.

FIG. 34.19

WSArchie gives you fairly complete information regarding the results of your search. Note that the result of this search is a directory. To view the contents of the directory, click twice on the name, and WSArchie will retrieve the file listing.

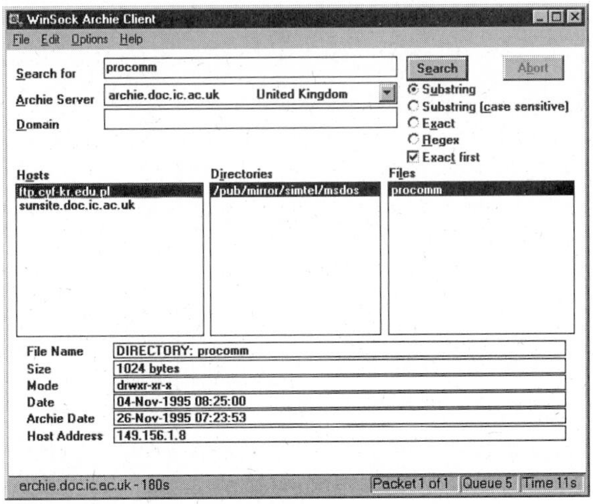

To examine the information about the files that were found, follow these steps:

1. Click the host you want to look at. The Directories area shows you the directories on that host that contain matching files.

2. Click the directories you want to examine. The files that match your search are listed in the Files area.

3. When you click each file, WSArchie shows you information about that file, including the following:

   - The name of the file
   - The size of the file, in bytes
   - The protection of the file
   - The date the file was last modified
   - The date the Archie server last checked the file's existence
   - The IP address of the host where the file resides

If any of the results shown in the Files area are directories, you can retrieve the contents of those directories. Click a directory item and choose File, Retrieve (or just double-click the directory item). The files in that directory are shown in the Files area.

You can save the results of a search in a text file. Choose File, Save. Use the file browser in the Save As window to specify the file where you want to write the results. The information is saved as a list of hosts. Each directory that contains matching files is listed under its host name, with the names of the matching files shown under each directory.

Part
VI

Ch
34

> **N O T E** The protection of each matching file is shown using the representation of the file system where it resides. If the file is a UNIX file (the most common anonymous FTP hosts), the protection will be shown as read, write, and execute (rwx) for each of three classes of users (for example, rwxr-xr-). If any of the three access modes is not permitted for a particular user group, a hyphen (-) is in that position instead of the letter. The first protection shown is for the owner of the file. The second is for users in the owner's group. The third is for all other users. Any file you want to retrieve must have read protection set for all other users. ▪

Retrieving Files

Now that you have the results of your WSArchie search, you can retrieve any files that interest you. To do this, you could always write down the name of the host and the directory path of the file that interests you, and then use any FTP program to connect to the host's anonymous FTP account and retrieve the file. If you have WS_FTP, however, retrieving the file is a much simpler process.

After you have set up your WS_FTP information, you can automatically retrieve a file from WSArchie. To do so, follow these steps:

1. Select the file that you want to retrieve in the Files area of the WinSock Archie Client window.

2. Choose File, Retrieve (or double-click the file you want to retrieve).

3. The FTP Command dialog box confirming the location of the file and the program you've specified to retrieve it appears (see Fig. 34.20). Choose OK to start the file retrieval, or Cancel if you don't want to go ahead with the transfer.

FIG. 34.20

The FTP Command dialog box displays the complete specification for retrieving the file. If you set up your FTP program correctly, the rest is automatic.

WS_FTP is started iconified. If the connection to the host is made successfully and the file is found, a Transfer Status dialog box is available to show you the progress of the transfer if you maximize the WS FTP program (see Fig. 34.21).

When the transfer is complete, the WS_FTP icon disappears. You can check the incoming directory you specified to see if the file was transferred successfully.

FIG. 34.21
WS_FTP's Transfer
Status dialog box gives
you the lowdown on
your file-retrieval
request.

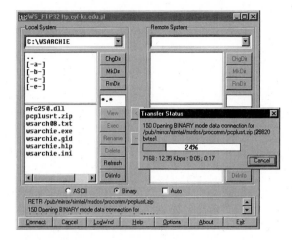

Setting Your Default Search Parameters

You can set default values for the search parameters so that every time you start WSArchie,
these values are set to the ones most useful to you. To set your default search parameters,
follow these steps:

1. Choose Options, User preferences. The User Preferences dialog box appears (see Fig.
   34.22).

FIG. 34.22
If you use a particular
set of settings
repeatedly, set them as
the program defaults
using the User
Preferences dialog box.

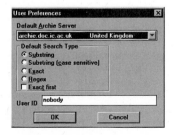

2. Select your default Archie server from the Default Archie Server drop-down list.
3. Select the radio button that corresponds to the type of search you do most frequently
   (Substring, Substring [case sensitive], Exact, or Regex).

Part
VI

Ch
34

4. If you want to try exact matches first, click the Exact First check box.

It is not necessary to change the User ID field.

Exiting WSArchie

When you have all your Archie searches, choose File, Exit to close WSArchie.

Gopher

Gophering is a big part of searching the Internet. Gopher searches are menu-based, and therefore highly structured according to someone else's sense of logic. You don't have the direct simplicity of FTP and Telnet.

What you do have is access to lots of servers loaded with information, and you have to do very little work to get to that information. Underneath the smooth Gopher interface is a constant switching of sites, computers, and remote logins. When you cruise Gopherspace, you're cruising the Internet, with the hard part hidden. Veronica and Jughead are just another two ways to extend the power of Gopher searches. Most Web browsers will also handle Gopher and these search tools as well.

▶ **See** "Why Use Gopher," **p. 834**

▶ **See** "Searching Gopherspace with Veronica," **p. 851**

Interactive Communication

CHAPTER 35

How Internet Relay Chat Works

by Dick Cravens

This chapter introduces Internet Relay Chat (IRC) and explains what it is and how it works. If you have a basic understanding of IRC and want to get connected right away, then skip ahead to Chapter 36, "Using mIRC, Netscape Chat, and Comic Chat."

Internet Relay Chat provides the electronic equivalent of a telephone party line. Instead of dialing up with your telephone, you use your computer's Internet connection to access the IRC system. Because the IRC uses the Internet, you can talk to people all over the world about hundreds of different subjects at any time. The usual style of IRC is more like a friendly gathering than a business or organizational meeting. However, IRC allows the use of private one-on-one or multiparty conversations that can be a lot more in-depth and controlled. Usually, though, IRC is much more social than any other part of the Internet. ■

What you can do with IRC

You can visit with thousands of people all over the world on just about any topic you can imagine.

How IRC clients and servers work

Learn about IRC clients and servers and how they work to connect you with other people.

What is an IRC nickname

You'll learn about nicknames, channels, and a host of other buzzwords that are unique to IRC.

The Basics of IRC

Internet Relay Chat might become one of the most useful and enjoyable parts of the Internet for you. It allows you to talk to people from all over the world about a wide variety of topics. At its core, IRC was made for you to meet people and have some fun. But before getting into the details of how to use IRC, you need to know how IRC started and what its major uses are.

What Is the Purpose of IRC?

IRC is used mostly as a recreational communication system. It allows you to communicate with people all over the world about thousands of different topics and subjects. Because of its interactive nature, an IRC conversation is much more chaotic than the one-at-a-time, debate-style conversations you might see on UseNet newsgroups. It is possible with IRC, though, to create private, invitation-only conversations that can be as controlled and in-depth as anything that can be done over the phone— even more so in some cases because IRC also allows the transfer of files and other information.

N O T E Although most uses of IRC are currently recreational, there is nothing stopping business from using this form of communication for conducting business meetings, seminars, and other activities. ▪

Many college students use IRC as a substitute for making long- distance telephone calls because once you have an Internet connection, using IRC is free. There is no limit to how many people can be on IRC or how many topics of conversation may be active simultaneously.

Some recreational and educational organizations hold meetings online at specified times. There are writing and philosophy groups and even an acting group that performs online. There are some business organizations that take advantage of the long-distance conferencing ability IRC provides. As with any other communication on the Internet, however, information is not necessarily secure; and some companies prefer to interact within a more controlled medium.

N O T E Any information sent across the Internet gets passed through many intermediate computer sites on its way to its destination. There is no way to be sure that someone is not looking at the information as it is passed along. IRC does provide some means for adding privacy to your conversations. For information about securing general Internet activity, see Chapter 40, "Privacy and Security on the Internet." ▪

History of IRC

IRC was developed in the late 1980s by a Finnish college student looking to improve the quality of interactive communication on his computer bulletin board. The project eventually moved in focus from private bulletin board systems to the Internet. The initial versions of IRC allowed for only simple communication among users. As time passed, more features were added; and improvements in performance were made. Today's IRC offers many interesting features, is programmable, and gives access to users all over the world.

Internet Relay Chat has grown steadily with the Internet. The activity on the hundreds of IRC channels has increased greatly over the last few years. Initially, you needed to be on a UNIX workstation to use IRC because the Internet has its roots in the UNIX operating system. Over the last few years, the amount of software available for PCs and Macintoshes that provides access to IRC services has grown significantly.

To get connected to IRC, you need to have at least some way of connecting to the Internet. The quality of service you get is dependent on the quality of your Internet connection. For more information about the types of Internet connections you can get, see Chapter 3, "The Various Ways to Connect: Which One Is Right for You?"

How Internet Relay Chat Works

Internet Relay Chat relies on TCP/IP, the networking protocol upon which the Internet is based. IRC uses two of the basic components of a TCP/IP-based network—*servers* and *clients*. The only part of the system you deal with directly is the client.

IRC Clients

The *client* is just a fancy name for the software you run on your computer to connect to IRC. The client software allows you to connect to the IRC server, which accepts connections from many IRC clients at the same time. The various IRC servers across the Internet are interconnected—from an IRC server you can access the conferences and users connected to many other IRC servers.

IRC clients provide varying levels of control over how much you can customize your IRC sessions. In the next chapter, you learn about an IRC client that runs under Microsoft Windows. In all cases, the client you use greatly affects your perception of IRC. The best clients are very flexible and still remain simple to use. Some IRC clients restrict you from performing certain functions that IRC servers provide.

IRC Servers

The *servers* are the core of the IRC system. IRC servers provide all of the supporting structure that allows Internet Relay Chat to work. The servers maintain information on the current available channels. Every time a new channel is added, the information about it has to be passed to every other IRC server. Servers also administer which users are currently connected and what options and features they have set up. All of this information is exchanged between servers as it is changed, and the technical details of how this is accomplished are quite complicated.

IRC servers are maintained by people called IRCops, short for IRC operators. These individuals run the servers and keep everything on IRC running properly.

There are more than one hundred IRC servers running on the Internet. When you first start your IRC client, you will probably be asked to enter the Internet address of the server to which you want to connect. If your Internet service provider maintains an IRC server of its own, it's generally a good idea to try that one first. Otherwise, you should pick an Internet server that exists geographically close to where you are. The reason for this is that the farther away the IRC server is from your connection, the longer messages between your client and server have to travel. The following is a short listing of some IRC servers. (There should be one in the general region in which you are located.)

Server Address	Location
irc.netsys.com	California
irc.caltech.edu	Cal-Tech University
irc.indiana.edu	Indiana University
csa.bu.edu	Boston University
wpi.wpi.edu	Massachusetts
irc.tc.umn.edu	University of Minnesota
mothra.syr.edu	Syracuse, New York
irc.nada.kth.se	Sweden

N O T E When you connect to an IRC server, you will usually be asked for a port number in addition to the Internet address. This port number specifies additional information that might be needed by the IRC server. Most of the time, the port number will be 6667. So unless it is specified to be something else, you should use this number as the default. Some clients will assume this value for the port number if you do not enter one. ■

There are listings available on the Net of current IRC servers. For various reasons, IRC servers are sometimes shut down. Many of the IRC servers are set up by universities and colleges. When computing resources are scarce, these organizations take the least necessary systems offline first. These usually include IRC, network games, and other recreational programs.

Telneting to IRC

If you do not have full access to the Internet, but do have access to the Internet program Telnet, you still can use IRC. There are systems that allow you to Telnet in to them to access IRC (see Fig. 35.1). However, using Telnet access to IRC is fairly limited. There are only a handful of IRC Telnet sites available. The ones that do exist can handle only a certain number of users at a time. You can't customize your interaction with IRC and will get fairly poor performance when compared to more direct IRC access. It is definitely advisable to pursue other means of accessing IRC before using Telnet. If you can't get better access, however, here is a short listing of some Telnet IRC sites with the IRC port number:

Site Address	Port Number
skyhawk.ecn.uoknor.edu	6677
vinson.ecn.uoknor.edu	6677
sci.dixie.edu	6677
caen.fr.eu.undernet.org	6677
obelix.wu-wien.ac.at	6677

FIG. 35.1

Telnet IRC access can be slow and very restrictive, and you sometimes end up in an IRC backwater such as the dungeon shown here!

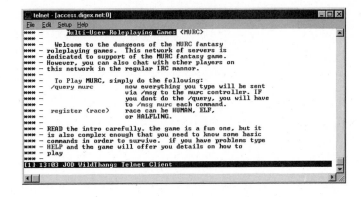

Net Splits

Sometimes while using IRC there suddenly will be no activity on any of the channels. If the connection to your server is still running, you may see a message explaining that a *Net split* has occurred. As you might have guessed, a Net split refers to a discontinuation of Internet service from one site to another.

The IRC system uses mostly direct links from one server to another. For example, say there are two servers, X and Y. Each has a direct link on the IRC system. Each of these servers supports three other servers on its respective side of the link between them. If the connection between X and Y goes down, the servers on each side of the X to Y connection are cut off from each other (see Fig. 35.2).

FIG. 35.2

The effect of a Net split is to isolate part of the IRC network.

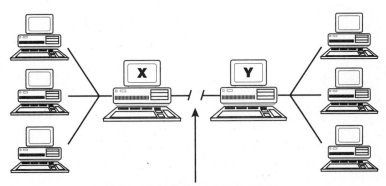

A break in the connection here
cuts off all four servers on the right side
from all four servers on the left

The best indicator of a Net split is the sudden disappearance of everyone in the channel or conversation group that you were talking in. Unfortunately, as a user of IRC there is no way to speed up the recovery from a Net split. Often it is a physical problem with parts of the Internet and must be serviced by whomever maintains that part of the Internet.

N O T E   The Internet was designed to minimize the effects of a Net split, allowing connections to be rerouted through different pathways. IRC, however, does not take advantage of these abilities. ▆

Talking on IRC

Getting adjusted to conversations on IRC might take some time. Because everything is typed instead of spoken, the use of language and expression of opinion are different from normal conversation. Using the IRC system is often referred to as IRCing (pronounced urk-ing). You will learn about the details of communicating on IRC in the next chapter.

The format that IRC is based on is topic-specific channels. When you connect to IRC, you will be able to see a listing of the current active channels and the topics being discussed on them. The channel names cannot be changed once they are created. The topic of each channel is changed fairly frequently, however, and gives a better indication of what is being discussed there.

Nicknames

IRC provides a mechanism for identifying yourself by a nickname. Nicknames are extremely encouraged and help to add color to the text-based world of IRC. Nicknames are limited to nine characters, but you will be surprised at how creative people are with so few. Many people use animal and food names in combination with their own. In Chapter 36, "Using mIRC, Netscape Chat, and Comic Chat," you learn how to pick and set your nickname. If you don't pick a nickname, IRC will usually use your computer account name instead.

IRC Channels

Channels are a lot like local pubs or night clubs. Depending on the time of day you stop by, the number and type of people who are there will be different. On many of the popular channels, most of the users know each other and tend to connect to IRC at the same time of day. Some channels are friendlier to new users than others. In Chapter 36, you learn about some of the more well-known channels as well as good places to get started.

The Undernet

The *Undernet* is a term often used to describe the entire IRC system. The Undernet, however, is actually an IRC system separate from a standard IRC system. A few years ago, several IRC operators started to feel that the major IRC system (sometimes referred to as EFNet) was becoming overloaded with users and needed some significant improvements. There were too many IRC servers that were not interested in making major changes, so these operators went off and improved the system on their own. The result is a separate, and arguably better, IRC system called the Undernet.

To connect to the Undernet, all you have to do differently is connect to an Undernet server instead of an EFNet server. All of the Undernet IRC servers have the word Undernet in their Internet address. Here is a listing of several Undernet IRC servers:

Undernet Internet Address	Location
caen.fr.eu.undernet.org	Europe
ca.undernet.org	Canada
au.undernet.org	Australia
us.undernet.org	USA
pasadena.ca.us.undernet.org	West-USA
boston.ma.us.undernet.org	East-USA

The designers of the Undernet rebuilt several parts of the networking communication system on which IRC is based. They have fixed many of the annoying bugs that the EFNet IRC currently has and have made an effort to make the Undernet a friendlier place. The Undernet is at this point much smaller than the EFNet, but it is still large enough to carry a variety of topics of conversation.

Other Sources of Information on IRC

With the growth of the World Wide Web, there are now several Web sites with great information about Internet Relay Chat. For starters, take a look at the Web site **http://www.yahoo.com/Computers_and_Internet/Internet/Chatting/IRC/**. This site provides an index of World Wide Web sites that have information and frequently asked questions about IRC. For information about how to connect to a Web site, see Chapter 16, "How the World Wide Web Works." ●

Part
VII

Ch
35

CHAPTER 36

Using mIRC, Netscape Chat, and Comic Chat

by Jerry Honeycutt

In Chapter 35, "How Internet Relay Chat Works," you learned about Internet Relay Chat, the Internet equivalent of CompuServe's CB or America Online's chat rooms—a place to chat with other folks about a particular topic of interest. IRC has a collection of discussions, called channels, for discussion of information on literally thousands of different topics. Chances are, if you're interested in it, you can find a group on IRC that is discussing it.

Traditionally, though, many of the programs for accessing IRC, called IRC clients, that are available on Internet access systems reflect their UNIX heritage—shell accounts running the UNIX operating system. They tend to be very powerful but are based on command-line prompts and command codes, and are extremely difficult to become proficient at.

For many PC-based systems, a new generation of IRC clients is being developed with a much more intuitive, graphical interface. The mIRC program for Windows 95 is just such a program. ■

Learn how to get and install mIRC

mIRC is the most popular IRC client available on the Internet, and it's free. This chapter shows you how to get it and how to install it.

Chat on IRC with mIRC

On the surface, mIRC is a very simple IRC client. It lets you do things that other IRC clients don't, however, such as customize to fit your needs.

Chat on IRC with Netscape Chat

The newest version of Netscape's Chat is hot. They've made significant improvements that make it a real contender for one of the best IRC clients.

Chat on IRC with Microsoft Comic Chat

Microsoft Comic Chat is a new IRC client from Microsoft that lets you see the other participants as cartoon characters.

Why Use mIRC or Netscape Chat?

As we discussed in Chapter 35, Internet Relay Chat has been around for a long time and is a very popular place for people on the Internet to hang out. At any given time, there may be as many as eight or nine thousand people from all over the world connected with IRC.

UNIX system IRC clients have been around for a long time as well. So, why do you need mIRC or Netscape Chat, a relative newcomer that allows you to connect to IRC from Windows 95?

The answer to that question is the same as the answer to the question: why use Windows 95 when you can use MS-DOS, which has been around for a long time as well? Both MS-DOS and UNIX IRC clients can provide you with powerful tools for doing their respective function...but they're not very easy or a lot of fun to use. Sure, everything you might want to do is somewhere in there, but it'll take forever to learn how to do it all.

mIRC and Netscape Chat take all of the command-line drudgery out of accessing IRC, giving an easy, intuitive Windows interface to the process of joining discussions, having private conversations, and exchanging files over IRC.

Installing mIRC

The version of mIRC used in this book is mIRC version 4.1. The archive that mIRC is distributed in includes both 16- and 32-bit versions. With Windows 95 you'll want to use the 32-bit version. Use the 16-bit version with Windows 3.1. This version of mIRC does not have an automated installation procedure, but doing the steps manually is not very difficult.

To install mIRC, follow these steps:

On the CD

1. You'll find MIRC41.ZIP on NetCD. You can also download the MIRC41.ZIP file from one of the following locations and put the following into the directory from which you want to run mIRC (for example, C:\Mirc\):

   ftp://ftp.undernet.org/pub/irc/clients/windows/mirc41.zip

   ftp://ftp.onramp.net/pub/ibm/IRC/mirc41.zip

   ftp://ftp.demon.co.uk/pub/ibmpc/win3/winsock/apps/mirc/mirc41.zip

2. Unzip Mirc41.zip. This gives you the following files (if you have your Windows Explorer set up to hide MS-DOS file extensions for registered file types, this list might look a little different, but the files will still be there):

   Mirc.exe (16-bit version)

   Mirc32.exe (32-bit version)

   Mirc.hlp

   Aliases.ini

   Mirc.ini

   Popups.ini

   Remote.ini

Readme.txt

Versions.txt

3. Add an entry for mIRC in the Start or Programs menu, or create a shortcut to it on your desktop (or any combination of the three). Since mIRC tends to get pretty involved with lots of windows, you might want to set it up to always start up maximized (see Fig. 36.1).

FIG. 36.1
Because you will want to use the whole screen when running mIRC, set up your shortcut to run the program maximized.

That's it! Your installation is complete! You might want to take this opportunity for a quick look at the Readme.txt and Versions.txt file, which gives some history for the program and other information.

Setting Up mIRC

When you first start mIRC, there's some setup information that you need to fill in to connect. To access this screen, click the Setup Information toolbar button or select the Setup item under the File menu. You will get the setup screen shown in Figure 36.2.

On this screen, fill in the real name you want to appear in IRC, along with your e-mail address, and a main and alternate choice of nickname. The nickname is what you will be identified by on IRC. If you have a dedicated local host name and IP number, click the Local Info tab and fill in that information (see Fig. 36.3).

If your Internet service provider furnishes you an IP number upon connection, click one of the choices in On Connect, always get:. You access the list of IRC servers by clicking Add Server, as shown in Figure 36.4—you can choose one of those shown or you can choose one supplied by your Internet service provider. See Chapter 35, "How Internet Relay Chat Works," to learn more about IRC servers.

FIG. 36.2

This is the setup screen after I have filled in all of the necessary information.

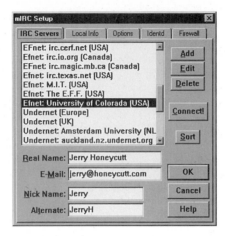

 TIP   The IRC servers shown are publicly available servers and tend to be pretty busy. If your Internet service provider has an IRC server of its own, you should add it to the mIRC server list and use it.

FIG. 36.3

You can enter your local info in this dialog box.

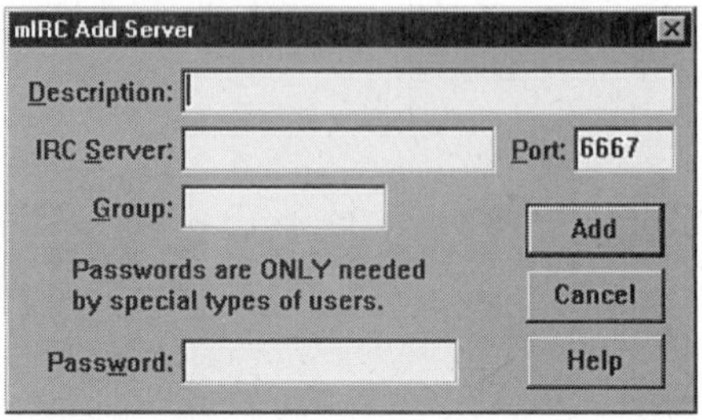

FIG. 36.4

If your Internet service provider has its own IRC server, make sure you add it to the list!

Accessing the IRC Using mIRC

Once you have set up mIRC, you are ready to connect. After you have closed the setup window (and any time you start mIRC), you see the mIRC Status window, which remains empty until you connect to IRC.

Connecting to IRC

To connect to IRC, click the Connect to IRC server toolbar button or select the Connect item from the File menu. If you fill out the setup information correctly, you are connected to IRC. You see a screen similar to that shown in Figure 36.5—the mIRC status window. This is the IRC server's Message Of The Day (MOTD).

Disconnect from
IRC Server

Setup
Information

Connect to
IRC Server

Channels
Folder

FIG. 36.5

Once you have connected to an IRC server, you get a Message Of The Day (MOTD) similar to the one shown here.

Status window

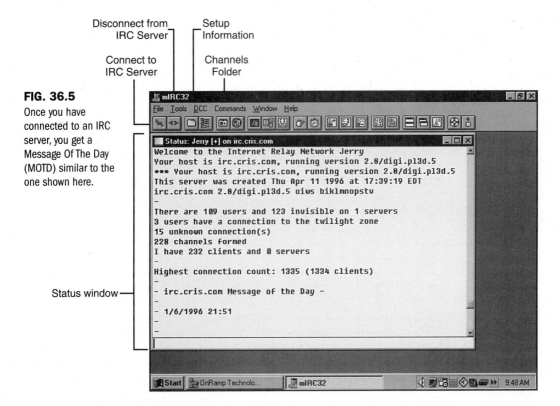

Joining the Discussion

Once you have connected to an IRC server, you are ready to join the conversation. But which one? IRC often has thousands of channels—the IRC term for discussion groups—how can you find out which to join?

If you are completely new to IRC (and mIRC), there are a few places you can start. If you click the Channels folder toolbar button, you get the window shown in Figure 36.6. By default, mIRC comes with a list of channels listed in this window that are good places for new IRC users to join to get a feel for the system. Once you have found other channels to join, you can add them to this list for easy access in the future.

FIG. 36.6

Clicking the Channels folder toolbar button gives you this list of IRC channels to choose from, or you can add your own.

But how do you find other groups to join? mIRC allows you to get a list of the names of all of the available public channels by clicking the List channels toolbar button. Because there may be thousands of channels, it might take a few minutes for mIRC to list them all in the list window that pops up.

You should wait until all of them are listed before trying to browse through this list—mIRC continuously sorts the groups alphabetically as it adds them to the list, so it's impossible to scroll through the list until they are all there.

N O T E To narrow down your list of groups, you can type a phrase in the window as shown in Figure 36.7. For example, if you type **irc** in that window, mIRC lists only those channels with irc in their names. If you want to narrow your search to the more (or less) popular groups, you can specify a minimum and/or maximum number of users for the listed groups. ▪

 You can join a channel by double-clicking its name in the Channel List window.

What if you can't find a channel for what you want to discuss? You can just start your own channel! The procedure for this is the same as for joining an existing channel. If you join a channel that doesn't exist, IRC creates the channel with you as its only member. If your topic is pretty obscure, you might have to wait awhile before anyone else joins your channel.

Once you have joined a channel through any of the methods just mentioned, you see a window for that channel similar to Figure 36.8. The left side of the window is the main part where everything everyone in the channel says (including you) appears.

FIG. 36.7
If you click the List Channels toolbar button, mIRC gives you a list of the channels that are available.

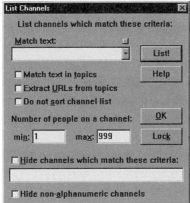

The right side shows a list of the nicknames for everyone in the channel. The input line on the bottom of this (and most mIRC) windows is the area where you type what you want to send.

FIG. 36.8
Once you're in a channel, you can join the conversation!

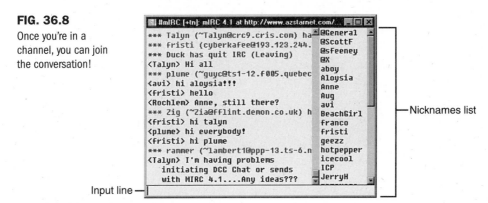

Nicknames list

Input line

Private Conversations

Once you have joined a channel and entered a discussion, or after you have been on IRC for awhile and have gotten to know other folks, you might want to have a one-on-one discussion with someone. There are two ways of doing this in IRC, and mIRC allows you to access them both.

The first is to use private messages via the IRC /msg or /query commands. The second is to use the Direct Client-to-Client protocol, which is described in the next section.

If you want to send a message to your friend Rochlem, instead of just typing a message, you preface it with **/msg Rochlem** in the input line of any window. This sends a message only to the IRC user whose nickname is Rochlem. You also can type the command **/query Rochlem** with no message, to open an mIRC Query window (see Fig. 36.9). Everything you type in this window is sent to Rochlem only.

FIG. 36.9
If you want to have a
private conversation with
someone, mIRC allows
you to do that with a
Query window.

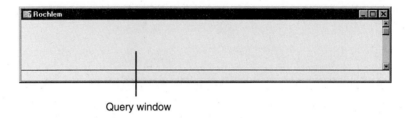

Query window

N O T E   If you send a message using /msg Rochlem <message>, a query window is not created
but the message is sent only to Rochlem. If Rochlem replies to your message by sending a
private message back, mIRC then automatically creates a query window. ■

CAUTION
Be careful about having private conversations on IRC. Normally, when having a one-on-one conversation with
someone on IRC you can assume it will be private—just between the two of you. However, because of the
nature of IRC, there is no guarantee. Using DCC Chat (see next section) is *more* secure but is not a
guarantee of privacy. Don't say anything you might regret (particularly if you expect to be a Supreme Court
nominee someday)!

A Little More Privacy Using DCC

As mentioned in the previous section, IRC offers a way to have a one-on-one conversation with
someone else using something called a Direct Client-to-Client (DCC) connection. To have a
conversation with someone, you can use DCC Chat. You can also send and receive files from
someone over IRC using DCC Send and DCC Receive.

To initiate a DCC Chat with someone, either hit the DCC Chat toolbar button or select the Chat
item in the DCC menu. mIRC gives you a dialog box in which to select the nickname of the
person you want to talk to.

Then you get a screen similar to that shown in Figure 36.10. You'll notice that the chat window
has the message Waiting for acknowledgement—that is because a DCC connection can only
be initiated with the agreement of both IRC clients.

Once the DCC Chat is accepted, the chat window behaves the same way as the query window
discussed in the previous section. Everything you type in the input line is sent only to the other
person. However, because this is a direct connection between your IRC client (mIRC) and
theirs, bypassing any IRC servers, it should be quicker and more secure (though not completely secure!).

As just mentioned, a DCC connection can also be used to send and receive files from another
user on IRC. To send a file to someone, click the DCC Send a File to Someone toolbar button
or select the Send item in the DCC menu. You see a dialog box similar to that shown in Figure
36.11, allowing you to select the IRC user and the file (or files) that you want to send. Once you
have selected the files, a mIRC pop-up window informs you of the progress of your DCC Send.

FIG. 36.10

A Direct Client to Client (DCC) Chat with someone is usually a faster, more private way to communicate one on one.

DCC Send a File to Someone ⌐ DCC Chat with Someone

DCC Options

Chat window

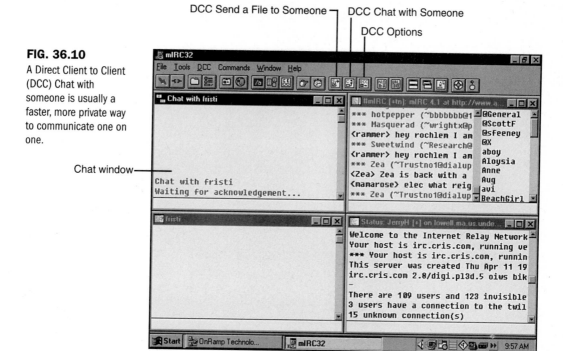

FIG. 36.11

You can send a file to someone else on IRC using DCC Send.

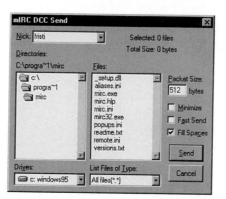

What about receiving files? Didn't I mention something called DCC Get? You may have noticed that there isn't a DCC Get a File from Someone toolbar button or a Get item in the DCC menu. The reason for this is that when someone uses DCC Send to try to send you a file, mIRC recognizes this and automatically asks you if you wish to receive the file (see Fig. 36.12)—click Get to do so. If you do, a DCC Get window pops up to show you the progress.

N O T E When you receive a file via DCC Get, the file is given the name it had on the sending computer, and it is put in the mIRC directory (for example, C:\Mirc). You can change this default location (along with other aspects of mIRC's DCC behavior) by clicking the DCC Options toolbar button or by selecting the Options... item in the DCC menu. ▪

FIG. 36.12
If someone else on IRC wants to send you a file, mIRC asks if you want to accept it. If you do, mIRC retrieves it with DCC Get.

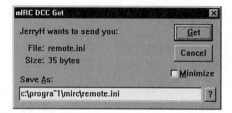

Setting mIRC Options

You can customize the behavior and look of mIRC by setting the different IRC options. You do this by clicking the appropriate toolbar button (see Fig. 36.13).

FIG. 36.13
You can access and change mIRC options by using these toolbar buttons or choosing File, Options from the Misc menu.

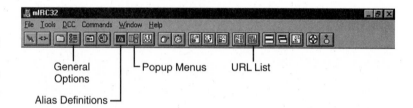

General Options

The bulk of the options you can use to customize mIRC's settings are accessed by clicking the general options toolbar button or selecting the Options item from the File menu. In the general options window are several categories of options that you can access and change by selecting the appropriate tab.

IRC Switches The first mIRC general options window is called IRC Switches (see Fig. 36.14). The default settings for most of these options are good, and you can experiment with them to see what you like. There are a few in particular that you might want to change.

The two options in the upper left relate to mIRC's connection with an IRC server. Checking the top box causes mIRC to connect automatically with its default IRC server upon startup of the program—if you always use the same server, you might want to check this box. If you have or are using an IRC server that frequently disconnects you, check the second box, which causes mIRC to attempt to reconnect with the server if it is disconnected.

Two other options that you might want to change are also on the left side and relate to mIRC's response to private messages from other users. The top box in this group of options, Iconify query window, starts a private message window as an icon in mIRC.

I usually like to see these messages right away, so I uncheck this option. The last option in this group, Whois on query, displays the nickname, address, and server in the status window of any user who sent you a private message.

FIG. 36.14

IRC options allow you to change some of mIRC's general settings.

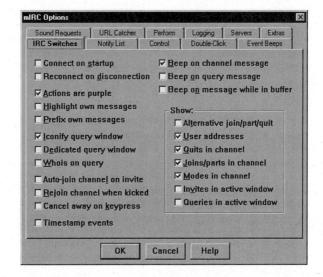

Feel free to experiment with the other options in this window to see if you like the way they change mIRC's behavior.

Perform   The Perform general option window (see Fig. 36.15) allows you to define IRC commands that execute when you connect to an IRC server. If you type a series of words in this window, separated by commas, these words will be highlighted when they appear in any mIRC window. This is a good way to highlight messages from certain people or about certain topics.

Control   The Control general option window (see Fig. 36.16) lets you define how you want mIRC to handle certain user nicknames:

- Auto-Op—Any IRC user nicknames entered in this box cause mIRC to automatically make those users an operator in an IRC channel in which you are an operator.

- Ignore—Any IRC user nicknames in this box cause mIRC to ignore anything those users say—you will not even see messages from them.

Notify List   A list of IRC nicknames entered in a Notify list (shown in Fig. 36.17), separated by spaces, causes mIRC to notify you by displaying a message in the status window whenever one of the users named is on IRC. This is a great way to keep an eye out for friends on IRC with whom you want to chat (or not-so-good-friends whom you want to avoid).

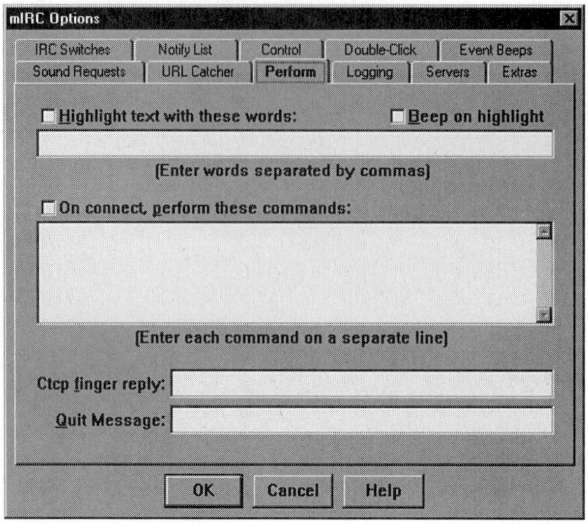

FIG. 36.15

Perform allows you to specify words that you want mIRC to highlight.

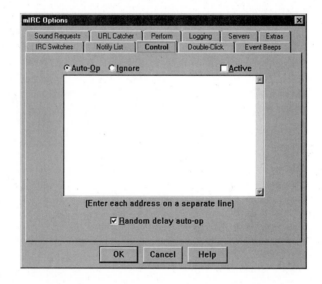

FIG. 36.16

Make sure that Active is selected to enable Auto-Op and Ignore.

URL Catcher   A very handy feature of mIRC is its URL Catcher (see Fig. 36.18). If the Enable URL catcher box is checked, mIRC scans all incoming messages to see if they contain World Wide Web (WWW) URLs, and Internet FTP and Gopher addresses.

FIG. 36.17
Use this list to keep an eye out for close friends and problem IRC users.

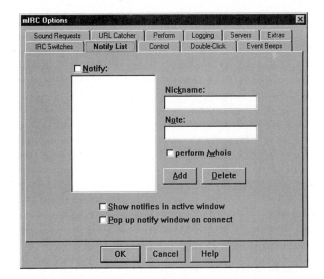

FIG. 36.18
The URL Catcher scans all incoming text for Internet and WWW addresses, and saves them to your URL list.

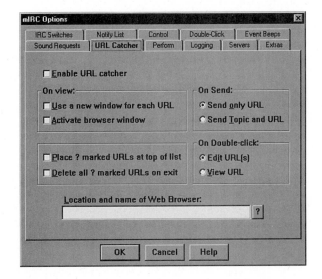

For instance, if someone sends me the URL of Microsoft's home page, as shown in Figure 36.19, mIRC grabs the URL and puts it in its URL list, which is accessed by clicking the URL List toolbar button. Also, by filling in the Location and name of WWW browser: field with a supported browser (currently only Netscape Navigator), you can use mIRC to automatically view a URL from the URL list.

FIG. 36.19

Whenever someone sends you a WWW URL or FTP address, the mIRC URL Catcher sees it and puts it in your URL list.

> ▶ **See** "Important WWW Concepts," **p. 366**
> ▶ **See** "Using Netscape 3," **p. 399**

Other General Options   The other general option windows allow you to control the following aspects of mIRC's operation:

- *Event Beeps*—Controls what events mIRC notifies you of using audible beeps.

- *Logging*—Allows you to have mIRC automatically log channel or one-on-one (Query or DCC Chat) discussions to files on your computer, as well as specify the path where the log files are put.

- *Sound Requests*—Specifies how mIRC handles incoming and outgoing sound requests— basically allowing mIRC to send, receive, and play .WAV sound files.

- *Servers*—Setting this up allows mIRC to act as an ident server and to send the specified User ID and System as identification. The default values mIRC puts in this box are usually fine, and you should never need to look at it.

- *Double-click*—Allows you to set up actions mIRC will take when you double-click in its different windows.

- *Extras*—Miscellaneous extra mIRC options. These are pretty self-explanatory—go ahead and experiment with them if you'd like.

Fonts

By default, mIRC displays text in all of its windows using the fixed system font. Clicking on any window's control menu, as shown in Figure 36.20, allows you to specify a different font for that window. Choose Font from this menu to display the font selection dialog box.

FIG. 36.20

mIRC allows you to select what font to use for the different types of windows.

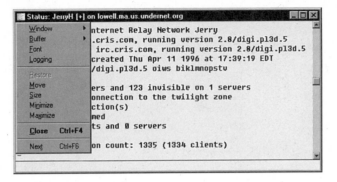

Pop-up Menus

mIRC has a very powerful and useful feature called pop-up menus. These are user-defined menus that appear when you right-click the mouse in different mIRC windows. While you can define each of these menus by clicking the pop-up menus toolbar button or selecting the pop-up item in the Tools menu, the default menus provided with mIRC are very useful. The best way to modify these menus would be to use the defaults as a starting point.

Figure 36.21 shows a sampling of how one of the pop-up menus is defined. The one shown appears when you right-click in either the main part of a channel or in the status window. Although this definition looks kind of complicated, it is pretty easy to figure out by comparing the definition with the actual menus (see Fig. 36.22).

FIG. 36.21

mIRC allows you to define pop-up menus with a right-click in the different windows. These pop-up menus allow you to perform mIRC actions easily.

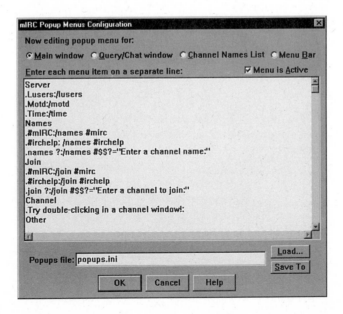

FIG. 36.22
Once the pop-up menus are defined, they can be accessed in mIRC. The default pop-up menu for the main window is shown here.

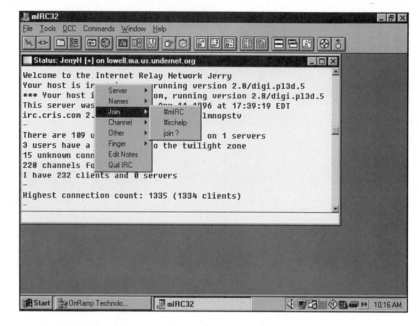

Netscape Chat and IRC

The Netscape Chat program also allows you to connect to IRC from Windows 95. The latest version of Netscape Chat provides most of the features you need to use IRC effectively. It's not as customizable as mIRC, however, but for some folks its simplicity is an attractive feature in itself.

Installing Chat

Netscape Chat can be installed on your Windows 95 system by following these steps:

1. Download the nc3220.EXE file for Windows 95 or NT and nc1620.EXE for Windows 3.1. To do so, point your browser to **http://home.netscape.com/comprod/mirror/index.html** and follow the instructions you see on the Web page.

2. Run the self-extracting NC3220.EXE file or NC1620.EXE. The default setup options put the program in the C:\Program Files\Netscape\NSCHAT directory.

Connecting to IRC Using Chat

If Netscape Chat can't find Navigator on your computer, it pops up the dialog box shown in Figure 36.23. You can either click on Configure to specify the location of Navigator, or you can click on Disable to turn off this feature.

FIG. 36.23
Netscape Chat is designed to work alongside Netscape Navigator, so you must enter Navigator's location in the Chat Preferences dialog box.

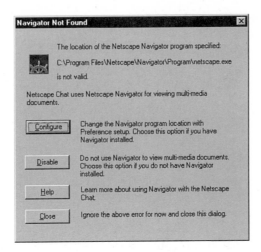

Netscape Chat comes loaded with a handful of IRC servers. The default is davis.dal.net. To connect to an IRC server, you need to enter the information for the server in the Server Connection dialog box, shown in Figure 36.24, which comes up when you start Chat or when you click the Connect toolbar button.

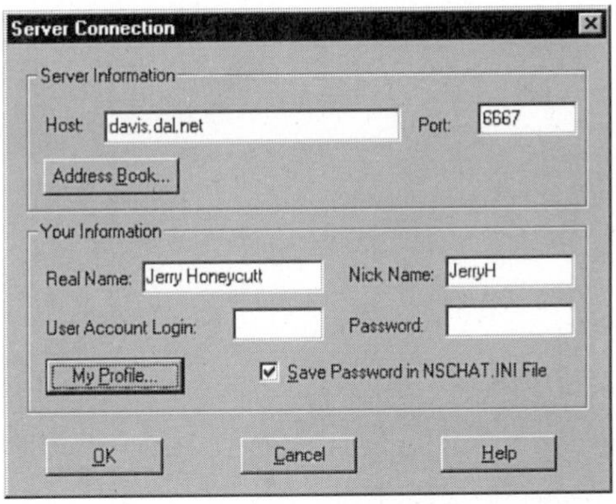

FIG. 36.24
You can connect Netscape Chat to IRC by entering your IRC server information in the Server Connection dialog box.

Group Conversation   To join an IRC channel, select the Show Rooms item under the File menu. Netscape Chat puts up the Conversation Rooms window, as shown in Figure 36.25. You can scroll through the list to find a channel you are interested in, click it, and then click the Join button. For example, Figure 36.26 shows the window after I have connected to the #WorldWideChat channel.

FIG. 36.25

The Netscape Chat Conversation Channels dialog box shows you what IRC channels are available for you to join.

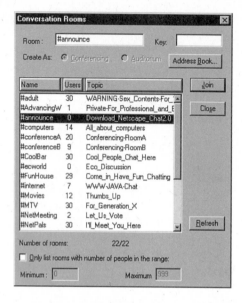

FIG. 36.26

Here I am connected to the #WorldWideChat channel.

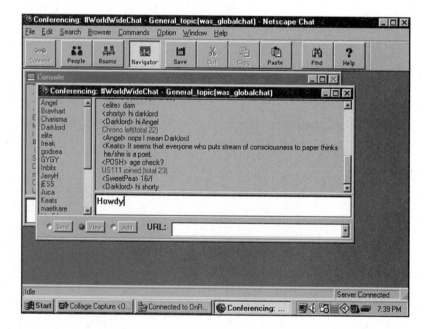

> **N O T E** When the Conversation Channel's window pops up, Netscape Chat loads the names of all the channels into the window. Because there may be thousands of channels, this can take a couple of minutes. Since the list is alphabetized as entries are loaded in, you won't be able to scroll through the list to find a channel of interest until the list has been fully loaded. ∎

Personal Conversation Just as private conversations are possible with mIRC, you can also have them with Netscape Chat. When you select the Show People item under the File menu, the Show People window appears (see Fig. 36.27). By entering a filter in the lower-right (where * is a wildcard) and clicking Refresh, you can list the names of users with certain groups of letters in their names.

For instance, if I am looking for my friend MysticSky, I can use the string My* in the filter. As shown in Figure 36.28, if MysticSky is listed, I can initiate a personal conversation with him by clicking his name and then the Talk button. If he accepts my invitation to a personal conversation, we can then talk one-on-one (see Fig. 36.28).

FIG. 36.27
I can use Netscape Chat's Show People dialog box to look for folks on IRC. Here I am looking for my friend Damone.

FIG. 36.28
Netscape Chat allows you to have personal, one-on-one conversations.

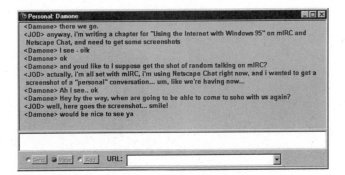

CAUTION

Just as with mIRC and all current IRC programs, you should assume that even private, one-on-one IRC conversations are not completely secure.

Netscape Chat Versus mIRC

Though Netscape Chat works with IRC, it was originally designed to work with the Netscape Chat server, where its ability to work closely with Netscape Navigator can be used to full advantage. Some of the advantages of a dedicated program such as mIRC over Netscape Chat are as follows:

- IRC can have thousands of channels at any one time. mIRC allows you to list channels containing a given phrase or group of letters (such as irc), while Netscape Chat can only list all of them.

- If you are looking for a person on IRC, Netscape Chat does allow you to list all of the users with a given group of letters in their names (for example, My* to look for MysticSkye). mIRC, on the other hand, allows you to use the IRC "notify" system that automatically tells you whenever any of a list of other users are on IRC.

- Private conversations are possible through both mIRC and Netscape Chat. mIRC gives you a couple of different ways of doing this, using either the IRC Query or more secure DCC Chat methods. Netscape Chat's method is to create a private, invite-only channel and then issue an invitation to the other person to join that channel. If the other person is not using Netscape Chat as well, this method can be a little confusing.

Using Microsoft Comic Chat

Microsoft Comic chat is a cute, new IRC client that lets you see cartoon representations of the folks you're chatting with. In fact, the whole chat session looks like a comic strip you'd see in the Sunday morning paper. This section shows you how to download and install Comic Chat. I don't recommend using it if you're serious about IRC, however, because it's just too basic. It doesn't provide the features (DCC chat, for example) that you find in mIRC or Netscape Chat.

You download Microsoft Comic Chat from Microsoft's Web site. Point your Web browser at **http://www.microsoft.com/msdownload/ieadd/0500.htm**, then click on one of the cchat10.exe links you see on the Web page to download Comic Chat. You can save this file into any folder you want, because it expands its contents into Windows' temporary folder. Installing Comic Chat is easy, too. Double-click on the file you downloaded and follow the instructions you see on the screen.

When you start Comic Chat, it asks you for the name of the chat server and the chat room you want to visit. Type the name of the chat server in Server or accept the default, which is Microsoft's chat server. You can type the name of a chat room in Go to chat room, or you can select Show all available chat rooms and click on OK to pick a chat room from a list. Figure 36.29 shows you Microsoft Comic Chat. You can see the current chat session in the viewing pane, which Comic Chat represents as cartoon strips. You add your own comments to the current chat session by typing them in the compose pane, and pressing Enter.

FIG. 36.29
You can change your cartoon character, user profile, and other settings by choosing <u>V</u>iew, <u>O</u>ptions from the main menu.

Self-View pane

Member List pane

Viewing pane

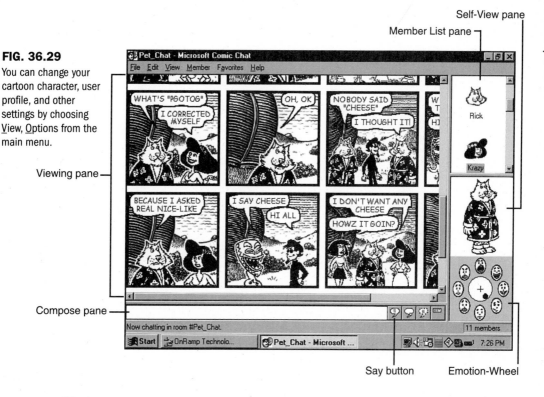

Compose pane

Say button

Emotion-Wheel

Viewing pane	Displays current chat session.
Member List pane	Displays chat participants.
Self-View pane	Displays your character.
Emotion-Wheel	Click in wheel to change facial expression.
Compose pane	Type your message and click the Say button.

Talking on the Internet

by Lori Leonardo

The Internet is about communication. Every improvement made on the Net relates to increasing speed, improving capabilities, or aiding communication in some other way. The Information in Information Superhighway is the stuff of communications. People still need to communicate often, even in this technological world in which we now live. So it should come as no surprise that the Internet is being increasingly used for just that—interpersonal communication.

It is interesting that it has taken so long for the Internet to employ the oldest form of human communication—speech. But many new applications apply the data transfer power of the Internet to let people actually hear and speak to one another in real-time. It's a far cry from e-mail, which seems impersonal in comparison. ■

Voice communications

Whether or not it is realistic to have the ability to make a "call" thousands of miles away over the Internet.

System requirements

The hardware and software requirements for setting up your computer to talk on the Internet.

Internet "phone" applications

How to get and configure the applications that you need to use the Internet for "phone" conversations.

Voice applications

How to choose which Internet voice application is best for you.

Using the Internet as a "Phone"

The science behind using the Internet as a vocal communication platform is not very complicated. Computers don't know what kind of data they're handling, and the Internet is certainly not aware of what kind of data is being transferred across it. It doesn't matter if the data being uploaded is a program file, image, digitized movie, or voice. Data is nothing more than data, zeros and ones. The Internet simply moves this data from one point to another, then back again. If that data is voice, then you have the ability to make a "call" thousands of miles away—and escape the highly unpleasant long-distance tolls of the phone company!

All you really need is a way to digitize your speech for transmission across the Net, a way to convert the digitized speech you receive back into sound, and software to handle all the details in between.

This is how people can speak to each other via the Internet: On one end, a user speaks into a microphone. The sound card in his computer converts the analog signal of the speaker's voice into digital data. This data is stored for a very short time in the computer's memory, where it is broken down by a voice communications program into chunks of data called *packets*. From the local computer, the data is transferred through a modem out to the Internet. The Internet is designed to get data packets from point A to point B, so the packets show up where they are supposed to. Once the data enters the remote computer via its modem, the data is put back together in memory. It is then fed through that computer's sound card, where the data is converted back into an audio signal, which is output through the speakers. This whole process happens very fast, and there is nothing really extra special about it. Most computer programs do exactly the same thing: change information into digital data, process it, transfer it, then convert it back into information again.

System Requirements

There are two obvious hardware requirements for engaging in voice communications over the Internet: a sound card and a modem (or a direct connection to the Internet). We'll discuss each in a moment. But there are some other hardware and software requirements and considerations to keep in mind. The following lists what you need to run a phone emulator on the Internet:

- A fast processor (50 MHz, minimum)
- A fair amount of RAM (12-16M is best)
- A good set of speakers with a built-in amplifier and volume, bass, and treble controls
- A microphone with an on/off switch and a long cord
- A TCP/IP connection to the Internet

If you don't have a direct TCP/IP Internet connection, you'll also need a Winsock-compatible SLIP or PPP dial-up connection

> **CAUTION**
>
> Chatting in real-time on the Internet uses a lot of system resources. Many applications, such as Netscape, use near-continuous disk access, which can use enough system resources to "break up" your voice communications. When using any of the Internet voice applications discussed in this chapter, avoid using Netscape or other "disk hogs" at the same time.

Your Sound Card

Since a voice conversation involves both speaking and listening, you have to have a way to get sound into your computer and a way to get it back out again. Fortunately, most computers these days already come with a device built specifically for this purpose—a sound card.

All sound cards are capable of converting digital data to audible audio, and most can digitize audio in real-time from a microphone input. Any card that can do both is capable of being used for voice communications over the Internet.

A 16-bit stereo sound card is best. Though an 8-bit card may work with some of the programs mentioned in this chapter, a 16-bit card will work with all of them. Creative Labs' Sound_Blaster 16 is the industry standard; if you have a Sound_Blaster card (or compatible) hooked up to a compatible microphone and a set of speakers or headphones, you're all set for holding conversations on the Internet.

> **CAUTION**
>
> Windows 95 gives you great multitasking capabilities, but you still can't do two things that access the same hardware device at the same time. For example, you can't listen to a music CD while chatting on the Internet, since both use your audio card.

Unfortunately, most of the sound cards in the world today operate in *half duplex* mode; that is, you can record audio or play audio, but you can't do both simultaneously. This means that your Internet conversations will be limited to a one-way-at-a-time mode. Most people have experienced this type of conversation when using a CB radio or speakerphone; while one person is talking, the other listens. Participants in a conversation must take turns.

There are very few sound cards on the market that support *full-duplex* mode; that is, that can record and play sound simultaneously. With such cards, some of the programs mentioned in this chapter support full telephone-style two-way conversations. Unfortunately, full duplex sound cards are relatively rare and expensive. Four that are currently on the market are the Gravis UltraSound Max, the ASB 16 Audio System, the Spectrum Office F/X (which is an all-in-one fax, modem, and sound card) and the Sound Blaster AWE32. As DSP (digital sound processor) chip technology becomes more prevalent in the PC marketplace, we're bound to see more, less expensive, full-duplex sound cards. (As a side benefit, most will double as modems, since DSP chips are capable of handling both tasks equally well—even simultaneously.)

You can easily test your sound card to see if it supports full-duplex operation by using Sound Recorder, an application included with all versions of Windows. To test your sound card, follow these steps:

1. Open the Multimedia folder which is located in your Accessories directory. Open a copy of Sound Recorder. Then load in a .WAV file choosing File, Open.

2. Open a second copy of Sound Recorder, and press the Record button on the toolbar of this second copy.

3. Now press the Play button on the toolbar of the first copy of Sound Recorder, the one that you loaded the .WAV file into in step 1.

4. If you get the warning dialog box shown in Figure 37.1, you have a half duplex sound card, like most of us. Sorry. However, if the .WAV file plays okay, you're one of the lucky ones—your card is working in full-duplex mode!

FIG. 37.1

Run two copies of Windows Sound Recorder to test whether you have a full-duplex audio card. If you see this warning dialog box, your card is only half duplex.

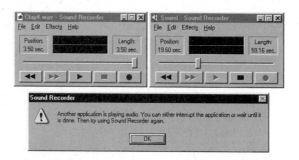

N O T E Some of the programs discussed in this chapter support using two half duplex sound cards to simulate full-duplex operation. However, unless you are a real whiz at setting up PC cards, with a complete understanding of IRQs, and such, don't even think about trying it. ■

Your Modem

If you're lucky enough to have a direct TCP/IP connection to the Internet from work or school, voice communications will be a joy. If not, don't despair—you can still communicate over a SLIP or PPP dial-up connection via modem. You'll find that voice doesn't use nearly the bandwidth that graphics and video do, so chatting over the Internet on a dial-up connection is not only realistic, but is usually indistinguishable from communicating over a direct connection.

The term *"modem"* is short for "modulator-demodulator"; it's a device that converts digital data from the computer to analog signals (audio beeps) the phone lines can handle. If you have ever listened to your modem as it is working, you've gotten an ear full of annoying screeches from your phone. That sound is the converted data being sent along the phone lines.

The most common modem now in use is the 28.8 Kbps (kilobits per second) modem. The number refers to how fast it is; that's a rate of 28.8 Kbps, which simply means that a 28.8 Kbps modem can transmit a little over 28,000 pieces of information (bits) over the phone lines each second. Older modems of 9600 baud (9.6 Kbps) or less are too slow to use on the Internet.

Most modern modems are actually capable of sending data much faster than their rated speed by using built-in data compression techniques. When a 28.8 Kbps modem uses compression, it can transfer over 114K of information per second. However, if you have noisy phone lines (hissing and the like) compression becomes less useful. Noises on the phone line are confusing to modems; line noise can be misinterpreted as data, resulting in erroneous information. That's why most modems have built-in error correction capabilities, too.

A normal phone conversation turned into digital data requires five to eight times the data transmission bandwidth of the original conversation. Without software data compression techniques, real-time voice communication via the Internet would be unfeasible.

N O T E Here's a "Mr. Wizard" explanation of how data compression works: Imagine a series of little sponge balls. If those balls (representing data) have to move through a plastic tube (representing the phone line) via the efforts of gravity alone, they will line up just barely touching and flow slowly out the other end. But if you take a ramrod and push quite hard and fast, the rate that the sponge balls come out increases rather dramatically. The sponge balls compress, but retain their original shape when they pop out the other end. ■

Internet Telephone Software

Voice communications is one of the fastest-developing application areas on the Internet. Why? The reason is simple, and familiar: money. Long-distance phone conversations are costly when they are handled by AT&T, MCI, or Sprint; they're free when placed over the Internet.

Though the technology is only a few short years old, there are already several good Internet voice communications programs available. We'll cover a couple of the most popular, then take a quick look at some of the up-and-comers. Most work very similarly, differing in only a few details and features, and to some degree in their look and feel.

T I P Most of the Internet voice applications discussed in this chapter can be downloaded from the Consummate Winsock Applications List site at **http:// www.stroud.com/**.

CoolTalk

CoolTalk by InSoft is an Internet telephone software plug-in included with Netscape Navigator 3.0. CoolTalk provides full duplex sound for audio conferencing as well as a shared work area where you and a fellow associate can view and edit the same document in real time. Since CoolTalk is part of Netscape 3.0, it is also easy to send and receive calls directly from the browser. Here are a list of features you will get with CoolTalk:

- Audio conference calling in full-duplex
- High-quality audio, low-bandwidth operation
- Phonebook directory of online CoolTalk users

- Answering machine records messages while away
- Shared Whiteboard allows multiple viewing and editing in real time
- Chat tool lets you send and receive text messages

Installing CoolTalk

1. If you have the minimum version of Netscape 3.0 that does not include the CoolTalk plug-in, you can download the program Ctalk32.exe by going to **http://home. netscape.com/comprod/products/navigator/cooltalk/download_cooltalk.html**, and following the steps shown there, and putting the program into a temporary directory on your hard drive.

2. Run Ctalk32.exe—this is a self-extracting file that will unpack itself into the temporary directory.

3. Run setup.exe. If you installed Netscape Navigator 3.0 in the default location and wish to do the same for CoolTalk, you may select the defaults for the CoolTalk setup process.

4. During the Setup process you will be asked to enter your login name, company info, and email address (see Fig. 37.2, the Setup Wizard screen).

5. After running the Setup program, double-click the CoolTalk icon to run CoolTalk (see Fig. 37.3).

FIG. 37.2

Setup Wizard for Entering Login, Company Information, E-mail Address, and Photo.

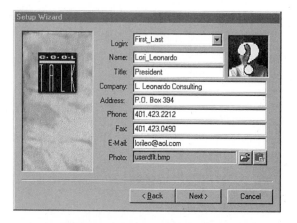

FIG. 37.3

CoolTalk, a built-in plug-in for Netscape Navigator 3.0, is the most popular "phone" application today.

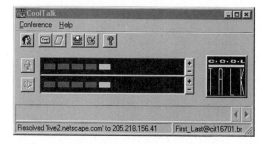

Configuring CoolTalk

To configure CoolTalk, follow these steps:

1. Select Conference Options, IS411 Server: Enter the hostname of the IS411 server you wish to use. The IS411 Server is a service that maintains a list of users currently running CoolTalk.

2. If you wish to make yourself available to other users connected to the IS411 Server you have specified, select Make Me Available Through Server.

   - Bandwidth: CoolTalk's audio communications include two options, 28,800 bps and 14,400 bps. If you are connected at 28,800 bps and you connect to a user who has 14,400 bps selected, you will automatically step down to their bandwidth.

   - Accept Invitation: There are three settings for CoolTalk's behavior when you are invited to conference, Always accept, Ask before accepting, and Never accept. Note that when the Answering Machine is on, this setting is ignored.

3. From the Audio Options page you can set which audio devices CoolTalk will use, and adjust other audio settings. CoolTalk automatically determines whether you have full-duplex audio capability. If you are using half-duplex audio, you can set CoolTalk to automatically switch between send and receive modes to simulate full duplex operation.

4. Using the selection boxes on the Audio Options page, you can select which devices you wish to use to send and receive audio. If your audio is too loud for the other user in the conference, you should turn down the amplification.

Now you're ready to start a new conference with CoolTalk. The following steps explain how:

1. Select Start from the Conference Menu. The Open Conference window will appear. There will be two tabs at the top of the window, Address Book and IS411 Directory.

2. Select Address Book. The window contains an input field where you can enter the user address of a user whom you wish to conference with, and a listing of the users contained in your Address Book.

3. Enter the user name and hostname of the user whom you wish to conference with in the field provided, and hit the OK button. For instance, to invite me, user "lorileo" at the hostname "aol.com", you would enter **lorileo@aol.com** in the field. When you press the OK button, the user you have invited will be sent an invitation to conference with you. Depending on whether they are in another conference, and whether they currently have the software loaded, your invitation will be accepted or refused, or their Answering Machine could pick up.

Once your call is answered, you can begin speaking or using CoolTalk's other communication tools, the Whiteboard and Chat Tool.

The Internet Phone

The Internet Phone by VocalTec was one of the first large-scale marketed software packages to use the Internet. With the right hardware, the I-phone allows full-duplex voice conversations.

Part
VII

Ch
37

N O T E VocalTec is now also working on a new audio software project, I-Wave, which promises to use audio on the Web in new and different ways. Watch this company; they are on the right track for your ears. ■

The Internet Phone is shareware. Though it does not expire after a trial period, you are limited to just 60 seconds of chatting before you get unceremoniously kicked out of a conversation. However, one minute is enough to see just how useful this product is. The $30 registration fee isn't much for what it does.

Installation and Configuration

Anyone with FTP or Web access can download the Internet Phone from a wide variety of Internet sites, including VocalTec's home page at **http://www.vocaltec.com/**.

To install it, follow these steps:

1. The program you downloaded is a self-extracting EXE file; in its current incarnation, it's called Iphone40.exe.

2. Double-click Iphone40.exe to extract the program files. Three subdirectories are created under the /Setup directory: Disk1, Disk2, and Disk3 (see Fig. 37.4, WinZip Self-Extractor screen).

   Setup.exe (which can be found in /Setup/Disk1 subdirectory) is automatically launched. The Internet Phone is installed on your system, and a program group is created for it.

FIG. 37.4

WinZip Self-Extractor—
Iphone40 exe.

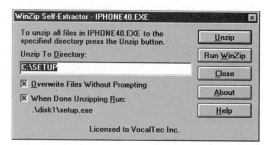

How Internet Phone Works

The I-phone piggybacks on the Internet's preexisting IRC (Internet Relay Chat) servers. Unbeknownst to many IRC users, their IRC host computers are thus pulling double duty. VocalTec allows the user to choose from a number of servers that already exist, so they don't have to charge you to use a special server of their own. The I-phone uses on-the-fly compression, so you don't really notice any lag when online, no matter which IRC server you're connected through. IRC servers simply receive and retransmit I-phone data; at this time the servers lack the capability to discriminate between voice transfer or text. As long as IRC servers continue to house Internet Phone transfers, VocalTec has a sure winner. However, the Internet Phone's use of IRC servers puts VocalTec in the position of looking for friendly IRC servers to keep up with the growth of the I-phone.

Although using IRC servers for Internet phone traffic is a truly inspired idea, there could eventually be a problem with usage of the I-phone bogging down IRC servers. Although I-phone comes preprogrammed to use several friendly IRC servers, there is nothing to stop users from deciding to meet via a particular IRC server. In cases such as this, the organization that owns the server may not want to act as an I-phone host. This is understandable, as hosting I-phone sessions is not what IRC servers were designed for.

After the I-phone is installed on your system, you can be online in seconds.

If you're not connected to the Internet via a "land-line" TCP/IP connection, the first thing you need to do is establish a SLIP or PPP TCP/IP dial-up connection. Once online, you can fire up the Internet Phone program.

At this point, establishing a conversation is easy (see Fig. 37.5). I-phone automatically connects to an IRC server and lets you start chatting.

Text Chat Session

Send Voice Mail

FIG. 37.5

The layout of the Internet Phone has all the controls the user needs accessed from one screen. The ten "tiles" keep track of the last ten people accessed. With one touch, you can automatically connect to them if they are online.

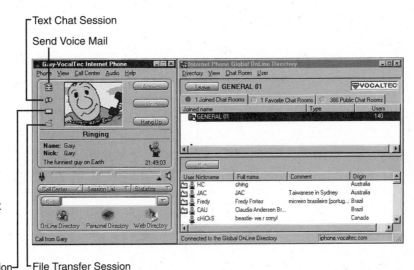

Whiteboard Session — File Transfer Session

Of course, it is best to take a few minutes to configure the I-phone first to get optimum results.

Configuration involves the following few steps:

1. Under View menu, choose Options. Click Global Online Directory. A list is displayed of phone servers shown in Figure 37.6.

2. The default IRC servers are checked, or you can uncheck any IRC servers from the list.

3. Under Options, choose Audio (see Figs. 37.7 and 37.8). Confirm that the audio settings are what you want.

4. Choosing Set Voice Activation (VOX) Level from the Audio Settings tab allows you to set the threshold where your microphone kicks on and off as you speak (refer to Fig. 37.8).

(This is also done via the little button to the left of your readout—bottom right of the main I-phone box.)

FIG. 37.6

The Internet Phone lets you set up many IRC servers as your default phone connections.

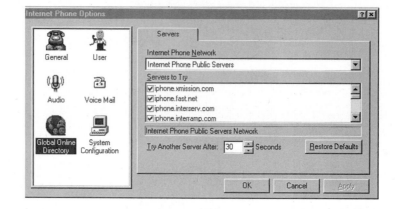

FIG. 37.7

The Audio/Sounds dialog box lets you configure sound options.

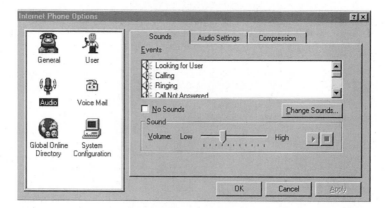

FIG. 37.8

The Audio/Audio Settings dialog box lets you configure audio options.

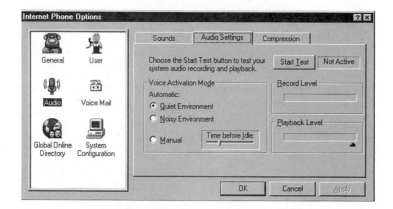

5. It's a good idea to choose Start Test from the same Audio Settings dialog box to make sure everything is working together properly.

6. Under the same Option menu, choose User. Fill out your personal information. After all, everyone is just as curious about who they are speaking to as you are (see Fig. 37.9).

Part

VII

Ch

37

FIG. 37.9
From the View Options menu, choose User, you can enter a little information that you would like other Internet Phone users to see.

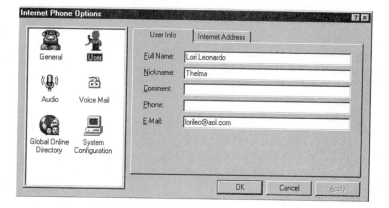

Making a Call

Now you are ready to talk to someone online. Connecting is super easy. When you start the application, you'll see the main program window shown. The I-phone will automatically connect to the IRC servers you checked in step 2 of the configuration procedure listed in the previous section.

Finding someone to chat with is very easy, too. By clicking the Call icon (the telephone in the upper-left corner of the I-phone window), you will see a list of people and topics, Global OnLine Directory, that is just like a list of IRC (Internet Relay Chat) channels (see Fig. 37.10). You can join several topics at once. General is the best topic to join; it's also the default topic. To get a list of topics, click the Public Chat Rooms button. Be prepared for some wild topic names out there. Below a list of users will be displayed with a little bit of information about themselves.

FIG. 37.10
The Call dialog box (Global OnLine Directory) shows people and groups you can chat with.

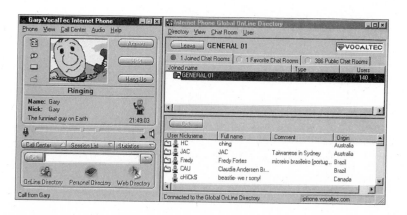

To initiate a call, double-click the person you are interested in chatting with. You'll hear a tone signifying that an attempt to connect is being made. If the target of your conversation is already talking to someone, you'll get a traditional busy signal along with a message that tells you they are busy.

When you find someone to talk to, you'll find that the voice quality is quite similar to a speaker phone. The only lag that you'll really notice is from distance. Just as a transatlantic phone call experiences a bit of lag, the same lag exists with the Internet. After all, it's the same cable (or satellite link).

 When speaking to people from different countries, remember to avoid odd slang or excessive contractions. Also remember to speak slowly and very clearly— accents are magnified when you can't see the person speaking.

N O T E   The I-phone has some nice extras that you will find very useful. You can choose the View Statistics option under the Options menu to display some very useful information. The stat sheet shows incoming and outgoing packets, but what I really find useful are the lost packet indicators and the average round-trip delay display (see Fig. 37.11). The higher the percentage gets on the lost packet indicator, the worse the quality. I have found the most loss you can handle without the conversation becoming nearly impossible is around 30 to 35 percent. After 35 percent, incoming audio is in short bursts with long gaps separating them. The round-trip delay number is in milliseconds, so if the statistic window shows a delay of 684, the round trip is .684 seconds. That may seem like a long time for computers, but it is subjectively very fast. ■

FIG. 37.11

When speaking with someone using the Internet Phone, you can pull up a display on the remote user you are speaking to and information on the quality of the connection.

If you wish to send Voice Mail to a friend, click the Send Voice Mail icon in the upper left hand corner of the main VocalTec Internet Phone screen. A dialog box (similar to an E-mail message) will be displayed (see Fig. 37.12).

FIG. 37.12

If a user is not available to speak to when using Internet Phone, you can pull up a Voice Mail dialog box and send a voice message.

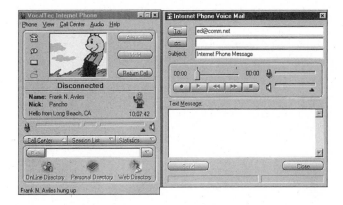

Part

VII

Ch

37

Not every communication has to be audio. You can communicate through text by choosing the TextChat Session button on the upper left corner of the main Internet Phone screen (under the Send Voice Mail button). See Fig. 37.13.

FIG. 37.13

You can have a chat session (text) by choosing the TextChat Session button on the main Internet Phone screen.

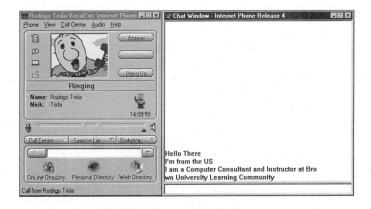

You can also view and work on projects with fellow associates in real time by choosing the Whiteboard Session button from the main Internet Phone screen (under the TextChat Session button). See Fig. 37.14.

For troubleshooting and technical support, select Support Wizard from the Help menu. I-phone will bring up their own browser with troubleshooting and technical support information (see Fig. 37.15).

FIG. 37.14
View and work on projects with fellow associates in real time by choosing the Whiteboard Session button from the main Internet Phone screen.

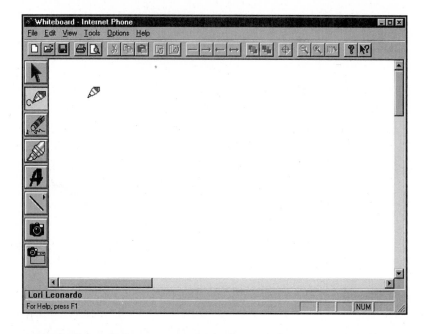

FIG. 37.15
Internet Phone technical support screen.

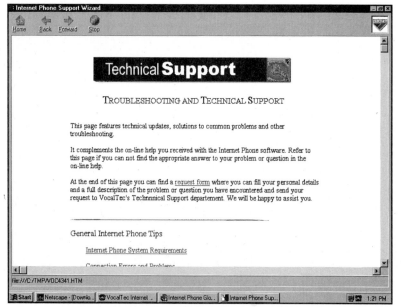

Digiphone

Another major Internet phone application is Obicom's Digiphone (see Fig. 37.16), distributed by Third Planet Publishing. Where the I-phone uses IRC servers, Digiphone uses direct point-to-point connections to other users with Digiphone software.

Part

VII

Ch

37

FIG. 37.16
To begin contacting users, type in the remote person's e-mail name in the Connect To box. From this box, Digiphone resolves the individual's IP address.

Without having to go through a central server of any kind, Digiphone is immune to server problems. When you use a server of any kind, your transmissions have to be received and re-transmitted by the server computer. Though problems at the server end do not happen very often, they can. It's just one more thing to worry about.

Digiphone is a commercial application, however, you can download a 30-day trial version of the program at **http://www.planeteers.com/**. You will find the instructions for downloading the trial version further along in this chapter.

Installation and Configuration

When you get Digiphone on CD-ROM, installation is easy. The install program runs very quickly due to the fact that the vast majority of information on the CD-ROM is extra (wave files) and is not really needed. The actual Digiphone program fits on just one 1.44M disk.

Digiphone features a compact user interface (refer to Fig. 37.16). Each option is actually launched via the taskbar. Digiphone automatically registers each user the first time it is used.

To set up Digiphone, select Settings, then Connection from the menu, then enter your e-mail name and mail server. Digiphone automatically resolves the IP addresses involved. Keep in mind that you need to enter the e-mail address of the ISP you are going to use Digiphone with. For the mail server address, you can enter the IP address or name of the mail server. If you don't know either, you will have to contact your ISP (Internet service provider) and obtain this information. Remember that mail servers have a unique name associated with them (such as mailserver.domain.com). Simply entering your domain name will not be enough for Digiphone to work with.

N O T E If your ISP assigns you an IP address each time you log on, that means you have a dynamic IP address, not a static IP address. With a dynamic IP address, you will not know what address the rest of the Internet knows your computer by until you log on. To find out if you have a static or dynamic IP, contact your Internet service provider. ■

The Provider Settings window allows users with dynamic IP addresses to use Digiphone. This is done by entering a range that your IP address will fall under. Internet service providers set aside a block of IP addresses to be used over and over as people log on to the Internet via their server. Contact your ISP to find out what range they use for dynamic IP addresses. To enter the range of dynamic IP addresses, use Advanced Direct Dial Configuration from the Provider Settings window.

When Digiphone is launched, your taskbar shows the main Digiphone minimized button along with a TCP/IP connected indicator. To do anything with the Digiphone, you need to right-click the minimized Digiphone to get a list of actions you can take. From here, you can configure the Digiphone. Right-click the minimized Digiphone, and choose the Connection settings. A nice feature allows the user to choose to employ compression, encryption, or both (see Fig. 37.17). On this same screen there is a sampling rate, which shows how much data is used per second as you send data. Using the default sampling rate is good if you feel you can squeeze higher fidelity; increase the number by blocks of one thousand. The higher the number, the better the quality, but the performance will begin to suffer. This is something that needs to be set for each computer, as no two systems are the same.

FIG. 37.17
Each user of the Digiphone can set compression or encryption. As encryption and security are becoming important issues, this is a very nice feature.

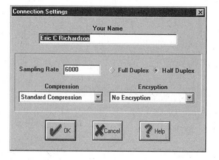

If you have a Sound Blaster card, Digiphone will work in Full Duplex which is really nice. If you don't have an application that is 100-percent SoundBlaster-compatible, you are stuck with Half Duplex.

CAUTION

Be careful not to select Full Duplex mode if you don't have a Sound Blaster (or an application 100-percent compatible) when installing Digiphone. I accidentally knocked out my sound driver by testing this. The program won't auto-seek your soundcard type. It would be nice to see it do so and automatically adjust the settings on Digiphone. If you are not sure what card you have and cannot find any supporting literature, select Half Duplex.

From the minimized Digiphone on the taskbar, choosing VOX settings will bring up the VOX dialog box. The VOX level sets the threshold to activate the microphone. If you set the number higher, you will have to make quite a bit of noise for your mike to begin transmitting; if it is set very low, you will have to whisper to avoid your mike locking open. Setting the VOX to be less sensitive is better; many people find it useful to keep background noise to a minimum and the microphone from transmitting when it really shouldn't. If the person you are speaking to says that the first syllable of speech always seems to be cut off, that is an indicator that you need to make the microphone a bit more sensitive. The alternative to that is to make a noise right before you begin to speak; any very short grunt will actually work quite well.

Included on the Digiphone CD-ROM is a very nice collection of .wav sounds. Open Explorer and move to the CD-ROM; from there move to the ringers folder where you will find many interesting files to copy into you main sound files folder.

The Digiphone CD came with two accessory disks. These disks hold what may be some of the best reasons to go out and buy Digiphone. They contain a high-quality suite of Internet access applications that are designed to get anyone up and running on the Internet (see Fig. 37.18). The cornerstone of this collection is the DigiSock TCP/IP dial-up stack, which can get you set up with a SLIP or PPP Internet connection. If you are looking for some new connection software to access the Internet. look no further.

FIG. 37.18

The additional undocumented applications that come with Digiphone make up a substantial addition to your purchase.

As I mentioned before, you can download a 30 day trial version at **http://www.planeteers.com/**. Follow the steps below to download and obtain a 30-day registration number (necessary to install the software).

1. Create a temporary directory on your hard drive.

2. Download the self-extracting .exe file Dptrial.exe by going to **http://www.planeteers.com/** and select the 30-day trial button (see Fig. 37.19) or go directly to **http://www.digiphone.com/download/dptrial.exe**.

3. Obtain a 30-day registration number at **http://www.digiphone.com/rexx-bin/timelcns.cmd**.

4. From Windows Explorer, double-click Dptrial.exe to extract the program files.

5. Double-click Setup.exe and follow the instructions on your screen. Make sure you have obtained your 30-day registration number.

FIG. 37.19
DigiPhone home page located at **http://www.planeteers.com/** where you can select a 30-day trial version.

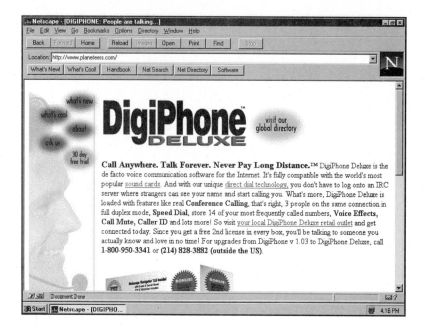

Making a Call

If you know the e-mail address of a friend with whom you wish to chat, enter her name in the Connect To field on the main Digiphone control panel. Then enter her domain name and hope she is online. By entering the domain name, a general search is made of people within that domain. If people are online with Digiphone, you see their e-mail addresses displayed on a list; from that list you can choose the names of those you'd like to chat with. If you don't already know whether a friend is online, there is no simple way to check in advance.

When I tested the Digiphone, I didn't know anyone specific to try to speak with. The manual suggested that I download a list of users from their Web site. While exiting to a second application to retrieve a list of information isn't my idea of ease of use, it did get me up and running. Digiphone does let you search a list of users from the Directories menu option. Choosing Global lets you get information about a specific name, country, state, or time zone.

Receiving a call is a lot easier than making one. A question box pops up indicating the person who wishes to speak to you and an Accept or Reject button. One feature I find neat is the ringing sound file that comes with Digiphone is actually a phone bell ringing. Odd how a program that is so modern would use a traditional ringing phone sound that has not existed for most people for the past 15 years.

Internet Global Phone

Internet Global Phone is strictly for those who are interested in becoming skilled programmers. The IGP is nowhere near ready to run when you download it—in fact, you have to finish it to suit your own needs.

In real estate, they have what they call "fixer uppers." This pretty much describes IGP. Written in Microsoft Visual C++, IGP requires that you build your own user interface. On the other hand, it is totally free. You can get the software by starting an FTP session to **ftp.cica.indiana.edu/win3/demos/IGP**. If you want the source code, FTP to **ftp.cs.tu-berlin.de/pub/local/kbs/tubmik/gsm/ddj**. This is a good example of college students doing a lot of work on their own and subsequently developing something on the Internet for all to use. In its current state, Internet Global Phone is really more of a learning tool. If you are asked for a username and password, log on as username Anonymous with your password being your actual username.

Speak Freely

Speak Freely supports three forms of data compression as well as secure communications using data encryption with DES, IDEA, and/or a key file (see Figs. 37.20 and 37.21). If the PGP (Pretty Good Protection) program is available on your system, it can be invoked automatically.

FIG. 37.20

Though it looks plain, Speak Freely packs a lot of power under the hood, including built-in data encryption and several compression options.

FIG. 37.21
Connection Options
Screen enabling built-in
data encryption.

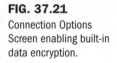

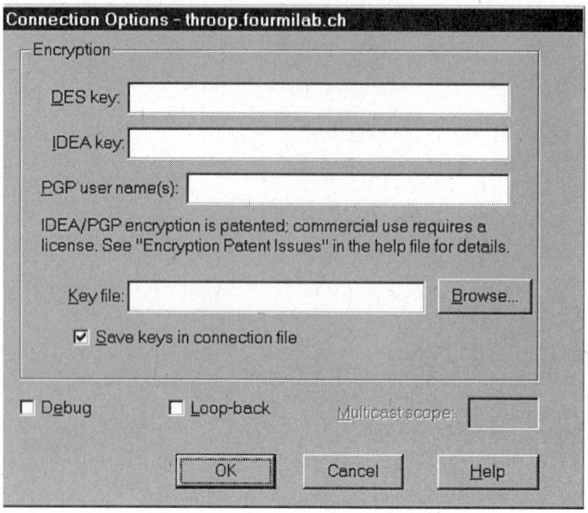

There are Windows and UNIX versions of Speak Freely. Users of the program for both plat-forms can find one another by communicating with a phone book server.

Multicasting is also implemented, which allows you to create multi-party discussion groups users can subscribe to or drop at their discretion. For those without access to multicasting, a broadcast capability allows transmission of audio to multiple hosts (at least, it does on a fast local network).

Speak Freely was written by John Walker, the founder of AutoDesk and the programmer who created AutoCAD. The latest version of Speak Freely can be downloaded from his home page at **http://www.fourmilab.ch/**.

WebTalk

WebTalk is the first Internet voice communications program to come from a major, established player in the software industry: Quarterdeck, the publishers of the QMosaic WWW browser. Intended as an add-on to QMosaic, WebTalk has released a full version of its program and promises to be a major force in defining the future of voice communications on the Internet, if for no other reason than the marketing muscle behind it.

For the latest on WebTalk, including an online shop, check out Quarterdeck's home page at **http://www.quarterdeck.com/**.

WebPhone

If there were an award for "Flashiest User Interface Design for an Internet Voice Communica-tions Program," WebPhone would win it hands down. This program is configured to look and work like a sexy high-tech cellular telephone (see Fig. 37.22).

FIG. 37.22
If looks were everything, WebPhone would have it all. The user help is just as classy looking, and it is complete and genuinely helpful.

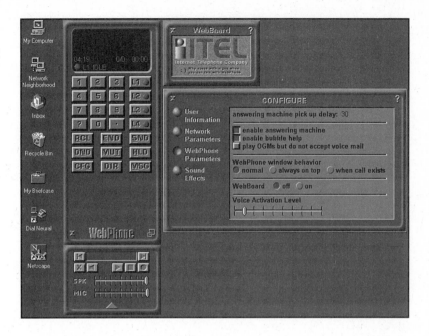

Because its user interface is based on a common, everyday item, WebPhone is uncommonly easy to use. What you can't figure out right away is clearly explained in WebPhone's truly helpful (and downright fun to use) online Help pages.

WebPhone (from the Internet Telephone Company—honest!) gives you a plethora of user options, plus four phone lines. It offers full-duplex operation with the right sound card and half duplex for the rest of us.

ITEL's Directory Assistance Server connects you to other WebPhone users worldwide, and you also have a local phone book. Integrated Voice Mail is included from NetSpeak.

You can try out the latest version of WebPhone for free by downloading it from ITEL's home page at **http://www.itelco.com**. WebPhone's one-time "activation fee" is $49.95.

PowWow

"Unique" is an overused word, but PowWow (see Fig. 37.23) really is a unique personal communications program for the Internet. Besides voice chat (our topic at hand), PowWow lets you chat with up to seven people by keyboard (as well as voice), send and receive files, play .WAV format sound files, and browse the World Wide Web together as a group. It is probably the most sociable Internet application I have ever seen.

FIG. 37.23

PowWow is optimized for friendly use by small groups.

Perhaps it comes as no surprise that this program is of Native American origin (a very social people). It was created through the auspices of Tribal Voice, an organization run by Native Americans from many tribes, which is dedicated to providing a Native American presence in the high-tech industry through free and low-cost computer software and services. All Tribal Voice products are "Native American in concept, architecture, and implementation."

PowWow connects to users through their e-mail addresses. All that's necessary is that they are running PowWow, too.

PowWow enables you to be very personable. You can send the URL of your home page to the people you're chatting with, and they can click the link to view it. You can set it up to send a JPEG image of yourself along to those who want to view it. You can chat with one or many, using voice or text. You can ask others to tag along with you as you browse the Internet as a group—a really neat feature that I haven't seen in any other software, anywhere.

There's even an Answering Machine mode where you can enter a message (up to 255 characters) that you would like displayed to those who try to connect to you when you have the Answering Machine mode turned on.

This program is well worth a look, if only to check out its truly unique features. The latest version can be found at **http://www.tribal.com/**. This site also includes a comprehensive phone book of PowWow users.

TeleVox

TeleVox, formerly Cyberphone (see Fig. 37.24), is an Internet phone application that supports both full- and half-duplex operation. It even comes with a set of drivers that purport to give you full-duplex operation with a SoundBlaster-compatible sound card, which usually only supports half-duplex operation.

FIG. 37.24

TeleVox sports a user-friendly interface window with big, colorful, clearly labeled, easy-to-understand buttons.

With versions available for Windows, Linux, and Solaris, TeleVox can claim to be one of the few cross-platform-compatible Internet voice communication applications. It also supports multiple users, and saves different user information files (including passwords) for each. TeleVox is server-based, which means that e-mail addresses and IP addresses are not required to initiate conversations—you just click the recipient's name in your phone book. (You can manually dial to an IP address if you want to, though.)

TeleVox can be downloaded from the VoxWare home page at **http://www.voxware.com/voxmstr.htm**.

TS Intercom

Telescape's TS Intercom (see Fig. 37.25) not only allows people to talk over the Internet, it also lets them view images and transfer files while they talk.

FIG. 37.25

The TS Intercom program window displays two images, one specified by you, and one by the person you're chatting with.

The most finely tuned part of TS Intercom seems to be the installation file, which has a slick interface and nice graphics. It makes unzip-and-install-it-yourself style shareware programs look anemic by comparison.

On the techie side of things, TS Intercom lets you set Word Length and Fidelity options, both of which affect audio transmission quality, which can improve performance over a slow connection.

One slick feature of TS Intercom is its ability to let you set up a signature image file in .gif, .jpeg, or .bmp format. While this picture can be of you (if you're of the type who wants everyone to know what you look like), it can also be an image of a project, design, or other topic under discussion.

Setting up a chat session is pretty easy. You can e-mail your intended recipient using a built-in link to your favorite mail program before starting up. TS Intercom maintains a phone book of people you've chatted with in the past.

Perhaps TS Intercom's most useful feature is its ability to send and receive files during a chat session. This has its fun aspects (sending picture and sound files, and so on) but it can also be very useful when you need to exchange documents, CAD files, or spreadsheets in a business environment.

The latest version of TS Intercom can be downloaded from **http://www.telescape.com/**.

Real-Time Audio Player Programs

What if you have no desire to talk to someone else over the Web? What if all you want to do is listen—in real-time?

Real-time audio is an emerging technology on the Internet, and there are a couple of relatively new programs that will get you involved and show you what the excitement is all about. The two top contenders right now are Progressive Networks' RealAudio and DSP Group's TrueSpeech.

RealAudio

RealAudio (see Fig. 37.26) was designed to allow real-time, one-way sound transfer over the Internet. RealAudio is currently freeware; you can look at it and download it from the RealAudio home page at **http://www.realaudio.com**.

RealAudio plays RealAudio format sound files, which have the filename extension .ram. RealAudio can be installed as a Web browser helper application, or it can load RealAudio files directly from disk or from a World Wide Web URL address. After launching, RealAudio sets up a buffer of several seconds that it uses to keep a few seconds of reserve time in case something disrupts the audio stream.

FIG. 37.26

When a RealAudio file is accessed from a Web browser, the RealAudio player pops up. Once installed, RealAudio is designed to allow the Internet user to just sit back and listen.

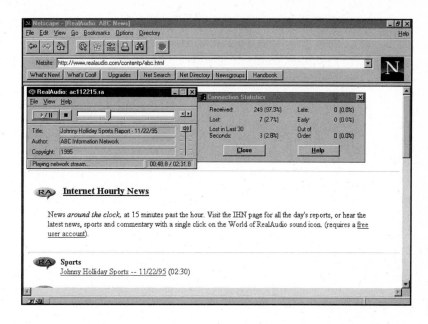

Using the buffer technique makes the mass broadcasting of audio files possible. You can connect to one of many live Net broadcasting sites. It is still very early in RealAudio's history, but even now many radio stations are moving to set up live feeds. From talk radio to sports to music, RealAudio is getting noticed as a way to send audio information on the Web. The ABC Information Network broadcasts news, sports, and commentaries from Peter Jennings. A favorite of many people is the National Public Radio site, where you can listen to your favorite PBS radio show. Links to these and other sites can be found on the RealAudio home page listed earlier.

While RealAudio is playing, you can multitask fairly well. Even using Netscape is possible while an audio feed is transferring. Real Audio is proving to be a very stable audio Internet utility.

Currently, it is necessary to obtain a user name and password to access many of the RealAudio pages. The service is free, so the real inconvenience is only felt the first time you use the service. An e-mail with your user name and password confirmation arrives very soon after applying for access.

From the RealAudio home page, you can also download utilities to create your own RealAudio .RAM files.

Netscape Corporation apparently has a high opinion of RealAudio—they have included it in Netscape Power Pack ($54.95), their CD-ROM collection of five Netscape support utilities. The Real Audio Player is in good company; the other applications on the Power Pack CD-ROM are Netscape Chat, Smartmarks, Adobe's Acrobat Reader, and Apple's QuickTime movie viewer. With Netscape support, Real Audio is bound to have a bright future on the Web.

TIP A good place to find .RA files is the Internet Radio Network at **http://town.hall.org/radio/**. They have over 200 hours of files online, and regularly broadcast the proceedings of Congress over the Web in real time. (The files are available in .WAV format, too.)

RealAudio is an application to watch; it is changing nearly as fast as the Internet itself. After all, if major radio stations and television networks notice RealAudio, you should too.

TrueSpeech

Any sound can be digitized, including speech. But sounds digitized in the proprietary TrueSpeech format by DSP Group, Inc., can be compressed and still retain excellent quality. DSP says that its technology can compress one minute of digitized speech to a file only 64K in size. It licenses this technology to developers (for a fee), but provides a free real-time player called TSPlay32 (see Fig. 37.27) to users who want to play them. It can be downloaded from **http://www.dspg.com/**.

FIG. 37.27

The TrueSpeech Internet Player plays wave files, and is optimized for playing digitized speech.

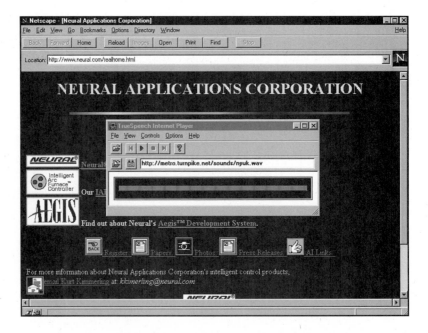

TSPlay32 is a Win95 program that plays TrueSpeech files and regular wave files to boot. (This program can also easily be configured as a Web browser helper application for playing all the waves that come its way over the Web.)

One of its best features is that it can play sound files in real time, as they are downloading; you don't have to wait for a file to download first. If you don't like what you hear, you'll know right away and can cancel the transfer in mid-stream. This can save you lots of expensive connect time if you're previewing many sound files, but keeping only a few. Of course, nothing is perfect—TrueSpeech sometimes gets ahead of a download and has to pause and wait for it to catch up, but you can always hit the Play button to start the file playing over again from the beginning.

TrueSpeech is unique in that it is on the forefront of a new World Wide Web technology: programs that can access the Web independently of a browser. You can run TSPlay32 all by itself and choose to load and play a file from your disk or network; but you can also tell it to load a URL and it will connect to the Web and play a file directly from the site where it is stored, all without the aid of Netscape or any other browser. This kind of independent program is going to open up the Web and make it seem more like a wide-area network than a communications service. Look for more programs like TSPlay32 in the near future.

Part
VII
Ch
37

Changes Voice Communication Is Making on the Net

Speaking by way of the Internet is still in its early stages, but there is a tremendous amount of potential in such technology.

Just as the telephone revolutionized conversation early in this century, Internet talk software could initiate another revolution in the way we converse. Voice communications on the Internet is still in its "hobbyist" stage, much as radio was in the 1920s. Though it is currently not practical to make initial contact with people in the business world with Internet phone utilities, that day may come sooner rather than later.

For personal communications, where price is a major factor in limiting long distance calls, Internet voice chat utilities are already unmatched in economy, if not usefulness.

Long distance phone companies have already indicated that they are not amused with this emerging technology. Expect to see it challenged in the courts, especially when the money to be made becomes substantial and the money lost by the phone companies makes it worth their while.

The Future

In the near future, we'll see fiber optic data lines in every home. One fiber optic cable running into your house could handle phone, live video feeds, cable TV, and Internet WAN (Wide Area Network) connections, and still be ready to accommodate lots more data. Until we see widespread fiber optic data distribution, however, there is still much more that can be done with existing technology. Refinements are being made to the electronic hardware we are all using now. In conjunction with the hardware improvements, programmers are always making better and better software.

The future of audio on the Internet includes the following possibilities:

- Conference calling in full duplex
- The Internet answering machine ("Sorry, I'm not online now")

- Talk forwarding to other terminals
- Sending files to each other as you talk about something
- Remote talking, so you don't have to be sitting in front of your computer

What will happen in the future is still just speculation. The many different voice utility applications will probably settle into one standard (or a very few).

Voice communications on the Internet has the potential of becoming as popular as the World Wide Web. It is a very possible that on business cards, people will someday have Internet voice contact information right under their e-mail address.

N O T E For more information on the topic of voice communications on the Internet, check out the Internet Phone FAQ (Frequently Asked Questions) file on UseNet. This file is posted on the 5th and 19th of each month to the UseNet newsgroups **alt.internet.services**, **alt.bbs.internet**, **alt.culture.internet**, **alt.winsock.voice**, **alt.winsock.ivc**, **comp.sys.mac.comm**, **comp.os.ms-windows.apps.comm**, **alt.answers**, **comp.answers**, and **news.answers**. The latest version of the FAQ is also available on the World Wide Web at **http://www.northcoast. com/~savetz/voice-faq.html** and **http://rpcp.mit.edu/~sears/voice-faq.html**. ▨

CHAPTER 38

Video Conferencing on the Net

by Mark R. Brown

The Internet is, in its raw form, communication. It should come as no surprise, then, that those of us who use the Internet have pushed progress in the direction of better and faster ways to transmit data.

Previous chapters have shown you that there's a move to make communicating via the Internet more natural. Voice communications have made great strides in that direction, and real-time video conferencing—which was fiction just a few years ago—is quickly becoming a reality on the Internet. ■

The history of video conferencing

This chapter shows you the technology behind video conferencing and the motivation for its evolution.

The advantages of video conferencing

You can get a lot of business done and save a lot of money by video conferencing. You can also have a lot of fun.

Install and configure CU-SeeMe

CU-SeeMe is one of the most popular video conferencing programs for the Internet. You'll learn where to get it, how to install it, and how to use it.

What the future holds for video conferencing

Video conferencing is still a very young technology. You need to understand where it's going and what the possibilities are. This chapter shows you.

Communications and Video Conferencing

The Internet has recently become quite popular with the business community; this interest has spawned a large amount of capital investment in the Internet and is beginning to reap rewards. The commercial community is now busily working to develop ways of information exchange that duplicate face-to-face conversation.

The private market (including colleges and universities) has been the major driving force behind the Internet in the past. However, as both the business and private sectors see advantages to video conferencing via the Internet, the world can expect this technology to grow rapidly.

We are now poised on the verge of finally making Dick Tracy-like gadgetry available to anyone on the Internet. With the strong multitasking power of Windows 95, simply downloading software may be all that is needed to implement useful video conferencing capabilities via the Internet.

Many previous attempts to bring video conferencing into the mainstream have failed because of the extreme cost of the hardware involved. Purchasing such equipment is still beyond the budget of most companies. An approach that uses inexpensive off-the-shelf consumer hardware in combination with innovative new software is much more practical and affordable.

The History of Video Conferencing

Twenty years ago, AT&T made an attempt to create a device that would allow two-way communication that went beyond the telephone. It was called the Picturephone. Although it worked, it never made it beyond the "odd new developments" segment of the evening news.

At that point, the technology simply was not in place to create a worldwide network of Picturephone terminals—which would have been very large and impossibly expensive to manage, anyway.

However, the Picturephone did start many people thinking about how to better transmit data and voice in a real-time environment. It is interesting to note that although the Internet did exist in the form of ARPANET at that time, it would still be quite a few years before serious work would go into merging it with video conferencing.

In the latter part of the 1970s, satellites offered the next chance for real-time video conferencing. There have been communications satellites in orbit around Earth since the very early days of orbital launches, but until the '70s it was nearly impossible for anyone to use a satellite communications *transponder* because of the extreme costs. (Most people over 30 can still remember how novel it was to watch a live broadcast from the other side of the world for something such as the 1972 Winter Olympic Games.)

Unless you happened to be a television network or the government, you simply couldn't afford it. In the late '70s and early '80s, with so many new satellites going up, renting a transponder became much less expensive. Video conferencing then became practical for larger companies;

in most ways, it was no different from setting up a closed circuit television system with a camera at each end.

N O T E A *transponder* is analogous to a modem, but it communicates over a channel on a satellite rather than on a telephone line. Most modern satellites used for TV have 24 transponders each for video, with a large and variable number of audio channels. ■

Video conferencing is still expensive when using the older technology, though high-speed phone lines or fiber-optic links are now used in lieu of satellites.

What may very well make long distance audiovisual communication commonplace on the Internet is modern digital technology—the same technology that was used in large part to create the computers that make up the Internet.

The Advantages of Video Conferencing

Part
VII

Ch
38

Companies worldwide share one common mantra: "Save Money." If anything pushes the development of video conferencing on the Internet, it will be this concept.

Many Kinko's and other copy stores nationwide have video conferencing suites available for rent. It is far less expensive to rent one of these suites for $150-$200 an hour and have people out of the office for a part of a day than it is to send a delegation to the other side of the world. This saves time as well as money, and time is still the most important commodity in business.

Video conferencing can foster better feelings in the people taking part in a long-distance conference than mere phone conferences can. Simply simulating a face-to-face meeting puts people at ease, even though everyone involved is aware of the distances being spanned. As with e-mail, IRC, or even the telephone, there exists a natural curiosity about what someone looks like (which is a subject worthy of its own book!).

Besides satisfying curiosity, video conferencing lets people convey meanings beyond what is being verbalized. All the speakers (and nonspeakers) in a meeting are constantly giving visual cues about what they may be feeling or thinking.

Simply put, body language has always been important and observing body language is a superb way to get "gut feelings" about situations. Ask any long-time salesperson about body language—you may be surprised what they can tell just by reading a person for subtle signs.

Then, too, when group effort becomes important and colleagues are scattered over a great distance, video conferencing shines. When talking about physical objects, such as when architects need to confer on a three-dimensional model of a proposed building, seeing something is far better than trying to describe it.

Data sharing can also be integrated into some video conferencing schemes, which lets people remotely work on the same spreadsheet, program code, document, or design. The old adage says that a picture is worth a thousand words, but a three-minute video conference can be worth a day of discussion when everyone can see and manipulate the same data.

T I P A good way to keep up to date on what is going on with video conferencing is to use IRC. There are many useful channels for video conferencing information. Try contacting the CU-bot for up-to-date information—just send the bot a private message (**/msg cu-bot help**).

For more information on the topic of video conferencing, you might want to check out links to this topic on the CU-SeeMe Web site at **http://cu-seeme.cornell.edu** (see Fig. 38.1).

FIG. 38.1
The CU-SeeMe home page on the Web is a wonderful source of information on video conferencing on the Internet.

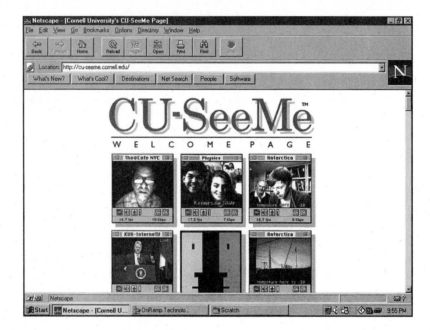

The Problem of Bandwidth

To understand how the Internet can transmit and receive the volumes of data that are involved in video conferencing, you need to comprehend the concept of *bandwidth*. Most people think bandwidth is the amount of data that can be transferred. While this is essentially correct, the true definition is a bit more complicated than the popular view.

My father, an electrical engineer, told me of a good analogy between current (amps) and voltage (volts). It's like the relationship between a hose and the water that flows through it. It is possible to have a hose with a huge diameter but just a moderate amount of water moving through it—the water trickles out of the hose.

On the other hand, if you have a hose with a small diameter and the same flow of water, you get a high-pressure jet. That is, the water has to move faster through the small diameter host to produce the same amount of output at the end. If you connect a bunch of hoses that can move water at different rates end to end, the water can only flow through the whole length at the speed allowed by the slowest hose in the system.

I've found that this same concept pretty much applies to digital bandwidth. Keeping with this analogy, the water flow rate (meters/second) is equivalent to data rate (bits/second). (Bits per second is the basis for rating of the speed of modems.) The data line (hose) limits how much data (water) can pass. The more constricted the data line is, the less data can flow in a given time period.

The Internet as a whole is made up of very dissimilar data lines: Some are as slow as regular phone lines while others are very fast. The Achilles heel of transfer speed on the Internet is wherever a step down in the speed of the data lines takes place. This is a "choke point" where the data traffic jam piles up.

From the choke point all the way down to the end user, data transmission is slowed to the speed of the choke point. This is why someone working on a computer directly connected to the Internet (such as an Internet service provider) has tremendous transfer rates. With a fast connection and no choke points, data flows better than water over Niagara Falls.

Part **VII**

Ch **38**

When you try to send both video and sound over the Internet, you are sending a huge amount of data down your data line. When this raw data is fired out into the Internet, the first choke-point hit disrupts the flow of data. The result is slow data reception, and choppy video and audio at the receiving end.

Hardware for Video Conferencing

The hardware needed for setting up desktop video conferencing is widely available. For high-end equipment, it is possible to spend in excess of $1,000, but a budget under $500 will do nicely (assuming you already have the computer). For example, take a look at Connectix's QuickCam. You can find more information by pointing your Web browser at **http://www.connectix.com/connect/catalog.html**.

Your Computer

The first and most important piece of equipment you should already have is your computer. If it is running Windows 95 relatively quickly and with no problems, you should have smooth sailing.

Usually, Windows 95 likes to reside in a fairly fast PC with a good amount of memory. Those general parameters also match up to the requirements of video conferencing.

Video Capture Board

The only piece of equipment you have to buy for two-way video conferencing is a video capture board (VCB). A VCB allows your computer to take an image from a video source (like a video camera) and translate it to digital data.

It's how you'll get a live video image of you into your machine and onto the Internet. You need one that handles live video in real time, not just single images.

VCBs are easy to install, but *first read the instructions.* (It's amazing how many people think instructions are to be read only as a last resort.)

A VCB can usually be installed in just a few minutes by taking the cover off your computer, finding an empty expansion slot, and placing the board in it. Sometimes the VCB replaces your video card, so be aware of that.

Using Windows 95 does not necessarily excuse you from having to install any driver software that comes with a video capture board. After the board is installed, power up your computer.

If Windows 95 does not automatically detect anything new, go to My Computer, open the Control Panel, and double-click on the Add New Hardware icon. You see a screen that says "To begin installing your new hardware, click Next." Try to click Next and let Windows 95 try to find the changes you made.

I have had pretty good luck with letting Windows 95 tell me about the changes I made. If your computer cannot find the new device (sometimes it thinks it is just a video card), install the drivers. Keep the number of the manufacturer's tech support line nearby in case you get into a bind.

Camera

The next piece of equipment is not as vital as you may think. The camera for your computer simply plugs into the video capture board you just installed.

Here again, after reading over the literature that comes with your camera, try to get Windows 95 to see if a new piece of equipment has been added to the system. Don't be surprised if it doesn't, as VCBs and cameras are not standardized for computers.

One point to look for when you purchase your camera is how physically stable the thing is. If it has double-sided tape on its feet, don't buy it.

It should be stable and preferably bottom heavy so it won't tip over if you bump into your desk. (Think about how many times you whack your knees into your desk during the average day!)

The camera should have some nice options, such as letting you control the zoom and aperture setting. There are really nice cameras out there that come with a remote to let the sender sit back and control the zoom and pan so viewers won't end up with a tight shot of someone's nose looking back at them. The camera should also be somewhat portable.

A camcorder is an alternative to using a special camera to video conference. With virtually no effort, you can attach a camcorder to a video capture board. If you purchased a VCB that has an audio and video input, you can probably just hook the camcorder into it.

To get an idea of just what audio and video connectors are, look at the back of your VCR. The little circular connectors labeled "Audio" and "Video," in and out, are the very same.

If your camcorder has an audio and video connector, just go to any electronics store and buy a length of VCR dubbing cable. More than likely it will be color coded. The two popular schemes are a combination of red and black or white and yellow.

Using a camcorder is great if you don't want to buy a special one-use-only camera. The video quality you will end up transmitting is quite like a tape recorded on the camcorder.

Sound Card

The sound card is something you probably already have. Cards that seem to work well are the higher-end, 16-bit cards. Cards that use 32-bit sound are really great, but if you have an older computer, odds are you won't have VESA or PCI slots (high-bit slots, 32 and 64, respectively) anyway, so just make sure you have a good 16-bit sound card.

There are many good sound cards on the market today. Finding a sound card with good bundled software makes the audio portion of video conferencing much more manageable. A software package that has a mixer incorporated into it allows the end user to better control the audio environment.

A microphone is used with the sound card to transmit audio with the video. Microphones are not very expensive: Good ones are usually less than $25.

Monitor

A monitor is the interface to your eyes when you are video conferencing on the Internet. For the purpose of video conferencing, a killer monitor doesn't really bring you any great advantages as technology stands now. Most applications used by Windows 95 need a good monitor anyway.

As the technology driving the Internet is growing quickly, a good monitor will probably be needed in the near future! If you are buying a new monitor, go for a 15-inch or larger monitor capable of displaying a resolution of 1024–768. A monitor with a non-glare screen is less fatiguing to look at for long stretches of time.

You can see that the hardware needed for video conferencing is nothing rare or unusual. Setting up your system is as easy as putting in your video capture card, connecting your camera or camcorder, and loading any special drivers that Windows 95 may need.

CU-SeeMe: A "Free" Video Conferencing Program

On the CD

With video conferencing for the Internet still in its infancy, there are very few software packages to connect people to each other available via the Internet. One of the best and most widely available programs currently available is CU-SeeMe (see Fig. 38.2). It's a free video conferencing program that is available from the CU-SeeMe Web site at **http://cu-seeme.cornell.edu**. You can also find CU-SeeMe on the NetCD.

Part
VII

Ch
38

FIG. 38.2

The CU-SeeMe main program title bar. As soon as the program starts, CU-SeeMe begins waiting for a connection to be made.

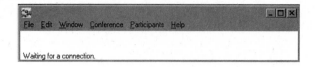

Besides the version for Windows 95/Windows 3.1, there is also a version of CU-SeeMe available for the Macintosh and UNIX. This way, almost anyone accessing the Internet from home, school, or the office can video conference with someone else doing the same.

Besides the hardware requirements, a PPP/SLIP account is a must. As for modems, 14,400 bps is the slowest you can get away with as long as the modem is using compression to "fake" a 57,600 connection. A 9600 modem or slower simply does not get the job done (but no one really has 9600 modems anymore, do they?).

A good quick way to judge if you are able to run CU-SeeMe well is to check how well you can access the Web. Using your Web browser as a diagnostic tool is actually a pretty good idea. If you are waiting eons for your browser to download complex files, you'll also have problems with CU-SeeMe.

Not much video equipment has been fully tested to work with CU-SeeMe. A list of tested hardware is available on the CU-SeeMe Web server (**http://cu-seeme.cornell.edu**).

But you already have a video capture board and camera hooked up, right? Sure you do, because you want to try CU-SeeMe yourself.

Reflectors

Just as IRC uses one computer to host many individual users, CU-SeeMe uses the one-to-many concept. CU-SeeMe uses very powerful UNIX computers to handle the job of actually connecting individual users together.

UNIX is just an operating system, but it is far more powerful than Windows 95 and a whole lot less user-friendly to those without lots of UNIX experience.

The centralized CU-SeeMe server computers are called *reflectors*. A reflector keeps track of who is connected to it, what data is coming in from people sending video, and what data is going out.

Reflectors are like the air traffic controllers of the Internet except they don't take coffee breaks. When connected to a reflector site, you can view up to eight different people sending video at once. (Of course, the more you are trying to watch, the more likely you are to bog down your system.)

When using a reflector, you can choose either to transmit data and become a sender or to simply sit back and watch what is going on. This makes you a *lurker* just like those who read but never type on IRC.

Many colleges have their own reflectors. Usually when there is a NASA mission, you can connect to a college reflector and view what is going on at NASA.

Having a cable TV system that is still in the dark ages, I am very happy to link to a CU-SeeMe site during a shuttle mission to watch and listen to what is going on. (The other alternative is to drive to someone's house with a better cable provider, which I have also done in the past!)

When there is a constant feed, such as during a NASA mission, most colleges ask people not to transmit data. This is done so only the NASA information is going out, allowing more people to lurk. Lurking at times like this is not only acceptable but preferable.

It is possible to use CU-SeeMe without a reflector—if both participants have a stable IP address, private conferencing is possible. Each user just needs to type in the other's address. Of course, as this is not encrypted at all, it is not secure but it is still better than chatting via a reflector.

Installation

CU-SeeMe is not a hard program to use or obtain. The version I have was downloaded from the CU-SeeMe Web home page (**http://cu-seeme.cornell.edu**).

N O T E   There is also a commercial version of CU-SeeMe. Check out White Pine Software's site at **http://www.wpine.com/cuseeme.html** for information. ▬

The file is zipped so unzip it in its own folder. Remember, you can pretty much name the folder anything you want (some of us still have to break the habit of keeping folder and file names to eight or fewer characters).

Once it is unzipped, bring up Windows Explorer and drag the icon into the folder that you have all your Internet utilities in. (If you bought this book, it's more than likely that you spend a lot of time using the Internet, so just keep a folder on your desktop with your Net goodies inside.)

Once you start CU-SeeMe, you see the main program window. In just a few minutes, you will be able to set it up and start receiving information from people. If you decided against getting the camera and capture board, all you can do is watch, but that's okay, too.

Configuration

Configuring CU-SeeMe is fast—just open the Edit menu, choose Preferences (see Fig. 38.3), and type your name or handle into the Preferences dialog box.

Part
VII

Ch
38

FIG. 38.3

The Preferences box, which is an option under the Edit menu, shows everything you need to configure CU-SeeMe.

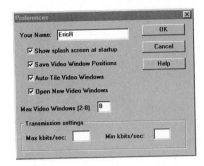

The Show Splash Screen at Startup option tells you which reflector you are connected to. Save Video Window Positions keeps your daughter windows where you want them next time.

Auto Tile Video Windows spaces them at a nice distance every time a new window is opened or started. Open New Video Windows does not ask your permission to pop open a display as soon as someone on the reflector begins transmitting from his or her camera.

Operation

When pulling up the Connect window from the Conference menu option (see Fig. 38.4), you see the Connect box. From here, you enter the IP address of the site or reflector you want to connect to. Just type the IP address of a reflector there, and you're off and running. The drop-down box has a list of IP addresses in it if you don't know any.

FIG. 38.4

The Connect box is the most-used option in CU-SeeMe. If you have a camera, you can select to send video or not; you should always leave the I Will Receive Video check box enabled.

Once you connect to a reflector, anyone who is already set up to transmit data does so automatically. As soon as a new sender connects, the standard video startup screen appears.

The square with "CU-SeeMe for Windows" displayed is where the image of the participant with a camera appears (see Fig. 38.5). The eye indicates if he or she has the receive video option turned on: "Yes" if the eye is open (and he or she has a camera), "no" if the eye is closed.

The speaker tells the status of the person's audio panel. If there is an "\" through the speaker, the person has all sounds muted. If the microphone is pressed, it means you can chat verbally with that person in private mode.

This is not as good as the Internet Phone program but you can still communicate verbally, albeit not as clearly as with the Internet voice utilities. It is also possible to speak to someone who is sending video even if you do not have a camera set up.

The last two buttons are to display information such as bytes transmitted and the IP address of the sender. The bottom numbers display frames per second (fps) and kilobytes per second (kps).

FIG. 38.5

This is a good example of the features incorporated into an incoming video window. The window usually ends up being roughly two inches by two inches.

A few seconds after the new video window pops into existence, an image of the sender appears. Besides verbal and video, those sending video have the option of typing messages at the same time they send video.

These messages appear across the bottom of their video window. Sometimes when data is missing or there is a bottleneck somewhere, partial information comes across.

As is pretty obvious from the figures, the picture quality isn't astounding. The images are about 120×120 pixels in size and are not updated very often. In fact, if you achieve a transfer rate of over 15 fps, consider yourself blessed by the gods of the Internet.

I have tested CU-SeeMe on a Pentium 100 with a direct connection to a server off a T1. I did not get much above 15 fps myself in those situations.

The images are rather low resolution. Not only do the images need to be small, but keeping the resolution down keeps the data outbound to a minimum. CU-SeeMe does use compression, but when sending even low-end audio and images, there is still a large amount of information being compressed.

Until compression on the fly gets a little better, we have to be satisfied with these resolution and audio limitations.

Audio is controlled by choosing the Conference option on the main menu and selecting Show Audio Panel. The audio panel has only a few options, but this option is all you really need.

Figure 38.6 shows the basic audio panel. The line through the microphone button mutes outgoing audio. Lurkers can speak to each other; if you don't want to hear them, just uncheck that option. When listening to someone, the intensity shows on the bar.

Part VII

Ch 38

FIG. 38.6
CU-SeeMe's basic audio panel lets you choose who—and who not—to listen to. Uncheck the Hear Lurkers box to cut off audio from lurkers.

The audio has a bad habit of popping and hissing a lot. Sometimes 30–50 percent of the audio is distorted to the point of being impossible to understand. Although this can get annoying, one needs to remember this is still new software in a totally new field of the Internet.

Pulling up the Participants menu allows you to choose the Show All command to view all the senders and lurkers. From here, you can get a good idea of what is going on.

If you want to chat with just one lurker, press the microphone button on his or her line. If you want to know a bit more about the lurker, click the information buttons (see Fig. 38.7).

FIG. 38.7
This figure shows a full site with NASA sending and many lurkers watching.

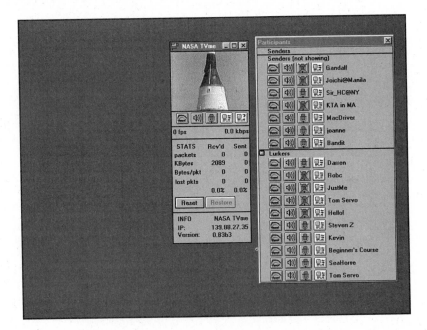

Limitations

Reflectors can't handle very many people at once; it is somewhat common to get an error message about too many lurkers being connected. When this happens, there is no recourse but to wait and try again later.

Lag time is also something that we all deal with on the Internet. As it is caused by many independent variables, it is a sure bet that Internet lag will continue to haunt us for generations.

> **N O T E** One subtle but ubiquitous annoyance with video conferencing is the human element. Until the day we embed a small camera in the middle of all monitors, people in video conferences will either appear to be looking away from the person they are speaking to or will have that weird look of staring directly into the camera.
>
> When exposed to cameras, most people tend to act differently—not necessarily goofy like when we were kids with uncontrollable desires to mug for the camera, but just a bit stiff. ▨

The Future of Video Conferencing

The problems inherent in transmitting real-time video and audio on the Internet won't slow the growth that video conferencing on the Net is beginning to experience. In fact, video con-ferencing looks to be a bright star of the Net for years to come.

The MBONE

The Multicast Backbone, commonly called the MBONE, is the newest gun in the arsenal of video conferencing. The MBONE has existed for a few years, but is still not very well known. The MBONE is able to multicast video and audio, which lets one person video conference with just one person or many people with great ease.

The MBONE supports multiperson conferencing at the same time, and it is being used for live Internet video broadcasts of events like rock concerts and conferences as well. The MBONE is basically a combination of improved equipment and tweaking of the current technology in use. You will undoubtedly hear more about the MBONE in the future.

> **N O T E** The MBONE is a more-or-less permanent arrangement, and it needs a commitment at the network administration level. If you would like your workstation-based LAN to become part of the MBONE, the IP multicast software is available by anonymous FTP.
>
> To find out how to download and set up the MBONE software, get the document called "mbone-connect" from **ftp://genome-ftp.stanford.edu/pub/mbone/**. But first, read the MBONE FAQ (frequently asked questions) list at **http://www.best.com/~prince/techinfo/** for more details about how MBONE works. ▨

The Virtual Meeting Room

AT&T is back at it from the Picturephone a few decades ago to the virtual meeting room today. The virtual meeting room's purpose is to try to fool our senses into thinking we are in a real meeting, interacting with other people.

The theory is that even when the mind knows something is not real, if the five senses say otherwise, the mind just might allow itself to be fooled. Virtual reality is the driving force behind this, as it is in many innovative Internet applications. Many futurists think the two will end up being the same thing.

Holographic Video Conferencing

Holography is a very exciting area of science. When we are able to project realistic holograms, the virtual meeting room will be outdone. The hardware and software for *Star-Trek: The Next Generation* holodeck-type, three-dimensional holography is quite a while off, but we are making rapid strides in that direction.

Maybe someday we will just plug into the Net and stay there. Video conferencing then will be our best way of communicating over distance. In fact, it might be almost indistinguishable from meeting in the flesh.

What to Do

Video conferencing is currently being used as a toy for the technologically curious and as a legitimate tool for business. Many software manufacturers are looking into writing more commercial software such as CU-SeeMe.

The history of software and applications for the Internet has shown that usually college students and hackers start working on something, and then it becomes popular. A company eventually gets involved because there is profit to be made.

Keep on the prowl for new and potentially interesting software as it comes out. However, with the complexity of video conferencing software, even an early beta version of a new program without a lot of nice extras still takes up a large amount of hard drive space.

Having a hard drive of one gigabyte or larger is generally a prerequisite for exploring video conferencing. Windows 95 can help with good compression software built right into it via the DriveSpace utility. I download lots of software, play around with it, and then archive it on a pile of floppies.

For my archiving purposes, I use all those nice free disks mailed to me by America Online, CompuServe, and PRODIGY. I get about 70 free disks a year. Just slap a new label on and erase the disk via Explorer to make it ready for useful service.

Whenever you are importing lots of new software, it is imperative that you do regular backups of your data and check for virus problems. With that said, go out of your way to try to find great repositories of software that are updated often.

Once you find yourself downloading every new piece of video conferencing software just to see what new goodies have been incorporated, you will know there is no going back to being satisfied with the telephone. ●

CHAPTER 39

Gaming on the Net: MUDs, MOOs, and MUSHes

by Faisal Jawdat

This chapter discusses Internet-based gaming. We'll look at how personal computers and UNIX systems fit in with traditional Internet games and see some of the new games that are taking advantage of the Internet. Most of the games discussed here require that you have TCP/IP access to the Internet—via PPP (or SLIP), a direct connection (such as ISDN or a T-1), or your online service.

There are far too many games on the Internet for us to cover in one chapter, so this chapter only goes into the specifics of the most popular online games. We look at traditional Internet games such as MUDs and Netrek, and more recent PC-based games such as Stars!, SubSpace, Bolo, and Quake. ■

How MUDs work

MUDs contain entire virtual worlds where you can meet and interact with other players. This chapter covers the basics of finding, connecting to, and using MUDs.

How Netrek works

Netrek is a complex space battle strategy game. You learn the basics of joining and playing Netrek games.

Quake, Stars!, Bolo, and more

We go over the basics of Internet games for personal computers, including Quake, Stars!, Bolo, and SubSpace.

DOOM, Descent, Warcraft

How to use traditional PC network games on the Internet.

The Beginnings of Internet Games

The first Internet games were developed on UNIX systems, where they were very popular. The most popular of these "traditional" games has always been the MUD (Multi User Dungeon, Multi User Dimension, or Multi User Dialogue, depending on who you talk to)—any of a breed of virtual worlds ranging from social fantasies to high adventure. MUD players create a character who interacts with the world and other player-controlled characters.

Another popular "traditional" game on the Internet is Netrek, a real-time, multiplayer arcade and strategy game with a theme loosely based on *Star Trek*. Netrek was developed for the X Window System beginning in the late 1980s, and offers players the opportunity to command starships, travel the galaxy, and blow up their friends.

While MUDs and Netrek are now available for Macs and PCs, many new Internet games are being developed for personal computers first and aren't making their way to the UNIX platform. Many new games for PCs and Macs are being released with Internet-based, multiplayer support, and tools are becoming available to allow traditional IPX based games for MS-DOS to be played over the Internet.

> **CAUTION**
> Experience has shown that the interactive nature of Internet games can be highly addictive. Internet gamers are frequently known to log several hundred hours of game play per year.

Online Gaming Concepts

Internet games differ from other games in that they use the Internet to allow multiple players to participate in the game. How they use the Internet to do this varies from game to game, but most Internet games use one of three general styles to communicate: e-mail, client-server, or peer-to-peer.

E-mail Games

E-mail games are usually turn-based strategy games that work by saving each player's turn and then using e-mail to send the saved game file to the game coordinator or the next player.

Client-Server Games

In client-server games, each player's computer runs software (called *the client*) which communicates with a central coordinating computer (called *the server*).

Peer-to-Peer Games

In peer-to-peer games, every player's computer communicates directly with every other player's computer on an equal basis.

Traditional and Multiplatform Games

This part of the chapter concentrates on traditional Internet games (such as MUDs and Netrek) that are available for all platforms, as well as some new multiplatform games designed for Internet play.

MUDs

MUDs are possibly the oldest and most popular multiplayer games on the Internet. Simply put, MUDs are virtual worlds where players control characters who interact with other players' characters. There are many forms of MUDs and it is practically impossible to create a description that applies to all MUDs.

Most MUDs present a fantasy or science fiction setting; others provide no theme or serve as virtual meeting places for business or educational users. Some MUDs concentrate on adventure and combat, while others are designed for socializing. Most MUDs are text-based but work is being done on graphical MUDs.

People familiar with classic, text-based adventure games such as *Adventure* or *Zork* should feel right at home in a MUD. Similarly, IRC users might feel quite comfortable in a MUD.

> **N O T E** Many descendants of the MUD now go by different names. In this chapter we use *MUD* to describe all members of the family of MUD-related games—including MUD, MUCK, MUSE, MUSH, MOO, etc. In instances where we refer to a specific form of MUD, we refer to it by a more precise name. ■

A History of MUDs The first MUD was written in the late 1970s by two Essex University students. After several rewrites and ports to more powerful computers (the original version ran on a DEC microcomputer and used 50K of RAM), the system was hooked up to an experimental ARPANET gateway and began serving users from around the world.

MUD development progressed slowly until the late 1980s when several people began development of new MUD servers for use with UNIX-based systems. Most of the MUD servers in use today owe at least part of their design to the MUDs designed in the late 1980s.

Types of MUDs Most of the MUDs in use today fall into one of two categories:

> *AberMUD, LPMUD, DikuMUD*—These MUDs are the most "lightweight" of the MUDs, with less support for "world building" than their more full-featured cousins. AberMUDs are among the oldest MUDs in use today and the simplest. LPMUDs are more powerful and are among the most popular MUDs around. LPMUDs are often used for combat-oriented games.

> *TinyMUD* (and variants)—TinyMUD and its descendants (most specifically, TinyMUSH) have rich world-building capabilities, allowing players to extend the MUD beyond the original design. TinyMUDs are often used for socially oriented systems.

There are also several other MUD systems in use today. One of the more interesting systems out there is *MOO*—a MUD based on an object-oriented programming system. MOO is very powerful, though slower than other (simpler) MUD systems.

How MUDs Work MUDs are based on the client-server model of communication. MUD administrators set up the MUD server—the Internet host to which players connect. Players run the MUD client—the program used to connect to and play on the MUD. All the action on the MUD is calculated on the server, and players use the client program to control their characters. Note that when people talk about connecting to the MUD, they generally are referring to the MUD server.

MUD Clients Most MUDs are based on simple commands such as "go north" or "kill bob," so players can use a MUD almost as easily from a UNIX terminal as from a graphical client for Windows 95 or the Macintosh.

In general, any MUD client (such as MUDDweller, GMud32 or TinyFugue) works with any MUD server, but some clients have special features that work only with some types of MUDs (for example, some clients provide special combat features that only work on LP MUDs). Figure 39.1 shows the GMud32 client for Windows 95.

FIG. 39.1
GMud32 for Windows 95 in action.

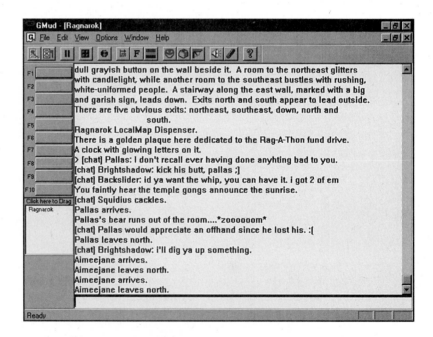

MUD Servers MUD servers run on large computer platforms and consume large amounts of resources. Most of these resources are devoted to the MUD's database, which describes the world, its inhabitants, contents, and more.

Most MUDs fall into one of the types previously discussed and generally have custom modifications (the "world" is what makes the MUD succeed or fail, so most MUD administrators put a lot of work into describing and expanding the database before the MUD is opened to the public). Customizing the database allows the MUD's creators to set the tone for the MUD and determine what characters can do there.

MUD servers are accessible via a standard Internet address with the addition of a port number. The port number is generally 4 digits and tells the client where to find the MUD on the server machine. For instance, the former ZenMOO was located at **cheshire.oxy.edu** and the port number is **7777**.

There are many MUD servers on the Internet to suit a wide variety of tastes. Rather than giving you a specific MUD to try out, we recommend that you check out **http:// www.mudconnect.com/**—an Internet site that catalogs MUDs so you can search for the one that is right for you. Take a few minutes to look through it now and find a MUD with a theme you find interesting, then record that address to use in the examples below.

MUD Culture   MUDs represent virtual worlds with fictional characters and plots so it should come as no surprise that MUDs have developed a culture of their own. It is important to be aware of MUD traditions and jargon. Conversely, people who ignore MUD etiquette will often get a bad reputation.

MUD Jargon   Over the years, MUDs have developed a jargon of their own. Some important terms include:

> *Bot*—A bot is a character that is controlled by a computer program rather than by a human being.
>
> *Furry*—This is anything cute and fuzzy. Generally this means a human/animal crossover character but it has other implications as well.
>
> *God*—This is the owner of the MUD, the person who set it up.
>
> *Lag*—This is the elapsed time between when you enter a command and when it's actually executed. Lag can come from heavy usage of the server or heavy usage of network bandwidth.
>
> *Tiny*—This is a prefix indicating that something is related to MUDs or based in MUD-life rather than real life. Many MUD dwellers have been known to have TinyFriends and perhaps a TinyGirlfriend or TinyBoyfriend.
>
> *Spam*—a Spam occurs when someone (or something) suddenly outputs large amounts of material to the screen, thereby messing up everyone's terminal. Spams are highly frowned upon.
>
> *Wizard*—Wizards are the leaders of the MUD, though their role varies from MUD to MUD. In general, Wizards are responsible for building the world appropriately and keeping the game enjoyable while keeping the regular players from getting out of line. The Wizards generally report to the God of the MUD.

MUD Etiquette   The first thing to realize about MUD culture is that it isn't uniform. What might annoy one group of people might amuse another. However, there are some general guidelines:

- Many people take MUDding very seriously. Always keep this in mind while playing.

- It is considered bad form to speak out of character without explicitly stating that you are doing so. Even if you do make this clear, don't expect people to pay attention to you— many players don't want to bring real life into the game at all. Accordingly, don't ask other players about their real life.

- Don't do anything you wouldn't do in real life unless it's something appropriately in character. In particular, unwarranted obnoxious behavior and flames will get you a reputation as a jerk.

- Always read the appropriate help and news files on the MUD to get an idea of the theme and current status of the MUD. Ask Wizards and experienced players for help when you need it but otherwise try to stay out of their hair.

- Don't be a dork. Trite as this might seem, this advice is necessary because many of the problems that people have with MUDs could be solved easily if one person wasn't being silly or stubborn about something he or she has no business being involved with in the first place. If something seems as if it will cause trouble, it probably will.

Choosing a Character Name   In a MUD your character is known by a name that is typically different from your real name. Your character's name provides a way to identify you uniquely on each MUD. In general, you should pick one character name and stick with it. On the other hand, don't be afraid to change your name if it becomes necessary. There are several issues to consider in picking a name:

- Many people use the same character name across multiple MUDs, especially in the case of social MUDs. You might find that your name conflicts with the name of someone who is well known, which can lead to all sorts of problems.

- In heavily themed MUDs, character names usually have something to do with MUD background. "ElfBane" makes sense in "Enraged Goblins MUD" but doesn't fit so well in "BattleStar Galactica." Likewise, "Starbuck" doesn't fit so well in "Enraged Goblins MUD."

- Don't pick a name that is either obnoxious or one that will annoy others.

N O T E   Some MUDs require you to register your character before you begin playing. This ensures that only serious players are involved in the MUD.

Information on how to register is usually displayed when you first connect to the MUD. Send your registration information to the contact person once and wait a week or two for a response—MUD administrators are often quite busy and they don't like impatience. ■

MUDs and Real Life   With MUDding, the line between real life and fantasy can get blurred fairly quickly. While we won't suggest that dragons really could jump out of your computer and eat you, it's quite possible for you to find that your personal emotions and life get entangled with your character's virtual emotions and life.

For this reason, many MUDders feel very strongly about how much they do and do not mix up real life and online life. It is important to respect other people's desires in this manner—while some MUD users are very friendly and eager to meet other MUD users in person, other MUD users have no interest in meeting other players offline and will get *very* annoyed if you press the issue.

MUD Software   Originally, a MUD player would connect to a MUD by using the Telnet application to connect directly to the MUD server. As MUDs evolved, people developed special software for connecting to MUDs.

We discuss a few of these specialized MUD clients here but there are many others available. We recommend that you experiment with the various clients available for your system and choose the one that suits you best.

Telnetting to MUDs   If you don't have access to a MUD client, you can Telnet to connect to the MUD server. How you access Telnet depends on your system:

Part
VII
Ch
39

- On a UNIX system, type **telnet** [host] [port] and press Enter. Replace [host] and [port] with the host name and port number of the MUD server—don't type [host] or [port] exactly.

- On a Windows 95 system, use the built-in Telnet application. From the Start menu's Run... command, enter **telnet** and press Enter. When Telnet has launched, choose the Remote System... command from the Connect menu and fill in the fields for Host Name and Port (you can ignore the TermType field). Press Enter and you should be connected to the MUD within a few seconds.

- On the Macintosh, use a program like NCSA Telnet. Open NCSA Telnet, and select Open Connection... from the File Menu. Fill in the host name and port in the Host/Session Name field of the connection dialog box and press Enter. The connection should open momentarily.

If you've found an appropriate MUD from http://www.mudconnect.com/, try connecting to that MUD now. For example, the former ZenMOO was located at cheshire.oxy.edu, on port 7777. UNIX users wanting to connect to ZenMOO would type:

telnet cheshire.oxy.edu 7777

Macintosh and Windows 95 users would launch their Telnet application and then fill in **cheshire.oxy.edu** and **7777** in the appropriate fields to connect to the MUD server. Figure 39.2 shows a Windows 95 Telnet session to a MUD.

FIG. 39.2

Connecting to a MUD
with Windows 95's
Telnet.

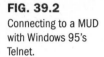

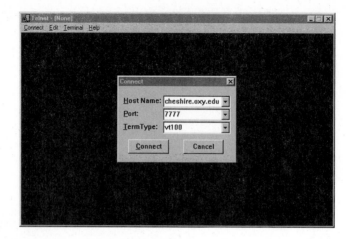

MUD Clients for Windows and Windows 95 There are several MUD clients for Windows and Windows 95. These clients make it easier to store lists of frequently visited MUDs and allow you to record macros for complex commands.

Many clients also allow you to enter multiple MUDs simultaneously so you can "lurk" on one while chatting or moving around on another. Our favorite client is GMud (available from the MUD section of the Papa WinSock archive at **ftp://papa.indstate.edu/winsock-l/mud/**). You can also find GMud on the Net CD included with this book.

To connect to a MUD using GMud, click the Connect button, which brings up the Connect to a Mud Server dialog box. Click the Add button, then enter the appropriate information for the server you want to connect to. Once the information is entered, the MUD appears on the list and you can double-click the name to connect. Figure 39.3 shows GMud connecting to a server.

MUD Clients for the Macintosh One of the more popular clients for the Macintosh is MUDDweller. MUDDweller has a quirky interface but it offers a lot of power and makes it easy to hold a conversation while many people are talking. Figure 39.4 shows a typical MUDDweller session. You can find MUDDweller at the Info-Mac HyperArchive at **http://hyperarchive. lcs.mit.edu/HyperArchive.html** and on the Net CD included with this book.

To connect to a MUD using MUDDweller, launch MUDDweller and select TCP/IP Address... from the Configure menu. Enter the host name and port number, click OK, then select Open Connection from the Configure menu. The connection should open momentarily.

MUD Clients for UNIX Not surprisingly, there are a lot of MUD clients for UNIX-based systems. One of the oldest and most popular is the text-based TinyFugue package. TinyFugue gives you the same line-by-line display that Telnet gives you but adds the ability to create macros and play on multiple MUDs at once.

FIG. 39.3
Using GMud to connect
to a MUD.

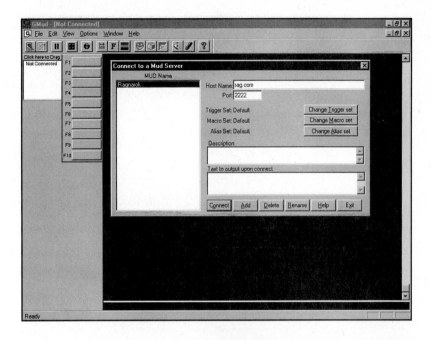

FIG. 39.4
Dwelling with
MUDDweller.

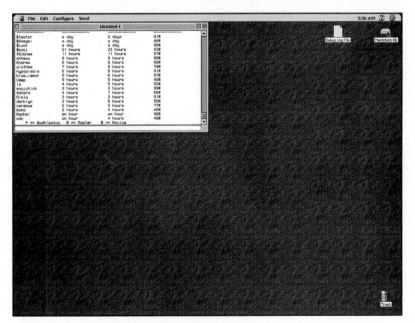

Also, TinyFugue can store your preferences for various MUDs. TinyFugue is available on many UNIX systems under the commands tf or tinyfugue. For example, to connect to the former ZenMOO, you would type:

> **tf cheshire.oxy.edu 7777**

or

> **tinyfugue cheshire.oxy.edu 7777**

If neither command works, you might want to ask your system administrator about installing TinyFugue.

Joining a MUD   Before joining a MUD, you'll have to find one you are interested in. UseNet users can check out **rec.games.mud.announce** for posts detailing the latest and greatest MUDs. You can also find lists of MUDs at one of several Web sites.

Web users can also check out a listing of sample MUD sites at **http://www.mudconnect. com/**. If this site is inaccessible, try using a Web search engine (such as Lycos—**http:// www.lycos.com/**) to find the type of MUD you are looking for—many MUDs now have a home page devoted to them. Another valuable resource is the Yahoo MUD list at **http:// www.yahoo.com/Recreation/Games/Internet_Games/MUDs__MUSHes__MOOs__ etc_/**.

Connecting to the MUD   When you have a site in mind, launch your MUD client and open a connection using the directions listed above (of course, if you're using a MUD client not discussed above, you should follow the directions from documentation for that client).

Once you have successfully connected to the MUD, you should see some form of login banner or list of possible commands. At this point, you are directed to enter your name and a password. This process varies depending on the type of MUD and whether you have a character there already.

On an LPMUD, you are commonly asked for your character name, then your password. If your character name is new, you might also be asked some supplementary information for the administration's sake. On a MUSH and some other TinyMUD variants, you will need to type different commands depending on whether you already have a character.

If you want to create a new character, you would type:

> **create [character] [password]**

If you want to connect to an existing character, you would type:

> **connect [character] [password]**

N O T E   As above, replace the words in [] brackets as appropriate (in this case, with the character name and password). ■

For example, to create ElfBane with the password BuzzCut! you would type:

create ElfBane BuzzCut!

You would then be able to access this character by typing

connect ElfBane BuzzCut!

> **N O T E** If you do not have access to a graphical client such as GMud or if you are accessing the
> Internet via a shell account, remember that you can always connect to a MUD via Telnet or
> TinyFugue, as previously described in the section "Telnetting to MUDs." ▪

Getting Help The first thing to do after connecting to a MUD and getting a character is to find local Help. The best place to start is the MUD's own online Help system, which lists the administrators and how to get in touch with them.

The Help files also describe how a particular MUD is set up, what the theme is, and what rules of behavior are in effect. Once you are familiar with the files, you can begin asking questions of other MUD users.

Getting Help is easy but the commands often vary by system. The most common command is

help

or

help [topic]

If Help doesn't work, try substituting @help. On some systems you might also want to try .help and +help to view help files on advanced commands.

More experienced MUD users are an excellent source of information—many are friendly and willing to help out a new player. In general, the nicer you are towards experienced players, the nicer they will be to you.

The less you ask of an experienced player, the more help they will give you when you need it. See the section "Dealing with Other Users," later in this chapter for more information on interacting with other users.

The MUD administrators can give you some help but keep in mind that they are very busy. Further, while MUD administrators are more willing to put up with "newbie" questions, they can also kick you out if you annoy them.

Administrators are best at answering technical questions and solving problems with the MUD, so it might be best to ask those questions of the administrators and save the rest for your fellow players.

Exploring the MUD Much of the MUD fun comes from exploring new and unfamiliar parts of the world. Navigating the MUD is extremely simple but there are a few points that are worth remembering in case you ever get in a jam.

MUDs are generally made of rooms that are connected by *exits*. Exits, in turn, point to other rooms. Common exits are north, south, east, and west. To access an exit, you need only type the name of the exit (on some systems you might need to type go before the name of the exit).

Conventionally, most rooms have exits in the cardinal directions (north, south, east, west) and they are often abbreviated (n, s, e, w) as well. There are six other common exits: northeast (ne), southeast (se), northwest (nw), southwest (sw), up (u), and down (d). While few rooms have all of these exits, most rooms have at least one.

It is sometimes hard to determine what all the exits from a room are. On many MUDs you can enter the exits command to see a list of all the exits from the current room.

Some MUDs use the technique of *teleporting*, which allows you to jump to another room without navigating there by hand. This technique is mostly a tool for Wizards but some MUDs also leave the option open to players in some circumstances. The most common variant of this is the home command, which takes you to your starting room.

Dealing with Other Users Another important aspect of many MUDs (especially social MUDs) is the interaction between players' characters. MUDs offer many different ways for characters to interact and this chapter barely scratches the surface. A good place to start is to determine who is on the MUD. The command for this is system-dependent, but is generally either WHO, who, or @who.

One of the first things to do on meeting another character is to see what he looks like. Easy enough:

>   look [player name]

For example:

>   look ElfBane

would return the description of ElfBane. Some systems use different syntax—look at ElfBane and ElfBane are both common variants. For more detailed information, some systems have additional commands such as examine and @examine.

Now you know how to view other players, but what about when they look at you? Use look to view your own character and you'll probably find that you need a description. Again, this varies from system to system. Common variants include:

>   describe me as "This is a description of me"
>
>   @desc me="This is a description of me"

Read the online Help for "description" and "gender" for more help on this matter.

The next step is to have a conversation with another user. You should automatically hear everything said in the same room so you need to worry only about what you say to others. The syntax:

>   say [sentence]

works on most systems. For example:

> say "Hi, I'm Bob!"

would cause everyone else in the room to see:

> Bob says, "Hi, I'm Bob!"

Sometimes you don't want everyone in the room to hear what you're saying. Many systems support the whisper command, allowing you to talk in the room without being overheard. Unfortunately, other players can sometimes tell that you are whispering to each other.

If that is the case or if you want to hold a conversation with someone who isn't in the room, consider the page command, which sends a message to anyone on the MUD. Unfortunately, pages cost "money" (see the next section, "Objects, Possessions, and Money") on some servers. Please see your server's Help files for more information on paging and whispering.

Objects, Possessions, and Money What would a virtual world and virtual characters be like without virtual possessions? MUDs support all sorts of activity with objects and many of the commands you might expect work for objects as well. Simple examples include:

> get keys
>
> examine keys
>
> give keys to Sean
>
> drop mug
>
> give 35 coins to Sean

If you entered the above commands in order, you would pick up the keys, look at them in detail, give them to a character named Sean (assuming Sean was in the same room), put down your mug, and give 35 of your coins to Sean.

The funds and objects you start with are usually at the discretion of your site administrator. You'll have to beg, borrow, steal, or earn the rest.

Combat Combat-oriented MUDs are populated with monsters (and occasionally other players) who will try to kill you unless you kill them first—use the kill command to attack a monster or another character. After eliminating enough opponents, you might rise in level and become more powerful. Combat-oriented MUDs generally use kill in the form of:

> kill [target]

Kill also works in some social MUDs, though the results vary. A common example is the MUSH, which requires you to spend a number of coins equal to the desired percentage chance of actually killing the target. For example, if you wanted to have a 50% chance of killing Sean, you would have to spend 50 coins to try it:

> kill Sean = 50

To up your odds to 75%, you'd have to spend 75 coins. 100 coins buy Sean a certain death.

Part

VII

Ch

39

N O T E   Player-character "death" means different things in different places. Some MUDs treat it lightly, while others treat it very seriously. As always, know the local conventions before you go around killing people. ■

Leaving the MUD   When you are ready to leave the MUD, take care to clear up any short-term business with other players and be sure to return home. Then sign off of the MUD, generally using the QUIT command (though it might be logout, quit, or @quit, depending on the system).

Advanced Concepts   There's too much development and history behind MUDs to cover everything here—even if we had an entire book to work with. We hope that you'll learn more about MUDs via the online help system. Eventually you might want to become a builder and maybe even a Wizard.

Most TinyMUDs, TinyMUD variants, MUSHes, and MOOs support *building* to some extent. This allows MUD users to extend the world to their own tastes, creating new objects to use and areas to explore. Generally, building needs approval from a Wizard and you are generally given a task area in which to build.

Building is both a privilege and a responsibility, but some people find it to be one of the most rewarding parts of MUDding. Experienced builders are often in demand to work with MUDs that are in development but even they need work before they can go online.

Being a Wizard means different things on different MUDs. In combat MUDs, players with the most combat experience become Wizards and serve somewhere between the administrator and high-powered players.

On social MUDs, Wizards are needed to help maintain the MUD and oversee the building of new areas. Wizards on social MUDs behave as social caretakers rather than military leaders.

More Information on MUDs   Not surprisingly, there is a lot of online information regarding MUDs. The **rec.games.mud** newsgroups on UseNet cover many aspects of MUDding. There are also several Web sites devoted to MUDding, including the following:

The MUD FAQ:

> **http://www.math.okstate.edu/~jds/mudfaq-p1.html**

MUD Information and resources:

> **http://www.cis.upenn.edu/~lwl/mudinfo.html**

Netrek

Netrek is a client-server, real-time, interactive, multiplayer action and strategy game with a theme loosely based on the *Star Trek* universe. Players control starships and fly around the galaxy conquering planets and blowing each other up. The object is for one team to conquer all the opposition's planets.

Netrek has a large following in the academic community and is now making its way into the home with software versions written for Windows 95 and the Macintosh. Figure 39.5 shows a Netrek game.

FIG. 39.5
Netrek: boldly game where no gamer has gamed before.

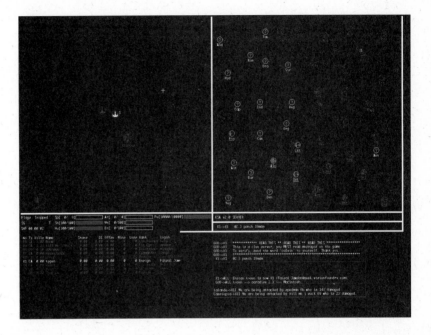

How Netrek Works

Netrek uses an extended version of the client-server architecture:

- You start your Netrek client by connecting to a specific server or by connecting to the "MetaServer"—an Internet site that lets you pick from currently available games in progress.

- The client and server use encryption to verify that all the players are human beings. This measure was added because people started using lightning-fast computer-controlled "bots" to beat slower human opponents, which was no fun for the human players.

Once connected to the server, you authenticate your character and begin playing. Each Netrek server keeps track of the players who use the server regularly, including running tallies of time spent online as well as combat statistics.

Netrek Software

Netrekwas created on UNIX workstations running the X Window System, and has only recently been ported to Windows 95 and the Macintosh. Because these ports are fairly new, they're not as developed as the ports on the UNIX side and don't use proper Windows 95 and Macintosh interface conventions as much as they should. However, they're still quite playable.

You can find most Netrek clients and lots of helpful Netrek material at the Netrek home page: **http://www.isn.net/~farnorth/netrek.html**.

Netrek on Windows 95   As of this writing, the Windows 95 ports of Netrek are still in development and are just now starting to get Windows 95 features such as sound. The ports are quite stable and playable, but have a few quirks in the interface.

One word of warning: these clients are designed to fit on a monitor with at least 1024×768 resolution and things will be cramped if your graphics card can't handle it. Further, these clients expect you to have your display set for "small fonts" and they get very confused if you have set "large fonts" or a custom font size.

There are three main *Netrek* clients available for Windows 95 and all are ports from the UNIX-based clients (versions of Swine, Cow, and Cow-Lite). All three versions have similar interfaces and they start in similar ways, so our instructions here should apply to all three.

At the time of this writing, all three versions were still in development and they still bore much of the legacy of their UNIX roots. In particular, they all need to be started from the command line and they all have peculiar problems with the mouse (they expect a three-button mouse and they accept only key presses when the mouse is in the active window).

Perhaps the quirkiest trait of the Windows 95 Netrek clients is that they prefer to be started from an MS-DOS shell rather than from the more familiar Explorer or Run... interface. This quirk comes from the clients' UNIX roots and will probably disappear in newer releases.

Netrek on the Macintosh   As of this writing, the Macintosh port of Netrek is in its first beta release. The program is fairly stable but has a very un-Mac-like interface. On the other hand, the software has sound capabilities that aren't in many other versions of Netrek.

Netrek on UNIX   Netrek was developed on UNIX so it makes sense that most Netrek clients are available for UNIX. Netrek clients are right at home in the UNIX environment and there are many versions of the software that allow you to configure the software to suit your tastes. Rather than go into all the clients in detail, we suggest you check out the Netrek home page at **http://www.isn.net/~farnorth/netrek.html**.

Joining a Game   To join a Netrek game, you'll first need to launch the Netrek client software, a procedure that varies from platform to platform.

On the Macintosh, all you need to do is double-click the Netrek application—the rest will be handled for you.

On UNIX, make sure Netrek is in your command path and type

> **netrek -h [host]**

to join a specific game or

> **netrek -m**

to connect to the MetaServer. The MetaServer allows you to pick from a list of open games and shows the current number of players in each game.

The procedure for starting Netrek under Windows 95 is similar to the procedure for UNIX: open an MS-DOS shell, change directory to the directory in which the Netrek client is stored, and type **netrek -h [host]** to connect to a specific host or **netrek -m** to connect to the MetaServer.

When you're connected to the server, the full *Netrek* window comes up. If you have a 1024×768 resolution monitor, this window covers most of the screen. If you have less resolution, you may get a compressed or cropped display, depending on the client (you can still play the game but you won't get the full effect).

As in MUDs, you must first enter your character name and password. After you have signed on, you see four colored boxes for various races at the bottom of the top-left quadrant of the window. Center the mouse over a race and type the letter of the ship type you want:

> **S** for Scout
>
> **D** for Destroyer
>
> **C** for Cruiser
>
> **B** for Battleship
>
> **A** for Assault Ship

Once you select your ship type, the window changes to the game display. The local area is displayed on the upper left, with the entire galaxy displayed on the upper right. The lower right contains a message box for talking with other players, while the lower left contains statistics on the game.

Getting Killed Unless you're lucky and very nimble, you're probably going to get thoroughly beaten when you first start playing *Netrek*. Unlike traditional arcade games in which you begin with easy opponents before graduating to the difficult challenges, *Netrek* drops you right into the middle of things and you'll often be facing opponents with years of practice.

With that said, we encourage you to practice and get used to the game, gaining skill and watching how other ships maneuver. Use the right mouse button to change direction and use the number keys to set your speed. The left button fires photon torpedoes, while clicking both the left and right button at once (or clicking the middle button if you have a three-button mouse) fires a phaser blast.

Notice how your speed affects your turns and just about everything affects your energy display in the lower left. Try attacking a few enemies (races are easily distinguishable by color) to see how they react and to see what kinds of maneuvers they perform.

Pressing h brings up a window that lists all the key commands. You can change the key settings by editing the netrekrc file, which is located in the same directory as the *Netrek* client.

It's also a good idea to pay attention to the message display in the lower right-hand corner of the screen. Because of the popularity of the Internet, some Netrek servers now use a "clue check" to keep out players who aren't seriously interested in the game.

The clue check works by asking you questions and kicking you out of the game if you don't answer them correctly within a certain amount of time. This is designed to encourage you to read the manual and learn about the game so both you and your opponents will get the most enjoyment out of it.

When you die, you'll go back to the startup screen to pick another ship.

When you're ready to quit, press **q** to self-destruct. Then press the quit box on the startup screen.

More Information on Netrek   You can find more information on *Netrek* on the UseNet **rec.games.netrek.*** newsgroups. You can also find more information at the *Netrek* home page on the Web (at the time of this writing, it was **http://www.isn.net/~farnorth/netrek.html**).

Additional Gaming Resources

The Net contains what is perhaps the world's largest library (unorganized as it may be) of information for gamers in the world. These days, every major game release is accompanied by press, support, and demonstration software released on the Internet. Most of the popular games have dozens of Web pages devoted to them and it becomes a chore to separate useful information about your favorite game from rehashed material that you've already seen.

Two new gaming-oriented Web sites have appeared to help you find the best of the gaming material that you want to see: Happy Puppy and The Games Domain. Located at **http://www.happypuppy.com/** and **http://www.gamesdomain.com/**, respectively, these sites have lots of reviews, rumors, tips, links, and freeware and shareware files related to your favorite games.

Windows 95 Games

When Microsoft designed Windows 95, it included multimedia, networking, and display support features designed to encourage game publishers to start writing for Windows 95 instead of DOS and to make Windows 95 the best game yet.

At the time of this writing, this vision is beginning to become real for the Windows 95 gaming world. Between Windows and DOS games that have found new life in Windows 95, and brand new games that take advantage of new features in Windows 95, the Windows gaming world is more exciting than ever.

Three good examples of the sorts of Windows 95 games that are popular on the Internet now are Quake, SubSpace, and Stars!

Quake

Quake is a new game from iD Software, the creators of DOOM! Quake extends the DOOM! system by offering Internet-based client-server games with fully configurable game worlds. Quake is available in shareware form from the iD servers at **http://www.idsoftware.com/**.

Currently, Quake is an MS-DOS-based game with special support for Internet games in Windows 95 only. To start Quake in Windows 95 Internet mode, download and install it, then run Q95 (Q95.bat if you have file type extensions showing) in the Quake directory.

After the game has started running, press ESC to bring up the menu. Choose "Multiplayer," followed by "Join A Game" and "TCP/IP." You'll see a screen that asks you for your player name and some game configuration details. Enter your name and the server you'd like to join. You'll enter the game immediately unless the server is full or unavailable, in which case you'll see an error message explaining the problem.

If you don't have a server in mind, you can view a list of currently running servers at the Quake Stomping Grounds at **http://www.stomped.com/**.

SubSpace

SubSpace is a new client-server arcade style shoot-'em-up where you can go head-to-head against many other players in a large arena. SubSpace looks something like the classic Asteroids game in which you fly a spaceship inertially and shoot at nearby objects. At the time of this writing, SubSpace was in late beta test, soon to be released. SubSpace is available from Virgin Interactive Entertainment, at **http://www.vie.com/subspace/**.

To provide the best display while handling a lot of players, SubSpace takes advantage of Microsoft's new DirectX display technology, which is currently only available on Windows 95. Because it uses DirectX, SubSpace may be incompatible with some graphics cards and slow on 486-class machines.

Playing SubSpace   After installing SubSpace, launch the SubSpace application. You'll be prompted for a name and password, and asked to select the arena to join from the active list of arenas. New players should enter a new player name so their statistics are valid on the games they play in and so they won't be mistaken for someone else by other players. Figure 39.6 shows the SubSpace connection process.

Once you have entered the information, the game pauses and then the display takes over your screen. You should see your ship in the center of the screen, a map in the lower right, and a listing of messages and helpful hints in the lower left.

When you have your bearings, you can begin to fly around and engage in wanton destruction. Unfortunately we can't show you a screen shot of SubSpace because it's based on DirectX, so you'll have to check out the game for yourself.

Stars!

Stars! is a strategic conquest game that uses Internet e-mail to communicate between players. Stars! was originally designed to work over LAN network, but became wildly successful with Internet game players.

Stars! is a shareware program, available from **http://beast.webmap.com/stars!/**. To give you a taste of what the full version is like, Stars! lets you run a small, multiplayer game with the unregistered version. Figure 39.7 shows a Stars! game in progress.

FIG. 39.6
Getting ready to launch with SubSpace.

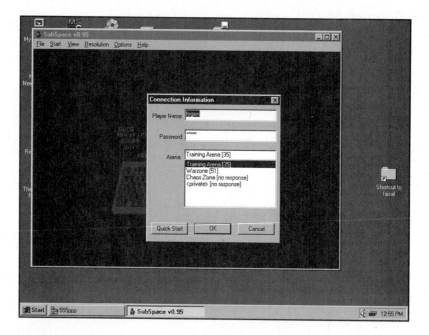

FIG. 39.7
Take over the galaxy in Stars!

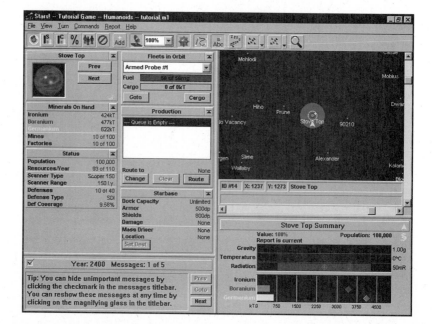

To run a multiplayer game, open Stars! and select a new game. Choose the advanced options, which allow you to add more players. The advanced options also allow you to pick races and configure the style of the game. The registered version also allows for customizable alien races in your Stars! game.

Once you've added the players you want, you can begin the game as normal. You will see a multiplayer game hosting window entitled Stars! Host Mode, which lets you run the game and generate new turns.

Kali

If you are hoping to be able to get a traditional LAN-network-based game like DOOM! or Descent to run on the Internet but never knew how before, we've got good news for you. A new piece of software called Kali allows you to play many of the traditional LAN-style network games over the Internet.

Kali is available from the Kali home page at **http://www.axxis.com/kali/**. The Kali home page also contains useful information about using Kali, and discusses how to use specific games with Kali.

How Kali Works Traditional LAN-style network games use Novell's IPX network system to communicate between machines. The IPX network protocol is different from the Internet's TCP/IP network protocol but the two can coexist on the same network.

Kali takes advantage of this fact by "tunneling" the IPX network protocol through TCP/IP to give you a LAN connection to another player. In other words, Kali uses the Internet to create a virtual traditional LAN between two machines on the Internet.

Kali 95 (the Kali version for Windows 95) is even easier to use than earlier versions of Kali because it simply coordinates between Windows 95's built-in TCP/IP and IPX network systems, so you don't have to set up either network yourself (earlier versions of Kali needed some work to set up the network).

At the time of this writing, Kali supports DOOM!, Descent, Warcraft/Warcraft II, Command & Conquer, Duke Nukem 3D, and most other games that support network mode over IPX networks.

Setting Up and Running Kali To set up Kali, start by running the installer. You will be asked some simple registration questions. Fill in your name, nickname, and e-mail address for contact information. Leave the "serial" and "skey" questions blank: you will need to fill them out when you register your copy of Kali.

From the Servers menu, choose Connect. Pick a server from the list to connect to. Figure 39.8 shows the process of hooking up to Kali.

Once you are connected, choose List Names from the Players menu to view who else is connected to the system. If you'd like to talk with some of the other players online at the time, select Chat Window from the View menu. Figure 39.9 shows a list of Kali players.

FIG. 39.8
Find other Internet gamers with Kali.

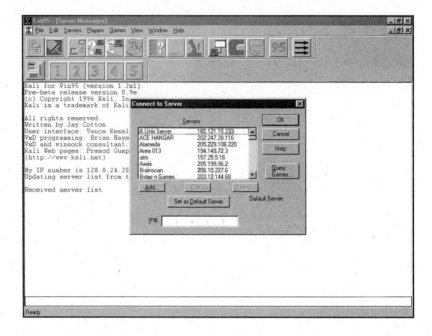

FIG. 39.9
The Kali players list: so many potential targets, so little time.

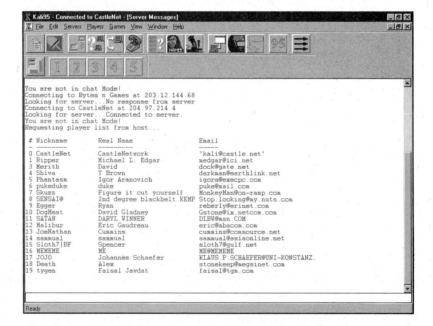

When you are ready to begin playing a game, leaving Kali running makes the computer "think" that it's on a local IPX network with all the players connected to that Kali server.

More Games on the Way

As we've said, the current wave of Internet-capable games is only beginning. More and more games are supporting Internet play every day. A notable upcoming game is Monster Truck Madness, from Microsoft. Although it isn't as well known as games such as Quake, Monster Truck Madness promises to be interesting because it is published by Microsoft and Microsoft is heavily promoting the technologies that Monster Truck Madness is based on. Monster Truck Madness includes support for play over the Internet and a central Internet site to coordinate between players.

Macintosh Games

The Macintosh was the first personal computer to have built-in networking and one of the first systems to have network games, so it should come as no surprise that it was one of the first systems to have Internet games. The classic Internet game for the Mac is Bolo, a multiplayer, peer-to-peer, tank battle game that blends elements of arcade action with complex strategy and tactics.

Beyond Bolo, you can look forward to new Mac network games in the near future. In part this is because of ports on Windows 95 games and in part it is because of a new programming system called Sprockets that is in development at Apple. The Sprockets system is designed to make game creation easier for developers and includes support for easy creation of Internet games.

Part

VII

Ch

39

Bolo

Bolo was developed by Stuart Cheshire as a study in both strategy and the design of network games. Over the past few years, Bolo has become very popular in the Mac gaming community, particularly with Internet players. Bolo players have even gone so far as to set up Bolo Trackers—Internet servers that keep track of the open Bolo games so you can know where to find a match. Figure 39.10 shows a Bolo game in progress.

Bolo is a complicated and subtle game, so we recommend reading the manual before playing. Accordingly, this section covers the basics of getting into an Internet game of Bolo.

First start by launching the Bolo Finder application to ask the Bolo Tracker for information. You may need to select the Preferences... item from the File menu to ensure that your settings are correct. At the time of this writing, the North American Bolo Tracker was at bolo.usu.edu, port 50000.

When you have found a game to join, launch the Bolo application. You are asked what type of game to join. Select UDP/IP and press Enter.

Next, you are asked what address you want to connect to. Enter the address information from the Bolo Tracker and click on the Join button. Alternatively, you can start a new Internet game by selecting the New button instead.

If you're starting a new game, you'll want to select the Tracker button to ensure that your game is registered with the Bolo Tracker so you can attract players (unless, of course, you want to keep the game private). Figure 39.11 shows an example of the join screen from Bolo.

FIG. 39.10
Bolo: strategy, tactics, and firepower.

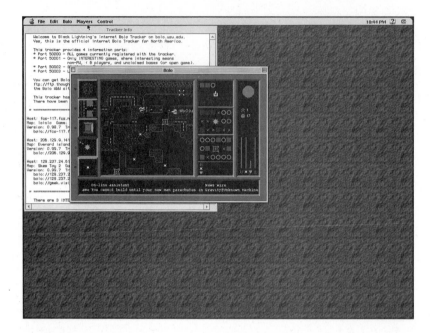

FIG. 39.11
Meeting new and interesting people (to shoot) in Bolo.

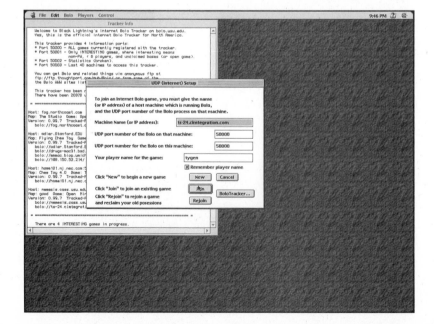

If you are joining a game, the game screen should come up, with the map area filling with white to show that the map is downloading, until the map is completely downloaded. If you're starting a new game you'll be asked to choose the parameters for the game and then you'll get the game window.

Marathon

Marathon is one of the most popular AppleTalk network games for the Mac. Many players ask how they can play Marathon over the Internet. Unfortunately, the answer is currently "not easily."

With no product like Kali for the Macintosh, it is a chore to set up AppleTalk network games over the Internet. However, people are still working on the problem. We suggest that you periodically monitor the comp.sys.mac.games newsgroup until a workable solution to the problem is found.

Outland

Outland is a Macintosh-based gamer's network service. Outland members can connect to Outland via the Internet, allowing them to play Outland-supported games (such as the popular space conquest game Spaceward Ho!) over the Internet. For more information, see Outland's Web page at **http://www.outland.com/**.

Ambrosia Software and the Mac Network Games Page

Ambrosia Software is one of the most respected game developers in the Macintosh world and the publisher of many shareware titles, including the mega-hit "maelstrom ." Ambrosia mostly develops arcade games and some of its current games in development feature Internet play.

As a service to the Macintosh community, Ambrosia provides a listing of Macintosh network games. The listing is available at Ambrosia's Web site at **http://www.ambrosiasw.com/**.

UNIX

Unfortunately, professional game developers have largely ignored the UNIX market. However, there are still some excellent freeware games available for UNIX that aren't available for any other system.

- Xtank—a classic game for the X Window system, Xtank features head-to-head arcade-style tank combat over the Internet.

- SpellCast—SpellCast is an abstract Internet game that simulates combat between rival magicians.

- Xpilot—similar to SubSpace, XPilot features arcade-style action in the form of spaceship combat over the Internet.

Internet Security

CHAPTER 40

Privacy and Security on the Internet

by Lori Leonardo

The Internet continues to grow exponentially. Where once only large computer facilities—universities, the government, and Fortune 500 corporations—were interconnected, today any individual with a personal computer can hook into the Internet. With the introduction of Windows 95, all a computer owner has to do is subscribe to the Microsoft Network or any other commercial online service and *voilà,* another member of the Internet community. With this growth comes security and privacy risks that were only of concern to larger facilities a few years back.

This chapter discusses the risks that you, as an individual computer user, will face when you travel the electronic superhighway. We will also give you tips on how you can protect your computer and yourself against unauthorized intrusion into your right to privacy. ■

What risks your Internet host faces

The security of Internet host sites is doubtful at best.

How the host's risks affect you

The moment you connect your computer to any other computer, you subject yourself to some risk of compromising your data.

Methods of protecting your computer

Netscape is more aware of security than other browsers and includes several options for protecting your computer.

Methods of protecting your privacy

Protect yourself against unauthorized intrusion into your right to privacy.

Internet Security Overview

The moment you connect your computer to any other computer, whether by Local Area Network with coworkers or by a dial-up connection to an Internet provider, you subject yourself to some risk that your data could be compromised. Your data could be stolen or destroyed. Your communications could be intercepted or misdirected.

The security of Internet host sites is nebulous at best. Eventually all of them will face some sort of break-in. It might be a hacker trying to prove that he or she can gain unauthorized access to an Internet site, or it might be a malicious attempt to destroy data. Being forewarned is your best defense against your data being corrupted or used in an unauthorized fashion.

Classic Hacking Methods

Almost every computer that supports multiple users is protected to some degree by the use of a login name and password. This serves two functions. First, users can be restricted to using only certain functions on the host. For example, each user can be restricted from accessing another user's files. Even if one user is allowed to read some common files, that user can be restricted to changing or replacing those files. The second function of the login name and password is to make sure that whoever uses the computer is authorized to do so.

Password Attacks

Passwords are the main point of security for most Internet sites against unauthorized access. Unfortunately, most users don't realize the importance of passwords and choose easily guessed combinations of letters. A proper password should contain letters, numbers, punctuation marks, and symbols. An intruder counts on the fact that users often choose passwords that are combinations of their name, common names, or even just the word "password."

How does an intruder obtain a login name and a password? Obtaining a login name is easy. Every post to a UseNet newsgroup contains the name and Internet address of the person who posted it. Guessing a password may be just that, a guess. A hacker can even use the power of his own computer to run through a list of common passwords in the hope that one of them works

N O T E On operating systems used by hosts on the Internet there is a root or supervisor account that can access every file and program on the system. This "super account" is the target of most hackers who want to do something more than read someone's files. New computers have a default name and password that is the same for every installation. Some administrators never get around to changing the default password, making it easy for someone to gain access with supervisor status. ■

Any system that allows access through the use of passwords has to store the passwords somewhere. The password file is usually encrypted by a one-way encryption routine. This means that your password is encrypted in such a manner that it cannot be decrypted. When you log on, the password that you enter is encrypted and compared with the password stored in the file. This method is more secure than decrypting the stored password and comparing it to the one you type at logon. Hackers rely on the fact that the password file, since it is encrypted, is easily obtained. They can then use a crypt-and-compare program to try various combinations of passwords until they find one that matches. There are programs available that can crypt and compare every word in the dictionary in an amazingly short period of time.

Another method commonly used by hackers is simply being aware that the more difficult a password is to guess, the more likely the user is to write it down. If you can't remember that your password to your Internet host is "BLxtj63JRB" you might be tempted to write it on a "yellow stickie" and attach it to your monitor. All a visitor has to do is look, no guesswork involved.

You might get a phone call from a purported representative of your Internet host. "We have had a serious break-in by a group of hackers and have to check all our accounts. Would you give me your current password so we can see if anyone has cracked your account." You might be tempted to give it, but don't! Instead, get a name, not just a number, hang up and call the company back. You are probably the victim of a hacker attack known as social engineering. Remember, no Internet or online service provider would really ask for your password. Never give your password out!

Data Interception

As you have seen in previous chapters, the data you send to someone else on the Internet, or even on a local network, is placed in data packets with the address of both the recipient and the sender. On the local network, all machines get all the packets but usually read only the ones intended for them. On the Internet, a packet is routed from one Internet site to another until the final destination is reached.

Just because a packet is addressed to another site or network node does not prevent someone along the way from examining the contents of that data packet. You have no way of knowing if the data packet you sent was even received by the intended recipient. You also have no way of knowing that a data packet your computer receives is the same one that was sent to you. Somewhere along the way, someone may be intercepting your communications and reading your messages.

Keyboard Logging

Windows 95 is a multitasking operating system. The task bar shows you what programs are running, but a program can hide that icon so you can't be sure which programs are running at any one time. Every time you move or click the mouse, press or release a key, get a packet of data from the modem or network, or use a file, Windows 95 records that *event*. The event is then placed in a message queue and sent to the running programs. Just as Windows 95 watches these events, so could a hacker's program. There might be a program running in the background that monitors keystrokes and places them in a hidden file. All the hacker has to do is get access to this file and read everything you typed.

Logging programs are not restricted to just the programs you are running at that time. There might be a hackers program out there that intercepts the communications stream to the modem and logs all incoming and outgoing calls. Maybe the entire communication is written to a hidden file as it is being sent to the modem.

Firewalls

In order to increase security, many network administrators have installed firewalls on their systems. In a building, a firewall prevents the spread of a fire from one part of a building to another. In computer terms, a *firewall* can be thought of as a way of isolating different parts of a system. A firewall can limit access to and from the network or between computers on the same network. Some systems have a dedicated gateway computer that routes all incoming and outgoing packets between the network and the Internet. Other firewalls consist of routers that filter out unwanted packets.

The most common firewall blocks all incoming TCP traffic with the exception of mail and FTP. Both of these services are routed to a dedicated host rather than every host on the network. Other filters block RIP, BGP, and other routing information except from trusted sources. ICMP redirects are blocked from all sources.

Routers have all the tools necessary for a network administrator to implement security measures if configured properly. Unfortunately, many administrators configure the router improperly, leaving holes in the firewall. For example, a router may be set to block all incoming connections to the range of privileged ports (0–1023), allowing an intruder access to all the ports from 1024 and higher. This particular "backdoor" implementation allows an intruder to add another Telnet daemon at one of the higher ports and reinitialize the Internet services managed by *inetd*.

One of the disadvantages of installing firewalls is the cost. Firewall implementations can consist of a combination of hardware and software costing hundreds of thousands of dollars just to install. Administrative costs of firewalls can also be considerable. Yet even the best firewall money can buy is no guarantee that an intruder can't gain access. The only way to make a system truly safe from intrusion is by turning the Internet connection off.

Password Security

The best and most expensive firewall in the world may not stop an intruder who possesses a valid ID and password. Just because a user has a password does not mean that it is secure. A would-be intruder can guess a password or try a list of frequently used passwords until he or she hits the proper one. The key to security is choosing and guarding a proper password.

Password Guidelines   It's generally easier to say what a proper password is not rather than what it is. Passwords should not be one of the following:

- Any word that can be found in the dictionary
- Less than 6 characters long
- A name
- Related to the user in any way

Some systems have programs to help the user choose a password. These programs tend to enforce some or all of the above rules. In general, a password should be as meaningless as possible, yet easy to remember so that you don't have to write it down.

One-Time Passwords   Passwords are often the weakest link to security. Although they may be encoded at the destination, they are rarely encoded at the source. Any time a password is transmitted in plain text, the potential exists for interception. One-time dynamic passwords are only good for one login, and then expire. Even if they are intercepted, they are no longer valid and of little use to a would-be intruder. One-time dynamic password schemes can be accomplished by hardware, software, or a combination of both.

Hardware   Security devices from vendors such as Security Dynamics, Digital Pathways, and Enigma Logic can provide almost the ultimate security for a host. Each user possesses a device about the size of a credit card that has an LED display. When a user logs in to the host, he or she must enter a Personal Identification Number (PIN) and the number displayed on the LED. The number displayed on the LED changes over time, so once a user logs in, the password is never used again. Even if the security card is lost or stolen, the thief needs the user's PIN in addition to the number displayed on the security card.

Software   Several different software schemes are available to implement a type of dynamic one-time passwording. One of these systems is the S-Key program. When a user logs in to the host system, the host issues a challenge in the form of a string of letters or numbers. The user then enters this string into the S-Key client, and the program displays an answer to the challenge in the form of a string that the user can send back to the host. If the challenge is not answered properly, the host terminates the connection.

Your Risk

Part VIII
Ch
40

You might think that a break-in on an Internet host does not affect you. Don't hackers break into government, university, or business computers? If you merely use your computer to browse the World Wide Web over a dial-up connection you might suppose that a break-in would have no consequences for you. In most cases you would be right. But there is a risk, although small, that you might be compromised too. Figure 40.1 shows a message sent to all users by an Internet host advising them that a hacker has attempted to penetrate the mail system.

If you pay for your Internet services by the hour and a hacker obtains your ID and password, you could wind up paying for the hacker's computer time. If a hacker has gained access to an Internet site that relays your messages, he or she might be able to read those messages and use the information. Suppose you ordered a left-handed sprocket bevel from the International House of Hardware using your Internet connection and you sent it your Visa card number over the computer so it could send you the merchandise by next day air. You always run the risk that an employee of the International House of Hardware will send his mother-in-law on a vacation to Hong Kong using your Visa number. But, you also face the risk of having Harry the Hacker intercept your Visa number from an intermediate Internet site.

FIG. 40.1
Security information
from an Internet
provider.

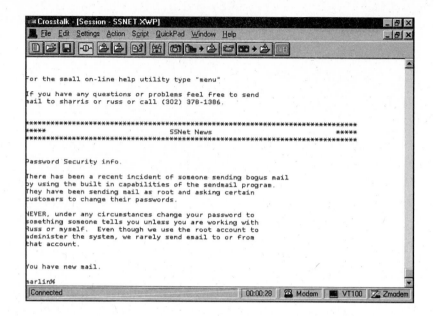

```
Crosstalk - [Session - SSNET.XWP]                               _ 8 X
File  Edit  Settings  Action  Script  QuickPad  Window  Help      _ 8 X

For the small on-line help utility type "menu"

If you have any questions or problems feel free to send
mail to sharris or russ or call (302) 378-1386.

********************************************************************
*****                       SSNet News                       *****
********************************************************************

Password Security info.

There has been a recent incident of someone sending bogus mail
by using the built in capabilities of the sendmail program.
They have been sending mail as root and asking certain
customers to change their passwords.

NEVER, under any circumstances change your password to
something someone tells you unless you are working with
Russ or myself.  Even though we use the root account to
administer the system, we rarely send email to or from
that account.

You have new mail.

marlin%

Connected                    00:00:28   Modem    VT100   Zmodem
```

Your communication over the Internet can also be subject to what is known as the "man in the middle." Harry the Hacker may not be satisfied with just intercepting and reading your communication with the International House of Hardware. He could just stop your data packets and pretend he was the International House of Hardware. He ends up with your Visa number, and you don't get anything in the next Fed-Ex delivery. Or he gets a left-handed sprocket bevel by next-day air, and you get a Visa bill in next month's mail.

Rest assured that most hosts on the Internet go to extraordinary lengths to prevent unauthorized usage. But it seems that every time one security hole is discovered and fixed, the hackers come up with yet another method for obtaining access. Common sense should tell you, however, that giving your Credit Card number over the phone is not any more secure than transmitting it over the Net. It is a risk you take when giving out any personal information.

Risks from Common Internet Utilities

When you sign up for Microsoft Network, available to all Windows 95 users, you are in touch with the wonderful and risky world of the Internet. Almost any Internet host can give you access to the World Wide Web, FTP, Gopher, Mail, and Telnet. These are the most common utilities used for surfing the Net. Other services include Archie, UseNet News readers, and IRC (Internet Relay Chat). How to use these utilities is covered in other chapters; let's discuss what risks are involved with using them.

You might be tempted to think of these services as one-way streets. Unless you have an Internet node set up on your computer and allow others to use one of these services to access your computer, it would seem that you are in control. You request data from someone else, but no one can get data from you that you do not send. This is not always the case. If you use one of the TCP/IP daemon programs provided on the CD in the back of this book, be aware that you are opening up your computer to almost everyone in the world.

World Wide Web

This graphics-based utility is quickly becoming the method of Net cruising most favored by PC users. The flashy graphics and point-and-click links make it easy to visit Internet sites around the world. However, the program that produces all of these wonders also makes it the most risky for your computer and your data.

The HyperText Markup Language (HTML) that makes your World Wide Web browser work also places your computer at serious risk. Windows 95 browsers are able to read and write files, launch applications, and even run a DOS session in the background. The very functions that make the World Wide Web so versatile make it vulnerable.

The browser included with Windows 95 is the Microsoft Internet Explorer. There are no security options available with this browser, and the help file makes no mention of any security problems with the World Wide Web.

One of the most popular World Wide Web browers is the Netscape Navigator. Netscape is more aware of security than other browsers and includes several options for alerting you to possible security risks. Netscape tries to establish a secure link using encrypted packets between the two linked sites. A small key icon, shown in Figure 40.2, and the color bar across the top of the content area indicate whether the link is secure. If the key is broken on a gray color bar background, then text is being sent in the clear, but if the key icon is connected with a blue color bar background, the link has been encoded and only the two machines can understand what is happening between them.

There is also another way that Netscape recognizes a secure document. This is the specification of a secure server URL address. A secure server URL address will begin with https:// instead of http://. These secure documents are protected with SSL (Secure Sockets Layer). Those with SSL, have a URL that begins with https://. Those without SSL have a URL that begins with http://.

Netscape Navigator identifies secure documents in several ways. You can tell whether a document comes from a secure server by looking at the location (URL) field. If the URL begins with https://instead of http://), the document comes from a secure server. You need to use https:// for HTTP URLs with SSL and http:// for HTTP URLs without SSL.

You can also verify the security of a document by examining the security icon in the bottom-left corner of the Netscape Navigator window and the colorbar across the top of the content area. The icon consists of a doorkey on a blue background to show secure documents and a broken doorkey on a gray background to show insecure documents. The colorbar across the top of the content area is blue for secure and gray for insecure.

Netscape includes a whole package of security options that you can set by clicking Options and Security menu choices. Many times there is nothing the browser can do to make a connection secure. In this case, the Netscape Navigator displays a warning before you submit information that be compromised and gives you a chance to cancel before the data is sent as shown in Figure 40.3.

FIG. 40.2

The Netscape security key.

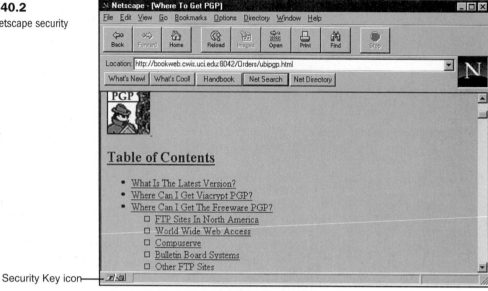

Security Key icon

FIG. 40.3

A Netscape security warning.

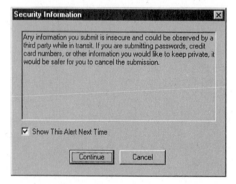

FTP

If you use FTP to access files from another site, there are certain risks you take. The program you obtain from the FTP site might contain a virus or be a Trojan horse. Although most reputable site managers make sure the programs they offer for downloading are free from viruses, if you don't personally know how the site is screened, you risk getting a program that contains a virus. See Chapter 41, "Avoiding Computer Viruses," for a discussion of viruses and how to protect yourself from them.

Certainly the FTP site is more at risk than a user who merely downloads a file from the site. The security holes in the FTP site itself may place you at risk when you download a file. If a hacker has penetrated the FTP site, the file that is logged on the site's index may not be the file you download.

There is also the possibility of a "man in the middle" intercepting your FTP request and furnishing a program that is nothing like the one you are trying to download from the FTP site. This risk is small, but it does exist.

Gopher

Like FTP sites, Gopher sites can contain files that are available for downloading. Unlike FTP and World Wide Web, some Gopher programs give you no indication as to which site you are connecting. If you use a World Wide Web browser to connect to a Gopher, at least you can see the URL in the address window. The Microsoft Internet Explorer, as well as other World Wide Web browers, shows the site in the lower left corner of the screen before a connection is made. The Microsoft Internet Explorer says "Shortcut to..." and then lists the document name followed by the site name. Other Internet browsers show the complete URL that lists the type of connection, site name, and document path. After the connection is made, Microsoft Internet Explorer shows the URL in the window near the top of the screen labeled "Connected to:".

Downloading a document or program from a Gopher site carries the same risk as with FTP sites. The only difference is the potential break-in methods that a hacker might employ when compromising the site.

Telnet

The biggest risk with Telnet is if you allow Telnet access to your computer. Telnet allows a remote user access to the site just as if he or she was at a console at the site itself. This is the method used by hackers to log in to a remote computer. If you don't allow Telnet sessions on your computer, you can rest assured that a hacker can't log in to your system by that method.

If you use Telnet to contact a remote computer on which you have an account, you can be at risk from a keystroke logging program running on your computer or an interception of your Internet packets by a third party. Of special interest to a hacker would be your logon sequence since you send your login ID and password in the clear over the Internet. If this communication was intercepted somehow, there is nothing to prevent a hacker from subsequently logging on to that computer as you.

Mail

One of the most tempting targets of an intruder is e-mail. Your e-mail may contain credit card information, passwords, or maybe even intimate personal information. Your e-mail is delivered to your host and stored in a file until you retrieve it. There is a certain level of security on most host computers so that only you can read what is in your e-mail file—actually, you and the system administrator, who has access to all files on the system. If an intruder has your account ID and password or the administrator's password, he or she could also read your mail.

Keeping Your Communications Private

I'm sure you are aware that your telephone conversations may be overheard by someone listening in. If not, you should be. Law enforcement agencies can tap phone conversations with the approval of a judge, but there are strict laws governing when and how an agency of the government can tap a phone line. If you are not engaged in any illegal activities, the risk is minimal that the government is listening in. Anyone with a portable phone and a set of alligator clips can tap the phone line between you and the local switching office. Yes, it's illegal, but it's easy to do.

The increased use of cellular phones has made the task of listening even easier and less risky for the perpetrator. Cellular phones are transmitted by radio, and anyone with a radio receiver set to the correct frequency can listen in—and it's not even illegal if the contents of the conversation are not divulged.

So, too, can the communications between computers be tapped. We have already discussed how the packets sent over the Internet can be intercepted, but there are other ways that someone could listen in on your computer conversations.

A phone tap can work just as well with a modem as with voice. A modem is merely a device that modulates and demodulates a digital signal on a carrier tone. With the proper equipment to demodulate the carrier tone, computer communication can be tapped just like voice conversations. Likewise any digital information sent over a cellular phone equipped with a modem can be intercepted. In fact, intercepting cellular calls is even easier because the call is broadcast by radio.

As a matter of fact, if someone were really interested in what you were doing with your computer, he or she could intercept radio frequency signals emitted from your computer even when you are not connected to the outside world. Your keyboard controller emits a certain frequency as does your video monitor. These radio frequency emissions can be picked up and analyzed by someone equipped with sophisticated detection gear. It may sound like grist for a James Bond spy movie, but it can and does happen—but probably not to you.

For the Truly Paranoid

Is a person paranoid if people are really out to get him or her? That is an interesting question. There is a high probability that no one has planted a keyboard logger in your computer, or is intercepting your e-mail. You probably don't see anyone lugging equipment up the nearest telephone pole, or mysterious vans with a roof full of antennas parked in front of your house. Still, there are some people for whom even the possibility of someone intercepting what is thought to be a private message is anathema. For you there is hope.

Encryption Programs

One of the ways in which you can ensure the privacy of your data is by encryption. Encryption is as old as government and armies; with computer technology it's now available to everyone.

As a matter of fact, encryption has become important enough that the government has gotten into the act and developed a standard called Data Encryption Standard or DES. In fact, the U.S. government thinks that DES is so good that it has prohibited the export of programs that use RSA algorithms.

Phil Zimmerman may have started out paranoid when he brought military grade encryption to the general public when he created Pretty Good Privacy (PGP). Certain governmental agencies blanched at the thought that average citizens could now encrypt messages using methods that take years of supercomputer time to crack. This and the fact that PGP was distributed free over the Internet took Phil Zimmerman out of the realm of the paranoid. People were out to get him, especially the U.S. Government. The government has accused Zimmerman of distributing a government-approved encryption standard outside of the United States, which is a violation of federal statutes.

Phil's legal troubles aside, his program is more than pretty good. It is an easy way for anyone to encrypt data into an almost unbreakable form. Additionally, PGP uses the concept of Private Key/Public Key encryption—something that can only be done by computers.

Cypher Keys

The basis of any encryption scheme is to change a message into a form that is meaningless to anyone who does not have the key to change it back. Simple substitution of one letter for another, something we all see in newspaper cryptograms, is the easiest form of key to crack. Once you know that every occurrence of the letter "E" in the original message is replaced by the letter "Y," decoding the message is easy. Another method would be to change the words in the original message into numbers. These numbers could signify the page, line, and word count in a book. If you know the code and have the book, you just go to the page and line and count the number of words in that line until you get to the substituted word. The key is the book. If you don't know which book to use, then you can't decode the message.

With the advent of computers, elaborate algorithms can be developed to substitute one letter for another. These algorithms are so sophisticated that reversing the process without the key becomes almost impossible. If you have the key, then the message can be decoded almost instantaneously.

Public Key

The problem with a public key is that anyone who has it cannot only decode the message, but can also encode a message using that key. If everyone has the key, then encoding is worthless. The concept of Public Key encoding solves the problem. There are two keys for every encryption, a public key and a private key. You can send your public key to anyone who wants to send a message to you. They encrypt the message using your public key, but the only way to decode the message is to use your private key. Even if everyone in the world has your public key, they cannot decode a message to you that was built using that key.

There are a few caveats associated with public key encoding. You must be sure that the public key you get is the public key of the person for whom the message is intended. Key exchange is, if you pardon the expression, the key to secure communications. Once a public key exchange has been made and verified, further communication between the two parties is for all intents and purposes *absolutely* private. There are even methods built into the exchange to verify the public and private keys of the originator and sender of the message.

PGP

A testament to the popularity of PGP encoding is the fact that the Internet world took to it rather rapidly. Check almost any UseNet newsgroup and you will see many messages signed with "PGP public key…" followed by the public key for that person. If you are paranoid, or if people are out to get you, you too can use PGP. Unfortunately, while PGP is available for almost any operating system—and Phil Zimmerman has even published the source code—it is not available for Windows 95. However, it is available for MS-DOS, and several Windows interfaces are available to help with DOS dysfunction.

The latest program PGP 2.6.2 for DOS is available free of charge from an FTP site maintained by MIT. You can reach this site by World Wide Web at

http://bs.mit.edu:8001/pgp-form.html

Once you answer a series of questions, you can download the ZIP file that contains the software and documentation. The file we downloaded was named Pgp262.zip. This represents PGP version 2.6.2. Always get the latest version.

On the CD

The first thing you must do is unzip the file. If you don't have an unzip program, you should also download PKZIP. This program is available worldwide and is usually distributed as a self-extracting archive with an .exe extension. The PKZIP program is also included on the CD in the back of this book.

The Pgp262.zip file contains two other zipped files, plus a text file called Setup.doc. The text file tells you how to install PGP for almost any type of computer. Scroll through the text until you find the setup instructions for MS-DOS. Some of the DOS terms are slightly different than the Windows 95 terms. For instance a subdirectory is a folder in the DOS world. You can run an MS-DOS session in Windows 95 and follow the instructions in the PGP setup file, or point and click your way around My Computer until you create the appropriate folders.

Now comes the fun part if you have never worked from the DOS prompt. You have to change your Autoexec.bat file and add a few lines. After you change the file, you have to restart your computer so that the lines you added to your Autoexec.bat file will take effect. The documentation that comes with the program tells you what to do, but remember that it was written for a DOS user and not a Windows 95 user. You can use the Notepad to edit the Autoexec.bat without having to use the DOS prompt. Add the lines indicated in the PGP documentation Setup.doc and restart the computer. Click Start and choose Shut Down from the menu. Click Restart Windows and wait while Windows 95 closes and restarts.

Unzip the file Pgp262I.zip, which contains the actual PGP program. Remember that this is a DOS program and will only work in the MS-DOS session that is a part of Windows 95.

Don't neglect the documentation that comes with PGP, especially the first part where Phil Zimmerman discusses why your file should be encrypted. The next part of the documentation tells you how to set up and use the software—written from a DOS point of view. If your entire knowledge of PCs is with Windows or Windows 95, you should print the documentation if you want to use PGP from the MS-DOS command line. If you don't do DOS, there is help.

WinPGP

There are some Windows programs that form an interface with the DOS version of PGP. Basically, the Windows interface merely sends the proper DOS commands to PGP depending on what options you choose from the Windows program. When this chapter was written, only one program was designed to work with Windows 95 and that was WinPGP. The latest archive file, version 4.1a, is Pgpw41.zip and is available from

ftp://ftp.coast.net/SimTel/win3/security/

Work your way down the FTP menu structure until you find the correct directory. There are several programs available that are Windows overlays for PGP.

After you have downloaded the archive file, Pgpw41.zip, extract the executable file by using PKUNZIP. The extracted files include the setup program Winpgp41.exe. Click Start, Run. Either browse to Winpgp41 or enter the name and click OK. The setup program will install the file in a new folder (or an old one if you so choose). Choose a program group for WinPGP in the Start menu.

Once WinPGP is up and running, you never have to use the PGP DOS command line again; it is done for you. Just choose the operation you want from the menu, or buttons shown in Figure 40.4. WinPGP will run the PGP program in a DOS window. When PGP is finished with an operation, you will have to press a key to exit the DOS window. Clicking the mouse will not work.

FIG. 40.4

The main screen for WinPGP.

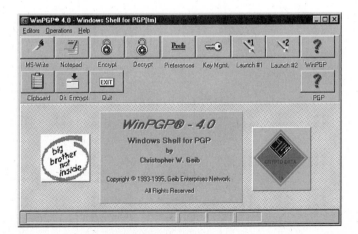

Your first task is to generate your private and public keys. Click the Key Management button and then choose Create Keys from the dialog box. WinPGP runs PGP with the proper parameters in a DOS box. Just read and follow the instructions.

> **CAUTION**
>
> You need to supply a key phrase (password) in order to generate your key. This phrase should be kept absolutely private. You will not see the phrase as you type, so choose a phrase that reflects your typing skills. Make it easy to remember, easy to type, and difficult to guess.

Once you have generated your own key, you should save your key to a file so you can send it to others. Click the Key Management button again and choose Extract a key from your key ring from the dialog box. Then pick the key you want to extract and the name of a file for the key. The default extension is .pgp.

When someone sends you their key, add it to the public key ring by pressing the Key management button and choosing Add key (public or private) to key[ring]. Note that the dialog box is not big enough for the entire phrase. Enter (or browse for) the name of the file containing the key, and then choose a key ring. The default key ring is Public.

Sending encoded messages is a multi-step process. First, compose a message using your favorite word processor. WinPGP has buttons that will launch Windows Write or Windows Notepad. Write your message, and save it with a .txt extension.

Click the Encrypt button and choose the type of encryption. See the documentation for the differences in types. Enter the name of the document in the box. You can browse for the document if you can't remember the file name. Then enter the recipient's name in the box. You can browse a list of keys on your public key ring and click the recipient's name if that is easier for you.

After you click OK, WinPGP launches PGP in a DOS box. PGP asks for your pass phrase and then encrypts the message to a file with the extension .pgp. Once this message is encrypted, it can only be decrypted by the recipient using his or her private key. You can't even decrypt the message, even though you were the one who encrypted it in the first place.

 If you are worried about the security of your own computer, be sure you erase the clear text file after you encrypt the message. Even erasing the file is not enough to ensure privacy unless you reuse the space. Remember, deleted files are not overwritten and can be recovered. WinPGP has an option to overwrite and then delete the original file once the encryption is complete. The truly paranoid will want to make sure the clear text has also been removed from memory and Windows 95 virtual memory.

If you receive an encrypted message, reverse the process. Save the message to disk with the extension PGP. Launch WinPGP and click the Decrypt button. Enter or browse for the name of the file (usually with a .pgp extension). You can also name the output file for the clear text file. It's a good idea to use this option since PGP writes the clear text to a file with the same basic name as the PGP file, but with no extension. If you choose a file name with a .txt extension, you can read the clear text directly from WinPGP by launching the Ms-Write or Notepad buttons. Once you have entered the file names, WinPGP launches PGP with the proper parameters and switches in a DOS box. Enter your pass phrase, and PGP decrypts the message and writes the clear text to a file. Press a key to close the DOS box and return to WinPGP.

There are many other features offered by WinPGP. Be sure to read the help files before you choose an option. Figure 40.5 shows a PGP-encrypted message in the Windows 95 word processor before decryption. Care to try your hand at decryption?

FIG. 40.5
A PGP-encrypted message.

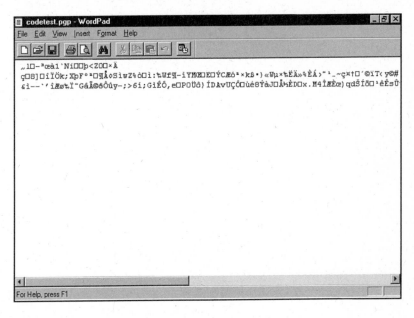

Part
VIII

Ch
40

N O T E WinPGP is shareware, meaning you can use it before you buy it. However, until you register your copy, you will often see a message box that reminds you that you are only trying it. Once you register your copy, these annoying messages disappear. ■

Network Security

If your computer is connected to a Local Area Network, you can restrict access to your resources. Windows 95 and Windows for Workgroups have built-in networking capabilities. Your Windows 95 computer probably has a Network Neighborhood icon on the desktop if you are connected to a network.

You can decide which of your computer's resources you want to share with others on the network. Click Network Neighborhood, then select your own computer from the list of people on the Net. A typical example of the resources available on a small network is shown in Figure 40.6.

FIG. 40.6

Windows 95 network
resources for a typical
small network.

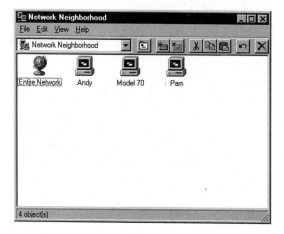

To select the computer resources you wish to share, click the My Computer icon on the desktop. As you click each item in the list, you can select File, Properties. When the properties
dialog box appears, click the Sharing tab and see how sharing is enabled for that item. You can
choose to share the resource with everyone on the network, as shown in Figure 40.7, or set up
a password so only some of the people on the network have access to the resource. You can
grant either full or read-only privilege to the network users. You always have the option of not
sharing with others on the network.

FIG. 40.7

Sharing network
resources through
Windows 95.

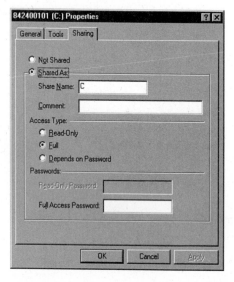

Remember the tree-like structure of the file system when you let others on the network share
your files. If you share your C drive, others on the network can access every folder on your
disk. However, when you choose File, Properties for one of your folders, you will notice that

sharing is not enabled (see Fig. 40.8). This does not mean that others cannot access that folder, it only means that the folder is not available on the network as a separate resource. Notice that the dialog box in Figure 40.8 does indicate that the folder is included in the shared resource C:\.

FIG. 40.8
Folder Not Shared.
Or Is It?

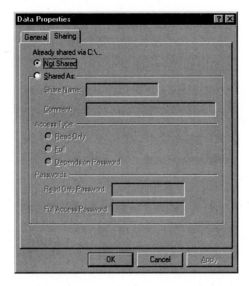

NetWare

If your LAN is part of a NetWare LAN, there are individual protections you can place on your files. Each NetWare folder and file can be set with Read, Write, Create, Modify, Erase, File Scan, Access Control, and Supervisory attributes. Files and folders can have any or all of these attributes. Since the rights attributes vary among different versions of NetWare, check your documentation or with your network administrator to find out how to set them up on your situation. ●

Part
VIII

Ch
40

CHAPTER 41

Avoiding Computer Viruses

by Bill Brandon

One of the charms of the Internet is the availability not just of information, but of thousands of programs you can run on your own computer without paying a dime up front. The downside is that you don't know whether you're getting a little extra something—a computer virus—along with what might be a very useful program.

In the entire world of routine computer use, no single subject is more arcane—or more misunderstood—than computer viruses. Almost the entire body of knowledge is owned by a very few: those who write viruses and those who find them.

And yet, the security of every computer system is potentially threatened by these miniature programs. If you use a PC, whether running DOS, Windows, or even UNIX (under certain circumstances that will be explained in this chapter), the chances are quite good that you will eventually see a virus in action or will know someone whose system has been infected. If you use Microsoft Word 6.0 or higher, or Excel 7.0 or higher, whether on a PC or on a Mac, and regardless of the operating system (in the case of Word), there is an excellent chance that you have already been affected by the so-called "macro viruses" that began appearing in 1995. In fact, whether your system is a stand-alone or part of a network, a Mac, a PC, or any other

Understanding what a virus is

There is a lot of debate about exactly what makes one program a virus and another one a desirable piece of software, but the easiest way to understand viruses is to learn what they do.

Understanding what a virus isn't

Users often think that they have been attacked by a virus when they haven't been, and sometimes panic causes more damage than a virus would ever be capable of doing.

How viruses spread

Thanks to misconceptions spread in the popular press, many people believe that viruses are spread through game files downloaded from the Internet.

How to protect yourself

While the chances of getting your computer infected by a virus aren't very large, and the consequences usually aren't serious, you do need to take certain measures on a regular basis. Fortunately, these precautions help you recover from disasters totally unrelated to viruses, too.

computer type, somewhere someone is writing or has written a virus program to exploit any weakness of your system or any lack of vigilance on your part.

Fortunately, many viruses do not do any serious or permanent damage. And there is plenty that you can do to reduce your vulnerability to these annoyances. In most cases, it is possible to recover from a virus infection no worse for the experience, other than losing time in the disinfection process. The keys are preparation, vigilance, and keeping your cool. ■

What Is a Virus?

Even the best virus-busters haven't been able to agree on the perfect definition of a virus. Two words—program and replicate—are key. In order to get from place to place (computer to computer, disk to disk) or *replicate*, some program must operate to make that happen. There are two other elements that are present in some but not all viruses, a *trigger* and a *payload*. A trigger is a section of program that looks for a certain event such as a date, a particular number of disk accesses, or a set number of duplications. The trigger can be used to activate the payload section of the virus. The payloads of some viruses are relatively benign. The "Stoned" virus, for example, simply announces that your computer is "stoned." Some versions carry an additional message urging reform of laws relating to the possession and use of marijuana (in case "stoned" is a new term to you). Others carry more dangerous payloads such as erasing all data on a drive, scrambling the file allocation table (FAT), or rendering a drive unreadable. A virus does not need a payload and trigger to be classified as a virus, but it must replicate.

Besides the obvious symptoms that virus writers sometimes put in their products, such as music, graphics, and message boxes, here are some of the common signs that a virus may be at work:

- File sizes or contents change
- More RAM is used than is expected
- Less RAM than actual is reported to be installed
- The boot sector on the hard drive changes
- Interrupt vectors change
- "Strange" behavior from the hardware
- "Strange" behavior from the software

Changes like these can happen as the virus replicates and hides itself, or as a result of the payload. Of course, these can result from hardware problems and from legitimate software, too. Be careful before crying, "Wolf!"

 TIP If you discover that a file has been deleted or is missing, or if a program does not seem to run correctly, don't assume that a virus is responsible. It's important not to panic. Far more damage is done by slips of the finger or mouse, or by badly-written software, than by all the computer viruses in the world.

So in the simplest terms, a virus is a program that replicates. It doesn't have to do any damage, it just has to spread. In order to spread, a virus must somehow get the user to run it. This is easily accomplished by appending the virus programming code to another program that the user is certain to run. Because almost all computer programs are stored on hard or floppy disks, all a virus has to do is change the file that contains the program without the user being aware of what is being done. No matter what computer or operating system is involved, nearly all viruses will take one of two paths to achieve that objective. They infect files, or they infect boot sectors on disks.

File Infectors

This class of virus is the simplest to write and the easiest to find. All executable programs share certain characteristics on any given system. For example, all executable programs running under any given operating system have file names that end with certain extensions. Most people have become so accustomed to clicking a colorful screen icon that they don't remember—or never knew—that there are some strict parameters for what goes on behind the scenes and screens.

A *file infector* is passed when an infected program is run and appends the virus code to another executable file. When the second program is run, it appends the virus code to a third program, and so on until every program stored on the disk is infected. As a general rule, each time an infected program is run, it will infect another one. However, general rules are often broken. Some viruses will infect multiple programs when they are run. With viruses, it's important to remember the general rule: There are no rules.

Emulation programs are becoming fairly common (for example, programs that allow you to run PC software on a Mac). You should realize that a Mac can pass a PC virus to PCs, although the Mac itself may not be affected by the virus. In certain cases, a PC program running under emulation on a Mac may be affected by a PC virus.

Another potential area for trouble is discussed in the section "Macro Viruses," later in this chapter. Macro viruses run on any system that will run the macros involved. For example, if you receive an MS Word 6.0 document that originated on a PC and load it into MS Word on your Mac, any macro viruses in that document will run in the Mac version. They may not cause the same kind of trouble that they do on a PC, but they will affect your files.

Boot Sector Infectors

Every hard disk and diskette contains what is known as a *boot sector*. This is the first physical sector on the disk. It stores a small program designed to get a computer up and running. Every time you reboot your computer, this small program runs. A boot sector infector (BSI) can only be "caught" by booting up your PC with an infected disk (see note). If you never have a disk in drive A or set your computer to always boot from the hard disk, you cannot be infected with a boot sector virus.

Part
VIII

Ch
41

> **N O T E** Remember the rule that there are no rules when it comes to computer viruses. A type of
> virus, called a *dropper*, places a virus in the boot sector. These viruses can infect a boot
> sector even if the computer is never started from an infected floppy. In addition, some viruses, referred
> to as *multipartite* viruses, infect both files and the boot sector. An example of this type is the PC virus
> called "Tequila." ▪

Boot sector viruses are hard to catch, but easy to spread. Once a PC is infected, any disk access—even a simple folder check—can pass a BSI from a hard disk to a floppy. If that floppy is used to boot another computer, the virus spreads.

Remarkable as it may seem, 90 percent of reported virus "hits" in mid-1995 were BSI viruses. Even computers using Windows 95 begin by reading the first sector on the disk to start the operating system loading. BSIs may be the most prevalent form of virus for the next several years.

Protecting against most BSI viruses is simple. Tell your computer *never* to boot from a floppy drive. Most computers can be set to boot from the hard drive by changing the boot configuration stored in ROM. Check your computer's manual to see if the configuration can be changed on your model. Please note the word "most" in the first sentence above; there are very few absolute certainties when it comes to virus protection.

There is a variant of the BSI type virus in the PC world that is important to understand. This is the master boot record (MBR) virus. It might be better referred to as a "BIOS virus." Because of the way this virus attacks a PC system, it is not operating-system specific. In other words, PCs running DOS, Windows, or UNIX can all be infected by an MBR virus. Well-known MBR viruses include Brain, Stoned, Empire, Azusa, and Michelangelo.

Macro Viruses

Another now broken rule of computer viruses is that only programs, not data, can contain a computer virus. A *macro* is data that affects the way a program operates. In a way, a macro is a program within a program. Usually macros are a way to save keystrokes when using a program such as a word processor, database, or spreadsheet. Several programs have within their macro language the capability to perform many of the functions of a virus—replication and possibly destruction. Some programs even have the macro equivalent of the Autoexec.bat file, a macro that runs whenever the program is started.

Macros are now being favored by some virus writers. If you use sophisticated programs with a rich macro language, such as Microsoft Word, you should be aware of the existence of macro viruses. Microsoft Word has the capability of embedding a macro right in the file. As operating systems get more diverse and "suite" applications continue to develop cross-platform interoperability, macro viruses may become more of a problem than program viruses. There are already several Word macro viruses, and a demonstration Excel macro virus has been reported. Macro viruses can be transferred across platforms, from PC to Mac, and back. Microsoft Word isn't the only application program exploited by macro virus writers; recently, an Ami Pro macro virus was reported.

NOTE How big is the virus threat? One way to look at this question is to ask how many computer viruses are known. While the number is increasing all the time, researchers report around 6,000 PC viruses, fewer than 50 Macintosh viruses, and about four UNIX viruses. Not many of these viruses are widespread—in fact most of them are in the category of lab experiments. Fewer than 40 of the known PC viruses cause most of the reported infections. Fewer than 200 PC viruses have been found "in the wild" (i.e., outside the lab). However, some viruses, such as the new Word macro virus called "Concept," have infected tens of thousands of systems (if not more) worldwide. ▪

What a Virus Is Not

It often seems that there are more myths associated with computer viruses than truth. The problem is that with the exception of those who develop viruses, few people really know how they work. Most of these people are the anti-virus researchers who develop programs to combat viruses. For those who market anti-virus products, the worse the scare, the better the sales. One wonders who can be trusted to provide accurate and objective information about viruses.

The media get most of their information from people who sell anti-virus products. Seldom does a person who writes viruses come forward and tell the media why and what he is doing. Users who have no concept of what a computer virus is often blame a virus for anything that makes them lose data. Legends are grown from the fruits of ignorance.

The truth is that most computer viruses (there are thousands of different ones) do not destroy a computer or its data. Most viruses do nothing more than replicate and waste space and time. But there are several widespread viruses that do have a destructive phase known as a payload, which was introduced earlier in the section, "What Is a Virus?" The payload can vary from erasing files to formatting a hard disk and destroying all the data on it. Often the payload, if present, will be triggered on a certain date or by certain actions. Payloads and triggers vary from one virus to another.

If you get a computer virus, the odds are that you won't lose all of your data. Of the thousands of viruses that have been written, only a few become successful in replicating throughout the computing community. Most are spotted quickly and eliminated before becoming widespread. The most successful (if that's the right term) viruses are those with no payload. They merely replicate themselves and go relatively unnoticed. A virus with a payload announces its presence in dramatic fashion and can be eliminated once spotted.

Many myths about computer viruses have built up since the first ones were discovered in the late 1980s. There have been stories of burning monitors and viruses transmitted by the control signals of modems. Recently, the Internet community was hit by the pseudo "Good Times" virus. Supposedly, mail and newsgroup messages that contained the words "good times" would release a virus and destroy the files of anyone who read the message. The virus itself was a myth, but Internet users replicated the warning message in virus-like proportions.

My favorite virus myth came from a tongue-in-cheek story written in *PC World* on April 1, 1991, shortly after the Gulf War. The story told of an American manufacturer of printers who, at the behest of the military, sent a shipment of printers to Iraq with a computer virus embedded in

Part

VIII

Ch

41

the read-only memory. The Coalition forces delayed the invasion of Iraq until the virus took hold in the Iraqi air defense system. When the air war began, the Iraqis could not shoot down the U.S. planes. True? Not a bit. Funny? Very.

A year later, a reputable national news magazine reported the exact same story. The magazine reported the story almost verbatim, but as absolute truth from an unnamed source deep within the Pentagon. When confronted by those who had read the original story in *PC World*, the magazine refused to admit that the story was an April Fool's joke and never printed a retraction or correction. In fact, they printed a confirmation. Because that particular magazine has a much wider distribution than *PC World*, many more people think the story is true than know it's a hoax.

Now that you know the basics of what a virus is and isn't, let's see how these little beasts came into being and how the public has been led and misled by the media.

A History Lesson—The Virus Wars

The opening salvos were fired in the fall of 1987 when the Brain virus was found at the University of Delaware in October, the Lehigh virus at the university of the same name the following month and, in December, the Jerusalem virus was discovered at Hebrew University. In early 1988, the Stoned virus popped up. In October of 1988, the first computer virus conference was held. The virus writers and anti-virus "experts" were at war.

But it was pretty much kid stuff until 1989, when the so-called "Dark Avenger" came on the scene with the first fast-infecting virus. Hot on Dark Avenger's heels came *polymorphic* viruses—viruses whose code changed with every iteration, so standard anti-virus techniques couldn't find them. Then along came multipartite viruses, stealth technique viruses, and, in 1995, macro viruses that break all of the existing rules.

N O T E Most viruses attempt to hide their actions from the user. The most common technique is for the virus to intercept error messages, such as the write-protect error, and to not report it to the user. Other viruses adjust the memory size of the computer so that the memory space it uses is hidden from other programs. Advanced stealth technique viruses include intercepting all queries about file size and reporting the uninfected size instead of the real size. Even more advanced viruses can set the processor into single-step mode and monitor each and every processor instruction and memory access. The virus is written this way to protect itself from discovery and removal. ▪

N O T E The most common kind of anti-virus software looks for a virus in a file or on the boot sector by comparing the bytes in the file with a known sample of the virus. To counter this technique, some viruses change form from one replication to another. The virus part of the file is encrypted differently each time the virus replicates to another file. A small portion of the code remains unencrypted and is used to decrypt the virus as it is loaded into memory. This unencrypted portion of the virus is often interspersed with random do-nothing instructions. The program operates in the same way each time it is run, but even this portion of the file contains an almost infinite variation of bytes. ▪

War Games

In the late 1980s, newly minted "virus experts" began to pump out anti-virus products as fast as the virus writers could get new viruses into distribution. The careful, generic approaches of some of the first anti-virus products were pushed aside by "scanners," most of which purported to "find all known viruses." There was speculation that some of the less honorable anti-virus types were writing their own viruses and distributing them so *only* their products would find the newest addition to the virus army.

The stakes were high, particularly for those who hoped to amass a fortune from selling their products. The virus writers had little more at stake except tweaking the most outrageous vendors with yet another variant of an "old standard" that the latest scanner couldn't find.

Apocalypse Now

The date was set for Friday, October 13th, 1989. On that date, the relatively benign Jerusalem virus and the heavily payloaded Columbus Day virus were scheduled to bring a halt to the world of computing as we knew it. Or that's what the media, fed by disinformation and misinformation would have had us believe.

The show, as the old saying goes, didn't live up to its advance reviews. The Jerusalem virus has a payload that will erase any program run on any Friday the 13th. The Columbus Day virus will erase all data on a hard disk on any date after Columbus Day, October 12. Friday, October 13, 1989, came and went, and computers kept on working. Few had been infected with those viruses.

The really big media show was two and a half years later.

Armageddon

The so-called Michelangelo virus, an MBR virus with a payload that destroys all the data on a hard disk every year on March 6 was discovered in 1991. Fifty million—that's right, 50,000,000—PCs were predicted to roll over and succumb to data death on March 6, 1992, 517 years after the birth of Michelangelo. With one notable exception, the Associated Press, which "considered the source" of the information, the media fell back in love with the concept of imminent destruction. Perhaps as a result of the extensive publicity and the almost overnight production of anti-Michelangelo products, there were very few reported "hits."

> **NOTE** Naming computer viruses began as soon as the first one was discovered. Often the name associated has nothing to do with the virus itself. A case in point is the Michelangelo virus. It's doubtful that the person who devised the virus had the Italian Renaissance painter Michelangelo, born in 1475, in mind when he or she chose the trigger date of March 6. The Michelangelo virus was named by a European anti-virus researcher who was not familiar with the history of Texas—"Remember the Alamo," March 6, 1835. ■

Hype or Help?

It's unlikely that the media, twice-burned by hyping an empty fear, will ever cover computer viruses with quite the intensity of the Jerusalem/Columbus Day and Michelangelo scares. Nevertheless, the list of known viruses, both lab viruses and those "in the wild," continues to grow, and virus incursions are almost commonplace today. The war is by no means over, but it's being fought in a quieter fashion.

Representing the Defense

There are three basic ways to combat the most common viruses:

- Known virus scanners
- Validity checkers
- Behavior blockers

Of the three, known virus scanning has developed into the most prevalent form of virus protection for the PC. Why? When asked at an international virus conference, one well-known speaker uttered one simple word: "Marketing."

Known Virus Scanning

The principle of *virus scanning* is simple. Viruses are program code, which is nothing more than a set of numeric values that tells the computer what to do. Each and every virus has a specific *signature*, a set of numbers in a particular order unique to the virus. A scanner can examine a program file or boot sector and determine if there is a signature of any one of the known viruses present. If there is, the scanner identifies the virus and notifies the user.

While it sounds simple enough, there are some drawbacks. First, the operative word is "known." The person who programs the scanner must know the signature of a particular virus. This is not always easy. To obtain a signature, the programmer must have a sample of the virus and select a series of program instructions that occur only in that virus. If the programmer does not have a sample of the virus, he or she cannot write a scanner that identifies that particular virus. With the geometric increase in the number of viruses being released, the work involved can rapidly overcome the energy of even the most avid anti-virus programmer. Every time a new virus is discovered, the anti-virus program must be updated to reflect the additional knowledge.

Another problem faced by scanners is the proliferation of a type of virus known as *polymorphic* viruses. These are viruses that change their own programming code from generation to generation. No two samples of the same virus contain the same series of programming instructions. It then becomes very difficult for a scanner to identify the virus from a series of programming instructions.

Scanning programs are convenient and popular. Within the limitations mentioned in this section, they do work. However, you should not rely solely on a scanning program to guard the security of your system and your data. It would be a very good idea to also install another kind of anti-virus program as well, with the best choice being a validity checker.

Validity Checks

Because the computer stores programs as files on a disk, any change in the file can be noted. This is the principle that guides the anti-virus technique of *validity checking*. A mathematical formula calculates a valid signature for the program file and stores the number in a separate data file. If a virus changes the contents of the program file, the calculated signature will no longer match the stored signature.

An advantage of validity checks over scanners is that the virus does not have to be known by the anti-virus program. The fact that the file has changed can be used to alert the user to the presence of a virus. This means that even mutating viruses and new viruses can be easily noted by a validity checking anti-virus program.

The disadvantage is that you don't know the name of the virus that is present in the system or how it got there. Also a validity check requires that the program file be uninfected with a virus when the signature is first calculated. If the file is already infected, a validity check will show no change.

Behavior Blockers

The third class of anti-virus software is programs that prohibit any virus-like activity. For example, there is seldom, if ever, a need to change the boot sector of a disk. A *behavior blocker* prevents this particular sector from being changed. Once a program has been installed, the basic executable file should never need to be changed. A behavior blocker can monitor this type of activity too.

Behavior blockers quickly fell into disfavor as a means of preventing viruses simply because they are subject to many false alarms. Because there are legitimate programs that may appear to have virus-like activity, a behavior blocker usually displays a warning and allows the user to either proceed with the questioned activity or not. For many reasons, the behavior blockers are the weakest form of anti-virus protection. For example, an unsophisticated user may often proceed where he or she should stop, or stop a perfectly legitimate function.

What Anti-Virus Programs Are Available?

As you might imagine, the anti-virus software business is booming. New anti-virus software (AVS) comes on the market frequently, and existing AVS is updated frequently. There are three Web sites that are worth visiting as you search for AVS.

The Antivirus Software Page:
http://www.cabot.nf.ca/general_links/virus-software.html

The A-Z Antivirus Page (Macintosh Antivirus):
http://isteonline.uoregon.edu/istehome/

Part VIII
Ch 41

Computer Virus Information and Resource Page:
http://lipsmac.acs.unt.edu/virus/index.html

In addition, Table 41.1 identifies some common anti-virus software by platform and type.

Table 41.1 Common Anti-Viral Software by Platform and Type

Type	Mac	PC
Virus Scanners	Disinfectant, SAM	VirusScan, F-PROT
Validity Checkers	(none)	ASP Integrity Toolkit
Behavior Blockers	Gatekeeper	Secure, Flu Shot+

When You're at Risk

Every personal computer is equipped with a piece of hardware that will guarantee that no computer virus will infect your machine. It's called a *plug*. Remove it from the wall socket and you will never get a computer virus. However, if you choose to use your computer, you run the risk of computer viruses.

Your risk depends on *how* you use your computer. If you never place a disk in the A drive, never add new programs, and are not connected to a network, you should worry more about lightning strikes than about computer viruses. This is safe computing. A virus is a social disease. Only contact with a program from an outside source can infect your computer. This program could be on the boot sector of a disk or contained in a new program added to your mix.

Any new program adds to the computer virus risk, no matter where it comes from. There have been cases where brand new computers with bundled software have been shipped with a computer virus. Even shrink-wrapped new software packages have been known to contain viruses. Computer stores often accept returns from unhappy customers, take the software package into the back room, redo the shrink wrap, and place it back on the shelves for another customer.

Software programs that you download from a bulletin board or obtain from an Internet FTP site can also be infected with a computer virus. Most reputable sites check and double-check a program before offering it for downloading, but sometimes a virus is a new one that is not trapped by their scanner. Some sites couldn't care less if you are infected by one of their programs. There are even some sites that deliberately distribute viruses. Your best defense is to know the site's reputation before downloading.

The highest risk is from your friendly computer repair person. That's right. The person who is supposed to fix your computer is the one that is most likely to infect you. When something goes wrong and you call the repair people, they bring with them a whole package of utility programs to try to repair any data damage. They place the disk in drive A, reboot the computer, and run a set of diagnostic programs. These utility disks travel from one sick computer to another. It is highly probable that one of the problems has been a computer virus. If the technician's diagnostic disk has become infected by one of these computers, that disk could introduce the virus to your system.

What to Do *Before* the Worst Happens

Most computer users will spend a happy life of computing without ever being hit by a computer virus. For this reason, only a small percentage are prepared when a computer virus does hit. The three most important steps you can take to prevent disaster in the event of a computer virus hit are

1. Back up!
2. Back up!!
3. Back up!!!

Back Up!

The roving mouse pointer may be a far worse enemy than the most dreaded computer virus. A click of the wrong icon means delete. That click can cause your precious document to disappear. You even get a chance to confirm that you want your document to go away, and you just might do it. I know. It happened to this chapter. Back up.

Back Up!!

That 1.5G (gigabytes) hard disk can be a disaster waiting to happen. Mechanical things can break down in use, and a hard disk is a *very* delicate instrument mounted in a shock-proof sealed case. How sturdy is that hard disk when confronted by earthquakes in California, hurricanes in Florida, or tornadoes in Kansas? Could your data survive a fire? Probably not. Back up.

Back Up!!!

In the rare event of a computer virus, your only hope may be a backup. If it is one of the viruses that have a destructive payload, your backup could be the only way to restore your data. The programs on your backup may be infected, but at least your data files will be safe. It's far easier to reinstall the software from the original disks and restore the backed-up data files than it is to re-create all the data from scratch. Back up.

Restoring a Virus-Infected Computer

There are many programs that can attempt to repair a virus-infected file or boot sector. Because some viruses overwrite the original information in the host, repair is not always possible. Still, a good number of viruses retain all the information of the host, and a repair program can remove the virus code from the file and restore it to the original condition.

Sometimes, the repair can be worse than the virus. Most boot sector viruses replace the original boot sector with a virus sector and move the original to another sector on the disk. After the virus runs its own code, it loads the original boot sector into memory and lets the computer complete the boot process as usual. To effect a repair, all you have to do is move the original boot sector back into the proper place. Repair programs must know where the original boot sector is located, or they might move the wrong sector. Then the computer won't work at all. You can't even use another repair program that will do it right.

Some file-infecting viruses destroy a portion of the original program and cannot be removed. In this case, the only option is to delete the file and reinstall the program from the original disks. Even if a virus can be removed from a program, your best choice is to reinstall the program from the original disk. Only use a repair program if you are unable to locate a disk version of the program.

Viruses and Windows 3.1

Most of the nearly 6,000 reported viruses that run on PCs are designed to run under MS-DOS. Most of these cannot run under Windows 3.1 because they are not compatible with the way Windows manages memory. For an average MS-DOS virus to work, it must load itself into memory, and Windows denies this opportunity. If an MS-DOS virus tries to infect a Windows application the same way it would infect a DOS executable, the Windows application simply will not run. This is a good indicator to an alert operator that something is wrong.

However, note that most MS-DOS viruses will run perfectly well and happily in an MS-DOS window. They will be able to replicate, too, and be passed on to other users.

You should not become over-confident, however. There are at least three viruses that are Windows 3.1-specific. They can correctly infect a Windows application. You can also "catch" a boot sector or MBR virus, which will interfere with Windows.

Windows 95 and Computer Viruses

A funny thing happened on the way to Windows 95. There is no anti-virus software included with the operating system. Could it be that Windows 95 is such a secure operating system that no virus could ever get through? No. The people at Microsoft, when asked, responded that they didn't want to be in the anti-virus business. Windows 95 is vulnerable to many of the existing MS-DOS and Windows 3.1 viruses.

Don't be fooled by the sales pitch. Under all the icons, Start buttons, and long file names, Windows 95 is still very similar to MS-DOS. The hard disk still contains a master boot record (MBR) in sector 1 and a DOS boot record on the first sector of the second side. The familiar Io.sys and Msdos.sys files are still present in the root directory as hidden system files, although they are not the same as the MS-DOS files of the same name. The disk directory structure and file allocation table (FAT) are still in the same place on the drive as under

MS-DOS. The Config.sys and Autoexec.bat files, if present, still begin the process of starting the computer.

The difference with Windows 95 and MS-DOS lies in the Io.sys program, which contains the basic function calls for the disk operating system. Without getting too technical, MS-DOS is an unprotected operating system that allows any program to have access to all areas of memory. A truly protected operating system isolates the memory allocated for programs from the memory used by the operating system. Windows 95 is a hybrid of the two.

At this point, specific Windows 95 viruses have appeared. Anti-virus researchers have not been able to study the effects of every DOS and Windows 3.1 virus on Windows 95, but of those that have been studied, a few pleasant surprises have developed.

Boot Sector Self Check

First, the good news. Windows 95 has a built-in integrity check for the boot sector. When Windows 95 detects a change in the boot sector, it displays a window and informs you that you may have a virus. The scheme that Windows 95 employs is not foolproof. Technically, a hard disk has two boot sectors, the MBR, which is the first sector of the disk, and the DOS boot sector (DBS), which is the first sector of the partition. Windows 95 displays the warning message if either of these sectors is infected, but always identifies it as the MBR.

Windows 95 misses some viruses that definitely change the MBR. Apparently, Windows 95 does not perform an integrity check of the entire sector, but only checks the vector (address) of interrupt 13h, the disk I/O vector. Windows 95 issues no warning for a virus such as "Jumper B," which does not change the vector of interrupt 13h. At this time, most boot sector viruses change the vector of interrupt 13h, but as Windows 95 becomes more popular, more viruses that circumvent the built-in check are likely to appear.

MS-DOS and Windows 3.1 Viruses under Windows 95

Now the bad news. Most of the MS-DOS viruses work under Windows 95. When you run one of your old MS-DOS programs under Windows 95, you run it in an MS-DOS window. Windows 95 sets up a separate DOS environment for the program and runs it just like it would under the old MS-DOS system. When you look at the technical aspects of a DOS program running under Windows 95, you find that Windows 95 tries to manage the DOS interrupts. DOS programs that use undocumented interrupt functions may fail (crash) under Windows 95. Although Microsoft tried to make all older DOS and Windows 3.1 programs compatible with Windows 95, not all will operate properly. A side effect of the incompatibility is that not all viruses will work properly either. This is good.

While you are working in an MS-DOS window with older DOS programs, any virus infection will spread just as it did under the older DOS system. When you exit the MS-DOS window, however, if you have inadvertently introduced a *resident* virus (a virus that acts like a terminate-and-stay-resident (TSR) program), Windows 95 assumes that you have run a pop-up utility and refuses to close the DOS session until you disable the pop-up. Even though this

Part
VIII

Ch
41

feature is not designed as a virus behavior blocker, it acts as one. When you exit the DOS box, the resident virus is disabled.

Just as in the previous version of Windows, every Windows 95 program has a DOS stub program. If you try to run a Windows program from DOS, the stub program runs and informs you that the program must be run under Windows. If you have a virus active in the DOS session when you run a Windows stub, the stub can become infected. The DOS program is not Windows-aware, and the virus could overwrite a portion of the file that contains the Windows program. The next time you run the program from Windows, you will find that the file is corrupted and either will not operate or will crash the system.

Windows 95 treats the DOS stub program a bit differently than the previous versions of Windows. In the older versions, if you attempted to run a Windows program from the DOS box, the stub would run instead. When Windows 95-specific programs are started from the DOS box, the stub is bypassed and the Windows 95 program runs normally. Because Windows 95 does not load and run the DOS stub, many viruses, even if memory resident, will not infect the program.

Any virus that ran under Windows 3.1 will run under Windows 95. Just as with DOS viruses, in some cases these may not be capable of doing damage.

Specific Windows 95 Viruses

The first Windows 95 virus appeared within two months of the release of the new operating system. Called Boza, it is a weak, badly written virus that infects only program files written in one specific format. It does not become resident in the computer's memory. Very few, if any, Windows 95 users are in any danger from this virus. Boza contains no harmful payload, but it is defective and sometimes damages files it infects.

Eventually more potent Windows 95 viruses will appear. Your best bet to avoid problems is to back up frequently and install anti-virus software designed specifically to meet the challenges of the Windows 95 environment.

Viruses and the Macintosh

There are around 50 viruses that infect the Macintosh. Most of the comments in this chapter about the way viruses work and about their symptoms are applicable to viruses on the Mac. There is nothing unusual or unique about the Macintosh or its operating systems in this regard.

However, Mac users should be aware of one peculiar problem area. Any program that can emulate MS-DOS so that MS-DOS programs or Windows can be run, can also host MS-DOS viruses. If an MS-DOS virus is activated in this way, it will most likely spread to any other DOS programs available to it in the emulator environment.

In general, viruses are not as large a problem for the Macintosh community as they are for PC users. This has not always been the case. In the late 1980s, viruses were a major concern if you owned a Mac. The shift to System 6 and then to System 7 has done much to decrease the occurance and spread of viruses in Macs.

One effect of this somewhat more benign atmosphere is that there are fewer anti-virus programs for Macs than for PCs. The most common Mac anti-virus programs—SAM (Symantec Antiviral for Macintosh) and Disinfectant—are scanners. There is one blocker-type anti-virus program, called Gatekeeper, but it is no longer updated and may fade from the scene in the near future.

Many Mac viruses are actually HyperCard viruses and are not detected by SAM and Disinfectant. HyperCard viruses propagate only between HyperCard stacks.

Viruses, UNIX, Windows NT, and NetWare

For a number of reasons, there are no known non-experimental UNIX viruses. This does not mean that such viruses are not possible (the very first experimental virus was implemented on a UNIX system); they just wouldn't spread very well.

However, this doesn't mean that UNIX users should move on to the next chapter. In certain cases, you will want to scan your UNIX system for *non*-UNIX viruses.

For example, all PCs are vulnerable to PC MBR (master boot record) infectors, regardless of the operating system in use. If you are running a UNIX OS on a PC, never boot from a floppy. If the floppy is infected with an MBR virus (Michelangelo, Stoned), the virus will pass to the PC's MBR and run despite the UNIX operating system.

A UNIX system that is acting as a file server for PC systems can hold PC-file infecting viruses. These will spread to the PC clients. In this case, the UNIX system must be scanned for PC viruses (not for UNIX viruses).

If you are running a file integrity checker (such as Tripwire), you may detect unauthorized changes to executable files on your UNIX system. Most of the time this is due to common circumstances, not to viruses, but it is a good idea anyway.

Windows NT is similar to UNIX because it is fairly secure from virus attack. However, PCs running NT are also vulnerable to MBR viruses. In addition, such a PC can host and pass along MS-DOS viruses.

Network operating systems are a special case worth looking at. While the network operating system itself is not DOS, there are some circumstances under which the server could become infected with a DOS virus. NetWare, and any other network operating system that boots from a DOS disk, loads a DOS executable that then takes control of the system. Even though there are no viruses that attack the NetWare kernel, the DOS executable (Server.exe in the case of NetWare) can be infected by a variety of means. If this happens, the server will fail at the next restart.

Protecting Your Computer

In looking at the various anti-virus programs offered for PCs running under Windows 3.1, you will notice that most of them are scanners. You will also notice that many of them are DOS products. This makes sense because the vast majority of computer viruses are also DOS programs. There is no problem at all in running your anti-virus program under DOS rather than Windows 3.1. The DOS version of the anti-viral may even run faster. McAfee and other antiviral publishers even offer MS-DOS anti-virus programs that stay memory resident after Windows starts. These TSRs will provide a warning if they detect certain types of virus activity or virus code in a file while Windows is running. The important thing is to use more than one kind of anti-viral product.

Each of the major anti-virus publishers offers one or more programs that are written specifically for the Windows 95 system. All of them are scanners. If you are running Windows 95, consider obtaining one of these as part of your protection plan, rather than running a Windows 3.1 or MS-DOS anti-viral product. That way, the anti-viral will run faster and should be better able to repair any damage caused by the virus.

If you prefer to run an MS-DOS based anti-viral on your Windows 95 machine, you should always start your computer in MS-DOS instead of Windows 95 before running the anti-virus program.

To protect your Macintosh from viruses, do the same basic things that PC owners do:

- Install and use antiviral software (and keep it up to date)
- Make regular backups
- Do not start your system from a floppy
- Keep the floppies with your original software on them locked

Finally, no matter what operating system and machine you run on, if you download files from the Internet, look for anti-viral software that inspects files for viruses *while they are being downloaded*. These programs will warn you before saving the program to disk if they find anything suspicious. The NetScape PowerPack, for example, contains the Norton Internet Anti-Virus.

Which Anti-Virus Programs Are Best?

The short answer to this question is, "Nobody knows." There are some good reasons for this unsatisfactory reply.

First, no one single anti-viral does the whole job. Earlier it was suggested that you should always choose a combination of products, such as a scanner and a validity checker. This combination will catch more viruses.

Second, some specific products are targeted by specific viruses. These viruses ignore other anti-viral products. It is hard to know which *one* product to choose, since this creates a vulnerability for your system.

Finally, the industry has not yet agreed on how to test anti-virus programs (although the National Computer Security Association has started its own certification program). Scanners can reliably test for 100 percent of the viruses programmed into their database. The only question is what virus signatures are in the database, and that is the basis for an industry standard.

Getting Reliable Virus Information

One of the more reliable sources of anti-virus information is the UseNet newsgroup comp.virus and its e-mail newsletter Virus-l. Other Internet sources of information are the **alt.com.virus** newsgroup and **http://www.yahoo.com/Computer** and Internet/Security and Encryption/ Viruses. Finally, you may wish to consider these Web pages:

Page Name	URL
Antivirus Software Page	**http://www.cabot.nf.ca/general_links/virus-software.html**
A-Z Antivirus (Macintosh)	**http://isteonline.uoregon.edu/istehome/edtechnews/antivirus/vir.MacSoft.html**
Computer Virus Information and Resources	**http://lipsmac.acs.unt.edu/virus/index.html**
HAVS Home Page ("Anti-Virus Site")	**http://www.valleynet.com/~joe/**
Mac Virus Information	**ftp://ftp.acs.ucalgary.ca/pub/Archivesmicros/mac/virus**

A Couple of Recommendations for PC Users

Surprisingly enough, some of the best anti-virus products are free. If you feel more comfortable with a commercial product, there are several good ones on the market. Most of the better anti-virus programs originate in Europe because the virus problem is greater there than in the United States. By reading the comp.virus newsgroup over the years, I have found that two PC products stand out as the best of the lot—Doctor Solomon's Anti-Virus Toolkit, a commercial product from England, and F-Prot by Frisk Software International of Iceland, which is free to individual users and also offers a commercial version.

Dr. Solomon's Anti-Virus Toolkit   Because the term "virus" is disease related, it's no wonder that many of the anti-virus product names are doctor related. But Dr. Alan Solomon is a real doctor, a Ph.D., anyway. He began producing anti-virus products in England when the threat was new, and he has continued producing one of the best commercial anti-virus products ever since. Dr. Solomon is one of the foremost computer virus researchers in the world today.

Dr. Solomon's Anti-Virus Toolkit can both find and repair viruses. The scanner, Findviru.exe, is one of the fastest and best in the business. The latest version of the Toolkit has a Windows interface that lets you select features from menus and buttons.

Dr. Solomon's Toolkit contains several features that aren't found on other scanners. It can scan a file that's in compressed format, such as .zip and .air. When you download programs from an Internet site or from a BBS, they are most likely in some compressed format. With the Toolkit, you can look inside these files without going through the process of decompression first. If you find a virus, you can delete the compressed file and never expose your computer to danger.

Some computers use a compression program for program files. Programs such as PKLite and LZExe make a program file smaller by compressing it and adding a small program to the beginning of the file that decompresses it at runtime. Dr. Solomon's Anti-Virus Toolkit can scan inside compressed programs.

Dr. Solomon takes particular care when it comes to the repair of virus-infected files. The program must be 100 percent sure that the virus is the *exact* same virus for which the repair is made. The Toolkit does not rely on just a virus signature. A Cyclical Redundancy Check or CRC determines if the virus is the same as the one for which the repair routine is written.

Dr. Solomon's Anti-Virus Toolkit is a commercial product and is available in many computer outlets. It is distributed by S&S International. The address is

S&S International PLC

Alton House

Gatehouse Way

Aylesbury, Buckinghamshire HP19 3XU

United Kingdom

The telephone number is

Voice: +44 (01)296 318700

Fax: +44 (01)296 318777

S&S International maintains a World Wide Web site at

http://www.sands.com

F-PROT   If you like the idea of getting something for nothing, then F-PROT is the program for you. Frisk International distributes one of the best anti-virus programs free to non-commercial individual users. They also have a professional version that's available for a reasonable fee to individuals, companies, and educational institutions.

The free version of F-PROT is DOS-based, but has a nice user interface with a point-and-press menu system. The professional version comes with a Windows interface. A Windows 95-specific version may be in the works.

The scanner is fast and accurate and consistently ranks among the best in identifying viruses, even when the tests are performed by competing companies. F-PROT includes a repair module, as well as a fairly complete description of most common viruses.

F-PROT is widely distributed on the Internet. The official distribution is by FTP through Simtel Mirror sites, although many online services carry the program, too. Rather than reading about it, download it and try it for yourself. It costs you nothing more than connect time.

F-PROT comes in a zipped file named FP-*nnn*.ZIP, where *nnn* is the latest version number. An official Simtel mirror site is **ftp://oak.oakland.edu/SimTel/msdos/virus**.

Check in the directory /pub/msdos/virus for the program. If you need to find another site, you can FTP Frisk International at **ftp://complex.is/pub/README** for a list of official sites. Frisk International does not distribute the program from its FTP site.

Disinfectant for the Macintosh

Your choices for an anti-virus program on the Mac are fairly limited, but one of the best ones also has the advantage of being free. Disinfectant can be downloaded from a number of sites, including its official site, **ftp://ftp.acns.nwu.edu/pub/disinfectant/**. You can also download the program and the manual from **http://lipsmac.acs.unt.edu/virus/macvirinf.html**. The manual is one of the best, most authoritative sources of information around on Mac viruses.

As mentioned earlier, Disinfectant is a scanner that recognizes all of the known non-HyperCard viruses, along with their clones and known variations. It attempts to repair infected files when it finds them. In addition, Disinfectant includes a virus protection extension (INIT) that protects uninfected systems against the known non-HyperCard viruses.

Disinfectant is updated periodically to include any newly discovered viruses. Unlike the PC programs (which issue data files containing new virus signature information), you must download the complete program each time you update. ●

Web Server

CHAPTER 42

Running a Web Server on Windows 3.1

by Mark Surfas

This is the first of three chapters discussing the installation and management of Web servers utilizing the Microsoft Windows family of operating systems. Rejoice! Providing information and services on the Internet is no longer the exclusive domain of UNIX gurus and educational institutions! Corporations and individuals are now free to publish and create their own presence without the need to learn or adapt to the freakish Unix Operating System. (Okay, freakish is a little strong. How about ornery?) Publish your own homepage! Create an on-line store! Set up an on-line club for fellow enthusiasts of whatever hobby you love! Whatever your needs, views, or interests, go forth and publish!

Operating a public Web server is a fun and exciting endeavor. It is absolutely true that whatever your imagination can conceive, you can deliver. This chapter and the following chapters will help you get started on the way to harnessing the power of Microsoft Windows as a robust base for your public and private Web servers. ■

The pros & cons of using Windows 3.1 as your server operating system

The operating system you run a server under can limit your capabilities or enhance them.

The best Web servers available for Windows 3.1

There are a limited number of Web servers for 3.1—we highlight the top two.

How to install the popular Win-HTTPD server

Quick and easy installation gets you up and running in 5 minutes!

How to administer the Win-HTTPD server

A short overview of system administration and considerations will label you "Webmaster" in no time!

Using Windows 3.1 as a Web Operating Platform

Windows 3.1 changed the computing landscape by becoming the de-facto graphical user interface (GUI) on the Intel platform. It is the first true operating system for the masses and has
enjoyed tremendous success as a single-user operating system. As of this writing, Windows 3.1
is the single most popular operating system on the planet in terms of numbers of existing
users.

A follow-up product, Windows for Workgroups, is often referred to as Windows 3.11 (note the
additional 1 at the end) and also WFW. Windows 3.11 is Windows 3.1 with some enhancements
in the area of networking. Running a Web server is largely about networking, and it is highly
recommended that you upgrade to Windows 3.11 if you are thinking about running a Web
server under Windows 3.1.

> **CAUTION**
>
> Many of the advanced features of the Web world are unavailable to 16-bit Web servers. Most notable are:
>
> - The inability to set up "virtual Web servers"
> - Lack of a 16-bit Java port
> - Lack of 16-bit CGI programs
>
> For low-volume Web sites, Windows 3.1 can be adequate. If your Web site needs to handle transaction
> processing or has extensive database links, you need to consider a 32-bit environment such as Windows 95
> or Windows NT. Also, you can perform multihoming or virtual servers under Windows NT. Windows 95 and
> Windows 3.1 do not support multiple IPs assigned to a single machine.
>
> Windows NT is a true 32-bit multithreaded environment that is perfect for serving large quantities of
> transactions. Windows 95 is a 32-bit operating system that still relies on a 16-bit base. While Windows 95 is
> a remarkable operating system, it is not as rock-solid as Windows NT.

Windows 3.1—The Logical Choice

The sheer popularity of Windows 3.1 makes it a logical first choice for millions of potential Web
publishers. Anyone can now connect to an Internet provider and launch Web servers. This
ease of use and setup could position the Windows 3.1 Web server as an information appliance
as valuable as the office fax machine.

Windows 3.1—The Illogical Choice

Running a server of any type can place great demands on the resources of the computer configured as a server. A brief discussion of the drawbacks of Windows 3.1 is therefore in order. This
discussion is not meant to dissuade you from using Windows 3.1, but just to give you an understanding of why there are problems here.

Windows 3.1 and 3.11 are both in a class of operating systems referred to as 16-bit. This literally means two things:

- The operating system communicates in 16-bit chunks. Intel processors beginning with the 386 are capable of processing 32 bits at a time.

- The computer is limited to using a 16-bit memory model that equates to roughly 16 megabytes of accessible RAM. The lack of available RAM is often the cause of slow performance.

Both of these issues merit serious consideration, but that isn't where the problems end.

- Windows 3.1 is not a true multitasking or multithreaded operating system. Using your server for tasks besides Web serving would greatly impact the running server and cost a painful performance penalty. If your server received many requests, it could quickly become overloaded.

Windows 3.11—A Better Choice

Windows 3.11 is a network-optimized version of Windows 3.1 and offers more efficient memory management and 32-bit performance. Windows for Workgroups builds on the architecture of Windows 3.1 by providing integrated networking capability in the base operating system.

In laymen's terms, WFW is faster and more stable—less likely to crash. In fact, all manufacturers of 16-bit Web servers recommend its use.

NOTE There are a number of excellent mailing lists for Windows users. Two such lists are:

- WFW-L (Windows for Workgroups)

WFW-L is a mailing list for discussions of user and developer issues regarding Microsoft Windows for Workgroups. To subscribe to the list, send e-mail with the message:

SUBSCRIBE WFW-L <YourFirstName> <YourLastName>

to this address:

LISTSERV@UMDD.UMD.EDU (Internet)

To post messages to the mailing list, e-mail messages to:

WFW-L@UMDD.UMD.EDU (Internet)

- WIN3-L (Windows 3.x)

WIN3-L is a mailing list for discussions of user and developer issues regarding Microsoft Windows 3.x products. To subscribe to the list, send e-mail with this message:

SUBSCRIBE WIN3-L <YourFirstName> <YourLastName>

to this address:

LISTSERV@UICVM.UIC.EDU (Internet)

To post messages to the mailing list, e-mail messages to:

WIN3-L@UICVM.UIC.EDU (Internet) ■

Part
IX

Ch
42

Recommended Hardware and Software

Running a stable and robust Web server under Microsoft Windows 3.1 and 3.11 requires that you optimize your environment to the greatest extent possible in terms of both hardware and software.

- Intel 386 CPU or better
- At least 8M of RAM
- 28,800 bps or faster Internet connection
- Windows for Workgroups 3.11
- Microsoft TCP32 3.11 or other 32-bit TCP/IP stack
- Windows in enhanced mode

N O T E We've mentioned that you should run Windows in Enhanced Mode. There are three different operating modes of Microsoft Windows version 3.1: real mode (similar to Windows/286 versions 2.x), 286 standard mode (also known as 286 protected mode), and 386 enhanced mode (also known as 386 protected mode).

WIN.COM automatically starts up Windows 3.0 in the proper mode for the configuration. However, Windows can be forced into one of the three modes through the following command-line switches:

Command Line	Mode
WIN /R	Real mode
WIN /S or WIN /2	Standard mode
WIN /3	Enhanced mode

The requirements for Win.com to automatically start up in enhanced mode are as follows:

a. 80386 processor or above

b. 1024K of free extended memory

c. Himem.sys loaded in the Config.sys file

T I P Windows operating system version 3.1 features 32-bit disk access as an option that is off by default when Windows 3.1 is installed on your system. You can enable it by going into the 386 Enhanced Mode dialog box in the Windows Control Panel. 32-bit access will give your system speed a considerable boost when the hard disk is accessed.

Web Servers

The vast bulk of Windows-based Web server development is taking place in the land of 32-bit computing: Windows 95 and Windows NT. There is, however, a small handful of servers available, all of them free or shareware!

The Webmasters Library

The most comprehensive reference of Web-related software is, of course, the Web itself. A number of excellent lists of available server software are out on the Web.

■ *Webcompare*   Here you'll find an up-to-date and exhaustive list of server software, categorized by features. This site is the most brutally honest server comparison, literally feature for feature, that you can find on the net or anywhere else.

   http://www.webcompare.com/server-main.html

■ *Yahoo Internet Directory*   Here you'll find links to commercial server software packages that have elected to register. You will also find terrific links to additional utilities and services that will help speed you on your way to running a perfect Web site.

   http://www.yahoo.com/Computers_and_Internet/Internet/World_Wide_Web/HTTP/

■ *The World Wide Web Consortium (W3C)*   You'll find in-depth information, white papers, and links to additional resources regarding all aspects of the Web.

   http://www.w3.org/pub/WWW/

Available Servers

One important distinction between the servers listed here is whether support and development of the software is continuing. This is an important issue if your web server is more than just a hobby. It's also important to note the size of the user base to see if there are other Webmasters that you can network with.

News Groups!

The Internet is a terrific resource for information related to running servers and utilizing the power of this incredible communications medium. Nowhere is this more evident than in the rich resource of news groups. Specifically related to WWW issues and development are

■ COMP.INFOSYSTEMS.WWW.Authoring.*

■ COMP.INFOSYSTEMS.WWW.Browser.*

■ COMP.INFOSYSTEMS.WWW.Server.*

■ COMP.INFOSYSTEMS.WWW.Misc.

■ COMP.INFOSYSTEMS.WWW.Advocacy

■ COMP.INFOSYSTEMS.WWW.Announce

Each of the Authoring, Browser, and Server groups branches into groups that are specific to the issues relevant to that arena.

Windows Httpd 1.4c

   URL: http://www.city.net/win-httpd

FREEWARE/SHAREWARE

Cost: U.S. $99.00 for commercial use. Free for personal/educational users.

Last revised: June 1995

The first released and best known Web server for Windows 3.1 is Windows Httpd, written by Bob Denny, a pioneer in Windows-based Web servers and systems (among other things!). If you are interested in the newest Windows-related Web developments, catch up with the ever insightful Bob at **http://solo.dc3.com**.

The Windows Httpd server is the precursor to the extremely popular 32-bit Windows-based Web server Web site from O'Reilly. However, Windows Httpd has not been updated or improved since late 1995, and there is no indication that fixes or improvements are forthcoming. Nevertheless, there are many Web sites to be found that are powered by HTTPD 1.4.

The server is free for personal and educational use, but there is a license fee for corporate use.

A number of add-on tools are available for the server and a great many enthusiastic Webmasters to network with. Highly recommended.

ZB Server 1.5

URL: **http://www.zbserver.com**

SHAREWARE

Cost: U.S. $25.00

Last Revised: December 1995

A combination of Web and Gopher servers!

Features include:

- An easy-to-use GUI control program (see Fig. 42.1)
- User/group security server macros
- Built-in Gopher server
- DOS/Win CGI script capability
- JAVA compatibility

FIG. 42.1
ZB Server features GUI administration tools.

Installing and Running Win-Httpd 1.4

You must first obtain the server software at **http://www.city.net/win-httpd**. (see Fig. 42.2).

1. Follow the links to download the server at
   http://www.city.net/win-httpd/lib/whttpd14.zip, and the upgrade at
   http://www.city.net/win-httpd/lib/upg14c.zip.

FIG. 42.2
The Win-HTTPD home page.

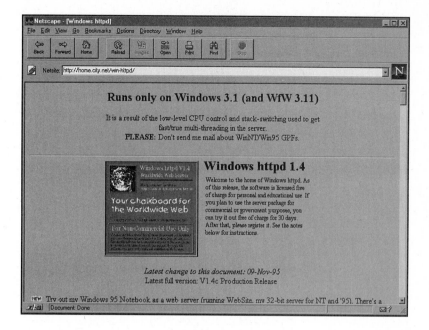

2. Edit your Autoexec.bat file and insert a line that tells the server what time zone you are in (hey, now that you're global, these things are important!):

   `SET TZ=EST5EDT`

   This line is for a server in the eastern time zone in the United States. The 5 in the example is for 5 hours west of GMT. If you don't use daylight-savings time in your state, omit the second 3-letter time zone abbreviation.

3. Reboot your PC.

4. Create a directory named "C:\HTTPD" (Don't pick a different name!).

5. Place this HTTPD zip file into the new directory.

6. Unzip the file using an unzip tool that preserves the directory structure stored in the zip file (see the example in Fig. 42.3). If you use PKUNZIP, be sure to use version 2.04g or later with the "-d" option.

7. Start a Web browser and open the local file "C:/HTTPD/HTDOCS/INDEX.HTM" as shown in Figure 42.4. This provides you with access to the online documentation.

8. You must have a WinSock 1.1 compliant TCP/IP package available. This does not refer to Trumpet (one of many WinSock packages); it means that your WinSock package must comply with the Windows Sockets Specification, Version 1.1. Httpd checks the WinSock version at startup.

Part
IX
Ch
42

 TIP If you have communication problems, add "-n" to the httpd command line to disable all multithreading and asynchronous I/O. If this fixes the problem, you have a broken WinSock package. See the online documentation for more information.

FIG. 42.3
Using WinZip, turn on Use Directory Names.

FIG. 42.4
Open the Index file to browse the documentation.

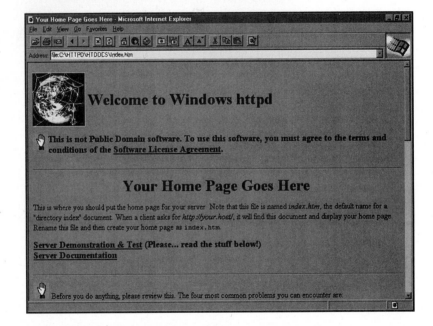

9. Execute HTTPD.exe and your server launches as shown in Figure 42.5.

Managing Your Win-Httpd Web Server

The Win-HTTPD server is extremely simple to manage, yet flexible enough to get the job done! Here we'll run down the major issues you deal with in the day to day management of the server.

FIG. 42.5
The Win-HTTPD splash
screen.

Shutting the Server Down To shut down the server, click once on its icon and choose Close in the pop-up "system" menu. The beep indicates that the server has received your request to shut down. The server quits immediately.

Keep in mind that users may be in the process of reading a document consisting of multiple linked pages and inline images or sounds. Each page or inline item is read with a separate transaction. Therefore, watch the server icon until the server counter reaches zero before deciding to shut down your server.

If the server window is open, choose Exit in the Control menu (see Fig. 42.6), Close in the "system" menu (click once in the upper left corner control box), or double click the control box. Again, the server acknowledges your request with a beep and then exits.

Managing the Log Files The server keeps three log files:

- The console log—httpd.log
- The access log—\logs\access.log
- The error log—\logs\error.log

Part
IX

Ch
42

FIG. 42.6
Use Exit to shut the
server down.

The access and error logs accumulate indefinitely. The server has a feature where it can "cycle" either or both of the logs on command while it is running. To do this simply run the logcycle.exe program in the /support directory. The command line arguments control which logs get cycled. There is also a DLL in the /support directory that signals the server to cycle the log(s) and which can be used from Windows programs such as Visual Basic.

The cycled logs are renamed .001, .002, and so forth. The server keeps a maximum of 30 logfile cycles. Older ones are deleted.

For servers running in a production mode, you can use the WinCron program that comes with Win-httpd to schedule logfile cycling. If you schedule a daily run of logcycle, only the past 30 days' (30 cycles) log data are kept.

CAUTION
The console log is cleared each time the server is started.

Overview of Web Publishing

Newcomers to the Web are often tempted to take existing literature and marketing materials and simply translate them to HTML to create Web pages. There is nothing wrong with getting your feet wet through this approach, but it doesn't take full advantage of the possibilities of HTML for turning large amounts of information into a fun and interactive journey. The following sections teach you how to make the most of your server's capabilities.

Planning Your Journey

You wouldn't dream of attempting to efficiently drive a car from Los Angeles to New York without first plotting your course, would you? If you would, then be prepared for the worst! Ugliness, long periods of time where you are seemingly driving in circles, and you haven't even left the driveway yet! Developing a Web site is a creative journey, and it is a journey that is rarely complete.

Planning Concepts

Designing the Web site starts with understanding the goals that have moved you or your organization to undertake this venture. A mission statement is the anchor for any sound business plan, and it is the same with your Web site. Define your mission!

Some sample mission statements:

- This Web site will be a shopping mall that is fun for the user and easily provides access for the purchase of goods and services.

- Our Web site is an internal Web server that serves the entire corporate community of XYZ industries, from the president to the stock room. It is THE source of corporate information.

- This Web site is a groundbreaking experiment in online publishing, aimed squarely at the 25 to 35 post-college demographic.

Audience Considerations

Acknowledgement of your intended audience is a must during the planning process. Who is the Web site for? Who are the likely users? Consider the answers to these questions against the goals you have set for your site. Do you need to broaden your approach to attract a larger audience? Is the Web site plan strong enough to attract the core audience you desire?

Beware the Browser!

As a Web designer you must remain aware of the universe of browsers that currently exists at all times. There was a great parody regarding the number of browsers in existence in the Dilbert cartoon strip recently where a rat dances on a keyboard hoping to destroy information, only to discover that he has authored a Web browser. At least 100 browsers are currently in use on the Web!

Understand that the latest extensions are NOT universally implemented, and that standard HTML is often interpreted differently from browser to browser. We keep 10 or so browsers available in addition to utilizing the built in browsers for the major online services—AOL, Compuserve, and Prodigy. The major online services represent a challenge: often they have the weakest browsers but by far the most users. Many client log analyses reveal that the vast majority of their "hits" are from AOL!

Test your site often and understand the trade-offs you must make to utilize that hot new Netscape or Microsoft extension. ●

CHAPTER 43

Running a Web Server on Windows 95

by Mark Surfas

You may be surprised to learn that you can run a robust personal or corporate Web server using the Windows 95 operating system. We'll discuss the reasons that make Windows 95 a fine base from which to transmit your Web signals across the planet as well as the drawbacks. Our earlier discussion, in Chapter 42, of running a Web server under Windows 3.1, covered many of the same issues. The 32-bit multitasking nature of Windows 95 offers more of the sturdiness and other features you need in a Web system.

The fact is that serving straight Web pages is a relatively simple matter for a multitasking operating system. The main concern is that the system be stable and powerful enough to serve the pages quickly and continuously for long periods of time. Windows 95 fits this bill perfectly. ■

The pros and cons of using Windows 95 as your server operating system

Using Windows 95, you can have a low-volume professional Web site for your business 24 hours a day.

The best Web servers available for Windows 95

You learn how to find more information on Web-related software.

How to install the popular WebQuest 95 server

You learn about system requirements for installing WebQuest 95.

How to administer the WebQuest 95 server

You see how to stop and run WebQuest 95 server.

Using Windows 95 as a Web Operating Platform

Windows 95 is the first operating system to truly become a consumer phenomenon. The $200,000,000 promotional launch by Microsoft heralded the arrival of an operating system destined to make its way into the lives of unsuspecting consumers around the globe. The unprecedented promotional spectacle does not diminish the fact that Windows 95 is a powerful, robust, and easy-to-use 32-bit operating system.

N O T E   If you say "Windows is a 32-bit operating system," some purists might argue that some of the underlying code base is, in fact, 16-bit code held over from the original DOS, and therefore not really 32-bit. They may be right technically, but you don't really care—you can run 32-bit programs. ■

> **CAUTION**
>
> Many of the advanced features and programs of the Web server world are unavailable to Windows 95 Web servers. Prepare yourself to find that most mainstream Web products today are released for the Windows NT environment. The most notable problems encountered with Windows 95 are:
>
> - Inability to set up "virtual Web servers"
> - Lack of server add-ons for Windows 95
> - Relative lack of security of Windows 95

The Power of Windows 95

For low to medium volume Web sites, Windows 95 is adequate. If your Web site needs to handle transaction processing or has extensive database links, move up to a true server environment such as Windows NT. Also, you can only perform multi-homing virtual servers under Windows NT. Windows 95 and Windows 3.1 don't support multiple IP's assigned to a single machine.

Windows NT is a true 32-bit multi-threaded environment that is perfect for serving large quantities of transactions. Windows 95 is a 32-bit operating system that still relies on a 16-bit base. While Windows 95 is a remarkable operating system, it is not as rock-solid as Windows NT.

Windows 95—A Reasonable Choice

The sheer popularity of Windows 95 makes it a logical first choice for millions of potential Web publishers. It is relatively stable and certainly has the power to serve plenty of Web pages.

In fact, using Windows 95 you can have a low-volume professional Web site for your business running 24 hours a day! The trick is to find a dial-up Internet Service Provider offering flat rate access (AT&T offers unlimited use for $19.95 per month: check out **http://www.att.com/worldnet/wis/index.html** or call 1-800-worldnet). Simply use the robust dial-up networking and keep your server on the Web for literally pennies a day! If you choose to follow this route, be sure to keep your pages relatively graphics free to increase the speed perceived by users accessing your site.

> **CAUTION**
>
> When using local dial-up access, check with your phone company to determine whether the number you are calling is in your local calling area. If it is, also check that you are not charged by the length of your calling time.

Windows 95—A Few Drawbacks

While Windows 95 is a solid base to use as a personal server, the most exciting server advances are taking place in the Windows NT environment. Windows 95 Web servers are a niche market at best, and this niche is ignored by most of the major players. Microsoft and Netscape have both declined to release a Windows 95-based server.

If you intend to serve databases via the Web or to run extensive back-end scripts you would be well advised to explore the option of Windows NT as your server environment. Windows NT server offers a more stable and robust platform optimized for network applications. Information security is also much greater—often a critical issue in the corporate environment.

N O T E If you want to know more about running Web servers in the Windows environment, take a look at Que's *Running a Perfect Web Site with Windows*. This comprehensive compendium covers the entire subject of designing, building, and running a terrific Web site using Windows 95 or Windows NT. ■

Survey of Web Server Software

At last count, there were at least 15 Web server packages for Windows 95. Shareware is prevalent, as are Timeware (software that disables after a period of time or number of uses) and Featureware (software that lacks important features found in the registered product).

A number of Web servers, most notably O'Reilly's Web Site, run under both Windows 95 and Windows NT. This is the exception rather than the rule. Most NT-based Web servers run only on NT. Some products also have separate Windows 95 and NT versions such as Questar's WebQuest.

N O T E The most complete reference of Web-related software is, of course, the Web itself. A number of excellent lists of available server software are out on the Web.

- *Webcompare*—Here you find an up-to-date and extensive list of server software, categrized by features. This site provides the most brutally honest server comparison (literally feature for feature) that you can find on the Net or anywhere else. **http://www.webcompare.com/server-main.html**.

continues

continued

- *Yahoo Internet Directory*—Here you find links to commercial server software packages that have elected to register. You also find terrific links to additional utilities and services that help speed you on your way to running a perfect Web site.

  http://www.yahoo.com/Computers_and_Internet/Internet/ World_Wide_Web/HTTP/

- The World Wide Web Consortium (W3C)—Here you find in-depth information, white papers, and links to additional resources regarding all facets of the Web.

  http://www.w3.org/pub/WWW/ ■

Folk Web Server 1.01

URL: http://www.ilar.com/folkweb.htm

SHAREWARE

Last Revised: December 1995

The Folk Web server (see Fig. 43.1) is a low-cost yet full-featured server available for free evaluation. The server supports all standard Web server features and includes some database connectivity extensions.

FIG. 43.1
Visit the Folk Web home page to download the software.

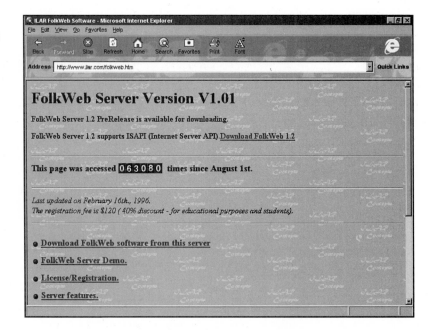

Purveyor for Windows NT and 95

> URL: **http://www.process.com**

The Purveyor Web server (see Fig. 43.2) from Process Software has its origins in the EMWACs server listed previously, but has quickly grown to become a full-featured server with advanced administration tools.

Purveyor was one of the earliest commercial-strength NT Web servers and is highly regarded. One of the three servers to offer Proxy services, Purveyor also features advanced database publishing capabilities. The Purveyor product line spans Windows NT, Windows 95, Netware, and VMS. An SSL-enhanced server for secure transactions is in the works as well.

FIG. 43.2

The Purveyor home page.

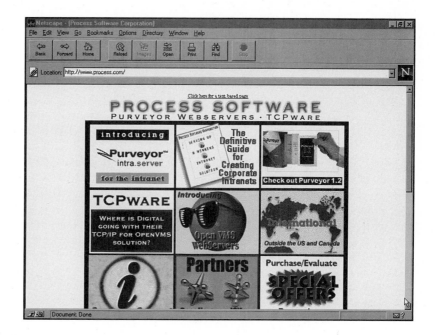

WebQuest 95

> URL: **http://www.questar.com**

WebQuest 95 and WebQuest NT are two servers published by Questar Microsystems (see Fig. 43.3).

These servers feature simple GUI-driven installation and management software along with a bevy of additional features, including the following:

- The only implementation of the Server Side Includes + (SSI+) 1.0 specification. SSI+ 1.0 provides a major enhancement to SSI with "CScript."

- CScript provides a complete "C"-like object-oriented language for HTML pages. Very complex operations can now be performed right on the HTML page without any compiler or external programs.

- "Load Sensor" technology intelligently maximizes the balance between resources and speed, based on access history.

- Full suite of remote administration and monitoring tools

- The software is built from the ground up for Windows NT and Windows 95—it is not a port.

- True preemptive multitasking with symmetric multiprocessor support

- Capable of managing and serving Web spaces on remote machines and mounted volumes

- Complex WAIS Web space indexing with graphical generation and administration

- Built-in PERL support

- Win-CGI supports legacy Windows 3.1 WinCGI scripts popularized by WebSite.

- Allows OLE 2 calls directly from HTML pages.

FIG. 43.3

The WebQuest home page.

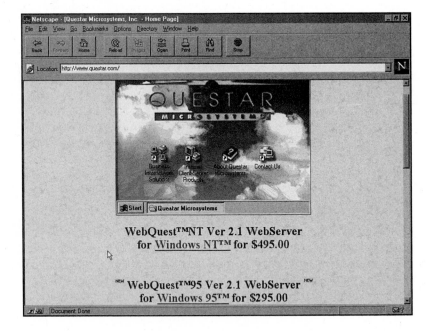

WebSite

URL: http:// website.ora.com

WebSite, from O'Reilly & Associates (see Fig. 43.4) was one of the first commercial NT & 95 Web servers to be released.

FIG. 43.4
The WebSite home page.

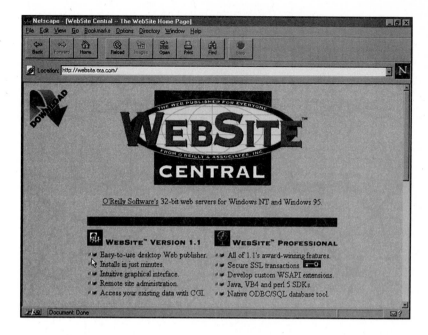

WebSite was written by Bob Denny, who wrote an extremely popular Web server for 16-bit Windows, WIN-HTTPD (covered in Chapter 42, "Running a Web Server on Windows 3.1").

Features   WebSite is a 32-bit multithreaded server with a tremendous number of important features:

- Support for a Visual Basic 4 framework (CGI32.BAS) with sample applications as well as server-push applications (WebSite 1.1)

- A graphical interface for creating virtual servers and for remote administration, password authentication, and access control.

- SSL for encrypted transactions (WebSite Pro)

- A GUI tool, Webview, which provides a tree-like display of the documents and links on your server

- Wizards that allow you to automatically create common Web documents

- Indexing and search tools that allow your users to locate items anywhere on your site

- Server Side Includes (SSI) that lets you combine static and programmed documents on the fly, and makes common document components easier to maintain.

Installing and Running WebQuest95

Choosing a Web server is a highly subjective task. The leading servers are continually adding new features and seeking to differentiate themselves. The basic issues regarding server setup and administration generally vary only in the implementation from server to server. We have chosen the WebQuest server as the implementation example because of its speed, flexibility, and ease of use. The concepts we cover will apply to any server you decide to implement under the Windows 95 environment.

Requirements for Windows 95 Version

For WebQuest95 to run on your system you must have

- A network (or dial-up) adapter configured to support TCP/IP
- An IP address assigned to your computer
- ODBC 32-bit driver(s) installed on your system
- Windows 95 1.0 or later
- 3 MB available hard drive space for WebQuest95
- 486 DX2 66
- 8M of RAM

Installation of WebQuest for Windows 95

To prepare for installation, you must close all programs that are running on your workstation or server. If ODBC is being used by another application, WebQuest does not install properly.

To install WebQuest95 simply launch setup.exe and follow the dialog prompts.

WebQuest95 follows standard Windows 95 conventions, so the server installation is configured exactly the same as any standard Windows 95 program installation (see Figs. 43.5 and 43.6).

FIG. 43.5
The WebQuest95
directory dialog box.

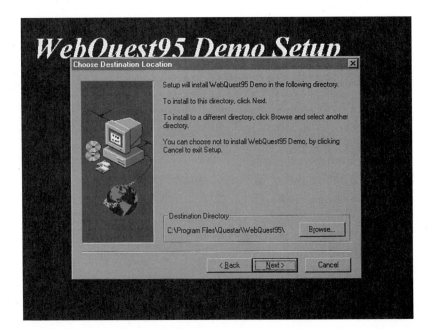

FIG. 43.6

The WebQuest95 installation dialog box.

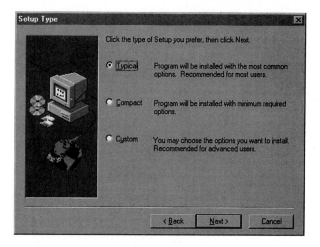

Unless you are reinstalling the software, select the Typical option in the Setup Type dialog box.

When complete, WebQuest will have installed its own program group called (remarkably) WebQuest, as shown in Figure 43.7. All files relevant to WebQuest95 are located in this group.

FIG. 43.7

The WebQuest95 program group.

Starting and Stopping the WebQuest95 Server

Starting the WebQuest95 server is a two-part operation. The WebQuest server is loaded into the Windows 95 environment by double-clicking on the WebQuest95 Icon in the WebQuest program group, as shown in Figure 43.8. You can also navigate to the program by using the Start button menus.

When you double-click the WebQuest95 icon in the WebQuest program group, you see the WebQuest95 icon in the bottom right-hand corner of your screen (as shown in Fig. 43.8) in the area referred to as the "tray." This doesn't mean that the server is actually running.

FIG. 43.8
Note the WebQuest icon in the lower right-hand corner of your screen.

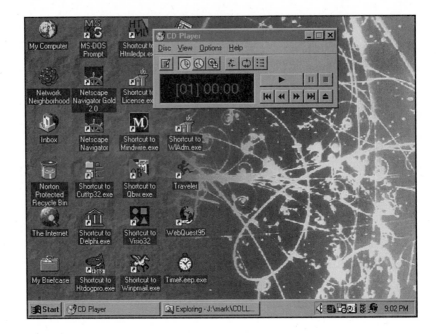

To actually run the server, right-click now on the icon to bring up the WebQuest95 start menu that you see in Figure 43.9.

FIG. 43.9
The WebQuest start menu displays after a right-click.

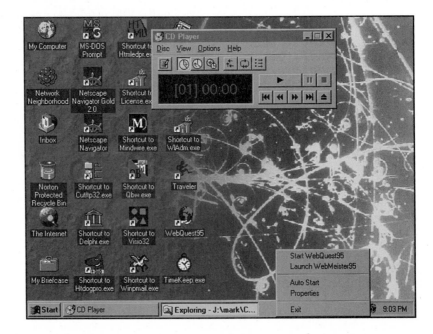

To start the Server using the default Web setup, simply click on Start WebQuest95. Your server is now up and running. To verify this, right-click again on the WebQuest Icon and note that the top menu selection now reads, Stop WebQuest95 as shown in Figure 43.10. This indicates that the server is in fact running.

FIG. 43.10
This time the menu reads stop, not start.

Configuring the WebQuest Server for Windows 95

Managing the configuration of WebQuest95 is achieved through two utilities. The Web server itself is configured through the Domain Manager. Security and link management are administered in a utility known as WebMeister.

Domain Managers   Basic server configuration and MIME-types are set up via the Domain Manager. To launch the Domain Manager (see Fig. 43.11), click the right mouse button on the WebQuest95 icon and select the Properties menu item.

FIG. 43.11
The Properties menu item launches the Domain Manager.

The Properties menu item

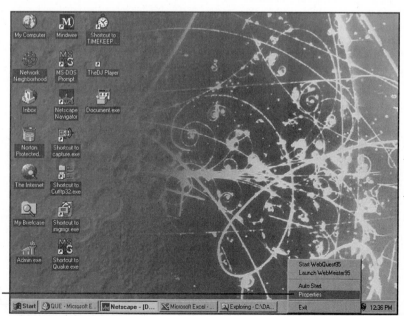

You can also launch the Domain Manager (see Fig. 43.12) by simply double-clicking on the WebQuest Icon.

Changes made using the domain manager take effect the next time the WebQuest service is started.

The Domain Manager is divided into six different areas, each with a border around it: Web-Space, Default Page Script, Log File Directory, Log Database (ODBC), Load Sensor, and AutoStart. Each area can be configured to meet your needs:

■ Webspace Name—This is an internal name for you to identify your Web. Enter a name that you will (hopefully) associate with the mission of this particular WebSpace.

■ Address—This is filled upon initial setup with the IP address entered in the Network settings in the Windows 95 control panel.

■ Directory—Select the directory that is to be associated with this WebSpace. Default file requests will be filled here.

■ Default Filename—If a user accesses this WebSpace, by either Domain Name or TCP/IP address, without requesting a specific file, this file is called. The WebQuest default is Default.htm but you can configure it to your liking. This is particularly useful when you are importing an existing WebSpace from another server with links that are already in place for a different default page.

■ Port—Each TCP/IP service that runs on your server is tuned to monitor a particular port for requests. Each service must have its own port—it can't share that port with other services. This is actually how multiple services coexist on one machine: when a request comes in from the Internet, the server looks at what port is requested and forwards the request to the appropriate service for processing. The standard HTTP port is 80.

Don't change the port number from 80 unless you have good reason to!

■ Proxy—Check this box if you wish this Web to act as a proxy server. Proxy services are used as part of an overall network security implementation that is beyond the scope of this chapter. To learn more about proxy services check out the firewall FAQ at **http:// www.cis.ohio-state.edu/hypertext/faq/usenet/firewalls-faq/faq.html**.

■ Browsing—This checkbox determines whether directories in this WebSpace are browseable. If browsing is allowed, then a directory that doesn't contain a file with the default file name (see Default Filename earlier) if accessed without a file name returns a list of files in the directory. This list of files contains an icon next to each name and is a hypertext link. Double-clicking on the file name causes the file to be retrieved. This is a valuable feature, because it makes creating lists of files easy and requires virtually no maintenance. To update the directory, simply add or delete files as appropriate.

If you select directory browsing be aware that this is a potential security hole. A user is free to look at all files in a directory that doesn't include the default file name.

■ Access Control—When Access Control is checked, file and directory-specific security is activated. The specifics of your security implementation are defined in the Admin function, Directory display. Access control is an extra layer of overhead, and is therefore a performance inhibitor. Only select access control if you need it.

■ Default Page Script—Not implemented in this version of the server.

■ Log File Directory—If you activate file logging, each hit on your server is recorded in a text file. This is often valuable information if you need to keep statistics on your WebSpace, or when troubleshooting.

CAUTION

If you store your logfiles within your WebSpace directory structure and directory browsing is enabled, your logfiles can be viewed by outside browsers. Be sure that you have a page with the appropriate default file name in the same directory.

■ Log Database (ODBC)—Instead of logging hits to a text file you can log access, error, and request events to an ODBC database. Click the dotted dialog box next to Source and the Domain Manager presents a list of available ODBC data sources.

FIG. 43.12
The WebQuest Domain Manager.

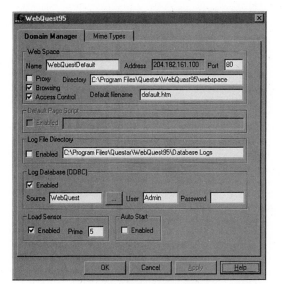

During the installation process WebQuest sets up a Microsoft Access database and a properly configured ODBC driver entitled WebQuest. You may select this database or configure another database and ODBC driver to use. If you configure another data source, be sure to utilize the same format as the database provided with WebQuest.

CAUTION

The amount of data captured in the ODBC data logs is significantly greater than that captured in the text log. This is a trade-off against the additional overhead required by the server to access the database. Additionally, the databases grow much larger and much faster than the text log. It's possible to crash your server if your database consumes all the available hard drive space.

- Load Sensor—This is another special feature of WebQuest95. Load Sensor allows the server to tune itself and respond to changing conditions. When usage goes up, WebQuest allocates additional resources to keep performance at an optimum level. Check the Enabled box to activate Load Sensor and set prime to the minimum number of threads that WebQuest will maintain. For my medium-load server a prime of 5 works well.

- Autostart— Select this check box if you want to launch the server every time you start Windows 95.

Select OK to save this new WebSpace.

MIME Type Configuration   Click the Mime button to display the Mime Types dialog box as shown in Figure 43.13. The WebQuest 95 server comes preconfigured with a list of standard MIME types. While you may add and delete MIME types here, do not delete any existing MIME types unless you are sure you know what you are doing.

Administration of Your WebSpace

The WebMeister tab of the WebQuest dialog box opens the Access Control Administrator as shown in Figure 43.14. The Administrator performs two functions: access control and link validation.

Access Control

The Access Control Administrator controls access to documents and to directories. This way you can set security for all files in a particular directory or for just a few. To set an access control for a document or directory, first select it in the list box. Select Enabled and then type in the user name and password required to retrieve the contents of the document or to gain access to the directory. Directory access can be based on AND or OR. AND access specifies that, to access a document, a user must be granted access to both the directory and the document. OR access specifies that the user may access a document if granted access to either the directory or the document.

FIG. 43.13
WebQuest is pre-
configured with all
standard Mime Types.

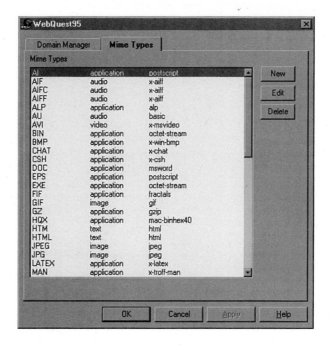

Note that a stoplight icon appears next to all documents and directories for which access control is enabled.

Hyperlink Validation

The Admin button on WebMeister is used to launch the administrator to maintain the WebSpace documents and directories. From here you view the layout of your Web and edit and delete documents.

Directory Display The right-hand side of the Administrator window is the WebSpace list box presenting an alphabetized listing by document type. Each document is identified and graphically represented with an icon.

You can double-click on a document to open into the viewer configured for that file type, or you can right-click on a document to produce a pop-up menu giving you the choice of editing, launching a viewer, or validating the link (see Fig. 43.15).

FIG. 43.14
WebMeister makes
document management
a snap!

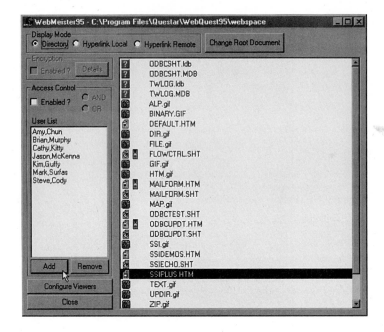

FIG. 43.15
Right-clicking launches
the Edit, Launch, or
Validate menu.

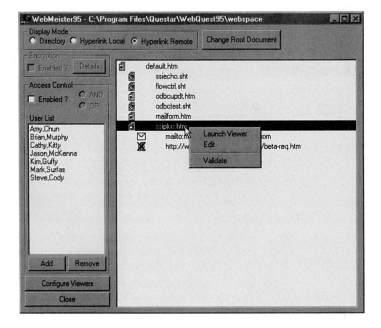

If you double-click on a directory, it opens and displays the files it contains.

Selection of the display mode radio buttons determines how documents are acted upon and displayed. One of three views can be selected: Directory, Local Hyperlink, and Remote Hyperlink.

The hyperlink local view as shown in Figure 43.16 displays the hierarchy of your WebSpace as defined by the hyperlinks in your HTML documents. All hyperlinks to files local to your machine are evaluated when you open the WebSpace for administration. Remote hyperlinks are left unvalidated. You can double-click on a document to open and display the hyperlinks, which may in turn be opened, viewed, or edited. If a hyperlink refers to a document on the local server, the WebSpace Administrator tries to validate its existence. If the document cannot be located, a red X (see Fig. 43.17) is superimposed over the document's icon.

FIG. 43.16

HyperLink Local Display is used to validate local links.

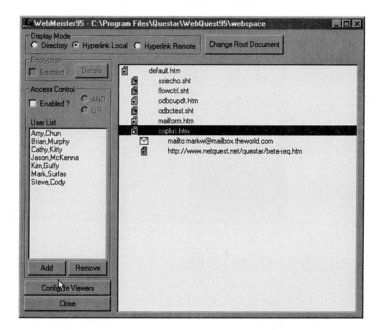

The hyperlink remote view shown in Figure 43.16 displays the hierarchy of your WebSpace as defined by the hyperlinks on your HTML documents. All local and remote hyperlinks are validated in real time. WebQuest creates a thread for each remote link and resolves all links simultaneously. This results in extremely fast validation of very large numbers of remote hyperlinks. If you right-click on a local document a pop-up menu appears, giving you the choice to edit or view. If you double-click on a local document, the document opens to display the hyperlinks, which may in turn be opened, viewed, and edited.

If a hyperlink refers to a document on another server, the WebSpace Administrator attempts to contact that document.

If the document is located, a green check mark is superimposed over the document's icon.

If the remote server does not respond, or if the document cannot be located on the remote server, a red X is superimposed over the document's icon.

FIG. 43.17

HyperLink Remote Display allows validation of remote links.

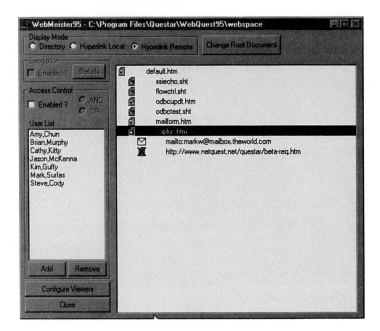

Viewer and Editor Configuration

Select the Configure Viewers button from the main panel to configure the editors and viewers you use to manipulate files from within the Administrator. As seen earlier, when you right-click on a document in the Administrator, you are offered a menu that lets you manipulate the document. This is where you define the viewers for the various document types.

Upon selecting Configure, the Viewers and Editors dialog box appears. Simply browse for the editors and viewers of your choice as shown in Figure 43.18.

FIG. 43.18
Notepad is the programmer's HTML editor.

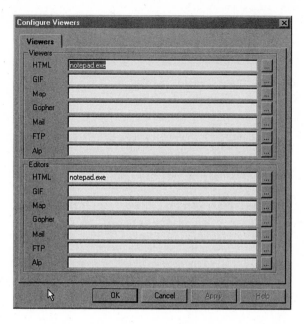

Logs

WebQuest95 supports two different types of logs: File and ODBC Database.

File Logs   File logs are simple ASCII text files that are added to incrementally every time the server receives a hit. This is the standard way of recording server activity. Most Webmasters then run these logs through statistical generation programs to create reports.

WebQuest logs all requests to files specified in the Log file directory box. Each day at midnight a new log file is created. The format of the log file name is WM<yy><mm><dd>.LOG, where <yy> is the year, <mm> is the month, and <dd> is the day of the month. The log file follows the standard EMWAC format. The following details are logged:

- Date
- Time

- Server IP
- Client IP
- HTTP Method
- URL
- HTTP Version

Here is an example line from a WebQuest log file:

Mon Jul 17 15:34:25 1995 204.96.64.171 204.96.64.51 GET /default.htm HTTP/1.0

While enabling this log file requires overhead, it's an important capability. If you don't care about the contents of the logs, don't enable the file log. However, the log files do contain useful information for tracing the cause of a server crash. Using the log file you can identify which site was hit last, and from there you can identify a problem with the page/site.

> **N O T E** Bear in mind that logs keep track of the number of requests made of the elements on a site. Each page can have more than one element that needs to be requested in order to send the whole page to the client. Therefore, this log is not an accurate representation of the number of hits a site has received. You will often hear outrageous claims of "millions of hits per day." When evaluating the popularity of a site, listen for the count of unique clients and unique pages. ∎

ODBC Database Logs WebQuest ODBC database logging is a way to record, in greater detail, what transpires in your site. This is invaluable information for the serious Webmaster. But as noted earlier, this feature comes with a significant performance penalty: for each element that is accessed on one of your pages, a record is inserted in a database.

ODBC Database Layout The sample database structure contains three tables: access, operations, and errors.

Errors The errors table lists errors that have occurred during the processing of requests. Errors can occur in many different phases of processing a request; the subsystem involved in the error is indicated in the log. Examples of subsystems are: HTTP, e-mail, and ODBC. The following details are logged:

- Subsystem—The subsystem in which the error was detected
- Error—The error that occurred
- Peer IP—The client IP address
- Detail—Detailed error information
- Time: Year, Month, Day, Hour, Minute, Second—The same format as in the operations table
- Index—Unique identifier (a counter) used as a key field

Access   The access table lists authorization details for access controlled documents. The following details are logged:

- Name—The username
- Password—The password of the user
- Time—A record of the time that access is attempted: Year, Month, Day, Hour, Minute, Second
- URL—The URL that was accessed
- Status—The result of the access check
- Index—A unique identifier (a counter) used as a key field

Operations   The operations table lists requests from clients and certain internal operations. The following details are logged:

- Operation—The type of call made to the server
- PeerIP—The IP address of the client
- URL—The URL for every item in every page requested by the client
- Year—The current year (1996)
- Month—The current month (1–12)
- Day—The day of the month (1–31)
- Hour—The hour of the request made by the client of the server (24 hour format, 1–24)
- Minute—The minute of the request made by the client (0–59)
- Second—The second of the request made by the client (0– 59)
- Index—A unique identifier (a counter) used as a key field

The following is an example from an Operations log file:

```
Operation   PeerIp        URL      Year    Month   Day    Hour    Minute    Second
                  Index
GET      204.96.64.101/studioe3/ 1996    8       11     13      5       55    7
GET      204.96.64.101/          1996    8       11     13      9       5     8
```

Each complete line written into the log file represents one request made of the server by the client. ●

CHAPTER 44

Running the Microsoft IIS

by Mark Surfas

Microsoft debuted the Internet Information Server (IIS) in early 1996 and is shipping version 2.0 of the IIS as part of the Windows NT Server 4.0 operating system. The IIS is an integral part of the Microsoft Internet product rollout for 1996 and beyond.

The IIS has matured quickly from version 1.0 to 2.0 and is evolving into a major force both on the Internet and on the corporate intranet. Third party add-ons are pouring forth to help Web developers enhance and extend the services they are offering with a minimum of effort.

But like a bad TV advertisement the Microsoft IIS is more than just a Web server—it's three, yes, three servers in one:

- World Wide Web (WWW)
- File Transfer Protocol (FTP)
- Gopher

Although we touch on the FTP and Gopher servers during our operations, this chapter focuses on the specifics of configuring the Web server component of the Microsoft IIS. ■

Set up and secure Windows NT for Internet access

You can use the powerful built-in NT security system to secure your system.

Install the IIS

The Internet Information Server has set the new standard for NT-based Internet services.

Establish logon requirements for remote clients

Use Internet Information Server for open public access and as a closed and secure Intranet.

Configure access permissions for remote clients

Just as you use the File Manager for LAN-based directory and file level security, you can set up Internet user controls.

Create multiple virtual servers on a single computer

The Internet Information Server will support hundreds of virtual Web sites that each appear to be a stand-alone server.

Configure logging options

Tailor the log files to your specifications or dump them directly into Microsoft SQL server.

Configuring Windows NT for the IIS

The Windows NT Web servers depend on the configuration of the underlying operating system to varying degrees. We'll examine all the necessary steps for configuring Windows NT to maximize the performance and security of your site.

This chapter assumes that you have already successfully installed Windows NT on your system.

 TIP You can stay up to date on Windows NT Server through the Windows NT Server home page at **http://www.microsoft.com/NTServer/**. The Windows Workstation home page is located at: **http://www.microsoft.com/NTWorkstation/**.

Windows NT Versions

There are two versions of Windows NT: NT Server and NT Workstation. The major differences between the two involve networking, which is an important issue for you to consider. With the standard NT operating system you get peer-to-peer networking, server networking, remote access services, and all the administration tools typically needed to maintain and manage a network server.

Both versions are built around the same core NT kernel and both feature C2-level security. NT Workstation is meant to be used as an individual computing environment or as a small workgroup server. NT Server is meant to be used as an enterprise-wide server platform.

The NT Server feature set includes more fault tolerance and greater network capabilities. Remote administration is an outstanding benefit for the busy Webmaster who is coordinating among remote sites.

N O T E Although NT Server and NT Workstation use the same basic kernel, NT Server is optimized to be a file and print server, and NT Workstation is optimized as a single-user operating system. ▪

If you are a serious Web publisher, you should run NT Server rather than NT Workstation. Also note that some Web servers, including the Microsoft IIS server, run on NT Server only and not on NT workstation.

N O T E Microsoft publishes upgrades and enhancements to the NT operating systems through distributions called *service paks*. Be sure to stay current with service pack distributions as they often solve common problems. Many of the Web servers for NT do not operate without the latest service paks installed. ▪

N O T E There is much confusion over whether or not users of Internet services are considered clients and therefore need licenses. Microsoft has recently clarified its position and has stated that users connecting to your Web server essentially do not need to be licensed. ▪

Basic Concepts

The basics of setting up and maintaining Windows NT for your Web server consist of:

- Network setup
- Security
- Administration
- Troubleshooting

Network and TCP/IP Setup

The Internet is a worldwide collection of individual transmission control protocol/Internet protocol (TCP/IP) networks. Each computer on the Internet has a unique IP address. Information is transmitted on the Internet in data packets. Each packet is addressed to a specific computer's IP address, such as 10.212.57.189.

Because IP addresses are hard to use and remember, the domain name system (DNS) was created to pair a specific IP address, such as 205.182.161.5, with a friendly domain name, such as www.Criticalmass.com (a shameless plug for my own Web server!). When a user browses the Internet by using a domain name, the browser first must contact a DNS server to resolve the domain name to an IP address, then contact the computer with that address.

This has three implications for your Web Server:

- You must install TCP/IP on your server.
- You must have a permanent IP address assigned to your server on the Internet.
- You should register a domain name in the DNS for your permanent IP address. Without a domain name your users need to access your site by remembering your IP address. Ugh!

N O T E   Your Internet service provider (ISP) generally provides your IP addresses and may also register your domain names. Contact the Internet Network Information Center (InterNIC) at **http://rs.internic.net** or your ISP for more information about DNS registration. ▓

Since the language of the Internet is TCP/IP, you have to install the TCP/IP and bind the TCP/IP protocol to your network adapter.

Like other networking software for windows NT, TCP/IP is installed through the network settings applet on the control panel. Before beginning installation you need to gather some information:

- The IP address(es) to be assigned to your network card
- The IP address of your default gateway
- The IP address of the DNS servers you will use
- Your domain name

If you are building an intranet-based system you may also need:

- Your primary and secondary WINS server IP addresses (if any)
- The LMHOST file for your network (if any)

To install TCP/IP:

1. Open the network applet on the control panel and click the Protocols tab (see Fig. 44.1).

FIG. 44.1

The network control panel applet in NT Server 4.0.

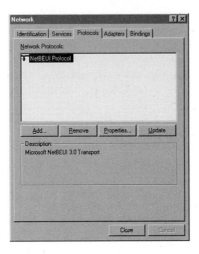

2. Click Add and the dialog box in Figure 44.2 appears. Select the TCP/IP protocol and click OK. You are prompted for the location of the files (most likely the CD-ROM distribution disk of your NT software).

FIG. 44.2

Select the TCP/IP protocol.

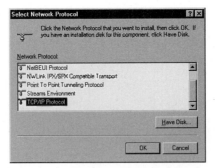

3. After you have the TCP/IP protocol, click the OK button and NT begins the binding analysis as it searches your network adapters. You see the TCP/IP properties dialog box shown in Figure 44.3.

FIG. 44.3
The TCP/IP properties
have not changed
much since NT 3.51.

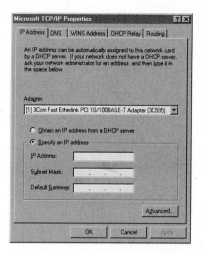

4. If you're using DHCP to assign an IP address—which is highly unlikely unless you are on a corporate NT-based local area network (LAN) or wide area network (WAN)—check the Enable Automatic DHCP configuration check box.

   Otherwise, enter the TCP/IP address for the network card shown in the Adapter field. If you don't know the TCP/IP address, contact your ISP or corporate network manager. Your TCP/IP address MUST BE UNIQUE. Do not enter in a random TCP/IP address: It will cause unpredictable behavior.

N O T E DHCP is used on corporate LANs to dynamically assign TCP/IP addresses to computers that need them. This is done to lower the amount of network administration needed. If you aren't sure whether your network uses a DHCP server, check with your network administrator. ■

N O T E If you intend to host multiple Webs on this host that are accessed via separate domain names, you need to attach multiple IP addresses to your network adapter. This is partly how "virtual Web servers" are implemented. Each IP address is matched up with a domain name and when we configure the Web server, we specify which files are to be "served" for each domain. ■

 You can attach up to 256 IP addresses per network adapter, but the TCP/IP dialog box only configures 5 per adapter. To go beyond this requires you to edit the Windows NT registry directly. This is recommended only if you have experience editing the registry! Improper changes to the registry can cause your system to fail.

Many users have reported that using more than 15 or 16 IP addresses per network adapter has resulted in unstable system behavior. Others have reported using hundreds with no ill side effects. Be warned: your mileage may vary!

5. Enter your subnet mask in the appropriate field. You get the mask from the same entity that provided your TCP/IP address. The most common scenario is that you are using a class C address. The subnet mask is then 255.255.255.0. The subnet mask is a 32-bit combination used to describe which portion of an address refers to the subnet and which part refers to the host.

6. In the Default Gateway field, enter in the TCP/IP address of the router or computer that connects your Web host to the Internet. See Figure 44.4 for an example of a filled-in TCP/IP dialog box.

FIG. 44.4

Be sure that the network addresses are valid before you use them.

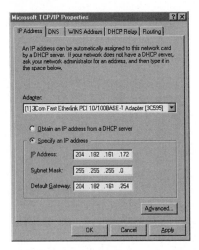

7. If you have access to a domain name server (DNS)—if you are on the Internet, you will need this—click the DNS tab (shown in Fig. 44.5) to configure the DNS addresses.

 You will want to use the DNS servers that are the fewest possible network hops away. Don't pick a DNS server that a friend happens to be using in Duluth. Ask your ISP or your network administrator for the closest DNS server. Your computer may communicate with the DNS server frequently, so you are wise to minimize the time this takes.

8. Enter a name for your system in the Host Name field. If you have not been assigned one, simply put in a descriptive name such as "web host."

9. In the Domain field, enter the name of the DNS domain that this host will be part of. Be careful not to confuse this with an NT Server domain, which is entirely different. Be sure to clarify the domain with your network administrator.

FIG. 44.5

Use the closest
available DNS servers.

10. In the DNS Search Order box, enter the IP addresses of the domain servers on your
    network. Place the DNS server closest to this station on the network (or Internet) to
    speed up name resolution.

11. Click the OK button and NT binds the new protocol to the adapter. You are then
    prompted to reboot the NT operating system for these changes to take effect.

Securely Configuring Windows NT Server

The Internet is often described as a cyber frontier, wilder and woolier than even the wild, wild
west of yesteryear. This may be somewhat overblown by slanted media coverage, but it is a
serious topic for all Webmasters. Windows NT provides user-account security and Windows
NT File System (NTFS) file-system security.

You can use the topics that follow as a checklist to ensure that you have effectively used user
accounts and NTFS to secure the Windows NT server. Additionally, you can prevent security
breaches by properly configuring the services running on your computer.

Preventing Intrusion by Setting Up User Accounts Windows NT security helps you protect
your computer and its resources by requiring assigned user accounts. You can control access
to all computer resources by limiting the user rights of these accounts.

Every operation on a computer running Windows NT identifies who is doing the operation. For
example, the username and password that you use to log on to Windows NT identify who you
are and define what you are authorized to do on that computer.

What a user is authorized to do on a computer is configured in User Manager by setting User
Rights in the Policies menu. User rights authorize a user to perform certain actions on the
system. Your Web service should be logged on "locally" with a username that is restricted
to access only what is necessary to provide services. Create an account (I call mine
WEBLOGON) specifically for this purpose.

Choose Difficult Passwords   The easiest way for someone to gain unauthorized access to your system is with a stolen or easily guessed password. Make sure that all passwords used on the system, especially those with administrative rights, have hard-to-guess passwords.

In particular make sure to select a good administrator password (a long, mixed-case, alphanumeric password is best) and set the appropriate account policies. Passwords can be set with the User Manager utility or at the system logon prompt.

Maintain Strict Account Policies   The User Manager utility provides a way for the Webmaster to specify how quickly account passwords expire (which forces users to regularly change passwords), and other policies such as how many bad logon attempts are tolerated before locking a user out. Use these policies to manage your accounts, particularly those with administrative access, to prevent exhaustive or random password attacks.

Limit the Membership of the Administrator Group   By limiting the members of the Administrator group, you limit the number of users who might choose bad passwords and expose your system.

NTFS File Security   In addition to user accounts, you should place your data files on an NTFS partition. NTFS provides security and access control for your data files. You can limit access to portions of your file system for specific users and services by using NTFS. In particular, it is a good idea to apply Access Control Lists (ACLs) to your data files for any Internet publishing service.

The NTFS file system gives you very granular control on files by specifying users and groups that are permitted access, and the kind of access they have for specific files and directories. For example, some users may have Read-Only access, while others may have Read, Change, and Write access. You should ensure that the WEBLogon account or authenticated accounts are granted or denied appropriate access to specific resources.

N O T E   Note that the Everyone group contains all users and groups. By default the Everyone group has full control of all files created on an NTFS drive. You will want to change this to suit your needs. ▪

You should review the security settings for content and CGI directories, and adjust them appropriately. Generally, you should use the settings in the following table:

Directory Type	Suggested Access
content	Read access
programs	Read and Execute access
databases	Read and Write access

Enable Auditing   You can enable auditing of NTFS files and directories on Windows NT Server through the File Manager. You can review the audit records periodically to ensure that no one has gained unauthorized access to sensitive files.

Running Other Network Services   You should review all the network services you are using on any computer connected to the Internet. When reviewing, consider three things:

- Is this service necessary?
- Does it create any security holes?
- Is it running under an account name with appropriate security?

N O T E Run only the services that you need! The fewer services you are running on your system, the less likely an administrative mistake will be made that can be exploited. Use the Services applet in the Windows NT control panel to disable any services not absolutely necessary on your Internet server.

 Unbind unnecessary services from your Internet adapter cards to improve performance and security.

Use the Bindings feature in the Network applet on the Windows NT control panel to unbind any unnecessary services from any network adapter cards connected to the Internet. For example, you might use the Server service to copy new images and documents from computers in your internal network, but you might not want remote users to have direct access to the Server service from the Internet.

If you need to use the Server service on your private network, you should disable the Server service binding to any network adapter cards connected to the Internet. You can use the Windows NT Server service over the Internet; however, you should fully understand the security implications and licensing issues.

Check Permissions on Network Shares   If you *are* running the Server service on your Internet adapter cards, be sure to double-check the permissions set on the shares you have created on the system. It is also wise to double-check the permissions set on the files in the shares' directories to ensure that you have set them correctly.

NT Management Tools

NT ships with two management tools that come in extremely handy during the day-to-day management of your Web server. These are the Event Log and the Performance Monitor. Take the time to understand the information these services can report back to you and you will go a long way toward gaining complete control of your system.

Tracking Problems with Event Viewer   Event Viewer, in the Administrative Tools program group, can notify administrators of critical events by displaying pop-up messages or by simply adding event information to log files. The information allows you to better understand the sequence and types of events that led up to a particular state or situation. You can use Event Viewer to view and manage three separate types of logs:

- System
- Security
- Application

The System log (shown in Fig. 44.6) reports information regarding system-level events.

FIG. 44.6
The System log reports information such as system startup and shutdown.

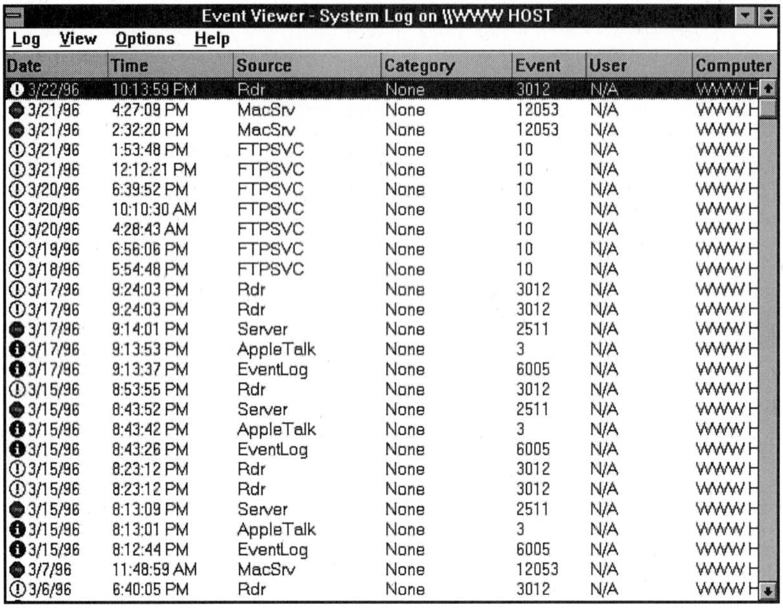

Event Viewer - System Log on \\WWW HOST

Log View Options Help

Date	Time	Source	Category	Event	User	Computer
3/22/96	10:13:59 PM	Rdr	None	3012	N/A	WWW H
3/21/96	4:27:09 PM	MacSrv	None	12053	N/A	WWW H
3/21/96	2:32:20 PM	MacSrv	None	12053	N/A	WWW H
3/21/96	1:53:48 PM	FTPSVC	None	10	N/A	WWW H
3/21/96	12:12:21 PM	FTPSVC	None	10	N/A	WWW H
3/20/96	6:39:52 PM	FTPSVC	None	10	N/A	WWW H
3/20/96	10:10:30 AM	FTPSVC	None	10	N/A	WWW H
3/20/96	4:28:43 AM	FTPSVC	None	10	N/A	WWW H
3/19/96	6:56:06 PM	FTPSVC	None	10	N/A	WWW H
3/18/96	5:54:48 PM	FTPSVC	None	10	N/A	WWW H
3/17/96	9:24:03 PM	Rdr	None	3012	N/A	WWW H
3/17/96	9:24:03 PM	Rdr	None	3012	N/A	WWW H
3/17/96	9:14:01 PM	Server	None	2511	N/A	WWW H
3/17/96	9:13:53 PM	AppleTalk	None	3	N/A	WWW H
3/17/96	9:13:37 PM	EventLog	None	6005	N/A	WWW H
3/15/96	8:53:55 PM	Rdr	None	3012	N/A	WWW H
3/15/96	8:43:52 PM	Server	None	2511	N/A	WWW H
3/15/96	8:43:42 PM	AppleTalk	None	3	N/A	WWW H
3/15/96	8:43:26 PM	EventLog	None	6005	N/A	WWW H
3/15/96	8:23:12 PM	Rdr	None	3012	N/A	WWW H
3/15/96	8:23:12 PM	Rdr	None	3012	N/A	WWW H
3/15/96	8:13:09 PM	Server	None	2511	N/A	WWW H
3/15/96	8:13:01 PM	AppleTalk	None	3	N/A	WWW H
3/15/96	8:12:44 PM	EventLog	None	6005	N/A	WWW H
3/7/96	11:48:59 AM	MacSrv	None	12053	N/A	WWW H
3/6/96	6:40:05 PM	Rdr	None	3012	N/A	WWW H

The Security log (shown in Fig. 44.7) can be used to monitor all logons to your server.

FIG. 44.7
The Security log is a critical log for you to monitor if your server is on the Internet.

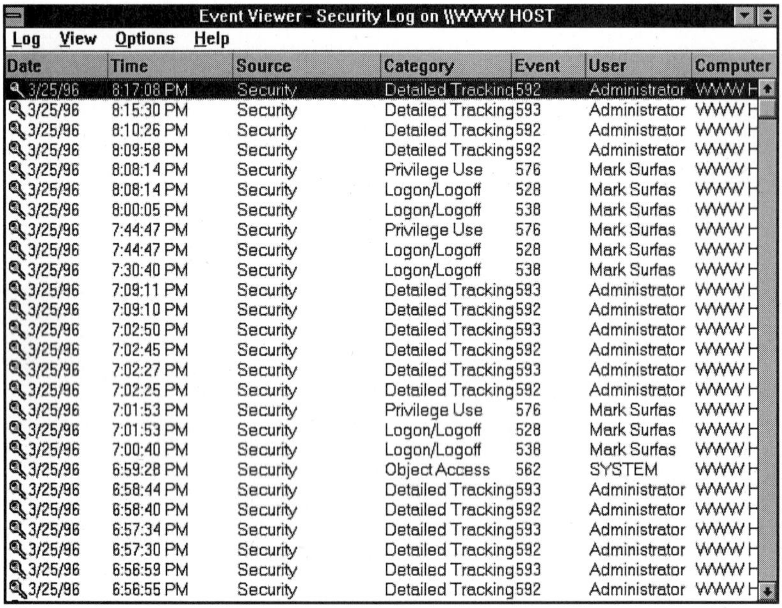

Event Viewer - Security Log on \\WWW HOST

Log View Options Help

Date	Time	Source	Category	Event	User	Computer
3/25/96	8:17:08 PM	Security	Detailed Tracking	592	Administrator	WWW H
3/25/96	8:15:30 PM	Security	Detailed Tracking	593	Administrator	WWW H
3/25/96	8:10:26 PM	Security	Detailed Tracking	592	Administrator	WWW H
3/25/96	8:09:58 PM	Security	Detailed Tracking	592	Administrator	WWW H
3/25/96	8:08:14 PM	Security	Privilege Use	576	Mark Surfas	WWW H
3/25/96	8:08:14 PM	Security	Logon/Logoff	528	Mark Surfas	WWW H
3/25/96	8:00:05 PM	Security	Logon/Logoff	538	Mark Surfas	WWW H
3/25/96	7:44:47 PM	Security	Privilege Use	576	Mark Surfas	WWW H
3/25/96	7:44:47 PM	Security	Logon/Logoff	528	Mark Surfas	WWW H
3/25/96	7:30:40 PM	Security	Logon/Logoff	538	Mark Surfas	WWW H
3/25/96	7:09:11 PM	Security	Detailed Tracking	593	Administrator	WWW H
3/25/96	7:09:10 PM	Security	Detailed Tracking	592	Administrator	WWW H
3/25/96	7:02:50 PM	Security	Detailed Tracking	593	Administrator	WWW H
3/25/96	7:02:45 PM	Security	Detailed Tracking	592	Administrator	WWW H
3/25/96	7:02:27 PM	Security	Detailed Tracking	593	Administrator	WWW H
3/25/96	7:02:25 PM	Security	Detailed Tracking	592	Administrator	WWW H
3/25/96	7:01:53 PM	Security	Privilege Use	576	Mark Surfas	WWW H
3/25/96	7:01:53 PM	Security	Logon/Logoff	528	Mark Surfas	WWW H
3/25/96	7:00:40 PM	Security	Logon/Logoff	538	Mark Surfas	WWW H
3/25/96	6:59:28 PM	Security	Object Access	562	SYSTEM	WWW H
3/25/96	6:58:44 PM	Security	Detailed Tracking	593	Administrator	WWW H
3/25/96	6:58:40 PM	Security	Detailed Tracking	592	Administrator	WWW H
3/25/96	6:57:34 PM	Security	Detailed Tracking	593	Administrator	WWW H
3/25/96	6:57:30 PM	Security	Detailed Tracking	592	Administrator	WWW H
3/25/96	6:56:59 PM	Security	Detailed Tracking	593	Administrator	WWW H
3/25/96	6:56:55 PM	Security	Detailed Tracking	592	Administrator	WWW H

The Application log in Figure 44.8 is used by programs running on the server to report information. Your Web server probably reports startups and shutdowns, as well as statistics and errors.

FIG. 44.8

The Application log reports information for the programs.

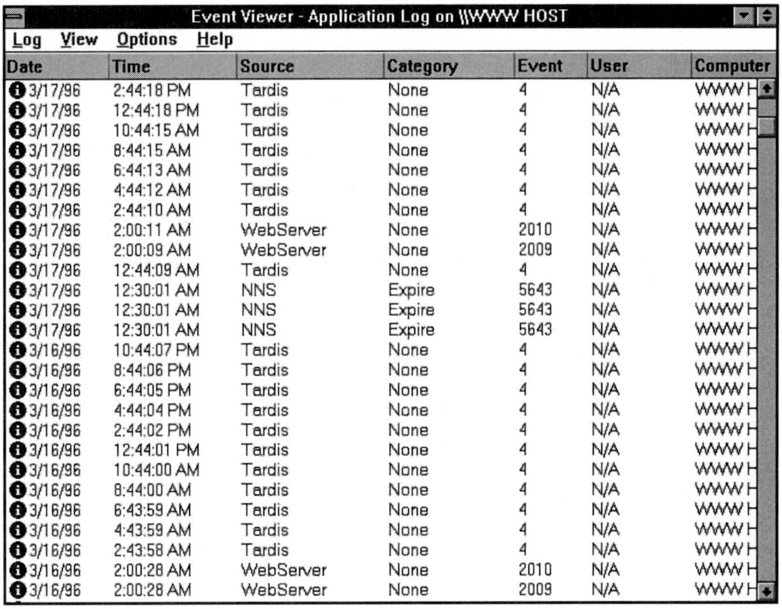

	Event Viewer - Application Log on \\WWW HOST						
Log **View** **Options** **Help**							
Date	**Time**	**Source**	**Category**	**Event**	**User**	**Computer**	
3/17/96	2:44:18 PM	Tardis	None	4	N/A	WWW H	
3/17/96	12:44:18 PM	Tardis	None	4	N/A	WWW H	
3/17/96	10:44:15 AM	Tardis	None	4	N/A	WWW H	
3/17/96	8:44:15 AM	Tardis	None	4	N/A	WWW H	
3/17/96	6:44:13 AM	Tardis	None	4	N/A	WWW H	
3/17/96	4:44:12 AM	Tardis	None	4	N/A	WWW H	
3/17/96	2:44:10 AM	Tardis	None	4	N/A	WWW H	
3/17/96	2:00:11 AM	WebServer	None	2010	N/A	WWW H	
3/17/96	2:00:09 AM	WebServer	None	2009	N/A	WWW H	
3/17/96	12:44:09 AM	Tardis	None	4	N/A	WWW H	
3/17/96	12:30:01 AM	NNS	Expire	5643	N/A	WWW H	
3/17/96	12:30:01 AM	NNS	Expire	5643	N/A	WWW H	
3/17/96	12:30:01 AM	NNS	Expire	5643	N/A	WWW H	
3/16/96	10:44:07 PM	Tardis	None	4	N/A	WWW H	
3/16/96	8:44:06 PM	Tardis	None	4	N/A	WWW H	
3/16/96	6:44:05 PM	Tardis	None	4	N/A	WWW H	
3/16/96	4:44:04 PM	Tardis	None	4	N/A	WWW H	
3/16/96	2:44:02 PM	Tardis	None	4	N/A	WWW H	
3/16/96	12:44:01 PM	Tardis	None	4	N/A	WWW H	
3/16/96	10:44:00 AM	Tardis	None	4	N/A	WWW H	
3/16/96	8:44:00 AM	Tardis	None	4	N/A	WWW H	
3/16/96	6:43:59 AM	Tardis	None	4	N/A	WWW H	
3/16/96	4:43:59 AM	Tardis	None	4	N/A	WWW H	
3/16/96	2:43:58 AM	Tardis	None	4	N/A	WWW H	
3/16/96	2:00:28 AM	WebServer	None	2010	N/A	WWW H	
3/16/96	2:00:28 AM	WebServer	None	2009	N/A	WWW H	

Monitoring Your Server with Performance Monitor   The Performance Monitor, also found in the Administrative Tools program group, provides a way of measuring and monitoring system performance. Many NT-based servers and services automatically install Windows NT Performance Monitor counters. With these counters, you can use the Windows NT Performance Monitor for real-time measurement of your Internet service use.

An excellent example of this is the Web service included in the Microsoft IIS package. This server provides counters to monitor a vast array of performance elements, including:

- Bytes Sent/sec
- Bytes Total/sec
- CGI Requests
- Connection Attempts
- Connections/sec
- Current Anonymous Users
- Current ISAPI Requests
- Current CGI Requests
- Current Connections

- Current NonAnonymous Users
- Files Received
- Files Sent
- Files Total
- Get Requests
- Head Requests
- Logon Attempts
- Maximum Anonymous Users
- Maximum ISAPI Requests
- Maximum CGI Requests
- Maximum Connections
- Maximum Non Anonymous Users
- Not Found Errors
- Other Request Methods
- Post Requests
- Total Anonymous Users
- Total Non Anonymous Users

While running your server, you should get to know the performance monitor and establish benchmarks for standard behavior. When there is deviation from these performance benchmarks, you can decide whether action is warranted.

Optimizing Windows NT Performance

One of the advantages of Windows NT is that much of the work to optimize it is done for you automatically by the system. We'll quickly cover a few of the most common methods for boosting performance.

RAM   Most NT gurus will tell you that the easiest way to boost system performance is to add RAM. You should have a minimum of 16M megabytes to run Windows NT Server and 32 are highly recommended. If you are running a highly active server that uses CGI scripts and heavy database access, you will likely see nice performance increases with each addition of RAM. Consider using at least 64M if your server receives constant daily use. Many of the popular NT Web sites that I know of use 128M of RAM and sometimes more.

Hard Disk   A Web site lives and dies by its hard disk. The first rule in hard disks today is to get a hard drive with a fast access rating. Drive speeds are usually rated in milliseconds (ms), and in today's environment a 5- to 9-ms rating is pretty good.

The second rule in hard drives is to connect it to your system through a 32-bit interface. Your server should have a 32-bit disk controller either built in or available via a 32-bit slot.

The third rule is to defragment your hard drive. This can greatly speed up file access by placing your files in contiguous blocks on the hard drive. Unfortunately there are only a few defragmenters on the market for Windows NT and all of them are expensive.

 TIP Many experts will tell you that increasing the performance of NT is simply a function of adding RAM. My experience has shown that RAM is definitely your best value when speeding up your system.

CPU   Serving Web is generally not much of a strain on the microprocessor. The CPU is only likely to become a factor as you start running sophisticated CGI-type applications. If you plan on a busy Web site, use a fast Pentium processor and consider the Pentium Pro.

Virtual Memory   Windows NT uses a virtual memory system. This means that when necessary, NT uses hard disk space as RAM, allowing more and larger applications to run. NT uses a paging file on each logical drive for virtual memory.

The size and location of these files are configurable through the system applet on the control panel. Be sure that you have plenty of available hard disk space. If you notice that your NT system is constantly accessing the hard drive during normal activity, this is an indication that you need more RAM.

 TIP Run only 32-bit applications. Windows NT is a 32-bit operating system that is backwards-compatible to allow you to run 16-bit applications. 16-bit applications cause NT to run a subsystem for compatibility. This slows down all the applications that are currently executing on your system.

Getting Started with Your Microsoft IIS

The Microsoft IIS is predestined to become one of the most popular Web servers on the Internet and on corporate intranets. The reasons for this are simple: It's powerful. It's fast. It runs on the most popular corporate server operating system today, Windows NT Server. And it's free.

You can get IIS in four ways:

1. Customers who don't own Windows NT Server can purchase Windows NT 4.0, which includes the IIS 2.0.
2. Customers who already own Windows NT Server 3.51 can get IIS 1.0 on disk for approximately $99.00.
3. You can sign up for the Microsoft Developer Network (MSDN) program.
4. You can download it for *free* from the Microsoft WWW site.

Requirements

The IIS 2.0 server is available only for Windows NT Server 4.0.

The IIS 1.0 server is available for both NT server 3.51 and 4.0.

Part
IX

Ch
44

You need a computer with at least the minimum configuration to run Windows NT Server.

When running Windows NT Server version 3.51, you must include Service Pack 3, which is provided on the IIS 1.0 CD.

> **N O T E**   You can administer IIS remotely from a computer running Windows NT Workstation version 3.51 and Service Pack 3, or NT Workstation 4.0. ■

You need a CD-ROM drive for the installation CD.

How to Install IIS

To install the IIS services, you must be logged on with administrator privileges. In addition, to configure the IIS services by using the Internet Service Manager, your user account must be a member of the Administrators group on the target computer.

 T I P   Before beginning installation, close all running applications. This lessens the chance that an application is keeping a file open that the installation process needs to update.

1. To start setup from File Manager or Explorer, double-click the file named Setup.exe in the root directory of either the CD or the directory to which you have expanded the downloaded server.

> **N O T E**   During setup, you can choose the Help button in any dialog box to get assistance. When you do, a Help topic is displayed that explains the choices you have at that point and the procedure to complete the dialog box. ■

2. The Microsoft IIS installation welcome dialog box appears (see Fig. 44.9). Click OK.

FIG. 44.9

The Installation Welcome dialog box.

The second dialog box appears, displaying the installation options shown in Figure 44.10.

FIG. 44.10

The Installation Options dialog box.

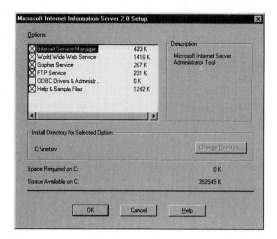

3. The Installation Options dialog box displays a dialog box for three types of Internet servers and some support systems. All the options are selected for installation by default. Here's a brief description of each option:

- Internet Service Manager installs the administration program for managing the services. This is necessary for system setup and maintenance.
- WWW services are for HTML publishing.
- Gopher Service creates a Gopher server.
- FTP Service creates an FTP publishing server.
- ODBC Drivers and Administration installs Open Data Base Connectivity (ODBC) drivers. These are needed for logging on to ODBC files and for enabling ODBC access from the WWW service.
- Help and Sample files installs online Help and sample HyperText Markup Language (HTML) files.
- Microsoft Internet Explorer installs the Web browser, Microsoft Internet Explorer.

N O T E The Gopher service is a powerful system for accessing textual information. Gopher existed before HTTP but has not seen the same popularity. Here's a snippet from the gopher FAQ (**http://www.cis.ohio-state.edu/hypertext/faq/usenet/gopher-faq/faq.html**):

Internet Gopher is a distributed document search and retrieval system. It combines the best features of browsing through collections of information and fully indexed databases.

The protocol and software follow a client-server model and permit users on a heterogeneous mix of desktop systems to browse, search, and retrieve documents residing on multiple distributed server machines. ▓

N O T E   If you have an application running that uses ODBC, you may see an error message telling you that one or more components are in use. Before continuing, close all applications and services that use ODBC. ■

You can also use the Setup program later to add or remove components. Setup can also be used to remove all IIS components. You can accept the default installation directory (C:\Inetsrv) or click the Change Directory button and enter a new directory. Be sure to check this directory against your security setup to ensure that you aren't creating any holes for mischief.

> **CAUTION**
>
> If you've installed IIS but want to reinstall it in another directory, you must remove the following key from the Registry: \HKEY_LOCAL_MACHINE\SOFTWARE\Microsoft\INetStp. If you don't delete this key, the Change Directory button is dimmed and you are unable to change the default directory.

The Publishing Directories dialog box appears next and offers a default directory for each type of service you are installing, or changes the directories (see Fig. 44.11).

FIG. 44.11
Set the default directory for each service.

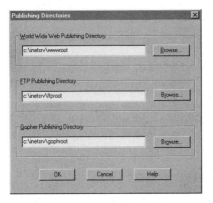

4. If you already have files ready to publish, you can enter the full path to their current location or move them into the default directories later. If your files are on a network drive, you should accept the default directory.

5. After setup is completed, use Internet Service Manager (see Fig. 44.12) to change your default home directory to the path for the network directory containing your files; for example, \\Servername\Sharename\WWWfiles. Be sure to carefully check the permissions on the network drive: there may be security implications.

6. When prompted to create the service directories (Wwwroot, Gophroot, and Ftproot by default), click Yes.

7. The Create Internet Account dialog box appears. This is the account used for all anonymous access to the IIS. You should monitor the access permissions for this

account carefully. Enter a password and confirm the password for this account. Choose OK, and the installation copies all remaining IIS files.

8. If you selected the ODBC Drivers and Administration option box, the Install Drivers dialog box appears.

9. To install the SQL Server driver, select the SQL Server driver from the Available ODBC Drivers list box and choose the OK button.

The preceding steps are all that is needed for a simple installation. You're now ready to publish on the Internet or your intranet. The server is up and running! You can use the Services applet in Control Panel to confirm successful installation of the WWW publishing service.

Part
IX

Ch
44

FIG. 44.12
The IIS Manager application is launched from the Start button menu.

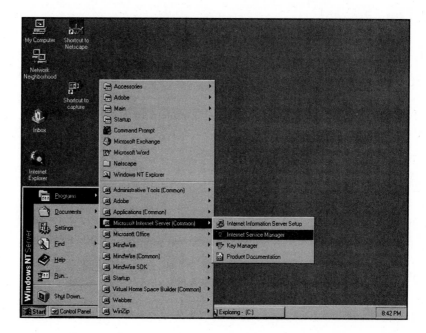

There is no need to start IIS unless you want to make configuration and security changes.

Configuring the IIS WWW Server

The IIS configuration is implemented via the Internet Service Manager, a simple yet powerful tool. One of the strengths of this tool is that it functions as both a local and a remote administrator.

The Microsoft Internet Service Manager

The Internet Service Manager is the tool that you use to configure and monitor your IIS (see Fig. 44.13). You can use the Service Manager to administer both locally running services and remote servers elsewhere on your network.

FIG. 44.13

The Internet Service Manager lists the status of available services.

There are three views available in Internet Service Manager: Reports, Servers, and Services.

Report View   Report view is the default view. This view alphabetically lists the selected computers, with each installed service shown on a separate line. Click the column headings to alphabetically sort the entire list. Report View (shown in Fig. 44.14) is probably most useful for sites with only one or two computers running IIS.

FIG. 44.14

The IIS Manager Report view.

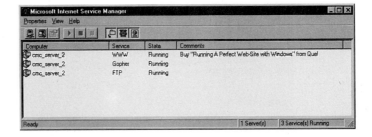

Servers View   Servers view (shown in Fig. 44.15) displays by computer name the services running on network servers. Click the plus symbol next to a server name to see the status of the services that server is running. Double-click a service name to see its property sheets. The Servers view is most useful for sites running a large number of servers when you need to know the status of the services installed on a specific computer.

FIG. 44.15

The Servers view listing available servers.

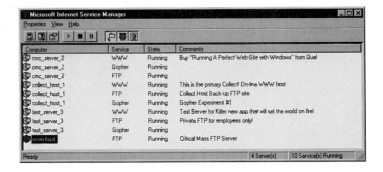

Services View   Services view (shown in Fig. 44.16) lists the services on every selected computer, grouped by service name. Click the plus symbol next to a service name to see the servers running that service. Double-click the computer name under a service to see the property sheets for the service running on that computer. Services view is most useful for sites with widely distributed servers when you need to know which computers are running a particular service.

FIG. 44.16

The Services view.

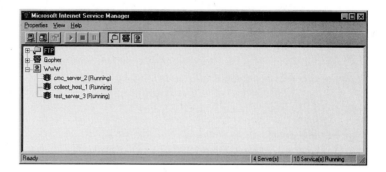

Property Sheets

Double-clicking the service icons launches the property sheets associated with that service instance. The Internet Service Manager service property pages are used to configure and manage the WWW and other services. There are four property pages for the WWW server:

- Service
- Directories
- Logging
- Advanced

Service The Service tab (shown in Fig. 44.17) is used to control high-level access to your server including the user account that non-authenticated browsers use.

FIG. 44.17

The WWW Service tab.

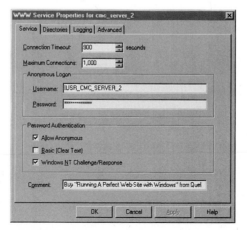

The IIS uses the native NT security permissions to control access to your WWW server. This is a nice benefit if you have an existing NT server setup that you now use to serve Web. No access control files, etc., are needed, and you use the existing NT user manager and file manager to set up your security.

You use the service properties page to control who can use your server and to specify the account used for anonymous client requests to log on to the computer. If yours is like most sites, you allow some (or many!) anonymous connections.

If you allow anonymous connections, then all user permissions for the user, such as permission to access information, use the IUSR_*computername* account. To use a different default user from your current security system to control information access, change the anonymous logon account to an existing account on your network.

The IUSR_computername Account   The IUSR_*computername* account is created during IIS setup. For example, if the computer name is marketing1, then the anonymous access account name is IUSR_marketing1.

By default, all IIS client requests use this account. In other words, IIS clients are logged on to the computer using the IUSR_*computername* account. The IUSR_*computername* account is permitted only to log on locally. No network rights are granted that could allow an unauthorized user to damage your server or its files.

> **N O T E**   The IUSR_*computername* account is also added to the Guests group. If you have changed the settings for the Guests group, those changes also apply to the IUSR_*computername* account. You should review the settings for the Guests group to ensure that they are appropriate for the IUSR_*computername* account. ▪

If you allow remote access only by the IUSR_*computername* account, remote users do not provide a username and password, and have only the permissions assigned to that account. This prevents hackers from attempting to gain access to sensitive information with fraudulent or illegally obtained passwords. For some situations this can provide the best security.

Password Authentication   You can require users to log on and become "authenticated" clients by specifying that users must supply a valid Windows NT username and password. This all happens through the native NT tools that you already know and love. The File Manageror Explorer dictates which areas are secured and the NT User Manager becomes your WWW User Manager! The following lists the various types of password authentication:

- **Allow Anonymous**—Anonymous browsing is the *modus operandi* for most Web surfing. You click, you connect, you surf. For most purposes, this works fine. Many Web sites are a combination of anonymous access and secured access. If this is the case for you, select Allow Anonymous to allow anonymous access via the IUSR_computername account.

- **Basic Authentication**—Basic authentication is used by all modern browsers. When a document or directory is accessed that is not accessible via the anonymous account, the user must log on and authenticate the session. Basic authentication does not encrypt your username and password before transmission. Basic authentication is encoded only by using UUEncode and can be decoded easily by anyone with access to your network, or to a segment of the Internet that transfers your packets.

Part

IX

Ch

44

> **CAUTION**
>
> Using Basic authentication means that you send your Windows NT username and password unencrypted over public networks. Intruders could easily learn usernames and passwords.

- **Windows NT Challenge/Response**—The WWW service also uses the Windows NT Challenge/Response encrypted password transmission. This method encrypts the username and password, providing secure transmission of usernames and passwords over the Internet. Unfortunately, Windows NT authentication can currently be used only by the Microsoft Internet Explorer.

With both basic authentication and Windows NT authentication, no access is permitted unless a valid username and password are supplied. Password authentication is useful if you want only authorized individuals to use your server or specific portions controlled by NTFS. You can have both IUSR_*computername* access and authenticated access enabled at the same time.

Directories Tab   The Service Directories (shown in Fig. 44.18) is a straightforward means of defining Webs and their directories.

FIG. 44.18

The WWW Directories tab.

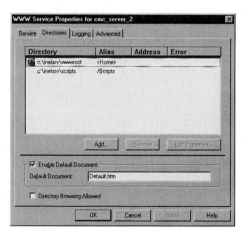

Directories   You start with one initial Web space and directory specified (see Fig. 44.19). All the immediate directories underneath this directory are accessible to the Web browser (security permitting). To add additional directories from outside this immediate directory tree to this Web structure, click on the Add button.

FIG. 44.19

Configure a virtual server or directory.

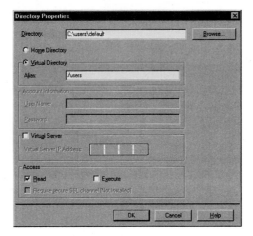

In the Directory box, you indicate the directory to add to this Web space. Remember that the security for this directory is dictated by NTFS and set it accordingly.

Each directory must be given an alias. The directory alias allows you to mask long directory names with a simple concise name. This alias is called by the browser immediately after the computer domain name. In this example, the c:\inet\test\excitement directory is accessible by the URL **http://www.scoop.com/coolthing/**.

If the physical location of the directory is on a remote network drive, use the Account Information box to provide a valid username and password to log on to that network drive.

> **CAUTION**
>
> If you connect to a remote network drive, all security access is governed by the logon name you supply. Be careful!

Virtual Servers   Virtual servers are set up through the same Add button we use to set up additional directories for our Web space. Setting up a virtual server is a similar process with a few differences.

Enter in the name of the directory that will be the home or default directory. If you specify a directory on a remote server, you need to enter a valid username and password to log on.

Select the Home Directory radio button, and the Alias radio button and text box gray out. Since this is the default directory, no alias is needed.

You need to select the Virtual Server check box to let IIS know that this is not just another directory but a distinct Web space. The IP address box becomes available for the IP address that will access this Web space.

N O T E If you have assigned multiple IP addresses to your network interface card, you will likely want to specify which IP address has access to each directory you create. If no IP address is specified, the directory becomes available to all virtual servers—which could come in handy in some cases. ▪

N O T E The default Web space works for all TCP/IP addresses specified on your network interface card unless you begin to specify additional virtual webs. ▪

Default Directory Behavior   In the bottom half of the directories page you can specify the default document name. This is the document the server looks for when a URL is noted that does not contain a specific document name. This is a nice way to keep your URLs short and your users out of trouble.

If a URL is called without a specific document and a default document does not exist, then the server checks to see if directory browsing is allowed. If it's allowed, then a hypertext listing of directories and files is presented to the browser.

Directory browsing (sometimes called *automatic directory indexing*) can only be allowed or disallowed for all directories and Webs on the server. You cannot allow it for some and not for others. If you turn on directory browsing, be sure that you have a default document in the directories in which you don't want browsing.

Logging Tab   The IIS server shines when it comes to control over logging (see the tab in Fig. 44.20). Perhaps this is a result of the corporate nature of Microsoft software…it understands that businesses love to analyze!

FIG. 44.20
The WWW Service
Logging tab.

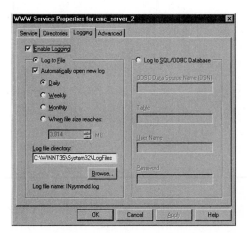

Part

IX

Ch

44

You can send log files to either a text file or to an ODBC-connected database. One really neat feature here is that multiple servers can log activity to a single file or database anywhere on the network. This has powerful implications for popular sites and for Web service providers that bill according to usage levels.

Log to File   When logging to file, you can specify how often the server should close the file and create a new one. This is usually called *log-file cycling*. IIS lets you cycle your logs according to a periodic schedule: daily, weekly, or monthly as well as when the log file reaches a certain size. This is a rare feature among NT Web servers.

If you fail to specify a log cycle event, the log file grows indefinitely.

> **N O T E**   Try not to let your log files grow too large. Most of the statistical report generators today refuse to give up the goods when confronted with a 100-MB log file. ▪

SQL/ODBC Logging   You can use any ODBC-supported database to log server activity. Logging to a database can allow you to direct the logging of all IIS services to a single source. This also means that you can use any ODBC-compliant application to view the log data in your database. In addition, you can use the Internet Database Connector to view log data in a Web browser.

Converting Log File Formats   The Microsoft Internet Log Converter converts Microsoft Internet Server log files to either European Microsoft Windows NT Academic Centre (EMWAC) log file format or the Common Log File format. Convlog.exe is located by default in the \Inetsrv\Admin directory. At the command prompt, type **convlog** without parameters to see syntax and examples, or to see Help.

Advanced Tab   The Advanced tab (shown in Fig. 44.21) is used to throttle access to your server based on IP addresses and transfer rates.

FIG. 44.21
The WWW Service
Advanced tab.

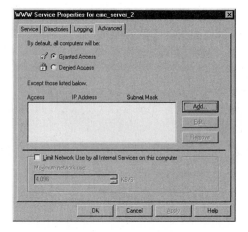

IP Access Control   You can control access to the IIS Web service by specifying the IP address of the computers to be granted or denied access.

If you choose to grant access to all users by default, you can then specify the computers to be denied access. For example, if you have a form on your WWW server and a particular user on the Internet is entering multiple forms with fictitious information, you can prevent the computer at that IP address from connecting to your site. Conversely, if you choose to deny access to all users by default, you can then specify which computers are allowed access.

Limiting Network Use   You can throttle the drain on your network and server bandwidth by limiting the network bandwidth available to the server. Although this feature has some value, it would be a fantastic feature for a Web service provider if it could be configured by individual webspace.

The FTP and Gopher Services

The FTP and Gopher services are essentially *last generation* or *legacy* services. They are from an era that predates the Web and have largely been superseded. They do offer some functionality that the Web does not and, therefore, merit some discussion.

The FTP Service

File transfer protocol (FTP) is a method of transferring files between client and server. The key advantage of FTP is that *clients can send files to the server.* HTTP lacks this extremely useful capability.

FTP servers offer you a nice way for your users to browse file directories and to download what they need, with no configuration needed on your part. While this is similar to the automatic directory indexing that most Web servers offer, there are a few advantages.

Any FTP client can connect to your server (including most web browsers). FTP clients are optimized for file management and make it extremely easy to move files between the client PC and the server. FTP servers can set a longer timeout period to ensure that file transfer is successfully completed in the allotted time period.

The Gopher Service

Gopher is the precursor to the Web. While Gopher is entirely text-based, it remains a powerful way to deliver information to client browsers. Like FTP, Gopher serves directories of existing files. Although more elegant than its FTP cousin, Gopher falls short in presentation compared to the WWW. Most WWW browsers today also connect to a Gopher server. ●

CHAPTER 45

Running an E-mail Server

by Mark Surfas

Internet usage statistics show that the most popular service on the Internet is not the World Wide Web, but plain old electronic mail! It is rapidly becoming necessary for a business to have e-mail addresses for most employees as well as the business e-mail address. ■

An overview of Internet e-mail

Interconnecting the millions of systems on the Internet today would not be possible without a set of standard protocols. You will learn about protocols such as POP (post office protocol) and SMTP.

A review of e-mail servers

By reviewing the available mail servers, you will find the right combination of features for your implementation.

Installation and configuration of NT-Mail

You learn how to install and run NT-Mail.

Internet E-mail

The basic concepts behind e-mail parallel those of regular mail. You send mail to people at their particular addresses, and they in turn write to you at your address. You can subscribe to the electronic equivalent of magazines and newspapers. Sooner or later, you'll probably even get the electronic equivalent of junk mail.

E-mail has distinct advantages over regular mail. The most obvious is speed: instead of taking several days, your message can reach the other side of the world in hours, minutes, or even seconds (depending on the state of the connections between where you drop off your mail and your destinee). In addition, e-mail is cheaper and handles more diverse forms of information than regular mail.

E-mail also has advantages over the telephone. You send your message when it's convenient for you, and your recipients respond at their convenience—no more telephone tag. A phone call across the country or around the world can quickly result in huge phone bills; e-mail lets you exchange vast amounts of mail for only a few pennies even if the recipient is on the other side of the earth.

Internet e-mail is governed by a group of standards, as are all standard services available on the Internet.

Internet Standards and Protocols

Interconnecting the millions of systems on the Internet today would not be possible without a set of standard protocols. Each Internet standard is described in a document called a request for comment (RFC). RFCs date back to 1969 and are the working notes of the Internet research and development community. Generally, an RFC is a description of a protocol, procedure, or service; a status report; or a summary of research. There are approximately 1,600 published RFCs to date.

RFCs are reviewed by the community of Internet users before they become standards. Most of the standard protocols on the Internet got started as RFCs. They are considered public domain documents, with a few exceptions, and are available online from several repositories. RFCs are numbered sequentially. Once given a number, they're never revised; new versions of the documents are issued instead. More information on RFCs and the Internet protocol standards process can be found in RFC 1310.

On the CD   The RFCs for Internet e-mail can be found on the CD included with this book.

Post Office Protocol Mail Server (POP)

The post office where Internet mail is stored and retrieved from is known as a POP server. The POP3 protocol governs how a mail client retrieves waiting mail from a mail server. A POP server is also designed to be compliant with the vast number of POP-compatible mail clients available. The POP3 protocol is defined in RFC 1460.

Simple Mail Transfer Protocol (SMTP)

Simple Mail Transfer Protocol, (SMTP), governs the exchange of electronic mail between two message transfer agents (MTAs) on the Internet. In essence, SMTP is the underlying transmission mechanism for most of the mail on the Internet. The standard (defined in RFC 821) was established in 1982; it has received a few extensions since then but is largely unchanged.

SMTP is a simple peer-to-peer model. Each host that wants to send mail sets up an SMTP server. When the host sends mail it contacts the appropriate server, which then acts as an SMTP receiver.

Overview of Mail Server Software

To set up an effective mail server, you need a system that has both an SMTP server and a POP-3 server. Fortunately, there are a great number of mail server packages available for the Windows 3.1, 95, and NT environments. By reviewing the available mail servers you will find the right combination of features for your implementation.

Part
IX
Ch
45

Windows 95 and NT

There is a growing contingent of excellent e-mail servers for both the Windows 95 and Windows NT environments. The number is growing quickly and the feature/price combinations are diverse. Traditional corporate e-mail systems are also quickly adding Internet e-mail functionality. Microsoft's Exchange server is an example of a product that originally shunned the Internet, but has been quickly adapted to operate as a mail gateway to the Internet. Expect to see this happen with every corporate level e-mail product.

MERCUR

Version Number: 1.84

Revision Date: April 9, 1996

License: Shareware

Cost: U.S. $50.00 to U.S. $640.00 depending on number of licenses.

HomePage: **http://www.atrium.de/mercur/mcr_eng.htm**

MERCUR is a full-featured SMTP/POP3 Server for Windows NT and Windows 95. The server runs as a system service and is easy to install and configure with the aid of the Control panel. MERCUR features easy administration and the ability to handle multiple domains.

SLMail95 & NT

Version Number: 2.0

Revision Date: April 9, 1996

License: Shareware 14-day test version

Costs: NT version: U.S. $325.00. 95 version: U.S. $189.00

Home Page: **http://www.seattlelab.com**

SLMail95 is a strong SMTP/POP3 server with auto-responders, mailing lists, and many other features. There is no restriction on the number of users or mailing lists.

Mail Coach

Version Number: 1.0

Revision Date: June 6, 1996

License: Shareware—limited to three users.

Cost: First 5 users: U.S. $210. Additional 5 user licenses: $90

Home Page: **http://www.multi.se/ymex/mailcoach.htm**

Mail Coach is an SMTP/POP3 server with UUCP mail transport. This means that it can receive and deliver mail via LAN, to and from clients who are using standard Internet mail software as well as batch upload outgoing mail to an Internet service Provider. This capability is less and less useful as the Internet grows up.

For more information, check the Mail Coach Web site.

Cmail

Version Number: 1.7

Revision Date: April 17, 1996

License: Commercial

Cost: 10 users: £325.00

Home Page: **http://www.computalynx.co.uk**

The Cmail mail server runs on both Windows 95 and NT 3.51. It services multiple e-mail accounts from one ISP connection.

NT-Mail 3.0

Version Number: 3.02d

Revision Date: May 11, 1996

License: Limited use Trial Key

Home Page: **http://www.net-shopper.co.uk**

NT-Mail was the first full-featured NT-based mail system. NT-Mail combines POP, SMTP, and list services in an easy-to-use package. You receive a trial key each month for a limited number of users.

Post Office

Version Number: 1.93B

Revision Date: May 22, 1996

License: 45-day trial

Home Page: **http://www.software.com/prod/po/po.html**

Post Office is a solid and popular SMTP, POP3, and Finger mail server, configured and administered via a Web-driven interface.

Windows 3.1

There are a small handful of mail servers that run in the Windows 3.1 environment. These servers are not recommended for a robust e-mail server in the corporate environment. However, if you have a need to use multiple e-mail addresses or would like to control all the e-mail for a domain you may want to consider this. Keep in mind that if you run an e-mail server it is critical that the server run continuously 24 hours a day, 7 days a week.

TIP If you are running an e-mail server be sure that either you or your ISP is running a backup mail server. In the event that your primary mail server fails, the backup will receive mail intended for your server. When your primary server is back online the backup server will forward the mail it is holding.

SLMail for Windows 3.1

Version Number: 2.0

Revision Date: April 9, 1996

License: Shareware

Cost: U.S. $100.00
Home Page: **http://www.seattlelab.com**

SLMail for Windows 3.1 is a nice SMTP/POP3 server with auto-responders, mailing lists, and many other features. This server lacks the administration utilities of its big brothers for 95 and NT and supports a maximum of two virtual domains.

Installing and Running NT Mail

NT Mail is a straightforward implementation with configuration examples and concepts that will apply to any mail server you eventually choose. The server is robust and sturdy enough for high-level corporate use, and mild enough on resources to use as a personal mail server.

The list of features for NT Mail is impressive and extensive.

Major features:

- RFC-compliant SMTP and POP servers that operate as 32-bit services designed to work using the advanced features of Windows NT
- Remote configuration and control
- NT Control Panel configuration utility
- All services multithreaded to take advantage of multiprocessor platforms
- Full logging, allowing mail misuse to be detected (including where the mail claims to have come from and where it really came from) and projection of mail loads to be determined
- Message Forwarding for people who move and holiday messages for those who are on holiday (to alert the sender that the reply may be delayed)
- Auto Responder, enables mail to be sent automatically (saving or dumping the original request)
- Utilities for dial-up support
- Optional Integral List Server
- Auto-launch executable option to start programs in response to mail
- Mail-delivery receipt messages to sender
- Message sizes capped to a user-defined limit
- Logging of all through-traffic
- Link to *LG-Fax,* allowing e-mail to FAX gateway to be designed for people without Internet access
- User ability to configure holiday message and plans via e-mail or WWW forms
- Finger server
- Password server

NT Mail is produced by Internet Shopper Ltd., located in the UK. The home page for NT Mail is **www.net-shopper.co.uk**. Be sure to check there for software updates, news, and so on.

Installing NT Mail

Once you have successfully downloaded the interNeTmail install file, you have to obtain a license key (either demonstration or full commercial key). Upon receipt of the key, you are ready to begin the installation process. During the installation you are asked to provide the following:

- The activation key
- Your Internet service provider's mail server/gateway, if your link is via a dial-up connection
- Your local domain name, if one has not already been configured (with TCP/IP)

To start the installation, copy the .ZIP file to a temporary location and then, via the COM-MAND PROMPT window, use PKZIP to decompress the distribution set. Next, either type SETUP at the command line or double-click on the SETUP.EXE icon using FILE MANAGER. The setup program then guides you through the installation process.

> **N O T E** The location of the SETUP.EXE is not important as it creates target directories as required. The environment variable temp must be set to a valid location. ■

The Target Directory

After the initial welcome dialogues have been displayed you are prompted to specify a directory into which interNeTmail is to be installed. The default is C:\NTMAIL if interNeTmail has not previously been installed. Otherwise, use the location of the current installation.

The Activation Key

When prompted, enter the license key and then OK. The key is then validated; three attempts are allowed before the installation automatically terminates. Once the key has been validated, the install program displays the number of licensed users and the expiration date of the key. You are only asked to enter the key on a first-time installation. Should you be required to enter the key again, you can use the interNeTmail control panel configuration utility as shown in Figure 45.1.

FIG. 45.1
The Key Management tab for NT mail.

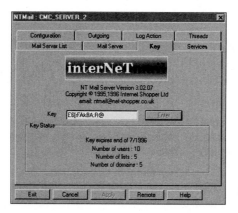

Local Domain Name

If performing a first-time installation, the interNeTmail installation program attempts to auto-detect the local domain name from the NT Registry. If a domain name cannot be found, you are prompted to provide your domain name. This acts as a default, i.e., the address that is added to any outgoing mail address if only a username is specified.

Dial-Up Connections

If performing a first-time installation, you are asked if the Internet connection is via a dial-up link. If it is, select OK and then enter the address of your provider's mail server—for example, mail.provider.com. The default configuration attempts to send all mail to the provider's mail server. You are only asked to enter the remote server name on a first-time installation.

Program Manager Groups

Once interNeTmail has been successfully installed, a Program Manager group called interNeTmail is created. It contains all the interNeTmail documentation, the configuration utility, the readme file, and the Windows help file.

User and Administrator Control Panel Configuration

Three configuration program icons are installed in the Windows NT Control Panel (as shown in Fig. 45.2): interNeTmail, interNeTmail users, and interNeT list. InterNeTmail is for use by the system administrator to configure the system-wide aspects of interNeTmail; interNeTmail users is used by account holders that the administrator has set up. InterNeT list provides a convenient way to configure the list server.

FIG. 45.2
The Control Panel after installation.

Testing the Installation

To test the interNeTmail installation, use the following procedure:

Mail yourself at **mark@criticalmass.com**.

Mail someone else at the same domain: cathy**@criticalmass.com**.

Mail someone at a different domain requesting a reply. If your connection is dial-up, you also need to manually ring the service provider or wait until any automatic connection is scheduled and then enter the command MAIL —k to send the message. A special account at Internet Shopper Ltd. can be used: **test@net-shopper.co.uk**. This replies with full details of the message sent. Verify that the reply is received.

Setting Up and Managing Mail Accounts

The following sections provide an introduction to setting up interNeTmail after installation. All of the actions covered are performed using the interNeTmail *C*ontrol *P*anel App*L*et (or CPL utility). After installation, the interNeTmail CPL utility can be started by double-clicking on the NT Control Panel icon as shown in Figure 45.3 or on the Configuration icon in the interNeTmail Program Manager group.

FIG. 45.3

The NT Mail CPL utility—there's a lot going on here!

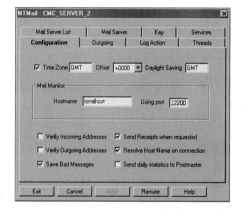

Part

IX

Ch

45

In addition to interNeTmail, there is also an interNeTmail users CPL as shown in Figure 45.4. This is identical to the interNeTmail CPL except that only a subset of operations is available, i.e., only those that are of interest to the account holders specified by the interNeTmail CPL. The tabs provided are *Accounts*, *Fax*, *Forward*, *Executable*, *Users,* and *Auto Responder*.

FIG. 45.4

The NT Mail users CPL.

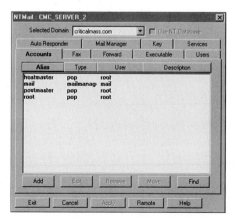

Details of interNeTmail users can be held in two distinct places: the NT Registry and the NT User Database. The pros and cons of each method are given in Table 45.1.

Table 45.1   Comparing NT User Database and NT Registry

NT User Database

Advantages	Disadvantages
Users may already have accounts set up for RAS.	Users must be given login privilege in order to collect their mail.
Adding a user to the user Database automatically provides a mail account.	Must actively lock out user by creating an entry in the Registry.

NT Registry

The ability to log onto an NT machine without an NT account.	Services must be updated when users are added.
Script-based configuration (via MAIL command).	
Password server allows passwords to be changed.	
Registry keys are easily saved and restored.	

The following description of the interNeTmail CPL assumes user information is added to the NT Registry. If you elect to use the NT User Database, you may want to set up additional mail accounts and aliases in the same way. Note that NT User Database accounts are not shown in the interNeTmail CPL.

When mail arrives, interNeTmail checks the NT Registry entries first and then the NT User Database, if enabled. This allows the addition of options and accounts for users who cannot log onto your machine.

If you use the interNeTmail CPL to make configuration changes to services running on a local machine, you will be asked whether the services should be updated. If you elect to update the services immediately, there may be a small delay while the services re-read their setup values.

The interNeTmail CPL is split into several pages each with a selectable tab. Each of the tabs has these buttons:

- Exit—Saves the currently edited data and then exits.
- Cancel—Discards the currently edited data and exits. Discards all the edits since the last time the Apply button was selected.

- Apply—Saves the currently edited data.

- Remote—Invokes a dialogue prompting for the name of the remote machine (connection must be NetBIOS and not TCP/IP). When entered, the CPL attempts to connect to the named machine and to display the setup of interNeTmail on the remote machine. For this to work, you must have access privilege to the NT Registry on the remote machine. It is possible to configure everything remotely except the contents of any files and the updating of services; they must be stopped and then restarted.

- Help—Displays a Windows help file containing some notes about available configuration options and parameters.

The Accounts tab displays a list of every maildrop (excluding NT user Database entries) known to interNeTmail. Across the top of the list are a set of title buttons: Alias, Type, User, and Description. They can be used to sort the list on the particular option selected (refer to Fig. 45.4.)

To add an account, simply select the Users tab and fill in the username for the account. Each account can have an unlimited number of *aliases*. To clarify, the account name and any aliases are used to receive mail from other Internet e-mail users. When configuring a client e-mail package, you use only the account name to retrieve e-mail. In Figure 45.5, the username testuser is the account name used to retrieve mail. This account accepts mail sent to both MR. Pumpkin and mr. test.

Part IX

Ch 45

FIG. 45.5

The Users tab.

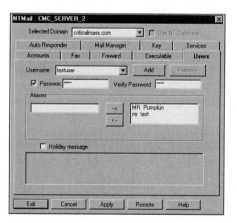

The holiday message is checked when a user wishes to continue to receive mail and also send an immediate response back containing the customized holiday message. This is useful when the user is on vacation or holiday, as well as in other situations when an auto-response is desired.

Activity Logging

The ability to log activities and errors is a key management tool shown in Figure 45.6.

Both the SMTP and POP servers offer a host of options. In this figure, the options selected are adequate for a complete understanding of the server activity. With these options you can monitor how heavy the traffic is as well as server startups, shutdowns, and errors. The logs themselves are text files and are located in the \log directory.

FIG. 45.6

Log Action tab.

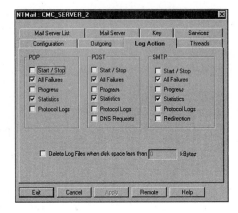

The logs (see Fig. 45.7) are generated continuously throughout the day and a new log is started each night at 12:00 a.m.. Log files are named with the date and prefixed by PO for the POP server and SM for the SMTP server.

FIG. 45.7

The logs are in ASCII format.

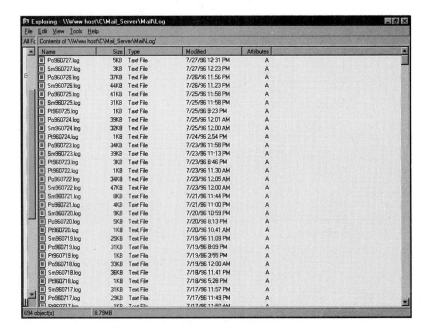

CHAPTER 46

Running an FTP Server

by Mark Surfas

File Transfer Protocol (FTP) is one of the original foundation services of the Internet. The ability to transfer files from one computer to another is a basic need of everyday computing. Today FTP is still one of the most popular services on the Internet. Although statistics are hard to come by, the last available NSF stats indicate that FTP traffic in April of 1995 was 21% of all traffic.

There are other ways of transferring files including HTTP and via e-mail, but FTP remains the most used and most reliable method. Perhaps this is due to the extensive standard set of server and client features. FTP can transfer anything: ASCII, executable binaries, images, sound files, and literally any other file format available. Why is this important? WWW and gopher servers like to know the type of file so they can handle it correctly. You often have to configure the server to handle binary data properly. With FTP you simply load in your files and they are ready to go.

Most WWW and Gopher browsers support links to FTP servers. This means that you can make files available for download in your FTP directory by FTP clients and relieve stress on your WWW server by linking browser downloads there as well. FTP is definitely a cooperative service that a Webmaster finds invaluble. ■

What features are desirable in an FTP server

FTP has a set of standards for interaction between client and host. However, there is plenty of room for a rich diversity of features and services on the host end.

An overview of available FTP servers

A number of reliable and robust FTP servers are available for the Microsoft Windows environment.

How to install an FTP server

We discuss the installation and management of an FTP server.

FTP Server Basics

A tremendous number of FTP servers are available for the entire span of Windows operating systems. Windows NT ships with an FTP server as part of the operating system! For all this diversity, an FTP server can, in practicality, provide only two types of access: Anonymous and User.

Anonymous FTP

Anonymous FTP is the form most commonly used by Internet publishers. An FTP server configured for anonymous access lets anyone access the server without having a preconfigured account. A user who uses the account name Anonymous or FTP is allowed to log in to an anonymous FTP server. The server does not check for a particular password, but instead takes whatever password is offered and logs it. It has become standard practice for users to submit their e-mail addresses as passwords, so the system administrator can find out who is using the server.

Anonymous FTP users are generally restricted to seeing only a part of the file system on the server. This is often referred to as the "anonymous ftp area" of the file system. This segmentation and tight security make an Anonymous FTP server an excellent candidate for providing public access to documentation and free or shareware software.

 The monster of all free shareware FTP servers is located at FTP.CDROM.COM. This service offers gigabyte upon gigabyte of freeware and shareware and is a model of a well-run FTP server. The service also has a Web interface at **http://www.cdrom.com**.

User FTP

FTP servers support user accounts and password level security features. This enables you to keep data and software secure within a privileged user group. User accounts can log in and gain free access to authorized locations of the file system. It's important to note that an account only allows access to FTP services. Users cannot execute operating system-level commands or other binary executables. They are limited to the commands that the FTP server provides, such as listing and changing directories, and sending and receiving files.

User account FTP creates a security problem. When users log in, their passwords travel across the Internet in clear text. This means that computers with sniffer programs located between the user and the server can grab the username and the password. This important point leads to two security rules:

1. Don't store confidential data on your FTP server.
2. Don't allow FTP users to use the same username and password combinations for other logins, such as e-mail or network access.

Available FTP Servers

A number of reliable and robust FTP servers are available for the Microsoft Windows environment. Microsoft made an FTP server available for Windows NT 3.51 and actually ships an FTP server with NT 4.0 as part of the Internet Information Server. The features that will guide your selection include:

- Operating system version
- Access logging

Several popular FTP servers for the Windows environment are Serv-U, WFTPD, Vermillion, and the Microsoft IIS FTP service.

 TIP Looking for Windows shareware, reduced-feature shareware, and freeware? Check out **http://www.tucows.com**. TUCOWS (The Ultimate Collection of Winsock Software) is one of the best run software archives on the Internet. With many mirror sites around the globe, access is fast and easy. These FTP servers and others can be found at TUCOWS.

Server Features

FTP has a set of standards for interaction between client and host. However, there is plenty of room for a rich diversity of features and services on the host end. Here is a list of features to consider:

- Security rich: Passwords, read/write/modify rights per directory or file for each user (including ANONYMOUS).
- Access on the basis of IP-number.
- Multiple simultaneous users and transfers.
- Available in 16- and 32-bit forms.
- Users can be grouped for easy maintenance of large numbers.
- Server works well with Web browsers.
- Access to all drives on your server, including network drives.
- Complete and strict implementation of RFC959 (FTP protocol specification—see **http://www.w3.org/hypertext/WWW/Protocols/rfc959/2_Overview.html** and RFC1123 (see **http://www.cis.ohio-state.edu/htbin/rfc/rfc1123.html**), including PASV.
- Supports "links" like those in UNIX.
- Supports the "resume" option, to continue interrupted file transfers.
- Configurable greeting messages, for signon, signoff, and login.
- Configurable directory change messages.
- Can run "invisible"—with no user access to the program.
- Has a "time-out" feature, so connections are automatically cleared when idle or hung.

- Easy to set up and maintain through menus.
- Logs all transactions to file and screen that can be read by other applications. Includes unique session IDs, time, and date stamps.

Serv-U

URL: **http://catsoft.dorm.duke.edu/**

Cost: U.S. $25.00

Serv-U is a full-featured FTP server for MS Windows in all its forms (Win3.1, WFW3.11, Win95, and NT). It offers a simple setup, yet is powerful and has extensive security features.

WFTPD

Home Page: **http://www.eden.com/~alun/**

Cost: U.S. $20.00

WFTPD is a WinSock FTP Daemon that works with Windows 3.*x*, Windows 95, and Windows NT. A new 32-bit version takes advantage of the latter two platforms. Like FTP Serv-U, WFTPD supports multiple simultaneous access, anonymous logins, extensive start-up instructions, and online Help documentation.

Vermillion FTP Server

Home Page: **http://jhunix.hcf.jhu.edu/~mbk/**

The Vermillion server is a 32-bit FTP server for Windows 95 and NT. It is full-featured and distributed as Timed shareware. Vermillion installation and setup are featured later in this chapter.

Microsoft FTP Servers

Home Page: **http://www.microsoft.com**

The FTP server released as part of the Microsoft Internet Information Server is a robust application, with the appropriate features for both an anonymous FTP and user FTP server. This server requires Windows NT 3.51 with Service Pak 3 or later, or Windows NT 4.0.

Installing and Managing Vermillion FTP Server

From this point forward we will be discussing the installation and management of an FTP server. I have chosen the Vermillion server as a well-rounded representative of the FTP server population. By reading about the Vermillion installation issues, you will be well-versed in the issues encountered when installing any Windows-based FTP server.

Installing the Vermillion FTP server couldn't be simpler; download the zip file from your favorite shareware source, unzip it, and launch the Vftpd.exe program.

The VFTPD interface utilizes the Windows 95 standard tab interface. The entire control panel is at your fingertips as shown in Figure 46.1. To switch between tabs, click on the tabs at the top of the window.

FIG. 46.1

The initial VFTPD screen status.

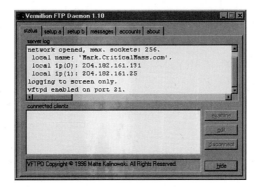

The first tab, Status, is concerned primarily with providing the current status of the server. At a glance, you can see the current status and user activity of the server.

On the Status tab there are two windows and two groups of buttons. The top list box, Server Log, provides a history of the last 1,000 events. You can actually filter which events appear in the log during server setup.

The bottom window, Connected Clients, shows a list of users currently connected to your system. The left column shows the unique session ID code, which can be matched with a corresponding code in the Server Log list box to identify which user is responsible for the event shown. The middle column lists the account under which the client has logged in, and the right column shows the address (or hostname if available) of the computer from which the client is connected.

By selecting a client from the Connected Clients window and clicking one of the top three buttons, you can perform several useful tasks.

The first button, Examine, brings up the dialog box shown in Figure 46.2 and contains a variety of useful information relating to the client. The information includes a log of the commands and replies sent over the control connection, time online, idle time, total number and size of files received and stored, and the status of the current transfer, including file name, size, current position, and transfer rate.

The second button, Edit, brings up the user editor and enables you to make any changes to the account. Note that most changes do not take effect until the user's next login.

The third button, Disconnect, does just that—it sends a Server "shutting down" message to the client and closes the control connection.

FIG. 46.2

Examine a client
connection.

The last button, <u>H</u>ide, has nothing to do with connected clients, but is one of most useful features of VFTPD. If you are finished examining the system status and wish to put the server window aside while you work on other things, you can click <u>H</u>ide to make the window disappear. It leaves only a tiny icon at the far right of the taskbar in the tray (see Fig. 46.3). This is very handy, because it keeps the program out of the way, but enables you to bring it back any time you wish.

FIG. 46.3

The Vermillion icon.

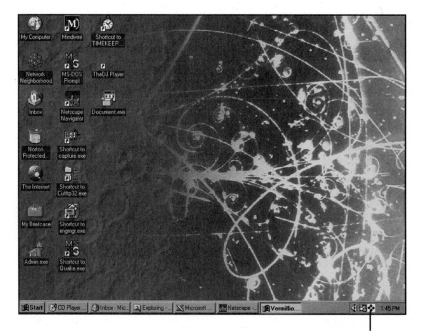

The Vermillion icon

A single click on this icon provides a quick status report shown in Figure 46.4, and displays information on the current number of users online, percent of capacity, and the combined data transfer rate of all clients. Double-clicking the icon "un-hides" the main program window and allows you to get a more detailed view of system activity, to change configuration options, or to edit user accounts.

FIG. 46.4

The Vermillion quick status window.

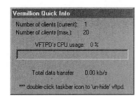

System Configuration

The actual system configuration page shown in Figure 46.5 is located on the Setup A tab. This tab contains all the variables used to run the server. Note that changes made on this tab are saved or become active only when you click the OK button in the lower-right corner. If you make a mistake, you can restore the last saved configuration by clicking Cancel.

FIG. 46.5

The Setup A tab for system configuration.

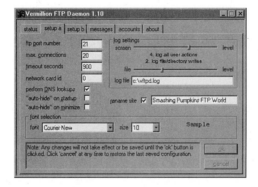

Setup A   These configuration options are available:

FTP port number: Port number on which VFTPD should listen for connections.

Max. connections: Limit to the number of simultaneous clients.

Timeout seconds: How long VFTPD should wait before disconnecting an idle user.

Start Hidden: Whether to start VFTPD "hidden."

Use DNS: Whether to use DNS to resolve remote addresses into hostnames. This is useful for administrators who like to monitor the logs and better understand who is utilizing the server.

Logging: Filters which events to show in the Server log and/or to save to disk. The log filters are applied through two slider controls, one for the written log and one for the log displayed on the status tab. The level of information in each option includes the infomation in all previous options.

- Level 0: None
- Level 1: Security messages, including successful and failed logins
- Level 2: File writes (created, modified, deleted, etc.)
- Level 3: File reads (retrieved, etc.)
- Level 4: All other actions, including directory changes
- Level D: Debug-level logging, including commands and replies

Messages   There are four methods of displaying messages to users as they interact with your server. Two of these are configured from the Messages tab shown in Figure 46.6.

FIG. 46.6

The Messages tab for configuring welcome and good-bye messages.

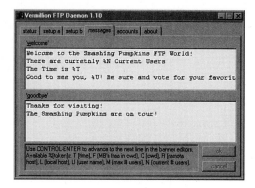

The Welcome banner is the first thing displayed to a connecting user, even before logging in.

The Good-bye banner is displayed when a client logs off gracefully (issues the QUIT command).

 TIP Use Ctrl+Enter to advance to the next line in either window. If you prefer a larger workspace, you can create the messages using a program, such as Notepad, and paste them into the window.

The other two messages are read from files located in the server directories.

Welcome.msg is placed in the home directory of a user and is displayed as part of the User logged in message. This means that after a successful login and after the display of the Welcome banner, a custom message can be displayed to the FTP client.

A message can also be displayed whenever a user moves into a new directory. If a file named .message (note the initial period) is placed in a directory, it is displayed when a user changes to that directory.

Note that all messages should be limited to 75 characters per line to be displayed correctly.

Message Tokens   Any of the four types of messages can contain special tokens, which are replaced with system information. They enable you to create more personalized or informative messages. The following tokens are available (they are not case-sensitive):

%T: Current time and date, e.g. Fri Apr 12 05:34:16 1996.

%F: Megabytes of free space in current directory, e.g. 212.

%C: Current directory, e.g. /pub/incoming/.

%R: Remote host, e.g. ppp123.rmt.critical.com.

%L: Local host, e.g. FTP.smashing.com.

%U: User name, e.g. Pumpkin.

%%: Percent character, e.g. %.

N O T E Not all tokens are valid in all situations, such as %U in the Welcome banner. In those situations, the token is ignored. For convenience, a quick reference of available tokens appears at the bottom of the Setup page. ▪

Account Setup

The user account editor is available from either tab three, Accounts, or from the Edit button on tab one, Status. The Accounts tab (shown in Fig. 46.7) is much more flexible, however, because it enables you to create, delete, and edit any user or template.

FIG. 46.7
Accounts tab.

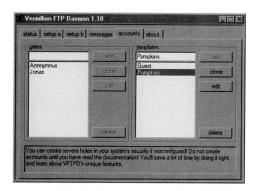

There are two ways to set up an account: individual user and template-based.

To create a new user individual account, type a name for the user in the edit box at the top of the window, and click the Add button. To create a user based on an existing account, select the existing account and click the Clone button. To edit an account, select Account and click Edit, or simply double-click on the account name.

If you add, clone, or edit an account, an edit window appears (shown in Fig. 46.8) for you to specify the following information:

Username: The name of the account; enter a new name if you wish to rename the account.

Password: Specifies a password for the account (users only).

Template: Select from a list of templates (users only).

Disable account: Disables any logins to this account (users only).

Guest account: A guest user and doesn't require a password (users only).

Priority login: Ignore "max. connection"; handy for administrators (users only).

File Security: List of directory permissions.

IP Security: A list of remote systems that are allowed to connect using this account.

FIG. 46.8

Editing a user account.

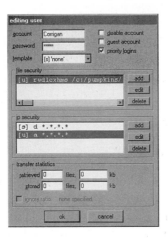

N O T E   In order for a user to log in, you must specify file and IP security permissions. The easiest way to do this is to create a template and set up the user as a member of that template. The permission lists display where the permissions are specified with the letter s for system defaults, t for template, and u for user. As you change templates for a user, the permission lists are updated to prevent mistakes in configuration. To set up permissions, simply click the appropriate buttons to the right of the list—Add, Edit, or Delete. Add and Edit bring up the appropriate Permissions edit window. ■

As mentioned previously, you can use templates to make account setup an easier process. Follow the same procedure for editing a template as for a user account.

When adding a new user you can now select a template instead of individually assigning IP addresses and directory level security permissions. These templates (one is shown in Fig. 46.9) can then be used whenever adding a new user. This reduces the amount of time it will take to add a new user as well as decreasing security risks through mistakes.

File Permissions   The File permissions edit window in Figure 46.10 contains a number of check boxes with which you can grant or remove rights for a pathname, specify the home directory, etc. Each permission is assigned a letter, which appears next to the pathname in the list if that permission is granted. The syntax for specifying directories is very specific, so be sure to follow the instructions given in the File permissions edit window.

FIG. 46.9
Use a template to ease user administration.

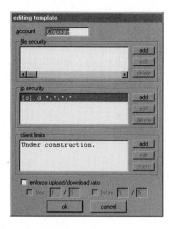

FIG. 46.10
The Editing File Permissions window specifies directory security.

IP Permissions   The IP permissions edit window shown in Figure 46.11 contains just one check box—Allow. If the IP mask that you specify should be allowed access using the current account, set the check box. If the IP mask should be denied access, clear the check box.

> **CAUTION**
>
> The system default is to deny all access, so for the account to become active you must set at least one IP permission; allow *.*.*.* is fine, and is appropriate for anonymous access. For user accounts, however, it is beneficial to be more restrictive.

FIG. 46.11
Editing IP address permissions.

Permission Conflicts   When a question of permissions arises, each setting is ranked according to how closely it matches the situation. For example, suppose a user wants to create a file in a directory called /c:/ftp/pub/games/arcade/ and there are different permissions given for /c:/ftp/pub/ and /c:/ftp/pub/games/. Both permissions match, but since the second is a closer match it takes priority.

A similar rule works with IP security. Suppose a user connects from a computer with IP 123.4.5.6, and there are settings to deny 123.*.*.*, allow 123.4.5.*, and deny 123.4.5.4-8. Each setting registers as a match, but the user is denied access, because the third permission is the most specific match and it specifies a deny.

However, if a conflict in permissions arises because a match is found in both the user's settings and the settings inherited from the template, the user's settings take priority even if the template's settings provide a closer match.

Anonymous Access   Unlike most FTP servers, there are no hard-coded accounts for anonymous access. However, it is very easy to configure the VFTPD server to accept anonymous logins. The simplest way is to set the desired permissions in a template, e.g., guest, and create two users belonging to that template: ftp and anonymous. Make sure that the Guest account is checked for both accounts and the IP permissions are sufficient.

TIP   One confusing feature of VFTPD is that, if an IP address is rejected for login, the message printed to the client says User <name> unknown, exactly as if the user really is unknown. This is by design, and although it may be confusing at first, it makes it more difficult for hackers and doesn't reward them for trying random names in their attempts to gain access.

CHAPTER 47

Using NT as a Dial-Up Internet Server

by Mark Surfas

Windows NT server has proved to be a robust and reliable server of information to the Internet. Windows NT is also a reliable and cost-effective way to provide dial-up Internet connectivity.

Remote Access Service (RAS) was originally Microsoft's strategic solution for connecting the mobile workforce to corporate networks. Quoting from Microsoft's corporate RAS backgrounder:

"Optimized for client-server computing, RAS is implemented primarily as a software solution, and is available for all of Microsoft's operating systems. Microsoft's goal for RAS is to enable remote networking out of the box with the Microsoft® Windows® operating system, thus making Windows the best platform for mobile computing."

The only item lacking from RAS in the beginning was the ability to use the all-important TCP/IP protocol. Once this was included RAS became a way to provide Internet access to dial-up users via modem.

Dial-up access to the Internet is most often provided via a piece of hardware known as a *terminal server*. This is basically a box that efficiently holds a lot of modems and assigns IP addresses, handles routing, and often works with a UNIX server to handle authentication. If you

The basics of remote access server

RAS is a powerful way to extend the connectivity options for the users of your LAN/WAN.

How to set up RAS for dial-in service

Set up RAS to enable LAN users to connect to your resources wherever they may be.

RAS security

Allow your users to dial in, but keep intruders out. Find out the issues and answers.

are using Windows NT you can forgo all of this and simply connect modems to serial ports on your server. ■

Overview of RAS

The goals in designing RAS were to make it

- Secure
- Interoperable
- Economical
- Scalable
- High performance
- Easy to use
- Extensible

Capabilities/Functionality

The RAS server, running on a Windows NT Server-based PC connected to the Internet or a corporate network, authenticates the users and services the sessions until terminated by the user or network administrator.

Large Capacity

Windows NT Server 3.51 and 4.0 support up to 256 simultaneous connections, up from 64 in version 3.1. Windows NT Workstation provides only a single RAS connection, rendering it unsuitable for anything other than personal use.

Software Data Compression

Software data compression in RAS enables users to boost their effective throughput. Data is compressed by the RAS client, sent over the wire in a compressed format, and decompressed by the server. In typical use, RAS software compression doubles effective throughput.

Data Encryption

RAS now provides data encryption in addition to password encryption, which ensures a high measure of privacy for sensitive data. Although most customers may choose not to enable encryption, government agencies, law enforcement organizations, financial institutions, and others can take advantage of it. Microsoft RAS uses the RC4 encryption algorithm of RSA Data Security, Inc. Visit their Web site at **http://www.rsa.com**.

Security

Corporate and government organizations deploying remote access solutions across the enterprise require varying degrees of security, from virtual public access to total discreet control.

Microsoft's Windows NT, with its RAS, offers all the tools necessary to implement any desired degree of security.

Microsoft's RAS provides security at the operating system, file system, and network levels, as well as data encryption, and event auditing. Some of the security features are inherited from the Windows NT operating system, while others are specific to RAS itself. Every stage of the process—such as user authentication, data transmission, resource access, logoff, and auditing—can be made secure. The next section describes RAS security in detail.

Security of Windows NT

First and foremost, Windows NT Server, the host for RAS, must be understood as a secure operating environment. Windows NT was designed to meet the requirements for C-2 level (US Department of Defense) security, meaning that access to system resources can be discretely controlled, and all access to the system can be recorded and audited. A Windows NT server-based computer, provided it is secured physically, can be totally locked down from a software perspective—any access of the system requires a password and leaves an audit trail.

Windows NT provides for enterprise-wide security using a *trusted domain, single network logon* model. A domain is simply a collection of servers that are administered together. Trusted domains establish relationships whereby the users and groups of one domain can be granted access to resources in a trusting domain. This eliminates the need for duplicate entry of user accounts across a multi-server network. Finally, under the single network logon model, once users are authenticated they carry with them their access credentials. Any time they attempt to gain access to a resource anywhere on the network, Windows NT automatically presents their credentials for them. If trusted domains are used, users never have to present a password after initial logon, even though their account exists only on one server in one domain.

The single network logon model extends to RAS users. RAS access is granted from the pool of all Windows NT user accounts. An administrator grants a single user, group of users, or all users the right to dial into the network. They then use their domain logon to connect via RAS. Once RAS authenticates the users, they can use resources throughout the domain and in any trusted domains.

Finally, Windows NT provides the Event Viewer for auditing. All system, application, and security events are recorded to a central secure database that, with proper privileges, can be viewed from anywhere on the network. The Event Log contains a record of any attempts to violate system security, start or stop services without authorization, or gain access to protected resources. Microsoft's RAS makes full use of the Event Viewer in Windows NT.

Authentication and Security

Authentication is one of the most important concerns that corporate customers express regarding security. Common questions include

How can we ensure the privacy of passwords?

Can we use our own security mechanism in addition to that provided by the RAS feature of Windows NT?

Is callback supported?

We'll explore these issues and tackle a few more by taking a look at the robust and secure environment provided by NT for remote connections. Microsoft has had several years to study the needs of the corporate customer and has developed a dynamic and flexible product.

Authentication Protocols   RAS uses the Challenge Handshake Authentication Protocol (CHAP) to negotiate the most secure form of encrypted authentication supported by both server and client. CHAP uses a challenge-response mechanism with one-way encryption on the response, the most secure form of encrypted authentication available. CHAP enables the RAS server to negotiate downward from the most secure to the least secure encryption mechanism, and protects any passwords that are transmitted in the process.

Network Access Restrictions   Remote access to the network under RAS is under the complete control of the system administrator. In addition to all the tools provided with Windows NT Server (authentication, trusted domains, event auditing, C2 security design, etc.), the RAS Administrator tool and the User Manager give the administrator the ability to grant or revoke remote access privileges on a user-by-user basis. This means that, even though RAS is running on a Windows NT Server-based PC, access to the network must be explicitly granted for each user who is authorized to enter the network via RAS.

In order to further protect customers' networks, RAS provides an additional measure of security. The RAS Administrator provides a switch that allows access to be granted either to all resources that the RAS host machine can see, or just to resources local to that PC. This enables a customer to tightly control the information that is available to remote users, and to limit their exposure in the event of a security breach.

Flexible Hardware Options   RAS offers the broadest hardware support of any remote access vendor. Currently, they support more than 1700 PCs, 300 modems, and 11 multi-port serial adapters. By selecting a remote access solution with very broad hardware support, customers gain flexibility in their system design. For a complete listing of the hardware devices supported by RAS, look in the Windows NT Hardware Compatibility List (HCL) located at **http://www.microsoft.com/ntserver/hcl/hclintro.htm.**

PPP but No SLIP   Internet dial-in services typically offer one or more of three types of service accounts:

- Shell
- SLIP
- PPP

Shell accounts are a terminal host paradigm commonly found in the UNIX environment. These accounts are generally undesirable for Internet access and RAS does not support them.

SLIP, the serial line internet protocol, is an older communications standard also found in UNIX environments. SLIP does not provide automatic negotiation of network configuration, but it requires user intervention. RAS does not provide a SLIP server in any release of Windows NT Server.

If you want to use Microsoft RAS for PPP dial-in support, you also need one client access license per connection. In other words, if the site supports 10 concurrent connections, you need to purchase a Server License and 10 Client Access Licenses for basic network services in the Per Server mode. If the site supports workstations in the Per Seat mode, you need to purchase a Server License and Client Access Licenses for basic network services for each workstation. If you increase the number of concurrent connections allowed, you must then purchase additional Client Access Licenses in the Per Server mode up to the maximum number of concurrent RAS users.

Secure Internet Transfer with New PPTP Technology

With Windows NT Server 4.0, RAS enables remote users to access their network via the Internet by using the new Point-to-Point Tunneling Protocol (PPTP). PPTP is a new networking technology integrated with RAS that supports multiprotocol virtual private networks (VPNs). PPTP uses the Internet as the transfer mechanism instead of long distance telephone lines, or a toll-free (1-800) service, greatly reducing transmission costs.

PPTP enables remote users to access their networks securely across the Internet in two ways: by dialing into an Internet Service Provider (ISP), or by connecting directly to the Internet. In either case, PPTP provides one essential benefit: secure over-the-Internet data transfer. Using an ISP offers additional benefits.

PPTP enables modems and ISDN cards to be separated from the company's RAS server. They can now be located at an ISP's modem bank or a front-end processor (FEP). This greatly reduces costs because modems, ISDN cards, etc., are loaded on the ISP's server, not the company's server. PPTP means less administrative overhead because the ISP, rather than the network administrator, manages the connection hardware.

For companies that want to manage their own networks entirely, and connect directly to the Internet through their own software and hardware, PPTP offers the security they need.

The PPTP connection over the Internet is encrypted and secure, and works with IP, IPX, NetBEUI, and other mainstream protocols.

Part
IX

Ch
47

Setting Up Remote Access Server for Internet Dial-in

This chapter makes several key assumptions:

- You have Windows NT Server 4.0 or later installed
- The server has a network interface card installed
- The server is on a network with routed access direct to the Internet
- The server has one or more active modems

Setting up a remote dial-in server is no small task. For many years and even today this is an area of computing where corporations employ specialists to get dial-in servers running efficiently. Windows NT has simplified the process into a number of clearly defined steps:

1. Install and configure serial port cards and modems.

2. Load the drivers for any intelligent multi-port serial cards.

3. Install RAS.

4. Configure the network protocols.

5. Grant dial-in access to appropriate users.

RAS is installed and set up via the Network Control Panel applet. As the name implies, RAS runs as a service on the server. To successfully install RAS, you need to have your installation CD-ROM handy and follow these steps:

1. Select the Network applet in the Windows NT control panel, shown in Figure 47.1. This opens up the Network dialog box, as shown in Figure 47.2.

FIG. 47.1

Your Control Panel may contain a slightly different set of icons.

FIG. 47.2

Select the Add button from the Network dialog box.

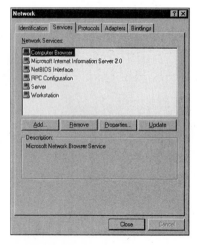

2. Click the Add button.

3. Once the Select Network Service dialog box is open, scroll down to the Remote Access Service entry, as shown in Figure 47.3. Select it and then click the OK button.

FIG. 47.3

Scroll down to Remote Access Service.

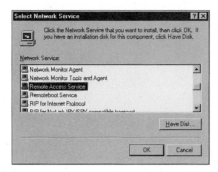

4. The Windows NT Setup dialog box, as shown in Figure 47.4, prompts you for the location of your setup files. If you are installing from CD-ROM, enter the drive letter of the CD and the directory path "\i386." The server installs all the necessary files and components.

FIG. 47.4

The Windows NT Setup dialog box.

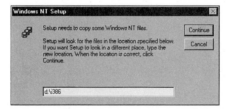

5. The server immediately proceeds into RAS setup mode and prompts you to configure an initial COM port. If you have previously set up a COM port for a particular modem, it is displayed in the list (as shown in Fig. 47.5). Select a suitable port from the RAS Capable Devices drop-down list.

FIG. 47.5

Pick a COM port, any COM port.

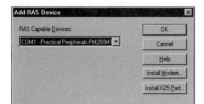

Part
IX

Ch
47

6. If you need to configure a modem, RAS prompts you to attempt automatic modem configuration, as shown in Figure 47.6. Automatic detection is useful because the server picks the settings that the modem best responds to. If you are using a newer modem, not supported in the default list, this is a strong choice.

T I P If you have a modem that does not appear in the list of modems supported by RAS, check your modem documentation: the modem manufacturer may have included a disk with the appropriate driver. If not, call the manufacturer's tech support, or check their Web site. It's always best to use the right driver for the right equipment.

FIG. 47.6

Install New Modem
dialog box.

Whether you opt for automatic detection or manual configuration, each port must be configured using the Configure Port Usage dialog box shown in Figure 47.7.

FIG. 47.7

The Configure Port
Usage dialog box.

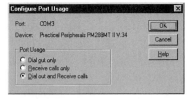

7. After configuring your COM ports, click OK, and then proceed to network setup. This is where you assign the desired network protocols, as well as their routing behaviors.

Click on the <u>N</u>etwork button (in Fig. 47.8) to configure the network protocols and encryption options, as shown in Figure 47.9.

FIG. 47.8

Modem settings.

FIG. 47.9

The Network Configuration dialog box.

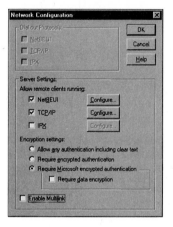

8. Since you are configuring this server as an Internet dial-up server, disable the NetBEUI Protocol and set up to allow any authentication, including clear text.

   The next step is to configure TCP/IP. Click the Configure button next to the TCP/IP check box.

9. Again, to serve as an Internet dial-up access point, you need to make sure you set up TCP/IP properly (see Fig. 47.10). Configure client access to the entire network: otherwise, users dialing in cannot be routed out to the Internet. If you are using a static address pool, be sure to allocate as many IP addresses as there are modems available.

10. After you have completed the installation and modem configuration, restart your server. You now have a new program group with an essential tool for completing the RAS installation—the Remote Access Administrator.

Part

IX

Ch

47

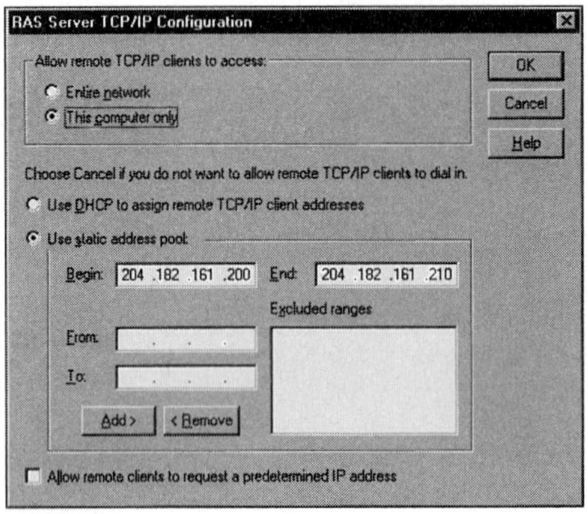

FIG. 47.10
Configure RAS TCP/IP options.

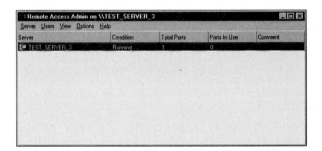

Configuring RAS

The Remote Access Administrator, as shown in Figure 47.11, is the tool you use to stop, pause, and resume RAS. If you have multiple RAS servers set up on your network, you can use this tool to manage all of them, assuming that you are a member of the administrator group in your domain.

FIG. 47.11
The Remote Access Administrator.

> **CAUTION**
>
> You must explicitly assign to each user the right to dial in using the Remote Access Administrator tool or the User Manager. This is the number one cause of confusion among beginning RAS administrators!

The first step in administering your RAS server is to launch the Remote Access Administrator and grant the appropriate users the right to dial in to the server. Choose Users, Permissions and you see the dialog box shown in Figure 47.12.

FIG. 47.12

In the Remote Access Permissions dialog box you can authorize (or not) each user in your domain for dial-in access.

N O T E Using Windows NT 3.51 you MUST use the Remote Access Administrator tool to set dial-in permissions. Windows NT 4.0 enables you to grant dial-in access in the User Manager. ▪

By clicking the Grant All button you instantly authorize all members of the domain for dial-in access. (Clicking the Grant All button will include guest accounts as well. So be cautious.) By the same token, click the Revoke All button to instantly wipe the remote access right from all users. This is a handy feature if you have a poorly managed domain and need to start from the ground up to rebuild your security.

RAS offers a call-back option, which is not likely to be applicable to most Internet dial-in situations. If you have high security needs for your network, you may want to consider using call-back: this makes it more difficult for a hacker to gain unauthorized access.

By double-clicking one of the communication ports in your list, you can monitor the status and activity of the port (see Fig. 47.13).

FIG. 47.13

The Communication Ports dialog box.

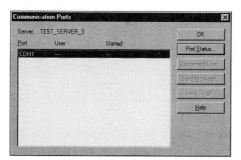

Part

IX

Ch

47

CHAPTER 48

Using NT as a TCP/IP Router

by Mark Surfas

Many Companies are looking for a leased-line type of connection to the Internet, without the high price. A typical T-1 connection to the Internet costs $2,000 to $3,000 per month, several thousand dollars in setup charges, and another $3,000 to $5,000 in equipment.

While this expense is justified in some cases, in most it is not. In fact, if you have a small network you may be surprised to discover that you can maintain a 24-hr-a-day connection to the Internet for less than a dollar per day.

You probably have an Internet service provider (ISP) in your area offering unlimited Internet access for a reasonable monthly fee. This chapter shows you how to use Remote Access Server (RAS) to maintain a dial-up gateway to the Internet that looks and feels to the outside world just like the big boys T-1 connection. ▪

Installing RAS

RAS is a powerful tool for extending your network services to the Internet.

Configuring dial-up networking

By using dial-up networking, you can use your modem as a bridge between your local area network (LAN) and the Internet—excellent solution for low-cost and low-traffic connectivity.

Editing the registry

Controlling the registry is critical to setting up TCP/IP routing. You learn exactly what to do.

Keeping the connection alive

Once connected, it's critical to stay connected. Learn to maintain your link without administrative headaches.

Setting Up Dial-Up Routing

Windows NT RAS version 3.5, or later, was not designed to route packets from a large LAN over a dial-up link. You can, however, use a computer running Windows NT RAS as a simple router to the Internet by correctly configuring both the RAS computer and the other computers on your small LAN with a static network configuration.

The following are requirements for using Windows NT RAS as a dial-up router between your LAN and the Internet:

- A Windows NT computer with a high-speed modem and a network adapter card
- A point-to-point protocol (PPP) connection to the Internet
- A valid network, or a subnet different from the subnet of the ISP
- The proper Registry and Default Gateway configurations on the computer acting as a router and on the LAN clients (the configurations are described later in this chapter)
- A small LAN that does not require the automatic routing configuration provided by RIP. (You probably do not need RIP functionality if you have a small LAN that is not expected to grow or change)

To be identified using names rather than IP addresses, you also need a domain name. Your ISP can usually help you obtain a domain name.

The Dial-Up Account

You need a PPP dial-up account from an ISP. All things being equal, the optimal account has the following features:

- Unlimited access at a flat monthly rate
- A 28.8 Kbps modem to dial into
- IP addresses for your computers
- A service that isn't oversaturated

The first two items are easily discernible. The last item, oversaturation, can usually only be determined by experience. If you are using dial-up routing for your business, you are in luck: Peak dial-up Internet activity typically occurs at the end of the business day. Loads increase dramatically starting at 5:00 p.m. and last until 11:00 p.m. For most businesses utilizing dial-up access, this does not present a problem.

Once you have a PPP connection, IP addresses for your subnet (and correct subnet mask) and (optionally) a domain name, you can then configure the RAS and LAN computers for Internet gateway, as described in the following procedure.

N O T E Contact your ISP in advance to arrange for a subnet to be relocated to your site. This will take time and effort by the ISP and is available at an extra cost. ■

Setting Up Remote Access Server for Internet Routing

This chapter makes several key assumptions:

- ■ You have Windows NT Server 4.0 or later installed
- ■ The server has a network interface card installed
- ■ The server is on a network with routed access direct to the Internet
- ■ The server has one or more active modems

Setting up routing to the Internet server often requires the purchase of expensive and complicated hardware solutions. However, by using the built-in routing capabilities of Windows NT, we can bypass this and use a modem for low speed access to the Internet. By utilizing an ISDN modem you can achieve enough bandwidth to run a well-used Web site!

There are a number of clearly defined steps needed to set up routing between the modem and the network interface card in your server.

1. Install and configure serial port cards and modems
2. Load the drivers for any intelligent multi-port serial cards
3. Install RAS
4. Configure the network protocols
5. Grant dial-in access to appropriate users

RAS is installed and set up via the Network Control Panel applet. As its name implies, RAS runs as a service on the server. To successfully install RAS have your installation CD-ROM handy and follow these steps:

1. Select the Network applet in the Windows 95 control panel (see Fig. 48.1). This opens up the Network dialog box, as shown in Figure 48.2.

FIG. 48.1
Your Control Panel may contain a slightly different set of Icons.

FIG. 48.2

Select the Add button from the Network dialog box.

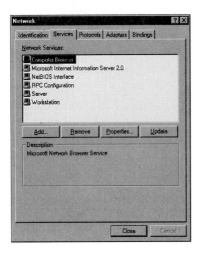

2. Click the Add button. This opens the Select Network Service dialog box, as shown in Figure 48.3.

3. Scroll down to the Remote Access Service entry. Select it and then click the OK button.

FIG. 48.3

Select Remote Access Service.

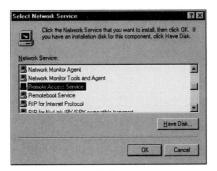

4. The Windows NT Setup dialog box, as shown in Figure 48.4, prompts you for the location of your setup files. If you are installing from CD-ROM, enter the drive letter of the CD and the directory path "\i386." The server installs all the necessary files and components.

5. The server immediately proceeds into RAS setup mode and prompts you to configure an initial COM port. If you have previously set up a COM port for a particular modem, it displays in the list (as shown in Fig. 48.5). Select a suitable port from the drop-down pick list.

FIG. 48.4

The NT Setup dialog box.

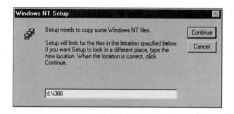

FIG. 48.5

Pick a COM port, any COM port.

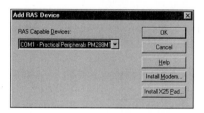

6. If you need to install and configure a modem, RAS prompts you to invoke the Modem Installer as shown in Figure 48.6. Automatic detection is useful, in that the server picks the settings that the modem best responds to. If you are using a newer modem not supported in the default list, this is a strong choice.

 TIP If you have a modem that does not appear in the list of modems supported by NT, check your modem documentation. The modem manufacturer may have included a disk with the appropriate driver. If not, call the manufacturer's tech support or check their Web site. It's always best to use the right driver for the right equipment.

FIG. 48.6

RAS will invoke the Modem Installer if needed.

Whether you opt for automatic detection or manual configuration, each port must be configured. Using the Remote Access Setup dialog box (shown in Fig. 48.7) you do the following:

- Configure each port for receiving and/or originating calls
- Set up network behaviors for any dial-in ports

Part

IX

Ch

48

FIG. 48.7

The RAS Setup dialog box.

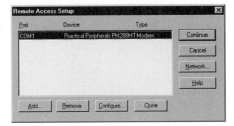

7. Click Configure to elect whether the modem is available for dial-in, dial-out, or both. (see Fig. 48.8). This is where you assign the desired network protocols. Click OK.

FIG. 48.8

The Configure Port Usage dialog box.

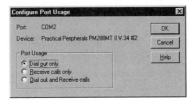

8 Click the Network button (refer to fig. 48.7) to configure the network protocols available for dial-out (see Fig. 48.9).

9. Select the TCP/IP dial-out protocol.

10. After you have completed the installation and modem configuration, reboot your server.

FIG. 48.9

Configure RAS TCP/IP options.

Configuring Dial-out Networking

To dial out, you utilize an application accessible via both the Start button menu and the Explorer—Dial-up Networking (shown in Fig. 48.10). This is an easy-to-use applet that connects your computer to a host and enables you to communicate on a network level with IPX, TCP/IP, and NetBEUI. This is true networking on demand and also enables you to connect your computer to the Internet. As described in the steps listed previously in this chapter, this connection also connects your LAN to the Internet.

The first step is to launch Dial-Up Networking (as shown in Fig. 48.11) and configure a phone book entry. This phone book entry requires you to know the following:

- The phone number of the ISP
- The TCP/IP address assigned to you (if any)
- The DNS (domain name server) address
- The remote gateway address

Static versus Dynamic IP Addressing

If you are setting up for Internet routing, you need to consider whether you are going to use the connection for out-bound access or for outside users to access services on your LAN. This often means Web or FTP access. For in-bound users, it's important that you have an account with a static IP address. In other words, every time you connect to your ISP you receive the same IP address.

Most dial-up accounts today use dynamic addressing. This allocates IP addresses to the available modems rather than to each specific user. ISP would rather maintain a limited pool of addresses for users actually online at the moment than maintain an ever-growing system of assigning an individual IP address to each user with an account.

Dynamic addressing would wreak havoc with your ability to have in-bound users locate your server. You would need to communicate a new address every time you restarted the connection.

FIG. 48.10

The dial-up networking applet can be launched from Explorer.

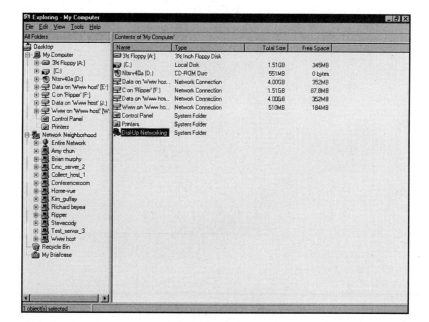

Part
IX

Ch

48

FIG. 48.11

The dial-up networking applet is the front end for RAS dial-out.

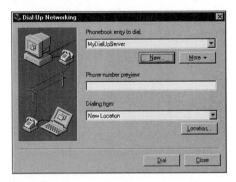

Click the New button to add the new entry to the phone book. This brings up the New Phonebook Entry dialog box shown in Figure 48.12. If you don't see this tabbed notebook and instead see a Wizard dialog box, click the button that reads "I already know how to set up a phone book entry". This tabbed notebook is the key to correctly setting up the network connection.

First, configure the modem by clicking the Configure button, which opens the Modem Configuration dialog box shown in Figure 48.13. This is where the physical connection properties are set. For Internet dial-up purposes, the recommended settings are to enable hardware Flow Control, Error Control, and Modem Compression.

FIG. 48.12

This tabbed dialog is crucial to dial-out success.

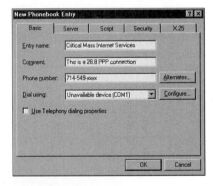

FIG. 48.13

Ask your Internet provider which settings are appropriate.

Next, click on the server tab. This reveals the dialog box to configure the network protocols, as shown in Figure 48.14. The first selection to make is the type of dial-up server you are connecting to. You essentially have two choices:

- PPP: Windows NT, Windows 95 Plus, Internet
- SLIP: Internet

The SLIP server type is quickly fading into obscurity and you are most likely to be selecting PPP. Check with your ISP if you are unsure.

FIG. 48.14

Server tab of the New Phonebook Entry dialog box.

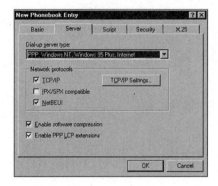

The next selection to make is the protocol. For Internet connectivity you must select the TCP/IP protocol. You can select either the IPX or NetBEUI protocols, but do NOT select these unless you have good reason to do so: selecting these protocols may open your system to unnecessary security holes. If you are connecting to an ISP that doesn't support these protocols they should have no effect (in theory). As I often say, "I want to move to Theory. Everything works in Theory."

Also at the bottom of this dialog box are two check boxes. These two options are fairly standard: software compression and LCP extensions. Again, contact your ISP to ascertain whether they support these extensions.

Next, click on the TCP/IP Settings button on this page. This opens the dialog shown in Figure 48.15. This is where you enter the TCP/IP addresses discussed at the beginning of this chapter.

Part
IX

Ch
48

FIG. 48.15

TCP/IP configurations are often set by the remote server.

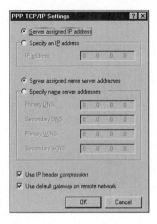

In the old days (pre-1996) dial-up connections required a fair amount of sophistication on the part of the user. As you can see in this dialog, setup is becoming easier. Most modern ISPs can actually send the settings to the user upon dial-in. If your ISP doesn't provide this service, fill in the necessary addresses.

So far, you have configured the physical parameters for dial-in and now need to configure the actual logon to the remote system. You have three options. You can

- Log on to a Windows NT based service, using your system username and password
- Open a terminal window and log on interactively
- Configure a script to automate logon

Setting up for logon to an NT based service is an unlikely Internet scenario. However, if this is the case for you, consult with your dial-in provider to create a secure authentication scenario.

If you are like most dial-up users, you log on either interactively or using a script.

Interactive logon is a poor choice if you expect to be logging on regularly to maintain an Internet routing scenario.

Every time you connect to your provider, you need to log on by entering a username and password. If you lose your connection and need to redial, you need to be standing by to enter the username and password.

The best choice is to use a login script that automatically performs the login to the ISP upon successful connection. All scripts are located in the Switch.inf file, accessible via the Edit Scripts button. When utilizing RAS scripts, you have a full set of commands and macros at your disposal. You can review full documentation at url: **http://www.microsoft.com/kb/bussys/ winnt/q125975.htm.**

Configure Routing to the Internet over a Dedicated PPP Account

To set up RAS as an appropriate route for computers attached to the same network as your dial-out server, you need to edit some registry settings. This is accomplished via the Regedt32.exe program.

> **CAUTION**
>
> The registry contains the basic configuration information used to start up and run the Windows NT server. Always be aware that by editing the wrong registry key you risk disabling the server or causing undesirable behavior. That said, most advanced NT configurations require you to edit the registry. Be careful!

1. On the RAS computer that routes packets from the LAN to the Internet, add the value **DisableOtherSrcPackets** to the Registry path shown below, and then set the value to 0.

    By default, the header of each packet sent by the RAS computer over the PPP link uses the IP address of the RAS computer as the source. Since the packets that come from LAN clients are not originating from the RAS computer, you must set **DisableOtherScrPackets** to 0 so that the packets are forwarded over the PPP link.

    ```
    \HKEY_LOCAL_MACHINE\System\CurrentControlSet\Services

    \RasArp\Parameters

    DisableOtherSrcPackets          REG_DWORD
    Range: 0-1
    Default: 1 (not in Registry)
    ```

2. If the subnet you have is in the same network class as your ISP (which is very likely in this scenario), you must also add the value **PriorityBasedOnSubNetwork** to the registry of the RAS computer that routes packets from the LAN to the Internet. Then set **PriorityBasedOnSubNetwork** parameter to 1.

    A computer can connect to the LAN using a network card and a RAS connection. If the RAS connection and the LAN network adapter card are assigned addresses with the same network number, and the Use Default Gateway On Remote Network check box is selected, then all packets are sent over the RAS connection. This is the case even though the two addresses are in different subnetworks within the same network.

    For example, if the network adapter card has IP address 17.1.1.1 (subnet mask 255.255.0.0) and the RAS connection is assigned the address 17.2.1.1, RAS sends all 17.x.x.x packets using the RAS connection. If the parameter is set, RAS sends 17.2.x.x packets using the RAS connection and 17.1.x.x packets using the network adapter card.

    ```
    \HKEY_LOCAL_MACHINE\System\CurrentControlSet\Services

        \RasMan\PPP\IPCP

      PriorityBasedOnSubNetwork          REG_DWORD
      Range: 0-1
      Default: 0 (not in Registry)
    ```

Part

IX

Ch

48

3. Configure the default gateway of all the computers on the LAN using the Network option in Control Panel.

The default gateway is set when you configure the TCP/IP protocol.

Use the IP address of the network card adapter in the RAS computer acting as a router to the Internet as the default gateway for all computers on the LAN except this computer. The default gateway for the computer acting as the router to the Internet should be left blank.

Staying Connected

One of the challenges of dial-up routing is staying connected. Your line may disconnect for a number of reasons, including excessive line noise. Additionally most ISP set a time-out period: if your line doesn't carry traffic for a set period of time (sometimes as little as 10 minutes), you are automatically disconnected.

This is highly disruptive behavior for users attempting to access your server from the Internet, and also for users attempting to surf the Internet from your LAN.

Keep the Connection Alive

The key to keeping your ISP from closing your connection is to ensure that some activity takes place at a regular interval. It doesn't matter how much activity takes place—it just needs to happen. There are many ways to achieve this goal.

The bottom line is that you need a software package to regularly create activity across the dial-up line. One method is to use the TARDIS package to synchronize your server's system clock with the atomic clock at NIST. Set it to retrieve the time as often as needed and it keeps the connection open. TARDIS is available at the NT software center at **www.bhs.com.**

Open the Connection If It Fails

If you do lose your connection, it's a great idea to have a software watchdog that immediately redials and reestablishes the connection. Somar software produces a watchdog utility called Somar Redial.

Somar Redial V1.1 is a Windows NT service that maintains a full-time dial-up PPP Internet, or other RAS connection, by redialing whenever the connection is lost. This service can optionally cycle the EMWAC HTTP server and other WINSOCK services, which lock up when the RAS connection is stopped and restarted. Redial can also be set to throttle redialing attempts: this is appropriate for cases where there is a cost to redialing.

You can get this valuable utility at **www.bhs.com.** ●

What's on the CD

The CD-ROM included with this book is packed full of valuable programs and utilities. This appendix gives you a brief overview of the contents of the CD. For a more detailed look at any of these parts, load the CD-ROM and browse the contents. ■

Contents Overview

- Several browser plug-ins to extend Netscape and Internet Explorer's capabilities.
- HTML Editors to help you create and maintain your online Web presence.
- Internet Mail and Newsreader clients to help maximize your online time.
- VRML browsers and utilities to view online worlds and make your own 3-D landscape.
- Graphics viewers/other utilities to supplement the resources for your online treks.
- Internet gaming and chat clients that get you connected to play or chat with other Internet users.
- The Java Developer Kit that contains the development tools and applet viewer for Windows, Solaris, and Mac platform.
- Web server software so you can set up your own presence on the Internet.

  Windows Httpd 1.4

  WebQuest 95 & NT

  Email and FTP servers

  NT-Mail 3.0

  Vermillion FTP

- The CD also contains additional reference material. You will find a listing of country codes, a time zone code table, vendor contact information, and a glossary of terms used in the book.

Loading the CD

The CD is designed to be used in conjunction with your Web browser. Simply pull down your browser's File menu selections and select "Load File" or its equivalent. Select the file "INDEX.htm" and it will load the beginning page, which then gives you the choices of software found on the CD. This CD supports frame-capable browsers and non-frame browsers alike. Once you have found a file you want to use, simply download it to your own hard drive (clicking on a link) and then use a decompression utility.

Web Utilities, Helper Applications, and Other Useful Utilities

This CD-ROM contains a collection of software programs that allow you to create and edit your own Web pages. We have also included a carefully selected collection of the best additional utilities that you can use when working with Netscape Navigator or Microsoft Internet Explorer.

FTP/Archie

FTP Icon Collection   QVTNet

Serv-UWFTP   Daemon

WS_FTPWS   Archie

Gopher

WS Gopher

HTML Editing Tools

Hot Dog   HoTMetaL Free

HTML Assistant   HTMLEd

HTML NotePad   HTML Writer

Kenn Nesbitt's WebEdit   LiveMarkup

Webber   Web Easy/Help

HTML Utilities

Microsoft Internet Assistants
for Word, Excel, and GT_HTML
(plug-in for MS Word; freeware)

MapEdit (shareware)   Map This!

Color Manipulation Device   HTML Library

WebForms   WebMania

Graphics Utilities

LView Pro   Paint Shop Pro

Alchemy Mindworks GIF
Construction Set (for GIF
89a animation)

Internet Relay Chat

mIRC 4.0

Web Server Software

Microsoft Internet Information Server

Web Browser

Microsoft Internet Explorer 3.0

Internet Connection Utilities

Dunce (free)   Duca (free)

E-mail

Eudora Lite (free)   Pegasus Mail (free)

Qbik Mail Monitor (free)

News Readers

News Xpress 32 (free)   Trumpet Newsreader (free)

Helper Applications for Sound

MIDI Jukebox 2 (shareware)   TrueSpeech for Windows 95 (free)

Sound Gadget Pro (free)   Awave (free)

Windows Play Any File (free)   StreamWorks client program for Windows (free)

Waveform Hold and Modify   Midi Gate (Free)
(shareware)

VRML

Terraform   VR Scout

VRWeb   Worldview

Fountain   ActiveVRML

Live3D

PDF Viewers

Adobe Acrobat Reader   Envoy Viewer

Common Ground Mini Viewer   Aladdin Ghostscript

Compression and Encoding

WinZip (shareware)   VisualZIP (shareware)

WinPack Deluxe (shareware)   WinCode (shareware)

Internet Gaming

Kali 95   Mud Software

Free HTML Versions of Popular Que Books

The final piece of this CD makes owning this book like getting five books in one. The CD contains the entire text of four popular best-selling books from Que in HTML format:

- *Special Edition Using Java*
- *Special Edition Using HTML*, Second Edition
- *Special Edition Using JavaScript*
- *Special Edition Using CGI*

We think that you'll find each of these books in HTML to be valuable additions to your reference library. You'll find these books in the \quebooks directory. ●

Index

N

Licensing Agreement

By opening this package, you are agreeing to be bound by the following:

0181-7516676

Mrs. Fodskatt